OXFORD PRIVATE INTERNATIONAL
LAW SERIES

GENERAL EDITOR: JAMES J FAWCETT
Professor of Law
University of Nottingham

THE ROME II REGULATION:
THE LAW APPLICABLE TO
NON-CONTRACTUAL OBLIGATIONS

OXFORD PRIVATE INTERNATIONAL LAW SERIES

General Editor: James J Fawcett

The aim of the series is to publish work of quality and originality in a number of important areas of private international law. The series is intended for both scholarly and practitioner readers.

THE ROME II REGULATION: THE LAW APPLICABLE TO NON-CONTRACTUAL OBLIGATIONS

ANDREW DICKINSON

Solicitor Advocate (Higher Courts—Civil)
Consultant, Clifford Chance LLP
Visiting Fellow in Private International Law,
British Institute of International and Comparative Law

www.romeii.eu

OXFORD
UNIVERSITY PRESS

OXFORD

UNIVERSITY PRESS

Great Clarendon Street, Oxford OX2 6DP

Oxford University Press is a department of the University of Oxford.
It furthers the University's objective of excellence in research, scholarship,
and education by publishing worldwide in

Oxford New York

Auckland Cape Town Dar es Salaam Hong Kong Karachi
Kuala Lumpur Madrid Melbourne Mexico City Nairobi
New Delhi Shanghai Taipei Toronto

With offices in

Argentina Austria Brazil Chile Czech Republic France Greece
Guatemala Hungary Italy Japan Poland Portugal Singapore
South Korea Switzerland Thailand Turkey Ukraine Vietnam

Oxford is a registered trade mark of Oxford University Press
in the UK and in certain other countries

Published in the United States
by Oxford University Press Inc., New York

British Library Cataloguing in Publication Data

Data available

Library of Congress Cataloging in Publication Data

Data available

Typeset by Cepha Imaging Private Ltd., Bangalore, India
Printed in Great Britain
on acid-free paper by
CPI Antony Rowe Ltd, Chippenham

ISBN 978–0–19–928968–4

1 3 5 7 9 10 8 6 4 2

General Editor's Preface

The Rome II Regulation on the law applicable to non-contractual obligations represents yet another step in the relentless process of the Europeanization of private international law. It can hardly be said to be a surprising development; the harmonization of choice of law rules in the EC was first mooted over thirty years ago. It can be seen as the third side of a triangle made up of the Brussels system, which deals with jurisdiction and the recognition and enforcement of judgments in civil and commercial matters, and the Rome I system, which deals with choice of law for contractual obligations. Nonetheless, Rome II is in some ways different from earlier measures. The need for such a Regulation is less obvious, the legal justification more suspect, its provisions more uncertain and alien, at least to English lawyers. The Rome Convention on the law applicable to contractual obligations enshrined basic concepts that were familiar to English private international lawyers. This is much less apparent with the Rome II Regulation. Its provisions look to be based on codifications of private international law to be found in civil law countries, such as Switzerland and Germany, with, for example, their special rules for particular torts. Understanding the Regulation requires a considerable understanding of the substantive law background in civil law systems. The introduction of the civil law concepts such as unfair competition, *negotiorum gestio* and *culpa in contrahendo* raise obvious questions of what English concepts might be said to fall within these concepts. Where do equitable obligations fit, if at all, within the Regulation? The difficult classification problems that existed under the pre-Regulation law have another twist added because the question is now how a matter is to be classified for the purposes of the Regulation, rather than for the purposes of English private international law.

Andrew Dickinson's book *The Rome II Regulation* is an invaluable guide to solving the challenges in interpretation that lie ahead. It looks in impressive depth at the legislative history of each provision, allowing the author to come to a conclusion on what the intention underlying that provision is. It examines the substantive law background to provisions and very importantly the influence of EC law on shaping the content of the Regulation. The format of setting out each article and then commenting on it makes the book especially practitioner friendly. At the same time broad themes such as the legal basis of the Regulation are examined in detail. This then will be an indispensable work of reference for private international lawyers across Europe, and, indeed, for private international lawyers from outside the EC who are interested in EC developments.

The aim of the *Oxford Private International Law Series* is to publish work of high quality and originality in a number of important areas of private international law. *The Rome II Regulation* meets these criteria and is an essential addition to the Series.

James Fawcett
Nottingham
28 August 2008

Foreword

This is a timely work, by which Andrew Dickinson performs a service that will be of enduring value for many years to practitioners and the business and financial community. The EC Regulation on the law applicable to non-contractual obligations ('Rome II') will come into force from 11 January 2009. It will supplement and interrelate with the existing Regulations on the law applicable to contractual obligations ('Rome I') and on civil jurisdiction and judgments ('Brussels I'). It continues the pattern of those Regulations by regulating relations between jurisdictions, rather than seeking to harmonize substantive law. However, as Andrew Dickinson explains, this does not mean that the European Community's competence to introduce it (or even Rome I) is uncontroversial; or that there may not be future moves to harmonize substantive law in the contractual field.

The book starts with the history and philosophy of Rome II, against the background of a survey of the current rules of private international law in England and other European states. Rome I is the first example of an instrument adopted under Title IV of the EC Treaty reaching the 'conciliation' stage of the process of co-decision between the Council and European Parliament introduced in this area by the Treaty of Nice in 2003. So its history gives interesting insights into the operation of co-decision, which would be further expanded if the Treaty of Lisbon comes into force.

The author identifies substantial arguments (many also raised by the House of Lords Select Committee on the European Union and by the United Kingdom during the Regulation's negotiation) for the view that Rome II exceeds Community competence, at least on the basis and in the width ultimately adopted. However, he voices understandable doubts about the likelihood of the European Court of Justice accepting such arguments, pointing to the series of that Court's decisions establishing expansive Community competence in the area.

The meat of the book lies in its systematic and comprehensive consideration of the Regulation's general scope, the general rules established and the specific subject-matters covered. Taking but two examples of topics covered under general scope: arbitration practitioners will be glad to read his conclusion that the concept of 'court or tribunal' does not cover arbitration, though perhaps slightly concerned by the absence of any express exclusion to that effect mirroring the exclusions in the Rome I and Brussels I Regulations and by the contrary arguments which Andrew Dickinson examines; while those interested in bailment will find a scrupulous discussion of the extent to which this can, on an autonomous European view, be described as contractual (within Rome I) or non-contractual (within Rome II).

The sections on the general rules applicable to wrongfully-inflicted damage are followed by sections on the specific heads covered by the Rome II Regulation. These include familiar heads such as product liability, environmental damage and intellectual property, together with other heads which may (to an English lawyer) appear more esoteric or uncertain in scope, such as unfair competition, *negotiorum gestio* and *culpa in contrahendo*. In each case, Andrew Dickinson carefully relates the likely impact of the Regulation to the various wrongs or heads of recovery which might be suggested to be relevant under English law.

An important section on choice of law (where the applicable law will generally parallel that which would apply in a contractual situation under Rome I) is followed by a section on the scope of the law applicable whenever the Regulation does in principle apply. Thus, in relation to the assessment of damages, the Regulation will reverse *Harding v Wealands* [2006] UKHL 32; [2007] 2 AC 1, assuming at least that the European Court of Justice is likely to take a narrower view of the autonomous concept of procedure (under Art 1(3) of the Regulation) than the view taken at common law by the House of Lords in that case. A matter left deliberately unspecific by the Regulation is the proper approach to pleading and proof of foreign law in domestic courts. The European Parliament has made clear its interest in requiring domestic courts to act on their own motion in this area, but Andrew Dickinson concludes that the deliberate exclusion from the Regulation of any such provision means that the European Court of Justice is likely to regard this at least as a matter currently within the procedural discretion of national courts. The work concludes with sections on public policy and on the Regulation's inter-relationship with other international instruments.

Andrew Dickinson's book is not only timely and likely to be of enduring interest, but is well-informed, practical and readable at the same time as being scholarly in content. It will be a pleasure to consult in the many cases in which reference to it will no doubt be made, and it is a pleasure to commend it now.

Lord Mance
London
1 October 2008

Preface

The Rome II Regulation is the product of almost forty years work by the institutions of the European Community and its Member States. My own interest in the project is of more recent memory. The public hearing organized by the European Commission in January 2003 to consider its preliminary draft proposal for a Regulation on the law applicable to non-contractual obligations was my first close-up view of the Community's legislative processes. I was not alone among those present in finding the experience disenchanting. Suffice it to say that the hearing, and the process leading up to it, cannot be seen as a model for better regulation. That said, the Commission's proposal, published in June 2003, was unquestionably an improvement on the preliminary draft, suggesting that the consultation process had served some useful purpose.

That proposal, with input from the Council and European Parliament, shaped the final version of the Rome II Regulation adopted in July 2007. Despite its flaws, the Regulation is undoubtedly a landmark in private international law, the first EC instrument of general application harmonizing rules of applicable law and the most comprehensive instrument of its kind anywhere in the world. With its younger sibling, the Rome I Regulation (adopted in June 2008), and with the Brussels I Regulation, it forms a substantial part of a Community rulebook that now covers much of the legal territory formerly occupied by national private international law rules in civil and commercial matters. We do not yet have a Community code of private international law, but (for better or worse) the Rome II Regulation has brought the day of reckoning for English private international law ever closer. It may also have dampened, temporarily, the ambitions of those who would prefer to see the Member States applying a unitary law of obligations, in all but name a European Civil Code. For that, many will be grateful.

It was the Regulation's novelty, and the variety of its subject-matter, that first attracted me to the idea of writing a commentary on it. What I failed to grasp or wilfully ignored, however, was that a blank canvas of this kind has the tendency to expand every time one applies a brushstroke to it. With each new insight comes a stark reminder as to the extent of one's ignorance of other matters. As a result, the book, started on the day after the Regulation was published in the Official Journal, is longer and, in places, more tentative than I had first anticipated. Out of necessity, I have drawn heavily on the *travaux préparatoires* and the case law of the ECJ in relation to the Brussels I regime in an attempt to describe the scheme and effect of the Regulation. I hope that the end product will be useful to practising lawyers grappling with its complexity, and will encourage debate among a wider audience.

If I have fallen short in these objectives, it is not through a want of encouragement or assistance from others. In particular, I have valued the support of my colleagues at Clifford Chance in London and elsewhere in Europe, with particular thanks to Simon James, Frédérick Lacroix, Sarah Shearer, Claire Killeen and Maria Dolan (London), Rick Verhagen (Amsterdam), Yves Herinckx and Gilles Teerlinck (Brussels), Felix Schmidt, Fabian von Schlabrendorff and Alexandra Isaakidis (Frankfurt), José Luis de la Calle Sánchez and Jose Antonio Caínzos (Madrid), Elena Calvo and Paola Ciabotti (Milan) and Sandrine Colletier and Peter Rosher (Paris). I would also like to thank Claudia Hahn (Commission), Oliver Parker (UK Ministry of Justice), Françoise Peemans (Belgian Foreign Ministry), Professor Adrian Briggs, Professor Derrick Wyatt, Adam Rushworth and Andrew Scott (University of Oxford), Jacob van de Velden (University of Groningen), Carolina Saf (Stockholm University), Adeline Chong (Singapore Management University), Professor James Fawcett (University of Nottingham) Professor Jonathan Harris and Martin George (University of Birmingham), Giorgio Buono (University of Rome) and Professor Paul Beaumont (University of Aberdeen), all of whom have responded patiently and helpfully to my questions and requests. Publication of this work in time for the Regulation's start date at the beginning of 2009 would not have been possible without the combined skills and efforts of the editorial and production team at OUP, with particular mention to Chris Rycroft, his successor Luke Adams, Kirsty Allen, Sandra Sinden and Fiona Stables. Lord Mance kindly agreed to write the foreword, and I am grateful to him for this.

For all this support, there are others without whom this book would never have seen the light of day. In particular, I would also like to pay tribute to the two men who, above all others, shaped my education in and way of thinking and writing about legal matters. In their inimitable ways, my tutor at St Edmund Hall, Professor Adrian Briggs, and the late Professor Peter Birks inspired me during my time in Oxford and have greatly influenced my approach to the subject-matter of this book. My admiration and gratitude towards each of them has only increased with time, and I can but hope that a little of their clarity of thought and writing-style has rubbed off. If it has not, the responsibility is mine alone.

Finally, my immersion in this project has meant that in the past fifteen months I have not been the easiest person to live with and have frequently been missing in body, mind and spirit from family life. Without the love and support of my wife, Ann Marie, and our children, Jonathan and Nell, and the promise of 'life after Rome II', I could not have reached this point. This book is dedicated to them.

The text takes account, principally, of developments up to 31 July 2008. Summaries of later developments and links to materials and other sites relating to the Regulation will appear on the companion website, <www.romeii.eu>.

Andrew Dickinson
Manningtree
1 October 2008

Contents—Summary

Contents

Table of Cases

Table of Legislation

Table of Legislation

Treaties and Conventions

National Legislation

Austria

Abbreviations

BGB	*Bürgerliches Gesetzbuch* (German Civil Code)
Brussels Convention	Convention on jurisdiction and the enforcement of judgments in civil and commercial matters (Brussels, 27.9.1968 (consolidated version at OJ C27, 1 [26.1.1998]))
Brussels I Regime	The Brussels Convention and the Brussels I Regulation
Brussels I Regulation	Regulation (EC) No 44/2001 on jurisdiction and the recognition and enforcement of judgments in civil and commercial matters (OJ L12, 1 [16.1.2001], as amended)
Brussels II *bis* Regulation	Regulation (EC) No 2201/2003 concerning jurisdiction and the recognition and enforcement of judgments in matrimonial matters and the matters of parental responsibility (OJ L338, 1 [23.12.2003], as amended)
Brussels Salvage Convention	Convention for the unification of certains rules of law relating to assistance and alvage at sea (Brussels, 23.9.1910)
CFR	Common Frame of Reference (see also DFCR in list of Books, Journals and Official Reports below)
Civil Procedure Rules	Civil Procedure Rules 1998 (SI 1998/3132) (England and Wales)
Commission Amended Proposal	European Commission, Amended proposal for a Regulation on the law applicable to non-contractual obligations (Rome II) (COM (2006) 83 final [27.7.2003])
Commission Market Notice	European Commission Notice on the definition of relevant market for the purposes of Community competition law (OJ C372, 5 [9.12.1997])
Commission Proposal	European Commission, Proposal for a Regulation on the law applicable to non-contractual obligations (Rome II) (COM (2003) 427 final [21.2.2006])

Common Position	Common position adopted by the Council with a view to the adoption of a Regulation on the law applicable to non-contractual obligations (OJ C289E, 68 [28.11.2006])
Community Design Regulation	Regulation (EC) No 6/2002 on the Community design (OJ L3, 1 [5.1.2002])
Community Plant Variety Regulation	Regulation (EC) No 2100/94 on Community plant variety rights (OJ L227, 1 [27.9.1994])
Community Trade Mark Regulation	Regulation (EC) No 40/1994 on the Community trade mark (OJ L11, 1 [14.1.1994]), as amended by Regulation (EC) No 422/2004 (OJ L70, 1 [9.3.2004])
COREPER	Committee of Permanent Representatives (EEC/EC)
DG JLS	European Commission Directorate General for Freedom, Security and Justice (*Justice, liberté et sécurité*) (formerly the Directorate General for Justice and Home Affairs (JAI))
DG Markt	European Commission Directorate General for Internal Market and Services
DG SanCo	European Commission Directorate General for Health and Consumer Protection
EAT	Employment Appeals Tribunal (England and Wales)
E-Commerce Directive	Directive (EC) 2000/31 on certain legal aspects of information society services, in particular, electronic commerce in the Internal Market (OJ L178, 1 [17.7.2000])
EC	European Community (1993–)
ECJ	European Court of Justice
ECtHR	European Court of Human Rights
EEC	European Economic Community (1958–1993)
EESC	European Economic and Social Committee
EESC Opinion	Opinion of the EESC on the Commission Proposal (OJ C241, 1 [28.9.2004])

EGBGB	*Einführungsgesetz zum Bürgerlichen Gesetzbuch* (Introductory Act to the Germen Civil Code)
Environmental Liability Directive	Directive (EC) No 2004/35 on environmental liability with regard to the prevention and remedying of environmental damage (OJ L143, 56 [30.4.2004]), as amended by Directive (EC) No 2006/21 (OJ L102, 15 [11.4.2006])
EP	European Parliament
EP 1st Reading Report	1st Reading Report of the EP JURI Committee (rapporteur: Diana Wallis MEP) on the proposal for a Regulation on the law applicable to non-contractual obligations (EP document A6-0211/2005 FINAL [27.6.2005])
EP 1st Reading Position	Position of the European Parliament adopted at 1st reading on 6 July 2005 with a view to the adoption of a Regulation on the law applicable to non-contractual obligations (OJ C157E, 371 [6.7.2006])
EP 2nd Reading Recommendation	Recommendation on 2nd Reading of the EP JURI Committee (rapporteur: Diana Wallis MEP) on the proposal for a Regulation on the law applicable to non-contractual obligations (EP document A6-0481/2006 FINAL [22.12.2006])
EP 2nd Reading Position	Position of the European Parliament adopted at 2nd reading on 18 January 2007 with a view to the adoption of a Regulation on the law applicable to non-contractual obligations (OJ C244E, 194 [18.10.2007])
EP 3rd Reading Report	Report on the joint text approved by the Conciliation Commitee for a regulation on the law applicable to non-contractual obligations (EP document A6-0257/2007 [28.6.2007])
EU	European Union
EWCA	Court of Appeal, England and Wales
EWHC	High Court, England and Wales

First Motor Insurance Directive	Directive (EEC) No 72/166 on the approximation of the laws of Member States relating to insurance against civil liability in respect of the use of motor vehicles, and to the enforcement of the obligation to insure against such liability (OJ L103, 1 [2.5.1972]), as amended
Fourth Motor Insurance Directive	Directive (EC) No 2000/26 on the approximation of the laws of the Member States relating to insurance against civil liability in respect of the use of motor vehicles (OJ L181, 65 [20.7.2000], as amended by Directive (EC) No 2005/14 (OJ L149, 14 [11.6.2005]))
GEDIP	European Group for Private International Law (*Groupe européen de droit international privé*)
Hague Product Liability Convention	Convention on the law applicable to products liability (The Hague, 2 October 1973)
Hague Traffic Accident Convention	Convention on the law applicable to traffic accidents (The Hague, 4 May 1971)
Hague Trusts Convention	Convention on the law applicable to trusts and on their recognition (The Hague, 1 July 1985)
HC Aus	High Court of Australia
HL Report	House of Lords European Union Committee, 'The Rome II Regulation', 8th Report of Session 2003–2004, HL Paper 66
Insolvency Regulation	Regulation (EC) No 1346/2000 on insolvency proceedings (OJ L160, 1 [30.6.2000])
IP Enforcement Directive	Directive (EC) 2004/48 on the enforcement of intellectual property rights (OJ L195, 16 [2.6.2004])
IPR	Intellectual property right
JHA	Justice and Home Affairs
JURI Committee	European Parliament Committee on Legal Affairs and the Internal Market

LIBE Committee	European Parliament Committee on Civil Liberties, Justice and Home Affairs
London Salvage Convention	International convention on salvage (London, 29.4.1989)
Lugano Convention	EC/EFTA Convention on jurisdiction and the enforcement of judgments in civil and commercial matters (Lugano, 16.9.2008 (OJ L319, 9 [25.11.1988]))
PC	Privy Council
PILA (UK)	Private International Law (Miscellaneous Provisions) Act 1995 (1995 c 42) (UK)
Product Liability Directive	Directive (EEC) No 85/374 on the approximation of the laws, regulations and administrative provisions of the Member States concerning liability for defective products (OJ L210, 29 [7.8.1995]), as amended by Directive (EC) No 1999/34
Rome Convention	Convention on the law applicable to contractual obligations, opened for signature in Rome on 19 June 1980 (OJ L266, 1 [9.10.1980])
Rome I Regime	The Rome Convention and the Rome I Regulation
Rome I Regulation	Regulation (EC) No 593/2008 on the law applicable to contractual obligations (Rome I) (OJ L177, 6 [4.7.2008])
Rome II Committee	Council Committee on Civil Law Matters (Rome II)
Rome II Proposal	Commission Proposal (see above)
Rome II Regulation	Regulation (EC) No 864/2007 on the law applicable to non-contractual obligations (Rome II) (OJ L199, 40 [31.7.2007])
TEU	Consolidated, re-numbered version of the Treaty on European Union, as constituted by the Treaty of Lisbon (not yet in force) (Cm 7310, p 3)
TFEU	Consolidated, re-numbered version of the Treaty on the Functioning of the European

	Union, as constituted by the Treaty of Lisbon (not yet in force) (Cm 7310, p 36)
Third Motor Insurance Directive	Directive (EC) No 90/232 on the approximation of the laws of the Member States relating to insurance against civil liability in respect of the use of motor vehicles (OJ L125, 93 [19.5.1990], as amended by Directive (EC) No 2005/14 (OJ L149, 14 [11.6.2005]))
UK	United Kingdom
UKHL	House of Lords, United Kingdom
Unfair Commercial Practices Directive	Directive (EC) No 2005/29 concerning unfair business-to-consumer commercial practices in the internal market (OJ L149, 22 [11.6.2005])
Unfair Terms in Consumer Contracts Directive	Directive (EC) No 93/13 on unfair terms in consumer contracts (OJ L95, 29 [21.4.1993])
WCOD	*Wet Conflictenrecht Onrechtmatige Daad* (2001) (Dutch Act regarding conflict of laws for unlawful acts)

Books, Journals and Official Reports Referred To in Abbreviated Form

AJCL	American Journal of Comparative Law
Arb Int	Arbitration International
Basedow, *Intellectual Property*	J Basedow, J Drexl, A Kur and A Metzger (eds), *Intellectual Property in the Conflict of Laws* (Tübingen: Mohr Siebeck, 2005)
Bellamy & Child	P Roth and V Rose (eds), Bellamy & Child: European Community Law of Competition (6th edn, Oxford: Oxford University Press, 2008)
Briggs & Rees	A Briggs and P Rees, *Civil Jurisdiction and Judgments* (4th edn, London: Informa, 2005)
Brook J Int L	Brook Journal of International Law
BYBIL	British Yearbook of International Law

California L Rev	California Law Review
Common Market L Rev	Common Market Law Review
DFCR	C von Bar and others (eds), *Principles, Definitions and Model Rules of European Private Law: Draft Common Frame of Reference* (2008)
Dicey, Morris & Collins	Sir L Collins and others (eds), *Dicey, Morris & Collins on The Conflict of Laws* (14th edn, London: Thomson Sweet & Maxwell, main work 2006 and 1st supplement 2007[1])
EBLR	European Business Law Review
Edinburgh L Rev	Edinburgh Law Review
Eur L Rev	European Law Review
Eur Rev Priv L	European Review of Private Law
Faull & Nikpay	J Faull and A Nikpay, *The EC Law of Competition* (2nd edn, Oxford: Oxford University Press, 2007)
Georgia J Int Comp L	Georgia Journal of International and Comparative Law
German LJ	German Law Journal
Giuliano & Lagarde Report	Report of Professors M Giuliano and P Lagarde on the 1980 (Rome) Convention on the law applicable to contractual obligations (OJ C282, 1 [31.10.1980])
Giuliano, Lagarde & van Ysselt Report	Report of Professors M Giuliano and P Lagarde and Mr Th van Sasse van Ysselt on the draft convention on the law applicable to contractual and non-contractual obligations (Commission document XIV/408/72 – E (provisional version))
ICLQ	International and Comparative Law Quarterly
Industrial LJ	Industrial Law Journal

---

[1] Unless otherwise stated, references in this book to Dicey, Morris & Collins are to the main work.

Int J L & IT	International Journal of Law and Information Technology
IPRax	*Praxis des Internationalen Privat- und Verfahrensrechts*
J Int Arb	Journal of International Arbitration
J Priv Int L	Journal of Private International Law
Jenard Report	Report of Mr P Jenard on the 1968 (Brussels) Convention on jurisdiction and the enforcement of judgments in civil and commercial matters
JIBLR	Journal of International Banking Law and Regulation
JIPLP	Journal of Intellectual Property Law and Practice
Lasok, Millett & Howard	K P E Lasok, T Millett and A Howard, *Judicial Control in the EU* (Richmond: Richmond Law & Tax, 2004)
LMCLQ	Lloyd's Maritime and Commercial Law Quarterly
Louisiana L Rev	Louisiana Law Review
LQR	Law Quarterly Review
Malatesta, *Unification*	A Malatesta, *The Unification of Choice of Law Rules on Torts and Other Non-Contractual Obligations in Europe* (Padova: CEDAM, 2006)
Neth Int L Rev	Netherlands International Law Review
Restitution L Rev	Restitution Law Review
Sydney L Rev	Sydney Law Review
von Bar, *Common European Law*	C von Bar, *The Common European Law of Torts* (Oxford: Clarendon Press, 2 vols: vol 1 – 1999 reprinted 2003; vol 2 – 2000 reprinted 2005)
Wyatt & Dashwood	D Wyatt and others, *Wyatt & Dashwood's European Union Law* (5th edn, London: Thomson Sweet & Maxwell, 2006)

Part I

Introductory Topics

1

Background

A. INTRODUCTION

1.01 The EC Regulation on the law applicable to non-contractual obligations (Rome II)[1] was adopted on 11 July 2007 and will apply[2] from 11 January 2009.[3] When, in September 1967, the Belgian permanent representative to the EEC, Joseph van der Meulen, wrote to the Commission urging it to consider possible measures to unify conflict of law rules in the (then) six Member States,[4] he can scarcely have foreseen that his letter would trigger a diplomatic and legislative process stretching over thirty years and resulting in a legislative instrument re-writing private international law rules in twenty-six European States.[5] Indeed, the letter emphasized an element of urgency in his proposal, noting the prospect of imminent reforms in some Member States with the consequent risk of crystallizing existing differences. Moreover, while Ambassador van der Meulen and his colleagues might well have anticipated that the co-ordination of rules of applicable law, particularly those for torts and other non-contractual obligations, would not be free from political difficulty,[6] the adoption of the Rome II Regulation undoubtedly has a wider legal and political significance than any multilateral convention of the kind that they contemplated could have had. As the first piece of Community legislation laying down uniform rules of applicable law of a general nature, the Regulation not only laid down a marker for later instruments in this area[7] but also tested the

---

[1] Regulation (EC) No 864/2007, OJ L299, 40 [31.7.2007], reproduced in **Appendix 1** and referred to in the following commentary as the **Regulation** or the **Rome II Regulation**. For a list of other books and materials dealing with the Regulation and the negotiations leading to its adoption, see **Appendix 6**.

[2] For discussion of the temporal application of the Regulation, including its apparent effect in relation to events occurring on or after 20 August 2007 but before 11 January 2009, see **3.315–3.324** below.

[3] Unless otherwise stated or the context otherwise requires, the commentary on the Regulation in the following chapters addresses the foreseeable state of the law on or after 11 January 2009.

[4] **1.45** below.

[5] The Regulation applies to all Member States except Denmark (**3.288** below).

[6] Indeed, in early discussions, the German delegation reported 'certain hesitancies concerning the matter in scientific and legal circles', adding that such differences of opinion need not bias their further deliberations from the outset (Report of Professor M Giuliano, Professor P Lagarde and Mr T van Sasse van Ysselt on the draft convention on the law applicable to contractual and non-contractual obligations (Commission document XIV/408/72 – E (provisional version)) (**Giuliano, Lagarde & van Ysselt Report**), 4).

[7] Not least, Regulation (EC) No 593/2008 on the law applicable to contractual obligations (Rome I) (OJ L177, 6 [4.7.2008]) (**Rome I Regulation**), which followed it and which (for contracts

legislative competence of the Community in the field of civil justice.[8] Thus, in the view of one commentator:[9]

Rome II is a dramatic step in the federalization or 'Europeanization' of private international law in the EU member states, a step that has been aptly characterised as the European conflicts revolution.

From a political viewpoint, the legislative process highlighted tensions **1.02** between the Commission Directorates General as to the relationship between Community law and private international law, as well as between the Community organs participating in the legislative process as to the structure and content of the instrument. The end product marks the ascendancy of the Council and the Commission positions over that of the European Parliament,[10] and is closer to the aspirations of private international law 'traditionalists' than those advocating a 'country of origin'[11] approach. At the same time, consumer protection and other policy objectives of the Community have shaped the final form of the Regulation, most obviously in the formulation of tailored rules of applicable law for specific torts.[12]

The Regulation, and the Rome I Regulation with which it is closely linked,[13] **1.03** will likely also play a significant role in the debate as to whether the substantive law of obligations in the Member States should be harmonized by a Community instrument. On the one hand, as instruments that use the techniques of private international law to promote greater harmony in the Member States' widely diverging[14] systems of civil liability for contractual and non-contractual obligations, the two Regulations might be thought to

concluded after 17 December 2009) will replace the 1980 Rome Convention (OJ L266, 1 [9.10.1980]).

[8] This topic is examined more closely in **Ch 2**.
[9] S C Symeonides, 'Rome II and Tort Conflicts: A Missed Opportunity' (2008) 56 AJCL 173, 174. For a different view, see P J Kozyris, 'Rome II: Tort Conflicts on the Right Track' (2008) 56 AJCL 471, 479–80.
[10] **1.86** and **1.94** below.
[11] For further discussion of the so-called 'country of origin' principle', see **1.59–1.61, 1.85** and **16.04–16.31** below.
[12] In particular, Arts 5 (product liability), 6 (unfair competition), 7 (environment), 8 (intellectual property), discussed in **Chs 5 to 8**. The general *lex loci damni* rule for torts in Art 4.1 (**4.21–4.74** below) is also focused on the position of the victim and, to this end, may be said to serve the objective of protecting consumers.
[13] Text to n 7 above.
[14] For comparative surveys of European tort law, see C van Dam, *European Tort Law* (2004); C von Bar, *The Common European Law of Torts*, 2 volumes (1998, 2000); W van Gerven, *Tort Law (Ius Commune Series)* (2001). For other non-contractual obligations, see D Johnston and R Zimmermann (ed) *Unjustified Enrichment: Key Issues in Comparative Perspective* (2002); C von

apply a (welcome) brake to the ambitions of those who advocate a European civil code.[15] On the other hand, the creation of uniform applicable law rules for torts, unjust enrichment and other civil obligations (and the accompanying interpretative competence of the European Court of Justice[16] and external Community competence[17]) will undoubtedly cast a greater light on the common ground among, and differences between, civil liability rules in the Member States. Furthermore, if the two Regulations do not prove successful in their objective of securing greater predictability in the outcome of litigation before Member State courts, the clamour for a root and branch reform of the law of obligations within the European Community will no doubt increase, with ominous consequences for the independence of the English common law and other Member State legal systems.

1.04   In January 2008, the Study Group for a European Civil Code (chaired by Professor Christian von Bar) published an 'interim outline' version of the 'Draft Common Frame of Reference' (DFCR) containing 'principles, definitions and model rules of European private law'.[18] Despite its unambitious title, it is a prototype European civil code. Books V to VII of the DFCR deal, respectively, with benevolent intervention in another's affairs, noncontractual liability arising out of damage caused to another, and unjustified enrichment. These three topics cover most of the subject matter of the Rome II Regulation and, if adopted, would represent a seismic shift in European private law. Whatever the future may hold, even the staunchest opponents of the civil code movement must admit a grudging respect for the tenacity of its disciples and of Professor von Bar, its high priest.

1.05   While maintaining, at least for the time being, the diversity of European legal culture, the Regulation may influence the future development of Member States' systems of non-contractual liability in a different way. As will be seen, its outlook, particularly the general rule for torts[19] and the special rules for product liability and environmental damage,[20] approaches

---

Bar, *Benevolent Intervention in Another's Affairs* (2005); J Beatson (ed), *Cases, Materials and Texts on Unjustified Enrichment (Ius Commune Series)* (2003).

[15]   In particular, the Study Group for a European Civil Code chaired by Professor Christian von Bar of the University of Osnabrück (<http://www.sgecc.net/> and its rival in the present area of study, the European Group on Tort Law (<http://www.egtl.org/>). Also C von Bar, *Common European Law*, n 14 above, vol 1, Part 4.

[16]   **3.02–3.03** below.

[17]   **16.43–16.46** below.

[18]   C von Bar et al. (eds), *Principles, Definitions and Model Rules of European Private Law: Draft Common Frame of Reference* (2008), available at <http://www.law-net.eu/en_index.htm>.

[19]   Art 4.

[20]   Arts 5 and 7.

the problem from the perspective of the 'victim' and favours the philosophy that tort law, in particular, should take as its primary objective the
distribution of loss among members of society, rather than the regulation
of conduct.[21] As a consequence, it may be supposed that, in cross-border
situations, a Member State's rules will more often be applied to its own
residents (whether by its own courts or by those of another Member State)
as persons suffering, rather than causing, injury. This in turn may focus
political minds on increasing the level of protection afforded to the injured
party. In this respect, the common law systems of the UK and Ireland have
further to travel than their continental cousins. As Professor van Dam
notes:[22]

France and England represent two opposite policy approaches to tort law. Whereas
French tort law primarily focuses on compensation and the principle of distributive justice (strict liability), the predominant focus of English tort law is on conduct
regulation and the principle of corrective justice (fault liability). These differences
are particularly, though not solely, recognizable in the area of accident law and in
the way that the liability of public authorities is dealt with. German tort law takes
a somewhat intermediate position; on the one hand it formally and dogmatically
often applies the tools of conduct regulation (fault liability), but at a policy level it
is strongly inspired by the principle of distributive justice.

Finally, the Regulation has a broader international significance. First, in **1.06**
crystallizing the external competence of the Community (and excluding
that of the participating Member States) to negotiate and conclude treaties
within its area of application.[23] Secondly, as a possible trigger for renewed
efforts to conclude an international treaty on the law applicable to torts
and other non-contractual obligations, most obviously under the auspices
of the Hague Conference on private international law. The issues of jurisdiction and applicable law with respect to torts were suggested as items to
be placed on the agenda of the Hague Conference in the late 1960s, an
option that was investigated by the Permanent Bureau and the Special
Commission.[24] At that time the Special Commission concluded that
'the field of torts was too wide and heterogeneous to be dealt with in one
single convention', and recommended that the Conference focus, first,

[21] Commission Proposal for the Rome II Regulation (**1.69–1.70** below), 12.
[22] C van Dam, n 14 above, 8.
[23] Opinion 01/03 on the *Competence of the Community to conclude the new Lugano Convention on jurisdiction and the recognition of judgments in civil and commercial matters* [2006] ECR I-1145, discussed at **16.43** below.
[24] See the summary at Report of Eric W Essén on the 1971 (Hague) Convention on the Law Applicable to Traffic Accidents, 1 (reproduced at <http://www.hcch.net/upload/expl19e.pdf>).

on traffic accidents[25] and, subsequently, on product liability.[26] Since then, the Hague Conference has not (at least so far as the author is aware) given further consideration to the possibility of a convention dealing with torts or non-contractual obligations generally, preferring to focus its efforts on specific areas of liability.[27]

1.07 This book consists of a commentary on the Rome II Regulation, and the process that led to its adoption. It is divided into four Parts. The first Part considers certain introductory topics, including (in this chapter) an overview of the pre-existing rules of applicable law in selected Member States and an account of the legislative history of the Regulation, (in Chapter 2) analysis of the treaty basis for the Regulation, and (in Chapter 3) discussion of the approach to interpretation, the scope of the Regulation, and certain key concepts and terms. The second Part considers the rules of applicable law for torts and delicts, including the special rules for product liability, competition law, violations of the environment, intellectual property, and industrial action. The third Part considers the rules of applicable law for other non-contractual obligations (unjust enrichment, *negotiorum gestio*, and *culpa in contrahendo*). The final Part considers topics common to all non-contractual obligations falling within the scope of the Regulation, including party choice of law, scope of the law applicable under the Regulation, public policy and mandatory rules, and the Regulation's relationship with EC and international law.

B. THE PRE-REGULATION POSITION: A COMPARATIVE OVERVIEW

1.08 It cannot be doubted that when the Regulation was adopted the Member States of the European Community had reached widely differing solutions to the question as to which country's rules concerning non-contractual

---

[25] Leading to the Convention on the Law Applicable to Traffic Accidents (4 May 1971, reproduced at <http://www.hcch.net/index_en.php?act=conventions.text&cid=81>) (the **Hague Traffic Accidents Convention**) (**4.114–4.120**).

[26] Leading to the Convention on the Law Applicable to Products Liability (2 October 1973, reproduced at <http://www.hcch.net/index_en.php?act=conventions.text&cid=84>) (the **Hague Products Liability Convention**) (**5.49–5.53**).

[27] Most recently, cross-border environmental damage (C Bernasconi, 'Civil liability resulting from transfrontier environmental damage: a case for the Hague Conference?' Preliminary document No 8 of May 2000, available at <http://www.hcch.net/upload/wop/gen_pd8e.pdf>) and unfair competition (Permanent Bureau of the Hague Conference, 'Note on Conflicts of Laws on the Question of Unfair Competition', Preliminary Document No 5 of April 2005, available at <http://www.hcch.net/upload/wop/gen_pd5c.pdf>).

liability should be applied by their courts in cross-border situations. The following (partial) survey is offered by way of illustration of this point, and should not be taken as a comprehensive statement of the law in force in each Member State. The law is described as it stood at the time of writing, prior to the date of application of the Regulation. The rules described below will be largely superseded by those in the Regulation, but will continue to apply to cases falling outside the Regulation's scope.[28]

UNITED KINGDOM[29]

The pre-Regulation rules of applicable law for torts or (in Scotland) delicts[30] are principally contained in the Private International Law (Miscellaneous Provisions) Act 1995. This legislation, which entered into force on 1 May 1996, largely replaced[31] the formerly applicable common law rule of 'double actionability' under which, in order to be actionable in the UK, conduct abroad[32] must generally both (a) have constituted a tort under the law of the forum, and (b) have been civilly actionable (although not necessarily as a tort) according to the place where, in substance, the tort occurred.[33] In later years, flexibility was introduced into this rule by an exception which (on the view that gained general acceptance) permitted either or both limbs to be displaced in relation to a particular issue by the law of the country which had the most significant relationship with the occurrence and the parties with respect to that issue.[34]

1.09

---

[28] For other surveys of the Member States' former rules, see T Kadner Graziano, *La responsabilité délictuelle en droit international privé européen* (2004); K Kreuzer in A Malatesta (ed), *The Unification of Choice of Law Rules on Torts and Other Non-Contractual Obligations in Europe* (2006), 46–9 and the (then 15) Member States' responses to the questionnaire circulated by the Commission in 1998 (Council document 12544/98 [11.11.1998]).

[29] Comprising, for these purposes, the separate legal systems of (1) England and Wales, (2) Scotland, and (3) Northern Ireland.

[30] Characterization of an issue as an issue relating to tort or delict being a matter for the law of the forum: Private International Law (Miscellaneous Provisions) Act 1995 (**PILA (UK)**), s 9(2)).

[31] Ibid, s 10. Defamation claims were excluded from the scope of PILA (UK) and the double actionability rule continues to apply to such claims (s 13) (**3.222–3.224** below).

[32] For torts committed in the UK, the practice of the English courts had been to apply English law (*Szalatnay-Stacho v Fink* [1947] KB 1 (EWCA)). The PILA (UK) probably also applies to these torts, although its drafting in this regard is highly unsatisfactory (see s 9(6) and the commentary in Sir L Collins et al. (eds), *Dicey, Morris & Collins: The Conflict of Laws* (14th edn, 2006) (**Dicey, Morris & Collins**), para 35-020).

[33] *Boys v Chaplin* [1971] AC 356 (UKHL); L Collins et al. (eds), *Dicey & Morris on The Conflict of Laws* (12th edn, 1993), Rule 203(1) and commentary.

[34] *Red Sea Insurance Co Ltd v Bouygues SA* [1995] 1 AC 190 (PC). For the position in Scotland, see E Crawford and J Carruthers, *International Private Law in Scotland* (2nd edn, 2006), para 16-05.

1.10   In contrast, the general rule under section 11 of the PILA (UK), the law generally applicable to issues relating to tort or delict is the (domestic[35]) law of the country in which the events constituting the tort or delict occur.[36] Where elements of those events occur in different countries, different sub-rules identify the applicable law as follows: (a) in cases of personal injury, the law of the country where an individual was when he sustained injury, (b) in cases of property damage, the law of the country where the property was when it was damaged, and (c) in other cases, the law of the country in which the most significant element or elements, weighed together,[37] of those events constituting the tort or delict occurred.[38] Under section 12 the general rule may be displaced with respect to the case as a whole or a particular issue if it appears from a comparison of the significance of (a) the factors that connect the tort or delict with the country whose law would apply under the general rule, and (b) the factors that connect the tort or delict with another country, that it is substantially more appropriate for the law of the latter country to determine the case or that issue.[39] The PILA (UK) contains no provision allowing party choice of law, although a choice of law provision in a contract related to the tort or delict may be taken into account in applying the rule of displacement in s 12.[40]

1.11   A public policy exception applies to the application of foreign law under the rules outlined above.[41] Further, matters of evidence and procedure remain governed (as at common law) by the law of the forum.[42] Most controversially, the law of the forum has been held to apply to the quantification of damages.[43]

1.12   Non-contractual obligations other than torts/delicts remain subject to judge made rules, which were still developing at the time of adoption of the Regulation. For obligations based on unjust enrichment, the most recent edition of *Dicey, Morris & Collins: The Conflict of Laws*, the leading

---

[35]   Any possibility of *renvoi* is excluded by PILA (UK), s 9(6).

[36]   Ibid, s 11(1).

[37]   *Morin v Bonhams & Brooks Ltd* [2004] EWCA Civ 1802; [2004] 1 Lloyd's Rep 702, [16] (Mance LJ, EWCA).

[38]   PILA (UK), s 11(2).

[39]   Ibid, s 12(1). A (non-exhaustive) list of the factors that may be taken into account is set out in s 12(2).

[40]   *Morin v Bonhams & Brooks Ltd*, n 37 above, [23]; *Trafigura Beheer BV v Kookmin Bank Co* [2006] EWHC 1450 (Comm); [2006] 2 Lloyd's Rep 455 (Aikens J, EWHC).

[41]   Ibid, s 14(3)(a)(i).

[42]   Ibid, s 14(3)(b).

[43]   *Harding v Wealands* [2006] UKHL 32; [2007] 2 AC 1 (**14.19** below). In contrast, identification of the recoverable heads of damage is a matter for the *lex causae* (*Boys v Chaplin*, n 33 above).

English work on the conflict of the laws, summarizes the current state of the case law in the following way:[44]

(1) The obligation to restore the benefit of an enrichment obtained at another person's expense is governed by the proper law of the obligation.
(2) The proper law of the obligation is (*semble*) determined as follows:
    (a) If the obligation arises in connection with a contract, its proper law is the law applicable to the contract;
    (b) If it arises in connection with a transaction concerning an immovable (land), its proper law is the law of the country where the immovable is situated (*lex situs*);
    (c) If it arises in any other circumstances, its proper law is the law of the country where the enrichment occurs.

As indicated by the tentative nature of the second paragraph, it has not always been possible for practitioners to predict with confidence how the principle of the proper law of the obligation would be applied to the facts of an individual case. In 2005, Sir Lawrence Collins, the senior editor of the work referred to above, while acting in a judicial capacity, described this as 'an uncertain and developing area of the law' and the place of enrichment connecting factor (sub-para (c) above) as a 'tentative formulation' of the proper law approach 'where the parties have no prior connection'.[45]   **1.13**

Finally, beyond the province of the law of torts and (common law) unjust enrichment, English law recognizes a wide variety of 'equitable obligations', being obligations of a kind formerly recognized by the Courts of Equity.[46] It was formerly suggested that, putting to one side trust obligations to which the 1985 Hague Convention on the law applicable to trusts and on their recognition and the UK legislation implementing that Convention   **1.14**

---

[44] Dicey, Morris & Collins, Rule 230. For the position in Scotland, see E Crawford and J Carruthers, n 35 above, para 16-31; *Baring Bros & Co v Cunninghame DC*, 1996 GWD 25-1405; Restitution L Rev §190 (Court of Session) (noted J Bird [1997] LMCLQ 182; R Stevens (1997) 113 LQR 249; A Dickinson [1997] Restitution L Rev 66). For commentaries on the pre-existing rules of applicable law for unjust enrichment claims under English law, see e.g. J Bird and R Stevens, ch 3 and 5 in F Rose (ed), *Restitution and the Conflict of Laws* (1995); G Panagopoulos, *Restitution in Private International Law* (2000); A Burrows, *The Law of Restitution* (2nd edn, 2002), 608–25; A Briggs, 'The conflict of laws and restitutionary issues: misappropriated and misapplied assets and the conflict of laws', paper presented at the conference on Restitution in Commercial Law held at the Faculty of Law, University of New South Wales from 3–5 August 2007.

[45] *Barros Mattos Junior v Macdaniels Ltd* [2005] EWHC 1323 (Ch); [2005] ILPr 630, [117], [119].

[46] The Courts of Equity and Common Law were combined as a result of the Judicature Acts 1873–1875, but the law applied by those courts survived subject to the proviso that rules of equity should prevail in case of conflict (a rule now contained in Supreme Court Act 1981, s 49).

applies,[47] only the forum's rules of equity could apply to equitable obligations, even if they arose from conduct abroad.[48] The modern trend, however,[49] favours the rejection of a separate category of 'equitable obligations'
in private international law and instead seeks to allocate its subject matter
between other, well-recognized categories (contract,[50] tort, trusts, restitution,[51] company law[52]).

BELGIUM

1.15   By Art 99§1 of the Belgian Code of Private International Law,[53] obligations
resulting from a harmful act (*fait dommageable*) are governed (a) by the law
of the State[54] of common habitual residence of the person liable and the
injured person at the time that the act occurs, (b) otherwise, by the law of
the State in which both the fact giving rise to damage and the damage
itself occurred in their entirety or are likely to occur, and (c) in all other
cases, by the law of the State to which the relevant obligation has its closest connection. Specific rules are contained in Art 99§2 for cases of defamation or violation of privacy or personality rights,[55] unfair competition,[56]

---

[47] Recognition of Trusts Act 1987; Dicey, Morris & Collins, ch 29. The relationship between
the Rome II Regulation, the Hague Trusts Convention, and the 1987 Act is considered at
3.201–3.207 below.

[48] See the authorities cited by Dicey, Morris & Collins, para 34-033, footnote 11.

[49] T M Yeo, *Choice of Law for Equitable Doctrines* (2004). Also Dicey, Morris & Collins, paras
34-033 to 34-050.

[50] e.g. *Rickshaw Investments Ltd v Baron von Uexkull* [2007] 1 SLR 377 (Singapore Court of
Appeal) (breach of fiduciary duty).

[51] e.g. *Douglas v Hello! Ltd (No 3)* [2005] EWCA Civ 595; [2006] QB 125, [97] (EWCA) (a
questionable characterization of a claim for breach of confidence).

[52] e.g. *Base Metal Trading Ltd v Shamurin* [2004] EWCA Civ 1316; [2005] 1 WLR 1157, [56]–
[57] (Tuckey LJ), [65]–[77] (Arden LJ) (equitable duty of company director; noted A Dickinson
(2005) 121 LQR 374 and discussed at **3.162–3.169** below).

[53] *Loi du 16 Juillet 2004 portant le Code de droit international privé*. An English translation is
available at <http://www.ipr.be/data/B.WbIPR[EN].pdf>. Also F Rigaux and M Fallon,
Droit International Privé (2005), 917–63 and, more generally, A Fiorini, 'The Codification of
Private International Law: The Belgian Experience' (2005) 54 ICLQ 499; P Wautelet, '*Le nou-
veau droit international privé belge*' (2005) *Droit bancaire et financier* 111.

[54] See Art 17 relating to States with more than one legal system.

[55] Art 99§2, sub-rule 1, apparently giving a choice between the law of the State in which
the act leading to the damage and the law of the State in which the damage occurred or is
likely to occur, unless (in the latter case) the person liable proves that he could not have
foreseen the damage would occur in that State.

[56] Ibid, sub-rule 2, designating the law of the State in which the damage occurred or is
likely to occur.

pollution of the environment,[57] product liability,[58] and road traffic accidents.[59] These general and specific rules are, however displaced in favour of the law applicable to an existing legal relationship between the parties which is closely connected to the obligation deriving from a harmful act.[60] Further, the parties may, after the dispute has arisen, expressly choose the law applicable to such obligation.[61] By Art 103 the law applicable to an obligation resulting from a harmful act extends (among other matters) not only to the existence and nature of the damage which is taken into account for compensation but also to the specific rules regarding the method and extent of compensation (i.e. including quantification).

Quasi-contractual obligations are governed by the law with which they **1.16** have their closest connection, generally presumed to be the law of the State in which (having regard to existing and envisaged relations between the parties) the fact resulting in the obligations occurred.[62] Again, the parties may expressly choose the applicable law after the dispute has arisen.[63]

The Code gives overriding effect to Belgian public policy and mandatory **1.17** rules,[64] as well as facilitating the discretionary application of the public policy and internationally mandatory rules[65] of a third State with which the situation has a close connection.[66] The doctrine of *renvoi* is expressly excluded.[67]

FRANCE

There is no specific provision in the French Civil Code concerning the law **1.18** applicable to non-contractual obligations.[68] Case law points towards the

---

[57] Ibid, sub-rule 3, designating (for damage to assets or persons only) the law of the State in which the damage occurred or is likely to occur.

[58] Ibid, sub-rule 4, designating the law of the State in which the injured person has his habitual residence at the time that the damage occurs.

[59] Ibid, sub-rule 5, deferring to the rules of applicable law contained in the Hague Traffic Accidents Convention.

[60] Ibid, Art 100.

[61] Ibid, Art 101. Such choice is, in any event, without prejudice to the Hague Traffic Accidents Convention and the rights of third parties.

[62] Ibid, Art 104§1. For obligations resulting from the payment of someone else's debt, the (rebuttable) presumption lies in favour of the law governing the debt.

[63] Ibid, Art 104§2.

[64] Ibid, Arts 20, first para and 21.

[65] i.e. rules which apply irrespective of the law otherwise applicable.

[66] Ibid, Art 20, second para.

[67] Ibid, Art 16.

[68] *Code Civil* (as amended). Art 3, first sentence (within the preliminary section dealing with the application of statutes) provides 'Statutes relating to public policy and safety are binding on all those living on the territory'.

application of the law of the place of delict,[69] which in practice may lead to the application of either the country where the event triggering the damage occurred (*'fait générateur du dommage'*) or the law of the country where the damage crystallized (*'lieu de réalisation du dommage'*),[70] the choice between these two possible conclusions depending on which of the two laws is seen to have the closest connection to the situation.[71] France is a party to the Hague Traffic Accidents and Products Liability Conventions[72] and, for situations falling within their scope, the rules of the relevant Convention apply instead.[73]

1.19 For quasi-contractual obligations, French case law supports the application of the law of the place of the fact which gave rise to them.[74]

1.20 The application of a law other than French law may be displaced for reasons of public policy (*ordre public international*) or on the ground of incompatibility with overriding *lois de police*, being rules considered necessary for safeguarding the political, social, or economic organization of the country, whether France or (more rarely) a third country.

<h2 style="text-align:center">G<small>ERMANY</small>[75]</h2>

1.21 By Art 40(1) of the Introductory Act to the German Civil Code,[76] claims arising from delict (*'unerlaubter Handlung'*) are subject to the law of the State where the person liable acted (*'in dem der Ersatzpflichtige gehandelt hat'*). Nevertheless, the injured person may elect that the law of the State

---

[69] *Cour de cassation, Ch civ*, 25 May 1948 (*Lautour*).

[70] *Cour de cassation, 1ère Ch civ*, 14 January 1997 (*Gordon and Breach Science Publishers*).

[71] *Cour de cassation, 1ère Ch civ*, 11 May 1999 (*Société Mobil North Sea*).

[72] nn 25–26 above.

[73] According to a decision of the *Cour de cassation, 1ère Ch civ*, 7 March 2000 (*Torfwerke*), the Product Liability Convention applies whether the obligation is properly characterized as contractual or non-contractual.

[74] *Cour de cassation, 1ère Ch civ*, 1 June 1976 (*Luccantoni*).

[75] Also C W Fröhlich, *The Private International Law of Non-Contractual Obligations According to the Rome II Regulation* (2008).

[76] *Einführungsgesetz zum Bürgerlichen Gezetzbuch* (EGBGB), as amended. The applicable law regime for non-contractual obligations was substantially amended in 1999. Previously, both the law of the State where the person liable acted (*Rechts des Handlungsorts*) and the law of the State where the results of that action came into effect (*Recht des Erfolgsorts*) were equally applicable. According to this principle, known as the *Günstigkeitsprinzip*, the injured person had the opportunity to choose between two legal regimes and decide which was more convenient. If he did not make a choice, it was up to the court to decide which law should apply (*Bundesgerichtshof 23.6.1964 NJW 1964*, p 2012). For comment on the 1999 amendments to the EGBGB, see M Reimann 'Codifying Torts Conflicts: The 1999 German Legislation in Comparative Perspective' (1999) 60 Louisiana L Rev 1297; P Hay, 'From Rule-Orientation to

where the result of that action came into effect ('*in dem der Erfolg einge-treten ist*') should be applied instead.[77] If, however, the person liable and the injured person had their usual residence (or, in the case of legal persons, head office or relevant branch) in the same State, the general rules in Art 40(1) are displaced in favour of the law of that State.[78] A further rule of displacement applies if a substantially closer connection exists to the law of another State,[79] in particular one arising from a special legal or factual relation between the parties that is connected with the obligation.[80] German courts have invoked this rule of displacement, for example, in applying the law of the affected market to competition law claims, and the law of the place where industrial action takes place to claims that are directly connected with that action.[81] In any event, delict claims subject to the law of another State are unenforceable if they (a) reach substantially beyond that which is necessary to provide reasonable compensation for the injured person, (b) manifestly serve purposes other than providing such compensation, or (c) contradict liability regulations of an international treaty binding on Germany.[82]

By EGBGB Art 38, claims for unjust enrichment resulting from performance with respect to a legal relationship ('*Leistungskondiktion*') are generally governed by the law applicable to that relationship.[83] Claims for unjust enrichment caused by interference in a protected interest ('*Eingriffskondiktion*') are generally governed by the law of the State where the interference occurred.[84] In other cases, unjust enrichment claims are governed by the law of the State where the enrichment occurred.[85] By Art 39, (a) statutory claims arising from the management of another's business without mandate are subject to the law of the State where the business was carried out,[86] and (b) claims arising from the discharge of

1.22

"Approach" in German Conflicts Law: the Effect of the 1986 and 1999 Codifications' (1999) 47 AJCL 633; W Kennett (2000) 49 ICLQ 502.

[77] EGBGB, Art 40(1), second sentence. The election (*Bestimmungsrecht*) must be made before the end of the first hearing (German Civil Procedure Code (*Zivilprozessordnung* or *ZPO*), §275) or written pre-trial proceeding (ZPO, § 276) in the court of first instance. Art 40(1) applies analogously to claims arising from the adverse effects of emissions from real estate (Art 44).

[78] Ibid, Art 40(2).
[79] Ibid, Art 41(1).
[80] Ibid, Art 41(2)(a).
[81] C W Fröhlich, n 75 above, 82–3, 95.
[82] Ibid, Art 40(3).
[83] Ibid, Art 38(1).
[84] Ibid, Art 38(2).
[85] Ibid, Art 38(3).
[86] Ibid, Art 39(1).

another's obligation are subject to the law applicable to that obligation.[87] The law applicable under these rules may also be displaced if there exists a substantially closer connection to the law of another State, including from a special legal or factual relation or (for cases other than unjust enrichment by performance rendered) from the common usual residence of the parties at the time of the legally relevant event.[88]

1.23 For all these non-contractual obligations, the parties may (pursuant to Art 42) choose the law governing the non-contractual obligation, but only after the event giving rise to the obligation has occurred.[89]

1.24 A foreign rule will not be applied under these provisions if it is manifestly inconsistent with the fundamental principles of German law, particularly fundamental (constitutional) rights (*Grundrechte*).[90] Unusually,[91] the EGBGB contains a general *renvoi* provision whereby, in case of referral to the law of another State (other than by choice of the parties), the private international law rules of that State shall be applied, unless this contradicts the meaning of the referral.[92] If that State's rules of applicable law refer back to German law, the substantive rules of German law will apply, breaking the chain of referrals and avoiding an inescapable circularity (*circulus inextricabilis*). If, however, the applicable law is determined by reference to a party choice of law (as in Art 42 and, indirectly, Arts 38(1) and 39(2)), there is no *renvoi*, the reference being to the material provisions of the relevant legal system exclusive of its rules of private international law.[93]

ITALY

1.25 By Art 62(1) of the Italian Law No 218/1995 concerning the reform of the Italian system of private international law,[94] liability for unlawful acts[95] is governed by the law of the State in which the 'event' ('*evento*') occurred. Nevertheless, the injured person may demand application of the law of

---

[87] Ibid, Art 39(2).

[88] Ibid, Art 41.

[89] Ibid, Art 42.

[90] Ibid, Art 6.

[91] Compare, for example, s 9(6) of the PILA (UK) and Art 16 of the Belgian Code of Private International Law as well as Art 24 of the Rome II Regulation (**3.41–3.43** below).

[92] Ibid, Art 4(1).

[93] Ibid, Arts 3(1) and 4(2).

[94] Law of 31 May 1995, no 218 '*Riforma del sistema italiano di diritto internazionale privato*'. An English translation is contained in M Beltramo, *The Italian Civil Code and Complementary Legislation* (1991, looseleaf), Appendix X.

[95] Italian Civil Code (Codice Civile), Arts 2043ff.

the State where 'the fact which caused the damage' (*'il fatto che ha causato il danno'*) occurred. This language suggests that the former connecting factor is, more naturally, to be equated with the place where the effects of the injurious act are suffered by the injured person.[96] By Art 62(2), however, if the unlawful act only involves persons who are citizens of the same State and are habitually resident there, the law of that State shall apply instead. Special rules apply to non-contractual liability for damages caused by a product[97] and to fundamental rights of the person.[98]

By Art 61 of the 1995 Law, obligations deriving from management of another's affairs[99] (*negotiorum gestio*), unjust enrichment, undue payments, and other legal obligations not regulated by a specific rule of applicable law are governed by the law of the State where 'the fact from which the obligation derives' (*'il fatto da cui deriva l'obbligazione'*) occurred. **1.26**

Art 13 of the 1995 Law concerns questions of *renvoi*, but does not apply to non-contractual obligations. By Art 16, foreign law must not be applied if its effects are contrary to public policy.[100] Art 17 gives effect to overriding mandatory provisions of Italian law. **1.27**

Netherlands

By Art 3(1) of the Dutch Act regarding conflict of laws for unlawful acts[101] obligations arising from an unlawful act are governed by the law of the State on whose territory[102] the act took place. Nevertheless, by Art 3(2), in cases of harmful effects to persons, things, or the natural environment in **1.28**

---

[96] See the response of the Italian delegation to the questionnaire circulated by the Commission in 1998 (Council document 12544/98 [11.11.1998], 6, 14).

[97] Law 218/1995, Art 63 giving a choice to the injured person between the place of domicile or management of the manufacturer or the place of purchase of the product, unless the manufacturer proves that the product was introduced into the market at that place without his consent.

[98] Ibid, Art 24, designating the national law of the person concerned to govern the existence and content of the fundamental rights of the person (including, e.g., privacy and reputation), the legal consequences of infringement being governed by the law applicable under Art 62.

[99] Italian Civil Code, Arts 2028ff.

[100] In such case, the foreign law in question will (if possible) be applied with reference to other criteria applicable to the same situation, failing which Italian law will apply.

[101] *Wet Conflictenrecht Onrechtmatige Daad* (2001) (**WCOD**). P Vlas, 'Dutch Private International Law: The 2001 Act Regarding Conflict of Laws on Torts' (2003) Netherlands Int L Rev 221. An English translation is available at <http://www.nblonline.com/nbl/nbl. exe?location=none&language=en>.

[102] 'Territory' is widely defined by WCOD, Art 1 to include (a) installations on the continental shelf over which a State exercises sovereign rights, and (b) vessels and aircraft registered by that State or, in default or registration, belonging to a national of that State.

another country, the law of that other country shall apply instead, unless the wrongdoer could not reasonably foresee the effect in that territory. According to further rules of displacement, if the wrongdoer and victim have their ordinary residence or establishment in the same State, the law of that State shall apply instead,[103] while if the unlawful act is closely connected with a juridical relationship between wrongdoer and victim the law applicable to that relationship shall apply.[104] A special rule applies to unfair competition designating the law of the State on whose territory competitive relations were affected.[105] In all cases, the parties may instead, expressly or otherwise with sufficient clarity, choose the law applicable to obligations resulting from unlawful acts.[106] By Art 7, the scope of the applicable law extends (among other matters) not only to the existence and nature of damage qualifying for compensation but also to the extent of the damage and the manner of its compensation (including, it would appear, matters of quantification). By Art 8, the rules just described do not prevent account being taken of traffic and safety rules existing at the place of the unlawful act, or of other comparable rules intended to protect persons or things.

1.29 The Netherlands is a party to the Hague Traffic Accidents and Products Liability Conventions[107] and, for situations falling within their scope, the rules of the relevant Convention will apply instead.[108]

1.30 Outside situations regulated by the Rome Convention,[109] the law governing unjust enrichment claims under Dutch law remains unsettled, although the law of the State where the enrichment occurred is often reverted to in decisions of the lower courts and legal writing.[110] In the absence of party choice and in the absence of a pre-existing legal relationship between the parties, claims based on management of another's affairs (*negotiorum gestio*) are governed by the law where the manager acted, or—when the manager has acted in several countries—by the law with which the *negotiorum gestio* is most closely connected.[111] If there is a pre-existing relationship between the parties, the law applicable to that relationship applies.

---

[103] WCOD, Art 3(3).

[104] Ibid, Art 5.

[105] Ibid, Art 4(1). By Art 4(2) this rule does not apply to acts aimed at a single competitor. Art 4(1) may also be displaced by the law governing the relationship of the wrongdoer and victim in accordance with Art 5.

[106] Ibid, Art 6.

[107] nn **25–26** above.

[108] WCOD, Art 2(1).

[109] **3.108–3.109** below.

[110] For more detailed analysis, see H Verhagen, 'Ongerechtvaardigde verrijking' in S Kortmann et al. (ed), *Op recht (liber amicorum Struycken)* (1996), 367–401.

[111] HR 23 February 1996, NJ 1997, 276 (*Total Liban/Blue Aegean Shipowners*).

Under Dutch law, public policy is not used to exclude objectionable for- **1.31**
eign laws from being applied. It may, however, serve as a means to
prevent enforcement where the outcome of the application of foreign law
is unacceptable.[112]

SPAIN

By Art 10, para 9 of the Spanish Civil Code,[113] 'non-contractual obliga- **1.32**
tions' are governed by the law of the place where the event from which
they arise occurred, without distinguishing obligations arising in tort or
delict from other obligations. By way of exception, however, (a) management of another's affairs (*negotiorum gestio*) shall be governed by the law
of the place where the manager undertakes the principal activity, and
(b) in unjust enrichment cases (including the recovery of payments not
due[114]), the law by virtue of which the transfer of patrimonial value in
favour of the enriched person took place shall apply. Further, although
Art 10, para 9 is expressed in broad terms, it does not apply to every other
non-contractual obligation. It has, for example, been doubted whether the
rule applies to obligations concerning the fundamental rights of privacy
and freedom of expression.[115] In this connection, it has been noted that:[116]

[S]uch rigid and undifferentiated legislation calls for a response adapted to the
special nature of the case, either by way of interpretation or even through
development of the law by the courts.

Spain is a party to the Hague Traffic Accidents and Products Liability **1.33**
Conventions[117] and, for situations falling within their scope, the rules of
the relevant Convention will apply instead.

Under Art 12.3 of the Civil Code, foreign law shall not be applied when it **1.34**
is contrary to public order. Further, under Art 12.4, the use of a conflicts

---

[112] See the response of the Dutch delegation to the questionnaire circulated by the
Commission in 1998 (Council document 12544/98 [11.11.1998], 26).

[113] *Código Civil español* of 24 June 1889 (as amended). For an English translation, see
J Romanach, *Civil Code of Spain* (1994). Also A Calvo Caravaca, *Derecho Internacional Privado*
(2004), vol I, 693 and following; M Amores Canradi, *Comentario del codigo civil* (1993),
127–30.

[114] See the response of the Spanish delegation to the questionnaire circulated by the
Commission in 1998 (Council document 12544/98 [11.11.1998], 72).

[115] Ibid, 49. Note also the comments (ibid, 17 and 79) concerning the trend in the case law
of the Supreme Court towards the application of (substantive) rules of contractual liability to
situations of non-contractual liability.

[116] Ibid, 3.

[117] nn **25–26** above.

rule for the purpose of evading a Spanish imperative law shall be considered a fraud of the law (*fraude de ley*). Finally, the Spanish Law on Unfair Competition[118] applies to all acts of unfair competition that produce or may produce substantial effects on the Spanish market, giving it overriding effect in such cases.

SWEDEN

1.35 The law applicable to tortious acts in Sweden is regulated by case law, designating the law of the place of the tort, without exception.[119] The identification of the applicable law gives rise to greater difficulty, however, if the wrongful acts have occurred in more than one country or have produced effects in one or more other countries. Various solutions have been suggested by legal writers.[120] In the situation where an act in one country causes damage in another, the leading case suggests that the place of the act is the most important connecting factor.[121]

1.36 Sweden is not a party to the Hague Products Liability Convention or the Hague Traffic Accidents Convention, but is (together with Denmark and Finland, among Member States, and Norway) a party to the Nordic Environmental Protection Convention.[122] Art 3 of that Convention appears to provide for sole application of the law of the place of the activity giving rise to actual or potential damage, although in practice it appears that the claimant is given the choice between that law and the law of the forum, being the place in which he is affected by that activity.[123] By virtue of the participation of two states not bound by the Rome II Regulation, (Denmark and Norway), the Convention will continue to apply to matters within its scope, in accordance with Art 28(1) of the Regulation.

1.37 The division of non-contractual obligations into torts/delicts, on the one hand, and other non-contractual obligations, on the other is not reflected in Swedish law.[124] While unjust enrichment, *negotiorum gestio*, and *culpa in*

---

[118] *Ley 3/1991 de Competencia Desleal*, Art 4.

[119] See, in particular, NJA 1933 s 364; NJA 1969 s 163 (both Supreme Court of Sweden).

[120] See the response of the Swedish delegation to the questionnaire circulated by the Commission in 1998 (Council document 12544/98 [11.11.1998], 7, 10).

[121] The 1969 decision of the Supreme Court of Sweden referred to above (the so-called 'Cronsioe case').

[122] Concluded at Stockholm, 19 February 1974. An English translation of the Convention is available at <http://sedac.ciesin.org/entri/texts/acrc/Nordic.txt.html>.

[123] Bogdan, *Svensk internationell privat- och processrätt*, (6th edn, 2004), 280.

[124] See the comments of the Swedish delegation in Council document 9009/04 ADD 8 [18.5.2004], 15.

contrahendo are all recognized bases of legal obligations,[125] no clearly established rules of applicable law has been established by case law for such cases,[126] although relationships bearing a resemblance to contracts will likely be characterized as such for the purposes of determining their applicable law.

Application of foreign law to non-contractual obligations is objectionable **1.38** on public policy grounds.[127] Further, in the case of traffic accidents, Swedish citizens and persons habitually resident in Sweden injured in an accident involving a car registered in Sweden may always claim compensation under the Swedish system, which imposes strict liability and gives an independent right to compensation from the insurer of the Swedish vehicle.[128]

Switzerland

Although not a Member State of the European Community, the Swiss **1.39** Federal Code of Private International Law[129] provides an interesting comparative model as, at least until the adoption of the Belgian Code[130] in 2004, it provided the most comprehensive model for a possible European private international law code and may have influenced the formulation of the Rome II Proposal, at least in terms of the matters which it addresses. The rules described below are unaffected by the Rome II Regulation.

Under the Swiss Federal Code, claims founded on an unlawful act (*acte* **1.40** *illicite*) are governed (a) by the law of the State in which the person responsible and injured party have their common habitual residence,[131] and (b) otherwise, by the law of the State in which the unlawful act was committed unless the person responsible should have foreseen that injury would result in another State, in which case the law of the State in which injury occurred shall apply instead.[132] If, however, the wrongful act violates an existing relationship between the person responsible and the injured

---

[125] Ibid.
[126] Council document 12544/98, 31.
[127] Ibid, 27.
[128] Council document SN 2852/04 ADD 5 [9.9.2004], 3–4.
[129] *Loi fédérale sur le droit international privé du 18 décembre 1987* (as amended). An English translation is available at <http://www.umbricht.ch/pdf/SwissPIL.pdf>. For a commentary in English, see A Imhoff-Scheir and P M Patocchi, *Torts and Unjust Enrichment in the New Swiss Conflict of Laws* (1990).
[130] **1.15–1.17** above.
[131] Art 133(b), sub-rule 1.
[132] Ibid, sub-rule 2.

party, claims founded on an unlawful act are governed instead by the law applicable to that legal relationship.[133] There are special rules for traffic accidents,[134] product liability,[135] unfair competition,[136] restraint of competition,[137] damaging emissions from immovable property,[138] and infringements of personality rights by the media.[139] In addition, the parties may agree at any time after the harmful event occurred to apply the law of the forum (Swiss law).[140]

1.41 Unjust enrichment claims are governed by the law that governs the existing or supposed legal relationship from which the enrichment results or (absent such relationship) by the law of the State in which the enrichment occurs.[141] Again, the parties may agree that the law of the forum shall apply.[142]

1.42 The Code gives overriding effect to Swiss public policy and internationally mandatory rules.[143] In addition, a mandatory provision of a system of

---

[133] Ibid, sub-rule 3.

[134] Ibid, Art 134, deferring to the rules of applicable law contained in the Hague Traffic Accidents Convention.

[135] Ibid, Art 135, sub-rule 1, giving the injured party a choice between (a) the law of the State in which the person responsible has his place of business/habitual residence, and (b) the law of the State in which the product was purchased, unless the person responsible proves that the product was marketed in that State without his consent. By sub-rule 2, awards in such claims are limited to the amount that would have been awarded under Swiss law.

[136] Ibid, Art 136, designating the law of the State in whose market the effects occur or (if the act affects a single competitor) the law of the State where the injured party has his place of business, subject (in either case) to displacement under Art 133, sub-rule 3 (text to n 133 above) in the case of an existing relationship between the parties.

[137] Ibid, Art 137, designating the law of the State in whose market the direct effects of the restraint on the injured party occur, but again limiting awards to the amount that would have been awarded under Swiss law.

[138] Ibid, Art 138, giving the injured party a choice between (a) the law of the place where the immovable is situated, and (b) the law of the place in which the effects of the damaging emissions occur.

[139] Ibid, Art 139, sub-rule 1, giving the injured party a choice between (a) the law of the State in which he has his habitual residence, to the extent that the person responsible should have foreseen that the infringement would produce effects in that State, (b) the law of the State in which the person responsible has his habitual residence/place of business, and (c) the law of (another) State in which the effects of the infringement occur, again to the extent that the person responsible should have foreseen such effects. By sub-rule 2 the right to reply shall be governed exclusively by the law of the State in which the publication appeared or from which the radio or television programme was broadcast. By sub-rule 3, the rule also applies to claims concerning personal data and its processing.

[140] Ibid, Art 132(a).

[141] Ibid, Art 128.

[142] Ibid.

[143] Ibid, Arts 17 and 18.

law other than that designated by the Code may be taken into account if the circumstances of the case are closely connected with that system and if, under Swiss law, the legitimate and manifestly preponderant interests of a party so require.[144]

OVERVIEW

Although, at least structurally, there are similarities between the applic- **1.43** able law solutions for non-contractual obligations adopted by European countries, it will be evident even within the narrow confines of the preced-ing survey that the differences between them far outweigh the common features. Indeed, these differences have increased in recent years with the adoption of detailed legislation in Italy (1995), the United Kingdom (1995), Germany (1999), The Netherlands (2001), and Belgium (2004). In view of the wide divergences between the Member States' substantive approaches to non-contractual liability[145] and in the absence of any international agree-ment of a general character in this field, the lack of uniformity is unsur-prising. It is, however, a feature that played a significant role in the Commission's case for legislative intervention and in the following debate as to the competence of the European Community to adopt the Rome II Regulation.[146]

C. THE ROAD TO ROME II

Appendix 5 contains a chronology of key developments in the process **1.44** leading to the adoption of the Rome II Regulation, with references to the principal documents.

CONCEPTION — A CONVENTION ON THE LAW APPLICABLE TO CONTRACTUAL AND NON-CONTRACTUAL OBLIGATIONS?[147]

By a letter dated 8 September 1967, Joseph Van Der Meulen, the permanent **1.45** representative of Belgium to the EEC invited the Commission to organize a collaboration of Member State experts with a view to unifying private

---

[144] Ibid, Art 19.
[145] **1.03** and **1.05** above.
[146] **2.64–2.65, 2.68, 2.70–2.71, 2.81, 2.92** and **2.96–2.97** below.
[147] Giuliano, Lagarde & Van Ysselt Report, 1–8 and the final Report of Professors M Giuliano and P Lagarde on the 1980 (Rome) Convention on the law applicable to contractual obligations (**Giuliano & Lagarde Report**) (OJ C282, 1 [31.10.1980], 4–7).

international law rules within the Community. That invitation was the product of an initiative by the governments of Belgium, Netherlands, and Luxembourg, whose joint efforts in this area had already resulted, in 1951, in the Benelux convention on private international law, although this had not yet entered into force.[148] The invitation came during the latter stages of the negotiations leading to the adoption by the Member States, in 1968, of the Brussels Convention on jurisdiction and the enforcement of judgments in civil and commercial matters.[149] Indeed, collaboration between the Member States in the area of reciprocal recognition of judgments had been specifically contemplated by Art 220 (now Art 293) of the EEC (now EC) Treaty. Although that provision made no specific mention of wider harmonization or unification of private international law rules, such coordination was in the view of the Benelux delegations a matter of some urgency having regard to likely reforms in 'some Member States' and the 'danger that existing divergences would become more marked'.[150]

1.46 As a result, the Commission engaged in a study as to the possible benefits of greater uniformity in private international law rules. Having reached a favourable conclusion in this study, it invited a group of experts to meet to consider possible future action, and circulated a questionnaire to facilitate the discussion. That meeting took place from 26 to 28 February 1969. In his opening address, the Commission's representative, Mr T Vogelaar, stated:[151]

This proposal should bring about a complete unification of the rules of conflict. Thus in each of our six countries, instead of the existing rules of conflict and apart from cases of application of international agreements binding any Member State, identical rules of conflict would enter into force both in Member States' relations *inter se* and in relations with non-Community States. Such a development would give rise to a common corpus of unified legal rules covering the territory of the Community's Member States. The great advantage of this proposal is undoubtedly that the level of legal certainty would be raised, confidence in the stability of legal relationships fortified, agreements on jurisdiction according to the applicable law facilitated, and the protection of rights acquired over the whole field of private law augmented.

[148] For an English translation of the text of the convention, concluded on 11 May 1951, see (1951) 1 ICLQ 426. Also E M Meijers, 'The Benelux Convention on Private International Law' (1953) 2 AJCL 1. Also the later Benelux treaty concerning a uniform law on private international law (3 July 1969), as to which see K H Nadelmann, 'The Benelux Uniform Law on Private International Law' (1970) 18 AJCL 406.
[149] Report of Mr P Jenard on the Brussels Convention (**Jenard Report**) (OJ C59, 3 [5.3.1979]). For the text of the original Brussels Convention, see OJ L299, 32 [31.12.1972]; for the text of the Convention as amended, see OJ C27, 1 [29.1.1998].
[150] Giuliano & Lagarde Report (OJ C282, 4 [31.10.1980]).
[151] Minutes of the meeting of experts, 26–28.2.1969, quoted in Giuliano & Lagarde Report, ibid, 4.

He continued:

According to both the letter and spirit of the Treaty establishing the EEC, harmonization is recognized as fulfilling the function of permitting or facilitating the creation in the economic field of legal conditions similar to those governing an internal market. I appreciate that opinions may differ as to the precise delimitation of the inequalities which directly affect the functioning of the common market and those having only an indirect effect. Yet there are still legal fields in which the differences between national legal systems and the lack of unified rules of conflict definitely impede the free movement of persons, goods, services and capital among the Member States.

Some will give preference to the harmonization or unification of substantive law rather than the harmonization of rules of conflict. As we know, the former has already been achieved in various fields. However, harmonization of substantive law does not always contrive to keep pace with the dismantling of economic frontiers. The problem of the law to be applied will therefore continue to arise as long as substantive law is not unified. The number of cases in which the question of applicable law must be resolved increases with the growth of private law relationships across frontiers.

At the same time there will be a growing number of cases in which the courts have to apply a foreign law. The Convention signed on 27 September 1968 on jurisdiction and the enforcement of judgments in civil and commercial matters uniformly governs the international jurisdiction of the courts within the Community. It should help to facilitate and expedite many civil actions and enforcement proceedings. It also enables the parties, in many matters, to [reach][152] agreements assigning jurisdiction and to choose among several courts. The outcome may be that preference is given to the court of a State whose law seems to offer a better solution to the proceedings. To prevent this 'forum shopping', increase legal certainty, and anticipate more easily the law which will be applied, it would be advisable for the rules of conflict to be unified in fields of particular economic importance so that the same law is applied irrespective of the State in which the decision is given.

To sum up, there are three main considerations guiding our proposal for harmonizing the rules of conflict for a few well-defined types of legal relations. The first is dictated by the history of private international law: to try to unify everything is to attempt too much and would take too long. The second is the urgent necessity for greater legal certainty in some sectors of major economic importance. The third is the wish to forestall any aggravation of the differences between the rules of private international law of the various Member States.[153]

Pausing there, it may be noted that these arguments are strikingly similar **1.47** to those that would be adopted by the Commission almost thirty-five years later to support its Rome II Proposal and that were subsequently carried

---

[152] Original: 'teach'.
[153] Ibid.

forward into the recitals of the Rome II Regulation.[154] Although Mr Vogelaar
and his colleagues did not, of course, have the opportunity to consider the
way in which the legislative competence of the Community in the field
of civil justice would develop as a result, in particular, of the 1997 Treaty
of Amsterdam,[155] the influence of their work in relating private international law rules to the economic objectives of the EEC is evident in the
Regulation in its final form.

1.48 At their second meeting, the group of experts recommended that follow-
up work should focus on areas that they considered to be closely involved
in the proper functioning of the common market, i.e. (a) the law applicable
to corporeal and incorporeal property, (b) the law applicable to contractual
and non-contractual obligations, (c) the law applicable to the form of legal
transactions and evidence, and (d) general matters of private international
law relevant to the foregoing topics (*renvoi*, characterization, application
of foreign law, acquired rights, public policy, capacity, representation).[156]
In October 1970, the Committee of Permanent Representatives (COREPER)
mandated the group to continue its work on this basis. As regards the second subject area, with one element of which this book is concerned, the
group of experts (led by Paul Jenard, of the Belgian Ministry of Foreign
Affairs, and the author of the official report on the Brussels Convention)
appointed Professor Mario Giuliano of the University of Milan as rapporteur. He was assisted on this project by Professor Paul Lagarde (University
of Paris), rapporteur on the subject of legal transactions and evidence, and
Mr Th van Sasse van Ysselt (Netherlands Ministry of Justice), rapporteur
on the general topics. Their work, and that of the group of experts, in the
period from 1970 to 1972 resulted in the submission to the Member States
of the preliminary draft EEC convention on the law applicable to contractual and non-contractual obligations[157] and the accompanying report of
Professors Giuliano and Lagarde and Mr van Sasse van Ysselt.[158]

1.49 So far as non-contractual obligations are concerned, the key features of the
preliminary draft convention were as follows:[159]

1. The draft convention contained separate rules for (a) non-contractual
liability resulting from 'an event which has resulted in damage or

---

[154] **2.62–2.78** and **2.106–2.109** below.

[155] **1.52, 1.56–1.57** below.

[156] Giuliano & Lagarde Report, 5.

[157] Commission document XIV/398/72.

[158] Commission document XIV/408/72 (French original; provisional English version also
available).

[159] For comment, see the materials cited in **Appendix 6** under 'Historical Background'.

injury'[160] (in the French original, *un fait dommageable*[161]), and (b) non-contractual obligations resulting from 'an event which does not result in damage or injury' (*un fait autre qu'un fait dommageable*).[162]

2. For category (a) (including torts), there was a general rule that the law of the country in which the relevant event 'occurred'[163] should apply,[164] subject to a rule of displacement in favour of another country with which the situation has a closer connection, provided that the situation has no significant link with the former country.[165]

3. During their discussions leading to the 1972 draft convention, the group of experts posed the question: 'If the event entailing damage occurs in a country other than that in which its damaging effects are felt, which shall be considered the one in which the event occurs?', but declined to give an answer 'in order not to impede ongoing developments in the jurisprudence of the Community countries'.[166]

4. For category (b) (encompassing, at least, *negotiorum gestio*, unjust enrichment, and the payment of money not owed),[167] the draft convention provided that the law of the country in which the relevant event occurred should again govern, subject again to displacement in favour of the law of another country with which there is a closer connection by reason of a connecting factor common to the interested parties.[168]

---

[160] 1972 preliminary draft convention, Art 10. The expression '*un fait dommageable*' appears in the English translation of the Giuliano Lagarde & van Ysselt Report as 'an event entailing damage'

[161] As the Giuliano Lagarde & van Ysselt Report noted (at 49), this was the same term used in the (French) version of Art 5(3) of the 1968 Brussels Convention (jurisdiction in matters relating to tort etc.) (n 166 below).

[162] 1972 preliminary draft convention, Art 13.

[163] Point 3 below.

[164] 1972 preliminary draft convention, Art 10, para 1.

[165] Ibid, Art 10, para 2. The relevant connection should normally be based on a connecting factor common to the victim and the author of the injury or, as the case may be, between the victim and a third party allegedly responsible for the acts of the author (Art 10, para 3). Also Arts 11 (scope of applicable law) and 12 ('rules issued on grounds of security or public order').

[166] Giuliano, Lagarde & van Ysselt Report, 50. Subsequently, the Court of Justice held, in its leading decision on Art 5(3) of the Brussels Convention (matters relating to tort, delict, or quasi-delict), that the term '*fait dommageable*' (in the English version, 'harmful event') was capable of referring both to the event giving rise to damage and to the resulting damage (Case 21/76, *Handelskwekerij G J Bier BV v Mines de Potasse d'Alsace SA* [1976] ECR 1735, paras 13–17, discussed at **4.02** below).

[167] K Siehr, 'General Report on Non-Contractual Obligations' in O Lando et al. (eds), *European Private International Law of Obligations* (1975), 62.

[168] 1972 preliminary draft convention, Art 13.

5. Matters excluded from the scope of the draft convention, or the rules concerning non-contractual obligations, included (a) nuclear damage,[169] and (b) liability of the State or other legal persons governed by public law, or the liability of their organs or agents, for acts of public authority performed by the organs or agents in the exercise of their official functions.[170]

1.50 Overall, particularly when compared to the provisions of the draft convention concerning contractual obligations and to the Rome II Regulation itself, the approach to non-contractual obligations in the 1972 draft seems awkward and to lack sophistication, although this may be explained by economic priorities at the time as well as the underdeveloped state of the private international law of non-contractual obligations. Whatever the explanation, this aspect of the draft was strongly criticized.[171] Perhaps unsurprisingly, in March 1978 (following the accession to the EEC of Denmark, Ireland, and the UK), the group of experts decided 'for reasons of time'[172] to focus their work on the area of contractual obligations. The resulting (Rome) Convention on the law applicable to contractual obligations was opened for signature on 19 June 1980.[173] For the time being, the project for the harmonization of rules relating to non-contractual obligations lay dormant. Even so, the close historical link with the Rome Convention would lead to it being branded with the short title 'Rome II'.[174]

Treaty on European Union — Picking Up Tools

1.51 Twenty years after submission of the draft convention, the project was reinvigorated by the Treaty on European Union, signed at Maastricht on 7 February 1992 and coming into force on 1 January the following year. This Treaty created, albeit outside the framework of what would be redesignated as the EC Treaty, a framework for cooperation between the Member States in, among other areas, matters of civil justice.[175]

---

[169] Ibid, Art 1(e).

[170] Ibid, Art 14. Also Arts 19 (presumptions, burden, and mode of proof), 21 (exclusion of *renvoi*), 22 (public policy), 24 (universal application).

[171] See the materials cited in **Appendix 6** under 'Historical Background'.

[172] Giuliano & Lagarde Report, 7.

[173] OJ L266, 1 [9.10.1980] (**Rome Convention**). Also the extract from the Commission opinion on the draft of that Convention quoted at **3.125** below, regretting that it had not been possible to cover non-contractual obligations as well.

[174] The earliest reference to the 'Rome II' terminology found by the author is in a Council Presidency communication in July 1998 (Council document 9755/98 [15.7.1998]), but the usage may originate from within the Commission.

[175] Treaty on European Union (**TEU**) (OJ C191, 1 [29.7.1992]), Art K.1(6) referring to 'judicial cooperation in civil matters'.

Subsequently, by a resolution dated 14 October 1996 laying down priorities for cooperation in this area, the Council stated that it intended to launch discussions on the possibility of a convention on the law applicable to 'extra-contractual obligations'.[176]

IMPACT OF THE TREATY OF AMSTERDAM

Before work could begin in earnest, however, the constitutional pendulum **1.52** had swung away from collaborative action of the Member States and towards the competence of the European Community and its institutions. An inter-governmental conference, launched at the Turin European Council in March 1996, led to agreement the following summer in Amsterdam on the text of an amending treaty, signed on 2 October 1997 by the foreign Ministers of the (then) fifteen Member States. Arguably, the most significant initiative in the Treaty was the transfer of competence with respect to certain aspects of the area of justice and home affairs from the TEU framework into the main body (Title IV) of the EC Treaty, conferring on the European Community the specific power to adopt rules in this area, including rules of private international law.[177] The surrender was not, however, total. Art 65 (initially Art 73m) of the EC Treaty, which refers to measures to promote the compatibility of rules applicable in the Member States concerning the conflict of laws and of jurisdiction, contains a number of restrictions on the legislative power of the European Community in this area. The nature and scope of these restrictions on the Community's legislative power in this area will be examined further in **Chapter 2** below. At the same time, Denmark declined to be bound by the new Title IV of the EC Treaty,[178] and the UK and Ireland hedged their position by means of a protocol preserving the right to opt-in or not to particular proposals on a case-by-case basis.[179]

EARLY WORK ON A POSSIBLE 'ROME II' CONVENTION

In February 1998, the Commission circulated among the Member States a **1.53** questionnaire asking them to identify their applicable national rules of private international law concerning non-contractual obligations. Based on the replies of the Member States,[180] the Austrian Presidency circulated

---

[176] OJ C319, 1 [26.10.1996], para 3.1(c).
[177] EC Treaty, Title IV and, in particular, Arts 61, 65(c), and 67.
[178] Treaty of Amsterdam, Protocol No 5 (Denmark: Border Controls and Defence).
[179] Treaty of Amsterdam, Protocol No 4 (United Kingdom and Ireland: Visas, Asylum etc).
[180] Council document 12544/98 [11.11.1998].

a document setting out initial views on the principal questions to be addressed by any convention,[181] and organized four working group meetings to discuss the issues. This document was first discussed at the meeting of the working group in November 1998.

PROPOSAL OF THE EUROPEAN GROUP FOR
PRIVATE INTERNATIONAL LAW (GEDIP)

1.54 The Commission had also funded through the GROTIUS programme a study on the feasibility of a convention by the European Group for Private International Law (GEDIP). Subsequently, GEDIP adopted the final version of its proposal for a convention on the law applicable to non-contractual obligations in June 1998. Its principal features were as follows:[182]

1. Separate rules for (a) non-contractual obligations 'arising out of a harmful event,'[183] and (b) non-contractual obligations 'arising out of an event other than a harmful event'.[184]

2. For non-contractual obligations arising out of a harmful event, a general rule that the applicable law should be the law of the country with which the non-contractual obligation is most closely connected,[185] combined with (a) rebuttable[186] presumptions in favour of (i) the law of the country of common habitual residence of the author of the damage and the person who suffers damage at the time of the harmful event,[187] alternatively (ii) the law of the country where both the event causing the damage and the damage occurred,[188] and (b) special presumptions in cases of (i) invasion of privacy or rights in personality,[189] (ii) unfair competition or restrictive trade practices,[190] and (iii) environmental damage.[191]

---

[181] Council document 9755/98 [15.7.1998].

[182] The text of the proposal is reproduced in (1998) 45 Neth Int L Rev 465 and on the Group's website at <http://www.drt.ucl.ac.be/gedip/documents/gedip-documents-8pe .html>.

[183] GEDIP proposal, Arts 3–4.

[184] Ibid, Art 7.

[185] Ibid, Art 3(1).

[186] Ibid, Art 3(4)–(5).

[187] Ibid, Art 3(2).

[188] Ibid, Art 3(3).

[189] Ibid, Art 4(a).

[190] Ibid, Art 4(b).

[191] Ibid, Art 4(c). Also Art 5 (scope of applicable law) and Art 6 (direct action against the insurer).

3. For non-contractual obligations arising out of an event other than a harmful event, an identical general rule,[192] with rebuttable[193] presumptions in favour of (a) the law which governs or which would govern a pre-existing or contemplated relationship to which the non-contractual obligation is connected,[194] alternatively (b) in the case of an obligation to make restitution based on unjust enrichment, the law of the country in which the enrichment occurs,[195] and (c) in the case of an obligation relating to management of the affairs of another (*negotiorum gestio*), the law of the country of the beneficiary's habitual residence at the relevant time or (in the case of protection of the person or tangible property) of the country where the person or property was situated at the relevant time.[196]

4. The parties would be allowed to choose the law applicable to a non-contractual obligation, but only by an express agreement entered into after the dispute had arisen and without prejudice to the rights of third parties.[197]

5. Matters excluded from the scope of the proposed convention included (a) non-contractual obligations arising out of a family or analogous relationship, (b) the personal liability of officers, members, and auditors of statutory accounts for the obligations of a company or other body, (c) liability arising out of events resulting from the exercise of public authority, and (d) nuclear damage.[198]

The GEDIP proposal has been described by Professor Symeonides as **1.55** 'an elegant, sophisticated, flexible document which has influenced the general content and coverage of Rome II, although not where it matters most'.[199] He also suggests that:[200]

The proposal was a sophisticated document drafted for sophisticated judges capable of, and entrusted with the discretion necessary for making the fine balancing the proposal envisioned. In contrast, Rome II is a pragmatic document that aims

---

[192] Ibid, Art 7(1).

[193] Ibid, Art 7(5).

[194] Ibid, Art 7(2).

[195] Ibid, Art 7(3).

[196] Ibid, Art 7(4).

[197] Ibid, Art 8. Also Arts 2 (universal application), 9 (mandatory rules—third country and forum), 10 (rules of safety and conduct), 11 (subrogation), 12 (habitual residence), 13 (exclusion of *renvoi*), 14 (public policy).

[198] Ibid, Art 1.

[199] S C Symeonides, n 9 above, 177. In Professor Symeonides' view (at 217), the GEDIP proposal was 'close to perfection'.

[200] Ibid, 217–18.

for simplicity and uniformity and primarily seeks to preserve the status quo rather than dramatically to alter it.

Overall, however, the differences between the approach of the GEDIP proposal and that of the Rome II Regulation do not appear as significant as Professor Symeonides suggests. Further, although the Regulation is undoubtedly conditioned to a large degree by the demands of legal certainty, the description of it as seeking to preserve the status quo seems questionable. Professor Symeonides recognizes elsewhere the divergences in the Member States' pre-existing rules of private international law and describes the Regulation as a 'dramatic step' and as part of the 'European conflicts revolution'. In the final analysis, whether it is considered superior to the final text of the Rome II Regulation or not, the GEDIP proposal marks one of a number of reference points in the legislative history of the Regulation, but it cannot be said to have been nearly as influential as might have been expected given its provenance.

The Vienna Action Plan and the Tampere European Council

1.56 Before the Amsterdam Treaty came into force, representatives of the European institutions set about making plans for the exercise of their new powers. In October 1998, the Council adopted (in Vienna) a joint Action Plan of the Commission and the Council on how best to implement Title IV of the Amsterdam Treaty.[201] Ambitiously, given the project's prior history, the drawing up of a legal instrument on the law applicable to non-contractual obligations was identified as a priority measure, to be taken within two years after the entry into force of the Treaty.[202] Perhaps predictably, when that deadline passed in May 2001, the Commission had not even got as far as publishing a text for consultation.[203]

1.57 Subsequently, political weight was added to these plans by the declarations of the Member States at the 1999 Tampere European Council, endorsing the principle of mutual recognition as the cornerstone of judicial cooperation in both civil and criminal matters within the European Union.[204] In the following year, the programme of measures for the implementation of that

---

[201] OJ C19, 1 [23.1.1999]. Also 1998 EU Bull No 1, point I.12.84.
[202] Ibid, 10, confusingly referring to this measure as 'Rome I'.
[203] **1.62** below.
[204] Presidency Conclusions, 15–16 October, para 33.

principle suggested a link, albeit not a compelling one, to measures for the harmonization of conflict of law rules, stating that:[205]

The measures relating to harmonisation of conflict-of-law rules . . . actually do help facilitate the mutual recognition of judgments.

Lastly, implementation of the mutual recognition principle *may* be facilitated through harmonisation of conflict-of-law rules.

THE COUNCIL'S WORK CONTINUES . . .

In the midst these developments, and despite the coming into force of the **1.58** Treaty of Amsterdam on 1 May 1999, the Council's working group continued to discuss the text of the proposed convention in further meetings throughout 1999. A heavily annotated, internal 'state of play' draft dated 9 December 1999[206] reveals the grainy, embryonic form of what was to emerge as the Rome II Regulation. In particular:[207]

1. The draft instrument categorizes non-contractual obligations using the terms 'tort or delict',[208] 'unjust enrichment',[209] and '*negotiorum gestio*',[210] all of which appear in the Rome II Regulation, as well as '*actio pauliana*'[211] which does not.[212]

2. The general rule for tort/delict refers to 'the law of the country where the injury occurs irrespective of where the consequences of that injury arose' (the *lex loci damni* or *lex laesionis*).[213] This accords with Art 4(1) of the Rome II Regulation.[214]

---

[205] OJ C12, 1 [15.1.2001], 2, 6. The programme nevertheless made clear that '[i]t in no way prejudges work that will be undertaken in other areas under judicial cooperation in civil matters, particularly with regard to conflicts of law' (ibid, 6).

[206] Council document 11982/99 [9.12.1999]. Also Council document 10231/99 [28.7.1999].

[207] Also Council document 11982/99, Arts 2 (universal application), 4 (areas not subject to territorial sovereignty), 14 (subrogation), 15 (right of direct action), 16 ('safety and police regulations'), 18 (burden of proof), 19 (mandatory rules of the forum), 20 (public policy), 21 (scope of applicable law), 22 (exclusion of *renvoi*).

[208] Ibid, Art 3 and 3A.

[209] Ibid, Art 8.

[210] Ibid, Art 9.

[211] Ibid, Art 10 (cf **3.249–3.258** and **4.98** below).

[212] Ibid, Art 11 contains a residual rule for 'Remaining non-contractual obligations' for which there is no equivalent in the Regulation in its final form (**3.248** below).

[213] Ibid, Art 3(1). However, by the square bracketed Art 3(3), it proposed that if injury is sustained by a person in more than one country, and proceedings are brought before the courts of the country in which the act or omission giving rise to injury occurred, the law of that country shall apply instead.

[214] **4.21–4.74** below.

3. The generally applicable law is subject to a rule of 'exceptional displacement' if, having regard among other matters to the parties' common habitual residence at the time when the injury occurred or a special relationship between the parties, it appears that the tort or delict is substantially more closely connected with another country, in which case the law of that other country would apply.[215] In contrast, Art 4(2) of the Rome II Regulation contains a separate rule of displacement for the habitual residence of the parties.[216]

4. Freedom of choice would be permitted, but only after the occurrence of the event giving rise to injury and without prejudice to the rights and obligations of third parties or to non-derogable rules of the law of the country with which the situation is otherwise (ignoring also any choice of forum) exclusively connected.[217]

5. Special rules are proposed for product liability[218] and unfair competition and unfair practices.[219] In contrast to the Regulation in its final form, however, there is no special rule for environmental damage and intellectual property is (tentatively) excluded from scope.[220] Defamation appears only as a heading.[221]

6. Other areas excluded (in some cases, tentatively) from scope include wills and succession, matrimonial property rights, rights and duties arising out of a family or analogous relationship, bills of exchange, cheques, promissory notes and other negotiable instruments, obligations governed by the law of companies and other similar bodies, trust obligations, matters of evidence and procedure not specifically brought within scope,[222] liability for acts and omissions performed in the exercise of public authority and nuclear injury.[223]

---

[215] Council document 11982/99, Art 3A.
[216] **4.80–4.83** below.
[217] Council document 11982/99, Art 3B. Cf Regulation, Art 14.
[218] Ibid, Art 5. Cf Regulation Art 5.
[219] Ibid, Art 6. Cf Regulation Art 6.
[220] Ibid, Art 1(h). Cf Regulation, Art 8.
[221] Ibid, Art 7.
[222] Cf ibid, Art 18.
[223] Ibid, Art 1(b)–(g), (i). Cf Regulation, Art 1(2).

Shortly after, the Council suspended its activities pending the submission of **1.59** a Community legislative proposal.[224] In fact, during 1999, the Commission had been considering whether to pre-empt the coming into force of the Treaty of Amsterdam and to seize the initiative from the Council by publishing its own legislative proposal.[225] A draft text was produced[226] and circulated by DG Justice and Home Affairs (since renamed Freedom, Security and Justice (JLS)) to other Directorates General within the Commission in 1999. Comments received included that (a) the document should take the form of a Green Paper and should consult on the necessity of a Community instrument regulating the law applicable to non-contractual obligation, (b) the text should be more open and analytical, (c) a section should be added dealing with electronic commerce, and (d) the text should note that private international law could not override 'internal market clauses' in certain Directives. This last point, raised specifically by DG Internal Market and Services (Markt), was based on the idea that relevant Directives,[227] as well as the Treaty provisions concerning the free movement of goods, persons, and services, required application of the law of the 'country of origin' as a rule of private international law. That view, shared by some other Directorates General (notably DG Information Society (INFSO), DG Enterprise and Industry (ENTR), and DG Education and Culture (EAC)) was opposed by DG JLS and DG Health and Consumers (SANCO). As appears below, debate as to the so-called 'country of origin' principle would dominate discussions within the Commission, and would almost de-rail the entire process.

THE COMMISSION'S GREEN PAPER—A DISAPPEARING ACT

In response to these criticisms, DG JLS briefly considered whether to defer **1.60** to the Member States' right of initiative. Having decided to press ahead, DG JLS prepared a draft Green Paper on a possible instrument concerning the law applicable to non-contractual obligations. At a meeting of the

---

[224] Council document 7563/1/00 REV1 [22.5.2000].

[225] Following the Amsterdam Treaty, the Commission shared the right of initiative under Title IV with the Member States (EC Treaty, Art 67(1)).

[226] An early draft dated 2 March 1999 appears on file.

[227] As the E-Commerce Directive had not been adopted at the date of the note above, the reference may have been, for example, to the 'Television without Frontiers Directive' (Directive (EC) No 97/36 (OJ L202, 60 [30.7.1997]). Also **16.23** below, n 45.

Council's Committee on Civil Law Matters in June 2000, the Commission's representative announced the forthcoming publication of that Paper.[228] Thereafter, however, the train hit the buffers. In response to an informal internal consultation, DG Markt raised almost exactly the same objections to the content of the draft Green Paper as it had made to the earlier draft proposal (**1.59** above), focusing its attention on the role of the 'country of origin'.

1.61 In January 2001, a formal Commission inter-service consultation was launched on a revised draft.[229] Among other elements, the draft contained questions as to the necessity of adopting an instrument laying down uniform rules of private international law on non-contractual obligations[230] and the approach to be adopted for non-contractual obligations arising in connection with computers etc.,[231] as well as an annex containing a short summary of the Member States' existing rules of applicable law for torts and delicts.[232] Two months later, the Commission reported to the Council's Committee on Civil Law Matters that it intended to prepare and publish a Green Paper during the first quarter of the year.[233] The Green Paper never appeared. In their responses to the inter-service consultation, DGs EAC, INFSO, and ENTR took the point that the E-Commerce Directive, adopted in June 2000,[234] regulated the law applicable in relation to the information society services. Similar comments were made with respect to other Directives. DG Markt also requested significant changes to the Green Paper to give what it saw as a more balanced explanation of the relationship between private international law and EC law. In the face of an apparent deadlock, DG JLS again considered whether to abandon the dossier and instead leave the right of initiative to the Member States.

1.62 By May 2001, the Commission had once again changed tack, telling the Council's Committee on Civil Law Matters that it had instead decided to create a proposal for an instrument on the law applicable to extra-contractual obligations.[235] The UK delegation queried this, concerned by the lack of consultation of practitioners concerned with this area of work.[236] At the

---

[228] Council document 7975/00 [5.6.2000], 4.
[229] Green Paper on the law applicable to non-contractual obligations, Commission draft, 18 January 2001.
[230] Ibid, para 1.5.
[231] Ibid, para 1.7.
[232] Ibid, Annex 2.
[233] Council document 5479/01 [9.3.2001], 4.
[234] Directive (EC) No 2000/31 on certain legal aspects of information society services (OJ L178, 1 [17.7.2000], discussed at **16.12–16.16** below.
[235] Council document 8398/01 [16.5.2001], 3.
[236] Ibid.

following meeting of the committee, the UK formally recorded its objection to the Commission's conduct, in the following terms:[237]

The United Kingdom delegation expressed surprise at the fact that the Commission had announced the presentation of a Regulation concerning the law applicable to non-contractual obligations (Rome II) without first preparing a green paper. This would have allowed interested parties at all levels to contribute to the discussions which concerned them very directly.

The Commission, on the other hand, appeared to consider that sufficient consultation with interested parties had already taken place.

The Commission's Preliminary Draft Proposal

During the remainder of 2002, discussions within the Commission centred on the relationship between the proposed Rome II instrument and internal market instruments, particularly the E-Commerce Directive. Views remained polarized, but the Directorates General eventually agreed to patch up their differences on the basis that clarification of the E-Commerce Directive should be left to the ECJ and should not be a matter for the Rome II Regulation. **1.63**

In announcing its plan to move forward to a proposal without a Green Paper, DG JLS had explained that it intended to consult on the text with stakeholders. Eventually, it agreed to make a draft available on the Internet. On 3 May 2002, three years after it had first attempted to formulate a proposal, DG JLS published what it described as a 'preliminary draft proposal' for a Regulation on the law applicable to non-contractual obligations,[238] without any explanatory memorandum. In the words of the Commission, the draft was 'no more than a Commission staff working paper for the sole purpose of consulting interested parties'. In its detailed response to the document, the UK Government raised the following objection to the form of the consultation:[239] **1.64**

The United Kingdom Government welcomes the opportunity to comment on draft proposals from the European Commission before any formal proposal is made. It is important that such an opportunity should always be made available. However it is also important that consultation should not be only on the basis of a draft instrument without any accompanying memorandum explaining the

[237] Council document 8342/01 [27.5.2001], 9.
[238] See <http://ec.europa.eu/justice_home/news/consulting_public/rome_ii/news_hearing_rome2_en.htm>.
[239] See document at <http://ec.europa.eu/justice_home/news/consulting_public/rome_ii/govern_uk_en.pdf>, paras 1–2.

policy behind that draft. This is likely to give rise to difficulty and misunderstanding where provisions in the draft text can reasonably be understood in different ways. It would have been better at this stage if the Commission's consultation had been focused more clearly on the underlying policy considerations in this technically complex area of private international law; this should be a standard part of the consultation procedure. . . .

The absence of any explanatory material means that the Commission has not made any attempt to justify the need for any harmonised rules in this area. In the view of the United Kingdom there has not so far been any demonstrated need for such an instrument which in order to comply with the requirements of Article 65 must be 'necessary for the proper functioning of the internal market'. In order to satisfy this requirement, and to justify the allocation of resources, the Commission should present evidence of difficulties currently arising in this context which constitute practical obstacles to cross-border trade and the movement of persons. It should only be on the basis of sufficient evidence of this kind that the Commission should proceed with a formal proposal for a draft Council Regulation.

1.65   In substance, the preliminary draft proposal marks a further stage in the development of the Rome II Regulation. In particular, the structure (if not the language) of the general rule for tort/delict in Art 3 is aligned to that in Art 4 of the Regulation,[240] combining a basic preference for application of the *lex loci damni*[241] with rules of displacement in favour of (a) the law of the parties' country of common habitual residence,[242] and (b) the law of another country with which the situation has a substantially closer connection, but only if there is no significant connection with the country whose law would be applicable under the preceding elements of the rule.[243] That general rule is combined with special rules for product liability,[244] unfair competition and other unfair practices,[245] violation of the environment,[246] and (most controversially) defamation/privacy,[247] the latter rule favouring the law of the country where the victim is habitually resident at the time of the tort. For other non-contractual obligations, a series of rules set out in Art 10, giving priority to the law applicable to a prior relationship between the parties

---

[240] **Ch 4** below.

[241] Preliminary draft proposal, Art 3(1) ('. . . the law of the country in which the loss is sustained, irrespective of the country or countries in which the harmful event occurred and irrespective of the country in which the indirect consequences of the harmful event are sustained . . .'). Cf Regulation, Art 4(1) ('. . . the law of the country in which the damage occurs irrespective of the country in which the event giving rise to damage occurred and irrespective of the country or countries in which the indirect consequences of that event occur . . .').

[242] Ibid, Art 3(2).

[243] Ibid, Art 3(3). Cf Regulation, Art 4(3).

[244] Ibid, Art 5.

[245] Ibid, Art 6.

[246] Ibid, Art 8.

[247] Ibid, Art 7.

out of which the obligation arose, is followed by separate rules for unjust enrichment[248] and 'actions performed without due authority in connection with the affairs of another person' (*negotiorum gestio*),[249] the law applicable under these latter rules being capable of being displaced only in favour of the law of the parties' common habitual residence at the time that the obligation arose.[250] Significantly, for the first time, Art 11 would allow that the parties should be permitted to choose the law applicable to a non-contractual obligation without any limit in time, so as to permit a choice before the obligation arose (*ex ante*).[251] Matters excluded from the scope of the preliminary draft Regulation include (a) non-contractual obligations arising out of a family or equivalent relationship, (b) succession, (c) obligations arising under bills of exchange, cheques, promissory notes, and other negotiable instruments,[252] (d) the personal liability of officers, members, and auditors of statutory accounts for the obligations of a company or other body, (e) liability incurred in the exercise of public authority, (f) trust obligations, and (g) matters of evidence and procedure not specifically brought within scope.[253]

The Commission invited written comments on the document by September 2002. In its follow-up document,[254] the Commission noted that around 80 contributions were received from academics, governments, business, and practitioners[255] and that: **1.66**

The reaction ranged from blunt refusal of the draft Regulation as a whole to approval with some points of criticism. It is worth noting that business was more critical of the draft than representatives of legal professions, academics and Member States, who in general welcomed the draft.[256]

---

[248] Ibid, Art 10(2), designating 'the law of the country in which the enrichment takes place'.
[249] Ibid, Art 10(3), designating 'the law of the country in which the action takes place'.
[250] Ibid, Art 10(4).
[251] Ibid, Art 11(1), subject to the rights of third parties, non-derogable rules of a country with which the situation is otherwise exclusively connected (Art 11(1)) and non-derogable rules of Community law in circumstances where 'the other elements of the situation were located in one (*sic*) of the Member States of the European Community at the time when the obligation came into being'.
[252] The latter only to the extent that such obligations arise out of their negotiable character (**3.157** below).
[253] Preliminary draft proposal, Art 1(2).
[254] <http://ec.europa.eu/justice_home/news/consulting_public/rome_ii/news_summary_rome2_en.htm>.
[255] Many of the submissions can be accessed from the link set out in the previous note.
[256] It is also worth noting that more than half of the published responses came from businesses or business organizations, and that UK legal practitioners (in particular) were more critical of the proposal than their continental counterparts. For the author's initial reaction, see <http://ec.europa.eu/justice_home/news/consulting_public/rome_ii/andrew_dickinson_en.pdf> and, subsequently, 'Cross-Border Torts in EC Courts—A Response to the Proposed "Rome II" Regulation' (2002) 13 EBLR 367. Also V C Noirissat and E Treppoz,

1.67 The second stage of the Commission's consultation process, a public hearing, took place in Brussels on 7 January 2003. The items on the agenda[257] did not include any assessment of the treaty basis or desirability of the proposed Regulation. It became evident that the Commission's position was that these matters had already been determined for it by the political declarations of the Member States in the Vienna Action Plan and the Tampere conclusions.[258] On other issues, the delegates were sharply divided, with representatives of business generally strongly critical of the proposal and consumer organizations generally in favour, but advocating greater victim protection.

The Treaty of Nice—Joint Competence of the Council and Parliament

1.68 On 1 February 2003, the Treaty of Nice came into force.[259] From that date, it was required that all measures in the field of judicial cooperation in civil and commercial matters within EC Treaty, Art 65 be taken in accordance with the co-decision procedure set out in Art 251 of that Treaty, giving the European Parliament joint legislative competence with the Council, as opposed to a mere right to be consulted.[260] As will be seen, that increase in the Parliament's powers would have a significant effect on the legislative process leading to the adoption of the Rome II Regulation, as it was the first instrument in this area to reach conciliation, the final stage of the co-decision procedure.[261]

The Commission's Proposal

1.69 Having reflected on the outcome of the consultation process, the Commission published its proposal for a Regulation on the law applicable to non-contractual obligations (Rome II) on 22 July 2003. This was accompanied by a detailed explanatory memorandum. The Commission explained the general purpose of its proposal as follows:[262]

The purpose of this proposal for a regulation is to standardise the Member States' rules of conflict of laws regarding non-contractual obligations and thus extend the

---

'*Quelques observations sur l'avant projet de proposition de règlement du Conseil sur la loi applicable aux obligations non contractuelles "Rome II"'* (2003) *Journal du Droit International* 7.

[257] <http://ec.europa.eu/justice_home/news/consulting_public/rome_ii/ordre_jour_en.pdf>.

[258] **1.56–1.57** above.

[259] OJ C80, 1 [10.3.2001].

[260] EC Treaty, Art 67(5) introduced by Art 2(4) of the Treaty of Nice.

[261] See, in particular, **1.94–1.95** below.

[262] COM (2003) 427 final (**Commission Proposal**), 4–5. Particular aspects of this key document, reproduced in full in **Appendix 2**, will be considered, as appropriate, in the following chapters. For comment see the materials cited in **Appendix 6** under 'Commission Proposal'.

harmonisation of private international law in relation to civil and commercial obligations which is already well advanced in the Community with the 'Brussels I' Regulation[263] and the Rome Convention of 1980.

The harmonisation of conflict rules, which must be distinguished from the harmonisation of substantive law, seeks to harmonise the rules whereby the law applicable to an obligation is determined. This technique is particularly suitable for settling cross-border disputes, as, by stating with reasonable certainty the law applicable to the obligation in question irrespective of the forum, it can help to develop a European area of justice. Instead of having to study often widely differing conflict rules of all the Member States' courts that might have jurisdiction in a case, this proposal allows the parties to confine themselves to studying a single set of conflict rules, thus reducing the cost of litigation and boosting the foreseeability of solutions and certainty as to the law.

. . .

This proposal for a Regulation would allow parties to determine the rule applicable to a given legal relationship in advance, and with reasonable certainty, especially as the proposed uniform rules will receive a uniform interpretation from the Court of Justice. This initiative would accordingly help to boost certainty in the law and promote the proper functioning of the internal market. It is also in the Commission's programme of measures to facilitate the extra-judicial settlement of disputes, since the fact that the parties have a clear vision of their situation makes it all the easier to come to an amicable agreement.

The Proposal contained a number of significant changes, both in terminol-   **1.70**
ogy and substance, from the preliminary draft proposal. In particular:[264]

1. In the general rule for tort/delict (Commission Proposal, Art 3), the term 'loss' was replaced by 'damage'[265] and the rule of displacement in Art 3(3) of the proposal now appeared, more or less, in the form which it would

---

[263] Regulation (EC) No 44/2001 on jurisdiction and the recognition and enforcement of judgments in civil and commercial matters (OJ L12, 1 [16.1.2001]) (**Brussels I Regulation**), as amended; consolidated text as of 1 January 2007 at <http://eur-lex.europa.eu/LexUriServ/site/en/consleg/2001/R/02001R0044-20070101-en.pdf>.

[264] Also Commission Proposal, Arts 2 (universal application), 11 (scope of applicable law), 13 (rules of safety and conduct), 14 (direct action against insurer), 15 (subrogation and multiple liability), 16 (formal validity), 17 (burden of proof), 18 (assimilation to the territory of a State), 19 (assimilation to habitual residence), 20 (exclusion of *renvoi*), 21 (States with more than one legal system), 22 (public policy), 23 (relationship with other provisions of Community law), 25 (relationship with existing international conventions), 27 (entry into force and application of time).

[265] Commission Proposal, Art 3(1). This change would appear to have been one of linguistic preference rather than substance, arising from difficulty in selecting an English term corresponding to the French '*dommage*' (see the evidence given in January 2004 by Ms Claudia Hahn of the Commission to the House of Lords select committee considering the Rome II proposal (House of Lords' European Union Committee, 'The Rome II Regulation', 8th Report of Session 2003–2004, HL Paper 66, answers to Q31–33)).

take in Art 4(3) of the final Regulation,[266] without the requirement that there be no significant connection between the non-contractual obligation and the law which would otherwise govern under paragraph 1 or 2.

2. The special rules for product liability,[267] unfair competition,[268] violations of privacy/personality rights (defamation),[269] and violation of the environment[270] had been re-written, and a new special rule introduced for infringement of intellectual property rights.[271]

3. The rules for non-contractual obligations other than those arising out of tort/delict were made more flexible by the introduction of a rule of displacement referring to the law of a country with which the non-contractual obligation was manifestly more closely connected.[272]

4. The right of parties to choose the law applicable to non-contractual obligations was restricted to agreements entered into after the dispute arose, and was excluded in the case of intellectual property rights.[273]

5. A new provision (Commission Proposal, Art 12(1)) was inserted, reflecting Art 7(1) of the Rome Convention, allowing discretionary application of overriding mandatory rules of a third country (i.e. other than the forum and that whose law would apply to the non-contractual obligation under the general or specific rules of applicable law) with which the situation had a close connection.[274]

6. Art 24 of the proposal provided that '[t]he application of a provision of the law designated by this Regulation which has the effect of causing non-compensatory damages, such as exemplary or punitive damages, to be awarded shall be contrary to Community public policy'. Not only was the concept of non-compensatory damages potentially very broad (including, for example, restitutionary and nominal damages), but also the concept of 'Community public policy', at least in the area of private law, was unprecedented and unwelcome. Happily, it was also short-lived.[275]

---

[266] **4.84–4.95** below.
[267] Commission Proposal, Art 4.
[268] Ibid, Art 5.
[269] Ibid, Art 6.
[270] Ibid, Art 7.
[271] Ibid, Art 8.
[272] Ibid, Art 9(5).
[273] Ibid, Art 10(1).
[274] Ibid, Art 12(1). The rule preserving overriding mandatory rules of the forum (Art 12(2)) remained.
[275] **14.22–14.23** below.

7. Consistently with the Brussels I Regulation, the proposed Regulation was restricted to 'civil and commercial matters'.[276] Revenue, customs and administrative matters,[277] matrimonial property regimes,[278] and non-contractual obligations arising out of nuclear damage[279] were added to the list of excluded matters. The specific exclusions of liability incurred in the exercise of public authority[280] and evidence and procedure[281] were removed.

ASSESSMENT OF THE PROPOSAL BY THE UK HOUSE OF LORDS' SELECT COMMITTEE

In early 2004, before any of the European institutions had formally responded, the European Union Committee of the UK House of Lords launched a public consultation to support its scrutiny of the Commission Proposal. In the following two months, it received several written contributions[282] and heard oral evidence from representatives of the Commission,[283] professional[284] and senior academic[285] lawyers, representatives of the media,[286] and of the UK Government.[287] The reaction to the Commission's proposal was generally, if not universally, hostile. Most significantly, two leading experts, the senior editors of the leading

1.71

---

[276] Commission Proposal, Art 1(1).

[277] Ibid, Art 1(1).

[278] Ibid, Art 1(2)(b).

[279] Ibid, Art 1(2)(f).

[280] Cf Preliminary draft proposal, Art 1(2)(e), apparently no longer necessary in light of the specific restriction to civil and commercial matters (cf **3.271–3.279** below).

[281] Cf Preliminary draft proposal, Art 1(2)(g).

[282] See Written Evidence annexed to Committee's final report, 'The Rome II Regulation', 8th Report of Session 2003–2004 (HL Paper 66) (**HL Report**), report (with links to evidence) available at <http://www.publications.parliament.uk/pa/ld200304/ldselect/ldeucom/66/6602.htm>

[283] Mario Tenreiro and Claudia Hahn, 21 January 2004 (HL Report, Evidence, 1–18).

[284] The Hon Mr Lawrence Collins, William Blair QC (COMBAR) and the author, 11 February 2004 (HL Report, Evidence, 46–69).

[285] Sir Peter North, 29 January 2004 (HL Report, Evidence, 19–30).

[286] Alastair Brett (The Times), Santha Rasaiah (Newspaper Society), Clare Hoban (Periodical Publishers Association), and Glenn del Medico (BBC), 4 February 2004 (HL Report, Evidence, 31–45).

[287] Lord Filkin CBE (Parliamentary Undersecretary of State), Oliver Parker (Legal Adviser), Louise Miller (Scottish Executive Justice Department), and Professor Paul Beaumont (University of Aberdeen) (HL Report, Evidence, 70–87).

general English works on private international law, expressed their strong opposition to the proposal. Sir Peter North[288] concluded that:[289]

[N]o clear and convincing need for this proposed Regulation had been identified by the Commission in terms of the operation of the internal market. It looks rather like harmonisation on the basis of tidiness. Furthermore, no convincing case has been made or justification given for the scope of any Regulation to be world wide. That said, a new Regulation limited in territorial scope could be regarded as acceptable, not least in the broader context of European co-operation, if it was well drafted and did not raise significant concerns as to its substance, even though its acceptance would mean a further change in our tort choice of law rules. . . . [M]y personal conclusion is that the current text is neither clear enough nor, substantively, satisfactory enough, however, for the proposed Regulation to be acceptable.

In similar fashion, Sir Lawrence Collins[290] commented:[291]

The arguments for adoption of a Regulation are wholly unconvincing. The Commission's website on harmonisation makes it clear that its aim is the ultimate harmonisation of rules relating to applicable law. Although the effect of the revised EC Treaty is that the Community has the power to take measures harmonising rules of private international law, it is fanciful to suppose . . . that a regulation to harmonise private international rules for non-contractual obligations is 'necessary for the proper functioning of the internal market'. . . .

1.72 The Committee, in its final report, did not pull any punches. Its main conclusions were as follows:[292]

The Regulation raises a serious question of *vires*. The Commission has not shown a convincing case of 'necessity' within the meaning of Article 65 TEC. Further, on any construction of Articles 61 and 65 of the EC Treaty there must be the most serious doubts that the proposal can have universal application and can be used to harmonise substantive rules of damages (Articles 2 and 24 respectively). We urge both the Council and the Parliament to give the most careful consideration to the issue . . .

There is no evidence of which we are aware that there are such problems in the application of the Member States' conflicts rules in this area as require the introduction of a Community measure. The justification provided by the Commission in its Explanatory Memorandum is unconvincing and fails to pay due regard to

---

[288] Co-editor, *Cheshire & North's Private International Law* (13th edn, 1999); Chair, Ministry of Justice Departmental Advisory Committee on Private International Law Matters (the North Committee).

[289] Memorandum, para 20 (HL Report, Evidence, 21).

[290] Senior editor, Dicey, Morris & Collins. At the time, a Justice of the High Court and now a Lord Justice of the Court of Appeal, England and Wales.

[291] Memorandum, para 1 (HL Report, Evidence, 46).

[292] HL Report, paras 184–5. For more detailed analysis, see HL Report, paras 66–79.

the views of industry, commerce, the media and legal practitioners. We invite the Council and the Parliament to look critically at the question whether there is a real practical need for the Regulation. . . .

The Committee also recommended deletion, or substantial revision, of **1.73** several provisions of the Commission's proposal.[293]

THE EUROPEAN PARLIAMENT (FIRST READING PROCEDURE)

As a result of the Treaty of Nice, the European Parliament would enjoy, **1.74** constitutionally at least, equal billing with the Council in the adoption of the proposed Regulation. After some discussion as to whether the Committee on Civil Liberties, Justice and Home Affairs (LIBE) or the Committee on Legal Affairs and the Internal Market (JURI) would take the lead, the latter claimed the prize and in late 2003 appointed Diana Wallis MEP[294] as rapporteur for the proposal.[295] Within a short timeframe, the rapporteur produced a working document in two parts[296] followed, in March 2004, by a draft report.[297] That report went through several further drafts[298] before being adopted by the JURI Committee on 21 June 2005.[299]

---

[293] Deletion: Art 2 (universal application: see HL Report, para 191), Art 4 (product liability: para 194), Art 6 (unfair competition: para 195), Art 7 (violations of the environment: para 197), Art 9 (non-contractual obligations other than tort or delict: para 199), Art 14 (direct actions against insurers: para 201), Art 24 (non-compensatory damages: para 201). Deletion or revision: Art 8 (intellectual property: para 198); Art 12(1) (third country mandatory rules: para 201). Revision: Art 1(2)(d) (auditors' liability: para 189); Art 1(2)(e) (trusts: para 190); Art 3 (general rules for torts: para 192); Art 6 (violations of privacy etc: para 196); Art 23 (relationship with other provisions of Community law: para 202). For more detailed analysis, see HL Report, paras 83–170. The Committee also criticized the UK Government's decision in October 2003 to opt-in to the Rome II proposal (text to n 339 below and HL Report, paras 80–2).

[294] Liberal Democrat, Yorkshire and the Humber (UK) since 1999. Mrs Wallis is a solicitor and currently holds the position of Vice President of the European Parliament.

[295] Mrs Wallis was reappointed in September 2004. LIBE appointed Barbara Kudrycka MEP (Poland) as the draftswoman for its opinion on the Rome II proposal, which (as adopted on 17.5.2005 – EP document reference A6-0211/2005 FINAL [15.4.2005], 41–43) deals principally with issues relating to violations of privacy and rights relating to the personality, matters subsequently excluded from the scope of the Regulation.

[296] EP document reference PE 338.502 [drafts dated 26.1.2004 (Part 1); 5.2.2004 (revised Part 1 and Part 2)].

[297] EP document reference PE 338.465 [15.3.2004].

[298] See, e.g., EP document references PE 338.465 [5.4.2004], PE 349.977v01-00 [11.11.2004], PE 349.977v02-00 [23–29.3.2005].

[299] EP document reference A6-211/2005 FINAL [27.6.2005], 1–40 (**EP 1st Reading Report**).

1.75 With relatively minor amendments in the plenary session,[300] the report formed the basis of the European Parliament's position at first reading on 6 July 2005.[301] By that time, clear water had emerged between the Parliament's position and the position of the Commission, towards which the Council would also ultimately steer. In particular,[302] the Parliament favoured greater flexibility in the general rule for torts/delict, with less reliance on special rules for particular torts.[303] Indeed, at one point,[304] the rapporteur recommended that the general rule should refer to the law of the country with which the non-contractual obligation is most closely connected, coupled with a series of rebuttable presumptions. She subsequently returned to the place of damage as a starting point, but substantially modified the Commission's rules of displacement. The significance of the parties' common habitual residence was downgraded from a factor of displacement in its own right[305] to an element in the more flexible 'escape clause' requiring a manifestly closer connection with another country.[306] The factors cited as potentially supporting the application of this flexible rule of displacement were greatly expanded by the Parliament to include:

(a) as far as loss-distribution and legal capacity are concerned, the fact that the person claimed to be liable and the person sustaining loss or damage have their habitual residence in the same country or that the relevant laws of the country of habitual residence of the person claimed

---

[300] 51 of the 54 amendments tabled by the JURI Committee were adopted in plenary (Council document 10812/05). In addition (a) there was an oral amendment deleting the (expired) dates in Arts 26 and 27 of the Proposal, and (b) more significantly, the plenary adopted Amendments 56 and 57 tabled by the rapporteur concerning the law applicable to non-contractual obligations arising out of violations of privacy or rights relating to the personality, in preference to those put forward by the JURI Committee in its report.

[301] OJ C157E, 371 [6.7.2006] (**EP 1st Reading Position**).

[302] See also amendments in EP 1st Reading Position to Arts 1(1)–1(2) (material scope), 1(3) (relationship with Community legislation, replacing Commission Proposal, Art 23), 9 (unjust enrichment), 10 (*negotiorum gestio*), 11 (scope of applicable law), 25 (relationship with international conventions), 27 (review).

[303] The Commission's special rules for product liability (Commission Proposal, Art 4), unfair competition (ibid, Art 5), and violation of the environment (ibid, Art 7) were removed (for criticism, see, e.g. the papers presented by A Saraville, 'The Law Applicable to Products Liability: Hopping Off the Endless Merry-Go Round'; C Honorati, 'The Law Applicable to Unfair Competition'; and F Munari and L Schiano di Pepe, 'Liability for Environmental Torts in Europe' at a conference held in December 2004 at the University of Castellanza, reproduced in Malatesta, *Unification*, n 28 above, 107–26, 127–58 and 173–220 respectively). Against this, the rule concerning violations of privacy and rights relating to the personality was retained in modified form (EP 1st Reading Position, Art 5) and a new special rule was introduced for industrial action (EP 1st Reading Position, Art 6). See EP 1st Reading Report, 39.

[304] Draft Report, Art 3 (EP document reference PE 349.977v01-00 [draft dated 11.11.2004]).

[305] Cf Commission Proposal, Art 3(2).

[306] EP 1st Reading Position, Art 4(3).

to be liable and of the country of habitual residence of the person sustaining loss or damage are substantially identical;

(b) a pre-existing legal or *de facto* relationship between the parties, such as, for example, a contract, that is closely connected with the non-contractual obligation in question;

(c) the need for certainty, predictability, and uniformity of result;

(d) protection of legitimate expectations;

(e) the policies underlying the foreign law to be applied and the consequences of applying that law.

The rapporteur explained:[307]

Your rapporteur takes the view that the complexity of many cases is such that a flexible regime is more appropriate than rigid rules for each class of non-contractual obligation. Small factual differences in cases can substantially alter the parties' expectations and the policy considerations at stake.

In this approach, the rapporteur was undoubtedly influenced by developments in American choice of law theory, and it would appear to be no coincidence that two weeks before publication of a new draft of her report in March 2005,[308] the rapporteur had organized a working group entitled 'Rome II—the international perspective', the speakers at which had included prominent modern US conflict of laws theorists.[309] The role envisaged for 'governmental interest analysis', which had previously been rejected as a basis for reform of the UK applicable law regime for torts[310] and was widely thought to be antithetical to the continental approach to conflict of laws,[311] was the most striking, and objectionable, element of the European Parliament's 1st Reading Position. Particularly when coupled with the universal application of the Regulation[312] and the Parliament's

---

[307] EP 1st Reading Report, 39.

[308] EP document reference PE 349.977v02-00 [23–29.3.2005].

[309] See the papers by S C Symeonides, 'Tort Conflicts and Rome II: A View from Across' published in H-P Mansel et al. (eds), *Festschrift für Erik Jayme* (2004), 935–54 and 'Impromptu Notes on the Rapporteur's Draft'; R J Weintraub, 'Discretion Versus Strict Rules in the Field of Cross-Border Torts', P J Borchers, 'The Proposed "Rome II" Regulation and the US Experience in Tort Choice of Law', to which links appear on the rapporteur's website, <http://www.dianawallismep.org.uk/pages/Rome-II-seminars.html>.

[310] Law Commission Working Paper No 87 and Scottish Law Commission Consultative Memorandum No 62, Private International Law: Choice of Law in Tort and Delict (HMSO, 1984), paras 4.35–4.54.

[311] J Fawcett, 'Is American Governmental Interest Analysis the Solution to English Tort Choice of Law Problems?' (1982) 31 ICLQ 150, concluding (p 166) that '[i]nterest analysis has nothing to offer the English or Continental lawyer'.

[312] EP 1st Reading Position, Art 2.

proposed reforms to pleading and proof of the applicable law,[313] the requirement that Member State courts consider the policies underlying the potentially relevant rules of all connected systems to determine whether the connection was or was not 'manifestly closer' than that to the system whose law would otherwise apply was open to criticism as being liable to increase the burden on judges as well as the costs of litigation, at the same time as reducing significantly the foreseeability of legal decisions, the primary stated objective of the Rome II Proposal.[314] It was, it is submitted, at least one step too far in the rapporteur's global search to find suitable models for the Rome II regime.[315]

1.76   Other key aspects of the EP 1st Reading Position include the following:

1. The flexibility of the general rule was further increased by recognizing the possibility of more than one applicable law, each issue being potentially subject to a separate analysis to determine its applicable law.[316] According to the rapporteur:[317]

[I]n disputes which take place in a Community of States without borders, all having different legal systems but sharing a common heritage of human rights provisions and Community law, justice will often be served by applying *dépeçage*. It is for this reason, that Article 3(3) provides that the court seised must, where necessary, subject each issue of the dispute to separate analysis. This may prove necessary, *inter alia*, in order to avoid having to apply *statuta odiosa* of non-Community countries. What is essential is that courts are provided with a clear instrument which allows them the necessary flexibility in order to do justice to the parties in individual cases.

2. In commercial contracts, the possibility of a valid *ex ante* choice of the law applicable to non-contractual obligations was recognized, subject to certain restrictions.[318]

3. Special rules were introduced to protect the victim in the case of traffic accidents.[319] Thus, Art 4(2) and Art 7(2) of the Parliament's 1st Reading

---

[313] Text to n 322 below.

[314] EP 1st Reading Position, Recital (9). Professor Fawcett (n 311 above, 165) suggests that 'it would be hard to think of an approach which is less likely to produce uniformity of law than interest analysis'.

[315] EP 1st Reading Report, 40.

[316] EP 1st Reading Position, Art 4(4).

[317] EP 1st Reading Report, 39. For discussion of the rejection of *dépeçage* within the Regulation, see **4.78–4.79**.

[318] EP 1st Reading Position, Art 3.

[319] For discussion, see A Malatesta, 'The Law Applicable to Traffic Accidents' and M Bona, 'Personal Injuries, Fatal Accidents and Rome II: Can the Law of the Country where the Victim Suffers Provide Full and Fair Compensation?', papers from the December 2004 Castellanza

Position recommended that the individual victim's place of habitual residence should govern both the type of claim for damages (heads of damage) and quantification of damages, 'unless it would be inequitable [to the victim[320]] to do so'.[321]

4. It was proposed to harmonize Member State rules concerning the introduction and ascertainment of foreign law, by requiring (a) the claiming party to identify the law(s) which he claimed to apply to his claim, and (b) the Member State court seised of the dispute to establish the content of the foreign law of its own motion, with the parties' collaboration if required.[322]

5. The concept of 'Community public policy'[323] in Art 24 of the Commission Proposal was rejected in favour of a clarification of the public policy exception, to the effect that an award of non-compensatory damages may be regarded as being contrary to public policy.[324]

The rapporteur did not attempt to hide the motivation behind some of these amendments. In a comment written in August 2005, she stated:[325] **1.77**

Historically we have been used to these types of proposals being worked on by the Commission and in Council working groups in a very technical way; Rome II is historic because it is the first time that the European Parliament has had the power of co-decision in such an area as private international law in a field with no pre-existing Convention. It was therefore important that Parliament should challenge and question some of the Commission's basic suggestions and also seek to extend the ambit of the text where the results will touch so directly on the daily lives of our citizens such as with damages in cross-border road traffic and other personal injury accidents.

Conference (n 303 above), reproduced in Malatesta (ed), *Unification*, n 28 above, 85–106 and 249–70 respectively. See also the proposal by the Swedish delegation in the Council's Rome II Committee that the person sustaining damage be given the right to choose, as an alternative to the law of the place of damage, the law of the place in which the vehicle was registered (Council document SN 2852/04 [9.9.2004], 2–7).

[320] The words in square brackets appear in Art 4(2), but do not appear in Art 7(2), of the EP 1st Reading Position.

[321] See also EP 1st Reading Position, Art 7(1) giving Member States the option to apply the rules set out in the 1971 Hague Traffic Accidents Convention (n 25 above). On its face, the option was not limited to those States party to the Convention, although it appears that this was the rapporteur's intention (EP 1st Reading Report, 40).

[322] Ibid, Arts 12–13.

[323] Text to n 275 above.

[324] EP 1st Reading Position, Art 25(3).

[325] 'The Future "Communitarization" of the Choice of Law Rules on Non-Contractual Obligations' in Malatesta, *Unification*, n 28 above, 3–4.

However the European Parliament is not challenging or raising a debate merely to justify its own existence but rather to add a very different dimension to the legislative process; as private international law becomes communitarised, so it must come out of the technical working groups and into the political debating chamber. Some will argue that politicians should not interfere in 'technical' law, but unless law is grounded in a political process with full and open debate, it will never be acceptable to our citizens. At this difficult time in the European Union's development,[326] this is surely acceptable.

THE REPORT OF THE EUROPEAN ECONOMIC AND SOCIAL COMMITTEE

1.78 In June 2004, following a request by the Council on 8 September 2003, the European Economic and Social Committee (**EESC**)[327] delivered its opinion on the Rome II Proposal.[328] The EESC Opinion was largely favourable, both as to the lawfulness of the proposed Regulation[329] and the overall substance of the Commission Proposal.[330] The EESC recommended certain adjustments to the text put forward[331] but otherwise urged the Commission 'to complete its initiative as rapidly as possible'[332] on the basis that the proposed Regulation would 'bring inestimable benefits in terms of simpler application of the law' and that 'instead of having to establish in each individual case which system of rules on conflict of laws will apply and familiarise themselves with these rules which, at least in detail, differ from one Member State to another, users of the law will in future be able to use a single set of rules . . .'.[333]

THE COUNCIL DELIBERATES

1.79 The Council was taking longer than its legislative partner to deliberate on the merits of the proposed Regulation. Between the Commission Proposal in July 2003 and September 2006, when the Council adopted its common position,[334] the Council was presided over by seven Member States.[335]

---

[326] A reference, no doubt, to the rejection of the proposed European Constitution by French and Dutch voters in May/June 2005.

[327] Under EC Treaty, Arts 257 to 262, the EESC, which consists of representatives of economic and social components of society (including producers, workers, professionals, and consumers), has an advisory role in the legislative process.

[328] OJ C241, 1 [28.9.2004] (**EESC Opinion**).

[329] EESC Opinion, para 3 (**2.93** below).

[330] Ibid, paras 4 to 8.

[331] Ibid, para 9.

[332] Ibid, para 1.2.

[333] Ibid, para 1.3.

[334] OJ C289E, 68 [28.11.2006] (**Council Common Position**) (**1.88** below).

[335] 2003 (2nd part) Italy; 2004 Ireland, Netherlands; 2005 Luxembourg, United Kingdom; 2006 Austria, Finland.

From 2004, the work programme of every Presidency specifically identified the Rome II proposal as an item requiring attention, yet progress was evidently slow.[336]

The Council's Committee on Civil Law Matters (Rome II)[337] first met to **1.80** discuss the proposal in September 2003. Most delegations expressed support, at least in principle, for the Regulation.[338] There were two significant early developments. First, in October 2003, both the United Kingdom[339] and Ireland[340] chose to opt-in to the Regulation in accordance with the Protocol arrangements governing their participation in Title IV measures under the Treaty of Amsterdam.[341] Secondly, in March 2004, the Council Legal Service presented to the Council's Rome II Committee an opinion on the legal basis for the proposed Regulation.[342] That advice, and its consequences in terms of the discussions in Council, will be examined more closely as part of the discussion of treaty basis in the following chapter.[343]

At the invitation of the General Secretariat of the Council,[344] 18 Member **1.81** States submitted written comments on the Commission Proposal.[345] In light of these comments, and the Rome II Committee's discussion at its early meetings, the outgoing Irish and incoming Dutch Presidencies prepared a revised text, with modest amendments to the Commission Proposal.[346] A further draft from the Dutch Presidency followed in September 2004,[347] in which the principal innovation was the tentative insertion, for discussion purposes, of a separate rule of applicable law for non-contractual obligations arising from industrial action. This was the result of a proposal by the Swedish delegation.[348]

---

[336] For snapshots as to the state of play at particular points in the process, see the drafts produced by the following Presidencies: Ireland/Netherlands (Council document 10173/04 [14.6.2004]); Netherlands (Council document 12746/04 [27.9.2004]); Netherlands/ Luxembourg (Council document 16231/04 [20.12.2004]); UK/Austria (Council document 16027/05 [22.12.2005]); Austria (Council document 8417/06 [21.4.2006]).

[337] Hereafter, the 'Rome II Committee'.

[338] Council document 14010/03 [17.12.2003].

[339] Council document 13903/03 [27.10.2003].

[340] Council document 14199/03 [30.10.2003].

[341] Text to n 179 above.

[342] Council document 7015/04 [2.3.2004] (partly accessible).

[343] **2.94–2.103** below.

[344] Council document CM1222/04 [26.3.2004].

[345] Council document 9009/04 + ADD1-17 [29.4.2004–2.6.2004].

[346] Council document 10173/04 [14.6.2004].

[347] Council document 12746/04 [27.9.2004].

[348] Discussed at **9.02–9.03** below.

1.82 On 5 November 2004, the Council endorsed the so-called 'Hague Programme', sub-titled 'Strengthening Freedom Security and Justice in the European Union', setting out priorities in that policy area.[349] The Programme required work on the Rome II proposal to be actively pursued as part of the programme of measures on mutual recognition.

1.83 In December 2004, the outgoing Dutch and incoming Luxembourg Presidency produced a joint revised text[350] in the light of comments made during meetings of the Rome II Committee on civil law in the preceding two months.[351] This document was in the nature of a discussion draft, setting out alternative proposals for addressing such matters as the scope of the Regulation,[352] product liability,[353] violations of privacy and defamation,[354] and violation of the environment.[355]

1.84 During the United Kingdom Presidency in the second half of 2005, the Council's Rome II Committee considered the amendments proposed by the European Parliament at first reading, accepting some but rejecting many of the novel aspects of the Parliament's position, including (a) the more flexible rules for tort/delict generally, (b) the proposed deletion of the special rules for product liability, unfair competition, and violations of the environment, (c) the compromise proposal for violations of privacy and defamation, (d) the proposed special rules for traffic accidents, and (e) the rules concerning introduction and ascertainment of foreign law.[356] A further draft, reflecting those discussions, was circulated by the outgoing UK and incoming Austrian Presidencies in December 2005.[357]

THE RISE AND FALL OF THE 'COUNTRY OF ORIGIN PRINCIPLE'

1.85 In the meantime, the debate that had already taken place within the Commission[358] as to the relationship between private international law

---

[349] OJ C53, 1 [3.3.2005].

[350] Council document 16231/04 [20.12.2004].

[351] Meetings of the Council's Rome II Committee were held in September, October, and November 2004. Minutes of these meetings have not been published, but the Commission representatives prepared notes.

[352] Council document 16231/04, Art 1(1a).

[353] Ibid, Art 4.

[354] Ibid, Art 6.

[355] Ibid, Art 7, including a proposal that the special rule be deleted.

[356] Council documents 11515/05 [27.7.2005], 13001/05 [10.10.2005] and 15643/05 [22.12.2005]. The EP 1st Reading Position is described at **1.75–1.76** above.

[357] Council document 16027/05 [22.12.2005].

[358] **1.58–1.61** and **1.63** above.

and EC law was played out before a wider audience. The course of that debate, centred on the so called 'country of origin principle', will be considered in **Chapter 16** below.[359] For present purposes, it suffices to note that the 'principle', which at the time of the Commission's proposed Directive on services in the internal market threatened to reduce the Rome II Regulation to a subordinate role in determining the law applicable to non-contractual obligations in intra-Community cases, met with strong opposition and was ultimately shut firmly back in its box.

THE COMMISSION'S AMENDED PROPOSAL

On 21 February 2006, the Commission published an Amended Proposal   **1.86**
with the objective of adapting its original Rome II Proposal in light of the EP 1st Reading Position while reflecting proceedings in the Council.[360] Of the 54 amendments adopted by the Parliament, the Commission accepted 16 as tabled, another 13 in modified form, and 5 in part only (including the general rule for tort/delict, substantially reversing the Parliament's position) but rejected the remaining 20 (including, most notably, (a) the proposed abolition of the special rules for product liability, unfair competition, and environmental damage, (b) the modified rule for violations of privacy,[361] (c) the newly proposed special rule relating to industrial action, (d) the special rules concerning traffic accidents, and (e) the proposals concerning pleading and proof of the applicable law).[362] On almost every significant point of dispute, the Commission's approach, if not its preferred wording, would ultimately prevail over that of the Parliament.

POLITICAL AGREEMENT AND COMMON POSITION OF THE COUNCIL

In February 2006, the Austrian Presidency presented to COREPER com-   **1.87**
promise proposals for certain of the Articles for discussion at a political level at the JHA Council.[363] That discussion took place on 21 February,[364] after which the Austrian Presidency circulated a further draft of the Regulation for comment.[365] Following a further meeting of the Rome II

---

[359] **16.04–16.31**.

[360] COM (2006) 83 final (**Commission Amended Proposal**), reproduced in **Appendix 3**.

[361] The Commission instead proposed a limited exclusion of 'violations of privacy and of personal rights by the media' (Commission Amended Proposal, Art 1(2)(h)).

[362] For a summary of the EP's position on these points, see **1.75–1.76** above.

[363] Council documents 5864/06 [3.2.2006] and 6165/06 [10.2.2006].

[364] Council document 6490/06 [23.2.2006], 3 referring to an 'exchange of views'; Council document 6598/06 [4.5.2006], 4.

[365] Council document 7432/06 [16.3.2006].

Committee on 27–28 March 2006,[366] the Presidency submitted a complete compromise package first to COREPER,[367] and then to the JHA Council.[368]

1.88 At its meeting on 27–28 April 2006, the JHA Council reached political agreement on the text as a whole, with the exception of the recitals.[369] That agreement was reflected in the Common Position adopted by the Council on 25 September 2006.[370] The Council took its decision by quali-fied majority: Estonia and Latvia alone voted against, due to reservations on the special rule for industrial action.[371] In general, the Common Position followed the approach of the Commission in its Amended Proposal, rather than that of the European Parliament.[372] The principal differences from the Amended Proposal were (a) the total exclusion of violations of privacy and rights relating to privacy from the scope of the proposed Regulation,[373] (b) the adoption of a special rule for industrial action designating the law of the country in which the relevant action was taken,[374] and (c) the dele-tion of the provision favouring discretionary application of third country mandatory rules.[375]

1.89 The Commission, somewhat grudgingly, accepted the Council's Common Position, while specifically reserving its position as to the law applicable in competition cases.[376]

---

[366] Council document 7709/06 [3.5.2008].

[367] Council documents 8076/06 and 7629/06 [both 10.4.2006].

[368] Council documents 8416/06 and 8417/06 [both 21.4.2006]. Also Council document 8417/06 ADD 1 [26.4.2006] setting out further amendments in light of the work of COREPER.

[369] Council document 9033/06 [10.5.2006], 3 and Council document 9417/06 [19.5.2006]. Also Council documents 8417/06 ADD 2 [2.5.2006] (final amendments), 8498/06 [2.5.2006] and 9143/06 [19.5.2006] (text, with recitals).

[370] OJ C289, 68 [28.11.2006] (**Common Position**), with accompanying statement of reasons (originally Council document 9751/7/06 REV 7 ADD 1 [25.9.2006]) and annex linking the provisions of the Commission Proposal to those of the final Regulation. The statement of rea-sons and annex are reproduced in **Appendix 4**.

[371] Common Position, Art 9. See the Joint Declaration of Latvia and Estonia and the state-ment by the Cypriot and Greek Delegations expressing reservations about Art 9, reproduced at **9.10–9.11** below.

[372] Statement of reasons accompanying the Council's Common Position (OJ C289E, 76 [28.11.2006]).

[373] Common Position, Art 1(2)(g).

[374] Ibid, Art 9.

[375] Cf Commission Amended Proposal, Art 13(2).

[376] Commission Communication concerning the Council's Common Position (COM (2006) 566 final [27.9.2006]), 3. The Commission was, at that time, consulting on its Green Paper on 'Damages actions for breach of EC antitrust rules' (COM (2005) 672 final), as to which see **6.05–6.06** below.

The European Parliament (Second Reading Procedure)

If at first you don't succeed, try, try, again.[377] Having been rebuffed by the   **1.90**
Commission and the Council, the European Parliament flexed its legislative muscles. In its second reading resolution on the Council's Common
Position, adopted on 18 January 2007,[378] the Parliament joined issue with
the other institutions on what it regarded as key points. In particular, the
EP 2nd Reading Position (a) accepted the text of the Common Position
general rule for tort/delict but added a recital emphasizing the need for a
'margin of discretion' to do justice in individual cases,[379] (b) insisted on the
deletion of the special rule for unfair competition,[380] while accepting,
at the same time the Common Position special rules on product liability
and violations of the environment,[381] (c) restated its proposal for a special
rule on violations of privacy and rights relating to the personality,[382] and
(d) retained recitals (without any accompanying substantive provision)
dealing with introduction and ascertainment of foreign law.[383] In addition,
and more controversially, the Parliament proposed what appeared,
somewhat eliptically, to be a rule of substantive tort law to address its
concern regarding the quantification of damages in personal injury cases

[377] Attributed to T H Palmer, *Teacher's Manual* (1840).

[378] EP legislative resolution on the Council Common Position (OJ C244E, 194 [18.10.2007])
(**EP 2nd Reading Position**). Also the 2nd reading recommendation of the JURI Com-
mittee (EP document reference A6-0481/2006 FINAL [22.12.2006]) (**EP 2nd Reading
Recommendation**).

[379] EP 2nd Reading Position, Recital (14), discussed at **3.24–3.28** below. In her draft
Recommendation for 2nd Reading (EP document reference PE 378.852v01-00 [8.11.2006]),
the rapporteur had proposed a linked amendment (16) to the general rule requiring the court
seised to have regard to 'the need for certainty, predictability and uniformity of result, the
protection of legitimate expectations and the policies underlying the foreign law to be
applied and the consequences of applying that law'. That proposed amendment was not carried forward into the JURI Committee's final Recommendation. So ended the rapporteur's
dalliance with 'governmental interest analysis', **1.75** above.

[380] EP 2nd Reading Position, Amendment 17.

[381] The JURI Committee's re-statement of its proposal to delete this rule (EP 2nd Reading
Recommendation, Amendment 18) was rejected in the plenary session.

[382] EP 2nd Reading Position, Art 7.

[383] EP 2nd Reading Position, Recitals (35) and (37). The linked substantive provision
requiring the court itself to establish the foreign law of its own motion (EP 2nd Reading
Recommendation, Amendment 21) was defeated in the plenary session, but curiously the
recitals remained. A second provision proposed by the rapporteur, requiring litigants to
notify the court of the law or laws which they considered applicable (draft Recommendation
for Second Reading (EP document reference PE 378.862v01-00 [8.11.2006])), was rejected by
the JURI Committee.

(a provision principally but not exclusively aimed at protecting the victims of traffic accidents). The proposed new Art 21a provided:

> In quantifying damages in personal injury cases, the court seised shall apply the principle of *restitutio in integrum*, having regard to the victim's actual circumstances in his country of habitual residence.

1.91 During debate, Diana Wallis, the rapporteur, was forceful in her defence of the Parliament's position, emphasizing the importance attached to the proposal being '[t]he ground plan, or roadmap, which will provide clarity and certainty for the basis of civil law claims across Europe'.[384] She added:[385]

> We need this, and we, here in Parliament, want to get it done, but it has to be done in the right way. This has to fit the aspirations and needs of those we represent. This is not just some theoretical academic exercise; we are making political choices about balancing the rights and expectations of parties before civil courts.

> I am sorry that we have not reached an agreement at this stage. I still believe that it could have been possible, with more engagement and assistance. Perhaps it is because both the other institutions are not used to Parliament having codecision in this particular area—I am sorry, but you will have to get used to it!

1.92 The rapporteur addressed the special rules for unfair competition and violations of the environment, before continuing:

> Now I come to the two big issues for this Parliament. The first is defamation. Please understand that we know only too well how difficult an issue this is. However, we managed to get a huge majority at first reading across this House, and you will likely see a similar pattern repeated here today. That the Commission decided to exclude this issue before we could consider it again was disappointing, to say the least. That it did so on the basis of a clear two-year review clause, which has now been abandoned, is unacceptable. We know the issues surrounding this area of media and communication will only increase and continue to haunt us. Maybe we cannot deal with it now, but we will soon be looking at Brussels I again, and it is imperative that jurisdiction and applicable law remain in step. So, would we deprive ourselves of the opportunity to look at this again? Exclusion may truly be the only answer, but this Parliament wants to try a little bit more to see if we cannot resolve this.

> I turn to the issue that my colleagues have been most tenacious in their support for (and I am very grateful for that): damages in road-traffic accidents. Commissioner, we have the support of insurers, the support of legal practitioners, the support

---

[384] EP document CRE 18/01/2007 – 4, available at <http://www.europarl.europa.eu/sides/getDoc.do?type=CRE&reference=20070118&secondRef=ITEM-004&language=EN&ring=A6-2006-0481>.
[385] Ibid.

of victims, the support of those we represent, but somehow we cannot transmit these concerns to the Commission or to the Council. Even last week, I was confronted by a very senior justice ministry official who thought that what we were trying to do was the equivalent of applying German law to determine liability in respect of a road-traffic accident which had happened in the UK, where, of course, we drive on the 'wrong' side of the road. Do you really think we are that stupid? I wish people would have the courtesy to read and understand what we are suggesting: merely the accepted principle of *restitutio in integrum*—to put victims back in the position they were in before the incident. There should be nothing so fearful in this. Indeed, the illogical approach would be for a judge in the victim's country to be able to deal with the case by virtue of the Motor Insurance Directives[386] and Brussels I,[387] and then have to apply a foreign, outside law in respect of damages. This, indeed, would be illogical—and that is the situation we are currently in. Please look at what we are saying and appreciate that, given the even the greater mobility of our citizens on Europe's roads, this matter needs attention, sooner rather than later, and a four-year general review clause just will not do.

She concluded:

My last hope is that our debates will have brought the subject of private international law out of the dusty cupboards in justice ministries and expert committees into the glare of public, political, transparent debate. Therefore, all we ask is that you bear with us a little longer so that, together, the institutions of Europe can get this right.

Franco Frattini, Vice-President of the Commission and JLS Commissioner, reacted coolly.[388] Like Mrs Wallis, he regretted the lack of a special rule for privacy and defamation, but indicated that the Commission had accepted the Common Position on this point on the ground of political expediency, there being (in his view) no possibility of a compromise position.[389] He was, however, strongly opposed to the deletion of special rules, particularly that concerning environmental liability (a view that prevailed in the plenary session). As to the proposed Art 21a concerning quantification of damages in personal injury cases, he described the proposal as 'very interesting', but suggested that as a matter of harmonization of civil law, it fell **1.93**

---

[386] **14.100–14.106** below.

[387] i.e. Regulation (EC) No 44/2001 on jurisdiction and the recognition and enforcement of judgments in civil and commercial matters, n 263 above.

[388] For the full text of his address, see the hyperlink at n 384 above.

[389] 'I firmly believe that to accept a provision that cannot obtain even the slightest consensus between the institutions, as several members of the Committee on Legal Affairs have stated, would be to reopen a can of worms.' The original, French text refers more vividly to *la boîte de Pandore*.

outside the proper scope of the Rome II instrument.[390] He nevertheless expressed sympathy for the Parliament's concern with the position of victims in road traffic accidents.[391] These comments were reflected in the Commission's subsequent Opinion on the Parliament's 2nd Reading Position, together with other specific observations and drafting points.[392]

1.94   Predictably, on 19 April 2007, the Council unanimously[393] decided not to adopt the text of the Regulation as amended by the European Parliament in its 2nd Reading Position. As a result, the European Community equivalent of extra time, the conciliation process, was invoked. In this regard, Art 251(4) of the EC Treaty provides:

> The Conciliation Committee, which shall be composed of the Members of the Council or their representatives and an equal number of representatives of the European Parliament, shall have the task of reaching agreement on a joint text, by a qualified majority of the Members of the Council or their representatives and by a majority of the representatives of the European Parliament. The Commission shall take part in the Conciliation Committee's proceedings and shall take all the necessary initiatives with a view to reconciling the positions of the European Parliament and the Council. In fulfilling this task, the Conciliation Committee shall address the common position on the basis of the amendments proposed by the European Parliament.

1.95   Trilogues[394] between the representatives of the Council, Commission, and Parliament[395] took place in March and April 2007. Work on a compromise

---

[390] The Commission's March 2007 Opinion on the EP 2nd Reading Position (n 392 below) stated bluntly that the issue of damages 'is a complex point of substantive civil law, and Rome II is not the proper place for addressing it' (COM (2007) 126 final [14.3.2007], 4).

[391] For further discussion of this issue, see **14.26–14.32** below.

[392] Commission Opinion on the European Parliament's amendments to the Council Common Position (COM (2007) 126 final [14.3.2007]).

[393] Council document 8569/07 COR1 [4.6.2007].

[394] An ugly and ill-conceived term, which is also frequently spelled in official documents as 'trialogue'. The word 'dialogue', from which it appears to derive, is itself derived from the Greek διάλογος ('conversation' from διά meaning 'through, across') and has nothing to do with the Greek δι- ('twice') (R W Burchfield (ed), *New Fowler's Modern English Usage* (3rd edn, 1996), 210). The Oxford English Dictionary defines 'trilogue' as 'a group of three words or sayings'. Unfortunately, it seems that we are stuck with the term as a shorthand for tripartite meetings within the conciliation process (see Joint Declaration of the European Parliament, Council and Commission on practical arrangements for the co-decision procedure (OJ C143, 3 [30.6.2007])).

[395] Delegation led by Mechtild Rothe (Vice-President), Giuseppi Gargani (Chair, JURI Committee), and Diana Wallis.

solution had, however, begun before this.[396] In the run up to the Conciliation Committee meeting on 15 May 2007, agreement had been reached on the text of several recitals, but differences on the key points had yet to be bridged, with the Parliament in particular maintaining its demand for a special rule concerning violations of privacy and rights relating to personality.[397] At that meeting,[398] however, common agreement on the text of the Regulation was reached,[399] with most of the disagreements on substantive provisions (including exclusion of privacy etc) being resolved in the Council's favour. The European Parliament nevertheless secured the agreement of the Council and the Commission to a review clause requiring the Commission to examine and report on (a) the law applicable to non-contractual obligations arising out of violations of privacy and rights relating to personality, (b) the effects of the way in which foreign law is treated in the Member States, and (c) the relationship between the Regulation and the Hague Traffic Accidents Convention.[400] The Commission, in a separate statement, also promised to produce, before the end of 2008, a study on the options, including insurance aspects, for improving the position of cross-border victims of road traffic accidents, paving the way for a Green Paper.[401]

All that remained was for the agreed text to be approved by majority vote **1.96** of the European Parliament[402] and by a qualified majority in the Council.

---

[396] See Council documents DS 94/07 [6.2.2007], 6309/07 [13.2.2007], 7318/07 [19.3.2007], and 8241/07 [25.4.2007] and the EP working document dated 27 February 2007 (EP document reference PE 386.319). For later updates as to the progress of discussions, see EP documents references PE 386.589 [21.3.2007], PE 388.454 [18.4.2007], and Council documents 8215/07 [5.4.2007], 8408/07 [13.4.2007], 8552/07 [17.4.2007], SN 2494/07 [30.4.2007], 9137/07 [7.5.2007], and 9457/07 [10.5.2007].

[397] See Council document 9457/07 [10.5.2007]. As appears from this document, the EP had, by this time, conceded the need for a special rule concerning unfair commercial practices/competition (although the text remained to be agreed) and appeared to have accepted that questions of pleading and proof of foreign law and compensation for traffic accident victims would be addressed in the review clause.

[398] Chaired by Mechtild Rothe, Vice-President of the European Parliament, and Brigitte Zypries, German Justice Minister.

[399] See Press Release (Council document 9713/07 [16.5.2007]). The co-Chairmen of the Conciliation Committee formally confirmed that agreement on 25 June 2007 (EP document reference PE-CONS 3619/07).

[400] Regulation, Art 30. See the Commission's statements on the review clause and on the treatment of foreign law appended to the Regulation in its final form at OJ L199, 49 [31.7.2007].

[401] Ibid (**14.32** below).

[402] See the report of the EP JURI Committee on the joint text approved by the Conciliation Committee for a Regulation on the law applicable to non-contractual obligations (EP document A6-0257/2007 [28.6.2007]) (**EP 3rd Reading Report**).

The Council approved the Regulation in the Environment Council on 28 June 2007, with Latvia and Estonia again voting against due to their objections to Art 9 (industrial action).[403] The Parliament followed in adopting the Regulation on 10 July 2007. In recommending a favourable vote, Mrs Wallis felt able to claim at least a partial victory for the European Parliament:[404]

We left a clear mark, on behalf of Parliament, on the final text—a text which, thanks to Parliament, goes beyond the mere technical and legal, bringing private international law into the open to serve the practical needs of our citizens, particularly in the area of road traffic accidents.

However, we also dealt with technical issues: clarifying definitions on the environment or supplying a solution on the issue of unfair competition, and then grappling with the relationship between European conflict of law rules and internal market instruments. I am not entirely sure that we got it right. I find I have been congratulated from many quarters, which makes me a little nervous. Then we are still trying to have the same debates around Rome I and the review of the consumer *acquis*. We have, at some point, to get this relationship correct.

She continued:[405]

There are many leftovers from Rome II that form the basis of studies that I hope the Commissioner will mention in his declaration—studies on road traffic accidents, on defamation, and on the treatment of foreign law. All these issues are absolutely integral to the relationship between civil justice and the internal market. Indeed, we could say that the internal market will function only if we have a coherent system of civil justice.

Civil justice cannot just be an add-on to the internal market—some sort of limited competence where we tread only reluctantly at the invitation of Member States. I seem to remember a long time ago in 1999 in Tampere that there was a vision of an area of civil justice. Rome II was part of that. We need to refocus, to question whether we have a civil justice system in Europe that functions for all the users of the internal market and for our citizens, and is accessible and understandable. Rome II plays its part as forming the basis—the initial roadmap—but the following studies give us the chance to re-evaluate and make the next steps forward.

[403] See voting record in Council document 11313/07 [28.7.2007]. As to the position of Latvia and Estonia, see n 371 above.
[404] EP document CRE 09/07/2007 – 22, available at <http://www.europarl.europa.eu/sides/getDoc.do?type=CRE&reference=20070709&secondRef=ITEM-022&language=EN&ring=A6-2007-0257>. Also EP 3rd Reading Report, 8–9.
[405] Ibid.

D. CONCLUSION: END OF THE ROAD?

The Rome II Regulation was published in the Official Journal of the **1.97**
European Union on 31 July 2007,[406] and thereby (apparently) entered into
force on 20 August 2007.[407] As noted, it will apply from 11 January 2009.
The process of development of the law applicable to non-contractual obligations seems, however, unlikely to stand still for long. Even before the
Rome II Regulation is applied by any Member State court, the Commission
is required by 31 December 2008 to submit the first, and perhaps most
important, of its studies under the review clause, that concerning the law
applicable to obligations arising out of violations and privacy. Further
developments can be expected, in due course, in the areas of (a) interaction between contractual and non-contractual obligations,[408] (b) unfair
competition,[409] (c) pleading and proof of foreign law,[410] and (d) traffic accidents,[411] as well as a report on the general functioning of the Regulation
due in 2011.[412] Those advocating reform of private international law rules
within the European Community must also compete with those promoting harmonization of substantive law, including advocates for a European
Civil Code. As such, the Regulation may be no more than a pit stop on
what is already a very long journey.

---

[406] OJ L199, 40.

[407] EC Treaty, Art 254(1), there being no entry into force date specified in the Regulation.
For further discussion of this point, see **3.315–3.324** below.

[408] The Regulation on the law applicable to contractual obligations (the so-called 'Rome I'
Regulation) was adopted on 17 June 2008 and will apply to contracts concluded after 17
December 2009.

[409] Following the Commission's White Paper on damages in anti-trust cases (**6.09** below).

[410] Regulation, Art 30(1)(i).

[411] Ibid, Art 30(1)(ii).

[412] Ibid, Art 30(1).

2

Treaty Base

A. INTRODUCTION

In considering whether the European Community had legislative compe- **2.01** tence to adopt the Rome II Regulation, it must be acknowledged from the outset that, however strong particular arguments might appear when canvassed on paper, the prospects of the European Court of Justice being persuaded that the Regulation is *ultra vires* or otherwise unlawful are very small indeed. However unpalatable it may be,[1] the institutions of the European Community have long sought to test the limits of their powers, perhaps in the fear that they would otherwise be eroded by the passage of time. The Rome II Regulation is but one example of this phenomenon of

---

[1] S Weatherill, 'Why Object to the Harmonization of Private Law by the EC?' (2004) 12 Eur Rev Priv L 633.

'competence creep', and onlookers should not be surprised by the confidence with which representatives of the Member States,[2] the Commission,[3] and the Parliament[4] have asserted that the Regulation is a natural step in the development of a coherent system of private law within the Community legal framework.

2.02 Equally, the European Court is becoming an inhospitable forum for those who seek to question newly asserted competences, particularly in the area of private law. In recent years, the ECJ has adopted an expansionist approach both to the reach of EC law,[5] and to the legislative and other powers of the Community organs.[6] Moreover, in the event of a challenge to the Rome II Regulation, the ECJ would no doubt be alert to the potential legal, political, and economic consequences of a negative decision in terms of its impact upon existing[7] and planned[8] measures in the area of judicial cooperation in civil matters.

2.03 Accordingly, it would be a courageous litigant who accepted the gauntlet thrown down by the arguments presented in the following paragraphs.[9] Whether a case will arise in which the subject matter is sufficiently valuable, financially or otherwise, to justify that course of action (with the attendant tactical advantage or disadvantage that the delay produced by a reference to the ECJ would involve) remains to be seen.

---

[2] Council document 12544/98 [11.11.1998], 120–4.

[3] **1.69** above.

[4] e.g. **1.96** above, text to n 405.

[5] e.g., Case C-281/98, *Angonese v Cassa di Riparmio di Bolzano* [2000] ECR I-4139 (extension of EC Treaty requirements to private persons); Case C-60/00, *Carpenter v Secretary of State for the Home Department* [2002] ECR I-6279 (expansive view of required connection to cross-border activity).

[6] e.g., Case C-176/03, *Commission v Council* [2005] ECR I-7879 (annulling Council Framework Decision 2003/80/JHA of 27 January 2003 on the protection of the environment through criminal law on the ground that the Community was competent to require criminal penalties in this area); Opinion 01/03, *Competence of the Community to conclude the new Lugano Convention on jurisdiction and the recognition of judgments in civil and commercial matters* [2006] ECR I-1145 (confirming, in emphatic terms, the Community's external competence to conclude the Convention)). Also the Commission's Communication on the implications of the decision in Case C-176/03 (COM (2005) 583 final [28.11.2005]) and the Court's subsequent decision in Case C-440/05, *Commission v Council* [2007] ECR I-000 (annulling Council Framework Decision 2005/667/JHA of 12 July 1995 to strengthen the criminal-law framework for the enforcement of the law against ship-source pollution).

[7] Most obviously, the Brussels I Regulation and the Rome I Regulation.

[8] e.g. the proposals in the area of family law and wills and succession referred to at **3.149** and **3.154** below.

[9] For techniques of judicial restraint, see **2.44–2.45** below.

B. THE EC LAW FRAMEWORK[10]

Introduction

In considering whether the Rome II Regulation was validly adopted, the **2.04** starting point is that the European Community is an international organization (or, rather, a grouping of international organizations) established by treaty. As such, it has only the competences assigned to it by its Member States by treaty, specifically the EC Treaty.[11] That relationship is confirmed by Art 5, para 1 of the EC Treaty which provides:

The Community shall act within the limits of the powers conferred upon it by this Treaty and of the objectives assigned to it therein.

The legal basis for the Regulation must, accordingly, be found within the **2.05** EC Treaty as it stood on 11 July 2007, the date on which the Regulation was adopted.[12]

Relevant Provisions of Title IV to the EC Treaty

The opening words of the preamble to the Rome II Regulation identify as **2.06** its specific legal basis Arts 61(c) and 67 of the EC Treaty. Art 61 lies within Title IV of the EC Treaty, introduced with effect from 1 January 1999 by the Treaty of Amsterdam,[13] and provides that:

In order to establish progressively an area of freedom, security and justice,[14] the Council shall adopt: . . .

(c) measures in the field of judicial cooperation in civil matters as provided for in Art 65.

---

[10] For a wider discussion of Community competence in matters of private international law, see A Dickinson, 'European Private International Law: Embracing New Horizons or Mourning the Past?' (2005) 1 J Priv Int L 197, in which some of the material in this chapter first appeared; S Bariatti, 'The Future Community Rules in the Framework of the Communitarization of Private International Law', 5–32 in A Malatesta (ed), *The Unification of Choice of Law Rules on Torts and Other Non-Contractual Obligations in Europe* (2006).

[11] P Sands and P Klein, *Bowett's Law of International Institutions* (5th edn, 2001), 292–6.

[12] References in Sections B to E of this chapter are to the provisions of the EC Treaty which were in force at the time the Regulation was adopted. The changes that would result from the Lisbon Reform Treaty, if ratified by all Member States, are considered at **2.41–2.43** below. The legality of the Regulation must, however, be judged according to the state of the law and the facts as they stood at the date of its adoption (Case C-449/98, *International Express Carriers Conference v Commission* [2001] ECR I-3875, para 87).

[13] **1.52** above.

[14] For discussion of this concept, see **2.11–2.15** below.

2.07 The power to legislate in the field of judicial cooperation in civil matters is, accordingly, expressly tied to the provisions of Art 65.[15] Art 65 itself provides:

> Measures in the field of judicial cooperation in civil matters having cross-border implications, to be taken in accordance with Art 67 and insofar as necessary for the proper functioning of the internal market, shall include:
> (a) improving and simplifying:
> —the system for cross-border service of judicial and extrajudicial documents;
> —cooperation in the taking of evidence;
> —the recognition and enforcement of decisions in civil and commercial cases, including decisions in extrajudicial cases;
> (b) promoting the compatibility of the rules applicable in the Member States concerning the conflict of laws and of jurisdiction;
> (c) eliminating obstacles to the good functioning of civil proceedings, if necessary, by promoting the compatibility of the rules on civil procedure applicable in the Member States.

2.08 By Art 67(5), introduced in 2003 by the Treaty of Nice, measures falling within the scope of Art 65 (other than family law measures) are subject to the 'co-decision' procedure prescribed by EC Treaty, Art 251.[16]

RESTRICTIONS ON COMMUNITY COMPETENCE

2.09 Art 65 contains a number of potential restrictions on the competence of the EC to legislate upon matters of private international law. Significantly, these restrictions were not part of the initial proposal for a Community competence in this subject area, which itself came at a relatively late stage of negotiations leading to the Treaty of Amsterdam.[17] As one commentator notes:[18]

> The idea to also include the provisions of Art K.3 [of the Treaty of European Union] dealing with cooperation in civil justice matters came late in the negotiations and

---

[15] The effect of those provisions cannot, therefore, be avoided by omitting reference to Art 65 in the recitals to a Community legislative instrument (as, for example, in Council Regulation (EC) No 2201/2003 of 27 November 2003 concerning jurisdiction and the recognition and enforcement of judgments in matrimonial matters and the matters of parental responsibility).

[16] **1.68** above.

[17] C Kohler, 'Interrogations sur les sources du droit international privé européen après le traité d'Amsterdam' (1999) 88 *Revue critique de droit international privé* 1, 9–14, esp footnote (20) setting out the text of the proposal of the Netherlands Presidency for an article creating Community competence in the field of civil justice. Also Council documents CONF/4000-4002/97.

[18] P E Herzog, commentary on Art 65 in D Campbell and S Cotter (ed), *The Law of the European Community, a Commentary on the EC Treaty* (New York, Matthew Bender, looseleaf), para 65.01. Also M den Boer 'A New Area of Freedom, Security and Justice: the Shaping of a Hybrid Compromise' in F Laursen (ed) *The Amsterdam Treaty: National Preference, Formation, Interstate Bargaining and Outcome* (2002), pp 509–34; A Duff (ed), *The Treaty of Amsterdam* (1997), 21. Also **2.25** below.

encountered some misgivings by a number of Member States. This may explain the somewhat awkward and ambiguous language of Art 65.

For present purposes, three aspects of Art 65 are of particular significance. **2.10** First, and most significantly, the reference to measures being taken 'insofar as necessary for the proper functioning of the internal market'. Secondly, the requirement that measures adopted must have 'cross-border implications'. Thirdly, the restriction in Art 65(b) to measures aimed at 'promoting the compatibility' of the rules applicable in Member States. In addition, other more general restrictions on the Community's competence to legislate apply here, including the requirements of subsidiarity and proportionality.

ESTABLISHING AN 'AREA OF FREEDOM, SECURITY AND JUSTICE'

EC Treaty, Art 61 refers to the progressive creation of an 'area of freedom, **2.11** security and justice'. As in the case of the Rome II Regulation,[19] the recitals to Title IV instruments invariably contain a reference to this 'aim' or 'objective', specifically linked in some instances to the free movement of persons.[20] Yet there is no other reference to the 'area' in the EC Treaty, and it is nowhere defined. In particular, the statement of the objectives and activities of the European Community in Arts 2 to 4 contains no specific reference to it. In contrast, Art 2 of the Treaty on European Union states that one of the objectives of the Union established by that Treaty is 'to maintain and develop the Union as an area of freedom, security and justice, in which the free movement of persons is assured in conjunction with appropriate measures with respect to external border controls, asylum, immigration and the prevention and combating of crime'.[21]

In the (Vienna) Action Plan of the Council and Commission following the **2.12** Amsterdam Treaty,[22] the two institutions sought to develop the interlinking concepts of 'freedom', 'security', and 'justice', noting that '[f]reedom loses much of its meaning if it cannot be enjoyed in a secure environment

---

[19] Recital (1).

[20] e.g. Recital (1) to the Brussels I Regulation; Recital (1) to Regulation (EC) No 1348/2000 on the service in the Member States of judicial and extra-judicial documents in civil or commercial matters (OJ L160, 37 [30.6.2000]) (the Service Regulation).

[21] Consolidated version, OJ C325, 1 [24.12.2002]. For discussion of the relationship between the 'area of freedom, security and justice', the 'free movement of persons', and 'combating of crime' in the context of the TEU and Schengen Agreement, see the Opinion of Adv Gen Sharpston in Case C-476/04, *Criminal proceedings against Gasparini* [2006] ECR I-9199, paras 82–4, 97, but note that her reasoning on this point was not accepted by the ECJ in its decision (ibid, Judgment, paras 22–33).

[22] OJ C19, 1 [23.1.1999] (**1.56** above).

and with the full backing of a system of justice in which all Union citizens and residents can have confidence'.[23] As to the concept of 'an area of justice', the authors of the Action Plan stated:[24]

> Justice must be seen as facilitating the day-to-day life of people and bringing to justice those who threaten the freedom and security of individuals and society. This includes both access to justice and full judicial cooperation between Member States.

2.13 The following explanation is then given with respect to judicial cooperation in civil matters:[25]

> Law-abiding citizens have a right to look to the Union to simplify and facilitate the judicial environment in which they live in the European Union context. Here principles such as legal certainty and equal access to justice should be a main objective, implying identification of the competent jurisdiction, clear designation of the applicable law, availability of speedy and fair proceedings and effective enforcement procedures.

Similarly, the Presidency Conclusions of the 1999 Tampere European Council stated:[26]

> The enjoyment of freedom requires a genuine area of justice, where people can approach courts and authorities in any Member State as easily as in their own. . . . Judgements and decisions should be respected and enforced throughout the Union, while safeguarding the basic legal certainty of people and economic operators. Better compatibility and more convergence between the legal systems of Member States must be achieved.

2.14 Laudable as these objectives are, there is no textual basis in the EC Treaty for treating the 'area of freedom, security and justice' as anything more than an amalgam of the specific legislative competences set out in EC Treaty, Art 61, each of which must be considered in accordance with its terms. The concept cannot be used, therefore, as a source of higher level principles such as 'legal certainty' and 'equal access to justice', which may themselves be used to colour the legislative competence of the Community in this field. Accordingly the Vienna Action Plan and the 1999 Tampere Presidency Conclusions cannot themselves be taken to authorize any wider Community competence than that which appears on the face of the EC Treaty.[27]

---

[23] Ibid, para 5.
[24] Ibid, para 15.
[25] Ibid, para 16.
[26] Presidency Conclusions, Tampere European Council (15–16 October 1999) (**1.57** above).
[27] **2.59–2.62** below.

In *Leffler v Berlin Chemie AG*, a case concerning the original Service **2.15**
Regulation,[28] the ECJ stated that:[29]

The objective pursued by the Treaty of Amsterdam of creating an area of freedom
of security and justice, thereby giving the Community a new dimension, and the
transfer from the EU Treaty to the EC Treaty of the body of rules enabling measures in the field of judicial cooperation in civil matters having cross-border
implications to be adopted testify to the will of the Member States to establish such
measures firmly in the Community legal order and thus to lay down the principle
that they are to be interpreted autonomously.

Beyond the fact that competences were undoubtedly transferred from the
TEU to the EC Treaty by the Treaty of Amsterdam, it is unclear what 'new
Community dimension' the Court of Justice had in mind—it made no
attempt to explain what an 'area of freedom security and justice' involved.
It was not, in any event, a necessary for the Court to refer to these matters
to conclude that the provisions of the Service Regulation should be interpreted autonomously— the need for uniform application of its provisions
across the Community was a perfectly adequate justification.[30]

The Internal Market Connection

Art 65 authorizes the taking of measures 'insofar as necessary for the **2.16**
proper functioning of the internal market'. This wording has been widely
discussed, with particular reference to the Rome II Regulation. In this connection, Sir Lawrence Collins, the general editor of Dicey, Morris & Collins,
submitted:[31]

[I]t is fanciful to suppose . . . that a regulation to harmonise private international
rules for non-contractual obligations is 'necessary for the proper functioning of the
internal market'

---

[28] Text to n 20 above. From 13 November 2008, the Service Regulation will be replaced by
Regulation (EC) No 1393/2007 (OJ L324, 79 [10.12.2007]).
[29] Case C-443/03 [2005] ECR I-9611, para 45. Also the Opinion of Adv Gen Stix-Hackl,
para 62 ('This need for autonomous interpretation of specific instruments of Community law
can also be founded on the objectives of the legislation in question. The Regulation has the
objective of developing an area of freedom, security and justice, in which the free movement
of persons is assured. This objective alone requires approximation as far as possible of the
legal consequences of rights arising out of the Regulation, since divergent interpretation of
the legal consequences would lead to unacceptable legal uncertainty and fragmentation in
the area of civil procedure in particular, which is sensitive in terms of fundamental rights.')
[30] **3.05–3.09** below.
[31] Evidence to House of Lords' European Union Committee examining the proposed
Regulation (House of Lords' European Union Committee, 'The Rome II Regulation', 8th
Report of Session 2003–2004 (HL Paper 66) (**HL Report**), Evidence, 46).

Similarly, the European Union Committee of the House of Lords concluded in April 2004:[32]

> The Commission has not shown a convincing case of 'necessity' within the mean-
> ing of Art 65.

2.17 In contrast, Community institutions have frequently asserted that uniform
rules of applicable law, including rules relating to non-contractual obligations, are 'necessary' in this sense.[33] In the present connection, a section of
the Commission's unpublished draft 2001 Green Paper[34] headed 'The
need for a Community instrument' contained the following statement:[35]

> By harmonising substantive law and establishing uniform conflict rules, it will be
> possible to determine with certainty the rule applicable to a given situation. This
> will increase certainty as to the law and thus help the smooth operation of the
> internal market.

2.18 Similarly, with respect to the 1968 Brussels Convention, the predecessor to
the Brussels I Regulation containing uniform rules governing jurisdiction
and the recognition and enforcement of judgments, the ECJ has stated
(without supporting material) that:[36]

> In fact it is not disputed that the Brussels Convention helps to ensure the smooth
> working of the internal market.

2.19 The difficulty with statements of this kind, on both sides of the debate,
is that they generally provide no indication of the legal test which
their author considers should be applied to establish that a measure is
sufficiently linked to the functioning of the internal market. They
also appear to make unstated assumptions as to the type of evidence
required to satisfy that legal test.[37] These matters merit more detailed
consideration. In particular, (a) what is the 'internal market' and what,

---

[32] HL Report, para 72.

[33] See, e.g., the evidence of Mr Mario Tenreiro and Ms Claudia Hahn (DG JLS) to the
House of Lords' European Union Committee (HL Report, Evidence, 1–6), the passage from
the EESC Opinion on the Commission Proposal quoted at **2.93** below, and the EESC's opinion on the proposal for a Regulation on the law applicable to contractual obligations (Rome I)
(OJ C318, 57 [23.12.2006]).

[34] **1.60–1.62** above.

[35] Draft Green Paper on the law applicable to non-contractual obligations' [18.1.2001],
para 1.5.

[36] Case C-281/02, *Owusu v Jackson* [2005] ECR I-1383, para 33. Also the ECJ's comments in
para 143 of its Opinion 01/03 on *Competence of the Community to conclude the new Lugano
Convention on jurisdiction and the recognition of judgments in civil and commercial matters* [2006]
ECR I-1145, quoted at text to n 86 below.

[37] The author admits his own prior culpability on both counts (HL Report, Evidence,
54–5).

from a legal viewpoint, is needed for it to function properly, and (b) how strict is the requirement of 'necessity' in Art 65?

The Internal Market and its Proper Functioning

By Art 3.1 of the EC Treaty, the activities of the Community 'shall include, **2.20** as provided in this Treaty':

... (c) an internal market characterised by the abolition, as between Member States, of obstacles to the free movement of goods, persons, services and capital ...

(g) a system ensuring that competition in the internal market is not distorted ...

By Art 14.1, the EC was required to adopt measures with the aim of pro- **2.21** gressively establishing the internal market over a period expiring on 31 December 1992. By Art 14.2:[38]

The internal market shall comprise an area without internal frontiers in which the free movement of goods, persons, services and capital is ensured *in accordance with the provisions of this Treaty.*

The Treaty contains separate sections on the free movement of goods **2.22** (Arts 23 to 31), workers (Arts 39 to 42), services (Arts 49 to 55), and capital (Arts 56 to 60) and on freedom of establishment (Arts 43 to 48).

The Required Connection to the Internal Market under Art 65

At the outset, it is necessary to consider the argument that the internal **2.23** market wording in Art 65 does not impose any additional qualification upon the competence of the Community legislator, but instead involves the overt recognition by the authors of the Treaty of Amsterdam that the measures described in Art 65 were, in fact, essential to the proper func- tioning of the internal market.[39] In an Opinion delivered in 1999, shortly before the coming into force of the Treaty of Amsterdam, Advocate General Cosmas stated:[40]

First, the entry into force of the Treaty of Amsterdam, if it occurs, will lead, under the new Article *[61]* et seq,[41] to the Community being vested with a number of

---

[38] Emphasis added.

[39] J Basedow, 'The Communitarization of the Conflict of Laws under the Treaty of Amsterdam' (2000) 37 Common Market L Rev 687, 703.

[40] Case C-378/97, *Criminal proceedings against Wijsenbeek* [1999] ECR I-6207, para 69 (footnotes added).

[41] **2.06–2.07** above. The numbering of Articles in the original refers to Arts 73i and following, being the original numbering in the Amsterdam Treaty.

powers[42] directly linked to the implementation of the general obligation under Article *[14]* of the EC Treaty[43] on the progressive establishment of the internal market. Article *[61]* et seq will in reality clarify and deal with on the regulatory plane the most important of the factors of the freedom of movement of persons to which Article *[14]* refers. In other words, the Treaty of Amsterdam provisions in question are the indispensable complement to the system intended to be created by Article *[14]* with which we are dealing in the present case.[44]

2.24 In the final footnote in the passage quoted above, the Advocate General suggested:

In other words, the 'area without internal frontiers' which the legislature of the Single European Act intends to create by means of Article *[14]* . . . presupposes, as a condition *sine qua non* of its existence, the establishment of an 'area of freedom, security and justice', the creation of which is mentioned only in the Treaty of Amsterdam.

2.25 The argument is forcefully presented. It is, however, difficult to reconcile with what is known of the course of the negotiations leading to the conclusion of the Treaty of Amsterdam.[45] The internal market wording appears for the first time in a conference document[46] circulated by the Council Presidency to delegations during the last session of the inter-governmental conference in Amsterdam on 17 June 1997. It was evidently part of a compromise package presented with a view to securing agreement on the provisions of what was to become Title IV, transferring competences from the Member States to the EC. Moreover, it is significant that the language used was similar (although not identical) to the language deployed in what, at that time, were Arts 3(h) and 100a of the EC Treaty[47] (now Arts 3(h)

---

[42] Footnote text in original: 'I do not wish, by reason of my observations, to participate in the debate whether the said Community powers are appropriate or sufficient in view of the creation of a framework of complete freedom of movement for persons or whether obstacles exist, particularly because of the maintenance of parallel powers of the Member States in the fields of asylum and immigration. Some of these matters continue to come within the realm of intergovernmental cooperation in accordance with Article K.1 et seq. of the Treaty on European Union (in the version amended by the Treaty of Amsterdam). I shall merely note that, by transferring a regulatory matter from the third pillar to the first, the Treaty of Amsterdam as a matter of principle lays the basis for the implementation of the general requirements of Article *[14]* of the Treaty, which in any case have not been achieved at the current stage of European unification.'

[43] **2.21** above. The numbering in the original refers to Art 7a, being the pre-Amsterdam Treaty numbering.

[44] Footnote text quoted in the following paragraph.

[45] **2.09** above.

[46] Council document CONF/4000/97 ADD 1 [17.6.1997].

[47] Introduced by the Maastricht Treaty on European Union (OJ C191, 1 [27.7.1992]), Art G.

and 95) and which, as appears below,[48] are far from empty of legal meaning. If the words were merely declaratory, they could easily have been omitted and an affirmation as to the legitimacy of the provisions of Title IV in the European project added to the conclusions of the conference.

On the premise that the internal market wording in Art 65 is not mere verbiage, possible interpretations include the following:[49] **2.26**

- First, that the Community legislator need only establish (by objective criteria amenable to judicial review[50]) some connection between the proposed measure and the cross-border movement within the EC of persons, goods, services, or capital (for convenience, this possible interpretation will be referred to in the following paragraphs as the 'low threshold').

- Secondly, that the legislator must establish (again by reviewable objective criteria) that the proposed measure removes 'restrictions' on the cross-border movement of persons, goods, services or capital within the meaning of EC Treaty, Arts 28 to 29 (ex-Arts 30 and 34) (goods), Art 39 (ex-Art 48) (workers), Art 43 (ex-Art 52) (establishment), Art 49 (ex-Art 59) (services), and Art 56 (ex-Art 73b) (capital) ('high threshold').[51]

- Thirdly, that the legislator must establish (again by reviewable objective criteria) either that the proposed measure removes 'restrictions' (in the sense described in the previous paragraph) or that it removes distortions of competition in the internal market for goods, persons, services, or capital. As Professor Barnard notes:[52]

To a certain extent this second ground overlaps with the first: any obstacle to trade is also likely to distort competition. However, this second ground is broader, covering situations where, owing to the absence of Regulation in State A, the producers or service providers established there enjoy a competitive advantage in terms of production costs over their competitors in State B who face substantial regulation. A harmonisation directive would iron out these cost differences.

---

[48] **2.30–2.32** below.

[49] There may be other possible variations, but the following illustrate the range of possible views.

[50] Case C-491/01, *R v Secretary of State for Health, ex p British American Tobacco (Investments) Ltd* [2002] ECR I-11453, para 93 (a case concerning EC Treaty, Art 95).

[51] It is not relevant for this purpose whether such restrictions are capable of being justified, so as to escape the conclusion that they are incompatible with the Treaty.

[52] C Barnard, *The Substantive Law of the EU* (2nd edn, 2007), 575. The comment is equally apposite in the case of harmonization by EC regulation.

This possible interpretation is, therefore, broader than the second, but narrower than the first, and will be referred to in the following paragraphs as the 'medium threshold'.

2.27 The number of possible interpretations doubles if one recognizes that, in each case, the required connection with the internal market may be applied strictly (so that the Community has no competence to legislate for situations in which the connection does not exist) or with greater latitude (so that the Community may legislate for situations in which the connection does not exist, as an incidental consequence of legislating for situations in which the connection does exist). This aspect of the Community competence will be considered separately below.[53]

2.28 It will be readily apparent that, if a low threshold is applied, the EC's competence under Art 65 to legislate in matters of private international law is unlikely to be materially hindered by the requirement of a connection to the internal market.

2.29 Conversely, if a high threshold is adopted, that requirement would constitute a potentially significant obstacle to Community legislation, such as the Rome II Regulation, laying down uniform rules of private international law. In general terms, although a rule of private international law may constitute an unlawful restriction on the free movement of goods, persons, services, and capital under the EC Treaty,[54] that is unlikely to be true in most cases[55] unless the rule in question is directly or indirectly discriminatory on grounds of nationality contrary to EC Treaty, Art 12.[56] Thus:

(a) Many rules operating in cross-border situations are of a procedural character, being inextricably linked with the process of litigation, and their effect appears too uncertain and indirect to be regarded as liable to hinder trade between Member States.[57]

---

[53] **2.34–2.39**.

[54] A notable example being the 'real seat' rule of applicable law considered by the Court of Justice in the *Überseering* case, discussed at text to nn 59–61 below. Note also the reasoning of Adv Gen Sharpston in Case C-353/06, *Grunkin and Paul v Standesamt Stadt Niebüll* Opinion (24 April 2008), paras 37–46.

[55] M Wilderspin and X Lewis, '*Les relations entre le droit communautaire et les règles de conflits de lois des États membres*' (2002) 91 *Revue critique de droit internationale privé* 1.

[56] e.g. Case C-323/95, *Hayes v Kronenberger GmbH* [1997] ECR I-1711; Case C-148/02, *Garcia Avello v Belgian State* [2003] ECR I-11613; *Grunkin and Paul*, n 54 above, Opinion, para 46.

[57] Case C-412/97, *ED Srl v Italo Fenochio* [1999] ECR I-3845, para 11. Also Case C-69/88, *Krantz v Ontvanger der Directe Belastingen* [1990] ECR I-583, para 11; Case C-339/89, *Alsthom Atlantique SA v Compagnie de construction mécanique Sulzer SA* [1991] ECR I-107, paras 14 and 15; Case C-93/92, *CMC Motorradcenter v Baskiciogullari* [1993] ECR I-5009, para 12. Adv Gen Kokott has argued against the use of the concepts of 'certainty' and 'directness' in this

(b) Rules of applicable law, such as those contained in the Rome II Regulation, are different. They are not rules of procedure. Instead, they define (positively or negatively) the content of national rules that regulate the status of and relationships between natural and legal persons in a cross-border context.[58] They do not themselves directly regulate cross-border activity, but they do play a central role in identifying the substantive rules regulating civil aspects of cross-border activity. Normally, however, it is those substantive rules (and not the rules of applicable law leading to their application) that are the proper subject matter of enquiry when it comes to assessing whether there is a restriction on free movement prohibited by the EC Treaty.

(c) Only if a rule of applicable law itself automatically or inevitably restricts or hinders cross-border movement of goods, persons, services or capital will it be correct to focus on that rule as constituting the objectionable restriction. For example, in *Überseering v Nordic Construction*,[59] the ECJ held that the refusal of the German courts to recognize the legal capacity of a company incorporated in another Member State was in violation of the right to freedom of establishment under Arts 43 and 48 of the EC Treaty. That non-recognition was based on the German rule of private international law under which a company's legal capacity was determined in accordance with the law of the country where its actual centre of administration was established.[60] In the circumstances, as the Court explained, that rule created a restriction on the freedom of establishment as a company validly incorporated under the law of, and having its registered office in, a Member State other than Germany but with its central administration in Germany would under German law have no alternative to reincorporation in Germany if it wished to enforce before a German court its rights under a contract entered into with a German company.[61]

(d) Cases of this type will be the exception rather than the rule. In other cases, the content and effect of the *substantive* rules that fall to be applied to determine the parties' rights and obligations must be examined for compliance with the EC Treaty. An example may serve to

---

context as 'they are difficult to clarify and thus do not contribute to legal certainty' (Case C-142/05, *Åklagaren v Percy Mickelsson* Opinion dated 14 December 2006, para 47).

[58] **3.38–3.40** below.

[59] Case C-208/00, *Überseering BV v Nordic Construction Company Baumanagement GmbH* [2002] ECR I-9919. Also *Grunkin and Paul*, n 54 above, Judgment of 14 October 2008.

[60] *Sitztheorie* or company seat principle, as opposed to the *Gründungstheorie* or incorporation principle (ibid, para 4).

[61] *Überseering v Nordic Construction*, n 59 above, para 79.

illustrate this point. Assume that X, a law firm based in Member State A, is asked by its client to provide an opinion to Y, a bank based in Member State B. Subsequently, Y asserts that X was negligent in preparing its opinion and thereby committed a tort. Assuming, for present purposes, that Y may sue X in the courts of either Member State A or Member State B,[62] a question arises as to the law applicable to X's non-contractual obligation. Depending on their respective rules of applicable law, courts in each of the two Member States may apply the same law (most likely, that of A or B) or different laws to determine the existence and scope of that obligation. Public policy and mandatory rules of the forum or of another state may also influence the content of the substantive rules applied in each Member State. It is, however, only once those rules have been identified that a conclusion can be reached as to whether the regulation of the situation by Member State A and/or Member State B constitutes a restriction on X's freedom to provide services.[63] The fact that the existence of different rules of applicable law may result in disparate treatment of the situation in two or more Member States does not of itself lead automatically to the conclusion that there is an unlawful restriction.[64]

(e) The existence of divergent rules of applicable law among the Member States leading to disparity of substantive treatment is, however, liable to increase the risk that cross-border commerce will be impeded by the phenomenon of 'double regulation'. Further, by the nature of the connecting factors that they employ, some rules of applicable law may inevitably result in different substantive treatment within a legal system either (i) between goods/services for domestic consumption and exported goods/services (i.e. according to country of destination) or (ii) between domestically sourced goods/services and imported goods/services (i.e. according to country of origin). Even if such differences do not themselves create unlawful restrictions under the EC Treaty, it may be argued that their effect is to distort competition in the internal market by subjecting different manufacturers/service providers operating within a single Member State to different non-contractual obligations. If a low or medium threshold were to be

---

[62] Brussels I Regulation, Arts 2 and 5.3.

[63] i.e. whether 'it is liable to prohibit or otherwise impede the activities of a provider of services established in another Member State where he lawfully provides similar services' (Case C-76/90, *Manfred Säger v Dennemeyer & Co Ltd* [1991] ECR I-4221, para 12).

[64] Case C-177/94, *Criminal Proceedings against Perfili* [1996] ECR I-161, para 17.

adopted, removal of such distortions (if appreciable) would be sufficient to justify legislative intervention.

(f) That said, the adoption of uniform applicable law rules cannot, at the same time, ensure identical substantive treatment of operators in both the country of origin and the country of destination of goods and services. Indeed, harmonization of applicable law rules gives a Community sanction to distinct treatment based on the connecting factors chosen. For example, applying the law of the country of damage to product liability cases will tend to lead to the application of different rules to exported goods. Nevertheless, by reducing disparities[65] in substantive treatment of the same situation by different Member State courts, the creation of uniform rules of applicable law has the *potential* to remove or prevent genuine[66] restrictions on cross-border trade or distortions in competition resulting from 'double regulation' even though the Member State rules of applicable law that are thereby replaced do not, viewed individually, constitute unlawful restrictions under the EC Treaty.

Some commentators support a low threshold for Art 65, treating the inter- **2.30**
nal market wording as having little or no significance.[67] This view, however, is difficult to reconcile with the case law of the ECJ concerning the similar wording in Art 95 of the EC Treaty and, in particular, the reasoning of the Court and its Advocate General in the landmark decision in 2000 concerning the validity of the Tobacco Advertising Directive.[68] That decision, as will be seen in the following paragraphs, provides strong support for the application of what has been described above as the medium threshold, requiring that the legislator establish by objective criteria that the existing Member State rules in the area to be harmonized either restrict the free movement of goods, persons, services, or capital, or otherwise distort competition, within the internal market.

---

[65] The impact of public policy and overriding mandatory provisions (Regulation, Arts 16 and 26) would mean that disparities cannot be eliminated without also excluding the potential overriding effect of the law of the forum.

[66] The need to support the case for legislation by evidence or other materials capable of being reviewed judicially remains.

[67] e.g., P Herzog, n 18 above, para 65.02 ('Commentators are, however, generally agreed that this requirement should not receive a narrow interpretation.'); G Vitellino, 'Rome II from an Internal Market Perspective' in Malatesta, *Unification*, n 10 above, 277–9 ((ibid, 278) '[T]he criteria of applicability of freedoms of movement are not very useful in order to outline the scope of uniform conflict rules in a general and abstract way').

[68] Case C-376/98, *Germany v European Parliament and Council* [2000] ECR I-8419 (Tobacco Advertising).

Regulating the Internal Market—The Tobacco Advertising Decision

2.31 The Tobacco Advertising Directive[69] was adopted under Art 100a (now Art 95) of the EC Treaty. Like Art 65, Art 95 requires that measures be linked to the functioning of the internal market, as follows:[70]

> The Council shall . . . adopt the measures for the approximation of provisions laid down by law, regulation or administrative action in Member States *which have as their object the establishment and functioning of the internal market.*

2.32 The Directive banned all forms of tobacco advertising and sponsorship in the EC. Germany, which had voted against the measure, successfully challenged its validity. The opinions of the Court of Justice and of the Advocate General (Fennelly) with regard to the nature and scope of the Community's legislative competence under Art 95 are, it is submitted, equally instructive in the case of Art 65. In summary, they analysed the nature and effect of the required connection to the internal market in the following terms:[71]

(a) The selection and evaluation of the legal basis for a measure must be based on objective factors which are amenable to judicial review. Those factors include, in particular, the aim and content of the measure.[72]

(b) Art 95 of the EC Treaty does not vest in the Community legislature a general power to regulate the internal market.[73] By parallel reasoning, Art 65 EC cannot be considered to create a general Community competence to regulate the area of civil justice.

(c) If a mere finding of disparities between national rules and of an abstract risk of resulting obstacles to the exercise of fundamental freedoms or of distortions of competition were sufficient to justify the choice of Art 95 as a legal basis, judicial review of compliance with the proper legal basis might be rendered nugatory.[74] Accordingly, the ECJ specifically rejected the low threshold for the internal market requirement.

---

[69] Directive (EC) No 98/43 (OJ L213, 9 [30.7.1998]).

[70] Emphasis added.

[71] References in the following footnotes to 'Court' and 'Adv Gen' are to the judgment of the ECJ and the Opinion of Adv Gen Fennelly in the *Tobacco Advertising* case, n 68 above.

[72] Court, para 59; Adv Gen, para 61. Also *R v Secretary of State for Health, ex parte British American Tobacco (Investments) Ltd* (Case C-491/01) [2002] ECR I-11453, para 93.

[73] Court, para 83; Adv Gen, para, 82.

[74] Court, para 84.

(d) The Court must verify whether a measure adopted under Art 95[75] actually contributes to eliminating obstacles to the free movement of goods and to the freedom to provide services, *or* to removing (or preventing[76]) distortions of competition.[77] The limited competence contemplated by what has been described as the high threshold was therefore also expressly rejected in favour of a test which seems in line with the medium threshold suggested above.[78]

(e) Measures may have as their object the prevention of future obstacles to trade resulting from multifarious development of national laws. Such future development must, however, be likely.[79]

(f) Distortions in competition which a measure seeks to remove must be 'appreciable'.[80]

Applying the reasoning in the *Tobacco Advertising* decision to Art 65, it is **2.33** submitted that the first question that the ECJ should ask itself in checking whether the Rome II Regulation has a sufficient connection to the proper functioning of the internal market is as follows:

Has it been established (by objective criteria amenable to judicial review) either (a) that the proposed measure removes appreciable existing restrictions on the cross-border movement of goods, persons, services or capital within the meaning of EC Treaty, Arts 28 to 29, 39, 43, 49 or 56 (as applicable), (b) that the proposed measure prevents likely future restrictions on the exercise of these fundamental freedoms, or (c) that the proposed measure removes appreciable distortions on competition within the internal market or prevents such distortions where they are likely to occur?

---

[75] And, by parallel reasoning, Art 65.

[76] Case C-300/89, *Commission v Council (Titanium Dioxide)* [1991] ECR I-2867, para 15. Such distortions must be 'likely' to occur.

[77] Court, para 95; Adv Gen, paras 83, 88. Also Case C-154/04, *R (Alliance for Natural Health) v Secretary of State for Health* [2005] ECR I-6541, paras 28–32.

[78] **2.26** (third bullet point). Note that the ECJ did not expressly align the concept of 'obstacles' with its case law concerning the operation of the fundamental freedoms. Nevertheless, that reading of its decision seems consistent not only with the concept of the internal market, requiring that free movement of goods etc. be ensured 'in accordance with' the provisions of the EC Treaty, but also with the cross-references to Art 30, one of the Treaty provisions defining the free movement of goods, in Art 95(6) and (10). Also D Wyatt, 'Community Competence to Regulate the Internal Market', Oxford Legal Studies Research Paper No 9/2007, available at <http://papers.ssrn.com/sol3/papers.cfm?abstract_id=997863>, 23, 41–6, recognizing that, in practice, the Community legislator has taken a wider view.

[79] Court, para 86. In the case of existing restrictions, it appears that, although a slight effect on trade may be enough (Adv Gen, para 104; also Case 8/74, *Procureur du Roi v Dassonville* [1974] ECR 837, para 5), the effect must be appreciable and not abstract (Court, para 84) or too uncertain and indirect (Case C-190/98, *Graf v Filzmoser Maschinenbau GmbH* [2000] ECR I-493 and the cases cited at n 57 above).

[80] Court, paras 106–7; Adv Gen, para 90.

Can Art 65 Measures Extend to Situations Having No Connection to the Internal Market?[81]

2.34 A further question arises as to whether the Community's legislative power under Arts 61 and 65 extends to situations that have no overt connection to the exercise of any of the freedoms comprising the internal market. That question is of particular significance for the Rome II Regulation, which purports to have 'universal application' in two different senses. First, the law applicable under the Regulation's rules of applicable law may be that of a non-Member State.[82] Secondly, the Regulation does not contain any express restriction upon its scope designed to ensure that the non-contractual obligations to which it applies are connected to the territory of one or more Member States or, more specifically, to the functioning of the internal market created by them under the EC Treaty.

2.35 In its response to the Commission's preliminary draft proposal, the UK Government expressed the view that the Community's legislative competence under Art 65 only extended to regulating situations connected to the functioning of the internal market. It offered, by way of example, 'a case where the English court has jurisdiction pursuant to a prorogation agreement entered into by two South Korean nationals domiciled in South Korea and the claim relates to an alleged tort committed by the defendant in that country'. In the view of the UK Government:[83]

> The link between such a case and the European Union, let alone the proper functioning of the internal market, would appear to be highly tenuous. There is therefore a treaty base issue in relation to any proposed Regulation which seeks to legislate in respect of parties with no connection with the European Union. In addition, it is also uncertain that all cases involving only one party who is habitually resident in the European Union (ie where the other is habitually resident in a third State) should be covered by the Regulation; so in the example given above if one of the Koreans, the plaintiff, is domiciled in the UK, it is unclear what relevance the application of the choice of law in tort to his claim has in relation to the proper functioning of the internal market.

2.36 The Commission's reasoning on this point and the subsequent course of the debate in relation to the Rome II Regulation will be examined more closely in **Section C** below. The question is addressed in this section at a

---

[81] For other views on this issue, see B von Hoffmann, 'The Europeanization of Private International Law' in B von Hoffmann (ed), *European Private International Law* (1998), 34; J Basedow, n 39 above, 702–4; O Remien, 'European Private International Law, The European Community and its Emerging Area of Freedom, Security and Justice' (2001) 38 CML Rev 53, 76–7; S Bariatti, n 10 above, 15–19; G Vitellino, n 67 above, 277–9.

[82] Regulation, Art 2. Also Commission Proposal, 9–10.

[83] Response of the Government of the United Kingdom, available at <http://ec.europa.eu/justice_home/news/consulting_public/rome_ii/govern_uk_en.pdf>, para 4.

higher level: does Art 65 require a connection to the internal market to be sufficiently established in all situations regulated by a Community civil justice measure? Again, the ECJ's case law on the internal market wording in Art 95 of the EC Treaty might be argued to provide a compelling analogy. The Court of Justice has held on more than one occasion that measures adopted under Art 95 may apply (and may, therefore, be validly adopted) even in situations which have no link with the exercise of the fundamental freedoms guaranteed by the EC Treaty.[84] This line of authority has subsequently been deployed by the Court of Justice in *Owusu v Jackson* in order to reject a restrictive interpretation of the rules of jurisdiction contained in the Brussels Convention.[85] Moreover, in its Opinion on the competence of the Community to conclude the Lugano (II) Convention on jurisdiction and the recognition and enforcement of judgments in civil and commercial matters, the ECJ referred to its reasoning in *Owusu* as supporting the following statement with reference to the Brussels I Regulation, an instrument with the same treaty basis as the Rome II Regulation:[86]

The purpose of that regulation, and more particularly Chapter II thereof, is to unify the rules on jurisdiction in civil and commercial matters, not only for intra-Community disputes but also for those which have an international element, with the objective of eliminating obstacles to the functioning of the internal market which may derive from disparities between national legislations on the subject . . .

The ECJ's reasoning in *Owusu v Jackson* and in its Lugano Convention **2.37** Opinion may appear to provide a template for future decisions on the extent of the Community's competence to harmonize rules of private international law under Art 65, including with respect to any challenge to the legality of the Rome II Regulation. Professor Briggs has suggested that, in *Owusu*, the ECJ was marking its territory 'to prevent those who may advance similar arguments to cast doubt on the treaty basis of Regulations, present and to come governing choice of law in contract, tort and unjust enrichment and family law etc' from doing so, with the consequence that:[87]

[C]areful and precise legal arguments about the legal basis for such legislation will be impotent against a boilerplate paragraph, bolted into every judgment, which will say that any disparities between national legislation will impede the

[84] Joined Cases C-465/00 & C-138–139/01, *Rechnungshof v Östereichischer Rundfunk* [2003] ECR I-4989, paras 42–43; *Lindqvist* (Case C-101/01) [2003] ECR I-12971, paras 40–1; Case C-380/03, *Germany v Parliament and Council* [2006] ECR I-11573, para 80. For comment, see D Wyatt, n 78 above, 36–40.
[85] Case C-281/02, *Owusu v Jackson* [2005] ECR I-1383, paras 34–5.
[86] Opinion 1/03 [2006] ECR I-1145, paras 143, referring also to the 2nd Recital to the Brussels I Regulation. Also paras 144–7.
[87] A Briggs, 'The Death of Harrods: *Forum Non Conveniens* and the European Court' (2005) 121 LQR 535, 539.

functioning of the internal market, and that legislation to eradicate such disparities is therefore within the competence of the organs of the European Union.

2.38 There is, however, a significant difference between the internal market
wording in Art 95 and that in Art 65, and neither *Owusu* (which concerned
the interpretation of a provision of an international convention raising no
question of Community competence) nor the Lugano Convention Opinion
(which concerned the Community's treaty making power to which the
restrictions on the Community's legislative competence under Title IV were
considered irrelevant[88]) can be seen as the final word on this issue. Whereas
Art 95 refers only to 'measures . . . which have as their *object* the establishment and functioning of the internal market' and appears to contemplate
the possibility that a measure might have a wider *effect*, Art 65 (by using the
words 'insofar as necessary') strongly suggests that the EC's legislative
competence goes no further than the proper functioning of the internal market requires. Nor is this simply a quirk of the English text of the EC Treaty.
The same difference in language appears also, for example, in the French[89]
and German[90] texts. Unlike Art 95, therefore, the internal market wording in
Art 65 can be seen as imposing its own independent proportionality requirement as a pre-condition to the exercise of Community competence.

2.39 On this view, if there were to be a challenge to the validity of the Rome II
Regulation on this ground, the Court of Justice must ask itself whether the
measures contained in the Regulation, insofar as it purports to have 'universal application' in the two senses described above, go no further than
necessary to eliminate the restrictions on the fundamental freedoms or
remove distortions of competition in the internal market which have been
identified as resulting from the Member States' pre-existing rules. The
Commission answered that question in the affirmative, although its reasoning appears open to doubt.[91]

The Treaty Establishing a Constitution for Europe and the Reform Treaty

2.40 Although not directly relevant to the questions surrounding the legitimacy of the Rome II Regulation, it is instructive to compare the text of Art
65 of the EC Treaty in its present form with the corresponding provisions

---

[88] Opinion 1/03, n 36 above, para 131. For discussion of the Community's external competence arising by reason of the adoption of the Rome II Regulation, see **16.43–16.46** below.

[89] Art 95: '*pour object l'éstablissement et le fonctionnement du marché intérieur*'; Art 65: '*dans la
mesure nécessaire au bon fonctionnement du marché intérieur*'.

[90] Art 95: '*welche die Errichtung und das Funktionieren des Binnenmarktes zum Gegenstand
haben*'; Art 65: '*soweit sie für das rebungslose Funtionieren des Binnenmarktes erforderlich sind*'.

[91] **2.79–2.88** below.

of the ill-fated Treaty establishing a Constitution for Europe[92] and its successor, the imperilled Lisbon (Reform) Treaty.[93]

Art III-269.1 of the Treaty establishing a constitution for Europe referred to **2.41** the creation of Community competence in the area of judicial cooperation in civil matters 'based on the principle of mutual recognition of judgments and decisions in extrajudicial cases'. Insofar as it would have conferred power to legislate in matters of private international law, the terms of Art III-269 were not dissimilar to those of Art 65. Significantly, however, Art III-269.2 referred to the adoption of measures *'particularly* when necessary for the proper functioning of the internal market'. As the UK Foreign and Commonwealth Office noted at the time,[94] this diluted the internal market wording contained in Art 65, with the result that any fetter on the scope of the Community's legislative competence resulting from that wording would unquestionably be removed.[95]

Art III-269 of the constitutional Treaty is reflected, almost word for word, **2.42** in Art 81 of the Treaty on the Functioning of the European Union (TFEU), as the amended EC Treaty would be known if the Lisbon Reform Treaty were to overcome its rejection in the Irish referendum. In its report on the Treaty of Lisbon, the House of Lords European Union Committee noted:[96]

New Article 81 no longer contains any absolute requirement that measures adopted be 'necessary for the functioning of the internal market'. Mrs Durand[97] *[of the Commission]* was of the view that the change to this Article was a deliberate one to separate cooperation in civil matters from the proper functioning of the internal

---

[92] OJ C310, 1 [16.12.2004].
[93] OJ C306, 1 [17.12.2007]. For a consolidated version of the EU treaties, as they would be amended if the Lisbon Treaty were ratified by all Member States, see OJ C115, 1 [9.5.2008].
[94] Commentary on Art III-269 at <http://collections.europarchive.org/tna/20080205132101/www.fco.gov.uk/Files/kfile/Commentary_Part2_Part3.pdf>.
[95] The fate of the internal market wording in the successor to Art 65 was uncertain throughout the negotiations for the draft Constitution. The Working Group (X) recommended its retention (European Convention Document CONV 426/02 [2.12.2002]). It was, however, removed entirely from the draft Articles dealing with the 'area of freedom security and justice' (CONV 614/03 [14.5.2005], Art 14 and commentary). The UK representatives (and others) subsequently sought its reintroduction (CONV 644/1/03 REV 1 [7.5.2003]). The internal market wording was not contained in the final draft of the Convention (CONV 850/03 [18.7.2003], Art III-170), but was reintroduced in the modified form described above during the inter-governmental negotiations leading to agreement on the constitutional Treaty.
[96] House of Lords European Union Committee, 'The Treaty of Lisbon: an impact assessment' (10th Report of Session 2007–08), HL Paper 62-I, para 6.134.
[97] Claire-Françoise Durand, Acting Director-General, Commission Legal Services.

market and enable cooperation in any case which had cross-border implications. However, she noted that in practice, it was difficult to come up with examples of measures which would be excluded under the current wording but could fall within the new wording, particularly given that the overriding consideration here is the cross-border dimension. . . .

2.43 Other witnesses before the Committee disputed the significance of the changes in the formulation of the Community competence in this area.[98] The Committee concluded, while noting the differences in language between Art 65 of the unamended EC Treaty and Art 81 of the amended and renamed TFEU, that:[99]

> In lieu of the present absolute requirement that measures taken be necessary for the proper functioning of the internal market, Article 81 provides that measures may be taken 'particularly when' so necessary. But, under both existing Article 65 and new Article 81, such measures are only permissible in civil measures 'having cross-border implications', itself a significant limitation. Both the existing and the new articles are capable of giving rise to differences of view regarding the scope of their application in particular situations, and we doubt whether this is much affected by the changes in Article 81.

> In light of the troubled state of the Reform Treaty project, that view may never be tested.

Facing Reality—Judicial Restraint in the Review of Internal Market Measures

2.44 It is, of course, one matter to define the questions that a court must ask itself and another to predict how it will answer those questions. Such a prediction requires a detailed understanding not only of the procedures and rules of evidence that the court deploys, but also the political and social influences on its decisions. In this connection, it has already been noted that very significant obstacles will face any litigant wishing to present a challenge to the validity of the Rome II Regulation.[100] More particularly, in examining the legality of measures regulating the internal market, the ECJ has shown a marked tendency towards judicial restraint, which in itself is unsurprising in view of the nature of the proceedings before the Court.

2.45 Thus, when engaging in a review of complex legislative choices affecting diverse economic and other interests, the Court will normally accept the

---

[98] HL Paper 62-I (2007–2008), n 96 above, paras 6.135–6.139.

[99] Ibid, para 6.141. For further discussion as to this requirement, see ibid, paras 6.227–6.234.

[100] **2.01–2.03** above.

assessment of the Community legislator that a measure is effective to ensure the proper functioning of the internal market.[101] As highlighted on several occasions since the *Tobacco Advertising* decision,[102] the ECJ will not lightly second guess the legislator's assessment of the need for a particular measure. Furthermore, the ECJ's approach in assessing the presence (or absence) of appreciable distortions of competition resulting from existing Member State rules has appeared largely impressionistic, not being based on an empirical assessment of any kind.[103] In a similar vein, albeit in a different context, the ECJ also willingly accepted the Community legislator's assertion that the Brussels I Regulation, a measure having the same treaty basis as the Rome II Regulation, contributed to the functioning of the internal market by removing disparities between national rules.[104] Finally, the ECJ has accepted that, although Art 253 of the EC Treaty requires the Community legislator to present its reasons for adopting a particular measure clearly and unequivocally, so as to enable the Court to exercise its power of review, the legislator is not required to go into every relevant point of fact and law.[105] Indeed, the question whether a statement of reasons is sufficient must be assessed with reference not only to the wording of the measure but also to its context and to the whole body of legal rules governing the matter in question. If the contested measure clearly discloses the overall objective pursued by the Community institution concerned, it would (in the view of the ECJ) be excessive to require a specific statement of reasons for each of the technical choices made by the institution.[106] Even if, therefore, the submissions outlined above as to the meaning and effect of the internal market wording in Art 65 are accepted, a successful challenge to the legality of the Rome II Regulation on the ground that its necessity for the proper functioning of the internal market was not sufficiently established or explained seems a remote prospect.

---

[101] *Tobacco Advertising*, n 68 above, Adv Gen, para 98.

[102] e.g. Case C-491/01, *R v Secretary of State for Health, ex p British American Tobacco (Investments) Ltd* [2002] ECR I-11453; Case C-210/03, *R (Swedish Match AB) v Secretary of State for Health* [2004] ECR I-11893; Joined Cases C-154–155/04, *R (Alliance for Natural Health) v Secretary of State for Health* [2005] ECR I-6541; Case C-380/03, *Germany v Parliament and Council*, n 84 above (an unsuccessful challenge to the measure replacing the Tobacco Advertising Directive). For further discussion, see D Wyatt, n 78 above.

[103] Case C-491/01, *Ex p British American Tobacco*, ibid, paras 74–5; Case, C-380/03, *Germany v Parliament and Council*, ibid, paras 69–75; Case C-158/00, *Leitner v TUI Deutschland GmbH & Co KG* [2002] ECR I-2631, para 21. For comment, see D Wyatt, n 78 above, 20, 29–36.

[104] Opinion 01/03 on *Competence of the Community to conclude the new Lugano Convention on jurisdiction and the recognition of judgments in civil and commercial matters* [2006] ECR I-1145, para 143 (quoted at text to n 86 above).

[105] Case C-380/03, *Germany v Parliament and Council*, n 84 above, para 107.

[106] Ibid, para 108.

Other Potential Restrictions on the Community's Legislative Competence

2.46 The following paragraphs consider possible restrictions on the Community's legislative competence under Arts 61 and 65 other than those deriving from the internal market wording.

Cross-Border Implications

2.47 For an instrument such as the Rome II Regulation, the requirement of 'cross-border implications' adds little, if anything, to an account of the Community's legislative competence.[107] As a measure harmonizing rules of private international law, the Regulation undoubtedly has cross-border implications, as the object of such rules is to deal with situations that are connected with more than one legal system.[108] Art 1(1) of the Regulation affirms that it applies 'in situations involving a conflict of laws'. It is, of course, possible that the situation requiring application of rules of private international law may be connected only with two or more legal systems within a particular State (e.g. England and Scotland) so that there would be no 'cross-border implications' if the expression were held to require an effect on inter-State relations. Art 25(2) of the Rome II Regulation makes clear, however, that it has no claim to apply to purely 'internal' cases. Even if, which seems improbable,[109] the expression 'cross-border' in Art 65 were construed by the ECJ as meaning 'across Member State borders',[110] this requirement would still appear to impose a less rigorous standard than the internal market requirement, discussed above.

Measures Promoting the Compatibility of Member State Rules

2.48 It has been suggested that the reference in Art 65(b) to measures 'promoting the compatibility of the rules applicable in the Member States concerning

---

[107] For the contrary view, that this wording provides the dominant restriction on the Community's legislative power in this area rendering the internal market wording of secondary importance, see HL Paper 62-I (2007–2008), n 96 above, paras 6.132–6.141, 6.227–6.234.

[108] C Kohler, n 17 above, 17 (footnote 26).

[109] Having regard, in particular, to the reasoning of the Court of Justice in Case C-281/02, *Owusu v Jackson* [2005] ECR I-1383, paras 25–9, echoed in Opinion 01/03 on the *Competence of the Community to conclude the new Lugano Convention on jurisdiction and the recognition of judgments in civil and commercial matters* [2006] ECR I-1145, paras 145–6.

[110] Cf J Basedow, n 39 above, 701–3.

the conflict of laws and of jurisdiction',[111] as contrasted with the more general language of Art 65(a),[112] does not allow for the possibility of creating a uniform set of rules of applicable law (or, for that matter, jurisdiction[113]) by means of an EC legislative instrument.[114] On a literal reading of Art 65(b), this argument carries some appeal. The verb 'promoting' (in French, '*favoriser*') and the noun 'compatibility' suggest measures short of unification by directly applicable Community law. It seems unlikely, however, that this argument would find favour with the Court of Justice. Further, notwithstanding the creation of Community private international law rules in particular areas (including rules of applicable law for non-contractual obligations), Member States will for the foreseeable future retain their own rules in other areas (e.g. civil status and property) and questions of compatibility between them will continue to arise. Accordingly, although the European Community may have no competence to create a single, complete system of European private international law (a private international law code), that restriction does not impinge on the Community's ability to adopt the Rome II Regulation.

Relationship between Article 65 and Article 95

It has also been suggested that Art 65 applies only to measures concerning **2.49** the free movement of persons, whereas Art 95 applies to measures concerning the free movement of goods and services.[115] Indeed, Professor Basedow, writing in 2000, argued:[116]

If the Community institutions endeavour, for example, to draw up a legal instrument on the law applicable to non-contractual obligations (Rome II), they intend to create a horizontal instrument which will have an impact on several freedoms in the areas of libel and slander, traffic accidents, infringement of intellectual property rights, anti-competitive conspiracies etc. Its proper basis would be Article 95.

That argument is unpersuasive. Arts 61 and 65, although contained in **2.50** a section of the EC Treaty entitled 'Visas, Asylum, Immigration and

[111] Art 65(c), concerning rules of similar procedure, contains the same wording.
[112] Referring to measures 'improving and simplifying' the system for cross-border service, cooperation in the taking of evidence or the recognition and enforcement of decisions in civil and commercial cases.
[113] Although the uniform rules of jurisdiction in the Brussels I Regulation might be seen as an integral, and subordinate, part of a scheme to simplify rules on the cross-border enforcement of judgments within the Community and so justified by Art 65(a).
[114] B von Hoffmann, n 81 above, 31; C Kohler, n 17 above, 19–21; compare J Basedow, n 39 above, 705–6; O Remien, n 81 above, 76–7.
[115] J Basedow, n 39 above, 697–9. Also C Kohler, n 17 above, 15–17.
[116] J Basedow, n 39 above, 698.

Other Policies Related to the Free Movement of Persons', contain nothing to suggest that they are limited to measures concerned with the free movement of persons.[117] As Art 61 provides a specific competence for measures, inter alia, in the area of civil justice, it is submitted that it (as qualified by Art 65) provides the correct treaty basis for measures adopted in this area, which have as their primary object the development of Community rules of private international law.[118] Moreover, with the exception of aspects relating to family law,[119] Art 61 is no less democratic than Art 95.[120] Finally, when read together with Art 65, Art 61 contains more extensive protections than Art 95 for the competence of Member States to legislate in this area.[121] Those protections should be respected, and not subverted by recourse to Art 95. Art 95 remains the appropriate Treaty basis in circumstances where creation or modification of rules of private international law is a subsidiary or incidental part of sectoral or general legislation affecting the internal market more broadly,[122] but that does not affect the priority to be given to Art 65 for a general instrument such as the Rome II Regulation.

Subsidiarity and Proportionality

2.51 Art 5, paras 2 and 3 of the EC Treaty explain the requirements of subsidiarity and proportionality in the following terms:

> In areas which do not fall within its exclusive competence, the Community shall take action, in accordance with the principle of subsidiarity, only if and in so far as the objectives of the proposed action cannot be sufficiently achieved by the Member States and can therefore, by reason of the scale or effects of the proposed action, be better achieved by the Community.

> Any action by the Community shall not go beyond what is necessary to achieve the objectives of this Treaty.

---

[117] There is also no suggestion that the former Art K.3 of the former Treaty on European Union, which contained provisions for cooperation in the field of civil justice, was so limited.

[118] Case C-491/01, *R v Secretary of State for Health, ex p British American Tobacco (Investments) Ltd* [2002] ECR I-11453, para 94; Case C-533/03, *Commission v Council* [2006] ECR I-1025, para 45.

[119] Art 67(5).

[120] In any event, the reasoning based on democratic process in the *Titanium Dioxide* decision (Case C-300/89, *Commission v Council* [1991] ECR I-2867) has been heavily criticized (C Barnard, n 52 above, 581–3).

[121] **2.09–2.48** above.

[122] Such as the Directives which, at least until the coming into force of the Rome I Regulation (Art 7), govern the law applicable to many insurance contracts (Directive (EEC) No 88/357 (Second Non-Life Insurance Directive) (OJ L172, 1 [4.7.1988]), Art 7 as amended; Directive (EEC) No 90/619 (Second Life Insurance Directive), (OJ L330, 50 [29.11.1990]), Art 4 as amended).

The treaty text is supplemented by a Protocol, introduced by the Amster- **2.52**
dam Treaty, which provides the following guidance:[123]

1. The reasons given for Community legislation must show compliance
   with the principles of subsidiarity and proportionality. In the case of the
   former principle, the reasons for concluding that a Community objective can be better achieved by the Community must be substantiated by
   qualitative or, wherever possible, quantitative indicators.
2. In applying the subsidiarity principle, consideration should be given to
   whether:
   (a) the issue under consideration has transnational aspects which
       cannot be satisfactorily regulated by action by Member States;
   (b) actions by Member States alone or lack of Community action would
       conflict with the requirements of the Treaty (such as the need to
       correct distortion of competition or avoid disguised restrictions on
       trade or strengthen economic and social cohesion) or would
       otherwise significantly damage Member States' interests; and
   (c) action at Community level would produce clear benefits by reason
       of its scale or effects compared with action at the level of the Member
       States.
3. The form of any Community action should be as simple as possible and
   consistent with satisfactory achievement of the objective of the measure
   and the need for effective enforcement. The Community shall legislate
   only to the extent necessary. Other things being equal, directives should
   be preferred to regulations and framework directives to detailed
   measures.
4. Community measures should leave as much scope for national decision as possible, consistent with securing the aim of the measure and
   observing the requirements of the Treaty. While respecting Community
   law, care should be taken to respect well established national arrangements and the organization and working of Member States' legal
   systems.

The Court of Justice has emphasized, however, that the principles of sub- **2.53**
sidiarity and proportionality in Art 5, particularly the former, operate mainly
at a political level, with the result that that the Community legislature has
a broad discretion in their application. Accordingly, a measure will only
be reviewed on either these grounds if it is manifestly inappropriate.[124]

---

[123] EC Treaty, Protocol No 30 on Subsidiarity and Proportionality, paras (4) to (7).
[124] e.g. Case C-491/01, *R v Secretary of State for Health, ex parte British American Tobacco
(Investments) Ltd* [2002] ECR I-11453, para 123; Case C-380/03, *Germany v Parliament and
Council* [2006] ECR I-11573, para 145.

Although each case must be considered on its merits, there seems very little prospect of a successful challenge to the Rome II Regulation on either of these grounds, given that Recital (38) asserts that the requirements of subsidiarity are satisfied. Further, if (as has been submitted above[125]) the internal market requirement in Art 65 imposes its own independent proportionality requirement, which prevents it from being used as a treaty base to regulate situations which have no connection with the proper functioning of the internal market, the relevance here of the general requirement of proportionality as a possible ground of challenge is further diminished.

Objectives beyond the Proper Functioning of the Internal Market

2.54 The Recitals to the Rome II Regulation make clear that its objectives extend beyond ensuring the proper functioning of the internal market. For example, Recital (20) refers to the objective of 'protecting consumers' health' and Recital (25) to Art 174 of the EC Treaty, providing that there should be a high level of protection for the environment based on the precautionary principle and on the principles that protective action should be taken, that environmental damage should as a priority be rectified at source, and that the polluter should pay. These objectives do not, however, prevent reliance on Art 65 as a treaty basis. In this connection, it may be pointed out that (a) Art 6 of the EC Treaty requires environmental protection requirements to be integrated into the definition and implementation of Community policies, and (b) in considering the Community's more general power to regulate the internal market, the ECJ has held that the fact that a measure may also pursue the objective of promoting public health does not take that measure outside the scope of Art 95 if it has as its principal object the establishment and functioning of the internal market.[126] That reasoning, it is submitted, applies with equal force to Art 65. Accordingly, the *vires* of the Rome II Regulation almost certainly cannot be questioned on the ground that the content of its rules takes into account other Community policies.

PROCEDURE FOR CHALLENGE

2.55 Under Art 230 of the EC Treaty, the legality of an act adopted by the Council and the European Parliament is reviewable on various grounds in an action brought by a Member State or a Community institution or a

---

[125] **2.34–2.39**.

[126] e.g. Case C-491/01, *R v Secretary of State for Health, ex parte British American Tobacco (Investments) Ltd* [2002] ECR I-11453, para 62; Case C-380/03, *Germany v Parliament and Council* [2006] ECR I-11573, paras 39, 92–8.

natural or legal person directly and individually concerned by the act in question.[127] Proceedings under this Article must, however, be instituted within two months of the publication of the measure.[128] No challenge of this kind has been brought with respect to the Rome II Regulation. The possibility remains, however, of a reference by a court of a Member State seised of proceedings to which the Regulation applies for a preliminary ruling on one or more questions concerning its validity.[129] If, following such a reference, the ECJ were to rule that the Regulation had not been validly adopted, the Regulation would not thereby automatically be annulled, as the decision would in theory be addressed only to the national court that made the reference. In these circumstances, however, the continued application of the Regulation could not be maintained in practice in the face of such a ruling.[130]

CONCLUSION

The restrictions on the Community's competence, under Arts 61 and 65 of **2.56** the EC Treaty, to adopt new rules of private international law must be taken seriously. Of the grounds for challenge considered in this section, two stand out as having some prospect of success. First, that the reasons given for the Regulation do not demonstrate that there exists a sufficient connection between the harmonization of rules of applicable law for non-contractual obligations and the proper functioning of the internal market. Secondly, that the Regulation goes beyond that which is necessary to ensure the proper functioning of the internal market by purporting to regulate the law applicable to non-contractual obligations which have no objective connection to the exercise of any of the fundamental freedoms which the concept of an internal market is intended to guarantee.

The foregoing discussion also confirms, however, the difficult task facing **2.57** any litigant wishing to challenge the legality of the Rome II Regulation in proceedings before the ECJ. The decisive manner of the Court's rejection, in *Owusu v Jackson* and in its Opinion on the Lugano Convention, of arguments pertaining to the territorial reach of Community measures and competence (albeit in different contexts),[131] as well as the restraint shown by the Court in its review of internal market measures since the landmark

---

[127] EC Treaty, Art 230, paras 1–3.
[128] Ibid, Art 230, para 4.
[129] Ibid, Art 234.
[130] H Schermers and D Waelbroek, *Judicial Protection in the European Union* (6th edn, 2001), 514–17.
[131] **2.36–2.38** above.

decision in the *Tobacco Advertising* case[132] make it unlikely that any challenge to the *vires* of the Regulation would succeed.

2.58 Against this background, the justifications advanced for the Regulation during its legislative passage (**Section C**) and in its final text (**Section D**) may now be examined more closely

C. THE CASE FOR COMMUNITY LEGISLATION

THE COMMISSION'S PROPOSAL

General Approach to Legal Basis

2.59 In the explanatory memorandum accompanying its Proposal, having stated the purpose of the proposed Regulation,[133] the Commission turned to consider the question of its legal basis. Referring to Art 65(b) of the EC Treaty, the Commission stated:[134]

> The Community legislature has the power to put flesh on the bones of this Article and the discretion to determine whether a measure is necessary for the proper functioning of the internal market. The Council exercised this power when adopting the Vienna action plan of 3 December 1998[135] on how best to implement the provisions of the Treaty of Amsterdam on an area of freedom, security and justice, point 40(c) of which calls expressly for a 'Rome II' instrument.

2.60 With respect, the second sentence of this paragraph does not follow from or support the first. As an organ of the European Community, the Council is, of course, entrusted with certain legislative competences, including (together with the European Parliament) the power to adopt measures under Title IV of the EC Treaty. While the 'Community legislature' as a composite body undoubtedly enjoys a margin of appreciation in the exercise of those powers,[136] its constituent organs cannot, whether acting unilaterally or individually, extend those powers by their own acts.[137] Nor, it is submitted, is it open to the Council to put 'flesh on the bones' of a Treaty provision conferring legislative power otherwise than by enacting measures in accordance with the procedures laid down in the EC Treaty, with the full cooperation of the European Parliament.

---

[132] **2.45** and **2.53** above.
[133] **1.69** above.
[134] Commission Proposal, 6.
[135] **1.56** above.
[136] **2.45** above.
[137] Cf EC Treaty, Art 5 (**2.04** above).

Further, although the Council consists of representatives of the Member **2.61**
States,[138] the assent of those representatives to a legislative programme or
statement of policy goals amounts to no more than a statement of collective intent and cannot, of itself, be taken to authorize any wider Community
competence than that appearing on the face of the EC Treaty. Although Art
31(3) of the Vienna Convention on the law of treaties[139] provides that, in
interpreting a treaty, there may be taken into account together with the
context 'any subsequent agreement between the parties regarding the
interpretation of the treaty or the application of its provisions' (sub-para
(b)) and 'any subsequent practice in the application of the treaty which
establishes the agreement of the parties regarding its interpretation' (sub-
para (c)),[140] neither the Vienna Action Plan nor any statement of policy or
legislative objectives which followed it[141] in any way constitute or evidence any 'agreement' for this purpose. In particular, (1) the question of
Community competence to adopt particular measures was not specifically
addressed by any of these documents, but was assumed or ignored,[142]
(2) more generally, there is no indication of an intention on the part of the
authors or participants to affect the international legal relations between
them,[143] (3) before July 2003, there was no legislative proposal to which
any agreement on the competence of the Community to adopt a regulation on the law applicable to non-contractual obligations could relate,
(4) even the unanimous adoption[144] in Council of a specific legislative
proposal could not override the obligation of the Court of Justice to ensure
compliance with the EC Treaty[145] or prevent a particular Member State
from subsequently challenging Community competence;[146] *a fortiori*, assent
to or acquiescence in a communication of a political or administrative

---

[138] EC Treaty, Art 203.

[139] Concluded 23 May 1969, 1155 UNTS 331; Cmnd 7964.

[140] For discussion, see A Aust, *Modern Treaty Law and Practice* (2nd edn, 2007), 238–43.

[141] Including, specifically, the Tampere summit conclusions (1999), the joint programme of
measures for implementation of the principle of mutual recognition (2000), or the Hague
Programme (2004), all of which are referred to in the recitals to the Rome II Regulation (**2.107**
below). There is no reference in the Recitals to the Vienna Action Plan.

[142] Thus, the phrases 'proper functioning' and 'internal market' do not appear in the
Vienna Action Plan, the Tampere Presidency Conclusions, or the Hague Programme.

[143] Indeed, para 23 of the Vienna Action Plan recognizes: 'The entry into force of the Treaty
of Amsterdam also raises a number of legal questions resulting from the transition of certain
policies from the third pillar to the first pillar as well as from the transition to new forms of
acts and procedures in the third pillar', without addressing those questions.

[144] The Rome II Regulation did not command universal support of the Member States
(**1.88** and **1.96** above).

[145] EC Treaty, Art 220.

[146] Case 166/78, *Italian Republic v Council* [1979] ECR 2575.

nature should not have this effect, and (5) any other conclusion would enable Member State representatives to circumvent national constitutional requirements relating to adoption of treaties conferring additional powers on the Community.

2.62 Accordingly, the Commission's reference to the Vienna Action Plan does not advance the legislative case for the Rome II Regulation. It is nonetheless possible to extract from other passages within the Commission's explanatory memorandum the following five reasons why, in the Commission's view, the Regulation fell within the powers conferred on the Community by Arts 61 and 65 of the EC Treaty:

(a) legal certainty;
(b) removal of obstacles to the exercise of fundamental freedoms;
(c) removal of distortions of competition;
(d) deterrence of forum shopping; and
(e) facilitating the free movement of judgments.

2.63 Whether taken individually or collectively, however, these reasons seem inadequate to support the Commission's choice of treaty basis. In the following paragraphs, each will be considered in turn:

2.64 (a) *Legal certainty*: As a principle of EC law, legal certainty takes many forms.[147] The argument presented by the Commission in its explanatory memorandum identified two forms of uncertainty in the existing situation within the Member States. First, that resulting from disparity between Member State rules of applicable law for non-contractual obligations, hindering the ability of economic operators to predict the outcome of litigation. Secondly, that resulting from the difficulty in identifying the Member States' rules, particularly in those systems relying on the decisions of courts rather than legislation.[148] As to the first form of uncertainty, the Commission explained:[149]

A comparative law analysis of the rules of conflict of laws reveals that the present situation does not meet economic operators' need for foreseeability and that the differences are markedly wider than was the case for contracts before the harmonisation achieved by the Rome Convention. Admittedly, the Member States

---

[147] **3.19–3.20** below.

[148] The assumption that judicially created law is less certain than that resulting from the hand of the legislator seems questionable. Unusually, in the present case, the UK had adopted legislation, in the form of the Private International Law (Miscellaneous Provisions) Act 1995, whereas some civilian code-based systems (notably, France) relied mainly on judicial decisions for the development of their rules of applicable law for torts and other non-contractual obligations.

[149] Commission Proposal, 5.

virtually all give pride of place to the *lex loci delicti commissi*, whereby torts/delicts are governed by the law of the place where the act was committed. The application of this rule is problematic, however, in the case of what are known as 'complex' torts/delicts, where the harmful event and the place where the loss is sustained are spread over several countries. There are variations between national laws as regards the practical impact of the *lex loci delicti commissi* rule in the case of cross-border non-contractual obligations. While certain Member States still take the traditional solution of applying the law of the country where the event giving rise to the damage occurred, recent developments more commonly tend to support the law of the country where the damage is sustained. But to understand the law in force in a Member State, it is not enough to ascertain whether the harmful event or the damage sustained is the dominant factor. The basic rule needs to be combined with other criteria. A growing number of Member States allow a claimant to opt for the law that is most favourable to him. Others leave it to the courts to determine the country with which the situation is most closely connected, either as a basic rule or exceptionally where the basic rule turns out to be inappropriate in the individual case. Generally speaking most Member States use a sometimes complex combination of the different solutions.

As to the second form of uncertainty, it was suggested that:[150]

Apart from the diversity of solutions, their legibility is not improved by the fact that only some of the Member States have codified their conflict-of-laws rules; in the others, solutions emerge gradually from the decisions of the courts and often remain uncertain, particularly as regards special torts/delicts.

Given the wealth of comparative material available, not least as a result of **2.65** the survey which it had instigated in 1998,[151] it is surprising that the Commission did not attempt to present a more detailed account of the (well documented) disparities between the Member States' existing applicable law regimes for non-contractual obligations. In contrast, the (unpublished) draft 2001 Green Paper[152] had annexed a summary of the rules of applicable law in force in each of 14 of the (then) Member States.

More fundamentally, if the ECJ's decision in the *Tobacco Advertising* **2.66** case[153] establishes anything, it is that the existence of disparities between Member State laws does not, standing alone, support the conclusion that a harmonization measure is necessary for the proper functioning of the internal market. Instead, those disparities must generate (or be likely to generate) appreciable obstacles to the exercise of the freedoms guaranteed by the internal market, or appreciable distortions of competition between

[150] Ibid.
[151] **1.53** above.
[152] **1.60–1.62** above.
[153] **2.30–2.32** above.

economic operators in that market. The same, it is submitted, can be said of uncertainty resulting from the lack of precision in the formulation of Member State laws, the second type of legal uncertainty on which the Commission relied. The fact, therefore, that the application of the Rome II Regulation may serve to improve legal certainty is not enough to establish Community competence. If it were otherwise, any harmonization measure could be said to contribute to the proper functioning of the internal market, by replacing 27[154] different sets of rules with a single Community rulebook.

2.67 Finally, although not directly relevant to the question of treaty basis, it may be noted that the Regulation's effectiveness in terms of the enhancement of legal certainty will likely be delayed until (at the very least) the ECJ has had the opportunity to define and refine the key concepts in the Regulation, and until after the review process[155] is completed. Moreover, as experience with the Brussels I Regulation and its predecessor Convention has demonstrated, it would be unrealistic to expect that disparities between the practice of different Member States will disappear even in the medium to long term.[156]

2.68 (b) *Removal of obstacles to the exercise of fundamental freedoms*: According to the Commission:[157]

> The approximation of the substantive law of obligations is no more than embryonic. Despite common principles, there are still major divergences between Member States, in particular as regards the following questions: the boundary between strict liability and fault-based liability; compensation for indirect damage and third-party damage; compensation for non-material damage, including third-party damage; compensation in excess of actual damage sustained (punitive and exemplary damages); the liability of minors; and limitation periods. During the consultations undertaken by the Commission, several representatives of industry stated that these divergences made it difficult to exercise fundamental freedoms in the internal market. They realised that harmonisation of the substantive law was not a short-term prospect and stressed the importance of the rules of conflict of laws to improve the foreseeability of solutions.

2.69 This, so far as the author is aware, is the sum total of the empirical evidence presented by the Commission as to the existence of obstacles to the

---

[154] 26, if one excludes Denmark.

[155] Art 30.

[156] See, generally, the Report of Professors Hess, Pfeiffer, and Schlosser on the application of the Brussels I Regulation in the Member States (Study JLS/C4/2005/03, September 2007), available at <http://ec.europa.eu/civiljustice/news/docs/study_application_brussels_1_en.pdf>.

[157] Commission Proposal, 5.

functioning of the internal market as a consequence of disparities in Member State law concerning non-contractual obligations. It is clearly lacking in specificity, both in terms of the identity of the consultees referred to and the nature of their businesses and in terms of the obstacles created by the pre-existing rules. Further, it will be noted, the difficulties which these consultees are said to have encountered in exercising their fundamental freedoms concerned divergences between the Member States' substantive rules for regulating non-contractual liability. Those divergences are unaffected by the Rome II Regulation.[158]

(c) *Removal of distortions of competition*: In this connection, the Commission argued that:[159] **2.70**

Harmonisation of the conflict rules helps to promote equal treatment between economic operators and individuals involved in cross-border litigation in the internal market. It is the necessary adjunct to the harmonisation already achieved by the 'Brussels I' Regulation as regards the rules governing the international jurisdiction of the courts and the mutual recognition of judgments. Given that there are more than fifteen different systems of conflict rules, two firms in distinct Member States, A and B, bringing the same dispute between them and a third firm in country C before their respective courts would have different conflict rules applied to them, which *could* provoke a distortion of competition.

The conclusion that disparities between Member States' rules of applicable law for non-contractual obligations *could* provoke a distortion of competition is unsupported by empirical evidence and, in any event, falls short of the requirement, supported by the decision of the ECJ in the *Tobacco Advertising* case,[160] that distortions of competition must be 'appreciable' and either existing or likely to occur. **2.71**

(d) *Deterrence of forum shopping*: In similar fashion, the Commission asserted that the diverse solutions adopted by Member States in this area '*could* also incite operators to go forum-shopping'.[161] So it could, but it is unclear why that observation directly supports the conclusion that a measure that deters forum shopping falls within the Community's competence in this area. Further, in many cases, the phenomenon of forum shopping is facilitated by the alternative bases of jurisdiction provided by the Brussels I Regulation and, in particular, the (uncharacteristically) broad manner in which the ECJ has applied Art 5(3) of that Regulation and its predecessor Convention concerning matters relating to tort, delict, or quasi-delict. **2.72**

---

[158] **1.03** and **1.05** above.
[159] Commission Proposal, 7 (emphasis added).
[160] **2.30–2.32** above.
[161] Commission Proposal, 7.

As the Commission itself recognized in an earlier passage in its explanatory memorandum:[162]

Apart from the basic jurisdiction of the courts for the place of the defendant's habitual residence, provided for by Article 2 of the 'Brussels I' Regulation, Article 5(3) provides for a special head of jurisdiction in relation to torts/delicts and quasi-delict in the form of *'the courts for the place where the harmful event occurred. . .'* . The Court of Justice has always held that where the place where the harmful act occurred and the place where the loss is sustained are not the same, the defendant can be sued, at the claimant's choice, in the courts either of the place where the harmful act occurred or of the place where the loss is sustained.[163] Admittedly, the Court acknowledged that each of the two places could constitute a meaningful connecting factor for jurisdiction purposes, since each could be of significance in terms of evidence and organisation of the proceedings, but it is also true that the number of forums available to the claimant generates a risk of forum-shopping.

2.73 If forum shopping were necessarily a 'bad thing' to be avoided at all costs, the Commission's attempt to present the Rome II Regulation as a solution to problems generated by the Brussels I Regulation, a measure itself adopted under Title IV of the EC Treaty, could be likened to the swallowing of a spider to catch a fly.[164] If the existing rules of jurisdiction present a problem to the functioning of the internal market, then the solution to that problem should lie in reform of those rules. Moreover, forum shopping cannot be condemned as unacceptable in every case:[165] claimants may choose the venue for proceedings for many reasons,[166] some of which are legitimate[167] and some of which are not. That observation, in turn, begs the question as to whether it can ever be legitimate for a claimant to choose his

---

[162] Ibid, 6.

[163] Referring here to Case 21/76, *Handelskwekerij G J Bier BV v Mines de Potasse d'Alsace SA* [1976] ECR 1735.

[164] For those unfamiliar with this cautionary tale, see <http://kids.niehs.nih.gov/lyrics/oldlady.htm>.

[165] *The Atlantic Star* [1974] AC 436, 471 (Lord Simon, UKHL: '"Forum-shopping" is a dirty word; but it is only a pejorative way of saying that, if you offer a plaintiff a choice of jurisdictions, he will naturally choose the one in which he thinks his case can be most favorably presented: this should be a matter neither for surprise nor for indignation'). Also F Juenger, 'What's Wrong with Forum Shopping?' (1994) 16 Sydney L Rev 5; B R. Opeskin, 'The Price of Forum Shopping: A Reply To Professor Juenger' (1994) 16 Sydney L Rev 14; F Juenger, 'Forum Shopping: A Rejoinder' (1994) 16 Sydney L Rev 28–31.

[166] A Bell, *Forum Shopping and Venue in Transnational Litigation* (2003), ch 2.

[167] Indeed, they may be entirely consistent with the objectives of the internal market, such as the quality of the court system or legal services provided by lawyers practising in a particular jurisdiction. This brings to mind the much cited (and sometimes criticized) comment of Lord Denning MR in *The Atlantic Star* [1973] QB 364, 382 (EWCA) ('You may call this "forum-shopping" if you please, but if the forum is England, it is a good place to shop in, both for the quality of the goods and the speed of service').

forum on the basis that it will apply a more favourable set of rules in deciding the case and, if not, why not. The Commission's assumption seems to be that such a choice would not be legitimate, but it does not explain its reasoning. The impeachment of forum shopping, standing alone, does not advance the Commission's case.

(e) *Facilitating the free movement of judgments*: In this connection, the **2.74** Commission argued that:[168]

[T]he harmonisation of the conflict rules also facilitates the implementation of the principle of the mutual recognition of judgments in civil and commercial matters. The mutual recognition programme[169] calls for the reduction and ultimately the abolition of intermediate measures for recognition of a judgment given in another Member State. But the removal of all intermediate measures calls for a degree of mutual trust between Member States which is not conceivable if their courts do not all apply the same conflict rule in the same situation.

This argument must also appears tenuous. The 'free movement of judg- **2.75** ments' is not one of the freedoms constituting the internal market; the impact of obstacles to the free circulation of judgments has, therefore, only an indirect effect on the functioning of the internal market. Further, the requirement that '[u]nder no circumstances may a foreign judgment be reviewed as to its substance' lies at the heart of the Community regime for the enforcement of Member State judgments, as set out in the Brussels I Regulation and its predecessor, the 1968 Brussels Convention.[170] In this connection, the ECJ has emphasized that:[171]

The court of the State in which enforcement is sought cannot, without undermining the aim of the [Brussels] Convention, refuse recognition of a decision emanating from another Contracting State solely on the ground that it considers that national or Community law was misapplied in that decision.

Assuming, therefore, that the Member States are meeting their obligations **2.76** under the Brussels I Regulation, the link between the creation of uniform rules of applicable law and achievement of the objective of mutual recognition of Community judgments would appear remote at best. The Commission admits elsewhere in its explanatory memorandum that 'the law under which the judgment was given . . . has very little impact'.[172]

---

[168] Commission Proposal, 7.
[169] OJ C12, 8 [15.1.2001].
[170] Brussels I Regulation, Art 36; Brussels Convention, Art 29.
[171] Case C-38/98, *Régie Nationale des Usines Renault SA v Maxicar SpA* [2000] ECR I-2973, para 33.
[172] Commission Proposal, 10 (in a passage quoted at text to n 180 below). Also the evidence of Mr M Tenreiro (DG JLS) to the House of Lords' European Union Select Committee (8th Report of Session 2003–2004 (HL Paper 66), Evidence, 6).

Moreover, neither the Rome II Regulation nor the Brussels I Regulation prevent Member States from invoking overriding reasons of public policy to justify refusal, in the case of the former instrument, to apply a rule of another Member State's law[173] or, in the case of the latter instrument, to recognize a Member State judgment.[174] These conflicts, more than any other, may involve sensitive matters liable to create tensions between the Member States' legal systems, but they are not addressed by the Rome II Regulation.

2.77 If, on the other hand, it can be demonstrated that the Member States (or any of them) are not meeting their obligations to recognize and enforce other Member State judgments under the Brussels I Regulation, the appropriate step would be for the Commission or another Member State or a private litigant to take action to remedy that non-compliance, rather than shoring up the system with additional regulation.

2.78 Accordingly, none of these reasons given in the Commission Proposal provides an entirely satisfactory basis for the adoption of the Rome II Regulation under Arts 61 and 65 of the EC Treaty.

Approach to Scope of Regulation

2.79 As noted in **Section B**,[175] the proposal for the present Regulation also raised a question whether the Community's competence under Arts 61 and 65 extends to situations that have no connection to economic or other activity falling within the purview of the internal market. This question is related to but must be kept separate from the question whether the Regulation should apply only if its rules would result in the application of the law of a Member State. Confusingly, the concept of 'universal application' has been used to describe both questions.[176] As to the second of these questions, the Commission's position, reflected in Art 2 of its proposal, was that the Regulation should apply even if its rules of applicable law designated the law of a non-Member State. That recommendation was not, in itself, inconsistent with the argument that the Regulation should include a restriction designed to ensure its application only to 'intra-Community' matters, and it is not difficult to conceive of situations in which, under the rules of applicable law contained in the Regulation in its

---

[173] Rome II Regulation, Art 26. Also Art 16 (overriding mandatory provisions).

[174] Brussels I Regulation, Art 34(1).

[175] **2.34–2.39** above.

[176] A point recognized by Mr Tenreiro (DG JLS) in his evidence to the House of Lords' European Union Select Committee (HL Report, Evidence, 6 (response to Q21)).

final form, (a) the law of a Member State might fall to be applied to a situation having no direct connection to economic or other cross-border activity within the EC,[177] or (b) the law of a non-Member State might fall to be applied to a situation which has a clear connection to such activity.[178] On this, the first question identified above, the Commission argued that the application of the proposed Regulation to all cross-border situations was itself necessary for the proper functioning of the internal market 'as avoiding distortions of competition between Community litigants'.[179] Pointing to the intention that the proposed Regulation should complement the Brussels I Regulation, the Commission put its case as follows:[180]

If the 'Brussels I' Regulation distinguishes *a priori* between situations in which the defendant is habitually resident in the territory of a Member State and those in which he is habitually resident in a third country,[181] it still governs both purely 'intra-Community' situations and situations involving a 'foreign' element. For the rules of recognition and enforcement, first of all, all judgments given by a court in a Member State that are within the scope of the 'Brussels I' Regulation qualify for the simplified recognition and enforcement scheme; the law under which the judgment was given [*whether*] the law of a Member State or of a third country therefore has very little impact. As for the rules of jurisdiction, the 'Brussels I' Regulation also applies where the defendant is habitually resident outside Community territory: this is the case where the dispute is within an exclusive jurisdiction rule,[182] where the jurisdiction of the court proceeds from a jurisdiction clause,[183] where the defendant enters an appearance,[184] and where the *lis pendens* rule applies;[185] in general, Article 4(2) specifies that where the defendant is habitually resident in a third country, the claimant, if habitually resident in a Member State, may rely on

---

[177] e.g. (1) a person habitually resident in England is injured in Ruritania by a product purchased there, but also marketed in England (Regulation, Art 5(1)(a), leading to the presumptive application of English law); (2) two Korean incorporated businesses with no EC connections agree that non-contractual claims arising out of their relationship are to be governed by English law and jurisdiction (Regulation, Art 14, leading to the application of English law).

[178] e.g. (1) a person habitually resident in Ruritania is injured in Member State A by a product purchased there (but also marketed in Ruritania) and manufactured in Member State B by a company incorporated in Member State C (Regulation, Art 5(1)(a), leading to the presumptive application of the law of Ruritania); (2) businesses established in Member State A and Member State B agree that non-contractual claims arising out of their relationship based in Member State C are to be governed by New York law and (non-exclusive) jurisdiction (Regulation, Art 14, leading to the application of New York law).

[179] Commission Proposal, 9.

[180] Ibid, 9–10 (footnotes adapted).

[181] Brussels I Regulation, Art 2(1).

[182] Ibid, Art 22.

[183] Ibid, Art 23.

[184] Ibid, Art 24.

[185] Ibid, Art 27.

exorbitant rules of the law of the country where he is habitually resident, irrespective of his nationality. It follows from all these provisions that the 'Brussels I' Regulation applies both to 'intra-Community' situations and to situations involving an 'extra-Community' element.

2.80 That reasoning is logically flawed. Even if the Brussels I Regulation and the Rome II Regulation are analogous instruments (which should not be assumed), the Commission's premise is that the Brussels I Regulation was validly adopted under Arts 61 and 65 of the EC Treaty even though it regulates 'situations involving an "extra-Community element"', the Commission's euphemistic label for circumstances having no evident link to the functioning of the internal market. That conclusion, however, is no more self-evident in the case of the Brussels I Regulation than it is in the case of the Rome II Regulation. The same questions must be asked, and answered, for both instruments. Further, although statements made by the ECJ in the course of its decision in *Owusu v Jackson* and in its Opinion on the Lugano Convention suggest that the Court has pre-destined the answer that it would give in the event of a challenge to the *vires* of the Brussels I Regulation,[186] those statements cannot be regarded as conclusive for the reasons already given.[187]

2.81 The Commission continued by recycling, in slightly different terms, an argument that it had already presented to support its choice of treaty basis:[188]

> What must be sought, therefore, is equal treatment for Community litigants, even in situations that are not purely 'intra-Community'. If there continue to be more than fifteen different systems of conflict rules, two firms in distinct Member States, A and B, bringing the same dispute between them and a third firm in country C before their respective courts, would have different conflict rules applied to them, which could provoke a distortion of competition as in purely intra-Community situations.

2.82 The Commission here refers to 'Community litigants' which, in contrast to the description 'economic operators and individuals involved in cross-border litigation in the internal market' used when presenting this 'distortion of competition' argument for the first time,[189] thinly disguises the fact that not all litigation in Member State courts pertains to economic or other

---

[186] Both the judgment and the opinion post-dated the Commission Proposal.

[187] **2.38** above.

[188] Commission Proposal, 10. Also **2.70–2.71** above, where the Commission's conclusion that divergences between the Member States' pre-existing rules of applicable law 'could provoke a distortion of competition' is criticized as weak.

[189] Ibid, 7 (**2.70** above).

activity within the European Community. The example given by the UK Government of the two South Korean nationals choosing a neutral forum[190] illustrates this. Individuals and companies operating entirely outside the EC frequently choose the law and jurisdiction of a Member State without intending that their relationship should have any other connection to that Member State.

If these arguments fail to convince, the next argument presented by the **2.83** Commission on this question is undoubtedly stronger. In the Commission's view:[191]

[T]he separation between 'intra-Community' and 'extra-Community' disputes is by now artificial. How, for instance, are we to describe a dispute that initially concerns only a national of a Member State and a national of a third country but subsequently develops into a dispute concerning several Member States, for instance where the Community party joins an insurer established in another Member State or the debt in issue is assigned. Given the extent to which economic relations in the internal market are now intertwined, all disputes potentially have an intra-Community nature.

On this view, the potential for any situation to develop into one having a **2.84** connection to the functioning of the internal market is seen as justifying the regulation of all situations whether such connection exists in the first place or not.[192] That, undoubtedly, is a more straightforward solution; attempts to formulate a rule that separates 'internal market' and 'non-internal market' situations immediately run into difficulty.[193] It is submitted, however, that the problem is overstated. The same difficulty exists in separating situations that have a sufficient cross-border connection for the purposes of the Regulation from those which concern only a single Member State. That, however, did not prevent the Commission, the Council, and the European Parliament from concluding that purely domestic situations should fall outside the scope of the Regulation, or from formulating a rule[194] to be applied by Member State courts in drawing the line. That rule, referring to 'conflicts solely between the laws of' different territorial units within a Member State, can be adapted for present purposes so as to exclude from the scope of the Regulation 'conflicts solely between the laws of the forum State and one or more non-Member States'. This test does not provide a bright line, and difficult cases would no doubt

---

[190] **2.35** above.
[191] Commission Proposal, 10.
[192] For a similar argument, see J Basedow, n 39 above, 704. Cf O Remien, n 81 above, 74–5).
[193] A Dickinson, n 10 above, 223–7.
[194] Commission Proposal, Art 21(2); Regulation, Art 25(2) (**3.292** below).

present themselves. The rule is, however, no less certain than that for domestic situations, now contained in Art 25(2) of the Regulation.

2.85 Further, it may be questioned whether the potential (however remote) for any situation to develop into one having a relevant connection to the Community justifies the absence of any restriction on the application of the Rome II Regulation to 'extra-Community' situations. In its case law on Art 95 of the EC Treaty, the ECJ has made clear that, to support the need for legislation, it must be *likely* that obstacles to free movement or distortions to competition will arise in the future.[195] The Commission's approach takes no account of the likelihood that what begins as a situation having no Community connection, other than (for example) the parties' choice of law or jurisdiction of a Member State, will subsequently develop such a connection. In any event, if such a connection has not manifested itself by the date on which a Member State court is called upon to determine a dispute, it may be doubted whether the Rome II Regulation has a legitimate claim to apply.[196]

2.86 Finally, the Commission resorts to the following practical argument:

> Evidence presented to the Commission by the legal professions—both bench and bar—in the course of the written consultation emphasised that private international law in general and the conflict rules in particular are perceived as highly complex. This complexity would be even greater if this measure had the effect of doubling the sources of conflict rules and if practitioners now had to deal not only with Community uniform rules but also with distinct national rules in situations not connected as required with Community territory. The universal nature of the proposed Regulation accordingly meets the concern for certainty in the law and the Union's commitment in favour of transparent legislation.

2.87 The fact, however, that a single set of rules for all situations would be more straightforward, and thereby produce greater certainty as to the law applicable, does not justify overriding the stated limitations upon the Community's competence to adopt legislation under Arts 61 and 65 of the EC Treaty. The existence, in parallel, of two separate sets of rules of applicable law for non-contractual obligations in each Member State may be inconvenient, but that fact cannot be said to affect the proper functioning of the internal market in circumstances where (a) all situations raising a genuine conflict between the laws of two or more Member States are regulated by a single set of harmonized rules (i.e. those contained in the Rome

---

[195] Text to nn 76 and 79 above.

[196] For a situation in which the subsequent creation of a link to a Member State did not mandate the application of the 1968 Brussels Convention, see Case C-129/92, *Owens Bank Ltd v Bracco* [1994] ECR I-117.

II Regulation), and (b) the Regulation does not, in any event, purport to regulate purely domestic situations.[197] Given that Member States could, in any event, elect to extend the field of application of the Regulation's rules to domestic and 'extra-Community' situations, that conclusion also accords with the principle of subsidiarity.[198]

Accordingly the Commission's case for rejecting any restriction on the application of the Rome II Regulation to situations having no connection to cross-border activity within the EC is also unpersuasive. **2.88**

Approach to Questions of Subsidiarity and Proportionality

As to subsidiarity and proportionality, the Commission stated:[199]   **2.89**

The technique of harmonising conflict-of-laws rules fully respects the subsidiarity and proportionality principles since it enhances certainty in the law without demanding harmonisation of the substantive rules of domestic law.

Recognizing that the Protocol on subsidiarity and proportionality[200] had expressed a preference for directives over regulations, the Commission sought to justify its choice of legislative instrument as follows:[201] **2.90**

[F]or the purposes of this proposal a Regulation is the most appropriate instrument. It lays down uniform rules for the applicable law. These rules are detailed, precise and unconditional and require no measures by the Member States for their transposal into national law. They are therefore self-executing. The nature of these rules is the direct result of the objective set for them, which is to enhance certainty in the law and the foreseeability of the solutions adopted as regards the law applicable to a given legal relationship. If the Member States had room for manoeuvre in transposing these rules, uncertainty would be reintroduced into the law, and that is precisely what the harmonisation is supposed to abolish. The Regulation is therefore the instrument that must be chosen to guarantee uniform application in the Member States.

These reasons, so far as they go, appear unobjectionable. The Commission, however, did not specifically address in this section the question whether the subject matter and territorial scope of the proposed Regulation went further than was necessary to meet the objectives of Title IV of the Treaty, as the Commission perceived them.[202] **2.91**

---

[197] Regulation, Art 25(2), discussed at **2.47** and **2.84** above.
[198] **2.51–2.52** above.
[199] Commission Proposal, 7.
[200] **2.52** above, point 3, reflecting para (b) of the Protocol.
[201] Commission Proposal, 7.
[202] Cf **2.79–2.88 above**.

THE EESC OPINION

2.92 The EESC, in its opinion,[203] endorsed the Commission's view on the Community's competence to adopt a Regulation in the terms set out in the proposal. In the EESC's view:[204]

> Conflict of laws regarding non-contractual obligations is still governed by the rules of the Member States which, although often based on a common understanding of the subject matter, differ significantly, at least in their details, and have been differently shaped by national case law and academic interpretation. This results in many difficulties for users of the law, including problems in obtaining the relevant rules, language problems, and problems of familiarisation with a foreign legal culture and academic and case-law interpretation. Because these areas are closely interrelated, the law on obligations covers both the contractual and non-contractual kind, and the provisions of the Rome Convention, while representing a major improvement, have always been considered incomplete. The Convention has always lacked a section dealing with non-contractual obligations. The harmonisation of the rules on conflict of laws regarding non-contractual obligations promises considerable progress vis-à-vis the current situation in the Community in view of the greater certainty and predictability it will bring to the process of determining the applicable substantive law.

2.93 In the section of its opinion entitled 'Legal basis', the EESC concluded:[205]

> The purpose of the regulation is the unification of the rules on conflict of laws regarding non-contractual obligations. The harmonisation of conflict rules falls under Article 65(b) TEC. This means that the Commission is empowered to act where this is necessary for the smooth operation of the internal market. In the Committee's view, this is the case, as harmonisation will help to ensure equal treatment of economic operators in the Community in cross-border cases, increase legal certainty, simplify application of the law and thus promote willingness to enter into cross-border business, as well as promote the mutual recognition of legal acts of the Member States by making it easier for nationals of other Member States to check that they are legally correct.

This reasoning pithily summarizes the Commission's case, but does not add to it.

---

[203] **1.78** above.
[204] EESC Opinion (OJ C241, 1–2 (para 2.1) [28.9.2004]).
[205] Ibid, 2–3 (para 3).

ADVICE OF THE COUNCIL LEGAL SERVICE

In March 2004, following doubts expressed by a minority of Member **2.94**
States,[206] the Council Legal Service presented to the Council's Rome II
Committee an opinion on the legal basis for the proposed Regulation.[207]
The substantive advice contained in that opinion has only recently been
made public following the decision of the ECJ in *Sweden and Turco v
Council*,[208] concerning the disclosure of legal advice under Regulation (EC)
No 1049/2001 regarding public access to European Parliament, Council
and Commission documents.[209]

The content of the opinion confirms the impression given in other parts of **2.95**
the *travaux préparatoires*,[210] that the Council Legal Service, while giving a
generally favourable view as to the Community's competence to adopt
the Rome II Regulation, expressed concerns as to its application to situations having no substantial Community connection. Having summarized
the aim and content of the proposed Regulation[211] and identified the
proposed legal basis,[212] the Legal Service dealt quickly with the argument
raised above[213] as to the effect of the words 'promoting the compatibility
of the rules applicable in the Member States' in Art 65(c). The Opinion
noted that the examples in sub-paras (a) to (c) of Art 65 are introduced
by the words 'shall include' and concluded, on this basis, that they are

[206] Council document 14010/03 [17.12.2003], 4.
[207] Council document 7015/04 [2.3.2004].
[208] Cases C-39/05 and C-52/05, *Sweden and Turco v Council* [2008] ECR I-0000 (Judgment of 1 July 2008).
[209] OJ L145, 43 [31.5.2001]. Under Art 4(2) of this Directive, the institutions are required to refuse public access to a document if disclosure would undermine the protection of court proceedings and legal advice, unless there is an overriding public interest in disclosure. In *Sweden and Turco*, n 208 above, the ECJ emphasized that the public interest in disclosure should normally prevail, even for legal advice. Neither concerns that the availability of legal advice might undermine confidence in the lawfulness of the measure in question, nor the possibility that the Community's lawyers might be pressurized to change their advice to present matters more favourably, provided general reasons for non-disclosure.
[210] e.g. Council documents 9009/04, ADD 1 [3.5.2004], 1 (Austria); ibid, ADD 4 [4.5.2004], 1 (Belgium); ibid, ADD 11 [24.5.2004], 1 (Germany); ibid, ADD 15 [26.5.2004], 2 (United Kingdom); Council document, 8026/05 [13.4.2005], 2 (United Kingdom). Also letter dated 7 June 2004 from Lord Filkin, Parliamentary Under Secretary of State in the (former) Department for Constitutional Affairs (DCA) to Lord Grenfell, responding to the HL Report (n 31 above) and letter dated 25 April 2006 from Baroness Ashton of Upholland, Parliamentary Under Secretary of State, DCA to Lord Grenfell.
[211] Council document 7015/04, paras 3–7.
[212] Ibid, para 8.
[213] **2.48**.

not exhaustive.[214] The Legal Service then turned to consider the meaning and effect of the requirement in Art 65 that measures have 'cross-border implications'.[215] In concluding that this requirement was satisfied, the Legal Service reasoned that:[216]

The proposed Regulation applies, according to its Article 1, paragraph 1, to situations involving a conflict of laws. Such situations arise only if a cross-border element is involved.

It is true that the Regulation applies also to conflicts of laws in situations where the cross-border element involves third States. But the scope of application of Article 65 of the EC Treaty is not limited to measures having cross-border implications exclusively within the Community. This follows from the wording of Article 65 which refers merely to 'cross-border implications' and not to internal cross-border implications.

2.96 Finally, the Legal Service turned to consider the meaning of the internal market wording in Art 65.[217] In its view:[218]

The Community legislator has a margin of appreciation in this respect and can reasonably conclude that a measure is necessary within the meaning of Article 65 if it facilitates the proper functioning of the internal market. . . .

It is clear from Article 65, point b), that the authors of the Treaty considered that the different rules of the Member States on the conflict of laws might, under certain circumstances, have the effect of putting obstacles to the free movement within the internal market. Otherwise, they would not have included measures 'promoting the compatibility of the rules applicable in the Member States concerning the conflict of laws' among the possible measures in the field of judicial cooperation in civil matters necessary for the proper functioning of the internal market. It remains, however, to be examined in the present context whether the adoption of uniform rules on the law applicable to non-contractual obligations, including uniform rules on the law applicable to events occurring entirely outside the Community, would indeed help eliminating obstacles to the free movement within the internal market.

2.97 The Legal Service referred, in particular, to the possibility that the outcome of Community litigation concerning non-contractual obligations may vary depending on which court was seised and that this fact might

---

[214] Council document 7015/04, para 9.
[215] **2.47** above.
[216] Council document 7015/04, paras 13 and 14. In the view of the Legal Service (ibid, para 12), 'the cross-border element can arise, inter alia, from situations where the relevant facts of a case, the domicile or residence of the litigants or the competent courts are located in more than one Member State'.
[217] **2.16–2.39** above.
[218] Council document 7014/04, paras 16, 18.

encourage forum shopping and increase legal uncertainty and the costs and complexity of resolving disputes.[219] The Commission's argument concerning possible distortions of competition was also cited, with apparent approval,[220] alongside an argument (not raised by the Commission) as to the possible impact of disparities between Member States' laws on the decision of an undertaking as to its place of establishment.[221] Finally, the Legal Service referred to the possible role of harmonized rules of applicable law in facilitating abolition of obstacles to the free movement of judgments between Member States.[222]

Having noted that these arguments were equally relevant whether the law **2.98** applicable under the Regulation was that of a Member State or a non-Member State (i.e. the first of the two meanings of 'universal application' considered above),[223] the Legal Service concluded that:[224]

The cumulative effect of the above series of arguments leads the Legal Service to consider that the establishment of uniform rules on the law applicable to non-contractual obligations would, in principle and without prejudice to the remainder of this opinion, facilitate the proper functioning of the internal market.

Accordingly, the Council Legal Service considered that the exercise of the **2.99** Community's legislative competence under Arts 61 and 65 to adopt a Regulation on the law applicable to non-contractual obligations was, in principle, justified. In the following paragraphs, however, the Legal Service doubted whether a Regulation could be validly adopted in the form set out in the Commission Proposal, without any restriction excluding its application to 'situations in which most or all of the relevant elements are situated outside the Community'.[225] Having noted that the Commission Proposal 'is drafted in a way that it would also apply to cases where none of the parties is domiciled or habitually resident in a Member State, where both the damage and the event giving rise to the damage occurred in a third State, and where there is no apparent relationship with the exercise by the applicant or the defendant of any of the freedoms on which the internal market is founded',[226] the Legal Service reviewed the arguments raised earlier in its Opinion and concluded that none of these was sufficient to justify the application of a Community instrument on the law

---

[219] Ibid, paras 19–20. Cf **2.64**–**2.65** and **2.72**–**2.73** above.
[220] Ibid, para 21. Cf **2.70**–**2.71** above.
[221] Ibid, para 22.
[222] Ibid, paras 23–5. Cf **2.74**–**2.77** above.
[223] Ibid, para 26; **2.34** above.
[224] Ibid, para 27.
[225] Ibid, para 28.
[226] Ibid, para 29.

applicable to non-contractual obligations to what it described as 'extra-Community cases'.[227] In its opinion:[228]

[I]t cannot be established that the application of the proposed Regulation to extra-Community cases would facilitate the proper functioning of the internal market. For such cases, the recourse to the legal basis of Articles 61, point c), and 67 of the EC Treaty would therefore not be appropriate. . . .

It is true that that the establishment of an additional layer of Community rules applying to intra-Community disputes only, added to the different national rules applying to extra-Community disputes, would make the application of conflict rules, which are in any case highly complex, even more difficult in practice. However, this additional complexity is a consequence of the EC Treaty itself. By limiting the scope of Article 65 to measures which are *'necessary for the proper functioning of the internal market'*, the drafters of the Treaty chose not to establish an all-embracing legal basis for measures in the field of judicial cooperation in civil matters in general and conflict rules in particular. In doing so, they accepted that the Community powers in this area are fragmentary and might need to be supplemented by national rules of the Member States. The Community legislator [has] to comply with this choice. It would be contrary to the principle of specific referral of powers to the Community and its institutions, laid down in Articles 5 and 7, paragraph 1, second subparagraph, of the EC Treaty, if the Community legislator, for mere considerations of convenience, deprived of their meaning the limits which the legal bases of the Treaty impose on the Community's powers.

2.100 The Legal Service recommended that the Council's Rome II Committee consider possible ways to restrict the scope of the proposed Regulation so as to address this concern, noting that the Community legislator enjoyed a margin of appreciation in this respect.[229]

Discussions in Council

2.101 Despite the concerns raised by the Council Legal Service, proposals to limit the scope of the Regulation by a provision requiring a sufficient connection to the internal market were ultimately rejected by the Council. The first attempt to formulate a suitable restriction on the Regulation's scope was contained in Art 1(1a) of the Irish/Dutch Presidency text circulated in June 2004, which proposed excluding cases where jurisdiction is based solely on a choice of court agreement.[230]

---

[227] Ibid, paras 30–1, in line with the conclusion at **2.34–2.39** and **2.79–2.88** above.

[228] Ibid, paras 32 and 34 (emphasis in original). The word 'has' in square brackets has been substituted for 'have' in the original.

[229] Ibid, para 33.

[230] Council document 10173/04 [14.6.2004]. For discussion of this provision in the Council's Rome II Committee, see Council document 11104/04 [2.7.2004], 3. Also Council document

Subsequently, the revised text produced by the outgoing Dutch and incom- **2.102**
ing Luxembourg Presidencies in December 2004[231] contained four suggested options for dealing with the Regulation's sphere of application.
These were (1) excluding the operation of the Regulation if the only connection to the EC results from a choice of court agreement designating a
Member State court (with the possible additional requirement that none of
the parties to the dispute be domiciled in a Member State), (2) excluding
the operation of the Regulation where a Member State court has assumed
jurisdiction solely on the basis of its national law,[232] (3) expressly applying
the Regulation in all cases where a Member State court has jurisdiction (on
whatever basis), and (4) making no express provision for the sphere of
operation of the Regulation. None of these options seemed apposite to
resolve the difficulty presented by the exclusionary effect of the internal
market requirement.[233]

In April 2005, the UK delegation presented its own proposal for restricting **2.103**
the scope of the proposed Regulation in order to give effect to the internal
market wording in Art 65, in line with its understanding of the Opinion
given by the Council Legal Service.[234] Under this proposal, the Regulation
would not have applied if jurisdiction were assumed by the Member State
court otherwise than pursuant to a Community instrument,[235] unless both
(a) at least one of the claimants were habitually resident in a Member State
when the damage occurred, and (b) the damage occurred in a different
Member State.[236] The UK proposal sank almost without trace, perhaps
because it was considered too complex or because the decision of the
Court of Justice in *Owusu v Jackson*[237] in the preceding month had strengthened the hand of the delegations within the Rome II Committee opposing
any restriction of this kind. Whatever the reason, the text circulated at the
conclusion of the UK Council Presidency in December 2005, which retained
the four options described above, did not refer to the UK proposal[238] and,
when it was tabled for debate the following month, it does not appear to

SN 2851/04 [20.7.2004], Art 1(1a), adding the further requirement that none of the parties to
the dispute is domiciled in a Member State.

[231] Council document 16231/04 [20.12.2004]. Options (1)–(3) were first presented in
Council document 12746/04 [27.9.2004].
[232] i.e. in accordance with Art 4 of the Brussels I Regulation.
[233] A Dickinson, n 10 above, 223–7.
[234] **2.94–2.100** above.
[235] Principally, the Brussels I Regulation.
[236] Council document 8026/05 [13.4.2005]. Although this is not the effect of the proposal as
drafted, the draftsman's intention appears in the examples given on p 5 of that document.
[237] **2.36** above.
[238] Council document 16027/05 [22.12.2005], Art 1(1a).

have attracted any support. Instead, by this time, many delegations favoured Option (4), i.e. making no express provision.[239] After this set-back, the UK presented a more straightforward proposal that the Regulation should apply if both the habitual residence of one of the parties and the damage were located in a Member State.[240] That proposal, in turn, was also considered and rejected by the Council's Rome II Committee.[241] In terms of the legislative process, the debate as to the Community's competence to adopt the Rome II Regulation was effectively at an end. In a communication to COREPER, the Austrian Presidency acknowledged that in the course of the negotiations 'a number of proposals have been made suggesting a different scope or logic to the text of the Regulation', before noting that 'in the light of the debates, the Presidency has the impression that these proposals have not gained majority support'.[242] It remained only for the Irish delegation, supported by the UK, to express regret at the failure to agree an appropriate restriction.[243] The UK delegation invited the Council Legal Service to express an opinion as to whether the absence of any restriction on scope would be in conformity with Community law.[244] It does not appear that the Legal Service responded to that invitation.

THE EUROPEAN PARLIAMENT

2.104 It appears that the European Parliament did not specifically address the question of treaty basis.

D. THE TEXT OF THE REGULATION

2.105 The preamble to the Regulation makes clear that it is based on Art 61(c) and, in terms of legislative procedure, Art 67 of the EC Treaty. It refers expressly to the 'proposal from the Commission'[245] and to the EESC Opinion.[246]

---

[239] Council document 6161/06 [10.2.2006], 5 recording discussions at the meeting of the Council's Rome II Committee held on 24–25 January 2006.

[240] Council document 7212/06 [10.3.2006].

[241] Council document 7551/06 [22.3.2006], 5.

[242] Council document 8076/06 [10.4.2006], 2.

[243] Council document 7709/06 [3.5.2006], 8.

[244] Ibid.

[245] A reference, presumably, to both the Commission Proposal and the Commission Amended Proposal.

[246] **1.78** above.

Recitals (1) and (2) to the Regulation, reflecting Art 61 and 65 of the EC **2.106**
Treaty,[247] state that:

(1) The Community has set itself the objective of maintaining and developing an
area of freedom, security and justice. For the progressive establishment of such an
area, the Community is to adopt measures relating to judicial cooperation in civil
matters with a cross-border impact to the extent necessary for the proper functioning of the internal market.

(2) According to Article 65(b) of the Treaty, these measures are to include those
promoting the compatibility of the rules applicable in the Member States concerning the conflict of laws and of jurisdiction.

Recitals (3), (4), and (5) refer respectively to the Presidency Conclusions of **2.107**
the Tampere European Council, the Council and Commission's joint programme of measures for implementing the principle of mutual recognition, and the Hague Programme.[248]

The following reasons for the Community's competence to enact the Rome **2.108**
II Regulation are given in Recitals (6), (13), (14), and (15):

(6) The proper functioning of the internal market creates a need, in order to
improve the predictability of the outcome of litigation, certainty as to the law
applicable and the free movement of judgments, for the conflict-of-law rules in the
Member States to designate the same national law irrespective of the country of
the court in which an action is brought.

(13) Uniform rules applied irrespective of the law they designate may avert the
risk of distortions of competition between Community litigants.

(14) The requirement of legal certainty and the need to do justice in individual cases
are essential elements of an area of justice. This Regulation provides for the connecting factors which are the most appropriate to achieve these objectives. . . .[249]

(15) The principle of the *lex loci delicti commissi* is the basic solution for non-contractual obligations in virtually all the Member States, but the practical application
of the principle where the component factors of the case are spread over several
countries varies. This situation engenders uncertainty as to the law applicable.

Save that there is no explicit claim that disparities between the Member **2.109**
States' existing rules of applicable law for non-contractual obligations
create obstacles to the exercise of fundamental freedoms within the
internal market, these reasons reflect the arguments presented by the
Commission in its Proposal,[250] and do not enhance the case for intervention

[247] **2.06–2.07** above.
[248] **1.56–1.57, 1.82, 2.12–2.13,** and **2.59–2.62** above.
[249] The remainder of Recital (14) summarizes the general scheme of rules of applicable law
contained in the Regulation.
[250] Discussed at **2.59–2.78** above.

by the Community. Even if taken at face value, despite the lack of support-ing material, the assertion in Recital (13) that 'uniform rules applied irre-spective of the law they designate *may* avert the risk of distortions of competition between Community litigants' falls short of the standard dic-tated by the ECJ in its *Tobacco Advertising* decision, requiring the likelihood that appreciable future distortions of competition result from disparities between Member State laws.[251] Further, the attempt to buttress this conclu-sion with references to legal certainty and the free movement of judgments seems inadequate, in the absence of a demonstrated link between these fac-tors and the functioning of the internal market in the present case.[252] At best, therefore, the stated reasons are unsatisfactory. Arguably, however, their deficiency provides a ground for challenging the validity of the Rome II Regulation in the course of a future reference to the ECJ.

2.110 In relation to the scope of the Regulation, Art 3 of the Regulation (entitled 'Universal application') provides that '[a]ny law specified by this Regulation shall be applied whether or not it is the law of a Member State'.[253] Recital (13), quoted above, seems to confirm that, in the absence of any express restriction intended to exclude from the Regulation's scope situations that have no connection to cross-border activity within the Community, the legislator's intention was that the rules of applicable law in the Regulation should apply to all situations, other than to situations raising conflicts solely between the laws of different territorial units of a single Member State.[254] For the reasons given above, and those set out in the Opinion of the Council's Legal Service, the absence of any restriction designed to give effect to the specific internal market wording in Art 65 of the EC Treaty presents another ground upon which the *vires* of the Rome II Regulation may be open to challenge in a future case.[255]

2.111 Finally, the questions of subsidiarity and proportionality[256] are addressed by Recital (38), as follows:

> Since the objective of this Regulation cannot be sufficiently achieved by the Member States, and can therefore, by reason of the scale and effects of this Regulation, be better achieved at Community level, the Community may adopt measures, in accordance with the principle of subsidiarity set out in Article 5 of the Treaty. In accordance with the principle of proportionality set out in that Article, this Regulation does not go beyond what is necessary to attain that objective.

---

[251] Text to n 80 above.
[252] **2.64–2.67** and **2.74–2.77** above.
[253] **3.294–3.295** below.
[254] Art 25(2).
[255] **2.34–2.39**, **2.79–2.88** and **2.99–2.100** above.
[256] **2.25–2.53** and **2.89–2.91** above.

However unsatisfactory this formulaic assertion may be, there is very **2.112** little prospect of it being successfully challenged before the ECJ.[257]

E. CONCLUSION

This chapter has identified two possible grounds on which a future chal- **2.113** lenge to the validity of the Rome II Regulation might be based. The first possible ground for challenge is the inadequacy of the reasons set out in the Recitals to the Regulation, when read together with the Commission Proposal and other *travaux préparatoires*. That is not to say that a convincing case could not have been made for a Community instrument harmonizing the Member States' rules of applicable law for non-contractual obligations. That case, however, is not made out in the Regulation or the Commission Proposal that led to it. The second possible ground for challenge, supported by the Opinion of the Council Legal Service, is the absence of any restriction designed to give effect to the specific internal market wording in Art 65.

Even so, a litigant presenting a challenge to the Regulation on either of **2.114** these grounds, or indeed any other, could not be confident of success. Indeed, the judicial restraint shown by the Court of Justice in the face of recent challenges to internal market measures[258] and its apparent willingness to confirm the aggrandizement of Community competence[259] provide obvious reasons for caution, and will likely require that the stakes be high before a challenge is even considered. Most significantly, in its recent jurisprudence concerning private international law measures, the ECJ has displayed an overt hostility to arguments that might impact on the scope of the Community's power to legislate in this area.[260] The statements in question may not be conclusive, but they send the message that the Court has steered a particular course from which it will not easily be diverted.

[257] **2.53** above.
[258] **2.44–2.45** above.
[259] **2.02** above.
[260] **2.36** above.

3

Foundations and Scope

A. INTERPRETATION

INTRODUCTION[1]

The Rome II Regulation has effect in the United Kingdom under s 2(1) **3.01**
of the European Communities Act 1972,[2] without the need for specific

---

[1] See, generally, D Wyatt et al., *Wyatt & Dashwood's European Union Law* (5th edn, 2006), paras 12-014 to 12-015; K P E Lasok, T Millett, and A Howard, *Judicial Control in the EU* (2004), ch 8; H Schermers and D Waelbroek, *Judicial Protection in the European Union* (6th edn, 2001), 10–27.

[2] *R v Secretary of State for Transport, ex p Factortame (No 2)* [1991] 1 AC 603 (UKHL).

implementing legislation.[3] Nevertheless, its provisions must be construed in accordance with the principles and guidelines laid down by the Court of Justice. In particular:[4]

[1] To begin with, it must be borne in mind that Community legislation is drafted in several languages and that the different language versions are all equally authentic. An interpretation of a provision of Community law thus involves a comparison of the different language versions.

[2] It must also be borne in mind, even where the different language versions are entirely in accord with one another, that Community law uses terminology which is peculiar to it. Furthermore, it must be emphasized that legal concepts do not necessarily have the same meaning in Community law and in the law of the various Member States.

[3] Finally, every provision of Community law must be placed in its context and interpreted in the light of the provisions of Community law as a whole, regard being had to the objectives thereof and to its state of evolution at the date on which the provision in question is to be applied.

3.02 Each of these three aspects of the approach to be taken in interpreting the Regulation will be considered in turn. Before embarking on that exercise, the following comment on the approach of the ECJ to the construction of Community legislation is worthy of note:[5]

The majority of cases in which a legal provision is construed contain no statement of the principle of construction used by the Court. Usually, that is because no particular problem of construction arises that demands recourse to, or the articulation of a principle: it is sufficient to read the provision and to take into account the matters that the Court normally takes into account as to the correct meaning of the text. Thus, where the language used is tolerably clear and apparently consistent with the purpose of the provision and the overall legislative context, the Court may simply remark that the true meaning follows from the words used and not disclose in express terms that it has taken into account the purpose and context of the provision. In cases in which some pronouncement is made disclosing the method of interpretation used, it is more often the case that the pronouncement is directed to the particular problem arising in the case in point: where the language used is less than clear, the reader may well be treated to an examination of whatever it is that, in that particular case, the Court regards as the most reliable pointer to the true meaning of the provision, which may be any one (or any combination)

---

[3] Under EC Treaty, Art 249, a regulation 'shall have general application. It shall be binding and directly applicable in all Member States.' As a corollary to this, national legislation that simply duplicates EC legislative instruments, as opposed to making supplemental provision to give effect to them in national law, is prohibited by the Treaty.

[4] Case 283/81, *CILFIT Srl v Ministry of Health* [1982] ECR 3415, paras [18]–[20] (numbering in italics added).

[5] Lasok, Millett & Howard, n 1 above, para [658].

of a number of factors, such as its purpose, the overall legal context, the practicalities of applying the legislation, the legislative history and so forth. A careful search through the cases is therefore capable of dredging up all manner of dicta or apparent statements of principle that can be used to support the most diverse approaches to the problem of the construction of legislative texts; and many of those statements may appear to be mutually inconsistent.

On occasion, the approach of the ECJ in construing particular provisions **3.03** of EC legislation may appear somewhat haphazard. That is not because the Court is engaging in a judicial lottery, but because the interpretative tools available to it are so many and so varied that, in combination with the Court's tendency to focus on the case before it and the need for several judges from widely differing professional and legal backgrounds to produce a unanimous opinion, their application produces the legal equivalent of an expressionist painting. These matters must be borne in mind in interpreting the Regulation.

The First Aspect—Equal Authenticity of Different Language Versions[6]

The need for a uniform interpretation of Community regulations makes it **3.04** impossible for the English language text of a provision of the Regulation to be considered in isolation. Instead, that provision should be interpreted and applied in the light of the versions existing in the other official languages of the Community.[7] All the language versions must, in principle, be recognized as having the same weight and this cannot vary according to the size of the population of the Member States using the language in question.[8] Thus, in theory, although the Commission Proposal was prepared in the French language and the legislative process (particularly in the Council) was conducted mainly in English, all 23 language versions of the Regulation[9] must be taken into account in determining the single meaning and effect to be given to each provision. An interpretation that is reconcilable with all the language versions must be preferred to one compatible with only some of them.[10] In practice, parties to legal proceedings

---

[6] Lasok, Millett & Howard, n 1 above, para [662]; H Schermers and D Waelbroek, n 1 above, 12–13.

[7] Case 9/79, *Koschniske v Raad van Arbeid* [1979] ECR 2717, para 6.

[8] Case C-296/95, *R v Commissioners of Customs and Excise, ex p Emu Tabac* [1998] ECR I-1605, para 36.

[9] Including Danish, although Denmark is not bound by the Regulation.

[10] *R v CCE, ex p Emu Tabac*, n 8 above, paras 34–36; Case C-306/98, *R v Ministry of Agriculture, Fisheries and Food, ex p Monsanto* [2001] ECR I-3279, paras 37–41. If a large majority of the language versions point to a particular meaning, the fact that the remainder cannot be reconciled with that meaning may be left out of account (see, e.g., Joined Cases C-283/94,

and national courts are likely (if only for reasons of cost and procedural efficiency) to prefer their own language version, unless alerted to a particular ambiguity or peculiarity in the text.

THE SECOND ASPECT—AUTONOMOUS MEANING OF PARTICULAR TERMS

3.05 The autonomy of the text of the Regulation from the content of the laws of individual Member States is essential to ensure its consistent interpretation throughout the EC.[11] That reasoning has consistently been deployed in the case law of the ECJ concerning the Brussels Convention.[12] In one of the first references decided by the Court under the Convention protocol, *Tessili v Dunlop*, the Court stated:[13]

> The Convention frequently uses words and legal concepts drawn from civil, commercial and procedural law and capable of a different meaning from one Member State to another. The question therefore arises whether these words and concepts must be regarded as having their own independent meaning and as being thus common to all the Member States or as referring to substantive rules of the law applicable in each case under the rules of conflict of laws of the court before which the matter is first brought.

> Neither of these two options rules out the other since the appropriate choice can only be made in respect of each of the provisions of the Convention to ensure that it is fully effective having regard to the objectives of Article 220 of the Treaty.[14] In any event it should be stressed that the interpretation of the said words and concepts for the purpose of the Convention does not prejudge the question of the substantive rule applicable to the particular case.

3.06 In *Tessili*, the Court took the view that, having regard to the differences obtaining between national laws of contract and to the absence of any unification of the applicable substantive law, it was not possible to provide an autonomous concept of 'place of performance' of a contractual obligation in Art 5(1) of the Brussels Convention, with the result that the determination of that connecting factor should be left to each Member State court applying its own rules of private international law.[15] A little more than a week later, however, the ECJ made clear that such an approach would

---

C-291/94, and C-292/94, *Denkavit International BV, VITIC Amsterdam BV and Voormeer BV v Bundesamt für Finanzen* [1996] ECR I-5063, para 25).

[11] Lasok, Millett & Howard, n 1 above, para [679].

[12] J A Pontier and E Burg, *EU Principles on Jurisdiction and Recognition and Enforcement of Judgments in Civil and Commercial Matters* (2004), 72–8.

[13] *Industrie Tessili Italiana Como v Dunlop AG* [1976] ECR 1473, paras 10–11.

[14] Now EC Treaty, Art 293.

[15] *Tessili v Dunlop*, n 13 above, paras 13–15. This approach was confirmed in Case C-440/97, *Groupe Concorde v The Master of the Vessel 'Suhadiwarno Panjan'* [1999] ECR I-6307.

be the exception rather than the rule and set itself on the path that would predominate in its later case law on the Brussels Convention. In the *Eurocontrol* case,[16] the Court was asked to consider the concept of 'civil and commercial matters' in Art 1 of the Convention, a concept also used to define the material scope of the Rome II Regulation.[17] The Court commented:[18]

As Article 1 serves to indicate the area of application of the Convention it is necessary, in order to ensure, as far as possible, that the rights and obligations which derive from it for the Contracting States and the persons to whom it applies are equal and uniform, that the terms of that provision should not be interpreted as a mere reference to the internal law of one or other of the states concerned.

By providing that the Convention shall apply 'whatever the nature of the court or tribunal' Article 1 shows that the concept 'civil and commercial matters' cannot be interpreted solely in the light of the division of jurisdiction between the various types of courts existing in certain states.

The concept in question must therefore be regarded as independent and must be interpreted by reference, first, to the objectives and scheme of the Convention and, secondly, to the general principles which stem from the corpus of the national legal systems.

In *Kalfelis v Schröder*,[19] the ECJ was required to consider the meaning of the **3.07** concept of 'matters relating to tort, delict or quasi-delict' used in Art 5(3) of the Brussels Convention.[20] Before attempting a definition, the Court noted:

With respect to the first part of the question, it must be observed that the concept of 'matters relating to tort, delict or quasi-delict' serves as a criterion for defining the scope of one of the rules concerning the special jurisdictions available to the plaintiff. . . . [I]t is important that, in order to ensure as far as possible the equality and uniformity of the rights and obligations arising out of the Convention for the Contracting States and the persons concerned, that concept should not be interpreted simply as referring to the national law of one or other of the States concerned.

Accordingly, the concept of matters relating to tort, delict or quasi-delict must be regarded as an autonomous concept which is to be interpreted, for the application of the Convention, principally by reference to the scheme and objectives of the Convention in order to ensure that the latter is given full effect.

---

[16] Case 29/76, *LTY Lufttransportunternehmen GmbH v Eurocontrol* [1976] ECR 1541.
[17] Art 1(1) (**3.263–3.269** below).
[18] Ibid, para 3.
[19] Case 189/87, *Kalfelis v Bankhaus Schröder, Münchmeyer, Hengst & Co* [1988] ECR 5565.
[20] **3.234–3.242** below.

3.08 In *Shearson Lehman Hutton*,[21] the Court referred to 'the principle, established by case-law[22] . . . according to which the concepts used in the Convention, which may have a different content depending on the national law of the Contracting States, must be interpreted independently, by reference principally to the system and objectives of the Convention, in order to ensure that the Convention is uniformly applied in all the Contracting States'.

3.09 The same approach, that is to say a strong presumption in favour of the concepts in the Regulation being given an autonomous EC law interpretation, will apply also to the Rome II Regulation.[23] It is particularly important that provisions concerning the scope of the Regulation, and of its rules of applicable law, should carry a single, uniform meaning across the Member States. If there were any doubt as to the approach to be taken, it is removed by Recital (11)[24] which makes clear that:

> The concept of a non-contractual obligation varies from one Member State to another. Therefore for the purposes of this Regulation non-contractual obligation should be understood as an autonomous concept. The conflict of law rules set out in this Regulation should also cover non-contractual obligations arising out of strict liability.

3.10 Similarly, Recital (30), addressing the scope of Art 12 of the Regulation,[25] provides:

> *Culpa in contrahendo* for the purposes of this Regulation is an autonomous concept and should not necessarily be interpreted within the meaning of national law. It should include the violation of the duty of disclosure and the breakdown of contractual negotiations. Article 12 covers only non-contractual obligations presenting a direct link with the dealings prior to the conclusion of a contract.

3.11 Although there are no corresponding Recitals for the Regulation's other rules of applicable law, that should not be taken as an indication that their scope is to be left to the individual brushes and palettes of Member State courts, applying their own national concepts. It is to be expected, therefore, that the giving of a non-uniform meaning to a term used in the

---

[21] Case C-89/91, *Shearson Lehman Hutton v TVB Treuhandgesellschaft für Vermögensverwaltung und Beteiligungen mbH* [1993] ECR I-139, para 13.

[22] Referring to Case 150/77, *Bertrand v Ott* [1978] ECR 1431, paras 14–16 and 19, and Case C-26/91, *Handte v Traitements Mécano-chimiques des Surfaces* [1992] ECR I-3967, para 10.

[23] Also Case C-443/03, *Leffler v Berlin Chemie AG* [2005] ECR I-9611, para 45, a passage quoted at **2.15** above.

[24] **3.86–3.87** below.

[25] **Ch 12** below.

Regulation will be exceptional. The only clear example in the Regulation is provided by Recital (27), which emphasizes that, for the purposes of Art 9 of the Regulation:[26]

The exact concept of industrial action, such as strike action or lock-out, varies from one Member State to another and is governed by each Member State's internal rules.

Nevertheless, as the ECJ recognized in its *Eurocontrol* decision,[27] general principles stemming from the corpus of the Member States' national legal systems do have a role to play in the shaping of concepts used in EC legislation.[28] A comparative survey of the meaning given to particular concepts across the EC may be useful in defining the boundaries of the individual rules of applicable law for which the Regulation provides.[29] This reference to 'general principles' does not require a precise correlation, or unanimity, between Member State legal systems. Instead, the object must be to identify features common to the legal systems of a significant majority of the Member States.[30] It remains to be seen whether the work products of those who have studied the Member States' legal systems for inspiration in developing a common substantive law of obligations across the European Community will be influential in this area, insofar as they identify common ground between the Member States in their treatment of non-contractual obligations.[31]

3.12

---

[26] Also **13.11–13.19** below, discussing the law applicable to agreements on the law applicable to non-contractual obligations.

[27] Text to n 18 above.

[28] Cf Pontier and Burg, n 12 above, 73–4.

[29] i.e. the meaning of terms such as 'tort/delict' (Art 4), 'unjust enrichment' (Art 10), and *negotiorum gestio* (Art 11). As to the techniques involved in the characterization process, see **3.62–3.74** below.

[30] For the approach in other subject areas, see for example Case 155/79, *AM & S Europe Ltd v Commission* [1982] ECR 1575, paras 18–28; Joined Cases T-125/03 and T-253/03, *Akzo Nobel Chemicals Ltd v Commission* [2007] ECR II-5049, paras 77–8, 170–1 (both cases concerning lawyer-client privilege in relation to Commission investigatory powers); Joined Cases C-122/99P and C-125/99P, *D and Sweden v Council* [2001] ECR I-4139, paras 33–7 (concept of 'marriage' within Staff Regulations).

[31] **1.03–1.04** above.

THE THIRD ASPECT—CONTEXT AND OBJECTIVES

3.13 The proposition that the provisions of the Regulation must be construed having regard to their context and objectives is uncontroversial. Thus, the Court has consistently affirmed that:[32]

> [T]he need for uniform application of Community law and the principle of equality require that the terms of a provision of Community law which makes no express reference to the law of the Member States for the purpose of determining its meaning and scope must normally be given an autonomous and uniform interpretation throughout the Community; that interpretation must take into account the context of the provision and the purpose of the legislation in question.

3.14 Countless examples of the application of these techniques can be given in relation to other Community instruments.[33] They have been used not only to discover the 'true' meaning of Community law where the different language versions conflict, but also to confirm the apparent meaning of the words used or to fill in gaps in the legislative framework.[34]

3.15 Even so, the proposition stated above provides little in the way of helpful guidance as to the approach to be taken in interpreting individual provisions of the Rome II Regulation—the 'objectives' of the Regulation and of particular provisions must be identified and their 'context' defined. Indeed, the statement may be liable to mislead insofar as it underestimates the weight to be given within the interpretative process to the ordinary meaning of the words actually chosen by the legislator. Whether that meaning is seen as the starting point for analysis,[35] or as a factor to be taken into account alongside context and purpose,[36] it must be recognized that context and purpose cannot stand alone but are merely tools to be used in selecting, finessing, shaping, or (on occasion) contorting the meaning which the words appearing in the Regulation must bear. In particular, the meaning and scope of terms for which Community law provides no definition must be determined by considering their usual

---

[32] Case C-321/02, *Finanzamt Rendsbug v Detlev Harbs* [2004] ECR I-7101. See, more recently, Case C-195/06, *Kommunikationsbehörde Austria v Österreichischer Rundfunk* [2007] ECR I-8817, para 24; Case C-98/07, *Nordania Finans A/S v Skatteministeriet* [2008] ECR I-0000 (Judgment of 6 March 2008) para 17.

[33] Their use can be traced back to the earliest decisions given in relation to the Treaty Establishing the European Coal and Steel Community (see the cases cited by Lasok, Millett & Howard, 378, footnote 2792).

[34] Wyatt & Dashwood, n 1 above, 405–6.

[35] Lasok, Millett & Howard, n 1 above, para [661] and the cases there cited.

[36] Case C-162/91, *Società Tenuta il Bosco Srl v Ministero delle finanze dello Stato*, para 11. See, more recently, Case C-98/07, *Nordania Finans A/S v Skatteministeriet* n 32 above , para 17.

meaning in everyday language, while also taking into account the context in which they occur and the purposes of the rules of which they are part.[37]

The following paragraphs consider the materials that may fall to be taken **3.16** into account in interpreting the provisions of the Regulation.

Recitals

The Recitals in the preamble to the Regulation are relevant for two pur- **3.17** poses. First, in identifying its objectives. Secondly, as an aid to construction. It must, however, be recognized that the Recitals do not themselves constitute binding legal rules,[38] with the result that words in the preamble that do not correspond to any substantive provision in the Regulation have no operative effect.[39] Recital (33) to the Regulation[40] falls within this category.

General Objectives of the Regulation

The following general objectives may be detected in the Recitals to the **3.18** Regulation: 'predictability of the outcome of litigation',[41] 'certainty as to the law applicable',[42] 'the free movement of judgments',[43] 'legal certainty',[44] 'the need to do justice in individual cases',[45] and ensuring 'a reasonable balance between the interests of the person claimed to be liable and the person who has sustained damage'.[46] These objectives can be subdivided into two main groups: those focusing on legal certainty and those focusing on fairness as between the persons involved. Recital (16) to the Regulation neatly sums up these elements, as follows:[47]

Uniform rules should enhance the foreseeability of court decisions and ensure a reasonable balance between the interests of the person claimed to be liable and the person who has sustained damage.

---

[37] Case C-336/03, *easyCar (UK) Ltd v Office of Fair Trading* [2005] ECR I-1947, para 21.
[38] Case 215/88, *Casa Fleischhandels-GmbH v Bundesanstalt für landwirtschaftliche Marktordnung* [1989] ECR 2789, para 31.
[39] Case C-1/98P, *British Steel plc v Commission* [2000] ECR I-10349, para 29.
[40] Discussed at **14.26–14.32** below.
[41] Recital (6). Recital (16) also refers to the 'foreseeability of court decisions'.
[42] Recital (6).
[43] Recital (6).
[44] Recital (14).
[45] Recital (14).
[46] Recitals (16) and (34). Recital (19) also refers to 'a reasonable balance . . . between the interests at stake'.
[47] See also the opening words of Recital (14), quoted at **3.22** below.

The overriding principle of legal certainty?

3.19 If the recent case law of the European Court of Justice in relation to the Brussels I Regulation and its predecessor Convention is a reliable guide, the demands of legal certainty are likely to predominate over the other general objectives identified in the Recitals to the Regulation. Within the Brussels I Regime, legal certainty has developed from a subsidiary principle supporting the objective of strengthening the legal protection of persons established in the Community into a freestanding principle said to form 'the basis of the Convention'.[48] The principle of 'legal certainty' is, however, anything but certain in its meaning and application. It is an extremely malleable concept and can be used to support contradictory conclusions in the same case. As Professor Tridimas contends:[49]

Legal certainty is by its nature diffuse, perhaps more so than any other general principle, and its precise content is difficult to pin down. The case law has used it with creativity, invoking it in diverse contexts to found a variety of propositions both in the substantive and procedural plane. . . . The cynic may argue that the principle is devoid of legal content because it can be used to support contradictory results. . . . [L]egal certainty rarely dictates a specific result in itself. It is a conceptual tool which must not be viewed in isolation but in the context of judicial reasoning taken as a whole.

3.20 The requirements of legal certainty may also vary according to the point in time at which it is considered. In the context of the Rome II Regulation, legal certainty will always, in some sense, be concerned with predictability of the outcome of litigation, but different considerations apply at different times. At the time of planning business and other activities, the demands of certainty will focus on the foreseeability of particular events and their connection to a particular country or its legal system (i.e. the parties' legitimate expectations[50]). After a dispute has arisen, however, and when litigation in one or more Member State courts is in prospect, the focus will switch to whether particular connecting factors are readily ascertainable.

---

[48] A Dickinson, 'Legal Certainty and the Brussels Convention—Too Much of a Good Thing?', in P de Vareilles-Sommières (ed), *Forum Shopping in the European Judicial Area* (2007), 116–23. For recent case law, see Case C-281/02, *Owusu v Jackson* [2005] ECR I-1383, paras 40–1; Case C-104/03, *St Paul Dairy Industries NV v United Exser BVBA* [2005] ECR I-3481, para 19; Case C-292/05, *Lechouritou v Federal Republic of Germany* [2007] ECR I-1519, para 44; Case C-04/03, *Gesellschaft für Antriebstechnik mbH & Co KG v Lemellen und Kupplungsbau Beteiligungs KG* [2006] ECR I-6509, para 28; Case C-539/03, *Roche Nederland BV v Primus* [2006] ECR I-6535, para 37. Compare Case C-103/05, *Reisch Montage AG v Kiesel Baumaschinen Handels GmbH* [2006] ECR I-6827, paras 24 describing legal certainty as 'one of the objectives of Regulation 44/2001'.

[49] T Tridimas, *General Principles of EC Law* (2nd edn, 2006), 243–4.

[50] T Tridimas, ibid, 242–5, 251–2.

The link between the Regulation and the functioning of the internal market suggest that certainty at the planning stage should take on a greater significance. The ECJ, however, has not always taken this view.[51]

The relationship between certainty and fairness

The desire for legal certainty may compete with other objectives, in partic- **3.21** ular the achievement of justice and fairness for the persons involved. In the words of Lord Wilberforce:[52]

[T]he present . . . rule produces certainty—but it is often simpler to produce an unjust rule than a just one. The question is whether, in order to produce a just, or juster, rule, too high a price has to be paid in terms of certainty.

Recital (14), in the following terms, suggests that the balance between **3.22** legal certainty and the interests of justice has already been struck by the Community legislator in framing the Rome II Regulation:[53]

The requirement of legal certainty and the need to do justice in individual cases are essential elements of an area of justice. *This Regulation provides for the connecting factors which are the most appropriate to achieve these objectives.* Therefore, this Regulation provides for a general rule but also for specific rules and, in certain provisions, for an 'escape clause' which allows a departure from these rules where it is clear from all the circumstances of the case that the tort/delict is manifestly more closely connected with another country. This set of rules thus creates a flexible framework of conflict-of-law rules. Equally, it enables the court seised to treat individual cases in an appropriate manner.

This combination of rules of applicable law deploying specific, geo- **3.23** graphical connecting factors to identify the law of a particular country (or countries) as applicable to a non-contractual obligation, with rules of displacement based on the existence of a 'manifestly closer connection' to another country can be seen not only in Art 4, the principal provision relating to tort/delict, but also Art 5 (product liability), Art 10 (unjust enrichment), Art 11 (*negotiorum gestio*), and Art 12 (*culpa in contrahendo*), but not in Art 7 (environmental damage), Art 8 (infringement of intellectual property rights), or Art 9 (industrial action). Arts 4 to 5 and 9 to 12 also contain or incorporate by reference rules of displacement favouring, in certain circumstances, the law of the parties' common habitual residence. Art 6 is described by Recital (21) as a clarification of the general rule in Art 4(1)

---

[51] In Case C-116/02, *Erich Gasser GmbH v Misat Srl* [2003] ECR I-14693, the claims of certainty at the post-dispute stage were preferred to those at the planning stage (A Dickinson, n 48 above, 121–2).

[52] *The Despina R* [1979] AC 685, 698 (UKHL).

[53] Emphasis added.

rather than a separate applicable law in its own right. Accordingly, it might be expected that the rules of displacement contained in Art 4 would also apply to non-contractual obligations arising from acts of unfair competition and restrictions of competition.[54] On closer examination, however, it appears that the rules in Arts 6(1) and 6(3) of the Regulation, which take a market-oriented approach, were intended to stand alone.[55] Article 6(3) stands alone in containing a restricted rule of displacement in favour of the law of the forum.

3.24 Recital (14) emerged from the conciliation process, the product of a Council compromise proposal in light of its objection to the following recital added by the European Parliament at the second reading stage:[56]

> Nevertheless, the need to avoid distortions of competition and the requirement of legal certainty must be tempered by the need to do justice in individual cases, and consequently the courts must have a margin of discretion.

3.25 The intention behind the Parliament's amendment was unclear, as the substantive amendment put forward by the rapporteur to which it was linked had been rejected by the EP JURI Committee.[57]

3.26 Professor Symeonides, approaching the regulation from a US perspective, has suggested that the references in Art 14 to 'the need to do justice in individual cases' and to the ability of courts 'to treat individual cases in an appropriate manner' ought to be seen 'as providing instruction to courts on when and how to use the escape . . . Thus, a court should resort to the escape[58] when the law designated as applicable by the general rule leads to a result that is incompatible with "the need to do justice in individual cases"'.[59] That suggestion, attractive as it might seem to a writer immersed

---

[54] **6.02** below.

[55] **6.01–6.03** below.

[56] EP 2nd Reading Position, Recital (14).

[57] EP document reference PE 378.852v01-00 [8.11.2006], Amendment 16 ('In resolving the question of the applicable law, the court seised shall have the need for certainty, predictability and uniformity of result, the protection of legitimate expectations and the policies underlying the foreign law to be applied and the consequences of applying that law'). This marked the last stand in the rapporteur's dalliance with 'governmental interest analysis' (**1.75** and **1.90** above).

[58] Referring to Regulation, Art 4(3).

[59] S C Symeonides, 'Rome II and Tort Conflicts: A Missed Opportunity' (2008) 56 AJCL 173, 199–200. As the title of his article suggests, Professor Symeonides is critical of several aspects of the Regulation in its final form. For a more favourable transatlantic view on the Regulation, see P J Kozyris, 'Rome II: Tort Conflicts on the Right Track! A Postscript to Symeon Symeonides' "Missed Opportunity"' (2008) 56 AJCL 471.

in the intricacies of US conflict theory,[60] cannot be accepted. Not only is the introduction of a subjective, discretionary element in the rule of displacement inconsistent with the language and legislative history of Recital (14), it is inimical to the approach taken by the ECJ in its case law concerning the Brussels Convention, an instrument closely linked to the Rome II Regulation.[61] In that context, it is clear that, although the rules of jurisdiction contained in the Convention must be construed by reference to their objectives, those objectives cannot serve as a justification for departing from those rules in individual cases. Thus, in addressing the rules conferring special jurisdiction as an alternative to suit in the courts of the defendant's domicile,[62] the ECJ has explained that the justification for conferring jurisdiction on a court other than that of the defendant's domicile in particular cases lies in the existence of a close connecting link between the type of dispute and the court having jurisdiction: the connecting factors linking the dispute to the place in which that court sits are thus to be interpreted having regard to that justification.[63] In *Custom Made Commercial Ltd v Stawa Metallbau GmbH*,[64] the defendant pointed out that the criteria laid down in these rules[65] may in certain cases have the effect of conferring jurisdiction on a court having no connection with the dispute. The defendant argued that, in such cases, the chosen jurisdictional connecting factor should be departed from on the ground that the result that it produces would be contrary to the aim of Art 5.[66] That argument was flatly rejected by the Court, which held that the need for certainty in the application of the Brussels Convention rules took precedence over the desirability of

[60] Or, to use Professor Symeonides' own words, one who 'has spent the last three decades laboring in the American conflicts vineyard'. For the fruits of this work, see S C Symeonides, *The American Choice-of-Law Revolution: Past, Present and Future* (2006).

[61] The relationship between the Rome II Regulation and the Brussels I Regime is considered at **3.34** below.

[62] Brussels Convention, Arts 5 and 6.

[63] Jenard Report, (OJ C59, 22 [5.3.1979]); Case 12/76, *Tessili v Dunlop* [1976] ECR 1473, para 13 (Art 5.1); Case 21/76, *Handelskwekerij G J Bier BV v Mines de Potasse d'Alsace* [1976] ECR 1735, paras 11, 17 (Art 5.3); Case 33/78, *Somafer SA v Saar-Ferngas AG* [1978] ECR 2183, para 7 (Art 5.5); Case 266/85 *Shenevai v Kreischer* [1987] ECR 239 (Art 5.1); Case 218/86, *SAR Schotte v Parfums Rothschild* [1987] ECR 4905, paras 9, 16 (Art 5.5); Case C-365/88, *Kongress Agentur Hagen GmbH v Zeehaghe BV* [1990] ECR I-1845, para 11 (Art 6.2); Case C-439/93, *Lloyd's Register of Shipping v Société Campenon Bernard* [1995] ECR I-961, para 21 (Art 5.5); Case 364/93, *Marinari v Lloyd's Bank plc* [1995] ECR I-2719, paras 12, 20 (Art 5.3).

[64] Case C-288/92, [1994] ECR I-2913.

[65] The reference in *Custom Made Commercial* concerned Art 5(1) (matters relating to a contract) but the reasoning applies equally to other rules of special jurisdiction contained in Arts 5 and 6.

[66] [1994] ECR I-2913, para 16.

assigning jurisdiction to a court having a close connection to the dispute.[67] Subsequently, in *Owusu v Jackson*,[68] the ECJ strongly opposed the deployment within the framework of Brussels Convention of discretionary rules[69] having as their object the selection of an appropriate forum in individual cases. According to the Court:[70]

> Application of the *forum non conveniens* doctrine, which allows the court seised a wide discretion as regards the question whether a foreign court would be a more appropriate forum for the trial of an action, is liable to undermine the predictability of the rules of jurisdiction laid down by the Brussels Convention, in particular that of Article 2, and consequently to undermine the principle of legal certainty, which is the basis of the Convention.

3.27 Unlike the rules of jurisdiction that were the subject of the decision in *Custom Made Commercial*, some of the rules of displacement in the Rome II Regulation do permit, and indeed require, an assessment of the relative connections of the non-contractual obligation in question to two or more countries, with a view to identifying whether there is a manifestly closer connection to a country other than that whose law is identified by the primary connecting factor. Even so, and recognizing the differences between the object and scope of the Brussels I Regime and those of the Rome II Regulation, the decision in *Custom Made Commercial* strongly supports the proposition that the rules contained in the Regulation (like those in the Brussels Convention) must be interpreted and applied having regard to the achievement of their objectives generally, across the spectrum of cases falling within their scope, rather than with reference to the outcome of individual cases. Further, the requirement that a non-contractual obligation be 'manifestly more closely connected' to another country leaves no room for assessing the impact that the application of that country's law would have in terms of satisfying the 'ends of justice' in a specific case. The Regulation identifies the legal system whose rules will apply to non-contractual obligations by reference to objective connecting factors, not the content of their rules.[71] Instead, the overall objective of the Regulation to achieve justice in individual cases is but one factor, alongside (and, in all probability, subordinate to) legal certainty, that will assist courts in moulding the concept of a 'manifestly closer connection', as well as other concepts used in the Regulation.

---

[67] Ibid, paras 17–19.
[68] Case C-281/02 [2005] ECR I-1383.
[69] Specifically, the *forum non conveniens* rules applied by UK courts.
[70] *Owusu v Jackson*, n 68 above, para 41.
[71] P J Kozyris, n 59 above, 473–6, 478–9.

That view, it is submitted, is entirely consistent with the language of **3.28** Recital (14) itself. As the second and third sentences make clear, the twin objectives of legal certainty and justice in individual cases have been taken into account in determining the connecting factors used in the Regulation's rules of applicable law.[72] Significantly, the final sentence does not injunct courts to do justice in individual cases, or confer any discretion on them to do so, but merely asserts that the framework thereby established enables the court seised of a dispute to determine the applicable law 'in an appropriate manner'. The Recital thus combines propaganda[73] with a description of the Regulation's structure, but it cannot support the emphasis that Professor Symeonides seeks to place on it.

Influence of Certainty and Fairness on the Approach to the Connecting Factors
Having regard to the twin aims of increasing the foreseeability of court **3.29** decisions and striking a reasonable balance between the interests of the parties, the factors that connect a non-contractual obligation to a particular country or its legal system should, whenever possible, be capable of being objectively ascertainable by those involved[74] and incapable of manipulation by one of them, at least after the dispute has arisen.[75]

Objectives of Specific Rules of Applicable Law
The following specific objectives for particular rules contained in the **3.30** Regulation appear from the Recitals:

- **The rules for product liability (Art 5):** 'fairly spreading the risks inherent in a modern high-technology society, protecting consumers' health, stimulating innovation, securing undistorted competition and facilitating trade'.[76]
- **The rules for unfair competition (Arts 6(1)–(2)):** 'protect consumers and the general public and ensure that the market economy functions properly'.[77]
- **The rules for environmental damage (Art 7):** 'a high level of protection based on the precautionary principle and the principle that preventative

---

[72] P J Kozyris, n 59 above, 482–3.

[73] Professor Symeonides (n 59 above, 199) calls it 'self-congratulatory'.

[74] For a similar approach in relation to other Community instruments, see *SAR Schotte GmbH*, n 63 above, para 15 (Brussels Convention, Art 5(5)); Case C-51/97, *Réunion Européenne SA v Spliethoff's Bevrachtingskantoor BV* [1998] ECR I-6511, paras 33–7 (Brussels Convention, Art 5(3)); Case C-341/04, *Eurofood IFSC Ltd* [2006] ECR I-3813, paras 33–4 (Insolvency Regulation).

[75] See Case C-1/04, *Staubitz-Schreiber* [2006] ECR I-701 (Insolvency Regulation). See further **4.67** and **4.87** below.

[76] Recital (20).

[77] Recital (21).

action should be taken, the principle of priority for corrective action at source and the principle that the polluter pays'.[78]

- **The rule for industrial action (Art 9):** 'protecting the rights and obligations of workers and employees'.[79]
- **Freedom of choice of the law applicable (Art 14):** 'the principle of party autonomy and . . . legal certainty' and 'protection . . . to weaker parties'.[80]

Recitals as an Aid to Interpretation

3.31 **Appendix 7** contains a table showing the Articles of the Regulation and the Recitals relating to each of them. The following Recitals contain definitions of particular terms used in the Regulation:

- Recital (10): 'family relationships' (partial definition)[81]
- Recital (11): 'non-contractual obligation' (partial definition)[82]
- Recital (17): 'country in which the damage occurs' (partial definition)[83]
- Recital (23): 'restrictions of competition'[84]
- Recital (24): 'environmental damage'[85]
- Recital (26): 'intellectual property rights'[86]
- Recital (30): *'culpa in contrahendo'* (partial definition)[87]
- Recital (32): 'public policy (*ordre public*)' (partial definition)
- Recital (33): 'rules of safety and conduct'[88]

Relevance of *Travaux Préparatoires*

3.32 Preparatory legislative materials (*travaux préparatoires*) play an increasingly important role in the interpretation of Community legislation,[89]

---

[78] Recital (25).

[79] Recital (28).

[80] Recital (31).

[81] **3.150–3.151** below.

[82] **3.86–3.87** below.

[83] **4.47** below.

[84] **6.32–6.33** below. It is unclear whether the definition, which refers only to EC law and the law of the Member States, is total or partial.

[85] **7.08** below.

[86] **8.10–8.13** below.

[87] **12.03–12.08** below.

[88] **15.30–15.32** below.

[89] Wyatt and Dashwood, n 1 above, 406; S Schønberg and K Frick, 'Finishing, refining, polishing: on the use of *travaux préparatoires* as an aid to the interpretation of Community legislation' (2003) 28 Eur L Rev 149. For a recent example of the use of preparatory legislative

reflecting the approach to the interpretation of treaties generally.[90] The ECJ has, however, placed restrictions as to the type of materials that can be taken into account. It appears that preparatory materials may be used as an aid to interpretation only if they clearly cast a positive[91] light as to the intention of the authors of the Regulation,[92] whether as to purpose or the meaning of a particular provision. In the interests of transparency, the materials must also be publicly available to those affected by the measure,[93] although the accessibility through the Internet of documents recorded on the registers of the Community institutions (particularly the Council) means that this requirement is now less significant.[94] However, whether or not publicly available, declarations made by individual Member States or by the EC institutions, acting individually or in concert, during negotiations[95] or at the time of adoption of the Regulation[96] are inadmissible unless referred to specifically in the text of the Regulation. For present purposes, the most significant documents, at least to the extent that the proposals that they contain were accepted, are likely to be the Commission Proposal,[97] the Commission Amended Proposal,[98] the Council's Common Position[99] and, to a lesser extent, the EP 1st Reading Report and 2nd Reading Recommendation adopted by the JURI Committee[100] and the EESC Opinion.[101]

---

materials to construe EC legislation, see C-306/06, *Telecom GmbH v Deutsche Telekom AG* [2008] ECR I-0000, para 25.

[90] Convention on the law of treaties, adopted at Vienna, 23 May 1969 (1155 UNTS 331; Cmnd 7964), Art 32; A Aust, *Modern Treaty Law and Practice* (2nd edn, 2007), 244–8.

[91] Cf Case C-307/98, *Commission v Belgium* [2000] ECR I-3933, para 40 in which wording contained in the original legislative proposal but which was not carried forward into the text of a Directive was held irrelevant.

[92] Joined Cases C-68/94 and C-30/95, *France v Commission* [1998] ECR I-1375, para 167.

[93] Lasok, Millett & Howard, n 1 above, para [671].

[94] Regulation (EC) No 1049/2001 regarding public access to European Parliament, Council and Commission documents (OJ L145, 43 [31.5.2001]).

[95] Case C-375/98, *Ministério Público and Fazenda Pública v Epson Europe BV* [2000] ECR-I 4243, para 23; Case C-402/03, *Skov Æg v Bilka Lavprisvarehus A/S* [2006] ECR I-199, para 42 (both cases concerning statements in Council minutes); Joined Cases C-283/94, C-291/94, and C-292/94, *Denkavit International BV v Bundesamt für Finanzen* [1996] ECR I-5063, para 29.

[96] Case C-292/89, *R v Immigration Appeal Tribunal, ex p Antonissen* [1991] ECR I-745, para 18 (statement in Council minutes); Case C-404/06, *Quelle AG v Bundesverband der Verbraucherzentralen und Verbraucherverbände* [2008] ECR I-0000 (Judgment of 17 April 2008), para 32 (statement in minutes of Council-Parliament conciliation committee).

[97] **1.69–1.70** above.

[98] **1.86** above.

[99] **1.88** above.

[100] **1.74–1.76** and **1.90** above.

[101] **1.78** above.

Relevance of Other EC Instruments

3.33 It follows from the general approach to interpretation outlined above that terms that are common to the Rome II Regulation and to another EC legislative instrument will not necessarily bear the same meaning in both instruments, as their context and objectives will differ.[102] If, however, there is a close connection between two instruments then, at least insofar as their objectives are consistent, it is proper to take one into account as part of the legislative context in construing the other.[103]

3.34 Recital (7) to the Regulation provides:

> The substantive scope and the provisions of this Regulation should be consistent with Council Regulation (EC) No 44/2001 of 22 December 2000 on jurisdiction and the recognition and enforcement of judgments in civil and commercial matters (Brussels I) and the instruments dealing with the law applicable to contractual obligations.

The link between the Rome II Regulation, on the one hand, and the Brussels I and Rome I Regimes was one that the Commission emphasized at the very outset in putting its case for a harmonized set of rules of applicable law for non-contractual obligations.[104] The Commission described the Rome II Regulation as 'the natural extension of the unification of the rules of private international law relating to contractual and non-contractual obligations in civil or commercial matters in the Community'[105] leading to the formation of a 'coherent set of instruments covering the general field of private international law in matters of civil and commercial obligations'.[106] Professor Légier vividly describes the Regulation as *'le troisième volet d'un vast triptyque que constitue le droit international privé européen des obligations'*.[107]

---

[102] e.g. the observations of Adv Gen Tizzano in Case C-168/00, *Leitner v TUI Deutschland GmbH & Co. KG* [2002] ECR I-2631, paras 34–5 of opinion concerning the concept of 'damage' in EC Directives concerning product liability and package travel. Also Case C-435/06, *C* [2007] ECR I-10141, Judgment, paras 42–6 and Opinion of Adv Gen Kokott, paras 35–8, interpreting the concept of 'civil matters' in the 'Brussels II'*bis* Regulation without reference to its case law concerning the meaning of 'civil and commercial matters' in the Brussels I Regime.

[103] e.g. Case 102/86, *Apple and Pear Development Council v Commissioners of Customs and Excise* [1988] ECR 1443, para 10.

[104] **1.69** above.

[105] Commission Proposal, 3.

[106] Commission Proposal, 8.

[107] G Légier, 'Le réglement "Rome II" sur la loi applicable aux obligations non contractuelles', *JCP/La Semaine Juridique—Edition Générale*, 21 November 2007, I-207, para 1.

Accordingly, in considering the scope of the Regulation and in construing **3.35**
its provisions, it will not only be legitimate but essential to refer to
the provisions of the Brussels I Regulation, the Rome Convention and
the Rome I Regulation, as well as to relevant case law of the ECJ.[108]
The reference to the Brussels I Regulation, in turn, leads to the provisions
of the Brussels Convention and to the Court's case law on that
Convention.[109]

In its Amended Proposal, the Commission introduced recitals[110] linking **3.36**
the special rules of applicable law for product liability,[111] 'unfair commercial practices',[112] and environmental damage[113] to particular Community
legislative instruments, specifically the Product Liability Directive,[114] the
Unfair Commercial Practices Directive,[115] and the Environmental Liability
Directive[116] respectively. Those references were not incorporated in the
Regulation in its final form.[117] Nevertheless, it is suggested that there is a
sufficiently close connection between these instruments and the Rome II
Regulation to take them into account as part of the context in construing
the Regulation and to seek to construe them, if possible, in a consistent
manner.

B. KEY CONCEPTS AND TERMS

Before turning to consider the material, territorial, and temporal scope of **3.37**
the Rome II Regulation, it seems useful to define certain key concepts and
terms that it deploys.

---

[108] For the time being, there are no ECJ decisions relating to the Rome Convention or the Rome I Regulation, the latter being not yet in force.
[109] Recitals (5) and (19) to the Brussels I Regulation refer to the need for continuity between the Brussels Convention and the Regulation as its successor. Also Case C-167/00, *Verein für Konsumentinformation v Henkel* [2002] ECR I-8111, para 49.
[110] Commission Amended Proposal, Recitals (12)–(14).
[111] Ibid, Art 6 (now Regulation, Art 5).
[112] Ibid, Art 7. Cf Regulation, Art 6(1) (unfair competition).
[113] Ibid, Art 8 (now Regulation, Art 7).
[114] Directive (EEC) No 374/1985 on the approximation of the laws, regulations and admin-istrative provisions of the Member States concerning liability for defective products (OJ L210, 29 [7.8.1985]) (as amended).
[115] Directive (EC) No 29/2005 concerning unfair business-to-consumer commercial prac-tices in the internal market (OJ L149, 22 [11.6.2005]).
[116] Directive (EC) No 35/2004 on environmental liability with regard to the prevention and remedying of environmental damage.
[117] Cf Regulation, Recitals (20), (21), (24)–(25).

'LAW APPLICABLE TO A NON-CONTRACTUAL OBLIGATION'

3.38 Each of Arts 4 to 12 provides that 'the law applicable to a non-contractual obligation' falling within its individual scope 'shall be' the law of a country identified by reference to specific connecting factors. These rules take the form, therefore, of directions to Member State courts as to the 'law' that they are to apply in determining matters involving non-contractual obligations. Two points follow from this. First, as an instrument regulating the conduct of Member State courts, the Regulation should not be understood to have any horizontal direct effect between Community litigants, entitling them (for example) to take action to restrain attempts to procure the determination of matters outside the European Community by a law other than that identified by the Regulation.[118] In this connection, it may be noted that Art 14 is expressed differently to the other rules, enabling actual or potential litigating parties to agree to submit non-contractual obligations to the law of their choice. In such cases, as Arts 6(4), 8(3), 14(2), and 14(3) make clear, the law that would otherwise apply under Arts 4–5, 7, and 9–12 is supplanted by the law chosen by the parties. Although the Regulation thereby gives effect to the parties' agreement to a limited extent, it does not, of itself, validate any contractual obligation, enforceable by injunction or otherwise, to ensure that the chosen law is applied in the determination of disputes between the parties. An action of that kind must be based on the law of contract, having regard to the rules contained in the Rome I Regulation, and not on Art 14 of the Rome II Regulation.[119]

3.39 Secondly, the direction to 'apply' the 'law' of a particular country must not be understood as requiring the Member State court to put itself in the position of a court of that country and to decide the case as that court would have decided it. Instead, it requires the Member State court to take from the legal order of the country whose law applies rules of the kinds specified, in particular, in Art 15 (scope of the law applicable) and to import those rules into its own legal order. This proposition is supported not only by the express exclusion in Art 24 of *renvoi*, (i.e. a reference to the rules of private international law of the country whose law applies under the Regulation),[120] but also by Art 3 under which the law applicable may

---

[118] Cf *Samengo-Turner v J & H Marsh & McLennan* [2007] EWCA Civ 723; [2007] 2 CLC 104, noted A Briggs [2007] LMCLQ 433; A Dickinson (2008) 57 ICLQ 465.

[119] Agreements on choice of court, but not agreements on choice of law, are excluded from the Rome I Regulation by Art 1(2)(e).

[120] **3.41–3.43** below.

be that of a non-Member State.[121] This latter provision negates any possible counter-argument that the Regulation constitutes a mutual transfer by the Member States of the sovereign right to apply their own laws concerning non-contractual obligations.

This view of the nature of the rules contained in the Rome II Regulation[122] **3.40** rejects the idea that the 'non-contractual obligations' to which it refers exist independently of litigation before Member State courts, leaving it to those courts to find and give effect to them. Rather, the Regulation empowers and requires a Member State court seised of the dispute to determine the parties' obligations in the case before it by reference to rules that have their origin in the country or countries to which its connecting factors point. Although the difference between these two accounts may appear technical, an understanding of what the Regulation means when it directs the court as to the law applicable to a non-contractual obligation may inform the approach to be taken to specific provisions of the Regulation that refer to 'the law of' a country or to its 'application'.[123]

RENVOI EXCLUDED

Article 24

Exclusion of renvoi

The application of the law of any country specified by this Regulation means the application of the rules of law in force in that country other than its rules of private international law.

Art 24, reflecting Art 15 of the Rome Convention,[124] excludes the doctrine **3.41** of *renvoi*. This reflects the pre-Regulation position under English law, at least in relation to tortious obligations.[125] Given the precedent in relation to contractual obligations, the quest for legal certainty,[126] and the modern

---

[121] **3.294–3.295** below.

[122] W W Cook, *Logical and Legal Bases of the Conflict of Laws* (1949), 19–42 and ch XIII, esp 323–4. Also *Caldwell v Vanvlissengen* (1851) 9 Hare 415, 425 (Turner V-C); *John Pfeiffer Pty Ltd v Rogerson* [2000] HCA 36; (2000) 203 CLR 503, [39]–[41] (Gleeson CJ, Gaudron, McHugh, Gummow, and Hayne JJ, HC Aus).

[123] For example, in considering the point in time at which the Regulation 'applies' under Arts 31 and 32 (**3.320–3.322** below).

[124] Also Rome I Regulation, Art 20.

[125] Private International Law (Miscellaneous Provisions) Act 1995, s 9(5). *Renvoi* in relation to an unjust enrichment claim was left (just about) alive in *Barros Mattos Jr v MacDaniels* [2005] EWHC 1323 (Ch); [2005] ILPr 630, at [112], [120] (Lawrence Collins J), where the argument for its application was described as 'weak'. Compare the pre-Regulation position in Germany (**1.24** above).

[126] Commission Proposal, 28.

hostility to the doctrine, that outcome was inevitable. There was no debate as to whether Art 24 contains a theoretically satisfactory rule.[127]

3.42 The exclusion of a country's rules of private international law does not prevent the application of so-called 'self-limiting provisions' in legislation,[128] which apply that legislation to part only of the territory of a country or to selected persons, things, or activities (e.g. nationals of the country in question), provided that such provisions are not an inseparable part of a rule that may operate in such a way as to require a court sitting in the country whose law is identified by the Regulation to apply another country's rules rather than rules of local origin. A rule of this latter character would plainly be a rule of private international law whose application is excluded by Art 24. If, however, the non-application of legislation containing a self-limiting provision will, under the law of the country whose law is identified by the Regulation, always result in the application of a (normally more general) rule of local origin, effect may be given to that self-limiting provision as part of the reference under the Regulation to the law of that country.

3.43 Art 24 applies within the limits of the Regulation. It does not apply to matters falling outside the scope of the Regulation (including, in particular, questions of status) even if they are instrumental to the determination of a claim based on a non-contractual obligation. For example, if, in a tort/delict claim involving alleged interference with an item of movable property, the law applicable under the Regulation requires that the claimant be the owner of the property, the court seised of the claim may apply its own rules of private international law (including the doctrine of *renvoi*, if applicable) in determining that question of title.[129]

DAMAGE

Article 2

Non-contractual obligations

1. For the purposes of this Regulation, damage shall cover any consequence arising out of tort/delict, unjust enrichment, *negotiorum gestio* **or** *culpa in contrahendo.*

---

[127] Contrast the sometimes over-elaborate analysis of the High Court of Australia in *Neilson v Overseas Projects Corp of Victoria Ltd* [2005] HCA 54; (2005) 221 ALR 213 (noted A Dickinson (2006) 122 LQR 183).

[128] Sir L Collins et al. (eds), *Dicey, Morris & Collins: The Conflict of Laws* (14th edn, 2006) (Dicey, Morris & Collins), paras 1-049 to 1-052.

[129] The relationship between matters of obligation and matters of status (including property) is considered at **3.88–3.103** below.

2. This Regulation shall apply also to non-contractual obligations that are likely to arise.

3. Any reference in this Regulation to:
(a) an event giving rise to damage shall include events giving rise to damage that are likely to occur; and

(b) damage shall include damage that is likely to occur.

Art 2 is a product of the Council's work on the Rome II Regulation.[130] The **3.44** Article first appeared in this form in the compromise package presented to COREPER by the Austrian Presidency in April 2006.[131] Arts 2(2)–(3), in particular, reflect the product of discussions in the JHA Council meeting held in February 2006.[132]

In its Communication on the Council's Common Position, the Commission **3.45** described Art 2 as 'a provision of a technical nature which intends to provide definition of certain concepts used throughout the Regulation with the intention to simplify the drafting of its individual provisions'.[133] Art 2 achieves that objective. Thus, (a) Art 2(1) makes sense of references to 'damage' in provisions of general application that extend to non-contractual obligations for which loss or injury to the claimant is not an essential element, most obviously those arising out of unjust enrichment, and (b) Arts 2(2) and 2(3) enable the Regulation to be applied to threatened wrongs and other non-contractual obligations that may arise in the future, without the need to refer repeatedly to obligations as being 'likely to arise' and damage as being 'likely to occur'.[134] The concerns of, among others, the German delegation were thereby satisfied.[135]

It would be wrong, however, to dismiss Art 2 as a mere tidying up provi- **3.46** sion. Art 2(1), in particular, seems significant in that it gives an autonomous meaning to the concept of 'damage' for the purposes of the entire Regulation, including the rules of applicable law for tort/delict in Art 4,[136] and thereby controls the need for Member State courts and the ECJ to

---

[130] Common Position, Art 2.

[131] Council document 7929/06 [10.4.2006], Art A.

[132] Council document 6623/06 [23.2.2006], 2.

[133] COM (2006) 566 final [27.9.2006], 5.

[134] Compare the text of Council document 16027/05 [22.12.2005]. Also Commission Proposal, 11 ('The expression "likely to arise" shows that the proposed Regulation, like Article 5(3) of the "Brussels I" Regulation, also covers preventative actions such as actions for a prohibitive injunction').

[135] The German delegation had criticized the indiscriminate use of the expression 'likely to arise' in an early Council draft (Council document 16240/04 [23.12.2004], 2–3).

[136] **Ch 4** below.

attempt that task themselves.[137] The provision neatly sidesteps the questions whether a particular injury or loss is to be regarded as legally significant, and replaces it with a broad, fact-based concept requiring identification of the consequences arising out of tort/delict, unjust enrichment, *negotiorum gestio*, or *culpa in contrahendo*. Equally, the location of those consequences involves a question of fact, albeit not one which will always be easy to answer.[138] As a result, the task of Member State courts in applying the general rule for tort/delict in Art 4(1) seems more straightforward than it might otherwise have been. Having identified the chain of events giving rise to the claim, it will be necessary for the court seised to identify and exclude (having regard to the autonomous meaning of each concept within the Regulation) (a) the event(s) that constitute the 'event giving rise to the damage', and (b) the 'indirect consequences of that event', leaving only the consequences of the tort/delict whose location(s) is/are significant for the purposes of Art 4(1). This approach will be considered in further detail in **Chapter 4** below.[139]

HABITUAL RESIDENCE

Article 23

Habitual residence

1. For the purposes of this Regulation, the habitual residence of companies and other bodies, corporate or unincorporated, shall be the place of central administration.

Where the event giving rise to the damage occurs, or the damage arises, in the course of operation of a branch, agency or any other establishment, the place where the branch, agency or any other establishment is located shall be treated as the place of habitual residence.

2. For the purposes of this Regulation, the habitual residence of a natural person acting in the course of his or her business activity shall be his or her principal place of business.

Introduction

3.47 The concept of 'habitual residence' appears in several places in the Rome II Regulation as an element in rules linking the law applicable to a

---

[137] See, in the context of the 1968 Brussels Convention, Case C-68/93, *Shevill v Press Alliance SA* [1995] ECR I-415, paras 28–9, 38–9 and, subsequently, *Shevill v Presse Alliance SA* [1996] 1 AC 959 (UKHL).

[138] **4.46–4.68** below.

[139] **4.29–4.74** below.

non-contractual obligation to a country of common habitual residence[140] and as the primary connecting factor in determining the law applicable to non-contractual obligations in cases of product liability.[141] Art 23 contains a partial definition of that concept. A similar interpretative provision, albeit using different connecting factors,[142] appeared in Art 19 of the Commission Proposal. As the Commission explained:[143]

In general terms the proposed Regulation is distinguished from the 'Brussels I' Regulation by the fact that, in accordance with the generally accepted solution in conflict matters, the criterion used here is not domicile but the more flexible criterion of habitual residence.

Habitual Residence of Natural Persons (Art 23(2))

For natural persons, Art 23 only defines 'habitual residence' for situations **3.48** in which the event giving rise to damage occurs, or the damage arises, in the course of a business activity. In these cases, habitual residence is equated with the natural person's principal place of business,[144] irrespective of whether the circumstances giving rise to the non-contractual obligation in question are connected with a branch, agency, or other establishment in another country.

Although 'habitual residence' does not appear as a connecting factor in **3.49** the Brussels I Regulation, it is used in the Rome I Regime[145] and in the so called 'Brussels II *bis*' Regulation concerning jurisdiction and the recognition and enforcement of judgments in matrimonial matters and the matters of parental responsibility.[146] It seems reasonable to suppose that case

---

[140] See Arts 4(2), 10(2), 11(2), and 12(2).

[141] Art 5(1)(a) (**5.29–5.33** below).

[142] For companies etc., the Commission proposed that the habitual residence should be the 'principal establishment', unless the event giving rise to the damage occurs or the damage arises in the course of the operation of a subsidiary, branch or other establishment, in which case that establishment should take the place of the habitual residence. For natural persons, where the event giving rise to the damage occurs or the damage arises in the course of business activity, the natural person's establishment was to take the place of his/her habitual residence.

[143] Commission Proposal, 27.

[144] Cf Rome Convention, Art 4(2); A G Guest et al., *Benjamin's Sale of Goods* (7th edn, 2006), para 25-064.

[145] Rome Convention, Arts 4(2), 5, 8(2), and 9(5); Rome I Regulation, Arts 4(1), 5, 6, 7, 10(2), 11. Art 19 of the Rome I Regulation contains a definition of 'habitual residence', which differs in certain respects from that in Art 23 of the Rome II Regulation.

[146] Regulation (EC) No 2201/2003 (OJ L338, 1 [23.12.2003]); R Lamont, 'Habitual Residence and Brussels II *bis*: Developing Concepts for European Private International Family Law' (2007) 3 J Priv Int L 261.

law of Member State courts and any future case law of the ECJ[147] concerning the general concept of 'habitual residence' in these instruments, and the Rome I Regulation in particular,[148] will be influential in determining the meaning to be given to the concept in the Rome II Regulation where it is not defined. Decisions of the ECJ concerning the meaning of the concept in other Community instruments may also be influential.

3.50 In the recent English High Court decision of *M v M*,[149] Munby J held (it is submitted, correctly) that, in the Brussels II *bis* Regulation, the expression 'habitual residence' must be given an autonomous meaning, independent of the meaning that it has under the law of the individual Member States.[150] Relying on ECJ case law concerning social security and staff regulations[151] and on the explanatory report of Professor Borràs on the original EC (Brussels II) Convention on jurisdiction and the recognition and enforcement of judgments in matrimonial matters,[152] his Lordship concluded that:[153]

> [T]he phrase 'habitually resident' in Article 3(1) [*of the Brussels II bis Regulation*] has the meaning given to that phrase in the decisions of the ECJ, a meaning helpfully and accurately encapsulated by Dr Borràs in para [32] of his report:[154]
>
>> the place where the person had established, on a fixed basis, his permanent or habitual centre of interests, with all the relevant facts being taken into account for the purpose of determining such residence
>
> and by the Cour de Cassation in *Moore v McLean*:[155]
>
>> the place where the party involved has fixed, with the wish to vest it with a stable character, the permanent or habitual centre of his or her interests.

---

[147] As yet, there is no decision of the ECJ concerning the meaning of the concept of 'habitual residence' in the Brussels II *bis* Regulation. See reference for a preliminary ruling from the *Korkein hallinto-oikeus* (Finland) lodged on 23 November 2007 in Case C-523/07, *A*.

[148] Existing case law concerning the concept of 'habitual residence' in the Rome Convention would appear to provide very little guidance (J Fawcett, J Harris, and M Bridge, *International Sale of Goods in the Conflict of Laws* (2005), paras 13.117–13.118).

[149] [2007] EWHC 2047 (Fam); [2007] 2 FLR 1018. See also *L-K v K (No 2)* [2006] EWHC 3280 (Fam).

[150] Ibid, [17]–[18].

[151] In particular, Case 76/76, *Silvana di Paulo v Office national de l'emploi* [1977] ECR 315; Case C-102/91, *Knoch v Bundesanstalt für Arbeit* [1992] ECR I-4341; Case C-452/93P, *Pedro Magdalena Fernández v Commission* [1994] ECR I-4295; Case C-90/97, *Robin Swaddling v Adjudication Officer* [1999] ECR I-1075.

[152] OJ C221, 37–8 (paras 30–2) [16.7.1998].

[153] *M v M*, n 149 above, [33] (footnotes added).

[154] n 152 above.

[155] 1ère Ch civ, 14 December 2005.

Munby J also recognized that, in deciding where the habitual centre of some- **3.51** one's interests has been established, the court must have regard to the aim and scheme of the Community legislation concerned.[156] Thus, in social security cases, the place of a worker's stable employment was likely to be a significant factor and, in matrimonial cases, the place of the matrimonial home may take on a greater importance. The broader scope of the Rome II Regulation may mean that no single fact will take on an overriding importance, and it will be necessary to consider all relevant facts including (for example) the relevant person's 'family situation; the reasons which have led him to move; the length and continuity of his residence;[157] the fact (where this is the case) that he is in stable employment; and his intention as it appears from all the circumstances'.[158]

Finally, his Lordship decided that, for the purposes of the Brussels II *bis* **3.52** Regulation, a person could only have a single place of habitual residence.[159] This seems correct and accords with the position under the Rome II Regulation for companies.[160] It would appear possible, however, that a person (such as a refugee) may have no stable or permanent centre of his interests. If so, there appears no compelling reason to look to establish an artificial connection to a particular country for the purposes of the Rome II Regulation. Insofar as Art 5(1)(a) of the Regulation refers to the victim's habitual residence as part of the cascade of rules to determine the law applicable in product liability claims,[161] that element in the cascade can be ignored for a person lacking a sufficient connection to any country without distorting the overall effect of Art 5.

Habitual Residence of Companies etc. (Art 23(1))

For companies and other bodies, corporate or unincorporated (including **3.53** partnerships), Art 23 provides a full, two-part definition of 'habitual residence'. This, in contrast to the autonomous concept of 'domicile' in Art 60 of the Brussels I Regulation,[162] points to a single 'habitual residence' of a company for the purposes of determining the law applicable to a non-contractual obligation under the Regulation.[163]

---

[156] *M v M*, n 149 above, [34]–[36].

[157] Ibid, [31]–[32] referring, with approval, to the approach of Singer J in *L-K v K (No 2)*, n 149 above.

[158] *Robin Swaddling v Adjudication Officer*, n 151, para 29 (footnote added).

[159] *M v M*, n 149 above, [40]–[44], not following *Armstrong v Armstrong* [2003] EWHC 777 (Fam); [2003] 2 FLR 357 (Butler-Sloss P).

[160] **3.53** below.

[161] Text to n 141 above.

[162] Commission Proposal, 27.

[163] Cf Dicey, Morris & Collins, paras 30-005 to 30-007, dealing with the pre-existing English law.

3.54 As a starting point, the 'habitual residence' of a company etc. is to be equated with its 'place of central administration', a concept that appears as one of the elements of the definition of 'domicile' in Art 60 of the Brussels I Regulation. In the latter context, it has been said that:[164]

> The notion 'central administration' (in French: *'administration centrale'*, in German *'Hauptverwaltung'*, in Dutch *'hoofdvestiging'*[165]) means the management and control centre (the 'real seat'). Although every company or other legal person has a central administration, this notion is . . . easier to ascertain than the statutory seat. The location of the central administration depends on factual circumstances, which have to be known to the plaintiff in order to decide in which Member State the company or other legal person can be sued. In practice problems could arise in determining the place of central administration. The notion has to be understood in an autonomous way and ought not to be treated [*as*] identical to the concepts of the national systems of private international law.

3.55 If, however, the event giving rise to the damage occurs, or the damage arises, in the course of operation of a branch, agency, or any other estab-lishment, the 'habitual residence' of a company etc. is to be equated with the place of that branch, agency, or establishment. The concept of a 'branch, agency or other establishment' also appears in Art 5(5) of both the Brussels Convention and the Brussels I Regulation[166] and it is highly likely that the case law of Member State courts and the ECJ concerning these provisions will be followed in the present context. In *Somafer v Saar Fern Gas AG*, a decision concerning Art 5(5) of the Brussels Convention, the ECJ stated:[167]

> [T]he concept of branch, agency or other establishment implies a place of business which has the appearance of permanency, such as the extension of a parent body, has a management and is materially equipped to negotiate business with third parties so that the latter, although knowing that there will if necessary be a legal link with the parent body, the head office of which is abroad, do not have to deal directly with such parent body but may transact business at the place of business constituting the extension.

---

[164] U Magnus and P Mankowski, *Brussels I Regulation* (2007), Art 60, para 5. Also *King v Crown Energy Trading AG* [2003] EWHC 163 (Comm); [2003] ILPr 28; *Ministry of Defence and Support of the Armed Forces of Iran v FAZ Aviation* [2007] EWHC 1042; [2008] 1 All ER (Comm) 342; Benjamin's Sale of Goods, n 144 above, para 25-063.

[165] These terms are also used in the French, German, and Dutch texts of Art 23 of the Rome II Regulation.

[166] Art 5(5) provides: 'A person domiciled in a Member State may, in another Member State, be sued: . . . as regards a dispute arising out of the operations of a branch, agency or other establishment, in the courts for the place in which the branch, agency or other estab-lishment is situated'.

[167] Case 33/78, [1978] ECR 2183, para 12.

In the following paragraph of its judgment in *Somafer*, the ECJ suggested **3.56** further restrictions concerning the requirement in Art 5(5) that the dispute 'arise out of the operations of' the branch etc.[168] For contractual obligations, the suggested requirement that the contractual undertaking must be performed in the Contracting State where the branch etc. is established was subsequently disowned by the ECJ in *Lloyd's Register of Shipping v Société Campenon Bernard*.[169] Equally, for non-contractual obligations, the English Court of Appeal has rejected the suggestion that activities of the branch etc. in that State must either constitute or directly bring about the harmful event.[170] As to the required relationship between the dispute and the operations of the branch etc., Lord Phillips MR suggested a flexible approach, noting that:[171]

The events which give rise to liability in tort can vary widely—compare the liability of the publishers of a defamatory book with the vicarious liability of a company for the negligent driving of an employee in the course of his employment. In these circumstances, I do not think it desirable to attempt to formulate any test to determine whether a dispute has arisen out of the activities of a branch.

His Lordship appeared to accept, however, that it was instructive, in applying Art 5(5) of the Brussels I Regime, to consider whether the dispute was more closely connected to the Contracting State of the branch etc. than to the Contracting State in which the company etc. was domiciled.[172] Within Art 23(1) of the Rome II Regulation, the relevant comparison would be between the connections of the non-contractual obligation to the country of the branch etc. and the connections to the country in which the central administration of the company etc. is situated.

In contrast to the wording of Art 5(5) in the English language version of **3.57** the Brussels I Regulation,[173] Art 23(1) of the Rome II Regulation requires either that the event giving rise to damage occurs, or the damage arises, *in the course of operation of* the branch etc. This, as well as the objective of

---

[168] Ibid, para 13.

[169] Case C-439/93 [1995] ECR I-961, paras 16–20.

[170] *Anton Durbeck GmbH v Den Norske Bank ASA* [2003] EWCA Civ 147; [2003] QB 1160, [38]–[46] (Lord Phillips MR).

[171] Ibid, [41].

[172] Ibid, [45]–[46].

[173] A comparison of the French texts of Art 5(5) of the Brussels I Regulation and Art 23(1) of the Rome II Regulation shows a similar difference in language (Brussels I: '*relative à l'exploitation*' / Rome II: '*dans le cadre d'exploitation*'), but the German texts of these two instruments describe the required link using the same words ('*aus dem Betrieb*').

improving foreseeability of court decisions,[174] suggests that there must be an objectively ascertainable, direct link between the activities of the branch etc. and the events constituting the non-contractual obligation.

3.58 Ships and aircraft do not fulfil the criteria for recognition as a branch, agency, or other establishment for these purposes, as they lack a permanent location. They may, however, be linked to a branch etc. for these purposes. If, for example, an incident should occur on board an aircraft involving a passenger and a member of the air-crew, resulting in a non-contractual claim against the airline or the passenger, the relevant place of business of the airline for these purposes will, arguably, be that having operational control over the aircraft.

C. SCOPE OF THE REGULATION—INTRODUCTION AND APPROACH TO CHARACTERIZATION

INTRODUCTION

3.59 This section considers the material, geographical, and temporal scope of the Regulation. So far as the first aspect is concerned, it must be noted at the outset that the material scope of the Regulation cannot be determined by reference only to the provisions that appear under the heading 'Scope' in Chapter I, and in particular sub-paragraphs (1) to (3) of Art 1. Instead, these provisions are closely linked to Arts 15 to 22 (Chapter V, under the heading 'Common Rules') and Art 26 (public policy), which define the matters for which and the extent to which the Regulation controls the law to be applied by a Member State court in determining a claim based on a non-contractual obligation to which it applies. For these purposes, Arts 1(1) and (2), which define the obligations to which the rules of applicable law contained in the Regulation (i.e. Arts 4 to 14) must be applied, can be said to fix the Regulation's 'horizontal material scope', whereas Arts 15 to 22 and 26 can be said to fix the Regulation's 'vertical material scope'. Art 1(3), excluding matters of evidence and procedure, also addresses the Regulation's vertical scope. In order to define the sphere of application of the Regulation, and its likely impact on private law in the Member States, each of these two dimensions and their combined effect must be more fully appreciated. The following paragraphs, which consider the horizontal scope of the Regulation, must therefore be read together with **Chapters 14 and 15** below, which consider the vertical scope of the Regulation.

---

[174] Recital (16).

The material scope of the Regulation also has positive and negative **3.60**
aspects. On first reading, it appears that Art 1(1) defines the scope of the
Regulation in positive terms whereas Art 1(2) and (3),[175] which are
expressed to exclude specified matters, define it in negative terms. On
closer inspection, however, it can be seen that Art 1(1) is also substantially
expressed in negative terms. First, certain matters[176] are expressly removed
from the scope of the Regulation, by way of clarification to the concept of
'civil and commercial matters'.[177] Secondly, the Regulation's leading concept, that of 'non-contractual obligations' must itself be defined, at least in
part, negatively, as excluding any 'contractual obligation'.[178]

Questions as to the territorial and temporal scope of the Regulation are **3.61**
considered separately below.[179]

APPROACH TO QUESTIONS OF CHARACTERIZATION[180]

Before proceeding, it seems appropriate to consider briefly how questions **3.62**
of characterization must be approached under the Rome II Regulation.
Both the horizontal and the vertical aspects of the Regulation's material
scope, as defined above, raise problems of characterization of a kind familiar to all students of private international law.[181] Thus, it may in a particular case be necessary for a Member State court to determine:

1. whether a given situation involves a 'non-contractual obligation' or a
'civil or commercial matter' (Art 1(1));[182]

---

[175] Art 1(3), this restricts the extent to which the law identified by Arts 4 to 14 must be
given effect in the determination of non-contractual obligations under the Regulation. It concerns, therefore, the vertical scope of the Regulation, and it seems appropriate to consider it
alongside other provisions of that kind (see **3.229** and **14.54–14.62** below).
[176] Revenue, customs and administrative matters, and the liability of the State for *acta iure
imperii*.
[177] **3.270–3.286** below.
[178] **3.104–3.105** below.
[179] **3.287–3.314** (territorial scope) and **3.315–3.324** (temporal scope).
[180] Also A Rushworth and A Scott, 'Rome II: Choice of law for non-contractual obligations'
[2008] LMCLQ 274, 296–7.
[181] See generally Sir L Collins et al (eds), *Dicey, Morris & Collins: The Conflict of Laws* (14th
edn, 2006), ch 2 and, in particular, the materials there cited at footnote 1. For summaries of
the approach taken by the English courts to questions of characterization generally, see
Macmillan Inc v Bishopsgate Investment Trust plc (No 3) [1996] 1 WLR 407, at 391–2 (Staughton
LJ), 407 (Auld LJ), 417–8 (Aldous LJ) (CA); *Raiffeisen Zentralbank Österreich AG v Five Star
General Trading LLC* [2001] EWCA Civ 68; [2001] QB 825, at [26]–[33] (Mance LJ).
[182] **3.86–3.145** and **3.230–3.286** below.

2. if there is a non-contractual obligation, whether it falls within any of the categories of obligation excluded by Art 1(2);[183]

3. if not, whether that obligation falls within any of the categories for which a rule of applicable law is prescribed in Chapter II (Tort/Delict) or Chapter III (Unjust Enrichment, *Negotiorum Gestio*, and *Culpa In Contrahendo*);[184]

4. whether the Regulation fixes the law to be applied in determining the particular matters in issue between the parties in the proceedings (Arts 1(3) and 15 to 22).

3.63 In almost every case, these problems fall to be addressed in a uniform manner through a process of construction of the provisions of the Regulation,[185] not by reference to concepts used within the law of obligations in the forum state, nor (insofar as they differ) by reference to those deployed by the forum within its own pre-existing rules of private international law, nor somehow by reference to the law that would apply to an obligation or specific question under the Regulation. Accordingly, the 'characterization process' should not be seen as possessing a mystical aura rendering it inaccessible to all but private international law specialists. Instead, it describes a specific set of questions concerning the interpretation of the Regulation's rules and their application to an actual or hypothetical dispute. In this connection, the categories of obligation and other legal concepts used in the Regulation are not only 'man made',[186] they are unquestionably of European origin. In shaping the concepts deployed within the Regulation to define its horizontal and vertical material scope, regard must be had (in particular) to (a) the objectives underlying the Regulation and individual rules within it, and in particular the twin objectives of foreseeability of court decisions and the need to ensure a reasonable balance between the interests of the parties,[187] (b) principles common to the legal systems of the Member States,[188] and (c) the content of the Brussels I and Rome I Regimes.[189] To promote consistency in the application of the Rome II Regulation, the borderline between the different categories that it recognizes must be defined as clearly as

---

[183] **3.146–3.228** below.

[184] **Chs 4–12** below.

[185] See, for example, Recitals (11) and (30), which it is submitted are illustrative of, rather than exceptions to, the general approach to characterization under the Regulation (**3.09–3.11** above).

[186] *Raiffeisen Zentralbank Österreich v Five Star General Trading,* n 181 above, at [27] (Mance LJ).

[187] **3.13–3.30** above.

[188] **3.12** above.

[189] Recital (7) (**3.34–3.35** above).

possible and legal terms of art or technical concepts must, whenever possible, be eliminated.

A review of Arts 1 to 22 of the Rome II Regulation suggests that the Member **3.64** State courts will be called upon to characterize *matters, liability, obligations, rules,* and *issues.* As to the concept of a *matter,* Art 1(1) refers to 'civil and commercial matters' and 'revenue, customs or administrative matters'. These phrases also qualify the subject matter scope of the Brussels I Regulation and its predecessor, the Brussels Convention, as well as the Rome I Regulation.[190] As the Rome II Regulation requires that its substantive scope be consistent with the Brussels I Regime,[191] the approach taken by the ECJ in its case law addressing the subject matter scope of that regime will likely be followed in relation to the Rome I and Rome II Regulations. That case law will be considered in further detail later in this chapter, in defining the concept of 'civil and commercial matters' within the Rome II Regulation.[192] For present purposes, two points are of particular note. First, in order to determine whether a claim falls within the subject matter scope of the Brussels I Regime (and, in particular, in considering whether it concerns a 'civil' or 'commercial' matter) only the subject matter of the claim itself, and not any plea raised by way of defence, is to be taken into account.[193] Secondly, although the concept of 'civil and commercial matters' must be given an autonomous interpretation and is not to be defined by reference to the concepts used within national law,[194] the application of that concept in individual cases requires the court seised of the dispute to examine the basis and the detailed rules governing the bringing of the action in order to determine whether a public authority that is a party to the dispute is acting in the exercise of its public powers, in the sense of powers falling outside the scope of rules applicable to relationships between private individuals.[195] In considering, therefore, whether a matter may be characterized as a 'civil' or 'commercial' matter for the purposes of the Brussels I Regulation, a Member State court's focus will be upon the legal *and* factual basis of the claim advanced by the claimant.

---

[190] Brussels Convention, Art 1, first para; Brussels I Regulation, Art 1(1); Rome I Regulation, Art 1(1).

[191] **3.34–3.35** above.

[192] **3.263–3.268** below.

[193] Case C-266/01, *Préservatrice foncière TIARD SA v Staat der Nederlanden* [2003] ECR I-4867, paras 42–3.

[194] Case C-172/91, *Sonntag v Waidmann* [1993] ECR I-1963, para 25.

[195] Case C-271/00, *Gemeente Steenbergen v Baten* [2002] ECR I-10489, para 30; Case C-266/01, *TIARD*, n 193 above, para 23; Case C-265/02, *Frahuil SA v Assitalia SpA* [2004] ECR I-1543, para 20.

3.65 That approach seems equally suited to the concept of 'civil and commercial matters' in the Rome II Regulation, and requires, therefore, that the
Member State court consider both the factual and legal basis of the claim
presented to it in order to determine whether it falls within the Regulation's
scope. At the outset, before the court has been able to reach a conclusion as
to the law that would apply under the Regulation if the matter fell within
its scope, the factual basis of the claim put forward by the claimant is likely
to dominate. That alone may enable the court to conclude that the claim is
based on the exercise of public powers. For example, in *Lechouritou v
Federal Republic of Germany* (a Brussels Convention case),[196] the claim concerned operations of the defendant's forces during the Second World War.
In the view of the Court of Justice:[197]

> [T]here is no doubt that operations conducted by armed forces are one of the
> characteristic emanations of State sovereignty, in particular inasmuch as they are
> decided upon in a unilateral and binding manner by the competent public authori-
> ties and appear as inextricably linked to States' foreign and defence policy.

> It follows that acts such as those which are at the origin of the loss and damage
> pleaded by the plaintiffs in the main proceedings and, therefore, of the action for
> damages brought by them before the Greek courts must be regarded as resulting
> from the exercise of public powers on the part of the State concerned on the date
> when those acts were perpetrated.

3.66 In other cases, however, the court must proceed to examine the relevant
rules of the country whose law would apply under the Regulation to see
if the action is concerned with the regulation of a private law relationship
rather than with the exercise of public law powers.[198] That question must
be approached from a wider Community perspective and not merely by
reference to the label and procedural categorization given to the applicable
rules within their legal system of origin.[199] The same approach must be
adopted in considering whether a matter is a 'revenue, customs or administrative matter'[200] or involves *liability* 'of the State for acts and omissions
in the exercise of State authority' under Art 1(1).[201] As appears below, these
are best seen as specific examples of matters that do not fall within the
scope of the Rome II Regulation for the reason that they are not 'civil and
commercial matters'.[202]

---

[196] Case C-292/05, [2007] ECR I-1519.
[197] Ibid, paras 37–8.
[198] See the cases referred to at n 195 above.
[199] *Sonntag v Waidmann*, n 194 above; *Lechouritou v Germany*, n 196 above, para 41.
[200] **3.270** below.
[201] **3.271–3.286** below.
[202] **3.270** and **3.274** below.

Equally, it may strongly be argued that the categories of *obligation* in Arts 1 **3.67**
and 4 to 12 of the Regulation, which in almost every case must be interpreted autonomously,[203] must be defined under the Regulation in terms of
factual *and* legal characteristics that the specific *obligation* that a litigating
party claims to exist (the 'obligation in question'[204]) must possess (or omit)
to fit within the scope of the Regulation (in the case of the concept of
'non-contractual obligation' in Art 1) or a particular rule of applicable law
(Arts 4 to 12). A non-contractual obligation, which cannot exist in a legal
vacuum, must be based on a factual situation triggering certain legal consequences under the law of one or more countries. The factual situation
and the civil law consequences flowing from it are linked by, and cannot
be understood without reference to, particular legal rules and an appreciation of those rules is essential if the character of the obligation in question
is to be understood. Those legal rules will shape the existence, content,
and consequences of a non-contractual obligation and identify the elements of the factual situation on which the obligation is founded. In every
case, therefore, the 'obligation in question' will combine legal elements
(i.e. rules regulating the content and consequences of the defendant's
supposed obligation) and factual elements (i.e. the facts which, under the
applicable legal rules, give rise to legal consequences).

Consider, for example, a situation in which the claimant (A) pays the **3.68**
defendant (B) a sum of money under a mistake which B through carelessness induces or fails to notice. A seeks to recover the amount of the
payment from B setting out in his claim the entire sequence of events
including his mistake and B's carelessness. At this stage, it may be
unclear whether, as a matter of law, A's mistake will suffice to give him
a legal remedy or whether he must also establish B's fault. That question
can only be answered by looking at the legal rules that are the source of
the putative obligation, an enquiry that is straightforward enough if the
problem is confined to a single legal system, but that becomes more complex in cross-border situations in which the rules of two or more countries may be claimed to apply to regulate B's obligation. Nevertheless,
the difficulty is one that must be faced if, as appears likely, identifying
the exact factual basis of A's claim may affect its characterization under
the Regulation.[205]

---

[203] **3.05–3.11** above.
[204] Case 14/76, *Ets A de Bloos SPRL v Société en commandite pour actions Bouyer* [1976] ECR
1497, paras 11–13, concerning the concept of 'obligation in question' in Art 5(1) of the 1968
Brussels Convention (matters relating to a contract).
[205] If A's claim is based on the mistake alone, it may be thought more likely to fall within
the province of Art 10 (unjust enrichment), whereas if it depends on proof of B's fault it may

3.69 The factual or legal characteristics that the obligation in question must possess (or omit) in order to constitute a 'non-contractual obligation' falling within the scope of the Regulation, or to fall within the scope of a particular rule of applicable law within the Regulation, will be considered in the commentary on individual Articles in this and the following chapters. In general terms, however, the formulation of the Regulation's rules of applicable law will allow the court in most cases to focus principally on factual elements of the obligation in question including, in particular, the event on which the defendant's liability is based or its consequences. For example, under Art 5 (product liability), the court must determine whether the obligation concerns 'damage caused by a product'[206] and under Art 12, the court must determine whether the obligation arises directly[207] 'out of dealings prior to the conclusion of a contract'.[208] Other rules (including, it is submitted, the general rule for tort/delict[209]) may be approached in the same way, by focusing on the fact(s) on which the claim is founded. That approach seems consistent with the principle of legal certainty, as it enables natural and legal persons more readily to reach a preliminary view at least as to the country or countries whose legal rules may apply to particular situations, whether existing or planned, and to take legal advice accordingly. For the reasons given in the preceding paragraph, however, the factual basis of the claim cannot be determined independently of the (potentially) applicable legal rules and these, in turn, may depend on how the claimant chooses to present his case.

3.70 Although normally insignificant, in a few instances, the Regulation's rules require the source or character of legal rules to be considered in order to place a particular obligation within the Regulation's scope or within a particular rule of applicable law. For example, (a) Art 1(2)(d) refers to non-contractual obligations arising out of 'the law of companies',[210] and (b) Art 8 concerns infringement of 'intellectual property rights', a concept that would appear to require analysis as to the nature of the protection given to the right-holder.[211] The remedy sought or available under the putative applicable law, will rarely, if ever, be a significant factor in characterizing *obligations* under the Regulation. Art 9 (industrial action) refers

---

be thought more likely to fall within Art 4 (tort/delict). Cf the discussion at **4.103–4.105** below as to the treatment under the Regulation of a claim under English law for 'knowing receipt'.

[206] **5.07–5.17** below.
[207] Recital (30).
[208] **12.03–12.08** below.
[209] **3.243–3.246** below.
[210] **3.158–3.172** below.
[211] **6.34** below.

to 'liability ... for damages', but the following reference to 'industrial action, pending or carried out' and other factors indicate that the rule cannot be restricted to monetary claims.[212] Otherwise, the Regulation's rules do not in terms appear to draw distinctions according to the nature of relief sought.[213]

Accordingly, in any situation calling, actually[214] or potentially,[215] for a **3.71** determination by a court in a Member State of the law applicable to a non-contractual obligation, the object of the process of characterization, involving construction of the Rome II Regulation's rules of applicable law, will be to (1) identify which of the rules of applicable law (if any) in the Regulation may be claimed to apply to the determination of the matters in issue between the parties, and (2) for each rule of applicable law within the Regulation that has been identified at the first stage, to consider whether the factual and legal basis of the obligation in question, in combination, bring the obligation within the scope of the relevant Regulation rule, so as to justify its application to the determine the parties' dispute. At the first stage, it is to be expected that the court will rely primarily on the way in which the claimant presents his claim. In the majority of cases, there is likely to be no doubt that a particular rule within the Regulation should apply. In the case of a road traffic accident between individuals with no prior relationship, for example, it will be clear from the factual basis of the claim alone that the only possible category is 'tort/delict' within Art 4 of the Regulation. In such cases, the court can proceed to identify the law applicable to the defendant's non-contractual obligation and to apply that law to determine the matters in dispute between the parties.

In other cases, however, there may appear to be more than one possible **3.72** characterization of the obligation in question under the Regulation (e.g. whether 'contractual' or 'non-contractual'; 'tort/delict' or 'unjust enrichment'). In these cases, the court should proceed to identify the law that would putatively apply to the obligation in question if it were to fall within each of the possible categories. If the connecting factors identified in the Regulation[216] for the competing categories point to the law of the same country, the court may be able to ignore the problem of

---

[212] **9.27** below; Dicey, Morris & Collins, 1st Supplement, para 535–242.

[213] See the discussion at **4.11–4.20** below as to the treatment under the Regulation of gain-based remedies for wrongdoing.

[214] i.e. in a situation in which proceedings have been brought.

[215] i.e. in a situation in which proceedings have not been brought, but with respect to which one or more Member State courts are competent according to the rules of jurisdiction contained in the Brussels I Regulation or otherwise.

[216] Or, in the case of a debate as to whether the obligation in question should be characterized as 'contractual' or 'non-contractual', in both the Rome II Regulation and the Rome I Regime.

characterization and proceed on the basis of an alternative analysis (e.g. to conclude that, whether the obligation in question is properly characterized as 'contractual' or whether it is not 'contractual', the law of [X] will apply and there is no material difference, so far as issues in the particular case are concerned, between the scope of the law applicable under the Rome I Regime and the Rome II Regulation). If, however, the characterization of an obligation matters, whether because a different law would apply under the Regulation to each of the competing categories or because differences in the scope of the applicable law in each case are material to the particular case, the proper way forward would appear to be for the court to refine its analysis in an attempt to fit the obligation within one of the categories to the exclusion of the others by highlighting particular features of the factual and legal framework as being 'fundamental' to an understanding of the obligation and putting others to one side. In the early years of the Regulation's application, without detailed guidance from the ECJ or courts within its own system as to the approach to be taken in deciding whether particular situations fall within one category, there is a risk that this process may appear arbitrary. In these circumstances, Member State courts must look elsewhere for inspiration in order to feel their way towards the correct answer. For example, they may look to identify principles common to the legal systems of the Member States, whether in their substantive laws governing obligations or in their pre-existing rules of private international law in this area, or consider the ECJ's approach to comparable questions of categorization in other areas, in particular in its case law with respect to the Brussels I Regime. In addition, if circumstances permit, the court should identify and examine the relevant rules of the law that would fall to be applied to each of the possible categories of obligation to see how they would regulate the parties' obligations towards each other on the particular facts of the case. Looking to the putative applicable law in this way cannot determine the factual and/or legal characteristics that an obligation in question must possess to fall within a particular category of obligation under the Regulation.[217] That will, in almost every case, be purely a matter of construction of the Regulation. Nor can it affect the court's (logically) prior determination of the country or countries to which the connecting factor points.[218] That would constitute a form of *renvoi*, which is not permitted under the Regulation.[219] Instead, the court's purpose in taking this step is to check that it has an accurate understanding of the obligation that is being

[217] *Sonntag v Waidmann*, n 194 above.
[218] Case C-364/93, *Marinari v Lloyd's Bank plc* [1995] ECR I-2719, paras 16–19.
[219] **3.41–3.43** above.

asked by the claimant to determine.[220] As will be seen, that technique has often been used by the ECJ in fitting claims within particular categories under the Brussels I Regime.[221] It may also allow the court to reach the conclusion that the claim can be supported on two independent bases, each of which should be considered to give rise to a separate obligation with its own governing law.[222] If so, the two obligations may eventually need to be reconciled with one another, principally through a detailed analysis of their content and relationship to other kinds of obligation within the legal systems from which they originate.[223]

Art 17 of the Regulation refers to 'rules of safety and conduct which were **3.73** in force at the place and time of the event giving rise to liability'. As appears from the commentary on that Article in **Chapter 15** below,[224] rules falling within this category may be taken into account as a matter of fact in the assessment of an element in the claim (e.g. a requirement of fault) or, possibly, of a defence to the claim (e.g. contributory fault). The expression 'rules of safety and conduct' suggests that the content of any rule which it is sought to invoke in this manner must be analysed to check that it actually regulates matters of safety or conduct (as opposed, for example, to matters of liability). Although certain questions arise as to the concept of a 'rule' for these purposes,[225] that enquiry should not be one that is difficult from a practical viewpoint.

Finally, Arts 1(3), 15, 18, and 19 to 22 define what has been described above **3.74** as the vertical material scope of the Regulation by describing the issues or questions to be determined by the law applicable to a non-contractual obligation under the Regulation, or a different law specified by the Regulation. Whether a particular issue arises for determination by a Member State will not become clear until the parties have had the opportunity to state their respective cases, whether in writing or orally. That, however, does not

---

[220] Cf A Rushworth and A Scott, n 180 above, 296 ('Given the questions asked by the Regulation's rules and concepts, such data must include an obligation's nature, incidents and the constitutive elements of the event from which it arises. It is submitted that the only law that can provide this data is the law by reference to which the claimant pleads his claim'). The court (having regard to its own rules governing the introduction and ascertainment of foreign law) may, however, need to go beyond the law pleaded or relied on by the claimant.

[221] e.g. the approach taken in *Reichert v Dresdner Bank (No 2)* (**3.252** below) and *Engler v Janus Versand* (**3.118–3.120** below). Also A Rushworth and A Scott, n 180 above, 296, footnote 158.

[222] For the possibility of separate, concurrent obligations in contract/'tort/delict' and 'tort/delict'/'unjust enrichment' see **3.124–3.139** and **4.20** below.

[223] e.g. **3.139** below.

[224] See, in particular, **15.33–15.34**.

[225] **15.30–15.32** below.

mean that the law applicable to particular issues cannot be ascertained in advance. Indeed, if the obligation in question falls within the scope of the Regulation, the country whose law applies to that obligation must be determined in accordance with the rules contained in its Chapters II to IV, without reference to the issues that actually arise for decision.[226] Once this has been done, the provisions of Chapter V, read together with Art 1(3), describe the functions that legal rules of the country whose law applies will perform under the Regulation in every case falling within its scope.

D. MATERIAL SCOPE

Article 1(1)

Scope

1. This Regulation shall apply, in situations involving a conflict of laws, to non-contractual obligations in civil and commercial matters. It shall not apply, in particular, to revenue, customs or administrative matters or to the liability of the State for acts and omissions in the exercise of State authority (*acta iure imperii*).

INTRODUCTION

3.75 Art 1(1) of the Rome II Regulation is the most important of the provisions defining the material scope of the Regulation. It is similar to Art 1(1) of the Brussels I Regulation[227] as well as Art 1(1) of the Rome I Regulation.[228] The first sentence makes clear that the subject matter of the Rome II Regulation is *non-contractual obligations*. More specifically, the title of the Regulation and its reference to 'situations involving a conflict of laws'[229] make clear that it is concerned with the law applicable to non-contractual obligations in circumstances where connections with two or more legal systems (including that of the forum) open up the possibility that the forum's own rules concerning non-contractual obligations should give

---

[226] **4.89** below.

[227] 'This Regulation shall apply in civil and commercial matters whatever the nature of the court of tribunal. It shall not extend, in particular, to revenue, customs or administrative matters.'

[228] 'This Regulation shall apply, in situations involving a conflict of laws, to contractual obligations in civil and commercial matters. It shall not apply, in particular, to revenue, customs or administrative matters.'

[229] Cf Art 1(1) of the Rome Convention referring to 'any situation involving a choice between the laws of different countries'. The French text *'comportant un conflit de lois'* is the same in the Rome Convention and the Rome II Regulation.

way to rules originating in another legal system.[230] In the Commission's view, the expression 'situations involving a conflict of laws' refers to *'situations in which there are one or more elements that are alien to the domestic social life of a country* that entail applying several systems of law'.[231] The italicized words in this passage would appear to provide a perfectly satisfactory working definition, but the following words add an unnecessary element of uncertainty as they beg the question whether a particular foreign connection justifies applying a rule originating in a legal system other than that of the forum. That said, the requirement that there be a 'conflict of laws' appears unlikely to cause significant difficulty in practice—the existence of a foreign connection should alert the Member State court to the possible need to apply the provisions of the Regulation in determining a civil claim raising questions of non-contractual liability.

The use of the passive voice in the opening sentence of Art 1(1) raises two **3.76** questions: to whom does the Rome II Regulation apply, and how does it apply? The formulation of many of the primary rules of applicable law contained in the Regulation ('the law applicable to a non-contractual obligation . . . shall be . . .'[232]), as well as the frequent references in the Recitals to terms such as 'court', 'action', 'litigants', 'cases',[233] emphasize that the Regulation is directed at judicial bodies within the Member States that may be called upon to determine disputes concerning non-contractual obligations, and that relations between natural and legal persons are regulated indirectly by creating a framework that will enable them to ascertain the rules that will be applied to determine their respective rights and obligations if (but only if) they are involved as parties in some form of judicial proceedings in a Member State. Accordingly, as noted above, the 'non-contractual obligations' to which Art 1(1) refers are tied to processes for the determination of disputes within the Member States.[234] They are fixed only when actually determined by a court. In the meantime, natural and legal persons may use the Regulation's rules of applicable law, in combination with the rules of jurisdiction in the Brussels I Regulation,[235] to predict the manner in which one or more Member State courts would regulate

---

[230] Giuliano & Lagarde Report (OJ C282, 10 [31.10.1980]). Also the report of Professors M Giuliano and P Lagarde and Mr T van Sasse van Ysselt on the draft convention on the law applicable to contractual and non-contractual obligations (Commission document XIV/408/72 – E (provisional version)), 12.

[231] Commission Proposal, 8 (emphasis added).

[232] Arts 4(1), 5(1), 6(1), 6(3)(a), 7, 8(1), 8(2), 9, 12(1).

[233] e.g. Recitals (6), (8), (13), (14), (22), (25), (32).

[234] **3.39–3.40**.

[235] As well as other instruments, such as the Lugano Convention, if applicable.

their legal relations if called upon to do so. They must also consider the possibility of a determination by a court or tribunal in a non-Member State that will not be bound by the Regulation's rules.

3.77 In this connection, Recital (8) provides:

> This Regulation should apply irrespective of the nature of the court or tribunal seised.

Even without this wording, the approach of the ECJ in its case law on the Brussels Convention would have provided powerful support for the view that the Regulation should apply without reference to the division of jurisdiction between the various types of courts existing in the Member States, whether dealing with civil, criminal, or administrative matters and whatever their title.[236] Notably, Art 5(4) of both the Brussels Convention and its successor instrument, the Brussels I Regulation, confers special jurisdiction:

> as regards a civil claim for damages or restitution which is based on an act giving rise to criminal proceedings, in the court seised of those proceedings, to the extent that that court has jurisdiction under its own law to entertain civil proceedings

3.78 It appears, however, that the court or tribunal in question must be exercising judicial functions of a Member State.[237] For this reason, proceedings before international courts and tribunals with their seats in the Community (including the European Court of Justice) are not affected by the Regulation. Equally, the case law of the ECJ concerning the right to make preliminary references under Art 234 of the EC Treaty, a right that is restricted to a 'court or tribunal of a Member State', supports the conclusion that the Regulation does not apply to a private arbitration tribunal sitting in a Member State. In this context, the Court has reasoned that:[238]

> In order to determine whether a body making a reference is a court or tribunal of a Member State for the purposes of Article 234 EC, the Court takes account of a number of factors, such as whether the body is established by law, whether it is permanent, whether its jurisdiction is compulsory, whether its procedure is *inter partes*, whether it applies rules of law and whether it is independent . . .
>
> Under the Court's case-law, an arbitration tribunal is not 'a court or tribunal of a Member State' within the meaning of Article 234 EC where the parties are under

---

[236] Case 814/79, *Netherlands State v Rüffer* [1980] ECR 3807, para 14.

[237] A Layton and H Mercer, *European Civil Practice* (2nd ed, 2004), para 12.026, in relation to wording in Art 1(1) of the Brussels I Regulation similar to that found in Recital (8) to the Rome II Regulation.

[238] Case C-125/04, *Denuit v Transorient–Mosaïque Voyages and Culture SA* [2005] ECR I-923, paras 12–13 (citations omitted). Also Case 102/81, *Nordsee Deutsche Hochseefischerei GmbH v Reederei Mond Hochseefischerei AG* [1982] ECR 1095; cf Case 61/65, *Vaassen v Management of the Beambtenfonds voor het Mijndedrijf* [1966] ECR 261.

no obligation, in law or in fact, to refer their disputes to arbitration and the public authorities of the Member State concerned are not involved in the decision to opt for arbitration nor required to intervene of their own accord in the proceedings before the arbitrator . . .'

On this view,[239] supported by specific references in the Regulation and **3.79** its Recitals to 'the Member State of that court'[240] and 'courts of the Member States',[241] an arbitral tribunal may continue to determine the law applicable to non-contractual obligations that are raised for determination by it having regard to rules of applicable law contained in national legislation governing arbitration and the parties' agreement to arbitrate, including any arbitration rules chosen by them. In the United Kingdom, for example, s 46 of the Arbitration Act 1996 provides, without distinguishing between contractual and non-contractual obligations, that the arbitral tribunal shall decide the dispute (a) in accordance with the law chosen by the parties as applicable to the substance, or (b) if the parties so agree, in accordance with such other considerations as are agreed between them or determined by the tribunal, or (c) if or to the extent that there is no such choice or agreement, by applying the law determined by the conflict of laws rules which it considers appropriate.[242] That section, as a non-mandatory provision of the Act, can be (and frequently is) excluded by contrary intention of the parties, often by the choice of a set of arbitration rules adopted by an international arbitration institution containing its own rules concerning the law applicable to the substance of the dispute.[243] Nor, on this view, will a Member State court generally be entitled, or obliged, to review an arbitral award on the ground that the law applied by the arbitral tribunal in determining a non-contractual obligation differed from that which would have been indicated by the Regulation. There would, on this reading of the Regulation, be no error of law on the part of the tribunal, let alone a failure to apply a mandatory provision of EC law.[244]

---

[239] For the avoidance of doubt, this does not amount to a submission that EC law cannot bind an arbitral tribunal with its seat in a Member State, a submission that would be untenable: Case 102/81, *Nordsee v Reederei Mond*, n 238 above, para 14 (quoted text to n 247 below); Case C-126/97, *Eco Swiss China Time Ltd v Benetton International NV* [1999] ECR I-3055, para 32.

[240] Art 6(3)(b).

[241] Recital (32), referring also to 'Member State of the court seised'.

[242] For further discussion, see A Tweeddale and K Tweeddale, *Arbitration of Commercial Disputes: International and English Law and Practice* (paperback edition, 2007), paras 6.48–6.77.

[243] e.g. UNCITRAL Arbitration Rules (1976), Art 33; ICC Rules of Arbitration (1998), Art 17; LCIA Arbitration Rules (1998), Art 22.3.

[244] For cases in which the failure by an arbitral tribunal to apply a mandatory provision of EC law triggered an absolute or qualified obligation upon a Member State court to review an

3.80 There are, however, arguments that support a broader construction of the words 'court or tribunal' so as to include a private arbitral tribunal. First, an early draft of the Regulation produced by the Dutch Presidency in September 2004 contained a footnote in the following terms:[245]

> A recital should indicate that this Regulation should apply irrespective of the nature of the court or tribunal. *This means that the Regulation is also applicable in arbitration cases.*

The second sentence was, however, deleted from the corresponding footnote in the following draft[246] and was never reinserted. There is no mention of any discussion of this point in the Commission's notes of meetings of the Council's Rome II Committee held at the time. Against this background, the deletion of the statement would appear at least as significant as its appearance in the first place, depriving the statement of any probative value.

3.81 Secondly, the ECJ in considering the question of the power of an arbitral tribunal to make preliminary references, has stated that:[247]

> Community law must be observed in its entirety throughout the territory of all the Member States; parties to a contract are not, therefore, free to create exceptions to it . . .

3.82 In this connection, the arguments may be presented that:

1. The Rome II Regulation contains no specific exclusion relating to arbitration, in contrast to the Brussels I Regulation (excluding 'arbitration'[248]) and the Rome I Regime (excluding 'arbitration agreements'[249]).

2. The Rome II Regulation's rules of applicable law, particularly the special rules for tort/delict in Arts 5–9, serve specific policy objectives of the Community (including protecting consumers' health,[250] protecting competitors, consumers and the general public,[251] securing a high level of environmental protection,[252] and protecting the rights and obligations

---

arbitral award, see Case C-126/97, *Eco Swiss*, n 239 above; Case C-168/05, *Mostaza Claro v Centro Móvil Milenium SL* [2006] ECR I-10421.

[245] Council document 12746/04 [27.9.2004], 3 (emphasis added).
[246] Council document 16231/04 [20.12.2004], 3.
[247] Case 102/81, *Nordsee v Reederei*, n 238 above, para 14.
[248] Brussels I Regulation, Art 1(2)(d).
[249] Rome Convention, Art 1(2)(d); Rome I Regulation, Art 1(2)(e).
[250] Art 5 (see Recital (20)).
[251] Art 6 (see Recital (21)).
[252] Art 7 (see Recital (25)).

of workers and employers).[253] Achievement of those objectives may be jeopardized if the parties are allowed to 'contract out' of the Regulation by choosing arbitration.

3. Although Art 14 of the Regulation[254] enables the parties to agree to submit non-contractual obligations to the law of their choice, there are limits to that choice that also reflect policy choices made by the Community legislator for the protection of parties thought to be in a weaker bargaining position[255] and (in the case of competition law) other market participants.[256]

In response to these arguments, it may be countered that: **3.83**

(a) The specific exceptions for arbitration in the Brussels and Rome I Regimes were designed to ensure consistency between those instruments and the Member States' obligations under the 1958 New York Convention on the recognition and enforcement of arbitral awards.[257] That Convention regulates the validity and effect of arbitration agreements on the jurisdiction of Contracting State courts, but does not regulate the law applicable to the substance of disputes referred to arbitration. Accordingly, there was no need for the Rome II Regulation to contain a similar provision. Consistently with this view, the Rome I Regime does not exclude 'arbitration' in its entirety, but only 'arbitration agreements'.

(b) The policy interests referred to at points 2 and 3 above are adequately protected by the requirements that (i) arbitrators sitting in a Member State give effect to mandatory rules contained in the EC Treaty (such as those concerning matters of competition law[258]) and in Community legislative instruments (such as the Unfair Terms in Consumer Contracts Directive[259]), and (ii) Member State courts, in reviewing arbitral awards, must treat non-compliance with such rules as the

---

[253] Art 8 (see Recital (27)).

[254] **Ch 13** below.

[255] Art 13(1)(b), discussed at **13.37–13.41** below.

[256] Art 6(4), excluding party choice (**6.74** below). Party choice is also excluded for infringements of intellectual property rights (Art 8(3)), although the main reason for this appears to be one of practicality in the application of the rule favouring the *lex protectionis* (**8.54** below).

[257] Jenard Report (OJ C59, 13 [5.3.1979]); Giuliano & Lagarde Report (OJ C282, 11–12 [31.10.1980]).

[258] Case C-126/97, *Eco Swiss*, n 239 above.

[259] Directive (EEC) No 93/13 on unfair terms in consumer contracts (OJ L95, 29 [21.4.1993]); Case C-168/05, *Mostaza Claro*, n 244 above; N Shelkoplyas, *The Application of EC Law in Arbitration Proceedings* (2003), ch 9–11.

equivalent of a breach of public policy under national law,[260] including (if necessary to ensure the effectiveness of Community law[261]) by raising such non-compliance of their own motion.[262]

(c) Arbitration is in any event an essentially contractual process so the question as to the law applicable by an arbitral tribunal to determine a dispute between the parties to an arbitration agreement should be characterized as concerning the interpretation and performance of a 'contractual obligation',[263] even if an element of the dispute to be arbitrated concerns a matter that would be characterized by a Member State court faced with the same claim as being founded on a non-contractual obligation.

(d) A decision that the Regulation extends to private arbitration tribunals sitting in the Member States would place them at a competitive disadvantage, in terms of attracting arbitration business, with non-Member States that allow a liberal choice of law regime for arbitration claims.

3.84 Although Recital (8) is ambiguous, these points and the supportive indications in the text of the Regulation,[264] tip the balance in favour of excluding private arbitral tribunals from the concept of 'court or tribunal' under the Rome II Regulation. Whether that view will be accepted remains to be seen.

3.85 Other difficult questions may arise, for example as to the effect of the Regulation on determinations by ombudsmen and similar bodies of complaints concerning the conduct of regulated persons.[265] In many instances, the jurisdiction of the complaint handler is compulsory, in the sense that the regulated person, who will be bound in the result, need not voluntarily accede to the complaint handling process or consent to the determination

---

[260] Case C-126/97, *Eco Swiss*, n 239 above, paras 37–9. Also N Shelkoplyas, n 259 above, ch 12; F-B Weigand, 'Evading EC Competition Law by Resorting to Arbitration?' (1993) 9 Arb Int 249; J Werner, 'Application of Competition Laws by Arbitrators: The Step Too Far' (1995) 12 J Int Arb 21 and the papers collected in the special edition of the European Business Law Review, 'Arbitrating Competition Law Issues: A European and a US Perspective' (2008) 19 EBLR 1-231.

[261] Joined Cases C-222/05 to C-225/05, *van der Weerd and Others v Minister van Landbouw, Natuur en Voedselkwaliteit* [2007] ECR I-4233.

[262] Case C-168/05, *Mostaza Claro*, n 244 above. Also J Hill, *International Commercial Disputes in English Courts* (3rd edn, 2005), 677–9; W Brown, 'Commercial Arbitration and the European Economic Community' (1985) 2 J Int Arb 21; C Schmitthoff, *Arbitration and EEC Law* (1987) 24 Common Market L Rev 143.

[263] Albeit one that (probably) falls outside the Rome Convention and Rome I Regulation (see text to n 249 above).

[264] Text to nn 240–241 above.

[265] For example, by the Financial Ombudsman Service under Part XVI of the UK Financial Services and Markets Act 2000 (**FSMA**).

by that body of a particular dispute.[266] The complaint handing body may also apply procedures that are similar to those in court proceedings[267] and award remedies to prevent or terminate injury or damage or ensure the provision of compensation.[268] In situations of this kind, it is submitted that the key question will be whether the complaint handling body determines complaints by applying rules of law, or by reference to non-legal criteria (or a mixture of legal and non-legal criteria).[269] Only if the body applies exclusively legal criteria will the complaint handler be capable of constituting a 'court or tribunal' under the Regulation.

Non-Contractual Obligations

Recital (11)[270] recognizes that, as the concept of a 'non-contractual obliga- **3.86** tion' varies between Member States, a single, autonomous meaning must be given to that concept under the Rome II Regulation, extending to non-contractual obligations arising out of strict liability.[271]

This autonomous concept of a 'non-contractual obligation'[272] has both **3.87** positive and negative aspects. Its negative aspects are threefold. First, it concerns obligations, excluding matters of status. Secondly, it excludes obligations that are considered to be 'contractual obligations' within the 1980 Rome Convention and its successor, the Rome I Regulation. Thirdly, Art 1(2) of the Regulation excludes certain categories of obligation from scope. The positive aspect of the concept of 'non-contractual obligation' is perhaps less obvious—it arises from the need to fit 'obligations' that are not 'contractual' and that are not expressly excluded from the Regulation's scope into one of the rules of applicable law in Arts 4 to 12. In some cases, it is submitted, that will not be possible, with the consequence that the outer limits of those rules, in combination, provide a further restriction on the scope of the Regulation.

---

[266] e.g. FSMA, s 226.

[267] e.g. FSMA, Sch 7, paras 13–14 and FSA Handbook, DISP/3.

[268] e.g. FSMA, s 228.

[269] The Financial Ombudsman Service determines complaints by reference to what is, in the opinion of the ombudsman, fair and reasonable in all the circumstances of the case (FSMA, s 228(2)). The ombudsman is not required to apply the rules of the English common law governing, for example, claims in negligence (*R (Heather Moor & Edgcomb Limited) v Financial Ombudsman Service* [2008] EWCA Civ 642).

[270] **3.09** above

[271] For the use of autonomous concepts within the Regulation framework, see **3.05–3.11** above.

[272] In the French text, '*obligations non contractuelles*'. In the German text, '*außertragliche Schuldverältnisse*'.

Negative Content of 'Non-Contractual Obligations' I—Obligations, not Status[273]

3.88 Professors Giuliano and Lagarde, in their report on the Rome Convention, recognized that:[274]

> [S]ince the Convention is concerned only with the law applicable to contractual obligations, property rights and intellectual property are not covered by these provisions. An Article in the original preliminary draft had expressly so provided.[275] However, the Group considered that such a provision would be superfluous in the present text, especially as this would have involved the need to recapitulate the differences existing as between the various legal systems of the Member States of the Community.

3.89 The Rome Convention, it may be noted, also contained specific exceptions concerning 'questions involving the status or legal capacity of natural persons'[276] and 'questions governed by the law of companies and other bodies corporate or unincorporate such as the creation, . . . legal capacity, internal organisation or winding up of companies and other bodies corporate or unincorporate'.[277] Although it contains no express provision in the same terms,[278] it is clear that the Rome II Regulation is (subject to one arguable exception[279]) concerned only with the law applicable to non-contractual obligations, and not with the law applicable to matters of status, even if those matters arise in the course of the determination of obligations falling within the Regulation's scope.

3.90 Rules governing status may concern the legal attributes of (a) a natural or legal person, (b) the relationship between two or more persons, or (c) the relationship between a person and a thing. All of these categories of legal rule fall outside the Regulation's scope, but the third (which may, for convenience, be described as concerning matters of property) is perhaps the most important for present purposes. For example, if under the law applicable by virtue of the Regulation one of the requirements of a

---

[273] Also A Rushworth and A Scott, n 180 above, 301–3.

[274] Giuliano & Lagarde Report (OJ C282, 10 [31.10.1980]).

[275] Preliminary draft convention on the law applicable to contractual and non-contractual obligations (Commission document XIV/398/72), Art 9, referring only to the rules concerning the law applicable to contractual obligations.

[276] Rome Convention, Art 1(2)(a).

[277] Rome Convention, Art 1(2)(e).

[278] The exclusion for matters of company law in Art 1(2)(d) refers to 'non-contractual obligations arising out of the law of companies and other bodies corporate or unincorporated'. There is no specific exclusion of questions involving status or legal capacity of natural persons.

[279] **3.102** below.

non-contractual obligation is that the claimant must be the 'owner' of an item of tangible property with which the claim is concerned, the question whether the relationship between the claimant and the thing has the attributes necessary to qualify as 'ownership' under the law applicable to the non-contractual obligation falls outside the scope of the Regulation and must be determined by reference to the forum's rules of applicable law for property issues.[280]

That conclusion accords with Art 295 of the EC Treaty, which provides: **3.91**

This Treaty shall in no way prejudice the rules in Member States governing the system of property ownership.

Although the Court of Justice has held that Art 295 does not exclude all Community influence in relation to the exercise of national property rights, the power of Member States to define the rules governing the system of property ownership is unqualified.[281] This exclusive competence may be thought to extend to rules of applicable law relating to the acquisition and disposition of property rights.

Even so, it is no easy matter to separate matters of 'obligation' from mat- **3.92** ters of 'status'. Two types of problem arise. First, it may be argued that, in a given situation, a party is relying exclusively or predominantly on a particular status (most obviously, a 'proprietary right') so that, in terms of characterization, there is no recognizable 'obligation' or any 'obligation' should be treated as wholly subordinate to the question of status (according to the principle *accessorium sequitur principale*[282]). Secondly, if a given situation is characterized as involving both matters of 'obligation' and 'matters of status', the outer limits of the Rome II Regulation must be defined in order to identify the extent to which the forum's rules of applicable law for status matters remain applicable.

---

[280] For earlier English cases raising questions of this kind, see *Macmillan Inc v Bishopsgate Investment Trust plc (No 3)* [1996] 1 WLR 407 (EWCA); *Gotha City v Sotheby's* (1998) The Times, 18 October 1998 (EWHC); *Glencore International AG v Metro Trading International Inc* [2001] 1 Lloyd's Rep 284 (EWHC); *Kuwait Airways Corp v Iraqi Airways Co (Nos 4 and 5)* [2002] UKHL 19; [2002] 2 AC 883; *Islamic Republic of Iran v The Barakat Galleries Ltd* [2007] EWCA Civ 1374.
[281] Joined Cases 56/64 and 58/64, *Consten and Grundig v Commission* [1966] ECR 299, 345; Case C-491/01, *R v Secretary of State for Health, ex parte British American Tobacco (Investments) Ltd* [2002] ECR I-11453, para 147.
[282] For a case in which the ECJ invoked this principle applying one of the rules of special jurisdiction in the 1968 Brussels Convention, see Case C-266/85, *Shenevai v Kreischer* [1987] ECR 239, para 19.

3.93 As to the first point, the editors of Dicey, Morris & Collins point out that:[283]

> [I]t must, obviously, not be assumed that a claim that would be characterised as tortious in English law will necessarily be characterised as arising out of tort for the purposes of the [Rome II] Regulation. English domestic law treats claims for interference with property rights as belonging to the law of tort (eg conversion), whereas civil law systems often treat such claims as belonging to the law of property (*rei vindicatio*).

3.94 Although the editors express no concluded view either way on this question of characterization under the Regulation, the English tort of conversion should be considered to fall within the category of 'obligation', and within scope, as the claim rests not only on an assertion of the claimant's proprietary entitlement to a thing (i.e. a matter of status) but on an act of deliberate dealing with that thing in a manner inconsistent with that entitlement.[284] The essence of the claimant's action, therefore, is not to vindicate his proprietary entitlement, which may not be in doubt, but instead to establish the defendant's responsibility for the consequences of his own conduct in dealing with the claimant's property. It will be argued below that this element of responsibility for conduct or for an event attributable to the defendant is the principal identifying feature of the concept of 'tort/delict' under the Regulation.[285] In this connection, it may also be noted (although it does not appear necessary for the conclusion suggested above) that the main remedy available to a claimant in a conversion case is damages, whether standing alone or as an alternative (at the election of the defendant) to delivery up of the thing to which his claim relates.[286] Moreover, the editors of Dicey themselves suggest, in their most recent commentary on the pre-existing English rules of applicable law that:[287]

> Whether the right has been acquired depends on the *lex situs*, but whether it is protected in the English court by a claim for damages depends on the law applicable to the tort. Thus, no act can be an act of conversion unless it is regarded as such by the applicable law of the tort.

3.95 On the other hand, the editors' apparent assumption that an action such as the civilian *actio rei vindicatio* should be treated as falling outside the scope of the Regulation can be supported if, on closer examination, it appears

[283] Sir L Collins et al. (eds), *Dicey, Morris & Collins: The Conflict of Laws* (14th edn, 2006), 1st supplement, para S35-177.
[284] A M Dugdale and M A Jones (eds), *Clerk & Lindsell on Torts* (19th edn, 2006), para 17-07.
[285] **3.243–3.246**.
[286] Torts (Interference with Goods) Act 1977, s 3.
[287] Dicey, Morris & Collins, main work, para 35-027.

that the claimant's claim rests wholly or substantially upon the assertion by him of his proprietary entitlement to the thing, and not on establishing the defendant's responsibility for conduct or another event. That conclusion may be easier to reach if the claimant's sole or main remedy is the recovery of the thing itself, and not damages. Accordingly, although the tort of conversion and the *actio rei vindicatio* may serve similar protective functions within the legal systems of which they form part, it does not follow that they must be characterized in the same way under the Regulation.

The relationship between 'obligation' and 'property' under the Rome II **3.96** Regulation was addressed by the Swedish delegation in its initial response to the Commission Proposal. Advocating the express exclusion of 'property rights' from the scope of the Regulation, the delegation commented:[288]

To lawyers from countries outside the Roman law tradition, such as Sweden, a property right could be seen as a non-contractual obligation, i.e. a good bought with a retention of title clause must, under the laws of several Member States, if sold to a third person, be returned to the holder of the title (e.g. a bank). The duty of the third person to return the good to the holder of the title could be considered to be a non-contractual obligation and thus one that is within the scope of the proposed Regulation.

What is more, the Rome Convention and the proposed Rome II Regulation are often depicted as put together having the same scope as the Brussels I Regulation. In the Commission's Explanatory Memorandum,[289] . . . , it is stated that 'the Brussels I Regulation, the Rome Convention and the Regulation proposed here constitute a coherent set of instruments covering the general field of private international law in matters of civil and commercial obligations'. As we all know, property rights are within the scope of the Brussels I Regulation (see e.g. Art. 22) and the Swedish version of the Memorandum speaks of *'förpliktelser'*, which is a much more general term than 'obligations'.

Some guidance as to the delineation between 'obligation' and 'property' **3.97** in the Rome II Regulation can be derived from the case law of the ECJ concerning Art 16 of the Brussels Convention, the predecessor to Art 22 of the Brussels I Regulation to which the Swedish delegation referred in the passage quoted above. Art 16(1) refers to 'proceedings which have as their object rights *in rem* in immovable property', and confers exclusive jurisdiction with respect to such proceedings on the courts for the place where the immovable property is situated. In its case law, the Court has emphasized the need to give Art 16(1) a narrow definition in order to avoid

[288] Council document 9009/04 ADD 8 [18.5.2004], 3.
[289] Commission Proposal, 8.

depriving the parties of the choice of jurisdiction which is otherwise available to them under the Convention, having regard to the purpose of Art 16 in ensuring that the courts designated as having exclusive jurisdiction are best placed to determine the case.[290] Those reasons are not relevant in considering the material scope of the Rome II Regulation. Nevertheless, particularly given that the exclusion of 'property' from the Regulation is not express but instead is implicit in the term 'obligation', a narrow definition of the former concept seems equally justified in order to ensure the effectiveness of the Regulation in achieving its objective of increasing predictability in the outcome of litigation. That approach would also promote consistency between the Rome II Regulation and the Brussels I Regulation, the successor regime to the Brussels Convention.[291] In the circumstances, although there is no necessary correlation, it may be that the ECJ would seek to draw inspiration from its Brussels Convention case law in considering whether particular claims relating to property rights fall outside the scope of the Rome II Regulation.

3.98 Three cases are of particular interest, as follows:

1. In *Reichert (No 1)*,[292] the ECJ held that an action brought by a creditor in a French court seeking to have a contract of sale, or gift, of immovable property by his debtor to a third party rendered ineffective (*action paulienne*) fell outside the scope of Art 16(1). Having regard to its objectives, the ECJ concluded that Art 16(1) 'does not encompass all actions concerning rights *in rem* in immovable property but only those which both come within the scope of the Brussels Convention and are actions which seek to determine the extent, content, ownership or possession of immovable property or the existence of other rights *in rem* therein and to provide the holders of those rights with the protection of the powers which attach to their interest'.[293] In contrast, the *action paulienne* was, in the Court's view:

[B]ased on the creditor's personal claim against the debtor and seeks to protect whatever security he may have over the debtor's estate. If successful, its effect is to render the transaction whereby the debtor has effected a disposition in fraud of the creditor's rights ineffective as against the creditor alone. The hearing of such an action, moreover, does not involve the assessment of facts or the application of

---

[290] Case C-115/88, *Reichert v Dresdner Bank AG* [1990] ECR I-27, paras 9–10; Case C-343/04, *Land Oberösterreich v ČEZ* [2006] ECR I-4557, paras 27–8.

[291] Regulation, Recital (7), discussed at **3.34** above.

[292] *Reichert v Dresdner Bank*, n 290 above. For discussion of the second ECJ decision in the same case concerning the scope of Art 5(3) of the 1968 Brussels Convention, see **3.235–3.239** and **3.250–3.257** below.

[293] Ibid, para 11.

rules and practices of the *locus rei sitae* in such a way as to justify conferring jurisdiction on a court of the State in which the property is situated.[294]

Consequently, such an action, brought by a creditor to set aside a contract of sale of immovable property entered into, or a donation thereof made, by his debtor, did not fall within the scope of Article 16(1).[295]

2. In *Webb v Webb*,[296] the reference concerned an action before an English court for a declaration that the defendant held property as trustee for the claimant, his father, and for an order requiring him to vest ownership in the claimant. The ECJ held that the claim fell outside Art 16(1). Having referred to its decision in *Reichert (No 1)*, the Court stated that 'it follows that it is not sufficient, for Article 16(1) to apply, that a right *in rem* in immovable property be involved in the action or that the action have a link with immovable property: the action must be based on a right *in rem* and not on a right *in personam*, save in the case of the exception concerning tenancies of immovable property'.[297] Applying this reasoning, the Court concluded that:

The aim of the proceedings before the national court is to obtain a declaration that the son holds the flat for the exclusive benefit of the father and that in that capacity he is under a duty to execute the documents necessary to convey ownership of the flat to the father. The father does not claim that he already enjoys rights directly relating to the property which are enforceable against the whole world, but seeks only to assert rights as against the son. Consequently, his action is not an action *in rem* within the meaning of Article 16(1) of the Convention but an action *in personam*.

3. The third case, *Land Oberösterreich v ČEZ as*,[298] concerned an action before an Austrian court brought by an Austrian province, as the owner of land, against a Czech power company seeking to bring an end to nuisance caused by radiation emanating from the defendant's nuclear power station. Again, the ECJ held that the action fell outside Art 16(1). The ECJ noted that authors of the Schlosser Report[299] 'had no difficulty in clarifying that actions for damages based on infringement of rights *in rem* or on damage to property in which rights *in rem* exist do not fall within the scope of Article 16(1)(a) since the existence and content of such rights *in rem*,

[294] Ibid, para 12.
[295] Ibid, para 14.
[296] Case C-294/92 [1994] ECR I-1717.
[297] Ibid, para 14.
[298] Case C-343/04 [2006] ECR I-4557.
[299] Report on the Convention for the Accession of Denmark, Ireland and the United Kingdom to the 1968 Brussels Convention, OJ C59, 120 (para 163) [5.3.1979].

usually rights of ownership, are of only marginal significance in that context'.[300] Turning to the claim advanced by the claimant in the case before it, the Court concluded:[301]

> An action for cessation of a nuisance, possibly preventive in nature, such as that at issue in the main proceedings, does not constitute a dispute having as its object rights *in rem* in immovable property either. It is true that the basis of such an action is the interference with a right *in rem* in immovable property, but the real and immovable nature of that right is, in this context, of only marginal significance. As ČEZ and the Commission point out, the real and immovable nature of the right at issue does not have a decisive influence on the issues to be determined in the dispute in the main proceedings, which would not have been raised in substantially different terms if the right whose protection is sought against the alleged nuisance were of a different type, such as, for example, the right to physical integrity or a personal right. Just like the action at issue in the main proceedings, such actions essentially seek an order that the person causing the interference, actual or potential, to a right, for example by failing to comply with current generally recognised technological standards, put an end to it.

3.99 These cases suggest that, in considering whether a particular claim concerns matters of 'property' falling outside the Rome II Regulation, it will be relevant to consider (a) whether the 'right' on which the claimant relies specifically concerns the defendant (or a limited number of persons including the defendant), (b) whether any question as to the claimant's proprietary entitlement has a 'decisive influence' on the issues to be considered, and (c) the nature of the remedy sought. As to (a), if the claim is premised on an act or other event for which the defendant, in particular, is said to be responsible, it should not fall outside the Regulation simply because the claimant's entitlement to particular property will be in issue. As to (b), the same conclusion will follow if the claimant's proprietary entitlement is only one of a number of issues that the court will be required to determine. As to (c), the same conclusion may be thought to be more likely to follow if the remedy sought is damages or a mandatory order other than one requiring that the defendant deliver up property to which the claimant has established a proprietary entitlement.

3.100 For the avoidance of doubt, it is not suggested that any claim that is not a 'property' claim in the sense described above will fall within the scope of the Rome II Regulation. Indeed, the three cases discussed above emphasize that this is only the first stage in analysing the Regulation's scope. In *Reichert*, the ECJ in a later decision held that the *action paulienne* fell outside Art 5(3) of the 1963 Brussels Convention, concerning matters relating

---

[300] *Land Oberösterreich v ČEZ*, n 298 above, para 33.
[301] Ibid, para 34.

to tort, delict, or quasi-delict. In light of that decision, it is unclear whether an action of that kind is based on a 'non-contractual obligation' falling within the scope of the Rome II Regulation. That issue will be returned to below.[302] *Webb v Webb* concerned a trust created voluntarily, with the result that the claim would fall within the scope of the exclusion in Art 1(2)(e) of the Rome II Regulation, also discussed below.[303] Finally, the claim in *ČEZ* concerned nuclear radiation, probably falling within the scope of the exclusion in Art 1(2)(f).[304] These two cases strongly suggest, however, that similar claims (based, for example, on a non-voluntary trust or nuisance caused by smoke emissions) will lie within the material scope of the Rome II Regulation.

As to the second point, concerning the limits of the Regulation's rules **3.101** of applicable law and their relationship to rules of applicable law concerning matters of status, it is important that Member State courts should ensure that the law applicable under the Regulation defines the non-contractual obligation, with particular reference to the matters set out in Art 15, and that any residual reference to the forum's rules of applicable law concerning matters of status does not undermine the effectiveness of the Regulation's rules. Accordingly, although questions of status will normally fall to be determined by reference to rules of applicable law other than those contained in the Regulation, it is the law applicable to the relevant non-contractual obligation under the Regulation that must determine whether the recognition of a particular status satisfies any condition necessary to confer on the claimant, or to impose on the defendant, a non-contractual obligation. As the editors of Dicey, Morris & Collins note in their commentary on the pre-existing English rules of applicable law:[305]

The claimant must, however, show that the title acquired under the *lex situs* gives him a right which is protected by the law applicable to the tort and he cannot, it is submitted, rely on the *lex situs* with the object of showing that anything less than this right suffices to succeed, e.g. with a claim for conversion.

The Regulation touches on questions of status in four of its provisions. **3.102** First, Art 1(2)(a) excludes from the scope of the Regulation 'non-contractual obligations arising out of family relationships and relationships deemed by the law applicable to such relationships to have comparable effects'. Recital (10) makes clear that the reference to 'relationships having

---

[302] **3.249–3.258**.
[303] **3.173–3.207**.
[304] **3.208–3.216** below.
[305] Dicey, Morris & Collins, para 35-027.

comparable effects' to marriage and other family relationships should be determined in accordance with the law of the Member State in which the court is seised, including (presumably) its rules of private international law.[306] Secondly, Art 8 of the Regulation contains rules governing the law applicable to non-contractual obligations 'arising from an infringement of an intellectual property right'. Those rules are discussed in **Chapter 8** below. For present purposes, it suffices to note that the specific references in Arts 8(1) and (2) to 'infringement' assume the existence of an intellectual property right. Particularly when read together with the list of matters governed by the applicable law set out in Art 15, these references support the view that issues relating to the validity, ownership, and (if relevant) registration of intellectual property rights fall outside the Regulation's scope.[307] That accords with the view taken by Professors Giuliano and Lagarde in relation to the Rome Convention.[308] Thirdly, in relation to Art 9 of the Regulation (industrial action), Recital (28) emphasizes that the special rule contained in that Article is 'without prejudice to the legal status of trade unions or of the representative organisations as provided for in the law of the Member States'. Fourthly, Recital (12) makes clear that the law applicable should also govern the question of the capacity to incur liability in tort/delict. In the first three cases, the text of the Regulation seems consistent with the view taken above, that matters of status fall outside its subject matter scope. The fourth, which may be contrasted with the position under the Rome Convention,[309] must be taken as a specific qualification to that proposition, explicable on the basis that questions of capacity to incur non-contractual liability are an integral and inseparable part of the rules imposing responsibility on the defendant.[310]

3.103 The right of an individual to use a name is a matter of personal status falling outside the Regulation.[311]

---

[306] **3.150–3.151** below.

[307] M Pertagas, 'Intellectual Property and Choice of Law Rules' in A Malatesta (ed), *The Unification of Choice of Law Rules on Torts and Other Non-Contractual Obligations in Europe* (2006), 238–9.

[308] Text to n 274 above. The French delegation sought a specific Recital in the Rome II Regulation to put this point beyond doubt (see Council document 13074/04 [5.10.2004], 7).

[309] Rome Convention, Arts 1(2)(a) and 11.

[310] **14.09–14.12** below.

[311] Commission Proposal, 17. For the relationship between EC law and private international law rules concerning the right to use a name, see Case C-353/06, *Grunkin and Paul v Standesamt Stadt Niebüll* [2008] ECR I-0000, Opinion of Adv Gen Sharpston (24 April 2008) and Judgment of 14 October 2008.

Negative Content of 'Non-Contractual Obligations' II—Excluding 'Contractual Obligations'

Introduction

Despite the absence in the Rome II Regulation of any definition of a 'non- **3.104** contractual obligation', it can be confidently stated that the category is intended to be complementary to the category of 'contractual obligation' deployed in the Rome Convention and its successor, the Rome I Regulation, and that there is no overlap between the instruments dealing with 'contractual' and 'non-contractual' obligations. Thus, 'contractual obligations' fall outside the scope of the Rome II Regulation. That is clear not only from the choice of terminology to match that in the Rome Convention, but also from Recital (7) of the Regulation, which confirms that the substantive scope of the Rome II Regulation should be consistent with the instruments dealing with the law applicable to contractual obligations. It also accords with the approach taken by the Court of Justice in defining the relationship between Art 5(1) (matters relating to a contract) and Art 5(3) (matters relating to tort, delict, and quasi-delict) of the Brussels Convention. In *Kalfelis v Schröder*, the ECJ recognized that the latter category excluded any matter falling within the former, as follows:[312]

In order to ensure uniformity in all the Member States, it must be recognized that the concept of 'matters relating to tort, delict and quasi-delict' covers all actions which seek to establish the liability of a defendant and *which are not related to a 'contract' within the meaning of Article 5(1)*.

In *Kalfelis*, the claimant brought claims against his contractual counter- **3.105** party (a) for breach of a contractual obligation to provide information, (b) in tort, for damage caused by conduct *contra bonos mores*, and (c) in unjust enrichment, to recover sums paid under futures contracts claimed not to be binding. The Court concluded that:[313]

It must therefore be recognized that a court which has jurisdiction under Article 5(3) over an action insofar as it is based on tort or delict does not have jurisdiction over that action insofar as it is not so based.

---

[312] Case 189/87, *Kalfelis v Bankhaus Schröder Münchmeyer, Hengst & Co* [1988] ECR 5565, para 17 (emphasis added). Also Case C-261/90, *Reichert v Dresdner Bank AG* [1992] ECR I-2149, para 16; Case C-51/97, *Réunion Europeénne SA v Spliethoff's Bebrachtingskantoor BV* [1998] ECR I-6511, para 22; Case C-96/00, *Rudolf Gabriel* [2002] ECR I-6367, para 33; Case C-167/00, *Verein für Konsumenteninformation v Henkel* [2002] ECR I-8111, para 36; Case C-334/00, *Fonderie Officine Meccaniche Tacconi SpA v Heinrich Wagner Sinto Maschinenfabrik GmbH* [2002] ECR I-7357, para 21; Case C-27/02, *Engler v Janus Versand GmbH* [2005] ECR I-481, para 29. For further discussion of these cases, see **3.234–3.242** below.

[313] [1988] ECR 5565, para 19. Compare the reasoning of Adv Gen Darmon, ibid, Opinion, paras 25–30.

The Court did not, however, attempt to characterize the claimant's individual claims for the purposes of the Convention, leaving that task to the national court.

The concept of a 'contractual obligation'[314]

3.106 *Relationship with the Rome I Regime*   Without any decision of the ECJ concerning the subject matter scope of the Rome I Regime,[315] it is with diminishing confidence that one turns to the task of separating 'contractual' from 'non-contractual' obligations. In the explanatory memorandum accompanying its Proposal, the Commission pointed out that:[316]

> [T]he demarcation line between contractual obligations and obligations based on tort or delict is not identical in all the Member States, and there may be doubts as to which instrument the Rome Convention or the proposed Regulation should be applied in a given dispute, for example in the event of pre-contractual liability, of *culpa in contrahendo* or of actions by creditors to have certain transactions by their debtors declared void as prejudicial to their interests. The Court of Justice, in actions under Articles 5(1) and (3) of the Brussels Convention, has already had occasion to rule that tort/delict cases are residual in relation to contract cases, which must be defined in strict terms. It will no doubt refine its analysis when interpreting the proposed Regulation.

3.107 The report of Professors Giuliano and Lagarde on the Rome Convention provides little guidance as to what constitutes a 'contractual obligation' for the purposes of that instrument. The report suggests that (1) most of the delegations involved in negotiations leading to the Convention favoured the view that gifts arising from a contract fell within its scope,[317] (2) continental institutions that correspond to the English trust will normally fall within scope because they are contractual in origin,[318] and (3) unilateral acts intended to have legal effect and which are not connected with a contract (for example, a recognition of a debt not arising under a contract, or a unilateral act creating, transferring, or extinguishing a right *in rem*) fall outside scope.[319]

---

[314] Also A Briggs, *The Conflict of Laws* (2nd edn, 2008), 158–61; T M Yeo, *Choice of Law for Equitable Doctrines* (2004), ch 7; A Rushworth and A Scott, n 180 above, 299–301.

[315] The Brussels Protocol, which conferred on the ECJ power to give rulings on the interpretation of the Rome Convention, finally entered into force in 2005. No case has yet been decided, although the Dutch Supreme Court referred certain questions relating to Art 4 of the Convention in March 2008 (Case C-133/08, *Intercontainer Interfrigo (ICF) SC v MIC Operations BV*).

[316] Commission Proposal, 8.

[317] Giuliano & Lagarde Report (OJ C282, 10 [31.10.1980]).

[318] Ibid, 13.

[319] Ibid, 29.

It is, however, clear from the terms of the Rome Convention and the corre- **3.108** sponding provisions of the Rome I Regulation that their (vertical) material scope extends to cover matters that might otherwise be characterized as non-contractual under the Rome II Regulation, including certain claims to recover payments made under a void or terminated contract.[320] Under Art 10(1)(e) of the Rome Convention,[321] the law applicable to a contract under the Convention shall govern 'the consequences of the nullity of contract'. This, as the Giuliano & Lagarde Report makes clear, covers 'refunds which the parties have to pay each other subsequent to a finding of nullity of the contract subject to the applicable law'.[322] In the negotiations leading to the conclusion of the Convention, some delegations objected to this extension on the ground that, under their legal systems, the consequences of nullity are non-contractual in nature. The majority were nonetheless in favour of extending the scope of the Convention this far, although provision was made in Art 22(1)(b) for Contracting States who objected to this to enter a reservation. The UK, along with Italy, exercised this opt-out when it rati- fied the Convention. The basis of its decision to do so was that 'under English law the right to recover money paid under a void contract is part of the law of restitution and not the law of contract'.[323] That opt-out remains in force for the Rome Convention. For the purposes of the Rome II Regulation and the Rome I Regulation (which contains no opt-out), United Kingdom courts must now accept that such claims involve or con- cern 'contractual obligations'. Unjust enrichment claims arising from the nullity of contracts concluded before 17 December 2009, the date of appli- cation of the Rome I Regulation,[324] will continue to be governed by the applicable common law rules. The Commission's apparent view that the provisions of the Rome II Regulation would fill the gap in those Member States that have chosen to exercise the opt-out from Art 10(1)(e) of the Rome Convention[325] cannot be accepted: the concept of a 'non-contractual obligation' within the Rome II Regulation must be given a consistent and uniform meaning in every Member State.

Even within the Member States that exercised the right to opt-out of Art **3.109** 10(1)(e) of the Rome Convention, some claims that would ordinarily be

---

[320] See also the discussion at **14.38–14.40** below as to whether the Rome I Regime deter- mines the validity and effectiveness of assignments of rights to enforce non-contractual obligations.

[321] Rome I Regulation, Art 12(1)(e).

[322] Giuliano & Lagarde Report (OJ C282, 33 [31.10.1980]).

[323] Lord Fraser of Carmyllie in Hansard (Series 6), HL, vol 513, col 1271 (12 December 1989). See Contracts (Applicable Law) Act 1990, s 2(2).

[324] Rome I Regulation, Art 28.

[325] Commission Proposal, 13.

classified as restitutionary claims under English law fall within the scope of the Rome Convention and its successor Regulation[326] and beyond the reach of the Rome II Regulation. These included claims to recover payments made under a valid contract subsequently terminated for breach[327] or frustrated (for example) by impossibility or supervening illegality.[328] The editors of Dicey, Morris & Collins also suggest that claims arising from the mistaken performance of a valid contract fall within the scope of Art 10(1)(b) of the Rome Convention[329] ('performance').[330] That view, however, seems questionable, as in such cases the claim does not concern 'performance' of the contract but its antithesis, i.e. a transfer of value that was not contractually required. Moreover, Art 10 of the Rome II Regulation provides specific rules for non-contractual obligations arising out of 'unjust enrichment, including payment of amounts wrongly received'. As the primary rule in Art 10(1) refers to 'a relationship existing between the parties, such as one arising out of a contract', this appears to have been specifically designed to cover these situations. Claims to recover contractual payments made in error should, therefore, be seen as 'non-contractual', falling within the scope of the Rome II Regulation.

3.110 *'Matters relating to a contract' under the Brussels I Regime* Further guidance as to the concept of 'contractual obligations' and their relationship with 'non-contractual obligations' can be gathered from the case law of the ECJ concerning the special jurisdiction of Member State courts under Art 5(1) and (3) of the Brussels Convention. It is, nevertheless, important to proceed with caution in drawing analogies with the Brussels I Regime on these issues.[331] In particular, it should be noted that Art 5(1) of both the Brussels Convention and its successor Regulation refer not to 'contractual obligations' but to 'matters relating to a contract'.[332] Correspondingly,

---

[326] Dicey, Morris & Collins, 34-006. The suggestion in the 1st supplement to that work (para 34–014, at 167) that a claim for recovery of payments on the basis that there has been a failure of consideration after termination for breach of contract falls within Art 10(1) of the Rome II Regulation is difficult to reconcile with this statement in the main work.

[327] Falling within Rome Convention, Art 10(1)(c) as one of 'the consequences of breach'. Also Rome I Regulation, Art 12(1)(c) referring to 'the consequences of total or partial breach of obligations', which if anything makes the point more clearly.

[328] Falling within Rome Convention, Art 10(1)(d) (Rome I Regulation, Art 12(1)(d)) as concerning 'the various ways of extinguishing obligations', or within Art 10(1)(b) (Regulation, Art 12(1)(b)) as concerning 'performance'.

[329] Rome I Regulation, Art 12(1)(b).

[330] Dicey, Morris & Collins, para 34-006.

[331] Zheng Tang, 'The Interrelationship of European Jurisdiction and Choice of Law in Contract' (2008) 4 J Priv Int L 35, 36–41.

[332] In the French text, *'en matière contractuelle'*.

Art 5(3) of both the Brussels Convention and the Brussels I Regulation refer not to 'non-contractual obligations'[333] but to 'matters relating to tort, delict or quasi-delict'.[334] Finally, other than in relation to criminal proceedings,[335] the Brussels I Regime does not contain special rules of jurisdiction specifically corresponding to the rules of applicable law in Arts 10–12 of the Rome II Regulation which concern non-contractual matters treated as falling outside the concept of tort/delict. Accordingly, the Brussels I Regime, on the one hand, and the Rome I Regime and Rome II Regulation, on the other, use different terminology for different purposes and the relationship between contractual and extra-contractual matters under the two regimes will almost certainly not be precisely the same. Further, the characterization of a matter as, or as not, relating to 'tort, delict or quasi-delict' under the Brussels I Regime will not necessarily be reflected in its characterization as concerning a non-contractual obligation 'arising out of a tort/delict' within Art 4 of the Rome II Regulation.

As to the relationship between these two provisions of special jurisdiction **3.111** in the Brussels I Regime, it has already been noted that the ECJ has emphasized that the categories of 'matters relating to a contract' and 'matters relating to tort, delict or quasi-delict' are mutually exclusive.[336] In *Martin Peters v ZNAV*,[337] the Court confirmed that the concept of 'matters relating to a contract' in Art 5(1) should not be interpreted simply as referring to the national law of one or other of the States concerned but should instead be given an autonomous meaning based on the system of the Convention.[338] More significantly, for present purposes, the ECJ held that a relationship (in that case, membership of a Dutch unincorporated association) that 'creates between its members close links of the same kind as those which are created between the parties to a contract' may be regarded

---

[333] The Portuguese language version refers to '*em matéria extracontractual*' and the Danish to '*i sager om erstatning uden for kontrakt*'. This wording has been criticized as 'too wide' (U Magnus and P Mankowski, *The Brussels I Regulation* (2007), Art 5, para 194.

[334] In the French text, '*en matière délictuelle or quasi délictuelle*'.

[335] Brussels Convention and Brussels I Regulation, Art 5(4), which refer to 'a civil claim for *damages or restitution*'.

[336] *Kalfelis v Schröder*, text to n 312 above.

[337] Case 34/82, *Martin Peters Bauunternehmung GmbH v Zuid Nederlandse Aannemers Vereniging* [1983] ECR 987. Also Case 9/87, *SPRL Arcado v SA Haviland* [1988] ECR 1539, paras 10–15.

[338] *Martin Peters*, ibid, paras 9–10.

as contractual for the purposes of Art 5(1),[339] even thought it was not so regarded under Dutch law.[340]

3.112 Subsequently, in *Handte v TMS*,[341] the Court was asked to rule whether an action between a sub-buyer of goods and the manufacturer relating to defects in those goods or to their unsuitability for their intended purpose was a 'matter relating to a contract'. The action was based on French law, which (at that time) characterized the sub-buyer's claim as contractual in nature, the theoretical justification offered for this being that the intermediate supplier transmits to the sub-buyer his contractual rights against the manufacturer or the person who sold to him.[342] The ECJ did not consider that characterization under national, domestic law was decisive.[343] Having considered the purpose of the special rules of jurisdiction contained in Art 5 of the Brussels Convention, the Court concluded:[344]

It follows that the phrase 'matters relating to a contract', as used in Article 5(1) of the Convention, is not to be understood as covering a situation in which there is no obligation freely assumed by one party towards another.

Where a sub-buyer of goods purchased from an intermediate seller brings an action against the manufacturer for damages on the ground that the goods are not in conformity, it must be observed that there is no contractual relationship between the sub-buyer and the manufacturer because the latter has not undertaken any contractual obligation towards the former.

Furthermore, particularly where there is a chain of international contracts, the parties' contractual obligations may vary from contract to contract, so that the contractual rights which the sub-buyer can enforce against his immediate seller will not necessarily be the same as those which the manufacturer will have accepted in his relationship with the first buyer.

3.113 It is important to note that the Court does not go as far as saying that there will be a 'matter relating to contract' if there exists an obligation 'freely assumed by one party towards another'. The use of the double negative in

---

[339] Ibid, para 13.

[340] Ibid, Opinion of Adv Gen Mancini, para 5, contrasting the position under Dutch law to that prevailing in almost all of the other Contracting States. The Advocate General concluded (ibid) that 'the prevailing tendency of the legal systems of Community States is to consider that both the act by which an association is created and the relationships between the members and the association are governed by the law of contract'.

[341] Case C-26/91, *Jakob Handte & Co GmbH v Traitements Mécano-chimiques des Surfaces SA* [1990] ECR I-3967.

[342] Ibid, Opinion of Adv Gen Jacobs, para 20. Also ibid, paras 17–19, 21 contrasting the position under French, Belgian, and Luxembourg law with that under the law of other Contracting States.

[343] Ibid, Judgment, para 10.

[344] Ibid, paras 15–17.

the first quoted paragraph appears significant and suggests that something more is required to constitute a 'contract' for these purposes. In his opinion in *Handte v TMS*, Adv Gen Jacobs suggested the following basis of distinction between contract and delict:[345]

The distinction between contractual and delictual liability is an old one and doubtless exists in all developed legal systems. Contractual liability may be defined as civil liability for a failure to perform an obligation that one person owes to another by virtue of an agreement entered into by the parties. Delictual liability may be defined as civil liability for a failure to perform an obligation which the law imposes independently of any agreement between the parties, e.g. an obligation to exercise reasonable care when driving a motor vehicle.

Moreover, the Court's reasoning, quoted above, confirms its willingness **3.114** to look through the theoretical explanation given by the national court for the sub-buyer's claim to identify what it saw as the 'true' basis of the claim. In the penultimate paragraph of its judgment,[346] it referred to the manufacturer's lack of knowledge of the buyer's identity and to the fact that 'in the great majority of Contracting States the liability of a manufacturer towards a sub-buyer for defects in the goods sold is not regarded as being of a contractual nature'.[347] Accordingly, no doubt fortified by the treatment of similar claims in other Member States, the Court appeared to treat the transfer of contractual rights under French law as a fiction and ignored it in characterizing the claim under the Brussels I Regime.[348] Similar reasoning could be used, for example, to resist any argument based on the theory that English common law claims to recover payments made under a mistake were based on an 'implied contract' between the parties. That theory has now been identified and rejected as a fiction, revealing the true basis of claims of this kind as resting on the defendant's unjust enrichment.[349]

---

[345] Ibid, Opinion, para 16. For a definition of contract focused on 'agreement', see C von Bar et al. (eds), *Principles, Definitions and Model Rules of European Private Law: Draft Common Frame of Reference* (2008), Book II, Art I:101 available at <http://www.law-net.eu/en_index.htm>. ('A contract is an agreement which gives rise to, or is intended to give rise to, a binding relationship or which has, or is intended to have, some other legal effect. It is a bilateral or multilateral judicial act.')

[346] Ibid, Judgment, para 20.

[347] Ibid, Judgment, para 20. Also, Opinion, para 38, referring to the Product Liability Directive which, in the Advocate General's view, 'in effect requires the laws of the Member States to treat actions falling within its scope as in substance delictual, notably by precluding any contractual derogation'.

[348] Cf A Briggs and P Rees, *Civil Jurisdiction and Judgments* (4th edn, 2005), para 2.125, footnote 681. It appears (ibid, footnote 680) that the French courts have also since abandoned the 'contractual' analysis of the sub-buyer's claim.

[349] *Westdeutsche Landesbank Girozentrale v Islington LBC* [1996] AC 669 (UKHL).

3.115 The significance that the Court appeared to attach to the manufacturer's lack of knowledge of the sub-buyer's identity is, however, puzzling.[350] Although the manufacturer in *Handte* may not have been aware of the sub-buyer's purchase of the product, it is submitted that the fact the identity of a person claiming as assignee or as successor to the contractual rights of another may be unknown to the obligor before proceedings are brought should not prevent his claim from being characterized as 'contractual' for these purposes, provided that the assignment or succession is genuine and not merely a fictional device designed to secure particular legal consequences. The obligation owed by the original contracting party to the assignee or successor in such cases is the obligation that he freely assumed to his original counterparty.[351]

3.116 The tests proposed by the ECJ and the Advocate General in *Handte* are relatively straightforward to apply to situations in which there is no direct relationship, contractual or otherwise, between the parties to the action or their predecessors. Thus, in *Verein für Konsumenteninformation v Henkel*, an action by a consumer protection association to prevent a trader from using unfair contract terms in his dealings with customers was held not to constitute a 'matter relating to a contract' under Art 5(1) of the Brussels Convention.[352] In such cases, the trader's obligation must equally be treated as 'non-contractual' within the Rome II Regulation.

3.117 Greater difficulty arises, however, if the parties have established, or have at least attempted by direct dealings to establish, some form of consensual relationship and the supposed obligation relates in some way to that relationship. Here, it may be said (without unduly straining the language used) that the obligor's obligations towards the obligee were 'freely assumed', at least in the sense that they arise from the voluntary conduct of the former in his relations with the latter. From a different viewpoint, however, the concept of an 'obligation freely assumed' may be argued to be empty of content: all obligations, including those arising from contracts, are imposed by law and ignorance of that law or a subjective unwillingness to be bound do not generally provide defences to obligation-based claims. A party may protest that he did not intend to enter into contractual

---

[350] A Briggs and P Rees, n 348 above, para 2.126.

[351] For treatment of issues of succession under the Brussels Convention, see Case C-387/98, *Coreck Maritime GmbH v Handelsveem BV* [2000] ECR I-9337; A Briggs and P Rees, n 348 above, para 2.126.

[352] *VfK v Henkel*, n 312 above, paras 38–40. Also Case C-51/97, *Réunion Européenne SA v Spliethoff's Bevrachtingskantoor BV* [1998] ECR I-6511, paras 17–20; Case C-265/02, *Frahuil SA v Assitalia SpA* [2004] ECR I-1543, paras 24–5.

relations with another on particular terms but, if that is the court's interpretation of his conduct, it cannot be doubted that his obligation to perform his side of the bargain is 'contractual' in nature. Moreover, the specific obligation on which the claimant rests his claim may be a legal incident of the parties' contractual relationship from which they were not free to derogate by agreement. Whether described as an 'implied term' of the contract[353] or an independent legal duty,[354] obligations that adhere to a contractual or similar relationship can properly be described as 'contractual' whatever their origin.[355]

The ECJ's later decision in *Engler v Janus Versand GmbH*[356] brings **3.118** together key elements of the autonomous concept of 'contract' within the Brussels I Regime, and may also be thought to provide a basis for separating 'contractual obligations' (Rome I Regime), from 'non-contractual obligations' (Rome II Regulation). In that case, the claimant had received a letter from the defendant which led her to believe that she had won a substantial prize in a draw 'without obligation'. She claimed the prize, but the defendant refused to pay. The claimant brought an action to recover the prize based on a statutory rule of Austrian law in the following terms:[357]

Undertakings which send prize notifications or other similar communications to specific consumers, and by the wording of those communications give the impression that a consumer has won a particular prize, must give that prize to the consumer; it may also be claimed in legal proceedings.

The Court concluded that the action was a 'matter relating to a contract' **3.119** under Art 5(1) of the Brussels Convention. Having referred[358] to its

---

[353] e.g. the undertakings as to title implied under the UK Sale of Goods Act 1979, which cannot be excluded by reference to a contract term (Unfair Contract Terms Act 1977, s 6).

[354] e.g. an employer's duty not unfairly to dismiss (Employment Rights Act 1996, s 94) or to discriminate against his employee (Sex Discrimination Act 1975, s 6; Race Relations Act 1976, s 4; Disability Discrimination Act 1995, s 4) or a principal's duty to compensate his commercial agent on termination of his agency (Commercial Agents (Council Directive) Regulations (SI 1993/3053), reg 17; *Lonsdale v Howard & Hallam Ltd* [2007] UKHL 32; [2007] 4 All ER 1).

[355] *Agnew v Länsföräkringsbolakens AB* [2001] 1 AC 223, 240 (Lord Woolf), 246–7 (Lord Cooke), 253–4 (Lord Hope), 264 (Lord Millett) (UKHL), a case concerning Art 5(1) of the 1968 Brussels Convention, considered at **12.10** below.

[356] Case C-27/02 [2005] ECR I-1481.

[357] Austrian Consumer Protection Law (*Konsumentenschutzgesetz*) (BGBl I, 1979, p 140), para 5j.

[358] Case C-27/02, *Engler v Janus*, n 356 above, para 50.

earlier decision in *Handte*, and later case law, the ECJ reasoned as follows:[359]

Accordingly, the application of the rule of special jurisdiction provided for matters relating to a contract in Article 5(1) *presupposes the establishment of a legal obligation freely consented to by one person towards another and on which the claimant's action is based.*

In that regard, the national court held that in this case, first of all, a professional vendor sent on its own initiative to the consumer's domicile, without any request by her, a letter designating her by name as the winner of a prize.

Such a letter, *sent to addressees and by the means chosen by the sender solely on its own initiative*, may therefore constitute an obligation 'freely assumed' . . .

Furthermore, according to the national court, a prize notification made in such circumstances by a professional vendor who has not drawn attention to the existence of a loophole and has even used a formulation of such a kind as to mislead the consumer in order to induce him to enter a contract by acquiring the goods offered by that vendor, could reasonably lead the addressee of the letter to believe that a prize would be awarded to him if he returned the 'payment notice' attached.

Second, it is clear from the file submitted by the national court that *the addressee of the letter at issue expressly accepted the prize notification* made out in her favour by requesting payment of the prize she had ostensibly won.

From that moment at least, the intentional act of a professional vendor in circumstances such as those in the main proceedings *must be regarded as an act capable of constituting an obligation which binds its author as in a matter relating to a contract. Therefore, and subject to the final classification of that obligation, which is a matter for the national court*, the condition concerning the existence of a binding obligation by one party to the other, . . . , may also be regarded as satisfied.

3.120   Having suggested that characterization of the obligation was a matter for the national court, the ECJ proffered its own view that:[360]

Legal proceedings such as those brought in the main proceedings by the consumer are intended to claim, as against a professional vendor, the award of a prize ostensibly won and whose payment has been refused by the latter. *Therefore it is founded specifically on the prize notification, since the ostensible beneficiary invokes the failure to award the prize as the reason for bringing the proceedings.*

---

[359] Ibid, paras 51–6 (emphasis added). In the earlier part of its judgment (paras 34–43), the ECJ had concluded that there was not a 'contract' falling within any of the categories set out in Art 13 of the Brussels Convention (consumer contracts). It did not, however, consider that conclusion to be determinative of the question whether the obligation in question fell within Art 5(1), as to which it took a broader view (paras 45–9). Cf the Opinion of Adv Gen Trstenjak (11 September 2008) in Case C-180/06, *Ilsinger v Dreschers*, a case concerning the consumer contract provisions of the Brussels I Regulation.

[360] Ibid, paras 57–8 (emphasis added).

It follows that all the conditions necessary for the application of Article 5(1) of the Brussels Convention are satisfied in a case such as that in the main proceedings.

For good measure, the ECJ[361] added that 'the mere fact that the professional vendor did not genuinely intend to award the prize announced to the addressee of his letter is irrelevant in that respect. . . .'

Elements of a 'contractual obligation' under the Rome II Regulation and the Rome I Regime

Two key elements of a 'contractual obligation', to be identified from the **3.121** Court's reasoning in *Engler*, provide at least a starting point for defining that concept in connection with the Rome I Regime and the Rome II Regulation. First, that the concept of 'contract' requires an intentional and voluntary act by one person towards another and (probably) some reciprocal voluntary act by that other person with those acts in combination giving rise to a binding legal obligation (the 'contract'). The view that there must be some bilateral element in the parties' relations reflects the central case of 'contract', that of a binding agreement, although as the ECJ's decisions in *Martin Peters* and *Engler* demonstrate, it also covers other legal institutions. On this view, unilateral acts fall outside the Rome I Regime. Secondly, that this 'contract' must constitute the *foundation* of the claim under the putative applicable law. If these conditions are satisfied, the claim will likely fall within the scope of the Rome I Regime as a 'contractual obligation', irrespective of the source and description of the obligation under national law and the parties' subjective intentions. If, however, there is no 'contract'[362] in the sense described above or if a 'contract' between the parties does not constitute the foundation of the claim but is only part of the factual matrix within which the claim arose, an obligation-based claim will instead fall within the scope of the Rome II Regulation as a 'non-contractual obligation'.

Pre-contractual obligations

In the case of obligations which concern the pre-contract conduct of the **3.122** parties (including, for example, a misrepresentation made by one of them to the other), it might be thought to that self-evident that the test suggested above for the existence of a 'contractual obligation' will not be met,

---

[361] Ibid, para 59, referring to para 48 of the Opinion of Adv Gen Jacobs (in which the Advocate General concluded that 'the issue of the sender's intention thus expressed is itself, in such a context, a contractual matter').

[362] Or putative contract. Rome Convention, Art 8(1) and Rome I Regulation, Art 10(1) make clear that a dispute as to the existence of a contract is a matter of 'contractual obligation' for these purposes.

in that (a) the first limb will not be satisfied if both parties accept that no contract resulted from their negotiations,[363] and (b) the second limb cannot be satisfied if the claim is founded on an act or omission that pre-dated any contract, even if the 'injury' alleged consists of entry into and performance of the contract. In this connection, Art 12(1) of the Rome II Regulation (*culpa in contrahendo*) confirms that obligations arising out of dealings prior to a contract may be characterized as 'non-contractual', whether a contract was actually concluded or not.[364] The impression that this will be the usual characterization for claims of this kind is supported by Art 1(2)(i) of the Rome I Regulation, which excludes from its scope 'obligations arising out of dealings prior to the conclusion of a contract'. Even so, there will remain claims that relate back to conduct during the period prior to conclusion of a contract but in which an attempt is made, under national law, to fit the obligation within a contractual framework, for example as an implied promise that all material information has been disclosed[365] or a collateral contract arising from a representation made during the parties' negotiations.[366] The classification of an obligation as 'contractual' under its putative applicable law cannot, of course, be decisive and the ECJ's reasoning in *Handte*[367] suggests a need to look behind the description of the obligation under that law in order to ascertain its true basis. In the case of a collateral contract claim, however, it may strongly be argued that the true basis of the action is not the misrepresentation but a 'contract' established by the parties' conduct and that any damage results from the representor's failure to perform to the promised standard rather than from the representee's decision to enter the contract on the faith of the representation. It these respects, the basis of representor's obligation is analogous to that in *Engler*[368] and can justifiably be characterized as 'contractual' and within the Rome I Regime.

3.123 In other cases, a particular claim, although undoubtedly resting on a pre-contractual act, may be so closely linked to the determination of the material validity of that contract that it should be characterized as a 'contractual obligation' falling outside the scope of the Rome II Regulation. Examples

---

[363] Case C-344/00, *Fonderie Officine Meccaniche Tacconi SpA v Heinrich Wagner Sinto Maschinenfabrik GmbH* [2002] ECR I-7357, para 23 (another case concerning Art 5(1) of the 1968 Brussels Convention).

[364] **12.03–12.12** below.

[365] *Agnew v Länsföräkringsbolakens AB* [2001] 1 AC 223 (UKHL), where the action (raising a question of interpretation of the 1988 Lugano Convention) was to set aside a contract on the ground of a material non-disclosure.

[366] e.g. *Dick Bentley Productions Ltd v Harold Smith (Motors) Ltd* [1965] 1 WLR 623 (EWCA).

[367] **3.115**.

[368] **3.120** above.

include restitution and counter-restitution of benefits conferred under a contract set aside for misrepresentation or duress (falling within Art 10(1)(e) of the Rome Convention[369]) and, arguably, a claim to damages in lieu of rescission of a contract under Misrepresentation Act 1967, s 2(2)[370] or similar rule. A claim, such as a claim under s 2(1) of the Misrepresentation Act 1967, to recover damages from a contractual counterparty independently of both (a) any term of the contract, and (b) any claim that the contract should be set aside or declared null and void for pre-contractual conduct is 'non-contractual' and falls within the scope of Art 12 of the Rome II Regulation (*culpa in contrahendo*).[371]

The problem of concurrent liability

The most difficult questions in the separation of 'contractual' from 'non-contractual' obligations concern the treatment of claims arising between the parties to a contract that, under national law, are classified as non-contractual and may be pursued concurrently with a contractual claim arising from the same factual situation.[372] The possibility of concurrent liability is recognized by some but not all legal systems[373] and, for a regime such as the Rome II Regulation which creates rules of applicable law for cross-border situations, creates two types of problem. First, should all claims arising between the parties to a contract that relate to the contract or its performance be characterized according to applicable private international law rules as 'contractual' and determined in accordance with the rules of applicable law for contractual obligations. Secondly, if not, what is the relationship between the contractual and non-contractual obligations and, more generally, the terms of contract and the non-contractual obligation in circumstances where different laws apply to them.

3.124

---

[369] **3.108** above.

[370] **12.10** below. In *Morin v Bonhams & Brooks* [2003] EWHC 467 (Comm); [2003] 2 All ER (Comm) 36, [29], a claim under s 2(2) was held to be tortious under the pre-existing English rules of applicable law.

[371] **12.09** below. For the position under English law before the Regulation, compare *JMJ Contractors v Marples Ridgway* [1986] 31 Build LR 100 (EWHC), in which a claim under s 2(1) of the 1967 Act was treated by concession of counsel as contractual, with *Morin v Bonhams & Brooks*, n 370 above, [29], in which a claim under s 2(1) was treated as tortious.

[372] L Collins, 'Interaction Between Contract and Tort in the Conflict of Laws' (1967) 16 ICLQ 103; P Nygh, *Autonomy in International Contracts* (1999), ch 10; A Briggs, 'Choice of Choice of Law?' [2003] LMCLQ 12; J Fawcett, J Harris, and M Bridge, *International Sale of Goods in the Conflict of Laws* (2004), ch 20; A Briggs, *The Conflict of Laws* (2nd edn, 2008), 162–3.

[373] *Henderson v Merrett Syndicated Ltd* [1995] 2 AC 145, 184–94 (Lord Goff, UKHL). Also C von Bar, *The Common European Law of Torts* (1998, reprinted 2003), paras 413–58; C von Bar and U Drobnig, 'Study on Property Law and Non-contractual Liability Law as they relate to Contract Law' (SANCO B5-1000/02/000574), paras 280–315 (available at <http://ec.europa.eu/consumers/cons_int/safe_shop/fair_bus_pract/cont_law/study.pdf>).

3.125 The problem of concurrent liability in private international law was recognized by the Commission in its opinion, given in March 1980, on the draft convention on the law applicable to contractual obligations (i.e. what became known as the Rome Convention).[374] In that opinion, the Commission regretted that it had not been possible in the Convention to deal also with non-contractual obligations, adding that:

> Cases will in fact frequently occur where not only contractual but also non-contractual claims form the subject-matter of the same action. Other cases will turn on the question whether a claim is to be considered as contractual or non-contractual (delictual or quasi-delictual). The application of the Convention in its present form may therefore result in a situation in which if an action is brought in one Contracting State it will be decided in accordance with the rules contained in the Convention, whereas if it is brought in another Contracting State it will be decided in accordance with the conflicts rules of the *lex fori* which have not yet been unified.

3.126 The Commission also alluded in its Rome II Proposal to possible future difficulties in the application of the Regulation to situations of concurrent liability. Referring to the 'escape clause' in Art 4(3), which enables Member State courts to apply to a tort/delict the law applicable to a pre-existing relationship between the parties instead of the law otherwise applicable under Art 4(1) or 4(2), the Commission commented:[375]

> This solution is particularly interesting for Member States whose legal system allows both contractual and non-contractual obligations between the same parties. . . . On a more technical level, it means that the consequences of the fact that one and the same relationship may be covered by the law of contract in one Member State and the law of tort/delict in another can be mitigated, *until such time as the Court of Justice comes up with its own autonomous response to the situation.*

3.127 In their commentary on the Regulation, the editors of Dicey, Morris & Collins suggest that:[376]

> [W]hatever national law might say, at the European level it is unlikely to be held that a particular obligation may be treated as sounding, alternatively, say, as either contract or tort, or as tort or unjust enrichment.

3.128 Given that the Rome I Regime and the Rome II Regulation, as well as the individual rules of applicable law within the Rome II Regulation, are

---

[374] OJ L94, 39 [4.11.1980].

[375] Commission Proposal, 13 (emphasis added).

[376] Dicey, Morris & Collins, 1st supplement, para S35-177, citing *Source Ltd v TUV Rhineland Holding AG* [1998] QB 54 (EWCA), a case discussed at **3.136** below. Compare the description of the pre-existing position under English law in the main work of Dicey, Morris & Collins, para 35-66.

intended to complement one another, the editors' tentative rejection of the possibility of alternative characterization of a single obligation seems, if anything, too cautious. It should not be open to the claimant to select a particular rule of applicable law simply by the manner in which he labels his claim. That description should be no more significant than the label attached to a claim by a country whose law may apply under the Regulation, or the law of the forum. The foregoing proposition leaves open, however, the questions whether, in a particular situation arising in connection with performance of a contractual obligation, more than one obligation can be identified as being owed and, if so, whether separate obligations arising from the same situation can be characterized differently, with some falling within and some outside the scope of the Rome II Regulation. It is submitted that both questions should be answered affirmatively. That conclusion is supported by the terms of the Regulation, which contemplates in several places the possibility that a non-contractual obligation that has a close connection with a contractual or other pre-existing relationship may fall within the scope of the Regulation and may be governed by the law applicable to that relationship.[377] Furthermore, Art 14(1)(b) allows parties pursuing a commercial activity to choose the law applicable to a non-contractual obligation arising between them by an agreement freely negotiated before the event giving rise to damage occurred. Such rules would appear useless or, at the very least, of little significance if claims arising in connection with a contract must be characterized as 'contractual' and as falling beyond their reach. It is also evident from a comparison of the Recitals to the Rome II Regulation and those of the Rome I Regulation that the rules of applicable law in the two instruments strike a different balance, both (a) between the parties to the proceedings, and (b) between the interests of the parties, on the one hand, and broader public or policy interests, on the other. In the absence of any signal that the Rome II Regulation is to be seen as subordinate to the Rome Convention and its successor Regulation, the temptation to treat a contract as creating a single or principal obligation between the parties to which all claims arising from its performance must accede[378] should be resisted.

Accordingly, at least if the claimant presents his case on this basis, the **3.129** court may consider the possibility that the basis of an action arising against the background of a contract (or other pre-existing relationship) can be characterized in two (or more) different ways, with reference to the

---

[377] Rome II Regulation, Arts 4(3), 5(2), 10(1), 11(1).
[378] For application of the maxim *accessorium sequitur principale* for a different purpose within the 1968 Brussels Convention, see Case 266/85, *Shenevai v Kreischer* [1987] ECR 239, para 19.

categories of obligation recognized by the Rome II Regulation,[379] and that the defendant may, at the same time, owe overlapping 'contractual' and 'non-contractual' obligations to the claimant. Most obviously, the defendant's conduct may be something for which he would have been legally responsible independently of any contract between the parties. For example, a landowner may agree to allow his neighbour to carry out certain activities on his land subject to the latter agreeing to meet certain safety requirements. In the event that the neighbour's conduct violates both statutory and contractual standards of safety and causes damage to the landowner's property, the fact that (a) the contract provided the occasion for the defendant's acts or omissions, and (b) the same acts or omissions violate both the contractual and the statutory obligation should not prevent the court from recognizing the existence of a non-contractual (tortious) obligation alongside a contractual one.

3.130 The test of *independence* (reflecting the language used by Adv Gen Jacobs in *Handte*[380]) will not, however, produce a clear answer in every case. The English tort of negligence provides a good example of this. Here, in cases involving economic loss, the defendant's tortious duty to take care to avoid causing loss to the claimant will often be closely linked to a contract between the parties, although the terms of that contract may also negate the duty.[381] In other cases, in which there is no contractual relationship between the parties, the tortious duty can be based on an objective assumption of responsibility akin or equivalent to contract.[382] In cases where there is a contract, or a situation equivalent to contract, it can be said, without straining the meaning of the words used, that the defendant's liability in tort arises from his own voluntary[383] conduct towards the claimant, creating the objective impression that he accepts legal responsibility for the consequences of that conduct (although he may not subjectively intend to do so).[384] On this view, the elements that led the ECJ to

---

[379] Including, for present purposes, 'contractual obligations' as a category separate from 'non-contractual obligations'.

[380] **3.113** above.

[381] e.g. *Henderson v Merrett Syndicates Ltd*, n 373 above.

[382] e.g. *Nocton v Lord Ashburton* [1914] AC 932, 972 (Lord Shaw, UKHL); *Hedley Byrne & Co Ltd v Heller & Partners* [1964] AC 465, 428 (Lord Devlin, UKHL); *Smith v Eric S Bush* [1990] 1 AC 831, 846 (Lord Templeman, UKHL).

[383] i.e. 'conscious', 'considered', or 'deliberate' (*Customs and Excise Commissioners v Barclays Bank plc*, [2006] UKHL 28; [2007] 1 AC 181, [73] (Lord Walker, UKHL)). Also, ibid, [38] (Lord Hoffmann).

[384] *Williams v Natural Life Health Foods Ltd* [1998] 1 WLR 830, 835 (Lord Steyn, UKHL). Cf *Customs and Excise Commissioners v Barclays Bank*, [4]–[5] (Lord Bingham), [35] (Lord Hoffmann), [85]–[86], [93] (Lord Mance).

conclude that the claim in *Engler* should be characterized as 'contractual' may appear to be present.[385] The English courts have also recognized that, in cases where there is a relationship equivalent to contract, the tort of negligence performs an 'essentially gap-filling role' against the background of 'the restricted conception of contract in English law, resulting from the combined effect of the principles of consideration and privity of contract'.[386] The theoretical explanation of the defendant's liability as resting on a non-contractual (tortious) duty may, therefore, be argued to be a fiction, disguising the 'true' contractual nature of the action.

Against this background, there are undoubtedly respectable arguments **3.131** for looking behind the classification of the negligence claim as non-contractual under English private law and instead characterizing the defendant's obligation as 'contractual', falling outside the scope of the Rome II Regulation.[387] Powerful as these arguments may appear, however, it is submitted that the better view is that all claims based on the English tort of negligence should be characterized under the Rome II Regulation as 'non-contractual obligations arising out of a tort/delict', falling within Art 4[388] unless another rule in Chapter II or III of the Regulation applies. The foundation of these claims, even when brought between contracting parties, should be identified as being not the voluntariness of the defendant's conduct towards the claimant but his responsibility for careless conduct causing damage to the claimant. The existence of a contract, or relationship equivalent to contract, between the parties is undoubtedly a significant factor in many cases, but it is only one of many factors that may justify the conclusion that the defendant owes a tortious duty to take care to prevent the claimant from suffering loss of a particular kind, by reason of a relationship of 'proximity' between the parties.[389] That, in turn, is only one of three requirements that define the tort of negligence in English law, whatever the nature of the damage and the circumstances in which it arose. These are (1) foreseeability of damage resulting from the defendant's failure to take care, (2) sufficient proximity between the parties, and (3) fairness, justice, and reasonableness of imposing a duty.[390] Of these, the

---

[385] **3.121** above. It may be doubted, however, whether the bilateral element in the relations between claimant and defendant is present, if it is required.

[386] *Williams v Natural Life Health Foods Ltd*, n 384, 837 (Lord Steyn).

[387] A Rushworth and A Scott, n 180 above, 293–4.

[388] **Ch 4** below.

[389] *Customs and Excise Commissioners v Barclays Bank*, n 383 above, [4]–[8] (Lord Bingham), [35]–[39] (Lord Hoffmann), [49]–[53] (Lord Rodger), [69]–[74] (Lord Walker), [82]–[99] (Lord Mance) (UKHL).

[390] *Marc Rich & Co v Bishop Rock Ltd* [1996] 1 AC 211 (UKHL). For more detailed analysis, see A M Dugdale and M A Jones (eds), *Clerk & Lindsell on Torts* (19th edn, 2006), ch 8.

first should be seen as the most important. Liability for negligence is, arguably, the closest that English law gets to a general principle of tort law,[391] corresponding (for example) to Art 1382 of the French *Code Civil* or Art 823 of the German *Bürgerliches Gesetzbuch*. That the courts have sought to control that liability by reference to the concepts of proximity, fairness, justice, and reasonableness should not disguise the essential character of the defendant's liability as being for his (or another's) negligent conduct causing harm to the claimant.[392] Whether the tortious duty of care is imposed in a situation in which there is a contract between the parties, the defendant's only responsibility is to avoid injuring the claimant through conduct falling short of the standard that the law imposes. That should be seen as any freestanding, one-sided, non-contractual obligation and not as any incident of any contractual relationship that may exist between the parties.

3.132 Characterization of tortious negligence claims as falling within the scope of the Rome II Regulation in all cases avoids the difficulty of distinguishing cases in which the defendant has truly 'voluntarily assumed' responsibility for his actions from other cases in which the language of 'voluntariness' is used in a different sense or to disguise what is essentially a policy decision by the court to hold the defendant responsible for the consequences of his conduct.[393] It also avoids straining the concept of an obligation 'freely assumed' to include, for example, a duty of care owed by an employee of a contracting party, separately from that owed by his employer. As May LJ noted in *Merrett v Babb*, a case concerning the employee's liability in negligence:[394]

> In my view, it is very often a helpful guide in particular cases to ask whether the defendant is to be taken to have assumed responsibility to the claimant to guard against the loss for which damages are claimed. But I also think that it is reaching for the moon—and not required by authority—to expect to accommodate every circumstance which may arise within a single short abstract formulation. The question in each case is whether the law recognises that there is a duty of care.

3.133 Finally, the conclusion that such claims should be characterized as 'non-contractual' for these purposes would enable Member State courts to apply the common rules contained in Chapter V of the Rome II Regulation, which seem more suited to claims of this kind than those contained in Arts 12–18 of the Rome I Regulation. For example, if the claim were characterized as 'contractual', the claimant would not be able to rely on Art 18 of the

---

[391] *Donohue v Stevenson* [1932] AC 562, 580 (Lord Atkin, UHKL).

[392] C van Dam, *European Tort Law* (2005), para 804-1.

[393] e.g. *White v Jones* [1995] 2 AC 207 (UKHL).

[394] [2001] EWCA Civ 214; [2001] 1 QB 1174, [41] (May LJ).

Rome II Regulation to bring a direct claim against the defendant's insurer. The Rome I Regime and the Rome II Regulation also take different approaches to questions of capacity to incur 'contractual' or, as the case may be, 'non-contractual' liability.[395]

Even if, contrary to the view taken above, the obligation underlying a **3.134** tortious negligence claim between contracting parties is properly charac- terized as 'contractual' and as falling within the Rome I Regime, it should be seen as distinct from any obligation that arises from a term express or implied in the parties' agreement. On this view, there would be two possible 'contractual' obligations, the first generated by the parties' agreement and the second generated by the defendant's objective assump- tion of responsibility in the performance of the first obligation. The law applicable to those obligations must still, therefore, be determined separately.

From a practical viewpoint, these answers given to these questions of **3.135** characterization will in many cases make no difference to the law applica- ble to the claims arising between the parties. Whether there is a single 'contractual' obligation or two distinct 'contractual' obligations or one 'contractual' and one 'non-contractual' obligation, the rules of applicable law in the Rome I Regime and the Rome II Regulation will frequently lead to the conclusion that claims between contracting parties and relating to their contractual relationship are all governed by the law applicable to the contract. For 'tort/delict' claims under the Rome II Regulation, the 'escape clause' in Art 4(3) and the parties' ability to choose the law applicable under Art 14 facilitate that outcome.[396] That, however, should not be taken as a reason in itself for a unitary 'contractual' characterization. Determining the law applicable to non-contractual obligations on an 'accessory basis' is a very different thing from treating them as acceding for all purposes to contractual obligations with which they are connected. As the Rome II Regulation makes clear through its Recitals, as well as the balancing approach required by the 'escape clauses'[397] and the restrictions on the parties' ability to select the law applicable to non-contractual obliga- tions,[398] the priorities of EC private international law in the area of non- contractual obligations are very different from those pursued by the Rome I Regime.

---

[395] **14.09–14.12** below.
[396] **4.90–4.94** and **Ch 12** below.
[397] **4.84** and **4.95** below.
[398] **Ch 12** below.

3.136 The English courts have already considered similar arguments in two related areas. In *Source Ltd v TUV Rhineland Holding AG*,[399] the question arose as to whether a tortious negligence claim should be considered as a 'matter relating to a contract' under Art 5(1) of the Brussels Convention when the negligent conduct complained of occurred in the defendant's performance of a contractual obligation to inspect goods and the defendant owed a parallel contractual duty to take care in carrying out that task. The Court of Appeal held that both the contractual and tortious claims fell within Art 5(1). Staughton LJ, with whom the other members of the Court agreed, held that the expression 'matters relating to a contract' included 'a claim which may be brought under a contract or independently of a contract on the same facts, save that the contract does not need to be established'. This aspect of the decision in *Source* has since been followed by a different constitution of the Court of Appeal in *Barry v Bradshaw*, a professional negligence case.[400] Whether the reasoning of the Court of Appeal in *Source v TUV* and *Barry v Bradshaw* is upheld in a jurisdictional context,[401] having regard in particular to the objective of avoiding fragmentation of disputes arising on the occasion of the performance of a contractual obligation,[402] the single obligation recognized by the Court would appear insufficiently sensitive to the differences between the two claims, which may take on a greater significance when it comes to determine the law applicable to them.[403]

3.137 In *Base Metal Trading v Shamurin*,[404] the Court of Appeal considered a case concerning the interaction of the rules of applicable law in the Rome Convention with the pre-existing English rules of applicable law for torts and equitable obligations. The decision concerned claims against a Russian director of a Guernsey incorporated corporate vehicle based on allegations

---

[399] [1998] QB 54 (EWCA).

[400] [2000] CLC 455 (EWCA). Cf *Domicrest Ltd v Swiss Bank Corporation* [1999] 1 QB 548, 561 (Rix J, EWHC), where the claims presented were alternative claims.

[401] The editors of Briggs & Rees (n 348 above, paras 2.129 and 2.148–2.150) are strongly supportive. In *Raiffeisen Zentralbank Osterreich AG v National Bank of Greece* [1999] 1 Lloyd's Rep 408, 411 (Tuckey J, EWHC) doubted whether the decision in *Source v TUV* could be reconciled with the view taken by the House of Lords as to the scope of Art 5(1) of the Brussels Convention in *Kleinwort Benson Limited v Glasgow City Council* [1999] 1 AC 153 (UKHL), a case concerning recovery of payments under an *ultra vires* contract. Tuckey J's reasoning was, in turn, criticized by one of his former colleagues (*Rayner v Davies* [2002] 1 All ER (Comm) 620, [18]–[19] (Morison J, EWHC)).

[402] *Martin Peters v ZNAV*, n 337 above, para 12. Cf the approach taken by the ECJ in the later case of *Kalfelis v Schröder* in the passage quoted at text to n 313 above.

[403] **3.131** above.

[404] [2004] EWCA Civ 1316; [2005] 1 WLR 1157, noted A Briggs (2005) 75 BYBIL 572; A Dickinson (2005) 121 LQR 374.

of negligent trading in futures contracts. The company advanced claims for breach of contract, breach of a tortious duty of care, and breach of the director's equitable duty of care owed to it.[405] The contract was held to be governed by Russian law (under which the claim failed), and it was submitted by the defendant that the tortious duty of care based on the director's 'voluntary assumption of responsibility to the company' should also be characterized as a 'contractual obligation' under the Rome Convention.[406] The Court of Appeal rejected that submission. Tuckey LJ (with whom the other members of the Court agreed on this point) stated:[407]

> Interesting though [Counsel's] submissions are, I do not accept them. The language of the [Rome] Convention does not support them. A contractual obligation is by its very nature one which is voluntarily assumed by agreement. Terms may be implied into that agreement, but that is because they are necessary to make what has been agreed work and so this does not undermine the fact that the obligation is consensual. There is nothing consensual about the imposition of a tortious or equitable duty of care. It arises from a voluntary assumption of responsibility, but that is a state of affairs which is not dependent upon agreement.

Although the conclusion reached as to the characterization of the tortious **3.138** negligence claim as falling outside the Rome I Regime is consistent with the position taken above, the reasoning may not go far enough. In this connection, the distinction drawn by Tuckey LJ between obligations created by the parties to an agreement and those imposed by law seems unhelpful. In this connection, the ECJ's decision in *Engler* supports the view that a claim may be seen as 'contractual' for these purposes even if it is based on a statutory rule from which there is no ability to contract out.[408] The reasoning could be said to apply equally to judicially created rules imposing duties in tort or otherwise. Instead of a test based on the source of the obligation, the key question should be whether the foundation of the obligation on which the claimant relies is a 'contract' between the parties derived from the defendant's voluntary conduct towards the claimant and (probably) the claimant's reciprocal conduct. For the reasons given above,[409] it is submitted that a negative answer should be given to that question whenever the claim is based on the English tort of negligence.

If two or more separate obligations are identified as potentially existing, the **3.139** impact of the factual link between them should, in each case, be a matter for

---

[405] For further discussion of the equitable claim, and its relationship to company law, see **3.162–3.169** below.

[406] *Base Metal Trading v Shamurin*, n 404 above, [25].

[407] Ibid, [28].

[408] **3.121** above.

[409] **3.131** above.

the law applicable to the individual obligation. If, for example, a contractual obligation governed by the law of State X is claimed to arise concurrently with a non-contractual obligation governed by the law of State Y, the law of State Y must determine the effect of the concurrent contractual obligation on the basis and extent of the defendant's non-contractual liability and vice versa (although it may be supposed that the existence of a concurrent non-contractual obligation may be thought unlikely to negate a contractual obligation).[410]

Other problematic cases—fiduciary relationships and bailment

3.140 Issues of a similar complexity, although not confined to the problem of concurrent liability, arise in relation to other obligations that fall outside the English law of contract even though, in many but not all cases, they arise from a voluntary relationship between the parties. Two areas merit particular attention: fiduciary relationships and bailment. How are obligations to which these labels are attached to be characterized under the Rome I Regime and in the Rome II Regulation? Consistently with the approach taken above, it must again be considered whether the foundation of the obligation in question, in some or all cases, is a 'contract' having regard to the autonomous meaning given to that term.[411]

3.141 *Fiduciary relationships*[412] In *Bristol and West Building Society v Mothew*, Millett LJ described the nature and obligations of a 'fiduciary' as follows:[413]

A fiduciary is someone who has undertaken to act for or on behalf of another in a particular matter in circumstances which give rise to a relationship of trust and confidence. The distinguishing obligation of a fiduciary is the obligation of loyalty. The principal is entitled to the single-minded loyalty of his fiduciary. This core liability has several facets. A fiduciary must act in good faith; he must not make a profit out of his trust; he must not place himself in a position where his duty and his interest may conflict; he may not act for his own benefit or the benefit of a third person without the informed consent of his principal. This is not intended to be an exhaustive list, but it is sufficient to indicate the nature of fiduciary obligations. They are the defining characteristics of the fiduciary. As Dr. Finn pointed out in his classic work *Fiduciary Obligations* (1977), p. 2, he is not subject to fiduciary obligations because he is a fiduciary; it is because he is subject to them that he is a fiduciary.

---

[410] For more detailed discussion of this question, see J Fawcett, J Harris, and M Bridge, n 372 above, paras 20.28–20.52.

[411] **3.121** above.

[412] Also T M Yeo, n 314 above, paras 7.24–7.72.

[413] [1998] Ch 1, 18 (EWCA).

On this view, the essential basis of these fiduciary duties, therefore, is 'a **3.142** relationship of trust and confidence' and they are correctly viewed as incidents of that relationship, intended to protect the principal as a party vulnerable to abuse of that relationship by the party. 'Trust' here is used not to refer to the common law institution of a 'trust of property' but in the sense that 'one person is reasonably entitled to repose and does repose trust and confidence in another'.[414] The combination of the fiduciary's undertaking to act and the principal's reciprocal trust may be argued to qualify the relationship as 'contractual' for these purposes, within the Rome I Regime. It must be recognized, however, that there are situations in which the 'fiduciary relationship' is a fiction serving as a justification for imposing fiduciary duties on a defendant who is considered, innocently or wrongfully, to have interfered in the affairs of another, without that other's consent.[415] Further, efforts to produce a globally applicable definition of 'fiduciary relationship' have foundered,[416] and '[f]or the moment, it seems that the only safe course is to list those relationships which the courts have accepted to be fiduciary: trustee/beneficiary, director/company, solicitor/client, partner/partner and so on, whilst also remembering that a relationship may be fiduciary in relation to some of its incidents but not others'.[417] The better view, therefore, may be to characterize obligations of a fiduciary character as 'contractual' if they attach to a contractual relationship between the parties (e.g. solicitor/client; joint venture; banker/customer), but not otherwise. In principle, the relationships between partners and (where both the company and the director consent to the director's appointment) director and company also appear 'contractual' in nature, although they may fall outside the scope of the Rome I Regime through the exclusion of 'questions governed by the law of companies and other bodies, corporate or unincorporated'.[418] The scope of the similarly worded exclusion in Art 1(2)(d) of the Rome II Regulation is considered in the next section.[419]

Bailment Bailment, under English law 'is a legal relationship distinct **3.143** from both contract and tort. It exists whenever one person (the bailee) is

---

[414] *Estate Realties v Wignall* [1991] 3 NZLR 482, 492; *Zhong v Wang* [2007] NZ 242, [88] (both CA, New Zealand).

[415] e.g. the knowing recipient of trust property (**4.103–4.105** below), the de facto or shadow director, or a trustee *de son tort* (**3.193** below).

[416] J Edelman and J Davies, 'Torts and Equitable Wrongs' in A Burrows (ed), *English Private Law* (2nd edn, 2007), paras 17.346–17.348.

[417] Ibid, para 17.348.

[418] Rome Convention, Art 1(2)(e); Rome I Regulation, Art 1(2)(f).

[419] **3.158–3.172** below.

voluntarily in possession of goods which belong to another'.[420] 'Bailment imposes certain basic obligations on every bailee. The bailee must take reasonable care of the goods and abstain from converting them. He must not deviate from the terms of the bailment and becomes an insurer of the goods if he does so. In most cases he must also refrain from denying the bailor's title'.[421] The bailor, under certain circumstances, also owes duties to the bailee.[422] As to the separation of bailment from contract under English law, the following points were made by Mance LJ in *East West Corp v DKBS AF 1912 A/S*:[423]

First, it is now well established that the existence of claims in bailment does not depend on contract. What is fundamental is not contract, but the bailee's consent. . . . [I]t is the voluntary taking of another's goods into custody that constitutes the person taking such custody a bailee towards that other person (the owner) . . .[424]

Secondly, a bailee may owe duties not merely to his bailor, but to a third party owner. The classic example. . . is the case of a sub-bailee. He owes duties in bailment, not merely to his immediate bailor, but also to an owner and head bailor of the goods . . . .

Thirdly, as a matter of principle and because the essence of bailment is the bailee's voluntary possession of another's goods, an owner's remedies cannot necessarily be confined to situations involving either a direct bailment or a sub-bailment. . . .

3.144 As to the first point, the fact that the bailment relationship is not contractual under English law is not, of course, determinative for these purposes.[425] Having regard to the fundamental requirement that the bailee consent to take goods into his custody, it is submitted that bailment can be characterized as giving rise to 'contractual obligations', falling outside the scope of the Rome II Regulation and within the Rome I Regime, if the bailee can be said to have consented to hold goods *for* the bailor with the bailor's consent, with or without payment on either side, including (for example) situations in which (1) the bailor, or his representative, delivers goods to the bailee with the latter's consent, (2) a bailee in possession of goods (for example,[426] as seller to the bailor or as bailee under an earlier bailment) indicates to the

---

[420] N Palmer, 'Bailment' in A Burrows (ed), *English Private Law*, n 416 above, para 16.01.

[421] Ibid, para 16.02.

[422] Ibid, paras 16.39–16.40, 16.43, 16.54, 16.63–16.64, 16.74.

[423] [2003] EWCA Civ 83; [2003] QB 1509, [24]–[26]. Also *Kamidian v Holt* [2008] EWHC 1483 (Comm).

[424] Referring to *The Pioneer Container* [2004] 2 AC 324, 341–2 (Lord Goff, UKHL).

[425] **3.121** above.

[426] For the distinction between gratuitous bailments and bailments for reciprocal advantage, see N Palmer, n 420 above, paras 16.32–16.34.

bailor, by words or conduct, that he holds the goods for him,[427] or (3) a third party (including, for example, a seller of goods or an intermediate bailor) delivers goods to the bailee with the consent of the bailor and in circumstances in which the bailee is taken to consent to hold goods *for* the bailor instead of, or in addition to, holding them for the third party.[428]

In some cases, provided that mutual consent of the bailor and bailee is present, sub-bailment and similar situations of a kind referred to by Mance LJ in his second point will fall within the third type of situation listed in the preceding paragraph and may be treated as contractual.[429] In other cases, however, the obligations owed by the sub-bailee to the head bailor appear analogous to the obligation of the manufacturer of goods to a sub-buyer which, in *Handte v TMCS*,[430] was characterized by the ECJ as non-contractual.[431] Relevant examples given by Mance LJ, although not relevant to the facts of the case before him, are cases in which (a) the person to whom goods have been bailed is unaware that a person other than his immediate bailor is interested in the goods, or (b) the owner is unaware that his goods are or may be sub-bailed.[432] In cases of these kinds, the obligations of both bailor and bailee towards each other should be considered 'non-contractual obligations', falling within the scope of the Rome II Regulation. Finally, as to Mance LJ's third point, the obligations of a bailee or similar obligations may be imposed on a person who possesses goods in circumstances where he does not consent to hold them for the bailor and/or the bailor does not consent to him doing so. Such situations include, for example, (1) the finding of goods, (2) a person who comes into possession of goods without consent (e.g. the recipient of unsolicited goods), (3) a person who mistakenly believes that goods belong to him (e.g. the innocent purchaser of a stolen item), and (4) a person who is unaware that goods are in his possession.[433] Again, in these cases, the obligations of **3.145**

---

[427] For discussion of 'bailment by attornment', see N Palmer, ibid, paras 16.78–16.81.

[428] Cf *RPS Prodotti Siderurgici SRL v Owners and/or demise charterers of The Sea Maas (The Sea Maas)* [1999] 2 Lloyd's Rep 281 (EWHC). In that case, claims by the consignee of cargo against a shipowner for damage to the cargo were framed, in the alternative, in contract, tort, and bailment. Rix J (at 283) recorded that it was common ground that all three claims fell within Art 5(1) of the 1968 Brussels Convention as 'matters relating to a contract'.

[429] See N Palmer, n 420 above, paras 16.82–16.84 referring to the concepts of sub-bailment and substitutional bailment.

[430] **3.112** above.

[431] Cf *Dresser UK Ltd v Falcongate Ltd* [1992] 1 QB 502, 511 (Bingham LJ, CA) concerning the concept of an 'agreement' on jurisdiction within Art 17(1) of the 1968 Brussels Convention (now Art 23(1) of the Brussels I Regulation).

[432] *East West Corp v DKBS 1912*, n 423 above, [25].

[433] N Palmer, n 420 above, paras 16.03, 16.86–16.89. Given the basic requirement that the bailee must consent to hold goods for another, the description of a bailment as 'involuntary'

the bailee (and, where appropriate, the bailor) should be considered 'non-contractual' and falling within the scope of the Rome II Regulation.

Negative Content of 'Non-Contractual Obligations' III—Specific Excluded Matters

Article 1(2)

2. The following shall be excluded from the scope of this Regulation:

(a) non-contractual obligations arising out of family relationships and relationships deemed by the law applicable to such relationships to have comparable effects including maintenance obligations;

(b) non-contractual obligations arising out of matrimonial property regimes, property regimes of relationships deemed by the law applicable to such relationships to have comparable effects to marriage, and wills and succession;

(c) non-contractual obligations arising under bills of exchange, cheques and promissory notes and other negotiable instruments to the extent that the obligations under such other negotiable instruments arise out of their negotiable character;

(d) non-contractual obligations arising out of the law of companies and other bodies corporate or unincorporated regarding matters such as the creation, by registration or otherwise, legal capacity, internal organisation or winding-up of companies and other bodies corporate or unincorporated, the personal liability of officers and members as such for the obligations of the company or body and the personal liability of auditors to a company or to its members in the statutory audits of accounting documents;

(e) non-contractual obligations arising out of the relations between the settlors, trustees and beneficiaries of a trust created voluntarily;

(f) non-contractual obligations arising out of nuclear damage;

(g) non-contractual obligations arising out of violations of privacy and rights relating to personality, including defamation.

Introduction

3.146 Art 1(2) of the Rome II Regulation lists seven categories of non-contractual obligation as being specifically excluded from its scope. In the explanatory memorandum accompanying its Proposal, the Commission stated:

These being exceptions, the exclusions will have to be interpreted strictly.

---

or 'unconscious' is, accordingly, a contradiction in terms, although a person in possession of goods belonging to another without his consent or who is unaware that he holds goods belonging to another may owe more limited duties (N Palmer, n 420 above, paras 16.86–16.93; *Marcq v Christie Manson & Woods Ltd* [2003] EWCA Civ 731; [2004] QB 686).

That statement appears too emphatic. Under EC law, a provision which **3.147** limits the scope of a Community measure must be interpreted having regard to the objectives of the measure in question and must be interpreted restrictively insofar as it is liable to prevent attainment of those objectives.[434] Nevertheless, the reasons for excluding particular matters from the Rome II Regulation, so far as they are ascertainable, must be considered carefully, in order to determine whether the exclusion of those matters actually jeopardizes the attainment of the objectives of the Regulation. In the case of the exclusions in Arts 1(2)(a) (family relationships) and Art 1(2)(b) (matrimonial property regimes) regard must also be had to other legislative initiatives under Title IV that enable the Rome II Regulation's position in the developing EC system of private international law to be identified.[435] These points may be taken to support a more generous approach to the construction of the exceptions than that for which the Commission contended, considering their wording in light of their individual context and objectives.[436]

Family Relationships (Art 1(2)(a))

In the explanatory memorandum accompanying its Proposal, which con- **3.148** tained an exclusion in almost identical terms, the Commission noted that:[437]

[N]on-contractual obligations arising out of family or similar relationships: family obligations do not in general arise from a tort or delict. But such obligations can occasionally appear in the family context, as is the case of an action for compensation for damage caused by late payment of a maintenance obligation. Some commentators have suggested including these obligations within the scope of the Regulation on the grounds that they are governed by the exception clause in Article 3(3),[438] which expressly refers to the mechanism of the 'secondary connection' that places them under the same law as the underlying family relationship. Since there are so far no harmonised conflict-of-laws rules in the Community as regards family law, it has been found preferable to exclude non-contractual obligations arising out of such relationships from the scope of the proposed Regulation.

---

[434] Case C-287/98 *Luxembourg v Linster* [2000] ECR I-6917, para 49. For more detailed discussion, and reference to other case law of the ECJ on this point, see Lasok, Millett & Howard, n 1 above, para 690.

[435] **3.149** and **3.154** above.

[436] Cf Case C-190/89 *Marc Rich & Co AG v Società Italiana Impianti PA* [1991] ECR I-3855, para 16, commenting that 'it does not follow that the [*Brussels*] Convention, whose purpose is in particular the reciprocal recognition and enforcement of judicial decisions, must necessarily have attributed to it a wide field of application'.

[437] Commission Proposal, 8 referring to Art 1(2)(a) of the Proposal.

[438] Art 4(3) of the Regulation in its final form.

3.149 Following publication of its Proposal, the Commission embarked on several initiatives in the area of family law, none of which have yet to bear legislative fruit. In particular, the Commission presented (1) in April 2004, a Green Paper concerning maintenance obligations,[439] following this with a formal proposal for a Council Regulation on jurisdiction, applicable law, recognition and enforcement of decisions and cooperation in matters relating to maintenance obligations,[440] and (2) in April 2005, a Green Paper on applicable law and jurisdiction in divorce matters (the so-called 'Rome III' instrument),[441] again followed by a formal proposal.[442] As to item (1), at the JHA Council meeting on 5–6 June 2008, the Member States' representatives in Council agreed on a set of political guidelines for further work on a proposal for a Regulation on maintenance obligations and in particular on the principal goal of the Regulation: the complete abolition of exequatur on the basis of harmonized applicable law rules.[443] As to item (2), at the same meeting, the Council concluded that the unanimity required under Art 67 of the EC Treaty for the Rome III instrument could not be attained within a reasonable period.[444] The possibility remains of some Member States taking the proposal forward by the mechanism of enhanced cooperation under Title VI of the EC Treaty.[445] Neither the UK nor Ireland has chosen to opt-in to negotiations on the Rome III instrument. Ireland, but not the UK, chose to opt-in to the maintenance obligations proposal.

3.150 'Family relationships' is defined by Recital (10) of the Rome II Regulation as follows:

> Family relationships should cover parentage, marriage, affinity and collateral relatives. The reference in Article 1(2) to relationships having comparable effects to marriage and other family relationships should be interpreted in accordance with the law of the Member State in which the court is seised.

3.151 The reference to 'the law of the Member State in which the court is seised' presumably includes reference to that Member State's rules of private international law permitting the recognition of foreign institutions comparable to marriage. This, however, is an area in which the public policy of the forum is likely to play a significant role. For example, unless a similar

---

[439] COM (2004) 254 final [15.4.2004].

[440] COM (2005) 649 final [15.12.2005].

[441] COM (2005) 82 final [14.3.2005].

[442] COM (2006) 399 final [17.7.2006].

[443] See factsheet at <http://www.consilium.europa.eu/ueDocs/cms_Data/docs/pressData/en/jha/101000.pdf>.

[444] Ibid.

[445] Council document 11653/08 (Presse 205) (Provisional Version), 23–4.

institution exists under national law, a foreign same sex marriage may not be recognized within a legal system even if it otherwise meets the criteria for recognition of a foreign marriage between persons of different sexes. Under English law, foreign same sex marriages are recognized as civil partnerships and not as marriages.[446] There is, however, no doubt that such relationships, under English law, have comparable effects to marriage.[447] It must, however, be noted that a decision that a relationship does not have comparable effects to a family relationship within the meaning of Art 1(2)(a) will result in the application of the Regulation's rules of applicable law to non-contractual obligations arising out of that relationship. As the Regulation contemplates a very limited role for the forum Member State's public policy and overriding mandatory provisions,[448] judges in Member States may need to contort themselves in an attempt to ensure that the Rome II Regulation does not apply without at the same time being seen to validate family law institutions that are not recognized within their own legal system.

Art 1(2)(a) excludes only obligations that arise out of family relationships, **3.152** and not all obligations that concern such relationships. For example, the question whether a parent is responsible for the acts of a child,[449] or one spouse is responsible in tort/delict for the acts of another, falls within the scope of the Regulation.[450] Similarly, non-contractual obligations owed between family members will fall within the scope of the Regulation if the obligation in question is not based on that relationship (e.g. the duty owed by a car driver to his passenger).[451]

Matrimonial Property Regimes, Wills and Succession (Art 1(2)(b))

These obligations were excluded from the scope of the Commission **3.153** Proposal 'for similar reasons' to those given above for the exclusion of non-contractual obligations arising out of family or similar relationships.[452]

The Commission has also been active in this area. In March 2005 it pre- **3.154** sented a Green Paper on succession and wills[453] followed, in July 2006, by

---

[446] Civil Partnership Act 2004, s 215; *Wilkinson v Kitzinger (No 2)* [2006] EWHC 2022 (Fam); [2007] 1 FLR 295; K Norrie (2006) 2 J Priv Int L 137.
[447] *Wilkinson v Kitzinger (No 2)*, n 446 above, [20] (Sir Mark Potter P).
[448] Arts 16 and 26 (**15.03–15.18** below).
[449] Commission Proposal, 24.
[450] **14.45–14.47** below. Also Dicey, Morris & Collins, 1st supplement, para S35-179; Schlosser Report (OJ C59, 88 [5.3.1979]), para 46.
[451] Cf Case 25/81, *CHW v GJH* [1982] ECR 1189 (**3.158** below).
[452] **3.148** above. See further Commission Proposal, 8. Also Brussels Convention, Art 1(1); Jenard Report (OJ C59, 11 [5.3.1979]); Schlosser Report, n 450 above, paras 43-50.
[453] COM (2005) 65 final [1.3.2005]. Also J Harris, 'Reflections on the Proposed EU Regulation on Succession and Wills', available at <http://www.conflictoflaws.net/2008/

a Green Paper on conflict of laws in matters concerning matrimonial property regimes.[454] Neither consultation has yet resulted in a formal proposal, although at the end of June 2008, the Commission produced a discussion paper for a meeting of national experts containing a preliminary draft of the text of a Regulation on succession matters.

3.155 The editors of Dicey, Morris & Collins suggest that '[t]here are likely to be few, if any, situations which fall within this provision', adding that 'the reference to "wills" would not seem apt to exclude, for example an action against a lawyer for negligent drafting of a will'. Those observations seem in line with the reasons justifying the exclusion. It is, however, possible to envisage claims that may fall within Art 1(2)(b), for example, a claim by a disappointed beneficiary against the deceased's estate,[455] a claim by one beneficiary or by the estate to recover a sum overpaid to another beneficiary,[456] and a claim between spouses relating to the management of property, at least where the authority of one spouse arises from the marriage or its dissolution.[457]

3.156 The ECJ has held that the expression 'rights in property arising out of a matrimonial relationship' in the Brussels Convention includes 'not only property arrangements specifically and exclusively envisaged by certain national legal systems in the case of marriage but also any proprietary relationships resulting directly from the matrimonial relationship or the dissolution thereof'.[458]

Bills of Exchange, Promissory Notes and Other Negotiable Instruments (Art 1(2)(c))

3.157 Non-contractual obligations arising under financial instruments of these kinds were excluded from the scope of the Commission Proposal for the same reasons as were given by Professors Giuliano and Lagarde in their report on the Rome Convention for excluding their contractual counterparts from the scope of that Convention,[459] i.e. (a) that the provisions of the Regulation were not suited to the regulation of these types of obligation, (b) that such obligations are not dealt with uniformly in the

---

guest-editorials/guest-editorial-harris-on-reflections-on-the-proposed-eu-regulation-on-succession-and-wills/>.

[454] COM (2006) 400 final [17.7.2006].

[455] Inheritance (Provision for Family and Dependents) Act 1975.

[456] *Re Diplock* [1948] Ch 465 (EWCA).

[457] Case 25/81, *CHW v GJH* [1982] ECR 1189.

[458] Ibid, para 6.

[459] See Rome Convention, Art 1(2)(c); Giuliano & Lagarde Report (OJ C282, 11 [31.10.1980]).

Member States, (c) that their inclusion would have involved rather complicated special rules, and (d) that the Geneva Conventions of 1930[460] and 1931[461] (to which several Member States are parties) already contained detailed rules regulating these matters.[462] In view of the Commission's earlier emphasis on the importance of legal certainty,[463] one might have expected that this was precisely the type of subject area that might benefit from a harmonized, coherent, modern[464] system of rules of applicable law in all Member States.[465] One suspects, therefore, that the exclusion of these matters from the scope of the Rome Convention provided a convenient explanation for not dealing in this Regulation with a topic which, while remaining hideously complex, is of diminishing importance in the modern era of electronic communication and money transfer.[466]

The Law of Companies and Other Bodies Corporate and Unincorporate (Art 1(2)(d))

Art 1(2)(d) of the Commission Proposal excluded 'the personal legal liabil- **3.158** ity of officers and members as such for the debts of a company or firm or other body corporate or incorporate, and the personal legal liability of persons responsible for carrying out the statutory audits of accounting documents'.[467] In the Commission's view, these matters could not be separated from the law applicable to the company or other body in connection with whose management the question of liability arises.[468] In its final

---

[460] Convention for the Settlement of Certain Conflicts of Laws in connection with Bills of Exchange and Promissory Notes (Geneva, 7 June 1930), 143 LNTS 317. Of the Member States, Austria, Belgium, Denmark, Finland, France, Germany, Greece, Italy, Netherlands, Poland, Portugal, and Sweden are currently parties to this Convention (see <http://untreaty.un.org/ENGLISH/bible/englishinternetbible/partII/Treaty-8.asp>).

[461] Convention for the Settlement of Certain Conflicts of Laws in connection with Cheques (Geneva, 19 March 1931), 143 LNTS 407. Of the Member States, Denmark, Finland, France, Germany, Greece, Italy, Netherlands, Poland, Portugal, and Sweden are currently parties to this Convention (see <http://untreaty.un.org/ENGLISH/bible/englishinternetbible/partII/Treaty-9.asp>).

[462] Commission Proposal, 9.

[463] **2.64** above.

[464] The two Geneva Conventions are over 75 years old and have not stood the test of time.

[465] The Italian delegation initially argued for deletion of this exclusion (Council document 9009/04 ADD 17 [2.6.2004], 2).

[466] J Dalhuisen, *International, Commercial, Financial and Trade Law* (2nd ed, 2004), 692, 700–2.

[467] The Spanish and Italian delegation initially argued for deletion of this exclusion (Council document 9009/04 ADD 10 [18.5.2004], 1–2; ibid, ADD 17 [2.6.2004], 2).

[468] Commission Proposal, 9. For discussion in the Council's Rome II Committee, see Council document 7551/06 [22.3.2006], 4–5 noting that '[t]he question of qualification of company law appeared to cause difficulties to many delegations'.

form, however, the 'company law' exclusion in Art 1(2)(d) the Regulation follows very closely that contained in Art 1(2)(e) of the Rome Convention[469] with the addition of a reference to the personal liability of auditors in relation to statutory audits.

3.159 The report of Professors Giuliano and Lagarde on the Rome Convention justified and explained the corresponding exclusion in the Rome Convention as follows:[470]

> This exclusion in no way implies that this aspect was considered unimportant in the economic life of the Member States of the Community. Indeed, this is an area which, by virtue of its economic importance and the place which it occupies in many provisions of the Treaty establishing the EEC, appears to have the strongest possible reasons for not being separated from Community work in the field of unification of private international law, notably in conflicts of laws pertaining to economic relations.

> Notwithstanding the foregoing considerations, the Group had thought it inadvisable, even in the original preliminary draft, to include companies, firms and legal persons within the scope of the Convention, especially in view of the work being done on this subject within the European Communities. Confirming this exclusion, the Group stated that it affects all the complex acts (contractual, administrative, registration) which are necessary to the creation of a company or firm and to the regulation of its internal organization and winding-up, ie acts which fall within the scope of company law.

> . . .

> The subject may be a body with or without legal personality, profit-making or non-profit-making. Having regard to the differences which exist, it may be that certain relationships will be regarded as within the scope of company law or might be treated as being governed by that law (for example, *société de droit civil*, *nicht-rechtsfähiger Verein*, partnership, *Vennootschap onder firma*, etc.) in some countries but not in others. The rule has been made flexible in order to take account of the diversity of national laws.

3.160 The authors continued:[471]

> Examples of 'internal organization' are: the calling of meetings, the right to vote, the necessary quorum, the appointment of officers of the company or firm, etc. 'Winding-up' would cover either the termination of the company or firm as provided by its constitution or by operation of law, or its disappearance by merger or other similar process.

---

[469] Rome I Regulation, Art 1(2)(f).
[470] Giuliano & Lagarde Report (OJ C282, 12 [31.10.1980]).
[471] Ibid.

At the request of the German delegation the Group extended the subparagraph (e) exclusion to the personal liability of members and organs, and also to the legal capacity of companies or firms. On the other hand the Group did not adopt the proposal that mergers and groupings should also be expressly mentioned, most of the delegations being of the opinion that mergers and groupings were already covered by the present wording.'

On this view, the company law exclusion affects 'all the complex acts . . . **3.161** which are necessary to the creation of a company or firm and to the regulation of its internal organization and winding-up'. That said, it is submitted that it is not sufficient that a non-contractual obligation should arise during the management of the affairs of a company or other body; rather, the obligation must be characterized as 'arising out of the law of companies and other bodies corporate or unincorporated', a concept that must receive an autonomous interpretation.[472] The matters listed in Art 1(2)(d), as well as the examples given in the commentary in the Giuliano & Lagarde Report, provide the context within which the more general concept of the 'law of companies' etc. must be understood.

Directors' liability   One particularly problematic area concerns directors' **3.162** liability for breaches of their obligations as directors to the companies that they represent. Those obligations may in some circumstances at least (e.g. those of a de facto or shadow director) fall to be characterized as 'non-contractual'.[473] In *Base Metal Trading v Shamurin* (discussed at **3.137–3.138** above) one of the claims raised against the defendant was that he had breached an equitable duty that he owed as a director of the claimant company to exercise reasonable care and skill in the business he transacted on behalf of the claimant and in his conduct of the claimant's affairs. Arden LJ held that 'the liability of a director by virtue of his office' fell within the 'company law' exclusion in Art 1(2)(e) of the Rome Convention.[474] In her Ladyship's view:[475]

The company law exclusion is to be construed against the background that the European Union has made substantial progress on the approximation of the company laws of member states so that there is less need for the Rome Convention (which is of course a treaty of the European Union) to stipulate what the proper law should be . . .

---

[472] Cf Case 133/78, *Gourdain v Nadler* [1979] ECR 733, paras 3–5, a case concerning the exclusion of 'bankruptcy' from the 1968 Brussels Convention.

[473] **3.142** above.

[474] [2004] EWCA Civ 1316; [2005] 1 WLR 1157, [65].

[475] Ibid, [65]–[66].

Moreover, the matters mentioned in the company law exclusion are aspects of company law, which, under generally accepted principles of the conflicts of laws in the member states, are considered to be governed by the law of the place of incorporation. Thus, for example, the Statute for a European Company (which came into effect on 8 October 2004), regulating the new Societas Europaea ('SE'), leaves a number of matters, including matters as to the liability of the directors of the SE, to be governed by the law applicable to public limited companies of the member state in which the SE has for the time being its registered office (which must be in the state in which the SE is currently registered, i.e. then incorporated): see Council Regulation (EC) No 2157/2001, articles 9, 51.

The other members of the Court agreed with that reasoning.[476]

3.163 Art 51 of the Statute for a European Company, to which Arden LJ referred, provides:[477]

Members of an SE's management, supervisory and administrative organs shall be liable, in accordance with the provisions applicable to public limited-liability companies in the Member State in which the SE's registered office is situated, for loss or damage sustained by the SE following any breach on their part of the legal, statutory or other obligations inherent in their duties.

3.164 The views of Arden LJ in relation to company law matters must be treated with the utmost respect. There are, however, reasons to question whether the 'company law' exclusions in the Rome I Regime and the Rome II Regulation cover a claim of the kind advanced in the *Base Metal Trading* case by a company against its director. First, Art 1(2)(e) of the Rome Convention, followed in this respect by Art 1(2)(d) of the Rome II Regulation and Art 1(2)(f) of the Rome I Regulation, appears to have been carefully worded and refers in terms to 'the personal liability of officers . . . as such *for the obligations of the company*'. As appears from the Giuliano & Lagarde Report, in the extract quoted above,[478] this particular wording was added at the request of the German delegation to clarify the scope of the exception. Another amendment suggested by the same delegation, concerning mergers and groupings, was rejected on the ground that mergers and groupings were already considered to be covered by the original wording. In light of this, it could be argued that the authors of the Rome Convention did not consider that the 'company law' exclusion extended to other aspects of officers' liability.

3.165 Secondly, under English law as it stood at the time of the decision in *Base Metal Trading*, the director's liability to the company in equity for a failure

---

[476] Ibid, [57] (Tuckey LJ), [89] (Newman J).
[477] OJ L294, 1 [10.11.2001].
[478] **3.160** above.

to take reasonable care could be argued to arise not 'by virtue of his office' (the words used by Arden LJ to define the 'company law' exception in this context) but because he had undertaken the performance of an act in relation to the affairs of another. In *Bristol and West Building Society v Mothew*, Millett LJ explained:[479]

The common law and equity each developed the duty of care, but they did so independently of each other and the standard of care required is not always the same. But they influenced each other, and today the substance of the resulting obligations is more significant than their particular historic origin.

His Lordship referred approvingly to the following statement by Lord Browne-Wilkinson in *Henderson v Merrett Syndicates Ltd*:[480]

The liability of a fiduciary for the negligent transaction of his duties is not a separate head of liability but the paradigm of the general duty to act with care imposed by law on those who take it upon themselves to act for or advise others. Although the historical development of the rules of law and equity have, in the past, caused different labels to be stuck on different manifestations of the duty, in truth the duty of care imposed on bailees, carriers, trustees, directors, agents and others is the same duty: it arises from the circumstances in which the defendants were acting, *not from their status or description*. It is the fact that they have all assumed responsibility for the property or affairs of others which renders them liable for the careless performance of what they have undertaken to do, *not the description of the trade or position which they hold*.

Thirdly, although English courts typically have recourse to the law of the **3.166** country of the company's incorporation (*lex incorporationis*) in determining matters of company law (including 'the duties inherent in the office of director'),[481] it must be recalled that the *lex incorporationis* not universally accepted as a solution for the law applicable to matters of company law,[482] despite the supervention of EC law concerning freedom of establishment.[483] For this reason, and differing views as to the breadth of the

---

[479] [1998] Ch 1, 16 (EWCA). This passage was referred to by Tuckey LJ in *Base Metal Trading v Shamurin*, n 474 above, [19].

[480] [1995] 2 AC 145, 205 (UKHL) (emphasis added). Also the statement by J Edelman and J Davies in A Burrows (ed), *English Private Law*, n 416 above, para 17.349 that 'Their duty to protect the beneficiary from harm. . . is nothing but a requirement of positive action connoting a duty of care, with the consequence that the wrong committed by breach of that duty is not distinct from the tort of negligence.'

[481] *Base Metal Trading v Shamurin*, n 474 above, [67]–[69]. Also Dicey, Morris & Collins, para 30-024.

[482] For background, see S Rammeloo, *Corporations in Private International Law* (2001), chs 2 and 3.

[483] Case C-208/00, *Überseering BV v Nordic Construction Company Baumanagement GmbH* [2002] ECR I-9919; Case C-167/01, *Kamer van Koophandel en Fabrieken voor Amsterdam v Inspire Art Ltd* [2003] ECR I-10155.

category of 'company law' issues in a private international law context,[484] the law otherwise applicable to claims against directors may vary greatly between Member States. Against this background, and given that the obligations of directors may not differ greatly in nature or content from those of other functionaries, a more restrictive approach to the scope of this exception is arguably justified in order to promote the objective of certainty as to the law applicable to non-contractual obligations.[485]

3.167 These arguments do not, however, provide a convincing answer to the case presented for bringing the liability of a director by virtue of his office within the 'company law' exclusions in the Rome I Regime and the Rome II Regulation.[486] As to the first point (**3.164** above), it may be countered that the question of a director's liability for the obligations of the company concerns a relationship that is external to the company, whereas the directors' duties to the company arising by virtue of his office concerns an internal relationship between the company and one of its officers. The better view may, therefore, be that the former should be seen as an extension of the concept of 'company law' for this purpose but that the latter naturally falls within its scope. As to the second point (**3.165** above), it may be countered that there is an important difference between the concept of a 'duty of care' in equity and its common law counterpart in the tort of negligence. At common law, the duty of care is a device deployed to control liability for negligently caused damage and does not depend for its existence on a relationship of any kind between the claimant and the defendant.[487] In equity, the duty (whether it is properly described as a 'fiduciary duty' or not[488]) depends on the existence of a 'fiduciary' relationship between two persons, and can be seen one of the incidents of that relationship.[489] In the case of a director, that relationship and the precise obligations to which it gives rise may be argued to be inseparable from the director's appointment, [490] or other event that leads to his being treated as

---

[484] See e.g. the passage from the Giuliano & Lagarde Report quoted at **3.159** above.

[485] **3.18** above.

[486] The author was formerly persuaded by the first two arguments, despite the efforts of others to persuade him otherwise (A Dickinson, 'Applicable Law Arbitrage—An Opportunity Missed?' (2005) 121 LQR 374, at 377). *Mea culpa.*

[487] **3.131** above.

[488] Cf J Edelman and J Davies, n 416 above, para 17.349, footnote 663.

[489] **3.142** above. Also *Base Metal Trading*, n 474 above, [74] (Arden LJ: 'The equitable duty is not a mere mirror image of the common law duty of care, whose content the parties can control, and thus to be treated, as the judge thought, as of no independent significance').

[490] P Davies, *Gower and Davies: Principles of Modern Company Law* (8th edn, 2008), para 16.10.

an officer of the company.[491] As 'appointment' is one of the aspects of the internal organization of the company specifically mentioned in the Giuliano & Lagarde Report, a strong case can be made for treating this class of obligations as falling within the 'company law' exclusions and outside both the Rome I Regime and the Rome II Regulation. Other obligations owed by a director to his company that are not based on his appointment to office, e.g. in contract (Rome I Regime) or in the tort of negligence (Rome II Regulation), remain within the scope of these instruments. Further, since the decision in *Base Metal Trading*, the obligations that directors owe to companies have been codified in the new UK companies legislation.[492] Although the source of the obligation will not normally be influential in characterizing it under the Regulation,[493] this development emphasizes the link between the obligations of the director of a UK company and the legal and regulatory framework for companies generally.

Finally, as to the third point (**3.166** above), it may be countered that the **3.168** considerations that the authors of the Rome Convention had in mind when framing the exception in Art 1(2)(e)[494] support the view that the law applicable to the liabilities of directors as such should be a matter left to the Member States to regulate as they consider appropriate, subject to the powers of the Community to harmonize company law. In *Base Metal Trading*, Arden LJ advanced the following policy considerations for the application of the *lex incorporationis* 'to the duties inherent in the office of director':[495]

[T]hese duties can only be modified by contract to the extent that the law of the place of incorporation allows. It is not open to the company and the director to contend that they have contractually varied the liabilities imposed by the law of the place of incorporation by the terms of a contract for the appointment of the director governed by some other law, unless it is also shown that the law of the place of incorporation would allow this. In the matter of directors' duties—which are essential to good corporate governance and to any effective system of law regulating companies—party autonomy is the exception not the rule, and its scope is always a matter for the law of the place of incorporation. . . .

[T]he result protects creditors and shareholders against the risk of managers entering into agreements which dilute the minimum standards set for directors by the law of the place of incorporation and reinforces the role of that law in regulating the companies over whose formation and continued existence it has control . . .

---

[491] For example, in the case of de facto and shadow directors (P Davies, ibid, para. 16.8).
[492] Companies Act 2006, ss 170–81.
[493] **3.70** above.
[494] **3.159** above.
[495] *Base Metal Trading*, n 474 above, [69], [74]–[75].

Companies are increasingly trading across national borders and moving their trading operations from country to country. They must not by so doing escape proper regulation or otherwise creditors and shareholders will suffer. The only system of law that can consistently and effectively regulate such multinational companies is the law of the place of incorporation. Accordingly I would strongly disagree with any suggestion that the duties imposed on directors . . . by the law of the place of its incorporation should be regarded as irrelevant or 'mechanistic'.

3.169 The policy reasons given in the first two paragraphs may, it is submitted, equally be served by an approach that subjects the regulation of the company's affairs to the law of its 'real seat'.[496] Indeed, the only genuine disagreement between Member States adopting a country of incorporation approach to the law applicable to company law matter and those adopting a real seat approach, to the extent consistent with EC law, may be as to the most appropriate source of the 'proper regulation' to which Arden LJ referred. As both Art 3 of the Rome I Regulation and, to a more limited extent, Art 14 of the Rome II Regulation[497] allow the parties to choose the law applicable to contractual and non-contractual obligations arising between them, the desire to protect creditors and shareholders against 'regulatory arbitrage' of a kind described by Arden LJ may provide a further reason for excluding duties of the kind to which she referred from the scope of the Rome II Regulation.

3.170 *Auditors' liability* In contrast to the corresponding provision in the Commission Proposal, which referred to 'personal legal liability of persons responsible for carrying out the statutory audits of accounting documents', Art 1(2)(d) of the Rome II Regulation in its final form only applies to the 'personal liability of auditors to a company or to its members in the statutory audits of accounting documents'.[498] Auditors' liability to third parties (e.g. those considering a takeover bid or purchasing securities on

[496] See the arguments raised by the German government in *Überseering v Nordic Construction*, n 483 above, paras 87–90, which are similar to those raised by Arden LJ in *Base Metal Trading* (**3.168** above).
[497] **Ch 14** below.
[498] For a study, prepared for the Commission, of the liability of statutory auditors in the Member States, see <http://ec.europa.eu/internal_market/auditing/docs/liability/auditliability_en.pdf>. For other materials, including the Commission's 2008 Recommendation concerning the limitation of the civil liability of statutory auditors and audit firms, see <http://ec.europa.eu/internal_market/auditing/liability/index_en.htm>.

the market) or for other activities carried out by them (e.g. the preparation of management accounts) falls within the scope of the Regulation.

Liability relating to stock exchanges and financial instruments   During discus- **3.171** sions in the Council's Rome II Committee, the Finnish delegation suggested that non-contractual obligations relating to stock exchanges should be excluded from the Regulation's scope. That suggestion was not widely supported,[499] but was followed by a specific proposal from the UK delegation that the Regulation should exclude:[500]

Non-contractual obligations arising out of transactions, such as issuing, admission to trading, offering or marketing, relating to financial instruments, including transferable securities, moneymarket instruments, units in collective investment undertakings, options, futures and other derivatives instruments.

At a meeting of the Rome II Committee in March 2006, several delegations **3.172** agreed that the topic merited further consideration but others considered that (having regard to the late stage of negotiations) it was doubtful whether the exclusion could be justified.[501] The latter view prevailed. In his 2008 *Review of Issuer Liability*, commissioned by the UK Government, Professor Paul Davies commented:[502]

Many companies quoted on the British capital markets will have investors resident in a number of different jurisdictions. Which law governs claims brought by such investors is a complex subject, partly because the British rules determining the answer are not entirely clear and partly because courts in other jurisdictions may use different (but equally complex) rules to determine the answer. It is thus not impossible that such companies may be subject to investor claims under as many differing legal regimes as it has investors in different jurisdictions. This seems to me undesirable. A better result would be one in which a single legal regime applied to investor claims, possibly the law of the jurisdiction where the issuer is incorporated or possibly the law of the jurisdiction where the issuer has its primary listing . . . My understanding is that the Government did advance precisely this point in the discussions on the (now agreed) 'Rome II' Regulation on the law applicable to non-contractual obligations, but without success.

---

[499] Council document 7551/06 [22.3.2006], 5.
[500] Council document 7928/06 ADD 1 [30.3.2006], 1. Cf Rome I Regulation, Art 4(1)(h) identifying the law applicable, in the absence of choice, to 'a contract concluded within a multilateral system which brings together or facilitates the bringing together of multiple third-party buying and selling interests in financial instruments'.
[501] Council document 7709/06 [3.5.2006], 7.
[502] P Davies, *Davies Review of Issuer Liability*, Final Report (June 2007), para 61 (available at <http://www.hm-treasury.gov.uk/media/4/7/davies_review_finalreport_040607.pdf>).

Accordingly, however unsatisfactory this outcome may appear, the Regulation applies to prospectus liability and other, similar claims.[503]

Voluntary Trusts (Art 1(2)(e))

3.173 *Introduction*   Art 1(2)(e) excludes some non-contractual obligations concerning 'trusts created voluntarily'. In the explanatory memorandum accompanying its Rome II Proposal, the Commission reasoned that 'trusts are a *sui generis* institution and should be excluded from the scope of this Regulation as previously from the Rome Convention'.[504] Art 1(2)(g) of the Rome Convention excludes from its scope 'the constitution of trusts and the relationship between settlors, trustees and beneficiaries'. That language, in turn, is carried forward into Art 1(2)(h) of the Rome I Regulation.

3.174 At least from an English law perspective, this provision is probably the most complex in the Rome II Regulation. Indeed, the more that one thinks about it, the greater the number of problems and questions that arise. In particular, the terminology in Art 1(2)(e) establishes a link to the 1985 Hague Convention on the law applicable to trusts and their recognition[505] and brings with it difficulties arising not only from the unclear and unsatisfactory terminology used in the Convention but also inconsistencies between the text of the Convention and the way in which it was implemented by the UK Recognition of Trusts Act 1987. Given that the practical significance of Art 1(2)(e) in the overall scheme of the Regulation is likely to be relatively small, these difficulties should not be blown out of proportion. The following discussion attempts to identify and to offer solutions to some, but not all, of the questions that may arise in applying the Regulation's rules to trusts and analogous institutions.

---

[503] The relationship between the Rome II Regulation and Community instruments imposing liability for the contents of prospectuses is addressed briefly at **15.19–15.20** below. Also **4.112**, **12.05** and **12.07** below.

[504] Commission Proposal, 9.

[505] Convention on the law applicable to trusts and on their recognition (The Hague, 1 July 1985) **(Hague Trusts Convention)**, reproduced at <http://www.hcch.net/index_en.php?act=conventions.text&cid=59>). Among the Member States, only Italy, Luxembourg, Malta, Netherlands, and the UK have ratified the Convention (see <http://www.hcch.net/index_en.php?act=conventions.status&cid=59>). See the Explanatory Report by Professor A von Overbeck, Proceedings of the 15th Session (1984), tome II, available in the original French language and English translation at <http://hcch.e-vision.nl/upload/expl30.pdf> **(von Overbeck Report)**.

For other English language commentaries on the Convention, see J Harris, *The Hague Trusts Convention* (2002); M Lupoi, *Trusts: A Comparative Study* (1997; English translation, 2000), ch 6; D Hayton, P Matthews, and C Mitchell (eds), *Underhill and Hayton: Law of Trusts and Trustees* (17th ed, 2006), ch 25; J Mowbray et al. (eds), *Lewin on Trusts* (18th ed, 2008), paras 11-56 to 11-88. Also the materials listed at <http://www.hcch.net/index_en.php?act=conventions.publications&dtid=1&cid=59>.

The concept of a 'trust' The first problem is that the Regulation does not **3.175**
define 'trust'. In this connection, the Giuliano & Lagarde Report on the
Rome Convention supports the view that the corresponding exclusion in
that Convention concerns 'trusts' in the sense in which they are understood in common law countries, including England.[506] The authors of the
Report also recognized, however, that similar institutions existing under
other laws[507] may be characterized as 'trusts' for these purposes, at least if
they exhibit 'the same characteristics'.[508]

Having regard to the stated intention that the substantive scope of the **3.176**
Rome II Regulation should be consistent with the instruments dealing with
the law applicable to contractual obligations,[509] it would appear strongly
arguable that the same (narrow) definition should apply for the purposes
of the Rome II Regulation. This begs the question as to what are the essential characteristics of the common law institution of the trust, which must
be possessed by the similar institutions existing under other laws.

In this connection, Art 2 of the Hague Trusts Convention,[510] provides: **3.177**

For the purposes of this Convention, the term 'trust' refers to the legal relationships created—*inter vivos* or on death—by a person, the settlor, when assets have
been placed under the control of a trustee for the benefit of a beneficiary or for a
specified purpose.

A trust has the following characteristics –

a) the assets constitute a separate fund and are not a part of the trustee's own
    estate;
b) title to the trust assets stands in the name of the trustee or in the name of another
    person on behalf of the trustee;
c) the trustee has the power and the duty, in respect of which he is accountable, to
    manage, employ or dispose of the assets in accordance with the terms of the
    trust and the special duties imposed upon him by law.

The reservation by the settlor of certain rights and powers, and the fact that the
trustee may himself have rights as a beneficiary, are not necessarily inconsistent
with the existence of a trust.

Although this was not intended to constitute a definition of 'trust',[511] **3.178**
Professor Harris acknowledges that 'the detail contained within the Article
comes close to a definition and it is reasonable to suppose that it will be so

---

[506] OJ C282, 13 [31.10.1980].
[507] See, generally, M Lupoi, n 505 above, ch 4, 5, and 7.
[508] OJ C282, 13 [31.10.1980].
[509] Recital (7).
[510] von Overbeck Report, paras 36–47; J Harris, n 505 above, 103–22; M Lupoi, n 505 above,
333–41.
[511] von Overbeck Report, paras 36–7.

regarded in certain civil law systems'.[512] He suggests, however, that the characteristics of a 'trust' described in Art 2 'lack a certain ambition', adding:[513]

They are rather general. Certainly, they do not incorporate anything like all the features of the English trust. In particular, no stress is placed on the transfer of ownership to the trustee; nor on the proprietary entitlement[514] and other rights of the beneficiary; and reference to the fiduciary nature of the trust, so pivotal to its essence in the common law world, is excluded.

3.179 Professor Lupoi is even more critical of Art 2 of the Convention, and its consequences.[515] Noting that the authors of the Hague Trusts Convention appear to have started from the Anglo-American model of a 'trust', as emphasized by the reference in the preamble to 'the trust, as developed in courts of common law jurisdictions and adopted with some modifications in other jurisdictions', he submits that this focus was lost during negotiations through a combination of 'arrogance', 'ambivalence', 'defensiveness', and a 'fear of alarming civil law countries'. This leads him to conclude that, if the criteria set out in Art 2 are faithfully applied, 'trusts' (or 'shapeless trusts' to use Professor Lupoi's terminology) probably exist in every legal system. He adds:[516]

One interpretative result of the conclusion we have reached lies in emptying the provisions of the Convention referring to systems . . . 'which do not have the institution of the trust'[517] of any content. . . .

The failure to conduct a comparative analysis has led to the definition of a legal structure whose relevance was not understood, and which today has problems of acceptance. This is not, however, a criticism; it is an interpretation of the rules of the Convention.

3.180 Professor Lupoi argues forcefully that, when compared to the Anglo-American model, the concept of a 'trust' described in Art 2 of the Hague Convention is both too narrow and too wide. For example, (1) it requires only that assets be 'under the control' of the trustee, and not vested in him,[518] (2) it presupposes that the trustee and settlor are different persons leading to the conclusion that transactions by which a person declares

---

[512] J Harris, n 505 above, 104.

[513] Ibid, 111 (footnote added).

[514] In the present author's view, the beneficiary's entitlement, although it appears proprietary in certain respects, can equally be expressed, in the context of the present Regulation, using the language of obligation (cf **4.104** below).

[515] M Lupoi, n 505 above, 327–41.

[516] Ibid, 339–41.

[517] Hague Trusts Convention, Art 13. Also ibid, Arts 5 and 6.

[518] M Lupoi, n 505 above, 237, 333–5.

himself as trustee fall outside the Convention,[519] (3) it makes no reference to the relationship between the trustee and other parties (fiduciary or otherwise),[520] and (4) it cannot easily be reconciled with the concepts of resulting and constructive trusts recognized by common law systems.[521]

Professor Harris, although acknowledging the force of many of Professor Lupoi's arguments, concludes that:[522] **3.181**

All that said, the radical implications of Lupoi's cogent argumentation may be thought unlikely to be followed to their logical extreme by the courts of contracting states. The intention principally to regulate the common law trust is clear from the Preamble to the Convention, even if it was subsequently decided to make provision for the 'analogous' institutions existing elsewhere . . . Purposive interpretation of the Convention by common law states would suggest that the most irreducible core of the trust would be that ownership of the assets passes to the trustee, but that the assets do not form part of his personal patrimony. But this view cannot be stated with confidence; still less can it be confidently asserted that the scope of Article 2 will be uniformly interpreted from one contracting state to another.

In a different context, the Schlosser Report on the convention for the accession of Denmark, Ireland, and the UK to the Brussels Convention stated:[523] **3.182**

A distinguishing feature of United Kingdom and Irish law is the trust. In these two States it provides the solution to many problems which Continental legal systems overcome in an altogether different way. The basic structure of a trust may be described as the relationship which arises when a person or persons (the trustees) hold rights of any kind for the benefit of one or more persons (the beneficiaries) or for some object permitted by law, in such a way that the real benefit of the property accrues, not to the trustees, but to the beneficiaries (who may, however, include one or more of the trustees) or other object of the trust.

This description, focusing on the legal consequences of the 'trust', rather than the way in which it comes into existence, seems a useful starting point against which to analyse analogous legal institutions as fitting within or outside Art 1(2)(e). In view, however, of the observation in the Giuliano & Lagarde Report that the continental counterparts to the English law **3.183**

---

[519] Ibid, 335.

[520] Ibid, 336.

[521] Ibid, 238, referring to Art 20 of the Convention ('trusts declared by judicial decisions'), discussed at **3.201–3.202** below.

[522] J Harris, n 505 above, 115–16.

[523] OJ C59, 106 [5.3.1979], para 109. Professor Schlosser continues by separating what he describes as 'the external relationships of the trust' (i.e. dealings of the trustee with third parties) from the 'internal relationships of the trust' (i.e. disputes between trustees, or between trustees and beneficiaries).

trust are 'normally contractual in origin',[524] the question as to what characteristics a 'trust' must possess seems more likely to arise in relation to the Rome I Regulation than the Rome II Regulation. The following paragraphs focus on the English law concept of a trust.

3.184 *Trust 'created voluntarily'* The Art 1(2)(e) exclusion applies only to trusts 'created voluntarily'. The Commission Proposal contained no such restriction, referring to 'non-contractual obligations among the settlers, trustees and beneficiaries of a trust'.[525] The narrower wording in the Regulation in its final form, originating in the European Parliament's 1st Reading Position,[526] was evidently intended to ensure greater consistency with the Hague Trusts Convention, Art 3 of which limits its principal[527] sphere of application to 'trusts created voluntarily and evidenced in writing'.[528] Art 1(2)(e) does not, however, impose a requirement of writing.[529]

3.185 A further reason identified by the EP JURI Committee in its 1st Reading Report for recommending this change was 'to avoid difficulty or confusion arising from the employment of the trust in common-law jurisdictions as a device for dealing with situations such as unjust enrichment'. Unfortunately, as will be seen, the language chosen does little to resolve these difficulties. From the viewpoint of English law and that of other common law systems, difficult questions arise as to whether resulting, constructive, and other non-express trusts, which may arise in a variety of circumstances, constitute trusts 'created voluntarily' for these purposes.

3.186 In his report on the Hague Trusts Convention, Professor von Overbeck contrasted 'trusts created voluntarily' with those created 'by operation of law or by judicial decision'.[530] He commented:[531]

> The exclusion of judicial trusts extends to constructive trusts imposed by the courts and to trusts that the courts create by virtue of an express provision of law. . . .
>
> During the discussion on judicial trusts, the problem of the resulting trust was raised. This may be involved, for example, in cases where the purposes of an express trust have been fulfilled, but the trustee continues to hold certain assets under a resulting trust. The opinion was expressed . . . that such resulting trusts could fall under the coverage of the Convention. This interpretation also corresponds to

---

[524] OJ C282, 13 [31.10.1980].
[525] Commission Proposal, Art 1(2)(e).
[526] EP 1st Reading Position, Art 1(2)(e) (Amendment 21).
[527] See, however, Art 20, discussed at **3.201–3.202** below.
[528] EP 1st Reading Report, 15.
[529] Cf Commission Amended Proposal, Art 1(2)(e), which required writing.
[530] von Overbeck Report, para 49.
[531] Ibid, paras 49, 51.

that of the Special Commission which had specifically omitted the words 'constituted expressly' which would have excluded resulting trusts.

Professor Lupoi is strongly critical both of the reasoning that led the **3.187** authors of the Hague Trusts Convention to limit its primary scope to the 'trusts created voluntarily', an invented category unknown in English law,[532] and of the analysis by Professor von Overbeck of 'judicial' and 'resulting' trusts.[533] He suggests, however, that the category of 'voluntary' trusts includes constructive trusts 'which begin with a declaration of will by the settlor'.[534] In similar fashion, Professor Harris suggests:[535]

It appears that the trust must at the very least reflect the will of the settlor (even if he did not expressly declare and constitute that trust), so excluding constructive trusts imposed by the court irrespective of the settlor's will and trusts created by operation of law.

In the context of the Rome II Regulation, however, a slightly different **3.188** approach may be favoured. Consistently with the approach taken above to the concept of 'contractual obligation',[536] it is submitted that the test as to whether the trust arises 'by operation of law' is unhelpful. Instead, the focus should be on the event that gives rise to the trust, with the result that a 'trust' should be taken to be 'created voluntarily' and to fall outside the scope of the Rome II Regulation if it is founded on a voluntary act of a person (the settlor) with regard to specific assets with the object, however ascertained, that they be held by him or by another person to whom those assets have been or are to be transferred for the benefit of one or more persons or for some purpose permitted by law.

On this view, the following may be seen as examples of trusts 'created **3.189** voluntarily' for the purposes of the Regulation:[537]

1. Trusts constituted expressly by a written instrument or oral declaration of trust.

2. Constructive trusts arising when there is either an express declaration of trust which does not satisfy formal requirements, or when the court determines on the available evidence as to the parties' discussions and conduct that the parties intended that an asset should be held otherwise

---

[532] M Lupoi, n 505 above, 341.

[533] Ibid, 342–3.

[534] Ibid.

[535] J Harris, n 505 above, 125.

[536] **3.121** and **3.138** above.

[537] Cf Dicey, Morris & Collins, 1st supplement, para 34-044; M Lupoi, n 505 above, 342–3; J Harris, n 505 above, 124–34; *Underhill & Hayton*, n 505 above, paras 102.64–102.85

than by the legal owner for his own benefit or by joint owners on the basis prescribed by law (so called 'common intention constructive trusts').[538] These trusts are concerned to prevent 'inequitable'[539] or 'unconsciona-ble'[540] conduct by the defendant in invoking his legal title to defeat the parties' common intention. As the claim, if successful, gives effect to that common intention, the view that such constructive trusts are excluded from the Rome II Regulation by Art 1(2)(e) does not appear to stretch the concept of a 'voluntary trust' beyond its proper limits.[541]

The English law doctrine of proprietary estoppel operates on a similar principle to the common intention constructive trust,[542] but claims based on this doctrine may be argued to fall on the other side of the line. Again, the claim focuses on the defendant's 'unconscionable conduct', this time in specifically[543] denying the claimant's reasonable belief that he would acquire a certain interest in land in particular circumstances, provided that the claimant has acted to his detriment in reliance on that belief.[544] The proprietary estoppel doctrine is not concerned, however, with giving effect to the claimant's expectation, engendered by the defendant's con-duct, of a beneficial interest in land, but with avoiding injustice to the claimant in circumstances where that expectation has proved unfounded. That objective may be achieved otherwise than by declaring the defendant to be a trustee for the claimant of the land or an interest in it, including by an award of monetary compensation.[545] Accordingly, the primary equitable obligation, if it is properly described as such, to which the defendant's conduct gives rise is an obligation not to treat the claimant unfairly, rather than to hold property as trustee. Even if the equi-table claim is appropriately satisfied by a declaration that the defendant holds land, or an interest in land, as trustee for the claimant, it seems arti-ficial to describe that trust as having been 'created voluntarily'. Accordingly, claims based on the doctrine of proprietary estoppel would appear to fall outside the trusts exclusion in Art 1(2)(e) and potentially within the scope of the Rome II Regulation.[546]

---

[538] *Stack v Dowden* [2007] UKHL 17; [2007] 2 AC 432.

[539] *Gissing v Gissing* [1981] AC 886, 905 (Lord Diplock, UKHL).

[540] *Grant v Edwards* [1986] Ch 638, 656 (Browne-Wilkinson V-C, EWHC); *Yaxley v Gotts* [2000] Ch 162, 176 (Robert Walker LJ, EWCA).

[541] Compare the categories of constructive trust discussed at **3.192–3.193** below.

[542] *Lewin on Trusts*, n 505 above, paras 9-80 to 9-81.

[543] *Yeoman's Row Management Limited v Cobbe* [2008] UKHL 55.

[544] *Gillett v Holt* [2001] Ch 210, 225–6 (Robert Walker LJ, EWCA).

[545] *Stack v Dowden*, n 538 above, [37].

[546] **4.106** below.

3. So-called 'presumed' resulting trusts which arise where (within his life-time) one person (A) voluntarily transfers assets to another (B), or pays a third person to transfer assets to B, in circumstances which lead to the conclusion (based on an evidential presumption[547]) that A intended that B should hold the asset on trust for him.[548]

The status of so called 'automatic' resulting trusts (i.e. those arising when **3.190** the trust fails, whether because the trusts declared fail to deal with the beneficial entitlement to some or all of the trust property, or the object fails, or otherwise)[549] is less clear. The commentary in the von Overbeck Report[550] suggests that such trusts should be considered as having been 'created voluntarily' for the purposes of the Hague Trusts Convention, and this seems the better view, although the explanation given, that the trust is based on the settlor's implied intention, is unconvincing.[551] Trusts of this kind cannot easily be explained as resting on the settlor's inten-tion.[552] Nevertheless, the link in such cases between the 'automatic' trust and a trust which is undoubtedly 'created voluntarily' appears sufficiently close for the former to be considered as falling within the scope of Art 1(2)(e).[553] It may be appropriate here to draw an analogy with Art 10(1)(e) of the Rome Convention under which the consequences of nullity of a contract are referred to the law applicable to the contract. To similar effect, Art 8(h)(i) of the Hague Trusts Convention refers to the law applicable to the trust questions concerning 'termination of the trust' and 'distribution

---

[547] W Swadling, 'Explaining Resulting Trusts' (2008) 124 LQR 72, rejecting the attempts by others (including Professors Birks and Chambers to argue that such trusts rest not on the trans-feror's intention but on the law's response to 'non-beneficial transfers' falling within the con-cept of unjust enrichment). Swadling (at 73) prefers the descriptive terms 'voluntary conveyance' and 'purchase money' trusts to the term 'presumed' resulting trusts, the latter terminology originating in the decision of Megarry J in *Re Vandervell's Trusts (No 2)* [1974] 2 Ch 269, 294.

[548] Professor Harris reaches a different conclusion in the context of the Hague Trusts Convention (J Harris, n 505 above, 127).

[549] Again, the label 'automatic resulting trust' is that of Megarry J in *Re Vandervell's Trusts (No 2)*. Swadling prefers the descriptive term 'failed trust resulting trust' (for references, see n 547 above).

[550] Text to n 531 above.

[551] M Lupoi, n 505 above, 342; J Harris, n 505 above, 125–6; R Stevens, 'Resulting Trusts in the Conflict of Laws', ch 8 in P Birks and F Rose (eds), *Restitution and Equity, vol 1: Resulting Trusts and Equitable Compensation* (2000), 157. Also W Swadling, n 547 above, 96–101.

[552] W Swadling, n 547 above, 94–6 commenting on the reasoning of Lord Browne-Wilkinson in *Westdeutsche Landesbank Girozentrale v Islington LBC* [1996] AC 699, 708 (UKHL).

[553] Cf *Gomez v Gomez-Monche Vives* [2008] EWHC 259 (Ch), [56]–[59] (Morgan J) rejecting the argument that an 'automatic' resulting trust was 'created by' the original instrument which failed to dispose of the beneficial entitlement for the purposes of Art 5(6) of the Brussels I Regulation (see text to n 571 below). Also, on appeal, [2008] EWCA Civ 1065, [78]–[79] (Lawrence Collins LJ).

of the trust assets'. On this basis, a resulting trust arising in consequence of the failure of an express trust falls wholly outside the scope of the Rome II Regulation.

3.191 In the case of statutory trusts, for example those imposed on insolvency or the transfer of land, the fact that such trusts are created by legislation should not prevent them from being characterized as 'trusts voluntarily created' for these purposes.[554] Instead, the court must identify the event on which the statutory trust is founded, applying the test suggested at **3.188** above. If the statutory trust does not arise from a voluntary act of the settlor, Art 1(2)(e) will not apply. If it does, Art 1(2)(e) may apply to the trust, but only if the object of that act was that specific assets should be held by the settlor or by a transferee for the benefit of one or more persons or for some purpose permitted by law.

3.192 Moving to the other side of the line separating 'voluntary' from 'non-voluntary' trusts, constructive trusts based on the defendant's 'unconscionable' conduct, other than in the type of cases identified in categories 1 and 2 (**3.189** above), should not be considered to be trusts 'voluntarily created', as they operate against the parties' intentions.[555] This, it is submitted, includes the situation in which it is sought to recover misappropriated trust assets from a 'knowing recipient'.[556] This situation can be seen as being but one example of a case in which recognition of the trust should be treated as an involuntary consequence of a contractual or non-contractual obligation found to be owing by the defendant to the claimant. Other examples include (a) 'remedial constructive trusts' of a kind recognized by some common law systems but not currently recognized under English law,[557] (b) the duty of a defaulting fiduciary to hold a bribe and its proceeds on trust for his principal,[558] and (c) the trust arising as a result of the availability of the remedy of specific performance to enforce a sale contract or other transaction.[559] In the last two examples, the existence of the trust under English law depends on the availability of a

---

[554] Cf J Harris, n 505 above, 133.

[555] *Westdeutsche v Islington LBC*, n 552 above, 708 (Lord Browne-Wilkinson).

[556] J Harris, n 505 above, 129. For the characterization of such a claim under the Regulation, see **4.103–4.105** below.

[557] *Westdeutsche v Islington LBC*, n 552 above, 714–16 (Lord Browne-Wilkinson); *Re Polly Peck International plc (No 2)* [1998] 3 All ER 812 (EWCA); *London Allied Holdings Ltd v Lee* [2007] EWHC 2061 (Ch), [259]–[264], [273]–[274] (Etherton J, EWHC).

[558] *Attorney-General for Hong Kong v Reid* [1994] 1 AC 324 (PC).

[559] *Shaw v Foster* (1972) LR 5 HL 321, 338 (Lord Cairns, UKHL). Professor Harris, on the other hand, argues that the trust arising in such cases is a 'trust created voluntarily' under the Hague Trusts Convention (J Harris, n 505 above, 128).

specific remedy for the defendant's wrongdoing coupled with the application of the equitable maxim 'equity regards as done that which ought to be done'.[560] The trust is thus parasitic on the remedy and the remedy on the defendant's obligation, whether contractual or non-contractual. The 'constructive trust' imposed on the 'knowing recipient' appears to be of a similar character. [561] Whether that view is accepted, or whether the trust is seen as a direct response to the defendant's wrongful conduct (or, possibly, unjust enrichment), all of these trusts should be considered to fall outside Art 1(2)(e) and to be capable of giving rise to non-contractual obligations within the scope of the Rome II Regulation.

The obligations as 'constructive trustee' of a person who, by mistake or **3.193** otherwise, assumes the character of a trustee without having been validly appointed (the so-called trustee *de son tort*[562]) also fall outside Art 1(2)(e), as may those of the person (e.g. the solicitor or agent) who receives trust property lawfully but then misappropriates it.[563] In neither case is the trust created voluntarily.

Trusts arising in connection with matters of wills and succession Art 1(2)(e) **3.194** must be read with the exclusion in Art 1(2)(b) of 'wills and succession'.[564] In the report of Professor Schlosser on the Convention for the Accession of Denmark, Ireland and the United Kingdom to the Brussels Convention, the exclusion of 'wills and succession' from the scope of the 1968 Convention[565] was stated to cover:[566]

[A]ll claims to testate or intestate succession to an estate. It includes disputes as to the validity or interpretation of the terms of a will setting up a trust, even where the trust takes effect on a date subsequent to the death of the testator. The same applies to proceedings in respect of the application and interpretation of statutory provisions establishing trusts in favour of persons or institutions as a result of a person dying intestate. The 1968 Convention does not, therefore, apply to any disputes concerning the creation, interpretation and administration of trusts arising under the law of succession including wills. On the other hand, disputes concerning the relations of the trustee with persons other than beneficiaries, in other words the 'external relations' of the trust, come within the scope of the 1968 Convention.

---

[560] *Attorney-General for Hong Kong v Reid*, n 558 above, at 336; *Central Trust and Safe Deposit Co v Snider* [1916] 1 AC 266, 272 (PC).
[561] This argument is developed at **3.200,** point 3 below.
[562] Lewin on Trusts, n 505 above, paras 42–74 to 42–82.
[563] Ibid, paras 42-83 to 42-97.
[564] **3.153–3.156** above.
[565] Art 1(4).
[566] OJ C59, 89 [5.3.1979], para 52.

By virtue of Art 1(2)(b), these matters are outside the scope of the Rome II Regulation. Other situations connected with testamentary dispositions, for example trusts arising with respect to mutual wills and so called 'secret trusts', also fall within the Art 1(2)(b) exclusion, whether or not the trusts can be considered to have been 'voluntarily created' for the purposes of Art 1(2)(e).[567]

3.195 *Obligations of (or to) persons other than settlor, trustee, or beneficiary*   The Art 1(2)(e) exclusion also applies only to non-contractual obligations 'arising out of' relations between the settlors, trustees, and beneficiaries of non-voluntary trusts. Accordingly, non-contractual obligations owed by or to 'outsiders' (for example, the liability of a person assisting a breach of trust or a trustee's tortious liability to a person with whom he deals) are not excluded from the Regulation by Art 1(2)(e).[568] The rights and obligations of third party holders of trust assets are also carved out of the Hague Trusts Convention.[569]

3.196 The same conclusion may be reached with respect to obligations owed by or to other persons concerned in the administration of the trust, including protectors and the donees of fiduciary powers. In *Gomez v Gomez-Monche Vives*,[570] the position of an 'appointor' under an English law trust was not considered sufficiently analogous to the position of a 'trustee' so as to justify the conclusion that a person claiming to be the appointor was sued 'as trustee' under Art 5(6) of the Brussels I Regulation.[571] In this connection, Morgan J commented:[572]

> Based on the detailed analysis of the differences between mere powers, fiduciary powers and trusts in the two cases I have cited, I conclude that there are considerable differences between the office or the capacity of a trustee and the position of a donee of a fiduciary power. In some circumstances, it might conceivably be right to react to the word 'trustee' in an instrument, or even in a statutory provision, by holding that the parties to the instrument or the enacting authority intended to

---

[567] Cf M Lupoi, n 505 above, 342–3; J Harris, n 505 above, 128, 131.

[568] Cf *Gomez v Gomez-Monche Vives*, [2008] EWCA Civ 1065, [81]–[90] (Lawrence Collins LJ) concluding that claims to recover mistakenly sums paid to a person falling within the class of beneficiaries were claims against her as 'beneficiary' within Art 5(6) of the Brussels I Regulation. A 'knowing recipient' may hold assets as a constructive trustee (**3.200** below), but that (involuntary) trust is distinct from that under which the assets were originally held by the defaulting trustee.

[569] Hague Trusts Convention, Art 11(d). See J Harris, n 505 above, 129, 321–30.

[570] n 553 above.

[571] Art 5(6) provides: 'A person domiciled in a Member State may, in another Member State, be sued: . . . as settlor, trustee or beneficiary of a trust created by the operation of a statute, or by a written instrument, or created orally and evidenced in writing, in the courts of the Member State in which the trust is domiciled'.

[572] Ibid, [102]–[103]. The judge's ruling on this point was upheld by the Court of Appeal ([2008] EWCA Civ 1065, [91]–[99] (Lawrence Collins LJ)).

embrace not just trustees properly so called but also persons who had fiduciary duties where those duties were, in the wide spectrum of fiduciary duties, close enough to be regarded as analogous to or akin to the duties of a trustee.

However, I have no doubt that that liberal or expansive approach to the word 'trustee', which might conceivably be possible in some contexts, is not appropriate in the present context. I have already referred to the restrictive approach which I am required to adopt to the derogation provisions in Article 5(6). It seems to me it would be quite inconsistent with that restrictive approach to read the words 'as trustee' in the present case in the expansive way . . .

It remains to be seen whether a similarly restrictive approach will be taken **3.197** to the term 'trustee' in respect to Art 1(2)(e) of the Rome II Regulation.

The relationship between trusts and non-contractual obligations under the **3.198** *Regulation* It does not, of course, follow from the conclusion that a trust was created otherwise than 'voluntarily' that the Rome II Regulation will govern all aspects of the relationship between the 'settlors', 'trustees', and 'beneficiaries' or, indeed, that it will play any role in determining (a) whether a trust relationship has been created between the parties in the first place, or (b) whether a trust relationship governed by or created under a foreign law must be recognized by the Member State in which proceedings are brought for breach of trust or otherwise to enforce a non-contractual obligation arising out of the trust. In this connection, it must be emphasized that the Regulation can apply only to *non-contractual obligations*, whether arising before or after the trust relationship is constituted. As to the question whether a trust has been created,[573] it is submitted that the law applicable under the Rome II Regulation will govern to the extent that the trust relationship arises as a consequence of a non-contractual obligation not otherwise excluded from the scope of the Regulation by Art 1(2).

So far as recognition of a trust relationship is concerned, it is submitted **3.199** that trusts already created, or recognized as existing between the parties, by a foreign judicial decision require separate treatment. In such cases, the Member State court must apply rules concerning the recognition and enforcement of foreign judgments. In other cases where recognition of a foreign trust is sought,[574] the Member State court must apply other rules of private international law, including (as appropriate) those contained in the Regulation and, in the United Kingdom, the Recognition of Trusts

---

[573] Putting to one side questions as to the relationship between the Regulation, the Hague Trusts Convention, and the UK Recognition of Trusts Act 1987, which are dealt with at **3.201–3.207** below.

[574] J Harris, n 505 above, 135–6.

Act 1987.[575] Subject to the Hague Trusts Convention, the Regulation will require a trust to be recognized in such cases if it arises as a consequence of a non-contractual obligation falling within its scope.

3.200 The following propositions appear consistent with the foregoing analysis:

1. In accordance with Art 15(1)(d) of the Rome II Regulation,[576] any question as to whether a Member State court ought to impose a remedial trust [577]over property in response to a tort/delict or other non-contractual obligation falling within the scope of the Regulation should be determined by reference to the law applicable to that obligation under the Regulation.

2. A trust imposed by another Member State court by way of a remedy for a non-contractual obligation in a civil or commercial matter must be recognized and, if necessary, enforced in accordance with the Brussels I Regulation.

3. A trust that arises as a direct consequence of the award or availability of a particular judicial remedy for a non-contractual obligation may also, for present purposes, be seen as an integral part of that remedy rather than as a separate aspect of the parties' relationship governed by a different rule of applicable law. Thus, the law applicable to the obligation of a defaulting fiduciary who has received a bribe or other assets as a consequence of his 'wrongful' conduct towards his principal[578] should, in the absence of an earlier binding judicial decision and subject to any procedural limit on the court's powers,[579] determine not only the remedy to be awarded to the claimant, and whether that remedy imposes obligations with regard to specific property, but also the proprietary and other consequences of that remedy, including whether the defendant is thereby placed in the position of a trustee with respect to the property held by him. Here, the defaulting fiduciary's obligation, as recognized under English law, to account for property received by him as a result of his wrongful conduct constitutes a measure taken to prevent or terminate injury or damage, within Art 10(1)(d) of the Rome II Regulation, and the question whether a trust relationship is deemed to

---

[575] As to the relationship between the Regulation and the 1987 Act, see **3.203–3.207** below.

[576] Referring to 'the measures which a court may take to prevent or terminate injury of damage or to ensure the provision of compensation' (**14.33–14.36** below).

[577] Text to n 557 above.

[578] *Attorney-General v Reid*, n 558 and text to n 560 above. Although the obligations of the defaulting fiduciary in that case are more appropriately viewed for the purposes of the Regulation as an incident of a contractual relationship (**3.142** above), other cases involving breach of fiduciary duties will fall within the scope of the Rome II Regulation.

[579] Rome II Regulation, Art 15(1)(d) (**14.34** below). Also Rome Convention, Art 10(1)(c); Rome I Regulation, Art 12(1)(c).

have been created at the moment of receipt with regard to the bribe and its traceable proceeds seems inseparable from the remedy itself.[580]

4. On this view, recognition under the Brussels I Regulation of a judgment of another Member State court awarding a remedy for a non-contractual obligation should also arguably trigger recognition of any trust arising as a consequence of that remedy under the law of the Member State of origin.[581]

5. The Rome II Regulation should also apply to the question whether a recipient of property is to be placed in the position of a trustee with respect to that property in circumstances where his receipt or retention of that property involves a tort/delict or unjust enrichment under the Regulation.[582] For example, in the case of the 'knowing recipient' of trust property under English law, from the moment that the defendant's 'conscience' is affected by knowledge of the legally significant fact or facts affecting the transfer to him of specific assets,[583] he must hold those assets for the transferor or other person beneficially entitled, and will be compelled to account for their whereabouts. In the meantime, the court treats him as if he held the assets on trust for the beneficiary, but that is simply a consequence of the court's willingness to intervene to prevent equitable wrongdoing. Indeed, it has been said that '[i]n such a case the expressions "constructive trust" and "constructive trustee" are misleading, for there is no trust and usually no possibility of a proprietary remedy; they are "nothing more than a formula for equitable relief".'[584]

Relationship between the Regulation, the 1985 Hague Convention, and the UK **3.201**
Recognition of Trusts Act 1987   The final set of problems concerns the relationship between the Rome II Regulation, the Hague Trusts Convention,

---

[580] In the case of contractual obligations, by the same process of reasoning, the law applicable under the Rome I Regime to the consequences of breach (Rome Convention, Art 10(1)(c); Rome I Regulation, Art 12(1)(c)) will (again, in the absence of an earlier binding judicial decision and subject to the procedural powers of the court) determine whether a contracting party occupies the position of trustee with respect to the subject matter of the contract in cases where the trust is founded on the court's ability to enforce the contract by an order for specific performance (text to nn 559–560 above).

[581] Case 145/86, *Hoffmann v Krieg* [1988] ECR 645, para 10; Jenard Report (OJ C59, 43 [5.3.1979] ('Recognition must have the result of conferring on judgments the authority and effectiveness accorded to them in the State in which they were given').

[582] For the characterization of particular claims involving the receipt of property for the purposes of the Regulation as either 'tort/delict' or 'unjust enrichment', see **4.103–4.105** below.

[583] *Westdeutsche v Islington LBC*, n 552 above, 705 (Lord Browne-Wilkinson).

[584] *Paragon Finance plc v D B Thakerar & Co* [1999] 1 All ER 400, 409 (Millett LJ, EWCA).

and the UK legislation implementing the Convention, the Recognition of Trusts Act 1987. It has already been noted that the Hague Trusts Convention, in contrast to the Rome II Convention, principally applies only to trusts 'created voluntarily'[585] and does not purport to determine the law applicable to questions concerning the rights and obligations of third party holders of trust assets.[586] Against this background, and even taking account of possible differences in the approach to be taken in determining whether there is a 'trust created voluntarily' under the two instruments,[587] it might have been thought that the Hague Trusts Convention and the Rome II Regulation would pass each other like ships in the night. Unhappily, Art 20 of the Hague Trusts Convention permits Contracting States to declare that the provisions of the Convention will be extended to trusts 'declared by judicial decisions' (in the French text, *créés par une décision de justice*). Professor von Overbeck appears to have considered constructive trusts imposed by courts or created by them by virtue of an express provision of law to fall within this category of 'judicial trusts'.[588] His reasoning is criticized by Professor Lupoi who argues that the category will apply to a trust 'not simply because a judgment declares that it exists, but only when the decision condemns the defendant to behave like a trustee, usually with the aim of compensating the plaintiff for losses he has suffered'.[589] He continues:[590]

If the basis of the judgment is different, there may or may not be a 'voluntarily created' trust and the deciding factor for the purposes of recognition will not be the judgment itself, but its *ratio decidendi*.

3.202 Accordingly, Professor Lupoi considers resulting trusts and what might be described as 'institutional' (as opposed to 'remedial') constructive trusts,[591] to fall beyond the reach of Art 20 of the Hague Trusts Convention.[592] That view seems more consistent with the French than the English language version of the Convention. There may, however, be room for a wider view of the category of 'judicial trusts', consistent with the English and French texts, which embodies at least some constructive trusts of an 'institutional' character. On this view, Art 20 should be taken to extend not only to trusts that are imposed by the court by way of remedy, but also to other trusts

---

[585] **3.184–3.193** above.
[586] **3.195–3.197** above.
[587] **3.188** above.
[588] Text to n 531 above. Also von Overbeck Report, n 505 above, paras 166–9.
[589] M Lupoi, n 505 above 344.
[590] Ibid, 344–5.
[591] *Westdeutsche v Islington LBC*, n 552 above, at 714–15 (Lord Browne-Wilkinson).
[592] M Lupoi, n 505 above, 238. Also J Harris, n 505 above, 145–8, 402–3.

that are closely linked to the remedial consequences of an obligation owed by the claimant to the defendant.[593] In particular, if the availability of a particular court remedy is a pre-condition to the continuing existence of the trust (as it will be if the trust arises through the operation of the equitable maxim 'equity treats as done that which ought to be done'[594]), the trust should be seen as being 'declared' by judicial decision under Art 20 of the Hague Trusts Convention.

Among the Member States party to the Hague Trusts Convention, only **3.203** Luxembourg and the UK have made a declaration under Art 20. In this connection, s 1(2) of the UK Recognition of Trusts Act 1987 provides that the scheduled provisions of the Convention 'shall . . . have effect not only in relation to the trusts described in Articles 2 and 3 of the Convention but also in relation to any other trusts of property arising under the law of any part of the United Kingdom or by virtue of a judicial decision whether in the United Kingdom or elsewhere'. That seems to go significantly further than the limited extension contemplated by Art 20 of the Hague Convention, however broadly it is interpreted. Of course, at the time that the UK adopted the 1987 Act, there was no compelling reason why the UK could not choose to apply the rules of applicable law contained in the Hague Trusts Convention to whatever 'trusts' or other legal relationships it considered appropriate. From 11 January 2009, however, the mandatory nature of the Rome II Regulation, and the exclusion by Art 1(2)(e) only of trusts 'voluntarily created', creates the possibility of conflict between the Regulation and the 1987 Act.

In accordance with Art 28(1) of the Regulation,[595] the UK[596] may continue **3.204** to apply the provisions of the Hague Trusts Convention to non-contractual obligations arising out of trusts 'declared by judicial decision' within the meaning of Art 20 of the Convention. Although Art 20 takes the form of a provision that permits a declaration to be made extending the provisions of the Convention, the application of the Convention's rules to 'judicial trusts' by a court in a Contracting State that has made that declaration should be seen as involving 'the application of' an international convention and as being permitted by Art 28(1).[597]

In the case of 'judicial trusts', therefore, the rules of applicable law con- **3.205** tained in the 1987 Act will continue to apply in the UK to identify the law

---

[593] **3.200,** point 3 above.
[594] Text to n 560 above.
[595] Discussed at **16.36–16.40** below.
[596] As well, one assumes, as Luxembourg.
[597] Dicey, Morris & Collins, 1st supplement, para 29-063.

governing 'the validity of the trust, its construction, its effects, and the administration of the trust' including (for example) the relationships between the trustees and the beneficiaries, the personal liability of the trustees to the beneficiaries, the distribution of the trust assets, and the duty of the trustees to account for their administration.[598] Significantly, however, neither the Hague Trusts Convention nor the 1987 Act apply to 'preliminary issues relating to the validity of wills or other acts by virtue of which assets are transferred to the trustee',[599] and the editors of Dicey, Morris & Collins give this as a reason for concluding that the Regulation's rules of applicable law (and not those contained in the Hague Trusts Convention) will apply to 'the question whether a constructive trust arises' as a consequence of a non-contractual obligation.[600] That conclusion, although it is not clearly supported by the language of the Convention,[601] has an instinctive attraction, as the rules of applicable law in the Convention do not appear well-suited to determining the remedial or other legal consequences of non-contractual obligations.[602] The editors of Dicey, Morris & Collins recognize, however, that:[603]

> [I]t must be the case that once the trust is found to exist, its governing law is determined by Arts 6 and 7 of the Hague Convention. Moreover, the obligations imposed upon the trustee in relation to the trust must be a matter for the law determined by the Convention, rather than for the law under which the trust arose.

Accordingly, in the UK and Luxembourg, the Hague Convention (and not the Rome II Regulation) will determine the law applicable to obligations arising out of a 'judicial trust' from the date of the judgment that creates or confirms its existence.

3.206 Under Art 7 of the Hague Convention, in the absence of choice by the 'settlor', a trust shall be governed by the law with which it is most closely connected. In the case of 'judicial trusts', arguments may be presented for the application of either the law of the country whose court imposes the trust or the remedy that gives rise to the trust, or the law of the obligation from which the trust arises. That said, these questions have not yet been directly addressed by the English courts. Indeed, Professor Harris comments that 'it might be

---

[598] Hague Trusts Convention, Art 8(g), (i), and (j).

[599] Hague Trusts Convention, Art 4, as scheduled to the 1987 Act. See J Harris, n 505 above, 151–7.

[600] Dicey, Morris & Collins, 1st supplement, para 29-063. Also paras 29-063 to 29-065 of the main work.

[601] Cf J Harris, n 505 above, 147.

[602] A Chong, 'The Common Law Choice of Law Rules for Resulting and Constructive Trusts' (2005) 54 ICLQ 855, 858–9.

[603] Dicey, Morris & Collins, para 29-065 (main work) referred to in 1st supplement, para 29-063.

thought somewhat remarkable that the Hague Convention's choice of law rules receive almost no discussion in the few English cases where the existence of a constructive trust in a transnational context has been at issue'.[604]

Summary of conclusions (UK law)   Accordingly, to summarize the conclu- **3.207** sions in the preceding paragraphs, the Regulation will not apply to non-contractual obligations arising out of relations between settlers, trustees, and beneficiaries under 'trusts created voluntarily' (including express, implied, 'common intention', and resulting trusts), but will apply to obligations owed by or to other persons in connection with such trusts. In the case of 'judicial trusts' arising from non-contractual obligations falling within the scope of the Rome II Regulation, the law applicable to the relevant non-contractual obligation under the Regulation will apply to the question whether a trust arises in the first place, but not to the obligations of the trustee or any other person under that trust following its creation, to which the Hague Trusts Convention will apply. For other trusts that are not 'created voluntarily' under either the Hague Trusts Convention or the Rome II Regulation, the rules of applicable law contained in the Regulation will apply not only to the question whether a trust arises in the first place as a consequence of a non-contractual obligation falling within the scope of the Regulation but also to the (non-contractual) obligations of the trustee or any other person under or in connection with that trust. Finally, to the extent that the 1987 Act is also expressed to apply to 'trusts of property arising under the law of any part of the United Kingdom' other than trusts 'created voluntarily' and 'judicial trusts', the rules of applicable law contained in the Regulation for non-contractual obligations will prevail over those in the 1987 Act.

Nuclear damage (Art 1(2)(f))

Art 1(2)(f) of the Regulation excludes non-contractual obligations arising **3.208** out of nuclear damage. According to the Commission:[605]

This exclusion is explained by the importance of the economic and State interests at stake and the Member States' contribution to measures to compensate for

---

[604] J Harris, n 505 above, 140.
[605] Commission Proposal, 9 (footnotes added). For earlier discussion as to whether nuclear damage should be excluded from the scope of a Community instrument on the law applicable to non-contractual obligations, see Council document 10265/99 [30.7.1999]. Ireland initially opposed this exclusion (Council document 9009 ADD 13 [24.5.2004], 3).

For a summary of the international instruments regulating civil liability for nuclear activity, see C Bernasconi, 'Civil liability resulting from transfrontier environmental damage: a case for the Hague Conference?' Preliminary document No 8 of May 2000, reproduced at <http://www.hcch.net/upload/wop/gen_pd8e.pdf>, 5–6.

nuclear damage in the international scheme of nuclear liability established by the Paris Convention of 29 July 1960[606] and the Additional Convention of Brussels of 31 January 1963, the Vienna Convention[607] of 21 May 1963, the Convention on Supplementary Compensation of 12 September 1997[608] and the Protocol of 21 September 1988.[609]

3.209 *The 1960 Paris Convention* Art 3(a) of the 1960 Paris Convention (to which the UK is a party[610]) provides: [611]

The operator of a nuclear installation shall be liable, in accordance with this Convention, for:

i. damage to or loss of life of any person; and
ii. damage to or loss of any property other than
    1. the nuclear installation itself and any other nuclear installation, including a nuclear installation under construction, on the site where that installation is located; and
    2. any property on that same site which is used or to be used in connection with any such installation,

---

[606] Convention on Third Party Liability in the Field of Nuclear Energy (Paris, 29 July 1960), as amended by the Additional Protocol of 28 January 1964 and by the Protocol of 16 November 1982, reproduced at <http://www.nea.fr/html/law/nlparis_conv.html>. Of the Member States, the Convention, and 1964 and 1982 Protocols have been ratified by Belgium, Denmark, Finland, France, Germany, Greece, Italy, Netherlands, Portugal, Slovenia, Spain, Sweden, and the UK (Source: website of OECD Nuclear Energy Agency <http://www.nea.fr/html/law/paris-convention-ratification.html>). Austria and Luxembourg have signed but not ratified the Convention.

[607] Convention on civil liability for nuclear damage (Vienna, 21 May 1963), reproduced at <http://www.iaea.org/Publications/Documents/Infcircs/1996/inf500.shtml>. Of the Member States, the Convention is in force with respect to Bulgaria, Czech Republic, Estonia, Hungary, Latvia, Lithuania, Poland, Romania, and Slovakia. Spain and the UK have signed but not ratified the Convention (Source: website of the International Atomic Energy Agency (IAEA)<http://www.iaea.org/Publications/Documents/Conventions/liability_status.pdf>).

[608] Reproduced at <http://www.iaea.org/Publications/Documents/Conventions/supcomp.html>. Of the Member States, only Romania has ratified the Convention on Supplementary Compensation.

[609] Joint Protocol Relating to the Application of the Vienna Convention and the Paris Convention (Vienna, 21 September 1988), reproduced at <http://www.nea.fr/html/law/nljoint_prot.html>. Of the Member States, the Joint Protocol is in force with respect to Bulgaria, Czech Republic, Denmark, Estonia, Finland, Germany, Greece, Hungary, Italy, Latvia, Lithuania, Netherlands, Norway, Poland, Slovakia, Slovenia, and Sweden. France, Spain, and the UK have signed but not ratified the Joint Protocol (Source: website of IAEA <http://www.iaea.org/Publications/Documents/Conventions/jointprot_status.pdf>).

[610] For implementing legislation, see the Nuclear Installations Act 1965.

[611] The expressions 'nuclear incident' and 'nuclear installation' are defined in Art 2.

upon proof that such damage or loss (hereinafter referred to as 'damage') was caused by a nuclear incident in such installation or involving nuclear substances coming from such installation, except as otherwise provided for in Article 4.

Art 4 concerns the carriage of nuclear substances. The following provi- **3.210** sions, Arts 5 to 10, define the limits of the operator's liability and deal with insurance matters. Art 11 specifies that nature, form, and extent of the compensation, within the limits of this Convention, as well as the equitable distribution thereof, shall be governed by national law.[612] Art 13 contains rules of jurisdiction, generally favouring the courts of the Contracting State in whose territory the nuclear incident occurred, and provides for the enforcement of judgments between Contracting States.

The 1963 Vienna Convention   The 1963 Vienna Convention defines 'nuclear **3.211** damage' as:[613]

i. loss of life, any personal injury or any loss of, or damage to, property which arises out of or results from the radioactive properties or a combination of radioactive properties with toxic, explosive or other hazardous properties of nuclear fuel or radioactive products or waste in, or of nuclear material coming from, originating in, or sent to, a nuclear installation;

ii. any other loss or damage so arising or resulting if and to the extent that the law of the competent court so provides; and

iii. if the law of the Installation State so provides, loss of life, any personal injury or any loss of, or damage to, property which arises out of or results from other ionizing radiation emitted by any other source of radiation inside a nuclear installation.

Arts II to VII of the Convention make the operator of a nuclear installation **3.212** liable for 'nuclear damage' in certain circumstances and subject to certain limits, and provide for insurance. Art VIII specifies that the nature, form, extent, and equitable distribution of compensation are to be governed by the law of the competent court, defined to include conflict of laws rules.[614] Art XI contains rules of jurisdiction, generally favouring the courts of the Contracting Party within whose territory the nuclear incident occurred. Art XII provides for the recognition and enforcement of judgments between Contracting States.

---

[612] This appears to be a reference to the law of the forum (Paris Convention, n 606 above, Art 14(b)).

[613] Vienna Convention, n 607 above, Art I.1(k). The expressions 'Installation State', 'nuclear fuel', 'nuclear installation', 'nuclear material', and 'radioactive products' are also defined in Art I.1.

[614] Ibid, Art I.1(e).

3.213 *The 1988 Joint Protocol relating to the application of the Vienna Convention and the Paris Convention*   According to Art II of the 1988 Joint Protocol (to which Contracting States to both the 1960 Paris and 1963 Vienna Conventions are parties):

> The operator of a nuclear installation situated in the territory of a Party to the Vienna Convention shall be liable in accordance with that Convention for nuclear damage suffered in the territory of a Party to both the Paris Convention and this Protocol;

> The operator of a nuclear installation situated in the territory of a Party to the Paris Convention shall be liable in accordance with that Convention for nuclear damage suffered in the territory of a Party to both the Vienna Convention and this Protocol.

3.214 *Expanded definition of 'nuclear damage' under the Vienna and Paris Conventions*   The definition of 'nuclear damage' in the 1963 Vienna Convention (**3.211** above) is significantly expanded by a Protocol concluded between the contracting parties on 12 September 1997.[615] As yet, however, the Protocol has only been ratified by Latvia and Romania among Member States. In its modified form, the definition will encompass:[616]

   i. loss of life or personal injury;
  ii. loss of or damage to property;

and each of the following to the extent determined by the law of the competent court;

  iii. economic loss arising from loss or damage referred to in sub-paragraph (i) or (ii), insofar as not included in those sub-paragraphs, if incurred by a person entitled to claim in respect of such loss or damage;
  iv. the costs of measures of reinstatement of impaired environment, unless such impairment is insignificant, if such measures are actually taken or to be taken, and insofar as not included in sub-paragraph (ii);
  v. loss of income deriving from an economic interest in any use or enjoyment of the environment, incurred as a result of a significant impairment of that environment, and insofar as not included in sub-paragraph (ii);
  vi. the costs of preventive measures, and further loss or damage caused by such measures;
  vii. any other economic loss, other than any caused by the impairment of the environment, if permitted by the general law on civil liability of the competent court,

---

[615] For the text of the Protocol, see <http://www.iaea.org/Publications/Documents/Conventions/protamend.html>.

[616] Protocol to the Vienna Convention, 12 September 1997, Art 2.2.

in the case of subparagraphs (i) to (v) and (vii) above, to the extent that the loss or damage arises out of or results from ionizing radiation emitted by any source of radiation inside a nuclear installation, or emitted from nuclear fuel or radioactive products or waste in, or of nuclear material coming from, originating in, or sent to, a nuclear installation, whether so arising from the radioactive properties of such matter, or from a combination of radioactive properties with toxic, explosive or other hazardous properties of such matter.

By a Protocol to the 1960 Paris Convention, concluded on 12 February **3.215** 2004 (but not yet ratified by any Contracting State), this definition will also be incorporated into that Convention.[617]

Non-contractual obligations 'arising out of nuclear damage' In *Land* **3.216** *Oberösterreich v ČEZ as*,[618] the claim before the Austrian court concerned an alleged nuisance caused by ionizing radiation emanating from a nuclear power station situated in the Czech Republic. The Czech Republic is a party to the Vienna Convention and the 1988 Joint Protocol. Austria is a party to neither the Paris nor the Vienna Convention. In the circumstances, the question arises as to whether a claim such as this would fall within the Art 1(2)(f) exclusion. In particular, having regard to the reasons given by the Commission,[619] does the exclusion extend to situations in which the liability of the nuclear operator is not regulated by the Paris Convention, the Vienna Convention, or the 1988 Joint Protocol, whether because the Member State seised of the dispute is a party to neither Convention or because the claim falls outside the situations regulated by the Conventions and the Protocol in that State, whether by reason of the nature of the 'damage' suffered or the place where it was suffered or the location of the nuclear operator? One possible approach would be to construe the words 'nuclear damage' having regard not only to the definitions contained in the Conventions (as amended) but also to their sphere of application. That view, however, seems likely not only to give rise to greater uncertainty but also to give the words of Art 1(2)(f) a non-uniform meaning. Further, 'the economic and State interests at stake' to which the Commission refers are no less important for Member States that have not subscribed to either of the two principal international regimes. In the circumstances, it is submitted that the better view is that a wide, independent meaning should be given to the concept of 'nuclear damage', consistently with the

---

[617] Protocol to the Paris Convention, 12 February 2004, Art 1.B. For the text of the Protocol, see <http://www.nea.fr/html/law/paris_convention.pdf>.
[618] Discussed at **3.98** above.
[619] Text to n 605 above.

developments in the 1997 and 2004 Protocols referred to above[620] and with the broad meaning given to 'damage' in Art 2(1) of the Regulation.[621] It should extend, therefore, to claims for environmental and economic damage suffered as a consequence of a nuclear accident.

Violations of privacy and rights relating to personality (Art 1(2)(g))

3.217 *Introduction*   No subject matter proved more controversial in the discussions leading to the adoption of the Regulation than the non-contractual obligations excluded by Art 1(2)(g).[622] That this should be the case was entirely foreseeable. Not only are respect for private and family life and freedom of expression recognized as (competing) fundamental rights by the European Convention on Human Rights,[623] but both personal privacy and (in particular) press freedom have a high political profile. Indeed, the sensitivity of the political and constitutional issues raised by the latter led to a declaration by those adopting the Treaty of Amsterdam that the new Art 73m of the EC Treaty (which, following renumbering, became Art 65 and provides the treaty base for the Rome II Regulation) 'shall not prevent any Member State from applying its constitutional rules relating to freedom of the press and freedom of expression in other media'. At an early stage of the discussions in Council, the Swedish delegation took the position that there was no legal basis to regulate matters concerning freedom of expression and freedom of the press,[624] although this position does not appear to have been supported by other Member States.

3.218 During the consultation process, representatives of the broadcast and print media proved a powerful lobby group, with many openly advocating application of the so-called 'country of origin' principle.[625] There was overt hostility from media representatives[626] to the rules on defamation and privacy formulated by the Commission in both its preliminary draft

---

[620] **3.214–3.215**.

[621] **3.44–3.46** above.

[622] **1.92–193** and **1.95** above. Also A Warshaw, 'Uncertainty from Abroad: Rome II and the Choice of Law for Defamation Claims' (2006) 32 Brook J Int L 269, 291–302.

[623] Arts 8 (respect for private and family life) and 10 (freedom of expression).

[624] Council document 9009/04 ADD 8 [18.5.2004], 4.

[625] **16.23–16.25** below.

[626] See, for example, the evidence of Mr Alastair Brett (Times Newspapers), Santha Rasaiah (The Newspaper Society), Ms Clare Hoban (Periodical Publishers Association), and Mr Glenn Del Medico (BBC) to the House of Lords' European Union Committee, *The Rome II Regulation*, 8th Report of Session 2003–2004 (HL Paper 66), Evidence, 31–45.

proposal[627] and its Proposal,[628] but there was apparent support within the industry for the following 'compromise proposal' tabled by the European Parliament's rapporteur and adopted by the Parliament at its first[629] and second[630] reading stages:

1. As regards the law applicable to a non-contractual obligation arising out of a violation of privacy or rights relating to the personality, the law of the country in which the most significant element or elements of the loss or damage occur or are likely to occur shall be applicable.

Where the violation is caused by the publication of printed matter or by a broadcast, the country in which the most significant element or elements of the damage occur or are likely to occur shall be deemed to be the country to which the publication or broadcasting service is principally directed or, if this is not apparent, the country in which editorial control is exercised, and that country's law shall be applicable. The country to which the publication or broadcast is directed shall be determined in particular by the language of the publication or broadcast or by sales or audience size in a given country as a proportion of total sales or audience size or by a combination of those factors.

This provision shall apply *mutatis mutandis* to publications via the Internet and other electronic networks.

2. The law applicable to the right of reply or equivalent measures and to any preventive measures or prohibitory injunctions against a publisher or broadcaster regarding the content of a publication or broadcast shall be the law of the country in which the publisher or broadcaster has its habitual residence.

3. Paragraph 2 shall also apply to a violation of privacy or of rights relating to the personality resulting from the handling of personal data.

Following adoption of the Parliament's 1st Reading Position, the **3.219** Commission rejected this proposal as being 'too generous to press editors rather than the victim of alleged defamation' and as not reflecting the position taken by the large majority of Member States.[631] Adjusting its original position, the Commission's Amended Proposal favoured excluding 'violations of privacy and of personal rights by the media', but not

---

[627] Art 7, applying the law of the victim's habitual residence at the time of the tort or delict.

[628] Art 6, applying the law of the forum to situations in which the law otherwise applicable to the tort/delict under Art 3 would be contrary to the fundamental principles of the forum as regards freedom of expression and information and applying the law of the broadcaster or publisher's habitual residence to the issue of right to reply or equivalent measures. For comment, see G Wagner, 'Article 6 of the Commission Proposal: Violation of Privacy: Defamation by Mass Media' (2005) 13 Eur Rev Priv L 21.

[629] EP 1st Reading Position, Art 5.

[630] EP 2nd Reading Position, Art 7.

[631] Commission Amended Proposal, 6.

other violations of privacy and personality rights, from the scope of the Regulation. Subsequently, at the Parliament's second reading stage, Commissioner Frattini appeared more sympathetic to the Parliament's desire to keep these matters within the scope of the Regulation,[632] but the Commission had already resigned itself (like the Council in its Common Position) to their exclusion '[b]ecause it has not been possible to reach a compromise on the text'[633] and because of 'the ultimate inability to agree on the scope (definition) of *media* in this context'.[634] The Commissioner pointed out that 'over ten different options were on [the] Council's table in April 2006, not one of them has any chance of success, either now or, probably, in the future'.[635]

3.220 In the statement of reasons accompanying its Common Position, the Council explained that:[636]

Negotiations over violations of privacy and rights relating to personality caused difficulties to many delegations. The Council examined this issue on numerous occasions and carefully considered all options on the negotiating table, including the proposal by the European Parliament.

Nevertheless, as a final compromise and in an attempt to reconcile the conflicting interests, the Council decided to delete the special rule on violations of privacy and rights relating to personality at this stage.

3.221 During the conciliation process, the European Parliament's representatives reluctantly accepted the exclusion in Art 1(2)(g) in exchange for the inclusion of specific wording in the review clause (Art 30) requiring the Commission to undertake and submit not later than 31 December 2008 a study on the situation with respect to the law applicable to non-contractual obligations arising out of violations of privacy and rights relating to personality, 'taking into account rules relating to freedom of the press and freedom of expression in the media, and conflict-of-law issues related to

[632] EP document CRE 18/01/2007 – 4, available at <http://www.europarl.europa.eu/sides/getDoc.do?type=CRE&reference=20070118&secondRef=ITEM-004&language=EN&ring=A6-2006-0481>.

[633] Ibid.

[634] Commission Communication concerning the Council Common Position (COM (2006) 566 final [27.9.2006]), 3.

[635] For specific proposals and discussions in the Council's Rome II Committee, see Council documents 5430/04 [27.1.2004], 11801/04 [28.7.2004], 12997/04 [4.10.2004] (UK), 14193/04 [4.11.2004] (Spain), 14193/04 ADD 1 [4.11.2004] (Sweden), 14193/04 ADD 3 [18.11.2004] (France), 16240/04 [23.12.2004] (Germany), 12841/05 [3.10.2005] (Germany), 13001/05 [10.10.2005], 5419/06 [19.10.2006] (Germany), 5864/06 [3.2.2006], 6161/06 [10.2.2006]. Also the initial responses of individual Member State delegations to the Commission Proposal in Council document 9009/04 + ADD 1-17 [29.4.2004–2.6.2004]

[636] OJ C289E, 76–77 [28.11.2006].

Directive 95/46/EC . . . on the protection of individuals with regard to the processing of personal data and on the free movement of such data'. The Commission has undertaken to 'take into consideration all aspects of the situation and take appropriate measures if necessary'. Whatever conclusions it may reach, its report when published seems likely to reignite the controversy.[637]

The pre-existing UK rules   In this respect, the legislative history of the Rome **3.222** II Regulation mirrored that of the legislation introduced in the UK to reform the common law rules of applicable laws for torts, i.e. Part III of the Private International (Miscellaneous Provisions) Act 1995.[638] Defamation was not originally excluded from the draft legislation introduced into Parliament. Indeed, the Law Commission and the Scottish Law Commission, in their earlier report, had recommended that if a statement published abroad had simultaneously or previously been published in the UK, the law of the place of publication within the UK should apply to defamation claims.[639] The Law Commissions justified this special rule on the ground of 'the public interest in free speech and in the proper functioning of public institutions'.[640] Commenting on the debate that led, eventually, to the exclusion of defamation from the 1995 Act, Professor Morse comments:[641]

Rarely, if ever before, can a change in the rules of English private international law have given rise to such a furore!

The London *Evening Standard*, for example, demanded that 'Parliament must stamp hard on this pointless, wasteful and deeply dangerous Bill'.[642] In this case, Parliament yielded. Less than 10 years later, the battle lines would be re-drawn in a European arena, with a similar result.

Under s 13 of the PILA (UK), the new rules for torts were expressed not to **3.223** affect the determination of issues arising in any defamation claim, defined to include (a) any claim under the law of any part of the United Kingdom for libel or slander or slander of title, slander of goods or other malicious falsehood and any claim under the law of Scotland for verbal injury, and (b) any claim under the law of any other country corresponding to or

---

[637] See the Commission's statement on the review clause (OJ L199, 49 [31.7.2007]).

[638] Dicey, Morris & Collins, para 35-125.

[639] Law Com No 193, *Private International Law: Choice of Law in Tort and Delict* (1990), Draft Bill, cl 3(2).

[640] Ibid, para 3.31.

[641] C G J Morse, 'Torts in Private International Law: A New Framework' (1996) 45 ICLQ 888, 891.

[642] Evening Standard, 19 January 1995, quoted by P B Carter, 'The Private International Law (Miscellaneous Provisions) Act 1995' (1996) 112 LQR 190, 194.

otherwise in the nature of a claim mentioned in (a) above. In the view of the editors of Dicey, Morris & Collins, this exclusion 'would seem to be limited to statements or representations, which have legal effects associated with liabilities which are set out in the provisions' and would not extend to 'liabilities arising (even from statements) which would constitute, say, an invasion of privacy under a foreign applicable law'.[643] Accordingly, the s 13 exclusion does not correspond exactly to the exclusion in Art 1(2)(g) of the Regulation.[644]

3.224 The combined effect of s 13 of the 1995 Act and Art 1(2)(g) of the Rome II Regulation is that the law applicable to defamation claims before UK courts must still be determined by reference to the common law 'double actionability' rule.[645] The law applicable to privacy claims must be determined under the 1995 Act, at least insofar as they are characterized as involving issues relating to tort or (in Scotland) delict.[646]

3.225 *Scope of the Article 1(2)(g) exclusion*   As with other categories of obligation in the Regultion, the concepts of non-contractual obligations arising out of (a) violations of privacy, and (b) rights relating to the personality[647] must be given autonomous meanings, independently of the classification given to particular claims under the law of individual Member States. Thus, for example, the fact that, under English law, privacy is protected not by a single tort bearing that label but by several common law and statutory remedies,[648] in particular the equitable wrong of breach of confidence[649] does not mean that claims to obtain such remedies fall within the Regulation's scope. Indeed, a claim to prevent disclosure of information relating to the private life of an individual claimant, or to compensate an individual for

---

[643] Dicey, Morris & Collins, para 35-128. The editors query whether foreign claims based on an actionable true statement would also fall within the exception.

[644] **3.225–3.228** below.

[645] **1.09** above. For more detailed discussion, see Dicey, Morris & Collins, paras 35-129 to 35-157.

[646] Private International Law (Miscellaneous Provisions) Act 1995, ss 9(1) –(2). For a case in which a breach of confidence claim aimed, at least in part, at protecting the claimant's privacy was provisionally characterized as being a 'restitutionary' claim, see *Douglas v Hello! Ltd (No 3)* [2005] EWCA Civ 595; [2006] QB 125, [97]. That conclusion seems questionable (see T M Yeo, *Choice of Law for Equitable Doctrines* (2004), paras 7.76–7.84; 8.73–8.78). The decision in *Douglas v Hello!* was reversed in part, but not on this point, at [2007] UKHL 21; [2008] 1 AC 1, sub nom *OBG Limited v Allan*.

[647] During discussions in Council, the Spanish delegation suggested referring to 'rights to a good name and to one's image' instead of 'rights to the personality', but this proposal was not accepted (Council document 14193/04 [4.11.2004]).

[648] *Wainwright v Home Office* [2003] UKHL 53; [2004] 2 AC 406, [18] (Lord Hoffmann).

[649] *Douglas v Hello! Ltd (No 3)*, n 646 above, [47]–[53] (EWCA).

the consequences of unauthorized disclosure, seems at the very heart of the exclusion.[650]

In overview, the focus of the Art 1(2)(g) exclusion appears to be less on the **3.226** nature of the event on which the claim is based but on its consequences for the claimant, in terms of an invasion of his privacy or injury to his reputation.[651] The exclusion, which uses the same terminology as the rule of applicable law in Art 6 of the Commission Proposal, may be considered to cover very similar ground to its forerunner. In the explanatory memorandum accompanying its proposal, the Commission's focus was on defamation by the mass media.[652] The Commission, however, emphasized the close link between the two categories of obligation and the guarantees of privacy and freedom of expression in the Charter of Fundamental Rights of the European Union[653] and in the European Convention on Human Rights.[654] It may be noted, however, that the right to respect for private and family life in Art 8 of the ECHR concerns matters other than violations of privacy, including (for example) the impact on family life of environmental pollution.[655] Non-contractual obligations in situations of the latter kind remain within Art 7 of the Regulation (environmental damage).

Although it is unclear to what extent companies enjoy a right to privacy **3.227** under ECHR, Art 8,[656] there is no reason why claims by bodies corporate or unincorporate to protect their reputation against defamatory comments or to protect the privacy of their operations[657] (rather than, for example, to protect their employees or the integrity of their premises[658]) should not equally fall within the scope of the Art 1(2)(g) exclusion. One significant qualification must, however, be recognized to that proposition, namely that the disclosure of business secrets remains within the scope of the Regulation in circumstances where the recipient is in competition with the claimant. In the explanatory memorandum accompanying its Proposal, the Commission indicated that cases of this kind fall within what is now

---

[650] *Von Hannover v Germany* (Application 59320/00) (2004) 16 BHRC 545, [2004] EMLR 379 (ECtHR); *Murray v Big Pictures (UK) Ltd* [2008] EWCA Civ 446.

[651] A M Dugdale & A M Jones, *Clerk & Lindsell on Torts*, (19th edn, 2006), paras 1-28 to 1-29.

[652] Commission Proposal, 17–18.

[653] Arts 7, 8, and 11.

[654] Arts 8 and 10.

[655] *Powell v United Kingdom* (Application 9310/81) (1990) 12 EHRR 355; *Lopez Ostra v Spain* (Application 16798/90) (1994) 20 EHRR 277.

[656] A Lester and D Pannick, *Human Rights Law and Practice* (2nd edn, 2004), para 4.8.42.

[657] Cf *R v Broadcasting Standards Commission, ex p BBC* [2001] QB 885 (EWCA).

[658] e.g. *Oxford University v Broughton* [2008] EWHC 75 (QB).

Art 6(2) of the Regulation.[659] It is submitted that it should make no difference to the application of the Art 1(2)(g) exclusion in such cases that the defendant is not the competitor but the person responsible for the unauthorized disclosure (whether an employee or otherwise). For the same reason, other non-contractual obligations based on 'an act of unfair competition' should be considered to fall within Art 6(1) or (2), as appropriate, and not within the Art 1(2)(g) exclusion. This would seem to include, for example, a claim for slander of goods or, arguably, defamation of a competitor in relation to its business activities.[660]

3.228 Finally, the exclusion probably also extends to civil claims to enforce against data controllers legislation concerning the protection of personal data.[661] In both its 1st and 2nd Reading Positions, the European Parliament had included wording that specifically extended the special rule to 'violations of privacy or of rights relating to the personality resulting from the handling of personal data'.[662] Although that rule does not survive in the final version of the Regulation, specific reference to the Data Protection Directive appears in the review clause of the Regulation,[663] requiring the Commission to prepare a study on the law applicable to violations of privacy and rights relating to personality 'taking into account', among other matters 'conflict-of-law issues' relating to the Data Protection Directive. The view that such claims are excluded by Art 1(2)(g) is also supported by the close connection between matters of personal privacy and the protection of personal data.[664]

---

[659] Commission Proposal, 16 referring to Art 5 of the Proposal.

[660] **6.30** below. Also Dicey, Morris & Collins, 1st supplement, paras S35-215 and S35-219; A Thünken, 'Multi-State Advertising over the Internet and the Private International Law of Unfair Competition' (2002) 51 ICLQ 909, 916.

[661] Directive (EC) No 95/46 on the protection of individuals with regard to the processing of personal data and on the free movement of such data (OJ L281, 31 [23.11.1995]) (the **Data Protection Directive**). Art 4 of the Directive makes provision for its territorial application. For the UK implementing legislation, see the Data Protection Act 1998. Under ss 10–12 of the 1998 Act, individuals have certain rights to prevent the processing of data relating to them. Under s 13, individuals may claim compensation for damage suffered as a consequence of infringement of any of the requirements of the Act.

[662] EP 1st Reading Position, Art 5(3); EP 2nd Reading Position, Art 7(3). The European Data Protection Supervisor, Peter Hustinx, expressed concerns about this proposal in a letter to the Council President in February 2007 (Council document 6899/07 [28.2.2007]).

[663] Art 30(2).

[664] e.g. *Copland v United Kingdom* (Application 62717/00), [2007] IP & T 600, (2007) The Times, 24 April; *Wieser v Austria* (Application 74336/01), Judgment of 16 October 2007 (both ECtHR).

Evidence and Procedure

Art 1(3), excluding matters of evidence and procedure from the scope of **3.229**
the Regulation, will be considered in **Chapter 14** below, alongside Arts 21
and 22, to which it specifically refers. For present purposes, it suffices to
note that this exclusion, reflecting that contained in Art 1(2)(h) of the Rome
Convention, did not appear in the Commission Proposal. The Commission
considered that:[665]

> It is clear from Article 11[666] that, subject to the exceptions mentioned, these rules
> are matters for the *lex fori*. They would be out of place in a list of non-contractual
> obligations excluded from the scope of this Regulation.

The European Parliament disagreed,[667] leading the Parliament to revise its
position.[668] The final wording of Art 1(3) originates in the Council's
Common Position.[669]

Positive Content of 'Non-Contractual Obligations'—Chapters II and III of the Regulation

Introduction

In the explanatory memorandum accompanying its Proposal, the Commis- **3.230**
sion suggested that the scope of the Regulation covers 'all non-contractual
obligations except those matters listed in paragraph 2'.[670] Within the
Commision Proposal, 'non-contractual obligations arising out of a tort or
delict' (Arts 3–8) were contrasted with 'non-contractual obligations arising out of an act other than a tort or delict' (Art 9), giving the impression
at least of universal coverage. In its initial response, the German delegation approved this aim of encompassing all non-contractual obligations,
i.e. of covering unjust enrichment, agency without authority, *and other possible categories* in addition to tort or delict.[671] Member State delegations
recognized, however, that the stated rules of applicable law for obligations
arising out of an act other than a tort or delict[672] were not comprehensive,
as (having provided for non-contractual obligations arising out of a
pre-existing relationship or between parties habitually resident in the

---

[665] Commission Proposal, 9.
[666] Art 15 of the Regulation in its final form (scope of the law applicable).
[667] EP 1st Reading Position, Art 1((2)(g) (Amendment 22).
[668] Commission Amended Proposal, Art 1(2)(i).
[669] Common Position, Art 1(3).
[670] Commission Proposal, 8.
[671] Council document 9009/04 ADD 11 [24.5.2004], 2. Also ibid, ADD 7 [11.5.2004], 1 (Estonia).
[672] **10.02** below.

same country[673]) they provided no residual rule for non-contractual obligations other than those arising out of unjust enrichment or agency without authority (*negotiorum gestio*).[674] Neither the escape clause which followed[675] nor the general rule in Art 3 of the Commission Proposal (which, although not expressly limited to obligations arising in tort/delict, followed the heading 'Rules Applicable to Non-Contractual Obligations Arising Out of a Tort or Delict' and referred both to 'damage' and 'the event giving rise to damage') seemed suited for this purpose. The German delegation argued that 'a solution should be found for other categories of non-contractual obligations, possibly in the form of a general rule'.[676] The Swedish delegation, noting that 'Article 9 in its present form lacks a general rule for the non-contractual obligations other than a tort or delict that are not expressly described in the Article', suggested that the general rule in Art 3 should apply. The Italian delegation also recognized that it was not clear what further cases, apart from those specifically mentioned, Art 9 of the Commission Proposal was intended to cover.[677] Having mentioned 'pre-contractual liability, contract voidness[678] and agency' as examples of doubtful situations, the Italian response concluded:[679]

It would be better to lay down just one general rule for all sources of non-contractual obligations not arising from a tort or delict; should it then be decided to list individual sources of obligations, reference would also need to be made to unilateral promises and undue payments, which would not come within the provision as currently worded.

Other Member State delegations, for various reasons, recommended deletion of the special rules for non-tortious, non-contractual obligations.[680]

3.231 At an early stage in discussions in the Council's Rome II Committee, the Portuguese delegation suggested amending and simplifying the structure of the draft instrument by removing the division between non-contractual

---

[673] Commission Proposal, Art 9(1) –(2).

[674] Ibid, Arts 9(3)–(4).

[675] Ibid, Art 9(5), referring to the rules in the first four paragraphs.

[676] Council document 9009/04 ADD 11, 11. The point appears to have been widely acknowledged among Member States in their early discussions (see Council document 6518/04 [26.2.2004]).

[677] Council document 9009/04 ADD 17 [2.6.2004], 4.

[678] At the time, Italy along with the UK had exercised its right to opt-out of Art 10(1)(e) of the Rome Convention (see **3.107** above).

[679] Ibid, 5.

[680] **10.06** below.

obligations arising or not arising out of a tort or delict and deleting Art 9 of the Proposal.[681] In its submission:[682]

The advantage of this more pragmatic approach would be that it would circumvent the problems of characterisation encountered in certain judicial systems and linked to the definition of delict and quasi-delict. It would make it possible to govern adequately the two best-known cases of quasi-delict, which were unjust enrichment and *negotiorum gestio*, with other specific cases—in the absence of a specific text—being governed by the general rule . . .

This proposal, which appears to have been driven by problems under **3.232** Portuguese law in separating 'tort' from strict liability,[683] apparently met with broad support, 'subject to more in-depth examination',[684] and was reflected in a draft circulated by the Dutch Presidency in late July 2004.[685] This draft provoked a mixed reaction.[686] At the following meeting of the Council's Rome II Committee, some delegations welcomed the new structure but others voiced difficulties, asking for greater clarity in the relationship between the Regulation's rules of applicable law.[687] The Presidency called an informal meeting of delegations to discuss the problems of structure, but this did not deliver a solution. The Rome II Committee returned to this issue a month later, by which time there was support among the delegations for a proposal of the Dutch Presidency distinguishing between 'torts and delicts', on the one hand, and 'unjust enrichment and *negotiorum gestio*' on the other hand, without attempting to define the second group.[688] That consensus was reflected in the draft of the Regulation produced in December 2004 by the outgoing Dutch and incoming Luxembourg Presidencies, separating Chapter II (headed 'Torts or delicts') from Chapter III (headed 'Unjust enrichment and Negotiorum gestion[689] [and . . .]').[690] Chapter III in that draft included not only special rules for unjust enrichment and *negotiorum gestio*, but also a tentative proposal for a special rule

---

[681] Council document 11801/04 [28.7.2004], 5.

[682] Ibid.

[683] Council document 16240/04 [23.12.2004], 1.

[684] Ibid.

[685] Council document SN2851/04 [20.7.2004], in which Chapter II is headed 'Uniform Rules'. Also Council document 12746/04 [27.9.2004].

[686] Compare the favourable views of the Portuguese delegation (Council document SN2852/04 ADD 2), and the Spanish delegation (Council document SN2852/04 [9.9.2004]) with the strong criticism presented by the German delegation (Council document SN2852/04 [2.9.2004], 1–2).

[687] Commission note of meeting held on 5/6 October 2004 (Commission document JAI/C/1/CH/bv D(04) 10582 [29.10.2004]).

[688] Commission note of meeting held on 10–11 November 2004 (undated).

[689] *Sic.*

[690] Council document 16231/04 [20.12.2004].

concerning dealings prior to the conclusion of a contract (*culpa in contrahendo*).[691] With the addition of a specific reference in the title of Chapter III to *culpa in contrahendo*,[692] that structure survived intact to the Council's Common Position and the final version of the Regulation. In a parallel development, the Commission's Amended Proposal in February 2006 suggested the categories 'tort or delict', 'specific torts/delicts', and 'unjust enrichment and *negotiorum gestio*'. In its 1st Reading Position, the EP used the categories 'tort or delict' and 'specific torts/delicts and non-contractual obligations'. In its 2nd Reading Position, the EP accepted the structure in the Council's Common Position.

3.233 Accordingly, despite initial support for the Commission's objective of embracing all non-contractual obligations not specifically excluded from, the negotiations led for reasons of practicality to a Regulation containing rules of applicable law for 'torts/delicts' and, separately, for three specified categories of non-contractual obligation (unjust enrichment, *negotiorum gestio*, and *culpa in contrahendo*).[693] Those categories are mutually exclusive, so that (for example) an obligation cannot arise from a tort/delict and, at the same time, from unjust enrichment.[694] Equally, an obligation cannot fall within more than one of the rules governing tort/delict in Chapter II. The category of 'tort/delict' must also be understood to cover non-contractual obligations arising out of strict liability[695] and that of 'unjust enrichment' is expressed in Art 10(1) to cover 'payment of amounts wrongly received'. Despite these extensions, it is submitted that none of the rules of applicable law in Arts 4 to 12 of the Regulation is capable of acting as a residual rule defined in negative terms and of accommodating non-contractual obligations not specifically excluded and not falling positively within the scope of any other rule within the Regulation.

The concept of 'tort, delict or quasi-delict' under the Brussels Convention

3.234 Although Art 4, described as a 'general rule', performs the function of a residual rule within the category of 'tort/delict', it seems clear that the words 'arising out of a tort/delict' in Art 4(1) cannot be empty of meaning or have a negative meaning only. That view accords with the case law of the ECJ and of the English Courts concerning Art 5(3) of the Brussels Convention (matters relating to tort, delict, or quasi-delict). In *Kalfelis v Schröder*, the Court defined the concept of 'matters relating to tort, delict or

---

[691] Ibid, Art 9C.
[692] Council document 7929/06 [10.4.2006], 10.
[693] As the definition of 'damage' in Art 2(1) confirms.
[694] Dicey, Morris & Collins, 1st supplement, para S35-177.
[695] Recital (11).

quasi-delict' in Art 5(3) as 'all actions which seek to establish the liability of a defendant and which are not related to a "contract" within the meaning of Article 5(1)'.[696] Taken at face value, the words 'all actions which seek to establish the liability of a defendant' suggested a wide scope.[697] The French and German language versions of the judgment,[698] referring to *'la responsabilité d'un defendeur'* and *'eine Schadenshaftung des Beklagten'* respectively, provide support for a more restrictive interpretation. The German language version, in particular, gave the impression that the Court was concerned with claims that seek to establish the responsibility of the defendant for an event causing damage, a view consistent with the connecting factor identified in Art 5(3) (harmful event, *fait dommageable*, *schädigende Ereignis*).

That impression was confirmed by the ECJ in its subsequent decision in **3.235** *Reichert v Dresdner Bank AG (No 2)*, concerning an *action paulienne* under French law brought by a creditor to set aside the transfer by his debtor of property to a third party.[699] The argument was presented, based on the ECJ's earlier decision in *Kalfelis*, that the claim (not being contractual) must fall within Art 5(3) of the Convention. In his opinion, Adv Gen Gulmann referred[700] to the comment of Adv Gen Warner in *Netherlands v Rüffer* that:[701]

No-one has ever succeeded, even in the context of any national legal system, in formulating an accurate description of tort that did not beg one or more questions. Like the proverbial elephant, tort is easier to recognize than to define.

Adv Gen Gulmann commented:[702] **3.236**

There is an extensive field in which Article 5(3) may undoubtedly be used and where its application will give rise to no problems (apart from those which may be involved in the determination of the place where the harmful event occurred). That field is represented by the typical actions for damages in which a claimant has suffered economic loss by a tortfeasor's conduct giving rise to liability and in which it is clear that there is no contractual link between the parties in relation to the damage. But the provision gives rise in any event to difficulties of demarcation in two respects.

---

[696] Case 189/87, *Kalfelis v Schröder*, [1988] ECR 5565, para 18.

[697] For the exclusion of 'contractual' matters, see **3.104–3.145** above.

[698] As Professor Briggs notes, these are the original linguistic versions of the judgment in *Kalfelis* (Briggs & Rees, n 348 above, para 2.146).

[699] For discussion of the first *Reichert* decision, see **3.98** above, and for further discussion of the ECJ's treatment of the *action paulienne* in *Reichert (No 2)* see **3.250–3.257** below.

[700] Case C-261/90 [1992] ECR I-2149, 2168.

[701] Case 814/79 [1980] ECR 3807, 3834–5.

[702] *Reichert (No 2)*, n 700 above, 2169.

3.237 That comment seems equally apposite in the context of Art 4 of the Rome II Regulation, and Adv Gen Gulmann's attempt to wrestle with the boundaries of the category of 'tort, delict or quasi-delict' is deserving of closer attention. Having referred to difficulties 'in the demarcation between matters of contract and matters of tort, delict or quasi-delict as regards liability for damages', he continued:[703]

> On the other hand there may be difficulties in distinguishing actions which may be regarded as actions for compensation covered by either Article 5(1) or 5(3) from those which cannot be regarded as actions for compensation in matters either of contract or of tort, delict or quasi-delict . . . This case concerns a problem of that kind.

> The various language versions of Article 5(3)[704] have in any case two features in common. One is that there must have been 'wrongful' conduct, and the other that that conduct must have caused a 'harmful event'.

> If that is correct, it may also be seen that the scope of Article 5(3) is potentially very wide. . . .[705]

3.238 Adv Gen Gulmann then turned to consider the definition of 'matters relating to tort, delict or quasi-delict' in the Court's judgment in *Kalfelis*.[706] He was prepared to accept that 'an action such as the *action paulienne* to set aside a transaction cannot be directly regarded as an action which seeks to establish "*Schadenshaftung*" or "liability" of a defendant',[707] but did not think this wording conclusive, noting (correctly) that the ECJ in *Kalfelis* had not been asked to determine which of the claims advanced in that case fell within Art 5(3). Instead, he based his conclusion that the *action paulienne* was not a 'matter relating to tort, delict or quasi-delict' within Art 5(3) on an examination of the purpose and context of that provision. In particular, he considered that the jurisdictional connecting factor, 'the place where the harmful event occurred', had hardly any special significance in determining the factual and legal circumstances relevant for settling such an action.[708]

---

[703] Ibid.

[704] Cited earlier in the Advocate General's opinion, ibid, 2167. See also the Opinion of Adv Gen Warner in *Netherlands State v Rüffer*, n 701 above, 3833–4.

[705] The Advocate General referred at this point to the statement by the ECJ in Case 21/76, *Handelskwekerij G J Bier BV v Mines de Potasse d'Alsace SA* [1976] ECR 1735, para 18 that Art 5(3) of the Brussels Convention 'covers a wide diversity of kinds of liability'.

[706] Text to n 696 above.

[707] *Reichert (No. 2)*, n 700 above, 2170.

[708] Ibid, 2172. Cf **3.255–3.257** below.

Reaching the same conclusion, the Court, in its accustomed manner, dealt **3.239**
with the question more briefly:[709]

[I]n French law the *action paulienne* may be instituted both against dispositions
made for consideration by the debtor when the beneficiary acts in bad faith and
against transactions entered into without consideration by the debtor even if the
beneficiary acts in good faith.

The purpose of such an action is not to have the debtor ordered to make good the
damage he has caused his creditor by his fraudulent conduct, but to render ineffective, as against his creditor, the disposition which the debtor has made. It is
directed not only against the debtor but also against the person who benefits from
the act, who is not a party to the obligation binding the creditor to his debtor, even,
in cases where there is no consideration for the transaction, where that third party
has not committed any wrongful act.

In these circumstances an action such as the *action paulienne* in French law cannot
be regarded as a claim seeking to establish the liability of a defendant in the sense
in which it is understood in Article 5(3) of the Convention and therefore does not
come within the scope of that provision.

Professor Briggs argues that this reasoning, with its apparent insistence **3.240**
upon a wrongful act and damage, was unnecessary and should not be
taken at face value as the *action paulienne* 'was, if anything, part of the law
of credit and security, but did not seek to establish liability in any recog-
nisable form'.[710] He refers, approvingly, to the ECJ's later decision in *VfK v
Henkel*[711] concerning an action brought by a consumer protection organization for the purpose of preventing a trader from using unfair contract
terms. In that case, the Court held that the concept of 'harmful event'
within the meaning of Art 5(3) of the Brussels Convention 'is broad in
scope so that, with regard to consumer protection, it covers not only situations where an individual has personally sustained damage but also, in
particular, the undermining of legal stability by the use of unfair terms
which it is the task of consumer associations such as the VKI to prevent'.[712]
This leads Professor Briggs to suggest that 'if proceedings to prevent the
undermining of legal stability are within Art 5(3) . . ., it is almost impossible
to see what will not be'.[713] Further, in a separate aspect of the decision in
Henkel, the ECJ rejected the argument that Art 5(3), in referring to the place
where the harmful event occurred, presupposes the existence of damage
and cannot be applied to purely preventative actions brought before actual

---

[709] Ibid, Judgment, paras 18–20.
[710] Briggs & Rees, n 348 above, para 2.147.
[711] Case C-167/00, *Verein für Konsumentinformation v Henkel* [2002] ECR I-8111.
[712] Ibid, para 42.
[713] Briggs & Rees, n 348 above, para 2.147.

damage has occurred.[714] That conclusion was affirmed in *DFDS Torline*, a case concerning an action to determine the lawfulness of threatened industrial action.[715]

3.241 Although both aspects of the reasoning in *Henkel* undoubtedly broaden the category of 'tort, delict or quasi-delict' under Art 5(3) of the Brussels Convention, and cannot be read as applying only to cases involving consumer protection, this does not leave Art 5(3) as a repository for all non-contractual claims which in some sense seek to establish the liability of the defendant to the claimant.[716] Even taking the concept in this diluted from, there remain (at a minimum) the elements of (a) an act or omission of one person or other event having some kind of adverse consequence for another, and (b) an action before a court or tribunal whose object is to establish the defendant's legal responsibility for the consequences of that act, omission, or other event. In *Engler v Janus Versand*,[717] Adv Gen Jacobs thought it 'too sweeping to state that Article 5(3) covers all actions which seek to establish liability and are not covered by Article 5(1)'.[718] In his view:[719]

> [I]t is not enough simply to ask whether the proceedings relate to a contract. The category of tort, delict or quasi-delict *is not merely negative or residual, but has a positive content*. Particularly in cases which do not fall unequivocally within one category, it is helpful to examine both.

> Whilst any attempt to provide a comprehensive definition of the concept of 'tort, delict or quasi-delict' based on the laws of the Contracting States would be problematic, it is possible to identify certain generally recurring features.

> First, one usual element in a tortious, delictual or quasi-delictual act is that it is in breach of a legal rule. . . .

> Second, a claim in tort, delict or quasi-delict generally, perhaps always, requires at least an allegation of harm or damage suffered—reflected in the expression 'harmful event' in Article 5(3) of the Convention . . .[720]

> Third, it is commonly the case that any amount awarded by a court to a claimant in tort, delict or quasi-delict takes account, primarily, of the nature and degree of

---

[714] *Henkel*, n 711 above, para 44.

[715] Case C-18/02, *DFDS Torline A/S v SEKO Sjöfolk Facket för Service och Kommunikation* [2004] ECR I-1417, discussed at **9.02** below.

[716] U Magnus and P Mankowski, *The Brussels I Regulation* (2007), Art 5, para 194.

[717] Case C-27/02 [2005] ECR I-481, discussed at **3.118–3.120** above.

[718] Ibid, Opinion, para 56.

[719] Ibid, Opinion, paras 57–9, 61, 64 (emphasis added).

[720] The Advocate General also acknowledged in a footnote the possibility of proceedings relating to damage likely to be suffered, noting that the case before him was not of this character.

harm suffered and perhaps, secondarily, of the seriousness of the (unlawful) act giving rise to the claim. There is generally a central element of compensation, though the final award may in some cases be increased to a dissuasive, or reduced to a symbolic, level.

The Court, having concluded that the claimant's claim fell within Art 5(1) **3.242** of the Brussels Convention as a 'matter relating to a contract' did not consider the application of Art 5(3).[721] It remains to be seen whether Adv Gen Jacobs' analysis will be picked up in later cases. The presence of the three 'generally recurring features' suggested by him will almost certainly correspond with the obligation in question being characterized as a 'matter relating to tort, delict or quasi-delict' within Art 5(3). Having regard to the decision in *Henkel*, however, it seems doubtful whether they will provide a useful template in borderline cases.

The concept of 'tort/delict' in the Rome II Regulation

Although there is a need for caution in carrying forward concepts devel- **3.243** oped within the Brussels I Regime into similarly worded provisions in the Rome II Regulation,[722] these decisions undoubtedly provide part of the context within which the concept of 'tort/delict' within the Rome II Regulation must be considered. The following points are of note:

1. There is no doubt that the words 'non-contractual obligation arising out of a tort/delict' must be understood as an autonomous concept within the wider category of non-contractual obligations.[723]

2. As in Art 5(3) of the Brussels Convention, the terminology used in the different language versions of the Rome II Regulation to describe this concept in Art 4(1) in the heading which precedes it varies widely. The choice of wording in the English language version is, perhaps, the least helpful in defining the concept, as it uses terms that have specific meanings in English and Scots law, and which (at least in the case of English law) cast little light on the intended scope of the Article.[724] The authors of a recent commentary on civil wrongs in English law concede that 'a rational account of the law of civil wrongs cannot confine itself to torts'.[725] In order to present a 'more coherent picture' of the operation of civil wrongs under English law, the same authors consider it necessary to

---

[721] *Engler*, n 717 above, Judgment, para 60.

[722] **3.110** above.

[723] Recital (11) (**3.86** above).

[724] For a comparative survey of the concepts of 'tort' and 'delict' in European legal systems, see C von Bar, *The Common European Law of Torts* (vol 1, 1998; reprinted 2003), paras 1–9.

[725] J Edelman and J Davies, n 416 above, para 17.02.

consider not only torts,[726] but also 'those equitable wrongs that are motivated by identical concerns (such as deceit and negligence) as well as other breaches of duty in equity, namely breach of trust and fiduciary duty, dishonest assistance in a breach of trust or fiduciary duty, and breach of confidence'.[727]

3. Other language versions of the Regulation use either descriptive or technical language, or a combination of the two, as the following examples indicate:[728]

- French: *'fait dommageable'* (harmful (f)act)[729]
- German: *'unerlaubte Handlung'* (unlawful act)[730]
- Dutch: *'onrechtmatige daad'* (unlawful act)[731]
- Finnish: *'vahingonkorvausvastuun perustavasta'* (events grounding liability)

---

[726] The authors note elsewhere that '[t]he law of torts still appears to consist of a list of over seventy wrongs, distinct though sometimes overlapping, each with its own name and conditions of liability' (ibid, para 17.05).

[727] Ibid, para 17.03.

[728] The translations given in brackets reflect the author's understanding of the literal meaning of the words used.

[729] Art 1382 of the French Civil Code (*Code Civil*), the first under the heading *'Des délits et des quasi-délits'* provides: *'Tout fait quelconque de l'homme, qui cause à autrui un dommage, oblige celui par la faute duquel il est arrivé, à le réparer'*. Art 1383 provides: *'Chacun est responsable du dommage qu'il a causé non seulement par son fait, mais encore par sa négligence ou par son imprudence'*. Art 1384 begins: *'On est responsable non seulement du dommage que l'on cause par son propre fait, mais encore de celui qui est causé par le fait des personnes dont on doit répondre, ou des choses que l'on a sous sa garde.'* The following Articles (1384 to 1386-18) provide for liability for animals, buildings, and defective products. See C van Dam, *European Tort Law* (2005), esp ch 3.

[730] The title *'Unerlaubte Handlung'* is given to Title VII of the German Civil Code (*Bürgerliches Gesetzbuch* or BGB) containing the following headings for obligation imposing rules: (1) liability for damages (BGB, Art 823), (2) endangering credit (Art 824), (3) inducing others to sexual acts (Art 825), (4) intentional damage contrary to public policy (Art 826), (5) liability for vicarious agents (Art 831), (6) liability of a person with a duty of supervision (Art 832), (7) liability of animal keeper (Art 833), (8) liability of animal minder (Art 834), (9) liability of the owner of a plot of land (Art 836), (10) liability of building possessor (Art 837), (11) liability of person with a duty of maintenance of a building (Art 838), (12) liability in case of breach of official duty (Art 839), (13) liability of court appointed expert (Art 839). See C van Dam, n 729 above, esp ch 4.

[731] The title *'Onrechtmatige Daad'* is given to Book 6, Title 3 of the Dutch Civil Code (*Burgerlijk Wetboek*). Art 162-1 provides *'Hij die jegens een ander een onrechtmatige daad pleegt, welke hem kan worden toegerekend, is verplicht de schade die de ander dientengevolge lijdt, te vergoeden'* ('He who commits towards another one an unlawful act, which can be attributed to him, is obliged to compensate for consequential damage which the other one suffers').

- Italian: *'illeciti'/'fatto illecito'* (illegal/unlawful (f)act)[732]
- Polish: *'czynu niedozwolonego'* (unlawful act)
- Portuguese: *'responsabilidade fundada em acto lícito, ilícito ou no risco'* (responsibility founded in lawful, unlawful, or no risk acts)
- Spanish: *'hechos dañosos'* (harmful event)
- Swedish: *'skadeståndsgrundande händelse'* (events grounding amends/ compensation)

4. Art 4(1) defines the connecting factor by reference to the concepts of 'damage' and 'event giving rise to damage'. The concept of 'damage' is in turn defined broadly by Art 2(1) as covering, for present purposes, 'any consequence arising out of tort/delict'. This seems to support a wide concept of the kind recognized by Adv Gen Gulmann in *Reichert (No 2)* and the ECJ in *Henkel*, albeit one that requires a close link between the event and its consequences.

5. Consistently with the ECJ's decisions in *Henkel* and *DFDS Torline* (**3.240** above), Art 2(2) provides that the Regulation shall apply to non-contractual obligations that are likely to arise, and Art 2(3) provides that references to an event giving rise to damage, and to damage, shall include events giving rise to damage and damage that is likely to occur.

6. The content of the special rules in Arts 5 to 9, which also fall within Chapter II (Torts/Delicts), may also be taken into account as giving colour to the concept of 'tort/delict' in the Regulation. These rules deal, respectively, with damage caused by a product (Art 5), acts of unfair competition and restrictions of competition (Art 6), environmental damage (Art 7), infringements of intellectual property rights (Art 8), and liability for damages caused by an industrial action (Art 9). Consistently with the language used in Art 4 (see point 3 above), these categories suggest a focus on (a) unlawful or wrongful acts (Arts 6 and 8), or (b) consequences of a particular event which are in some sense adverse to the person affected (Arts 5, 7, 9).

7. Account may also be taken of the categories of obligation in Arts 10 to 12, which were considered to fall outside Chapter II (Torts/Delicts). For the first, unjust enrichment, it would appear that a defining feature of this category is that the event that forms the basis of the obligation (i.e. that giving rise to enrichment) must in some sense be attributable to the claimant.[733]

---

[732] The title *'Dei Fatto Illeciti'* is given to Book 4, Title IX of the Italian Civil Code (*Codice Civile*). Art 2043 (headed *'Risarcimento par fatto illecito'*) provides *'Qualunque fatto doloso o colposo, che cagiona ad altri un danno ingiusto, obbliga colui che ha commesso il fatto a risarcire il danno'* ('Any fact involving fault or negligence, which causes others damage, requires the person who committed the fact to compensate the damage').

[733] **10.21** below.

This contrasts with tort/delict, for which the event giving rise to damage is linked to the defendant. The second, *negotiorum gestio*, concerns a bilateral relationship, imposing obligations on both parties, resulting from the intervener's act.[734] The third, *culpa in contrahendo*, is less easy to isolate from tort/delict. Indeed, consistently with the decision of the ECJ in *Tacconi v HWS*, that breach of an obligation of good faith during negotiations fell within Art 5(3) of the Brussels Convention in circumstances where no contract had been concluded between the parties, it would have been possible to categorize non-contractual obligations arising out of pre-contractual dealings as a category of obligations arising out of a tort/delict subject to special rule within Chapter II.[735] The decision to deal with *culpa in contrahendo* separately in Chapter III reflects, perhaps, its special position at the intersection of the law of contractual and non-contractual obligations.

8. Recital (11) confirms that the Regulation 'should also cover non-contractual obligations arising out of strict liability'. The concept of 'tort/delict' cannot, therefore, be understood as requiring fault on the part of the defendant.[736]

9. It also seems clear that Chapter II, and Art 6 in particular, accommodate actions by consumer associations such as that brought in *Henkel*.[737] In this connection, Art 6(1) refers to the effects of an act of unfair competition on 'competitive relations' and the 'collective interests of consumers'.[738]

10. The law applicable under the Regulation may lead to the conclusion that the defendant is liable for the acts of another person (e.g. an employee or child).[739] This may include both direct liability, in which the defendant's breach of a non-contractual obligation is established by attributing to him the conduct of the third person, and vicarious liability, in which the defendant must answer for the third person's breach of a non-contractual obligation.[740] Equally, it is submitted, the Regulation and Art 4 in particular must accommodate situations in which responsibility (often on a strict liability basis) is imposed on the defendant for damage caused by a thing owned or controlled by him (e.g. a building, an aircraft, or an animal).[741]

---

[734] **11.04** below.

[735] **12.01** below.

[736] Cf *Reichert v Dresdner Bank (No 2)*, n 700 above, paras 18–20 (quoted at **3.239** above).

[737] Commission Proposal, 15.

[738] **6.17** and **6.49** below.

[739] Art 15(1)(g). For a comparative survey of English, French, and German law concerning liability for other persons, see C van Dam, n 729 above, ch 16.

[740] **14.46** below.

[741] C van Dam, n 729 above, ch 14–15.

Having regard to these points, the following definition of the concept **3.244**
'non-contractual obligation arising out of a tort/delict' within the Rome II
Regulation is, tentatively, suggested:

A non-contractual obligation establishing the defendant's responsibility to the
claimant for, or preventing the occurrence of, an act, omission or event which (1)
has adverse consequences for the claimant or one or more persons represented by
the claimant in the proceedings, and (2) is an act or omission of the defendant or a
person for whose conduct the defendant is liable, or is otherwise an act, omission,
or other event attributable to the defendant through his relationship with the
person or thing giving rise to those consequences.

It is unclear whether, in addition, the event must, in some respect at least, **3.245**
be unlawful, or whether rules that address the civil consequences of lawful acts (e.g. the erection of a building in accordance with a planning consent) also fall within scope.[742] This seems unlikely to be a significant issue
in practice, although the difficulty of separating liability for a lawful act
from strict liability for an act considered unlawful provides a pragmatic
reason for bringing both, and not just the latter, within scope.

Whether there is a requirement of 'unlawfulness' or not, it is not difficult **3.246**
to identify non-contractual obligations other than those addressed in
Chapter III that clearly, or arguably, fall outside the definition suggested
above. Examples include obligations arising from unilateral acts intended
to have legal effect, statutory fees and levies, liability for costs in civil proceedings, monetary incidents attaching to immovable property[743] and
non-contractual royalty obligations.[744] Whatever definition is adopted,
there will undoubtedly be obligations which lie at the boundaries and
which are difficult to characterize. For example, it is unclear whether the
obligation of airlines to compensate passengers, with whom they may
have no contractual relationship, for delays (by the payment of fixed sums
and the provision of food and other services) falls within the scope of the
Rome II Regulation.[745]

---

[742] Note the reference to 'lawful acts' (*acto lícito*) in the Portuguese text of Art 4(1) of the
Regulation, in contrast to other language versions using terminology corresponding to
'unlawful (f)acts' (**3.243** above, point 3).

[743] e.g. chancel repair liability (*Aston Cantlow Parish Church Council v Wallbank* [2003]
UKHL 37; [2004] 1 AC 546).

[744] **8.18** below.

[745] Regulation (EC) No 261/2004 establishing common rules on compensation and assistance to passengers in the event of denied boarding and of cancellation or long delay of flights
(OJ L46, 1 [17.2.2004]). Also Regulation (EC) No 1371/2007 of the European Parliament and
of the Council of 23 October 2007 on rail passengers' rights and obligations (OJ L15, 14
[3.12.2007]). See Case C-344/04, *R (International Air Transport Association) v Department for
Transport* [2006] ECR I-403.

Other non-contractual obligations in the Rome II Regulation

3.247 Moving from Chapter II of the Regulation to Chapter III, Recital (29) provides:

> Provision should be made for special rules where damage is caused by an act other than a tort/delict, such as unjust enrichment, *negotiorum gestio* and *culpa in contrahendo*.

3.248 The final wording, which reflects the Council's Common Position,[746] closely reflects Recital (15) of the Commission Proposal.[747] The use of the words 'such as' could be taken as an indication that the three identified categories of obligation for which Chapter III provides (unjust enrichment, *negotiorum gestio, culpa in contrahendo*) are merely examples of situations in which 'damage is caused by an act other than a tort/delict', and that other non-contractual obligations not arising out of a tort or delict are somehow capable of being fitted within Chapter III. In contrast to Chapter II dealing with 'tort/delict', however, Chapter III contains no 'general rule' of applicable law designed to accommodate non-contractual obligations arising otherwise than from a tort or delict which do not fall within one of the categories for which a specific rule is provided.[748] Further, the reference in Recital (29) to 'damage' is unfortunate. If, in this context, 'damage' bears the meaning set out in Article 2(1),[749] the imported reference (to the consequences of unjust enrichment, *negotiorum gestio*, or *culpa contrahendo*) leads to circularity. If, however, 'damage' is intended to mean 'harm' or 'loss' of some kind, it seems inappropriate, as unjust enrichment claims in particular may arise in circumstances in which the claimant has not been 'harmed' in any meaningful sense.[750] Recital (29) thus appears to signify nothing other than the intention of the framers of the Regulation that specified non-contractual obligations not characterized as 'arising out of a tort/delict' should nevertheless be brought within the scope of the Regulation. The reference to 'act other than a tort/delict' is a hangover from the original structure of the Regulation.[751]

---

[746] Common Position, Recital (26).

[747] 'Similar rules should be provided for where damage is caused by an act other than a tort or delict, such as unjust enrichment and agency without authority.'

[748] Arts 10–12 are considered in Chapters 10-12.

[749] i.e. 'any consequence arising out of tort/delict, unjust enrichment, *negotiorum gestio* or *culpa in contrahendo*' (see **3.44–3.46** above).

[750] A Burrows, *The Law of Restitution* (2nd edn, 2002), 28–9.

[751] **3.230** above.

Testing the Limits of the Regulation—The *Action Paulienne*

There can be no doubting that difficult questions will arise in determining **3.249** whether particular claims fall within the scope of the Regulation. The *action paulienne* and similar institutions recognized in both civil and common law jurisdictions provide a good example of these difficulties.

In *Reichert v Dresdner Bank (No 2)*,[752] the Bank brought an action in France **3.250** under Art 1167 of the French Civil Code, according to which creditors may 'on their own behalf, attack transactions made by their debtor in fraud of their rights',[753] with the object of rendering ineffective as against the Bank a disposition by Mr and Mrs Reichert to their son of a flat in France. That action is known in France as the *action paulienne* (deriving from the *actio Pauliana* recognized in Roman law), but this or a similar form of action exists in many countries.[754] In England and Wales, statutory rules for reversing transactions entered into by a debtor at an undervalue for the purpose of putting assets beyond the reach of creditors, or otherwise prejudicing the interests of creditors, are contained in s 423 of the Insolvency Act 1986.[755] Under this provision, an application may be made to court by any victim of the transaction, but he is treated as doing so not in his sole interest but on behalf of every such victim.[756] If the requirements of the action are made out, the court may make a wide variety of orders against those who benefited from the transaction, with certain exceptions for those who receive benefits in good faith without notice of the grounds for relief.[757]

In the explanatory memorandum accompanying its Proposal, the **3.251** Commission referred to 'actions by creditors to have certain transactions by their debtors declared void as prejudicial to their interests' as an example of a claim which might fall within either the Rome Convention or the Rome II Regulation.[758] Although contained in a section of the *Code Civil*

---

[752] Case C-261/90 [1992] ECR I-2149.

[753] '*Ils peuvent aussi, en leur nom personnel, attaquer les actes faits par leur débiteur en fraude de leurs droits.*'

[754] P Wood, *Principles of International Insolvency* (2nd edn, 2007), paras 17-035 to 17-037.

[755] Under English law, s 423 may have the status of an overriding mandatory provision which may apply irrespective of any foreign connection; the existence of a 'suffcient connection' to England and Wales will be a material factor in the exercise of the court's discretion in making an order (*Re Paramount Airways* [1993] Ch 223, 237–41 (Nicholls V-C, EWCA); *Jyske Bank (Gibraltar) Ltd v Spjeldnaes* [1999] 2 BCLC 101 (EWHC)).

[756] Insolvency Act 1986, s 424.

[757] Insolvency Act 1986, s 425.

[758] Commission Proposal, 8. A rule headed 'Actio Pauliana' appears in Art 10 of the Council's 'state of work' draft of the instrument on the law applicable to non-contractual obligations (Council document 11982/99 [9.12.1999]). It provides that: 'The conditions and effects arising from an obligation where a creditor may contest a contract concluded by a

concerning the effect of agreements on third parties,[759] it seems improbable that the action against the beneficiary of a transaction defrauding creditors would be characterized as based on a 'contractual obligation' within the Rome I Regime in cases in which the victim brings the action on his own behalf or on behalf of all victims, as in these circumstances there will be no voluntary undertaking by the beneficiary towards the victim.[760] This leaves the possibility that the action may be characterized as based on a 'non-contractual obligation' under the Rome II Regulation and, in particular, one based on tort/delict (Art 4) or unjust enrichment (Art 10). As to the latter category, it seems doubtful whether the claim can be characterized as arising from unjust enrichment, as the beneficiary's enrichment is not directly attributable to the victim.[761] No doubt, the beneficiary's enrichment by the debtor is, at the same time, prejudicial to the victim in reducing his prospects of being paid in full, but that would not appear sufficient to fit the obligation within the category of 'unjust enrichment' in Art 10.

3.252 It is a matter of debate whether the claim can be characterized as one arising in 'tort/delict' under Art 4. In *Reichert (No 2)*, the ECJ gave three reasons for excluding the *action paulienne* from the scope of Art 5(3) of the Brussels Convention (matters relating to tort, delict, or quasi-delict).[762] First, that the action did not require fault on the part of the beneficiary.[763] That, however, cannot be conclusive under the Rome II Regulation, which extends to non-contractual obligations arising out of strict liability.[764] Secondly, that the purpose of the action is not to have the debtor ordered to make good the damage he has caused to the creditor by his wrongful conduct, but to render ineffective, as against his creditor, the disposition that the debtor has made.[765] The first part of this reason is shown to be too narrow by the

---

debtor with a third party, endangering satisfaction of the creditor [fulfilment of the claim] shall be determined by the law applicable to the obligation existing between the creditor and his debtor'.

[759] French Civil Code (*Code Civil*), Arts 1165–7. Art 1165 appears as a qualification to the general rule, in Art 1165, that contracts may neither harm nor benefit third parties.

[760] *Reichert (No 2)*, n 752 above, Opinion of Adv Gen Gulmann, 2164.

[761] **10.21 below.**

[762] In *Reichert (No 2)*, n 752 above, the Bank argued that the *action paulienne* was 'quasi-delictual' in nature (Judgment, para 13), but this characterization (even if correct) makes no difference for present purposes, as matters of quasi-delict may also fall within Art 4 of the Rome II Regulation (**4.97 below**).

[763] *Reichert (No 2)*, ibid, Judgment, para 18.

[764] Recital (11). Further, as Philip Wood points out (n 754 above, para 17-037), creditor collusion is an element of the action in many civil code countries such as Austria, Belgium, Greece, and Switzerland.

[765] *Reichert (No 2)*, n 752 above, Judgment, para 19.

ECJ's later decisions in *Henkel* and *DFDS Torline*[766] and by the express extension of the Regulation to non-contractual obligations, events giving rise to damage, and damage that are likely to occur.[767] The second part, referring to the effectiveness of the transaction, suggests that the Court saw the *action paulienne* as raising a matter of status, as distinct from obligation (for example, as concerning the quality of the beneficiary's title to an asset or the debtor's capacity to contract or transfer assets in fraud of his creditors). If that is the correct characterization, the action can justifiably be seen as falling outside the Rome II Regulation.

There may, however, be reason to doubt that conclusion for (as Adv Gen **3.253** Gulmann noted in *Reichert (No 2)*[768] and the Court itself had pointed out in its earlier decision in that case[769]) the revocation of the transaction under French law takes effect only in relation to the creditor who has brought the claim: it appears, therefore, in the nature of a right *in personam*.[770] Treatment of the action as concerning matters of status would appear even less satisfactory in the case of the English statutory rules, which take effect not by declaring the transaction at an undervalue to be void but by making orders against the parties to the transaction and other beneficiaries with a view to restoring the position to what it would have been if the transaction had not been entered into, and protecting the interests of persons who are the victims of the transaction.[771] This seems to lie within the expanded concept of 'matters relating to tort, delict or quasi-delict' recognized by the ECJ in *Henkel*.[772] It should not matter, in this connection, that the claimant is acting not exclusively on his own behalf, but instead for the protection of all of the persons affected by the transaction. Further, it may be noted, the types of order that the court can impose on the defendant are mainly, but not exclusively, obligation imposing.[773]

The third reason given by the ECJ in *Reichert (No 2)* for excluding the *action* **3.254** *paulienne* from Art 5(3) of the Brussels Convention is that the beneficiary has not committed any wrongful act. Again, it may be doubted whether this provides a reason to exclude the action from the scope of Art 4 of the Rome II Regulation. Whether he is at fault or not, the beneficiary may be seen as an accessory to what is clearly a wrongful act on the part

---

[766] **3.240** above.
[767] Art 2(2)–(3).
[768] *Reichert (No 2)*, n 752 above, Opinion, 2163.
[769] *Reichert v Dresdner Bank (No 1)*, n 290 above, para 12.
[770] **3.98–3.99** above.
[771] Insolvency Act 1986, s 423(2).
[772] **3.240** above.
[773] Insolvency Act 1986, s 425(1).

of the debtor. The wrongful nature of the beneficiary's conduct will be clearer in those systems which require an element of collusion on the part of the beneficiary.[774] Otherwise, the action seems to confirm the difficulty of distinguishing between liability for a lawful act and strict liability for an unlawful act, and suggests that legal certainty would be improved if both were to be brought within the scope of the Regulation.

3.255 In his opinion in *Reichert (No 2)*, Adv Gen Gulmann resorted to a teleological construction of Art 5(3), concluding that the jurisdictional connecting factor of the 'place where the harmful event occurred' (referring both to the place of damage and the place of the event giving rise to damage) did not establish a strong connecting link between the dispute and the chosen forum. He argued:[775]

> In a case such as this the place where the harmful event occurred may well be either the place where the instrument of conveyance was drawn up or the place where the property conveyed is situated. But neither of these places seems to be of special significance in deciding whether the conditions for setting the transaction aside are met. The most essential such conditions are those concerning the existence of the debt owed to the creditor and the debtor's intention knowingly to restrict the creditor's opportunities for enforcement.

3.256 The Advocate General concluded that there was no need for a rule of alternative jurisdiction in cases of this kind, as the dispute could perfectly well be dealt with by the courts of the defendant's domicile, and comforted himself with the fact that this decision would remove the need to determine the location of the 'harmful event' in the case before him.[776]

3.257 In the context of the Rome II Regulation, such arguments are either unavailable or unappealing. Here, the court seised of the dispute must determine the law applicable to the claim by some means or other; the principal question is whether the rules of applicable law contained in Art 4 of the Regulation are appropriate for this purpose. It is submitted that they are: the country of damage for the purposes of Art 4(1) should be identified with the country in which the creditor has lost his opportunity to enforce his claim against assets of the defendant, being, normally, the country in which the asset (in the case of a transaction involving a specific asset) or the defendant's principal assets was or were located before the transaction giving rise to the action. Within the EC and those countries party to the Lugano Convention, at least, the courts of that country have exclusive

---

[774] n 764 above.
[775] *Reichert (No 2)*, n 752 above, Opinion, 2172–3. Also ibid, 2173–4.
[776] Ibid, 2173.

jurisdiction over matters of enforcement,[777] further reinforcing this link. The rules of displacement in Arts 4(2) and 4(3) would also apply. The latter, in particular, may be thought more likely to be used in circumstances in which the asset in question was in transit at the time of, or has been moved with a view to facilitating, the transaction in question.[778]

Overall, therefore, there seems no compelling reason why the *action pauli-* **3.258** *enne* and similar claims cannot be considered for the purposes of the Regulation to be based on a non-contractual obligation, in particular one arising out of tort/delict. In some cases, however, that obligation may be removed from scope by the provisions of Art 1(2), most obviously sub-paragraphs (a) and (b) in the case of marriage settlements and gifts by will. Finally, in an insolvency situation, the rules of applicable law contained in the Regulation may be overridden by those contained in the Insolvency Regulation.[779]

Non-Contractual Obligations—Summary of Conclusions

If, as submitted above, the concept of 'tort/delict' within the Rome II **3.259** Regulation must be defined positively, the absence of a residual rule of applicable law for non-contractual obligations not arising out of a 'tort/delict' leads inexorably to the conclusion that the horizontal material scope of the Regulation is no greater than the sum of its constituent parts, i.e. the individual scope of the rules of applicable law in Chapters II and III.

In considering whether the Rome II Regulation applies in a particular case, **3.260** both negative and positive aspects of its horizontal material scope must be considered.[780] During this enquiry, the following questions may arise. These are questions of characterization to be approached in the manner suggested above.[781] First, is the matter raised for determination one of obligation, as opposed to status?[782] If the latter, neither the Rome I Regime nor the Rome II Regulation will apply. Secondly, is the obligation in question a 'contractual obligation' falling within the scope of the Rome I Regime, and not the Rome II Regulation?[783] Thirdly, is the obligation within any of the categories

---

[777] Brussels I Regulation, Art 22(5); Lugano Convention, Art 16(5); *Kuwait Oil Tanker SAK v Qabazard* [2003] UKHL 31; [2004] 1 AC 300.
[778] **4.87** above.
[779] Regulation (EC) No 1346/00 on insolvency proceedings (L160, 1 [30.6.2000]) (**16.32** below).
[780] **3.87**.
[781] **3.62–3.72**.
[782] **3.88–3.103**.
[783] **3.104–3.145**.

excluded by Art 1(2)?[784] Fourthly, assuming the obligation in question is not 'contractual', does the obligation fall within the scope of the any of the rules of applicable law in Chapters II and III of the Rome II instrument:

- as 'arising out of damage caused by a product' (Art 5)[785];
- as 'arising out of an act of unfair competition' (Art 6(1));[786]
- as 'arising out of a restriction of competition' (Art 6(3));[787]
- as 'arising out of environmental damage or damage sustained by persons or property as a result of such damage' (Art 7);[788]
- as 'arising from an infringement of an intellectual property right' (Arts 8 and 13);[789]
- as concerning liability 'for damages caused by industrial action' (Art 9);[790]
- as 'arising out of unjust enrichment' (Art 10);[791]
- as 'arising out of an act performed without due authority in connection with the affairs of another person' *(negotiorum gestio)* (Art 11);[792]
- as 'arising out of dealings prior to the conclusion of a contract' *(culpa in contrahendo)* (Art 12);[793]
- as not falling within any of the preceding categories, but 'arising out of a tort/delict' (Art 4)?[794]

3.261 These categories must be defined autonomously having regard to the objectives of the Rome II Regulation as well as principles common to the legal systems of the Member States, and the meaning given to particular words will not necessarily accord with that used by the forum State in a domestic context.[795] Nor will the label given to an obligation under the Regulation necessarily correspond with that given to it, and to the rule creating it, by the system whose law applies under the Regulation (or would apply if the Regulation were applicable) or by the law of the forum: it is the basis of the obligation, and not its description, that matters in the process of characterization.

---

[784] **3.146–3.228**.
[785] **5.07–5.17** below.
[786] **6.15–6.41** below.
[787] **6.31–6.33** below.
[788] **7.03–7.14** below.
[789] **8.10–8.20** below.
[790] **9.17–9.30** below.
[791] **10.10–10.21** below.
[792] **11.02–11.17** below.
[793] **12.03–12.12** below.
[794] **3.243–3.245** above and **4.06–4.20** below.
[795] **3.05–3.11** and **3.63** above.

If the obligation in question does not fit within any of these categories, it **3.262** falls outside the scope of both the Rome I and Rome II Regulations, and must be addressed by reference to the residual rules of private international law of the Member State seised of the dispute. That said, the latter conclusion may be one which Member State courts and the ECJ will reach reluctantly, as it would create a further *lacuna* in the Community applicable law regime for the law of obligations not expressly provided for in Art 1(2), jeopardizing the objective of increasing certainty as to the law applicable. Accordingly, it is suggested, the courts will likely adopt a flexible approach (in particular) to the concept of a 'tort/delict' so as to bring cases within the scope of Art 4, the provision best suited as a repository for non-contractual obligations which may otherwise prove difficult to categorize.

CIVIL AND COMMERCIAL MATTERS

Introduction

Under Art 1(1), the Regulation applies only to non-contractual obligations **3.263** in 'civil and commercial matters'. This reference to 'civil and commercial matters' reflects the terminology used in the Brussels I Regime and the Rome I Regulation.[796] Given that the substantive scope of the Rome II Regulation is intended to be consistent with the Brussels I Regulation and the Rome I Regime,[797] it cannot be doubted that an autonomous meaning must be given to this concept in accordance with the case law of the Court of Justice in relation to the Brussels I Regime, as well as any future case law concerning the Rome I Regulation. In the Commission's view, this use of common terminology 'makes it clear that the "Brussels I" Regulation, the Rome Convention and the [*Rome II Regulation*] constitute a coherent set of instruments covering the general field of private international law in matters of civil and commercial obligations'.[798]

In its case law on the Brussels Convention, the ECJ has emphasized that **3.264** the concept of 'civil and commercial matters' has two aspects, focusing on (1) the parties to the action, and (2) the basis and nature of the action and the detailed rules underlying it. In *Lechouritou v Federal Republic of Germany*, the Court stated:[799]

---

[796] Brussels Convention, Art 1; Brussels I Regulation, Art 1.1; Rome I Regulation, Art 1(1).
[797] Recital (7).
[798] Commission Proposal, 8. Note that the 1980 Rome Convention is not expressly restricted to 'civil and commercial matters', although (as noted) this terminology appears in Art 1(1) of its successor, the Rome I Regulation.
[799] Case C-292/05, *Lechouritou v Dimosio tis Omospondiakis Dimokratias tis Germanias* [2007] ECR I-1519, paras 29–31, noted V Gärtner, 'The Brussels Convention and Reparations' (2007) 8

In order to ensure, as far as possible, that the rights and obligations which derive from the Brussels Convention for the Contracting States and the persons to whom it applies are equal and uniform, the terms of that provision should not be interpreted as a mere reference to the internal law of one or other of the States concerned. It is thus clear from the Court's settled case-law that 'civil and commercial matters' must be regarded as an independent concept to be interpreted by referring, first, to the objectives and scheme of the Brussels Convention and, second, to the general principles which stem from the corpus of the national legal systems.[800]

According to the Court, that interpretation results in the exclusion of certain legal actions and judicial decisions from the scope of the Brussels Convention, by reason either of the legal relationships between the parties to the action or of the subject-matter of the action.[801]

Thus, the Court has held that, although certain actions between a public authority and a person governed by private law may come within the scope of the Brussels Convention, it is otherwise where the public authority is acting in the exercise of its public powers.[802]

3.265 Further, as the Court explained:[803]

The fact that the plaintiff acts on the basis of a claim which arises from an act in the exercise of public powers is sufficient for his action, whatever the nature of the proceedings afforded by national law for that purpose, to be treated as being outside the scope of the Brussels Convention . . . [T]hat the proceedings brought before the referring court are presented as being of a civil nature in so far as they seek financial compensation for the material loss and non-material damage caused to the plaintiffs in the main proceedings is consequently entirely irrelevant.

German LJ No 4 (available at <http://www.germanlawjournal.com/article.php?id=815>); H Muir-Watt and E Pataut, 'Les actes *jure imperii* et le Règlement Bruxelles I—A propos de l'affaire Lechouritou', *Revue Critique de Droit International Privé* 2008, 61.

[800] The ECJ referred to Case 29/76, *LTU Lufttransportunternehmen GmbH v Eurocontrol* [1976] ECR 1541, paras 3 and 5; Case 814/79, *Netherlands v Rüffer* [1980] ECR 3807, para 7; Case C-271/00, *Gemeente Steenbergen v Baten* [2002] ECR I-10489, para 28; Case C-266/01, *Préservatrice foncière TIARD v Netherlands* [2003] ECR I-4867, para 20 and Case C-343/04, *Land Oberösterreich v ČEZ* [2006] ECR I-4557, para 22.

[801] Referring to *LTU v Eurocontrol*, para 4; *Netherlands v Rüffer*, para 14; *Steenbergen v Baten*, para 29; *TIARD v Netherlands*, para 21; *Land Oberösterreich v ČEZ*, para 22 (references in the preceding footnote); Case C-167/00, *Verein für Konsumentinformation v Henkel* [2002] ECR I-8111, para 29.

[802] Referring to *LTU v Eurocontrol*, para 4; *Netherlands v Rüffer*, para 8; *VKI v Henkel*, para 26; *Steenbergen v Baten*, para 30; *Préservatrice foncière TIARD v Netherlands*, para 22 (for references see nn 800–801 above); Case C-172/91, *Sonntag v Waidmann* [1993] ECR I-1963, para 20.

[803] *Lechouritou v Germany*, n 799 above, para 41.

Accordingly, if none of the parties to the action is a State or other govern- **3.266** mental or public authority or its representative, the matter will be a 'civil and commercial matter' under the Rome II Regulation.[804] For this pur- pose, a consumer organization or other representative body established under private law cannot be equated with a public authority.[805] Even if there is a State party in the proceedings, a matter will still fall within the scope of the Regulation if it involves a 'private law' relationship and the public body is not exercising its 'public powers', i.e. powers going beyond those existing under the rules applicable to relations between private indi- viduals.[806] Actions concerning a private law relationship between a State or public body, on the one hand, and a private person, on the other (or even between two States or public bodies[807]) will fall, therefore, within the scope of the Regulation, unless the subject matter of the action is the exer- cise of public powers.[808] In addressing this question, the court must iden- tify the legal relationship between the parties and examine the legal and factual basis of the action as presented by the claimant.[809] Consequently, the matter will not be removed from the scope of the Regulation by reason only of the fact that the defendant's case requires the court to investigate an exercise of public powers.[810]

Applying these principles, the following matters involving non-contractual **3.267** obligations have been held not to constitute 'civil and commercial matters' under the Brussels Convention:

- A claim by the agent responsible for policing public waterways to recover the costs of removing a wreck located in those waterways in the exercise of its public powers.[811]

---

[804] *VKI v Henkel*, ibid, para 30.

[805] Ibid.

[806] *Préservatrice foncière TIARD v Netherlands*, n 800 above, paras 22, 30, and 36; Case C-265/02, *Frahuil SA v Assitalia SpA* [2004] ECR I-1543, para 21.

[807] See thie Report of Professor Schlosser on the convention for the accession of Denmark, Ireland and the United Kingdom to the 1968 Brussels Convention (OJ C59, 84 (para 28) [5.3.1979]).

[808] *Préservatrice foncière TIARD v Netherlands*, n 800 above, paras 33–6.

[809] *Steenbergen v Baten*, n 800 above, para 31; *Préservatrice foncière TIARD v Netherlands*, n 800 above, para 23; *Frahuil v Assitalia*, n 806 above, para 20.

[810] *Préservatrice foncière TIARD*, n 800 above, paras 39–44 (validity of exercise of powers raised by way of defence to guarantee claim). In this connection, the suggestion by the editors of Dicey, Morris & Collins, 1st supplement, para 34-014 that a claim by a local authority to recover pay- ments under a contract held to be *ultra vires* (cf *Kleinwort Benson Ltd v Glasgow CC* [1999] 1 AC 153 (UKHL)) seems wrong. The claim concerns a private law relationship and even the relevant 'public law' rules regulate the authority's ability to enter into contracts under private law.

[811] *Netherlands v Rüffer*, n 800 above. The same reasoning applies, for example, to a claim by a public authority acting in the exercise of public powers to recover the costs of cleaning up a pollution incident (**7.03–7.07** below).

- A claim by representatives of victims and survivors of a wartime massacre by military forces seeking compensation from the State concerned.[812]
- A defamation claim against a central bank in relation to a report prepared by it in the exercise of its supervisory functions.[813]

3.268 The following matters have, on the other hand, been held to constitute 'civil and commercial matters' under the Brussels Convention:

- A civil claim, brought within criminal proceedings, against a teacher who, during a school trip, caused injury to a pupil through a breach of his duty of supervision.[814]
- A preventative action brought by a consumer protection organization to prevent a trader from using unfair contract terms in contracts with private individuals.[815]

3.269 Proceedings by a victim of a criminal act to obtain compensation from a competent authority in a Member State, as opposed to from the perpetrator or other person responsible for the perpetrator's acts, fall outside the scope of the Regulation.[816]

Revenue, Customs, and Administrative Matters Excluded

3.270 The specific exclusion of 'revenue, customs and administrative matters' in Art 1(1) of the Rome II Regulation also reflects the language used in the Brussels I Regime.[817] The wording adds little, if anything, to the concept of 'civil and commercial matters'. As the ECJ recognized in *Préservatrice foncière TIARD v Netherlands*, these words were added to Art 1 of the Brussels Convention on the accession of Denmark, the United Kingdom, and Ireland 'in order to clarify, by means of examples, which matters do not fall within the scope of the Brussels Convention'.[818] The Court added:[819]

That sentence seeks only to draw attention to the fact that customs matters are not covered by the concept of civil and commercial matters. That clarification did not

---

[812] *Lechouritou v Germany*, n 799 above.

[813] *Grovit v De Nederlandsche Bank NV* [2007] EWCA Civ 953; [2008] 1 WLR 51.

[814] *Sonntag v Waidmann*, n 802 above.

[815] *VFK v Henkel*, n 801 above.

[816] For EC/EU measures in this area, see Directive (EC) No 2004/80 relating to compensation of crime victims (OJ L261, 15 [6.8.2004]); Council Framework Decision (2001/220/JHA) on the standing of victims in criminal proceedings (OJ L82, 1 [22.3.2001]).

[817] Brussels Convention, Art 1; Brussels I Regulation, Art 1(1).

[818] *Préservatrice foncière TIARD v Netherlands*, n 800 above, para 38.

[819] Ibid, paras 38–9.

however have the effect of either limiting or modifying the scope of the latter concept.

It follows that the criterion for fixing the limits of the concept of customs matters must be analogous to that applied to the concept of civil and commercial matters.

Liability for Exercise of State Authority Excluded

The specific exclusion of liability of the State for acts and omissions in the **3.271** exercise of State authority (*acta iure imperii*) was the product of concerns raised at an early stage in discussions in the Council's Rome II Committee. The Luxembourg delegation noted, for example, that:[820]

Luxembourg wishes to see the civil liability of public authorities (State, local authorities, other public-law bodies) formally excluded from the scope. Under Luxembourg law, the liability of public authorities is a civil matter, thus it falls a priori within the scope of Rome II. A foreign law should not be applied where the state has acted in the exercise of its powers. Such a situation falls exclusively within the scope of the national law of the State whose liability is sought.

In the draft text circulated by the outgoing Irish and incoming Dutch **3.272** Presidencies in June 2004, it was suggested that a reference to the exclusion of liability of the State for acts and omissions in the exercise of State authority (*acta iure imperii*) should appear in a recital.[821] In the following draft, however, the wording transferred (in square brackets) to the text of Art 1(1), where it remained.[822] That change reflected, in part, a proposal advanced by the Spanish delegation by whom State liability was described as a 'red line' issue,[823] and ensured consistency with the language used in the Regulation creating a European Enforcement Order for uncontested claims, adopted in April 2004.[824] At the same time, Spain had proposed that State liability falling within the scope of the Regulation (i.e. for *acta*

---

[820] Council document 9009/04 [29.4.2004], 1. Also ibid, ADD 1 [3.5.2004], 2 (Austria); ibid, ADD 10 [18.5.4], 1–2 (Spain); ibid, ADD 11 [24.5.2004], 3 (Germany); ibid, ADD14 [24.5.2004], 2 (Lithuania). Compare, however, the views of the Polish delegation (ibid, ADD 3 [4.5.2004], 1) arguing that such claims should be brought within scope, and of the Netherlands delegation (ibid, ADD 16 [28.5.2004], 1), arguing that the exclusion of 'civil and commercial matters' was sufficient to cover *acta iure imperii*, without elaboration. The German delegation (ibid, ADD 11, 6) also suggested that it would be useful to stipulate that, in general, only the law of the country of office should apply to the liability of public officials falling within the scope of the Regulation.

[821] Council document 10173/04 [14.6.2004], 3.

[822] Council document 12746/04 [27.9.2004], Art 1(1). The square brackets were removed in the draft circulated by the outgoing UK and incoming Austrian Presidencies in December 2005 (Council document, 16027/05 [22.12.2005], Art 1(1)).

[823] Council document SN2852/04 ADD 3 [9.9.2004].

[824] Regulation (EC) No 805/2004 creating a European Enforcement Order for uncontested claims (OJ L143, 15 [30.4.2004]), Art 2(1). The same language has since been used in Regulation

iure gestionis) should be subject to the law of the State concerned. That proposal, and later Spanish proposals of a similar kind, [825] were not accepted.[826] In its 1st Reading Position, the European Parliament suggested excluding 'the liability of public administrations in respect of acts or omissions occurring in the performance of their duties' and 'liability for acts of public authority, including liability of publicly-appointed officeholders'.[827] Only two Member State delegations were specifically opposed in principle to the first amendment, but others preferred to keep the language consistent with the European Enforcement Order Regulation.[828] That approach was also favoured by the Commission.[829] The second amendment was considered unnecessary by most Member State delegations.[830]

3.273 This exclusion must be read together with Recital (9), which provides:

> Claims arising out of *acta iure imperii* should include claims against officials who act on behalf of the State and liability for acts of public authorities, including liability of publicly appointed office-holders. Therefore, these matters should be excluded from the scope of this Regulation.

3.274 As in the case of the specific reference to revenue, customs, or administrative matters,[831] it seems doubtful whether the specific reference in Art 1(1) to liability in the exercise of State authority does anything more than clarify the general exclusion of matters other than 'civil and commercial matters' from the scope of the Regulation. In *Lechouritou*, it was common ground among the Member States who made observations to the ECJ that the effect of the Court's earlier jurisprudence was that the exclusion of 'civil and commercial matters' from the Brussels Convention covered *acta iure imperii*, although differences existed between them as to the definition of such acts and whether they included the conduct of the armed forces of

---

(EC) No 1896/2006 of the European Parliament and of the Council of 12 December 2006 creating a European order for payment procedure (OJ L399, 1 [30.12.2006]), Art 2(1); and Directive (EC) No 2008/52 on certain aspects of mediation in civil and commercial matters (OJ L136, 3 [24.5.2008]), Art 1(2).

[825] Council document 7212/06 ADD 2 [10.3.2006]. See also the explanatory note by the Spanish delegation in Council document 7681/06 [22.3.2006].

[826] Council document 7551/06 [22.3.2006].

[827] EP 1st Reading Position, Arts 1(1) and 1(2)(h) (Amendments 18 and 23).

[828] Council document 11515/05 [27.7.2005], 2.

[829] Commission Amended Proposal, Art 1(2)(g).

[830] Council document 11515/05, 2.

[831] **3.270** above.

one Member State on the territory of another.[832] Having considered, with reference to the Court's case law, the reasons for the exclusion of *acta iure imperii* and the criteria on which the exclusion is based, Adv Gen Colomer concluded:[833]

> It may be deduced from the case-law cited that, in order to determine whether an act is an act *iure imperii* and, therefore, not subject to the Brussels Convention, regard must be had, first, to whether any of the parties to the legal relationship are a public authority, and, second, to the origin and the basis of the action brought, specifically to whether a public authority has exercised powers going beyond those existing, or which have no equivalent, in relationships between private individuals. The 'private' criterion refers to a formal aspect, while the 'subordination' criterion relates to the basis and nature of the action and to the detailed rules for exercise of the right of action.

In its judgment, the ECJ also referred to the concept of acts *iure imperii* as falling outside of the Brussels I Regime, referring to the wording of the European Enforcement Order Regulation.[834]

Earlier in his opinion in *Lechouritou*, Adv Gen Colomer had recognized that:[835] **3.275**

> [T]he difficulty is that it may not always be easy to distinguish between instances in which the State and its independent organs act in a private law capacity and those in which they act in a public law capacity, in particular if it is borne in mind that countries which have common law systems are not familiar with the distinction between public and private law, in the sense that civil law covers all matters which are not part of criminal law. Accordingly, although the legal systems of the Contracting States provide some guidance in this connection, the definition of a situation governed by public law may not be found in those systems, which in many instances are divergent and imprecise.

Although the continental distinction between 'public' and 'private' law **3.276** may be unfamiliar to common lawyers, the approach of the ECJ in deciding whether a matter is or is not a 'civil or commercial matter' is resonant of the distinction drawn in public international law between sovereign (immune) acts (*acta iure imperii*) and private (non-immune) acts (*acta iure*

---

[832] *Lechouritou v Germany*, n 799 above, Opinion of Adv Gen Colomer, para 29, referring in a footnote to the specific reference to *acta iure imperii* in Art 1(2)(g) of the Commission Amended Proposal for the Rome II Regulation.

[833] Ibid, Opinion, para 46.

[834] Ibid, Judgment, paras 40, 45.

[835] Ibid, Opinion, para 36 referring to the Opinion of Adv Gen Jacobs in Henkel, n 801 above, para 22.

gestionis), as applied by UK courts. In *Kuwait Airways Corporation v Iraqi Airways Co*, Lord Goff stated:[836]

> The ultimate test of what constitutes an *act jure imperii* is whether the act in question is of its own character a governmental act, as opposed to an act which any private citizen can perform.

3.277 Equally, Recital (9), which emphasizes that officials and public authorities (including office-holders) should be equated with the State for these purposes, is consistent not only with the case law of the ECJ under the Brussels Convention[837] but also with the approach taken in the context of State immunity. In *Jones v Ministry of Interior of Saudi Arabia*, a case involving allegations of torture by State officials, Lord Hoffmann stated:[838]

> I start with the proposition that, as a matter of international law, the same immunity against suit in a foreign domestic court which protects the state itself also protects the individuals for whom the state is responsible . . . The traditional way of expressing this principle in international law is to say that the acts of state officials acting in that capacity are not attributable to them personally but only to the state.[839] . . .

> Despite the undoubted authority for expressing the rule in this way, I do respectfully think that it is a little artificial to say that the acts of officials are 'not attributable to them personally' and that this usage can lead to confusion. . . . I would therefore prefer to say, as Leggatt LJ did in *Propend Finance Pty Ltd v Sing*,[840] that state immunity affords individual employees or officers of a foreign state 'protection under the same cloak as protects the state itself'. But this is a difference in the form of expression and not the substance of the rule.

3.278 In this connection, his Lordship referred to the 2004 UN Convention on jurisdictional immunities of States and their property.[841] Art 2(1)(b) of that

---

[836] [1995] 1 WLR 1147, 1160 (Lord Goff, UKHL). For a comparative survey of the approach taken to this question in different jurisdictions, see S Wittich, 'The Definition of Commercial Acts', ch 2 in G Hafner, M Kohen, and S Breau (eds), *State Practice Regarding State Immunities* (2006).

[837] *Sonntag v Waidman*, n 802 above, paras 20–1.

[838] [2006] UKHL 26; [2007] 1 AC 270, [66]–[68]. Also Lord Bingham, [10]–[11].

[839] His Lordship referred to the reasoning of the International Criminal Tribunal for the Former Yugoslavia in *Prosecutor v Blaskic* (1997) 110 ILR 607, 707 and to the decision of the German Federal Supreme Court in the *Church of Scientology Case* (1978) 65 ILR 193, 198.

[840] (1997) 111 ILR 611, 669 (EWCA).

[841] Adopted by the General Assembly of the United Nations on 2 December 2004, but not yet in force (General Assembly resolution 59/38, annex, Official Records of the General Assembly, Fifty-ninth Session, Supplement No. 49 (A/59/49)). Among Member States, Austria, Portugal, and Romania are parties to the Convention. Several other Member States have signed but not ratified the Convention (see <http://untreaty.un.org/ENGLISH/bible/englishinternetbible/partI/chapterIII/treaty38.asp>).

Convention defines a 'State' as including:[842]

(i) the State and its various organs of government;
(ii) constituent units of a federal State or political subdivisions of the State, which are entitled to perform acts in the exercise of sovereign authority, and are acting in that capacity;
(iii) agencies or instrumentalities of the State or other entities, to the extent that they are entitled to perform and are actually performing acts in the exercise of sovereign authority of the State;
(iv) representatives of the State acting in that capacity.

That definition also seems appropriate in the context of the Rome II **3.279** Regulation. Although, on a literal interpretation, Recital (9) could be taken as excluding all claims against officials and public authorities from the scope of the Regulation by irrebuttably treating such claims as 'arising out of *acta iure imperii*', it cannot have been the intention of the authors of the Regulation to put such persons in a more favourable situation than the State on whose behalf they act or to distinguish between situations in which the State, and those in which another person, is the correct defendant. In all cases, therefore, the test to be applied is whether the action is based on the exercise of public powers, i.e. powers going beyond those existing under the rules applicable to relations between private individuals.

Liability under International and EC Law

In *Lechouritou*, Adv Gen Colomer recognized that the question of State **3.280** responsibility under international law, whether under customary or written[843] rules, does not involve a 'civil' matter within Art 1 of the Brussels Regulation,[844] and that it is irrelevant to the classification of a matter as involving the exercise of public powers and as being 'civil' for this purpose whether the acts in question are unlawful under international law or were undertaken outside the territory of the State concerned.[845] The same reasoning should apply under the Rome II Regulation.

---

[842] Also the commentary on the corresponding provision in the International Law Commission's 1991 draft articles (YBILC (43rd session), vol II, Pt 2, 13), reproduced in A Dickinson, R Lindsay, and J Loonam, *State Immunity: Selected Materials and Commentary* (2004), para 2.005.
[843] International Law Commission draft articles on responsibility of States for internationally wrongful acts (2001), with commentary, available at <http://untreaty.un.org/ilc/reports/2001/english/chp4.pdf>.
[844] *Lechouritou*, n 799 above, Opinion, paras 59–61.
[845] Ibid, paras 62–9.

3.281 In many cases, claims arising on the plane of international law, including claims to enforce the provisions of a treaty, will not be justiciable before national courts, and are no concern of the Rome II Regulation.[846] Increasingly, however, individual natural and legal persons are subject to, and may seek in national courts to enforce, obligations arising by treaty and customary international law.[847] The most developed example of this phenomenon is the EC Treaty itself.[848] As the ECJ recognized in its judgment in *Courage v Crehan*:[849]

> It should be borne in mind, first of all, that the Treaty has created its own legal order, which is integrated into the legal systems of the Member States and which their courts are bound to apply. The subjects of that legal order are not only the Member States but also their nationals. Just as it imposes burdens on individuals, Community law is also intended to give rise to rights which become part of their legal assets. Those rights arise not only where they are expressly granted by the Treaty but also by virtue of obligations which the Treaty imposes in a clearly defined manner both on individuals and on the Member States and the Community institutions.

3.282 *Courage* concerned a claim to damages based on an alleged breach of the prohibition of agreements liable to restrict or distort competition within the meaning of Art 81 (formerly Art 85) of the EC Treaty. In its later decision in *Manfredi v Lloyd Adriatico*, the Court held that:[850]

> As regards the possibility of seeking compensation for loss caused by a contract or by conduct liable to restrict or distort competition, it should be recalled that the full effectiveness of Article 81 EC and, in particular, the practical effect of the prohibition laid down in Article 81(1) EC would be put at risk if it were not open to any individual to claim damages for loss caused to him by a contract or by conduct liable to restrict or distort competition . . .[851]

---

[846] *Buttes Gas and Oil Co v Hammer (No 3)* [1982] AC 888, 931–2 (Lord Wilberforce, UKHL); *JH Rayner (Mincing Lane) Ltd v Department of Trade and Industry* [1990] 2 AC 418, 499 (Lord Oliver, UKHL).

[847] R McCorquodale, 'The Individual and the International Legal System', ch 10 in M D Evans (ed), *International Law* (2nd edn, 2006).

[848] For claims involving allegations of human rights violations, see **15.09** below.

[849] Case C-453/99, *Courage Ltd v Crehan* [2001] ECR I-6297, para 19, referring to Case 26/62, *Van Gend en Loos v Nederlandse Administratie der Belastingen* [1963] ECR 1, Case 6/64, *Costa v Ente Nazionale per l'Enefia Elettrica (ENEL)* [1964] ECR 585 and Joined Cases C-6/90 and C-9/90, *Francovich v Italian Republic* [1991] ECR I-5357, para 31.

[850] Joined Cases C-295/04 to C-298/04, *Manfredi v Lloyd Adriatico Assicurazioni SpA* [2006] ECR I-6619, paras 60–2.

[851] Referring to *Courage v Crehan*, n 849 above, para 26.

It follows that any individual can claim compensation for the harm suffered where there is a causal relationship between that harm and an agreement or practice prohibited under Article 81 EC.

In the absence of Community rules governing the matter, it is for the domestic legal system of each Member State to designate the courts and tribunals having jurisdiction and to lay down the detailed procedural rules governing actions for safeguarding rights which individuals derive directly from Community law, provided that such rules are not less favourable than those governing similar domestic actions (principle of equivalence) and that they do not render practically impossible or excessively difficult the exercise of rights conferred by Community law (principle of effectiveness) . . .[852]

3.283 Actions of this kind brought between private parties, or between a private party and a public authority acting otherwise than in the exercise of its public powers, quite clearly fall within the scope of the Rome II Regulation. Indeed, Art 6(3) contains specific rules of applicable law for non-contractual obligations arising out of a restriction of competition and Recital (22) refers to 'infringements of both national and Community competition law'.[853] Art 81 is, however, by no means the only provision of EC law breach of which may entitle one private person suffering damage to bring a claim for compensation, or to bring a preventative action, against another. Thus, it is clearly established that, at least in certain circumstances, the fundamental freedoms guaranteed by the EC Treaty are capable of having 'horizontal direct effect' between private parties.[854] Further, in *Antonio Muñoz v Frumar*, the ECJ appeared to suggest a wider role for private enforcement, in giving effect to obligations imposed on traders by Community legislation in the form of a regulation. The case of *Muñoz* concerned an EC Regulation that prohibited the sale of grapes otherwise than in accordance with designated quality standards. Having referred to *Courage v Crehan*, the Court stated:[855]

The full effectiveness of the rules on quality standards . . . imply that it must be possible to enforce that obligation by means of civil proceedings instituted by a trader against a competitor.

3.284 It is unclear whether the Court in *Muñoz* was contemplating that, in bringing such proceedings, one trader would enforce an obligation owed

---

[852] Referring to Case C-261/95 *Palmisani v Istituto Nazionale Della Previdenza Sociale* [1997] ECR I-4025, para 27, and *Courage and Crehan*, n 849 above, para 29.

[853] **6.58** below.

[854] Case C-483/05, *International Transport Workers' Federation v Viking Line ABP* [2007] ECR I-0000, paras 56–66; N Reich, 'Horizontal Liability in EC Law: Hybridization of Remedies for Compensation in Case of Breaches of EC Rights' (2007) Common Market L Rev 705.

[855] Case C-253/00, *Antonio Muñoz y Cia SA v Frumar Ltd* [2002] I-7289, para 30.

directly to him by his competitor, or would be acting as a 'private enforcement authority' to enforce an obligation in the interest of traders or consumers generally.[856] If the former, such an action would appear clearly to fall within the scope of the Rome II Regulation as a 'civil and commercial matter'. Even on the latter view, the reasoning of the ECJ in *Henkel*[857] and the text of the Commission Proposal[858] suggest strongly that such private enforcement proceedings fall within the Regulation's scope. In either case, non-compliance with quality standards would appear in the nature of an act of unfair competition within Art 6(1).[859]

3.285 On the other hand, claims to enforce EC law, and other obligations arising under a treaty or rule of customary international law, fall outside the scope of the Rome II Regulation if the claimant's action is based on the exercise of public powers by the State or other public authority. This includes claims of State liability based on a failure to transpose EC legislation into national law,[860] the adoption of legislation contrary to the EC Treaty,[861] failure of a court correctly to apply EC law,[862] or other official acts.[863] For the same reason, civil claims against UK public authorities for failure to give effect to the provisions of the European Convention on Human Rights scheduled to the UK Human Rights Act 1998[864] or against a State or its official for war crimes,[865] torture, or other human rights violations involving acts of a peculiarly sovereign character fall outside the scope of the Regulation.[866]

3.286 For claims based on breaches of EC law that fall within the scope of the Rome II Regulation, Member State courts must always have regard to the principles of equivalence and effectiveness,[867] whether called upon to apply their own law or the law of another Member State. In this connection, the principle of equivalence may require some modification so that it refers to rules no less favourable than those governing similar domestic actions under the law of the Member State that applies under the Regulation

---

[856] D Wyatt et al., *Wyatt & Dashwood's European Union Law* (5th edn, 2006), para 5-004.

[857] **3.240** above.

[858] Commission Proposal, 15 (**3.243**, point 9 above).

[859] **4.112** below.

[860] *Francovich v Italian Republic*, n 849 above.

[861] Joined Cases C-46 and 48/93, *Brasserie du Pêcheur SA v Bundesrepublik Deutschland* [1996] ECR I-1029.

[862] Case C-173/03, *Traghetti del Mediterraneo SpA v Repubblica italiana* [2006] ECR I-5177.

[863] e.g. C-470/03, *AGM-COS.MET Srl v Suomen valtio* [2007] ECR I-2749; *Grovit v De Nederlandsche Bank*, n 813 above.

[864] Human Rights Act 1998, s 8.

[865] *Lechouritou v Germany*, n 799 above.

[866] **15.09** below.

[867] Text to n 852 above.

(as opposed to the law of the forum Member State). The principle of effectiveness of EC law, however, remains an overriding requirement which all Member State courts must observe whatever law applies under the Regulation.

E. TERRITORIAL APPLICATION OF THE REGULATION

Two aspects of the territorial application of the Regulation must be considered separately. First, location of the 'persons' regulated by the Regulation. Secondly, the territorial connections of the 'situations' regulated. **3.287**

The Persons Regulated—Courts or Tribunals of the EC Member States (Excluding Denmark)

Final clause

This Regulation shall be binding in its entirety and directly applicable in the Member States in accordance with the Treaty establishing the European Community.

Article 1(4)

Scope

For the purposes of this Regulation, 'Member State' shall mean any Member State other than Denmark.

The Regulation applies to Member State courts and tribunals in the determination of the law applicable to non-contractual obligations falling within the Regulation's material scope.[868] As the final clause of the Regulation, read together with Art 1(4), makes clear the Regulation applies in every EC Member State with the exception of Denmark (26 in total).[869] The Regulation applies in the UK and Ireland, both countries having exercised their right, conferred by Protocol to the EC Treaty, to opt-in to the negotiations leading to the Regulation.[870] **3.288**

The territorial limits of each Member State for these purposes fall to be determined in accordance with Art 229 of the EC Treaty. So far as the UK is concerned, the Regulation extends to England and Wales, Scotland, Northern Ireland, and Gibraltar but not to the Channel Islands, Isle of Man, the **3.289**

---

[868] **3.38** and **3.76** above.
[869] Title IV measures do not apply to Denmark (see **1.52** above and Recital (40)).
[870] **1.80** above and Recital (39).

Sovereign Base Areas in Cyprus, or non-European territories for whose external relations the UK is responsible.

The Situations Regulated—Application to Federal and Other Composite States

Article 25

States with more than one legal system

1. Where a State comprises several territorial units, each of which has its own rules of law in respect of non-contractual obligations, each territorial unit shall be considered as a country for the purposes of identifying the law applicable under this Regulation.

2. A Member State within which different territorial units have their own rules of law in respect of non-contractual obligations shall not be required to apply this Regulation to conflicts solely between the laws of such units.

3.290 This Article reflects very closely Art 19 of the Rome Convention,[871] which in turn appears to have been based on similar provisions contained in some of the Hague Conventions.[872] As the Commission explained:[873]

> The uniform rules also apply where several legal systems coexist in a single State. Where a State has several territorial units each with its own rules of law, each of those units is considered a country for the purposes of private international law. Examples of those States are the United Kingdom, Canada, the United States and Australia. For example, if damage is sustained in Scotland, the law designated by Article 3(1) [*of the Proposal*[874]] is Scots law.

3.291 The concept of a 'territorial unit' for these purposes does not, it is submitted, require a separate court system, but it does suggest a degree of constitutional separation.[875] Thus, the fact that certain rules concerning non-contractual liability apply only to specific regions within a State does not mean that those regions will automatically constitute one or more separate countries for the purposes of the Regulation.[876] If, however, the requisite degree of constitutional separation exists (most obviously, if a region has its own court system or a legislature with power to prescribe

---

[871] Also Rome I Regulation, Art 22.

[872] Professors Giuliano and Lagarde, in their report on the Rome Convention, refer to the Convention on the law applicable to matrimonial property regimes (14 March 1978), Arts 17 and 18 and the Convention on the law applicable to agency (14 March 1978), Arts 19 and 20 (OJ C282, 38 [31.10.1980]).

[873] Commission Proposal, 28.

[874] Regulation, Art 4(1).

[875] For the possible treatment of unrecognized states as 'territorial units' for these purposes, see **3.307–3.309** below.

[876] For the application of self-limiting provisions in legislation, see **3.42** above.

rules concerning non-contractual obligations), the territorial units must be treated as separate from each other, even if they largely share a 'common law', subject to local variations.[877] For these purposes, Scotland and Northern Ireland each constitute a separate country from England and Wales. It is, perhaps, a matter of debate whether Wales constitutes a separate country from England for these purposes.[878]

Under Art 25(2), the Regulation does not extend to 'conflicts solely between the laws of' different territorial units within a Member State. Each Member State consisting of one or more territorial units must, therefore, decide whether to apply the Regulation to situations of this kind. In practice, such situations may be most likely to arise from traffic accidents in border areas in which residents of one 'territorial unit' (e.g. Scotland) may cross regularly into another (e.g. England). If, however, there is a relevant connection to a State outside the Member State concerned, the restriction in Art 25(2) will not apply.[879] For these purposes, the objective of the Regulation in ensuring certainty as to the law applicable suggests that Art 25(2) should be given a narrow construction and that a connection to another State should be considered sufficient to escape its grasp if it (a) concerns the habitual residence of one of the parties or its insurer, or (b) is one which might be taken into account in determining the law applicable under the Regulation. Given that Arts 4(3), 5(3), 10(3), 11(4), and 12(2)(c) refer broadly to 'all the circumstances of the case' in determining the law applicable, Art 25(2) may be of very limited practical significance. **3.292**

The UK has yet to publish draft regulations to give effect to the Regulation. It is understood, however, that the Department of Justice plans to extend the application of the Regulation to conflicts arising solely between the constituent territorial units of the UK (including, for these purposes, Gibraltar). **3.293**

The Situations Regulated—Universal Application

Article 3

Universal application

Any law specified by this Regulation shall be applied whether or not it is the law of a Member State.

[877] For a comparative account of the role of the 'common law' in the legal systems of Australia, Canada, and the United States, see M Leeming, 'Common law within three federations', Sydney Law School Legal Studies Research Paper No 07/64, available at <http://papers.ssrn.com/sol3/papers.cfm?abstract_id=1027508>.
[878] Government of Wales Act 2006.
[879] Giuliano & Lagarde Report (OJ C210, 39 [31.10.1980]). Also Commission Proposal, 8 referring to 'one or more elements that are alien to the domestic social life of a country'.

3.294 The significance of Art 3 in the debate surrounding the Regulation's treaty base has been considered in **Chapter 2**.[880] Its effect within the Regulation, however, is uncontroversial—the Regulation applies irrespective of any connection with a country in a non-Member State that may result in the application of the law of that Member State to a non-contractual obligation falling within the Regulation's scope.

3.295 The provision reflects Art 2 of the Commission Proposal, a provision which the EESC welcomed in its opinion for the reason that:[881]

> In so doing [*the Proposal*] is following a generally recognised standard in conflict of laws, which in principle prohibits discrimination against other systems of law in conflict rules.

The Situations Regulated—Connection to the Territory of a State and other Situations

Introduction

3.296 The connecting factors used in the Regulation's rules of applicable law are principally, but not exclusively, geographical in character, pointing towards the place where a particular fact occurred. Thus, the Regulation refers (for example) to the country (a) 'in which the damage occurs',[882] (b) 'in which the product was acquired',[883] (c) 'where competitive relations or the collective interests of consumers are . . . affected',[884] (d) 'where the market is . . . affected',[885] (e) 'in which the event giving rise to damage occurred',[886] (f) 'in which the act of infringement was committed',[887] (g) 'where the [industrial] action is to be . . . taken',[888] (h) 'in which the unjust enrichment took place',[889] (i) 'in which the act [of *negotiorum gestio*] was performed'.[890] It also refers, in various places, to the country of habitual residence of one or more persons.[891] In terms of non-geographical, or potentially non-geographical,[892] connecting factors, the Regulation refers

---

[880] **2.110** above.
[881] EESC Opinion, para. 4.6 (OJ C241, 3 [28.9.2004]).
[882] Arts 4(1), 5(1)(c), and 12(2)(a). Also, by reference to Art 4(1), Arts 6(2), and 7.
[883] Art 5(1)(b).
[884] Art 6(1).
[885] Art 6(3).
[886] Art 7.
[887] Art 8(2).
[888] Art 9.
[889] Art 10(3).
[890] Art 11(3),
[891] Arts 4(2), 5(1)(a), 10(2), 11(2), 12(2)(b). Also, by reference to Art 4(2), Arts 5(1) and 9.
[892] **4.90–4.91** below.

to 'the country for which protection is claimed',[893] 'the law that applies to the contract',[894] 'the law of . . . choice',[895] and to 'a pre-existing relationship between the parties' or 'a relationship existing between the parties'.[896]

In the case of geographical connecting factors, the relevant fact will nor- **3.297** mally occur, without any doubt, within the undisputed land boundaries of a single State recognized under international law, or a territorial unit within a recognized State.[897] That, however, will not always be the case. In some cases, the fact may occur in, or cross the boundaries between, two or more States or territorial units. In others, the relevant event may occur (a) at sea, whether within a State's territorial waters or within its sector of the continental shelf outside its territorial waters[898] or on the high seas, or (b) in a disputed territory, including in the territory of an unrecognized State. Non-geographical connecting factors are also capable of pointing to the laws of more than one country.

Reference to more than one country/law—the concept of 'Mosaikbetrachtung' (mosaic view)

In its commentary on the proposed general rule for tort/delict, favouring **3.298** the law of the place of damage, the Commission addressed the problem of reference by one of the Regulation's rules of applicable law through its connecting factor to the law of more than one country. The Commission explained:[899]

The rule entails, where damage is sustained in several countries, that the laws of all the countries concerned will have to be applied on a distributive basis, applying what is known as 'Mosaikbetrachtung' in German law.

This idea of splitting a non-contractual obligation by reference to the sev- **3.299** eral places where damage has occurred is a familiar one to European practitioners. In *Shevill v Presse Alliance SA*, a case concerning Art 5(3) of the Brussels Convention (matters relating to tort, delict, or quasi-delict), the ECJ held that the victim of libel by a newspaper article printed in France by a French domiciled publisher but distributed in several Contracting States had the option of bringing an action against the publisher in the place

---

[893] Art 8(1).
[894] Art 12(1).
[895] Art 14(1).
[896] Arts 4(3), 5(2), 10(1), and 11(1).
[897] **3.291** above.
[898] e.g. on an offshore installation. For the pre-existing UK rules governing liability for acts occurring offshore in the UK area of the continental shelf and surrounding waters, see Civil Jurisdiction (Offshore Activities) Order 1987, SI 1987/2197.
[899] Commission Proposal, 11.

of the publisher's domicile (France) or before the courts of each Contracting State in which the publication had been distributed and where the victim claimed to have suffered injury to his reputation. The Court added, however, that the courts for each place of distribution had jurisdiction 'solely in respect of the harm caused in the State of the court seised'.[900] As a result, if the claimant chooses this option, the court seised must proceed on the basis that the non-contractual obligation only causes (direct[901]) damage within its territory and must give a ruling on that basis.

3.300 So expressed, the concept of the 'mosaic view' is beguilingly simple, although it has been criticized in Germany, its country of origin, mainly on the ground of complexity and procedural inefficiency.[902] It means that Member State courts should not react to a situation in which the connecting factor points to more than one country by concluding that the rule of applicable law has in some sense failed or by seeking to identify the country among those identified with which the situation is most closely connected or principally concerned. Instead, the court seised of the matter should first consider whether any rule of displacement applies or whether the initial identification of two or more laws as applying to the non-contractual obligation is confirmed. As part of this process in many cases, the court must ask itself the question whether the non-contractual obligation in question is 'manifestly more closely connected with a country *other than that indicated*' by the basic rule.[903] Although 'escape clauses' of this kind are intended to apply exceptionally,[904] the reference to a country 'other than that indicated' should not be taken to exclude the possibility of using a rule of displacement to select one among two or more countries or laws identified by the basic rule of applicable law on the ground that the circumstances (including the connecting factor) point overwhelmingly to that country.

3.301 If no rule of displacement applies, the court must give effect to the split governing law by applying each law 'on a distributive basis'. This is an expression into which all of the problems inherent in the 'mosaic view' principle are loaded. The Commission offered no guidance as to its application in practice. As the precise manner in which the principle is given

---

[900] Case C-68/93 [1995] ECR I-415, paras 28–31.

[901] **4.36–4.45** below.

[902] C W Fröhlich, *The Private International Law of Non-Contractual Obligations According to the Rome-II Regulation* (2008), 62–5 and the materials there cited. The Lithuanian delegation on the Council's Rome II Committee also raised concerns about the application of many laws on a distributive basis (Council document 9009/04 ADD 14 [25.5.2004], 3).

[903] Arts 4(3), 5(2), 10(4), 11(4), 12(2)(c).

[904] **4.84–4.85** below.

effect will depend on the nature of the connecting factor, the obligation in question, and the remedy sought, its application will be considered in further detail below in the commentaries on Arts 4 (tort/delict—general rule) and Art 6 (unfair competition/restriction of competition).[905] It is the latter rule that causes most difficulty, as the market-oriented rules in Arts 6(1) and 6(3) are inherently likely to point towards the application of the law of several countries and there is no generally applicable[906] escape clause that will allow courts to escape the uncertainty that will inevitably cause. That uncertainty may encourage Member State courts and the Court of Justice to construe and apply the connecting factors, legitimately or otherwise, in such a way as to avoid fragmentation of the law applicable under the Regulation.

Areas outside State sovereignty

Legislative history The Commission, in its preliminary draft proposal,[907] **3.302** proposed a separate rule of applicable law for torts or delicts 'occurring in areas not subject to the territorial sovereignty of a State' as follows:

Article 4—Areas not subject to territorial sovereignty

1. The law applicable to a tort or delict occurring in areas not subject to the territorial sovereignty of a State shall be the law of the country in which the means of transport or the installation connected with the tort or delict is registered or whose flag it flies or with which it has similar connections.

2. If there is no connection with a specific country or if there is a connection with several countries, the applicable law shall be that of the country with which the case is most closely connected.

In its Proposal, however, the Commission put forward a different solution **3.303** explaining:[908]

The text proposed by the Commission in the written consultation procedure in May 2002 contained a special conflict rule. One of the difficulties with this rule lay in the diversity of the situations concerned. It is by no means certain that a single rule will adequately cover the position of a collision between ships on the high seas, the explosion of an electronic device or the breakdown of negotiations in an aircraft in flight, pollution caused by a ship at sea etc.

The contributions received by the Commission have made it aware that the proposed rule made it all too easy to designate the law of a flag of convenience, which would be contrary to the more general objectives of Community policy.

---

[905] **4.69–4.74, 6.56–6.57** and **6.64** below.
[906] Art 6(3)(b) contains a limited exception in favour of the law of the forum in the case of restrictions of competition, but the claimant must elect for its application.
[907] **1.64** above.
[908] Commission Proposal, 27.

Many contributors had doubts about the value added by a rule which, where two or more laws are potentially involved, as in collision cases, merely refers to the principle of the closest connection.

Rather than introducing a special rule here, Article 18 *[of the Commission Proposal]* offers a definition of the 'territory of a State'. This solution is founded on the need to strike a reasonable balance between divergent interests by means of the different conflict rules in the proposed Regulation where one or more connecting factors are located in an area subject to no sovereignty. The general rule in Article 3 and the special conflict rules accordingly apply.

3.304 Art 18 of the Commission Proposal, in turn, provided that for the purposes of the Regulation, the following shall be treated as being the territory of a State:[909]

a) installations and other facilities for the exploration and exploitation of natural resources in, on or below the part of the seabed situated outside the State's territorial waters if the State, under international law, enjoys sovereign rights to explore and exploit natural resources there;

b) a ship on the high seas which is registered in the State or bears *lettres de mer* or a comparable document issued by it or on its behalf, or which, not being registered or bearing *lettres de mer* or a comparable document, is owned by a national of the State;

c) an aircraft in the airspace, which is registered in or on behalf of the State or entered in its register of nationality, or which, not being registered or entered in the register of nationality, is owned by a national of the State.

3.305 This provision, apparently inspired by Dutch private international law,[910] was welcomed by the EESC as 'closing certain undesirable gaps in the law and preventing fortuitous application of systems of law'[911] and was accepted, without amendment, by the European Parliament on first reading.[912] It was, however, deleted in the Commission's Amended Proposal and was not carried forward into the Council's Common Position. Its disappearance at an early stage in the Council's deliberations[913] appears to have

---

[909] See the detailed amendments proposed by the Swedish delegation in Council document 9009/04 ADD 8 [18.5.2004], 26–8 with reference to the provisions of the UN Convention on the law of the sea (opened for signature 10 December 1982; 1833 UNTS 397).

[910] Council document 8445/04 [19.4.2004], 4. See *Wet Conflictenrecht Onrechtmatige Daad* (2001) (Dutch Act regarding conflict of laws for unlawful acts), Art 1 and the explanation of that provision given by the Netherlands State Committee on Private International Law in its 1996 opinion on the draft legislation, annexed to the response of the Netherlands to the Commission's 1998 questionnaire (Council document 12544/98 [11.11.1998], 145–6).

[911] EESC Opinion, para 8.2.

[912] EP 1st Reading Position, Art 20.

[913] It is shown as deleted in the Dutch/Luxembourg Presidency draft circulated in December 2004 (Council document 16231/04 [20.12.2004]).

been on the basis that the subject matter was considered to be more related to 'public law' (a reference, presumably, to public international law) and might conflict with other (unspecified) provisions of the draft Regulation.[914] Solutions to the problems described above (**3.297**) must, therefore, be divined from other sources.

The territory of a State under the Regulation In some cases, the occurrence **3.306** of the relevant fact at sea will present little difficulty, as a sufficient connection to the territory of a State will be evident. Consistently with the case law of the ECJ with respect to the Brussels Convention, a State's territory for these purposes should, it is submitted, be taken to include not only its land boundaries but also its territorial waters and offshore installations situated in its sector of the continental shelf.[915] Other situations may require more detailed examination of the principles of public international law concerning the law of the sea, including the 1982 United National Convention on the law of the sea.[916]

Territory under the control of an unrecognized State or government In the **3.307** case of a dispute as to territorial sovereignty between a recognized and unrecognized State, it is suggested that only the former can (in accordance with established international law doctrines[917]) be treated as a 'State' under the Rome II Regulation. Nevertheless, it may be possible to argue that 'rules of law' promulgated by those[918] having effective control over a particular territory (although not recognized as having sovereignty) may be sufficiently coherent and effective within that territory to create a sufficiently identifiable, de facto 'territorial unit' for the purposes of Art 25 of the Regulation,[919] with the result that the territory in question may fall to be treated as a separate 'country' under the Regulation, allowing geographical connecting factors at least to point towards the application of

---

[914] Council document 10173/04 [14.6.2004], 14, footnote 1.

[915] Case C-37/00, *Hubert Weber v Universal Ogden Services Ltd* [2002] ECR I-2013, paras 29–36 (a case concerning the territorial scope of Art 5(1) of the Brussels Convention).

[916] Opened for signature 10 December 1982; 1833 UNTS 397. See M D Evans, 'The Law of the Sea', ch 8 in M Evans (ed), *International Law* (2nd edn, 2006). For the status of the law of the sea Convention under EC law, see Case C-308/06, *R (International Association of Independent Tanker Owners) v Secretary of State for Transport* [2008] ECR I-0000 (Judgment of 3 June 2008).

[917] Sir R Jennings and Sir A Watts, *Oppenheim's International Law* (9th edn, 1992), ch 2; C Warbrick, 'States and Recognition in International Law', ch 8 in M Evans (ed), *International Law* (2nd edn, 2006).

[918] Whether the government of an unrecognized State or an unrecognized government of a recognized State.

[919] **3.291** above.

the 'law' of that country. In this connection, Lord Wilberforce suggested that:[920]

[W]here private rights, or acts of everyday occurrence, or perfunctory acts of administration are concerned . . . the courts may, in the interests of justice and common sense, where no consideration of public policy to the contrary has to prevail, give recognition to the actual facts or realities found to exist in the territory in question.

3.308 In many parts of the world, regimes not recognized according to the principles of international law as having sovereign authority over a territory may make rules that govern the day-to-day conduct of persons resident in that territory. Those regimes, although not accorded international recognition, may provide a stable form of government and the application of those rules to relations between such persons may be said to reflect their legitimate expectations and to strike a fair balance between. The rules in question may regulate, for example, conduct on the road and deal with the legal consequences of road traffic accidents. The argument that the Rome II Regulation should recognize such 'actual facts or realities' can, therefore, be said to be consistent with the objectives of the Regulation.[921]

3.309 Against this, it may be pointed out that, like the Rome Convention, the language used in the Rome II Regulation suggests that the law to be applied must be the law of a State or one of the territorial units 'comprising' a State.[922] It must also be recalled that the relationship between the Republic of Cyprus and the so-called Turkish Republic of Northern Cyprus raises particularly sensitive issues for the European Community and its Member States. Although matters concerning the TRNC require special consideration in light of the terms on which Cyprus acceded to the European Community in 2004,[923] it may be thought unlikely that the ECJ would interpret the Regulation in such a way as to require a Member State

---

[920] *Carl Zeiss Stiftung v Rayner and Keeler* [1967] AC 853, 954 (Lord Wilberforce, UKHL) cited with approval by Lord Denning MR (at 218) in *Hesperides Hotels Ltd v Aegean Turkish Holidays* [1979] 1 QB 205 (EWCA). The Court of Appeal's decision in *Hesperides Hotels* was reversed in part by the House of Lords, but without considering this point ([1979] AC 508, 537 (Lord Wilberforce), 540 (Viscount Dilhorne), 545 (Lord Fraser) (UKHL)). See further, *Oppenheim's International Law*, n 917 above, 201–3; Dicey, Morris & Collins, paras 25-004 to 25-005; P Nygh, n 372 above, 63.

[921] In particular, Recital (16).

[922] Regulation, Arts 3 and 25; Rome Convention, Arts 2 and 19.

[923] Protocol 10 to the Act concerning the conditions of accession of Cyprus and other new Member States (OJ L236, 955 [23.9.2003]) suspends the operation of the Community *acquis* in those areas of the island over which the Republic of Cyprus does not have effective control (Art 1), without prejudice to the effect of the *acquis* in any other part of the Republic of Cyprus. The effect of the Protocol upon the Brussels I Regulation was considered by Jack J in

court (including in Cyprus) to apply, or refuse to apply, the 'laws' of the TRNC concerning non-contractual obligations. The argument for taking some account of the acts of an unrecognized regime may be at its strongest in relation to so-called 'rules of safety and conduct' to which Art 17 refers, which probably need not take the form of legal rules.[924] Art 17, it may be noted, refers not to the concept of 'country' but instead to the 'place . . . of the event giving rise to liability', which may be sufficiently flexible to permit account to be taken (for example) of highway regulations imposed by an unrecognized regime if a road traffic accident leading to proceedings before a Member State court takes place in territory under its control.

A dispute as to territorial sovereignty between two recognized States will cause greater difficulty as, at least if there is no consensus within the international community, such a dispute may be considered non-justiciable by national courts.[925] **3.310**

Events Above or Beyond State Territory, including on the High Seas The most problematic aspect of the Regulation's territorial application concerns situations in which the basic rule of applicable law yields no immediate answer as to the law applicable to a particular category of non-contractual obligation because the fact referred to as the connecting factor points to an area which is indisputably outside the territory, or extended territory, of any State. The high seas provide the most important example of an area outside State sovereignty, but the possibility cannot be excluded that polar regions and even outer space will raise similar issues in the future.[926] **3.311**

Situations of this kind must be distinguished, as least for the purposes of analysis, from those in which a difficulty in identifying the law applicable under the Regulation results from evidential uncertainty as to the country to which the connecting factor identified by the Regulation points.[927] This distinction can be illustrated by the example, given by the Commission (**3.303** above), of an aircraft in flight. If the aircraft's flight path takes it exclusively over land or over the territorial sea of one of more States, the geographical connecting factors in the Regulation's rules of applicable law can only point to the territory of a country. Evidential difficulties which may **3.312**

Orams v Apostolides [2006] EWHC 2226 (QB); [2007] 1 WLR 241 (Jack J), followed by a reference to the Court of Justice in Case C-420/07, *Apostolides* (OJ C297, 20–1 [8.12.2007]).

[924] **15.32** below.

[925] *Buttes Gas & Oil Co v Hammer (No 3)* [1982] AC 888 (UKHL). Compare *Kuwait Airways Corp v Iraqi Airways Co (Nos 4 and 5)* [2002] 2 AC 883 (EWCA and UKHL).

[926] *Oppenheim's International Law*, n 917 above, paras 256–7 and ch 7.

[927] Cf Giuliano, Lagarde & van Ysselt Report, 55, in which the two types of situation are treated together.

arise in some cases in determining over which country an event on board or an airborne collision occurred cannot justify treating such obligations or cases as outside the Regulation's scope.[928]

3.313 If, on the other hand, the aircraft's flight path or a ship's course takes it over the high seas as well as the territory of one or more States, the evidential difficulty in determining where the fact to which the Regulation refers occurred may still need to be tackled. A preliminary question arises, however, as to whether the Regulation can apply at all to non-contractual obligations arising from events occurring, or having consequences, on or over the high seas or another area outside State sovereignty.[929] The contention that the Regulation does not apply in these cases draws succour from the way in which the rules of applicable law are framed so as to require a factual connection to a 'country'.[930] The authors of the report on the 1972 draft convention concluded that, in these circumstances, the proposed rule for non-contractual obligations arising out of an event entailing damage (*fait dommageable*), referring principally to the country in which that event took place, could only operate if the place where the event occurred lay within the territorial jurisdiction of a State.[931] In the case of the Regulation, however, there are strong countervailing arguments. In particular, the objectives of the Regulation, of enhancing the foreseeability of court decisions and ensuring a reasonable balance between the parties, are equally important in cases of this type, which fall within the domain of private international law. The possible contention that, at least in ship collision cases, there is no 'conflict of laws' within Art 1 because maritime law applies universally, does not withstand close scrutiny[932] and, in any event, provides only a

---

[928] Cf Dicey, Morris & Collins, 1st supplement, paras S35-198 (maritime torts) and S35-199 (aerial torts), where the point is left open.

[929] M George, 'Choice of Law in Maritime Torts' (2007) 3 J Pr Int L 137, 170–1, rejecting the argument that the Regulation does not apply but raising a doubt as to whether the Regulation's rules are suited to maritime torts. Cf Dicey, Morris & Collins, 1st supplement, paras S35-198 and S35-199, where the point as to the application of the Regulation to maritime and aerial torts is left open.

[930] **3.296** above.

[931] Giuliano, Lagarde & van Ysselt Report, 55. After further discussion of possible solutions to this problem, the matter was left open by the working group (ibid, 56).

[932] *Owners of the Motor Vessel Toju Maru v NS Bureau Wijsmuller, The Tojo Maru* [1972] 1 AC 242, 290–1 (Lord Diplock) ('Outside the special field of "prize" in times of hostilities there is no "maritime law of the world," as distinct from the internal municipal laws of its constituent sovereign states, that is capable of giving rise to rights or liabilities enforceable in English courts. . . . [T]he fact that the consequences of applying to the same facts the internal municipal laws of different sovereign states would be to give rise to similar legal rights and liabilities should not mislead us into supposing that those rights or liabilities are derived from a

partial explanation for the non-application of the Regulation.[933] Significantly, given that the Commission's explanation of Art 18 of its Proposal made clear that it considered that the Regulation would apply to situations of this kind,[934] the reasons given by the Council Presidency for deletion of that provision do not suggest a fundamental disagreement with that assumption. That deletion, it may be noted, was not accompanied by the exclusion of situations formerly covered by Art 18 within Art 1(2) of the Regulation.[935] On balance, therefore, it seems probable that the Regulation will be held to apply to non-contractual obligations arising from events that occur, or have consequences, on or over an area outside State sovereignty, with the connecting factors being moulded to identify a link with a particular country.

These conclusions leave questions as to how the Regulation's rules of **3.314** applicable law should be applied if (a) there is uncertainty as to the location of the fact that provides the connecting factor to the applicable law, or (b) that fact appears to have occurred on or outside the territory, or extended territory, of a State. These questions will be returned to in the next chapter in considering the general rule in cases of tort/delict, on the assumption that the Regulation applies in both cases.[936]

F. TEMPORAL SCOPE

Article 31

Application in time

This Regulation shall apply to events giving rise to damage which occurs after its entry into force.

Article 32

Date of application

This Regulation shall apply from 11 January 2009, except for Article 29, which shall apply from 11 July 2008.

In considering the temporal effect of the Regulation under Arts 31 and 32, **3.315** it is important to appreciate that EC law distinguishes between the date of

---

"maritime law of the world" and not from the internal municipal law of a particular sovereign state.')

[933] It does not address situations of events occurring on a single vessel. For a survey of English law, see M George, n 929 above, 138–59.

[934] **3.303** above.

[935] **3.305** above.

[936] **4.47–4.57** below.

entry into force, the date from which a measure adopted by the Community is to have effect, and the date of application.[937] Thus, the 'entry into force' and 'application' of a measure do not necessarily coincide: the date of application may be set after or, where retroactive application is justified, before entry into force.[938] The technique of deferred application is used, for example, in the case of Regulations setting up common market organizations. In such cases, the purpose of the separation of entry into force and application of the Regulation may be to enable the new bodies to be set up immediately and to enable the Commission to adopt implementing measures on which those new bodies have to be consulted.[939]

3.316 Arts 31 and 32, read together, emphasize that the rules of applicable law contained in the Regulation will apply from 11 January 2009, to events giving rise to damage[940] that occur after its 'entry into force'. The earlier application of Art 29, requiring the Member States to provide by 11 July 2008 a list of the Conventions having priority over the Regulation's rules, does not affect this general proposition. Neither Art 31 nor Art 32, however, stipulates the date on which the Regulation is to enter into force. Art 31 does not refer to any date, and Art 32 refers in the English, French, German, and other versions not to the 'entry into force' but to 'application' of the Regulation.[941] The Dutch text, it may be noted, refers in the heading of Art 32 to '*inwerktreding*' (meaning 'entry into force'), but the following text ('*Deze verodening is van toepassing met ingang van 11 januari 2009*'; 'This Regulation will apply with effect from 11 January 2009') seems more in line with the other language versions. The Spanish and Romanian texts contain a similar mismatch between the terminology used in the heading of Art 32 ('*entrada en vigor*'; '*data intrării în vigoare*') and the content of the Article ('*El present Reglamento se aplicará* . . .'; '*Prezentul regulament se aplică începând* . . .'). This leaves an unsatisfactory muddle.

---

[937] Joint Practical Guide of the European Parliament, the Council and the Commission for persons involved in the drafting of legislation within the Community institutions (2003), available at <http://eur-lex.europa.eu/en/techleg/pdf/en.pdf>, para 20.1.

[938] Ibid, para 20.2.2.

[939] Ibid, para 20.10.

[940] 'Damage' being here used in the broad sense defined by Art 2 as including reference to the consequences of unjust enrichment, *negotiorum gestio*, and *culpa in contrahendo* (**3.44–3.46** above).

[941] The heading of Art 32 in other language versions is, e.g., (French) '*date d'application*', (German) '*Zeitpunkt des Beginns der Anwendung*', (Italian) '*data di applicazione*', (Portuguese) '*date de aplicação*'. In each case, Art 32 uses a different word to describe the temporal effect of the Regulation from that used in Art 31. For example, the French language version uses the words '*entrée en viguer*' in Art 31 but states in Art 32 that '*le présent règlement est applicable à partir du 11 janvier 2009*'.

According to Art 254(1) of the EC Treaty, Regulations adopted in accord- **3.317** ance with the cooperation procedure in Art 251 (including the Rome II Regulation) 'shall enter into force on the date specified in them or, in the absence thereof, on the twentieth day following that of their publication'. If it is correct that neither Art 31 nor Art 32 of the Regulation specify the date of entry into force of the Regulation, the Regulation must be considered to have entered into force on 20 August 2007, 20 days after its publication in the Official Journal. A period of almost 17 months will have elapsed, therefore, between that date and the designated date of application of the Regulation. This results not, as might be suggested, in retrospective effect of the Regulation but in a modified and complex form of prospective effect.

It may be asked whether this separation of the date of entry into force and **3.318** the date of application of the Rome II Regulation can possibly have been intended, given the uncertainty that it generates. The legislative history of Arts 31 and 32 supports the view that the Council, at least, recognized the distinction between 'entry into force' and 'application' in choosing to omit a specific entry into force date. Thus, the Commission Proposal contained a single Article (Art 27) deferring the entry into force of the Regulation, and applying its provisions to non-contractual obligations arising out of acts occurring after its entry into force. Subsequently,[942] the provision developed during the Council's deliberations in three stages. First, the elements dealing with 'Application in time' and 'Entry into force' were separated into two Articles.[943] Secondly, a new sub-rule was added providing for an application date 6 months after the stated entry into force date.[944] Thirdly, in the 'compromise package' presented by the Austrian Presidency to the Member States in April 2006, the sub-rule which provided expressly for an entry into force date was removed.[945] The minutes of the meeting of the Council's Rome II Committee held on 27–28 March 2006 show that the separation between the date of application and entry into force was

---

[942] The author is grateful to Giorgio Buono of the University of Rome and conflictoflaws. net for the following analysis of the Council's position (for further discussion, see <http://www.conflictoflaws.net/2007/legislation/rome-ii-and-small-claims-regulations-published-in-the-official-journal/>).

[943] Council document 16027/05 [22.12.2005], Arts 27 and 27A. At this stage, the Council applied the Regulation to damage or harm caused after the Regulation's entry into force. At the following stages, the link to the event giving rise to damage was restored.

[944] Council document 7432/06 [16.3.2006], Art 27A(2).

[945] Council document 7929/06 [10.4.2006], Art 27A.

appreciated by Member States at the time that this decision was taken, noting that:[946]

> Several delegations considered that the distinction between the date of entry into force and the date of application was confusing. The Presidency pointed out that the date of entry into force brought along obligations for Member States, which would have to be fulfilled prior to application (eg notification of Conventions).

It is unclear, however, whether the consequences of this decision in terms of the impact of Art 254(1) of the EC Treaty upon the relationship between what became Arts 31 and 32 were fully appreciated.

3.319 Whether deliberate or not, the end product must be regarded as extremely unsatisfactory for it creates the possibility that for certain non-contractual obligations (i.e. those for which the event giving rise to damage occurred on or after 20 August 2007 but before 11 January 2009), different rules of applicable law will operate depending on the date on which the Regulation is 'applied', whatever this may involve.[947] Some commentators have taken the view that the only escape from this is to read the Regulation in such a way as to conclude that it applies only to events occurring after 11 January 2009, whether by treating Art 31 as referring to the date of application or by treating Art 32 as also prescribing the date of entry into force.[948] Such an approach, although practical, is almost impossible to reconcile with the text of the Regulation and its legislative history, as described above. It cannot, with confidence, be predicted that the ECJ and Member State courts will be able to escape the conclusion that the Regulation has a partial, suspensory effect for events occurring between 20 August 2007 and 11 January 2009.

3.320 Against that background, it will be important to identify with precision the point in time at which the Regulation falls to be 'applied' for the purposes of Arts 31 and 32. Four candidates emerge, as follows:

1. The Regulation 'applies' only at the point at which the Member State court or tribunal finally determines the law applicable to a non-contractual obligation.

2. The Regulation 'applies' at the point at which proceedings based on a non-contractual obligation are commenced before a Member State court.

---

[946] Council document 7709/06 [3.5.2006], 6.

[947] **3.320–3.322** below.

[948] G Légier, *'Le réglement "Rome II" sur la loi applicable aux obligations non contractuelles'*, JCP/La Semaine Juridique—Edition Générale, 21 November 2007, I-207, para 8; A Heldrich, *Palandt Bürgerliches Gesetzbuch*, 67. Auflage, Vorb v EGBGB 38, 2566. In particular, it is understood that German commentators on the Regulation strongly favour this interpretation of Arts 31 and 32.

3. The Regulation 'applies' at the point at which there is not only 'an event giving rise to damage' but also 'damage', as defined in Art 2.

4. The Regulation 'applies' at the point at which the non-contractual obligation 'arises', with that question being determined either under the law which would apply to it under the Regulation or by reference to an autonomous concept developed for the purposes of the Regulation.

Of these possible solutions, the first appears most consistent with the language and approach of the Rome II Regulation, requiring Member State courts and tribunals to apply the law of a particular country to particular non-contractual obligations.[949] The second option, favoured by the editors of Dicey, Morris & Collins,[950] is less satisfactory, as it is difficult to see in what sense the Regulation is applied at the point of issue of proceedings. Had this been the legislator's intention, it would have been relatively straightforward to provide such a rule.[951] The third option is also difficult to justify, given that the concept of 'damage' appears in fewer than half of the Regulation's rules of applicable law. Finally, the fourth option, while arguably more consistent with the language of the Regulation than the second and third opinions,[952] seems too uncertain as it would require either that the rules of applicable law contained in the Regulation be applied on a provisional basis to determine its scope or that the ECJ and Member State courts develop, without guidance in the Regulation, autonomous rules fixing the point in time at which an obligation 'arises' for these purposes. **3.321**

Accordingly, the first solution seems preferable. On this view, the Regulation will apply to any situation in which a Member State finally determines on or after 11 January 2009 (whether following a trial or as a preliminary issue) the law applicable to a non-contractual obligation, provided that the event giving rise to damage occurred on or after 20 August 2007. Under this regime, there may well be cases in which the parties have sought, before the cut-off date, to expedite or delay the court's determination as to the law applicable. The opportunities for securing a tactical advantage would appear greater if the date of proceedings is treated as the relevant date for application of the Regulation, as it would increase the parties' ability to control the applicable law by submitting a claim (including, in the case of a person claimed to be liable, for negative declaratory relief) just before or just after the cut-off date. After 11 January 2009, there may be very little that courts can do in the exercise of their case **3.322**

---

[949] **3.38** and **3.76** above.
[950] Dicey, Morris & Collins, 1st supplement, para S35-168.
[951] Cf Brussels I Regulation, Art 66(1).
[952] The term 'arising' appears in Arts. 4, 5, 6(1), 6(3), 7, 8, 10, 11, 12, and 13, but not Art 9.

management powers to correct any perceived 'abuse', other than perhaps to reflect its disapproval in any order for costs following determination of the law applicable.

3.323 Happily, it seems that lessons have been learnt. In the case of the Rome I Regulation, the Council had originally suggested following the wording of the Rome II Regulation concerning its temporal application, with the result that the Rome I Regulation would have applied to contracts entered into after its entry into force date which (unlike the date of application) was not separately specified.[953] In the final version of the Rome I Regulation, however, Art 28 provides that the Regulation will apply to contracts entered into after 17 December 2009,[954] which is also the date of its application.[955]

3.324 Art 14 (freedom of choice) raises a specific issue concerning the effect under the Regulation of choice of law agreements concluded before 11 January 2009. That issue will be considered in the commentary below on Art 14.[956]

G. OVERVIEW AND THE WAY FORWARD

3.325 This chapter may be seen as the engine room of this book. Although only eight Articles of the Regulation (Arts 1–3, 23–25, and 31–32) have been considered in detail so far, the object of the foregoing sections has been to lay the foundations for the following commentary on the rules of applicable law contained in Arts 4–14, the common rules in Arts 15–22, and the other rules concerning the relationship between the Regulation, on the one hand, and the law of the forum, EC law, and international concentions, on the other. The topic of interpretation (**Section A**) is (of course) relevant to every provision of the Regulation, and the key concepts and terms (**Section B**) and the approach to characterization (**Section C**) will be important elements in the reasoning underlying the application of the Regulation in many cases.

3.326 At the outset, the first question that a Member State court must address is whether the claim which is raised for determination before it falls within the scope of the Rome II Regulation (**Section C**). Potentially, the court

---

[953] Council document 11150/07 [25.11.2007], Arts 25 and 26.

[954] Rome I Regulation, Art 28.

[955] Ibid, Art 29, which also expressly stipulates that the Regulation shall enter into force on the twentieth day following its publication in the Official Journal.

[956] **13.42** below.

must consider separately the questions of material, territorial, and temporal scope (**Sections D** to **F**), although the second of these will rarely be problematic and the last will become less and less relevant as time passes. So far as the material scope of the Regulation is concerned, the court must consider whether the subject matter of the claim is an obligation,[957] which is not 'contractual'[958] and is not specifically excluded from scope,[959] as well as whether it involves a civil or commercial matter.[960]

Chapters 4 to 12 below (which share the numbers of the Articles of the **3.327** Rome II Regulation to which they relate) consider the primary rules of applicable law for non-contractual obligations. **Chapter 13** considers the freedom of the parties to choose the applicable law (Art 15). **Chapter 14** considers the scope of the law applicable under the Regulation, the principal element in what has been described in this chapter as its 'vertical material scope'.[961] **Chapter 15** considers the residual role of the law and public policy of the forum, and of rules of safety and conduct. Finally, **Chapter 16** considers the relationship between the Regulation, EC law, and international instruments.

---

[957] **3.88–3.103** above.
[958] **3.104–3.145** above.
[959] **3.146–3.228** above.
[960] **3.263–3.286** above.
[961] **3.59** above.

Part II

Non-Contractual Obligations
Arising Out of Tort/Delict

4

Tort/Delict—General Rules

Article 4

General rule

1. Unless otherwise provided for in this Regulation, the law applicable to a non-contractual obligation arising out of a tort/delict shall be the law of the country in which the damage occurs irrespective of the country in which the event giving rise to the damage occurred and irrespective of the country or countries in which the indirect consequences of that event occur.

2. However, where the person claimed to be liable and the person sustaining damage both have their habitual residence in the same country at the time when the damage occurs, the law of that country shall apply.

3. Where it is clear from all the circumstances of the case that the tort/delict is manifestly more closely connected with a country other than that indicated in paragraphs 1 or 2, the law of that other country shall apply. A manifestly closer

connection with another country might be based in particular on a pre-existing relationship between the parties, such as a contract, that is closely connected with the tort/delict in question.

A. INTRODUCTION[1]

4.01 Subject to the rules of displacement contained in Arts 4(2) and (3), Art 4(1) provides that the law generally applicable to non-contractual obligations arising out of a tort/delict is the law of the country in which the damage occurs (*lex loci damni*).[2] Despite minor changes in wording, this outcome largely reflects the Commission Proposal.[3] The Commission's approach was challenged by the European Parliament during the passage of the Regulation,[4] but was supported by the Member State delegations in the Council.

4.02 In recommending this solution, the Commission rejected four alternatives to the country of the damage as the primary connecting factor. First, to refer to the country of the 'harmful event' (French '*fait dommageable*'), reflecting the language of Art 5(3) of the Brussels I Regulation and the Brussels Convention before it. Although that solution had appealed to the authors of the 1972 draft convention,[5] the ECJ had subsequently determined that the expression 'place where the harmful event occurred' in Art 5(3) of the Brussels Convention (matters relating to tort, delict, or quasi-delict) referred not only to the place where the event giving rise to damage occurred but also to the place where damage occurred, giving the claimant the right to choose between the courts of those two places.[6] In the Commission's view, that solution was acceptable within the Brussels I Regime dealing with the jurisdiction of Member State courts, 'but it does not enable the parties to foresee the law that will be applicable to their

---

[1] For earlier comparative surveys of the law applicable to torts, see A Ehrenzweig and S Strömholm, 'Torts Introduction', A Ehrenzweig, 'Enterprise Liability' and S Strömholm, 'Intentional Torts', chs 31–33 in K Lipstein (ed), *International Encyclopaedia of Comparative Law*, vol III (private international law).

[2] For a critical comment on Art 4, see H Koziol and T Thiede, '*Kritische Bemerkungen zum derzeitigen Stand des Entwurfs einer Rom II-Verordnung*' (2007) 106 *Zeitschrift für Vergleichende Rechtswissenschaft* 235 (with English summary at <http://www.conflictoflaws.net/2007/articles/austrian-article-on-rome-ii/>).

[3] Commission Proposal, Art 3.

[4] **1.74** and **1.90** above.

[5] **1.49** above.

[6] Case 21/76 *Handelskwekerij G J Bier BV v Mines de Potasse d'Alsace* [1976] ECR 1735. For discussion of this and later decisions on Art 5(3), see **4.26–4.27** below.

situation with certainty'.[7] Had this approach been adopted for tort/delict in the Regulation, it would have introduced a so-called 'principle of ubiquity' (*Günstigkeitsprinzip*) in a form adopted until 1999 in Germany, allowing the injured person to choose the law most favourable to him.[8] An express provision of that kind was the second alternative option rejected by the Commission. In its view, 'this solution would go beyond the victim's legitimate expectations and would introduce uncertainty in the law, contrary to the general objective of the proposed Regulation'.[9] The third alternative would have been to apply the law of the country of the act or other event giving rise to damage (*lex loci actus*). Finally, the Commission rejected the possibility of applying the law of the place where the event giving rise to damage occurred.[10]

The Commission argued that its preference for the law of the country of **4.03** the damage reflected recent developments in Member States' conflict rules, and suggested that the solution had been applied in the Netherlands, the United Kingdom, and France, as well as Switzerland.[11] As appears from the comparative survey in **Chapter 1**, however, that statement manifestly over-simplified the rules of applicable law in force in these countries, which essentially blend the *lex loci actus* and the *lex loci damni* albeit (a) in different ways, (b) using different terminology, and (c) subject to different exceptions.[12]

The Commission also argued that its favoured solution 'establishes an **4.04** objective link between the damage and the applicable law',[13] although each of the solutions that it rejected would also have achieved this. Further, in the Commission's view, the preference for the law of the country in which the damage occurred 'reflects the modern concept of the law of civil liability which is no longer, as it was in the first half of the last century, oriented towards punishing for fault-based conduct: nowadays it is the

---

[7] Commission Proposal, 11.

[8] **1.21** above. In the reform of the EGBGB in 1999, the *Günstigkeitsprinzip* was replaced by a rule designating the law of the place of conduct, but giving the injured person a right of election (*Bestimmungsrecht*) in favour of the law of the place of harm. A similar right of election, although working in the opposite direction (place of damage > place of harmful event) is now to be found in Art 7 of the Regulation for cases of environmental damage (**Ch 7** below). That solution reflects the former generally applicable law rule for torts under Italian law (**1.25** above).

[9] Commission Proposal, 10–11. Cf S C Symeonides, 'Rome II and Tort Conflicts: A Missed Opportunity' (2008) 56 AJCL 173, 191–2.

[10] **4.33–4.35** below.

[11] Commission Proposal, 11.

[12] **1.08–1.43** above.

[13] Commission Proposal, 12.

compensation function that dominates as can be seen from the proliferation of no-fault strict liability schemes'.[14]

4.05 In the following commentary, the term 'victim' is used as a convenient shorthand for the person sustaining the damage and the term 'tortfeasor' is used as a convenient shorthand for the person responsible for the event giving rise to damage. The terms 'claimant' and 'defendant' are generally used to describe, respectively, the likely procedural positions of the victim and tortfeasor (or the persons representing them or liable for their conduct, as the case may be). It is, of course, possible that those positions may be reversed, for example if the victim counterclaims against the tortfeasor[15] or if the tortfeasor seeks a declaration that he is not liable to the victim.[16]

B. NON-CONTRACTUAL OBLIGATIONS ARISING OUT OF A TORT/DELICT

THE CATEGORY OF 'TORT/DELICT' AND THE RELATIONSHIP OF ARTICLE 4 WITH OTHER RULES

4.06 The concept of a 'non-contractual obligation arising out of a tort/delict' has already been considered at length in **Chapter 3**, in assessing the subject matter scope of the Regulation.[17] In summary:

1. The concept of a 'tort/delict', like that of 'non-contractual obligation',[18] is an autonomous one under EC law, and its content does not fall to be determined by reference to the concepts of 'tort' or 'delict', or corresponding terminology, deployed within particular legal systems, including the legal system of the forum Member State and that of the putative applicable law.[19]

2. The concept of 'non-contractual obligation' potentially includes all civil obligations that are not 'contractual obligations'.[20] For these purposes, a 'contractual obligation' is one which has as its foundation a 'contract',

---

[14] Ibid. For the possible influence of the decision to favour the *lex loci damni* on the future development of Member State systems of non-contractual liability, see **1.05** above.

[15] Brussels I Regulation, Art 6(3).

[16] For the view that a claim for a declaration that there was not a tort falls within Art 5(3) of the Brussels I Regulation, see *Equitas Ltd v Wave City Shipping Ltd* [2005] EWHC 923 (Comm).

[17] **3.243–3.246**.

[18] Recital (11).

[19] **3.243,** point 1 above.

[20] **3.87** above.

consisting of an intentional and voluntary act by one person towards another and (probably) some reciprocal voluntary act by that other person with those acts in combination giving rise to a binding obligation.[21]

3. The Regulation also applies to non-contractual obligations arising from strict liability.[22] The concept of a 'tort/delict' cannot, therefore, be understood as requiring fault on the part of the tortfeasor.[23]

4. The source of the rule generating the obligation within the legal system is not a relevant factor in its characterization.[24] Thus, for example, statutory rules and rules developed by the Courts of Equity in England (e.g. breach of trust, breach of fiduciary duty) may create non-contractual obligations falling within the Regulation's scope.

5. Despite the Commission's suggestion that the Rome II Regulation should apply to all non-contractual obligations, there is a residual group of non-contractual obligations for which the Regulation does not provide any rule of applicable law. Such obligations (for example, monetary obligations attaching to immoveable property) fall outside the scope of the Regulation.[25]

6. Within the category of non-contractual obligations, the concept of 'tort/delict' should be given a broad construction so as to accommodate (so far as possible) non-contractual obligations that might otherwise fall outside the Regulation.[26]

7. The structure and language of the Regulation and common usage among the Member States' legal systems, as well as the approach taken by the Court of Justice to the concept of 'tort, delict or quasi-delict' in Art 5(3) of the Brussels Convention, support the definition of a non-contractual obligation arising from tort/delict as:[27]

A non-contractual obligation establishing the defendant's responsibility to the claimant for, or preventing the occurrence of, an act, omission or event which (1) has adverse consequences for the claimant or one or more persons represented in the proceedings by the claimant and (2) is an act or omission of the defendant or a person for whose conduct the defendant is liable, or is otherwise an act, omission or other event attributable to the defendant through a relationship with the person or thing giving rise to those consequences.

---

[21] **3.121** above.
[22] Recital (11).
[23] **3.243**, point 8 above.
[24] **3.63** and **3.243**, point 2 above.
[25] **3.246** above.
[26] **3.262** above.
[27] **3.244** above.

8. It is unclear whether it is an additional requirement that the relevant act, omission, or other event must, in some sense, be unlawful, so as to exclude rules imposing responsibility for lawful acts.[28]

4.07 As its opening words make clear, Art 4 also has a negative aspect to its scope, in that it does not apply to non-contractual obligations for which separate provision has been made elsewhere in the Rome II Regulation. Accordingly, Art 4 does not apply to:

- non-contractual obligations arising out of damage caused by a product (Art 5);[29]
- non-contractual obligations arising out of environmental damage or damage sustained by persons or property as a result of such damage (Art 7);[30]
- non-contractual obligations arising out of an infringement of an intellectual property right (Art 8);[31]
- non-contractual obligations in respect of the liability of workers, employers, or organizations representing their professional interests for damages caused by an industrial action (Art 9).[32]

4.08 The relationship between Art 4, on the one hand, and Arts 6 and 10 to 12, on the other, is less straightforward. In the case of Art 6, Recital (21) states that it is a clarification of the general rule in Art 4(1) rather than an exception to it. The intended meaning and effect of this statement are unclear.[33] Further, under Art 6(2), Art 4 applies without modification in cases which affect exclusively the interests of a specific competitor. In the case of Arts 10 to 12, the headings of Chapters II (containing Art 4) and III (containing Arts 10 to 12) in the Regulation, as well as Recital (29), confirm that tort/delict, on the one hand, and unjust enrichment, *negotiorum gestio*, and *culpa in contrahendo*, on the other, are mutually exclusive categories. Nevertheless, it may be argued that the rules contained in Chapter III must, to some degree, be given priority over, or at least equal status with, those in Chapter II in determining the non-contractual obligations to which they apply. The opposite view, giving the rules in Chapter II priority over those Chapter III and leaving Arts 10–12 to pick from the residue of non-contractual obligations not arising out of a tort/delict would be liable to deprive Art 12 (*culpa in contrahendo*), at least, of much

---

[28] **3.245** above.
[29] **Ch 5** below.
[30] **Ch 7** below.
[31] **Ch 8** below.
[32] **Ch 9** below.
[33] **6.11–6.13** below

of its content.[34] It would also remove from Art 11 (*negotiorum gestio*) claims by the principal or intervener against the other to recover compensation for harm resulting from the intervention, thereby splitting the claims arising from relations between principal and intervener into two.[35] The relationship between Art 4 (together with the special rules for tort/delict in Chapter II) and the special rules for *negotiorum gestio* and *culpa in contrahendo* will be returned to in the commentaries on Arts 11 and 12.[36] The relationship between Chapter II and Art 10 (unjust enrichment) will be addressed in the following section, in considering the treatment of claims for gain-based remedies based on tort/delict.

Non-Compensatory Remedies for Tort/Delict

Non-Compensatory Remedies Generally

The category of 'non-contractual obligations arising out of a tort/delict' **4.09** under the Rome II Regulation is not limited to actions to obtain damages compensating the claimant for the adverse consequences of the event giving rise to damage. It extends, for example, to claims for injunctive relief to prevent future breaches of non-contractual obligations.[37] Art 15(d) refers to the law applicable under the Regulation 'the measures which a court may take to prevent or terminate injury or damage'.[38]

Further, Recital (32), concerning the overriding effect of public policy and man- **4.10** datory provisions, specifically contemplates that law designated by the Regulation may provide for non-compensatory exemplary or punitive damages.[39]

Gain-Based Remedies

In many countries, the law provides remedies of various descriptions **4.11** (e.g. disgorgement, restitutionary damages, account of profits, remedial constructive trust) that have the object or the appearance at least of depriving the defendant of the profit of his wrongful conduct towards the claimant. In some cases, an award of this kind may sometimes justifiably be

---

[34] Cf Case C-334/00, *Fonderie Officine Meccaniche Tacconi SpA v Heinrich Wagner Sinto Maschinenfabrik GmbH* [2002] ECR I-7357, a case concerning Art 5(3) of the 1968 Brussels Convention discussed at **3.243,** point 7 above.

[35] **11.08** below.

[36] **11.08–11.12** and **12.06–12.08** below.

[37] Art 2(2).

[38] **14.33–14.36** below. Also Art 15(c) referring to 'the existence, the nature and the assessment of . . . the remedy claimed' (**14.20–14.25** below).

[39] **14.21–14.23** below.

described as compensating the claimant;[40] sometimes not.[41] Commentators on English law disagree as to whether cases falling within the description[42] of 'restitution for wrongdoing' should be seen as part of the law of obligations, or the law of unjust enrichment, or both. The late Professor Birks, the leading English scholar in this area, concluded that:[43]

> Unjust enrichment . . . requires a connection between claimant and enrichment which is independent of wrongdoing and a reason for restitution which is likewise not a wrong. . . . In unjust enrichment 'unjust' always denotes a reason for restitution which is not a manifestation of consent and not a wrong.

4.12 For Professor Burrows, on the other hand, 'the law of restitution may be regarded as having a central divide between unjust enrichment by subtraction . . . and unjust enrichment by wrongdoing. This division is marked by the two meanings of "at the expense of the claimant"; "by subtraction from" and "by a wrong to"'.[44] Professor Burrows acknowledges, however, that '[t]he divide is one between where unjust enrichment is the cause of action or event to which restitution responds and where a wrong is the cause of action or event to which restitution responds'.[45] The difference between these two schools of thought, therefore, may be more one of terminology than substance. Each accepts that it is the wrong that triggers the law's response in these cases.

4.13 Whether, as a matter of domestic law, a claim of this type can be fitted within the law of unjust(ified) enrichment and whatever label is attached to the remedy sought, such claims should be characterized as falling within Chapter II of the Regulation (tort/delict), not Art 10 (unjust enrichment), whenever the remedy sought responds to a tort/delict in the sense described above, i.e. an act or omission of or attributable to the defendant or other event for the consequences of which the defendant[46] is responsible to the claimant.[47] In such a case, even if it can also be said that there is 'unjust enrichment' within the autonomous meaning given to that term in the Regulation,[48] the defendant's non-contractual obligation should be

---

[40] Lord Scott of Foscote, 'Damages' [2007] LMCLQ 465.

[41] Most obviously, an award stripping the defendant of the entire profit of his wrongful conduct in circumstances in which the claimant would have been unable to earn those profits.

[42] Adopted here for convenience only.

[43] P Birks, *Unjust Enrichment* (2nd edn, 2005), 13. Also C Mitchell, 'Unjust Enrichment' in A Burrows (ed), *English Private Law* (2nd edn, 2007), paras 18.04–18.07.

[44] A Burrows, *The Law of Restitution* (2nd edn, 2002), 5. See further **10.11–10.12** below.

[45] Ibid.

[46] Or a person for whose acts the defendant is liable.

[47] Or a person represented by the claimant.

[48] **10.10–10.21** below.

considered to be founded not on that unjust enrichment but on the act, omission, or other event that constitutes the 'tort/delict' within Art 4 or one of the special rules in the following provisions of the Regulation.[49] To quote Professor Birks:[50]

Where a claimant identifies himself as the victim of a wrong he is relying on the wrong and, albeit in the language of unjust enrichment, asking the court whether that wrong is one which yields a right to a gain-based award. The law of unjust enrichment cannot answer that question. It belongs to the law of wrongs.

This view accommodates not only what an English lawyer might describe **4.14** as 'restitution for wrongdoing'[51] but also, for example, claims under the German law concept of the *Eingriffskondiktion* (literally 'interference/ encroachment condition') based on an interference with the claimant's right[52] even though they fall under the heading of 'unjustified enrichment' in the German Civil Code.[53] It accords with Art 15(c) of the Regulation referring to the law applicable under the Regulation 'the nature and assessment of the damage or the remedy claimed'.[54] Further, insofar as remedies that strip the defendant of some or all of the profit of his wrongful conduct serve a prophylactic purpose in disincentivizing that conduct, they can also be seen as measures 'to prevent or terminate injury or damage' (Art 15(d)), closely related to other measures of this kind, such as injunctions.[55] Finally, a test focusing on the basis for granting the remedy, rather than on the nature of the remedy granted, disposes of the need for further analysis as to whether, in substance, the remedy is 'compensatory' or 'restitutionary' in nature, and avoids making what may be seen as arbitrary distinctions, for example, between restitutionary damages and punitive damages against those who deliberately commit wrongs for profit.

Two aspects of the wording of Art 10(1) may be thought to provide **4.15** reasons to doubt the correctness of the above conclusion. First, this sub-rule refers specifically to 'payments of amounts wrongfully received', which at first sight might be thought to cover restitutionary claims based on wrongdoing. Secondly, the sub-rule also contemplates the possibility of

---

[49] Dicey, Morris & Collins, 1st supplement, para 34-032; A Rushworth and A Scott, 'Rome II: Choice of law for non-contractual obligations' [2008] LMCLQ 274, 286; A Chong, 'Choice of Law for Unjust Enrichment/Restitution and the Rome II Regulation' (2008) 57 ICLQ 1, 890–892.

[50] P Birks, n 43 above, 74.

[51] **4.11–4.12** above.

[52] B Markesinis, W Lorenz, and G Dannemann, *German Law of Obligations* (3rd edn, 1997), 740–9.

[53] *Bürgerliches Gesetzbuch* (BGB), §812.

[54] **14.20–14.25** below.

[55] **4.09** above.

a close connection between a non-contractual obligation arising out of unjust enrichment and a relationship existing between the parties 'such as one arising out of . . . a tort/delict'. The existence of that connection results in the application to the unjust enrichment claim of the law governing the tort/delict, which might be thought to make this question of characterization a largely theoretical one. As to the first aspect, this appears to be no more than an unfortunate choice of words in the English text of the Regulation, for which it appears the UK delegation on the Council's Rome II Committee must take some responsibility.[56] The French language version (referring to *'paiement indu'*) and the German (referring to *'Zahlungen auf eine nicht bestehende Schuld'*) indicate that the legislator's intention was to refer to claims to recover payments of a non-existing debt (*condictio indebiti*). This would appear to have been in order to remove doubts raised by Member State delegations as to whether these types of claim, dealt separately from unjust(ified) enrichment within some legal systems, were covered by the rule.[57] The second aspect is more problematic, as it is not clear what the addition of this wording, which first appeared in the draft produced by the outgoing Dutch and incoming Luxembourg Presidencies in December 2004,[58] was intended to achieve. It may be that the draftsman had in mind situations in which the prior commission of a tort/delict is an element in an unjust enrichment claim brought by the wrongdoer against the victim to prevent the latter from being over-compensated.[59] Whether that speculation is correct, the reference to a 'relationship existing' appears to require a liability in tort/delict of one of the parties to the other that is complete at the time of the unjust enrichment that is connected to it.[60] On this view, it would not suffice that there is factual connection between the circumstances giving rise to claims in tort/delict and unjust enrichment. The required element of separation between the tort/delict and the unjust enrichment cannot, in any event, be said to exist in the case of a claim for profit-based damages, which

---

[56] Council document 7551/06 [22.5.2006], 2 (minutes of a meeting of the Council's Rome II Committee held on 1–2 March 2006). The final wording first appears in a draft prepared by the Austrian Presidency shortly after that meeting (Council document 7432/06 [16.3.2006], Art 9A(1)). Earlier English language drafts of the Council text refer, more accurately if inelegantly, to 'undue payment' (see e.g. Council document 16231/04 [20.12.2004], Art 9A).

[57] See the comments of the Dutch, Italian, and Portuguese delegations in Council documents 9009/14 ADD 16 [28.5.2004], 4; ibid, ADD 17 [2.6.2004], 5; SN 2852/04 ADD 2 [6.9.2004], 4.

[58] Council document 16231/04 [20.12.2004], Art 9A.

[59] **10.25** below.

[60] The French text, in referring to *'une relation existante entre les parties . . . telle qu'une obligation découlant . . . d'un fait dommageable'*, is if anything clearer on this point.

constitutes an indissociable part of the tie[61] between victim and tortfeasor arising out of the latter's conduct towards the former.

The inclusion of Art 13 may also be thought to undermine the view that **4.16** claims to strip the defendant of the profits of his wrongdoing normally fall within Chapter II, not Art 10, of the Regulation. Under the heading 'Applicability of Article 8', this Article provides that:

For the purposes of this Chapter, Article 8 shall apply to non-contractual obligations arising from an infringement of an intellectual property right.

Art 13 reflects, in its effect if not its wording, Art 9(6) of the Commission **4.17** Proposal.[62] The proposed rule, as the Commission explained, was intended:[63]

To ensure that several different laws are not applicable to one and the same dispute, paragraph 6 excludes from this Article non-contractual obligations relating to intellectual property, to which Article 8 alone applies. E.g. an obligation based on unjust enrichment arising from an infringement of an intellectual property right[64] is accordingly governed by the same law as the infringement itself.

In light of this explanation, it could be suggested that, without a provision **4.18** corresponding to Art 13 for other obligations within Chapter II (Arts 4–7 and 9), claims to reverse the defendant's enrichment from a tort/delict other than an infringement of an intellectual property right must, by necessary inference, fall within Art 10. It is submitted that, having regard to the points made above, that inference is not justified. Art 13 should be considered as a clarification in the scope of Art 8, for the avoidance of doubt, and not as resolving the question as to how gain based remedies for wrongdoing should be characterized in other situations.

---

[61] The word 'obligation' derives from the Latin *ligare* (bind) (see C von Bar *The Common European Law of Torts* (vol 1, 1998; reprinted 2003), para 4).

[62] Contained in the provision dealing with the law applicable to non-contractual obligations arising out of an act other than a tort or delict, Art 9(6) stated: 'Notwithstanding the present Article, all non-contractual obligations in the field of intellectual property shall be governed by Article 8'.

[63] Commission Proposal, 20 (footnote added).

[64] The possibility of a restitutionary claim with respect infringement of a Community intellectual property right is explicitly acknowledged by Regulation (EC) No 2100/94 on Community plant variety rights (OJ L227, 1 [27.9.1994]), Art 97(1). Also Directive (EC) 2004/48 on the enforcement of intellectual property rights (OJ L195, 16 [2.6.2004]), Art 13. For the availability of an account of profits under English law, see e.g. *Celanese International Corp v BP Chemicals* [1999] RPC 203, [36]–[54] (Laddie J, EWHC). Also R Meagher, D Heydon, and M Leeming, *Meagher, Gummow and Lehane's Equity Doctrines and Remedies* (4th edn, 2002), 873–4.

4.19 Treating claims of this kind as falling within Chapter II not only ensures consistency between the remedies for tort/delict, whether compensatory or non-compensatory, it also prevents dilution of the special rules in Arts 6, 7, and 9 and supports the achievement of the particular objectives that they pursue. In particular, it should be noted that, even if (contrary to the author's view[65]) the reference in Art 10(1) to 'a relationship existing between the parties, such as one arising out of . . . a tort/delict' can be read sufficiently broadly to allow the conclusion that the law applicable to a tort/delict should also be applied to a restitutionary claim based on that tort/delict,[66] that law would be subject to displacement by the flexible escape clause in Art 10(4). An escape clause of this kind was not considered appropriate for obligations falling within Arts 6, 7, or 9, and it is difficult to see why the claimant's decision to seek a gain-based remedy for the defendant's wrongful conduct should make a difference. Further, the law applicable under Art 10 can be displaced by party choice under Art 14, a possibility that is excluded for non-contractual obligations arising out of acts of unfair competition and restrictions of competition (Art 6(1) and (3)).[67] The wider, market-oriented objectives pursued by these rules, and in particular by the exclusion of party autonomy,[68] do not support a distinction between loss-based and preventative remedies, on the one hand, and gain-based remedies on the other. Indeed, in some cases, the availability of a remedy stripping the defendant of the profits of anti-competitive conduct may provide a strong incentive for him to tailor his conduct to comply with laws and practices regulating the market in question.

4.20 Of course, the claimant may be able to frame his claim as an unjust enrichment claim without needing to rely on the defendant's legal responsibility for the event that caused his enrichment.[69] In such a case, as for concurrent contractual and non-contractual obligations,[70] there is no reason in principle why the same factual situation cannot, under the Regulation, give rise to both a non-contractual obligation arising in tort/delict (Art 4) and a

---

[65] **4.15** above. If the author's view, that these words require that the tort/delict and the unjust enrichment be separate, is accepted, the case for applying Art 10 to gain-based claims for wrongdoing is further weakened, as (absent a prior relationship between the parties) the place of enrichment (Art 10(3)) may not be foreseeable from the claimant's point of view, may be open to manipulation by the defendant, and does not appear to ensure a reasonable balance between the interests of the parties (cf Recital (16)).

[66] Ibid.

[67] Regulation, Art 6(4).

[68] **6.74** below.

[69] P Birks, n 43 above, 83–6. For an example in a cross-border situation, see *Berry Floor Ltd v Moussavi* [2004] EWHC 49 (Comm), [64] (Cooke J).

[70] **3.124–3.138** above.

non-contractual obligation arising in unjust enrichment (Art 10). The law applicable to each obligation must be determined separately: it appears unlikely, for the reasons given above, that the 'tort/delict' connector in Art 10(1) can be used to fix both claims with the same applicable law, although that result may be achieved through the more general rule of displacement in Art 10(4).

C. THE LAW GENERALLY APPLICABLE TO TORTS/ DELICTS—LAW OF THE COUNTRY OF (DIRECT) DAMAGE (ART 4(1))

INTRODUCTION

Art 4(1) provides: **4.21**

Unless otherwise provided for in this Regulation, the law applicable to a non-contractual obligation arising out of a tort/delict shall be the law of the country in which the damage occurs irrespective of the country in which the event giving rise to the damage occurred and irrespective of the country or countries in which the indirect consequences of that event occur.

This provision, the cornerstone of the Rome II Regulation, must be read **4.22** together with Recitals (16) and (17), as follows:

(16) Uniform rules should enhance the foreseeability of court decisions and ensure a reasonable balance between the interests of the person claimed to be liable and the person who has sustained damage. A connection with the country where the direct damage occurred (*lex loci damni*) strikes a fair balance between the interests of the person claimed to be liable and the person sustaining the damage, and also reflects the modern approach to civil liability and the development of systems of strict liability.

(17) The law applicable should be determined on the basis of where the damage occurs, regardless of the country or countries in which the indirect consequences could occur. Accordingly, in cases of personal injury or damage to property, the country in which the damage occurs should be the country where the injury was sustained or the property was damaged respectively.

According to the explanatory memorandum accompanying the Commis- **4.23** sion Proposal:[71]

[*Article 4(1)*] takes as the basic rule the law of the place where the direct damage arises or is likely to arise. In most cases this corresponds to the law of the injured party's country of residence.

---

[71] Commission Proposal, 11 (referring in the original to Art 3(1) of the Proposal).

It must not, however, be assumed that the victim's country of residence is the country in which the damage 'occurs'.

4.24 In this connection, the Commission Proposal had referred to the country in which the damage 'arises or is likely to arise'. The word 'occurs' seems preferable, being consistent with the English text of the leading decision of the ECJ in *Bier v Mines de potasse d'Alsace*, discussed below.[72] It emphasizes that the focus is on the place where the event giving rise to the damage 'produces its harmful effects on the victim', rather than where it originates.[73]

4.25 This aspect of the Commission Proposal was not universally well received.[74] Some Member States were critical of the vagueness of the distinction between consequences of the event giving rise to damage that are 'indirect' and those that are not.[75] In the main, these concerns seem to have been assuaged at an early stage in the process.[76]

LINK TO THE BRUSSELS CONVENTION

4.26 The language and structure of Art 4(1) reflects that used by the ECJ in its case law concerning Art 5(3) of the Brussels Convention (matters relating to tort, delict, or quasi-delict). In the first and most significant case on Art 5(3), *Bier v Mines de potasse d'Alsace*, discharges by the defendant mining company into the River Rhine in France were alleged by the claimant to have resulted in the excessive salination of the river, causing damage to its plantations in the Netherlands and obliging it to take expensive measures in order to limit that damage.[77] The Court was asked to identify whether the 'harmful event' (*fait dommageable*) referred to in Art 5(3) occurred in France or in the Netherlands. The Court, extraordinarily in light of its later restrictive approach to the construction of the rules of 'special jurisdiction' in Arts 5 and 6 of the Brussels Convention,[78] held that the courts for both the place of the event giving rise to damage and the place of damage had jurisdiction. The Court reasoned[79] that 'the place of the event giving rise to the damage no less than the place where the damage occurred can,

---

[72] **4.26–4.27.**

[73] Case C-68/93, *Shevill v Presse Alliance SA* [1995] ECR I-415, para 28.

[74] Council document 14010/03 [17.12.2003], 4.

[75] Council documents 9004/04 [29.4.2004], 2 (Luxembourg); ibid, ADD 6 [7.5.2004], 1 (Cyprus); ibid, ADD 16 [28.5.2004], 2 (Netherlands); ibid, ADD 17 [2.6.2004], 2 (Italy).

[76] Council document 11801/04 [28.7.2004], 2. Cf Council document 13047/04 [1.10.2004], 4 (France).

[77] *Bier v Mines de Potasse*, n 6 above, paras 3–4. A claim of this kind would now fall within Art 7 of the Rome II Regulation (**Ch 7**).

[78] e.g. Case C-168/02, *Kronhofer v Maier* [2004] ECR I-6009, paras 12–14.

[79] *Bier v Mines de Potasse*, n 6 above, para 15.

depending on the case, constitute a significant connecting factor from the point of view of jurisdiction', adding:[80]

Liability in tort, delict or quasi-delict can only arise provided that a causal connexion can be established between the damage and the event in which that damage originates.

Taking into account the close connexion between the component parts of every sort of liability, it does not appear appropriate to opt for one of the two connecting factors mentioned to the exclusion of the other, since each of them can, depending on the circumstances, be particularly helpful from the point of view of the evidence and of the conduct of the proceedings.

To exclude one option appears all the more undesirable in that, by its comprehensive form of words, Article 5(3) of the Convention covers a wide diversity of kinds of liability.

4.27 The references in Art 4(1) of the Rome II Regulation to 'the country in which the damage occurs' and 'the event giving rise to the damage' reflect the distinction drawn by the ECJ in *Bier*. In later cases, the ECJ sought to limit the effect of this decision in extending the jurisdiction of Member State courts under the Brussels Convention in matters relating to tort etc. In particular, it sought to restrict the concept of 'damage' by excluding the consequences of the event giving rise to damage that were thought to be indirect and too remote. That restriction was first identified in *Dumez France SA v Hessische Landesbank*[81] and subsequently applied in *Marinari v Lloyd's Bank plc*[82] and *Kronhofer v Maier*.[83] *Marinari* was referred to by the Commission as supporting the exclusion of the 'indirect consequences' of the event giving rise to damage from the connecting factor in its proposed general rule for tort/delict. The scope and effect of that exclusion, carried forward into Art 4(1) in its final form, will be considered, with reference to the ECJ's decisions in all three of these cases, at **4.36–4.45** below.

THE APPROACH TO BE TAKEN IN APPLYING ARTICLE 4(1)

4.28 In *Bier*, the ECJ was unable or unwilling to choose between the place of the event giving rise to damage and the place of damage as a connecting factor for jurisdiction purposes. The choice of the latter in Art 4(1) of the Rome II Regulation was described by the Commission as 'a compromise between the two extreme solutions of applying the law of the place where the event giving rise to the damage occurs and giving the victim the option' and seems to

---

[80] Ibid, paras 16–18.
[81] Case C-220/88 [1990] ECR I-49.
[82] Case C-364/93 [1995] ECR I-2719.
[83] Case C-168/02 [2004] ECR I-6009.

have been preferred to the country of the event giving rise to damage on the basis that it was more favourable to the victim, consistently with the Commission's view that the civil liability rules now had as their predominant object the compensation of those affected by the conduct of others rather than the punishment of fault-based conduct.[84] That view is reflected in Recital (16).[85] Nevertheless, as Recital (16) also makes clear, the primary object of the rule in Art 4(1) is to enhance the foreseeability of court decisions and to strike a reasonable balance between the interests of the person claimed to be liable and the person who has sustained damage. Thus, the concept of the 'country in which the damage occurs' in Art 4(1) must be applied so as, whenever possible, to base the identification of the law applicable to a tort/delict on factors objectively ascertainable by both parties.[86] To enhance legal certainty, those factors should also be applied uniformly with respect to similar types of claim. The strength of the connection to the country identified is a matter to be taken into account in moulding the concepts of 'damage' and 'indirect consequences', but the absence of a real connection in a particular case should not lead the court to refuse to apply Art 4(1).[87] Instead, if there is only a tenuous connection with the country of damage, it may be considered appropriate to apply the 'escape clause' in Art 4(3).[88]

THE CONCEPT OF 'DAMAGE' (ART 2(1))

4.29 Art 2(1) defines 'damage' as covering 'any consequence arising out of tort/delict [etc]'.[89] This clarification renders it unnecessary for the ECJ and Member State courts to develop an autonomous concept of 'damage' for the purposes of the Regulation[90] or to refer to the putative applicable law or the law of the forum.[91] Instead, it is submitted, Art 4(1) requires the court to consider the sequence of events giving rise to the claimant's claim, not limiting itself to those pleaded by the claimant, and to identify (1) the 'event giving rise to damage', (2) the consequences of that 'event' in terms of its (adverse[92]) effect on the victim,[93] and (3) which of those consequences may be considered as 'indirect consequences' excluded from having any

---

[84] Commission Proposal, 12.

[85] **4.22** above.

[86] **3.29** above.

[87] **3.27–3.28** above.

[88] Commission Proposal, 12 (**4.87** below).

[89] **3.44–3.46** above.

[90] Cf Case C-167/00, *Verein für Konsumentinformation v Henkel* [2002] ECR I-8111, para 42.

[91] Cf *Shevill v Press Alliance SA*, n 73 above, paras 34–9.

[92] The French text of Art 2(1), in which the words '*toute atteinte*' correspond to 'any consequences' conveys this idea more clearly.

[93] For cases in which the 'victim' may be somebody other than the claimant or a person represented by the claimant, see **4.39–4.45** below.

role in determining the law applicable under Art 4(1). Member State courts must take a broad view of what, for these purposes, may constitute 'damage', and must not restrict the meaning of the term to interests that would be protected under the law of the forum. In *VfK v Henkel*, for example, the ECJ held that the concept of 'damage' for the purposes of Art 5(3) of the Brussels Convention was capable of covering 'the undermining of legal stability by the use of unfair terms'.[94]

The concept of 'damage' within the Rome II Regulation is broader, for example, than that in the Product Liability Directive[95] or developed by the ECJ in its case law concerning the non-contractual liability of the Community.[96] **4.30**

THE APPROACH TO CAUSATION

Consistently with the reasoning of the ECJ in *Bier*,[97] both Art 2(1) and the language of Art 4(1) emphasize that the 'damage' must, in some sense, be caused by the event giving rise to damage.[98] Nevertheless, it is important that Member State courts should not take an unduly restrictive approach to causation, for example by applying a 'but for' test or by requiring that the consequence be foreseeable. Nor should the words 'consequence' and 'consequences' in Arts 2(1) and 4(1) respectively be given a technical meaning, contrasted (for example) with 'effects' or 'results'.[99] Indeed, for Art 4(1) to apply effectively, every 'event giving rise to damage' must be considered as causing some 'damage', the location of which will enable the law applicable to the non-contractual obligation arising in tort/delict to be identified. Art 4(1) must, therefore, be able to accommodate those cases in which the claim tests the boundaries of scientific knowledge or involves 'an unfamiliar tale about unfamiliar events',[100] as much as those in which the effect of a particular event is obvious to all. For example, if the claimant asserts that his illness resulted from exposure to asbestos while in the employ of several persons, **4.31**

---

[94] *VfK v Henkel*, n 90 above, para 42 (**3.240** above).
[95] Directive (EEC) No 1985/374 on the approximation of the laws, regulations and administrative provisions of the Member States concerning liability for defective products (OJ L210, 29 [7.8.1995]), as amended by Directive (EC) No 1999/34, Art 9 (**5.07** below).
[96] EC Treaty, Art 288, 2nd sentence. See A G Toth, 'The Concepts of Damage and Causality as Elements of Non-Contractual Liability', ch 10 in T Heukels and A McDonnell (eds), *The Action for Damages in Community Law* (1997), 180–91.
[97] *Bier v Mines de Potasse*, n 6 above, para 16 (quoted in full at text to n 80 above).
[98] Compare the approach taken by the ECJ in relation to the non-contractual liability of the EC under EC Treaty, Art 288: A G Toth, n 96 above, 191–8. Also F Smith and L Woods, 'Causation in *Francovich*: The Neglected Problem' (1997) 46 ICLQ 925.
[99] Cf H L A Hart and T Honoré, *Causation in the Law* (1985, reprinted 2002), 27–8.
[100] H L A Hart and T Honoré, ibid, 68. For more detailed discussion of the causal concept of 'consequence', see ibid, 68–81.

it should not matter that he cannot point to the 'guilty' fibres or say that, but for a particular period of exposure, he would still have been healthy.[101] The illness must, for the purposes of determining the law applicable, be taken as the consequence of each exposure. Equally, but more fancifully, if a land-owner claims that the flapping of butterflies kept on his neighbour's land resulted in damage to his property due to a change in air pressure, the court must proceed on the basis that the property damage is a consequence of the defendant's lepidoptery. Of course, the question of causation must be re-examined at the stage of considering the defendant's liability by reference to the law applicable to the tort/delict, once this has been identified.[102]

4.32 In accordance with Art 2(3)(b), the concept of damage must also include damage that is likely to occur. This suggests an element of foreseeability as to future consequences of the event giving rise to damage although, for the reasons just given, the threshold should not be set at a high level.

THE EVENT GIVING RISE TO DAMAGE[103]

4.33 The 'event giving rise to damage' should be the present or future[104] act, omission, or other event of or attributable to the tortfeasor on which the claimant's claim is founded. This will not necessarily correspond with the fact that the claimant, or the rules of any of the countries whose law may be apply, identifies as being 'unlawful'[105] or with the last act attributable to the defendant.[106] In the Brussels Convention case of *Shevill v Presse Alliance*, the ECJ held that the 'event giving rise to damage' in a case involving defamatory comments in a newspaper[107] was the issue and putting into circulation of the newspaper containing the libel (in France) rather than its publication to one or more persons (in several countries, including England).[108] It was able to reach that conclusion, although (a) under English law, as both the law of the forum and the law applicable to the tort in that case, it was publication of the defamatory statement to a third party that constituted the tort, and (b) the defendant had also been responsible

---

[101] Cf *Fairchild v Glenhaven Funeral Services Ltd* [2002] UKHL 22; [2003] 1 AC 32. Also *Gregg v Scott* [2005] UKHL 2; [2005] 2 AC 176.

[102] Art 15(a) (**14.06** below).

[103] For discussion of this concept within the 1968 Brussels Convention, see U Magnus and P Mankowski, *The Brussels I Regulation* (2007), Art 5, paras 214–28; A Briggs and P Rees, *Civil Jurisdiction and Judgments* (4th edn, 2005), paras 2.160–2.161.

[104] Art 2(3)(a).

[105] A Briggs and P Rees, n 103 above, para 2.160.

[106] U Magnus and P Mankowski, n 103 above, Art 5, para 214.

[107] Claims of this type are excluded from the Regulation by Art 1(2)(g), but this does not affect the point made in the text above.

[108] *Shevill v Press Alliance*, n 73 above,

for distribution of its newspaper in England after printing it and putting it into circulation.

Two English High Court decisions on the Brussels Convention support a **4.34** test expressed in terms of 'where in substance the cause of action in tort arises, or what the tort is most closely connected with',[109] a test reminiscent of the approach taken by the English courts in locating cross-border torts under the former common law rules.[110] That approach was, however, rejected by Rix J in *Domicrest Ltd v Swiss Bank Corporation* as not reflecting the wording of or philosophy behind the ECJ's case law on Art 5(3) (including *Shevill*).[111] Reasoning by analogy with *Shevill*, he held that the event giving rise to damage in a claim based on misrepresentation was the making of the representation and not its receipt.[112]

Having identified the event giving rise to damage, it is not necessary for **4.35** the purposes of the Regulation to identify where it occurred (at least for the purposes of Art 4(1), although this may be a relevant factor in carrying out the balancing exercise required by Art 4(3)[113]). In many cases, the event giving rise to damage and the (direct) damage will occur in the same country, and the reference to the former in Art 4(1) does no more than emphasize that its focus is not on the tortfeasor's conduct but on the effect that conduct has on the victim. It is not, therefore, a qualification to the concept of 'damage' but a clarification as to the nature of the connecting factor.

THE INDIRECT CONSEQUENCES OF THE EVENT GIVING RISE TO DAMAGE[114]

Financial and Other Non-Material Consequences of Injury Sustained Elsewhere

In the explanatory memorandum accompanying its Proposal, the Com- **4.36** mission explained:[115]

The place or places where indirect damage, if any, was sustained are not relevant for determining the applicable law. In the event of a traffic accident, for example,

---

[109] *Minster Investments v Hyundai Precision and Industry Co Ltd* [1988] 2 Lloyd's Rep 621, 624 (Steyn J) and *Modus Vivendi Ltd v The British Products Sanmex Company Limited* [1997] ILPr 654, [44] (Knox J). Also U Magnus and P Mankowski, n 103 above, para 216.

[110] e.g. *Distillers Co Ltd v Thompson* [1971] AC 458 (PC).

[111] [1999] QB 548, 567.

[112] Ibid, 567–8. For other English cases on the same point, see Dicey, Morris & Collins, para 11-303, footnote 418.

[113] **4.87** below.

[114] For discussion of this concept within the 1968 Brussels Convention, see U Magnus and P Mankowski, n 103 above, Art 5, paras 233–40; A Briggs and P Rees, n 103 above, para 2.157.

[115] Commission Proposal, 11.

the place of the direct damage is the place where the collision occurs, irrespective of financial or non-material damage sustained in another country.

4.37 The Commission referred, in this connection, to the ECJ's decision in *Marinari v Lloyd's Bank*. In that case Mr Marinari sought compensation in Italy following the Bank's refusal to return to him promissory notes that he had lodged with its branch in Manchester and its subsequent report to the British police leading to Mr Marinari's arrest and sequestration of the notes. He sought not only payment of the face value of the notes but also compensation for damage suffered by reason of his arrest and damage to his reputation.[116] The ECJ, responding to a preliminary question put to it by the Italian court, concluded that the concept of 'harmful event' within Art 5(3) of the Brussels Convention did not extend to 'the place where, as in the present case, the victim claims to have suffered financial damage following upon initial damage arising and suffered by him in another Contracting State'.[117] In the Court's view, this was inherent in the wider proposition that the connecting factor in Art 5(3)[118] 'cannot be construed so extensively as to encompass any place where the adverse consequences can be felt of an event which has already caused damage actually arising elsewhere'. In the preceding paragraphs of its judgment, the Court had explained the need for Art 5(3) to be applied so as to ensure a significant connection to the court having jurisdiction, and to avoid unduly favouring the courts of the claimant's domicile.[119] Although those objectives are specific to the Brussels I Regime, they are broadly consistent with the Commission's reasons for choosing the *lex loci damni* as the connecting factor under the Rome II Regulation.[120] There is little doubt, therefore, that financial or other consequences that reflect or follow from initial damage to the claimant must be treated as 'indirect consequences' within Art 4(1). For example, in the case of a claim for loss of earnings in State A following injuries suffered in a motor accident in State B, Art 4(1) will point exclusively towards application of the law of State B. Similarly, if the defendant's negligence leads to the loss of assets under management in State C, it matters not that the claimant's assets are concentrated in State D and that he feels the effects of that loss there.[121]

---

[116] Case C-364/93 [1995] ECR I-2719, paras 3–4.
[117] Ibid, para 15. Also the Opinion of Adv Gen Darmon, esp paras 28–48.
[118] Ibid, para 14.
[119] Ibid, paras 12–13.
[120] **4.04** above.
[121] Case C-168/02, *Kronhofer v Maier*, n 83 above.

Deterioration in the Physical Condition of the Person or Property

The examples given in the preceding paragraph are relatively straightfor- **4.38**
ward applications of the distinction between 'direct' and 'indirect' consequences of the event giving rise to damage in Art 4(1). Other situations
create greater difficulty. The second sentence of Recital (17) states that, in
cases of personal injury or damage to property, the country of damage
should be that where the injury was sustained or the property was damaged.[122] Ordinarily, therefore, it would appear that personal injury or
property damage must be treated as 'direct' damage. What if an injury
occurring in State E is followed by a deterioration in the victim's condition
after his return home to State F? In *Henderson v Jaouen*, the English Court
of Appeal (applying the reasoning in *Marinari* by analogy) held that
although aggravation in England of the claimant's injury gave a fresh
cause of action in France (where the traffic accident which had caused the
injury had occurred), it was not a separate 'harmful event' under Art 5(3)
of the Brussels Convention.[123] That conclusion also seems appropriate
under the Rome II Regulation, in terms of avoiding undue favour to the
law of the victim's habitual residence and enhancing foreseeability as to
the law applicable. The damage should be taken to have occurred in State E.

Consequences of Injury Sustained by Another (Reflective and Ricochet Losses)

More difficult questions arise in cases in which damage suffered by one **4.39**
person in one country causes financial or other loss to another person in a
different country. That was the situation in *Dumez France SA v Hessische
Landesbank*. In that case, two French companies sought in the French courts
compensation for losses suffered by them by reason of the insolvency of
their German subsidiaries. Those losses, in turn, were alleged to have been
caused by the defendant banks' unlawful cancellation of certain loan facilities relating to a project in which the subsidiaries were interested.[124]
Answering a preliminary question put by the French court, the ECJ ruled
that Art 5(3) of the Brussels Convention cannot be interpreted as permitting the claimant to pursue in the courts of the place in which he

---

[122] For discussion of problems in locating the place of injury or property damage, see
4.47–4.65 below.
[123] [2002] EWCA Civ 75; [2002] 1 WLR 2971. Cf *Cooley v Ramsey* [2008] EWHC 129 (QB),
a case concerning the English rules of jurisdiction for claims against foreign defendants not
domiciled in a Member State.
[124] Case C-220/88 [1990] ECR I-49, paras 2–3.

ascertained damage resulting from harm suffered by other persons as direct victims of the harmful act. In the Court's view:[125]

> The harm alleged by the parent companies . . . is merely the indirect consequence of the financial losses initially suffered by their subsidiaries following cancellation of the loans and the subsequent suspension of the works.

4.40 Adam Rushworth and Andrew Scott have argued that the reasoning in *Dumez* should not be replicated in the context of the Rome II Regulation.[126] They note that the Commission referred in the explanatory memorandum accompanying its Rome II Proposal only to the ECJ's decision in *Marinari* and not to *Dumez*. That observation, however, should carry little weight, especially as (a) the Court in *Marinari* referred to its earlier decision in *Dumez*,[127] and (b) the terminology used in Art 4(1) of the Regulation ('indirect consequence') comes from the decision in *Dumez* not that in *Marinari*. Further, in his Opinion in *Marinari*, Adv Gen Darmon quoted with approval the following statement from a comment by Professor Gaudemet-Tallon on *Dumez*:[128]

> Admittedly, in [*Dumez*] the Court of Justice is considering the case only of an indirect victim, but there is no reason for it to give a different answer regarding damage suffered by a direct victim, which later produces harmful consequences, located in most cases at the place where the victim is domiciled.

4.41 Rushworth and Scott also argue that the replication of *Dumez* within the framework established by Art 4(1) of the Rome II Regulation would create insuperable difficulties in determining whether a person claims as a 'direct' (primary) or 'indirect' (secondary) victim,[129] illustrating their argument with the following example:[130]

> [A] football match played in Athens is negligently stewarded by the defendants, causing serious injuries to supporters at the stadium. Where the events are broadcast in England to a local claimant's distress, which law will Art 4(1) apply to determine the defendant's liability for the claimant's psychiatric harm?

4.42 A short-cut to the answer to this particular example might be provided by Recital (17),[131] which states that, in cases of personal injury, the country in

---

[125] Ibid, para 14. See also the very detailed review in the Opinion of Adv Gen Darmon, paras 32–46 as to the treatment of 'indirect' or 'ricochet' victims in the Member States.

[126] A Rushworth and A Scott, n 49 above, 279.

[127] *Marinari v Lloyds Bank plc*, paras 7 and 10. Also the Opinion of Adv Gen Darmon in *Marinari*, esp paras 28, 38–9.

[128] Ibid, Opinion of Adv Gen Darmon, para 39.

[129] For discussion of this point in relation to the Brussels Convention, see U Magnus and P Mankowski, n 103 above, Art 5, paras 236–7.

[130] A Rushworth and A Scott, n 49 above.

[131] **4.22** above.

which the damage occurs should be the country where the injury was sustained. This may be argued to create a strong indication that a person suffering personal injury, however it may occur, should be considered to be a primary, direct victim of the event giving rise to damage, leading in the example to the application under Art 4(1) of English law.[132] That solution, however, creates its own problems as to the meaning of the (presumably) autonomous concept of 'personal injury'. If nervous shock or other psychiatric illness is to be considered as falling within this category, what about emotional distress or grief?[133] It also fails to address the wider problem. Suppose that an opera singer is injured in a traffic accident in State G leading to the enforced cancellation of his concert in State H. The concert organizer wishes to recover his losses from the person responsible for the accident.[134] The effect of *Marinari*, as the Commission explains,[135] is that the opera singer's claim to recover his own lost income, like his personal injury claim, would *prima facie* be governed by the law of State G. There seems no reason why his employer, the concert organizer, should be treated any differently. His own loss, although apparently sustained in State H, is an adverse consequence of an event that has already caused damage elsewhere, albeit to a different, primary victim. Applying the law of State G to the secondary victim's claim not only promotes consistency as to the law applicable to the claims of the two victims, it also links the applicable law to a tangible, recordable fact (the accident) the location of which can, without difficulty, be identified by both parties after the event. The location of that fact is also foreseeable to both the tortfeasor and the primary victim at the time of the event giving rise to damage. Although it may not be foreseeable to the concert organizer, the balance between the parties seems in favour of applying the law of State G (the country of damage to the primary victim) rather than that of State H (the country of damage to the secondary victim).[136]

The submission that, at least, financial or other non-material consequences **4.43** to the claimant that reflect or follow from the primary victim's damage should be treated as 'indirect consequences' of the event giving rise to

---

[132] See also the passage from the Commission Proposal quoted at text to n 138 below, referring to 'non-material' and 'financial' damage.

[133] For example, Professor van Dam notes that 'in French law the difference between mental harm and grief is fluid' (C van Dam, *European Tort Law* (2008), para 1211). Also *Dumez France v Hessische Landesbank*, n 124 above, Opinion of Adv Gen Darmon, para 37.

[134] Cf the decision of the *Cour de Cassation, 2ème Ch civ*, 14 November 1958 (see C van Dam, n 133 above, para 1105).

[135] Text to n 115 above.

[136] The concert organizer in the example would arguably be in a better position to insure against cancellation due to unavailability of his talent, than the driver for liability to the concert organizer.

damage within Art 4(1) may be supported by other examples. Thus, if the opera singer were a passenger in a car damaged in the accident, should his claim for lost earnings be treated any differently depending on whether he is injured or is the owner of the damaged vehicle or is merely delayed by the incident? What if he is driving a car caught in a traffic jam caused by an accident ahead of him in the road? In each of these cases, the opera singer's financial loss should be seen as an indirect consequence of personal injury or damage to property sustained, whether by him or by another victim, at the time and place of the accident.

4.44 The text of the Regulation and the *travaux préparatoires* also support this conclusion. One of the matters that Art 15 refers to the law applicable to a non-contractual obligation under the Regulation, including one arising out of a tort/delict, is 'persons entitled to compensation for damage sustained personally'.[137] According to the Commission:[138]

> [T]his concept particularly refers to the question whether a person other than the 'direct victim' can obtain compensation for damage sustained on a 'knock-on' basis, following damage sustained by the victim. Such damage might be non-material, as in the pain and suffering caused by a bereavement, or financial, as in the loss sustained by the children or spouse of a deceased person.

4.45 There seems no rational basis for distinguishing between relations of the primary victim and other indirect victims, such as the concert organizer in the example given above. Whether, by virtue of Recital (17) and the above statement of the Commission, a distinction can be drawn between 'financial' and other 'non-material' damage, on the one hand, and material damage (including personal injury and damage to property), on the other, with the latter always being taken into account in applying Art 4(1), remains to be seen.

Locating the 'Damage' under Article 4(1)[139]

4.46 Having identified the adverse consequences of the event giving rise to damage, and excluded those that are 'indirect', the next step is to locate the damage in a particular country (or countries[140]) in order to identify the law(s) applicable to the non-contractual obligation arising out of tort/delict under Art 4(1). That will, in many cases, involve a straightforward

---

[137] Art 15(f) (**14.42–14.44** below). Cf the French text, referring to '*les personnes ayant droit à réparation du dommage qu'elles ont personnellement subi*', but other language versions seem in line with the English language version.

[138] Commission Proposal, 24.

[139] For discussion of this topic within the Brussels Convention, see U Magnus and P Mankowski, n 103 above, Art 5, paras 243–57; A Briggs and P Rees, n 103 above, para 2.158.

[140] **4.69–4.74** below.

verification of a fact. In other cases, as appears below, it will be more difficult to locate the damage for the purposes of the Regulation.

Personal Injury and Damage to Property

As noted, Recital (17) provides that, in cases of personal injury or damage **4.47** to property, the country in which the damage occurs should be the country where the injury was sustained or the property was damaged respectively. In the case, for example, of road traffic accidents, this should cause no difficulty. The place where personal injury was 'sustained' or damage to property 'occurred' will not, however, always be certain. Two types of uncertainty may arise. First, evidential uncertainty as to the point in time and place at which the damage occurred. Secondly, legal uncertainty as to the meaning of 'personal injury' or 'damage to property' or resulting from the location of damage being outside the territory of a State. Neither the first nor, probably, the second type of uncertainty would seem to take a matter outside the scope of the Regulation (**3.311–3.314** above).

Both types of uncertainty may occur in cases concerning international **4.48** transport, by road, rail, air, or sea. In the case of the carriage of persons by road or rail, it will not usually be difficult to locate the place of injury arising by reason of an incident occurring on, or in relation to, the mode of transport. Such situations are not, it is submitted, isolated from the countries through which vehicles may pass merely because the passengers may not engage with the outside world. The carriage of persons by sea or air, however, seems different in character, and raises three particular issues. First, there may be a genuine practical difficulty in locating a vessel or aircraft at the time of a particular event, particularly one that occurred exclusively on board the aircraft (Issue A).[141] Secondly, particularly in the case of aircraft, the passengers are, in a very real sense, isolated from the countries through whose territorial waters or over which they pass (Issue B). Thirdly, the ship or aircraft may pass through, or across, areas not subject to the territorial sovereignty of a State, including the high seas, and it is possible that the event may occur during that passage (Issue C).[142]

It appears possible for Issue A, raising a problem of evidential uncertainty, **4.49** to be dealt with under the Regulation in one of two ways. The first solution would be to require the court, by considering evidence of factual and expert witnesses and applying its rules of evidence and the burden

---

[141] For the regulation by treaty and EC Regulation of the carrier's liability for accidents occurring on board aircraft, see **15.19** and **15.21** below.
[142] **3.313** above.

of proof, to reach a conclusion as to which State's territory the ship or aircraft was sailing through or flying over at the time that the damage occurred. The second solution would be to treat non-contractual obligations arising during the international transit of aircraft and ships as a special category and to mould the connecting factor so as to remove the evidential difficulty. Neither of these two solutions is obviously correct. From the standpoint of international law, the first solution has a powerful attraction. It accords, in particular, with Art 1 of the Chicago Convention on international civil aviation, which provides that 'every State has complete and exclusive sovereignty over the airspace above its territory',[143] and with Art 2 of the UN Convention on the law of the sea concerning sovereignty over the territorial sea.[144] Having regard, however, to the isolation of the ship or aircraft from its surroundings (Issue B), it seems artificial, especially for incidents occurring on board an aircraft, to conclude that damage occurring (for example) in an aircraft flying from Paris to Warsaw occurred 'in' Germany, even if it is established on the balance of probabilities that the event occurred over German territory.[145] Of course, in many cases, the Regulation, by providing an 'escape clause' such as that in Art 4(3), may allow the court to sidestep the evidential difficulty by concluding that, whatever country is identified as a result of the enquiry, the fact that the ship or aircraft was in transit significantly weakens the link with the country identified by the primary connecting factor and supports the conclusion that the non-contractual obligation is manifestly more closely connected with another country. Among the candidates for the country with which the obligation is more closely connected would be (a) the State of departure, (b) the State of (scheduled) destination, (c) the State in which the ship or aircraft is registered, or (d) the country of habitual residence of its operator.[146] That, however, leads one to question the sense of an evidential enquiry that requires the resources of the court to be deployed to produce a result which, if accepted, is unappealing and, if rejected, is worthless. An enquiry of this kind would also be fruitless if it were to result in a finding that the damage occurred on or over the high seas or another area not subject to the territorial sovereignty of a State (Issue C).

4.50 These issues must also be faced in the case of the carriage of goods by sea or air. The international carriage of goods by whatever means presents additional difficulties by reason of the fact that goods are not sentient and

---

[143] 15 UNTS 295 (7 December 1944); Sir R Jennings and Sir A Watts, *Oppenheim's International Law* (9th edn, 1992), para 141.

[144] 1833 UNTS 397 (10 December 1982); *Oppenheim's International Law*, n 143 above, para 187.

[145] Dicey, Morris & Collins, para 35-080.

[146] The habitual residence of ship and aircraft operators is discussed at **3.58** above.

cannot tell or protest when they have been damaged. That damage may be discovered days, weeks, or months later, for example when a container is opened for inspection on arrival of a vessel.

Liability of carriers of persons and goods by land, sea, or air, and some **4.51** other aspects of the civil liability of those concerned with international modes of transport (e.g. limitation of a shipowner's liability[147]), are regulated by international conventions to which EC Member States are party and which, in order to ensure their efficacy, will normally require to be given overriding (mandatory) effect by a State party, whether or not the law applicable to the obligation in question under the Rome I Regime or the Rome II Regulation (as applicable) is the law of another State party.[148] The law applicable under the Rome II Regulation will continue to apply to non-contractual obligations in situations not regulated in the forum Member State by international convention, or in which any relevant convention only partially harmonizes the civil liability rules. Accordingly, these international conventions do not provide a complete solution to the problems described above even within the areas to which they apply.

Issues of this kind have been addressed by the ECJ, within the framework **4.52** of Art 5(3) of the Brussels Convention, in *Réunion Européenne v Spliethoff's*.[149] In that case, pears carried by sea from Australia to The Netherlands and then by road to France were discovered by the consignee on arrival to have been damaged during transit. The consignee's insurers, exercising their right of subrogation, sought in the French courts to recover from the issuer of the bill of lading, the sea carrier, and the master of the vessel the amount that they had paid to the consignee. The Dutch owners and master of the vessel contested jurisdiction under the Brussels Convention. The insurers argued that jurisdiction existed under Art 5(3) of the Convention (matters relating to tort, delict, or quasi-delict) on the basis that 'damage' had occurred in France, where the goods were eventually delivered and the damage discovered. The ECJ rejected that argument. For this purpose,

---

[147] Convention on limitation of liability for maritime claims (Brussels, 19 November 1976), as amended by the Protocol signed 3 May 1996. All Member States with the exception of Austria, Czech Republic, Hungary, Italy, Portugal, Slovakia, and Slovenia are parties to the 1976 Convention in its original or amended form (Source: International Maritime Organisation website <http://www.imo.org/includes/blastDataOnly.asp/data_id%3D22499/status-x.xls>). Also International Convention relating to the Limitation of the Liability of Owners of Sea-Going Ships (10 October 1957); Case C-39/02, *Mærk Olie & Gas A/S v Firm M de Haan en W de Boer* [2004] ECR I-9657.

[148] **15.21** below.

[149] Case C-51/97, *Réunion Européenne SA v Spliethoff's Bevrachtingskantoor BV* [1998] ECR I-6511. For the subsequent decision of the French Cour de Cassation declining jurisdiction, see [1999] ILPr 613.

it might well have sufficed for the ECJ to point out that it was for the French court seised of the dispute to determine when, and where, 'damage' had occurred,[150] drawing attention to the requirement under the Convention (as now under the Rome II Regulation[151]) that the damage be the 'direct' consequence of the event for which the defendant was said to be responsible. On any view, given that the pears had already travelled halfway around the world, it is difficult to see how the French court could have concluded that the pears were 'damaged' only after they were unloaded and had entered France. Whatever the outcome, however, this question of fact would not have been a matter for the ECJ to determine.

4.53 The ECJ did not, however, choose to resolve the problem presented to it in *Réunion Européenne* in this way. It started by noting that 'in an international transport operation of the kind at issue in the main proceedings the place where the event giving rise to the damage occurred may be difficult or indeed impossible to determine'.[152] Although the Court referred here to difficulties in identifying 'the event giving rise to damage', its reference in the same paragraph to the Advocate General's analysis of evidential, and other, difficulties in locating the 'damage'[153] suggests that these difficulties were equally on its mind. Having then rejected both the place of final delivery and the place of inspection as being appropriate tests for the place of 'damage' for these purposes, mainly because they would give undue preference to the claimant's home court, the Court concluded that:[154]

[T]he place where the damage arose in the case of an international transport operation of the kind at issue in the main proceedings can only be the place where the actual maritime carrier was to deliver the goods.

4.54 The Court explained that this place 'meets the requirements of foreseeability and certainty imposed by the Convention and displays a particularly close connecting factor with the dispute in the main proceedings, so that the attribution of jurisdiction to the courts for that place is justified by reasons relating to the sound administration of justice and the efficacious conduct of proceedings'.[155] That reasoning appears consistent with the objectives underlying Art 4(1) of the present Regulation, to 'enhance the foreseeability of court decisions and ensure a reasonable balance between the interests of the person claimed to be liable and the person who has

---

[150] Following, in this respect, *Shevill v Press Alliance SA*, n 73 above, paras 34–40.
[151] **4.36–4.45** above.
[152] *Réunion Européenne v Spliethoff's*, n 149 above, para 33.
[153] Ibid, Opinion of Adv Gen Cosmas, para 55.
[154] Ibid, Judgment, paras 33–5. Also Opinion, paras 55–60.
[155] Ibid, Judgment, para 36.

sustained damage'.[156] With that in mind, there is every reason to believe that, if the ECJ were to be presented with a case under the Rome II Regulation involving international transport in a type of situation (such as that in *Réunion Européenne*) in which evidential difficulties commonly arise, it will direct its reasoning in such a way as to locate the damage in a particular country by reference to an objectively ascertainable factor present in all situations of that type that links the damage to a particular country.[157]

In other cases of damage occurring on board ships and aircraft, at least **4.55** where the event giving rise to damage is internal to the ship or aircraft, the connecting factor corresponding most closely to that identified in the decision in *Réunion Européenne* would appear to be the next scheduled destination of the ship or aircraft on which the damage occurred. That solution, however, may be thought unsatisfactory, particularly for ships that may be weeks or months away from their destination, and appears especially unsuited to dealing with claims arising from collisions between ships and aircraft, to which the country of destination seems irrelevant. It seems more likely, therefore, that Member State courts and the ECJ, if the matter were to be raised towards it, would steer towards a solution favouring the law of the flag State of a ship or the State of registration of an aircraft, on the basis that the ship or aircraft is deemed, for this purpose, to be part of the territory of the State.[158] A strong pointer towards that conclusion was given by the ECJ in its decision in *DFDS Torline*, in which the Court (considering the relevance of the nationality of a ship in determining the place of damage under Art 5(3) of the Brussels Convention) concluded:[159]

The nationality of the ship can play a decisive role only if the national court reaches the conclusion that the damage arose on board the [ship]. In that case, the flag State must necessarily be regarded as the place where the harmful event caused damage.

An autonomous solution to locating the country of damage in cases of **4.56** international transport has the added advantage that it addresses the third issue referred to above, i.e. the possibility that damage may be found, in

---

[156] Recital (16).

[157] Cf A Rushworth and A Scott, n 49 above, 272, favouring the distributive application of the laws of the country through which a cargo passes to the solution adopted in *Réunion Européenne*.

[158] Cf Dicey, Morris & Collins, 1st supplement, S35-198 to S35-199. If the flag State consists of two or more countries (as defined in Art 25 of the Regulation), the place of registration within that State may be applied instead.

[159] Case C-18/02, *DFDS Torline A/S v SEKO Sjöfolk Facket för Service och Kommunikation* [2004] ECR I-1417, para 44.

fact, to have occurred on or over an area not subject to State sovereignty. In such cases, application of the law of the flag or registration State would provide a workable, if not perfect, starting point in determining the law applicable to damage resulting from events on board ships or aircraft on or over the high seas. That outcome also seems consistent with international conventions concerning criminal jurisdiction.[160] In the case of collisions between ships and aircraft on or over the high seas, the logic and structure of Art 4(1) would appear to favour application of the law of the flag or registration State of the damaged ship/aircraft, not that of the ship/aircraft causing damage.[161]

4.57 Otherwise, the only viable solution in cases where damage, in fact, occurs on or over an area not subject to State sovereignty would be to neutralize Art 4(1), leaving the law applicable to the obligation in question to be determined solely by reference to Arts 4(2) and (3). That approach could not, it may be noted, be extended to other rules within the Regulation that contain no flexible rule of displacement, for example in a situation in which one ship releases pollutants which damage another ship (or crew member) (Art 7) or the crew of a ship threaten industrial action while the ship is on the high seas (Art 9). If the solution of applying the law of the flag or registration State were rejected in these cases, a default rule would be required, perhaps favouring the law of the forum, *faute de mieux*. This appears a less satisfactory solution.

4.58 Similar difficulties in identifying the country of damage will also arise in cases not involving international transport. For example, consider a case in which a contractor is exposed to asbestos in State J while working temporarily away from his home in State K and, many years later, moves to State L where he is diagnosed as suffering from an asbestos related disease. He sues the owner of the building in which he was working.[162] It is suggested that, in this case, the injury should be considered to have been 'sustained' in State J where the claimant was exposed to the asbestos, and not in State K (where the disease most likely developed), or State L (where the disease was diagnosed). This allows the applicable law to be identified by reference to an objective factor, ascertainable by both parties and appears, in particular insofar as it excludes the country of diagnosis,

---

[160] UN Convention on the law of the sea (1982), n 144 above, Art 94; Convention on offences and other acts committed on board aircraft (Tokyo, 14 September 1963), Art 3.

[161] For the exercise of criminal jurisdiction over collisions between ships on the high seas, see *The Lotus*, PCIJ, Series A, No 10, but compare UN Convention on the law of the sea (1982), n 144 above, Art 97 (*Oppenheim's International Law*, n 143 above, paras 140 and 291).

[162] Although this is a case of 'damage caused by a product' it does not fall within Art 5 (**5.13–5.14** below).

consistent with the approach of the ECJ in *Réunion Européenne*. The deterioration of the claimant's health in States K and L should be considered as indirect consequences of the original injury sustained in State J.

Another problematic area concerns the unborn child. Two types of situation may be contemplated. In the first, perhaps more likely to arise in cases of product liability,[163] an event affecting the child's mother may result in injury to the child,[164] with a claim being brought by it or on its behalf. If the child is *en ventre sa mère* at the time of the event (e.g. a car accident), it seems appropriate to conclude that the child has also been injured at that time and in that country. What if, however, the child has not been conceived at the time that damage is caused to the mother (e.g. by swallowing medication)? Four possible solutions may be suggested. First, the child should be deemed to have sustained injury at the same time and in the same place as the mother. Objection may be taken to that approach, however, on the ground that it does not treat the child as a separate life. Secondly, the child should be taken to have sustained injury at the moment and in the place of its conception. Thirdly, the child should be taken to have sustained injury in the country where the mother was habitually resident at the time of conception. Fourthly, the child should be taken to have sustained injury at the moment and in the place of its birth. **4.59**

In the second type of situation, an event (e.g. a sterilization or vasectomy) causes the unintended conception of a child, with a claim being brought by the parents of the child.[165] The second, third, and fourth options described above (i.e. country of conception, country of habitual residence at the time of conception, and country of birth) may also be suggested as candidates for the location of damage in this type of case. As a further alternative, it may be argued that the damage in this second category is purely economic, and that the conception of the child should not be treated as 'damage', and should be seen as an indirect consequence of the injury caused by the (failed) treatment at the time and place of treatment. **4.60**

It is submitted that, in both types of case, the country of birth should be rejected, as being too remote to the event giving rise to damage.[166] The country of habitual residence at the time of conception has its attractions, as it may avoid problems in identifying the place of conception. It may, however, be argued to be inconsistent both with the rejection by the ECJ in **4.61**

---

[163] **Ch 5** below.
[164] C van Dam, n 133 above, para 707.
[165] Ibid, para 706; A M Dugdale and M A Jones, *Clerk & Lindsell on Torts* (19th edn, 2006), paras 8-79 to 8-82, 29-57 to 29-63.
[166] For personal injuries sustained by the mother at birth, see **4.64** below.

Marinari and *Kronhofer* (**4.37** above) of the victim's country of habitual residence as a general connecting factor for jurisdiction purposes and with the use of *common* habitual residence as a connecting factor in Art 4(2). The better view, therefore, may be that the country of damage in both types of situation should be where the child was conceived, although the connection with that country may be a weak one (capable of being displaced under Art 4(3)) if, for example, the parents were travelling at the time. The economic loss suffered by the parents in supporting the child should be considered an indirect consequence of its conception, and left out of account for the purposes of Art 4(1).

4.62 There is, of course, a need for care so as to avoid describing the conception of a child as 'damage'. In *McFarlane v Tayside Health Board*, Lord Millett commented that:[167]

> It is morally offensive to regard a normal, healthy baby as more trouble and expense than it is worth.

4.63 That said, Art 2(1) of the Regulation defines 'damage' in terms of the consequences of a tort/delict and it would appear difficult to dispute that the conception of a child is a direct consequence of, for example, the negligent performance of a sterilization option. Nor does it stigmatize the child to describe its conception in this way. Further, if this seems too technical a point, the 'damage' to the parents may instead be described as a loss of autonomy in matters of family planning and upbringing,[168] a consequence that has its strongest connection to the moment, and the country, of conception.

4.64 The mother herself will sustain injury during birth. If she claims with respect to such injury, as well as pain, discomfort, and financial losses suffered earlier in her pregnancy, it may be argued that all such losses flow from the child's conception and that all claims arising from that event should be governed by the same law, whether by locating all of the 'damage' in the country of conception (which seems artificial, especially in view of the wording of Recital (17)[169]) or through application of the escape clause in Art 4(3).

4.65 The second type of situation has been considered by the Dutch courts on more than one occasion in the context of the Brussels I Regulation.[170]

---

[167] [2002] 2 AC 59, 114 (UKHL). Professor van Dam (n 133 above, 157) refers to a statement by the French Cour de Cassation that *'l'existence de l'enfant qu'elle a conçu ne peut, à elle seule, constituer pour sa mère un préjudice juridiquement réparable'*.

[168] *Rees v Darlington Memorial Hospital* [2003] UKHL 52; [2004] 1 AC 309, [123] (Lord Millett).

[169] **4.22** above.

[170] U Magnus and P Mankowski, n 103 above, Art 5, para 251.

In 2003, a district court held that the damage sustained from the child's birth was economic and occurred in the country where the parents' accounts were located.[171] In a later case, an appellate court held that, so far as material damage is concerned, damage was suffered in the place where the child was conceived.[172] The court, however, ruled that the non-material damage arising from the breach of the mother's right to self-determination was located in the place where the mother was when she became aware of the pregnancy. That conclusion is difficult to reconcile with the ECJ's rejection in *Reunion Européenne* of the place of discovery of damage as identifying the place of damage within Art 5(3) of the Brussels Convention.[173] On balance, the country of conception seems the more appropriate connecting factor under Art 4(1) of the Rome II Regulation.

Financial and other Non-Material Loss

The task of locating, for the purposes of the Regulation, the financial or **4.66** other non-material consequences of an event giving rise to damage raises a different set of problems. First, these consequences may lack an immediate, physical manifestation. For example, a credit balance in an Internet bank account may be recorded on a server in a country that has no direct connection with either the customer or the bank. An electronic transfer from that account to a third party's account consists of nothing more than a stream of electrons.[174] Other forms of non-material damage, such as damage to reputation and to goodwill are equally intangible. Secondly, particularly in the case of transfers of financial assets, the location of damage may be open to manipulation by both tortfeasor and victim. A fraudster may lure his victim to a country whose laws provide a lower level of protection, or a company may decide to concentrate its assets in, or channel transfers through, a particular country on the basis that the laws of that country provide stronger protection against fraud. Thirdly, the tortfeasor's act may trigger a chain of events involving the victim. At what point is it to be said that the victim has sustained 'damage' and that later consequences following on from that 'damage' are to be considered as 'indirect consequences'[175] to be left out of account in determining the applicable law?

---

[171] *Rechtbank Middelberg*, NIPR 2003 No 53, 104.
[172] *O v G, Gerechtshof's-Gravenhage*, Judgment of 14 October 2004, NIPR 2005 No 50. For an English summary of the decision, see <http://curia.europa.eu/common/recdoc/convention/en/2006/40-2006.htm>.
[173] **4.53** above.
[174] *Agip (Africa) Ltd v Jackson* [1990] Ch 285, 286 (Millett J, EWHC).
[175] **4.36–4.37** above.

4.67 The most common situation raising problems of this kind concerns the effects of a negligent or fraudulent misrepresentation. The misrepresentation may be initiated by the tortfeasor in one country (State M), received by the victim or the victim's representative in a second (State N), and present in the mind of the victim at the time that one or more decisions are taken in a third country (State P), leading to particular acts or omissions by the victim or its representatives in a fourth country or set of countries (State Q). Of these, only State M can be immediately disregarded under Art 4(1), as the initiation of the misrepresentation by the tortfeasor constitutes the event giving rise to damage and not damage.[176] The possibility of applying the law of State N can also be dismissed with relative ease, as the misrepresentation is at this stage only latent. Decisions of the English courts have, for the most part, also rejected the possibility of applying the law of State P, instead requiring some form of 'concrete transaction' as a result of the victim's reliance on the misrepresentation.[177] There is eminent good sense in that requirement, as the adverse consequences of the misrepresentation would appear to be reversible until that point. Indeed, it is submitted that the test of 'reversibility' is helpful in terms of identifying the transaction or other act or omission on the faith of the misrepresentation that constitutes 'damage' to the victim for this purpose, and in reconciling the earlier decisions of the English courts concerning the location of the place of damage under Art 5(3) of the Brussels Convention. If, on the faith of the representation, the victim enters into a contract or other transaction with the tortfeasor, it may be appropriate to look through that transaction and instead to identify the country of damage with that in which the victim or his representative irreversibly incurred expenditure or liability or in which he lost control of assets or other resources in the performance of the contract.[178] The fact that the victim may undertake a liability towards the tortfeasor at the moment he signs the contract should be ignored, on the basis of a strong presumption at least that the contract, while executory, is reversible either by setting it aside or by a refusal to perform on the basis of misrepresentation. If, however, the victim performs, or fails to perform, some act towards a

---

[176] **4.33–4.35** above.

[177] *Raiffeisen Zentralbank Osterreich AG v Tranos AG* [2001] ILPr 9, [15] (Longmore J, EWHC).

[178] *Alfred Dunhill Ltd v Diffusion Internationale de Maroquinerie de Prestige SARL* [2002] 1 All ER (Comm) (EWHC). Also *ABCI v Banque Franco-Tunisienne* [2003] EWCA Civ 205 [2003] 2 Lloyd's Rep 146, [44]–[46].

third party, whether by entering into a contract[179] or by transferring an asset[180] or otherwise,[181] resulting in a diminution in the victim's assets or in his incurring liability to that third party then that act or omission should be considered to have caused him 'damage' at the moment, and in the country, where the act or omission becomes irreversible by his own actions. In the case of entry into a contract, the country of damage should be that of the country in which the contract was concluded. Although this fact may be open to manipulation and does not in any event appear to provide a particularly powerful connecting factor,[182] it can be objectively ascertained and seems preferable (for example) to the place where the third party may enforce the contract against the victim or the place of performance of the victim's obligations towards the third party. In the case of transfer of an asset, the country of damage should be that in which the asset was located immediately prior to transfer (and not the place where the victim gives instructions for its transfer). In the case of transfers from bank accounts, this country should be that in which the branch at which the account is held is situated or, in the case of Internet or other delocalized accounts, the bank's habitual residence determined in accordance with Art 23. The intangible nature of financial and other material loss, and the propensity for the connecting factors to be manipulated, may be factors to be taken into account in applying the 'escape clause' in Art 4(3) (**4.87** below).

Similar problems must be addressed in other situations involving non-material consequences of an event giving rise to damage. For example, what of a situation in which the first defendant (D1) in State R hacks into a computer server located in State S, steals information confidential to the claimant (C, a company habitually resident in State T), and transfers it electronically to the second defendant (D2) in State V, who then puts it to use in the manufacture of products sold in competition with C's products around Europe. Here, the consequences of the event(s) giving rise to damage are beyond the claimant's control. As against D1, there would appear to be a **4.68**

[179] *Raiffeisen Zentralbank v Tranos*, n 177 above; *London Helicopters Ltd v Heliportugal LDA-INAC* [2006] EWHC 108. Although the judge in the latter case formulated his test in terms of the place of receipt and reliance, the claimant had relied on the defendant's certificate in purchasing the helicopter engine from, and selling it to, third parties.

[180] *Minster Investments Ltd v Hyundai Heavy Industry Co Ltd* [1988] 2 Lloyd's Rep 621 (EWHC), as explained by Rix J in *Domicrest Ltd v Swiss Bank Corporation* [1999] QB 548, 566 (Rix J) (cf *Alfred Dunhill Ltd v Diffusion Internationale de Maroquinerie de Prestige SARL*, n 178 above, 960–1 (Mr K Rokison QC)).

[181] *Domicrest v Swiss Bank Corporation*, n 180 (release of secured assets).

[182] It has long been rejected as being significant in terms of identifying the law applicable to contractual obligations, even in the absence of choice by the parties (P Nygh, *Autonomy in International Contracts* (1999), 49–50).

strong case for identifying State S as the country of damage, as this is where the confidentiality of the claimant's information was first compromised and diluted by that defendant's actions. That, in a case such as this, the location of the server may provide only a tenuous connection to the tort/delict is again a factor to be taken into account in applying the Art 4(3) 'escape clause'. As against D2, it is not clear whether Art 4 applies at all, or if D2's obligation must be considered to arise out of an act of unfair competition falling within Art 6(1) and not excluded from its scope by Art 6(2).[183] If Art 4 does apply, there are arguments for locating the 'damage' in (1) State S (if it is sought to hold D2 responsible for D1's conduct), (2) State R (on the basis that this is the country from which the unauthorized disclosure was made by D1 to D2), (3) State V (on the basis that this is the country in which the confidential information was misused in the manufacture of goods), or (4) the countries in which the markets on which D2's products were sold in competition with C's products were located. Of these, State R, as the country in which D2's conduct directly interfered with the obligations that D1 owed to the claimant, appears the strongest candidate (and would have the advantage of fixing the damage in D2's case in a single country), but the position is far from clear.[184] The only country that can be safely excluded from consideration is State T, as any damage suffered there by the claimant must be seen as an indirect consequence of damage occurring elsewhere.[185]

Damage in More than One Country—the 'Mosaic View'

4.69 If the relevant damage is located in more than one country, the rule of applicable law in Art 4(1) requires the law of each of those countries to be applied on a distributive basis (the so-called mosaic view or *Mosaik-betrachtung*).[186] Having regard to the ECJ's decision in *Shevill v Presse Alliance SA*,[187] which applies the same concept in the context of the Brussels Convention, this distributive approach would appear to require the Member State court seised of the dispute to apply a country's law only with respect to damage occurring in the territory of that country (as well, presumably, as damage in other countries that is considered to be an 'indirect consequence' of the damage occurring in that country) and then to combine the

---

[183] **6.27–6.30** below.

[184] For critical analysis of the application of Art 4 to trade secrets cases, see C Wadlow, 'Trade secrets and the Rome II Regulation on the law applicable to non-contractual obligations' [2008] EIPR 309. The author (at 319) likens the challenges presented by the Regulation in such cases to those of a computer game designed by a 'warped and malevolent genius'.

[185] *Kitetechnology BV v Unicor GmbH* [1994] ILPr 598 (EWCA), a Brussels Convention case.

[186] **3.298–3.301** above.

[187] n 73 and **3.299** above.

results of applying each country's law to determine the outcome of the case before it. That seems straightforward enough if what the claimant seeks is compensation for his injury, and such an award is available in all of the countries whose law applies. In this type of case, the court (assuming that it has jurisdiction over the entire claim[188]) must proceed as if there were as many different obligations as the number of countries whose law applies and must combine the compensation awarded under the law of each country in a single award.

The mosaic view approach is, however, much less satisfactory in cases in **4.70** which the claimant seeks a remedy, whether monetary or non-monetary, which is available and would be given to him under the rules of one or more, but not all, of the countries concerned. Particular difficulties arise in the case of claims to prohibit future breaches of non-contractual obligations or to prevent further damage from an existing breach. One specific criticism leveled at the approach is that the distributive application of laws to a non-contractual obligation is unsatisfactory in its application to claims to prevent an activity (such as marketing via the Internet[189]) which produces its effects simultaneously in many countries, or globally, and in such a way that those effects cannot easily be controlled by reference to national boundaries.[190] In such cases, it is argued, fragmentation of the applicable law allows a claimant to select the law most favourable to him from among those that apply and to seek an injunction to prohibit the harmful effects of the activity in that country, an order that in practice will compel the defendant to cease his activity even in countries where it is entirely lawful. These concerns, however, may be overstated. In particular, the defendant in an injunction case of the type referred to above can legitimately seek to rely on the law of other countries where his activity produced its effects to argue that an injunction is an inappropriate measure to terminate injury or damage in the circumstances of the case.[191] Further, the prohibition by a Member State court of cross-border activity must be consistent with the requirements of the EC Treaty and, where applicable, the E-Commerce Directive.

It may be more difficult to avoid problems in applying the mosaic view **4.71** approach in the mirror image situation, in which the non-availability of injunctive or similar relief in one out of several countries may render

---

[188] **4.74** below.
[189] A Kur, 'Trademark Conflicts on the Internet: Territoriality Redefined', in J Basedow, J Drexl, A Kur, and A Metzger (eds), *Intellectual Property in the Conflict of Laws* (2005), 187–91.
[190] U Magnus and P Mankowski, n 103 above, Art 5, para 213.
[191] Regulation, Art 15(d).

worthless the protection afforded to the defendant in the other countries. This problem can perhaps be seen most clearly in the case of claims concerning the unlawful disclosure of confidential information.[192] As Sir John Donaldson noted in the *Spycatcher* case:[193]

> Confidential information is like an ice cube. Give it to the party who undertakes to keep it in his refrigerator and you still have an ice cube by the time the matter comes to trial. Either party may then succeed in obtaining possession of the cube. Give it to the party who has no refrigerator or will not agree to keep it in one, and by the time of the trial you just have a pool of water which neither party wants. It is the inherently perishable nature of confidential information which gives rise to unique problems.

4.72 As a result, it may be feared that the claimant's ability to protect his confidential information would, in practice, be limited to the lowest common denominator among the remedies available under the laws applied on a distributive basis. It would not appear open, except perhaps on the basis of public policy, for the court to award a remedy for a non-contractual obligation with respect to 'damage' likely to occur in a particular country that is not available under the law of that country.

4.73 In the face of the challenges of applying several potentially conflicting laws in a harmonious and just manner, it will be interesting to see whether Member State courts will seek to interpret the connecting factor in Art 4(1) in such a way as to locate the damage in a single country or will resort to the escape route provided by Art 4(3), allowing a single law to be applied with respect to all of the consequences of the tort/delict. In the case of confidential information, for example, it might be possible to identify the country of damage as being that in which the confidentiality of the claimant's information was or would be originally compromised as a result of the defendant's conduct and to treat later disclosures or abuses of that damage as indirect consequences of that original damage, to be left out of account. Alternatively, Art 4(3) may be relied on to displace the otherwise applicable law(s) in cases where there is a pre-existing relationship between the parties. Finally, if the obligation to protect the claimant's confidential information arises from an agreement between the parties, whether as an express or implied term, the matter may be treated as involving a 'contractual obligation' falling outside the scope of the Rome II Regulation and governed by the law applicable to the contract under the Rome I Regime.

---

[192] C Wadlow, 'Trade secrets and the Rome II Regulation on the law applicable to non-contractual obligations' [2008] EIPR 309, 314 describing the result of applying the 'mosaic view' approach to trade secrets cases as a 'culminating disaster'.

[193] *A-G v Newspaper Publishing plc* [1988] 1 Ch 333, 358 (EWCA).

The foregoing discussion has proceeded on the basis that the Member **4.74** State court has jurisdiction over the entire dispute between the parties. Under the Brussels I Regulation, however, a court other than those of the defendant's domicile or the place where the event giving rise to damage occurred may have jurisdiction only with respect to damage occurring within its territorial jurisdiction.[194] In such a case, Art 4(1) will point in practice towards application of the law of the forum.

D. EXCEPTIONS TO THE GENERAL RULE

SPECIAL RULES WITHIN CHAPTER II

Art 4(1) opens with the words 'unless otherwise provided for in this **4.75** Regulation'. According to Recital (19) to the Regulation, 'specific rules should be laid down for special torts/delicts where the general rule does not allow a reasonable balance to be struck between the interests at stake'. The relationship between Art 4 and the other provisions in Chapter II has been considered at **4.07–4.08** above.

RULES OF DISPLACEMENT

Recital (18) provides: **4.76**

The general rule in this Regulation should be the *lex loci damni* provided for in Article 4(1). Article 4(2) should be seen as an exception to this general principle, creating a special connection where the parties have their habitual residence in the same country. Article 4(3) should be understood as an 'escape clause' from Article 4(1) and (2) where it is clear from all the circumstances of the case that the tort/ delict is manifestly more closely connected with another country.

In the explanatory memorandum accompanying its proposal, the Com- **4.77** mission suggested that these rules of displacement reflect the concern that 'application of the basic rule might well be inappropriate where the situation has only a tenuous connection with the country where the damage occurs'.[195]

No *Depeçage*

Professor Symeonides has argued that the principal defect of the rules of **4.78** displacement in Arts 4(2) and 4(3) of the Rome II Regulation is that they do not allow the general rule to be departed from on an issue-by-issue

---

[194] Case C-68/93, *Shevill v Presse Alliance SA* [1995] ECR I-415 (**3.299** above).
[195] Commission Proposal, 12.

basis (*depeçage*).[196] The issue-by-issue approach would have been allowed by the single rule of displacement adopted by the European Parliament in its 1st Reading Position,[197] following (in this respect at least) the pre-existing UK statutory rules.[198] This aspect of the Parliament's proposal was criticized as '[e]xtremely dangerous for a consistent and homogeneous appreciation of a case',[199] a criticism that appears well-founded. There is, of course, no systemic reason why a legal system cannot, through its rules of private international law, combine rules originating in different legal systems in order to regulate a particular situation.[200] Indeed, the provisions of Chapter V and Art 26 of the Regulation[201] openly contemplate the possibility of more than one law applying to different aspects of a single case, and matters of evidence and procedure remain outside the Regulation's scope.[202] It is nevertheless desirable that the approach taken by a foreign legal system in regulating the civil consequences of particular events should, so far as possible, be treated as a coherent whole. The assumption, while not always reflecting constitutional reality, should be that choices made by a country's legislature or courts in relation to one element of its regulation of these matters are reflected in choices made in relation to other elements. Thus, for example, the imposition of a stricter standard of responsibility may be counterbalanced by limits on the level of liability.[203] Although cross-border situations undoubtedly present different challenges for legislatures and courts, and may justify different regulatory choices, the task of judges should be to apply the content of foreign law as it stands to the facts of the case before them and not to speculate as to whether different choices might have been made by a foreign legislature or court if it had the facts of the instant case in mind. Allowing the law applicable to non-contractual obligations to be determined on an

---

[196] S C Symeonides, n 9 above, 184–6, 195, 200–1. The author was also formerly of this view (see A Dickinson, 'Cross-Border Torts in EC Courts—A Response to the Proposed "Rome II" Regulation' (2002) 13 EBLR 367, 374–85). Professor Symeonides also criticizes the absence of a rule of displacement in situations where the habitual residence of the actors differs but their 'home' legal systems provide identical or functionally analogous rules (ibid, 196). For strong opposing views, see K Kreuzer in A Malatesta, *The Unification of Choice of Law Rules on Torts and Other Non-Contractual Obligations in Europe* (2006), 68; P J Kozyris, 'Rome II: Tort Conflicts on the Right Track! A Postscript to Symeon Symeonides' "Missed Opportunity"' (2008) 56 AJCL 471, 481.

[197] Art 4(4): 'In resolving the question of the applicable law, the court seised shall, where necessary, subject each specific issue of the dispute to separate analysis.'

[198] Private International Law (Miscellaneous Provisions) Act 1995, s 12(1).

[199] K Kreuzer in Malatesta, *Unification*, n 196 above, 68. Also P J Kozyris, n 196 above, 477–8.

[200] **3.39–3.40** above.

[201] See **Ch 15–16** below.

[202] Art 1(3).

[203] See, e.g., C van Dam, *European Tort Law*, n 133 above, paras 1206, 1216 comparing the different approaches of English and French law to civil liability for personal injury.

issue-by-issue basis creates the risk of either a 'slice and dice' approach to civil liability, creating a modified obligation that is unrecognizable to its legal system of origin, or of placing an unsupportable burden on individual judges requiring them to consider whether applying a different law to a particular issue would undermine the interests of the country whose law would apply to the remaining issues. Although the 'all or nothing' approach is not perfect, and it has given rise to genuine concerns in the context of traffic accidents,[204] it has the attraction not only of coherence but also of enhancing legal certainty.

In any event, it is now too late to re-write history. The current position is **4.79** clear: neither Art 4(2) nor Art 4(3) permits *depeçage*, which occurs under the Regulation only to the extent that it is mandated or permitted under Chapter V or as a result of the exclusion of matters of evidence and procedure. Under Art 15, the law applicable to non-contractual obligations under the Regulation applies to all of the matters set out. It is not possible for the court to divide those matters, with one law applying to some of them and another law applying to the others.

Displacement in Favour of the Country of Common Habitual Residence

Under Art 4(2), if the person claimed to be liable and the person sustaining **4.80** damage both have their habitual residence in the same country at the time when the damage occurs, the law of that country shall apply instead of the law applicable under Art 4(1). According to the Commission:[205]

Paragraph 2 introduces a special rule where the person claimed to be liable and the person who has allegedly sustained damage are habitually resident in the same country, the law of that country being applicable. This is the solution adopted by virtually all the Member States, either by means of a special rule or by the rule concerning connecting factors applied in the courts. It reflects the legitimate expectations of the two parties.

This last statement appears too sweeping.[206] Although the application **4.81** of the law of the country of habitual residence of the relevant actors to

---

[204] See **1.76** above for a summary of the European Parliament's proposals in this regard. See also the different views expressed by Professors Malatesta and Bona in their respective papers on this subject area in Malatesta, *Unification*, n 196 above, 85–106, 249–70. Art 30(1) requires the Commission to present, not later than 20 August 2001, a report on the application of the Regulation, including a study of the relationship between the Regulation and the Hague Traffic Accidents Convention.

[205] Ibid.

[206] See also T Petch, 'The Rome II Regulation: An Update' [2006] JIBLR 449, 455; S C Symeonides, n 9 above, 195. CF TW Dornis, '"When in Rome, do as the Romans do"—A Defense of the *Lex Domicilii Communis* in the Rome II Regulation' (2007) 4 The European Legal Forum 152.

determine certain aspects of non-contractual liability between them may in some circumstances reflect their reasonable expectations, particularly if they have a pre-existing relationship, it is not difficult to dispel the notion that this is a universal truth. Take, for example, the situation in which the claimant (A) is struck by a car driven by the defendant (B) while crossing a road in France. A and B are both habitually resident in England. Under the French *loi Badinter*, liability for traffic accidents is strict.[207] Under English law, liability is based on negligence, albeit subject to a high standard of care.[208] Damages for personal injury in England are typically higher than those in France.[209] In these circumstances, it can scarcely be said to reflect the parties' legitimate expectations that the basis and extent of B's liability should be governed by English law. Even if one supposes that A is a passenger in the car and that A and B are husband and wife (or employee and employer), the application of English law to judge B's responsibility for his conduct might well come as a surprise to A, although both parties would perhaps be more willing (at least in principle) to accept the proposition that questions of compensation should be determined by their place of common habitual residence.[210] If the facts are reversed, with the incident occurring in England and A and B being habitually resident in France, B might be similarly surprised to find that he owes a higher standard of responsibility when he runs over a fellow countryman than when he injures an Englishman or another foreigner in England.

4.82 In these, and similar circumstances, it may be argued that the 'escape clause' in Art 4(3) provides a solution for any situation in which Art 4(2) may be thought to depart from the parties' reasonable expectations. The difficulty with this argument, as both the language of the Regulation and the Commission recognize,[211] is that Art 4(3) imposes a very high threshold for the displacement of the law applicable under Art 4(1) or Art 4(2). That threshold would almost certainly not be reached in the second scenario contemplated above (where A is a passenger and has a relationship with B based in England). It would provide a more promising argument in

---

[207] C van Dam, n 133 above, para 1404-1.

[208] C van Dam, ibid, para 1404-3. The majority of Member States impose liability without fault in traffic accident cases, subject to defences of varying width. For a comparative survey of liability rules, see para 2.1 of the background note prepared by the EP Policy Department in March 2007 ('Compensation of Victims of Cross-Border Road Traffic Accidents in the EU: Assessment of Selected Options', EP document IP/C/JURI/FWC/2006-171 LOT 2 PE 378.94, available at <http://www.europarl.europa.eu/comparl/juri/hearings/20070319/background_en.pdf>).

[209] C van Dam, ibid, paras 1202-7.

[210] Cf *Boys v Chaplin* [1971] AC 356 (HL).

[211] **4.84** below.

the first scenario (where A has no prior relationship with B), but this identifies the principal weakness of the 'common habitual residence' rule in Art 4(2), that it automatically displaces the general rule on the basis of a connection between the parties that is much weaker than the type of pre-existing relationship that, in Art 4(3), provides only a possible basis for displacing the otherwise applicable law. In other words, Art 4(2) gives too much weight to the commonality of the parties' residence. It would have been preferable if a 'common habitual residence' had been identified in Art 4(3) as a factor that might, depending on the circumstances, justify displacement of the general rule.[212] Again, however, it is too late to re-write the regulation.

Other aspects of this rule of displacement require further explanation, as follows: **4.83**

1. *Habitual residence:* The concept of 'habitual residence', partly defined in Art 23, is considered at **3.47–3.58**.

2. *'Person claimed to be liable':* Art 4(2) refers to 'person claimed to be liable' (in the French text, *'la personne dont la responsabilité est invoqée'*), a term appearing also in Arts 5(1) and 17. Four possible meanings of this expression may be canvassed, each of which may produce different results in individual cases. First, that it refers, individually, to each person (usually in the position of a defendant[213]) whose responsibility it is sought to establish in the proceedings, the test being applied on a party-by-party basis. Secondly, that, notwithstanding the use of the singular 'person', it is capable of referring, collectively, to all of the persons whose responsibility it is sought to establish in the proceedings. Thirdly, that it is capable of referring to every person against whom a claim for particular damage has been or might in the future be made, whether or not that person is sued in the proceedings. Fourthly, that it refers to the person (or, possibly, persons) whose conduct caused the damage, whether or not that person is sued.[214] Of these, the first is to be preferred, as being more easily reconciled

---

[212] This solution was suggested, for example, by Austria (Council document 9009/04 ADD 1 [3.5.2005], 2), Spain (ibid, ADD 10 [18.5.2004], 2), Ireland (ibid, ADD 13 [24.5.2004], 4), and the UK (ibid, ADD 15) [26.5.2004]). The EP 1st Reading Position, Art 4(3)(a) identified the common habitual residence of the person claimed to be liable and the person sustaining loss or damage (alongside the fact of their residence in countries having substantially identical laws) as a factor which might justify displacement, but only 'as far as loss-distribution and legal capacity are concerned'.

[213] But not, for example, if the claim is for a declaration of non-liability or a direct action against an insurer.

[214] This last view receives some support from Art 17, which refers to 'the conduct of the person claimed to be liable'.

not only with the legislator's choice of words but also with Recital (18),[215] with the view of the Commission,[216] and with the demands of legal certainty. It also appears consistent with the approach taken by the ECJ in applying the *lis alibi pendens* rules under the Brussels Convention.[217] The second and third possible meanings, on the other hand, would generate uncertainty: the second would potentially allow the claimant to manipulate the applicable law by choosing which defendants to sue and the third is unworkable, as there appears no basis for assessing whether a particular claim is justified or not. The fourth possible meaning seems inadequate, as a claim of responsibility in tort/delict may be based on an event that is not an act or omission of a particular person (e.g. injury caused by an animal or building). Further, Art 15(g), which applies the law applicable under the Regulation to *'liability* for the acts of another person' appears inconsistent with this meaning.

Even so, the need to adopt a party by party approach highlights further deficiencies in Art 4(2), as (unless the court intervenes by deploying the escape clause in Art 4(3)) the application of the common habitual residence rule may result in claims arising from the same event and with respect to the same damage being governed by different laws. In particular, in cases of joint, common, or vicarious liability, Art 4(2) may displace the generally applicable law for claims against one defendant, habitually resident in the same country as the person sustaining damage, but not another. If, in the example given above, a French resident driver (C) had also been involved in the accident or if B had been acting in the course of his employment for his French-based employer (D), Art 4(2) would apply to a claim by A against B but not against C or D. This, in turn, may raise complex issues when it comes to assessing questions of joint responsibility and contribution.[218]

3. *'Person sustaining damage'*: Art 4(2) also refers to the 'person sustaining damage'.[219] At first sight, it might appear possible to argue that this choice of wording supports the view that Art 4(2) applies only to cases of damage to the person. In this connection, it may be noted that Art 7 refers to 'damage *sustained by* persons or property' in restricting the kinds of damage that fall within the scope of that Article. There is, however, no suggestion in the *travaux préparatoires* that the habitual residence exception was intended to be so restricted. Further, the French language version of the

---

[215] **4.76** above, referring to 'the parties'.
[216] Text to n 205 above, referring to 'the two parties'.
[217] Case C-406/92, *The Tatry/The Maciej Rataj* [1994] ECR I-5439, paras 29–36.
[218] **14.17** and **14.115–14.120** below.
[219] See also Art 5(1)(a) referring to the 'person sustaining the damage'.

Regulation uses the expression '*la personne lésée*' in Art 4(2), while referring instead in Art 7 to '*dommages . . . subis par des personnes ou causés à
des biens*'. Art 4(2) should apply, therefore, whatever the nature of the
damage.

Although Recital (18) refers to 'the parties', the choice of terminology here
and elsewhere in the Regulation suggests that the identity of the 'person
sustaining damage' will not necessarily correspond to the party (usually
in the position of claimant) who seeks to establish the responsibility of
another in the proceedings. In this connection, a contrast may be drawn
with the expression 'the person seeking compensation' which appears in
Arts 6(3)(b) and 7. Against this background, the expression 'person sustaining damage' appears capable of bearing one of two possible meanings,
depending in turn on the meaning given to the term 'damage' in Art 4(2).
If 'damage' bears the (broader) meaning given to it in Art 2(1), it would
seem to follow that the 'person sustaining damage' is the person affected
by the consequences of the tort/delict in respect of which the proceedings
have been brought, whether those consequences are characterized as
direct or indirect. If, however, 'damage' bears the (narrower) meaning
given to it in Art 4(1) (excluding indirect consequences of the harmful
event), the 'person sustaining damage' will be the person who is the primary victim of the tort/delict. On the view taken above as to the basis for
separating direct and indirect consequences within Art 4(1),[220] that person
may be neither a claimant nor a person represented by a claimant.

For consistency, it is suggested that 'damage' should bear the same meaning in Art 4(2) as it does in Art 4(1) and that the term 'person sustaining
damage' should be read as referring to the primary victim of an event giving rise to damage. For example, if, in the example given above,[221] A had
been killed in the traffic accident and A's widow E (habitually resident in
Poland) had sued B both as A's personal representative and, in her own
right, claiming damages for loss of support and bereavement, A would
remain the 'person sustaining damage' for the purpose of all of the claims
brought by E, with the consequence that Art 4(2) would apply (leading to
the application of English law) notwithstanding her habitual residence in
Poland. The common habitual residence of the person claimed to be liable
and the actual claimant may, however, be a factor to be taken into account
in applying the more flexible rule of displacement in Art 4(3).

4. *Timing:* The test of common habitual residence must be applied at the
time when the relevant[222] damage occurs, not (for example) the date of the

---

[220] **4.39–4.45** above.
[221] **4.81**.
[222] See point 3 above.

harmful event or the date of proceedings. If that damage is sustained over a period of time, it is submitted that the earliest point in time should be taken. A change in habitual residence after that point in time will not affect the application of the rule of displacement in Art 4(2),[223] although it may be a factor to be taken into account in applying Art 4(3).

Displacement in Favour of a Country having a 'Manifestly Closer Connection'

Application generally

4.84 Under Art 4(3), where it is clear from all the circumstances of the case that the tort/delict is *manifestly* more closely connected with a country other than the country where damage occurred (Art 4(1)) or the country of the parties' common habitual residence (Art 4(2)), the law of that other country shall apply instead. In the explanatory memorandum accompanying its Proposal, the Commission emphasized the narrow ambit of this exception:[224]

> Like Article 4(5) of the Rome Convention, paragraph 3 is a general exception clause which aims to bring a degree of flexibility, enabling the court to adapt the rigid rule to an individual case so as to apply the law that reflects the centre of gravity of the situation.

> Since this clause generates a degree of unforeseeability as to the law that will be applicable, it must remain exceptional. Experience with the Rome Convention, which begins by setting out presumptions, has shown that the courts in some Member States tend to begin in fact with the exception clause and seek the law that best meets the proximity criterion, rather than starting from these presumptions.[225] That is why the rules in Article 3(1) and (2) of the proposed Regulation[226] are drafted in the form of rules and not of mere presumptions. To make clear that the exception clause really must be exceptional, paragraph 3 requires the obligation to be 'manifestly more closely connected' with another country.

4.85 Art 4(3) must, therefore, be considered as exceptional, requiring strong and clear reasons for displacing the law otherwise applicable under Arts 4(1) and (2). The addition of the word 'manifestly', which does not appear in Art 4(5) of the Rome Convention but has been added to the

[223] Cf Case C-1/04, *Staubitz-Schreiber* [2006] ECR I-701 (Insolvency Regulation).
[224] Commission Proposal, 12 referring to Art 3(3) of the Proposal in very similar terms to Art 4(3) of the Regulation. The footnotes have been added.
[225] For the UK experience, see J Hill, 'Choice of Law in Contract under the Rome Convention: The Approach of the UK Courts' (2004) 53 ICLQ 325; S Attrill, 'Choice of Law in Contract: The Missing Pieces of the Article 4 Jigsaw' (2004) 53 ICLQ 549.
[226] Reflected in Arts 4(1) and 4(2) of the Regulation in its final form.

corresponding provision in the Rome I Regulation,[227] suggests a test focusing on objective factors, including outward expressions of the law applicable to the parties' relationship, rather than the subjective intentions or expectations of the parties. In this connection, it may be noted that the Commission suggested in its Amended Proposal (responding to the EP 1st Reading Position) that the following additional wording be added to paragraph 3:[228]

For the purpose of assessing the existence of a manifestly closer connection with another country, account shall be taken *inter alia* of the expectations of the parties regarding the applicable law.

That suggestion was not accepted by the Council in its Common Position,[229] and did not find its way into the Regulation in its final form.

Art 4(3) requires the Member State court, in applying the rule, to consider **4.86** 'all the circumstances of the case'. For this purpose, the court should not limit itself to considering the matters relied on by the claimant to support the claim. As the following words indicate, however, those circumstances must be relevant to the question whether the tort/delict is manifestly more closely connected with a country (State B) other than that whose law applies under Art 4(1) or (2) (State A). The court cannot, therefore, apply a different test, by considering (for example) whether justice would be better served by the application of the rules of State A than those of State B.[230] The reference in Art 4(3) to 'the tort/delict' (in the French text, '*fait dommageable*')[231] should here be taken to refer in combination to the event giving rise to damage and all of the consequences of that event, including indirect consequences. Against this background, and having regard to Art 24 which excludes *renvoi*, it would not appear to be permissible for a court to have regard to the rules of applicable law that would be applied by the courts of State A (or State B) if they were to be seised of the matter.[232] Such rules are extraneous to the question that the court that is actually seised of the dispute between the parties must ask itself under Art 4(3).

---

[227] Rome I Regulation, Art 4(3) ('Where it is clear from all the circumstances of the case that the contract is manifestly more closely connected with a country other than that indicated in paragraphs 1 or 2, the contract shall be governed by the law of the country with which it is most closely connected').

[228] Commission Amended Proposal, Art 5(3).

[229] Common Position, Art 4(3). The Commission, in its response to the Common Position (COM (2006) 566 final) did not take any point on this.

[230] **3.26–3.28** above.

[231] Compare Art 4(1) referring to 'an obligation arising out of a tort/delict', which appears more legalistic.

[232] Cf A Rushworth and A Scott, n 49 above, 273.

4.87 The case for applying State A or State B may be strengthened (or weakened), for example, by:

1. The existence of circumstances linking the tort/delict to State A or State B, including, without limitation, (a) the presence (or absence) of factual connectors other than damage (Art 4(1)) or common habitual residence (Art 4(2)) linking the tort/delict to State A, (b) any factual connectors linking the tort/delict to State B, (c) any pre-existing relationship between the parties,[233] and (d) the personal connections of the persons involved, including (where applicable) (i) the parties, (ii) the tortfeasor, if not the defendant, (iii) the victim, if not the claimant, (iv) any primary victim not represented by the claimant, and (v) any other person whose conduct is closely connected to the tort/delict (including a person claimed to be jointly liable).

2. The permanence (or transience) of the circumstances that link the tort/delict to State A or State B.

3. The nature of the circumstances linking the tort/delict to State A or State B and, in particular, whether those linking factors were foreseeable, tangible, accidental, artificial, or open to manipulation.

4. The occurrence of personal injury or damage to property (as opposed to non-material damage) in State A.

4.88 If, in all the circumstances of the case, there is any room for doubt as to whether the tort/delict is more closely connected to State A than State B, the law of State A should be applied. The burden of proving the existence of circumstances establishing a manifestly closer connection should be on the party who seeks to displace the law applicable under Art 4(1) or 4(2).[234]

4.89 The following additional points may be made:

1. *No* depeçage: Art 4(3), like Art 4(2), operates on an 'all or nothing', and not an issue-by-issue, basis.[235] The court must look for connections to the 'tort/delict' and not to the particular issues which the parties have presented for determination. Whether, for example, the defendant has admitted liability or quantum is agreed between the parties should not be a relevant factor in the application of the 'escape clause'.[236] It follows that Art 4(3) is significantly less flexible than the rule of displacement in s 12 of the UK Private International Law (Miscellaneous Provisions)

---

[233] **4.90–4.95** below.
[234] Dicey, Morris & Collins, 1st supplement, para S35-197.
[235] **4.78–4.79** above. The Council's Rome II Committee considered and rejected the European Parliament's proposal to allow *depeçage* (see Council document 11515/05 [27.7.2005]).
[236] Cf Dicey, Morris & Collins, 1st supplement, para S35-197.

Act 1995,[237] which is capable of being applied to the determination of a particular issue.

2. *Relationship with Arts 4(1) and 4(2)*: Art 4(3) refers to the application of the law of a country 'other than that indicated in paragraphs 1 or 2'.[238] The use of the plural, 'paragraphs', might be thought to suggest that Art 4(3) cannot be invoked to displace the law applicable under Art 4(2), by reason of common habitual residence, in favour of the law originally identified by reference to Art 4(1).[239] On this view, Art 4(3) also could not be applied to select one of a number of laws applicable under Art 4(1) by reason of the occurrence of damage in more than one country.[240] Neither argument can be accepted. The Commission described this as a 'general exception clause' and its sphere of operation should not be restricted without clear words. The reference should be to a country different from that (or those) indicated by whichever of paragraphs 1 or 2 has identified the law from which it is sought to escape.

3. *Timing*: Unlike Art 4(2), Art 4(3) does not specify the time when the relevant circumstances connecting the tort/delict to State A or State B are to be compared. As a result, it should be applied at the time that the law applicable to the non-contractual obligation is determined. Indeed, Art 2(3)(b) would appear to contemplate that the court will have regard not only to fresh consequences of the event giving rise to damage, occurring between the date of issue of proceedings and the date on which it finally determines the applicable law but also any further consequences that are likely to occur in the future.

A pre-existing relationship between the parties[241]

Art 4(3) gives only one example of circumstances in which a manifestly **4.90** closer connection *might* exist with a country other than that whose law applies under Art 4(1) or Art 4(2), referring to 'a pre-existing relationship between the parties, such as a contract, that is closely connected with the tort/delict in question'. The wording of the Regulation, however, is not specific as to whether this connecting factor points towards application of the law of the country in which the pre-existing relationship is based or the law applicable to the pre-existing relationship. Although in many cases, a relationship will be governed by the law of the country in which

---

[237] **1.10** above.
[238] Compare Recital (18) referring to 'an "escape clause" from Article 1 and 2'.
[239] A Scott and A Rushworth, n 49 above, 281; cf Dicey, Morris & Collins, 1st supplement, para S35-197.
[240] **3.300** above.
[241] Also A Scott and A Rushworth, n 49 above, 303–5.

it is based, that will not always be the case. Some support for the view that the reference should be exclusively to the law of the country in which the relationship is based is provided by (a) the apparent contrast in the first sentence of Art 4(3) between 'country' and 'law of the country', suggesting perhaps that a geographical rather than legal connection was intended, and (b) the undoubted fact that not every pre-existing relationship will have an identifiable governing law.[242] On the other hand, it may be countered that (1) Art 25 links the concept of a 'country' to a territorial unit of a State with its own rules of law, thereby weakening any inference to be drawn from the different terminology used in Art 4(3), and (2) more significantly, the explanatory memorandum accompanying the Commission Proposal strongly supports the conclusion that the rule is capable of, and indeed will usually be taken to, connect the tort/delict with the law applicable to the relationship in question.[243] Thus, the Commission Proposal refers repeatedly to 'the law applicable to the pre-existing relationship' as well as to a 'choice of law clause'.[244]

4.91 Accordingly, the fact of a pre-existing relationship would appear capable of supporting a manifestly closer connection to either the country whose law applies to that relationship or the country in which the relationship is centred. That is consistent with the approach taken under the pre-existing English statutory rules.[245] On this view, as the law applicable to a preexisting relationship[246] cannot be determined by reference to the Regulation's rules of applicable law for non-contractual obligations, that law must be identified by reference to the forum's other rules of private international law. For relationships other than contractual relationships falling within the scope of the Rome I Regime, which provides a common set of rules across the Community for contractual obligations, that creates the possibility of a lack of consistency between Member State courts in their application of Art 4(3).[247]

---

[242] S C Symeonides, n 9 above, 203–4.

[243] Commission Proposal, 11–12.

[244] See, e.g., the extracts quoted at text to nn 249 and 258 below.

[245] *Morin v Bonhams & Brooks Ltd* [2003] EWCA Civ 1802; [2004] 1 Lloyd's Rep 702, [23] (Mance LJ); *Trafigura Beheer BV v Kookmin Bank Co* [2006] EWHC 1450 (Comm); [2006] 2 Lloyd's Rep 455, [101]–[104] (Aikens J); cf A Briggs, *Agreements on Jurisdiction and Choice of Law* (2008), paras 10.64–10.68.

[246] Other than those arising from a non-contractual obligation, such as a tort/delict. The absence of specific reference in Art 4(3) to a relationship of this character, in contrast to Arts 10 and 11 (**10.25–10.26** and **11.19** below), may be thought to exclude the possibility that this type of relationship can be taken into account.

[247] G Carella, 'Other Non-Contractual Obligations' in Malatesta, *Unification*, n 196 above, 78–9.

One other aspect of the law applicable to a pre-existing relationship for the **4.92** purposes of the Regulation must be noted. The Regulation contains no specific provisions corresponding to those in the Rome I Regime[248] intended to protect parties considered to be in a weaker bargaining position, in particular consumers and employees. In the explanatory memorandum accompanying its Proposal, however, the Commission noted that:[249]

[W]here the pre-existing relationship consists of a consumer or employment contract and the contract contains a choice-of-law clause in favour of a law other than the law of the consumer's habitual place of residence, the place where the employment contract is habitually performed or, exceptionally, the place where the employee was hired, the secondary connection mechanism cannot have the effect of depriving the weaker party of the protection of the law otherwise applicable. The proposed Regulation does not contain an express rule to this effect since the Commission considers that the solution is already implicit in the protective rules of the Rome Convention: Articles 5 and 6 would be deflected from their objective if the secondary connection validated the choice of the parties as regards non-contractual obligations but their choice was at least partly invalid as regards their contract.

It remains to be seen whether and, if so, how this restriction will be given **4.93** effect to by Member State courts and the ECJ on the wording of Art 4(3). One possibility is that Art 4(3) must be taken to connect non-contractual obligations that are closely connected to a relationship arising from a consumer or employment contract falling within Arts 5 and 6 of the Rome Convention, or the corresponding provisions of the Rome I Regulation, not only to the country whose law is chosen by the parties to govern that contract but also to the consumer's country of habitual residence or, as the case may be, the country whose law would apply to the employment contract in the absence of choice. That dual connection may make it more difficult for the non-consumer or employer to rely on Art 4(3) to displace the law otherwise applicable under Arts 4(1) and 4(2). That does not mean, however, that the rules of applicable law for consumer and employment contracts in the Rome I Regime should be applied automatically to non-contractual obligations, so as (for example) to require the application of the law of the consumer's country of habitual residence. The flexibility inherent in Art 4(3) remains in all cases. Similarly, although the requirement in Art 14 that agreements on choice of law made before the event giving rise to damage occurred be 'freely negotiated'[250] cannot be read

---

[248] Rome Convention, Arts 5–6; Rome I Regulation, Arts 6, 8.
[249] Commission Proposal, 12.
[250] **13.38–13.41** below.

into Art 4(3), the fact that the relationship between the parties is governed by a non-negotiable contract containing a choice of law provision may be taken into account as a factor diluting the strength of the connection to the law applicable to that contract.

4.94 The Commission also suggested that the reference to a pre-existing relationship 'is flexible enough to allow the court to take account of a contractual relationship that is still only contemplated, as in the case of the breakdown of negotiations or of annulment of a contract, or of a family relationship'.[251] Elsewhere in its explanatory memorandum, the Commission suggests that 'the expression "pre-existing relationship" applies particularly to pre-contractual relationships and to void contracts'.[252] To a common lawyer, it may seem artificial to describe the exchanges between parties negotiating a contract as a 'pre-existing relationship', although the civil law doctrine of *culpa in contrahendo* rests on the idea that initiation of contractual obligations creates a relationship of obligation belonging or related to the law of contract.[253] A debate on whether this terminology is apt to describe the continuum of communications in contemplation of contract would, in any event, be largely academic as (a) the appearance in the final sentence of Art 4(3) of the words 'in particular' emphasizes that a connection between a tort/delict and a 'pre-existing relationship' is but one example of circumstances that may justify displacement of the otherwise applicable law, and (b) Art 12 contains a specific rule for 'non-contractual obligations arising out of dealings prior to the conclusion of a contract' (*culpa in contrahendo*),[254] which includes non-contractual obligations originating in a contemplated contractual relationship that would otherwise lie within Art 4.[255] So far as 'void contracts' are concerned, it seems appropriate to recognize a 'pre-existing relationship' as a matter of fact even if the law's response to the existence of the vitiating factor is to treat the contract as if it had never existed.[256] That relationship may establish a connection either to the putative applicable law or to the law of the country in which the contract was centred. Art 10(1)(e) of the Rome Convention and Art 12(1)(e) of the Rome Convention require the consequences of nullity of a contract to be treated

---

[251] Commission Proposal, 12.

[252] Ibid, 21.

[253] C von Bar, *The Common European Law of Torts* (vol 1: 1998; reprinted 2003), paras 471, 474–6; *Fonderie Officine Meccaniche Tacconi SpA v Heinrich Wagner Sinto Maschinenfabrik GmbH* [2002] ECR I-7357, para 25 (Brussels Convention).

[254] **Ch 12** below.

[255] **4.08** above.

[256] Cf *Baring Bros & Co Ltd v Cunninghame District Council* (1996) The Times, 30 September; [1997] CLC 108 (Court of Session (Outer House), Scotland).

as matters of contractual obligation falling outside the scope of the Rome II Regulation.[257] Nevertheless, there may still be a close connection between a void contract and a tort/delict committed, for example, in the course of 'performing' the supposed obligations.

As to the application of Art 4(3) in cases involving a pre-existing rela- **4.95** tionship, the Commission emphasized that 'the law applicable to the pre-existing relationship does not apply automatically and the court enjoys a degree of discretion to decide whether there is a sufficient connection between the non-contractual obligations and the law applicable to the relationship'.[258] The use of the word 'discretion' is unfortunate, as (taken out of context) it might be thought to suggest that the court, in making its decision, may take into account matters other than the relative connections to the country whose law otherwise applies under Art 4(1) or 4(2) and the country whose law applies to the parties' relationship (for example, the consequences of applying the rules of those two countries to the case before him[259] or the private international law of a non-Member State[260]). The requirement that the court focus solely on the link between the relationship and the tort/delict in question is, however, reinforced by the closing words of Art 4(3) requiring that the two be 'closely connected'. This requirement should be applied objectively and not by reference to the parties' private motives for the performance of a particular act.[261]

E. TORT/DELICT—SPECIFIC EXAMPLES

Against this background, this section considers certain types of claim to **4.96** which Art 4 may apply, and which raise particular problems. These categories are considered mainly from the viewpoint of English law but would, of course, extend to analogous claims under the law of another country.

Quasi-Delict

Unlike some language versions[262] of Art 5(3) of the Brussels Convention, the **4.97** Rome II Regulation does not specifically refer to 'quasi-delict'. That category is

---

[257] **3.108** above.
[258] Commission Proposal, 12.
[259] **4.86** above.
[260] Ibid.
[261] Cf A Rushworth and A Scott, n 49 above, 304.
[262] e.g. English, French, Spanish.

unknown in the English law of obligations. In Roman law, the category of quasi-delict included a residue of actions dealing, variously, with liability for persons and things, for example liability of occupiers to those on the street below, liability of ship-owners and publicans for damages caused by their business 'because they employed unreliable persons', the liability of animal keepers, and the liability of the *paterfamilias* for delicts by children of the house.[263] These actions appeared to have in common a stricter form of liability for events that could not, in most cases,[264] be directly attributed to the defendant's acts or omissions. In modern law, the term *quasi-délit* appears in the Civil Codes of France, Belgium, and Luxembourg 'where it has from the outset been a synonym for liability for negligence'.[265] Whatever the common denominator of obligations described under national law as quasi-delictual, there is little doubt that they fall within the scope of Chapter II of the Regulation, and principally within Art 4, at least insofar as they concern the defendant's responsibility for the adverse consequences of an event having harmful consequences for another person. Accordingly, the Commission's suggestion in the explanatory memorandum accompanying its Proposal that 'obligations relating to what in some jurisdictions is termed "quasi-delict" or "quasi-contract"' fall outside the category of 'tort or delict'[266] should be rejected. As Recital (11) makes clear, the Regulation extends to non-contractual obligations arising out of strict liability. As these obligations cannot comfortably be accommodated within any of the rules in Chapter III, Art 4 appears the natural home for them.

Action Paulienne

4.98 The question whether and, if so, where the *action paulienne* under French law, and similar claims recognized in other legal systems, fits within the Regulation has already been addressed in **Chapter 3**. In summary, there appears no compelling reason why these claims cannot be considered to fall within Art 4, with the place of damage for the purposes of Art 4(1) being the country in which the creditor has lost his opportunity to enforce against a particular asset or the assets generally of the defendant.[267]

---

[263] C von Bar, n 253 above, para 7. Also R Zimmerman, *The Law of Obligations: Roman Foundations of the Civilian Tradition* (1996), 16–18.

[264] The example given in Justinian's Institutes (Book IV, para 5) of liability of a judge for breach of his official duties seems impossible to reconcile with this generalization

[265] C von Bar, n 253 above, para 8.

[266] Commission Proposal, 8.

[267] **3.249–3.258** above.

Equitable Obligations[268]

It will be clear from the preceding discussion,[269] as well as the restricted nature **4.99** of the exclusion of trust obligations in Art 1(2)(e), that the Rome II Regulation may apply to obligations that an English lawyer would recognize as 'equitable obligations', i.e. as originating in the jurisprudence of the courts of equity prior to their union with the common law courts.[270] Accordingly, for example, claims for breach of trust, breach of fiduciary duty, and breach of confidence[271] may fall within the scope of the Regulation, although whether they do so in a particular case will depend on whether (a) the obligation in question is 'contractual' or 'non-contractual',[272] and (b) a non-contractual obligation falls within the scope of any of the exclusions in Art 1(2).[273] Further, in those Member States party to the Hague Trust Convention (and, in particular, the UK and Luxembourg that have chosen to extend the Convention to trusts declared by judicial decisions) the rules of applicable law contained in the Regulation may be displaced by those in the Convention.[274]

Of those equitable claims falling within the scope of the Regulation, it **4.100** seems likely, however curious the juxtaposition may seem to an English lawyer, that many[275] will be characterized as arising in tort/delict and subject to the general rule in Art 4. In the main, the essential basis of these claims is that the defendant's conduct falls short of that expected of him by rules of equitable origin (in terms of honesty, loyalty, diligence, or otherwise) and that he should be restrained from further 'inequitable' conduct and/or required to compensate the claimant or to account to him for the consequences of his conduct. This fits the pattern of responsibility for conduct that is the hallmark of a tort/delict under the Rome II Regulation.[276]

---

[268] For more detailed analysis, focussing mainly on the pre-existing rules of English law, see T M Yeo, *Choice of Law for Equitable Doctrines* (2004), ch 8.

[269] See, in particular, **3.63**, **3.243** and **4.06** above.

[270] T M Yeo, n 268 above, para 8.58.

[271] For the application of the Regulation's rules to claims concerning the disclosure of confidential information, see **4.71–4.73** above and **6.29** below.

[272] For discussion of this aspect in relation to fiduciary duties, see **3.141–3.142** above.

[273] **3.162–3.169** (director's equitable duties), **3.173-3.207** above (breach of trust), **3.225** and **3.227** above (breach of confidence/privacy).

[274] **3.201–3.207** above.

[275] But not all. For example, the fiduciary duties of a trustee *de son tort* or a shadow director (**3.142** above) may more appropriately be regulated by Art 11 (*negotiorum gestio*) and Art 12 (*culpa in contrahendo*) will apply to non-contractual, equitable claims arising out of dealings prior to the conclusion of a contract.

[276] **4.06** above.

Dishonest assistance

4.101 A good example of an equitable obligation falling within Art 4 is the accessory liability of a person who dishonestly assists a breach of trust or fiduciary duty to the beneficiary of the trust or duty.[277] In *Grupo Torras SA v Al
Sabah*, the Court of Appeal, in considering the law applicable to a claim of
this kind under the pre-existing English rules, endorsed the view that
equitable wrongdoing, such as dishonest assistance, had 'marked similarities' to a tort in that it imposed liability to pay damages for fault.[278]
Subsequently, in *Casio Computer Co Ltd v Sayo*,[279] the English Court of
Appeal held that a dishonest assistance claim fell within Art 5(3) of the
Brussels Convention as a 'matter relating to tort, delict or quasi-delict'.
The Court rejected the argument that the claim lacked the necessary
element of a causal connection between the damage suffered and an
event attributable to the defendant.[280]

4.102 For this type of claim, the country of damage should be considered to be
the country in which the asset misappropriated by the defaulting trustee/
fiduciary was situated at the time of the misappropriation facilitated by
the defendant's conduct. That is the country in which relations between
the claimant and the trustee/fiduciary are affected by the defendant's
interference.[281] Insofar as decisions of the English courts concerning
Art 5(3) of the Brussels Convention may favour (without accepting as correct) the view that the place of 'dissipation' of the assets is the place of
damage for these purposes,[282] it is respectfully submitted that they should
not be followed in the context of the Rome II Regulation. The laundering
of assets appears to be an indirect consequence of the defendant's involvement in their misappropriation in the first place.

Knowing receipt

4.103 The editors of Dicey, Morris & Collins agree that 'a claim for dishonest
assistance is likely to be classified as tortious for Regulation purposes'.[283]

---

[277] *Royal Brunei Airlines Sdn Bhd v Tan* [1995] 2 AC 378 (PC). The defendant's liability is
often, but inaccurately, referred to as the liability of a constructive trustee (*Dubai Aluminium
Co Ltd v Salaam* [2003] 2 AC 366, [141]–[142] (Lord Millett, UKHL)).

[278] [2001] Lloyd's Rep Bank 36; [2001] CLC 221, [125] (EWCA) referring to the judgment of
Rix J in *Dubai Aluminium Co v Salaam* [1999] 1 Lloyd's Rep 415, 467 (EWHC). For analysis of
this and earlier English cases on the same point, see T M Yeo, n 268 above, paras 8.22–8.47.

[279] [2001] EWCA Civ 661. Also *Dexter Ltd v Harley* (2001) The Times, 2 April (EWHC).

[280] *Casio Computer v Sayo*, ibid, [11]–[16] (Tuckey LJ), [47]–[53] (Pill LJ).

[281] *Casio Computer Ltd v Sayo* (2001) The Times, 6 February, [22] (Anthony Mann QC),
although this reasoning was doubted by Tuckey LJ in the Court of Appeal (n 282 below).

[282] *Dexter Ltd v Harley*, n 279 above, [17] (Lloyd J); *Casio Computer v Sayo* (EWCA), n 279
above, [22] (Tuckey LJ).

[283] Dicey, Morris & Collins, 1st Supplement, para 34-033.

In so doing, they distinguish non-contractual obligations for which the remedy is compensation for loss (including dishonest assistance) from non-contractual obligations for which 'the measure of damages is usually restitutionary'. They argue that the latter category, including so-called 'knowing receipt' claims,[284] is likely to be classified for the purposes of the Rome II Regulation as arising out of unjust enrichment within Art 10.[285] That distinction, however, seems questionable. First, the characterization of an obligation within the scheme of the Regulation should not require the court to identify the 'usual remedy' within a legal system for the claimant in the circumstances of the case before it. Instead, the court must identify the foundation of the claimant's claim in order to fit it within one of the categories of obligation for which the Regulation provides. Within this process, the principal determinant will be the factual basis of the claim put forward by the claimant, shaped by the legal rules relied on. The remedy sought, or available under the putative applicable law, will rarely, if ever, be a significant factor.[286] Secondly, the editors of Dicey, Morris & Collins consider that a claim to a gain-based award for a tort/delict probably falls within Art 4 rather than Art 10 of the Regulation.[287] The need to distinguish 'knowing receipt' claims from cases of 'restitution for wrongdoing' may explain the editors' preference for the 'usual remedy' criterion, for which there is no apparent basis in the Regulation. Thirdly, the remedy available against a 'knowing recipient', the obligation to account in equity for property received and retained by him, is available in aid of both equitable and legal claims which, in many cases, will be founded on wrongdoing (e.g. a breach of trust) on the part of the defendant.[288] Fourthly, for the time being at least, the liability of a 'knowing recipient' under English law is based not solely on receipt by the defendant of assets disposed of in breach of trust or fiduciary duty but also on the defendant having sufficient knowledge of the circumstances as to make it 'unconscionable' for him to retain the benefit or pay it away for his own purposes.[289] A senior English judge has called for this requirement of fault on the part of the knowing recipient to be removed and for knowing receipt to be accommodated within the English law of restitution/unjust

---

[284] *Bank of Credit and Commerce (Overseas) Ltd v Akindele* [2001] 1 Ch 437 (EWCA).

[285] Dicey, Morris & Collins, 1st Supplement, para 34-033.

[286] **3.70** above.

[287] Dicey, Morris & Collins, 1st Supplement, para 34-032 referring to the same paragraph in the main work. **4.11–4.20** above.

[288] R Meagher, D Heydon, and M Leeming, *Meagher Gummow and Lehane's Equity Doctrines and Remedies* (4th edn, 2002), ch 25.

[289] *BCCI (Overseas) v Akindele*, n 284 above, 448–456 (Nourse LJ); *City Index Limited v Gawler* [2007] EWCA Civ 1382; [2008] 2 WLR 950, [7]–[8], [32] (Carnwath LJ) (compare the views of Arden LJ, [64]–[71]).

enrichment rather than the law of equitable wrongs.[290] Others have argued for a non-fault, receipt based claim to be recognized alongside 'knowing receipt'.[291] For the time being, however, those calls have not been answered, and the 'knowing receipt' claim appears to have more in common with the English torts of conversion[292] and inducing breach of contract than common law claims to reverse unjust enrichment.[293] The basis of the claim remains, therefore, the wrongful retention or disposal of assets that are the subject of a pre-existing relationship between the claimant and the defaulting trustee/fiduciary, which have been transferred to the defendant in breach of the trustee/fiduciary's obligations towards the claimant. From the moment that the defendant's 'conscience' is affected by knowledge of the legally significant fact or facts affecting the transfer to him of specific assets,[294] he must hold those assets for the transferor or other person beneficially entitled, and will be compelled to account for them. On this basis, the English courts have been willing, without finally deciding the point, that 'knowing receipt' and similar claims fall within Art 5(3) of the Brussels Convention.[295]

4.104 Finally, even if English law were to move to a position where the liability of the recipient of misappropriated trust assets is strict and arises at the moment of receipt, it may still be doubted whether the defendant's obligation should be characterized for the purposes of the Regulation as arising in unjust enrichment (Art 10) rather than as arising out of a tort/delict (Art 4). The imposition of strict liability does not automatically take an obligation outside Art 4.[296] More significantly, there may be some difficulty in fitting the recipient's liability within Art 10, which appears to be concerned with reversing transfers of value to the defendant that are attributable, in some way, to the claimant. Here, the transfer to the defendant comes not from the claimant but from the defaulting trustee/fiduciary.

---

[290] *Twinsectra Ltd v Yardley* [2002] UKHL 12; [2002] 2 AC 164, [105] (Lord Millett).

[291] Lord Nicholls of Birkenhead, 'Knowing Receipt: The Need for a New Landmark' in W R Cornish and others (eds), *Restitution Past, Present and Future* (2005), 231–46; P Birks, *Unjust Enrichment* (2nd edn, 2005), 156–8. The Australian High Court has strongly opposed the introduction of a general remedy based on 'unjust enrichment' in such cases, see *Farah Constructions Pty Ltd v Say-Dee Pty Ltd* [2007] HCA 22, [130]–[155].

[292] This analogy was accepted by Morison J in *Cronos Containers Ltd v Palatin* [2002] EWHC 2819 (Comm); [2003] 2 Lloyd's Rep 489, [18].

[293] Cf *El Ajou v Dollar Land Holdings Plc (No 1)* [1993] 3 All ER 717, 736 (Millett J); *Grupo Torras SA v Al-Sabah* [2001] Lloyd's Rep Bank 36; [2001] CLC 221, [122] (EWCA).

[294] *Westdeutsche v Islington LBC*, [1996] AC 669, 705 (Lord Browne-Wilkinson, UKHL).

[295] *Cronos Containers v Palatin*, n 292 above, [18] (Morison J); *Dexter v Harley*, n 279 above, [13] (Lloyd J). Cf *Casio Computer v Sayo* (EWCA), n 279 above, [22] where the point was described by Tuckey LJ as 'debatable'. Also *Bank of Tokyo-Mitsubishi Ltd v Baskan Gida Sanayi Ve Pazarlama* [2004] EWHC 945 (Ch); [2004] 2 Lloyd's Rep 395, [218] (Lawrence Collins J).

[296] Recital (11).

As a matter of English law, it suffices to pass to the defendant the trustee/fiduciary's interest in the asset concerned but does not extinguish the claimant beneficiary's 'equitable interest' (unless the defendant is a bona fide purchaser of a legal interest for value without notice, in which case the equitable claim against him will fail). For the purposes of the Rome II Regulation, this 'equitable interest' may be understood in one of two ways, as a true proprietary interest or as a bundle of personal rights against the trustee/fiduciary which are protected from interference by third parties. Although its existence was historically based in the willingness of the Courts of Equity to enforce trust and similar obligations against third parties whose 'conscience' was affected, the English courts now clearly consider the beneficiary's equitable interest in trust property to be a form of 'ownership'.[297] In its one skirmish to date with the English trust, however, the ECJ refused to characterize it as creating rights *in rem*, at least as between trustee and beneficiary.[298] Whichever view is taken, the defendant's receipt of the asset does not, except in the case mentioned of the bona fide purchaser, who would have a defence to an equitable receipt-based claim, transfer anything from the claimant to the defendant. On the first view, the claimant may seek to recover his 'property' from the defendant, if the defendant still has it. Such a claim may, depending on its precise basis, fall outside the Regulation as concerning a matter of status (property) not obligation.[299] Although it may be possible to describe a claim to vindicate the claimant's equitable title as within the province of the law of restitution,[300] its object does not appear to be reversing the defendant's unjust enrichment.[301] If the defendant no longer has the asset, or refuses to return it, the basis of the claimant's equitable claim still appears to be the defendant's conduct, akin to the English tort of conversion for which liability is strict, rather than the defendant's enrichment. On the second view, supported by the approach taken by the ECJ in *Webb v Webb*, the 'receipt' claim would appear to be based on the defendant's interference (albeit, in some cases, innocent) with relations between the claimant and the trustee/fiduciary through his participation in a transaction with the latter defrauding the claimant. Viewed in this way, it is not dissimilar from the *action paulienne*.[302]

---

[297] *Tinsley v Milligan* [1994] 1 AC 340, 371 (Lord Browne-Wilkinson, UKHL; J Martin, *Hanbury & Martin: Modern Equity* (17th edn, 2005), paras 1-018 to 1-019.

[298] Case C-242/92, *Webb v Webb* [1994] ECR I-1717, discussed at **3.98**, point 2 above.

[299] **3.88–3.101** above.

[300] *Nabb Brothers Limited v Lloyd's Bank* [2005] EWHC 405 (Ch), [75]–[76] (Lawrence Collins J).

[301] *Foskett v McKeown* [2001] 1 AC 102, 127–9 (Lord Millett).

[302] **4.98** above. In *Cronos v Palatin*, n 292 above, Morison J (at [15]) thought the analogy with the *action paulienne* was 'false and unhelpful' in terms of defining the scope of Art 5(3) of the Brussels Convention.

4.105 In many cases, the choice between Art 4 and Art 10 for 'knowing receipt' claims will not affect the law applicable under the Regulation. In particular, if there is a pre-existing relationship between the claimant and the defendant[303] or if the claimant and defendant are habitually resident in the same country at all material times,[304] the outcome should be the same. In the absence of these factors, however, the basic rule in Art 4(1) refers to the country of damage[305] whereas the residual rule in Art 10(3) refers to the country in which the unjust enrichment took place.[306] For 'knowing receipt' claims, Art 10(3) would appear to point towards the place where the defendant first obtained control of the asset from the defaulting trustee,[307] whereas (whether or not the defendant's liability is strict) Art 4(1) may be thought to point to the place where the asset was situated at the time that the defendant disposed of it, or refused to deliver it to the claimant.[308] Alternatively, and consistently with the approach suggested above for the *action paulienne*, it may be preferable to characterize the event giving rise to damage uniformly as the transaction by which the defendant received the asset from the defaulting trustee/fiduciary, or other intermediate holder, and the country of damage as the location of the misappropriated asset(s) immediately prior to this transfer, being the country in which relations between the claimant and the defaulting trustee/fiduciary were interfered with by the defendant's participation in the transfer. This solution would tie in with the solution suggested above (**4.102**) for cases of accessory liability (dishonest assistance), which would have a practical benefit as such claims are often brought alongside 'knowing receipt' claims. Given that all of these connectors may be open to manipulation by the defendant and other participants in fraudulent schemes, which often give rise to claims of this kind, none of the solutions may be entirely satisfactory and the court should have regard to any artificiality in the location of the assets in applying the 'escape clause' in Art 4(3).

Proprietary estoppel

4.106 Claims based on the equitable doctrine of proprietary estoppel may also be thought to fit the description of a 'non-contractual obligation arising out of a tort/delict' above, in that the defendant's liability rests on his unconscionable conduct in denying the belief that, by his own acts, he has

---

[303] Arts 4(3) and 10(1).

[304] Arts 4(2) and 10(2). Note, however, that Art 4(2) refers to the time when damage occurs whereas Art 10(2) refers to the time when the event giving rise to unjust enrichment occurs.

[305] **4.21–4.74** above.

[306] **10.29–10.34** below.

[307] **10.34** below.

[308] Case C-364/93, *Marinari v Lloyd's Bank plc* [1995] ECR I-2719; *Dexter v Harley*, n 279 above, [20] (Lloyd J). Also *Cronos Containers v Palatin*, n 292 above, [18].

engendered in the claimant as to the claimant's entitlement to an interest in land. Although it may generate interests in land that are capable of binding third party purchasers, the claim is personal in nature and may entitle the claimant to no more than monetary compensation for the detriment that he has suffered.[309] On this view, Art 4 should apply. In line with the approach suggested in misrepresentation cases (**4.67** above), the country of damage should be that in which the claimant has acted to his detriment, in reliance on the belief engendered by the defendant. The fact that the estoppel relates to land situated in another Member State and that the parties contemplated a relationship involving the transfer between them of an interest in that land may provide good reasons for displacing the law otherwise applicable under Art 4(1) or Art 4(2) in favour of the *lex situs*.

Anti-Suit Injunctions[310]

A different set of problems is presented by claims for what an English **4.107** lawyer would describe as an anti-suit injunction, i.e. an order restraining the defendant from commencing or continuing proceedings in a country other than the forum.[311] In some cases, the basis of the injunction is the defendant's breach of a promise contained in a contract to bring proceedings before the courts of, or an arbitral tribunal in, the forum. In these cases, the defendant's obligation is contractual and falls outside the scope of the Rome II Regulation. It also, by express exclusion, falls outside the scope of the Rome Convention and its successor Regulation.[312] According to the prevailing view among the English judiciary,[313] there are two further categories of cases. First, those in which the anti-suit injunction is an ancillary measure granted in support of existing English proceedings in order to protect the jurisdiction of the English court in those proceedings.[314] Within this category, it is not necessary for the claimant to show that the defendant's conduct in starting foreign proceedings infringes

---

[309] **3.189,** point 2 above, where the argument that proprietary estoppel is excluded from scope by Art 1(2)(f) (voluntary trusts) is considered and rejected.

[310] For detailed analysis, from an English law perspective, of the issues raised below, see A Briggs, 'Anti-Suit Injunctions in a Complex World', in F D Rose (ed), *Lex Mercatoria: Essays on International Commercial Law in Honour of Francis Reynolds* (2000), 219–44; T M Yeo, n 268 above, paras 4.49–4.75.

[311] For the relationship between anti-suit injunctions and the Brussels I Regime, see Case C-159/02, *Turner v Grovit* [2004] ECR I-3565. Also the pending reference by the UK House of Lords in Case C-185/07, *Allianz SpA (formerly Riunione Adriatica Di Sicurta SpA) v West Tankers Inc* ([2007] UKHL 4; [2007] 1 Lloyd's Rep 391) and the Opinion of Adv Gen Kokott (5 September 2008) in that case.

[312] Rome Convention, Art 1(2)(d); Rome I Regulation, Art 1(2)(e).

[313] *Masri v Consolidated Contractors* [2008] EWCA Civ 625; [2008] 2 Lloyd's Rep 301.

[314] Ibid, [59], [83]–[96] (Lawrence Collins LJ).

a legal or equitable right.[315] Secondly, those in which the injunction is based on 'unconscionable conduct' of the defendant amounting to breach of an equitable obligation.[316] Doubts remain as to whether this division is justified in principle or consistent with earlier authority.[317] In any event, it is unclear whether claims for an anti-suit injunction not involving a breach of contract fall within the scope of the Rome II Regulation and, if so, how its rules are to be applied.

4.108 In *Turner v Grovit*, in the English courts' first fruitless attempt to persuade the ECJ that anti-suit injunctions restraining proceedings in another Member State are consistent with the Brussels Convention, the late Lord Hobhouse argued that, from a European perspective, all anti-suit injunctions should be seen as being based on personal wrongdoing by the defendant towards the claimant. In his view:[318]

> The power to make the order is dependent upon there being wrongful conduct of the party to be restrained of which the applicant is entitled to complain and has a legitimate interest in seeking to prevent. In *British Airways Board v Laker Airways Ltd*,[319] Lord Diplock said that it was necessary that the conduct of the party being restrained should fit 'the generic description of conduct that is "unconscionable" in the eye of English law'. The use of the word 'unconscionable' derives from English equity law. It was the courts of equity that had the power to grant injunctions and the equity jurisdiction was personal and related to matters which should affect a person's conscience. But the point being made by the use of the word is that the remedy is a personal remedy for the wrongful conduct of an individual. It is essentially a 'fault' based remedial concept. Other phrases have from time to time been used to describe the criticism of the relevant person's conduct, for example, 'vexatious' and 'oppressive', but these are not to be taken as limiting definitions; it derives from 'the basic principle of justice': per Lord Goff, *Société Nationale Industrielle Aérospatiale v Lee Kui Jak*.[320] Sometimes, as in the present case, the phrase 'abuse of process' (borrowed from another context) is used to express the same general ideas but with particular reference to the effect of the unconscionable conduct upon pending English proceedings.

4.109 On that view, which was not questioned by the ECJ in its judgment on the reference,[321] it may appear that claims for anti-suit injunctions outside a contractual context fall within Art 4 of the Rome II Regulation. If that view

---

[315] Ibid, [45]–[54].

[316] Ibid, [39]–[44], [56].

[317] A Briggs and P Rees, n 103 above, para 40.

[318] [2001] UKHL 64; [2001] 1 WLR 107, [24].

[319] [1985] AC 58, 81 (UKHL).

[320] [1987] AC 871, 893 (UKHL).

[321] *Turner v Grovit*, n 311 above, para 28.

is accepted, however, it presents a further difficulty in that the connecting factor of 'damage' in Art 4(1) appears to point towards the application of the law of the country in which proceedings are brought against the claimant seeking an anti-suit injunction, and not that of the forum which the claimant asserts is the natural and proper forum for the resolution of, or is otherwise closely connected to, the dispute between the parties.[322] It is in the former country in which the defendant's conduct in bringing proceedings has its immediate effect on the claimant, by placing him under an obligation to appear to defend himself and to instruct lawyers to do so. Any 'vexation' or 'oppression' of the claimant in his ability to continue English proceedings would appear to be an indirect consequence of the foreign proceedings, which ought therefore to be left out of account in identifying the country of 'damage' under Art 4(1).[323] Further, the claimant's ability to invoke the jurisdiction of the English court is unaffected by foreign proceedings in these circumstances.[324] In particular, the existence of proceedings brought 'wrongfully' will not be given any weight if the defendant applies for a stay of English proceedings.[325] It cannot, therefore, be argued that impairment of the jurisdiction of the court granting the injunction is a separate, independent consequence of the defendant's conduct that supports the conclusion that the claimant sustains relevant 'damage' in that country.

If there were proceedings pending between the parties in the courts of **4.110** the forum State at the time that the foreign proceedings were started, it might be possible to avoid these difficulties by treating the relationship of claimant and defendant in those proceedings as a 'pre-existing relationship' between the parties, governed by the law of the forum, that justifies application of the escape clause in Art 4(3). It would appear artificial, however, to extend that approach to cases in which the defendant's foreign proceedings respond only to a threat by the claimant to issue proceedings in the forum's courts, still less to 'single forum' cases in which the only remedy lies in the foreign court.[326]

If the courts of the forum Member State have jurisdiction with respect to the **4.111** substance of the dispute between the parties, the most obvious 'way out' of

[322] *Airbus Industrie v Patel* [1999] 1 AC 119 (UKHL).

[323] **4.36–4.45** above.

[324] For the (problematic) view that the Brussels I Regulation confers a statutory right on persons domiciled in a Member State to be sued in the EC, see *Samengo-Turner v J & H Marsh & McLennan* [2007] EWCA Civ 723; [2007] 2 CLC 104. For comment on this case, see A Briggs [2007] LMCLQ 433; A Dickinson (2008) 57 ICLQ 465.

[325] e.g. *Sohio Supply Co v Gatoil (USA) Inc* [1989] 1 Lloyd's Rep 588 (EWCA); *Meridien Biao Bank GmbH v Bank of New York* [1997] 1 Lloyd's Rep 437 (EWCA).

[326] *Masri v Consolidated Contractors*, n 313 above, [56] (Lawrence Collins LJ).

these problems would be to reject the view of Lord Hobhouse that, in a Community context, anti-suit injunctions should be seen as being based on 'wrongful conduct' and instead to treat them as procedural measures ancillary to an existing or future claim before the courts of the forum State. That appears to be the direction in which the English courts are now moving. Indeed, in *Masri v Consolidated Contractors*, Lawrence Collins LJ expressed the *(obiter)* view that an interim anti-suit injunction qualifies as a 'protective measure' within Art 31 of the Brussels I Regulation, being designed to protect the claimant's underlying rights and the integrity of the English substantive proceedings in which it was granted.[327] On this view, anti-suit injunctions outside a contractual context can be characterized as being procedural in nature and falling outside the Rome II Regulation, by reason of the exclusion of matters of evidence and procedure in Art 1(3).[328] Even on this view, there would remain a troublesome rump of cases (i.e. the 'single forum' cases[329]) to which the Regulation would, apparently, continue to apply.

Breaches of EC Law

4.112 Some claims based on breach of EC law fall within the scope of the Rome II Regulation as non-contractual obligations in civil or commercial matters.[330] Most of these claims will be properly characterized as arising out of a tort/ delict within Chapter II.[331] Art 4 will, therefore, apply to situations not falling within any of the special rules in Arts 5 to 9. Given that the EC Treaty and measures adopted under it are principally concerned with regulating the conduct of those exercising economic activity in the internal market and protecting the interests of consumers, many breaches of EC law will fall within Art 6(1) (unfair competition). Other situations, for example claims relating to the compatibility of industrial action with the fundamental freedoms guaranteed by the EC Treaty or pre–contractual liability, will fall within one of the other special rules.[332] In practice, therefore, Art 4 may apply in relatively few cases.

4.113 The obligation of Member State courts to give effect to EC law requires that the law which applies under the Regulation to regulate the parties'

---

[327] Ibid, [66].

[328] **14.54–14.62** below.

[329] *Masri v Consolidated Contractors*, n 313 above, [42]–[44], [56].

[330] **3.281–3.286** above.

[331] For the possibility of an alternative claim based on unjust enrichment (albeit in a case involving the unlawful levying of taxes and falling outside the scope of the Rome II Regulation), see Joined Cases C-397 and 410/98, *Metallgesellschaft Ltd v Inland Revenue Commissioners* [2001] ECR I-1727; *Sempra Metals Ltd v Inland Revenue Commissioners* [2007] UKHL 34; [2008] 1 AC 561.

[332] Industrial action: Art 9 (**9.12–9.15** below); pre–contractual liability: Art 12 (**12.05** below).

relations must comply, in the case of a law of a Member State, with the principles of equivalence and effectiveness[333] and with any overriding mandatory provisions of EC law.[334]

F. RELATIONSHIP WITH THE HAGUE TRAFFIC ACCIDENTS CONVENTION[335]

In accordance with Art 28(1) of the Regulation,[336] Art 4 will not apply in those Member States party to the Hague Traffic Accidents Convention[337] to matters falling within the scope of that Convention. Currently, among the Member States, Austria, Belgium, Czech Republic, France, Latvia, Lithuania, Luxembourg, Netherlands, Poland, Slovakia, Slovenia, and Spain are parties to this Convention by ratification, succession, or accession.[338] Portugal has signed, but not ratified, the Convention. **4.114**

The Convention contains rules of applicable law for determining the law applicable to civil non-contractual liability arising from traffic accidents, in whatever kind of proceeding it is sought to enforce this liability.[339] For this purpose, 'traffic accident' is defined to mean an accident which involving one or more vehicles, whether motorized or not, and is connected with traffic on the public highway, in grounds open to the public or in private grounds to which certain persons have a right of access.[340] **4.115**

---

[333] **3.286** above.
[334] **15.19–15.20** below.
[335] Also A Staudinger, 'Rome II and traffic accidents' [2005] European Legal Forum I-61.
[336] **16.36–16.42** below.
[337] Convention on the Law Applicable to Traffic Accidents (4 May 1971), reproduced at <http://www.hcch.net/index_en.php?act=conventions.text&cid=81>. See also the Explanatory Report by Eric W Essén, *Actes et Documents de la Onzième Session* (1968), tome III. An English translation of Explanatory Report on the Hague Traffic Accidents Convention is available at <http://www.hcch.net/upload/expl19e.pdf>.
For commentary on the Convention, see K M H Newman, 'The law applicable to traffic accidents' (1969) 18 ICLQ 643; C S Armstrong, 'Hague Convention on the Law Applicable to Traffic Accidents: Search for Uniformity Amidst Doctrinal Diversity' (1972) 11 Columbia Journal of Transnational Law 74; V Brunner, *The Hague Convention on the law applicable to traffic accidents of 1971 in the light of the European practice*, unpublished thesis (Cornell University, 1972) and the other materials cited on the website of the Hague Conference at <http://www.hcch.net/index_en.php?act=conventions.publications&dtid=1&cid=81>.
[338] For the current status, see <http://www.hcch.net/index_en.php?act=conventions.status&cid=81>.
[339] Hague Traffic Accidents Convention, Art 1.
[340] Ibid.

4.116 Significantly, for present purposes, the Convention does not apply:[341]

(1) to the liability of manufacturers, sellers or repairers of vehicles;

(2) to the responsibility of the owner, or of any other person, for the maintenance of a way open to traffic or for the safety of its users;

(3) to vicarious liability, with the exception of the liability of an owner of a vehicle, or of a principal, or of a master;

(4) to recourse actions among persons liable;

(5) to recourse actions and to subrogation in so far as insurance companies are concerned;

(6) to actions and recourse actions by or against social insurance institutions, other similar institutions and public automobile guarantee funds, and to any exemption from liability laid down by the law which governs these institutions.

4.117 Items (1) to (5) remain within the scope of the Rome II Regulation. In particular, (a) item (1) concerns non-contractual obligations arising out of product liability and falls within Art 5, (b) item (2) (occupier's liability) falls within the general rule in Art 4, (c) item (3) falls within the scope of the law applicable under Art 4 (Art 15(g)), (d) item (4) falls either within Art 15(b) or Art 20, and (e) item (5) falls within Arts 18 and 19. Item (6), insofar as it involves the provision of compensation or other exercise of public powers by the social insurance institution, does not concern a civil or commercial matter and falls outside the scope of the Regulation. A claim by a social insurance institution to be subrogated to the rights of the victim against the tortfeasor may fall within Art 19.[342]

4.118 Arts 3 to 6 contain a complex cascade of rules of applicable law, as follows:

1. The starting point (Art 3) is that the law applicable to liability arising from traffic accidents is the internal law of the State where the accident occurred.

2. Under Art 4, that law is displaced as follows:

(a) If only one vehicle is involved in the accident and that vehicle is registered in a State other than that where the accident occurred, the internal law of the State of registration will apply to determine liability (i) towards the driver, owner, or any other person having control of or an interest in the vehicle, irrespective of their habitual residence, (ii) towards a victim who is a passenger and whose habitual residence

---

[341] Ibid, Art 2.

[342] Case C-433/01, *Freistaat Bayern v Blijdenstein* [2004] ECR I-981, paras 20–21 (a Brussels Convention case).

is in a State other than that where the accident occurred, and (iii) towards a victim who is outside the vehicle at the place of the accident and whose habitual residence is in the State of registration. Where there are two or more victims the applicable law is determined separately for each of them.

(b) If two or more vehicles are involved in the accident, and all the vehicles are registered in the same State, the internal law of the State of registration will apply to the same extent as under (a) above.

(c) If one or more persons outside the vehicle or vehicles at the place of the accident are involved in the accident and may be liable, the law of the State of registration will only apply under either (a) or (b) above if all these persons have their habitual residence in the State of registration (even though they may also be victims of the accident).

3. The law applicable under Articles 3 and 4 to liability towards a passenger who is a victim also governs liability for damage to goods carried in the vehicle and which either belong to the passenger or have been entrusted to his care.[343]

4. The law applicable under Articles 3 and 4 to liability towards the owner of the vehicle also governs liability for damage to other goods carried in the vehicle.[344]

5. Liability for damage to goods outside the vehicle or vehicles is governed by the internal law of the State where the accident occurred.[345]

6. Liability for damage to the personal belongings of the victim outside the vehicle or vehicles is governed by the internal law of the State of registration when that law would be applicable to the liability towards the victim according to Article 4.[346]

7. The internal law of the State in which a vehicle is habitually stationed shall replace the law of the State of registration (a) for unregistered vehicles or vehicles registered in several States, and (b) if neither the owner nor the person in possession or control nor the driver of the vehicle has his habitual residence in the State of registration at the time of the accident.[347]

[343] Art 5, 1st para.
[344] Art 5, 2nd para.
[345] Art 5, 3rd para.
[346] Art 5, 4th para.
[347] Art 6.

4.119 Art 7 requires account to be taken of rules relating to the control and safety of traffic that were in force at the place and time of the accident.[348] Other provisions of the Convention concern (a) the scope of the applicable law (Art 8), (b) direct action against insurers of the person liable (Art 9), (c) public policy (Art 10), (d) application within States comprising more than one territorial unit (Arts 12–14).

4.120 In view of the complexity of the Hague Traffic Accidents Convention, it is unsurprising that it did not commend itself as a model for regulating the law applicable to traffic accidents under the Regulation. Its continued application in almost half the Member States, leading to a sharp division in the rules regulating civil liability in this area, is deeply unsatisfactory.[349] It can only be hoped that this divergence will be addressed by the Commission in its report on the application of the Regulation, due in 2011, which requires it to study, among other matters, the effects of Art 28 with respect to the Hague Convention.

---

[348] **15.27–15.29** below.

[349] Also T Thiede and M Kellner, '"*Forum shopping*" *zwischen dem Haager Übereinkommen über das auf Verkehrsunfälle anzuwendende Recht und der Rom-II-Verordnung*' (2007) *Versicherungsrecht* 1624. An English summary of the article is available at <http://www.conflictoflaws.net/2007/articles/german-article-on-rome-ii-regulation/>.

5

Product Liability

Article 5

Product liability

1. Without prejudice to Article 4(2), the law applicable to a non-contractual obligation arising out of damage caused by a product shall be:

(a) the law of the country in which the person sustaining the damage had his or her habitual residence when the damage occurred, if the product was marketed in that country; or, failing that,

(b) the law of the country in which the product was acquired, if the product was marketed in that country; or, failing that,

(c) the law of the country in which the damage occurred, if the product was marketed in that country.

However, the law applicable shall be the law of the country in which the person claimed to be liable is habitually resident if he or she could not reasonably foresee the marketing of the product, or a product of the same type, in the country the law of which is applicable under (a), (b) or (c).

2. Where it is clear from all the circumstances of the case that the tort/delict is manifestly more closely connected with a country other than that indicated in paragraph 1, the law of that other country shall apply. A manifestly closer connection with another country might be based in particular on a pre-existing relationship between the parties, such as a contract, that is closely connected with the tort/delict in question.

A. INTRODUCTION

5.01   This Article, concerning non-contractual obligations arising out of damage caused by a product, must be read together with Recital (20), which provides:[1]

> The conflict-of-law rule in matters of product liability should meet the objectives of fairly spreading the risks inherent in a modern high-technology society, protecting consumers' health, stimulating innovation, securing undistorted competition and facilitating trade. Creation of a cascade system of connecting factors, together with a foreseeability clause, is a balanced solution in regard to these objectives. The first element to be taken into account is the law of the country in which the person sustaining the damage had his or her habitual residence when the damage occurred, if the product was marketed in that country. The other elements of the cascade are triggered if the product was not marketed in that country, without prejudice to Article 4(2) and to the possibility of a manifestly closer connection to another country.

5.02   The cascade of rules of applicable law in Art 5 of the Rome II Regulation bears a passing resemblance to the sequence of rules contained in the Hague Products Liability Convention. That Convention will continue to apply in several Member States in place of the Regulation's rules.[2]

5.03   Art 5 differs radically from the apparently more straightforward approach of the Commission in its Proposal and Amended Proposal,[3] and was the product of extensive discussion in the Council's Rome II Committee,

---

[1]   For criticism of this recital, see Sir L Collins et al. (eds), *Dicey, Morris & Collins: The Conflict of Laws* (14th edn, 2006), 1st supplement, para S35-202.

[2]   Hague Products Liability Convention, Arts 4–7, discussed at **5.49–5.53** below.

[3]   Commission Proposal, Art 4; Commission Amended Proposal, Art 6. For critical comment on the Proposal, see T Kadner Graziano, *The Law Applicable to Product Liability: The Present State of the Law in Europe and Current Proposals for Reform* (2005) 54 ICLQ 475.

in which widely diverging compromise proposals were considered.[4] In its 1st Reading Position, the European Parliament had advocated removal of the special rule for product liability[5] on the ground that its reformulated general rule for tort/delict was adequate.[6] At the second reading stage, however, the Parliament accepted the rule as formulated by the Council in its Common Position.[7] In its statement of reasons accompanying the Common Position, the Council explained:[8]

The Council considers that the application of the general rules in cases of product liability would not allow foreseeing[9] the applicable law with reasonable certainty. Creation of a cascade system of connecting factors, together with a foreseeability clause, appears to be a balanced solution in view of this objective.

The rules must also be understood against the background of the 1985 EC **5.04** Directive concerning liability for defective products, which lays down minimum standards for Member State product liability rules concerning defective products. [10]

Art 5 in its final form has not escaped criticism. The Commission in its **5.05** communication concerning the Common Position expressed its regret at the 'rather complex system of cascade application of connecting factors', favouring its own original proposal as offering 'an equally balanced solution for the interests at stake, while expressed in much simpler drafting'.[11] The language of Art 5 has also been justifiably criticized for the difficult questions that it leaves open.[12] Professor Symeonides, in turn, describes the rules, and in particular the 'foreseeability clause' as 'unduly generous

---

[4] See, for example, the proposal by the Dutch Presidency (Council document 13446/04 [3.11.2004], 2–3) and the separate proposals by the delegations from Spain (Council document SN 2852/04 [9.9.2004], 4–5), the UK (Council document 12997/04 [4.10.2004]), and Belgium (Council document 14193/04 [8.11.2004], 2). The Common Position reflects, in substance, the compromise proposal presented to COREPER in February 2006 (Council document 5864/06 [3.2.2006], 4–5; also Council documents 6623/06 [23.2.2006] and 7709/06 [3.5.2006]).

[5] EP 1st Reading Position, Amendment 27.

[6] EP 1st Reading Report, 20. For critical comment of the EP 1st Reading Position, see A Saravalle, 'The Law Applicable to Products Liability' in A Malatesta (ed) *The Unification of Choice of Law Rules on Torts and Other Non-Contractual Obligations in Europe* (2006), 107–25.

[7] Common Position, Art 5.

[8] OJ C289E, 79–80 [28.11.2006].

[9] *Sic.*

[10] Directive (EEC) No 85/374 on the approximation of the laws, regulations and administrative provisions of the Member States concerning liability for defective products (OJ L210, 29 [7.8.1995]), as amended by Directive (EC) No 1999/34 (**Product Liability Directive**) (**5.48** below).

[11] COM (2006) 566 final [27.9.2006], 3.

[12] P J Kozyris, 'Rome II: Tort Conflicts on the Right Track' (2008) 56 AJCL 471, 486–95.

to the defendant'.[13] He also suggests that 'the fact that Article 5 does not differentiate between cases in which the law of the victim's domicile favors and those in which it disfavors the victim raises additional questions. One such question is whether Article 5 favors residents of developed countries and disfavors residents of lesser developed countries.'[14] In this connection, he suggests that 'the German plaintiff who is injured in India by a Japanese product acquired in Egypt will get the benefit of German law. However, an Indian plaintiff who is injured in Austria by a German product acquired in Germany will be confined to the remedies provided by Indian law.'[15] The second part of this statement, however, appears to overlook the potentially overriding mandatory effect of the Product Liability Directive[16] in situations having a close connection to the EEA[17] or of the forum's product liability rules.[18]

5.06   Art 5 is undoubtedly complex. Whether it will give rise to significant problems, or produce unsatisfactory results, in practice remains to be seen. In all likelihood, 'the search for the perfect formula [*for product liability cases*] must continue. Article 5 of Rome II is far from the perfect formula, but the real question is whether it is good enough.'[19]

B. DAMAGE CAUSED BY A PRODUCT

'DAMAGE'

5.07   Art 2(1) defines damage as including 'any consequence arising out of a tort/delict'. In contrast, Art 9 of the Product Liability Directive defines 'damage' for the purposes of the Directive's principal rule rendering a producer liable for damage caused by a defect in his product[20] as meaning (a) damage caused by death or personal injuries, or (b) damage to, or destruction of, any item of property other than the defective product itself, with a lower threshold of 500 ECU, provided that the item of property

---

[13] S C Symeonides, 'Rome II and Tort Conflicts: A Missed Opportunity' (2008) 56 AJCL 173, 206–7.

[14] Ibid, 208.

[15] Ibid, 209.

[16] **5.48** below. It is also doubtful whether the Product Liability Directive would extend to the first of the scenarios suggested by Professor Symeonides.

[17] The Product Liability Directive extends to EEA members (Norway and Iceland) as well as the EC Member States.

[18] Art 16 (**15.14–15.18**).

[19] S C Symeonides, n 13 above, 209.

[20] Product Liability Directive, Art 1.

(i) is of a type ordinarily intended for private use or consumption, and (ii) was used by the injured person mainly for his own private use or consumption. The following words of Art 9, however, make clear that this definition is without prejudice to national provisions relating to non-material damage. In the explanatory memorandum accompanying its Rome II Proposal, the Commission emphasized that:

The scope of the special rule in Article 4 [*of the Proposal*[21]] is consequently broader than the scope of Directive 85/374, as it also applies to actions based on purely national provisions governing product liability that do not emanate from the Directive.

Against this background, there seems no reason to give the concept of 'damage' in Art 5 the restrictive interpretation that it is given in the Product Liability Directive. In particular, it seems capable of including financial and other non-material loss, as well as damage to the product itself.[22] **5.08**

Consistently with the Product Liability Directive, Art 5 is not restricted to claims by consumers or other end users. Indeed, a proposal by the UK delegation to this effect[23] was rejected in the Council Rome II Committee.[24] It may extend, for example, to claims by bystanders[25] or businesses sustaining damage falling within the scope of the Article. **5.09**

'PRODUCT'

In its Proposal, the Commission had suggested that the definition of 'product' in Art 2 of the Product Liability Directive should apply for the purposes of its proposed special rule governing product liability.[26] Although Art 5 in its final form differs significantly from the terms of that Proposal[27] and it does not necessarily follow that a term given a specific definition in one Community instrument should be given the same meaning in another **5.10**

---

[21] Regulation, Art 5.

[22] For the view that the words 'damage caused *by* a product' excludes damage caused *to* a product by itself, and that Art 4 should apply to such cases, see G Légier, '*Le réglement 'Rome II' sur la loi applicable aux obligations non contractuelles*', JCP/La Semaine Juridique—Edition Générale, 21 November 2007, I-207, para 55(3). This may be thought to be liable to produce an unnecessary split in the law applicable to product liability claims, and to encourage artificial distinctions between 'the product' and other property.

[23] Council document 12997/04 [4.10.2004], 1–2.

[24] Commission note of meeting of Council Rome II Committee held on 5–6 October 2004 (Commission document JAI/C/1/CH/bv D(04) 10582 [29.10.2004], 2).

[25] **5.40** below.

[26] Commission Proposal, 13.

[27] **5.03** above.

Community instrument where it is not defined,[28] the Commission's comments evidence the link between the Directive and the Rome II Regulation[29] and it seems sensible to treat the Directive definition as providing, at least, an inclusive definition of 'product' for the purposes of the Regulation.

5.11   Art 2 of the Product Liability Directive provides:[30]

> For the purpose of this Directive, 'product' means all movables even if incorporated into another movable or into an immovable. 'Product' includes electricity.

5.12   This broad concept, as implemented in the UK Consumer Protection Act 1987, includes 'substances, growing crops and things comprised in land by virtue of being attached to it and any ship, aircraft or vehicle'[31] and has been held to be capable of including transfused blood.[32] The reference to 'movables', however, and the supplementary reference to electricity suggest strongly that, electricity aside, the product must have some physical manifestation, with the result that (for example) information stored and transferred by electronic means,[33] ideas, the spoken word, and services fall outside the definition. Immovable assets are also excluded from the concept of a 'product' under the Directive, although movable assets incorporated into an immovable remain within its scope.

The Required Link between Product and Damage

5.13   Greater difficulty is likely to be encountered in defining the limits of the words 'damage caused by a product'. Taken literally, they might be capable of accommodating many non-contractual obligations that would not typically be regarded as involving 'product liability', for example liability for damage caused by vehicles in traffic accidents or of a professional adviser for the content of written advice.[34] Unlike the Product Liability

---

[28] **3.33** above.

[29] Note, however, that the Commission proposal to include a specific reference to the Directive in Recital (12) of its Amended Proposal was not included in the final version of the Regulation.

[30] See also Consumer Protection Act 1987, s 1(2) (UK). Compare Hague Products Liability Convention, Art 2(a) ('the word "product" shall include natural and industrial products, whether raw or manufactured and whether immovable or immovable').

[31] Consumer Protection Act 1987, s 45.

[32] *A v National Blood Authority* [2001] 3 All ER 289 (Burton J). The editors of *Clerk & Lindsell on Torts* suggest that '[i]t seems to follow that it also covers other biological products, such as semen, and presumably organs for transplant' (A M Dugdale and M A Jones, *Clerk & Lindsell on Torts* (19th edn, 2006), para 11-48).

[33] Although, possibly, not information supplied on a tangible medium such as a hard drive or disk (*Clerk & Lindsell on Torts*, n 32 above, para 11-50).

[34] A Rushworth and A Scott, 'Rome II: Choice of law for non-contractual obligations' [2008] LMCLQ 274, 283.

Directive, the scope of Art 5 is not expressly limited to liability of the 'producer' or persons treated as the 'producer'.[35] That said, the words 'damage caused by a product', when taken together with the definition of 'product' in the Directive[36] suggest that the relevant damage must be caused by the physical attributes of the product and not, for example, damage resulting from reliance on information contained in the product,[37] or its legal consequences.[38] 'Responsibility for products' may be a more apt description of the matters covered by Art 5. Further, the detail of the sub-rules in Art 5 suggests strongly that the liability must be of a person concerned in some way with the putting of the product on the market, including the producer, importer, or supplier, other persons in the chain of distribution (for example a repairer or warehouseman), and their employees and agents.[39] That restriction is consistent with the Commission's view that: [40]

The expression 'person claimed to be liable' does not necessarily mean the manufacturer of a finished product; it might also be the producer of a component or commodity, or even an intermediary or a retailer. Anybody who imports a product into the Community is considered in certain conditions to be responsible for the safety of the products in the same way as the producer.

On this view, the non-contractual liability (for example) of a building **5.14** owner with respect to injury to visitors caused by collapsing scaffolding falls outside Art 5, but the non-contractual liability of the manufacturer or supplier for damage caused by a physical attribute of the scaffolding (e.g. its propensity to collapse when erected) will fall within scope. If the supplier installs the product, Art 5 may also be argued to apply to a claim against him based (for example) on defective installation, on the basis that such claims are sufficiently linked to his role in the marketing of the product. Claims against the manufacturer or supplier based on inadequate instructions should arguably be treated in the same way. In the case of an independent contractor, however, a non-contractual claim

---

[35] Product Liability Directive, Art 3.

[36] **5.12** above.

[37] *Clerk & Lindsell on Torts*, n 32 above, para. 11-49. Alternatively, in the case of the professional adviser, it may be argued that the damage results from the provision of services, to which the written advice is merely an incidental product.

[38] For this reason, damage caused by financial instruments (insofar as they have a physical form) falls outside Art 5. Cf T Petch, 'The Rome II Regulation: An Update: Part 2' [2006] JIBLR 509, 509.

[39] Compare Hague Products Liability Convention, Art 3. If, however, the repair takes place after the product has been marketed to the person sustaining the damage, the repairer's non-contractual liability should fall within Art 4, not Art 5. Also Dicey, Morris & Collins, 1st supplement, para S35-211.

[40] Commission Proposal, 15.

for defective installation should be seen as based on the provision of services not linked to the marketing of a product and as falling within Art 4 not Art 5.

5.15 One important respect in which Art 5 in its final form appears (in the English language version, at least[41]) wider than the corresponding provision (Art 4) in the Commission Proposal is that the latter, following the EC Product Liability Directive,[42] referred to 'damage caused by a defective product'. That wording might have excluded (for example) liability for damage caused by products, such as cigarettes or firearms, which are inherently dangerous or harmful but not 'defective' in the sense described in the Directive.[43] Art 5, which omits the word 'defective', seems apt to cover the liability of a person involved in the marketing of the product in such cases, including situations in which liability is strict[44] or based on a failure to warn of dangers.

PRODUCT LIABILITY UNDER ENGLISH LAW

5.16 Under English law, Art 5 will cover not only claims made under Part I of the Consumer Protection Act 1987, implementing the Product Liability Directive, but also other claims against producers and other persons involved in the marketing of a product to establish their responsibility for damage caused, including (for example) claims for negligence,[45] or breach of statutory duty.[46]

THE RELATIONSHIP BETWEEN ARTICLE 5 AND OTHER RULES IN CHAPTER II

5.17 In cases falling within its scope, the rules of applicable law in Art 5 take priority over those in Art 4 (tort/delict). Questions may arise as to the

---

[41] The Spanish text and Portuguese texts of Art 5 refer in the heading to 'defective products' ('*productos defectuosos*'; '*productos defeituosos*'), but that language is not repeated in the main body of the Article. The French, German, Dutch, Italian, and Swedish texts, for example, are consistent with the English text on this point.

[42] Product Liability Directive, Arts 1 and 6. See the comments of the Swedish delegation in Council document 5041/04 [8.1.2004].

[43] *Clerk & Lindsell on Torts*, n 32 above, para 11-60.

[44] Recital (11).

[45] *Donohue v Stevenson* [1932] AC 562 (UKHL); *Clerk & Lindsell on Torts*, n 32 above, paras 11-08 to 11-43. Also Employer's Liability (Defective Equipment) Act 1969, attributing negligence to employers when an employee has been injured by a defect in equipment provided to him by his employer, if that defect is attributable to fault of a third party.

[46] *Clerk & Lindsell on Torts*, n 32 above, para 11-88.

relationship between Art 5 and other rules within Chapter II. The potential for conflict is greatest in relation to Art 7 (environmental damage).[47] What if a defect in a product results in the release of noxious fumes or chemicals causing pollution? It does not seem satisfactory to say that, as the non-contractual obligation cannot be said only to arise exclusively from damage caused by a product or environmental damage, neither rule can prevail,[48] as this solution (resulting, presumably, in the application of the rules contained in Art 4) fails to give effect to the policies underlying either special rule.[49] Instead, the question must be asked whether, in the type of claim that is before the court, the objectives of the Regulation are, on balance, better served by applying one rule instead of another. In cases of environmental damage, Art 7, which favours the victim as well as serving the policies of the EC concerning environmental protection, seems likely to prevail over Art 5.

C. PRODUCT 'MARKETED' IN A PARTICULAR COUNTRY

The common thread running through the cascade of rules in Art 5(1) is the concept of 'the product' being 'marketed' in the country in which (a) the person sustaining damage is habitually resident, (b) the product was acquired, or (c) the damage occurred. Unfortunately, this important concept is not defined in the Regulation.[50] Some guidance is provided in the explanatory memorandum accompanying the Commission Proposal, although it must be borne in mind that, under Art 4 of the Proposal, the country of 'marketing' was relevant only to the application of the escape clause from the primary rule favouring the victim's country of habitual residence in circumstances in which the defendant could show   **5.18**

---

[47] Cf A Rushworth and A Scott, n 34 above, 298 who suggest that 'cases of true overlap between the product liability rule and the environmental damage rule will be rare'. That conclusion, however, is based on a restrictive reading of Art 7 as applying only to cases in which 'environmental damage' is a necessary element of the claim advanced under national law. This seems too restrictive (**7.14** below).

[48] Cf A Rushworth and A Scott, n 34 above, 298.

[49] **5.01** and **7.16** below.

[50] P J Kozyris, n 12 above, 489.

that 'the product was marketed in that country without his consent'.[51] Commenting on this provision, the Commission stated:[52]

Given the requirement that the product be marketed in the country of the victim's habitual residence for his law to be applicable, the solution is foreseeable for the producer, *who has control over his sales network.* It also reflects the legitimate interests of the person sustaining damage, who will generally have acquired a product that is *lawfully marketed* in his country of residence.

Where the victim acquires a product in a country other than that of his habitual residence, perhaps while travelling, two hypotheses need to be distinguished: the first is where the victim acquired abroad a product *also marketed* in their country of habitual residence, for instance in order to enjoy a special offer. In this case the producer had already foreseen that his activity might be evaluated by the yardstick of the rules in force in that country . . .

In the second hypothesis, by contrast, where the victim acquired abroad a product that is not lawfully marketed in their country of habitual residence, none of the parties would have expected that law to be applied.

5.19 These comments suggest that the Commission had in mind the following points:

1. 'Marketing' includes, at least, selling products through a sales network.
2. The 'product' that is marketed need not be the exact product that caused damage to the victim. It may, at least, be an identical product.
3. The marketing of the product in a particular country must have been lawful.

5.20 As to point 1, there is no reason to suppose that other transactions by which products are made available through commercial channels[53] (e.g. hiring, the provision of free samples, by prescription) are excluded from the concept of 'marketing'. It is unclear whether stocking, advertising, or offering a product for sale (without actually selling it) would constitute 'marketing' for this purpose.[54] The editors of Dicey, Morris & Collins suggest that advertising a product, including by the Internet, should suffice,[55] a view that appears consistent with the objectives of

---

[51] **5.34–5.36** below. The Commission proposal did not deal explicitly with the situation in which the product had not been marketed at all in the victim's home state, but the Commission emphasized that pre-condition in its explanatory memorandum (see extracts from the Commission Proposal quoted at text to n 52 below).

[52] Commission Proposal, 14 (emphasis added).

[53] This is the language used in Art 7 of the Hague Product Liability Convention.

[54] Compare the view taken by the ECJ, in a different context, in Case C-16/03, *Peak Holding AB v Axolin-Elinor AB* [2004] ECR I-11313, para 42.

[55] Dicey, Morris & Collins, 1st supplement, para S35-210.

Art 5 provided that it is also required that potential end users/consumers in the country in question must be targeted by the advertisement with a view to sales (e.g. a sign in a border area displaying goods available for purchase in a different country). Otherwise, it may be argued, the sufficiency of displays or advertisements on the Internet would significantly water down the requirement of 'marketing'. An analogy may be drawn here with the requirement in Art 15(1)(c) of the Brussels I Regulation and Art 6(1)(c) of the Rome I Regulation that 'commercial or professional activities' be 'directed' to the country of the consumer's habitual residence.[56] It may also be thought necessary that at least one sale to a targeted person in the relevant country should result for 'marketing' to take place.

As to point 2, the view that it is the identical product, not merely a product **5.21** of the same type, that must be marketed in the country identified in Art 5(1)(a) to (c) seems to be confirmed by the reference in those sub-rules to 'the product', contrasted with the wider reference in the 'foreseeability clause' (**5.00** below) to 'the product, or a product of the same type'. Difficult questions remain, however, as to whether two products may be considered to be 'identical' if there are minor differences between them, for example in markings or packaging.[57] Products that have been modified in a material respect following manufacture and second-hand items[58] may be argued not to constitute identical products for this purpose, reflecting the more limited control that the manufacturer is able to exercise over the marketing of these items. In the case of the liability of component manufacturers, the marketing of a 'product' should be taken to refer to a product in which the component is contained.

Point 3, the requirement of lawful marketing, may well be explained by **5.22** the fact that the Commission formulated its escape clause in terms of the defendant's consent.[59] That aspect of the Proposal was criticized, in particular, on the ground of the practical difficulties of requiring the producer, or other defendant, to prove a negative.[60] During discussions in the

---

[56] See Rome I Regulation, Recital (24) referring to the Joint Statement of the Council and the Commission in relation to Brussels I Regulation, Art 15(1)(c).

[57] See, in a different context, Joined Cases C-427/93, C-429/93, and C-436/93, *Bristol-Myers Squibb Co v Paranova A/S* [1996] ECR I-3457. The concept of a 'product of the same type' is considered at **5.34–5.36** below.

[58] A re-sale may also be argued to lack the element of 'commercialisation' which appears to be required.

[59] For the concept of 'consent' to marketing at the intersection of EC law and intellectual property rights, see Joined Cases C-414/99 to C-416/99, *Zino Davidoff SA v A & G Imports Ltd* [2001] ECR I-8691; G Petursson and P Dryberg, 'What is Consent?' (2002) 27 Eur L Rev 464.

[60] Council document 5430/04 [27.1.2004], 2. Also Council document 5041/04 [8.1.2004], 2–3 (proposal of the Swedish delegation).

Council's Rome II Committee, all delegations preferred an escape clause based on reasonable foreseeability.[61] It remains to be seen whether the unlawful marketing of products (including infringing sales of 'grey market' products purchased outside the EC for sale in a Member State, as well as sales of smuggled products) may be capable of satisfying the marketing condition in Art 5(1).[62] If so, the lawfulness of the activity will be relevant only to the defendant's ability to foresee the marketing of the product in the country in question for the purposes of the escape clause.

5.23 In the German text of the Regulation, the words ('*in Verkehr gebracht wurde*') corresponding to the word 'marketed' in the English version also appear in Arts 7 and 11 of the German text of the Product Liability Directive. That coincidence is not, however, reflected in other language versions of the two instruments, which contrast the 'marketing' or 'commercialisation' of the product (Rome II)[63] with its being 'put into circulation' (Product Liability Directive).[64] In *O'Byrne v Sanofi Pasteur*, the ECJ held that, for the purposes of Art 11 of the Product Liability Directive, a product is 'put into circulation' when it leaves the production process operated by the producer and enters a marketing process in the form in which it is offered to the public in order to be used or consumed[65] and that, generally, it is not important in that regard whether the product is sold directly to the producer to the user/consumer or that the sale is carried out as part of a distribution process involving one or more operators.[66] The second part of the reasoning seems helpful in understanding the concept of 'marketing' under the Regulation: it is the commercialization of the product and not the precise method of its commercialization that is important. It seems doubtful, however, whether the Court's preferred definition of 'put into circulation' is helpful for present purposes: linking the concept of marketing to the time and place at which the production process ends and the marketing process begins appears likely to favour the manufacturer, and to reduce the objectivity and foreseeability of the law applicable under Art 5 from the user/consumer's perspective. In *Sanofi*, the ECJ was not concerned with identifying the place of marketing, but its timing for the purposes of the limitation defence

---

[61] Council document 6161/06 [10.2.2006], 2 (**5.34–5.36** below).

[62] For a broad view, in the context of the Hague Products Liability Convention, see H D Tebbens, *International Product Liability* (1979), 346.

[63] e.g. '*commercialisé*' (French); '*se comercializó*' (Spanish); '*commercializzato*' (Italian).

[64] e.g. 'put . . . into circulation' (English); '*mis . . . en circulation*' (French); '*puso . . . en circulación*' (Spanish); '*messo. . . in circolazione*' (Italian).

[65] Case C-127/04, *O'Byrne v Sanofi Pasteur MSD Ltd* [2006] ECR I-1313, para 27.

[66] Ibid, para 28.

contained in Art 11 of the Directive. In seeking to attribute a geographical location to the marketing process in order to establish a factor connecting that location to a tort/delict involving damage caused by the product
marketed, or a materially identical product, the focus should be on
the country or countries in which the persons who purchase or otherwise acquire products are directly affected by the marketing process
(which will often be their place of habitual residence), and not on the
beginning of that process from the manufacturer's viewpoint. This
approach, it is submitted, strikes a reasonable balance between producers
and purchasers, the groups from which claimants and defendants in product liability claims will most commonly be drawn. For distance marketing
(including via the Internet[67]), the product should be considered to have
been marketed in the country where the purchaser acted or where he was
targeted by the marketing with a view to a sale. If a purchaser was targeted in one country and travelled to another country to complete his purchase, the product should be considered to have been marketed in both
countries as a result of the transaction.

At an early stage of discussions in the Council's Rome II Committee, the   **5.24**
Spanish delegation suggested a rebuttable presumption that a product
marketed in one Member State is marketed in the other Member States.[68]
Later attempts at formulating a compromise solution for product liability
cases treated the fact of marketing in one Member State as sufficient to
establish the marketing of a product in all Member States.[69] These proposals may have been inspired by the principle of 'exhaustion of rights' developed by the ECJ in dealing with the relationship between the EC Treaty
provisions concerning the free movement of goods and intellectual property rights.[70] Eventually, however, the idea of introducing a rule or presumption that a product marketed in one Member State was also marketed
in all the other Member States was rejected.[71] Accordingly, in all cases, it
must be shown that the product was actually marketed, in the sense
described above, in the Member State to which the relevant sub-rule in

---

[67] **5.20** above.

[68] Council document 9009/04 ADD 10 [18.5.2004], 3.

[69] e.g. Council documents SN 2852/04 [9.9.2004], 4–6 (Spain); 13446/04 [3.11.2004], 2–3
(Dutch Presidency); 14193/04, ADD 1 [4.11.2004], 2–3 (Sweden); 16231/04 [20.12.2004], Art 4
(Dutch/Luxembourg Presidencies).

[70] Case C-10/89, *SA CNL-SUCAL NV v HAG GF AG* [1990] ECR I-3711, para 12; D Wyatt et
al., *Wyatt & Dashwood's European Union Law* (5th edn, 2006), paras 16-050 to 16-064;
C Barnard, *The Substantive Law of the EU* (2nd edn, 2007), ch 9. See, for example, the comments of the Portuguese delegation (Council document SN 2852/04 [6.9.2004], 3).

[71] Council document 6161/06 [10.2.2006] 2; Council document 7432/06 [16.3.2006], Art 4.

Art 5(1) points. If, however, that burden can be discharged[72] and it can also be shown that the defendant knew that the product, or a product of the same type, was being marketed in one Member State, the principle of free circulation of goods within the EC would make it very difficult, if not impossible, for him to establish that he could not reasonably foresee the marketing of that product in another Member State. Effectively, he would have to show that the market in the latter Member State was isolated from the market in the first Member State, there being no reasonable prospect that end users/consumers in one would desire or be able to acquire the product from the other.

5.25 Art 5 does not specify the point in time at which 'the product' must be marketed in the country whose law is indicated as being potentially applicable. In the case of the product causing the damage, this question would appear insignificant—the fact that the product has been marketed is sufficient.[73] Otherwise sub-rules (a) to (c) in Art 5(1) use the imperfect tense, suggesting that it will be sufficient if identical products were being marketed in the relevant country at the time that damage first occurred (in the case of sub-rules (a) and (c)) or the time that the product causing the damage was acquired (in the case of sub-rule (b)). The desire to ensure a continuing responsibility on the part of manufacturers may support the conclusion that the marketing of identical products at either of these times should suffice for all three sub-rules, subject to the 'foreseeability clause' (**5.34–5.36** below) being applied to marketing at the relevant time.

D. THE LAW APPLICABLE TO NON-CONTRACTUAL OBLIGATIONS ARISING OUT OF DAMAGE CAUSED BY A PRODUCT

5.26 Putting to one side the difficulties with the terminology used, as considered in **Sections B** and **C** above, the structure of Art 5 seems relatively straightforward. Art 5(1) provides three sub-rules in descending hierarchy, each of which requires the product (i.e. that causing the damage or a materially identical product[74]) to have been marketed[75] in the country identified by the relevant connecting factor. The connecting factors in these three

---

[72] For the burden of proof, see **5.28** below.

[73] Cf Explanatory Report by W L M Reese on the Hague Products Liability Convention, *Acts and Documents of the Twelfth Session* (1972), tome III, 264. The Report is available at <http://hcch.e-vision.nl/upload/expl22.pdf>.

[74] **5.21** above.

[75] **5.18–5.25** above.

sub-rules point to (a) the country of habitual residence of the person sustaining the damage at the time that the damage occurred, (b) the country in which the product was acquired, and (c) the country in which the damage occurred. In each case, the person claimed to be liable may resist the operation of any sub-rule for which the marketing condition is satisfied by showing that he could not reasonably foresee the marketing of the product, or a product of the same type, in the country identified by the sub- rule. If the person claimed to be liable successfully invokes this escape clause for each sub-rule that applies, or (probably) if none of the sub-rules applies, the law applicable will be that of his country of habitual residence.

The law identified under Art 5(1) may be displaced (1) if the person **5.27** claimed to be liable and the person sustaining damage both have their habitual residence in the same country at the time when the damage occurred, in favour of the law of that country, whether the product was marketed there or not, (2) otherwise, in favour of the law of a country with which the tort/delict is manifestly more closely connected in all of the circumstances of the case.

As to the burden of proof, the language used in Art 5 suggests that (a) the **5.28** burden of establishing that a product was marketed in the country identified by each sub-rule lies with the party who asserts that the sub-rule applies, (b) the person claimed to be liable must establish that he could not reasonably foresee that the product was marketed in the country indicated by any of the sub-rules, and (c) the party who invokes the escape clause in Art 5(2) must establish that it is manifestly more appropriate to apply a law other than that of the country identified by Art 5(1).[76]

First Level — Country of Habitual Residence of the Person Sustaining the Damage (Art 5(1)(a))

The Sub-Rule

Art 5(1)(a) points to the application of the law of the country in which the **5.29** person sustaining the damage[77] had his habitual residence when the damage occurred, if the product (i.e. that causing damage or a materially identical product[78]) was marketed in that country. In determining the habitual residence of that person, account must be taken of the definition of 'habitual residence' contained in Art 23, although in most cases

---

[76] **4.88** above.
[77] For the meaning of this term, see **4.83,** point 3 above.
[78] **5.21** above.

involving natural persons it will be necessary to look elsewhere for the test to be applied.[79]

5.30 The requirement that the victim's habitual residence be determined 'when the damage occurred' is problematic. First, unlike Art 4(1), Art 5(1) does not expressly exclude from the concept of 'damage' the indirect consequences of the event giving rise to damage.[80] The reason for this may be that the category to which the rule applies ('damage caused by a product') is defined using that concept.[81] If the Art 4(1) restriction of 'damage' is not read into Art 5(1)(a) and Art 5(1)(c), applying the law of the country in which damage occurred, these sub-rules may have the effect not only of fragmenting the applicable law in many cases but also of identifying the law of one or more countries that do not have a significant connection to the tort/delict, for example if the victim changes his habitual residence after sustaining personal injury and incurs expenses or loss of earnings in his new residence. As the considerations that justified restricting 'damage' as a connecting factor in Art 4(1)[82] seem no less powerful here, the argument that 'damage' in both Art 5(1)(a) and 5(1)(c) should be taken to exclude indirect consequences of the event giving rise to damage would appear a strong one. If that view is accepted, it may follow that the 'person sustaining the damage' can be a primary victim other than the claimant or a person represented by the claimant.[83]

5.31 Secondly, products may cause damage over a period of time, for example by exposure to a dangerous chemical or consumption of harmful medication.[84] In many cases, that fact will have no appreciable impact on the law applicable under Art 5(1). What, however, if the victim resided in, or otherwise travelled to, one or more countries other than his country of habitual residence while continuing to consume a product or otherwise being exposed to its harmful effects? At what time, and in which countries, will damage be considered to have occurred? This raises problems of a different kind from the situation, considered in **Chapter 4**, in which the victim is exposed to the harmful effects of a product (e.g. by swallowing medication) in one country (State A), and injury resulting from that exposure develops or manifests itself in a different country (State B). In that situation, it seems correct to conclude that the damage occurred in State A at

---

[79] **3.47–3.58** above.
[80] Art 4(1).
[81] **5.07–5.09** above.
[82] **4.36–4.37** above.
[83] **4.39–4.45** above.
[84] Cf Explanatory Report on the Hague Products Liability Convention, n 73 above, 260–1.

the time of the original exposure.[85] Here, however, it may be thought artificial to conclude that the damage occurred at one time or in one place. From the point of view of causation, even if there is no cumulative adverse effect on the victim's health, it will in most cases not be possible to conclude that the 'harmful' exposure occurred at a particular point in time and in a particular place.[86]

Within Art 5(1)(a), three possible solutions to this conundrum may be sug-   **5.32**
gested. First, to apply on a distributive basis (applying the so-called mosaic view[87]) the law of all countries in which the victim had his habitual residence while being exposed to the product's harmful effects. Secondly, to treat Art 5(1)(a) as having 'failed' if the person sustaining the damage was habitually resident in more than one country over the period of exposure, leading to the application (as the next step in the process) of Art 5(1)(b). Thirdly, to apply a tie-break rule in favour of the country in which the victim was habitually resident at the time that he first sustained damage or, possibly, at the time that the 'principal' damage was sustained or the damage first manifested itself. From a theoretical standpoint, having regard to the approach taken in relation to Art 4,[88] the first solution seems correct. In practice, however, it would appear too complex even before the difficulties inherent in the mosaic view approach[89] have been taken into account. For example, consider a case in which the claimant was habitually resident in two countries while taking a course of medication. For Art 5(1)(a) to apply on this interpretation, the product must be shown to have been marketed in each of those countries. If the product was marketed in only one of those countries, Art 5(1)(a) provides only a partial answer, requiring the law applicable to the balance of the damage to be determined in accordance with sub-rules (b) and (c). If the product was marketed in both of those countries, the defendant faces a dual burden of showing that he could not reasonably foresee the marketing of the product, or a product of the same type, in each of the countries. If he succeeds in discharging that burden only for one of the countries, Art 5(1)(a) again only provides a partial answer. This complexity is multiplied if the first solution is also preferred for locating the country of damage within Art 5(1)(c), as the damage may be considered to have occurred in several countries to which the claimant travelled while taking medication, each of which will need to

---

[85] **4.58** above.
[86] *Fairchild v Glenhaven Funeral Services Ltd* [2002] UKHL 22; [2003] 1 AC 32.
[87] **3.298–3.301** above.
[88] **4.69** above.
[89] **4.70–4.74** above.

be validated by marketing in that country and, potentially, rebutted by the defendant's inability to foresee that marketing.

5.33 The second or third solutions suggested above may, therefore, be thought more suited to the demands of legal certainty. Of these, the objectives of enhancing foreseeability as to the law applicable and of ensuring a reasonable balance between the interests of the parties would appear best served by the second solution, alternatively by fixing the damage at the time and (for the purposes of Art 5(1)(c)) in the place that the victim was first exposed to the harmful effects of the product.

The Foreseeability Clause

5.34 Art 5(1)(a) will not apply, however, if the person claimed to be liable[90] discharges the burden of showing that he could not reasonably foresee the marketing of the product, or a 'product of the same type', in the country of the victim's habitual residence.[91] 'Marketing' here corresponds with the references to 'marketed' in the sub-rules.[92] Equally, 'the product' need not be that which causes damage, but may be an identical product, subject (possibly) to non-material differences in markings or packaging.[93] The reference in the final paragraph of Art 5(1) to 'a product of the same type', wording that does not appear in the sub-rules, lacks certainty. On a literal interpretation, it appears capable of covering products produced by persons unrelated to the defendant, which may compete with the product causing damage.[94] There are, however, strong indications in the *travaux préparatoires* that the reference was intended to be to products of the same type of the person claimed to be liable.[95] This wording first appeared in proposals circulated within the Council's Rome II Committee which based the defendant's escape on his lack of consent to the marketing.[96] The requirement of consent, as opposed to one of reasonable foreseeability, could only be applied to products marketed by or through the defendant.

---

[90] For the meaning of this term, see **4.83,** point 2 above.
[91] Art 5(1), final para.
[92] **5.18–5.25** above.
[93] **5.21** above.
[94] P J Kozyris, n 12 above, 489. Cf Art 7 of the Hague Products Liability Convention (**5.49–5.53** below), referring to 'his own products of the same type'.
[95] Council document 9009/04 ADD 10 [18.5.2004], 4 (Spain) referring to 'products of the same type/class produced by the same liable person'. Also Council documents SN 2852/04 [2.9.2004], 2 (Austria); ibid, ADD 3 [9.9.2004], 5 (Spain); ibid, ADD 4 [9.9.2004], 1 (Sweden).
[96] The criterion of reasonable foreseeability first appears as an alternative to consent in Council document 13446/04 [3.11.2004], p 2 (Option 2).

Given that the foreseeability clause would appear to be concerned with striking a reasonable balance between the interests of persons involved in the marketing of a product, on the one hand, and persons injured by products marketed in particular countries, on the other, the conduct of unrelated third parties (such as competitors) should not be a relevant consideration in the process of identifying the law applicable under Art 5.

An expansive interpretation of the words 'a product of the same type', so **5.35** as to include competitor's products would also magnify the existing uncertainty as to the degree of similarity required between 'the product' and the non-identical 'product of the same type'. It is not difficult to see different versions of the same item produced by the same manufacturer (for example, with a different plug type or additional features) as being 'the same type'. When comparing different manufacturers' products, however, the differences in terms of manufacture and functionality are likely to increase greatly. These words cannot, it is submitted, be construed so broadly as to deprive a Korean manufacturer of hairdryers of the benefit of a reasonable foreseeability defence in a claim brought by a Latvian resident who purchased the defendant's hairdryer in China simply because he could foresee that comparable hairdryers would be marketed in Latvia. Instead, it is submitted, there must be substantial identity between the two products at least in terms of (1) the undertaking that produces them or is responsible for their production,[97] (2) their purpose, (3) their price, (4) their target market, and (5) the technology used in their manufacture.

Art 7 of the Hague Products Liability Convention contains a similar fore- **5.36** seeability clause, which applies 'if the person claimed to be liable establishes that he could not reasonably have foreseen that *the product or his own products of the same type* would be made available in that State through commercial channels'.[98] In his comment on this provision, the rapporteur on the Convention project, W L M Reese did not expand on the intended meaning of 'products of the same type'.[99] Nevertheless, case law on this Article of the Hague Convention, particularly from within the Member States party to it, may provide some guidance as to the application of the foreseeability clause in Art 5(1).

---

[97] This wording contemplates the possibility that products may be produced by different members of the same group or a licensee.

[98] **5.51** below (emphasis added). See H D Tebbens, 'Western European Private International Law and the Hague Convention relating to Product Liability' in TMC Asser Institute, *Hague-Zagreb Essays 2* (1978), 23–5; H D Tebbens, *International Product Liability* (1979), 345–50.

[99] Explanatory Report on the Hague Products Liability Convention, n 73 above, 263–4.

Second Level—Country in which the Product was Acquired
(Art 5(1)(b))

The Sub-Rule

5.37 If Art 5(1)(a) does not apply, whether because the product was not marketed in the country of the victim's habitual residence or because the person claimed to be liable could not reasonably foresee that fact or otherwise,
the possible application of the second sub-rule must be considered. This
rule points to the application of the law of the country in which the product was acquired, if the product was marketed in that country. Confusingly,
the two references in this sub-rule to 'the product' seem to refer to two
different things: the first must be taken to refer to the actual product
that caused the damage, the second must be taken to refer either to that
product or a materially identical product.[100]

5.38 The apparent simplicity of the reference to the country of acquisition con-
ceals difficulties in the application of the sub-rule in particular cases. The
first problematic area concerns distance sales.[101] Should the product be
considered to have been 'acquired' in (a) the country in which, under the
forum's rules of private international law, the person acquiring it obtained
title, (b) the country of despatch, or (c) the country of receipt (i.e. in which
the person acquiring a product obtained physical control)? An autonomous interpretation of the concept of acquisition seems preferable both in
terms of achieving uniformity in the application of the Regulation and in
increasing legal certainty. Option (b) or (c), therefore, should be preferred
over option (a). Of these two options, the place of receipt seems to strike a
fairer balance between producer and purchaser, especially as the producer
will usually not also be the immediate seller. It also accords with the point
in time at which a consumer's right of withdrawal from a distance sale
of goods arises under EC law.[102]

5.39 Secondly, it is unclear whether the acquisition must be on a commercial
basis, or whether (for example) a gift, private loan, or even theft might
suffice. Consistency with the concept of 'marketing' may be thought
to require an element of commerciality.[103] There may, however, be no

---

[100] **5.21** above. See the example given by the Swedish delegation in Council document
14193/04 [4.11.2004], 2–3.
[101] Directive 97/7 (EC) on the protection of consumers in respect of distance contracts (OJ
L144, 19 [4.6.1997]) (Distance Sales Directive). Also Directive 2000/31 (EC) on certain legal
aspects of information society services, in particular electronic commerce, in the Internal
Market (OJ L178, 1 [17.7.2000]), Arts 10–11.
[102] Distance Sales Directive, Art 6.
[103] **5.20** above.

necessary correlation between the two. Under the Hague Products Liability Convention, the concept of 'acquisition' would appear to refer simply to the acquisition of physical possession and control, as opposed to title.[104] Adopting this broader definition within Art 5(1)(b) of the Rome II Regulation, consistently with the approach taken above to distance sales, would establish in most cases a link between the victim and the product, although the degree of foreseeability to the manufacturer would be reduced.

Finally the position of the injured bystander must also be considered. **5.40** Bystanders, being persons to whom a product has caused damage but who did not acquire the product,[105] may or may not have a pre-existing relationship with the person who did acquire the product, who may have been injured at the same time. Should Art 5(1)(b) be capable of applying to claims brought by such persons and, if so, how?[106] If Art 5(1)(b) is to apply, it should be on the basis of the 'acquisition' by the person having control at the time that damage is caused to the bystander.[107] It would appear preferable, however, to treat Art 5(1)(b) as 'failing' if the person sustaining the damage did not acquire the product, leading to the application (as the next step in the process) of Art 5(1)(c). In such cases, the country of the bystander's habitual residence (Art 5(1)(a)) and the country of damage (Art 5(1)(c)) provide much stronger connecting factors than the country of acquisition by a third party. If, for any reason, there is a close connection between the bystander and the acquisition of the property (for example, because it was bought by a family member and kept in the place where he resides) this fact can be taken into account in the application of the escape clause in Art 5(2).[108]

The Foreseeability Clause

Art 5(1)(b) will not apply if the person claimed to be liable discharges the **5.41** burden of showing that he could not reasonably foresee the marketing of the product or a 'product of the same type'[109] in the country in which the product was acquired.[110]

---

[104] Explanatory Report on the Hague Products Liability Convention, n 73 above, 262.
[105] For the concept of 'acquisition', see **5.39** above.
[106] Arts 4(c) and 5(b) of the Hague Products Liability Convention (**5.51** below) refer to acquisition of the product by the person directly suffering damage.
[107] Assuming that the broader meaning of that concept suggested above is accepted
[108] **5.47** below.
[109] **5.34–5.36** above.
[110] Art 5(1), final para.

THIRD LEVEL—COUNTRY IN WHICH THE DAMAGE OCCURRED (ART 5(1)(C))

The Sub-Rule

5.42 If neither Art 5(1)(a) nor Art 5(1)(b) apply, for whatever reason, the possible application of the third sub-rule must be considered. This points to the law of the country in which the damage occurred,[111] if the product (i.e. that causing damage or a materially identical product) was marketed in that country. Certain difficulties in interpreting the concept of 'damage' as used in Art 5(1)(c) have been considered in the commentary on Art 5(1)(a) above.[112] Other situations involving legal or factual uncertainty in identifying the location of the 'damage' have been considered in the commentary on the damage-based general rule for tort/delict in Art 4(1) (**4.46–4.72** above).

The Foreseeability Clause

5.43 Again, Art 5(1)(c) will not apply if the person claimed to be liable discharges the burden of showing that he could not reasonably foresee the marketing of the product or a 'product of the same type'[113] in the country in which damage occurred.[114]

FIRST RULE OF DISPLACEMENT—COUNTRY OF HABITUAL RESIDENCE OF THE PERSON CLAIMED TO BE LIABLE (ART 5(1), FINAL PARA)

5.44 The law of the country of habitual residence[115] of the person claimed to be liable[116] will apply if that person is able to resist the application of any of the sub-rules (a) to (c) that would otherwise apply by discharging the burden placed upon him by the foreseeability clause.[117] It is clear from the words 'failing that' at the end of both Art 5(1)(a) and 5(1)(b) that is it not sufficient for him successfully to invoke the foreseeability clause in relation to the first sub-rule for which the marketing condition is satisfied. Instead, he must do so for each of the sub-rules that identifies a country in which the product was marketed.

---

[111] Cf Explanatory Report on the Hague Products Liability Convention, n 73 above, 260–1.
[112] **5.30–5.33** above.
[113] **4.21–4.74** above.
[114] Art 5(1), final para.
[115] **3.47–3.58** above.
[116] For the meaning of this term, see **4.83**, point 2 above.
[117] **5.34–5.36, 5.41** and **5.43** above.

Art 5 does not expressly deal with the situation if the product is not **5.45** marketed in any of the countries to which the sub-rules in Art 5(1) point. In such a case, which may be rare, the law of the country of habitual residence of the person claimed to be liable should apply as a default rule. The defendant should not be worse off if the product was not marketed at all in any of these countries, than if unforeseeable marketing had taken place in one or more of them. The alternative solution would be to conclude that Art 5 has 'failed' in this situation, and instead to apply the general rule in Art 4.[118] However, application of the law of the country in which the damage occurs under Art 4(1), without requiring that the product also be marketed in that country, would appear inconsistent with Art 5(1)(c).

SECOND RULE OF DISPLACEMENT—COUNTRY OF COMMON HABITUAL RESIDENCE (ART 5(1), OPENING WORDS REFERRING TO ART 4(2))

In accordance with its opening words, Art 5(1) is without prejudice to Art **5.46** 4(2). Accordingly, if the person claimed to be liable and the person sustaining damage both have their habitual residence in the same country at the time when the damage occurs, the law otherwise applicable under Art 4(1) will be displaced in favour of the law of the common habitual residence.[119] That appears to be the end of the line in terms of identifying the applicable law. Art 5(1) is not also expressed to be without prejudice to Art 4(3) (the escape clause within Art 4) and the escape clause in Art 5(2) may apply only to displace a law indicated 'in paragraph 1'.[120]

THIRD RULE OF DISPLACEMENT—COUNTRY HAVING A 'MANIFESTLY CLOSER CONNECTION' (ART 5(2))

The law of a country that applies under Art 5(1), including the rule of dis- **5.47** placement in favour of the country of habitual residence of the person claimed to be liable but not that in favour of the common habitual residence under Art 4(2), may be displaced if the tort/delict is manifestly more closely connected with a different country, including (in particular) by reason of a closely connected, pre-existing relationship between the parties. This mirrors the escape clause in Art 4(3) and should be applied

---

[118] Dicey, Morris & Collins, 1st supplement, para S35-203.
[119] **4.80–4.83** above.
[120] A Rushworth and A Scott, n 34 above, 283–4.

in the same way.[121] In particular, the words 'a country other than that indicated in paragraph 1' should not be read as preventing the application of Art 5(2) to displace the otherwise applicable law by reference to the connecting factors that appear in Art 5(1), or by the law identified under any of them.[122]

E. THE RELATIONSHIP BETWEEN ARTICLE 5 AND THE PRODUCT LIABILITY DIRECTIVE

5.48 In several respects, Art 5 of the Rome II Regulation is broader than the Product Liability Directive. Not only does it appear to define 'damage' more widely, it would appear to apply to damage caused by non-defective products and to claims against a wider class of persons.[123] It may also lead to the application of national product liability rules of a Member State or a non-Member State,[124] which may themselves impose a more onerous liability even in cases falling within the scope of the Directive. What if, however, the law of a non-Member State that applies under Art 5(1) of the Regulation does not meet the minimum standards laid down by the Directive as to the liability of a producer, or person treated as a producer, in a case having a material connection to the EEA? In particular, what would be the position if the product in question has been marketed and acquired in the EEA, but also marketed in the non-EEA country of habitual residence of the victim (leading to the application of the law of that country under Art 5(1)(a))? Assuming that Art 5(2) does not displace that law in favour of the law of a Member State, it will be necessary to consider whether the Community law requires that national regulations implementing the Directive be given overriding effect (for example) in situations in which (a) the producer is established in the EEA, (b) the product is acquired in the EEA, or (c) damage is sustained in the EEA. Neither the Regulation nor the UK Consumer Protection Act 1987 provide a clear answer to these questions.[125] It seems doubtful, however, whether the Rome II Regulation will be taken to define the territorial limits of the Product Liability Directive. As a measure whose

---

[121] **4.84–4.95** above.

[122] For discussion of similar issues in relation to Art 4, see **4.89**, point 2 above. Also Dicey, Morris & Collins, 1st supplement, para S35-207.

[123] **5.08, 5.13** and **5.15** above.

[124] Regulation, Art 3.

[125] Cf *Clerk & Lindsell on Torts*, n 32 above, para 11-74. For the approach to be taken generally in considering the territorial effect of EC legislation, see Case C-381/98, *Ingmar GB Ltd v Eaton Leonard Technologies Inc* [2000] ECR I-9305.

predominant object under its recitals would appear to be protection of the consumer, it would appear strongly arguable that it should apply (at a minimum) to all products sold or supplied within the Member States and causing damage there, irrespective of the place of habitual residence of the victim or of the producer. These questions remain, however, to be settled.

F. RELATIONSHIP WITH THE HAGUE PRODUCTS LIABILITY CONVENTION

In accordance with Art 28(1) of the Regulation,[126] Art 5 will not apply in those Member States party to the Hague Products Liability Convention[127] to matters falling within the scope of that Convention. Currently, among the Member States, Finland, France, Luxembourg, Netherlands, Slovenia, and Spain are parties to this Convention by ratification or succession.[128] Belgium, Italy, and Portugal have signed, but not ratified, the Convention.   **5.49**

The Convention contains rules of applicable law for determining the liability of manufacturers and certain other persons[129] for 'damage' caused by a 'product', including damage in consequence of a misdescription of the product or of a failure to give adequate notice of its qualities,   **5.50**

---

[126] **16.36–16.42** below.

[127] Convention on the Law Applicable to Products Liability (2 October 1973, reproduced at <http://www.hcch.net/index_en.php?act=conventions.text&cid=84>. See also the Explanatory Report by W L M Reese, *Acts and Documents of the Twelfth Session* (1972), tome III, 246–73. The Report is available at <http://hcch.e-vision.nl/upload/expl22.pdf>.

For commentary on the Convention, see G Kuhne, 'Choice of Law in Products Liability' (1972) 60 California L Rev 1; B Durham, 'Hague Convention on the Law Applicable to Products Liability' (1974) 4 Georgia J Int Comp L 178; M L Saunders, 'Innovative Approach to International Products Liability: the Work of the Hague Conference on Private International Law' (1972) 4 Georgetown J Int L 187; W L M Reese, 'The Hague Convention in the Law Applicable to Products Liability' (1974) 8 International Lawyer 606–25 and 'Further Comments on the Hague Convention on the Law Applicable to Products Liability' (1978) 8 Georgia J Int Comp L 311; H D Tebbens, 'Western European Private International Law and the Hague Convention Relating to Product Liability' in TMC Asser Institute, *Hague Zagreb Essays 2* (1978), 4–34 and *International Product Liability* (1979), 333–60. Other materials are listed on the website of the Hague Conference at <http://www.hcch.net/index_en.php?-act=conventions.publications&dtid=1&cid=84>.

[128] For the current status, see <http://www.hcch.net/index_en.php?act=conventions.status&cid=84>.

[129] Hague Products Liability Convention, Art 3.

its characteristics, or its method of use.[130] Liability between the transferor and transferee of a product is excluded.[131] For these purposes, (a) 'product' includes natural and industrial products, whether raw or manufactured and whether movable or immovable,[132] (b) 'damage' means injury to the person or damage to property as well as economic loss; however, damage to the product itself and the consequential economic loss is excluded unless associated with other damage,[133] (c) 'person' includes legal and natural persons.[134] To the extent that the Hague Convention is narrower than Art 5 of the Regulation, the latter provision will determine the law applicable to non-contractual product liability claims.[135]

5.51 Arts 4 to 6 of the Hague Convention contain a complex set of interrelated rules. In brief summary:

1. Under Art 5, the law of the country of habitual residence of the person directly suffering damage applies, if it is also either (a) the principal place of business of the person claimed to be liable, or (b) the place of acquisition of the product by the person directly suffering damage.

2. If Art 5 does not apply, Art 4 applies the law of the country of injury if it is also either (a) the country of habitual residence of the person directly suffering damage, (b) the principal place of business of the person claimed to be liable, or (c) the place of acquisition of the product by the person directly suffering damage.

3. If neither Art 4 nor Art 5 applies, Art 6 applies the law of the country of the principal place of business of the person claimed to be liable, but gives the claimant the option of basing his claim upon the law of the country of injury.

---

[130] Ibid, Art 1, 1st para.

[131] Ibid, Art 1, 2nd para. Such claims may fall, therefore, within the scope of the Regulation insofar as they involve non-contractual obligations.

[132] Ibid, Art 2(a). In covering immovable products, this is wider than the definition in the Product Liability Directive, which may apply under the Regulation (**5.11** above). Art 16(2) of the Hague Convention allows Contracting States to exclude the application of the Regulation in relation to raw agricultural products. Of the Member States, only Spain has made a declaration reserving its right under this Article.

[133] Ibid, Art 2(b). This seems narrower than the concept of 'damage' as used in the Regulation (**5.07–5.09** above).

[134] Ibid, Art 2(c).

[135] For the suggestion that Art 14 of the Regulation (freedom of choice) applies even to claims falling within the scope of the Hague Convention, see G Légier, n 22 above, paras 54, 56.

4. Art 7 contains a foreseeability clause similar to that in Art 5(1) of the Regulation,[136] excluding application of the law of the country of injury or the law of the victim's habitual residence if the person claimed to be liable establishes that he could not reasonably have foreseen that the product or his own products of the same type would be made available in that State through commercial channels.

Other provisions of the Convention concern such matters as (a) scope **5.52** of the applicable law (Art 8), (b) rules of conduct and safety (Art 9),[137] (c) public policy (Art 10), and (d) application within States comprising more than one territorial unit (Arts 12–14).

The continuing existence of two separate applicable law regimes for **5.53** product liability cases within the Member States is undoubtedly unsatisfactory. It is hoped that the Commission will address this divergence in its first report on the Regulation, due in 2011.

---

[136] **5.34–5.36** above.
[137] Considered at **15.27** below.

6

Unfair Competition/Restriction of Competition

Article 6

Unfair competition and acts restricting free competition

1. The law applicable to a non-contractual obligation arising out of an act of unfair competition shall be the law of the country where competitive relations or the collective interests of consumers are, or are likely to be, affected.

2. Where an act of unfair competition affects exclusively the interests of a specific competitor, Article 4 shall apply.

3. (a) The law applicable to a non-contractual obligation arising out of a restriction of competition shall be the law of the country where the market is, or is likely to be, affected.

(b) When the market is, or is likely to be, affected in more than one country, the person seeking compensation for damage who sues in the court of the domicile of the defendant, may instead choose to base his or her claim on the law of the court seised, provided that the market in that Member State is amongst those directly and substantially affected by the restriction of competition out of which the non-contractual obligation on which the claim is based arises; where the claimant sues, in accordance with the applicable rules on jurisdiction, more than one defendant in that court, he or she can only choose to base his or her claim on the law of that court if the restriction of competition on

which the claim against each of these defendants relies directly and substantially affects also the market in the Member State of that court.

4. The law applicable under this Article may not be derogated from by an agreement pursuant to Article 14.

A. INTRODUCTION[1]

6.01 To an English lawyer, Art 6 is the most outlandish of all the rules of applicable law in the Regulation. Not only have the English courts denied the existence of a general civil wrong of 'unfair competition',[2] but the rules contained in Arts 6(1) and 6(3) bear not even a passing resemblance to any pre-existing rule of English private international law. From a wider perspective it may also be considered, in terms of its drafting and practicality, the least satisfactory of the Regulation's rules of applicable law. Its poorly defined features seem likely to trouble Member State courts for many years to come.

6.02 Art 5 of the Commission Proposal, entitled 'unfair competition', contained provisions corresponding to those now appearing in Arts 6(1) and (2) of the Regulation in its final form.[3] In the accompanying explanatory memorandum, the Commission referred not only to conduct of a kind falling within the traditional domain of unfair competition law in the Member States[4] but also 'modern competition law' protecting consumers and the public in general.[5] Initially, that reference appeared capable of bringing within the scope of the proposed special rule claims for breach of Arts 81 and 82 of the EC Treaty and their national counterparts.[6] The EESC, for example,

---

[1] For earlier comparative surveys of the law applicable to non-contractual obligations falling within the scope of this Article, see A Troller, 'Unfair Competition' and I Schwartz and J Basedow, 'Restrictions on Competition, chs 34 and 35 in K Lipstein (ed), *International Encyclopaedia of Comparative Law*, vol III (private international law); Permanent Bureau of the Hague Conference, 'Note on Conflicts of Laws on the Question of Unfair Competition', Preliminary Document No 5 of April 2005, available at <http://www.hcch.net/upload/wop/gen_pd5e.pdf>.

[2] *L'Oreal SA v Bellure NV* [2007] EWCA Civ 968; [2008] RPC 9, at [92], [135]–[161] (Jacobs LJ).

[3] For comment on this aspect of the Commission Proposal, see C Honorati, 'The Law Applicable to Unfair Competition' in A Malatesta (ed), *The Unification of Choice of Law Rules on Torts and Other Non-Contractual Obligations in Europe* (2006), 127–58; M Leistner, 'Unfair Competition Law Protection Against Imitations', in J Basedow et al. (eds), *Intellectual Property in the Conflict of Laws* (2004), 135–57.

[4] See extract quoted at text to n 50 below.

[5] Commission Proposal, 15.

[6] For an opposing view, see J Adolphsen, 'The Conflict of Laws in Cartel Matters in a Globalised World: Alternatives to the Effects Doctrine' (2005) 1 J Pr Int L 151, 176.

recommended that the title of the provision be changed to 'Competition and unfair trade practices' in order 'to make it clearer that the regulation is intended to cover all infringements of competition comprehensively'.[7] In the meantime, however, the Commission had clarified its position, explaining that 'Article 5 was intended to apply to acts of unfair competition in the strict sense and not to measures restricting competition'.[8] A later note from the Commission's Competition Directorate General to the Member State delegations concluded that neither the proposed special rule for unfair competition nor the general rule for tort/delict was adequate for claims based on breaches of EC competition law, and set out possible options for the treatment of such claims within the Rome II Regulation, favouring application of the law of the forum.[9]

In their responses to the Commission Proposal, the Austrian[10] and German[11] **6.03** delegations suggested excluding anti-trust law from the scope of the Regulation entirely. Sweden, on the other hand, proposed a separate rule for restrictions of competition on the ground that the Regulation (EC) No 1/2003 on the implementation of Arts 81 and 82 of the Treaty 'foresees a shift from public enforcement of EC competition law to private enforcement'.[12] Despite early reservations of the UK delegation,[13] an agreement in principle that non-contractual obligations arising from restrictions of competition resulting from private law actions should be dealt with by a special rule in the Regulation, alongside unfair competition, was reached at an early stage of the Council's deliberations.[14] Subsequently, however, the need for *any* special rule in this area was questioned by the European Parliament's JURI Committee, which also complained of the lack of clarity in the Proposal as to the meaning of 'acts of unfair competition'.[15] Art 5 of the Commission Proposal was deleted by the Parliament in its 1st Reading Position.[16]

---

[7] EESC Opinion (OJ C241, 4 [28.9.2004]).

[8] Council document 5430/04 [27.1.2004], 2.

[9] Commission document COMP/A/1/AS/jw [16.12.2004].

[10] Council document 9009/04 ADD 1 [3.5.2004], 2 on the ground that anti-trust law 'is so close to public law'.

[11] Ibid, ADD 11 [24.5.2004], 4, 7.

[12] Ibid, ADD 8 [18.5.2004], 9. Spain suggested that the rule for unfair competition should apply also to acts restricting free competition (ibid, ADD 10 [18.5.2004], 4).

[13] Ibid, ADD 15 [26.5.2004], 3.

[14] Council document 11801/04 [28.7.2004], 4, but note the reservations of the German delegation (Council document SN2852/04, ADD 1 [2.9.2004], 3). Also Council document 6161/06 [10.2.2006], 2 indicating that some delegations continued to harbour doubts on this point.

[15] EP 1st Reading Report, 21.

[16] EP 1st Reading Position, Amendment 29.

6.04 In its Amended Proposal, rejecting the Parliament's deletion of Art 5, the Commission presented a modified provision under the new title 'Unfair commercial practices',[17] building on the terminology of the Directive on unfair business-to-consumer commercial practices, adopted in May 2005.[18] As the Commission explained:[19]

> [*The European Parliament's amendment*] would abolish the special rule for anti-competitive practices. The Commission cannot accept this amendment: Article 5 of the initial proposal did not seek to introduce a rule differing from the general rule on the substance but simply to determine more accurately the place where the damage arises, which is not always an easy matter. Article 7 has been slightly reworded in the amended proposal to make clear that the aim is solely to determine more accurately where the damage arises. To meet the European Parliament's requests regarding definitions, the Commission has also opted to use terminology in Article 7 of the amended proposal that is directly inspired by Directive 2005/29 of 11 May 2005. The result, *a contrario*, is that non-contractual obligations arising from anti-competitive practices outlawed under Articles 81 and 82 of the Treaty or equivalent rules in the Member States are not covered by Article 7; they are consequently subject to the general rule in Article 5 [*of the Amended Proposal*].[20] But in its Green Paper '*Damages actions for breach of the EC antitrust rules*', scheduled for publication in December 2005, the Commission is planning to provoke debate on the question of the law applicable to civil actions for compensation for damage arising from an anti-competitive practice. Depending on the replies, the Commission may wish to support a different solution in the course of the codecision procedure.

6.05 In fact, by the time that the Commission's Amended Proposal was published, the Commission had already finalized its Green Paper on damages actions for breaches of EC anti-trust rules.[21] A staff working paper prepared by the Commission's DG Competition to accompany the Green Paper confirmed the Commission's view that the special rule for unfair competition, in the form in which it would appear in Art 7 of the Amended Proposal, 'is applicable only to laws concerning unfair business practice, thus not covering claims based on an infringement of Articles 81 and 82 EC (or similar provision in national competition law)'.[22] Moreover, in the Commission's view, 'the application of the rule to antitrust litigation

---

[17] Commission Amended Proposal, Recital (13) and Art 7.

[18] Directive (EC) No 2005/29 concerning unfair business-to-consumer commercial practices in the internal market (OJ L149, 22 [11.6.2005]), Art 4 (**Unfair Commercial Practices Directive**). The relationship between Art 6 and the Directive is discussed at **6.35–6.41** below.

[19] Commission Amended Proposal, 6 (footnote added).

[20] Regulation, Art 4.

[21] COM (2005) 672 final [19.12.2005].

[22] Commission Staff Working Paper (SEC (2005) 1732), Annex to the Green Paper, 'Damages actions for breach of the EC antitrust rules' (COM (2005) 672 final [19.12.2005]), para 246.

would pose problems because it cannot be said in an action by a purchaser against a seller that there exists between them a competitive relationship. Purchaser and seller are not normally competitors.'[23]

The staff working paper considered in detail possible options for regulating the law applicable to anti-trust claims, suggesting as possible options (1) the general rule for tort/delict, with the place of damage as a starting point, (2) an effects-based test applying the law of the affected market, (3) the law of the forum,[24] and (4) giving the claimant a choice among the laws identified by options (1), (2), and/or (3) above.[25] **6.06**

A separate special rule for restrictions of competition, sitting alongside that for unfair competition and designating the law of the affected market, was proposed by the Swedish delegation at a meeting of the Council's Rome II Committee in January 2006.[26] At the time, there was no agreement on the terms of the rule, although the Committee rejected[27] a separate proposal by the UK delegation that the law of the forum should apply to certain anti-competitive practices corresponding to the prohibitions in Arts 81 and 82, and that otherwise there should be no special rule for matters of unfair competition.[28] Following that meeting, the 'affected market' rule was adopted by the Austrian Presidency and, apparently, accepted in principle by the JHA Council in February 2006, subject to possible review of the law applicable to breaches of EC competition law.[29] Continuing disagreement among the Member State delegations as to whether the law applicable to restrictions of competition should be the law of the forum or the law of the affected marked was resolved at a late stage in favour of the latter solution.[30] **6.07**

---

[23] Ibid. The argument seems weak, as neither Art 5 of the Proposal nor Art 7 of the Amended Proposal required that competitive relations be affected between claimant and defendant, and both referred also to 'the collective interests of consumers'. This connecting factor was generally understood as referring to the market affected by the act of unfair competition (see C Honorati, n 3 above, 148–54)

[24] Compare the proposal by the UK delegation in Council document 5460/06 [18.1.2006].

[25] Ibid, paras 242–54. See further **6.60** below.

[26] Council document 5805/06 ADD 1 [31.1.2006].

[27] Council document 6161/06 [10.2.2006], 2.

[28] Council document 5460/06 [18.1.2006]. A revised proposal by the UK delegation in Council document 7928/06 ADD 1 [30.3.2006] was also rejected.

[29] Council documents 6165/06 [10.2.2006], 6 and 6623/06 [23.2.2006], 3. Also Council document 7432/06 [16.3.2006], 7, retaining the law of the forum as a possible solution for breaches of Arts 81 and 82.

[30] Council document 7709/06 [3.5.2006], 3.

6.08 This aspect of the Council's Common Position,[31] carried forward almost exactly in Arts 6(1), (2), (3)(a), and (4) of the Regulation in its final form, was rejected in its entirety by the European Parliament at the 2nd Reading Stage.[32] Both the Council and the Commission[33] opposed the deletion of the special rules, which were duly reinstated as part of the final compromise in the conciliation process.[34] The additional wording in Art 6(3)(b) giving a person seeking compensation who sues in the court of domicile of one of the defendants the right to base his claim on the law of the forum resulted from a compromise proposal of the European Parliament in conciliation.[35] Despite initial misgivings by the Council delegation,[36] the suggested text was re-modelled to the satisfaction of both sides.

6.09 In a staff working paper accompanying its White Paper on damages actions for breaches of the EC anti-trust rules, published in 2008,[37] the Commission expressed satisfaction with the outcome of the Rome II process in relation to restrictions of competition:[38]

> The Commission believes that Article 6(3) of Regulation 864/2007 contains an appropriate applicable law rule enabling claimants to effectively use their right to obtain antitrust damages in case of an infringement of the EC competition rules. In particular, these new rules, read together with the rules on jurisdiction, allow for procedural economy as they provide claimants with the option to have their case for antitrust damages heard by one court applying one single law, even in situations where more than one defendant is involved and where the damages occurred in several Member States. The Commission therefore does not consider it necessary to further address the issue of applicable law in the White Paper.

6.10 Art 6 accordingly settles, at least for the foreseeable future, the rules of applicable law for both unfair competition, in its traditional sense, and restrictions of competition. Whether these rules will prove to be satisfactory, however, may be doubted. As appears from the following commentary, several aspects are uncertain and difficult to apply in practice.

---

[31] Common Position, Art 6.

[32] EP 2nd Reading Position, Amendment 17. Also EP 2nd Reading Recommendation, 7-8.

[33] Commission Opinion on the EP 2nd Reading Position (COM (2007) 126 final [14.3.2007]), 5. The Commission also reserved its position concerning the appropriateness of the Council's proposed rule for restrictions of competition, pending the outcome of its study on damages for breaches of EC anti-trust rules (**6.05–6.06** above and, for the outcome of that process, **6.76** below).

[34] Council document 9713/07 (Presse 111) [16.5.2007], 3.

[35] Council document 8215/07 [5.4.2007], 18.

[36] Council document 8408/07 [13.4.2007], 16.

[37] COM (2008) 165 final [2.4.2008].

[38] SEC (2008) 404 [2.4.2008], para 9 (footnotes omitted).

B. THE NATURE OF ARTICLE 6 AND ITS RELATIONSHIP TO ARTICLE 4

According to the first sentence of Recital (21), 'the special rule in Article 6 **6.11** is not an exception to the general rule in Art 4(1) but rather a clarification of it'. This wording originates in the Council's Common Position.[39] Neverthe-less, the relationship between Art 6 and Art 4 is not as straightforward as the Recital would appear to suggest. First, Art 6(2) expressly provides for the application of the rules in Art 4 and not the special rule in Art 6(1) if the act of unfair competition 'affects exclusively the interests of a specific competitor'. This suggests a difference in treatment between the two situ-ations. Secondly, Art 6(3)(b), which allows the claimant in certain circum-stances to elect that the law of the forum should be applied, cannot be explained as a clarification of Art 4(1). Thirdly, Art 6(4) excludes the par-ties' ability to choose the law applicable to a non-contractual obligation under Art 14, a possibility which exists for other obligations arising out of tort/delict falling within Art 4. Fourthly, as the Commission noted, the connecting factor used in Art 6(1)[40] will not necessarily correspond to that used in Art 4(1):[41]

The need for a special rule here is sometimes disputed on the ground that it would lead to the same solution as the general rule in Article 3 [*of the Proposal*[42]], the dam-age for which compensation is sought being assimilated to the anti-competitive effect on which the application of competition law depends. While the two very often coincide in territorial terms, they will not automatically do so: for instance, the question of the place where the damage is sustained is tricky where two firms from State A both operate on market B.

Overall, whatever Recital (21) may say, the rules of applicable law in Arts 6(1) and 6(3) appear sufficiently independent of the general rule for torts to be characterized as special rules in their own right.

If the Recital is taken at face value, and Arts 6(1) and 6(3) are to be treated **6.12** as mere refinements of the general rule for tort/delict, it would follow that Member State courts could rely on the rules in Arts 4(2) and 4(3) for the purpose of displacing the law that would otherwise apply under, at least, Arts 6(1) or 6(3)(a), which contain connecting factors corresponding to the

---

[39] See the Council's accompanying statement of reasons (OJ C289E, 80 [28.11.2006]).
[40] '[T]he law of the country where competitive relations or the collective interests of con-sumers are . . . affected'.
[41] Commission Proposal, 16.
[42] Regulation, Art 4.

country of damage in Art 4(1). It may be doubted whether this outcome was intended.[43] It would allow connecting factors personal to the parties involved, such as habitual residence or the law applicable to a pre-existing relationship, to trump rules of applicable law serving objectives going beyond the balancing of their individual interests, specifically the protection of competitors, consumers, and the general public (Art 6(1)) and the effective enforcement of EC and national competition rules (Art 6(3)).[44] The Commission, in particular, appears to be of the view that these rules did not apply to matters of unfair competition, commenting that:[45]

[T]he rules of secondary connection, of the common residence and the exception clause are not adapted to this matter in general.

6.13 Accordingly, the opening sentence of Recital (21) should probably be read as indicating no more than that the rules of Arts 6(1) and 6(3)(a) follow the methodology of Art 4(1) in focusing on the consequences of the tort/delict and not on the defendant's conduct. On this view, Arts 4(2) and 4(3) do not apply to non-contractual obligations arising out of acts of unfair competition and restrictions of competition, other than the category of claims specifically identified in Art 6(2) as falling within Art 4. It is unfortunate that this point was not settled more clearly.

6.14 A further potential difficulty concerns the relationship between the market-oriented rules in Arts 6(1) and 6(3) and the rule of jurisdiction contained in Art 5(3) of the Brussels I Regulation (matters relating to tort, delict, or quasi-delict). Under the latter rule, a Member State court (if it is not the court of the defendant's domicile or of the place where the event giving rise to damage occurred) may have jurisdiction only with respect to 'damage' occurring within its territory.[46] As the Commission noted,[47] although the connecting factors in Arts 6(1) and 6(3) may be seen as being functionally equivalent to the concept of 'damage', they will not necessarily point to the same country as a test framed in terms of the place of damage. If that view is accepted, this might lead to a mis-match between the 'damage' with respect to which a Member State court has jurisdiction under Art 5(3) of the Brussels I Regulation and the connecting factor that will determine the applicable law under Art 6(1) or 6(3) of the Rome II Regulation. This would be undesirable. One possible advantage of the

---

[43] The editors of Dicey, Morris & Collins (1st supplement, para S35-217) consider that Art 4(2) is not applicable to cases falling within Art 6(1).

[44] Recitals (21)–(23).

[45] Commission Proposal, 16.

[46] Case C-68/93, *Shevill v Presse Alliance SA* [1995] ECR I-415.

[47] Text to n 41 above.

curious wording in the opening sentence of Recital (21) is that it may enable Member States courts faced with cases falling within Art 6(1) or 6(3) to treat the effect on the market identified as the connecting factor in each of these rules as equivalent to 'damage' under Art 5(3) of the Brussels I Regulation.

C. THE LAW APPLICABLE TO NON-CONTRACTUAL OBLIGATIONS ARISING OUT OF ACTS OF UNFAIR COMPETITION (ARTS 6(1) AND 6(2))

SCOPE AND RELATIONSHIP WITH OTHER RULES

The Concept of 'Unfair Competition'

Arts 6(1) and (2) apply to non-contractual obligations 'arising out of an **6.15** act of unfair competition'. Art 6(2) applies to situations in which the relevant act affects exclusively the interests of a specific competitor, and Art 6(1) applies to other non-contractual obligations arising out of an act of this kind.

The concept of 'unfair competition' is well developed in civil law systems, **6.16** but it is less familiar to common lawyers. In a recent decision, the English Court of Appeal refused to develop the existing tort of passing off, which requires misrepresentation, into a general civil wrong of unfair competition. Jacobs LJ concluded:[48]

> I think the tort of passing off cannot and should not be extended into some general law of unfair competition. True it is that trading conditions have changed somewhat over time—but I cannot identify any particular change which makes a general tort of unfair competition desirable, still less necessary. If the courts (or indeed Parliament) were to create such a tort it would be of wholly uncertain scope—one would truly have let the genie out of the bottle.

Within the Regulation, the concept of 'unfair competition' must be inde- **6.17** pendent of the meanings, if any, given to it in national legislation, except

---

[48] *L'Oreal SA v Bellure NV*, n 2 above, [161]. Also M Leistner, n 2 above, 130–3; A M Dugdale and M A Jones, *Clerk & Lindsell on Torts* (19th edn, 2006), para 1-37. Also F Beier, 'The Law of Unfair Competition in the European Community—Its Development and Present Status' [1985] EIPR 284; F Henning-Bodewig and G Schricker, 'New Initiatives for the Harmonisation of Unfair Competition Law in Europe' [2002] EIPR 271; R de Vrey, *Towards a European Unfair Competition Law: A Clash Between Legal Families* (2005); R Hilty and F Henning-Bodewig (eds), *Law Against Unfair Competition* (2007).

insofar as these are consistent with principles common to all, or the large majority at least, of Member States.[49] According to the Commission:[50]

> The purpose of the rules against unfair competition is to protect fair competition by obliging all participants to play the game by the same rules. Among other things they outlaw acts calculated to influence demand (misleading advertising, forced sales, etc), acts that impede competing supplies (disruption of deliveries by competitors, enticing away a competitor's staff, boycotts), and acts that exploit a competitor's value (passing off and the like). The modern competition law seeks to protect not only competitors (horizontal dimension) but also consumers and the public in general (vertical relations). This three-dimensional function of competition law[51] must be reflected in a modern conflict-of-laws instrument. . . .

> Article 5 [*of the Proposal*] applies also to actions for injunctions brought by consumer associations.[52] The proposed Regulation thus sits well with recent decisions of the Court of Justice on the Brussels Convention holding, for instance, that 'a preventive action brought by a consumer protection organisation for the purpose of preventing a trader from using terms considered to be unfair in contracts with private individuals is a matter relating to tort, delict or quasi-delict within the meaning of Article 5(3) of that convention'.[53]

6.18 Commenting on Art 5(2) of it Proposal, which became Art 6(2) of the Regulation, the Commission added:[54]

> Paragraph 2 deals with situations where an act of unfair competition targets a specific competitor, as in the case of enticing away a competitor's staff, corruption, industrial espionage, disclosure of business secrets or inducing breach of contract. It is not entirely excluded that such conduct may also have a negative impact on a given market, but these are situations that have to be regarded as bilateral.

6.19 Although the examples in these paragraphs are helpful in understanding the types of claim that might fall within the concept of 'unfair competition', they do not provide a general definition which enables the outer

---

[49] **3.12** above.

[50] Commission Proposal, 15 (extract—footnotes added).

[51] For an explicit recognition of this triple purpose of modern competition law, see the German Act against Unfair Competition (*Gesetz gegen den unlauteren Wettbewerb*, UWG), §1. For commentary on the German Act, see M Finger and S Schmieder, 'The New Law Against Unfair Competition: An Assessment' (2005) 6 German LJ 201, available at <http://www.germanlawjournal.com/article.php?id=550>; J P Heidenreich, 'The New German Act Against Unfair Competition' (2005), available at <http://www.iuscomp.org/gla/literature/heidenreich.htm>; S Heim, 'Protection of competitors, consumers and the general public—The new German Act against Unfair Competition' (2006) 1 JIPLP 564.

[52] Referring to Directive (EC) No 98/27 on injunctions for the protection of consumers' interests (OJ L166, 51 [11.6.1998]).

[53] Referring to Case C-167/00, *Verein für Konsumenteninformation v Henkel* [2002] ECR I-8111, para 34.

[54] Commission Proposal, 16.

limits of Art 6(1) to be determined. In the search for that definition,[55] the Paris Convention for the Protection of Industrial Property may represent common ground between the Member States, including those with a common law tradition.[56] The second paragraph of Art 10*bis* of the Convention defines an act of unfair competition as:

Any act of competition contrary to honest practices in industrial or commercial matters constitutes an act of unfair competition.

The following paragraph gives the following examples of acts prohibited **6.20** by the Convention:

(i) all acts of such a nature as to create confusion by any means whatever with the establishment, the goods, or the industrial or commercial activities, of a competitor;

(ii) false allegations in the course of trade of such a nature as to discredit the establishment, the goods, or the industrial or commercial activities, of a competitor;

(iii) indications or allegations the use of which in the course of trade is liable to mislead the public as to the nature, the manufacturing process, the characteristics, the suitability for their purpose, or the quantity, of the goods.

Similarly, Art 1 of the World Intellectual Property Organisation's Model **6.21** Provisions on Protection Against Unfair Competition[57] defines an act of unfair competition as including 'any act or practice, in the course of industrial or commercial practices, that is contrary to honest practices', as well as the acts and practices listed in Arts 2 to 6. Those acts or practices are collected under the following headings (a) causing confusion with respect to another's enterprise or its activities (Art 2), (b) damaging another's goodwill or reputation (Art 3), (c) misleading the public (Art 4), (d) discrediting another's enterprise or its activities (Art 5), and (e) unfair competition with respect to secret information (Art 6). These provisions suggest a category that is, potentially, very broad indeed.

Professor Honorati has suggested that the Unfair Commercial Practices **6.22** Directive[58] provides 'a European and binding definition of what is

---

[55] On this question, see also the note prepared by the Permanent Bureau of the Hague Conference, n 1 above, 7–21.

[56] The Convention, originally concluded on 20 March 1883 and amended on several occasions since, is available at <http://www.wipo.int/treaties/en/ip/paris/trtdocs_wo020.html>. For an account of the influence of the UK delegation in the promotion of the unfair competition provisions in the Paris Convention, see C Wadlow, 'The British Origins of Article 10*bis* of the Paris Convention for the Protection of Industrial Property', Oxford Intellectual Property Research Papers (2002), available at <http://www.oiprc.ox.ac.uk/EJWP0403.pdf>.

[57] WIPO Publication No 832(E) (1996). Also 'Protection Against Unfair Competition—An Analysis of the Present World Situation', WIPO Publication No 825(E) (1994).

[58] n 18 above.

intended to be covered by "unfair competition'".[59] Art 5 of the Directive provides:

1. Unfair commercial practices shall be prohibited.
2. A commercial practice shall be unfair if:
   (a) it is contrary to the requirements of professional diligence, and
   (b) it materially distorts or is likely to materially distort the economic behaviour with regard to the product of the average consumer whom it reaches or to whom it is addressed, or of the average member of the group when a commercial practice is directed to a particular group of consumers.
3. Commercial practices which are likely to materially distort the economic behaviour only of a clearly identifiable group of consumers who are particularly vulnerable to the practice or the underlying product because of their mental or physical infirmity, age or credulity in a way which the trader could reasonably be expected to foresee, shall be assessed from the perspective of the average member of that group. This is without prejudice to the common and legitimate advertising practice of making exaggerated statements or statements which are not meant to be taken literally.
4. In particular, commercial practices shall be unfair which:
   (a) are misleading as set out in Articles 6 and 7, or
   (b) are aggressive as set out in Articles 8 and 9.
5. Annex I contains the list of those commercial practices which shall in all circumstances be regarded as unfair. The same single list shall apply in all Member States and may only be modified by revision of this Directive.

6.23 Claims brought by individuals or organizations to enforce the provisions of the Directive (if a Member State in its implementing regulations so provides[60]), or which otherwise concern a practice that it prohibits, should be considered to fall within Art 6(1) of the Regulation. As the Directive recognizes, the protection of consumer interests from unfair practices indirectly protects legitimate businesses from their competitors who do not play by the rules.[61] Its subject matter, therefore, fits squarely within the existing framework of unfair competition law. The Directive applies, however, only to 'business-to-consumer commercial practices', defined in Art 2(d) as 'any act, omission, course of conduct or representation, commercial communication including advertising and marketing, by a trader, directly

---

[59] C Honorati, n 3 above, 142.

[60] Unfair Commercial Practices Directive, Art 11(1). The UK has opted for enforcement by public authorities, through criminal sanctions and other powers (see Consumer Protection from Unfair Trading Regulations (SI 2008/1277), Parts 3 and 4). A similar approach has been taken in implementing Directive (EC) No 2006/114 concerning misleading and comparative advertising (OJ L376, 21 [27.12.2006]) (see Business Protection from Misleading Marketing Regulations (SI 2008/1276), Parts 2 to 4).

[61] Ibid, Recital (8).

connected with the promotion, sale or supply of a product to consumers'. According to the Recitals, '[i]t neither covers nor affects the national laws on unfair commercial practices which harm only competitors' economic interests or which relate to a transaction between traders'.[62] Even if the obvious differences in terminology between the Directive and the Rome II Regulation are put to one side,[63] it will be obvious that the Directive cannot possibly claim to provide an exhaustive definition of the non-contractual obligations falling within Art 6(1) or 6(2). In this connection, therefore, the examples in the Commission's explanatory memorandum and the definitions of an 'act of unfair competition' in the Paris Convention and WIPO Model Provisions (**6.19–6.21** above)would appear to provide more reliable guides as to the autonomous meaning to be given to the concept of 'unfair competition' within the Rome II Regulation.

Both the text of Arts 6(1) and 6(2) and the Commission's commentary on **6.24** its Proposal suggest that, in order for there to be an 'act of unfair competition', the defendant's conduct must have some impact on relations between the participants in a particular market, whether horizontally (between competitors) or vertically (as against consumers collectively). If the relevant act or course of conduct is directed at one or more of the defendant's competitors in a particular market, it will not be difficult to conclude that it constitutes an act of unfair competition, so as to fall within Art 6(1) or Art 6(2). If, more commonly, the conduct is directed at market participants other than competitors (including consumers and other customers, as well as suppliers) then, in order for Art 6(1) or Art 6(2) to apply, it must be shown that the act or course of conduct has some (appreciable) effect either on a specific competitor or upon a class of market participants, whether competitors or consumers. Otherwise, the law applicable to any resulting non-contractual obligations will fall instead to be determined by reference to the general rule in Art 4. Conduct directed at a single individual other than a competitor (e.g. a fraudulent representation by a business to a customer as to the properties of a product) seems unlikely to cross this threshold,[64] but there will clearly be circumstances in which it is capable of doing so (e.g. a fraudulent representation to a customer as to the

---

[62] Recital (6). Recital (8) to the Directive also recognizes that there are other commercial practices which, although not harming consumers, may hurt competitors and business customers, and urges the Commission to examine the need for further Community measures in the field of unfair competition.

[63] Regulation: 'unfair competition' (French: *'concurrence déloyale'*); Directive: 'unfair commercial practices' (French: *'pratiques commerciales déloyales'*).

[64] Neither Art 6(1) nor Art 6(2), it may be noted, refers to the interests of an individual consumer.

properties of a competitor's product, inducing a competitor's customer to break or terminate his contract). On the other hand, conduct directed at an entire class of market participants and which distorts the conditions for competition in the market, for example the use of unfair standard terms as referred to in the Commission's example, falls within Art 6(1). The rule may also be suited to dealing with civil actions for compensation based, for example, on insider dealing or market abuse and other rules of this character regulating behaviour of participants in particular markets.[65]

6.25 From an English law perspective, the concept of a non-contractual obligation 'arising out of an act of unfair competition' in Art 6(1) appears capable of accommodating (a) the tort of passing off,[66] (b) the tort of malicious falsehood as it applies to cases of comparative advertising,[67] and (c) actions by a non-public body (including the Consumer Association[68]) designated as an enforcer under Part 8 of the Enterprise Act 2002,[69] or otherwise, with respect to infringements of EC and domestic consumer protection legislation.

Matters Excluded from Article 6(1)

6.26 Art 6(1) must, however, be taken to exclude the following obligations, dealt with by separate rules:

- non-contractual obligations arising out of acts of unfair competition affecting exclusively the interests of a specific competitor (Art 6(2));
- non-contractual obligations arising out of a restriction of competition (Art 6(3));
- non-contractual obligations arising out of an infringement of intellectual property right (Art 8).

The following paragraphs consider these three (negative) aspects of the scope of Art 6(1).

---

[65] In such cases, it may be necessary to construe the concept of 'competitor' broadly so as to encompass participants competing for the same resources (e.g. shares) in the marketplace.

[66] e.g. *Consorzio del Prosciutto di Parma v Marks & Spencer plc* [1991] RPC 351 (EWCA); *L'Oreal v Bellure*, n 2 above.

[67] e.g. *De Beers v International General Electric Co of New York Ltd* [1975] 1 WLR 972 (EWHC); *McDonald's Hamburgers Ltd v Burgerking (UK) Ltd* [1986] FSR 45 (EWHC), reversed on other grounds [1987] FSR 112 (EWCA).

[68] Enterprise Act 2002 (Part 8) (Designation of the Consumers' Association) Order (SI 2005/917).

[69] The provisions of Part 8 give effect under UK law to the Injunctions Directive (n 52 above). Also Commission Communication concerning Article 4(3) of the Injunctions Directive, concerning the entities qualified under the Directive to bring an enforcement action (OJ C63, 5 08/03/2008 [8.3.2008]).

Relationship with Article 6(2)—acts exclusively affecting a specific competitor

For Art 6(1) or 6(2) to apply at all, there must be an act of unfair competi- **6.27** tion, in the sense described above,[70] having an appreciable effect on relations between market participants. Art 6(2) removes from Art 6(1) situations in which the act of unfair competition 'affects exclusively the interests of a single competitor'. In proposing this qualification, the Commission referred to similar exclusions from the general rule for acts of unfair competition in Art 136(2) of the Swiss Code of Private International Law,[71] in s 4(2) of the Dutch Act regarding conflict of laws for unlawful acts,[72] and in German case law.[73]

This test used in Art 6(2) is one that is easier to state than to apply, although **6.28** the language used and the status of Art 6(2) as a derogation from the rule in Art 6(1) suggest it should be construed restrictively.[74] As noted,[75] the Commission gave the following examples of acts of unfair competition falling within this sub-rule: (a) enticing away a competitor's staff, (b) corruption, (c) industrial espionage, (d) disclosure of business secrets, and (e) inducing breach of contract. The Commission suggested that what these situations had in common was that the defendant's act 'targets a particular competitor' and that, notwithstanding any negative effect on the marketplace, they were to be treated as 'bilateral'.[76] In the examples given by the Commission, any effect that the defendant's conduct has on the relevant market can be argued to be subordinate to its effect on the targeted competitor, so that it is more appropriate to apply the general rules in Art 4, which reflect the individual interests and connections of the parties, than the market-oriented rule in Art 6(1).[77]

The Commission's first concept of 'targeting' is, however, difficult to **6.29** reconcile with the language of Art 6(2), which focuses less on the defendant's underlying intention and more on the consequences of an act of

[70] **6.15–6.25** above.
[71] **1.40** above.
[72] **1.28** above.
[73] M Leistner, n 3 above, 146–50, referring also to s 48(2) of the Austrian Code of Private International Law and the unitary rule in Art 4 of the Spanish Law on Unfair Competition (**1.34** above).
[74] C Honorati, n 3 above, 157. For the suggestion that the difficulties inherent in the 'mosaic view' approach may lead to a more generous interpretation in some cases, see **6.57** below.
[75] **6.18** above
[76] Commission Proposal, 16.
[77] Cf C Honorati, n 3 above, 154–8, arguing that the law of the affected market should apply to all non-contractual obligations arising from acts of unfair competition.

unfair competition.[78] The Commission's second concept of 'bilaterality' also appears unpromising as a litmus test, as it suggests that either there must be a pre-existing relationship between the parties or that the act of unfair competition must not involve another market participant. On either view, the concept seems at odds some of the Commission's examples: there may be no pre-existing relationship, for example, in a case of industrial espionage and inducement of a breach of contract will necessarily involve a third party, such as a supplier or customer.[79] It may, therefore, be more helpful to consider the requirement of 'exclusivity' by asking the question whether the act of unfair competition gives a competitive advantage to the defendant solely at the expense of a single competitor,[80] without at the same time materially changing the conditions of competition in the market as a whole. If so, it may be said to affect that competitor's interests to the exclusion of others competing in the same market. If, however, an act of unfair competition has an appreciable effect upon the conditions upon which other persons compete with the defendant in the market, Art 6(1) rather than Art 6(2) will apply, although the act itself may directly affect and concern a particular competitor or its product. This approach seems consistent both with the overall objectives of Art 6, in terms of protecting competitors, consumers, and the general public and ensuring the proper functioning of the market, and with the specific examples given by the Commission. Situations involving passing off or misleading or comparative advertising provide examples of cases falling within Art 6(1) rather than Art 6(2), as the defendant's conduct is liable directly to distort competition in the market as a whole by using the get-up or characteristics of a particular competitor's product to enhance his position in the market, not only vis-à-vis the 'targeted' competitor but also against others. On the other hand, the act of inducing a competitor's customer to break his contract and to contract instead with the defendant seems unlikely to have a wider market effect. The answer to the question whether an act of unfair competition materially changes the conditions of competition in the market as a whole may be sensitive to the particular facts of the case. For example, if the defendant steals trade secrets from the claimant allowing him to produce and sell goods more cheaply in the market in competition

---

[78] M Leistner, n 3 above, 144.

[79] Matthias Leistner (ibid, at 145) is prepared to overlook this inconsistency and supports 'direct bilaterality' as the principle underlying Art 6(2), with the result that Art 6(1) would be disapplied only 'when the direct effects of an act of unfair competition prejudice exclusively the interests of a specific competitor, *without at the same time influencing the customer side of the market*'.

[80] Who may or may not be the claimant.

not only with the claimant but also with other market participants, it may be argued that Art 6(1) should apply.[81]

If Art 6(2) applies, the law applicable to the obligation in question will be **6.30** determined not by the law identified in Art 6(1), but by the general rule for non-contractual obligations arising out of a tort/delict in Art 4.[82] From the perspective of English law, Art 6(2) appears capable of accommodating claims arising between persons competing with one another based on the following torts or equitable wrongs: (a) causing loss by unlawful means,[83] (b) inducing breach of contract,[84] (c) intimidation,[85] (d) lawful and unlawful act conspiracy,[86] (e) some cases of malicious falsehood (including the causes of action sometimes referred to as 'slander of title' or 'slander of goods'),[87] (f) deceit (at least insofar as the giving of a bribe is concerned[88]), and some cases of (g) breach of confidence,[89] and (h) dishonest assistance in a breach of fiduciary duty.[90] Defamation of a person, including situations in which a defamatory statement concerning a thing casts a defamatory imputation on the reputation of a natural or legal person,[91] arguably falls outside the scope of the Regulation by virtue of Art 1(2)(g).[92]

Relationship with Article 6(3)—restrictions of competition

The structure of Art 6, as well as its drafting history,[93] emphasize that the **6.31** categories of 'non-contractual obligations arising from an act of unfair competition' and 'non-contractual obligations arising out of a restriction of competition' were intended to be mutually exclusive. In general terms,

---

[81] Cf C Wadlow, 'Trade secrets and the Rome II Regulation on the law applicable to non-contractual obligations' [2008] EIPR 309, 311–12, suggesting that all trade secrets cases fall within Art 4 of the Regulation, whether by virtue of Art 6(2) or directly.

[82] **Ch 4** above. As to the parties' ability to choose the law applicable under Art 14, see **6.75** below.

[83] See *OBG Ltd v Allan* [2007] UKHL 21; [2008] 1 AC 1.

[84] Ibid.

[85] *Rookes v Barnard* [1964] AC 1129 (UKHL).

[86] *Lonrho Ltd v Shell Petroleum Co Ltd (No 2)* [1982] AC 173; *Lonrho plc v Fayed* [1992] 1 AC 148; *Revenue and Customs Commissioner v Total Network SL* [2008] UKHL 19; [2008] 2 WLR 711 (all HL).

[87] A M Dugdale and M A Jones, n 48 above, para 24-01. See e.g. *London Ferro-Concrete Co Ltd v Justicz* (1951) 68 RPC 261 (CA); *Ratcliffe v Evans* [1991] FSR 62 (CA). Cases involving comparative advertising (see n 67 above) may be argued to have a more direct effect on the marketplace, so falling within Art 6(1).

[88] See e.g. *Arab Monetary Fund v Hashim* [1993] 1 Lloyd's Rep 543 (Evans J), affd [1996] 1 Lloyd's Rep 589 (CA).

[89] **6.29** above.

[90] *Royal Brunei Airlines Sdn Bhd v Tan* [1995] 2 AC 378 (PC) (**4.101–4.102** above).

[91] *Clerk & Lindsell on Torts*, n 48 above, para 23-41.

[92] **3.227** above.

[93] **6.02–6.08** above.

the distinction between the two categories may be said to be that the aim of the former is to repress falsification of competition whereas the aim of the latter is to ensure freedom of competition.[94] It has also been suggested that:[95]

Where there are overlapping areas, such as with respect to boycotts, discrimination and the protection of distribution systems, preference should be given to a regulating in the context of cartel law; a double regulation also within the framework of unfair competition law does not seem necessary.

6.32   By providing a detailed definition of the concept of 'restriction of competition' in Art 6(3), Recital (23) makes clear that the following matters are not to be treated as acts of unfair competition under Art 6(1):

'[P]rohibitions on agreements between undertakings, decisions by associations of undertakings and concerted practices which have as their object or effect the prevention, restriction or distortion of competition within a Member State or within the internal market, as well as prohibitions on the abuse of a dominant position within a Member State or within the internal market, where such agreements, decisions, concerted practices or abuses are prohibited by Articles 81 and 82 of the Treaty or by the law of a Member State

6.33   Accordingly, Art 6(3) covers not only breaches of EC Treaty law but also corresponding breaches of the competition law of individual Member States.[96] It is unclear whether the definition in Recital (23) is exhaustive or whether Art 6(3) is also capable of encompassing similar conduct that is prohibited by the anti-trust legislation of a non-Member State of the European Community.[97] As the Regulation has universal application under Art 3,[98] there seems no reason in principle why it should not.[99] The alternatives, which appear less satisfactory, would be to fit claims to enforce the competition laws of a non-Member State into Art 6(1) or to leave them to be regulated by the general rule for tort/delict in Art 4.

---

[94] F Henning-Bodewig and G Schricker, n 48 above, 272; A Thünken, 'Multi-State Advertising over the Internet and the Private International Law of Unfair Competition' (2002) 51 ICLQ 909, 910–11; Permanent Bureau of the Hague Conference, n 1 above, 7. Also Regulation (EC) No 1/2003 on the implementation of the rules on competition laid down in Articles 81 and 82 of the Treaty (OJ L1, 1 [4.1.2003]), Recital (9).

[95] F Henning-Bowedig and G Schricker, ibid.

[96] See UK Competition Act 1998, ss 2 (agreements preventing competition), 18 (abuse of dominant position).

[97] Subject to public policy considerations (Art 26). See, e.g., Protection of Trading Interests (US Antitrust Measures Order (SI 1983/900) (UK)).

[98] **3.294–3.295** above.

[99] Dicey, Morris & Collins, 1st supplement, para S35-220; Editorial Comment, 'Sometimes it takes thirty years and even more. . .' (2007) 44 Commn Market L Rev 1567, 1572–3.

Relationship with Article 8—intellectual property rights

The law concerning unfair competition is very closely related to the law **6.34** regulating intellectual property rights and their infringement,[100] a topic dealt with separately in Art 8 of the Regulation. Recital (26) gives, as examples of 'intellectual property rights' within Art 8, copyright, related rights, the *sui generis* right for the protection of databases, and industrial property rights (including patents and trademarks).[101] For example, an action based on infringement of the claimant's trademark by a competitor through comparative advertising[102] would fall within Art 8 not Art 6(1).[103] On the other hand, confidential information and goodwill cannot be regarded as 'intellectual property rights' for the purposes of the Regulation. Although both have a commercial value[104] and enjoy legal protection (under English law, for example, by the equitable wrong of breach of confidence and the tort of passing off), that protection is purely negative in terms of preventing injury to the relationship between confider and confidee or a trader and his customers. Intellectual property rights, on the other hand, are artificial legal concepts that positively enhance the value to the right-holder of the intangible products of the time and resources expended in developing ideas or expressions of ideas.

Relationship with the Unfair Commercial Practices Directive

The Commission's Rome II Proposal was published shortly after the Commis- **6.35** sion had separately proposed a Directive on unfair business-to-consumer commercial practices in the internal market, covering matters of substantive law falling within the traditional domain of unfair competition law.[105] This coincidence led to a debate as to the relationship between the rules to be contained in the two measures, centring upon the role of the 'country of origin' of goods and services in internal market instruments and their impact on measures, such as the proposed Rome II Regulation, containing uniform rules of private international law.[106] At an early stage in

---

[100] Permanent Bureau of the Hague Conference, n 1 above, 9.

[101] **8.10–8.13** below.

[102] Under English law, see Trade Marks Act 1994, s 10(6); *Cable & Wireless plc v British Telecommunications plc* [1998] FSR 383 (EWHC).

[103] C Hahn and O Tell, 'The Future "Rome I and II" Regulations' in *Basedow*, Intellectual Property, n 3 above, 16.

[104] See, in the case of confidential information, *Douglas v Hello! Ltd (No 3)* (sub nom *OBG Ltd v Allen*) [2007] UKHL 21; [2008] 1 AC 1.

[105] COM (2003) 356 final [18.6.2003].

[106] For the wider debate surrounding the so-called 'country of origin principle', see **1.58–1.61** and **1.85** above and **16.04–16.31** below.

the discussions in the Council's Rome II Committee, the Commission's representative expressed the view that, if the proposed Directive were adopted, the Rome II Regulation would then only cover business-to-business dealings.[107] It may be doubted whether this view was correct at the time. It must, in any event, be re-appraised in light of the wording of the Directive in its final form

6.36 Art 4 of the Commission's proposal (led by DG SanCo) for the Unfair Commercial Practices Directive provided that:[108]

1. Traders shall only comply with the national provisions, falling within the field approximated by this Directive, of the Member State in which they are established. The Member State in which the trader is established shall ensure such compliance.

2. Member States shall neither restrict the freedom to provide services nor restrict the free movement of goods for reasons falling within the field approximated by this Directive.

6.37 Both the EESC and the Council's Committee on civil law matters expressed concerns as to the relationship between this 'internal market clause' and Art 5 of the Commission Proposal for the Rome II instrument (unfair competition). The former, in its opinion on the Commission Proposal, contended:[109]

The provisions of the regulation on unfair competition (Article 5) are based on the principle traditionally applied in this area, namely that the applicable law shall be that of the country in which competition is directly and substantially affected. This rule entails equal treatment of domestic and foreign competitors in relation to the rules which they are required to observe. The same subject is, however, dealt with differently in Article 4(1) of the draft Directive on unfair business practices, with reference being made to the Member State of establishment principle. Although the explanatory memoranda to these two legal instruments do not address this difference, the disparity in the application of general principles of Community and internal market law can be resolved as follows: Article 5 of the regulation refers to external Community law relating to non-Member States (or in areas not covered by the directive), whereas Article 4(1) of the directive deals with relations between Member States in the internal market. If this is in fact the intention, the Commission would do well to make it clear in the explanatory memoranda to the two legal instruments. However, this still leaves an unacceptable situation whereby the same rules apply to EU and non-EU competitors within a given Member State, whereas different rules may apply if the competitors in question are from different EU Member States (this is, however, a question of the degree of harmonisation of substantive competition law brought about by the directive).

[107] Council document 5430/04 [27.1.2004], 4.
[108] COM (2003) 356 final [18.6.2003].
[109] EESC Opinion, para 5.3.

The Committee on civil law matters, in its opinion on the proposed Directive, **6.38** expressed concern 'that this Article 4 will create a choice of law rule designating the law of the country of establishment of the trader (country of origin) as applicable to matters of unfair commercial practices'.[110] Referring to the different solution adopted by Art 5 of the Commission's Rome II Proposal, the Committee suggested that '[i]f this solution is not retained, it would certainly affect the interests of competitors and the general public'.[111]

In the final version of the Unfair Commercial Practices Directive, Art 4(1) **6.39** of the Commission's Proposal (**6.36** above) was omitted, leaving the way clear for the Rome II Regulation to address the question of applicable law for acts of unfair competition by a rule of general application, subject to the overriding obligation of Member States to give effect to the requirements of the Directive, to EC Treaty provisions, and other measures regulating the internal market.[112] In presenting this compromise to the Member States, the Council Presidency stated:[113]

The compromise proposal by the Presidency retains in Article 4 the obligation for Member States [*under*] the free movement provision, in consideration of the proposal's legal basis, but it deletes the 'country of origin clause'. Article 3 aims at clarifying the relationship both with existing Community legislation and private international law.

Art 3(4) of the Directive in its final form provided: **6.40**

In the case of conflict between the provisions of this Directive, and other Community rules regulating specific aspects of unfair commercial practices, the latter shall prevail and apply to those specific aspects.

Art 6 of the Rome II Regulation is a Community rule regulating the law applicable to acts of unfair competition, including unfair business-to-consumer commercial practices. Following its adoption, and in accordance with Art 3(4) of the Unfair Commercial Practices Directive, it no longer seems possible to argue that the residual 'internal market clause' in Art 4 of the Directive mandates application of the law of the trader's country of origin.[114] Instead,

---

[110] Council document 5668/04 [28.1.2004], para 4.

[111] Ibid, para 8. Also the opinion of the Council legal service (Council document 7799/04 [25.3.2004] (partially accessible)) and the Committee's subsequent report (Council document 8821/04 [10.5.2004]).

[112] Recital (35) (**16.01**) below.

[113] Council document 9217/04 [10.5.2004], 3 (word in square brackets added for sense). The Commission agreed, reluctantly, to the deletion of what it described as 'the choice of law rule' in Art 4(1) (see COM (2004) 753 final [16.11.2004], 4).

[114] For further discussion of the rise and fall of the so-called 'country of origin' principle, see **1.85** and **16.11–16.31**.

the provisions of the Directive and implementing measures adopted by Member States, to the extent that they are relevant to civil matters at all,[115] must be applied as part of the law applicable to a non-contractual obligation under the Regulation (if it is the law of a Member State) or, possibly, as an overriding mandatory provision of the law of the forum.[116]

The Country where Competitive Relations or the Collective Interests of Consumers are Affected

6.42 Under Art 6(1), the law applicable to a non-contractual obligation arising out of an act of unfair competition is the law of the country where competitive relations or the collective interests of consumers are, or are likely to be, affected. Art 5 of the Commission Proposal had similarly referred to the law of the country where competitive relations or the collective interests of consumers are or are likely to be *directly and substantially* affected.

6.43 Recital (21) describes the objectives underlying this rule as follows:

> In matters of unfair competition, the conflict-of-law rule should protect competitors, consumers and the general public and ensure that the market economy functions properly. The connection to the law of the country where competitive relations or the collective interests of consumers are, or are likely to be, affected generally satisfies these objectives.

6.44 According to the Commission, its chosen connecting factor corresponded to 'the market where competitors are seeking to gain the customer's favour'. In the Commission's view:[117]

> This solution corresponds to the victims' expectations since the rule generally designates the law governing their economic environment. But it also secures equal treatment for all operators on the same market. The purpose of competition law is to protect a market; it pursues a macro-economic objective. Actions for compensation are purely secondary and must be dependent on the overall judgement of how the market functions.

6.45 This link to the market affected by the defendant's conduct, if accepted, may be thought likely to lead Member State courts to draw on principles and reasoning from the case law of the Court of Justice and the practice of the Commission concerning Arts 81 and 82 (ex-Arts 85 and 86) prohibiting,

---

[115] Recital (9) states that the Directive is without prejudice to individual actions brought by those who have been harmed by unfair commercial practices, and Art 11 gives Member States a choice between enforcement by legal action or by an administrative authority. The UK has chosen the latter option (n 60 above).

[116] **15.19** below.

[117] Commission Proposal, 16.

respectively, anti-competitive agreements and the abuse of a dominant market position. In particular, that case law and practice may be relevant insofar as it considers the definition and location of a 'market'. This aspect is considered in further detail in the commentary below on Art 6(3), in which the country of the 'market . . . affected' is expressly identified as the main connecting factor (see **6.62–6.63**). Elsewhere, however, it has been suggested that the concept of the 'affected market' bears a narrower meaning in the context of unfair competition law, referring to a marketplace solely within the territory of a single country.[118]

Even so, one cannot but take notice that both the Commission in its **6.46** Proposal and the Council in its Common Position avoided defining the connecting factor for acts of unfair competition in terms of the 'affected market'. By way of contrast, as noted above, Art 6(3) of both the Common Position and the Regulation expressly refer to the 'country where the market is . . . affected'.[119]

Professor Honorati, commenting on omission of the 'affected market' cri- **6.47** terion from the Commission Proposal, speculates that:[120]

[O]ne reason for abandoning wording that received strong support and is by now wide spread,[121] is because of an assumed vagueness and uncertainty of this criterion. The difficulties in applying the effect-doctrine, especially within its first applications to antitrust cases, are certainly well known. It is possible that it was thought that, by making clear that the relevant legal values are the competitive relations and the consumers' collective interests, the risk of uncertainty and vagueness would be reduced.

She suggests, however, that the language chosen by the Commission does **6.48** not improve legal certainty, and concludes that:[122]

[T]he criterion of the place where competitive relations and consumers interests are to be substantially affected . . . is to be interpreted as having the same meaning as the more traditional criterion of the affected market. Different textual formulation should not be considered as implying a different connecting factor.

A possible explanation for the words chosen to describe the connecting fac- **6.49** tor in Art 6(1) is that the Commission wanted to emphasize that its proposed

---

[118] Permanent Bureau of the Hague Conference, n 1 above, 27 referring to a commentary on Art 136 of the Swiss Code of Private International Law, which contains a provision similar to Art 6.
[119] **6.07–6.08** above.
[120] C Honorati, n 3 above, 149.
[121] e.g. Swiss Federal Code of Private International Law (**1.40** above), Art 136(1); Proposal of the European Group of Private International Law (**1.54** above), Art 4(b).
[122] C Honorati, n 3 above, 150.

special rule applied not only to actions between competitors (horizontal relations) but also actions between suppliers and 'consumers' (vertical relations),[123] and to bring within its scope actions brought by consumers' associations to enforce consumer protection legislation.[124] Thus, the Commission indicates in the explanatory memorandum accompanying its Proposal[125] that the concept of the 'collective interests of consumers' is inspired by a number of Community consumer protection directives, particularly the Injunctions Directive.[126] Within the framework of the Rome II Regulation, however, it is submitted that the concept of 'consumer' must be construed more widely, as referring to the person seeking to acquire products or services on the market, and not restricted, as elsewhere in EC law[127] to a person acting outside his trade or profession (normally, the ultimate consumer of a product or service). With this in mind, the twin elements of the connecting factor in Art 6(1) could be seen as descriptions of two different aspects of the market affected by the act of unfair competition, and not as departing from the 'affected market' solution favoured by Professor Honorati and others.

6.50 A possible alternative explanation for the choice of connecting factor in Art 6(1) is that it was recognized that an act of unfair competition may produce its effects not across the entire geographic area of a market for a particular product, but across a more restricted area. For example, a newspaper advertisement comparing the claimant's products unfavourably to those of the defendant may be distributed, wholly or exclusively, in a single State only.[128] In such a case, the effect of the defendant's act on competitive relations in the product market in question is restricted to the area of distribution of the newspaper, even if the geographic area of the market is wider. Equally, if the defendant uses particular unfair terms only in his dealings with customers in a particular Member State, the effect of that conduct on the collective interests of consumers will be limited to that

---

[123] M Leistner, n 3 above, 141 maintaining that the formulation 'is consistent with the modern institutional approach of the existing European Union directives in the field of unfair competition law, which follow the triple objective of protecting the interests of competitors, consumers, and the public in general in an undistorted competition'.

[124] *VFK v Henkel*, n 53 above.

[125] Commission Proposal, 15. In a note written in December 2004 to the Member State delegations (n 9 above), DG Markt made clear its view that 'the test provided by Art 5 [*of the Proposal*] is far from ideal' and suggested that 'the term "collective interests of consumers" was only intended to cover actions brought by consumer associations'.

[126] n 52 above.

[127] e.g. Brussels I Regulation, Art 15(1); Unfair Commercial Practices Directive, n 18 above, Art 2(a).

[128] Cf Case C-68/93, *Shevill v Presse Alliance SA* [1995] ECR I-415.

Member State even if the product market extends over a wider area. On this view, which seems more in line with the language used, the connecting factor in Art 6(1), although not departing entirely from the 'affected market' approach, must be taken to be sensitive to the particular act of unfair competition and the precise effect that it has on other market participants.

A final possibility is that the Community legislature intended that the concept of a 'market' should be confined within national frontiers, and not confused with the broader, economic concept developed within the framework of EC competition law.[129] Some support can be derived from the fact that, in the explanatory memorandum accompanying its Proposal, the Commission only addresses the problem of multiple applicable laws by reference to a situation in which the anti-competitive conduct 'has an impact on several markets',[130] and not by reference to the situation in which a single market covers the territory of more than one country. Nevertheless, that approach would seem unduly parochial and to conflict not only with the approach taken under Arts 81 and 82 of the EC Treaty but also with the existence and objectives of the internal market. The 'qualified affected market' approach suggested in the preceding paragraph would appear the better solution. **6.51**

Whether Art 6(1) is taken to point towards the entire geographic area of the affected market or only the specific area within that market that was affected by the defendant's act of unfair competition, two questions remain. First, what is to be considered a sufficiently material 'effect' for this purpose.[131] Secondly, what approach is to be taken if the geographic area identified by the connecting factor takes in the territory of two or more countries. **6.52**

As to the first point, Art 5 of the Commission Proposal, unlike the Regulation in its final form, expressly required that the act of unfair competition had a 'direct' and 'substantial' effect on competitive relations or the collective interests of consumers. The Commission commented that:[132] **6.53**

Regarding the assessment of the impact on the market, academic writers generally acknowledge that only the direct substantial effects of an act of unfair competition should be taken into account.

---

[129] **6.62–6.63** below.

[130] Commission Proposal, 16.

[131] For discussion of the same point in relation to Art 6(3), see **6.65–6.66** below.

[132] Commission Proposal, 16. Also the EESC Opinion (extract quoted at text to n 109 above).

6.54 This requirement of a 'direct substantial effect' is nebulous,[133] and the wording was deleted at an early stage in discussions in the Council's Rome II Committee.[134] In this connection, the Austrian delegation argued that:[135]

> It must also be clear which law is applicable even where claims are asserted on the grounds of anti-competitive effects that are not substantial. Whether the effects are so substantial that claims arise is a question of substantive law. The same applies to the question of directness.

6.55 The Commission's suggested approach may also be argued to sit uncomfortably with the approach taken by the ECJ in defining the territorial scope of the substantive rules concerning restrictions of competition in Arts 81 and 82 of the EC Treaty. Thus, in its leading decision on this point, the Court chose to focus on the requirement that the anti-competitive arrangement be 'implemented' within the Community, rather than on whether it had a sufficient effect on the Community market.[136] The debate as to whether EC law recognizes an 'effects-based' doctrine of competition law and the nature of that doctrine continues, although the Commission remains one of its main proponents.[137] Within the Rome II Regulation, a focus on the market, or sector of the market, in which the act of unfair competition was 'implemented' would appear, objectively, to achieve greater certainty than a requirement of 'direct and substantial effect'. On either view, it may be argued that 'spill over' effects of an act of unfair competition on other markets should be treated as 'indirect consequences' of that act, and left out of account in determining the law applicable under Art 6(1).[138]

---

[133] Dicey, Morris & Collins, 1st supplement, paras S35-217 ('these terms involve a not inconsiderable margin of appreciation in relation to particular measures').

[134] Council document 10173/04 [14.6.2004], Art 5(1). Cf the proposal of the German delegation that the words 'materially and imminently' should be inserted (Council document 16240/04 [23.12.2004], 4).

[135] Council document 9009/04 ADD 1 [3.5.2004], 2. Also ibid, ADD 14 [24.5.2004], 3 (Lithuania). Also **4.31** above.

[136] Joined Cases 89, 104, 116, 117, and 125 to 129/85, *Åhlström Osakeyhtiö v Commission* [1988] ECR 5193, paras 16–18 (the *Wood Pulp* case). Also UK Competition Act 1998, s 2(3).

[137] e.g. D Lange and J Sandage, 'The Wood Pulp Decision and its Implications for the Scope of the EC Competition Law' (1989) 26 Common Market L Rev 137; F A Mann, 'The Public International Law of Restrictive Practices in the European Court of Justice' (1989) 38 ICLQ 375; D Wyatt et al. (eds), *Wyatt and Dashwood's European Union Law* (5th edn, 2006), para 22-016; R Whish, *Competition Law* (5th edn, 2003), paras 12.54–12.55.

[138] For the exclusion of the 'indirect consequences' of an event giving rise to damage from the concept of 'damage' in Art 4(1), see **4.36–45** above.

As to the second point, the Commission suggested that its emphasis on a   **6.56**
direct, substantial effect was important 'since anti-competitive conduct
commonly has an impact on several markets and gives rise to the distributive application of the laws involved'. This refers back to the Commission's
reference, in its commentary on Art 4(1), to the *Mosaikbetrachtung* or
'mosaic view' approach, which applies when the connecting factor in the
Regulation points to the law of more than one country.[139] Difficulties in
applying this approach to cases falling within Art 4 have already been discussed.[140] Those difficulties are, however, magnified in the case of Art 6(1)
as (a) the connecting factor, unless it can be interpreted restrictively as
referring to several (artificial) national markets rather than a single economic market,[141] is more likely to point to a geographic area spanning the
territory of more than one country, or even an entire free trade area (such
as the EC/EEA), (b) the connecting factor does not focus on the location of
harmful consequences of the act of competition to an individual claimant,
and (c) Art 6(1) contains no escape clause on which a Member State court
may rely (legitimately or otherwise) to side-step the requirement to apply
the laws identified on a distributive basis.

Take, for example, a case in which the defendant markets goods in such a   **6.57**
way as to exploit the claimant's goodwill. The impact on the claimant's
sales may occur, principally, in one country and the claimant may be content to pursue a remedy only with respect to sales lost in that country. The
market for products of the relevant kind in which the parties compete
may, however, be much wider and Art 6(1) (assuming that it applies[142])
will lead to the application 'on a distributive basis' of the law of each
country within whose territory the market operates on a distributive basis.
In these circumstances, the wording of Art 6(1) does not appear sufficiently
flexible to allow the court to re-characterize the connecting factor as 'damage'
to or an 'effect upon' the individual claimant and to apply the law of each
country to sales lost by the claimant in that country. Instead, it is submitted,
the sales lost by one market participant must be treated as an indissociable
part of the effect of the act of unfair competition on competitive relations
in the entire market and the laws of all relevant countries applied to the
claim on some other distributive basis (for example, market share of sales by
country and producer) to determine the relief to which the claimant is entitled.
This is as impractical as it is unattractive, but it would appear a necessary

---

[139] **3.298–3.301** above.
[140] **4.69–4.74** above. For a defence of the application of the 'mosaic view' approach in this area, see M Leistner, n 3 above, 153–7.
[141] An argument rejected at **6.51** above.
[142] **6.15–6.34** above.

consequence of the decision by the Community legislator to adopt a rule that focuses not on the individual interests of the litigating parties but on the wider interests of the market participants and the general public. Against this background, Member State courts may be tempted to find ways of avoiding the problems inherent in the 'mosaic view' approach, for example (a) adopting a restrictive interpretation of the connecting factor so as to refer to a national market or sector of the market, whatever the economic reality, (b) finding reasons to define the geographic area of the economic market or the affected sector of that market within the borders of a single country, or (c) applying the exclusionary rule in Art 6(2) more generously, ignoring some effects on the market as a whole in order to reach the lifeboat represented by the escape clause in Art 4(3).[143]

D. THE LAW APPLICABLE TO NON-CONTRACTUAL OBLIGATIONS ARISING OUT OF RESTRICTIONS OF COMPETITION (ART 6(3))

6.58 Under Art 6(3)(a), the law applicable to a non-contractual obligation arising out a restriction of competition shall be the law of the country where the market is, or is likely to be, affected. Art 6(3)(b) contains a limited exception to that rule in favour of the law of the forum if (1) the person seeking compensation sues in the courts of a Member State in which at least one of the defendants is domiciled, (2) the market in that Member State is amongst those directly and substantially affected by the restriction of competition, and (3) the claimant chooses to base his claim on the law of the forum. These rules should be read together with Recital (22), as follows:

The non-contractual obligations arising out of restrictions of competition in Article 6(3) should cover infringements of both national and Community competition law. The law applicable to such non-contractual obligations should be the law of the country where the market is, or is likely to be, affected. In cases where the market is, or is likely to be, affected in more than one country, the claimant should be able in certain circumstances to choose to base his or her claim on the law of the court seised.

6.59 Recital (23), which provides a definition of the concept of restriction of competition for the purposes of the Regulation, has been considered in the commentary on Art 6(1) (acts of unfair competition) (**6.31–6.33** above). Arts 6(1) and 6(3) must be treated as mutually exclusive.

---

[143] **6.13** above.

The solution adopted in Art 6(3)(a), i.e. the law of the market affected by a **6.60** restriction of competition, was one of the options presented by the Commission in the working paper accompanying its Green Paper on damages actions for breaches of Arts 81 and 82 of the EC Treaty.[144] In this connection, the authors of the working paper submitted that:[145]

> Such claims could be governed by the law of the state on whose market the victim was affected by the anti-competitive practice. The civil remedy (damage claim) would thus be linked to the restriction or distortion of competition. . . .

> The application of such an effects-based test would lead to the application of one single law in those cases in which the market affected is either national or subnational. If, however, the affected market is bigger than one single state or where there are several national markets, special problems arise with the proposed rule as in such a case the laws of a number of different states could be applicable to a claim. The recovery of each loss would be governed by the law specifically applicable to it. This could render litigation very complex.

Difficulties of the kind described in the last paragraph led to the adoption of **6.61** Art 6(3)(b), giving the person seeking compensation the right, in certain cases, to choose to base his claim on the law of the court seised of the dispute. The Council press release, issued at the conclusion of the Rome II conciliation process, described this as a 'compromise solution' that 'will allow for the application of one single law, while at the same time limiting, as far as possible, "forum shopping" by claimants'.[146] In its subsequent White Paper on damages actions, the Commission has declared that compromise to be satisfactory in terms of achieving the objectives of EC competition law.[147]

THE LAW OF THE AFFECTED MARKET (ART 6(3)(A))

The connecting factor in Art 6(3)(a) raises questions of some complexity as **6.62** to the methods by which the location of the market affected by the restriction of competition is to be identified. In this connection, there are good reasons, in terms of predictability and consistency of approach (if not cost and convenience), for looking to the law and practice generated in applying the substantive rules of EC competition law in Arts 81 and 82 of the EC Treaty. In particular, it would appear appropriate to have regard to

---

[144] SEC (2005) 1732 [19.12.2005]. See F Marcos and A Sánchez Graells, 'Towards a European Tort Law? Damages actions for breach of the EC antitrust rules: harmonising Tort Law through the back door', available at <http://papers.ssrn.com/sol3/papers.cfm?abstract_id=1028963>.

[145] Ibid, paras 247–8.

[146] Council document 9713/07 (Presse 111) [16.5.2007], 3.

[147] Text to n 38 above.

the Commission's 1997 Notice on the definition of relevant market for the purposes of Community competition law.[148]

6.63 A detailed examination of this complex topic falls outside the scope of this work.[149] The following points may be noted:

1. In a competition law context, the concept of the 'relevant market' is different from other usages of the word 'market'. For example, a company often uses the term 'market' to refer to the areas where it sells its products or to refer broadly to the industry or sector where it belongs.[150] Here, it refers to a market defined by reference to a combination of legal and economic factors.

2. For present purposes, a relevant market should be considered as having at least two relevant dimensions, the product market and the geographic market. The relevant market within which to assess a competition issue is therefore defined by reference to the product and geographic dimensions in combination.[151] A third aspect, concerning the temporal scope of the market,[152] would appear to be of limited significance in the present context.

3. The relevant product market comprises all those products and/or services that are regarded as interchangeable or substitutable by the consumer, by reason of the products' characteristics, their prices, and their intended use.[153]

4. The relevant geographic market comprises the area in which the undertakings concerned are involved in the supply and demand of products or services, in which the conditions of competition are sufficiently homogenous, and which can be distinguished from neighbouring areas because the conditions of competition are appreciably different in those areas.[154]

5. Basically, the exercise of market definition consists in identifying the effective alternative sources of supply for the customers of the undertakings involved, in terms both of products/services and of geographic location of suppliers.[155]

---

[148] OJ C372, 5 [9.12.1997] (**Commission Market Notice**).

[149] For comprehensive accounts, see J Faull and A Nikpay (eds), *The EC Law of Competition* (2nd edn, 2007), paras 1.130–1.1184 (**Faull and Nikpay**); P Roth and V Rose (eds), *Bellamy & Child: European Community Law of Competition* (6th edn, 2008), ch 4 (**Bellamy & Child**).

[150] Commission Market Notice, n 148 above, para 3.

[151] Ibid, para 9.

[152] Bellamy & Child, n 149 above paras 4.001, 4.089–4.090.

[153] Commission Market Notice, n 148 above, para 7. Also Case T-504/93, *Tiercé Ladbroke v Commission* [1997] ECR II, 923, para 81.

[154] Commission Market Notice, n 148 above, para 8.

[155] Ibid, para 13.

6. This process involves considering both 'demand-side substitution', in which customers switch to alternative products or sources of supply, and 'supply-side substitution', in which suppliers change their behaviour to provide different products or to supply different areas. In general, at least for the product market,[156] demand-side substitution is more important than supply-side substitution.[157] A third source of competitive constraint, potential competition (i.e. the prospect of changes in the marketplace in the longer term[158]) is not generally taken into account for this purpose.[159]

7. The concept of the relevant product market 'presupposes that there is a sufficient degree of interchangeability between all the products forming part of the same market in so far as a specific use of such products is concerned'.[160] However, product characteristics and intended use are insufficient to show that two products are demand substitutes: the responsiveness of customers to price changes[161] may depend on other economic factors.[162]

8. Within a geographic market, it is not necessary for the conditions of competition to be perfectly homogenous, so long as they are similar or sufficiently homogenous.[163]

9. The starting point for the analysis of the geographic market is the activities of the party or parties concerned.[164] From this starting point, as the editors of Bellamy & Child explain:[165]

[A] working hypothesis can be developed regarding the geographic market, normally based on market shares and prices in different areas, before testing that hypothesis using demand- and supply-side analyses. On the demand side, it is necessary to consider purchasers' willingness to acquire products from other

---

[156] cf Bellamy & Child, n 149 above, para 4.071.

[157] Commission Market Notice, n 148 above, para 13. As to supply-side substitution, see ibid, paras 20–23.

[158] Bellamy & Child, n 149 above, paras 4.020 and 4.054.

[159] Commission Market Notice, n 148 above, para 24.

[160] Case 85/76, *Hoffmann-La Roche & Co AG v Commission* [1979] ECR 461, para 28.

[161] The Commission's methodology centres on the so-called SSNIP test which involves speculating on the reaction of consumers to a hypothetical, small lasting chance in relative prices (Commission Market Notice, n 148 above, paras 17–19; Bellamy & Child, n 149 above, paras 4.016, 4.024–4.032; Faull & Nikpay, n 149 above, paras 1.143–1.148).

[162] Commission Market Notice, n 148 above, para 36. For the Commission's evidential approach to product substitution, see ibid, paras 25–43. Also Bellamy & Child, n 149 above, paras 4.034–4.050; Faull & Nikpay, n 149 above, paras 1.135–1.142).

[163] Case T-229/94, *Deutsche Bahn AG v Commission* [1997] ECR II-1689, para 92; Bellamy & Child, n 149 above, para 4.070.

[164] Bellamy & Child, n 149 above, para 4.071. For the Commission's evidential approach, see Commission Market Notice, n 148 above, paras 44–52.

[165] Bellamy & Child, n 149 above, para 4.076.

areas. On the supply side, attention focuses on the willingness of suppliers in other areas to commence supply in (or into) the area in question.

10. The geographic market may be restricted by national measures imposing barriers to trade. On the other hand, removal of those barriers by internal market measures may result in a reappraisal of the geographic area of the market.[166] The geographic market may also be limited by linguistic requirements, cultural features, or customer preferences in particular countries.[167] Account may be taken of existing purchasing preferences, and suppliers' shares of the market, in particular countries in order to determine whether the market in that country is distinct from neighbouring countries.[168] The views of the market participants, both suppliers and customers, as to the geographic area of the market are also relevant.[169] Evidence of difference in prices between two areas is a significant, but not conclusive, factor.[170] Finally, differences resulting from artificial barriers erected by the market participants will be ignored.[171]

6.64 The requirement for individual litigants, and their legal advisers, to undertake legal-economic analysis of this kind in order to determine the law applicable to a non-contractual obligation is one of the least satisfactory aspects of the Rome II Regulation, and seems likely significantly to increase costs in cases of this kind. The escape clause in Art 6(3)(b) provides a partial antidote but, as will be seen,[172] it is by no means adequate. Moreover, a thorough analysis will in many cases lead to the conclusion that the geographical area of the affected market covers the territory of more than one country, or even an entire free trade area (such as the EC/EEA). As a result, subject to the Art 6(3)(b) escape clause, the Regulation will require the application of the law of each of the countries in which the affected market is located on a distributive basis, the so-called *Mosaikbetrachtung* or 'mosaic view' approach.[173] This approach is as complex and unsatisfactory for non-contractual obligations arising out of restrictions of competition as it is for non-contractual obligations arising out

---

[166] Commission Market Notice, n 148 above, para 32; Bellamy & Child, n 149 above, para 4.072.

[167] Bellamy & Child, n 149 above, para 4.076.

[168] Ibid, paras 4.077–4.088.

[169] Ibid, paras 4.081–4.082.

[170] Ibid, para 4.075.

[171] e.g. Case T-83/91, *Tetra Pak International SA v Commission* [1994] ECR II-755, para 96.

[172] **6.68** below.

[173] **3.298–3.301** above. See the comments of the authors of the Commission staff working paper quoted at text to n 144 above.

of unfair competition.[174] The requirement, at least in the English courts, to plead and prove each applicable foreign law will further drive costs up in cases of this kind. Having regard to these factors, it would be unsurprising if Member State courts adopted a less technical approach in defining the geographic area of the relevant market more restrictively for these purposes, being more willing to accept that (for example) national preferences or linguistic differences support the conclusion that a national market should be distinguished from that in neighbouring areas.

Further questions arise as to the nature of the link required, for the purposes of Art 6(3), between the restriction of competition and the affected market, and as to the time at which the geographic area of the affected market must be assessed. The first question has already been addressed in the commentary on Art 6(1).[175] In relation to Art 6(3), it may be noted that the escape clause in Art 6(3)(b) requires, as a condition of its application, a 'direct' and 'substantial' effect on the market in the Member State seised of the dispute,[176] but those words do not form part of the connecting factor in Art 6(3)(a). Nor is the requirement of a direct and substantial effect referred to in the Recitals. A compromise proposal presented to the Council's Rome II Committee by the Austrian Presidency in February 2006 raised the possibility of inserting a recital in terms that the effect of a restriction of competition on the market must be 'direct and foreseeable'.[177] That led to a statement in Recital (20) to the Council's Common Position that, so far as non-contractual obligations arising out of restrictions of competition were concerned, the effect must be 'direct and substantial'. Curiously, that wording survived the Parliament's deletion of the special rule for competition law matters,[178] but was altered during the conciliation process. That decision, coupled with the re-emergence of the wording in Art 6(3)(b) alone, supports the view that there is no general requirement in cases falling within Art 6(3) that the effect on the market of a restriction of competition be 'direct and substantial'. **6.65**

An alternative approach, consistent with the ECJ's decision in the *Wood Pulp* case concerning the territorial scope of Arts 81 and 82 (ex-Arts 85 and 86) of the EC Treaty,[179] would be to focus on the market on which the anti-competitive arrangement was implemented. As with Art 6(1),[180] **6.66**

---

[174] **6.56–6.57** above.
[175] **6.53–6.55** above.
[176] **6.71–6.72** below.
[177] Council document 6623/06 [23.2.2006], 3.
[178] EP 2nd Reading Position, Recital (22).
[179] Text to n 136 above.
[180] **6.55** above.

it may be argued that 'spill over' effects onto other markets should be treated as analogous to the 'indirect consequences' of an event giving rise to damage under Art 4(1) and left out of account in determining the law applicable to a non-contractual obligation arising out of a restriction of competition.

6.67 As to the point in time at which the affected market must be identified, it would seem sensible to consider the position either at the first point in time at which the restriction of competition has a relevant effect on the market, or at the first point in time at which the person seeking compensation is affected by the restriction in question. The former solution appears more consistent with the market-oriented approach in Art 6(3).

THE CLAIMANT'S RIGHT TO CHOOSE THE LAW OF THE FORUM (ART 6(3)(B))

6.68 The escape clause in Art 6(3)(b) applies 'when the market is, or is likely to be affected, in more than one country'. This language suggests that Art 6(3)(b) is primarily concerned with situations in which the geographic area of a single market covers the territory of two or more countries, leading to the application of the laws of each of those countries under Art 6(3)(a) on a distributive basis.[181] The following references to 'the market in [a] Member State' should, therefore, be taken as referring to (artificial) national sectors within the wider market. Art 6(3)(b) may also be capable of applying to a situation in which a single restriction of competition affects more than one market.[182]

6.69 Art 6(3)(b) gives the person seeking compensation the right to choose to base his claim solely on the law of the forum if two conditions are satisfied.

6.70 First, at least one of the defendants must be domiciled in the Member State of the forum. If that condition is satisfied, the claimant may also be able to choose the law of the forum to govern claims against all defendants joined to the proceedings in accordance with the applicable rules of jurisdiction. These rules include Art 6(1) of the Brussels I Regulation, which allows a defendant domiciled in a Member State to be sued in the courts of another Member State in which a co-defendant is domiciled, provided that the

---

[181] **6.64** above.

[182] The authors of the Commission staff working paper accompanying the Green Paper for damages actions for breaches of Arts 81 and 82 of the EC Treaty referred to cases in which 'the affected market is bigger than one single state *or* where there are several national markets'.

claims are so closely connected that it is expedient to hear and determine them together to avoid the risk of irreconcilable judgments resulting from separate proceedings.[183]

Secondly, the market in the Member State of the forum must be amongst **6.71** those directly and substantially affected by the restriction of competition on which the person seeking compensation relies (a) against the defendant domiciled in that Member State, or (b) if more than one defendant is sued, against each of the other defendants. The requirement that the effect on the market of the forum Member State must be both 'direct' and 'substantial' was introduced into Art 6(3)(b) at a very late stage in the conciliation process, on the initiative (apparently) of the Commission.[184] The Commission also prepared the following wording for a recital to clarify when a market is 'directly and substantially' affected, although this was not adopted:[185]

When determining whether or not a restriction of competition affects a market directly and substantially, in particular the prices, output, innovation or the variety of products on that market, due regard must be given to the position and the importance of the undertakings involved on the market for the products concerned.

Without further guidance, this causal test adds an element of uncertainty **6.72** to Art 6(3)(b),[186] but probably serves as a deterrent to forum shoppers, by emphasizing the need for a genuine link to the Member State in which proceedings are brought.

If these conditions are satisfied and the person seeking compensation **6.73** chooses, in accordance with the forum's procedural rules,[187] to base his claim on the law of the forum, that law alone will apply. The right to apply the law of the forum is, accordingly, one-sided. Nevertheless, a person against whom allegations of anti-competitive conduct are made may be able to exclude the possibility of the complainant's free choice of law by himself bringing an action for a declaration of non-liability in a Member State whose market is not affected by the restriction of competition or in which none of the persons alleged to be responsible is domiciled. If the person claimed to be liable takes that step, the complainant will no longer be able to bring proceedings against him in a court which meet the

---

[183] For a restrictive approach to this requirement, see Case C-539/03, *Roche Nederland BV v Primus* [2006] ECR I-6535.
[184] Council document 9137/07 [7.5.2007], 20.
[185] Commission document SPI (2007) 42 [3.5.2007], 9.
[186] **6.54** above.
[187] Cf **7.25–7.26** below.

conditions set out in Art 6(3)(b),[188] and he must instead counterclaim for a remedy and accept the consequences of the more complex rule in Art 6(3)(a). The price for this tactical manoeuvring may be that the person claimed to be liable must face the complainant on his home territory, relying on Art 2 of the Brussels I Regulation to establish the jurisdiction of the courts of the complainant's domicile.

E. EXCLUSION OF PARTY CHOICE (ART 6(4))

6.74 Under Art 6(4), the law applicable 'under this Article' may not be derogated from by an agreement between the parties even if it otherwise meets the requirements of Art 14.[189] The rules in the Commission Proposal allowing restricted party autonomy after the dispute arose had applied to all non-contractual obligations other than those arising out of infringements of intellectual property rights. The suggestion that freedom of choice should also be excluded for non-contractual obligations arising out of unfair competition was raised at an early stage of the discussions in the Council's Rome II Committee.[190] The Swedish delegation, for example, argued that 'laws on unfair competition and restrictions of competition (antitrust) are so strongly linked to governmental interests that a choice of law should not be allowed'.[191] The point was not settled in the Council until much later, due to the wish of some Member State delegations to debate whether there should be any limits on the parties' ability to choose the law applicable to a non-contractual obligation after the event.[192]

6.75 The words of limitation in Art 6(4) ('under this Article') suggest that the parties may choose the law applicable to a non-contractual obligation arising out of an act of unfair competition that affects exclusively the interests of a specific competitor.[193] Under Art 6(2), the law applicable to an obligation of this type must be determined in accordance with the rules in Art 4, rather than those within Art 6.

---

[188] Case C-406/92, *The Tatry/The Maciej Rataj* [1994] ECR I-5439.

[189] **Ch 13** below.

[190] A reference to what was then Art 5 of the proposed text as being excluded from the rule allowing party choice of law first appears in square brackets in Council document 10173/04 [14.6.2004], Art 3A.

[191] Council document 9009/04 ADD 8 [18.5.2004], 5. Also ibid, ADD 10 [18.5.2004], 6 (Spain); ibid, ADD 11 [24.5.2004], 13 (Germany).

[192] e.g. Council document 16027/05 [22.12.2005], 14 (footnote 2).

[193] **6.27–6.30** above.

F. THE PRIVATE ENFORCEMENT OF COMPETITION LAW—FUTURE DEVELOPMENT

In April 2008, the Commission adopted its White Paper on damages **6.76** actions for breach of the EC anti-trust rules.[194] As noted,[195] the Commission expressed satisfaction with the rules contained in Art 6(3) of the Rome II Regulation, and did not address this area further. Elsewhere, however, the Commission made several suggestions to enhance the role of private parties in the enforcement of EC competition law. These included, for example, development of opt-in collective actions by victims of competition law infringements, as well as representative actions brought by qualified entities,[196] more favourable rules of evidence and disclosure,[197] dilution of the fault requirement that exists under the laws of some Member States,[198] minimum standards for damages awards and further guidance on the calculation of damages,[199] and common limitation rules.[200]

In November 2007, the UK Office of Fair Trading had published its own **6.77** recommendations to the Government on steps to be taken to improve the effectiveness of civil law remedies for victims of breaches of competition law in the UK.[201] The OFT recommended modifying existing procedures concerning representative and group actions, or introducing new procedures, so as to allow representative bodies to bring stand-alone and follow-on representative actions for damages and applications for injunctions on behalf of consumers, either individually or collectively. The OFT also opened up the possibility of developing similar procedures for businesses, and recommended changes to the rules governing the measure of damages and costs.

---

[194] COM (2008) 165 final [2.4.2008], accompanied by a Staff Working Paper (SEC (2008) 404 [2.4.2008]).
[195] **6.09** above.
[196] Staff Working Paper (SEC (2008) 4004), ch 2.
[197] Ibid, ch 3.
[198] Ibid, ch 5.
[199] Ibid, ch 6.
[200] Ibid, ch 8.
[201] Office of Fair Trading, Private actions in competition law: effective redress for consumers and business, (OFT916resp, November 2007), available at <http://www.oft.gov.uk/shared_oft/reports/comp_policy/oft916resp.pdf>; Civil Justice Council, 'Improving Access to Justice through Collective Actions' (July 2008), available at <http://www.civiljusticecouncil.gov.uk/files/Improving_Access_to_Justice_through_Collective_Actions.pdf>.

6.78 These proposals come at a time when there is increasing interest in the use of collective and representative actions to ensure compliance by businesses, in particular, with rules governing competition and unfair business practices.[202] It remains to be seen whether they will lead to measures of the kind referred to above being adopted. If they do, the case for reviewing the complex rules in Art 6 and moving, for example, towards a wider application of the law of the forum Member State to collective actions may be irresistable sooner rather than later.

---

[202] See, e.g., the research paper prepared by Professor Rachel Mulheron for the UK Civil Justice Council entitled 'Reform of Collective Redress in England and Wales: A Perspective of Need', available at <http://www.civiljusticecouncil.gov.uk/files/collective_redress.pdf>.

7

Environmental Damage

Article 7

Environmental damage

The law applicable to a non-contractual obligation arising out of environmental damage or damage sustained by persons or property as a result of such damage shall be the law determined pursuant to Article 4(1), unless the person seeking compensation for damage chooses to base his or her claim on the law of the country in which the event giving rise to the damage occurred.

A. INTRODUCTION

Art 7 of the Rome II Regulation reflects closely the provision contained in **7.01** Art 7 of the Commission Proposal. The Commission justified the need for a special provision as follows:[1]

European or even international harmonisation is particularly important here as so many environmental disasters have an international dimension. But the instruments

---

[1] Commission Proposal, 19. Also F Munari and L Schiano Di Pepe, 'Liability for Environmental Torts in Europe: Choice of Forum, Choice of Law and the Case for Pursuing

adopted so far deal primarily with questions of substantive law or international jurisdiction rather than with harmonisation of the conflict rules. And they address only selected types of cross-border pollution. In spite of this gradual approximation of the substantive law, not only in the Community, major differences subsist—for example in determining the damage giving rise to compensation, limitation periods, indemnity and insurance rules, the right of associations to bring actions and the amounts of compensation. The question of the applicable law has thus lost none of its importance.

Analysis of the current conflict rules shows that the solutions vary widely. The *lex fori* and the law of the place where the dangerous activity is exercised play a certain role, particularly in the international Conventions, but the most commonly applied solution is the law of the place where the loss is sustained (France, United Kingdom, Netherlands, Spain, Japan, Switzerland, Romania, Turkey, Quebec) or one of the variants of the principle of the law that is most favourable to the victim (Germany, Austria, Italy, Czech Republic, Yugoslavia, Estonia, Turkey, Nordic Convention of 1974 on the protection of the environment, Convention between Germany and Austria of 19 December 1967 concerning nuisances generated by the operation of Salzburg airport in Germany). The Hague Conference has also put an international convention on cross-border environmental damage on its work programme, and preparatory work seems to be moving towards a major role for the place where the damage is sustained, though the merits of the principle of favouring the victim are acknowledged.

7.02 This aspect of the Commission's Proposal initially met with a mixed reaction from the Member State delegations in the Council's Rome II Committee.[2] Some supported the choice offered to the victim,[3] while others argued for the deletion of the rule, or expressed concerns, on the grounds that it was unnecessary and/or that it was too onerous.[4] The European Parliament, on the recommendation of its JURI Committee,[5]

Effective Legal Uniformity', in A Malatesta (ed), *The Unification of Choice of Law Rules on Torts and Other Non-Contractual Obligations in Europe* (2006), 173–219; C Bernasconi, 'Civil liability resulting from transfrontier environmental damage: a case for the Hague Conference?', Preliminary Document No 8 of May 2000, available at <http://www.hcch.net/upload/wop/gen_pd8e.pdf>; 2nd Report of the International Law Association's Committee on Transnational Enforcement of Environmental Law, Report of the 71st Conference (Berlin, 2004), 909–26; Final Report of the ILA Committee on Transnational Enforcement of Environmental Law, Report of the 72nd Conference (Toronto, 2006), 655–71.

[2] Council document 5340/04 [27.1.2004], 3; Council document 11801/04 [28.7.2004], 4
[3] Council documents 9009/04 [29.4.2004], 3 (Luxembourg); ibid, ADD 2 [3.5.2004], 3 (Czech Republic); ibid, ADD 7 [11.5.2004], 3 (Estonia); ibid, ADD 10 [18.5.2004] (Spain).
[4] Council documents 9009/04 ADD 1 [3.5.2004], 3 (Austria); ibid, ADD 5 [7.5.2004], 2 (Finland); ibid, ADD 11 [24.5.2004], 9–10 (Germany); ibid, ADD 13 [24.5.2004], 5 (Ireland); ibid, ADD 14 [24.5.2004], 4 (Lithuania); ibid, ADD 15 [26.5.2004], 6 (UK).
[5] EP 1st Reading Report, 24.

deleted the special rule at its first reading stage.[6] That position was not accepted, however, by either the Commission[7] or the Council's Rome II Committee, whose member delegations were slowly being persuaded by the merits of the rule.[8] That momentum was carried forward into the Council's Common Position, the wording of which is mirrored in Art 7 of the Regulation in its final form. The recommendation of the EP JURI Committee to delete this rule on second reading[9] was defeated in the plenary session.[10] The only issue remaining in the conciliation process was the Parliament's proposal to insert a recital defining the concept 'environmental damage' by reference to Art 2 of the Environmental Liability Directive.[11] This move, although not accepted by the Council, led to the compromise text now to be found in Recital (24).[12]

B. SCOPE OF ARTICLE 7

Civil or Commercial Matters—Claims by Public Authorities

Like the other rules in the Rome II Regulation, Art 7 applies only to 'civil **7.03** or commercial matters'.[13] This concept in Art 1(1), which also appears in the Brussels I Regime and Rome I Regulation, covers not only claims between private parties, but also claims by non-public bodies to enforce, for example, laws for the protection of consumers.[14] On the other hand, it excludes from the scope of the Regulation claims by or against States or other public bodies acting in the exercise of their public powers.[15] In *Netherlands State v Rüffer*, a claim by the State, as the authority responsible

---

[6] EP 1st Reading Position, Amendment 33. For criticism of the Parliament's position, see F Munari and L Schiano di Pepe, n 1 above, 193–204; G Betlem and C Bernasconi, 'European Private International Law, the Environment and Obstacles for Public Authorities' (2006) 122 LQR 125, 137–44.

[7] Commission Amended Proposal, 6.

[8] Council document 13001/05 [13.10.2005], 4; Council document 7709/06 [3.5.2006] 13.

[9] EP 2nd Reading Recommendation, Amendment 18.

[10] EP 2nd Reading Position, Art 6.

[11] Directive (EC) No 2004/35 on environmental liability with regard to the prevention and remedying of environmental damage (OJ L143, 56 [30.4.2004]), as amended by Directive (EC) No 2006/21 (OJ L102, 15 [11.4.2006]) (Environmental Liability Directive). Consolidated version availableat<http://eur-lex.europa.eu/LexUriServ/site/en/consleg/2004/L/02004L0035-20060501-en.pdf>.

[12] **7.08** below.

[13] **3.263–3.286** above.

[14] Case C-167/00, *Verein für Konsumentinformation v Henkel* [2002] ECR I-8111, para 30.

[15] Ibid, para 26.

for policing inland waterways, to recover the costs of removing a wreck was held not to constitute a civil matter within the Brussels Convention. On this basis, a claim by a public authority to recover its costs of remedying a pollution incident from the person responsible for that incident would also fall outside the scope of the Rome II Regulation if that action was based on a provision enabling it recover the costs of exercising its public powers.[16] The Regulation would, however, apply (for example) if the public authority based its claim on a right to compensation for damage suffered by it as the owner of land[17] or as transferee, by subrogation or otherwise, of the private law rights of an injured person.[18]

7.04 In relation to matters of jurisdiction and the enforcement of Member State judgments under the Brussels I Regime, Gerrit Betlem and Christophe Bernasconi have argued for a 'green' interpretation of the concept of 'civil and commercial matters' so as to cover claims by public authorities acting in the exercise of their public powers to ensure compliance with environmental law.[19] This argument is based on the objectives for environmental protection listed in Art 174 of the EC Treaty.[20] The authors note that in *Verein für Konsumentinformation v Henkel*,[21] the ECJ referred to the Unfair Terms in Consumer Contracts Directive[22] to support a broad construction of the connecting factor in Art 5(3) of the Brussels Convention (matters relating to tort, delict, or quasi-delict),[23] and suggest that the Environmental Liability Directive may require a similar approach to be taken to the concept of 'civil and commercial matters' in Art 1(1) of the Brussels I Regulation insofar as the civil enforcement of environmental protection measures are concerned.

7.05 With respect, this argument cannot be accepted, whether in relation to the Brussels I Regime or the Rome II Regulation. In *Henkel*, the claim before the Court had been brought by a consumer organization under the Austrian regulations implementing the Unfair Terms Directive, which in turn specifically contemplates that court proceedings may be taken by organizations of this kind to enforce the terms of the Directive.[24] It was the

---

[16] e.g. Environmental Liability Directive, n 11 above, Art 8(1).

[17] Case C-343/04, *Land Oberöstereich v ČEZ as* [2006] ECR I-4557 (a Brussels Convention case).

[18] Case C-271/00, *Gemeente Steenbergen v Baten* [2002] ECR I-10489; Case C-433/01, *Freistaat Bayern v Blijdenstein* [2004] ECR I-981 (both Brussels Convention cases).

[19] G Betlem and C Bernasconi, n 6 above, 135–7.

[20] Also Art 6 ('Environmental protection requirements must be integrated into the definition and integration of the Community policies and activities . . .').

[21] Case C-167/00 [2002] ECR I-8111 (also **3.240** above).

[22] Directive (EC) No 93/13 on unfair terms in consumer contracts (OJ L141, 27 [24.4.1993]).

[23] Ibid, para 43.

[24] Unfair Terms in Consumer Contracts Directive, n 22 above, Art 7(2).

claimant's status as a consumer organization, and the fact that it was not exercising public powers, and not the fact that it was pursuing an action to enforce EC law, that brought the claim within the concept of 'civil and commercial matters' under the Brussels Convention.[25] The Environmental Liability Directive, on the other hand, excludes any intention to affect civil liability regimes[26] and achieves its objectives by conferring enforcement powers on the Member States' designated competent authorities.[27] Natural or legal parties may request the competent authority to act,[28] and must be given access to a court or other independent and impartial body to review the competent authority's decisions, acts, or failure to act under the Directive.[29] The Directive does not, however, confer a direct right of action against the polluter on individuals or representative groups. Further, the Directive disclaims any intention to affect rules of private international law.[30] The Directive thus leaves the law applicable to non-contractual obligations arising out of environmental damage to be determined by reference to the rules of applicable law contained in the Rome II Regulation (principally, but not exclusively,[31] Art 7), subject to any overriding mandatory rules of the law of the forum[32] and to any international convention prescribing rules of applicable law.[33] It does not purport to affect the scope or content of that instrument or the Brussels I Regulation.

Against this background, the right of a Member State's competent author- **7.06** ity to recover the costs of taking preventative and remedial measures under the Directive,[34] and the exercise of any similar right conferred on it under national law,[35] should be seen as being based on the exercise of

---

[25] *VfK v Henkel*, n 21 above, para 30.

[26] Environmental Liability Directive, Recitals (11)–(14) and (29); Art 3(3) (see F Munari and L Schiano di Pepe, n 1 above, 187–90).

[27] Ibid, Recital (15) and Art 11.

[28] Ibid, Art 12.

[29] Ibid, Art 13.

[30] Ibid, Recital (10), referring specifically to the Brussels I Regulation (see F Munari and L Schiano di Pepe, n 1 above, 192–3).

[31] The parties may choose the law applicable in accordance with Art 14 (**Ch 13** below).

[32] Regulation, Art 16. Those rules may, in turn derive from an international convention (**7.31–7.34**).

[33] Regulation, Art 28. The best example of such a convention in the area covered by Art 7 of the Rome II Regulation is probably the Nordic Environmental Protection Convention, discussed at **1.36** above, between Denmark, Finland, and Sweden (Member States) and Norway (a non-Member State). Also n 96 below.

[34] Environmental Liability Directive, n 11 above, Art 8.

[35] If a public body invokes a right conferred by international treaty (cf G Betlem and C Bernasconi, n 6 above, 136–7), the nature of that right will need to be examined in detail to see whether it derogates from the rules of law applicable to private individuals (*VfK v Henkel*, n 21 above, para 40).

powers of a public nature conferred exclusively on it, and as falling outside the Brussels I Regime and the Rome II Regulation. The cross-border recovery by Member State authorities of clean up costs involves mutual legal assistance,[36] which is properly the subject of a Community measure under Art 175 of the EC Treaty. It is not appropriate for it to be shoehorned into instruments dealing with private international law rules adopted under Arts 61 and 65. Nor, in the case of the Art 7 of the Rome II Regulation, can it be said that the objectives set out in Art 174 of the EC Treaty have not been taken into account, as they are specifically referred to in Recital (25) as justifying the adoption of a rule favourable to the person sustaining the damage.[37] Accordingly, the concept of 'civil and commercial matters' in Art 1(1) of the Regulation should not be given a broader interpretation for matters falling within Art 7 than for matters falling within the other rules of applicable law in Chapters II and III.

Types of Damage to which Article 7 Applies

7.07 Art 7 applies to 'environmental damage or damage sustained by persons or property as a result of such damage'.

Environmental Damage

7.08 For the purposes of this Article, Recital (24) defines 'environmental damage' as meaning:

[A]dverse change in a natural resource, such as water, land or air, impairment of a function performed by that resource for the benefit of another natural resource or the public, or impairment of the variability among living organisms.

7.09 This broad and concise definition may be compared with the more detailed, and narrower,[38] definition contained in the Environmental Liability Directive, as follows:[39]

 1. 'environmental damage' means:
    (a) damage to protected species and natural habitats,[40] which is any damage that has significant adverse effects on reaching or maintaining the favourable

---

[36] The cooperation provisions in Art 15 of the Environmental Liability Directive are plainly inadequate for this purpose.

[37] **7.16** below.

[38] Cf EP 3rd Reading Report, 8, suggesting that the definition in Recital (14) is 'in line with other EU instruments, such as the Directive on Environmental Liability'.

[39] Environmental Liability Directive, n 11 above, Art 2 (footnotes added). See F Munari and L Schiano di Pepe, n 1 above, 190–1.

[40] 'Protected species and natural habitats' is defined in Art 2(3) of the Directive.

conservation status[41] of such habitats or species. The significance of such effects is to be assessed with reference to the baseline condition, taking account of the criteria set out in Annex I;

Damage to protected species and natural habitats does not include previously identified adverse effects which result from an act by an operator which was expressly authorised by the relevant authorities in accordance with provisions implementing Article 6(3) and (4) or Article 16 of Directive 92/43/EEC[42] or Article 9 of Directive 79/409/EEC[43] or, in the case of habitats and species not covered by Community law, in accordance with equivalent provisions of national law on nature conservation.

(b) water damage, which is any damage that significantly adversely affects the ecological, chemical and/or quantitative status and/or ecological potential, as defined in Directive 2000/60/EC,[44] of the waters[45] concerned, with the exception of adverse effects where Article 4(7) of that Directive applies;

(c) land damage, which is any land contamination that creates a significant risk of human health being adversely affected as a result of the direct or indirect introduction, in, on or under land, of substances, preparations, organisms or micro-organisms;

2. 'damage' means a measurable adverse change in a natural resource[46] or measurable impairment of a natural resource service[47] which may occur directly or indirectly.

The Environmental Liability Directive applies to (a) environmental dam-   **7.10** age caused by any of the occupational activities listed in Annex III to the Directive, and (b) damage to protected species and natural habitats caused by other occupational activities through the fault or negligence of the operator, as well as to any imminent threat of such damage occurring by reason of such activities.[48] Certain matters are also specifically excluded from the scope of the Directive.[49] The definition of 'environmental damage' in Recital (24) of the Rome II Regulation is not subject to these restrictions, although nuclear damage is excluded from the scope of the Regulation by Art 1(2)(f).[50]

---

[41] 'Conservation status' is defined in Art 2(4) of the Directive.

[42] Directive (EEC) No 92/43 on the conservation of natural habitats and of wild fauna and flora (OJ L206, 7 [22.7.1992], as amended).

[43] Directive (EEC) No 79/409 on the conservation of wild birds (OJ L103, 1 [25.4.1979]).

[44] Directive (EC) No 2000/60 establishing a framework for the Community action in the field of water policy (OJ L327, 1 [22.12.2000]).

[45] 'Waters' is defined in Art 2(5).

[46] 'Natural resource' is defined in Art 2(12) of the Directive.

[47] 'Natural resource services' are defined in Art 2(13) of the Directive.

[48] Environmental Liability Directive, n 11 above, Art 3(1).

[49] Ibid, Art 4.

[50] **3.208–3.216** above.

Damage Sustained by Persons or Property as a Result of Such Damage

7.11 Without prejudice to relevant national legislation, the Environmental Liability Directive accords no right of compensation to private parties as a consequence of environmental damage or of an imminent threat of such damage.[51] Nor does the Directive apply to cases of personal injury, to damage to private property, or to any economic loss; nor does it affect any right regarding these types of damages.[52]

7.12 Art 7 of the Regulation, on the other hand, expressly extends to 'damage sustained by persons or property' as a result of environmental damage. These words, initially suggested by the Belgian delegation,[53] were no doubt intended to emphasize that Art 7, unlike the Environmental Liability Directive,[54] applied to claims for personal injury and property damage resulting from environmental damage. Although the English language version is not as clear as it might be,[55] it may appear that liability for economic loss resulting from environmental damage, but not itself consequential on personal injury or property damage, falls outside Art 7, and within the general rule in Art 4. That impression is supported by Recital (14) to the Environmental Liability Directive[56] which refers to 'economic loss' alongside personal injury and damage to private property as a matter excluded from the scope of the Directive.

7.13 Against this view, it can be argued that the addition of the specific reference to 'damage sustained by persons or property' serves only to emphasize that personal injury or property damage must not be treated as 'indirect consequences' of the environmental damage from which they arise when applying the rule of applicable law in Art 4(1), to which Art 7 refers.[57] On this view, a claim to recover 'pure' economic loss consequential upon environmental damage may still fall within Art 7, although its location will not be a relevant factor in determining the law applicable under Art 4(1).[58] This seems the better view, as it avoids unnecessary

---

[51] Environmental Liability Directive, n 11 above, Art 3(3).

[52] Ibid, Recital (14).

[53] Council document 9009/04 [4.5.2004], 3

[54] Text to n 52 above.

[55] Compare the German language version (referring to *'einer solchen Schädigung herrührenden-Personen- oder Sachschaden'*) and the French language version (referring to *'dommages subséquents subis par des personnes ou causés à des biens'*).

[56] Text to n 52 above.

[57] **4.36–4.45** above. Also Recital (17).

[58] It is, however, difficult to conceive in circumstances in which personal injury will be sustained or damage to property will occur in a country other than that in which the environment was damaged (**7.19–7.20** below).

splitting of the applicable law between claims for environmental damage and economic loss flowing from it and is consistent with the objectives underlying Art 7, set out in Recital (25).[59]

APPROACH TO CHARACTERIZATION

In characterizing a claim as falling within or outside Art 7, it is the conse- **7.14** quences of the event giving rise to damage and not the event giving rise to damage itself that must be analysed. If the obligation in question concerns the responsibility of the defendant or a person for whose acts the defendant is liable for environmental damage or its consequences, Art 7 will apply whether that responsibility is strict or fault-based. Under English law,[60] the provision will accommodate many claims based on the tort of nuisance[61] or the related principle originating in the nineteenth century case of *Rylands v Fletcher*[62] as well, for example, as some cases of tortious negligence and breach of statutory duty.

C. THE LAW APPLICABLE TO NON-CONTRACTUAL OBLIGATIONS ARISING OUT OF ENVIRONMENTAL DAMAGE

INTRODUCTION

Art 7 provides that the law applicable to a non-contractual obligation **7.15** arising out of environmental damage or damage sustained by persons or property as a result of such damage shall be determined in accordance with Art 4(1), resulting in the application of the law of the country in which the damage occurred. The person seeking compensation for damage may, however, choose instead to base his or her claim on the law of the country in which the event giving rise to the damage occurred.

---

[59] **7.16** below.
[60] For a comparative survey of German, English, and French rules concerning environmental liability, see C van Dam, *European Tort Law* (2005), para 1414. Also C Bernasconi, n 1 above, 16–26.
[61] A M Dugdale and M A Jones, *Clerk and Lindsell on Torts* (19th edn, 2006), ch 20.
[62] (1866) LR 1 Ex 265, affirmed (1886) LR 3 HL 30. Also *Cambridge Water Co Ltd v Eastern Counties Leather plc* [1994] 2 AC 264 (UKHL); *Transco plc v Stockport MBC* [2003] UKHL 61; [2004] 2 AC 1.

7.16 These rules are to be read together with Recital (25), which provides:[63]

> Regarding environmental damage, Article 174 of the Treaty, which provides that
> there should be a high level of protection based on the precautionary principle and
> the principle that preventive action should be taken, the principle of priority for
> corrective action at source and the principle that the polluter pays, fully justifies
> the use of the principle of discriminating in favour of the person sustaining the
> damage . . .

THE BASIC RULE—THE LAW DETERMINED PURSUANT TO ART 4(1)

7.17 As a starting point, the law applicable to non-contractual obligations falling within the scope of Art 7 is determined by the provisions of Art 4(1),
pointing towards application of the law of the country in which the damage occurred (or is likely to occur).[64] Art 7 does not cross-refer to Arts 4(2)
or 4(3), allowing displacement of the law of the country of damage on the
basis of a common habitual residence or manifestly closer connection to
another country.[65] Nor is it a relevant consideration that the defendant could
not have foreseen that damage would occur in the country in question.[66]

7.18 In the view of the Commission:

> The basic connection to the law of the place where the damage was sustained is in
> conformity with recent objectives of environmental protection policy, which tends
> to support strict liability. The solution is also conducive to a policy of prevention,
> obliging operators established in countries with a low level of protection to abide
> by the higher levels of protection in neighbouring countries, which removes the
> incentive for an operator to opt for low-protection countries. The rule thus contrib-
> utes to raising the general level of environmental protection.

7.19 The structure of Art 7 suggests that the location of the environmental
damage and the location of resulting damage sustained by persons or
property must be determined separately for the purposes of determining
the basic applicable law, although it may be doubted whether this will
make any material difference to the outcome of the enquiry.[67] For personal
injury or damage to property, Recital (17) provides that the country in

---

[63] The remainder of Recital (25) concerns the procedure for exercise of the claimant's right
of election (**7.25–7.26** below).

[64] **4.21–4.74** above.

[65] Cf **4.76-4.95** above.

[66] The Netherlands' delegation in the Council's Rome II Committee made a proposal
along these lines, but it was not taken up (Council document 9009/04 ADD 16 [28.5.2004], 5).
Also S C Symeonides, 'Rome II and Tort Conflicts: A Missed Opportunity?' (2008) 56 AJCL
173, 210–11.

[67] n 58 above.

which the damage occurs should be the country where the injury was sustained or the property was damaged respectively. For environmental damage, the wording of Recital (24)[68] suggests that the damage will occur in any place in which there is an adverse change in a natural resource, such as water, land or air, impairment of a function performed by that resource for the benefit of another natural resource or the public, or impairment of the variability among living organisms (as applicable).

In the case of water or air pollution, in particular, the change may spread **7.20** itself over a wide area. In principle, damage must be considered to have occurred in every country in which there is an adverse change to water or air quality, even if this results from the diffusion of pollutants from their original source due, for example, to the flow of a river[69] or wind. If the claim relates to environmental damage in more than one country, the laws of those countries must be applied on a distributive basis.[70]

Economic loss consequential upon damage to persons or property or, if **7.21** within the scope of Art 7,[71] environmental damage must be considered to be an indirect consequence of the environmental damage and left out of account in determining the law applicable under Art 4(1).[72]

THE CLAIMANT'S RIGHT OF ELECTION—THE LAW OF THE COUNTRY IN WHICH THE EVENT GIVING RISE TO DAMAGE OCCURRED

The person seeking compensation, who will not necessarily be the same as **7.22** the person who originally sustained the damage, may elect that the law of the country in which the event giving rise to damage occurred should be applied instead of the law or laws to which Art 4(1) points. For this purpose, the 'event giving rise to the damage' should be taken as the event for which the defendant is alleged to be responsible, whether or not it consists of his own act or omission.[73]

According to the Commission:[74]   **7.23**

[T]he exclusive connection to the place where the damage is sustained would also mean that a victim in a low-protection country would not enjoy the higher level of

---

[68] **7.08** above.
[69] As occurred in the Brussels Convention case of *Bier* (Case 21/76, *Handelskwekerij G J Bier BV v Mines de Potasse d'Alsace* [1976] ECR 1735).
[70] **4.69–4.74** above.
[71] **7.12–7.13** above.
[72] **4.36–4.45** above.
[73] **4.33–4.35** above.
[74] Commission Proposal, 19–20.

protection available in neighbouring countries. Considering the Union's more general objectives in environmental matters, the point is not only to respect the victim's legitimate interests but also to establish a legislative policy that contributes to raising the general level of environmental protection, especially as the author of the environmental damage, unlike other torts or delicts, generally derives an economic benefit from his harmful activity. Applying exclusively the law of the place where the damage is sustained could give an operator an incentive to establish his facilities at the border so as to discharge toxic substances into a river and enjoy the benefit of the neighbouring country's laxer rules. This solution would be contrary to the underlying philosophy of the European substantive law of the environment and the 'polluter pays' principle.

Article 7 accordingly allows the victim to make his claim on the basis of the law of the country in which the event giving rise to the damage occurred. It will therefore be for the victim rather than the court to determine the law that is most favourable to him.

7.24 If the claimant elects to have applied the law of the country in which the event giving rise to damage occurred, that law will displace the law or laws otherwise applicable by reference to Art 4(1) for all purposes. The claimant may not, for example, seek to apply one law to the question of the defendant's liability and another to the question of available remedies. There is no room for *dépeçage*.[75]

7.25 Recital (25) provides that 'the question of when the person seeking compensation can make the choice of the law applicable should be determined in accordance with the law of the Member State in which the court is seised'. For example, under the pre-existing German law, which recognized a similar right of election for torts generally,[76] the election (*Bestimmungsrecht*) must be made before the end of the first hearing or written pre-trial proceeding[77] in the court of first instance. A similar rule is proposed in Art 46a of the German draft law to adopt the Rome II Regulation.[78]

7.26 Under current English procedural law, a party wishing to assert that a foreign law applies to the case must plead and prove (by expert evidence) that foreign law to the satisfaction of the judge.[79] Otherwise English law will usually be applied even in cross-border cases.[80] These rules, and their

---

[75] **4.78–4.79** above.

[76] Introductory Act to the German Civil Code (EGBGB), Art 40(1), second sentence.

[77] German Civil Procedure Code (*Zivilprozessordnung* or ZPO), §275–6.

[78] *Gesetz zur Anpassung der Vorschriften des Internationalen Privat-rechts an die Verordnung* (EG) Nr 864/2007, reproduced in (2008) 28 IPRax 364, Art 46a.

[79] See Sir L Collins et al. (ed), *Dicey, Morris & Collins, The Conflict of Laws* (14th edn, 2006), Rule 18(1) and commentary.

[80] Ibid, Rule 18(2) and commentary.

relationship to the rules of applicable law in the Regulation, are examined more closely in **Chapter 14** below.[81] In this connection, however, and subject to compliance with the relevant rules of procedure and to the court's discretion in case management matters, it remains open to a party to seek to amend his statement of case[82] and to adduce additional evidence[83] at any point up to and, in limited circumstances, following judgment or on appeal.[84] 'Decisions as to the form of the pleadings and the relief to be sought are not an election against reliance on other allegations of fact or law, or other claims, and a party may change his position subject to obtaining leave'.[85] Accordingly, in the absence of a specific procedural rule for the exercise of the right of a claimant before the English courts to choose that the law of the country in which the event giving rise to the damage occurred should apply to a claim under Art 7, it would appear to remain open to him to make that choice at any time, subject to the court's discretion as to whether to allow any amendment of his statement of case or additional evidence required for this purpose.

D. THE ROLE OF RULES OF SAFETY AND CONDUCT (ART 17)

Art 17 of the Regulation requires that 'account should be taken' by Member **7.27** State courts of the 'rules of safety and conduct which were in force at the place and time of the event giving rise to liability'. The origin and effect of that provision are considered in **Chapter 15**.[86] In view of the extensive regulation under national law of industrial and other processes liable to cause environmental damage, Art 17 may have a particular significance in the context of environmental claims falling within Art 7. In this connection, the Commission noted:[87]

A further difficulty regarding civil liability for violations of the environment lies in the close link with the public-law rules governing the operator's conduct and the safety rules with which he is required to comply. One of the most frequently asked

---

[81] **14.63–14.76**.

[82] Civil Procedure Rules, Part 17.

[83] Ibid, rr 32.10 (witness statements) and 35.13 (expert's report).

[84] Litigants will generally be held to the basis on which they have presented their case at trial, but this is not an absolute rule (see K R Handley, *Estoppel by Conduct and Election* (2006), para 15-041).

[85] K R Handley, ibid, para 15-027, referring to *United Australia Ltd v Barclays Bank Ltd* [1941] AC 1, 18-19 (Viscount Simon LC, UKHL).

[86] **15.26–15.34** below.

[87] Commission Proposal, 20.

questions concerns the consequences of an activity that is authorised and legitimate in State A (where, for example, a certain level of toxic emissions is tolerated)
but causes damage to be sustained in State B, where it is not authorised (and where
the emissions exceed the tolerated level). Under Article 13 [*of the Proposal*[88]], the
court must then be able to have regard to the fact that the perpetrator has complied
with the rules in force in the country in which he is in business.

7.28 It is, however, important to appreciate that the requirement to 'take
account' of rules of safety and conduct does not mean that those rules
must be *applied* to determine questions of civil liability, in particular insofar as they exonerate the defendant or authorize particular conduct that
has caused or may cause environmental damage. The Commission itself
emphasizes this point, as follows:[89]

> Taking account of foreign law is not the same thing as applying it: the court will
> apply only the law that is applicable under the conflict rule, but it must take
> account of another law as a point of fact, for example, when assessing the serious-
> ness of the fault of the author's good or bad faith for the purposes of the measure
> of damages.

7.29 With respect to Art 7, if the claimant chooses to base his claim on the law
of the country in which the event giving rise to damage occurred or if the
damage also occurred in that country leading to the application of its law
in any event, the defendant may rely (for example) on the fact that he complied with local emissions standards or on the terms of a public licence to
undertake certain activity, if those facts constitute a defence under that
law. If, on the other hand, the damage occurred in a country other than
that in which the defendant acted, and the claimant does not exercise his
right of election under Art 7, the defendant's compliance with regulatory
standards or the terms of a licence granted by the authorities for the place
where the defendant acted will assist him only if, having regard the law of
the country of damage, it is appropriate to take them into account under
Art 17 in assessing the defendant's fault (if liability is fault based) or if that
law recognizes his compliance as having equivalent effect to compliance
with its own regulatory requirements or to a public licence granted under
its own law and as providing him with a defence. Questions as to the recognition of a foreign licence, being a matter concerning the grounds of
exemption from liability, are governed solely by the law applicable under
the Regulation.[90] Art 17 does not extend this far.

---

[88] Regulation, Art 17.

[89] Commission Proposal, 25.

[90] Art 15(1)(b). For more detailed discussion of the effects of licence on liability in cross-
border cases, see 2nd Report of the International Law Association's Committee on Transnational
Enforcement of Environmental Law, n 1 above, para 3.5.

In the well-known case of *Bier v Mines de potasse d'Alsace*, following refer-   **7.30**
ence to the ECJ on the question of jurisdiction,[91] the French defendant
raised in its defence the fact that it had been authorized to carry out its
activities by permits granted under French law. That defence was rejected
both at trial and subsequently on appeal on the ground that the permits
expressly preserved the rights of third parties.[92] The Dutch first instance
court acknowledged, however, that the existence of the French permits
was 'not without importance to the question of liability'.[93]

E. REGULATION BY INTERNATIONAL CONVENTION

RELATIONSHIP WITH ART 7

Cross-border activities causing environmental damage are increasingly   **7.31**
regulated by international agreements.[94] Among other matters, some conventions regulate civil liability of those responsible for pollution or the
causes of pollution, particularly in relation to the marine environment.[95]
Typically, these conventions do not contain rules concerning the law applicable to civil claims.[96] Instead, they regulate substantive law and require
State parties to give effect to their provisions in all situations to which they
apply. Accordingly, if the Member State in which proceedings are brought
is a party to a relevant civil liability convention, the provisions of that convention will likely take precedence as overriding mandatory provisions of

---

[91] **4.26** above.

[92] *Hoge Raad*, Judgment of 23 September 1988, RvdW (1988); (1990) 21 Netherlands
Yearbook of International Law 434, 439. The Supreme Court judgment was followed by the
announcement of a settlement between the parties (ibid, 440).

[93] *Rechtbank Rotterdam*, Judgment of 16 December 1983, NJ 1984, No 341. For an English
translation, see (1984) Netherlands Yearbook of International Law 471.

[94] For detailed analysis of this subject area, see C Redgwell, 'International Environmental
Law', ch 22 in M Shaw (ed), *International Law* (2nd edn, 2006). Also P Birnie and A Boyle,
International Law and the Environment (2nd edn, 2002); P Sands, *Principles of International
Environmental Law* (2nd edn, 2003); E Louka, *International Environmental Law: Fairness,
Effectiveness, and World Order* (2006); J Brunnee, D Bodansky, and E Hey, *The Oxford Handbook
of International Environmental Law* (2007).

[95] Environmental Liability Directive, n 11 above, Art 4(2) and Annex IV. For a survey of
international conventions regulating civil liability for environmental damage, see C Bernasconi,
n 1 above, 4–16.

[96] A notable exception is the Nordic Convention on the protection of the environment (**1.36**
above). Also C Bernasconi, n 1, 26–8. It seems doubtful whether Art 4 of the Convention for the
prevention of pollution from ships (London, 2 November 1973) (MARPOL), to which Bernasconi
refers (ibid, 27), constitutes a rule regulating the law applicable to civil obligations, as these are
not addressed in the Convention, which deals only with State enforcement measures.

the law of the forum State under Art 16 of the Rome II Regulation, whether directly or through the measures taken by that State to implement the convention. If the Member State in which proceedings are brought is not a party to a relevant civil liability convention, then the convention will probably have effect only if the State whose law applies to the non-contractual obligation under Art 7 is a party and if the matters regulated by the convention fall within the scope of the law applicable, as defined in Chapter III of the Regulation,[97] excluding matters of evidence and procedure.[98]

THE OIL POLLUTION CONVENTIONS

7.32 Arguably, the most important of the conventions in force dealing with civil liability for environmental damage are the 1969 Convention on civil liability for oil pollution[99] and the 2001 Convention on civil liability for bunker oil pollution damage.[100] These contain detailed rules governing the liability of shipowners and related persons for pollution damage caused by the escape of oil from ships. All Member States with the exception of Austria, Czech Republic, Romania, and Slovakia are Contracting States under the Oil Pollution Convention.[101] Twelve Member States are States Parties under the Bunker Oil Pollution Convention.[102]

7.33 The Oil Pollution Convention in its amended form applies to oil pollution caused in the territory of a Contracting State, including in its territorial sea, or in a Contracting State's exclusive economic zone established under

---

[97] **Ch 14** below.

[98] Art 1(3).

[99] Adopted 29 November 1969, as amended by later protocols, including (in particular) the protocol adopted on 27 November 1992 which substantially revised the text (**Oil Pollution Convention**). See also the Convention on the establishment of an international fund for compensation for oil pollution damage, adopted on 18 December 1971, as amended by later protocols. The consolidated text of both Conventions is available at <http://www.iopcfund.org/npdf/Conventions%20English.pdf>. For the UK implementing legislation, see Merchant Shipping Act 1995, ss 152–71.

[100] Adopted 23 March 2001 (**Bunker Oil Pollution Convention**). The Convention entered into force in November 2008. See Council Decision 2002/762/EC of 19 September 2002 authorising the Member States, in the interest of the Community, to sign, ratify or accede to the International Convention on Civil Liability for Bunker Oil Pollution Damage, 2001 (the Bunkers Convention) (OJ L 256, 7 [25.09.2002]). The text of the Convention is available at <http://www.official-documents.gov.uk/document/cm66/6693/6693.pdf>. See Merchant Shipping (Oil Pollution) (Bunkers Convention) Regulations (SI 2006/1244).

[101] Source: International Maritime Organisation (<http://www.imo.org/includes/blast-DataOnly.asp/data_id%3D22499/status-x.xls>). See Merchant Shipping (Oil Pollution) (Bunkess Convention) Regulations (SI 2006/1244).

[102] Ibid. The Member States referred to are Bulgaria, Cyprus, Estonia, Germany, Greece, Latvia, Lithuania, Luxembourg, Portugal, Slovenia, Spain, United Kingdom.

international law.[103] The Convention provides for the liability of the ship-owner at the time of the pollution incident, excludes the liability of others,[104] permits the shipowner to limit his liability by establishing a limitation fund in a Contracting State court,[105] and protects shipowners who have taken this step.[106] The Convention also requires oil-carrying ships regis-tered in a Contracting State to take out insurance, and provides for a right of direct action against the insurer.[107] The Bunker Oil Pollution Convention, which has the same territorial scope,[108] is modelled along similar lines.[109] Both Conventions contain rules on jurisdiction and the recognition and the enforcement of judgments, but not as to the law applicable to matters not expressly regulated by the Convention.[110]

Neither Convention applies to oil pollution damage caused in a non- **7.34** Contracting State or on the high seas. The law applicable to claims with respect to such damage in a Member State court must be determined in accordance with Art 7 of the Rome II Regulation.[111]

---

[103] Oil Pollution Convention, Art II.
[104] Ibid, Art III.
[105] Ibid, Art V.
[106] Ibid, Art VI.
[107] Ibid, Art VII.
[108] Bunker Oil Pollution Convention, Art 2.
[109] Ibid, Arts 3–7.
[110] Oil Pollution Convention, Arts IX and X; Bunker Oil Pollution Convention, Arts 9 and 10.
[111] For discussion as to the application of the Regulation to events and damage occurring in an area outside State sovereignty, see **3.311–3.314** and **4.48** and **4.56–4.57** above.

8

Intellectual Property

Article 8

Infringement of intellectual property rights

1. The law applicable to a non-contractual obligation arising from an infringement of an intellectual property right shall be the law of the country for which protection is claimed.

2. In the case of a non-contractual obligation arising from an infringement of a unitary Community intellectual property right, the law applicable shall, for any question that is not governed by the relevant Community instrument, be the law of the country in which the act of infringement was committed.

3. The law applicable under this Article may not be derogated from by an agreement pursuant to Article 14.

A. INTRODUCTION[1]

8.01 No specific rule for intellectual property matters was to be found in the Commission's preliminary draft proposal.[2] Art 8(1) of the Commission Proposal, favouring the law of the country for which protection is sought (*lex loci protectionis*), appears to have been inspired by the comments[3] on that preliminary draft of the Hamburg Group for Private International Law, a collaboration of German scholars.[4]

8.02 In this connection, the Commission explained that:[5]

> The general rule contained in Article 3(1)[6] does not appear to be compatible with the specific requirements in the field of intellectual property. To reflect this incompatibility, two approaches were discussed in the course of preparatory work. The first is to exclude the subject from the scope of the proposed Regulation, either by means of an express exclusion in Article 1 or by means of Article 25,[7] which preserves current international conventions. The second is to lay down a special rule, and this is the approach finally adopted by the Commission with Article 8.

8.03 The Commission also recognized, however, that its special rule favouring the *lex loci protectionis* was not appropriate for Community intellectual property rights, which apply to the territory of the Community as a whole.[8] Accordingly, the Commission proposed that the law of the country in which the act of infringement is committed should apply to questions not determined by the Community instrument creating the right in question.

8.04 At an early stage in discussions in the Council's Rome II Committee, the German delegation proposed that non-contractual obligations relating to

---

[1] For detailed analysis of the relationship between private international law and intellectual property see the collected papers in J Basedow, J Drexl, A Kur, and A Metzger (eds), *Intellectual Property in the Conflict of Laws* (2005), Parts I and III; J Drexl and A Kur (eds), *Intellectual Property and Private International Law: Heading for the Future* (2005), Part 2. Also J Fawcett and P Torremans, *Intellectual Property and Private International Law* (1998), esp chs 9–13.

[2] **1.64** above.

[3] Hamburg Group for Private International Law, Comments on the European Commission's Draft Proposal for a Council Regulation on the Law Applicable to Non-Contractual Obligations, 21–5, reproduced at <http://www.mpipriv.de/de/data/pdf/commentshamburggroup.pdf>.

[4] C Hahn and O Tell, 'The European Commission's Agenda: The Future "Rome I and Rome II" Regulations', in Basedow, *Intellectual Property*, n 1 above, 13.

[5] Commission Proposal, 20.

[6] Regulation, Art 4(1).

[7] Regulation, Art 28.

[8] C Hahn and O Tell, n 4 above, 14–15.

intellectual property rights should be excluded from the Regulation entirely on the following grounds:[9]

- international arrangements opting in effect for the same connection already exist;
- intellectual property rights must be accorded special treatment in Article 9;[10]
- an overlap with the rules of applicable law with respect to acts of unfair competition[11] is conceivable;
- discussions are in progress concerning the appropriate connection for modern communication technologies, and their outcome should not be pre-empted.

As to the first of these reasons, it may be supposed that the German dele-   **8.05** gation had in mind the 'national treatment' provisions in Arts 2 and 3 of the 1883 Paris Industrial Property Convention,[12] Arts 5 and 6 of the 1886 Berne Copyright Convention,[13] and Arts 3 and 4 of the WTO Agreement on Trade-Related Aspects of Intellectual Property Rights (TRIPs).[14] Closer examination of these provisions suggests, however, that they do not lay down any rule of applicable law for infringements of intellectual property rights, let alone one that favours the *lex loci protectionis*.[15] Indeed, 'the only private international law implication of Article 3 TRIPs (and similar provisions in *inter alia* the Berne and Paris Conventions) is that nationality cannot be used as a connecting factor because this may lead to a different degree of protection granted to national and foreign right owners'.[16]

---

[9] Council document 9009/04 ADD 11 [24.5.2004], 4. Also ibid, ADD 12 [24.5.2004], 4–5 (France); ibid, ADD 17 [2.6.4] (Italy). Similar arguments were raised in response to the Commission's preliminary draft proposal (C Hahn and O Tell, n 4 above, 12).

[10] Art 9 of the Commission Proposal contained rules for determining the law applicable to non-contractual obligations arising out of an act other than a tort or delict, corresponding (in part) to those now found in Regulation, Arts 10 (unjust enrichment) and 11 (*negotiorum gestio*). Art 9(6) of the Commission Proposal contained a rule corresponding to that now found in Regulation, Art 13 (**8.19–8.20** below).

[11] Commission Proposal, Art 5; Regulation, Art 6(1) and 6(2).

[12] Paris Convention for the protection of industrial property, 20 March 1883, available at <http://www.wipo.int/treaties/en/ip/paris/trtdocs_wo020.html#P77_5133>.

[13] Berne Convention for the protection of literary and artistic works, 9 September 1986, last revised at Paris on 24 July 1971, available at <http://www.wipo.int/treaties/en/ip/berne/trtdocs_wo001.html>.

[14] Marrakesh, 15 April 1994, available at <http://www.wto.org/english/tratop_e/trips_e/t_agm2_e.htm>.

[15] M Pertagas, 'Intellectual Property and Choice of Law Rules' in A Malatesta (ed), *The Unification of Choice of Law Rules on Torts and Other Non-Contractual Obligations in Europe* (2006), 226–8.

[16] Ibid, 228.

8.06 In 2005, the ECJ endorsed that view in *Tod's v Heyraud*, a case concerning the Berne Copyright Convention:[17]

> As is apparent from Article 5(1) of the Berne Convention, the purpose of that convention is not to determine the applicable law on the protection of literary and artistic works, but to establish, as a general rule, a system of national treatment of the rights appertaining to such works.

8.07 Art 64(3) of the European Patent Convention (EPC)[18] raises slightly different considerations. It provides that:

> Any infringement of a European patent shall be dealt with by national law.

> In *Pearce v Ove Arup*, a copyright case, the English Court of Appeal suggested (*obiter*) that the reference to 'national law' in Art 64(3) was a reference to 'the law of the state in respect of which the patent was granted'.[19] As the Court contrasted this with the position under Art 5(2) of the Berne Copyright Convention (for which, in its view, there was no reason for concluding that the references to 'the laws of the country where protection is claimed' do not include that country's own rules of private international law), it appears that the Court took the view that Art 64(3) of the EPC required application of the *lex loci protectionis* without the possibility of *renvoi*. Professor Pertegás disagrees, however, with this interpretation of the EPC. She argues forcefully that:[20]

> In the first place, reference is made to 'national law' and not to 'substantive' or 'internal' law. In order to exclude the working of the choice of law rules, international conventions generally refer to the expression 'internal law', or state that the term 'law' does not include choice of law rules. In the absence of an express indication to the contrary, there is no reason to interpret Article 64(3) of the EPC as excluding the use of private international law rules in order to determine the relevant substantive rules.

---

[17] Case C-28/04, *Tod's SpA v Heyraud SA* [2005] ECR I-5781, para 32. In this case, the ECJ ruled, however, that Article 12 of the EC Treaty, prohibiting non-discrimination on grounds of nationality, must be interpreted as meaning that the right of an author to claim in a Member State the copyright protection afforded by the law of that State may not be subject to a distinguishing criterion based on the country of origin of the work., as contemplated by Art 2(7) of the Berne Convention.

[18] Convention on the grant of European patents (**EPC**), 5 October 1973, as revised by the Act revising Article 63 EPC of 17 December 1991 and the Act revising the EPC of 29 November 2000. The text of the Convention is available at <http://www.epo.org/patents/law/legal-texts/html/epc/2000/e/ma1.html>.

[19] *Pearce v Ove Arup Partnership Ltd* [1999] 1 All ER 769, 800.

[20] M Pertegás Sender, 'Patent Infringement, Choice of Laws and the Forthcoming Rome II Regulation', in *Basedow, Intellectual Property*, n 1 above, 161.

Furthermore, the harmonisation of the choice of law rules of the EPC Member State clearly goes beyond the ratio of Article 64(3) of the EPC. Indeed, this provision must be read in combination with Article 64(1) of the EPC, which provided that the European patent is to have the effects of a national patent in the designated states. Article 64(3) of the EPC ensures that the post-grant life of a European Patent is ruled by national law in the same way as a national patent. The private international law rules of the forum apply in disputes concerning the enforcement of national patents, and hence the same rules must apply in cases involving European patents.

Accordingly, it would have been possible, in theory at least, for the **8.08** Community to adopt a solution concerning the law applicable to intellectual property rights other than the one favoured in Art 8(1) of the Commission Proposal, for example in favour of the law of the country of infringement. Despite early hesitation among the members of the Council's Rome II Committee,[21] the Commission's view that the *lex loci protectionis* should apply to infringements of national intellectual property rights was never seriously challenged[22] and, subject to minor textual changes, the text of Art 8(1) of its Proposal was carried through the legislative process.[23] Doubts among the Member States about the need for a separate solution for Community intellectual property rights and the connecting factor proposed by the Commission for these rights[24] were also eventually dispelled.[25] The exclusion of party choice for intellectual property rights, originally contained within the text of Art 10 of the Commission Proposal (freedom of choice) was brought within Art 8 as a separate sub-rule.[26] The European Parliament did not make any material amendments to Art 8 at either the first or second reading stage.[27]

---

[21] Council document 6518/04 [26.2.2004], 1–2.

[22] Council document 11801/04 [28.7.2004], 5.

[23] The final text derives from the Council Common Position, Art 8.

[24] Council document 11801/04, 5. Also Council documents 13047/04 [5.10.2004], 7 (France); 16240/04 [23.12.2004], 6–7 (Germany). The law of the country for which protection is claimed, the law Member State in which the act of infringement was committed, the law of the Member State in which damage occurred and the law of the forum were put forward as possible options in the Council's Rome II Committee (Council documents SN2851/04 [20.7.2004], Art 8(2); 12746/04 [27.9.2004], Art 8(2)).

[25] Council documents 7551/06 [22.3.2006], 6 and 7709/06 [3.5.2006], 3.

[26] **8.54** below. Art 8(3) appears in its final form in Council document 8416/06 [21.4.2006], Art 8(3). In earlier drafts, it is combined with wording giving priority to Art 8 over the general rule for tort/delict and the rules for unjust enrichment, *negotiorum gestio* and *culpa in contrahendo* (see, e.g., Council document 7432/06 [16.3.2006]. The opening words of Art 4 and Art 13 of the Regulation (**8.19–8.20** below) now perform the latter function.

[27] EP 1st Reading Position, Art 8; EP 2nd Reading Position, Art 8.

8.09 In the following commentary, for convenience, the abbreviations 'IPR' and 'Community IPR' are used, respectively, to refer to national (non-Community) intellectual property rights and unitary Community intellectual property rights.

B. INFRINGEMENT OF INTELLECTUAL PROPERTY RIGHTS

NON-COMMUNITY INTELLECTUAL PROPERTY RIGHTS

8.10 Recital (26) contains the following (non-exhaustive) definition of 'intellectual property rights':

> For the purposes of this Regulation, the term 'intellectual property rights' should be interpreted as meaning, for instance, copyright, related rights, the *sui generis* right for the protection of databases and industrial property rights.

8.11 The reference to copyright confirms that Art 8 concerns registered as well as unregistered IPRs. Although the Recital does not refer specifically to trademarks or patents, two of the most important classes of IPRs, those rights fall under the description of 'industrial property rights'. In this connection, Art 1(1) of the Paris Industrial Property Convention[28] provides:

> The protection of industrial property has as its object patents, utility models, industrial designs, trademarks, service marks, trade names, indications of source or appellations of origin, and the repression of unfair competition.

8.12 Art 8(1) covers infringements of all of the rights named, but does not deal with matters of unfair competition generally, as these are dealt with separately within Art 6. The English tort of passing off should be considered as a non-contractual obligation arising out of an act of unfair competition, within Art 6(1) rather than one arising out of infringement of an intellectual property right, within Art 8(1).[29]

8.13 The use of the words 'for instance' in Recital (26) emphasize that the list is non-exhaustive. Although it is, no doubt, easier to identify an intellectual property right than to define one, the concept seems capable of encompassing any right arising under national law which positively enhances, rather than merely protects, the value to the right-holder of the intangible products of the time and resources expended in developing ideas or

---

[28] n 12 above.

[29] **6.34** above. Cf the views of the UK delegation in the Council's Rome II Committee (Council documents 9009/04 ADD 15 [26.5.2004], 6 and 5460/06 [18.1.2006], 2).

expressions of ideas. Examples under English law include patents,[30] copyright,[31] registered and unregistered design rights,[32] trade marks,[33] and plant breeders' rights.[34]

Community Intellectual Property Rights

Art 8(2) refers to 'unitary Community intellectual property rights'. The **8.14** following reference to 'the relevant Community instrument' confirms that the provision is concerned with rights generated by a Community legislative instrument. At present, the following Community IPRs have been created by Community Regulations:[35]

1. Community trademarks;[36]

2. Community design rights;[37]

3. Community plant variety rights.[38]

In addition to these rights, EC Directives have required the Member States **8.15** to create new kinds of national intellectual property right concerning, for example, the protection of databases[39] and the artist's resale right.[40] It is doubtful, however, whether non-contractual obligations arising out of

---

[30] Patents Act 1977.

[31] Copyright Act 1988.

[32] Registered Designs Act 1949; Copyright Act 1988, s 213.

[33] Trade Marks Act 1994.

[34] Plant Varieties Act 1997.

[35] Note also the provisions of Directive (EC) 2004/48 on the enforcement of intellectual property rights (OJ L195, 16 [2.6.2004]).

[36] Regulation (EC) No 40/1994 on the Community trade mark (OJ L11, 1 [14.1.1994]), as amended by Regulation (EC) No 422/2004 (OJ L70, 1 [9.3.2004]) (**Community Trade Mark Regulation**). A consolidated version of the Regulation is available at <http://oami.europa.eu/EN/mark/aspects/pdf/4094enCV.pdf>.

[37] Regulation (EC) No 6/2002 on the Community design (OJ L3, 1 [5.1.2002]) amended by Regulation (EC) No 1891/2006 to give effect to the accession of the European Community to the Geneva Act of the Hague Agreement concerning the international registration of industrial designs (**Community Design Regulation**). A consolidated version of the Regulation is available at <http://oami.europa.eu/EN/design/pdf/6-02-CV-en.pdf>.

Also Commission Regulation (EC) No 2245/2002 implementing Council Regulation (EC) No 6/2002 on Community designs (OJ L341, 28 [17.12.2002]).

[38] Regulation (EC) No 2100/94 on Community plant variety rights (OJ L227, 1 [27.9.1994]) (**Community Plant Variety Regulation**).

[39] Directive (EC) No 1996/9 on the legal protection of databases (OJ L27, 20 [27.3.1996]), as implemented in the UK by the Copyright and Rights in Databases Regulations (SI 1997/3032).

[40] Directive (EC) No 2001/84 on the resale right for the benefit of the author of an original work of art (OJ L272, 32 [13.10.2001]), as implemented in the UK by the Artist's Resale Right Regulations (SI 2006/46).

infringements of these rights[41] also constitute 'unitary Community intellectual property rights' falling within Art 8(2). In putting forward its proposal, the Commission appeared to have had in mind only rights created by means of a Regulation. Having referred to the *sui generis* right for the protection of databases as an example of an IPR falling within Art 8,[42] the Commission did not include this right in its list of examples of 'unitary' Community IPRs, instead referring only to the Community trade mark, Community designs and models, and the proposed Community patent. [43] Those rights, as well as the Community plant variety right, are explicitly described in the Regulations creating them as 'unitary' or 'uniform' rights.[44] Moreover, although rights arising from the implementation of EC Directives can justifiably be described as rights under EC law,[45] it seems artificial to describe IPRs arising from the implementation of a Directive as 'unitary' Community IPRs. As Directives leave to the Member States the form of choice and methods of implementation,[46] a separate right is created under the law of each Member State by its implementing rules. The non-unitary character of a right arising from a Directive becomes even clearer if, as in the case of the Directive for the legal protection of databases,[47] the legislation gives Member States a margin of appreciation as to the scope of the right itself. Desirable as it might be for Art 8(2) to apply to rights of this kind, identifying a single Member State whose rules apply to an infringing act, that interpretation does not appear open under Art 8(2) as it stands. Instead, Art 8(1) will apply.

8.16 Brief reference should also be made to the Commission's proposal, originally made in 2000, to create a Community patent.[48] Although the proposal led to a measure of political agreement between the Member States,[49] certain aspects of the Proposal have been strongly opposed by stakeholders on the grounds of high costs of translation requirements and

---

[41] This assumes that the right is defined in such a way as to be capable of being infringed. The artist's resale right, being simply a right to receive a fixed sum on resale of the artist's work, may not raise questions of 'infringement' at all (**8.18** below).

[42] Commission Proposal, 20.

[43] Commission Proposal, 21.

[44] Community Trade Mark Regulation, Art 1(2); Community Design Regulation, Art 1(3); Community Plant Variety Regulation, Art 2.

[45] Cf Art 14(3) of the Regulation referring to 'provisions of Community law, where appropriate as implemented in the Member State of the forum' (**13.32–13.33** below).

[46] EC Treaty, Art 249.

[47] n 39 above, Arts 6(2) and 9.

[48] COM (2000) 412 final [28.11.2000].

[49] Council document 7119/04 [8.3.2004].

the excessive centralization of the proposed jurisdictional system.[50] Negotiations have stalled since 2004, with little prospect of a successful outcome in the short term.[51]

This proposal to establish a unitary Community patent right is not to be **8.17** confused with the bundle of national rights that arises from registration of a European patent in accordance with the terms of the European Patents Convention.[52] The EPC is a separate initiative between the EC Member States and several non-Member States, and does not depend for its effectiveness on Community law.

'INFRINGEMENT' OF INTELLECTUAL PROPERTY RIGHTS

Both Art 8(1) and 8(2) concern 'infringement' of IPRs. It may be doubted, **8.18** therefore, whether IPRs that only generate a right to receive a sum of money on a particular event (for example, the resale right conferred by EC law for the benefit of artists[53]) fall within the scope of the Regulation, there being no relevant infringement even if the sums due are not paid. Neither provision applies, in any event, to questions concerning the creation, registration, validity, or transfer of IPRs. Not only are such matters logically prior to any question as to whether there has been an infringement, they are also matters of status, which fall outside the material scope of the Regulation.[54] Accordingly, if infringement proceedings are defended on the ground that the IPR relied on is invalid, the law applicable to the question of validity must be determined otherwise than by reference to Art 8. As questions of validity will almost certainly be referred to the law of the country of origin of the relevant IPR (coinciding with the *lex loci protectionis*) or, in the case of a Community IPR, EC law, this point as to the boundaries of Art 8 may be of largely theoretical significance.

---

[50] Commission Communication on Enhancing the Patent System in Europe (COM (2007) 165 final [3.4.2007]), 3. Also Commission Communication 'An Industrial Rights Strategy for Europe' COM (2008) 465/3.

[51] Ibid, 3–4. The creation of a harmonized jurisdiction regime may be the next step on the road to a common EC patent law (ibid, 5–11).

[52] n 18 above.

[53] Directive (EC) No 2001/84 on the resale right for the benefit of the author of an original work of art, n 40 above.

[54] **3.102** above. Also J Fawcett and P Torremans, n 1 above, 642.

PRIORITY OF ARTICLE 8

8.19 In considering the material scope of Art 8, it is also necessary to refer to Art 13, which provides as follows:

Article 13

Applicability of Article 8

For the purposes of this Chapter, Article 8 shall apply to non-contractual obligations arising from an infringement of an intellectual property right.

8.20 This provision, corresponding to Art 9(6) of the Commission Proposal, was explained by the Commission as being 'to ensure that several different laws are not applicable to one and the same dispute', with specific reference to the possibility of an 'obligation based on unjust enrichment arising from an infringement of an intellectual property right'.[55] This provision appears to have been influenced by the broader concept of unjustified enrichment recognized under German law.[56] It may be questioned, however, whether this provision was necessary, as both Art 8(1) and Art 8(2) refer generally to 'infringements' of intellectual property rights, without distinguishing according to the character or remedial consequences of the infringement and Art 15 refers to the law applicable under the Regulation both 'the existence, the nature and the assessment of damage or the remedy claimed' (Art 15(c)) and 'the measures which a court may take to prevent or terminate injury or damage or to ensure the provision of compensation' (Art 15(d)). That question is closely linked to the question whether claims for what an English lawyer might refer to as 'restitution for wrongdoing'[57] (i.e. gain-based responses to tort/delict) fall within Chapter II (as arising out of tort/delict) or Art 10 of the Regulation (as arising out of unjust enrichment). It has been submitted in **Chapter 4** that the tort/delict characterization is correct.[58] On this basis, Art 13 is best seen as a clarification, for the avoidance of doubt, that Art 8 has priority over the rules of applicable law in Chapter III.[59] It also has priority over the general rule for tort/delict in Art 4.[60]

---

[55] Commission Proposal, 22.
[56] C Hahn and O Tell, n 1 above, 13–14. Also **10.13** below.
[57] P Birks, *Unjust Enrichment* (2nd edn, 2005), 12–16.
[58] **4.11–4.20** above.
[59] i.e. Arts 10 (unjust enrichment), 11 (*negotiorum gestio*), and 12 (*culpa in contrahendo*).
[60] **4.07** above.

C. NON-COMMUNITY INTELLECTUAL PROPERTY RIGHTS—THE LAW OF THE COUNTRY FOR WHICH PROTECTION IS CLAIMED (ART 8(1))

Under Art 8(1), the law applicable to a non-contractual obligation arising **8.21** from an infringement of an IPR other than a Community IPR is the law of the country for which protection is claimed. This rule must be read together with the opening words of Recital (26), as follows:

Regarding infringements of intellectual property rights, the universally acknowledged principle of the *lex loci protectionis* should be preserved.

The suggestion that the *lex loci protectionis* is a 'universally acknowledged **8.22** principle' goes too far.[61] Indeed, prior to the Regulation, there was no consistent practice even among the Member States.[62] The 'principle', however, would appear to originate in the idea that intellectual property rights are sovereign in character and operate within territorial limits, with each State having the exclusive power to regulate such rights within its territory. As the editors of Dicey, Morris and Collins recognize:[63]

The essence of an intellectual property right is the owner's right to take action to prevent others from engaging in certain types of activity in a given territory without the owner's permission. Although patents, trade marks and copyright are classified as movables, they share some of the characteristics of immovables in the sense that the rights which they confer are territorially limited.

Although this argument based on sovereignty and territoriality has been **8.23** undermined in recent years, for example in matters of civil jurisdiction for IPRs,[64] it appears to have exerted a strong influence on the development of Art 8(1) of the Rome II Regulation. According to the Commission:[65]

The treatment of intellectual property was one of the questions that came in for intense debate during the Commission's consultations. Many contributions

---

[61] Cf A Kur, 'Applicable Law: An Alternative Proposal For International Regulation—The Max-Planck Project on International Jurisdiction And Choice Of Law' (2005) 30 Brook J Int L 951.

[62] M Pertegás, n 15 above, 229–35. For the pre-existing treatment of IPRs under English private international law, see Sir L Collins et al. (ed), *Dicey, Morris & Collins: The Conflict of Laws* (14th edn, 2006), para 35-030.

[63] Dicey, Morris & Collins, para 22-051.

[64] Dicey, Morris & Collins, para 35-031; *Satyam Computer Services Ltd v Upaid Systems Ltd* [2008] EWHC 31 (Comm), [91]–[104] (Flaux J), affd [2008] EWCA Civ 487.

[65] Commission Proposal, 20. It is, however, doubtful whether the Berne or Paris Conventions to which the Commission referred contain rules of applicable law favouring the *lex loci protectionis* (**8.05–8.06** above).

recalled the existence of the universally recognised principle of the *lex loci protectionis*, meaning the law of the country in which protection is claimed on which eg the Bern Convention for the Protection of Literary and Artistic Works of 1886 and the Paris Convention for the Protection of Industrial Property of 1883 are built. This rule, also known as the 'territorial principle', enables each country to apply its own law to an infringement of an intellectual property right which is in force in its territory: counterfeiting an industrial property right is governed by the law of the country in which the patent was issued or the trade mark or model was registered; in copyright cases the courts apply the law of the country where the violation was committed. This solution confirms that the rights held in each country are independent.

8.24 In addition, one cannot ignore the extent to which IPRs are also influenced by extra-legal considerations. In particular, they are used by States as a tool of economic policy for the promotion (or inhibition) of trade and enterprise. Professor Basedow, a member of the Hamburg Group,[66] makes the following point:[67]

> By their nature, intellectual property rights are legal artifacts, created by a given state as monopolies limited in time and designed to determine the competitive conditions in the relevant markets of that country.

8.25 For these reasons, it is perhaps inevitable that legal systems characterize and equip similarly named IPRs in different ways and that, in particular, the definition of an infringing act, the defences to infringement actions and the remedies may vary greatly. The rule of applicable law in Art 8(1) of the Rome II Regulation is neutral as to the achievement of those objectives in that it does not specify what element of activity connected with the territory of a country justifies the application of that country's laws regulating intellectual property. An important consequence of the application by Member State courts of the *lex loci protectionis* principle is that, so far as those courts are concerned, each State in defining its national IPRs may choose its own set of unilateral connecting factors describing, in each case, the required connection to its territory. As the product of a process engaging over twenty Member States, each of which sets its own economic priorities, Art 8(1) in its final form may owe more to pragmatism than to theories of sovereignty or jurisdiction under international law.

8.26 So far as Community litigants are concerned, the adoption of the *lex loci protectionis* principle allows claimants to choose the IPR (or bundle of IPRs) that best serves their interests and objectives, subject only to the requirement that the protection that they seek must pertain to the territory

---

[66] Text to n 4 above.
[67] J Basedow, 'Introduction' in Basedow, *Intellectual Property*, n 1 above, 2.

of the country whose law it is sought to apply. In other words, the national IPR relied on must apply to the facts relied on as establishing an infringement on the basis of a connection to the territory of its country of origin, and not because of an extra-territorial connection. The relevant connection may, however, relate to an act of the defendant or another person or to the consequences of such act. All that the claimant need show is that the protection is claimed 'for' a particular country. Although Art 8(1) refers to the law of the country for which protection is 'claimed', the rule should apply equally to actions by alleged infringers for declarations of non-infringement, a common tactic in intellectual property litigation. The connecting factor should here be taken to refer to the law of the country for which the availability of protection is denied.

Even in a straightforward cross-border case, an act in one country having **8.27** consequences in another may enable the claimant to claim protection under one or more national IPRs in each country. The court or courts seised of the dispute must of course take steps to avoid over-compensation of the claimant. In other cases, identical conduct or consequences in several countries may allow the claimant to pursue several distinct claims simultaneously, with each claim relating only to the conduct or its consequences in a particular country.[68]

Application of national IPRs under Art 8(1) must be consistent with the **8.28** requirements of the EC Treaty concerning, in particular, the free movement of goods. In particular, under the so-called 'exhaustion of rights principle' a right-holder who has consented to the marketing of goods in one Member State may not generally rely on a national IPR in order to restrict the importation marketing of those goods elsewhere in the Community.[69]

From the viewpoint of those advising the parties to intellectual property **8.29** litigation, there is no doubt that Art 8(1) produces greater certainty as to the law applicable, one of the primary objectives of the Regulation. The trade-off for that certainty, however, is an increased regulatory burden for commercial parties, requiring more extensive investigation of national IPRs both when planning new cross-border business activity and, in the event of a dispute, prior to commencing or defending litigation. Adoption in the Rome II Regulation of the *lex loci protectionis* principle may yet prove to be

---

[68] Cf Case C-539/03, *Roche Nederland BV v Primus* [2006] ECR I-6535.
[69] Case C-10/89, *SA CNL-SUCAL NB v HAG GF AG* [1990] ECR I-3711, para 12. For more detailed analysis of the relationship between national IPRs and the EC Treaty, see C Barnard, *The Substantive Law of the EU* (2nd edn, 2007), ch 9.

a stop-gap solution pending further consolidation of IPRs or the associated rules of private international law at a European or international level.[70]

D. COMMUNITY RIGHTS—THE LAW OF THE COUNTRY IN WHICH THE ACT OF INFRINGEMENT OCCURRED (ART 8(2))

8.30 Under Art 8(2), the law applicable to a non-contractual obligation arising from an infringement of a unitary Community intellectual property right is the law of the country in which the act of infringement was committed, but this law applies only to 'any question that is not governed by the relevant Community instrument'.[71] The effect of this rule must, therefore, be determined by reference to the terms of the legislative instrument creating the relevant Community IPR. For the time being, as noted above, there are three such instruments: (1) the Community Trade Mark Regulation, (2) the Community Design Regulation, and (3) the Community Plant Variety Regulation.[72] Each of these Regulations, and its relationship to Art 8(2), will be considered in turn.

(1) THE COMMUNITY TRADE MARK REGULATION

Relevant Provisions

8.31 The Community Trade Mark Regulation concerns trade marks for goods and services that are registered in accordance with its provisions.[73] A Community trade mark may consist of any signs capable of being represented graphically, provided that such signs are capable of distinguishing the goods or services of one undertaking from those of other undertakings.[74] Under Art 9(1) of that Regulation, and subject to the restrictions in Art 12 and the principle of exhaustion of rights[75] in Art 13,

---

[70] For a transatlantic view, see the American Law Institute's *Intellectual Property Principles Governing Jurisdiction, Choice of Law, and Judgments in Transnational Disputes*, published in June 2008.

[71] W Tilmann, 'Community IP Rights and Conflict of Laws', in Basedow, *Intellectual Property*, n 1 above.

[72] nn 36–38 above.

[73] Community Trade Mark Regulation, n 36 above, Art 1(1).

[74] Ibid, Art 7.

[75] **8.28** above.

the proprietor of the mark may prevent a third party from using in the course of trade, without the proprietor's consent:[76]

(a) any sign which is identical with the Community trade mark in relation to goods or services which are identical with those for which the Community trade mark is registered;

(b) any sign where, because of its identity with or similarity to the Community trade mark and the identity or similarity of the goods or services covered by the Community trade mark and the sign, there exists a likelihood of confusion on the part of the public; the likelihood of confusion includes the likelihood of association between the sign and the trade mark;

(c) any sign which is identical with or similar to the Community trade mark in relation to goods or services which are not similar to those for which the Community trade mark is registered, where the latter has a reputation in the Community and where use of that sign without due cause takes unfair advantage of, or is detrimental to, the distinctive character or the repute of the Community trade mark.

Art 9(2) prohibits the following acts in particular: **8.32**

(a) affixing the sign to the goods or to the packaging thereof;

(b) offering the goods, putting them on the market or stocking them for these purposes under that sign, or offering or supplying services thereunder;

(c) importing or exporting the goods under that sign;

(d) using the sign on business papers and in advertising.

Article 14 (entitled 'Complementary application of national law relating **8.33** to infringement') provides:

1. The effects of Community trade marks shall be governed solely by the provisions of this Regulation. In other respects, infringement of a Community trade mark shall be governed by the national law relating to infringement of a national trade mark in accordance with the provisions of Title X.

2. This Regulation shall not prevent actions concerning a Community trade mark being brought under the law of Member States relating in particular to civil liability and unfair competition.

3. The rules of procedure to be applied shall be determined in accordance with the provisions of Title X.

Within Title X of the Community Trade Mark Regulation, Arts 90–94 deal **8.34** with matters of jurisdiction, Art 95 creates a presumption of validity, and Art 96 regulates counterclaims for revocation or declaration of invalidity. As to remedies, Art 98(1) requires Member State trade mark courts, on a

---

[76] For particular issues concerning the use of signs on the Internet, see A Kur, 'Trademark Conflicts on the Internet: Territorality Redefined?', in Basedow, *Intellectual Property*, n 1 above.

finding of infringement, to prohibit infringements or threatened infringements unless special reasons exist. The same Article also requires that the
prohibition be enforced by measures available under national law. Art
99(1) requires Member States to offer the same provisional or protective
measures as are available for infringements of national trade marks.
Otherwise, Arts 97(2) and 98(2), in combination, require Member States to
apply national law, including private international law, to determine matters not covered by the Regulation. Art 97(2) provides:

> On all matters not covered by this Regulation a Community trade mark court shall
> apply its national law, including its private international law.

8.35 So far as sanctions are concerned, Art 98(2) provides:

> In all other respects the Community trade mark court shall apply the law of the
> Member State to which the acts of infringement or threatened infringement were
> committed, including the private international law.

Application of Art 8(2) of the Rome II Regulation

8.36 The first question to be addressed is whether Arts 97(2) and 98(2) of the
Community Trade Mark Regulation (**8.34–8.35** above) exclude Art 8(2) of
the Rome II Regulation. This argument that they do may be presented in
two ways. First, as Art 8(2) applies only to questions not governed by the
Regulation creating the IPR, it cannot apply if the Regulation exhaustively
regulates infringements of the right in question even if it does so by referring to national law.[77] Secondly, under Art 27, the Rome II Regulation cannot override provisions of Community law which, in relation to particular
matters, lay down conflict-of-law rules relating to non-contractual obligations.[78] Arts 97(2) and 98(2) may be argued to create rules of applicable
law, favouring the law of the country in which protection is sought (i.e. the
lex fori) with a *renvoi* in accordance with that country's rules of private
international law, and to have overriding effect under Art 27. Neither of
these arguments is convincing. As the opening words of Art 97(2) make
clear, the reference that these provisions make to national law specifically
concerns matters 'not covered by' the Community Trade Mark Regulation,
and the argument that the provision somehow incorporates by reference
rules of national law so as to create an exhaustive regulatory regime contradicts this wording. Further, with reference to Art 27 of the Regulation,

---

[77] This point was raised by the German delegation in the Council's Rome II Committee on
more than one occasion (see Council documents SN2852/04 ADD 1 [2.9.2004], 3; 16240/04
[23.12.2004], 6–7).
[78] **16.32–16.35** below.

it seems artificial to describe either Art 97(2) or 98(2) as laying down con-flict-of-law rules relating to non-contractual obligations, given that they expressly require the forum Member State to apply its own rules of private international law. Instead of creating harmonized Community rules of applicable law, the two provisions simply clear the way for Member States to choose and apply their own rules.[79] Finally, if Arts 97(2) and 98(2) were treated as containing rules of applicable law and as overriding Art 8(2), difficult questions would arise as to whether the private international law rules to which they refer now include the Rome II Regulation and, if so, how it should be applied. In particular, could the rule in Art 8(2) apply at this stage, or would it be necessary to apply the general rule in Art 4? Given that all of the existing Community IPR instruments contain provi-sions corresponding to Art 97(2)[80] there is no reason to believe that it was intended that Art 8(2) should not apply to any of them by reason of argu-ments of this kind. Instead, Art 8(2) should be seen as imposing a uniform rule as to the law applicable to infringement matters not dealt with in the Regulation, replacing the formerly applicable national rules.[81]

Turning to the application of the connecting factor in Art 8(2), pointing to **8.37** the law of the country in which the act of infringement was committed, the concept of an 'act of infringement' must be an autonomous one drawn from the provisions of the Regulation and, in particular, Art 9.[82] Under the Community Trade Mark Regulation, therefore, the law applicable will be that of the country or countries within the EC in which a third party uses or threatens to use the proprietor's mark. If the proprietor complains of unlawful use of his mark in more than one country, each country's law governing infringement must be applied separately to use in that country.[83]

(2) THE COMMUNITY DESIGN REGULATION

Relevant Provisions

The Community Design Regulation protects both registered and unregis- **8.38** tered designs, provided that they are new and have individual character.[84]

---

[79] C Hahn and O Tell, n 4 above, 9–10.
[80] **8.40** and **8.45** below.
[81] F Wenzel Bulst and C Heinze, 'Discussion: Non-Contractual Obligations' in Basedow, *Intellectual Property*, n 1 above, 212; M Pertegás, n 15 above, 246.
[82] **8.31–8.32** above.
[83] Prof Pertegás describes this solution for infringing acts in more than one Member State as undesirable (n 15 above, 246).
[84] Community Design Regulation, n 37 above, Arts 4–6.

For these purposes, 'design' means the appearance of the whole or a part of a product resulting from the features of, in particular, the lines, contours, colours, shape, texture, and/or materials of the product itself and/or its ornamentation.[85] A design that meets the requirements for protection enjoys protection, without registration, for a period of three years from the date on which it was made available to the public.[86] Protection for a longer period may be secured only by registration.[87] A registered Community design confers on its holder, subject to the restrictions in Art 20 and to the exhaustion of rights principle[88] in Art 21, the exclusive right to use it and to prevent any third party not having his consent from using it, in particular, by making, offering, putting on the market, importing, exporting, or using a product in which the design is incorporated or to which it is applied, or stocking such a product for those purposes.[89] An unregistered design confers more limited protection against use involving copying.[90]

8.39 Title IX of the Community Design Regulation contains provisions similar to those in Title X of the Community Trade Mark Regulation.[91] Arts 79–83 concern matters of jurisdiction. Art 84 regulates counterclaims for a declaration of invalidity. Art 85 creates a presumption of validity. Arts 86–87 deal with the consequences of judgments on invalidity. Art 89(1) requires Member State design courts, on a finding of infringement, to impose particular sanctions (including prohibiting infringement and seizing infringing products and equipment used in their manufacture) unless there are strong reasons for not doing so. Art 89(2) requires those sanctions to be enforced by measures available under national law. Art 90(1) requires Member States to offer the same provisional or protective measures as are available for cases involving national design rights.

8.40 The Community Design Regulation does not contain a provision corresponding to Art 98(2) of the Community Trade Mark Regulation. Art 88(2), however, follows the wording of Art 97(2) of the latter Regulation, as follows:

> On all matters not covered by this Regulation, a Community design court shall apply its national law, including its private international law.

---

[85] Ibid, Art 3(a).
[86] Ibid, Art 11.
[87] Ibid, Arts 12–13.
[88] **8.28** above.
[89] Community Design Regulation, n 37 above, Art 19(1).
[90] Ibid, Art 19(2).
[91] **8.34–8.35** above.

Application of Article 8(2)

The position under this Regulation would appear to correspond to that **8.41** under the Community Trade Mark Regulation. Accordingly:

- Art 88(2) of the Community Design Regulation should not be treated as excluding Art 8(2) of the Rome II Regulation.[92]
- The 'country in which the act of infringement was committed' under Art 8(2) will be each country in the EC in which a third party used the design without the proprietor's consent.[93]

(3) THE COMMUNITY PLANT VARIETY REGULATION

Relevant Provisions

The Community Plant Variety Regulation raises slightly different issues from **8.42** the other two Regulations. The right granted under the Regulation protects varieties of all botanical genera and species,[94] provided that they are (a) distinct, (b) uniform, (c) stable, (d) new, and (e) designated by a denomination.[95] Subject to certain qualifications[96] and the exhaustion of rights principle,[97] the right-holder may require authorization of the following acts in respect of variety constituents, or harvested material of the protected variety:[98]

(a) production or reproduction (multiplication);
(b) conditioning for the purpose of propagation;
(c) offering for sale;
(d) selling or other marketing;
(e) exporting from the Community;
(f) importing to the Community;
(g) stocking for any of the purposes mentioned in (a) to (f).

Under Art 93 ('Application of national law'):   **8.43**

Claims under Community plant variety rights shall be subject to limitations imposed by the law of the Member States only as expressly referred to in this Regulation.

Part Six of the Community Plant Variety Regulation, immediately follow- **8.44** ing Art 93 (above), contains provision relating to infringement proceedings that are far more detailed and sophisticated than those contained in

---

[92] **8.36** above.
[93] **8.37** above.
[94] Community Plant Variety Regulation, n 38 above, Art 5(1).
[95] Ibid, Arts 6–10.
[96] Ibid, Arts 13–15.
[97] Ibid, Art 16.
[98] Ibid, Art 13(1)–(2). Also Arts 17–18 concerning the use of variety denominations.

the Community Trade Mark or Design Regulations. In particular, (1) Art 94(1) confers a right of action on the right holder to enjoin infringement by, or to obtain reasonable compensation from, a person performing any of the proscribed acts without consent, (2) Art 94(2) requires a person who intentionally or negligently violates the right to compensate the holder for any further damage resulting from the act in question, (3) Art 95 provides for the payment of reasonable compensation for performance of any of the proscribed acts between publication of the holder's application for a plant variety right and grant of the right, and (4) Art 96 contains a uniform limitation period for claims under Arts 94 and 95.

8.45 Art 97 (entitled 'Supplementary application of national law regarding infringement') then provides as follows:

> 1. Where the party liable pursuant to Article 94 has, by virtue of the infringement, made any gain at the expense of the holder or of a person entitled to exploitation rights, the courts competent pursuant to Articles 101 or 102 shall apply their national law, including their private international law, as regards restitution.

> 2. Paragraph 1 shall also apply as regards other claims that may arise in respect of the performance or omission of acts pursuant to Article 95 in the time between publication of the application for grant of a Community plant variety right and the disposal of the request.

> 3. In all other respects the effects of Community plant variety rights shall be determined solely in accordance with this Regulation.

Application of Article 8(2)

8.46 Accordingly, the Community Plant Variety Regulation deals comprehensively with actions for injunctions and compensatory damages. The only infringement matters that it does not govern and which fall, therefore, within Art 8(2) of the Rome II Regulation are those matters listed in Art 97(1) and (2) and, in particular, claims for restitution (i.e. to reverse unjust enrichment). In cases falling within these two provisions, the law applicable under Art 8(2) of the Rome II Regulation will be the country or countries in which the defendant performed, without consent, an act requiring the holder's authorization under the Community Plant Variety Regulation (**8.42** above).

E. SCOPE OF THE APPLICABLE LAW

Remedies

8.47 The scope of the law(s) applicable under Art 8(1) or 8(2) of the Rome II Regulation, like other rules in Chapters II and III, will be fixed by Art 15 and the other common rules in Chapter V. In particular, the applicable law(s) will govern (1) the existence, the nature, and the assessment of damage or the remedy claimed (Art 15(c)), and (2) within the limits of the Member State court's procedural powers, the measures which a court may take to prevent or terminate injury or damage or to ensure the provision of compensation (Art 15(d)). These provisions are considered in further detail in **Chapter 15** below. One aspect of the vertical scope of the Regulation that may be of particular significance for IPRs generally is the question whether the claimant's entitlement to an interim injunction to restrain infringing conduct, or for the seizure of infringing articles pending trial falls, within the province of the law applicable under the Regulation, or should be considered as a matter of procedure excluded by Art 1(3). In the explanatory memorandum accompanying its Proposal, the Commission referred specifically to 'an interlocutory injunction' as an example of a measure to halt or prevent damage within what is now Art 15(d) of the Regulation.[99] This provides strong support for the view that the law applicable under the Regulation should be applied to determine the availability of all such measures, an approach which seems correct in principle given the significance that the grant or refusal of an interim restraining order may have in terms of putting pressure on a party to settle.[100] Although, in practice, arguments as to the law applicable may not play a significant role in pre-trial proceedings, claimants must be prepared to justify the grant of an interim injunction or temporary seizure by reference to the law of the country or countries whose national IPRs they wish to invoke.

RELATIONSHIP WITH THE IP ENFORCEMENT DIRECTIVE

For national IPRs of Member States, as well as Community IPRs, the meas-   **8.48**
ures, procedures, and remedies conferred under national law must meet
the requirements of the IP Enforcement Directive.[101] Art 9 of this Directive
(headed 'Provisional and precautionary measures') provides:

1. Member States shall ensure that the judicial authorities may, at the request of
the applicant:
(a) issue against the alleged infringer an interlocutory injunction intended to pre-
    vent any imminent infringement of an intellectual property right, or to forbid,
    on a provisional basis and subject, where appropriate, to a recurring penalty
    payment where provided for by national law, the continuation of the alleged

---

[99] Commission Proposal, 24.
[100] **14.35** below.
[101] Directive (EC) 2004/48 on the enforcement of intellectual property rights (OJ L195, 16 [2.6.2004]) (**IP Enforcement Directive**).

468 Chapter 8: Intellectual Property

infringements of that right, or to make such continuation subject to the lodging of guarantees intended to ensure the compensation of the rightholder; . . .[102]

(b) order the seizure or delivery up of the goods suspected of infringing an intellectual property right so as to prevent their entry into or movement within the channels of commerce.

2. In the case of an infringement committed on a commercial scale, the Member States shall ensure that, if the injured party demonstrates circumstances likely to endanger the recovery of damages, the judicial authorities may order the precautionary seizure of the movable and immovable property of the alleged infringer, including the blocking of his/her bank accounts and other assets. To that end, the competent authorities may order the communication of bank, financial or commercial documents, or appropriate access to the relevant information . . .[103]

8.49 Section 5 of the IP Enforcement Directive (headed 'Measures resulting from a decision on the merits of the case') provides for the recall and destruction of infringing articles,[104] injunctions,[105] and alternative measures.[106] Art 13 (entitled 'Damages') provides:

1. Member States shall ensure that the competent judicial authorities, on application of the injured party, order the infringer who knowingly, or with reasonable grounds to know, engaged in an infringing activity, to pay the rightholder damages appropriate to the actual prejudice suffered by him/her as a result of the infringement.

When the judicial authorities set the damages:

(a) they shall take into account all appropriate aspects, such as the negative economic consequences, including lost profits, which the injured party has suffered, any unfair profits made by the infringer and, in appropriate cases, elements other than economic factors, such as the moral prejudice caused to the rightholder by the infringement; or

(b) as an alternative to (a), they may, in appropriate cases, set the damages as a lump sum on the basis of elements such as at least the amount of royalties or fees which would have been due if the infringer had requested authorisation to use the intellectual property right in question.

2. Where the infringer did not knowingly, or with reasonable grounds know, engage in infringing activity, Member States may lay down that the judicial authorities may order the recovery of profits or the payment of damages, which may be pre-established.

---

[102] The Directive here deals separately with claims against intermediaries (words omitted).
[103] Art 9(3)–(7) deal with matters of evidence and procedure
[104] IP Enforcement Directive, n 101 above, Art 10.
[105] Ibid, Art 11.
[106] Ibid, Art 12.

Recital (18) to the IP Enforcement Directive provides that:[107]   **8.50**

The persons entitled to request application of those measures, procedures and remedies should be not only the rightholders but also persons who have a direct interest and legal standing in so far as permitted by and in accordance with the applicable law, which may include professional organisations in charge of the management of those rights or for the defence of the collective and individual interests for which they are responsible.

Claims by the organizations referred to in this Recital should also fall **8.51** within the scope of the Rome II Regulation. Their position, in this respect, is very similar to that of consumer associations who bring private proceedings to enforce the collective interests of consumers under laws established for their protection.[108]

The IP Enforcement Directive does not, however, have any direct impact **8.52** on the law applicable to intellectual property claims. Recital (11) to the Directive confirms that:

This Directive does not aim to establish harmonised rules for judicial cooperation, jurisdiction, the recognition and enforcement of decisions in civil and commercial matters, or deal with applicable law. There are Community instruments which govern such matters in general terms and are, in principle, equally applicable to intellectual property.

At the time that the IP Enforcement Directive was passed, the second **8.53** sentence referred, for example, to the rules of jurisdiction in the Brussels I Regulation. It may now, equally, be taken to refer to the Rome II Regulation.

F. EXCLUSION OF PARTY CHOICE (ART 8(3))

The law applicable under Art 8 may not be derogated from by an agree- **8.54** ment pursuant to Art 14.[109] This is consistent with the Commission Proposal, which expressly excluded obligations to which Art 8 applies from the scope of the provision allowing (limited) party choice.[110] The Commission considered that to allow such choice would be 'inappropriate'.[111] So far as Art 8(1) is concerned, that conclusion may be justified both on the grounds

---

[107] Also IP Enforcement Directive, Art 4.
[108] **6.49** above.
[109] Regulation, Art 8(3).
[110] Commission Proposal, Art 10(1). The German delegation argued that freedom of choice should apply to IPRs (see Council document 9009/04 add 11 [24.5.2004], 13).
[111] Ibid, 22.

that (a) it should not be open to the parties to derogate from rules that perform an important economic policy objective, and (b) the limited territorial effect of national IPRs[112] means that a choice in favour of any law other than that of a country for which protection is to be sought would result in a legal vacuum.[113] The second argument, however, overlooks that in some cases the protection afforded by IPRs of different countries will overlap, giving the claimant the option under Art 8(1) of relying on one or both national IPRs to support his claim. Here, in order to improve legal certainty, Art 8 might have allowed the parties to restrict the claimant's choice. Moreover, these arguments do not provide a convincing explanation why, in the case of Community IPRs, the parties are not allowed to choose the law of a particular Member State for all infringements.[114] Neither of these options was pursued.

---

[112] **8.22–8.23** above.

[113] C Hahn and O Tell, n 4 above, 17.

[114] C Hahn and O Tell, ibid, referring to the argument presented by Hausmann, 'Infringements of industrial property rights in European international private law and procedural law' [2003] European Legal Forum 278, 287. Also M Pertegás, n 15 above, 246–7.

9

Industrial Action

Article 9

Industrial action

Without prejudice to Article 4(2), the law applicable to a non-contractual obligation in respect of the liability of a person in the capacity of a worker or an employer or the organisations representing their professional interests for damages caused by an industrial action, pending or carried out, shall be the law of the country where the action is to be, or has been, taken.

A. INTRODUCTION

The Commission Proposal and the accompanying explanatory memorandum did not contain any provision for, or mention of, non-contractual obligations relating to industrial action. The addition of the special rule in Art 9 of the Rome II Regulation resulted from an initiative of the Swedish Government, with the support of the European Parliament. Its introduction, however, was strongly opposed by some Member State delegations and it was the only provision of the Council's Common Position that did not command the unanimous support of all Member States. **9.01**

In its initial response to the Commission Proposal, the Swedish delegation proposed that non-contractual obligations arising out of industrial action **9.02** should be governed by the law of the place where the action had been taken.[1] The Swedish proposal linked the perceived necessity for such a rule to the decision of the Court of Justice in the *DFDS Torline* case,[2] delivered in February 2004. In that case, DFDS, a Danish shipping company, had brought an action against a Swedish trade union in the Danish courts seeking to determine the lawfulness of threatened industrial action, consisting of the blacking of its ship by Swedish port workers preventing her from being unloaded in Swedish ports. To avoid that action, DFDS chartered another ship to operate between Gothenburg and Harwich, England. It sought, by separate Danish proceedings,[3] to recover from the trade union the costs of the charter. The ECJ held that both the lawfulness and damages actions fell within Art 5(3) of the Brussels Convention (matters relating to tort, delict, or quasi-delict).[4] The ECJ also held that, although the event giving rise to damage (notification of the industrial action) had occurred in Sweden, the damage consisted of DFDS' financial loss arising from the withdrawal of its ship from the Gothenburg–Harwich route and its replacement with another ship, leaving it to the Danish court to determine whether that loss could be regarded as having arisen in Denmark, taking into account (among other factors) the fact that Denmark was the flag State of the withdrawn ship.[5] Having summarized the facts of the case and the Court's ruling, the Swedish delegation commented:[6]

Since the wording of Article 3 of the proposed Rome II Regulation is very similar *[to Art 5(3) of the Brussels Convention]*, the consequence of this case is that the legality of an industrial action, carried out in order to secure that the working conditions in the state in which the work is to be performed, could be governed by another law.[7]

9.03 After noting that, under Swedish law, it is left to trade unions to secure from employers appropriate terms and conditions of employment, including for

---

[1] Council document 9009/04 ADD 8 [18.5.2004], 12–13.

[2] Case C-18/02, *Danmarks Rederiforening, acting on behalf of DFDS Torline A/S v LO Landsorganisationen i Sverige, acting on behalf of SEKO Sjöfolk Facket för Service och Kommunikation* [2004] ECR I-1417.

[3] Under Danish law, different courts had jurisdiction to determine the lawfulness and damages actions (*DFDS Torline*, ibid, paras 20–8).

[4] Questions 1(a), (b), and (c) (ibid, paras 19–38).

[5] Ibid, paras 39–45. The Court noted (para 45) that 'The nationality of the ship can play a decisive role only if the national court reaches the conclusion that the damage arose on board the [ship]'. For a similar argument under the Rome II Regulation, see **4.55–4.56** above.

[6] Council document 9009/04 ADD 8, 12.

[7] i.e. a law other than that of the country in which the action was taken.

posted workers,[8] and that this may involve the taking of industrial action, the Swedish delegation concluded that the decision in *DFDS Torline* made a special rule for industrial action essential from its point of view, adding:[9]

We are quite certain that other delegations will understand this and recognize that **the question is of paramount importance to Sweden.**

The following year, the European Parliament proposed the following rule **9.04** at its first reading stage:[10]

The law applicable to a non-contractual obligation arising out of industrial action, pending or carried out, shall be the law of the country in which the action is to be taken or has been taken.

According to the Report of the EP JURI Committee:[11]   **9.05**

The rights of workers to take collective action, including strike action, guaranteed under national law must not be undermined.

The Parliament's proposed rule was, however, rejected by the Commission **9.06** in its Amended Proposal on the ground that it was 'too rigid'.[12]

In the meantime, the Swedish proposal had attracted only limited support **9.07** in the Council's Rome II Committee. Indeed, by early 2006, it had attracted the explicit support of only one other delegation.[13] At this stage, Sweden re-presented its proposal, arguing:[14]

Industrial relations systems in different countries are often unique and protected by strong governmental interests. In this regard the situation differs significantly from other situations covered by Article 3.[15] Each national system balances the interests of the parties in the market. If industrial action that is taken in one country in compliance with the national system there could lead to liability under the law of another country, the proper balance of the national systems would be disturbed.

---

[8] Referring to Directive (EC) No 96/71 concerning the posting of workers in the framework of the provision of services (OJ L18, 1 [28.1.1997]), Art 3(1) of which requires that specified terms and conditions of employment of the host state be applied irrespective of the law applicable to the employment contract.

[9] Council document 9009/04 ADD 8, 13 (emphasis as in original text).

[10] EP 1st Reading Position, Art 6.

[11] EP 1st Reading Report, 23.

[12] Commission Amended Proposal, 6.

[13] Council document 6161/06 [10.2.2006], 5. Also Council document 13001/05 [10.10.2005], 3, where the EP amendment was considered, with no consensus being reached.

[14] Council document 6724/06 [23.2.2006]. See also the proposal in Council document 7212/06 ADD 3 [10.3.2006], supported by the Finnish and Netherlands delegations.

[15] i.e. the general rule for tort/delict, now Regulation, Art 4.

9.08 At the following meeting of the Council's Rome II Committee, a number of delegations indicated that they could support the proposal,[16] but other delegations remained opposed.[17] Nevertheless, the rule, by now in its final form, was adopted by a majority of the Member States as an element in the Council's Common Position.

9.09 The Commission, in its communication responding to the Common Position, reacted more favourably to the more detailed definition of the rule's scope, but was not entirely won over:[18]

> The text of the provision in the common position is a redraft which attempts to give effect to the main objections of the Commission during the discussions in the Council. Its scope is now defined more precisely and is, in particular, limited to the issue of liability of employers, workers and/or trade unions in the context of an industrial action. The text is, however, still unclear that it should not extend to relationships vis-à-vis third parties and the Commission regrets this lack of clarity.

9.10 For all the discussion concerning such matters as defamation and traffic accidents, it was Art 9 of the Rome II Regulation that created the greatest discord among the Member States.[19] In particular, Latvia and Estonia identified Art 9 as their sole reason for voting against both the Common Position and the Regulation in its final form. They were the only Member States to do so. A joint communication issued by the two States at the time of the vote on the Common Position explained their position as follows:[20]

> Latvia and Estonia recognise that industrial action is one of the essential rights of a worker, an employer or the organisations representing their professional interests. Thus the principle provided in Article 9 should apply only to the cases which arise directly from exercise of those essential rights. At the same time Latvia and Estonia stress that application of Article 9 should not constitute any further restrictions to the freedom to provide services within the Community.

9.11 Greece and Cyprus, although voting in favour of the Regulation, added:[21]

> The Greek and Cypriot delegations would like to point out that the application of Article 9 of the Regulation would probably cause problems for shipping, given

---

[16] Council document 7551/06 [22.3.2006], 6.

[17] Council document 7709/06 [3.5.2006], 8. Also the alternative proposal presented by the German delegation in Council document 7728/06 [30.3.2006], 1–2, which did not gain majority support.

[18] COM (2006) 566 final [27.9.2006], 4.

[19] See also the exchanges between MEPs from Estonia and Finland in the European Parliament's 2nd Reading debate (EP document CRE 18/01/2007 - 4, available at <http://www.europarl.europa.eu/sides/getDoc.do?type=CRE&reference=20070118&secondRef=ITEM-004&language=EN&ring=A6-2006-0481>.

[20] Council document 12219/06 ADD 1 [14.9.2006], 2.

[21] Ibid, 1.

that vessels would be exposed to rules which varied according to the laws of the Member States of their ports of call, irrespective of whether those vessels were in full conformity with the laws of the flag State.

The topicality and political sensitivity of this issue is illustrated, and **9.12** heightened, by two recent decisions of the ECJ, which have opened up the possibility of claims by employers against trade unions based on the restriction by industrial action of the fundamental freedoms guaranteed by the EC Treaty.[22] Claims for this type would appear to fall within the scope of the Regulation[23] and may, therefore, justify the application of the special rule in Art 9 to determine the law applicable to matters not regulated by EC law, including as to the available remedy (subject to the principles of equivalence and effectiveness). [24]

The first decision, in the case of *International Transport Workers' Federation* **9.13** *v Viking Line ABP*,[25] concerned the blacking of a ship operated by the claimant under the Finnish flag following its decision to re-flag the vessel by registering it in Estonia or Norway. The claimant sought and obtained an interim injunction from the High Court in England (where one of the defendant trade unions was based) on the ground that the threatened blacking action unlawfully restricted its freedom of establishment under EC Treaty, Art 43, as well as the free movement of workers and freedom to provide services under Arts 39 and 49 respectively.[26] On appeal by the trade unions, the Court of Appeal referred to the ECJ questions as to whether Arts 43 and 49 provided the employer with a remedy.

The ECJ answered those questions as follows: **9.14**

1. Article 43 EC is to be interpreted as meaning that, in principle, collective action initiated by a trade union or a group of trade unions against a private undertaking in order to induce that undertaking to enter into a collective agreement, the terms of which are liable to deter it from exercising freedom of establishment, is not excluded from the scope of that article.

2. Article 43 EC is capable of conferring rights on a private undertaking which may be relied on against a trade union or an association of trade unions.

---

[22] For comment on these decisions, see A Davies, 'One Step Forward, Two Steps Back? The Viking and Laval Cases in the ECJ' (2008) 37 Industrial LJ 126; N Reisch, 'Free Movement v Social Rights in an Enlarged Union—the Laval and Viking Cases before the ECJ' (2008) 9 German LJ 125

[23] **3.281–3.284** above.

[24] **3.286** above.

[25] Case C-438/05 [2007] ECR I-0000 (Judgment of 11 December 2007).

[26] *Viking Line ABP v International Transport Workers' Federation* [2005] EWHC 1222 (Comm); (2005) The Times, 22 June.

3. Article 43 EC is to be interpreted to the effect that collective action such as that at issue in the main proceedings, which seeks to induce a private undertaking whose registered office is in a given Member State to enter into a collective work agreement with a trade union established in that State and to apply the terms set out in that agreement to the employees of a subsidiary of that undertaking established in another Member State, constitutes a restriction within the meaning of that article.

That restriction may, in principle, be justified by an overriding reason of public interest, such as the protection of workers, provided that it is established that the restriction is suitable for ensuring the attainment of the legitimate objective pursued and does not go beyond what is necessary to achieve that objective.

9.15 The second case, *Laval un Partneri Ltd v Svenska Byggnadsarbetareförbundet*,[27] concerned industrial action taken by Swedish trade unions against the worksites in Sweden of the claimant, a Latvian company, with a view to securing more favourable conditions for the company's Latvian posted workers. The claimant brought proceedings in Sweden for a declaration that the action was unlawful, an order that the action should cease, and compensation for losses suffered by it by reason of the action. The decision in *Laval* focuses on the provisions of the Posted Workers Directive,[28] and it adds little to the earlier judgment in the *Viking Line* case so far as claims between employers and trade unions based on the EC Treaty provisions are concerned. Of greater interest for present purposes is the Court's description of the breadth of the industrial action that appears to be permissible under Swedish law. That action was summarized by the ECJ as follows:[29]

Blockading ('blockad') of the Vaxholm building site began on 2 November 2004. The blockading consisted, *inter alia*, of preventing the delivery of goods onto the site, placing pickets and prohibiting Latvian workers and vehicles from entering the site. Laval asked the police for assistance but they explained that since the collective action was lawful under national law they were not allowed to intervene or to remove physical obstacles blocking access to the site . . .

In December 2004, the collective action directed against Laval intensified. On 3 December 2004, Elektrikerna initiated sympathy action. That measure had the effect of preventing Swedish undertakings belonging to the organisation of electricians' employers from providing services to Laval. At Christmas, the workers posted by Laval went back to Latvia and did not return to the site in question.

In January 2005, other trade unions announced sympathy actions, consisting of a boycott of all Laval's sites in Sweden, with the result that the undertaking was no

---

[27] Case C-341/05 [2007] ECR I-0000 (Judgment of 18 December 2007).
[28] n 8 above.
[29] Judgment, paras 34, 37, 38.

longer able to carry out its activities in that Member State. In February 2005, the town of Vaxholm requested that the contract between it and Baltic[30] be terminated, and on 25 March 2005 the latter was declared bankrupt.

The breadth of this action, including blockading the claimant's sites and **9.16** sympathy action by other unions is, to an English lawyer, startling.[31] That comment is not intended as a criticism of the position of Swedish law, under which trade unions clearly play a more central role in the protection of workers' rights than they do under English law. This disparity in the approaches and attitudes between Member States, however, goes a long way to explaining why the Swedish delegation in the Rome II Committee was so troubled by the *DFDS Torline* decision and the possibility that, without a special rule, a law other than Swedish law might apply to industrial action taken by Swedish trade unions for the protection of workers based in Sweden. These matters must also be borne in mind in considering the meaning of 'industrial action' within Art 9.

B. SCOPE OF ARTICLE 9

Non-Contractual Obligations

Art 9 applies only to non-contractual obligations.[32] Accordingly, it does **9.17** not apply (for example) to the enforcement of the contract between worker and employer or between a trade union and its members. The law applicable to contractual obligations such as these must be determined in accordance with the Rome I Regime.[33]

Industrial Action

Recital (27) provides **9.18**

The exact concept of industrial action, such as strike action or lock-out, varies from one Member State to another and is governed by each Member State's internal rules. Therefore, this Regulation assumes as a general principle that the law of the country where the industrial action was taken should apply, with the aim of protecting the rights and obligations of workers and employers.

---

[30] A former Swedish subsidiary of the claimant.

[31] For the position under English law in relation to liability for trade disputes, see A M Dugdale and M A Jones, *Clerk and Lindsell on Torts* (19th edn, 2006), paras 25-138 to 25-205.

[32] **3.86–3.262** above.

[33] See, in particular, Rome Convention, Art 6 and Rome I Regulation, Art 8 concerning individual employment contracts.

9.19 Accordingly, and as an exception to the general approach to interpretation of the concepts used in the Regulation, 'industrial action' is not to be given an autonomous meaning. Instead, it would appear that it must be understood in accordance with the law of the country in which the relevant action is to be, or has been, taken, i.e. the putative applicable law under Art 9. Application of the law of the forum to answer that question would not serve the objectives identified in Recital (27). In particular, it may lead to Art 9 being construed more narrowly or broadly than is necessary to protect workers carrying out industrial action in another country. As the *Viking Line* case[34] illustrates, proceedings in a case with an international dimension may be brought otherwise than before the courts of the country where the industrial action takes place. Application of any law other than the law identified by Art 9 to determine the breadth of the concept of 'industrial action' would reduce the parties' ability to predict the law applicable to claims arising out of acts that might be argued to constitute industrial action.

9.20 Nevertheless, the outer limits of what may constitute 'industrial action' may still fall to be defined by reference to the terms of Art 9 and the accompanying Recitals. These suggest that, at a minimum, the action must in some sense be concerned with the relationship between workers and employers. Accordingly, action taken in protest at government policy (for example, a blockade of a port in protest at reductions in fish quotas or a motorway go-slow to raise awareness about fuel duties) falls outside Art 9.

9.21 Under the law of England and Wales (and Scotland), the principal statutory immunities from civil liability of trade unions and others in this area are defined in terms of whether the act in question is in contemplation or furtherance or of a trade dispute.[35] 'Trade dispute' is defined, for these purposes, as meaning a dispute between employers and workers which is related to one or more listed matters as follows:[36]

(a) terms and conditions of employment, or the physical conditions in which any workers are required to work;
(b) engagement or non-engagement, or termination or suspension of employment or the duties of employment, of one or more workers;

---

[34] **9.13–9.14** above.

[35] Trade Union and Labour Relations (Consolidation) Act 1992, ss 219–21. Note, however, the exclusions from protection in the following sections including, in s 224, for secondary action. The protection in s 220 for 'peaceful picketing' is very narrow and does not extend, for example, to blockading premises (*Clerk & Lindsell on Torts*, n 31 above, paras 25-185 to 25-186).

[36] Ibid, s 244.

(c) allocation of work or the duties of employment between workers or groups of workers;
(d) matters of discipline;
(e) a worker's membership or non-membership of a trade union;
(f) facilities for officials of trade unions; and
(g) machinery for negotiation or consultation, and other procedures, relating to any of the above matters, including the recognition by employers or employers' associations of the right of a trade union to represent workers in such negotiation or consultation or in the carrying out of such procedures.

Elsewhere in the same legislation, in defining the right of a trade union member to insist on a ballot, the term 'industrial action' is defined as 'a strike or other industrial action by persons employed under contracts of employment'.[37] A 'strike' for these purposes has been held to involve a concerted stoppage of work in connection with a grievance related to employment, as opposed to one brought about by an external event, for example by a fire or bomb scare.[38] The concept of 'other industrial action' is not defined in the legislation, but has been held to include (for example) (a) a refusal to work overtime, (b) a go-slow or work to rule, and (c) a refusal to work new machinery.[39] Trade union activities, such as meetings, have been held not to constitute 'other industrial action'.[40] In *Fire Brigades Union v Knowles*, Neill LJ commented:[41] **9.22**

Industrial action can take many forms, but, in the absence of any statutory definition, I do not think that any attempt at a paraphrase is likely to be useful. In my judgment, the question of what is industrial action for the purposes of s 65 of the 1992 Act is a mixed question of fact and law. In large measure it is a question of fact, but the facts have to be judged in the context of the Act which plainly contemplates that industrial action is a serious step.

It is necessary to look at all the circumstances. These circumstances will include the contracts of employment of the employees and whether any breach of or departure from the terms of the contract are involved, the effect on the employer

---

[37] Ibid, s 62(6).
[38] *Tramp Shipping Corp v Greenwich Marine Inc* [1975] 2 All ER 989, 991–2 (Lord Denning MR, EWCA). Cf the statutory definition, in a different context, in s 246 of the 1992 Act.
[39] *Halsbury's Laws of England* (2001 reissue, online version), vol 47, para 1502 referring to *Power Packing Casemakers Ltd v Faust* [1983] QB 471, [1983] ICR 292 (EWCA); *Drew v St Edmundsbury Borough Council* [1980] ICR 513 (EAT); *Secretary of State for Employment v Associated Society of Locomotive Engineers and Firemen (No 2)* [1972] 2 QB 455, [1972] ICR 19 (EWCA) and *Thompson v Eaton Ltd* [1976] ICR 336 (EAT).
[40] *Rasool v Hepworth Pipe Co Ltd (No 2)* [1980] IRLR 137 (EAT).
[41] [1996] 4 All ER 653 (EWCA).

of what is done or omitted, and the object which the union or the employees seek to achieve.

9.23 In terms of the employer's conduct, the concept of 'industrial action' under English law may include a lockout,[42] although civil liability issues arising from the employer's action will normally involve contractual obligations between employer and employee, falling outside the scope of the Rome II Regulation.

Liability in the Capacity of a Worker or an Employer or the Organizations Representing their Personal Interests

9.24 Art 9 is restricted to liability of persons 'in the capacity of a worker or an employer' or of the organizations representing their personal interests. As to the concept of liability 'in the capacity of a worker' this would appear capable, for example, of extending to former employees and to those employed by others who participate in secondary action, whether lawful or otherwise, but not to third parties (including, for example, relatives or friends of workers or interest groups) who may become involved.

9.25 As to the concept of liability in the capacity of an employer, it is submitted that this should extend to the liability of those representing the employer in a trade dispute (including, for example, senior management). Equally, the reference to the organizations protecting the interests of workers and employers should extend to officials representing these organizations. Otherwise, the protection that Art 9 affords to workers, employers and representative organizations may easily be circumvented by suing an individual responsible for implementing particular action.

9.26 The reference in Recital (27) to 'the rights and obligations of workers and employers' might be thought to suggest an element of mutuality that restricts the scope of Art 9 to claims arising between the categories of persons referred to, i.e. workers, employers, and representative organizations, and excludes claims brought by third parties. For example, what law should apply to a claim against a trade union responsible for blockading a port in an employment dispute with the port owner brought by the owner of cargo that deteriorated in another country as a result of delays due to the blockade? This appears to be an open question. As noted above,[43] the Commission in its response to the Council's Common Position expressed concerns as to the lack of clarity regarding the position of third parties.

---

[42] *Halsbury's Laws of England* (2001 reissue, online version), vol 47, para 1504.
[43] **9.09** above.

Although the Commission's view would appear to have been that Art 9 should not extend to liability otherwise than between the named parties, the objectives of foreseeability as to the law applicable[44] and the protection of the rights (and obligations) of workers under the law of the place of the industrial action may appear to point towards the application of Art 9, rather than the general rule in Art 4 in such cases. Whichever view is preferred, this may be one of the occasions on which it is not possible to strike a reasonable balance under the Regulation between the interests of the person claimed to be liable and the person who has sustained damage.[45]

DAMAGES CAUSED BY AN INDUSTRIAL ACTION

Art 9 refers to liability 'for damages caused by an industrial action'. The **9.27** choice of the plural 'damages', which appears also in other language versions of Art 9 of the Regulation,[46] may be contrasted with the use of the singular form 'damage' elsewhere in the Regulation, in particular in Art 4. Nevertheless, it is clear that Art 9 is not to be read as being restricted to an action for a monetary remedy corresponding to an award of 'damages'. In particular, (1) Art 9 contemplates a non-contractual obligation arising from industrial action that is 'pending' and 'is to be' taken in the future, which seems consistent only with a claim for injunctive or declaratory relief, (2) the *DFDS Torline* case, which prompted the original proposal by the Swedish delegation,[47] concerned monetary and non-monetary claims, and (3) the terminology used in other language versions (for example, in the French version, '*dommages*' rather than '*dommages-intérêts*' and, in the German version, '*Schäden*' rather than '*Schadensersatz*') suggests that what is contemplated is not a specific kind of remedy but separate elements of damage resulting from the same action. Although use of the plural in an EC legislative instrument should be taken to include the singular,[48] it would have been equally appropriate having regard to the concept of 'damage' as defined in Art 2 of the Regulation to refer in Art 9 to 'damage caused by an industrial action', avoiding the uncertainty resulting from the use of the plural form.

---

[44] Recital (16).

[45] Cf Recital (16).

[46] e.g. '*dommages*' (French); '*Schäden*' (German); '*danni*' (Italian); '*danos*' (Portuguese); '*danõs*' (Spanish); '*skador*' (Swedish).

[47] **9.02–9.03** above.

[48] H Schermers and D Waelbroek, *Judicial Protection in the European Union* (6th edn, 2001), 15.

9.28 Art 9 requires a causal link between the industrial action and the damage suffered by the claimant. During discussions in the Council's Rome II Committee, the French delegation presented a proposal to restrict, by a recital, the scope of the special rule to questions of 'remedy and compensation for direct economic damage caused or likely to be caused' by industrial action, so as to exclude 'peripheral situations (violence committed during a strike, attacks on property etc)'.[49] That proposal was not adopted, but a similar result can almost certainly be achieved by both a literal and a purposive construction of the words used in Art 9 to exclude situations that are not concerned with the protection of the rights of workers and employers acting in those capacities, even if the defendant's act is somehow related to industrial action (e.g. violence on a picket line). In cases such as those referred to by the French delegation, the defendant's liability should be characterized as arising otherwise than out of the exercise of his rights or of obligations imposed on him as a worker or an employer, as the case may be. The law applicable in such cases should accordingly be determined by the general rule in Art 4 (tort/delict), not Art 9.

Exclusion of Matters of Industrial Relations Law and Status of Trade Unions

9.29 Recital (28) emphasizes that certain matters fall outside the scope of Art 9 and, indeed, the Regulation as a whole:[50]

> The special rule on industrial action in Article 9 is without prejudice to the conditions relating to the exercise of such action in accordance with national law and without prejudice to the legal status of trade unions or of the representative organisations of workers as provided for in the law of the Member States.

9.30 The law applicable to these matters must be determined in accordance with other rules of private international law of the forum Member State. The law applicable under Art 9 will, however, apply to determine, for example, the legal and factual criteria that a trade union or other representative body must meet in order to be exempted from non-contractual liability for industrial action.

---

[49] Council document 9016/06 [4.5.2006].

[50] For the exclusion generally of matters of status from the Regulation, see **3.88–3.103** above.

C. THE LAW APPLICABLE TO NON-CONTRACTUAL OBLIGATIONS IN INDUSTRIAL ACTION CASES—LAW OF THE COUNTRY WHERE THE ACTION IS TAKEN

Under Art 9, without prejudice to Art 4(2), the law applicable to a non-contractual obligation of one of the listed categories of person for damages caused by an industrial action is the law of the country where the action is to be, or has been, taken. The connecting factor should be taken to refer to the country in which the acts of the workers collide with the interests of the employer, or vice versa. That will not necessarily be the same as the country in which the defendant acts, as the defendant's involvement may be limited to an act preparatory to industrial action (e.g. a trade union serving a notice of industrial action). For example, in the case of the blacking of a ship, the country of industrial action will be the place where port workers refuse to cooperate in the loading or unloading of the ship. In the case of a strike, it will be the place(s) where workers would ordinarily work but for the stoppage.[51] **9.31**

By reason of the reference to Art 4(2), the law otherwise applicable under Art 9 will be displaced if the person claimed to be liable and the person sustaining damage both have their habitual residence in the same country at the time when the damage occurs.[52] In this case, the law of the country of common habitual residence will apply. There being no reference in Art 9 to Art 4(3), it is not possible for that law, or the law which otherwise applies under Art 9, to be displaced on the basis of a manifestly closer connection to another country. The reason for including the common habitual residence rule without the more flexible escape clause is puzzling, but seems to be part of the overall conviction of the framers of the Regulation that application of the common habitual residence rule reflects the legitimate expectations of the parties. That will not always be the case[53] and, without any fallback, it may lead to unsatisfactory results. For example, if an international trade union based in London and acting from its headquarters organizes the blacking in Sweden of a ship owned by an English company, and operated from Harwich,[54] the law applicable under Art 9 to a claim against the union to prohibit the action will be English not Swedish law. **9.32**

---

[51] If a ship's crew engages in industrial action while the ship is at sea, the law of the flag may be argued to apply, at least if the ship is on the high seas (**4.55–4.57** above).

[52] **4.80–4.83**.

[53] **4.81–4.82** above.

[54] If the ship is operated from a port in another country, it may be argued that the shipowner's habitual residence under Art 23 should be that country if it has an establishment there responsible for the day-to-day operations of the ship (**3.58** above).

Part III

Other Non-Contractual Obligations

10

Unjust Enrichment

A. CHAPTER III OF THE REGULATION—UNJUST ENRICHMENT, *NEGOTIORUM GESTIO,* AND *CULPA IN CONTRAHENDO*

Articles 10 to 13, to be discussed in this and the following two chapters, **10.01** form Chapter III of the Regulation, entitled 'Unjust Enrichment, *Negotiorum Gestio* and *Culpa in Contrahendo*'.[1] These specific non-contractual obligations were deliberately segregated from Chapter II on the basis that, as Recital (29)[2] makes clear, they were not considered to arise out of a 'tort/delict'. Beyond this, however, the elongated title of the Chapter suggests that there is no other common element that unifies the rules of applicable law in Arts 10 to 12. Art 13 does not contain a separate rule of applicable law but confirms that Art 8 applies to non-contractual obligations arising from an infringement of an intellectual property right that might otherwise fall within the scope of Chapter III.

---

[1] For an earlier comparative survey of the law applicable to unjust enrichment and *negotiorum gestio*, see K Zweigert and D Müller-Gindullis, 'Quasi-Contracts', ch 30 in K Lipstein (ed), *International Encyclopaedia of Comparative Law*, vol III (private international law).

[2] Discussed at **3.247–3.248** above.

10.02 The structure and content of Chapter III in its final form are in marked contrast to the corresponding part (Section 2) of the Commission Proposal, entitled 'Rules Applicable to Non-Contractual Obligations Arising Out of an Act Other than a Tort of Delict'. That Section contained a single article with six sub-rules.[3] The first provided that a 'non-contractual obligation arising out of an act other than a tort or delict' (in the French version, *'une obligation non contractuelle dérivant d'un fait autre qu'un délit'*) which concerned a relationship previously existing between the parties was to be governed by the law that governs that relationship. The second, without prejudice to the first, provided for the application of the law of the country in which the parties had their common habitual residence. The third, without prejudice to the first two, provided that 'a non-contractual obligation arising out of unjust enrichment' was to be governed by the law of the country in which the enrichment takes place. The fourth, again without prejudice to the first two, provided that 'a non-contractual obligation arising out of actions performed without due authority in connection with the affairs of another person' was to be governed by the law of the beneficiary's habitual residence at the time of the unauthorized action, unless that action related to the physical protection of the person or specific tangible property, in which case the applicable law should be that of the country in which the beneficiary or (as the case may be) property was situated at the time of the action. The fifth, expressed to apply 'notwithstanding' the first four rules, provided for the application of the law of another country with which the non-contractual obligation was manifestly more closely connected. The sixth dealt with intellectual property rights and reflected, in its intent if not its wording, Art 13 of the Regulation in its final form.

10.03 The Commission described this collection of rules in the following terms:[4]

> In all the Member States' legal systems there are obligations that arise neither out of a contract nor out of a tort or delict. The situations that are familiar to all the Member States are payments made by mistake and services rendered by a person that enable another person to avoid sustaining personal injury or loss of assets.

> Since these obligations are clearly distinguished by their own features from torts and delicts, it has been decided that there should be a special section for them.

> To reflect the wide divergences between national systems here, technical terms need to be avoided. This Regulation refers therefore to 'non-contractual obligations arising out of an act other than a tort or delict'. In most Member States there are

---

[3] Commission Proposal, Art 9. For comment, see EESC Opinion, OJ C241, 4–5 [28.9.2004]; G Carella, 'The Law Applicable to Non-Contractual Obligations Other than Tort of Delict' in A Malatesta (ed), *The Unification of Choice of Law Rules on Torts and Other Non-Contractual Obligations in Europe* (2006), 73–84.

[4] Commission Proposal, 21.

sub-categories for repayment of amounts wrongly received or unjust enrichment on the one hand and agency without authority (*negotiorum gestion*[5]) on the other. Both the substantive law and the conflict rules are still evolving rapidly in most of the Member States, which means that the law is far from certain. The uniform conflict rule must reflect the divergences in the substantive rules. The difficulty is in laying down rules that are neither so precise that they cannot be applied in a Member State whose substantive law makes no distinction between the various relevant hypotheses nor so general that they might be open to challenge as serving no obvious purpose. Article 9 seeks to overcome the problem by laying down specific rules for the two sub-categories, unjust enrichment and agency without authority, while leaving the courts with sufficient flexibility to adapt the rule [to] their national systems.

This suggested a view of non-tortious, non-contractual obligations that **10.04** centred upon the twin institutions of unjust enrichment and *negotiorum gestio*, without requiring Member State courts to force rules generating non-contractual obligations into these categories and leaving scope for the sub-rules to apply to other kinds of non-contractual obligation. That view received support from the Commission's statement earlier in the explanatory memorandum accompanying its proposal that:[6]

The scope of the Regulation covers all non-contractual obligations except those in matters listed in paragraph 2.[7] Non-contractual obligations are in two major categories, those that arise out of a tort or delict and those that do not. The first category comprises obligations relating to tort or delict, and the second comprises obligations relating to what in some jurisdictions is termed 'quasi-delict' or 'quasi-contract', including in particular unjust enrichment and agency without authority or *negotiorum gestio*. The latter category is governed by section 2.

The Commission's contentions that (a) the Regulation covers all non- **10.05** contractual obligations except those specifically excluded in Art 1, and (b) quasi-delictual obligations fall within what is now Chapter III rather than Chapter II of the Regulation have been discussed, and rejected, in earlier chapters.[8] The Commission Proposal was, in any event, ill-equipped to deal with non-tortious/non-delictual obligations falling outside the two categories, unjust enrichment and *negotiorum gestio*, for which specific provision was made. Thus, although the first and second sub-rules could be read as rules of general application, Art 9 of the Commission's proposal contained no residual rule designed to catch obligations to which none of the

---

[5] The word 'gestion' rather than 'gestio' appears in the English and French but not, for example, the German and Italian language versions of the explanatory memorandum accompanying the Proposal.

[6] Commission Proposal, 8.

[7] A reference to what became Art 1(2) of the Regulation.

[8] **3.230–3.248** and **4.97** above.

first four sub-rules applied. It would, no doubt, have been possible in these circumstances to argue for the application of the fifth sub-rule as requiring the application of the law of the country with which the obligation was most closely connected, but this would be to turn it from an exceptional rule of displacement[9] to a free-standing rule of applicable law in its own right.

10.06 The process by which Art 9 of the Proposal was transformed into Chapter III of the Regulation in its final form is described more fully in **Chapter 3**.[10] In summary, this part of the Commission Proposal was rejected by the European Parliament, which at first reading favoured separate, more detailed rules for only unjust enrichment and *negotiorum gestio*.[11] These amendments were accepted by the Commission in its Amended Proposal,[12] subject to what the Commission described as adjustments to 'reflect certain technical improvements in the text emerging from Council proceedings'.[13] In early discussions, Member State delegations were divided as to the need for rules of applicable law for non-contractual obligations other than those arising out of a tort/delict,[14] but were soon persuaded that the Regulation should address at least the two specific categories of obligation identified by the Commission.[15] Criticisms that the rules put forward were overly complex and repetitive were also put to one side.[16] In its Common Position, the Council added the third category of '*culpa in contrahendo*'[17] and made one important change to the European Parliament's proposed set of rules for unjust enrichment, favouring the law of the place of enrichment over the law of the place of the event giving rise to enrichment.[18] The Parliament accepted those changes at its second reading stage.[19]

10.07 The rules of applicable law for the three specific categories of non-contractual obligation identified in Chapter III are considered in this and

---

[9] Commission Proposal, 22.

[10] **3.230–3.233** above.

[11] EP 1st Reading Position, Arts 9 and 10 (discussed at **10.09** and **11.01** below).

[12] Commission Amended Proposal, Arts 10 and 11.

[13] Ibid, 3.

[14] Council document 6518/04 [26.2.2004], 2. Compare, for example, the views of the delegations representing Germany (Council document 9009/04 ADD 11 [24.5.2004], 11–13) and France (ibid, ADD 12 [24.5.2004], 5) with those of the delegations representing the UK (ibid, ADD 15 [26.5.2004], 7) and The Netherlands (ibid, ADD 16 [28.5.2004], 4).

[15] Council document 11801/04 [28.7.2004].

[16] Commission note of meeting of the Council's Rome II committee on 5–6 October 2004 (Commission document JAI/C/1/CH/bv D(04) 10582 [29.10.2004]).

[17] Common Position, Art 12.

[18] Common Position, Art 10(3) and see the accompanying statement of reasons (OJ C289E, 79 [28.11.2006]), discussed at **10.31** below.

[19] EP 2nd Reading Position, Arts 10–12.

the two following chapters. This chapter deals with unjust enrichment (Art 10), **Chapter 11** deals with *negotiorum gestio* (Art 11), and **Chapter 12** deals with *culpa in contrahendo* (Art 12). Art 13 has been discussed elsewhere.[20]

Article 10

Unjust enrichment

1. **If a non-contractual obligation arising out of unjust enrichment, including payment of amounts wrongly received, concerns a relationship existing between the parties, such as one arising out of a contract or a tort/delict, that is closely connected with that unjust enrichment, it shall be governed by the law that governs that relationship.**

2. **Where the law applicable cannot be determined on the basis of paragraph 1 and the parties have their habitual residence in the same country when the event giving rise to unjust enrichment occurs, the law of that country shall apply.**

3. **Where the law applicable cannot be determined on the basis of paragraphs 1 or 2, it shall be the law of the country in which the unjust enrichment took place.**

4. **Where it is clear from all the circumstances of the case that the non-contractual obligation arising out of unjust enrichment is manifestly more closely connected with a country other than that indicated in paragraphs 1, 2 and 3, the law of that other country shall apply.**

B. NON-CONTRACTUAL OBLIGATION ARISING OUT OF UNJUST ENRICHMENT

As noted, the Commission Proposal contained a single sub-rule for unjust enrichment, designating the law of the country in which the enrichment takes place,[21] subject to two higher ranking rules of more general application[22] and a single rule capable of displacing the law applicable under the preceding rules.[23] That structure and hierarchy is retained within Art 10, which applies exclusively to non-contractual obligations 'arising out of unjust enrichment'.[24] **10.08**

---

[20] **4.17–4.18** and **8.19–8.20** above.

[21] Commission Proposal, Art 9(3).

[22] Designating the law governing a previously existing relationship between the parties with which the non-contractual obligation is concerned (ibid, Art 9(1)), otherwise the law of the country in which the parties have a common habitual residence when the event giving rise to the damage occurs (ibid, Art 9(2)).

[23] In favour of the law of another country with which the non-contractual obligation is manifestly more closely connected (ibid, Art 9(5)).

[24] **10.01–10.21** below.

10.09 The most significant issue debated during the passage of the Regulation was whether the basic rule should favour the law of the country of enrichment or the law of the country in which the event giving rise to enrichment occurred. The Commission, in its original Proposal, favoured the former view as being the 'conventional conclusion', being consistent (for example) with the approach of the GEDIP draft Convention[25] and German and Swiss Law.[26] The European Parliament, at first reading, disagreed with the Commission's view. It favoured 'the law of the country in which the event giving rise to unjust enrichment substantially occurred, irrespective of the country in which the enrichment occurred'[27]. The Council, in its Common Position, preferred the country of enrichment approach.[28] The effect of this sub-rule is considered at **10.29–10.34** below.

C. THE CONCEPT OF 'UNJUST ENRICHMENT'[29]

10.10 The sub-rules within Art 10 appear relatively straightforward to apply.[30] The most difficult issues, therefore, concern the material scope of these rules. What types of claim do they cover? As the Commission recognized in its Proposal,[31] the Member States' legal systems diverge in their treatment of non-contractual obligations outside the core category of tort/ delict. That is as much true for the substantive law governing unjust enrichment as it is for any other category. In some systems (e.g. Germany), the concept is both clearly developed and wide ranging. In others (e.g. France), it is clearly developed, but narrower. Elsewhere, the law of unjust enrichment is less well established. In England and Wales, the common law side of the subject has only recently shaken off its historical links

---

[25] GEDIP proposal for a convention on the law applicable to non-contractual obligations (1988) 45 Neth Int L Rev 465, Art 7(3) (**1.53** above).

[26] Germany: *Einführungsgesetz zum Bürgerlichen Gezetzbuch* (EGBGB), Art 38(3); Switzerland: *Loi fédérale sur le droit international privé du 18 décembre 1987*, Art 128 (**1.22** and **1.41** above). For the role of the law of the place of enrichment under the pre-existing English common law rules (and possible application of the doctrine of *renvoi*), see Sir L Collins et al. (eds), *Dicey, Morris & Collins: The Conflict of Laws* (14th edn, 2006), paras 34-030 to 34-031; *Barros Mattos Jr v Macdaniels Ltd* [2005] EWHC 1323 (Ch), [84]–[121].

[27] EP 1st Reading Position, Art 9(3). The Commission, in its Amended Proposal, followed the Parliament's line (Commission Amended Proposal, Art 10(3)).

[28] See the statement of reasons accompanying the Common Position at OJ C289E, 79 [28.11.2006].

[29] Also A Chong, 'Choice of Law for Unjust Enrichment/Restitution and the Rome II Regulation' (2008) 57 ICLQ 863, 864–872 and 890–896.

[30] **10.22–10.36** below.

[31] Text to n 4 above.

to the law of contract[32] and, like an escaped prisoner, is still struggling to come to terms with its independence and fearing re-capture. On the equitable side, a satisfactory separation of 'wrongs' and 'unjust enrichment' has yet to be achieved.[33] In Scandinavian systems, the concept would appear to be even less well developed.[34] These differences in development and approach are equally apparent in the treatment of unjust enrichment within private international law.[35] The need, within the Regulation, for an autonomous, non-technical meaning to be given to the concept of 'a non-contractual obligation arising out of unjust enrichment' is evident.[36]

In the English language version, Art 10 of the Regulation refers to 'a **10.11** non-contractual obligation arising out of unjust enrichment, including payment of amounts wrongly received'. At first sight, this appears[37] to give a broad scope to the provision and to be capable, at its widest, of spanning Professor Burrows' 'central divide between unjust enrichment by subtraction . . . and unjust enrichment by wrongdoing'.[38] For Professor Burrows, the two forms of 'unjust enrichment' reflect different senses of the idea of the defendant's enrichment *at the expense of* the claimant:[39]

The first and most natural meaning, is that the defendant's gain has come from the claimant's wealth: in Birks' terminology there has been a 'subtraction from' the

---

[32] The so-called 'implied contract' theory of common law unjust enrichment claims was not finally rejected in England until 1996 (*Westdeutsche Landesbank Girozentrale v Islington LBC* [1996] AC 669 (UKHL)).

[33] For detailed accounts of the theoretical underpinnings and current state of the English law of unjust enrichment, see P Birks, *Unjust Enrichment* (2nd edn, 2005); C Mitchell, 'Unjust Enrichment' in A Burrows (ed), *English Private Law* (2nd edn, 2007), ch 18.

[34] C von Bar, *The Common European Law of Torts* (vol 1, 1998; reprinted 2003), para 517, footnote 644.

[35] **1.08–1.43** above. For a, by now dated, survey of the law applicable to unjust enrichment, see K Zweigert and D Müller-Gindullis, n 1 above, 4–18. For discussion of the (underdeveloped) pre-existing English rules, see Sir L Collins et al. (eds), *Dicey Morris & Collins: The Conflict of Laws* (14th edn, 2006), ch 36; F Rose (ed), *Restitution and the Conflict of Laws* (1995); G Panagopoulos, *Restitution in Private International Law* (2000); Barros Mattos Jr v Macdaniels Ltd, n 26 above.

[36] A Rushworth and A Scott, 'Rome II: Choice of law for non-contractual obligations' [2008] LMCLQ 274, 285–6. Carine Brière, on the other hand, floats the idea of characterization according to the law of the forum ('*Le règlement (CE) no 864/2007 du 11 juillet 2007 sur la loi applicable aux obligations non contractuelles (Rome II)*' (2008) Journal du Droit International 31, 50. That seems incompatible with the objective of creating uniform rules across the Member States (Recitals (13) and (16)).

[37] So far as the words 'payment of amounts wrongly received' are concerned, the appearance is deceptive (**4.15** above).

[38] A Burrows, *The Law of Restitution* (2nd edn, 2002), 5.

[39] Ibid, 26.

claimant. The second, and less obvious meaning, is that the defendant's gain has been acquired by committing a wrong against the claimant.

10.12 The late Professor Birks, however, was never comfortable with the idea of 'unjust enrichment by wrongdoing'. He considered that it confused two categories of event triggering remedial responses, preferring the terminology 'restitution for wrongdoing' to that of 'unjust enrichment by wrongdoing'.[40] Before his untimely death in 2004, he had rejected the idea of a thematic link between these two categories. In his view, 'the "wrong" sense of "at the expense of". . . cannot be admitted to the law of unjust enrichment'.[41]

10.13 A broad interpretation of the concept of 'unjust enrichment' is also suggested by the reference in the German language version to *'ein außertragliches Schuldverhältnis aus ungerechtfertifter Bereicherung'*. This reflects the title heading above Section 812 of the German Civil Code (*Bürgerliches Gesetzbuch*). Section 812, itself entitled *'Herausgabeanspruch'* (claim to restitution), deals both with situations in which a person obtains something by performance of another person (*Leistungskondiktion*) and with other situations in which a person is enriched 'in another way', including by interference with another's rights (*Eingriffskondiktion*).[42] The Dutch version of the Regulation, in turn, refers to *'ongerechtvaardigde verrijking'*, the heading used in the Dutch Civil Code (*Burgerlijk Wetboek*) for a single provision (Art 6:212) dealing with unjustified enrichments at the expense of another other than undue payments. It would appear that, at the time of its adoption, this provision was intended to play a subsidiary role to the law of tort and that it has scarcely been relied on.[43]

10.14 The terminology used in other language versions of the Regulation, however, suggests a more restricted concept of 'unjust enrichment' concerning itself with the reversal of transfers of value from the claimant to the defendant for which there is no legal basis, and centred on (but not limited to) the civil law institution of the *condictio indebiti*. This is what an English lawyer might describe as subtractive unjust enrichment.[44] Thus, the French text refers to *'enrichissement sans cause'*,[45] the Italian to *'arricchimento*

---

[40] P Birks, *An Introduction to the Law of Restitution* (revd edn 1989), 40–4.

[41] P Birks, n 33 above, 74. Professor Birks continues with the passage quoted in the text to n 50 at **4.13** above).

[42] B Markesinis, W Lorenz, and G Danneman, *The German Law of Obligations* (3rd edn, 1997), ch 9.

[43] C von Bar, n 34 above, para 521.

[44] A Burrows, n 38 above, 25–31.

[45] Art 1376 of the French Civil Code (*Code Civil*) (under the Title *'Des Quasi-Contrats'*) deals with the specific situation of the *paiement de l'indu*, where a person who by error or knowingly

senza causa', and the Portuguese to *'enriquecimento sem causa'*. A third group, including the Spanish and Swedish language versions, contain a literal translation of the words 'unjust enrichment', which do not appear to correspond to any specific concept within their legal systems.[46]

Although the French text appears to reflect more closely than the English **10.15** or German texts the narrower understanding of 'unjust enrichment' in many continental legal systems,[47] as well as the view of Professor Birks as to the proper ambit of the subject under English law,[48] the preceding survey offers little by way of firm guidance as to the autonomous meaning to be given to the concept of 'unjust enrichment' within the Rome Regulation. Limited assistance is provided by the specific example given in Art 10 of 'payments of amounts wrongly received' (in the French text, *'paiement indu'*, and in the German text, *'Zahlungen auf eine nicht bestehende Schuld'*), apparently referring, despite the clumsiness of the English language text, to claims to recover payments not due (*condictio indebiti*). This wording, consistent with both the narrower and the wider views of 'unjust enrichment' referred to above, would appear to have been added for the avoidance of doubt in view of the separate treatment of such claims within some legal systems.[49] The words, accordingly, reveal very little. The connecting factors, in the main, also appear neutral, although the reference in Art 10(3) to the country of enrichment is more appealing as a connecting factor if that country can be identified by the claimant and the defendant at the time of the enrichment. That is more likely to be the case if the defendant's enrichment results from an act of the claimant.[50]

In light of this uncertainty, it may be best to approach the material scope of **10.16** Art 10 from the other direction by asking what it does not include. Three, possibly four, categories of excluded matter can be identified from the text of the Regulation itself. First, unjust enrichment claims arising from an

---

receives what is not due to him is obliged to make restitution to the person from whom he received it. That and the following Article, concerning mistaken payment of a debt, were widened by case law into a general law of *enrichissement sans cause* (see C von Bar, n 34, para 517, footnote 644).

[46] Professor von Bar notes (ibid) that (a) the relevant articles of the Spanish Civil Code are similar to those in the French Civil Code, and (b) under Swedish law the extent of the principle of liability linked with the concept of unjust enrichment is unclear.

[47] C von Bar, ibid.

[48] P Birks, n 33 above, 11–16 (see, in particular, the passage quoted at **4.11** above).

[49] **4.15** above.

[50] For discussion as to the meaning of the reference in Art 10(1) to 'a relationship existing between the parties, such as one arising out of . . . a tort/delict', see **4.15** above and **10.25–10.26** below.

infringement of an intellectual property right are excluded by Art 13.[51] Secondly, Art 11 extends to a claim for remuneration by a person who performs an act without due authority in connection with the affairs of another (*negotiorum gestio*).[52] Thirdly, claims for recovery of payments made under a contract that has been nullified or terminated for breach or otherwise must be treated as sufficiently closely related to the (putative/former) contractual obligation to fall within the scope of the Rome Convention and its successor Regulation,[53] and outside the reach of Art 10.[54] The editors of Dicey, Morris & Collins also suggest that obligations arising from mistaken performance of a valid contract also fall within the Rome I Regime, as a form of 'performance'.[55] It seems doubtful whether that view is correct, particularly as Art 10 of the Rome II Regulation refers specifically to the *paiement de l'indu*.[56] Fourthly, it may be possible to argue that claims to reverse unjust enrichment arising out of dealings prior to the conclusion of a contract (e.g. to recover a reasonable remuneration for work performed in anticipation of a contract or a pre-contractual deposit) fall within Art 12 (*culpa in contrahendo*), although the better view would appear to be that the latter provision concerns obligations based on the conduct of the person responsible and not on the claimant's own acts.[57]

10.17 These points chip away at the content of Art 10, without really telling us more about what is intended to be covered by the words 'non-contractual obligation arising out of unjust enrichment'. A more fundamental question is whether Art 10 of the Rome II Regulation extends to or excludes situations in which the claimant seeks a remedy to strip the defendant of a gain made by him and bases his claim on a tort/delict (i.e. an act or omission of, or an act, omission, or other event attributable to, the defendant or a person for whose acts the defendant is liable).[58] This question has been

---

[51] **4.17–4.18** and **8.19–8.20** above.

[52] **11.04** below.

[53] **3.108–3.109** above. Reversal of payments made under a void contract falls within 'the consequences of nullity of the contract' (Rome Convention, Art 10(1)(e); Rome I Regulation, Art 12(1)(e)). Reversal of payments made under a contract terminated for breach falls within 'the consequences of breach' (Convention, Art 10(1)(c); Regulation, Art 12(1)(c)). Reversal of payments made under a contract terminated for another reason (e.g. illegality, impossibility) should be considered as an aspect of 'performance' (Convention, Art 10(1)(b); Regulation, Art 12(1)(b)) or the extinction of obligations (Convention, Art 10(1)(d); Regulation, Art 12(1)(d)).

[54] Cf Dicey, Morris & Collins, 1st supplement, para 34-014, but this is difficult to reconcile with the statement in the main work, para 34-006.

[55] Rome Convention, Art 10(1)(b); Rome I Regulation, Art 12(1)(b).

[56] **3.109** above.

[57] **12.04** below.

[58] Or a person represented by the claimant.

considered in **Chapter 4**,[59] where it was proposed that claims of this kind should be characterized as falling within Chapter II of the Rome II Regulation (tort/delict), not within Art 10 (unjust enrichment), if the remedy responds to a tort/delict within the autonomous meaning given to that term under the Regulation, whether or not the defendant can be said at the same time to have been 'unjustly enriched'. On this view, both the English law category of 'restitution for wrongdoing' (based on a tort or equitable wrong) and the German law *Eingriffskondiktion* (based on interference with the claimant's rights) appear to fit more naturally within the tort/delict category (Chapter II) than the unjust enrichment category (Art 10). That view is consistent with the terms of Art 15, describing in broad terms the scope of the law applicable to a non-contractual obligation under the Regulation and, in particular, by Arts 15(c) and (d).[60] Further:

- A test focusing on the foundation of the claim rather than the nature of the remedy sought avoids the need to look behind a remedy to see if it is truly 'compensatory' or 'restitutionary' and avoids arbitrary distinctions between different kinds of remedy for the same wrong.

- Bringing gain-based remedies for tort/delict within Chapter II protects the special rules in Arts 6, 7 and 9, and the policies underlying them.

If, on the other hand, the claimant can frame his claim to reverse the **10.18** defendant's enrichment without relying on the defendant's tort/delict, that claim, being independent of the 'wrong', will fall within Art 10.[61]

The search for a positive definition of the concept of 'unjust enrichment' **10.19** within Art 10 must continue.[62] At a minimum, the words 'unjust enrichment' emphasize a need for the defendant to have, in some way, been enriched and for that enrichment to be considered unacceptable. It is also clearly desirable, given the different ways in which Member States approach the subject, to avoid technical restrictions, for example as to the nature of the enrichment, the ground(s) for restitution or the correspondence between the diminution in the claimant's assets and the defendant's enrichment.[63] This may be one area in which uniformity would be promoted

---

[59] **4.11–4.19**.

[60] **14.18–14.36** below.

[61] **4.20** above. For an example of 'alternative analysis' under the pre-existing English rules of applicable law, see *Berry Floor Ltd v Moussavi* [2004] EWHC 49 (Comm), [64] (Cooke J).

[62] See also the comments of Adv Gen Mazák in Case C-47/07P, *Masdar (UK) Ltd v Commission*, Opinion dated 12 June 2008 concerning the liability of the Community under EC Treaty, Art 288 on the basis of unjust enrichment and *negotiorum gestio* (**11.09–11.12** below).

[63] A Rushworth and A Scott, n 36 above, 285–6. Also, for perspectives on the substantive law in England and Germany, P Birks, n 33 above, chs 3–6; B Markesinis, W Lorenz, and G Dannemann, n 42 above, ch 9.

by a common understanding as to the Community law meaning of the terms used, and the Commission's wish to develop a Common Frame of Reference (CFR) as a 'tool box' for the European legislator may be one way of taking this forward.[64] Although it is not authoritative and pursues wider objectives than the intended CFR, the treatment of 'unjustified enrichment' in Book VII of the interim outline edition of the 'Draft Common Frame of Reference' (DFCR) published in 2008 by the Professor von Bar's Study Group on a European Civil Code[65] provides food for thought. The authors of the DFCR define 'unjustified enrichment' as:[66]

[A]n enrichment which is not legally justified, with the result that, if it is obtained by one person and is attributable to another's disadvantage, the first person may, subject to legal rules and restrictions, be obliged to that other to reverse the enrichment.

10.20 Book VII of the DFCR then proceeds as follows:

1. Art 1:101 contains a basic rule reflecting the description of unjustified enrichment given above.

2. Art 2:101 defines the circumstances in which an enrichment is 'unjustified'. In general terms, an enrichment is considered to be unjustified unless (a) the enriched person is entitled as against the disadvantaged person to the enrichment by virtue of a contract or other juridical act, a court order or a rule of law; or (b) the disadvantaged person consented freely and without error to the disadvantage.[67] An enrichment will also be considered to be unjustified if (a) the disadvantaged person conferred it (i) for a purpose which is not achieved, or (ii) with an expectation which is not realised, (b) the enriched person knew of, or could reasonably be expected to know of, the purpose or expectation, and (c) the enriched person accepted or could reasonably be assumed to have accepted that the enrichment must be reversed in such circumstances.[68] This adopts the civilian model of enrichment *sine causa*, rather than the traditional English model of requiring an individual 'unjust factor' to be identified in

---

[64] Commission, Second Progress Report on the Common Frame of Reference (COM (2007) 447 final [25.7.2007]). For further information on the Common Frame of Reference, see <http://ec.europa.eu/consumers/cons_int/safe_shop/fair_bus_pract/cont_law/index_en.htm>.

[65] C von Bar et al. (eds), *Principles, Definitions and Model Rules of European Private Law: Draft Common Frame of Reference* (2008), available at <http://www.law-net.eu/en_index.htm> (**DFCR**).

[66] DFCR, Annex 1 (at 343).

[67] DFCR, Art 2:101(1).

[68] Ibid, Art 2:101(4). Also Art 2:102 dealing with the justification of enrichment through performance of an obligation to a third person and Art 2:103 dealing with the concept of free consent.

each case.[69] As a general test, it is helpful, therefore, only at a high level of abstraction.

3. Arts 3:101 and 3:102 define the concepts of 'enrichment' and 'disadvantage' and, provided that they are not taken as exhaustive, may be more useful in creating an autonomous Community concept of 'unjust enrichment' under the Regulation. Both enrichment [and disadvantage][70] are defined broadly as referring to (a) an increase [or decrease] in assets or a decrease [or increase] in liabilities, (b) receiving [or rendering] a service or having work done, or (c) use of another's assets.

4. Chapter 4 of Book IV deals with the important concept of attribution, i.e. the link required between the disadvantage and the enrichment. Under Art 4:101, an enrichment is attributable to another's disadvantage in particular if (a) an asset of that other is transferred to the enriched person by that other, (b) a service is rendered to or work is done for the enriched person by that other, (c) the enriched person uses that other's asset, especially where the enriched person infringes the disadvantaged person's rights or legally protected interests, (d) an asset of the enriched person is improved by that other, or (e) the enriched person is discharged from a liability by that other. These appear to provide paradigm examples of situations falling within the concept of 'unjust enrichment' in Art 10. The remainder of Chapter IV deals with other, more specific situations (indirect representation, debtor's performance to a non-creditor, act of an intervener). Under Art 4:107, an enrichment may be attributable to another's disadvantage even though the enrichment and disadvantage are not of the same type or value.

5. Chapter 5 deals with the method of reversal of enrichment, dealing separately with the reversal of transferable and non-transferable enrichments. Chapter 6 deals with defences. Chapter 7 deals with the relation of unjustified enrichment to other legal rules. For present purposes, these rules do not appear to provide significant assistance in defining 'unjust enrichment' within the Regulation.

Overall, the model suggested by the DFCR points towards a broad concept of 'unjust enrichment' based on the idea of an accretion to the defendant's assets linked to a diminution in the claimant's assets in which the reason (or lack or reason) for that link underlies the defendant's obligation **10.21**

---

[69] P Birks, n 33 above, ch 5. For a possible shift in the direction of the English law of unjust enrichment, see *Deutsche Morgan Grenfell Group plc v Inland Revenue Commissioners* [2006] UKHL 49; [2007] 1 AC 448, [150]–[158] (Lord Walker), a tribute to Professor Birks.

[70] The square bracketed wording is taken from the definition of disadvantage in Art 3:102.

to restore to the claimant the enrichment or its value. At the very least, this provides a point of departure in defining the material scope of Art 10. It also seems consistent with the exclusion from Art 10 of gain-based remedies for tort/delict.[71] It would also support the exclusion from the category of 'unjust enrichment' of other non-contractual obligations that are founded on the defendant's conduct and/or disadvantage suffered by the claimant. The English law tort of conversion and the equitable claim of 'knowing receipt' may be cited as examples of claims that fall outside Art 10 for reasons of this kind, even if the law's response is aptly described as 'gain based'.[72] Accordingly, the territory occupied by unjust enrichment within the Regulation would appear narrower than that which the law of restitution currently occupies, or is claimed to occupy, under English law.

D. THE LAW APPLICABLE TO NON-CONTRACTUAL OBLIGATIONS ARISING OUT OF UNJUST ENRICHMENT[73]

10.22 Like Art 5, and in contrast to the structure of Art 4, Art 10 deploys a descending cascade of rules of applicable law subject to a single rule of displacement in Art 10(4).

Fɪʀsᴛ Lᴇᴠᴇʟ—Lᴀᴡ Gᴏᴠᴇʀɴɪɴɢ Rᴇʟᴀᴛɪᴏɴsʜɪᴘ Eхɪsᴛɪɴɢ ʙᴇᴛᴡᴇᴇɴ ᴛʜᴇ Pᴀʀᴛɪᴇs ᴡɪᴛʜ ᴡʜɪᴄʜ Oʙʟɪɢᴀᴛɪᴏɴ ɪs Cᴏɴᴄᴇʀɴᴇᴅ (Aʀᴛ 10(1))

10.23 Under Art 10(1), a non-contractual obligation arising out of unjust enrichment (including payment of amounts wrongfully received) which concerns and is closely connected to a 'relationship existing between the parties' shall be governed by the law applicable to that relationship. The concept of a 'pre-existing relationship' is also to be found in Art 4(3)[74] and Art 5(2)[75] and, although Art 10(1) uses slightly different wording, there is

---

[71] **10.17** above. Book VI, Art 6:101(4) of the DFCR (in the section dealing with 'non-contractual liability arising out of damage caused to another') provides that, as an alternative to reinstatement of the victim, reparation may take the form of recovery from the person accountable for the causation of the legally relevant damage of any advantage obtained by the latter in connection with causing the damage, but only where this is reasonable.

[72] **4.103–4.105** above. Also A Rushworth and A Scott, n 36 above, 286; cf Dicey, Morris & Collins, 1st supplement, para 34-033.

[73] A Chong, 'Choice of Law for Unjust Enrichment/Restitution and the Rome II Regulation' (2008) 57 ICLQ 863, 872–890.

[74] **4.90–4.95** above.

[75] **5.47** above.

(subject to the points, addressed in the following paragraphs) no reason to suggest that a broader or narrower meaning was intended in this context.[76]

It may appear that the two provisions differ in the connection required **10.24** between the relationship and the event giving rise to the non-contractual obligation in question. Art 4(3) requires that the pre-existing relationship be 'closely connected with' the tort/delict in question. In contrast, Art 10(1) requires that the non-contractual obligation 'concerns' the existing relationship. The following words in Art 10(1), however, confirm that a 'close connection' test is appropriate in both contexts.

Art 4(3) gives only one example of a pre-existing relationship, that of a **10.25** contract between the parties. In contrast, Art 10(1) gives two examples, adding the concept of a relationship arising out of a tort/delict to one arising out of a contract. The contract example is relatively straightforward, and Art 10(1) promotes a uniform applicable law for claims to reverse enrichments in connection with valid or void contracts, whether or not the non-contractual obligation is held to fall within the Rome II or Rome I Regulation.[77] The intention behind the tort/delict example is less clear.[78] One possibility, discussed and rejected in **Chapter 4**, is that it was intended to accommodate claims that seek to make the defendant give up the profits of a tort/delict (restitution for wrongdoing).[79] In that discussion, the reference to a 'relationship existing between the parties' was taken to require a temporal separation between the events constituting the obligation arising out of a tort/delict and those constituting the obligation arising out of unjust enrichment. In contrast, Adam Rushworth and Andrew Scott suggest that the tort/delict example in Art 10(1) could cover circumstances in which the sequence of events that constitute a tort/delict also support a discrete claim to reverse unjust enrichment, without reference the defendant's wrongful conduct.[80] That view, however, is not only incompatible with the proposition that Art 10(1) requires a pre-existing 'tort/delict', it also gives the coincidence of claims

---

[76] Commission Proposal, 21, linking its proposed rule in Art 9(1) (now Regulation, Art 10(1)) to that in Art 3(3) (now Regulation, Art 4(3)) (see the text of the following footnote).

[77] **10.16** above. The Commission suggested that 'As in the case of the general exception clause in Article 3(3) [*of the Proposal*], the expression "pre-existing relationship" applies particularly to pre-contractual relationships and to void contracts' (Commission Proposal, 21). This point is discussed at **4.94** above.

[78] The wording first appeared in a draft circulated by the outgoing Dutch and incoming Luxembourg Presidencies in late 2004 (Council document 16231/04 [20.12.2004], Art 9A).

[79] **4.15** above.

[80] A Rushworth and A Scott, n 36 above, 286.

in tort/delict and unjust enrichment a significance within the applicable law equation that (it is submitted) it cannot bear. Possible examples of situations to which the example of a relationship arising out of a tort/delict in Art 10(1) might, on the more restrictive view taken in **Chapter 4**, be applied include (a) if the defendant tortfeasor brings a restitutionary counterclaim seeking an allowance with respect to the value of services provided to the claimant,[81] (b) if the tortfeasor seeks to recover a voluntary payment made to the claimant in the mistaken belief that the claimant had suffered a particular loss, and (c) if two or more persons responsible for the same loss each compensate the victim to the full extent of his loss and then seek to claim back part of the sum paid to avoid overcompensation.[82]

10.26 If, contrary to the author's view, Art 10 accommodates claims for gain-based remedies for tort/delict, a more liberal reading of the requirement of a relationship existing between the parties would be required in order to secure the result that (at least as a starting point for analysis[83]) claims for compensatory and gain-based remedies based on a tort/delict are subject to the same applicable law.

10.27 Art 10(1), unlike Art 4(3),[84] expressly refers to the law governing the pre-existing relationship between the parties. In the case of a contractual relationship, that law must be determined by reference to the provisions of the Rome Convention and its successor Regulation. The reference to 'the law governing the pre-existing relationship' will likely include not only rules of the law chosen by the parties or applicable to the contract in the absence of choice, but also any non-derogable rules (for example, of a consumer's country of habitual residence[85] or the country in which an employee habitually carries out his work[86]) whose application in a contractual context is preserved by the Rome I Regime.[87]

Second Level—Country of Common Habitual Residence (Art 10(2))

10.28 Art 10(2), which applies if there is not a close connection between the obligation arising from unjust enrichment and a pre-existing relationship, is formulated in terms similar to Art 4(2), which contains a rule of

---

[81] *Guinness plc v Saunders* [1990] 2 AC 663 (UKHL).

[82] C von Bar, n 34 above, para 517, text to footnote 651.

[83] For difficulties arising from the differences between Art 10 and the special rules in Art 6, 7, and 9, see **4.19** above.

[84] Cf **4.90–4.91** above.

[85] Rome Convention, Art 5(2); Rome I Regulation, Art 6(2).

[86] Rome Convention, Art 6(1); Rome I Regulation, Art 8(1).

[87] Commission Proposal, 13, discussed at **4.92–4.93** above.

displacement in favour of the law of a country of common habitual residence for certain torts/delicts.[88] Two potential differences may be noted.
First, Art 10(2) requires that the test of common habitual residence[89] be
applied 'when the event giving rise to unjust enrichment occurs' and not,
as in Art 4(2), 'when the damage occurs'. Given the broad definition of
'damage' in Art 2,[90] it would have been possible to use the same test
although this would probably have led to a focus on the time at which the
enrichment (i.e. the 'consequence arising out of . . . unjust enrichment')
occurred. Nevertheless, as a result, the test of common habitual residence
in Art 10(2) must be applied at the time at which the claimant's disadvantage linked to the defendant's enrichment occurred.[91] Secondly, Art 10(2)
refers to the common habitual residence of the 'parties' whereas Art 4(2)
refers to the common habitual residence of the 'person claimed to be liable
and the person sustaining damage'. In this context, however, the context
suggests that 'parties' was intended to refer not to the named parties in the
litigation, but rather the persons between whom the non-contractual obligation was generated as a result of unjust enrichment. On this view, little,
if anything, seems to turn on the difference in language.

Third Level—Country in which Enrichment Took Place (Art 10(3))

If neither Art 10(1) (pre-existing relationship) nor Art 10(2) (common **10.29**
habitual residence) applies, the law applicable to a non-contractual obligation arising out of unjust enrichment is the law of the country in which
the 'unjust enrichment' took place.[92] The words 'unjust enrichment' must
be understood as a reference to the enrichment of the defendant that it is the
object of the action, and not to other elements forming part of the factual
basis of the claim.[93] That view, which promotes legal certainty and avoids
the need for a distributive application of laws whenever events take
place in different countries, is supported by the drafting history of Art 10.
In its initial response to Art 9 of the Commission Proposal, the French

---

[88] **4.80–4.83** above. Art 4(2) is also incorporated by reference within Art 5 (product liability) and Art 9 (industrial action).
[89] For the concept of 'habitual residence', see **3.47–3.58** above.
[90] **3.44–3.46** above.
[91] If, contrary to the author's view, Art 10 applies to gain-based remedies for tort/delict,
the event giving rise to unjust enrichment for such claims would remain the event giving rise
to damage.
[92] Art 10(3).
[93] A Rushworth and A Scott, n 36 above, 287.

delegation raised the following concern as to possible ambiguity in the meaning of the 'place where the enrichment occurred':[94]

> Enrichment may take place in the place where the *solvens* lost or the place where the *accipens* gained financially. For practical reasons, the preference must be given to the latter option.

10.30 According to the Austrian delegation:[95]

> [T]he wording 'in which the enrichment occurred' should be used instead of 'in which the enrichment takes place'.
>
> In any event the wording should refer as clearly as possible to the place in which the person obtaining the enrichment gained power of disposal, for instance where an amount was credited to him. The debiting of another account should not have any influence as a connecting factor.

10.31 The amendment proposed by the Austrian delegation was not accepted. As noted, however, the European Parliament at first reading rejected the place of enrichment as the basic connecting factor in the absence of a pre-existing relationship or common habitual residence, favouring instead 'the law of the country in which the event giving rise to unjust enrichment substantially occurred, irrespective of the country in which the enrichment occurred'.[96] The report of the EP JURI Committee explained that '[t]he place where enrichment takes place may be entirely fortuitous (e.g. dependent upon where a fraudster chooses to open the bank account to which monies are fraudulently paid over)'.[97] The Parliament's amendments to the special rules for unjust enrichment were, in turn, accepted by the Council's Rome II Committee 'subject to some technical modifications'.[98] The most important of those modifications was to keep, in the Council's working draft,[99] 'the country in which the enrichment takes place' as the connecting factor. That language (without the word 'unjust') was retained in the text approved by the JHA Council agreed in April 2006.[100] At some point in the following three months (it is not clear when or why) the wording was changed so that the Common Position referred instead, in the past tense, to 'to the country in which the *unjust* enrichment *took place*'.[101] In its accompanying statement of reasons, however, the Council explained its

---

[94] Council document 9009/04 ADD 12 [24.5.2004], 5.
[95] Ibid, ADD 1 [3.5.2004], 3–4.
[96] **10.09** above.
[97] EP 1st Reading Report, 26.
[98] Council document 13001/05 [10.10.2005], 4.
[99] Council document 16027/05 [22.12.2005].
[100] Council document 9143/06 [19.5.2006].
[101] Common Position, Art 10(3).

decision to differ from the Parliament's amendment on the basis that '*the law of the country in which enrichment took place* is a more appropriate connecting factor in case the applicable law cannot be determined on the basis of Article 10(1) or (2)'.[102] It appears, therefore, that the Council did not see any significance in the decision to refer in Art 10(3) to 'unjust enrichment' rather than 'enrichment'. Overall, these materials support the view that (a) 'the country in which the unjust enrichment took place' was intended to refer to the country in which the defendant was enriched as opposed to the country in which the event giving rise to enrichment occurred, and (b) the late changes to the text of the Common Position were no more than an attempt to use consistent language throughout Art 10 and were not intended to move away from the country of enrichment as the connecting factor.

Commenting on the different approaches to be taken by the Commission in its Proposal and the European Parliament at the first reading stage, Professor Carella suggests:[103] **10.32**

[S]ome drawbacks arise when the choice-of-law rule is only based on the enrichment factor. The law of the place of enrichment could be arbitrary and will not always necessarily be the one most closely connected with the unjust enrichment. The notion of a place of enrichment is rather fictitious where the enrichment is channelled through bank accounts. A place of enrichment rule in such a situation would be a blessing to fraudsters, who might wish to regulate their potential liability by channelling funds and thereby becoming 'enriched' in the desired locations.

Accordingly, she expresses a preference in situations involving money payments for a rule based on the country where the claimant acted, while maintaining the country of enrichment as the connecting factor in other cases.[104] That suggested distinction gives rise, however, to problems of definition. For example, should the special treatment be extended to securities accounts? What about payment in cash or by cheque? These situations appear no less important or open to manipulation by a fraudster. Further, Professor Carella's argument based on manipulation of the connecting factor seems compelling only within a framework within which the country of enrichment provides the only, or the primary, connecting factor. That is not the case within Art 10 of the Rome II Regulation. Even if neither of the two rules of applicable law taking priority over Art 10(3) **10.33**

---

[102] See the statement of reasons accompanying the Common Position at OJ C289E, 79 [28.11.2006] (emphasis added).

[103] G Carella, n 3 above, 83.

[104] Ibid.

is engaged,[105] the law that would apply under this sub-rule may be displaced under Art 10(4) in favour of the law of another country with which the non-contractual obligation arising out of unjust enrichment has a manifestly closer connection.[106] The intangible nature of the enrichment resulting from an electronic transfer of funds or securities, as well as any evidence that the account into which monies or securities were initially received was merely a cipher or a sham designed to make tracing more complicated, will reduce the significance of the country of enrichment and make it more straightforward to displace the application of that law through the operation of Art 10(4).[107] Further, in the case of the fraudster just cited, a question may arise as to whether the principle of abuse of right, which constitutes one of the general principles of EC law,[108] could be deployed (in addition or as an alternative to the escape clause in Art 10(4)) to defeat the defendant's claim to rely on the law of the country of enrichment to deny an obligation to restore the enrichment or its value.[109] Finally, the fraudster's conduct will also likely expose him to liability in tort/delict (including, possibly, for a gain-based remedy), the law applicable to which must be determined in accordance with Art 4, focusing on the place in which the victim of the fraud suffered damage.

10.34 Consistently with the approach taken in applying the concept of 'damage' in Art 4, the correct approach in locating the enrichment for the purposes of Art 10(3) should involve looking for a fact that is objectively ascertainable by both the person disadvantaged and the person enriched[110] that identifies the country in which the latter received a direct economic benefit, as opposed to the country in which that benefit was indirectly received or enjoyed[111] or in which his wealth is recorded.[112] In the case of receipt of a tangible asset, that will be the country in which the defendant or his representative assumed control over the asset. In the case of a transfer into a bank account, the country of enrichment will be that in which the branch from which the account is operated is located.[113] In the case of the

---

[105] Art 10(1)–(2) (**10.23–10.28** above).

[106] **10.35–10.36** below.

[107] For similar considerations regulating the escape clause in Art 4(3), see **4.67**, **4.87** and **4.105** above.

[108] K P E Lasok, T Millett, and A Howard, *Judicial Control in the EU* (2004), para 646.

[109] See, in a related context, A Nuyts, 'The Enforcement of Jurisdiction Agreements Further to Gasser and the Community Principle of Abuse of Right', ch 2 in P de Vareilles-Sommières (ed), *Forum Shopping in the European Judicial Area* (2007).

[110] **4.28** and **4.66–4.68** above.

[111] Cf Case C-364/93, *Marinari v Lloyd's Bank plc* [1995] ECR I-2719, discussed at **4.37** above.

[112] Cf Case C-168/02, *Kronhofer v Maier* [2004] ECR I-6009, discussed at **4.37** above.

[113] For the approach to be taken in relation to delocalized accounts, see **4.67** above.

provision of services, it will be the place where the claimant performed in favour of the defendant. Situations involving the discharge of a debt owed by the defendant to a third party are more problematic, as the involvement of a third party makes it more difficult to identify the country in which the defendant received the benefit of the enrichment. Three possible solutions may be suggested. First, the country in which the creditor received payment. Secondly, the country whose law applies to the debt. Thirdly, the country of the defendant debtor's domicile, as the primary place of enforcement of the debt, at least under the Brussels I Regime.[114] Of these, the first seems the most satisfactory. Although the defendant may be unaware of the payment, he may reasonably be expected to foresee the country in which his creditor will accept payment of the debt.

RULE OF DISPLACEMENT—COUNTRY HAVING A 'MANIFESTLY CLOSER CONNECTION' (ART 10(4))

Under Art 10(4), having determined the law that applies to the obligation **10.35** in question under the first three paragraphs, that law may be displaced in favour of the law of another country with which that obligation is manifestly more closely connected. This escape clause is very similar to that found in Arts 4(3) and 5(2) of the Regulation. Two initial comments may be made as to its application. First, the reference to 'a country other than that indicated in paragraphs 1, 2 and 3' should not be taken to exclude the possibility of applying the law of the country in which the enrichment took place in cases to which Art 10(1) (pre-existing relationship) or Art 10(2) (common habitual residence) applies. Art 10(3) applies only '[w]here the law applicable cannot be determined on the basis of paragraphs 1 and 2' and should not be taken to 'indicate' a law at all if either of those two paragraphs applies.[115] Secondly, it seems highly unlikely in practice that the law applicable under Art 10(1), requiring a pre-existing relationship between the parties with which the obligation is closely connected, will ever be displaced under Art 10(4).

Subject to these points, Art 10(4) should be applied in a like manner to **10.36** Art 4(3). Accordingly:

1. Art 10(4) must be considered as exceptional, requiring the party relying on it to show strong and clear reasons for displacing the law otherwise applicable under Art 10.[116]

---

[114] Brussels I Regulation, Art 2, although this rule is subject to several exceptions.
[115] For rejection of a similar argument relating to Art 4(3), see **4.89,** point 2 above.
[116] **4.85** above.

2. Art 10(4), like Art 4(3), requires the Member State court to consider 'all the circumstances of the case'. It should not limit itself to considering the matters relied on by the claimant to support the claim. Those circumstances must, however, be relevant to the question whether the obligation in question is manifestly more closely connected with a country (State B) other than that whose law would otherwise apply under Art 10 (State A). The court cannot, therefore, consider (for example) whether justice would be better served by the application of the rules of State A than by those of State B.[117]

3. The case for applying State A or State B may be strengthened (or weakened), for example, by:
(a) The existence of circumstances linking the obligation to State A or State B, including (without limitation) (a) the presence (or absence) of factual connectors other than the defendant's enrichment (Art 10(3)) or common habitual residence (Art 10(2)) linking the underlying events to State A, (b) any factual connectors linking those events to State B, (c) the personal connections of the parties and (where applicable) any other persons involved.
(b) The permanence (or transience) of the circumstances which link the obligation to State A or State B.
(c) The nature of the circumstances linking the obligation to State A or State B (and whether those linking factors were foreseeable, accidental, artificial, or open to manipulation).

4. If, in all the circumstances of the case, there is any room for doubt as to whether the obligation is more closely connected to State A than State B, the law of State A should be applied.[118]

5. Art 10(4) operates on an 'all or nothing', and not an issue by issue, basis. The court must look for connections to the 'obligation arising out of unjust enrichment' and not to the particular issues that the parties have presented for determination.[119]

---

[117] **4.86** above.
[118] **4.88** above.
[119] **4.89,** point 1 above.

11

Negotiorum Gestio

Article 11

Negotiorum gestio

1. If a non-contractual obligation arising out of an act performed without due authority in connection with the affairs of another person concerns a relationship existing between the parties, such as one arising out of a contract or a tort/delict, that is closely connected with that non-contractual obligation, it shall be governed by the law that governs that relationship.

2. Where the law applicable cannot be determined on the basis of paragraph 1, and the parties have their habitual residence in the same country when the event giving rise to the damage occurs, the law of that country shall apply.

3. Where the law applicable cannot be determined on the basis of paragraphs 1 or 2, it shall be the law of the country in which the act was performed.

4. Where it is clear from all the circumstances of the case that the non-contractual obligation arising out of an act performed without due authority in connection with the affairs of another person is manifestly more closely connected with a country other than that indicated in paragraphs 1, 2 and 3, the law of that other country shall apply.

A. INTRODUCTION

11.01 Art 11, under the heading *negotiorum gestio,* concerns non-contractual obligations arising out of acts performed without due authority in connection with the affairs of another. As in the case of unjust enrichment (Art 10),[1] Art 11 essentially retains the hierarchy of rules of applicable law within Art 9 of the Commission Proposal, which combined a provision dealing specifically with the law applicable to 'actions performed without due authority in connection with the affairs of another person'[2] with two higher ranking rules of more general application[3] and a single rule capable of displacing the law applicable under the preceding rules.[4] That said, the basic rule in the final version of Art 11, designating the law of the country in which the relevant act was performed in all cases of *negotiorum gestio,*[5] is significantly more straightforward than that contained in the Proposal, which dealt with situations involving physical protection of a person or tangible property separately from other cases.[6] The text of Art 11 corresponds substantially with that adopted by the European Parliament at its first reading stage,[7] subject to what were described as 'technical' amendments in the Amended Proposal[8] and the Common Position of the Council.[9] In particular, the Council chose to refer to 'an act performed without due authority' and to 'the country in which the act was performed'[10] rather than 'actions performed without due authority' and 'the country in which the action took place'.[11] This change, like the change in the wording of the rule for unjust enrichment referred to at **10.31** above, occurred between

---

[1] **10.08** above.

[2] Commission Proposal, Art 9(4).

[3] Designating the law governing a previously existing relationship between the parties with which the non-contractual obligation is concerned (ibid, Art 9(1)), otherwise the law of the country in which the parties have their habitual residence when the event giving rise to the damage occurs (ibid, Art 9(2)).

[4] In favour of the law of another country with which the non-contractual obligation is manifestly more closely connected (ibid, Art 9(5)).

[5] Regulation, Art 11(3).

[6] The Commission justified this distinction on the ground that 'protection' cases merited more favourable treatment for the 'agent' providing 'measures of assistance', whereas other cases involved 'interference' by the 'agent' in the affairs of the 'principal' and required the latter to be protected (Commission Proposal, 22).

[7] EP 1st Reading Position, Art 10. Also EP 1st Reading Report, 27.

[8] Commission Amended Proposal, 3.

[9] Council document 13001/05 [10.10.2005].

[10] Common Position, Art 11.

[11] EP 1st Reading Position, Art 10.

political approval of the text by the JHA Council in April 2006 and adoption of the Common Position in September 2006.[12]

B. NON-CONTRACTUAL OBLIGATION ARISING OUT OF AN ACT PERFORMED WITHOUT DUE AUTHORITY IN CONNECTION WITH THE AFFAIRS OF ANOTHER (*NEGOTIORUM GESTIO*)

As in the case of Art 10 (unjust enrichment),[13] the most difficult questions raised by Art 11 concern its material scope. In light of differences in approach between Member States whose legal systems recognize the institution of *negotiorum gestio*,[14] and the fact that other Member States (including England, Ireland, and to a lesser degree the Scandinavian systems[15]) do not collect rules dealing with situations of unauthorized intervention in another's affairs under a single heading, it is appropriate to give the concept of 'a non-contractual obligation arising out of an act performed without due authority in connection with the affairs of another' an autonomous meaning,[16] with regard to principles common to the majority of the Member States' legal systems in this area. **11.02**

The title of Art 11, *negotiorum gestio*, suggests that it is concerned with regulating non-contractual aspects of the legal relationship between two or more persons, or groups of persons, where one of them (the 'intervener') acts in connection with the affairs of another (the 'principal') in the interest of the principal, but without authority.[17] According to Professor von Bar:[18] **11.03**

The concept of *negotiorum gestio* is a solid component part of the codified civil law systems of continental Europe which have adopted it from Roman law and

---

[12] Compare Common Position, Art 11 with the corresponding text in Council document 9143/06 [19.5.2006].

[13] **10.10–10.21** above.

[14] **11.03–11.08** below.

[15] C von Bar (trans S Swann and MR McGuire), *Principles of European Law: Benevolent Intervention in Another's Affairs* (2006), paras 53–76.

[16] Cf C Brière, 'Le règlement (CE) no 864/2007 du 11 juillet 2007 sur la loi applicable aux obligations non contractuelles (Rome II)' (2008) *Journal du Droit International* 31, 50, floating the idea of characterization according to the *lex fori*.

[17] C von Bar, n 15 above, para 5 referring to the definitions in the Portuguese and Dutch Civil Codes, adding that 'The other civil codes have not expressly defined *negotiorum gestio*. However, it is possible to derive from the individual rules alone, taken as a whole, the same or at any rate a quite similar underlying basic concept.'

[18] Ibid, para 6.

continued its legal development. Among those jurisdictions there are admittedly a number of differences at the margins. That is in part attributable to the fact that the boundary to contract law is not drawn universally according to identical criteria. Some of these jurisdictions, furthermore, have demarcated the borderlines between the law of *negotiorum gestio* on the one hand and the law of tort and the law of unjustified enrichment on the other differently in response to particular issues. However, as regards the core questions of the law of benevolent intervention in another's affairs there is predominantly more common ground by far than there are points of difference.

11.04 This concept, as it is understood in continental European legal systems, is capable of embracing not only claims by the intervener against the principal (most obviously, for reimbursement of expenditure[19]) but also claims by the principal against the intervener with respect to damage caused[20] or to recover benefits received[21] by the intervener. *Negotiorum gestio* may thus be thought to describe a relationship that is essentially bilateral. As Professor Birks explains:[22]

> *Negotiorum gestio* is not properly regarded as a species of unjust enrichment. There is no doubt that the intervener's right to reimbursement turns on the utility of the intervention, not on its success. There is no inquiry at all into the enrichment of the beneficiary and hence no tie between enrichment of the beneficiary and the amount he must pay. The measure of recovery is not gain-based. Moreover, the event has wider consequences. It binds the intervener to execute his intervention with due care and skill and to surrender anything he obtains in the course of his intervention.

11.05 On the other hand, the institution of *negotiorum gestio* as it is recognized in civil law systems is generally taken to exclude:

1. Situations in which the intervener acts exclusively for his own benefit or with an intention to injure, rather than to act on behalf of, the intervener. Non-contractual obligations in such situations are generally treated as tortious, although the legal systems of a few Member States[23] recognize such situations as generating obligations analogous to those created by a 'true' *negotiorum gestio*.[24]

---

[19] Ibid, para 23. A claim of this kind, being one aspect of the relationship between intervener and principal, should not be considered to arise out of unjust enrichment within Art 10 (**10.16** above).

[20] Ibid, para 18.

[21] Ibid, para 21.

[22] P Birks,*Unjust Enrichment* (2nd edn, 2005), 23. Also C von Bar, n 15 above, para 41.

[23] Germany, Greece, Estonia, and Hungary.

[24] C von Bar, n 15 above, para 28,

2. Situations in which the intervener acts in connection with the affairs of another but in the mistaken belief that he is acting on his own behalf. Non-contractual obligations in such situations are normally categorized as tortious or as concerning unjust enrichment, although at least two Member States[25] recognize such situations as falling within *negotiorum gestio*.[26]

3. Claims by third parties against the intervener (or principal) for damage caused by the intervener's act.[27] A particular example of this is the liability of the so-called 'false procurator' who purports to create contractual relations between the principal and a counterparty. The counterparty's claim may lie in contract, for example if it rests on a separate undertaking by the agent to perform or a contractual warranty of his own authority, or be based on a non-contractual obligation, for example if the counterparty seeks compensation for damage suffered in the belief, induced by the agent's misrepresentation of his own authority, that a valid contract had been entered into.

In contrast, the English language of Art 11(1), in referring to 'a non-contractual obligation arising out of an act performed without due authority in connection with the affairs of another', might be thought to suggest a broader concept capable of embracing non-contractual obligations within all three of these categories. Although this lack of precision could be explained by the fact that 'the English legal language does not yet possess a native description for the legal obligation . . . which arises by operation of law out of the management of another's affairs',[28] it is not merely a quirk of the English text but appears in other language versions,[29] although the legal systems in the countries in question do recognize the concept of *negotiorum gestio* for which there are well-established terms of art. Other language versions, on the other hand, do use local terms of art (for example, the French ('*une gestion d'affaires*'[30]), German ('*Geschäftsführung ohne Auftrag*'[31]), Dutch ('*zaakwaarneming*'[32]), and Italian ('*una gestione d'affari altrui*'[33]) texts). When taken with the appearance of the words *negotiorum gestio* in the title of

11.06

---

[25] Italy and Portugal.

[26] C von Bar, n 15 above, para 29.

[27] Ibid, para 46 ('If the *gestor* in the course of his interventions causes damage to a third party, the claims of the third party will find their legal basis only in tort law').

[28] Ibid, para 3. The Study Group whose work is presented by Professor von Bar chose the description 'benevolent intervention in another's affairs'.

[29] For example, the Spanish ('*un acto realizado sin la debida autorización en relación con los negocios de otra persona*') and Portuguese ('*un acto relativamente a negócios alheios sem a devida autorização*').

[30] French Civil Code (*Code Civil*), Arts 1372–5.

[31] German Civil Code (*Bürgerliches Gesetzbuch*), §§677–87.

[32] Dutch Civil Code (*Burgerlijk Wetboek*), Arts 6:198–6:202.

[33] Italian Civil Code (*Codice Civile*), Arts 2028–32.

Art 11 and the text of Recital (29),[34] this terminology strongly suggests that Art 11 should be taken to exclude non-contractual obligations within the three categories described above.[35] Such cases must be dealt with under other provisions of the Regulation (most obviously, (for category 1) Art 4 (tort/delict), (for category 2) Art 4 or Art 10 (unjust enrichment), and (for category 3) Art 4 or, possibly, Art 12 (*culpa in contrahendo*).[36]

11.07 Another question on which the Member State's legal systems differ as to the requirements for *negotiorum gestio* is whether the intervention must be justified on reasonable grounds.[37] In practical terms, it would appear more difficult to define the concept of *negotiorum gestio* in the Regulation by reference to a criterion of reasonableness, and this restriction is not supported by the text of Art 11. Given that the basic requirement of an act in the interest of the principal is satisfied even if the intervention is not objectively justifiable, claims between the intervener and the principal should be considered to fall within Art 11 whether or not the intervention was objectively justified.

11.08 Further questions arise as to the relationship between Art 11 (*negotiorum gestio*) and Chapter II (tort/delict). As Professor von Bar points out, there are inconsistencies between the Member States' legal systems as to the inter-relationship between *negotiorum gestio* and tort law.[38] In order to ensure uniformity as to the law applicable to relations between the principal and the intervener, it would appear sensible to apply a single rule to all non-contractual obligations arising out of the intervener's unauthorized act, even if it concerns responsibility of the intervener or principal for damage caused to the other. Benevolent intervention may provide a defence against the principal's claims, in particular in respect of damage

---

[34] **3.247** above.

[35] Also A Rushworth and A Scott, 'Rome II: Choice of Law for Non-Contractual Obligations' [2008] LMCLQ 274, 288 who suggest a requirement that the purpose of the act be to transact the affairs of another, excluding cases within the first two categories; Max Planck Institute for Comparative and International Private International Law, Comments on the European Commission's Rome I Proposal, 133, available at <http://www.mpipriv.de/shared/data/pdf/comments_romei_proposal.pdf>.

[36] The question whether Art 12 applies to claims against the agent of a counterparty in contractual negotiations is discussed at **12.07–12.08** and **12.10,** point 3 below.

[37] C von Bar, n 15 above, paras 26–7. Book V of the Draft Common Frame of Reference (benevolent intervention in another's affairs) requires either than the intervener has a reasonable ground for acting or that the principal approves the act without such undue delay as would adversely affect the intervener (C von Bar et al. (eds), *Principles, Definitions and Model Rules of European Private Law: Draft Common Frame of Reference* (2008), available at <http://www.law-net.eu/en_index.htm>, Book V, Art 1:101(1)).

[38] C von Bar, n 15 above, para 46.

to property and personal injury,[39] and this protection, which avoids a potential disincentive to benevolent intervention, would potentially be undermined by characterizing a claim for damage, whether by principal or agent, as one in tort/delict (Art 4), potentially governed by a different law from a claim by the intervener for reimbursement of expenses or a claim by the principal for recovery of benefits falling within Art 11. Within the Rome II Regulation, therefore, the argument for giving priority to Art 11 over Art 4 and treating all non-contractual obligations arising from the intervener's unauthorized act as falling within Art 11 would appear, at first sight, to be a strong one.

There may, however, be reason to doubt the correctness of that conclusion. **11.09** In *Masdar (UK) Ltd v Commission*,[40] a case concerning the non-contractual liability of the Community under Art 288 of the EC Treaty, the claimant argued that 'the general principles common to the laws of the Member States' referred to in that article included actions for unjust enrichment and *negotiorum gestio*. In the case of *negotiorum gestio*, the claimant submitted that the principles common to the Member States' legal systems included the following elements:[41]

- the management of the principal's affairs, whether legal or material, must benefit the principal;
- at the relevant time the principal was unable to manage his own affairs, but there was a need for his affairs to be managed;
- the manager had no intention to act gratuitously—there was no *animus donandi*;
- the manager was under no contractual obligation to manage the affairs of the principal;
- the principal could reasonably have been expected to take the action undertaken by the manager had the principal been aware of the need for action.

The Court of First Instance accepted that the non-contractual liability of **11.10** the Community under Art 288 could, in principle, be based on *negotiorum gestio* but did not consider it necessary to consider these elements individually, ruling that (on the facts of the case before it) the fact that the claimant had provided services under a contract with a third party and had a contractual remedy against that party excluded the possibility of an action against the Commission based on *negotiorum gestio*.[42] The Court also held, however, that the action was precluded in the case before it by the fact that

---

[39] Ibid.
[40] Case T-333/07 [2006] ECR II-4377.
[41] Ibid, para 76.
[42] Ibid, paras 97–100.

(a) the claimant had contacted the Commission before acting, so it could not be considered to have acted benevolently, (b) the Commission was in a position to act in its own interests, and (c) the Commission was aware of the claimant's action whereas, according to the principles common to the Member States, the principal must either be unaware of the need to act or at least unaware of the need to act immediately.[43]

11.11 On the claimant's appeal against this decision, Adv Gen Mazár in his opinion rejected the *negotiorum gestio* claim for essentially the same reasons as the Court of First Instance.[44] His following comments may, however, be thought to bear upon the autonomous meaning to the words used to define the category of *negotiorum gestio* within Art 11:[45]

> [*Art 288 of the EC Treaty*] cannot be understood as meaning that the principles governing non-contractual liability applied by the Community Courts must—or even could—exactly correspond to those existing in the laws of all the Member States or that they could somehow be deduced 'mechanically' as common denominators from those laws. To a certain extent, therefore, as is generally the case with general principles of law as a legal source, until there is settled case-law on the matter discussing the concrete content of such a principle can be very much like discussing the shape of a ghost. *The solution applied by the Court of First Instance in the framework of Article 288 EC should, however, be inspired by the basic characteristics of the relevant concepts in the national legal orders, adapted, where necessary, to meet the specific requirements of Community law.*

> That being said, as to the *de in rem verso* and *negotiorum gestio* actions relied upon by in the present case, a comparison of the legal orders of the Member States reveals a great diversity as regards their recognition and application.

> In general, however, the attitude of the legal systems of the Member States in that regard can be characterised as very cautious, and this applies even more so to *negotiorum gestio* than to unjust enrichment. *Whilst the former principle, in particular, is even unknown in certain legal orders, it can be said that where those principles exist as a foundation of liability, it is generally possible to rely on them only under strict conditions and as a subsidiary means of redress.* As a rule, those actions or principles function as 'gap fillers' and pleas of last resort inspired by general considerations of justice and equity, which is why in many instances they have been recognised and developed mainly by the judiciary.

11.12 Although one must be wary of carrying over principles developed in one area of EC law into a different area and of confusing rules of substantive law with those of private international law, the Advocate General's view as to the principles common to the Member States' legal systems might be

---

[43] Ibid, para 101.
[44] Case C-47/07P, Opinion of 12 June 2008, paras 40–65.
[45] Ibid, paras 45–9 (emphasis added).

thought to support a restrictive and subordinate view of Art 11 and its role within the Rome II Regulation. Although *Masdar v Commission* concerned the relationship of *negotiorum gestio* with contract and not with tort,[46] the relationship between Art 4 and Art 11 within the Regulation remains to be settled along with other aspects of Art 11's material scope.

NEGOTIORUM GESTIO AND ENGLISH LAW

At this point, the question must be asked whether Art 11 has any possible **11.13** relevance for the English substantive law of obligations. The traditional view is that the English common law has rejected any notion of *negotiorum gestio*.[47] That view has recently been challenged.[48] In practice, English law recognizes a number of claims and defences that, collectively and in certain situations, replicate many of the features of the civilian doctrine. These include cases of agency of necessity that do not rest on a pre-existing agency relationship between the parties,[49] rules governing the duty of care owed by and to rescuers,[50] necessity as a defence in cases of trespass to the person[51] and other intentional torts when the necessity relates to saving the claimant's person or property,[52] cases dealt with under the law of bailment where (by finding or otherwise) the 'bailee' takes possession of property on behalf of but without the knowledge of the 'bailor',[53] and a miscellany of cases at common law and under statute.[54] From the former domain of

---

[46] Professor von Bar suggests (n 15 above, para 46) that '[b]y contrast *[with contract]* there is no scope for a subsidiarity of the law on benevolent intervention in relation to the other extra-contractual legal relationships—in particular in the relationship to tort law and unjustified enrichment law . . .'.

[47] *Re F* [1990] 2 AC 1, 44 (Butler-Sloss LJ (EWCA)) referring to *Falcke v Scottish Imperial Insurance Co* (1886) 34 Ch D 234, 248 (Bowen LJ (EWCA)). Compare the analysis of Lord Goff in the same case ([1990] 2 AC 1, 74–5 (UKHL)).

[48] P Birks, n 22 above, 23–4; D Sheehan, 'Negotiorum: A Civilian Concept in the Common Law' (2006) 55 ICLQ 253.

[49] F Reynolds, *Bowstead & Reynolds on Agency* (17th edn, 2006), ch 4; D Sheehan, n 48 above, 269–71; C von Bar, n 15 above, 66–7. Cases arising within an existing agency relationship are better viewed as concerning incidents of that relationship and as being contractual in nature,

[50] A M Dugdale and M A Jones (eds), *Clerk & Lindsell on Torts* (19th edn, 2006), paras 8-29 to 8-32.

[51] *Re F*, n 47 above.

[52] Cf *Clerk & Lindsell on Torts*, n 50 above, para 3-116.

[53] *Great Northern Railway Co v Swaffield* (1874) LR 9 Exch 132; C von Bar, n 15 above, 71. For the treatment of bailment under the Regulation, see **3.143–3.145**.

[54] e.g. payment of funeral expenses (*Jenkins v Tucker* (1788) 1 Hy Bl 90); the provision of necessaries to a lunatic (*Re Rhodes* (1890) 44 ChD 94); acceptance of a bill of exchange for honour (Bills of Exchange Act 1882, ss 65–8); payment of fees to professional medics following road traffic accidents (Road Traffic Act 1988, ss 157–9). For discussion of these and other suggested

the courts of equity, the rules concerning the rights and obligations of the trustee *de son tort* and of shadow directors[55] also concern interventions in the affairs of others.

11.14 Ultimately, whether situations covered by the English law rules described above can be fitted within Art 11 will depend on how broadly the concept of 'an act performed without due authority in connection with the affairs of another' is interpreted. The absence of the label *negotiorum gestio* in English law cannot be decisive. If it requires only that the obligation in question arises, in fact, from the performance by one of the parties on behalf of or otherwise for the benefit of another (even if it does not benefit him) then most of the situations just described will be sucked in. If, however, it requires that the intervener's act generates rights and obligations between principal and intervener that are reciprocal and not dissimilar from those arising under a contract, the territory occupied by Art 11 under English law will be much more limited. Arguably, only the cases of agency of necessity outside contract, involuntary bailment, the trustee *de son tort*, and shadow directors may fit within this narrower description.

SALVAGE

11.15 In its response to the Commission's preliminary draft proposal, the Hamburg Group, a collaboration of German scholars, commented:[56]

> The most commonly discussed case of *negotiorum gestio* in the conflict of laws was the case of a ship rendering help to another ship. Nevertheless it is not advisable to design a rule especially for this case. In modern times such cases mostly fall into the realm of contract and are not left to *negotiorum gestio*. The small remainder not ruled by contract will most likely be governed by the Convention on Salvage. It appears even more unnecessary to provide for a specific conflicts rule since there would be a kind of deadlock to choose between the flag of the helping ship and the flag of the ship to which help is rendered, as the appropriate connecting factor.

---

examples, see C von Bar, n 15 above, paras 60–76; D Sheehan, n 48 above, 269–78; A Burrows, *The Law of Restitution* (2nd edn, 2002), ch 9.

[55] **3.142, 3.162, 3.193** and **4.100** above.

[56] Hamburg Group for Private International Law, Comments on the European Commission's Draft Proposal for a Council Regulation on the Law Applicable to Non-Contractual Obligations, 34, reproduced at <http://www.mpipriv.de/de/data/pdf/com-mentshamburggroup.pdf>.

The Convention on Salvage to which the group refers is the London **11.16**
International Convention on salvage.[57] That Convention partly superseded the Brussels Convention for the unification of certain rules of law
relating to assistance and salvage at sea.[58] The two Salvage Conventions
contain detailed substantive rules regulating salvage claims. Art 15(2) of
the London Salvage Convention, however, contains rules of applicable
law regulating questions of apportionment between salvors, which may
apply to non-contractual obligations. Art 15 provides as follows:

1. The apportionment of a reward under article 13 between salvors shall be made
on the basis of the criteria contained in that article.

2. The apportionment between the owner, master and other persons in the service
of each salving vessel shall be determined by the law of the flag of that vessel. If
the salvage has not been carried out from a vessel, the apportionment shall be
determined by the law governing the contract between the salvor and his
servants.

Of the Member States, 18 are parties to the London Salvage Convention.[59] **11.17**
Of the remainder, six are parties to the Brussels Salvage Convention.[60]
Bulgaria, Czech Republic, and Slovakia are parties to neither Salvage
Convention. The last two named States are land-locked, although
ships may sail under their flag.[61] Accordingly, in proceedings arising
from non-contractual salvage on the high seas brought before the courts
of these States, which would not be required to give mandatory effect
to either Salvage Convention, Art 11 of the Rome II Regulation could
lead to the application of the law of a State not party to either Convention
if the owners of both ships had their habitual residence in the same
non-party State[62] or, arguably, if the salvaged vessel flies the flag of a

---

[57] Signed, 29 April 1989. In force, 14 July 1996 (the **London Salvage Convention**). The text
of the Convention is available at <http://untreaty.un.org/English/UNEP/salvage_english.
pdf>. For UK rules, see Merchant Shipping Act 1995, Part IX and Sch 11 (salvage and wreck);
Civil Aviation Act 1982, s 87.

[58] Signed, 23 September 1910, as amended by a Protocol dated 27 May 1967 (the **Brussels
Salvage Convention**). The text of the Convention is available at <http://www.admiralty-
lawguide.com/conven/salvage1910.html> and the Protocol at <http://www.admiralty-
lawguide.com/conven/protosalvage1967.html>.

[59] Belgium, Denmark, Estonia, Finland, France, Germany, Greece, Ireland, Italy,
Latvia, Lithuania, Netherlands, Poland, Romania, Slovakia, Spain, Sweden, United Kingdom
(Source: International Maritime Organisation <http://www.imo.org/includes/blastDataOnly.
asp/data_id%3D22499/status-x.xls>).

[60] Austria, Cyprus, Hungary, Luxembourg, Malta, Portugal. (Source: Swiss Confereration
website <http://www.admin.ch/ch/f/rs/i7/0.747.363.2.fr.pdf>).

[61] UN Convention on the law of the sea (1833 UNTS 397), Art 90.

[62] Art 11(2).

non-party State.[63] Art 11 may also apply to cases of salvage, or similar institutions recognized under national law, on inland waterways.[64] Even so, Art 11 would appear to be of limited significance in this context and the Hamburg Group was undoubtedly correct to reject the need for an additional special rule dealing with salvage matters.

C. THE LAW APPLICABLE TO NON-CONTRACTUAL OBLIGATIONS IN SITUATIONS OF *NEGOTIORUM GESTIO*

First Level—Law Governing Relationship Existing between the Parties with which Obligation is Concerned (Art 11(1))

11.18 Under Art 11(1), a non-contractual obligation arising out of an act performed without due authority in connection with the affairs of another person that concerns and is closely connected to a 'relationship existing between the parties' shall be governed by the law that governs that relationship. This sub-rule is in materially identical terms to Art 10(1), considered in the preceding chapter.[65] In this connection, the Commission suggests that this sub-rule will be important, for example, 'where an agent exceeds his authority or where a third-party debt is settled'. In the former example, it can readily be seen that the law applicable to the existing relationship between principal and agent has a strong claim to govern claims between the principal and agent with respect to the act performed in connection with the principal's affairs without authority, whether because the obligations underlying such claims are properly seen as being incidents of that relationship and as falling within the Rome I Regime and not the Rome II Regulation or because, as non-contractual obligations, they are very closely related to it. The latter example, however, is less compelling, as a claim may be brought arising from the discharge of a debt (for example, by acceptance of a bill of exchange for honour) if there is no pre-existing relationship between the parties.

11.19 It is also difficult to think of situations in which the example of a relationship existing between the parties 'arising out of . . . a tort/delict' will be relevant.[66] A possible example would be if the defendant's wrongful act towards the

---

[63] Art 11(3) (**11.21** below). In such a case, it would appear preferable to treat the act of salvage as having been 'performed' on board the salvaged vessel.

[64] Cf *The Goring* [1988] 1 AC 831 (UKHL).

[65] **10.23–10.27**.

[66] **10.25–10.26** above.

claimant has put both parties in danger and one of them takes steps to rescue the other. It may be the wording was copied from what is now Art 10(1) into Art 11(1) without considering whether it served any useful purpose.[67]

SECOND LEVEL—COUNTRY OF COMMON HABITUAL RESIDENCE (ART 11(2))

Art 11(2), which applies if there is no close connection between the obliga- **11.20** tion in question and a pre-existing relationship, refers to the law of the parties' common habitual residence. This sub-rule is materially identical to Art 10(2), also considered in the preceding chapter.[68]

THIRD LEVEL—COUNTRY IN WHICH THE ACT WAS PERFORMED (ART 11(3))

If neither Art 11(1) (pre-existing relationship) nor Art 11(2) (common **11.21** habitual residence) applies, the law applicable to a non-contractual obligation arising out of *negotiorum gestio* is the law of the country in which the intervener's act was performed.[69] This may be thought unlikely to give rise to any difficulty in its application, except perhaps in cases in which the act takes place in an area outside State sovereignty such as the high seas or on a ship or aircraft in transit, in which cases it may be argued that the law of the flag or registration State should apply.[70] As Art 11(3) is arguably the least significant, from a legal and economic viewpoint, of the rules of applicable law in Chapters II and III of the Regulation, these problems are scarcely worth worrying about unless and until they arise in practice.

RULE OF DISPLACEMENT—COUNTRY HAVING A 'MANIFESTLY CLOSER CONNECTION' (ART 11(4))

Under Art 10(4), having determined the law that applies to the obligation **11.22** in question under the first three paragraphs, that law may be displaced in favour of the law of another country with which that obligation is manifestly more closely connected. This sub-rule is in materially identical terms to Art 10(4), also considered in the preceding chapter.[71]

---

[67] The wording first appeared in a draft circulated by the outgoing Dutch and incoming Luxembourg Presidencies in late 2004 (Council document 16231/04 [20.12.2004], Art 9B).
[68] **10.28**.
[69] Art 11(3).
[70] **4.55–4.57** and text to n 63 above. Also A Rushworth and A Scott, n 35 above, 289.
[71] **10.35** above.

12

Culpa in Contrahendo

Article 12

Culpa in contrahendo

1. The law applicable to a non-contractual obligation arising out of dealings prior to the conclusion of a contract, regardless of whether the contract was actually concluded or not, shall be the law that applies to the contract or that would have been applicable to it had it been entered into.

2. Where the law applicable cannot be determined on the basis of paragraph 1, it shall be:
(a) the law of the country in which the damage occurs, irrespective of the country in which the event giving rise to the damage occurred and irrespective of the country or countries in which the indirect consequences of that event occurred; or
(b) where the parties have their habitual residence in the same country at the time when the event giving rise to the damage occurs, the law of that country; or
(c) where it is clear from all the circumstances of the case that the non-contractual obligation arising out of dealings prior to the conclusion of a contract is manifestly more closely connected with a country other than that indicated in points (a) and (b), the law of that other country.

A. INTRODUCTION

12.01 Art 12, under the heading *culpa in contrahendo*, concerns non-contractual
obligations arising out of dealings prior to the conclusion of a contract,
whether the contract was concluded or not. The Commission Proposal
contained no specific rule dealing with the category of obligations recognized in many civil law systems, albeit in different forms, under the title
or description *culpa in contrahendo*.[1] In *Tacconi v Wagner*, decided less
than a year before publication of the Proposal, the Court of Justice had
held that an obligation to make good the damage caused by the unjustified breaking off of contractual negotiations fell within Art 5(3) of the
Brussels Convention (matters relating to tort, delict, or quasi-delict).[2]
Referring to that decision, the Commission noted that there may be doubts
as to whether pre-contractual liability under the heading *culpa in contrahendo* was to be considered as a contractual obligation within the scope of
the Rome Convention and any successor instrument, or as a tort/delict
within the proposed Rome II instrument.[3] The Commission concluded
that the ECJ 'will no doubt refine its analysis when interpreting the proposed Regulation', and left matters there.

12.02 Art 12 emerged, therefore, from the work of the Council's Rome II Committee
leading to the adoption of the Common Position.[4] Some Member State
delegations pressed for separate treatment of *culpa in contrahendo* at an
early stage in discussions,[5] and a rule based on the wording suggested by
the Swedish and Spanish delegations first appeared (in square brackets) in
a draft circulated by the outgoing Dutch and incoming Luxembourg
Presidencies in December 2004.[6] Subsequently, the German delegation
proposed separating the law applicable to violations of pre-contractual
duties of disclosure/advice (which, under the German proposal, were to
be governed by the law that would have applied to the contract had it
been entered into) and other non-contractual obligations arising out of

---

[1] C von Bar, *The Common European Law of Torts*, vol 1 (1998, reprint 2003), paras 472–6;
C von Bar and U Drobnig, 'Study on Property Law and Non-contractual Liability Law as they
relate to Contract Law' (SANCO B5-1000/02/000574), paras 343–56 (available at <http://ec.
europa.eu/consumers/cons_int/safe_shop/fair_bus_pract/cont_law/study.pdf>).

[2] Case C-334/00, *Fonderie Officine Meccaniche Tacconi SpA v Heinrich Wagner Sinto
Maschinenfabrik GmbH* [2002] ECR I-7357.

[3] Commission Proposal, 8.

[4] Common Position, Art 12.

[5] Council document 11801/04 [28.7.2004], 2.

[6] Council document 16231/04 [20.12.2004]. Also Council document 9009/04 ADD 8
[18.5.2004], 14 (Sweden).

pre-contractual duties, for example duties to protect the integrity of the other person (which, under the proposal, were to be governed by the general rules of applicable law for torts/delicts).[7] That proposal was rejected.[8] Instead, the Rome II Committee (after some debate[9]) preferred a rule based on the law applicable to the contract or contemplated contract between the parties, following the original Swedish and Spanish proposal, with an additional default rule dealing with situations in which the law applicable 'cannot be determined' on that basis.

B. NON-CONTRACTUAL OBLIGATION ARISING OUT OF DEALINGS PRIOR TO THE CONCLUSION OF A CONTRACT (*CULPA IN CONTRAHENDO*)[10]

DEALINGS PRIOR TO THE CONCLUSION OF A CONTRACT

Art 12 must be read together with Recital (30), which provides: **12.03**

Culpa in contrahendo for the purposes of this Regulation is an autonomous concept and should not necessarily be interpreted within the meaning of national law. It should include the violation of the duty of disclosure and the breakdown of contractual negotiations. Article 12 covers only non-contractual obligations presenting a direct link with the dealings prior to the conclusion of a contract. This means that if, while a contract is being negotiated, a person suffers personal injury, Article 4 or other relevant provisions of this Regulation should apply.

The expression *culpa in contrahendo* that appears in the title but not in the   **12.04** text of Art 12 suggests that focus is on responsibility for blameworthy conduct occurring before the making of a contract.[11] The opposing view that fault should not be an essential element in non-contractual obligations falling within Art 12, the text of which refers more neutrally to 'a non-contractual obligation arising out of dealings prior to the conclusion of a contract', is supported by the statement in Recital (11) that 'the conflict-of-law rules set out in this Regulation should also cover non-contractual obligations arising out of strict liability'. Accordingly, on this view, Art 12 would be

---

[7] Council document 7928/06 [30.3.2006], 2.

[8] Council document 7709/06 [3.5.2006], 3–4.

[9] Ibid, 4, in which many delegations supported an option based on the law of the country in which damage occurred (see Council document 7432/06 [16.3.2006], Art 9C, option 2).

[10] R A Garcia, '*La regulación de la responsabilidad precontractual en el Reglamento Roma II*' (2007) Anuario Español de Derecho Internacional Privado, available at <http://adipr.files.wordpress.com/2008/04/responsabilidad-precontractual-adipr2.pdf> (Spanish language with English abstract).

[11] C von Bar, n 1 above, para 472.

capable of extending, for example, to liability for an innocent misrepresentation made during contractual negotiations. That said, reference in the title to *culpa in contrahendo* and the correspondence between the rules in Art 10(2) and those in Art 4 (tort/delict) may be taken to confirm that Art 12 concerns claims founded on the conduct of the defendant in the pre-contractual period. If so, a claim (for example) to recover reasonable remuneration for goods provided or services performed by the claimant in anticipation of a contract[12] would fall within Art 10 (unjust enrichment), not Art 12.[13]

12.05 The rules of applicable law contained in Art 12 apply 'regardless of whether the contract was actually concluded'. Thus, it extends beyond situations in which responsibility attaches to the avoidance of contractual obligations (e.g. through breach of a duty to act in good faith during negotiations or premature revocation of an offer) to include other situations in which pre-contractual dealings affect a contract actually concluded between the parties so as to attract civil liability (e.g. through misrepresentation, breach of a duty to disclose material facts,[14] or intimidation). Art 12 requires, however, a concluded or contemplated *contract* and does not apply to dealings leading to other types of transaction, for example in relation to the transfer of property or the creation or transfer of financial instruments not constituting contracts. Accordingly, a claim based on the English doctrine of proprietary estoppel, which has elements in common with the civil law doctrine of *culpa in contrahendo*,[15] would not fit within Art 12. If such a claim falls within the scope of the Regulation at all,[16] it must be dealt with under Art 4 (tort/delict).

12.06 According to Recital (30), there must be a direct link with the dealings prior to the conclusion of a contract, with the consequence that Art 4 or other relevant provisions of the Regulation will apply if a person suffers personal

---

[12] Under English law, a claim of this kind would be pursued by means of the common law action for a *quantum meruit* or *quantum valebat* (A Burrows, *The Law of Restitution* (2nd edn, 2002), 372–81; *Yeoman's Row Management Limited v Cobbe* [2008] UKHL 55).

[13] Cf A Rushworth and A Scott, 'Rome II: Choice of law for non-contractual obligations' [2008] LMCLQ 274, 290.

[14] This includes duties of pre-contractual disclosure imposed by national rules implementing EC legislation such as Art 3 of Directive (EC) No 94/47 on the protection of purchasers in respect of certain aspects of contracts relating to the purchase of the right to use immovable properties on a timeshare basis (OJ L280, 83 [29.10.1994]; Art 4 of Directive (EC) No 97/7 on the protection of consumers in respect of distance contracts (OJ L144, 19 [4.6.1997]); Arts 5–6 and 10 of Directive (EC) No 2000/31 on electronic commerce (OJ L178, 1 [17.7.2000]); Arts 3–5 of Directive (EC) No 2002/165 concerning the distance marketing of consumer financial services (OJ L271, 16 [9.10.2002]).

[15] C von Bar and U Drobnig, n 1 above, paras 353 and 355.

[16] **3.189** and **4.106** above.

injury while a contract is being negotiated or otherwise anticipated. The purpose of this statement would appear to be to exclude from Art 12 situations in which the parties' pre-contractual relationship provides only the context within which wider legal obligations to protect the person and property of a party are imposed.[17] For example, in a 1961 decision of the German Federal Supreme Court,[18] a customer entered a department store and slipped on a banana skin resulting in injury. The Court held that the obligation to examine the floor of the store for objects of this kind was part of the store's duty arising from *culpa in contrahendo*.[19] Under the Rome II Regulation, however, Recital (30) makes clear that a claim of this type should be characterized as arising out of a tort/delict and the applicable law determined by reference to Art 4. Equally, a claim with respect to damage caused by a product during pre-contractual testing should fall within Art 5 (product liability).

As the primary connecting factor within Art 12 is the law applicable to a **12.07** contract, either concluded or contemplated, there is a strong argument for restricting its scope to claims between the (intended) parties to the contract so as to exclude (for example) a claim for damages by one of the parties against the issuer of securities that he has purchased on the market or the agent of another for misrepresentation or as a false procurator.[20] There may, of course, be good reasons for concluding that claims against an agent, whether in contract or in tort/delict, should be governed under the Rome I Regime or Art 4 of the Rome II Regulation by the law of the contract (*lex contractus*), especially if he has taken an active part in negotiations conducted on the basis of drafts containing a choice of law provision. Art 12, however, would appear to contemplate an existing or contemplated contractual relationship between the parties to the non-contractual obligation.[21] That view is consistent, for example, with the approach taken under English law to liability for misrepresentation, providing a separate claim for damages as between the contracting parties only.[22] Section 311(3) of the German Civil Code (*Bürgerliches Gesetzbuch*) provides, however, that:

An obligation with duties under section 241(2)[23] may also come into existence in relation to persons who are not themselves intended to be parties to the contract.

---

[17] C von Bar, n 1 above, paras 190 and 477.

[18] *Bundesgerichtshof* (BGH), 26.9.1961, NJW 1962, 31.

[19] The summary is taken from C von Bar, n 1 above, para 190.

[20] **12.10** below.

[21] To the same effect, A Rushworth and A Scott, n 13 above, 290.

[22] Misrepresentation Act 1967, s 2(1) referring to 'a misrepresentation. . . by another party'; *Resolute Maritime Inc v Nippon Kaiji Kyokai (The Skopas)* [1983] 1 WLR 857 (EWHC).

[23] BGB, Art 241(2) refers to an obligation 'take account of the rights, legal interests and other interests of the other party'.

Such an obligation comes into existence in particular if the third party, by laying claim to being given a particularly high degree of trust, substantially influences the pre-contract negotiations or the entering into of the contract.

12.08 The language of Recital (30) (**12.03** above) reduces the significance of comparative analysis of this kind, which in any event is inconclusive. On balance, therefore, claims by or against the representatives of negotiating or contracting parties should be considered to fall outside Art 12, although the contract or supposed contract to which the agent's conduct relates should be considered as a circumstance to be taken into account in applying a flexible rule of displacement such as that in Art 4(3) of the Rome II Regulation or in identifying the law applicable under the Rome I Regime to any contract between agent and counterparty.

NOT A 'CONTRACTUAL OBLIGATION'—INTERACTION
WITH THE ROME I REGULATION

12.09 The subject matter of Art 12 will almost certainly place it at the heart of the debate as to the relationship between the Rome II Regulation and the Rome I Regime concerning the law applicable to contractual obligations.[24] In common with the other provisions of the Rome II instrument, Art 12 only applies to 'non-contractual obligations', a negative concept that excludes matters falling within the horizontal or vertical scope of the Rome I Regulation. For example, as the issue of the material or formal validity of a contract as well as the consequences of nullity of the contract fall within the scope of the Rome I Regime,[25] it seems likely that the rules of applicable law contained in that instrument, and not Art 12 of the Rome II Regulation, will apply to a claim to avoid a contract and to any other obligations, for example to restore benefits or compensate for losses, triggered by the success of that claim. Thus, under English law, rescission of a contract for misrepresentation or duress involves a 'giving back and a taking back on both sides'[26] and may require the defendant to indemnify the claimant with respect to obligations assumed by the latter in accordance with the terms of the contract.[27] These obligations to restore benefits, and resume burdens, should be considered as matters of 'contractual obligation' falling within the Rome I Regime.[28] On the other hand, a claim for

---

[24] For more detailed discussion, see **3.104–3.145** above.

[25] Rome Convention, Arts 8, 9, and 10(1)(e); Rome I Regulation, Arts 10, 11, and 12(1)(e).

[26] *Newbigging v Adam* (1886) 34 Ch D 582, 595 (Bowen LJ, EWCA).

[27] *Whittington v Seale-Hayne* (1900) 82 LT 49 (EWCA).

[28] **3.108** above. Cf *Dimskal Shipping Co SA v International Transport Workers Federation, The Evia Luck* [1992] 2 AC 152 (UKHL), discussed by J Bird (at 127–8), P Brereton (at 169–72) and R Stevens (at 199–202) in F Rose (ed), *Restitution and the Conflict of Laws* (1995). Also Sir

damages between contracting parties[29] that arises out of the same conduct as is relied on to avoid the contract but which does not depend for its success on the avoidance of the contract should be seen as 'non-contractual' and falling within Art 12 of the Rome II Regulation.[30]

Certain obligations recognized under English law raise more difficult **12.10** questions of characterization, as follows:

1. English law recognizes, for certain types of contract, a duty to make full disclosure of material facts. That obligation, which may lead to the setting aside of the contract but does not itself support a claim in damages, should be considered as a matter of contractual obligation. In *Agnew v Länsföräkringsbolakens AB*,[31] the House of Lords held that an obligation of this kind fell within Art 5(1) of the Brussels Convention as a matter relating to a contract. Lord Millett, who in a dissenting judgment concluded that neither Art 5(1) nor Art 5(3) of the Brussels Convention applied to a contractual condition precedent of this kind (whether express or implied),[32] commented:[33]

It is tempting to equate the duty of the insured to make a fair presentation of the risk with the obligation of good faith which obtains in civil law systems, but it would in my view be a mistake to do so. French law recognises a general '*obligation de bonne foi dans la formation des contrats*', breach of which gives rise to liability in delict. German law has embraced the concept of '*culpa in contrahendo*', which gives rise to liability whether or not a contract is concluded, and accordingly is also not considered to be based on contract. But both sound in damages, and thus differ from the English doctrine, which is incapable of giving rise to contractual or tortious liability whether or not a contract is concluded but merely serves to render any resulting contract voidable.

L Collins et al. (eds), *Dicey, Morris & Collins: The Conflict of Laws* (14th edn, 2006), para 34-022.

[29] e.g., as a matter of English law, under s 2(1) of the Misrepresentation Act 1967.

[30] A Rushworth and A Scott, n 13 above, 290.

[31] [2001] 1 AC 223 (UKHL).

[32] Ibid, 262–7. His Lordship took the view (at 266) that the reference in Art 5(1) of the Brussels Convention to an 'obligation in question' must be limited to an obligation non-performance of which gives rise to contractual liability, and does not extend to what, when properly analysed, is merely a condition precedent to the formation of a fully binding contract. He also doubted (ibid) whether the so-called obligation to make full disclosure has any place of performance within the meaning of that expression in Art 5(1). As to the second submission, see the later decision of the ECJ in Case C-256/00, *Besix SA v Wassereinigungsbau Alfred Krezschmar GmbH & Co KG* [2002] ECR I-1699. These arguments do not, however, impact on the relationship between 'contractual' and 'non-contractual' obligations in the Rome I Regime and the Rome II Regulation.

[33] Ibid, 265. Compare the approach of Lord Hope in his dissenting judgment (ibid, 253–4). The majority considered the disclosure obligation to be contractual.

Claims of this type to set aside a contract on the ground of non-disclosure fall within the Rome I Regime as concerning either the material validity of the contract[34] or the extinction of obligations.[35]

2. Under s 2(2) of the Misrepresentation Act 1967, an English court may award damages in lieu of rescission for misrepresentation, except in cases of fraud. In *Morin v Bonhams & Brooks Ltd* a claim under s 2(2) was treated as a claim in tort for the purposes of determining the law applicable to it under the pre-existing English statutory rules in the Private International Law (Miscellaneous Provisions) Act 1995.[36] It appears, however, artificial to separate the damages claim under s 2(2) from the question whether the contract should be set aside for misrepresentation in the first place, a question that is clearly a matter of contractual obligation.[37] The power to award damages under s 2(2) of the 1967 Act should be seen as subordinate to the power that the section confers on a court or tribunal to declare a contract as subsisting despite the existence of a misrepresentation that would otherwise justify its rescission. Both elements should be seen as contractual in nature falling within the Rome I Regime.

3. A claim by a party to a supposed contract against the agent of his counterparty who has acted in excess of his authority will fall outside Art 12 if, as suggested above, the rule is restricted to claims between the contracting parties.[38] Whichever view is taken on that point, the agent's liability may fall to be characterized as contractual, within the Rome I Regime,[39] or non-contractual, within the Rome II Regulation. If the claimant seeks to establish the agent's responsibility for his own or the principal's non-performance of obligations under the contract (for example, on the basis of a contractual warranty of authority[40]), the claim should be seen as contractual, having as its basis an obligation voluntarily assumed by the agent towards the claimant. If, however, the claimant seeks to recover damages for losses suffered by him in negotiating with the agent and in attempting

---

[34] Rome Convention, Art 8(1); Rome I Regulation, Art 10(1).

[35] Rome Convention, Art 10(1)(d); Rome I Regulation, Art 12(1)(d).

[36] [2003] EWHC 467 (Comm); [2003] 2 All ER (Comm) 36, [29] (Jonathan Hirst QC, EWHC). The judge's decision as to the law applicable was upheld on appeal ([2003] EWCA Civ 1802; [2004] 1 Lloyd's Rep 702) without considering this point.

[37] Rome Convention, Art 8(1); Rome I Regulation, Art 10(1) (material validity).

[38] **12.07–12.08** above.

[39] Art 1(2)(d) of the Rome Convention and Art 1(2)(g) of the Rome I Regulation exclude from their scope the question whether an agent is able to bind his principal to a third party. That exclusion, however, does not extend to relations between the principal and agent or the agent and third party which are included in so far as they are of a contractual nature (Giuliano & Lagarde Report (OJ C282, 13 [31.10.1980])).

[40] F Reynolds, *Bowstead & Reynolds on Agency* (18th edn, 2006), paras 9-060 to 9-072.

to perform the contract on the faith of the agent's misrepresentation as to his own authority, the claim should be seen as non-contractual, falling within Art 12 or (on the view taken above) Art 4.

The foregoing examples concern situations in which a contract has actually **12.11** been concluded. If, on the other hand, the claim is based on conduct of the defendant that has prevented a contract from being concluded,[41] the obligation in question should be considered as non-contractual, even if the Member State seised of the dispute or the State whose law would apply under Art 12 would adopt a different classification under its national law.[42]

In this context, the debate as to whether a particular obligation is 'contrac- **12.12** tual' or 'non-contractual' is largely academic, as the basic rule in Art 12(1) points strongly towards application of the law that applies to the contract under the Rome I Regime. Nevertheless, cases may arise in which the question of characterization will prove to be significant, for example, if there is said to be a difference as to the scope of the law applicable,[43] if one of the parties seeks to rely on rules of safety and conduct in the place where the defendant acted,[44] or if a claim is brought against the insurer of the person liable.[45]

C. THE LAW APPLICABLE TO NON-CONTRACTUAL OBLIGATIONS ARISING FROM *CULPA IN CONTRAHENDO*

In determining the law applicable to a non-contractual obligation arising **12.13** out of dealings prior to the conclusion of a contract (*culpa in contrahendo*), Art 12 operates in two stages. The first stage (Art 12(1)) refers, according to whether the contract was actually concluded, to the law that applies to the contract or the law that would have applied to the contract if it had been entered into. At the second stage (Art 12(2)), which applies only if the law applicable 'cannot be determined' at the first stage, the rules are almost identical to those in Art 4 for tort/delict generally.

---

[41] As in *Tacconi v Wagner*, n 2 above.
[42] In some Member States (including Germany and Greece), *culpa in contrahendo* is seen as contractual in character. For a comparative survey, see the materials referred to at n 1 above.
[43] Rome Convention, Arts 8-10; Rome I Regulation, Arts 10–12; Rome II Regulation, Art 15.
[44] Rome II Regulation, Art 17. Cf Rome Convention, Art 10(2); Rome I Regulation, Art 12(2).
[45] Rome II Regulation, Art 18.

FIRST STAGE—THE LAW THAT APPLIES (OR WOULD HAVE APPLIED)
TO THE CONTRACT (ART 12(1))

12.14 If a contract has been concluded between the parties,[46] a non-contractual
obligation arising out of dealings prior to the conclusion of the contract
will be governed by the law applicable to the contract, determined in
accordance with the rules of the Rome I Regime.[47] As every contract has a
governing law,[48] that law must be capable of being determined in every
case of this kind. Accordingly, in such cases, there is no possibility of a
different law being applied by reference to Art 12(2). The law applicable
to the contract between the parties can be displaced only by an agreement
between the parties under Art 14 to apply the law of a different country.

12.15 If no contract has been concluded between the parties, a non-contractual
obligation arising out of dealings in contemplation of the contract will be
governed by the law that would have been applicable to the contract if it
had been entered into, if that law can be determined. If not, the law applicable to the obligation in question must be identified in accordance with
the rules contained in Art 12(2).

12.16 This aspect of Art 12(1) appears, at first sight, similar to Art 8(1) of the
Rome Convention, which provides:[49]

> The existence and validity of a contract . . . shall be determined by the law which
> would govern it under this Convention if the contract or term were valid.

12.17 Art 8(1) of the Rome Convention, refers questions of the existence of consent and material validity of a contract to what can, for convenience and
according to preference, be described as the putative applicable law of the
contract or the law applicable to the putative contract.[50] Under the Rome I
Regime, this approach extends to the existence and validity of consent
to a choice of law provision.[51] Within Art 8(1), the connecting factor
is determined by the terms of the contract that is claimed to have been
concluded and, in the absence of a choice of law, by the surrounding
circumstances. There is much to be said for this approach, even if one of the
parties denies that he consented to a contract or that it was concluded on

---

[46] This will, in most cases, be a matter for the (putative) law applicable to the contract
(Rome Convention, Art 8; Rome I Regulation, Art 10).

[47] Rome Convention, Arts 3–6; Rome I Regulation, Arts 3–8.

[48] *Amin Rasheed Shipping Corpn v Kuwait Insurance Co* [1984] AC 50, 65 (Lord Diplock,
UKHL).

[49] Rome I Regulation, Art 10(1) is in materially identical terms.

[50] A Briggs, *The Conflict of Laws* (2nd edn, 2008), 175–7.

[51] Rome Convention, Art 3(4); Rome I Regulation, Art 3(5).

materially different terms. A positive result validates the connecting factor, whether the putative applicable law rests on an express or implied choice of law by the parties or a connection established by reference to the nature and terms of the contract and the circumstances surrounding its conclusion. A negative result in terms of the counterparty's consent undermines the connecting factor, but this does not weaken the case for applying the putative applicable law to determine contractual consent, as the conclusion that there is no contract between the parties on the terms proposed does not alter their legal relations and does not prevent either party from seeking to establish the existence of a contract on different terms, by reference to the same or a different law. The putative applicable law has done its job, and it is time to move on.

Despite the passing similarity to this rule, Art 12(1) of the Rome II **12.18** Regulation works differently. In terms of its connecting factor, it requires the court to identify the law that would, hypothetically, have applied to a contract that (in these cases) has not been and will never be concluded. Under any circumstances, this requires a measure of speculation as to the terms of that contract. The key question concerns the degree of certainty required for Art 12(1) to function, i.e. in what circumstances can the law applicable to the failed contract be determined? This, it is submitted, is an important point, as the reasons underlying the failure to conclude a binding contract may prevent the court from being able to determine the connecting factor under Art 12(1) in the first place. At least three scenarios may be contemplated. First, the failure to contract may result from a breakdown in negotiations as a result of which both parties accept that no binding agreement has been reached between them. Secondly, one of the parties may assert that a contract has been concluded on particular terms, in circumstances where the other denies that fact or asserts that a different contract has been concluded (most obviously, following a 'battle of the forms'). Thirdly, both parties may agree that an attempt has been made to conclude a binding contract on particular terms, but in circumstances in which one of them successfully asserts (or both accept) that the contract is invalid or can be set aside (e.g. for misrepresentation).

The third scenario differs from the first two in that the terms of the parties' **12.19** agreement can be argued to have been settled so that, in most cases, the court may consider that the law that would have governed the parties' hypothetical contract if the vitiating factor had not interfered is sufficiently certain.[52] If the agreement contains an express choice of law provision,

---

[52] Art 12(1) probably requires the court to assume that the parties would still have entered into a contract in these circumstances.

that provision will normally identify the law applicable to the hypothetical contract under Art 12(1). If not, it will be necessary to consider other terms of the agreement in order to determine the existence of an implied choice of law or to determine the law applicable to the contract in the absence of choice. In some cases, of course, the vitiating factor may destroy not only the parties' contractual bond but also the appearance of consent to the material terms of the contract. Most obviously, if one party successfully argues that his consent to a choice of law provision was induced by fraud or duress, it would no longer appear possible to conclude with sufficient certainty that the expressly chosen law would have applied to the contract if it had been successfully concluded, which in this connection should be taken to mean if it had been entered into *without fraud or duress*.[53]

12.20 In the first scenario, however, as well as in the second if the court concludes that neither party is correct to assert that a contract has been concluded, there is not even the appearance of a contract between the parties. In these circumstances, a determination for the purposes of Art 12(1) that the contract between the parties would have been concluded on particular terms (with or without a choice of law provision) and would, therefore, have been governed under the Rome I Regime by the law of a particular country requires the court to speculate as to how the parties would have conducted themselves if their negotiations had not broken down. It is unclear whether, in these circumstances, Art 12(1) allows the court to draw evidential inferences in order to reach a view as to the most likely outcome of negotiations or whether, in the absence of a high degree of certainty as to the law that would have applied to the contemplated contract, the rules in Art 12(2) must be applied instead on the ground that the law applicable cannot be determined. Whichever view is taken,[54] the contents of a draft agreement circulated by one party may in practice carry little weight, unless (1) the parties had expressly or by necessary implication settled on the choice of law provision or other term(s) by reference to which the law applicable to the hypothetical contract is to be identified, and (2) there is no reason to believe that the draft might subsequently have been altered in such a way as to change the law applicable.[55]

---

[53] For analysis of similar issues concerning the validity of jurisdiction agreements, see *Fiona Trust & Holding Corporation v Yuri Privalov* [2007] UKHL 40; [2007] 4 All ER 951.

[54] The second view seems more consistent with the need for certainty as to the law applicable. For a more flexible approach than the one taken here, see A Rushworth and A Scott, n 13 above, 291.

[55] Cf *Bols Distilleries v Superior Yacht Services Limited* [2006] UKPC 45; [2007] 1 WLR 12 (Brussels I Regulation).

SECOND STAGE—FOLLOWING THE APPROACH FOR TORTS/DELICTS GENERALLY (ART 12(2))

Art 12(2) applies only if the law applicable to a non-contractual obligation **12.21** arising out of dealings prior to the conclusion of a contract cannot be determined under Art 12(1). That possibility exists only if (1) no contract has been concluded,[56] and (2) the court is unable to determine, to the required standard (whatever this may be) the law that would have applied to the contract between the parties if it had been entered into.[57]

If these two conditions are satisfied, Art 12(2) requires that the law appli- **12.22** cable to a non-contractual obligation arising out of dealings prior to the conclusion of a contract be determined in almost exactly the same manner as for a non-contractual obligation arising out of tort/delict and falling within Art 4. In the first place, Art 12(2)(a) refers to the law of the country in which damage occurs, irrespective of the country in which the event giving rise to the damage occurred and irrespective of the country or countries in which the indirect consequences of that event occurred.[58] Under Art 12(2)(b), if the parties have their habitual residence in the same country at the time when the event giving rise to the damage occurs, the law of that country will apply instead.[59] The reference here to the parties should, it is submitted, be taken as a reference to the parties to the contemplated contract, and not the parties to the proceedings.

Finally, under Art 12(2)(c), the law applicable under Art 12(2)(a) or 12(2)(b) **12.23** (as the case may be[60]) may be displaced in favour of the law of another country with which the non-contractual obligation arising out of dealings prior to the conclusion of the contract is manifestly more closely connected. The test here is the same as that in Art 4(3), although no examples are given of circumstances in which a manifestly closer connection may exist.[61] Presumably, it was thought unnecessary to refer to the possibility of establishing a manifestly closer connection to a pre-existing relationship between the parties, as the nature of the parties' relationship will be evident. Although Art 12(2)(c), unlike Art 12(1), does not contain the words 'whether the contract was concluded or not', it should not be read as

---

[56] **12.14** above.
[57] **12.15–12.20** above.
[58] **4.21–4.74** above.
[59] Cf Art 4(2) referring to 'the person claimed to be liable' and the 'person sustaining damage' (**4.80–4.83** above).
[60] **4.89**, point 2 above.
[61] Cf **4.84–4.95** above.

requiring a contract to have been concluded between the parties.[62] That interpretation would deprive it of all effect given that Art 12(1) ought to be capable of being applied to every case in which a contract has actually been concluded.[63] The words 'non-contractual obligation arising out of dealings prior to the conclusion of a contract' in Art 12(2)(c) should, therefore, be read as referring to all non-contractual obligations to which Art 12(1) may extend.[64]

---

[62] Sir L Collins and others, *Dicey, Morris & Collins: The Conflict of Laws* (14th edn, 2006), 1st supplement, para S35-247.

[63] **12.14** above.

[64] **12.03–12.12** above.

Part IV

Freedom of Choice and Common Rules

13

Choosing the Law Applicable to Non-Contractual Obligations

Article 14

Freedom of choice

1. The parties may agree to submit non-contractual obligations to the law of their choice:

(a) by an agreement entered into after the event giving rise to the damage occurred; or

(b) where all the parties are pursuing a commercial activity, also by an agreement freely negotiated before the event giving rise to the damage occurred.The choice shall be expressed or demonstrated with reasonable certainty by the circumstances of the case and shall not prejudice the rights of third parties.

2. Where all the elements relevant to the situation at the time when the event giving rise to the damage occurs are located in a country other than the country whose law has been chosen, the choice of the parties shall not prejudice the application of provisions of the law of that other country which cannot be derogated from by agreement.

3. Where all the elements relevant to the situation at the time when the event giving rise to the damage occurs are located in one or more of the Member States,

the parties' choice of the law applicable other than that of a Member State shall not prejudice the application of provisions of Community law, where appropriate as implemented in the Member State of the forum, which cannot be derogated from by agreement.

A. INTRODUCTION

13.01 A notable feature of the Commission's preliminary draft proposal[1] was the very wide freedom that it offered to contracting and litigating parties to choose the law applicable to non-contractual obligations arising or existing between them. This extension of the principle of party autonomy from contractual to non-contractual obligations was welcome. It was, therefore, disappointing that the Commission in Art 10 of its Proposal moved to restrict the right to choose the law applicable to non-contractual obligations to the period after the dispute had arisen. The Commission explained only that it had followed recent developments in national private international law, referring to the recent Dutch and German codifications, neither of which supported a restriction in the terms put forward. The Dutch rule contained no temporal restriction on party choice,[2] whereas the German rule allowed party choice following the act giving rise to the non-contractual obligation.[3] In the Council's Rome II Committee, the Commission also expressed the view that sufficient account had been taken of an express choice of law made before the events giving rise to the non-contractual obligation by the specific references to a 'pre-existing relationship' in proposed rules for tort/delict and other non-contractual obligations.[4]

13.02 At first reading, the European Parliament supported the extension of party choice to agreements between commercial contracting parties made before the dispute arose. The Parliament's text required, however, not only that the agreement be 'freely negotiated' and that '[t]he choice must be expressed or demonstrated with reasonable certainty', requirements that remain in the final text of Art 14, but also that there be 'a pre-existing arms-length commercial arrangement between traders of equal bargaining power', words of such elasticity as to cast doubt on the usefulness of the principle.[5]

13.03 Initially, the UK and Spain stood alone among the delegations in the Council working group in favouring the right to choose the applicable law

---

[1] **1.65** above.

[2] *Wet Conflictenrecht Onrechtmatige Daad* (2001) (WCOD), Art 6 (**1.28** above), requiring that the choice of law must have been made explicitly or must otherwise be sufficiently clear.

[3] *Einführungsgesetz zum Bürgerlichen Gezetzbuch* (EGBGB), Art 42 (**1.23** above).

[4] Council document 6518/04 [26.2.2004], 3, referring to Commission Proposal, Arts 3(3) and 9(1).

[5] EP 1st Reading Position, Art 3. EP 1st Reading Report, 16–17.

before any dispute arose.[6] A Commission note of a meeting of the Council's Rome II Committee in October 2004 recorded that most Member State delegations did not agree with the proposal to allow party choice for business to business relationships.[7] Following the European Parliament's amendment at first reading, however, an overwhelming majority favoured allowing pre-dispute (*ex ante*) agreements in situations not involving employees and consumers.[8] Three delegations opposed this extension.[9] The general view at the time was that the conditions on party choice imposed by the Parliament were excessive,[10] and this view was reflected in the amended text produced by the Council's Rome II Committee[11] and adopted as part of the Council's Common Position.[12] That text was accepted by the Parliament at its second reading stage.

Art 14 must be read together with Recital (31), which emphasizes that the **13.04** principles of party autonomy and legal certainty underlie the freedom of choice given to the parties:

> To respect the principle of party autonomy and to enhance legal certainty, the parties should be allowed to make a choice as to the law applicable to a non-contractual obligation. This choice should be expressed or demonstrated with reasonable certainty by the circumstances of the case. Where establishing the existence of the agreement, the court has to respect the intentions of the parties. Protection should be given to weaker parties by imposing certain conditions on the choice.

The text of Recital (31) was agreed in conciliation[13] as a compromise between **13.05** the different language used in the Common Position[14] and the EP 2nd Reading Position.[15]

---

[6] See the comments of the Spanish delegation in Council document 9004/04 ADD 10 [18.5.2004], 6–7 and Council document SN 2852/04 ADD 3 [9.9.2004], 3 and those of the UK delegation in Council document 9004/04 ADD 15 [26.5.2004], 7.

[7] Meeting report of 5 and 6 October 2004 (Commission document JAI/C/1/CH/bv D(04) 10582 [29.10.2004]).

[8] Council document 11515/05 [27.7.2005], 3.

[9] Ibid. The delegations in question may have been France, Luxembourg, and Italy, all of whom had opposed *ex ante* agreements in their initial comments on the Commission Proposal (see Council documents 9009/04 [29.4.2004], 4; ibid, ADD 12 [24.5.2004], 5; ibid, ADD 17 [2.6.2004], 5). Lithuania sought to restrict the parties' choice to the law of the forum (Council document 9009/04, ADD 14 [24.5.2004], 4).

[10] Council document 11515/05 [27.7.2005], 4.

[11] Council document 7432/06 [16.3.2006], Art 3A.

[12] Common Position, Art 14. Also Commission Amended Proposal, Art 4(2) with comment at 3 (Amendment 25).

[13] See EP document PE 388.454 [18.4.2007] and Council document 9137/07 [7.5.2007].

[14] Common Position, Recital (28).

[15] EP 2nd Reading Position, Recital (32), referring to the possibility of inferring 'a choice as to the law applicable to an issue in tort/delict'.

B. PARTY CHOICE OF LAW FOR
NON-CONTRACTUAL OBLIGATIONS (ART 14(1))

13.06 Under Art 14(1), the parties may agree to submit non-contractual obligations to the law of their choice either (a) by an agreement entered into after
the event giving rise to the damage occurred, or (b) where all the parties
are pursuing a commercial activity, also by an agreement freely negotiated
before the event giving rise to the damage occurred. The choice must be
expressed or demonstrated with reasonable certainty by the circumstances
of the case and shall not prejudice the rights of third parties. This freedom
of choice makes an important contribution to legal certainty as to the
law applicable to non-contractual obligations in a commercial context.
The Regulation, however, seeks to balance the principle of legal certainty
with the perceived need to protect weaker parties against oppressive bar-
gains and the wider public interest by imposing certain limits on party
autonomy. These limits on party choice are considered in the following
paragraphs.

Non-Contractual Obligations to which Art 14 does not Apply

13.07 The freedom of choice conferred by Art 14 does not extend to non-
contractual obligations arising out of an act of unfair competition[16] or to
non-contractual obligations arising out of an infringement of an intellectual property right.[17]

The Parties' Agreement as to the Law Applicable

13.08 Art 14(1) requires an 'agreement' between 'the parties' as to the law applicable to non-contractual obligations. This raises two questions. First, does
Art 14(1) have in contemplation the parties to the agreement or the parties
to any proceedings that may be brought to enforce a non-contractual obligation for which such an agreement is made? Secondly, is the concept of
an 'agreement' to be given an autonomous meaning or must it be understood in accordance with the law applicable to the agreement determined
in accordance with the rules of private international law of the forum
Member State for contractual obligations, i.e. those contained in the Rome I
Regime?

---

[16] Art 6(4) (**6.74–6.75** above).
[17] Art 8(3) (**8.54** above).

Identity of the Parties

As to the first question, the need for certainty as to the effectiveness of a **13.09** choice of law provision in a concluded agreement supports the conclusion that 'the parties' should be taken to refer to the parties to the agreement as to the law applicable, rather than the parties to the proceedings.[18] Otherwise, if one or more of the parties to an agreement is not pursuing a commercial activity in entering the agreement, the effectiveness of that agreement may depend on the identity of the persons joined as parties to subsequent proceedings concerning non-contractual obligations arising out of that agreement. This view seems consistent with the use of the present tense in Art 14(1)(b) ('where all the parties are pursuing a commercial activity') and in the contrast that Art 14(1) makes between 'the parties' and 'third parties'. It also reflects the ECJ's view as to the meaning of 'the parties' in Art 17 of the Brussels Convention, which validates choice of court agreements.[19]

If one or more claimants or defendants in subsequent proceedings was **13.10** not a party to the original agreement as to the law applicable, the Member State court seised of the dispute must in each case determine (according to the law applicable to the agreement or other relevant rules of private international law[20]) whether the relevant claimant or defendant has succeeded to the rights and obligations of an original party to the agreement with respect to the non-contractual obligation that the claimant seeks to enforce or which it is sought to enforce against the defendant.[21] The requirement of succession should, probably, be considered to have been satisfied in the case of an assignee of a non-contractual obligation who seeks to enforce that obligation, even if there has been no separate assignment of the agreement containing the choice of law provision.[22]

---

[18] A Rushworth and A Scott, 'Rome II: Choice of Law for Non-Contractual Obligations' [2008] LMCLQ 274, 293.

[19] Case C-387/98, *Coreck Maritime GmbH v Handelsveem BV* [2000] ECR I-9337, para 17.

[20] For example, those governing universal succession (*National Bank of Greece and Athens SA v Metliss* [1958] AC 509 (UKHL)).

[21] *Coreck v Handelsveem*, n 19 above, paras 22–6.

[22] See, in relation to the Brussels Convention, *Glencore International AG v Metro International AG* [1999] 2 Lloyd's Rep 632 (EWHC); *Kolden Holdings Ltd v Rodette Commerce Ltd* [2008] EWCA Civ 10; [2008] 1 Lloyd's Rep 434; U Magnus and P Mankowski, *The Brussels I Regulation* (2007), Art 23, para 161. Cf A Briggs and P Rees, *Civil Jurisdiction and Judgments* (4th edn, 2005), para 2.97.

The Concept of an Agreement and the Relationship to National Law

13.11 As to the second question, Recital (31) provides that '[w]here establishing the existence of the agreement, the court has to respect the intentions of the parties'. That, however, does not resolve the question as to the law to be applied in determining the intentions of the parties. As noted, there appear to be two viable solutions.[23] First, to give an autonomous meaning under EC law to the concept of 'agreement' in Art 14(1). Secondly, to require the Member State court seised of the dispute to determine questions of consent and interpretation in accordance with the law applicable to the agreement, itself determined in accordance with the rules of applicable law for contractual obligations contained in the Rome Convention and its successor Regulation.

13.12 In this connection, the existing European private international law instruments in the area of civil justice point in different directions. Under the Rome Convention, the existence and validity of the consent of the parties to the choice of the applicable law must be determined in accordance with the law applicable to questions of material and formal validity and the capacity of natural persons in Arts 8, 9, and 11 of the Convention.[24] In the case of material validity, Art 8(1) refers to the law that would govern the contract or contractual term if it were valid (the so-called 'putative applicable law'). As to matters of interpretation, the English courts currently favour the view that the question whether a contractual provision amounts to or imports a choice of law under Art 3 of the Rome Convention 'should be looked at from a broad Convention-based approach, not constrained by national rules of construction'.[25] This view appears to treat the requirement that the parties' choice be 'expressed or demonstrated with reasonable certainty', a requirement that also appears in Art 14(1) of the

---

[23] The possibility of referring to the contract law of the forum can safely be rejected as resulting in a lack of uniformity and legal certainty (A Rushworth and A Scott, n 18 above, 292).

[24] Rome Convention, Art 3(4). To the same effect, Rome I Regulation, Art 3(5).

[25] Dicey, Morris & Collins, para 32-080. This statement in an earlier edition of that work was approved by Clarke J in *Egon Oldendorff v Libera Corporation (No 2)* [1996] 1 Lloyd's Rep 380, 387 (EWHC) and by the Court of Appeal in *Samcrete Egypt Engineers and Contractors SAE v Land Rover Exports Ltd* [2002] EWCA Civ 2019, [26]–[27] (Potter LJ).

For the test to be applied in inferring a choice of law by the parties, see *Aeolian Shipping SA v ISS Machinery Services Ltd* [2001] EWCA Civ 1162; [2001] 2 Lloyd's Rep 641, [16], but compare *American Motorists Insurance Co v Cellstar Corporation* [2003] EWCA Civ 206, [44] (Mance LJ) and J Hill, 'Choice of Law in Contract under the Rome Convention' (2004) 53 ICLQ 325, 326–32, both favouring an approach similar to that governing the implication of contract terms under English contract law.

Rome II Regulation,[26] as requiring the meaning of the words used in the contract that are said to constitute a choice of law to be interpreted in an autonomous manner. Even if that view is accepted, however, there appears a strong argument for looking to the law that is claimed to have been chosen, at least for the purpose of confirming the autonomous interpretation of the words used. As the words used by the parties can only be fully understood within the framework of the law that applies to the contract in question,[27] and as the distinction between questions of 'consent'/'validity' and questions of 'interpretation' may depend simply on the way that the question is presented to the court,[28] there is much to be said for applying the putative applicable law to questions of identification and interpretation of a choice of law provision under the Rome Convention, as well as to questions of the existence and validity of the parties' consent to that provision. On this view, the requirement in Art 3(1) of the Rome Convention that a choice of law be 'expressed or demonstrated with reasonable certainty by the terms of the contract or the circumstances of the case' should be seen as imposing a lower threshold in terms of the certainty required to demonstrate the parties' agreement and as requiring the court to take account of matters other than the words used by the parties in the supposed choice of law provision.

In contrast, under the Brussels I Regime, the ECJ and the United Kingdom courts have been moving slowly towards an autonomous concept of 'agreement' for questions concerning the existence and validity of a choice of court agreement under Art 17 of the Brussels Convention and Art 23 of the Brussels I Regulation,[29] while leaving questions of interpretation and certain other matters to the law applicable to the agreement. Five decisions of the ECJ are of particular significance: **13.13**

1. In *Estasis Salotti v RÜWA Polstereimaschinen*, the ECJ emphasized that the requirements set out in Art 17 of the Brussels Convention must be strictly construed. The Court explained that:[30]

By making such validity subject to the existence of an 'agreement' between the parties, Article 17 imposes on the court before which the matter is brought the duty of examining, first, whether the clause conferring jurisdiction upon it was in

---

[26] **13.21–13.26** below.

[27] Both Rome Convention, Art 10(1)(a) and Rome I Regulation, Art 12(1)(a) refer matters of interpretation of a contract to the law which applies to the contract.

[28] **13.15** below.

[29] For present purposes, there is no material difference between these two provisions.

[30] Case 24/76, *Estasis Salotti di Colzani Aimo v RÜWA Polstereimaschinen GmbH* [1976] ECR 1831, para 7.

fact the subject of a consensus between the parties, which must be clearly and pre-cisely demonstrated.

The purpose of the formal requirements imposed by Article 17 is to ensure that the consensus between the parties is in fact established.

2. In *Sancicentral GmbH v Collin*, the ECJ held that it was not open to a Member State court to invalidate a choice of court agreement meeting the requirements of Art 17 by reference to a pre-existing rule of national law excluding the possibility of such choice in employment contracts, even if the agreement in question had been made before the coming into force of the Brussels Convention in that Member State.[31]

3. In *Powell Duffryn plc v Petereit*, the ECJ ruled that:[32]

The concept of 'agreement conferring jurisdiction' is decisive for the assignment, in derogation from the general rules on jurisdiction, of exclusive jurisdiction to the court of the Contracting State designated by the parties. Having regard to the objectives and general scheme of the Brussels Convention, and in order to ensure as far as possible the equality and uniformity of the rights and obligations arising out of the Convention for the Contracting States and persons concerned, therefore, it is important that the concept of 'agreement conferring jurisdiction' should not be interpreted simply as referring to the national law of one or other of the States concerned.

Accordingly, as the Court has held for similar reasons as regards, in particular, the concept of 'matters relating to a contract' and other concepts, referred to in Article 5 of the Convention, which serve as criteria for determining special jurisdiction . . . ,[33] the concept of 'agreement conferring jurisdiction' in Article 17 must be regarded as an independent concept.

In *Powell Duffryn*, the Court concluded that a clause conferring jurisdiction in the statutes of a company was an 'agreement' within the meaning of Art 17 of the Brussels Convention, which bound any shareholder whether or not he had opposed the adoption of the clause or had become a shareholder after the clause was adopted.[34] In response, however, to other questions presented by the German court seised of the dispute, the ECJ held that questions of interpretation of the choice of court agreement were to be determined by the national court.[35] Accordingly, the Court did

---

[31] Case 25/79 [1979] ECR 3423, paras 6–7.

[32] Case C-214/89 [1992] ECR I-1745, paras 13–14.

[33] The ECJ referred to Case 34/82, *Martin Peters Bauunternehmung GmbH v Zuid Nederlandse Aannemers Vereniging* [1983] ECR 987, paras 9 and 10.

[34] *Powell Duffryn v Petereit*, n 32 above, paras 17–18.

[35] Ibid, paras 33, 36.

not consider that the autonomous concept of 'agreement' extended to questions of interpretation.

4. In *Benincasa v Dentalkit Srl*, the ECJ held that:[36]

A jurisdiction clause, which serves a procedural purpose, is governed by the provisions of the Convention, whose aim is to establish uniform rules of international jurisdiction. In contrast, the substantive provisions of the main contract in which that clause is incorporated, and likewise any dispute as to the validity of that contract, are governed by the *lex causae* determined by the private international law of the State of the court having jurisdiction . . .

Article 17 of the Convention sets out to designate, clearly and precisely, a court in a Contracting State which is to have exclusive jurisdiction in accordance with the consensus formed between the parties, which is to be expressed in accordance with the strict requirements as to form laid down therein. The legal certainty which that provision seeks to secure could easily be jeopardized if one party to the contract could frustrate that rule of the Convention simply by claiming that the whole of the contract was void on grounds derived from the applicable substantive law.

The Court added, referring to *Powell Duffryn v Petereit*, that it was for the national court to interpret the clause conferring jurisdiction, including as to whether that clause covers any dispute relating to the validity of the contract.[37]

5. Finally, in *Trasporti Castelletti v Trumpy*, the ECJ concluded:[38]

In *Benincasa*,[39] . . . , the Court explained that the aim of securing legal certainty by making it possible reliably to foresee which court will have jurisdiction has been interpreted, in connection with Article 17 of the Convention, by fixing strict conditions as to form, since the purpose of that provision is to designate, clearly and precisely, a court in a Contracting State which is to have exclusive jurisdiction in accordance with the consensus between the parties.

It follows that the choice of court in a jurisdiction clause may be assessed only in the light of considerations connected with the requirements laid down by Article 17. . . .

[I]n a situation such as that in the main proceedings, any further review of the validity of the clause and of the intention of the party which inserted it must be excluded and substantive rules of liability applicable in the chosen court must not affect the validity of the jurisdiction clause.

[36] Case C-269/95 [1997] ECR I-3767, paras 25 and 29.
[37] Ibid, para 31.
[38] Case C-159/97, *Trasporti Castelletti Spedizioni Internazionali SpA v Hugo Trumpy SpA* [1999] ECR I-1597, paras 49, 51. Also *Coreck Maritime v Handelsveem BV*, n 19 above, paras 13–15.
[39] The ECJ referred to paras 28–29 of the judgment in *Benincasa v Dentalkit*, n 36 above.

13.14 Subsequently, in a case before the English High Court in which the claimant sought to recover damages for the defendants' alleged anti-competitive conduct in violation of Arts 81 and 82 of the EC Treaty, Aikens J summarized the combined effect of these cases with respect to Art 23 of the Brussels I Regulation in the following way:[40]

> Given these pronouncements of the ECJ I must conclude that when a jurisdiction clause is subject to Article 23, then the court seised of the issue of whether it is valid and applicable in the instant case must not apply national laws at all to the issue of the validity of the clause. So national laws are irrelevant to the issue of whether a clause can be valid at all if invoked in a dispute where fraud is alleged or it is alleged that the dispute concerns a tort of intent.

> However the ECJ's judgment in the *Powell Duffryn* case establishes that relevant national laws will determine two issues. The first is whether the dispute concerned arises out of the legal relationship in connection with which the jurisdiction agreement was made. The second is the scope of the jurisdiction agreement when applied to the dispute before the court.

13.15 In that case, Aikens J was faced with the submission that, under German law, jurisdiction agreements were ineffective by reason of the nature of the allegations put forward.[41] It is in that context that his Lordship's reference to 'the issue of whether a clause can be valid at all if invoked in a dispute where fraud is alleged' must be understood. His Lordship was not required to consider the effect of fraud on a party's consent to the choice of court clause, and cannot be taken to have ruled as to how such an allegation should be addressed under Art 23 of the Brussels I Regulation. This case also demonstrates the difficulty, in practice, of distinguishing between questions of validity and questions of interpretation, as the judge relied on the restrictive approach taken under German law to the construction of choice of court agreements in cases of intentional wrongdoing to support his conclusion that the parties' choice of German jurisdiction did not extend to the case before him.[42]

13.16 The issue as to how, within the framework established by Art 23, the question of a party's consent to a choice of court agreement must be determined was directly addressed by the English courts in *Deutsche Bank v Asia Pacific Broadband Wireless*, a case in which the defendant argued that the individuals who had signed the contract containing the choice of court agreement did not have authority to represent it. The claimant argued that there was a sufficient 'agreement' for this purpose as the formal requirements of Art 23 were satisfied and there were objective indicia of the

---

[40] *Provimi Limited v Aventis Animal Nutrition SA* [2003] EWHC 961 (Comm); [2003] 2 All ER (Comm) 683, [80]–[81].

[41] Ibid, [75].

[42] Ibid, [84]–[102].

defendant's consent, including signature of the agreement, a board minute, and warranties in the contract as to the authority of the persons signing in the defendant's name. Both Flaux J and the Court of Appeal appeared to accept that questions of consent to a choice of court agreement were to be determined according to autonomous principles of EC law rather than national law,[43] but reached opposing conclusions. Flaux J rejected the claimant's submission but the Court of Appeal accepted it.[44]

In Longmore LJ's view:[45]   **13.17**

But I do not read the authorities as laying down any requirement that such clauses are not to apply if there is a (plausible) allegation that the contracts, in which such clauses are contained, are vitiated by mistake, misrepresentation, illegality, lack of authority or lack of capacity. That would be to deny the concept of separability which is as much part of European law as English law. Separability was indeed a doctrine in many European jurisdictions well before it was acknowledged in English law, see *Harbour v Kansa . . .*[46]. *Benincasa*[47] is a case in which jurisdiction was assumed under Article 5 by the courts of the place of performance despite allegations of illegality, fraud and misrepresentation. *Effer v Kantner . . .*[48] was a similar case in which the (plausible) allegation was that there was no contract with the claimant at all but rather with a third party. It is difficult to think that a different answer would have been given by the European Court in either case if there had been a written jurisdiction clause and Article 23 (rather than Article 5) was being relied on.

It remains to be seen how the concept of 'agreement' in Art 23 of the **13.18**
Brussels I Regulation will develop in the future and whether, in particular, Member State courts and the ECJ will accept the challenge of defining the conditions for establishing a party's consent for this purpose, or will resort expressly or by stealth to national law.[49] It is submitted, however, that

---

[43] *Deutsche Bank AG v Asia Pacific Broadband Wireless Communications Inc* [2008] EWHC 918 (Comm), [19] (Flaux J); [2008] EWCA Civ 1091, [23], [30] (cf [32]) (Longmore LJ). Also *Knorr-Bremse Systems v Haldex Brake Products* [2008] EWHC 156 (Patents), [30] (Lewison J).

[44] *Deutsche Bank v Asia Pacific Broadband Wireless*, [2008] EWHC 918 (Comm), [34]–[38]; [2008] EWCA Civ 1091, [23]–[32].

[45] [2008] EWCA Civ 1091, [29].

[46] [1993] 1 QB 701. Longmore LJ referred, in particular, to the judgment of Leggatt LJ in that case.

[47] Text to n 36 above

[48] [1982] ECR 825.

[49] For differing views as to the extent to which the concept of 'agreement' in Art 23 must be understood autonomously, see A Layton and H Mercer, *European Civil Practice* (2nd edn, 2004), paras 20.028–20.039; A Briggs and P Rees, n 22 above, para 2.105; U Magnus and P Mankowski, n 22 above, Art 23, paras 75–87; A Briggs, *Agreements on Jurisdiction and Choice of Law* (2008), paras 7.09–7.35.

there are good reasons for not following this approach in relation to Art 14(1) of the Rome II Regulation and for preferring the view that questions as to the parties' consent to an agreement on the law applicable to non-contractual obligations should be determined in accordance with the law applicable to that agreement under the Rome I Regime. First, unlike Art 14(1), both Art 17 of the Brussels Convention and Art 23 of the Brussels I Regulation contain detailed formal requirements for choice of court agreements. As the ECJ emphasized in *Estasis Salotti*[50] and *Trasporti Castelletti v Trumpy*,[51] it is those formal requirements that provide the foundation for the autonomous approach to Art 23 in terms of determining the validity of choice of court agreements. Within Art 14(1), neither the requirement that the parties' choice of law be expressed or demonstrated with reasonable certainty nor the requirement that the agreement be freely negotiated, which in any event only applies to agreements concluded before the event giving rise to damage, perform that role. Secondly, agreements on choice of court are excluded from the scope of the Rome Convention and the Rome I Regulation.[52] Agreements as to the law applicable to non-contractual obligations are not. Accordingly, an agreement within Art 14(1) could be seen as a contract or a term of a contract, the existence and validity of which ought, in principle, to be determined by the law that would govern it under the Rome I Regime if it were valid.[53] Thirdly, in practice, an agreement as to the law applicable to non-contractual obligations will frequently be combined in a single clause with an agreement as to the law applicable to contractual obligations.[54] It seems unsatisfactory for questions of consent to one part of the clause to be determined by reference to different principles from the other. Fourthly, the reference to the common rules of applicable law contained in the Rome I Regime provides greater certainty, and avoids the difficulties inherent in the autonomous approach to the concept of 'agreement' in the Brussels I Regime, of separating questions of validity from questions of consent and of developing an autonomous doctrine of consent. Accordingly, the question whether the parties have 'agreed' to submit non-contractual obligations to the law of their choice should be determined in accordance with the law applicable to the agreement in question, which will normally be the same law as that which the parties have chosen. Indeed, even if the parties have not chosen the law generally applicable to the contract, the choice of the law

---

[50] Text to n 30 above.
[51] Text to n 38 above. Also *Deutsche Bank v Asia Pacific Broadband Wireless* [2008] EWCA Civ 1091, [30] (Longmore LJ).
[52] Rome Convention, Art 1(2)(d); Rome I Regulation, Art 1(2)(e).
[53] Rome Convention, Art 8(1); Rome I Regulation, Art 10(1).
[54] For examples, see **13.24–13.25** below.

applicable to non-contractual obligations should (at the very least) amount to an implied choice as to the law applicable to that term of the contract under Art 3(1) of the Rome Convention and its successor Regulation. Subject to the threshold requirement that the choice of law must be expressed or demonstrated with reasonable certainty by the circumstances of the case,[55] that law should also govern the identification and interpretation of an agreement on choice of law, including identification of the non-contractual obligations to which the choice of law extends.[56]

That does not mean, however, that all questions concerning the existence **13.19** and effect of the parties' agreement under Art 14(1) will be left to national law. The principle of effectiveness under EC law requires Member State courts to ensure that applicable rules of national law do not render practically impossible or excessively difficult the exercise of rights conferred by Community law.[57] Accordingly, it will not be open to Member States to impose substantive restrictions as to the parties' ability to choose the law applicable to non-contractual obligations other than those set out in Art 14(1), including (for example) an absolute prohibition on agreements made before the event giving rise to damage occurred[58] or a requirement that the choice be express or in a particular language.[59] Formal requirements may equally be considered to undermine the effectiveness of Art 14(1). For the same reason, it may be argued that the objectives of Art 14 in terms of achieving greater legal certainty and respecting the principle of party autonomy would be undermined if a party could argue that the Art 14(1) agreement is ineffective because it is contained in a contract that is invalid under the law that applies to it, for reasons unrelated to the parties' consent to the choice of law provision.[60] The view that agreements on choice of law should be considered to be independent from the contract in which they are contained is consistent with Art 3(4) of the Rome Convention.[61]

---

[55] **13.21–13.26** below.
[56] The English court's current approach to the corresponding requirement in the Rome Convention suggests that they may prefer an autonomous approach to these questions (see discussion at **13.12** above).
[57] **3.286** above.
[58] For discussion as to whether such restrictions may be applied to agreements concluded before 11 January 2009, see **13.242** below.
[59] Case 150/80, *Elefanten Schuh GmbH v Jacqumain* [1981] ECR 1671, para 27 (Brussels Convention).
[60] Cf *Benincasa v Dentalkit*, text to n 36 above.
[61] **13.12** above. Also Rome I Regulation, Art 3(5); *Premium Nafta Products Ltd v Fili Shipping Co Ltd* [2007] UKHL 40; [2008] 1 Lloyd's Rep 254, [27] (Lord Hope).

THE LAW CHOSEN BY THE PARTIES

13.20 Art 14(1) allows the parties to submit non-contractual obligations to 'the law of their choice'. A number of points follow from this:

1. It seems clear that Art 14(1) only allows reference to the law of a country,[62] and not (for example) to general principles of law, Sharia law, or the provisions of the draft Common Frame of Reference concerning non-contractual obligations.[63] The same restriction applies under the Rome I Regime.[64]

2. Under Art 3(1) of the Rome Convention,[65] the parties to a contract may select the law applicable to the whole or part only of the contract. It is unclear whether, under the Rome Convention, it is also possible to split the law applicable to different issues arising from the same term of a contract, so that (for example) its material validity is governed by one law, its interpretation by a second law, and so forth.[66] Art 14(1) of the Rome II Regulation, on the other hand, does not expressly permit *dépeçage* in either of these senses, and this may be thought to reflect a general hostility to *dépeçage* within the Regulation.[67] Here, although the principle of party autonomy and the need to respect the wishes of the parties favour allowing the parties freedom to choose the law applicable to a non-contractual obligation on whatever basis they consider appropriate, considerations of legal certainty and the coherence of the law applicable to non-contractual obligations, as well as the use of the singular 'law' in Art 14(1) and Recital (31), support a more restrictive approach. Further, it may be noted that Recital (31) was amended in conciliation so as to remove the European Parliament's proposed reference to 'a choice as to the law applicable to an issue in tort/delict'.[68]

---

[62] For the meaning of 'country' within the Regulation, see **3.290–3.291** and **3.307–3.309** above.

[63] C von Bar et al. (eds), *Principles, Definitions and Model Rules of European Private Law: Draft Common Frame of Reference* (2008), available at <http://www.law-net.eu/en_index.htm>, Books V–VII.

[64] *Shamil Bank of Bahrain EC v Beximco Pharmaceuticals Ltd* [2004] EWCA Civ 19; [2004] 1 WLR 1784; *Halpern v Halpern* [2007] EWCA Civ 291; [2008] QB 195.

[65] Rome I Regulation, Art 3(1).

[66] Dicey, Morris & Collins, para 32-047 to 32-053; P Nygh, *Autonomy in International Contracts* (1999), 132–3.

[67] **4.78–4.79** above.

[68] EP 2nd Reading Proposal, Recital (32).

On balance, Art 14 should be taken to exclude the possibility of *dépeçage* for a single non-contractual obligation.[69] Accordingly, although the parties may, if they wish, choose to subject different non-contractual obligations to different laws, it seems unlikely that Art 14(1) will enable the choice of different laws to govern different parts of the same non-contractual obligation (e.g. damage occurring in different countries) or different issues (e.g. liability and the assessment of damage).

3. Although the parties will normally identify the country whose law is to apply to non-contractual obligations arising between them by name, there appears no reason why they may not do so by reference to objective factors, such as the place of habitual residence of one of them.[70]

OTHER RESTRICTIONS ON FREEDOM OF CHOICE

Expressed or Demonstrated with Reasonable Certainty by the Circumstances of the Case

Under Art 14(1), the choice of law must be expressed or demonstrated **13.21** with reasonable certainty by the circumstances of the case. This wording follows closely Art 3(1) of the Rome Convention, which requires that the parties' choice of law must be 'expressed or demonstrated with reasonable certainty by the terms of the contract or the circumstances of the case'.[71] In their commentary on that provision, Professors Giuliano and Lagarde refer to a number of factors that may justify the conclusion that the parties have made a 'real choice of law' although this is not expressly stated in the contract, including (a) the contract is in a standard form which is known to be governed by a particular system of law even though there is no express statement to this effect, (b) a previous course of dealing between the parties under contracts containing an express choice of law, provided that omission of the choice of law clause in a later contract does not indicate a deliberate change of policy by the parties, (c) in some cases, the choice of a particular forum for resolution of disputes between the parties, (d) references in a contract to specific provisions of the law of a particular system, (e) an express choice of law in related transactions between the same parties, or (f) the choice of a place where disputes are to be settled by

---

[69] For a different view, S C Symeonides, 'Rome II and Tort Conflicts: A Missed Opportunity' (2008) 56 AJCL 173, 186.

[70] *Coreck Maritime v Handelsveem*, n 19 above, para 15 (Brussels Convention).

[71] Art 3(1) of the Rome I Regulation requires that the choice shall be 'made expressly or clearly demonstrated by the terms of the contract'. The French language versions of Art 14(1) of the Rome I Regulation and Art 3(1) of both the Rome Convention and Rome I Regulation require that the choice be '*exprès ou résulte de façon certaine*'.

arbitration in circumstances indicating that the arbitrator should apply the law of that place. [72] The authors concluded:[73]

> This Article does not permit the court to infer a choice of law that the parties might have made where they had no clear intention of making a choice.

13.22 The possibility, under English law, of an implied choice of law for contractual obligations in circumstances such as those described in this passage is well-established.[74] In particular, the choice of English law to govern a contract may be inferred from an agreement that the English courts should have jurisdiction to determine disputes between the parties or from an agreement to arbitrate in England. In this connection, Recital (12) to the Rome I Regulation now provides:

> An agreement between the parties to confer on one or more courts or tribunals of a Member State exclusive jurisdiction to determine disputes under the contract should be one of the factors to be taken into account in determining whether a choice of law has been clearly demonstrated.

13.23 In the case of the choice of the law applicable to non-contractual obligations in other situations, a more cautious approach would seem to be required, if only because the principle of party autonomy for torts and other non-contractual obligations is currently less well developed than for contractual obligations.[75] If the parties to a commercial contract have limited themselves to saying 'this contract shall be governed by the law of X', it may be doubted whether, according to current practice, it can be inferred with reasonable certainty (French: *de façon certaine*) that they intended their choice to extend not only to contractual obligations but also to non-contractual obligations arising out of their contractual relationship. If, however, the parties have expressed their choice of law provision more broadly (e.g. 'any claim arising under [*or* in connection with] this agreement'[76]) or if they have coupled a short, standard form choice of law provision with a dispute resolution provision that, on its proper construction extends to non-contractual obligations,[77] a stronger case can be made for inferring that the

---

[72] Giuliano & Lagarde Report (OJ C282, 17 [31.10.1980]).

[73] Ibid.

[74] Dicey, Morris & Collins, paras 32-092 to 32-099.

[75] P Nygh, n 66 above, 14; A Briggs, *Agreements on Jurisdiction and Choice of Law* (2008), paras 10.43–10.48.

[76] *Kitchens of Sara Lee (Canada) Ltd v A/S Falkefjell (The Makefjell)* [1975] 1 Lloyd's Rep 528, 531–2 (EWHC), affd [1976] 2 Lloyd's Rep 29.

[77] For the rejection by the English courts of the technical approach to construction of particular words and phrases used in choice of court agreements in favour of a broader, more commercially focused approach (see *Premium Nafta v Fili Shipping*, n 61 above). That case concerned the question whether a choice of court or arbitration provision should be taken to

parties intended that all aspects of their relationship, or all claims that they had agreed should be brought before a particular court or arbitral tribunal, should be governed by the same law.[78]

However these principles may develop in the future, the only safe option **13.24** will remain for the parties to make a choice of law in such a way as to put beyond doubt that they intended that the identified law should govern non-contractual obligations between them arising from their relationship. Professor Briggs has suggested the following wording for a choice of English law:[79]

This Agreement, and the whole of the relationship between the parties to it, is governed by English law. The parties agree that all disputes arising out of or in connection with it, or with the negotiation, validity or enforceability of this Agreement, and the relationship between the parties, and whether or not the same shall be regarded as contractual claims, shall be exclusively governed by and determined only in accordance with English law.

If a more condensed form is preferred, the following wording may be con- **13.25** sidered appropriate:

This Agreement and all matters (including, without limitation, any contractual or non-contractual obligation) arising from or connected with it are governed by English law.

The parties should also consider techniques by which the benefit (and bur- **13.26** den) of their choice of law agreement may be extended to related parties, including associated companies, servants, and agents, against whom (or by whom) non-contractual claims might be brought in an effort to circumvent the terms of the contract, including as to the governing law. Again, the following wording is based on that suggested by Professor Briggs:[80]

(1) Each of the parties undertakes to use its best endeavours to prevent persons not party to this Agreement from bringing or continuing against another party to this Agreement, otherwise than in the English courts or in accordance with English law, any action or other proceeding which would, if brought by a party to this Agreement, have been required by this Clause to be brought in the English courts or, as the case may be, in accordance with English law.

---

extend to disputes as to the validity of the contract in which it was contained. There is no reason, however, to conclude that a different approach is required if the question is whether a choice of court or arbitration agreement extends to non-contractual obligations arising out of the parties' relationship.

[78] *The Pioneer Container* [1994] 2 AC 324, 342–4 (PC); *Premium Nafta v Fili Shipping*, n 61 above, [26] (Lord Hope); A Briggs, n 75 above, paras 10.59–10.63.

[79] A Briggs, n 75 above, para 5.17, with commentary at paras 5.18–5.22.

[80] A Briggs, n 75 above, para 5.17, with commentary at paras 5.47 to 5.50.

(2) Each of the parties hereby agrees and declares that the benefit of this Clause shall extend to and may be enforced by any officer, employee, agent, representative or [group company[81]] of each of them as if they were named as a party to this agreement.

No Prejudice to Rights of Third Parties

13.27 The parties' choice under Art 14(1) shall not prejudice the rights of third parties. For this purpose, third parties should be taken to exclude both the original parties to the agreement and persons succeeding to their rights and obligations with respect to the non-contractual obligation in question.[82] For example, (1) if a claimant agrees with one co-defendant that the law of State A should apply to non-contractual obligations between them, that agreement may not be taken into account in considering whether, in relation to an action brought by the claimant against another defendant, there is a manifestly closer connection to the law of State A, and (2) if claimant and defendant agree that the law of State B should apply to non-contractual obligations between them, that agreement will be ignored in determining the law applicable to the non-contractual obligation for the purposes of a direct action against the defendant's insurer under Art 18[83] or a contribution claim by the defendant against other persons (not parties to the choice of law agreement) liable to the claimant for the same claim.[84]

C. INSULATION OF THE APPLICABLE LAW (ARTS 14(2) AND 14(3))

13.28 Arts 14(2) and (3) constitute anti-avoidance provisions in the sense that, without requiring any deliberate intent on the part of the parties seeking to choose the applicable law, they prevent an agreement having effect under Art 14(1) from 'prejudicing' the application of certain rules that cannot be derogated from by agreement in situations in which the non-contractual obligation is otherwise internalized within a particular country (Art 14(2)) or the Member States party to the Regulation (Art 14(3)).

---

[81] This term should, ideally, be defined, for example by reference to the definitions of 'subsidiary' and 'holding company' in the Companies Act 2006, s 1159.

[82] **13.09–13.10** above.

[83] **14.87** below. This example is given in the Commission Proposal, 9.

[84] **14.116** below.

All Relevant Elements Located in a Single Country

Art 14(2) reflects very closely the terms of Art 3(3) of the Rome Convention,[85] **13.29** although, in contrast to the latter provision, the Community legislator avoided attributing the label 'mandatory' to rules that cannot be derogated from by contract, preferring to reserve that term for provisions that apply irrespective of the law otherwise applicable to the non-contractual obligation.[86]

Unlike its counterpart in the Rome Convention, Art 14(2) does not explicitly **13.30** state that the parties' choice of law is not to be taken into account in determining whether all the elements relevant to the situation at the time when the event giving rise to the damage occurs are located in a single country, although this is a necessary inference. It is less clear what other elements, if any, must be ignored for this purpose. Most significantly, perhaps, the requirement to apply the test prescribed by Art 14(2) 'at the time when the event giving rise to the damage occurs'[87] would appear to exclude reference to the country (or countries) in which damage has occurred after that event, unless (perhaps) such damage was likely to occur at the time. Presumably, however, the countries of habitual residence of the person claimed to be liable and the person sustaining damage, as well as the country or countries in which the event giving rise to damage occurs, are relevant elements of the 'situation'.[88] It is less clear whether the law applicable to a pre-existing relationship between the parties, or a choice of contractual forum, may be taken into account.[89] Whichever view is taken, it seems doubtful whether Art 14(2) will have any greater impact than the provision which inspired it.[90]

According to the Commission, the effect of applying Art 14(2) is that '[t]he **13.31** choice by the parties is not deactivated, but it may not operate to the detriment of such mandatory provisions of the law which *might* otherwise

---

[85] Commission Proposal, 22. Also Rome I Regulation, Art 3(3).

[86] Within the Regulation, this latter class of rules (described as 'overriding mandatory provisions') are dealt with in Art 16 (**15.14–15.21** below).

[87] In contrast, Art 10(2) of the Commission Proposal referred to 'the time when the loss is sustained'.

[88] Compare Giuliano-Lagarde Report on the Rome Convention OJ C282, 27 [31.10.1980] discussing Art 7(1) of the Rome Convention, which also uses the term 'situation'.

[89] Rome Convention, Art 3(3) also specifically excluded reference to a choice of foreign tribunal accompanying the parties' choice of law. That language is carried forward in Recital (15) to the Rome I Regulation, which suggests that the wording of its Art 3(3) 'is aligned so far as possible' with Art 14 of the Rome II Regulation.

[90] The English courts have applied Rome Convention, Art 3(3) very restrictively (see *Caterpillar Financial Services Corp v SNC Passion* [2004] EWHC 569 (Comm); [2004] 2 Lloyd's Rep 99 (Cooke J)).

be applicable'.[91] This suggests that, even if all relevant elements are located in a single country, Art 14(2) only preserves the application of provisions of the law of that country that cannot be derogated by contract if that country's law would have applied to the non-contractual obligation but for the parties' agreement under Art 14(1) to submit that obligation to a different law of their choice. That approach seems sensible, particularly if (as submitted above) the country of damage (the principal connecting factor for tort/delict) is not a factor that may be taken into account as 'relevant to the situation'. That said, the text of Art 14(2) does not clearly support that approach and, on the contrary, could be argued itself to operate as a rule of applicable law in favour of non-derogable rules of the identified country, partially overriding not only Art 14(1) but also any other rule in Chapter II or III that would otherwise apply to the situation.[92]

ALL RELEVANT ELEMENTS LOCATED IN THE MEMBER STATES

13.32 Unlike Art 14(2),[93] Art 14(3) is a novelty,[94] and a curious one at that. Its ostensible purpose is to prevent the parties frustrating the application of mandatory rules of Community law through the choice of the law of a third country.[95] That seems unobjectionable enough in itself, but an extension of the anti-avoidance rule in Art 14(2) appears unnecessary to achieve this end. Unlike the law of any single country identified by Art 14(2), rules of Community law must be applied by the courts of all Member States in accordance with their terms. Further, as the decision of the Court of Justice in *Ingmar v Eaton Leonard* demonstrates, EC law is well-equipped to prevent evasion of its legislative rules through the simple expedient of a choice of law clause in circumstances where the situation is closely connected with the Community.[96] That result can be achieved by a process of construction of EC rules themselves, having regard to their objectives,

---

[91] Commission Proposal, 22 (emphasis added).

[92] It is understood that this was the view taken by the Council's Rome II Committee during discussion of this provision. See also the discussion at **13.33** below of the corresponding wording in Art 14(3).

[93] **13.29–13.31** above.

[94] A materially identical provision has since been included in the Rome I Regulation, Art 3(4).

[95] Commission Proposal, 23.

[96] For techniques of construction, see Case C-381/98, *Ingmar GB Ltd v Eaton Leonard Technologies Inc* [2000] ECR I-9305, paras 16–26. For express provisions overriding the choice of law of a non-Member State, see Directive (EC) No 1999/44 on certain aspects of the sale of consumer goods and associated guarantees (OJ L171, 12 [7.7.1999], Art 7(2)); Directive (EC) No 2002/165 concerning the distance marketing of consumer financial services (OJ L271, 16 [9.10.2002]), Art 12(2).

it being necessary to refer to some dogmatic principle contained in the EC Treaty or another legislative instrument. If, as a matter of its proper construction, it appears that a provision of Community law was not intended to have this overriding effect, it is not clear why the fact that all of the elements relevant to the situation at the time when the event giving rise to the damage occurs (whatever they may be[97]) were located within the Member States (excluding Denmark[98]) should enlarge their scope. Further, if Community law has an overriding mandatory effect, irrespective of the law otherwise applicable to the non-contractual obligation, Art 16 of the Rome II Regulation[99] suffices to ensure that it takes priority.

This leads to the question as to how Art 14(3) works when the test that it **13.33** lays down is satisfied. On one view, it simply clears the way for Community law to be applied to a particular situation if (and only if) it would have applied but for the parties' choice of law, whether as part of the otherwise applicable law or, if the law of a non-Member State would otherwise apply, as an overriding mandatory provision of the law of the forum (this last possibility explaining, with reference to EC directives, the words 'where appropriate as implemented in the Member State of the forum'[100]). On the other hand, Art 14(3) could itself be argued to operate as a rule of applicable law giving overriding effect to Community law in all situations and referring (in the case of directives) to the implementing legislation in the forum State, irrespective of whether another Member State's law would otherwise apply to the non-contractual obligation. This outcome is difficult to defend, but the possibility that Art 14(3) will be taken to have this effect cannot be excluded.[101]

D. TIMING OF THE AGREEMENT

Art 14(1) presents two options in terms of the timing of the parties' agree- **13.34** ment. First, after the event giving rise to damage, any parties may choose the law applicable to non-contractual obligations arising between them as a result of that event (Art 14(1)(a)). Secondly, before the event giving rise to damage, parties pursuing a commercial activity may choose the law

---

[97] **13.30** above.
[98] Art 1(4).
[99] **15.19–15.20** below.
[100] It is unclear whether these words in Art 14(3) may require Member State courts to apply rules that go beyond the minimum harmonization standards required by a directive.
[101] It is understood that this was the view taken by the Council's Rome II Committee during discussion of this provision.

applicable to non-contractual obligations between them by an agreement freely negotiated (Art 14(1)(b)). The references in Art 14(1)(a) and (b) to 'event giving rise to damage' must not be understood as restricting Art 14(1) to non-contractual obligations arising out of tort/delict. Instead, 'damage' must, in accordance with Art 2(1), be taken to refer to 'any consequence arising out of tort/delict, unjust enrichment, *negotiorum gestio* or *culpa in contrahendo'*. On this basis, the 'event giving rise to damage', although not separately defined in Art 2, should be taken to refer:

(a) in the case of tort/delict, to the act, omission, or other event for the consequences of which the defendant, or a person for whose acts the defendant is liable, is claimed to be responsible;[102]

(b) in the case of unjust enrichment, to the event (normally a transfer of value from the claimant) giving rise to the defendant's enrichment;[103]

(c) in the case of *negotiorum gestio*, to the intervener's act;[104]

(d) in the case of *culpa in contrahendo*, to the act in the course of dealings prior to the conclusion of a contract for the consequences of which the defendant is claimed to be responsible.[105]

First Option—An Agreement Entered into after the Event Giving Rise to Damage Occurred

13.35 The reference to the time of the event giving rise to damage does not require that a dispute has arisen between the parties, or even that the parties are aware of that event. Nevertheless, it is to be expected that agreements of this kind will usually be concluded after a dispute has arisen, and in contemplation of litigation.

13.36 There is no reason, in principle, why an agreement of this kind cannot be made by an exchange of pleadings during litigation. Art 14(1) requires, however, that the parties' choice must be expressed or demonstrated with reasonable certainty by the circumstances of the case, and this may require some caution on the part of Member State courts. If, in a case involving a non-contractual obligation, the claimant asserts that the 'law of Y applies to this claim', the primary purpose of that statement is to assert that this is the law that applies to that obligation under the rules in Chapters II and III

---

[102] **4.33–4.35** above.
[103] **10.21** above.
[104] **11.03** above.
[105] **12.04** above.

of the Rome II Regulation. It may be, however, that the statement can also be taken as an offer, if the defendant will agree, to fix the law applicable by reference to Art 14(1) of the Regulation.[106] If, therefore, the defendant positively admits that the law of Y applies, that would arguably be enough to demonstrate with reasonable certainty a binding agreement between the parties to that effect. If the defendant responds to that assertion, without admitting that the law of Y applies, there can be no agreement. If the defendant does not respond, he should not, it is submitted, be treated as having agreed that the law of Y should apply under Art 14 of the Regulation, even if the rules of pleading treat his failure to respond as a deemed admission.[107]

SECOND OPTION — AN AGREEMENT FREELY NEGOTIATED
BETWEEN PARTIES PURSUING A COMMERCIAL ACTIVITY

Art 14(2)(b) requires all of the parties to the agreement (**13.09** above) to be **13.37** pursuing a commercial activity. That test must be satisfied with reference to the time, and having regard to the subject matter, of the agreement. For these purposes, 'commercial activity' should be considered to include any activity with a commercial or professional purpose. The absence of a reference to 'professional activity', in contrast to both Art 15 of the Brussels I Regulation and Art 6 of the Rome I Regulation, should not be taken to require a distinction to be drawn between those acting commercially and those acting in the pursuit of a profession. As Recital (31) and the Commission Amended Proposal makes clear,[108] the conditions imposed by Art 14(2)(b) are intended to protect weaker parties, primarily consumers and employees, and should not apply to commercial or professional contracts.[109] The ECJ's case law concerning the consumer contract provisions of the Brussels Convention also suggests that, if a person acts partly for commercial or professional purposes and partly for his own private purposes, the commercial purpose should predominate, unless it is so limited as to be negligible in the overall context of the agreement.[110]

---

[106] Such an offer is not possible in cases concerning anti-competitive conduct (Art 6) or infringements of intellectual property rights (Art 8).

[107] e.g. Civil Procedure Rules, r 16.5(5).

[108] The text of Recital (31) appears at **13.04** above. Also Commission Amended Proposal, 3 (comment on Amendment 25).

[109] **13.06** above. Art 14(2)(b) is not, however, one-sided and there seems no reason why a commercial or professional party cannot assert that its requirements are not satisified (cf Case C-89/91, *Shearson Lehman Hutton Inc v TVB* [1993] ECR I-139 (Brussels Convention, Art 13)).

[110] Case C-464/01, *Johann Gruber v Bay Wa AG* [2005] ECR I-439.

13.38 The requirement that the agreement be 'freely negotiated' originated in the Parliament's amendments to this element of the Commission Proposal at the first reading stage.[111] The Report of the EP JURI Committee explained that:[112]

> [T]here seems to be no reason why parties in an arms-length commercial relationship[113] should not be able to agree on the law applicable to any claim in tort/delict before any such claim arises. This may be convenient to businesses wishing to regulate all potential aspects of their relationship from the outset. However, the wording of this amendment is designed to exclude consumer contracts and agreements not freely negotiated (such as standard-form contracts—*contrats d'adhésion*) where the contracting parties do not have equal bargaining power (e.g. insurance, franchise and licensing contracts).

13.39 Accordingly, it appears that this wording was intended to exclude situations in which a choice of law provision was imposed by one party on another without giving the other a reasonable opportunity to negotiate the terms of that provision. It should not be taken to have any wider meaning, as requiring (for example) the absence of misrepresentation or any other factor affecting consent. These are primarily matters for the law applicable to the agreement.[114]

13.40 Further guidance may be sought in the approach taken by the Unfair Terms in Consumer Contracts Directive to the requirement that a contractual term be 'individually negotiated'.[115] During discussions in the Council's Rome II Committee, the Member State delegations suggested using these words instead of 'freely negotiated' in what became Art 14, but this was not followed up in the Common Position.[116] Even so, the two expressions appear sufficiently proximate for the terms of the Directive and relevant case law of Member State courts, as well as any future case law of the ECJ, to be taken into account in construing the Regulation. Art 3(2) of the Directive provides:

> A term shall always be regarded as not individually negotiated where it has been drafted in advance and the consumer has therefore not been able to influence the

---

[111] EP 1st Reading Position, Art 3 (Amendment 25).

[112] EP 1st Reading Report, 17.

[113] The EP's requirement that there be a 'pre-existing arms length commercial relationship between traders of equal bargaining power' was subsequently rejected by the Council (**13.02–13.03** above).

[114] **13.11–13.19** above.

[115] Directive (EC) No 93/13 on unfair terms in consumer contracts (OJ L95, 29 [21.4.1993]). For UK implementing legislation, see Unfair Terms in Consumer Contracts Regulations (SI 1999/2083).

[116] Council document 6161/06 [10.2.2006], 3.

substance of the term, particularly in the context of a pre-formulated standard contract. The fact that certain aspects of a term or one specific term have been individually negotiated shall not exclude the application of this Article to the rest of a contract if an overall assessment of the contract indicates that it is nevertheless a pre-formulated standard contract.

Where any seller or supplier claims that a standard term has been individually negotiated, the burden of proof in this respect shall be incumbent on him.

Accordingly, the fact that a contract containing a provision dealing with **13.41** the law applicable to non-contractual obligations is in a standard form (e.g. a market standard for a specific type of market instrument) will not automatically take it outside Art 14(1)(b) if every party had an opportunity to influence its terms, and in particular the choice of law provision.[117] The person presented with that form of agreement need not have taken up that opportunity. Indeed, in practice, there may be no discussion of boilerplate provisions such as jurisdiction and choice of law provisions. If, however, the party who presents a form of contract states, at the outset, that the choice of law provision or the boilerplate language generally is 'non-negotiable', that may provide a strong indication that the agreement as to the law applicable was not 'freely negotiated' under Art 14(1)(b) of the Regulation.

E. AGREEMENTS CONCLUDED BEFORE 11 JANUARY 2009

Under Arts 31 and 32, the Regulation shall apply from 11 January 2009 to **13.42** 'events giving rise to damage which occur after its entry into force'. The uncertainty generated by these provisions as to the temporal effect of the Regulation has been discussed in **Chapter 3**.[118] Art 14 raises its own problem, as to whether the rules that it contains should apply to determine the effectiveness of agreements as to the law applicable to non-contractual

---

[117] For English cases dealing with the requirement that a term be 'individually negotiated' under the UK legislation implementing the Unfair Terms in Consumer Contracts Directive, see *Heifer International AG v Christiansen* [2007] EWHC 3015 (TCC), [304] (Judge Toulmin QC), concerning the ability of a party through his lawyers to influence dispute resolution provisions in a construction contract. Also *Bryen & Langley Ltd v Boston* [2005] EWCA Civ 971, [46] (Rimer J), for a case in which the consumer through his professional advisers had required that a particular form of contract be used (for comment on this decision, see H Beale et al. (eds), *Chitty on Contracts* (29th edn, 2004), 3rd cumulative supplement (2006), para 15-032A).

[118] **3.315–3.324** above.

obligations concluded before 11 January 2009, or whether pre-existing national rules (for example, those under German and Dutch law to which the Commission referred[119]) should continue to apply. There appear to be strong reasons for applying Art 14 in all cases.[120] First, unlike the Rome Convention and the Rome I Regulation,[121] the temporal effect of the Rome II Regulation is not defined by reference to the date of conclusion of an agreement. Secondly, although it seems correct to test the validity of such agreements by reference to the circumstances prevailing at the time they were entered into and by reference to the law applicable to them under the Rome I Regime,[122] such agreements operate in a procedural context in relation to the enforcement of non-contractual obligations before Member State courts. The principal consequence of an agreement of this kind occurs when a Member State court seised of a dispute is asked to determine the law applicable to a non-contractual obligation in accordance with the rules contained in the Regulation, at which time the existence of an agreement within Art 14(1) may constitute one of several possible connecting factors pointing towards application of the law of a particular country. The date of that determination should, therefore, be the relevant date for the purposes of considering the effectiveness of the parties' choice of law. Very similar reasoning was deployed by the ECJ in *Sanicentral v Collin*[123] in rejecting the argument that pre-existing national rules should continue to determine the validity of a choice of court agreement entered into before the coming into force of the Brussels Convention. Thirdly, the continued application of national rules to agreements concluded before 11 January 2009 would result in wide differences in approach between Member States, jeopardizing the uniformity that the Rome II Regulation seeks to achieve. Some Member States do not validate such agreements at all; others impose conditions as to the nature of the agreement[124] or its timing.[125] That disparity of approach is unacceptable, particularly as non-contractual obligations may for many years continue to arise in relation to agreements concluded before 2009.

---

[119] **13.01** above.

[120] It is understood that German scholars disagree with this view.

[121] Rome Convention, Art 17; Rome I Regulation, Art 28.

[122] **13.09**, **13.11–13.19** and **13.37** above.

[123] Text to n 31 above.

[124] Under Dutch law, the agreement must be express.

[125] Under German law, an agreement of this kind may be concluded in all cases only after the act giving rise to the non-contractual obligation occurred.

F. APPRAISAL

The recognition that parties in a commercial relationship may choose the **13.43** law applicable to non-contractual obligations arising between them not only after but also before a dispute has arisen is undoubtedly one of the key defining features of the Rome II Regulation, which will likely give it a wider resonance internationally. It has been applauded by some, but criticized by others. One commentator has gone as far as suggesting that, as a result of Art 14:[126]

[P]arty autonomy has thereby become the *primary* conflicts rule for non-contractual claims in the commercial sector. No doubt, legal certainty for the parties is the winner.

On the other hand. Professor Symeonides regrets what he sees as 'only min- **13.44** imal scrutiny' of fairness of 'pre-tort' agreements on applicable law and suggests:[127]

As with some other freedom-laden ideas, Article 14 may well become the vehicle for taking advantage of weak parties, many of whom are 'parties' to 'commercial' relationships. The argument that the 'mandatory rules' of paragraphs 2 and 3 of Article 14, or the *ordre public* exception of Article 26 will protect the weak parties is overly optimistic because of the high threshold these provisions require before they become operable.

It may, however, be questioned whether either of these predictions will be **13.45** realized, at least in the short term. On the one hand, commercial practice concerning the drafting of agreements will likely take some time to adjust to the newly created freedom to choose the law applicable to non-contractual obligations. On the other, the application of national rules concerning consent to a choice of law provision and restrictions on party autonomy that Art 14 contains, particularly for *ex ante* agreements, appear more than sufficient to enable courts to protect weaker parties against the abuse of a dominant bargaining position.

[126] Editorial, 'Sometimes it takes thirty years and even more' (2007) 44 Common Market L Rev 1567, 1570.
[127] S C Symeonides, n 69 above, 216.

14

Scope of the Law Applicable under the Regulation

A. INTRODUCTION

14.01   The common rules in Chapter V of the Regulation are of three kinds. First, Arts 15 and 18–22 contain rules that positively define what has been described in **Chapter 3** as the vertical material scope of the Regulation,[1] by listing the matters governed by the law applicable to a non-contractual obligation determined in accordance with the rules in Chapters II to IV or otherwise as set out in the Regulation. Secondly, Art 16 (overriding mandatory provisions), alongside Art 26 in Chapter VI (public policy of the forum), defines the limits of the law applicable under the Regulation in terms of its relationship to the law of the forum. Thirdly, Art 17 recognizes a limited role for rules of safety and conduct in force at the place and time of the event giving rise to the liability in the assessment of the conduct of the person claimed to be liable. This chapter considers the first group of rules. Arts 16, 17, and 26 are considered in the following chapter.

B. SCOPE OF THE LAW APPLICABLE (ART 15)

Article 15

Scope of the law applicable

The law applicable to non-contractual obligations under this Regulation shall govern in particular:

(a) the basis and extent of liability, including the determination of persons who may be held liable for acts performed by them;

(b) the grounds for exemption from liability, any limitation of liability and any division of liability;

(c) the existence, the nature and the assessment of damage or the remedy claimed;

(d) within the limits of powers conferred on the court by its procedural law, the measures which a court may take to prevent or terminate injury or damage or to ensure the provision of compensation;

(e) the question whether a right to claim damages or a remedy may be transferred, including by inheritance;

(f) persons entitled to compensation for damage sustained personally;

(g) liability for the acts of another person;

---

[1] **3.59** above.

(h) the manner in which an obligation may be extinguished and rules of prescription and limitation, including rules relating to the commencement, interruption and suspension of a period of prescription or limitation.

INTRODUCTION

Art 15 is the most important provision determining the Rome II Regulation's vertical material scope. In large part, it corresponds to Art 11 of the Commission Proposal. The Commission suggested that this element of the Proposal was inspired by the 1980 Rome Convention:[2] **14.02**

Article 11 defines the scope of the law determined under Articles 3 to 10 of the proposed Regulation.[3] It lists the questions to be settled by that law. The approach taken in the Member States is not entirely uniform: while certain questions, such as the conditions for liability, are generally governed by the applicable law, others, such as limitation periods, the burden of proof, the measure of damages etc, may fall to be treated by the *lex fori*. Like Article 10 of the Rome Convention, Article 11 accordingly lists the questions to be settled by the law that is actually designated.

In line with the general concern for certainty in the law, Article 11 confers a very wide function on the law designated. It broadly takes over Article 10 of the Rome Convention, with a few changes of detail.

In terms of content, however, Art 11 of the Proposal and the Commission's explanation of it would appear to have been more directly influenced by the terms of Art 11 of the 1972 draft convention on the law applicable to contractual and non-contractual obligations and the commentary on that provision in the report of Professors Giuliano and Lagarde and Mr Th van Sasse van Ysselt.[4] That provision was, in turn, influenced by Art 8 of the Hague Traffic Accidents Convention and the explanatory report of Mr Eric W E Essén.[5] **14.03**

Although the language used by the Commission in the paragraph quoted above might be taken to suggest that the list of matters settled by the law applicable to a particular non-contractual obligation under Art 15 should be taken to be exhaustive, it may be noted that the opening sentence of Art 15 (like Art 11 of the Commission Proposal) concludes with the words 'in particular', which strongly suggest a non-exhaustive statement.[6] Instead, it is submitted, Art 15 must be read alongside not only the following **14.04**

---

[2] Commission Proposal, 23.

[3] Corresponding to Arts 4–14 of the Regulation in its final form.

[4] Giuliano, Lagarde & van Ysselt Report, 57–62.

[5] Ibid, 57. For references to the report of Mr Essén and other materials on the Hague Traffic Accidents Convention, see **4.114** above.

[6] Ibid.

provisions, Arts 16 to 22, but also Art 1(3), which excludes matters of evidence and procedure from the Regulation. The relationship between Art 15 and Art 1(3) is considered separately below.[7]

14.05 Each of the sub-paragraphs of Art 15 will be addressed in turn.

(A) The Basis and Extent of Liability, Including the Determination of Persons who may be held Liable for Acts Performed by them

Basis of Liability

14.06 The corresponding provision of the Commission Proposal[8] referred to 'the conditions and extent of liability', but the change in language from 'conditions' to 'basis' in Art 15(a) of the regulation does not seem particularly significant. The Commission explained that:[9]

> [T]he expression 'conditions . . . of liability' refers to intrinsic factors of liability. The following questions are particularly concerned: nature of liability (strict or fault-based); the definition of fault, including the question whether an omission can constitute a fault; the causal link between the event giving rise to the damage and the damage; the persons potentially liable; etc.

Extent of Liability

14.07 As to the meaning of this expression, the Commission suggested that:[10]

> 'Extent of liability' refers to the limitations laid down by law on liability, including the maximum extent of that liability and the contribution to be made by each of the persons liable for the damage which is to be compensated for. The expression also includes division of liability between joint perpetrators.

14.08 Given that Art 15(b) refers expressly to 'division of liability', the Regulation's treatment of questions of apportionment of liability is considered in the commentary on that sub-rule below.[11] Of course, whether these questions fall within Art 15(a) or Art 15(b) makes no difference to the law applicable. Questions of contribution between persons liable are considered in the commentary in Section I below on Art 20 (headed 'Multiple Liability').[12]

---

[7] **14.57–14.62.**
[8] Commission Proposal, Art 11(a).
[9] Commission Proposal, 23.
[10] Ibid.
[11] **14.16–14.17.**
[12] **14.115–14.120** below.

Capacity to Incur Liability

The reference in Art 15(a) to 'the determination of persons who may be **14.09** held liable for acts performed by them' seems apt to cover questions as to whether a natural or legal person has legal capacity to incur liability for breach of non-contractual obligations.[13] If any doubt remained that such questions fall within the Regulation's vertical scope, it is removed by Recital (12), which provides:

The law applicable should also govern the question of the capacity to incur liability in tort/delict.

A Recital to this effect was first introduced by the European Parliament at **14.10** first reading.[14] Although both the Commission[15] and Council[16] thought this unnecessary, the same Recital was re-introduced by the Parliament at the second reading[17] and accepted by the Council during the conciliation process.

This accords with the current position under English private international **14.11** law. According to the editors of Dicey, Morris & Collins:[18]

This principle applies, it is submitted, regardless of whether the alleged tortfeasor is a natural person or a legal person. As regards the latter, it matters not that, by the law of the place of incorporation, a corporation cannot be made liable for what, according to the law of that place, would be an *ultra vires* tort. For while what a corporation *may do* is properly governed by the law of the place of incorporation and by the law of the country which governs the transaction in question, the legal consequences which arise when the corporation *does* something which is *ultra vires* must surely be determined by the *lex causae*.

That reasoning applies with equal force in the context of the Regulation.

The treatment of capacity under the Rome II Regulation may be contrasted **14.12** with that under the Rome I Regime for contractual obligations. Under Art 1(2)(a) of the Rome I Regulation (in identical terms to the corresponding provision of the Rome Convention), 'questions involving the status of

---

[13] See the comments of the Swedish delegation in Council document 9009/04 ADD 8 [18.5.2004], 17–18, referring to Section 828(1) of the German Civil Code (*Bürgerliches Gesetzbuch*) under which a person who has not reached the age of seven is not responsible for damage caused to another person.

[14] EP 1st Reading Position, Recital (10) resulting from Amendment 5.

[15] Commission Amended Proposal, 2.

[16] Statement of reasons accompanying the Common Position at OJ C289E, 79 [28.11.2006].

[17] EP 2nd Reading Position, Recital (11).

[18] Sir L Collins and others (eds), *Dicey, Morris & Collins: The Conflict of Laws* (14th edn, 2006), para 35-040.

legal capacity of natural persons' are excluded from the scope of the Regulation, subject to the provisions of Art 13,[19] which restrict the right of natural persons to rely on incapacity arguments if they conclude a contract while in the same country as the contractual counterparty. Under Art 1(2)(f) of the Rome I Regulation (reflecting Rome Convention, Art 1(2)(e)), questions as to the legal capacity of companies and other bodies corporate or unincorporate are also excluded from the scope of the Regulation.

(B) THE GROUNDS FOR EXEMPTION FROM LIABILITY, ANY LIMITATION OF LIABILITY AND ANY DIVISION OF LIABILITY

14.13 The Commission described these as 'extrinsic factors of liability', adding:[20]

> The grounds for release from liability include *force majeure*; necessity; third-party fault and fault by the victim. The concept also includes the inadmissibility of actions between spouses and the exclusion of the perpetrator's liability in relation to certain categories of persons.

14.14 Accordingly, the law applicable to a non-contractual obligation under the Rome II Regulation will govern questions of causation relating to the intervention of third party acts and the availability of defences to a non-contractual obligation, whether total or partial, including contributory negligence[21] and set-off.[22] It will also govern the question whether the defendant, or a person for whom the defendant is responsible, may incur non-contractual liability to the claimant, or a person represented by the claimant. This includes, for example, the question whether a husband may be liable to his wife in tort or a parent liable to his or her child, or vice versa.[23] Although non-contractual obligations arising out of family relationships are excluded from the scope of the Regulation by Art 1(2)(a), this exclusion should not be taken to extend to non-contractual obligations which arise independently of such relationships, e.g. from the act of driving a car.[24]

---

[19] Rome Convention, Art 12.

[20] Commission Proposal, 23.

[21] Cf *Dawson v Broughton* (2007) unreported, 31 June (Manchester County Court).

[22] Also Art 15(h) referring to 'the manner in which an obligation may be extinguished' (**14.53** below). Under Rome I Regulation, Art 17, '[w]here the right to set-off is not agreed to by the parties, set-off shall be governed by the law applicable to the claim against which the right to set-off is asserted'. Whether this applies to set-off involving a non-contractual obligation is unclear. In the case of set-off as a defence to a non-contractual obligation, this rule produces the same result as Art 15(b).

[23] Dicey, Morris & Collins, para 35-041.

[24] **3.152** above.

Exclusion or Limitation of Liability by Agreement

Under Art 15(b), the law applicable to a non-contractual obligation under **14.15**
the Rome II Regulation will determine whether liability with respect to
that non-contractual obligation may be excluded or limited by a prior
agreement between the parties or by a unilateral act.[25] The agreement in
question may be embodied in a contract between the parties or may be
expressed or implied in circumstances where there is no intent to create a
legally binding relationship, for example in the case of participants in
sporting activities.[26] If the law applicable under the Rome II Regulation
requires a contract, the validity and construction of any contract will be a
matter for the law applicable to that contract under the Rome I Regime.
Otherwise, the effectiveness of an agreement or other act in excluding
or limiting liability will be a matter for the law that applies under the
Rome II Regulation,[27] without prejudice to the possibility that a contracting party may argue that the commencement of proceedings based on a
non-contractual obligation constitutes a breach of contract entitling it to
a remedy.[28]

Division of Liability

The Commission's commentary on Art 15(a) refers to 'division of liability **14.16**
between joint perpetrators'.[29] Questions of division of liability are not,
however, limited to cases of joint liability in the narrow sense understood
by English law, i.e. where two or more persons are responsible for the
same event and owe a single, indivisible obligation.[30] Thus, tortfeasors
may act with a common design or may act separately in such a way that
each is held liable for damage that is suffered by another.[31] For example, as
a consequence of s 3 of the UK Compensation Act 2006, all those persons
(usually employers) who have negligently allowed others to become

---

[25] The release of liability by subsequent agreement or other act falls within Art 15(h) (**14.53** below). Also Art 21 (**14.77–14.80** below).

[26] For the treatment of such situations under English law, see A M Dugdale and M A Jones (eds), *Clerk & Lindsell on Torts* (19th edn, 2006), paras 3-101 to 3-102.

[27] The law applicable to a contract in which the relevant agreement is said to be found may provide an essential part of the context within which the meaning of the words used will be determined by the court.

[28] *National Westminster Bank plc v Utrecht-America Finance Co* [2001] EWCA Civ 658; [2001] 3 All ER 733; *National Westminster Bank plc v Rabobank Nederland* [2007] EWHC 1742 (Comm); [2008] 1 Lloyd's Rep 16

[29] **14.07** above.

[30] Clerk & Lindsell on Torts, n 26 above, paras 4-03 and 4-04.

[31] C van Dam, *European Tort Law* (2005), para 1108.

exposed to asbestos resulting in the latter contracting mesothelioma in circumstances in which the exposure attributable to them materially increased the risk of that disease will be jointly and severally responsible for all of the damage suffered even though it is not possible to state whether a particular exposure triggered the disease.[32] In other cases, successive tortious events may be linked to the same damage, or a second event may exacerbate damage caused by the first.[33]

14.17 If, under the Regulation, the same law applies to the non-contractual obligations owed by all those responsible, no difficulty arises in applying that law to all questions of division of liability. What, however, if those non-contractual obligations are governed by two or more different laws? In these circumstances, it is submitted, the extent to which each person responsible will be liable to the person seeking compensation must be determined by reference to the law applicable to the non-contractual obligation owed by him, on the assumed basis (admittedly unsatisfactory) that the liability of the other persons responsible also falls to be determined by reference to that law. Questions of contribution between those liable must be dealt with separately according to the rules in Art 20 (multiple liability), at least in cases where one of them has satisfied the claim.[34]

(C) THE EXISTENCE, THE NATURE AND THE ASSESSMENT OF DAMAGE OR THE REMEDY CLAIMED

14.18 The Commission Proposal provided separately for 'the existence and kinds of damage for which compensation may be due'[35] and 'the measure of damages in so far as prescribed by law'.[36] The Commission explained that the first category concerned 'the damage for which compensation may be due, such as personal injury, damage to property, moral damage and environmental damage, and financial loss or loss of an opportunity'.[37] As to the second, its only comment was that 'if the applicable law provides for rules on the measure of damages, the court must apply them'.[38] These two elements of existence and assessment of damage were merged

---

[32] For earlier case law, to which the 2006 Act reacted, see *Fairchild v Glenhaven Funeral Services Ltd* [2002] UKHL 22; [2003] 1 AC 32 and *Barker v Corus (UK) Plc* [2006] UKHL 20; [2006] 2 AC 572.

[33] C van Dam, n 31 above, para 1109.

[34] **14.114–14.120** below.

[35] Commission Proposal, Art 11(c).

[36] Ibid, Art 11(e), reflecting, in part, Rome Convention, Art 10(1)(c).

[37] Commission Proposal, 23. Also Giuliano, Lagarde & van Ysselt Report, 59.

[38] Commission Proposal, 24.

in the Council's Common Position,[39] although the European Parliament had previously amended the Commission's text for the first category so as to reflect closely the final wording,[40] while leaving the second category intact.

The Assessment of Damages Generally

By requiring not only the existence of damage, but also its assessment, **14.19** to be determined in accordance with the law applicable under Chapters II to IV, the Rome II Regulation departs from the view taken by English law, both at common law and under the Private International Law (Miscellaneous Provisions) Act 1995, that the quantification or assessment of tortious damages is a matter of procedure to be governed by the law of the forum.[41] Accordingly, the law applicable under the Regulation and not the law of the forum must be applied to determine the *basis* of assessment of a monetary award. In this connection, 'the law applicable' should be understood in a broad sense to include judicial conventions and practices, which will facilitate the assessment of damages by the court seised of the dispute in a manner which reflects, as closely as possible, the result that would be achieved in a court of the country whose law applies.[42] Thus, for example, the court seised should look to particular tariffs, guidelines, or formulae[43] which are used in practice by foreign judges in the calculation of damages,[44] as well as the approach in calculating awards in individual cases. The applicable law will also determine the extent to which specific

---

[39] Common Position, Art 15(c).

[40] EP 1st Reading Position, Art 11(c) referring to 'the existence, the nature and the assessment of damages or the redress sought'.

[41] *Harding v Wealands* [2006] UKHL 32; [2007] 2 AC 1. See P Beaumont and Zheng Tang, 'Classification of Delictual Damages—*Harding v Wealands* and the Rome II Regulation' (2008) 12 Edinburgh L Rev 135.

[42] In their initial response to the Commission Proposal, the Austrian and Swedish delegations, in particular, opposed the words 'in so far as prescribed by law' in Art 11(e) of the Proposal on the ground that they might be taken to suggest a distinction between those legal systems that regulated the measure of damages by statute and those that did so by case law (Council documents 9009/04 ADD 1 [3.5.2004], 4; ibid, ADD 8 [24.5.2004], 18–19; also ibid, ADD 13 [24.5.2004], 11 (Ireland)). Those words do not appear in the final text of the Regulation.

[43] Cf A Rushworth and A Scott, 'Rome II: Choice of Law for Non-Contractual Obligations' [2008] LMCLQ 274, 294, arguing that (in certain circumstances) discount rates should be treated as an element in the factual assessment of the claimant's loss rather than as part of the legal framework for that assessment.

[44] The equivalent of the English Judicial Studies Board, *Guidelines for the Assessment of General Damages in Personal Injury Cases* (8th ed, 2006).

facts (for example, social and economic conditions in a particular place[45]) are relevant to the assessment of damages.[46] Proof of the underlying facts will, however, remain a matter for the law of the forum, in accordance with Art 1(3) of the Regulation. The law of the forum has a potentially greater influence on the *mode* of assessment, a topic addressed in the commentary on Art 15(d) below.[47]

14.20 The editors of Dicey, Morris & Collins suggest that the use in Art 14(c) of the word 'damage' as opposed to 'damages' appears to be a slip, noting that the French version of the Regulation uses the word *'dommages'*.[48] Other language versions vary in the use of the singular and plural form.[49] More appropriate English expressions to convey the intended meaning would perhaps be 'the damage' or 'the elements of damage', as the word 'damages' leads to confusion with the specific monetary remedy (for which the French term is *'dommages-intérêts'* and the German *'Schadensersatz'*).[50] On either view, the concept of 'the existence, the nature and the assessment of damage or the remedy claimed' should be taken to include not only questions relating to the award of compensatory damages in cases of tort/delict, but also (a) the award of damages with respect to a non-contractual obligation on a non-compensatory basis (e.g. a gain-based or punitive award[51]), (b) the measure of any monetary award in cases of unjust enrichment, *negotiorum gestio*, and *culpa in contrahendo*, and (c) the availability and scope of certain non-monetary remedies.

14.21 As to item (a), the application of rules concerning non-compensatory damages, and punitive damages in particular, may be restricted by the public policy of the forum, in accordance with Art 26 of the Regulation. In this connection, Recital (32) specifically addresses the topic of non-compensatory damages, as follows:

> In particular, the application of a provision of the law designated by this Regulation which would have the effect of causing non-compensatory exemplary or punitive damages of an excessive nature to be awarded may, depending on the circumstances of the case and the legal order of the Member State of the court seised, be regarded as being contrary to the public policy (*ordre public*) of the forum.

---

[45] M Bogdan, 'General Aspects of the Future Regulation' in A Malatesta (ed), *The Unification of Choice of Law Rules on Torts and Other Non-Contractual Obligations in Europe* (2003), 42.

[46] Giuliano & Lagarde Report (OJ C282, 33 [31.10.1980]).

[47] **14.34** below.

[48] Dicey, Morris & Collins, 1st supplement, para S35-257, footnote 52.

[49] Singular: German (*'Schadens'*); Italian (*'danno'*); Dutch (*'schade'*). Plural: Spanish (*'daños'*); Portuguese (*'danos'*); Swedish (*'skadorna'*).

[50] Also **9.27** above.

[51] For the treatment of claims for such remedies within the Regulation, see **4.09-4.20** above.

This Recital was all that remained of the sentiment that had led the **14.22** Commission originally to propose that:[52]

The application of a provision of the law designated by this Regulation which has the effect of causing non-compensatory damages, such as exemplary or punitive damages, to be awarded shall be contrary to Community public policy.

In this connection, the Commission noted concerns expressed during **14.23** its consultation at the idea of applying third country rules[53] awarding damages on a non-compensatory basis, and pointed to Art 40(3) of the German EGBGB,[54] which excludes enforcement of claims subject to the law of another State if they either reach substantially beyond that which is necessary to provide reasonable compensation for the injured person (sub-rule 1) or manifestly serve other purposes than providing reasonable compensation for the injured person (sub-rule 2). The Commission's conception of 'Community public policy'[55] was, however, rejected by both the European Parliament[56] (which instead proposed a new rule, similarly worded to Recital (32), clarifying the sphere of application of the forum's public policy[57]) and the Council (which denied the need for any clarification of the concept of public policy).[58] Recital (32) emerged from the conciliation process.[59] Its effect would appear to be that Member State principles of public policy concerning non-compensatory exemplary or punitive damages,[60] such as sub-rule 2 of EGBGB, Art 40(3), should be taken to satisfy the requirement, originating in Art 26 of the Regulation, that the public policy of the forum that is invoked to derogate from the law otherwise applicable under the Regulation must serve to protect a fundamental principle of the forum's legal system.[61] It will arguably still be necessary to show, in each case, that the application of law that applies under the Regulation to the non-contractual obligation in question to the assessment of damages would be *manifestly* incompatible with that public policy.[62] On its face, however, the Recital does not appear to grant similar

---

[52] Commission Proposal, Art 24 (headed 'Non-compensatory damages').
[53] i.e. those of the United States of America or its constituent States.
[54] *Einführungsgesetz zum Bürgerlichen Gezetzbuch* (**1.21** above).
[55] The expression 'Community public policy' appears in Giuliano & Lagarde Report (OJ C282, 38 [31.10.1980]), but has rarely been used by the Community courts and appears to have no settled meaning.
[56] EP 1st Reading Position, Amendment 52.
[57] Ibid, Art 24(3) introduced by Amendment 50.
[58] Statement of reasons accompanying the Common Position (OJ C289E, 80 [28.11.2006]).
[59] Council document 9137/07 [7.5.2007], 25.
[60] But not restitutionary damages, which can also be seen as non-compensatory (**4.11** above).
[61] **15.07** below.
[62] **15.10** below.

'white list' status to rules such as sub-rule 1 of EGBGB, Art 40(3) which concerns the level of compensatory damages or damage more generally.[63] The questions whether damages are 'compensatory' or 'non-compensatory' and, if the latter, whether 'exemplary or punitive' and 'excessive' or otherwise within the terms of Recital (32), are probably matters with respect to which the court seised will enjoy a margin of appreciation, provided that the principle of public policy concerned is not used as a device to impose the forum's view as to the appropriate level of compensation.

14.24   As to item (b), it should be noted that 'damage' here bears the wider meaning contemplated by Art 2(1) so as to cover 'any consequence arising out of tort/delict, unjust enrichment, *negotiorum gestio* or *culpa in contrahendo*'. The 'nature and assessment of damage' thus contemplates an examination of the consequences of the event giving rise to the relevant non-contractual obligation, insofar as those consequences are material under the law that applies to that obligation under the Regulation.

14.25   As to (c), it may be noted that Art 15(c), also refers to 'the remedy claimed', extending its scope to remedies falling outside Art 15(d), which concerns 'the measures which a court may take to prevent or terminate injury or damage or to ensure the provision of compensation'. It may cover, for example, declaratory relief or approval of a statement in open court.

The Assessment of Damages in Traffic Accident Cases

14.26   In its application to claims arising from road traffic accidents, Art 15(c) must be read together with Recital (33), which provides:

> According to the current national rules on compensation awarded to victims of road traffic accidents, when quantifying damages for personal injury in cases in which the accident takes place in a State other than that of the habitual residence of the victim, the court seised should take into account all the relevant actual circumstances of the specific victim, including in particular the actual losses and costs of after-care and medical attention.

14.27   Unsurprisingly, given its opaque wording, Recital (33) is the product of a compromise reached between the Council and the European Parliament during the conciliation process. In its 2nd Reading Position, the Parliament had proposed amendments to the Council's Common Position concerning the quantification of damages in personal injury cases. The effect of these amendments, in the form of a new Article[64] and supporting Recital,[65] was to

---

[63] Cf P Beaumont and Zheng Tang, n 41 above, 140.
[64] EP 2nd Reading Position, Art 22.
[65] Ibid, Recital (34).

impose a new rule requiring the court seised of a personal injury claim to 'apply the principle of *restitutio in integrum,* having regard to the victim's actual circumstances in his country of habitual residence'. In the view of the Parliament's rapporteur:[66]

Given that the Council has rejected Parliament's first-reading amendment seeking to have the victim's national law applied for the purposes of calculating the quantum of the claim in traffic accident cases, the rapporteur has drafted two new amendments (one to the preamble and one to the enacting terms) in which the same result is sought to be attained by different means. Given the criticism voiced about the original limitation to traffic accidents, the rapporteur has extended the provisions to cover personal injuries generally.

In the case of personal injuries, it is vital to take account of the circumstances in which the victim will find him or herself in his or her country of habitual residence: the actual cost of nursing and carers, medical aftercare and so on. This provision will assist in making free movement of persons within the internal market more attractive for citizens, while showing an awareness of citizens' concerns. It will also avoid placing an unfair burden on the social security and assistance schemes of the country of habitual residence of an accident victim.

14.28 Given that it attempted to impose a mandatory, substantive rule governing the measure of damages, the Parliament's proposal (although apparently designed to facilitate agreement with the Council[67]) was a non-starter. The Commission described it as 'a very interesting idea for improving the situation of road traffic victims' but one which 'constitutes harmonisation of the Member States' substantive civil law which is out of place in an instrument harmonising the rules of private international law'.[68] In conciliation, the Council took the position that these amendments were unacceptable because they referred to substantive law and might have economic repercussions, but indicated a willingness to address the problem outside the context of the Rome II Regulation.[69] At a late stage in the discussions, the Parliament indicated that it could accept a compromise text suggested by the Commission in the following terms:[70]

Given the different practices followed in the Member States as regards the level of compensation awarded to victims of road traffic accidents, it is appropriate, when

---

[66] EP 2nd Reading Recommendation, comment to Amendment (11).

[67] Ibid.

[68] Commission Opinion on the European Parliament's amendments to the Council Common Position (COM (2007) 126 final [14.3.2007]), 5.

[69] See, for example, Council Document 8215/07 [5.4.2007], 11, 20 and the comments of the German Presidency in Council document DS 94/07 [6.2.2007], 15.

[70] Council Document 9137/07 [7.5.2007], 11 (underlining in original).

deciding on the level of compensation, to take account of <u>the actual</u> circumstances under which the victim would recover from personal injuries in the country of his/her habitual residence.

14.29 Further work in the drafting committee led to agreement on Recital (33) in its final form, set out above.[71]

14.30 In Professor Symeonides' view, 'despite its precarious placement and equivocal wording, this recital does more than recognize the relevance of foreign facts (i.e., the costs of after-care and medical attention); it also recognises the relevance of foreign *law*'.[72] Noting that the Recital does not authorize the application of the law of the victim's habitual residence to questions of compensation, he suggests:[73]

> Nevertheless, unless one assumes that the Parliament got nothing in return for this 'compromise', the recital must mean *something*. What it may mean is that—consistently with the admonition to 'do justice in individual cases' in recital 14—a court should keep in mind (for example, in applying the closer connection escape) the need to adequately compensate victims of traffic accidents.

14.31 Professor Symeonides' views as to the meaning and effect of Recital (14) have been discussed, and rejected, in **Chapter 3**.[74] His view as to the meaning and effect of Recital (33) is equally difficult to reconcile with the language used and with its legislative history. The Recital focuses, not on the role of compensation in the applicable law equation, but on the substantive law of personal injury damages in the Member States. Even on the most favourable view, it is no more than an attempt, albeit at a very high level of generalization,[75] to summarize the damages principles currently applied by Member State courts and to identify a common thread. That statement is not without value, as it may serve as a plea or a reminder to judges required to assess damages in cross-border cases that they should not approach the problem without regard to the actual circumstances of the victim. Nevertheless, as a mere recital in an instrument dealing with rules of private international law, it cannot possibly modify the rules applicable to the assessment of damages in the Member States, and it should not alter the way in which the Rome II Regulation (through Art 14(c)) approaches these questions.

---

[71] **14.26.**

[72] S C Symeonides, 'Rome II and Tort Conflicts: A Missed Opportunity' (2008) AJCL 173, 183.

[73] Ibid, 206, (emphasis in original).

[74] **3.22–3.28** above.

[75] At least insofar as English law is concerned. See generally *Heil v Rankin* [2001] 1 QB 272 (EWCA); H McGregor (ed), *McGregor on Damages* (17th edn, 2003), ch 35.

In this connection, it should be noted that the Commission has undertaken **14.32** to prepare, by the end of 2008, a study on possible options for improving the position of cross-border victims of road traffic accidents, paving the way for a Green Paper.[76] In a statement accompanying the Rome II Regulation, the Commission acknowledged 'the different practices followed in the Member States as regards the level of compensation awarded to victims of road traffic accidents'[77] and indicated a willingness to examine 'the specific problems resulting for EU residents involved in road traffic accidents in a Member State other than the Member State of their habitual residence'.[78] This study may, therefore, lead to reform of the Member States' substantive rules regulating compensation for road traffic accidents, or to adjustment of the rules of applicable law in the Rome II Regulation.[79] In this process, Recital (33) should be seen as no more than the point of embarcation.

(D) WITHIN THE LIMITS OF POWERS CONFERRED ON THE COURT BY ITS PROCEDURAL LAW, THE MEASURES WHICH A COURT MAY TAKE TO PREVENT OR TERMINATE INJURY OR DAMAGE OR TO ENSURE THE PROVISION OF COMPENSATION

The final version of the text of Art 15(d) of the Regulation, although prob- **14.33** ably no different in its substantive effect, appears preferable to the, apparently circular, language of the original Commission Proposal.[80] According to the Commission,[81] the concept of 'measures . . . to prevent or terminate injury or damage or to ensure the provision of compensation' refers 'to forms of compensation, such as the question whether the damage can be repaired by payment of damages, and ways of preventing or halting the damage, such as an interlocutory injunction, though without actually obliging the court to order measures that are unknown in the procedural law of the forum'.

---

[76] A background note entitled 'Compensation of Victims of Cross-Border Road Traffic Accidents in the EU: Assessment of Selected Options' (EP document IP/C/JURI/FWC/ 2006-171/LOT 2 PE378.292) was prepared by the European Parliament's Policy Department and presented to a public hearing organized by the JURI Committee in March 2007. The note is available at <http://www.europarl.europa.eu/comparl/juri/hearings/20070319/ background_en.pdf>.

[77] See para 2.2 of the background note referred to in the preceding footnote.

[78] OJ L199, 49 [31.7.2007].

[79] EP 3rd Reading Report, 7.

[80] Commission Proposal, Art 11(d) ('within the limits of its powers, the measures which a court has power to take under its procedural law to prevent or terminate injury or damage or to ensure the provision of compensation').

[81] Commission Proposal, 24.

14.34 Such measures may be granted only 'within the limits of powers conferred on the court by its procedural law'. Thus, Art 15(d) does not require Member States to create new remedies or procedures in order to accommodate those recognized by the law applicable under the Regulation. Instead, it is submitted, the court seised of the dispute must adopt a 'best fit' approach, using the procedural and remedial powers that are available to it to reflect the remedial framework of the applicable law as closely as possible. If, for example, damages are assessed by jury in the country whose law applies under the Regulation, the court seised is not required to empanel a jury if, under the law of the forum, damages are assessed by judge alone. The judge must, however, consider the basis upon which juries are instructed to assess damages under the relevant foreign law as well as the practice of juries in similar cases, particularly where that practice has been approved by a supervising court in the foreign legal system. Similarly, if, under the applicable law, an application can be made to vary damages after trial whereas, under the law of the forum, damages can only be assessed 'once and for all' at trial,[82] it may be that the court seised of the dispute will be able to use the procedural powers that are available to it (for example, trial on a preliminary issue of liability and an order for interim payment of damages) to build a remedy that approximates to that available under the law that applies under the Regulation.

14.35 The phrase 'measures which a court may take to prevent or terminate injury or damage or to ensure the provision of compensation' seems apt to include, among other matters, the currency of any monetary award and the availability of interest on such award.[83] On the basis of the Commission's explanation, it also includes interim measures, including injunctions, to prevent or halt damage. That conclusion is supported by the importance that the grant or refusal of measures of this kind may have in practice in promoting settlement before trial. In its initial response to the Commission Proposal, the Polish delegation suggested that 'it is not clear whether the court can issue interim measure[84] under the *lex fori* where the applicable law indicated by the Regulation does not provide for that type of measure'.[85] If, however, it is correct to conclude that interim measures fall within Art 15(d), the Member State court seised of the dispute cannot award relief of this kind unless that possibility exists under the law applicable to the obligation in question.

---

[82] *Hulse v Chambers* [2001] 1 WLR 2386 (EWHC).

[83] Cf Dicey, Morris & Collins, paras 33-395, 33-396, and 36-023.

[84] *Sic.*

[85] Council document 9009/04 ADD 3 [4.5.2004], 4. Also Council document 6518/04 [26.2.2004], 4.

Again, the reference to 'damage' in Art 15(d) should, in accordance with **14.36** Art 2(1), be understood to refer to the consequences arising out of tort/ delict, unjust enrichment, *negotiorum gestio*, or *culpa in contrahendo*. For example, the law applicable under Art 10 to a non-contractual obligation arising out of unjust enrichment will determine whether (within the limits of the forum's procedural powers) the defendant can be required to deliver up a specific asset.

(E) The Question Whether a Right to Claim Damages or a Remedy may be Transferred, including by Inheritance

The corresponding provision in the Commission Proposal referred to 'the **14.37** question whether a right to compensation may be assigned or inherited'.[86] The Commission thought this 'self-explanatory', but nevertheless felt the need to explain that:[87]

In succession cases, the designated law governs the question whether an action can be brought by a victim's heir to obtain compensation for damage sustained by the victim. In assignment cases, the designated law governs the question whether a claim is assignable and the relationship between assignor and debtor.

Unlike the Commission Proposal, the final text of the Regulation (reflecting **14.38** the Council's Common Position[88]) does not refer specifically to assignment. The most likely explanation for this, consistent with the course of the discussions in the Council's Rome II Committee, is that it was considered that the effect of an assignment of a non-contractual obligation as between the claimant and defendant was adequately dealt with by the Art 12 of the Rome Convention, concerning 'voluntary assignment of a right against another person'.[89] At a meeting of the Council's Rome II Committee in November 2004, a Swedish proposal for a stand alone provision dealing with voluntary assignment, reflecting Art 12 of the Rome Convention,[90] was supported by some delegations[91] but opposed by others and by the Commission representatives on the ground that the provision concerned contractual obligations (assignment being viewed as a 'contract' irrespective

---

[86] Commission Proposal, Art 11(f).

[87] Commission Proposal, 24.

[88] Common Position, Art 15(e).

[89] See now Rome I Regulation, Art 13, referring to 'a voluntary assignment or contractual subrogation of a claim against another person'.

[90] Council document 14193/04 ADD 1 [4.11.2004], 7–8. Also Council documents 9009/04 ADD 8, 23 (Sweden); ibid, ADD 10 [18.5.2004], 7 (Spain).

[91] Spain, United Kingdom, and the Netherlands.

of the nature of the underlying obligation) and was outside the scope of the Regulation.[92] Subsequently, the draft text circulated by the Austrian Presidency in March 2006[93] referred (in what was then Art 11(f)) to 'assignment and inheritance', but the former term was deleted in the following draft.[94] A Spanish proposal to introduce an additional sub-paragraph, reflecting Art 12(2) of the Rome Convention,[95] in the list of matters governed by the law applicable under the Rome II Regulation did not win majority support. The only reason given in the minutes of the Council's Rome II Committee was that '[o]ther delegations considered that this should be left to the Rome I instrument'.[96]

14.39 It is debatable whether the view taken within the Rome II Committee and by the Commission as to the application of Art 12 of the Rome Convention to the assignment of a right corresponding to a non-contractual obligation is correct, given that the Rome I Regime applies only to contractual obligations.[97] An assignment may indisputably result from a contract, but it produces its effects on the right assigned. This might, however provide a further example of the vertical scope of the EC regime for contractual obligations extending into the sphere formerly occupied by the Member State's pre-existing rules of applicable law for torts and other non-contractual obligations.[98] In any event, the debate appears largely academic. Art 15(e) of the Rome II Regulation is drafted in sufficiently broad terms to encompass assignment of non-contractual rights if the Rome I Regime does not apply and both Art 15(e) and

---

[92] Commission note of meeting held on 10–11 November 2004 (undated).

[93] Council document 7432/06 [16.3.2006].

[94] Council document 8076/06 [10.4.2006], Art 11(f).

[95] Council document 7432/06 [16.3.2006], 13 (footnote 2).

[96] Council document 7709/06 [3.5.2006], 5. Also Council document 7551/06 [22.3.2006], 2.

[97] Hamburg Group for Private International Law, Comments on the European Commission's Draft Proposal for a Council Regulation on the Law Applicable to Non-Contractual Obligations, 51–52, reproduced at <http://www.mpipriv.de/de/data/pdf/commentshamburggroup.pdf>; Max Planck Institute for Comparative and International Private International Law, Comments on the European Commission's Rome I Proposal, 87, available at <http://www.mpipriv.de/shared/data/pdf/comments_romei_proposal.pdf>. Both sets of Comments note the lack of clarity as to whether the voluntary assignment provisions of the Rome I proposal covered the assignment of non-contractual rights. The Hamburg Group proposed a stand-alone article in the Rome II instrument dealing with assignment. The MPI working group urged a clarification in the recitals of both the Rome I and Rome II Regulations.

[98] See also the suggestion by the Commission representative during discussions in the Council's Rome II Committee (Council document 8445/04 [19.4.2004], 3) that the provision concerning subrogation (Regulation, Art 19) would partially govern. There seems no basis for this.

Art 12(2) of the Rome Convention require application of the law applicable to the assigned right (i.e. that corresponding to the non-contractual obligation in question) to relations between the assignee and the obligor. The relationship between assignor and assignee remains a matter of contractual obligation, falling within either Art 12(1) of the Rome Convention[99] or, if that provision does not apply to assignments of non-contractual rights, the Rome I Regime's rules of applicable law for contracts generally.

Accordingly, whether the Rome I Regime or the Rome II Regulation **14.40** applies, questions as to the assignability of rights to claim damages or another remedy based on a non-contractual obligation, and the validity of the assignment, will in principle be governed by the law applicable to that obligation. It is unclear what impact (if any) this will have on the application of rules (such as the English rules prohibiting maintenance and champerty[100]) designed to protect the administration of justice in a particular legal system. Rules of this kind are based on public policy, a policy however that may apply only if the right in question is enforced in the courts of the legal system of which the rule forms part. Thus, a rule of the country whose law applies to a particular non-contractual obligation under the Regulation, which prohibits trafficking in litigation through the assignment of the right to enforce a non-contractual obligation, may on closer examination be found to have no claim to apply if the proceedings to enforce that obligation take place in a different country. It may appear that the rule is designed solely to protect the integrity of courts of that country. Equally, the forum State's own rules of this character may have a claim to apply as overriding mandatory rules or as public policy of the forum under Art 16 or 26 of the Regulation,[101] although it must be considered, in each case, whether the rule in question protects a sufficiently important interest of the forum State to be capable of being applied under the Regulation.[102]

By virtue of Art 15(e), the law applicable under the Rome II Regulation **14.41** determines the question whether a non-contractual obligation is personal to the person sustaining damage or may be passed to his heirs. The question whether a right of action dies with the person claimed to be liable or can

---

[99] Rome I Regulation, Art 13(1).
[100] The extent to which a tortious claim for damages is assignable under English law today is unclear (see A M Dugdale and M A Jones (eds), *Clerk & Lindsell on Torts* (19th ed, 2006), paras 5-63 to 5-66; *Defries v Milne* [1913] 1 Ch 98 (EWCA)).
[101] Cf *Trendtex Trading Corp v. Crédit Suisse* [1982] AC 679 (UKHL).
[102] **15.04–15.18** below.

be asserted against his estate or its representatives falls within Art 15(h) concerning 'the manner in which an obligation may be extinguished'. The determination of the persons to whom the right to claim damages etc. passes by inheritance, or of the persons representing the estate of the person liable, raises questions of status, which fall outside the scope of the Regulation.[103]

(F) Persons Entitled to Compensation for Damage Sustained Personally

14.42 According to the Commission:[104]

> [T]his concept particularly refers to the question whether a person other than the 'direct victim' can obtain compensation for damage sustained on a 'knock-on' basis, following damage sustained by the victim. Such damage might be non-material, as in the pain and suffering caused by a bereavement, or financial, as in the loss sustained by the children or spouse of a deceased person.

14.43 A similar provision[105] appeared in Article 11(6) of the 1972 draft convention on the law applicable to contractual and non-contractual obligations. Referring to the possibility of claims by 'ricochet' victims, the authors of the Giuliano, Lagarde & van Ysselt Report commented:[106]

> It very often occurs that moral damage is one of the wrongs caused by an initial damage to someone else, eg accidental death causing affliction to another. A similar situation arises in respect of material damage. When the text states that the prejudice must be personal to the party seeking compensation this does not signify that a juristic person comprising a group of individuals may not seek compensation for injury to the interests it represents as a whole. The question of whether a claim by a juristic person is admissible also depends on the law declared applicable to liability.

14.44 Questions concerning the law applicable to claims by indirect/ricochet victims have been considered in the commentary of the general rule for torts/delicts in Art 4.[107]

---

[103] **3.89** above.

[104] Commission Proposal, 24 referring to the identically worded Art 11(g) of the Proposal.

[105] Referring to 'the persons who have a right to compensation for damage or injury which they personally have suffered'. This language is reflected closely in the French text of Art 15(f) of the Rome II Regulation *'les personnes ayant droit à réparation du dommages qu'elles ont personellement subi'*.

[106] Giuliano, Lagarde & van Ysselt Report, 60.

[107] **4.39-4.45**.

(G) Liability for the acts of Another Person

As a matter of first impression, this provision seems straightforward **14.45** enough. As the Commission explained:[108]

[T]his concept concerns provisions in the law designated for vicarious liability. It covers the liability of parents for their children and of principals for their agents.

Although the Commission refers to 'vicarious liability', Art 15(g) appears **14.46** broad enough to encompass both rules that establish liability by attributing one person's acts or omissions to another (e.g. where a principal has authorized or ratified his agent's tort) and rules that impose liability on a person for the non-contractual obligations of another (e.g. where an employee commits a tort in the course of his employment).

The nature of the relationship required, and the required connection to the **14.47** event giving rise to liability, are matters for the law applicable to the relevant non-contractual obligation under the Rome II Regulation. The question whether a particular relationship (e.g. principal and agent; employer and employee; parent and child) exists is one of status or contract, and falls outside the scope of the Regulation.

(H) The Manner in which an Obligation may be Extinguished and Rules of Prescription and Limitation, including Rules Relating to the Commencement, Interruption and Suspension of a Period of Prescription or Limitation

Art 15(h) reflects, in large part, the position reached under English law **14.48** following the adoption of the Foreign Limitation Periods Act 1984. Prior to that, English private international law differentiated in its treatment of two types of rule concerning the consequences of delay in bringing a claim to enforce a non-contractual obligation.[109] First, those extinguishing the right/obligation, which were treated as substantive and within the scope of the law applicable to the right/obligation in question. Secondly, those that only extinguished the remedy, which were treated as procedural in nature and a matter for the law of the forum. That distinction, and the application by the English courts of English limitation rules (most of which were of the second kind) to claims governed by foreign law, was

---

[108] Commission Proposal, 24.
[109] Sir L Collins et al. (eds), *Dicey, Morris & Collins: The Conflict of Laws* (14th edn, 2006), paras 7-045–7-049.

heavily criticized,[110] and led to the adoption of the 1984 Act.[111] For claims governed by foreign law, s 1 of that Act substituted the limitation rules of the relevant foreign law for the limitation rules of English law. That is also the result achieved by the second part of Art 15(h).

14.49 Three potential differences may be noted between the effect of Art 15(h), so far as it applies to rules of limitation and prescription, and the effect of the 1984 Act:

1. The 1984 Act excludes the application of foreign limitation rules to the extent that they conflict with public policy.[112] Although Art 15(h) is subject to a similar restriction, in the form of Art 26 of the Regulation,[113] the latter provision is more restrictive in two respects. First, Art 26 requires that the application of a provision of the applicable law be *manifestly* contrary to the forum's public policy. This almost certainly imposes a higher threshold than at common law.[114] Secondly, s 2(2) of the 1984 Act extended the statutory concept of public policy to any situation in which the application of a rule 'would cause undue hardship to a person who is, or might be made, a party to the action or proceedings'. That fact, of itself, seems unlikely to be enough for the purposes of Art 26, unless the rule interferes with the subject's right of access to justice under Art 6 of the European Convention on human rights.[115]

2. Section 2(3) of the 1984 Act requires the English courts to disregard rules of foreign limitation law that extend or interrupt the limitation period in respect of the absence of a party to the action or proceedings from a specified jurisdiction or country. In contrast, rules of this kind appear capable of falling within Art 15(h), which refers specifically to rules relating to the 'interruption' of a limitation period. Such rules, however, may produce curious results when applied by the courts of a different country. Take for example, a situation in which the courts of Member State A are called upon to apply a rule of State B suspending the running of the limitation period 'for any period during which the defendant is outside State B'. That rule may, for example, be intended to facilitate service on the defendant or to discourage those who may consider fleeing the country

---

[110] Ibid, paras 2-040–2-042; Law Commission Report No 114, *Classification of Limitation in Private International Law* (1982).

[111] P B Carter (1985) 101 LQR 68.

[112] Foreign Limitation Periods Act 1984, s 2(1).

[113] **15.03–15.13** below.

[114] **15.10** below.

[115] Cf *Stubbings v United Kingdom* (Application No 22083/93) (1996) 23 EHRR 213 (ECtHR).

to escape justice. In order for the rule to serve these purposes in proceedings before the courts of Member State A, the rule must be read as referring not to State B but to Member State A, as the place where the obligation in question is to be enforced. This, however, may stretch the interpretation of the rule under the law of State B beyond breaking point. One possible solution would be to treat rules concerned with facilitating service as being procedural, falling outside the Regulation under Art 1(3), allowing the court in Member State A (assuming that it applies the *lex fori* to matters of procedure) to apply a similar rule under its own law.

3. Under s 4(3) of the 1984 Act, its provisions do not have the effect of excluding English rules of equitable origin by virtue of which a court may, in the exercise of its discretion, refuse equitable relief[116] on the grounds of acquiescence or otherwise. In applying those rules to a case to which foreign law applies, the English court must, however, have regard to any relevant provision of the foreign law. Under the Regulation, rules relating to the availability of a specific remedy fall within Art 15(c) or Art 15(d)[117] and, given that they probably cannot be characterized for these purposes as 'limits of powers conferred on the court by its procedural law' under Art 15(d), the English equitable rules of *laches* and acquiescence should be applied only if English law is the law applicable to the non-contractual obligation in question.

Under s 1(3) of the 1984 Act, the law of England and Wales will determine **14.50** for the purposes of any applicable limitation rule whether, and the time at which, proceedings have been commenced. Given that the rules and procedures for commencing and continuing court proceedings may vary widely between different countries, the argument for also treating such matters as 'procedural' under the Regulation, with the result that they fall outside its scope[118] is a strong one. That said, the Regulation makes clear that 'rules relating to the commencement, interruption and suspension of a period of prescription or limitation' fall within the ambit of Art 15(h). Accordingly, for example, if the limitation regime of the country whose law applies to a particular non-contractual obligation under the Regulation specifies that an event prior to or following the commencement of legal proceedings is relevant for limitation purposes (for example, formal notification of a claim, commencement of a mediation procedure[119] or service

---

[116] Most commonly, an injunction or order for specific performance.
[117] **14.18–14.36** above.
[118] Art 1(3) (**14.54–14.62** below).
[119] Directive (EC) No 2008/52 on certain aspects of mediation in civil and commercial matters (OJ L136, 3 [24.5.2008]), Art 8(1) ('Member States shall ensure that parties who choose mediation in an attempt to settle a dispute are not subsequently prevented from initiating

of the claim document) the Member State court seised of proceedings must endeavour to give effect to that rule, having regard to its own corresponding procedures where appropriate.

14.51 One specific point merits closer attention. Section 1(3) of the 1984 Act refers specifically to s 35 of the Limitation Act 1980, concerning the introduction of new claims by way of amendment to a statement of case in a pending action before the English courts. If allowed, new claims introduced by amendment are treated for the purposes of the rules of limitation contained in the 1980 Act as having been brought on the date of the original claim.[120] As a counterbalance to this statutory back-dating (or 'relation back'), s 35(3) of the 1980 Act prohibits any new claim by way of amendment 'after the expiry of any time limit *under this Act* which would affect a new action to enforce that claim', unless the claim is permitted by rules of court which must themselves satisfy certain conditions. Under s 1(3) of the 1984 Act, s 35 of the 1980 Act and the Civil Procedure Rules that give effect to it apply equally to foreign time limits which fall to be applied *under* the 1984 Act. Section 35 does not, however, apply to new claims brought following expiry of any foreign limitation period that applies under Art 15(h) of the Rome II Regulation. In the circumstances, it is unclear how the powers that the English court has to amend existing claims, by adding new claims or new parties,[121] will apply to new claims falling within the scope of the Regulation. On a strict view, it could be argued that there is no possibility of an amendment to introduce a new claim or a new party after expiry of the primary limitation period otherwise than by reference to s 35 of the 1980 Act, which does not apply here.[122] Even if the country whose law applies under the Regulation has a rule that enables its courts to allow such an amendment after expiry of the relevant time limit, that may be argued to be a procedural rule and to be beyond the scope of Art 15(h).

14.52 The Civil Procedure Rules, however, expressly permit amendments to introduce a new claim or to change the parties to an existing claim following expiry of a period of limitation under 'any other enactment which

---

judicial proceedings or arbitration in relation to that dispute by the expiry of limitation or prescription periods during the mediation process').

[120] Limitation Act 1980, s 35(1).

[121] See further s 35(4)–(5) and Civil Procedure Rules, rr 17.4 (new claims) and 19.5 (new parties).

[122] *Rhone-Poulenc Rorer International Holdings Inc v Yeda Research and Development Co Ltd* [2006] EWHC 160 (Ch) [48]–[54] (affd [2006] EWCA Civ 1094 but reversed on other grounds [2007] UKHL 43), referring to *Ketteman v Hansel Properties Ltd* [1987] AC 189 (UKHL) and *Banks v CBS Songs Ltd* [1992] FSR 278 (EWCA).

allows such an amendment, or under which such an amendment is allowed',[123] and this has not only been upheld as a legitimate exercise of the rule making power but has also been construed broadly so as to be capable of referring to a limitation regime that does not either expressly or impliedly prohibit amendments of this character.[124] On this basis, the counter-argument can be presented that a foreign limitation regime applicable under Art 15(h) ought to be treated, whether standing alone or coupled with the Regulation, as a relevant 'enactment' for these purposes so as to enable the English court to allow an amendment after expiry of the applicable foreign limitation period if (a) an amendment of this kind is permitted or, at the very least, is not expressly or impliedly prohibited under the applicable foreign law, and (b) the other conditions laid down by the Civil Procedure Rules are satisfied.[125]

The first part of Art 15(h) also applies to other modes of discharge of non-contractual obligations, for example death,[126] accord and satisfaction, and release. Modes of discharge that are attributable to the effect of a judgment, including estoppel by record (*res judicata*) and the English doctrine of merger (or former recovery),[127] should probably be treated for the purposes of the Rome II Regulation as 'procedural' in character, to be addressed by other rules of private international law.[128] **14.53**

C. EVIDENCE AND PROCEDURE

Article 1(3)

3. This Regulation shall not apply to evidence and procedure, without prejudice to Articles 21 and 22.

---

[123] Civil Procedure Rules, r 17.4(1)(c) and r 19.5(1)(c).

[124] *Parsons v George* [2004] EWCA Civ 912; [2004] 1 WLR 3264.

[125] Civil Procedure Rules, r 17.4(2), for example, allows an amendment whose effect will be to add or substitute a new claim, only if the new claim arises out of the same facts or substantially the same facts as an existing claim. For cases involving the application of r 17.4 to claims governed by foreign law, see *Latreefers Inc v Hobson* [2002] EWHC 1696 (Ch) (Morritt VC); *Barros Mattos v MacDaniels Ltd* [2004] EWHC 1323 (Ch) (Lawrence Collins J).

[126] **14.41** above.

[127] See also Civil Jurisdiction and Judgments Act 1984, s 34.

[128] Most obviously, within the European Community, by Arts 33–36 of the Brussels I Regulation concerning the recognition of judgments. For more detailed discussion of these issues, see P Barnett, *Res Judicata, Estoppel and Foreign Judgments* (2001).

INTRODUCTION

14.54   Art 1(3) of the Regulation reflects Art 1(2)(h) of the Rome Convention.[129] Professors Giuliano and Lagarde, in their report on the Convention, thought that this exclusion required 'no comment'.[130] In its Rome II Proposal, however, the Commission suggested that it was not necessary to carry forward that exclusion into the Regulation, adding:[131]

> It is clear from Art 11,[132] subject to the exceptions mentioned, these rules are matters for the *lex fori*. They would be out of place in a list of non-contractual obligations excluded from the scope of this Regulation.

14.55   That reasoning sat uncomfortably with the use in Art 11 of the Commission Proposal of the words 'in particular', leaving its precise scope open,[133] and from the reference in that provision to a number of issues that could be considered procedural in nature (e.g. 'the measures which a court has power to take under its procedural law'[134] and 'rules of prescription and limitation'[135]). In its First Reading Position, the European Parliament sought to exclude matters of evidence and procedure from the scope of the Regulation, by adding to the list of excluded matters in Art 1(2) a new exclusion in terms materially identical to Art 1(3) of the Regulation in its final form.[136] The accompanying report of the JURI Committee observed:[137]

> This amendment takes account of the universal principle of *lex fori* within private international law that the law applicable to procedural questions, including questions of evidence, is not the law governing the substantive legal relationship (*lex causae*), but, rather, the procedural law of the forum.

14.56   This amendment was accepted by the Commission, albeit in slightly modified form,[138] and by the Council, introducing in its Common Position the text of Art 1(3) in its final form.[139]

---

[129]   Rome I Regulation, Art 1(2)(h).
[130]   Giuliano & Lagarde Report (OJ C282, 13 [31.10.1980]).
[131]   Commission Proposal, Art 9.
[132]   Now Regulation, Art 15 (**14.02–14.53** above).
[133]   **14.04** above.
[134]   Commission Proposal, Art 11(d).
[135]   Ibid, Art 11(i).
[136]   EP 1st Reading Position, Art 1(2)(h) (Amendment 22). At the same time, the Parliament also sought to harmonize procedures for the pleading and proof of foreign law (see EP 1st Reading Position, Arts 12–13. These proposed amendments, which were ultimately rejected, will be considered separately at **14.67–14.69** below.
[137]   EP 1st Reading Report, 15.
[138]   Commission Amended Proposal, Art 1(2)(i) removing the reference to what became Regulation, Art 21 (formal validity).
[139]   Common Position, Art 1(3).

SCOPE AND RELATIONSHIP WITH ART 15

Art 1(3) is expressed to be 'without prejudice to 'Arts 21 (formal validity) **14.57** and 22 (burden of proof)'.[140] It does not refer expressly to Art 15. This might be taken to suggest that the exclusion by Art 1(3) of matters of 'evidence' and of 'procedure', leaving Member States courts free to apply their own rules, may erode significantly the sphere of influence of the law that applies to non-contractual obligations under the Rome II Regulation. It is submitted, however, that this would be to approach the matter in the wrong way. First, it should be noted that Art 1(3) is solely a restriction on the (vertical) scope of the Regulation. It does not designate the *lex fori* as applicable. Instead, for matters to which Art 1(3) applies, Member State courts may continue to apply their pre-existing rules of private international law, which may or may not lead to application of the forum's own rules. Secondly, as with all matters that define the scope of the Regulation, the concepts of 'evidence' and 'procedure' must be understood as autonomous concepts, to be given a uniform meaning independent of the forum's notions as to the reach of the law of evidence and the law of procedure.[141] Thirdly, as noted above, the Commission suggested that restrictions on the scope of the Regulation should be interpreted strictly.[142] As a general proposition, that seems debatable.[143] In relation to Art 1(3), however, a strict interpretation of the concepts of 'evidence' and 'procedure' is justified, both by the Commission's view that Art 15 of the Regulation 'confers a very wide function on the law designated'[144] and by the stated objectives of the Regulation, namely that 'in order to improve the predictability of the outcome of litigation, certainty as to the law applicable' there is a need 'for the conflict-of-law rules in the Member State to designate the same national law irrespective of the country of the court in which an action is brought'.[145] A broad interpretation of either of the concepts used in Art 1(3), giving greater freedom to Member State courts to apply a law other than that applicable to non-contractual obligations under the Regulation, would put the achievement of these objectives in jeopardy. Further, in its case law on the Brussels Convention, the Court of Justice has repeatedly emphasized that 'the application of national procedural rules

---

[140] **14.77–14.86** below.

[141] **3.05–3.11** above.

[142] Commission Proposal, 9.

[143] **3.147** above.

[144] See the extract from the explanatory memorandum accompanying the Commission Proposal, cited at **14.02** above.

[145] Recital (6). For discussion of the specific mischief of 'forum shopping', see **2.72–2.73** above.

may not impair the effectiveness of the Convention'.[146] That proposition links closely to the generally recognized requirement that the detailed procedural rules governing rights conferred by Community law, although in principle a matter for the Member States' domestic legal systems, must (a) not be less favourable than those governing similar domestic actions (*principle of equivalence*), and (b) not render virtually impossible or excessively difficult the exercise of those rights (*principle of effectiveness*).[147] Finally, the scope of the exclusion must itself be defined partly by reference to the list of matters set out in Art 15. That Article makes clear that certain matters that might otherwise be considered to be matters of 'evidence' or 'procedure', fall squarely within the scope of law applicable under the Rome II Regulation. These include, in particular, (1) the assessment of damage (Art 15(c)[148]), (2) the available remedial measures (albeit 'within the limits of powers conferred on the court by its procedural law') (Art 15(d)[149]), and (3) rules of prescription and limitation (Art 15(h)[150]).

14.58 In recent years, the courts of common law jurisdictions outside England have moved hesitatingly towards the position that the rules of the forum's law will be characterized as procedural rules under private international law only in circumstances in which the corresponding foreign rule cannot, or cannot without difficulty, be accommodated within the forum's legal framework for the judicial determination of disputes. In *Harding v Wealands*[151] (a case concerning the substance/procedure distinction under the pre-existing UK statutory rules of applicable law for torts[152]) the majority of the English Court of Appeal adopted that approach in applying legislation adopted by an Australian state to control awards of damages in personal injury cases. Arden LJ expressed the following view:[153]

A principled approach requires the court to start from the position that it has already decided that the proper law of the tort is not the law of the forum, ie that

---

[146] See, e.g., Case C-159/02, *Turner v Grovit* [2004] ECR I-3565, para 29. The Brussels Convention and its successor, the Brussels I Regulation, do not expressly exclude matters of procedure from its scope. In Case 365/88, *Hagen* [1990] ECR I-1845, however, the ECJ noted that (para 17) 'the object of the Convention is not to unify procedural rules' and (para 19) 'as regards procedural rule, reference must be made to the national rules applicable by the national court', subject (para 20) to the 'principle of effectiveness'.

[147] Joined Cases C-222/05 to C-225/05, *van der Weerd v Minister van Landbouw, Natuur en Voedselkwaliteit* [2007] ECR I-4233, para 28.

[148] **14.18–18.32** above.

[149] **14.33–14.36** above.

[150] **14.48–14.53** above.

[151] [2004] EWCA Civ 1735; [2005] 1 WLR 1539.

[152] Private International Law (Miscellaneous Provisions) Act 1995, s 14(3)(b).

[153] Ibid, [52].

some other law applies to the tort, either because it is the *lex loci delicti* or because it is substantially more appropriate than the *lex loci delicti*. On this basis, a reference to the law of the forum must be the exception, and it must be justified by some imperative which, relative to the imperative of applying the proper law, has priority. It may, for instance, be appropriate to apply the law of the forum where the court cannot put itself into the shoes of the foreign court.

Both Arden LJ and Sir William Aldous, in turn, approved[154] the following **14.59** passage from the judgment of the majority of the High Court of Australia in *John Pfeiffer Pty Ltd v Rogerson*:[155]

Two guiding principles should be seen as lying behind the need to distinguish between substantive and procedural issues. First, litigants who resort to a court to obtain relief must take the court as they find it. A plaintiff cannot ask that a tribunal which does not exist in the forum (but does in the place where a wrong was committed) should be established to deal, in the forum, with the claim that the plaintiff makes. Similarly, the plaintiff cannot ask that the courts of the forum adopt procedures or give remedies of a kind which their constituting statutes do not contemplate any more than the plaintiff can ask that the court apply any adjectival law other than the laws of the forum. Secondly, matters that affect the existence, extent or enforceability of the rights or duties of the parties to an action are matters that, on their face, appear to be concerned with issues of substance, not with issues of procedure. Or to adopt the formulation put forward by Mason CJ in *McKain*,[156] 'rules which are directed to governing or regulating the mode or conduct of court proceedings' are procedural and all other provisions or rules are to be classified as substantive.

The approach to the substance/procedure distinction in the UK statute **14.60** taken by the majority of the Court of Appeal in *Harding v Wealands* was subsequently rejected by the House of Lords, which considered that the concept of 'procedure' within the UK statutory regime was to be understood in light of the common law authorities existing at the time that the legislation was enacted in 1995.[157] Further, following the decision in *Pfeiffer v Rogerson*, an almost identically constituted majority of the High Court of Australia had reserved for further consideration the question whether the test laid down in *Pfeiffer* (involving a conflict of laws solely between two Australian states) should also be applied to separate substantive from procedural rules in international cases (i.e. connected to a legal system

[154] Ibid, [54] (Arden LJ), [90], [95] (Sir William Aldous).
[155] [2000] HCA 36; 203 CLR 503, [99] (Gleeson CJ, Gaudron, McHugh, Gummow, and Hayne JJ).
[156] *McKain v RW Miller & Co (SA) Pty Ltd* (1991) 174 CLR 1, [30] (in a dissenting judgment).
[157] [2006] UKHL 32; [2007] 2 AC 1. For comment, see A Briggs (2006) 77 BYIL 565; P Rogerson [2006] CLJ 515; A Scott [2007] LMCLQ 44.

outside Australia).[158] Nevertheless, at least until Member State courts or the Court of Justice have had the opportunity to consider the question, the approach identified in the two passages quoted above may be thought helpful in assessing the scope of the exclusion of matters of evidence and procedure in Art 1(3) of the Rome II Regulation. Certainly, a restrictive approach to the concept of 'procedure' in Art 1(3) seems justified and (to use the words of the majority judgment in *Pfeiffer*) Art 15 may justifiably be seen as describing 'matters that affect the existence, extent or enforceability of the rights or duties of the parties to an action', while refraining from demanding that Member State courts 'adopt procedures or give remedies of a kind which their constituting statutes do not contemplate'.[159]

14.61 Without judicial guidance, the precise scope and effect of Art 1(3) remains unclear. Nevertheless, the nature and objectives of the Rome II Regulation, as well as the reasoning in the passages quoted above, support the view that a decision by a Member State court, in the determination of a non-contractual obligation, to refuse to apply a rule originating in the country whose law applies under the Regulation on the ground that the rule in question is 'evidential' or 'procedural' in character must be (1) exceptional, and (2) justified by reference to a feature of that rule that prevents its incorporation into the legal framework to be applied by the Member State court in that determination. Equally, a decision by a Member State court in the determination of a non-contractual obligation, to apply a rule of its own legal system on the ground that is 'evidential' or 'procedural'[160] within Art 1(3) should be justified by a feature of that rule that marks it as an integral and indispensable element of the forum's legal framework for the judicial determination of disputes. Rules falling within the category of 'evidence and procedure' on this basis would include, for example, those concerning (a) the creation, constitution, and domestic competences of courts, (b) requirements for the commencement of proceedings and any appeal process, (c) case management, (d) the power to grant a remedy of a particular kind,[161] (e) mode of trial, (f) mode of proof of facts,[162] and (g) costs.

14.62 On occasion, English judges have concluded that provisions of a UK statute that regulates non-contractual claims before the English courts should, as a matter of statutory construction, be applied in all cases before those

---

[158] *Régie Nationale des Usines Renault SA v Zhang* [2002] HCA 10; (2002) 210 CLR 491, [76] (Gleeson CJ, Gaudron, McHugh, Gummow, and Hayne JJ).

[159] See, in particular, Art 15(d) (**14.33–14.36** above).

[160] Assuming that the *lex fori* applies to such matters (**14.57** above).

[161] Art 15(d).

[162] For the position in relation to pleading and ascertainment of foreign law, see **14.63–14.76** below

courts (including those with a cross-border connection) even if the provision in question controls the existence or content of the defendant's non-contractual obligation. For example, in *Roerig v Valiant Trawlers*, the Court of Appeal concluded that s 4 of the Fatal Accidents Act 1976 (concerning the non-deductibility from a damages award of benefits accruing to the claimant from the estate of the deceased person or otherwise as a result of his death) was '"procedural" or "adjectival or non-substantive" in the sense that it is a part of the law which the English court must apply to actions brought under this particular statute'.[163] In *Harding v Wealands*, Arden LJ suggested that this aspect of the decision in *Roerig* rested on the Court's view that the relevant provision of the 1976 Act was an overriding mandatory rule of English law.[164] In light of the restrictive approach to the concept of 'procedure' that the Rome II Regulation is likely to require, classification as an overriding mandatory provision under Art 16 would now appear to be the only possible basis for explaining the continued application by the English courts of statutory provisions of this kind in circumstances in which the law of another country applies under the Regulation to the defendant's non-contractual obligation. Even so, the English courts may need to reconsider the approach taken in *Roerig*, and similar decisions, in light of likely restrictions on the deployment of overriding mandatory provisions of the law of the forum under Art 16.[165]

D. INTRODUCTION AND ASCERTAINMENT OF THE LAW APPLICABLE UNDER THE REGULATION

INTRODUCTION

The Regulation, in its final form, contains no rules dealing explicitly with **14.63** the introduction (pleading) and ascertainment of the applicable law. The review clause in Art 30 requires the Commission's first report on the application of the Regulation, due by 2011, to include 'a study on the effect of the way in which foreign law is treated in the different jurisdictions and on the extent to which courts in different Member States apply foreign law in practice pursuant to this Regulation'.[166] The treatment of foreign law is

---

[163] [2002] EWCA Civ 21; [2002] 1 WLR 2304, [28]–[30] (Waller J).
[164] *Harding v Wealands* [2004] EWCA Civ 1735; [2005] 1 WLR 1539, [48].
[165] **15.16–15.18** below.
[166] Art 30(1)(i).

also currently on the list of matters under active consideration by the Hague Conference on Private International Law.[167]

CURRENT POSITION IN THE MEMBER STATES—A COMPARATIVE OVERVIEW

14.64   As is well known, the legal systems of the Member States take widely differing approaches to the introduction and ascertainment of foreign law.[168] In this connection, '[d]ifferences prevail not only between common law and civil law judges, but also between the civil law judges, particularly between the German and Dutch judges on one hand, and the French and Belgian judges on the other'.[169] Under the English system, the parties play the primary role in the introduction and ascertainment of foreign law, which is treated as a question of fact, albeit of a special kind.[170] A party wishing to rely on a rule of foreign law to support his case must plead that rule in his statement of case and prove its content, usually by expert evidence.[171] If the content of any applicable foreign law is not pleaded, or is pleaded but not sufficiently proved, the court will normally apply the corresponding rules of English law, *faute de mieux*, to fill the vacuum.[172] This, it may be noted, treats foreign law unlike ordinary questions of fact, for a party who fails to discharge the burden of proving a fact will be considered to have failed to

---

[167]   Permanent Bureau of the Hague Conference, *Feasibility Study on the Treatment of Foreign Law* (Preliminary Documents No 21A of March 2007), available at <http://www.hcch.net/upload/wop/genaff_pd21ae2007.pdf>. The Permanent Bureau has been invited to report and, if possible, to make a recommendation as to future action to the Council of General Affairs and Policy of the Conference in 2009.

[168]   S Geeroms, *Foreign Law in Civil Litigation: A Comparative and Functional Analysis* (2003), esp ch 2; T C Hartley, 'Pleading and Proof of Foreign Law: The Major European Systems Compared' (1996) 45 ICLQ 271; R Fentiman, *Foreign Law in English Courts: Pleading, Proof and Foreign Law* (1998), ch 9.

Eighteen Member States responded to the questionnaire circulated by the Permanent Bureau of the Hague Conference on Private International Law in October 2007. The individual responses are available at <http://www.hcch.net/upload/wop/genaff_resp_pd09.html>, with summaries at <http://www.hcch.net/upload/wop/genaff_pd21be2007.pdf> (Preliminary Document No 21B of March 2007), <http://www.hcch.net/upload/wop/genaff_pd09ae2008.pdf> (Preliminary Document No 9A of March 2008) and <http://www.hcch.net/upload/wop/genaff_pd09be2008.pdf> (Preliminary Document No 9B of March 2008).

[169]   S Geeroms, n 168 above, 389.

[170]   *Morgan Grenfell & Co Ltd v SACE—Istituto per I Servizi Assicurativi del Commercio* [2001] EWCA Civ 1932, [45]. See Dicey, Morris & Collins, ch 9; A Layton and H Mercer (eds), *European Civil Practice* (2nd edn, 2004), ch 8.

[171]   *Morgan Grenfell v SACE*, ibid, [46]–[52].

[172]   *Dynamit AG v Rio Tinto Ltd* [1918] AC 260 (UKHL); Dicey, Morris & Collins, para 9-025. For a recent example, in a contractual context, see *Balmoral Group Ltd v Borealis (UK) Ltd* [2006] EWHC 1900 (Comm); [2006] 2 Lloyd's Rep 629, [427]–[434] (Christopher Clarke J).

establish that element of his case. Instead, applicable foreign rules of law that are sufficiently proved are assimilated into the legal framework for determining the matters in issue in a particular case and rules of English law are borrowed to fill gaps in that framework to avoid a legal vacuum. Even so, a new approach to questions of foreign law is slowly evolving. The English courts have shown an increased willingness to recognize exceptions to the principle that English law will be applied where foreign law is not proved,[173] and the Court of Appeal has expressed the hope that:[174]

[T]he time may not be far off when it will be permissible for the English courts to take judicial notice of decisions of foreign courts, including those in the European Union, (and perhaps academic writings) in deciding what the relevant foreign law is in cases of this kind.

As yet, however, that time has not come.

By way of contrast, in Germany, courts must generally apply foreign **14.65** law if the facts point towards its application, even if the parties have not raised its possible application.[175] In this connection, the courts have emphasized the mandatory character of the underlying rules of applicable law, whether based on statute or case law.[176] The court must also ascertain the applicable foreign law of its own motion.[177] In so doing, it is not confined to the information provided by the parties, but must consult all accessible sources.[178] To fulfil this duty, German courts are supported by an established infrastructure which is able to provide advisory opinions (*Rechtsgutachten*) on foreign legal issues. One of the main suppliers of these *Gutachten* is the Max Planck Institute for Comparative and International Law in Hamburg, founded in 1926.[179] No similar infrastructure currently exists in England, where each party is left to identify and brief a suitably qualified expert in the laws of the relevant foreign legal system to prepare a report and, if necessary, appear in court to give evidence.[180]

---

[173] *Shaker v Al-Bedrawi* [2002] EWCA Civ 1452; [2003] Ch 350, [64]–[72] (CA); Dicey, Morris & Collins, para 9-025.

[174] *Morgan Grenfell v SACE*, n 170 above, [53].

[175] S Geeroms, n 168 above, paras 2.08–2.20.

[176] Ibid, para 2.12–2.13.

[177] Ibid, paras 2.135–2.150.

[178] German Civil Procedure Code (*Zivilprozeßordnung* or *ZPO*), §293.

[179] See S Geeroms, n 168 above, paras 2.299–2.300. For the history of the Institute, see <http://www.mpipriv.de/ww/en/pub/research/research_profile/academic_history/academic_history.cfm>.

[180] H M Malek et al. (eds), *Phipson on Evidence* (16th edn, 2005), paras 33-57 to 33-58.

14.66   In certain circumstances, French courts are also obliged to apply foreign law of their own motion, even against the parties' wishes. Such cases are, however, limited to situations in which rights are considered to be 'non-waivable'. In other cases, the court must respect any procedural agreement reached between the parties and otherwise enjoys a discretion.[181] If non-waivable rights are involved, or if the court applies foreign law of its own motion, the responsibility for establishing the content of foreign law will lie with the court, although it may request assistance from the parties.[182] In other cases, the burden will lie on the party who claims the application of foreign law.[183]

The European Parliament's Proposed Rules

14.67   Against this background, the European Parliament proposed a partial harmonization of the Member States' rules for the pleading and proof of the law applicable under the Regulation. Arts 12 and 13 of the EP 1st Reading Position provided as follows:[184]

Article 12

Contentions as to applicable law

Any litigant making a claim or counterclaim before a national court or tribunal which falls within the scope of this Regulation shall notify the court or tribunal and any other parties by statement of claim or other equivalent originating document of the law or laws which that litigant maintains are applicable to all or any parts of his/her claim.

Article 13

Determination of the content of foreign law

1. The court seised shall establish the content of the foreign law of its own motion. To this end, the parties' collaboration may be required.

2. If it is impossible to establish the content of the foreign law and the parties agree, the law of the court seised shall be applied.

14.68   The Commission rejected these proposals in its Amended Proposal. As to the proposed Art 12, the Commission stated that, although it was in favour of simplifying procedures, the rule 'would be too difficult to implement as parties are not all capable of stating what law is applicable to their situation,

---

[181]   S Geeroms, n 168 above, paras 2.48–2.73 referring, in particular, to the 1999 decision of the *Cour de Cassation, Cass 1e civ fr*, 26 May 1999 (*Mutuelle du Mans*).

[182]   Ibid, paras 2.176–2.188.

[183]   *Cour de cassation, 1ère Ch civ*, 5 November 1991 (*Masson*).

[184]   Reflecting Amendments 42 and 43. Also EP 1st Reading Position, Recital (20).

in particular when they are not legally represented'. As to the proposed Art 13, the Commission expressed the view that most Member States would not be able to apply the rule as they do not have proper structures in place to enable the courts to apply the foreign law in this way. The Commission accepted, however, that special attention should be paid to this topic in the first report on the implementation of the Regulation.[185] The Council also opposed the introduction of rules concerning the application of foreign law, arguing that 'this question should be tackled in a different context'.[186]

Again, the Parliament's JURI Committee, and its rapporteur, were reluc- **14.69** tant to yield. In her draft 2nd Reading Recommendation, the rapporteur re-inserted the text of Arts 12 and 13 of the 1st Reading Position, and the accompanying Recital.[187] These suggested amendments did not, however, survive the committee vote. Instead, the JURI Committee favoured a single draft Article, requiring Member State courts to ascertain the foreign law of their own motion,[188] coupled with two new Recitals dealing with both introduction and ascertainment.[189] The Committee's draft Article was, in turn, rejected by the plenary vote in Parliament, leaving the curious (and untenable) result that the Recitals to the Parliament's position at the second reading stage[190] referred to procedural requirements that would have a significant effect upon the conduct of litigation in many Member States, without any corresponding substantive provision to back them up. Unsurprisingly, this position proved unacceptable to the Commission[191] and the Council.[192] The conciliation process resulted in the deletion of the Parliamentary Recitals and the insertion of a specific requirement in the review clause that the Commission consider the treatment of foreign law in its implementation report.[193]

---

[185] Commission Amended Proposal, 7.
[186] Statement of reasons accompanying the Common Position at OJ C289E, 80 [28.11.2006].
[187] EP document PE 382.852v01-00 [8.11.2006], Amendments 12, 21, and 22.
[188] EP 2nd Reading Recommendation, Amendment 21 ('The court seised shall of its own motion establish the substance of foreign law. To that end the court may in certain circumstances also ask the parties to provide assistance.')
[189] Ibid, Amendments 12 and 13.
[190] EP 2nd Reading Position, Recitals (35) and (37) reflecting Amendments 12 and 13.
[191] Commission Opinion on the EP 2nd Reading Position (COM (2007) 126 final [14.3.2007]), 5.
[192] EP document PE 386.319 [27.2.2007] stating, in each case, 'Not acceptable because this recital does not refer to a concrete article'.
[193] **14.63** above.

EVALUATION OF THE CURRENT PRACTICE OF THE ENGLISH COURTS

14.70 Against this background, the question remains whether the current practice of the English courts concerning the pleading and proof of foreign law[194] can be reconciled with the Regulation in its final form. This issue was, presciently, highlighted by the English and Scots Law Commissions in their 1974 consultative document on the 1972 draft convention. The authors noted that:[195]

> The Convention in general provides what in the various circumstances specified 'shall be' the applicable law. . . . Because of this mandatory form of words the question arises of whether the court will be held to be under a positive obligation to apply the law made applicable by the Convention. If it is, it may then become important to make provision one way or another for the proof of foreign law. Is the court itself to be charged with the duty of ascertaining the relevant provisions of a foreign law or, if this task is to be undertaken by the parties, what is to happen if they fail to do so? . . . In any event, there may be much to be said for including in the Convention some clear provision about the proof of foreign law and the respective duties in this regard of the court and the parties.

14.71 As Art 1(3) excludes matters of evidence and procedure from the scope of the Rome II Regulation, there may appear no difficulty in accommodating the English rules concerning the pleading and proof of foreign law. Unfortunately, the position is not so straightforward. In particular, it may be thought likely that the Court of Justice will, in the context of the Rome II Regulation, restate the view that it has expressed on several occasions in relation to the Brussels Convention that the application of national procedural rules may not impair the effectiveness of the rules of private international law that the Regulation lays down.[196] In this connection, it must be noted that (a) the rules of applicable law in Arts 4 to 12 of the Regulation are all expressed in mandatory terms ('the law applicable . . . shall be . . .'), and (b) the ability of the parties to choose a different law is restricted, both by the terms of Art 14[197] and by Arts 6(4) and 8(3), which exclude the possibility of party choice for obligations concerning unfair competition, acts restricting free competition, and infringement of

---

[194] **14.64** above.

[195] Law Commission and Scottish Law Commission, *EEC Preliminary Draft Convention on the Law Applicable to Contractual and Non-Contractual Obligations: Consultative Document* (August 1974), para 21.2.23.

[196] Text to n 146 above.

[197] **Ch 13** above.

intellectual property rights.[198] Under current English practice,[199] the introduction and ascertainment of English law is controlled, very largely, by the parties. Moreover, if none of the parties introduces foreign law or if foreign law is pleaded but not sufficiently proved, English law is applied instead. One cannot exclude the possibility that the ECJ would consider this to be in the nature of a disguised rule of applicable law, favouring the law of the forum and impairing the effectiveness of the Regulation rules described at points (a) and (b) above.

There are also clear parallels between this debate, and that which raged **14.72** for many years in relation to the compatibility with the Brussels Convention of the common law doctrine of *forum non conveniens*, and in particular the question whether it was open to UK courts to decline jurisdiction conferred by the Convention's substantive provisions, in mandatory terms, so as to allow determination of the matters in issue by a non-Contracting State. That debate was famously settled by the Court of Justice's decision in *Owusu v Jackson*,[200] which gave priority to the Brussels Convention's rules over the discretionary *forum non conveniens* rule of UK law. In the course of its judgment, the EC emphasized the mandatory nature of Art 2 of the Brussels Convention (on which jurisdiction in *Owusu* had been based) with the result that 'according to its terms, there can be no derogation from the principle it lays down except in the cases expressly provided for by the Convention'.[201] This reasoning could be argued to apply with similar force in the case of the relationship between rules of applicable law in the Rome II Regulation, also expressed in mandatory terms, and the English rules concerning pleading and proof of the law applicable to non-contractual obligations.

Against these arguments, it may be noted that the ECJ in *Owusu*, in reach- **14.73** ing its conclusion that Art 2 of the Brussels Convention had mandatory effect, relied on the *travaux préparatoires* leading to the UK's accession to the Convention, specifically the report of Professor Schlosser,[202] which indicated that the compatibility of the doctrine of *forum non conveniens* with the existing provisions of the Convention had been considered during the accession process and that the UK and Irish delegations had not pressed for any formal adjustment to the Convention in this respect. In contrast, the legislative history of the Rome II Regulation,

---

[198] **6.74–6.75** and **8.54** above.
[199] **14.64** above.
[200] Case C-281/02 [2005] ECR I-1383.
[201] Ibid, para 37.
[202] Ibid.

described above,[203] strongly supports the conclusion that the treatment by Member States of foreign law was deliberately left outside the scope of the Rome II Regulation. In this connection, (a) both the Council and the Commission considered that it was not appropriate to address in the Regulation any problems arising from disparities between Member States' current practices in the area of non-contractual obligations alone, (b) the Commission, in particular, recognized that the courts of some Member States may not possess the infrastructure necessary to determine the content of the applicable law of their own motion, and (c) the review clause in Art 30(1)(i) contemplates that Member State courts will continue to treat foreign law differently in applying the Regulation. To require Member States to establish that infrastructure (or to impose that burden on the parties against their wishes) appears disproportionate to the objectives of the Regulation. In England, such a change would require not only significant additional resources, but also a change in judicial thinking.[204]

14.74 Furthermore, the Court of Justice's approach to the relationship between Community law and national procedural law in other areas strongly suggests that (save in exceptional cases when the relevant rule of Community law is of an overriding mandatory character[205]), EC law does not impose a duty on national courts to raise a plea based on a Community provision of their own motion, irrespective of the importance of that provision to the Community legal order, if the parties are given a genuine opportunity to raise that plea themselves.[206] That opportunity exists under English law.

14.75 On balance, the current English procedural rules appear justifiable, as being consistent with both the principle of equivalence and the principle of effectiveness.[207] Even so, there may be ways in which (without significant reforms of the kind contemplated by the European Parliament) the current English practice might evolve to encourage the application of foreign law in cases falling within the scope of the Rome II Regulation. This, in turn, may deter criticism and avoid legal uncertainty of the kind that appears to have motivated the ECJ to act in *Owusu*.

14.76 Three aspects of practice, in particular, may be significant in future cases. First, judges dealing with cases involving non-contractual obligations

---

[203] **14.67–14.69.**

[204] S Geeroms, n 168 above, 389–90.

[205] e.g., in the field of consumer protection (Joined Cases C-240-98 to C-244/98, *Océano Grupo Editorial SA v Quintero and others* [2000] ECR I-4841; Case C-168/05, *Mostaza Claro v Centro Móvil Milenium SL* [2006] ECR I-10421).

[206] *van der Weerd v Minister*, n 147 above, para 41.

[207] **14.57** and **14.71** above.

with a cross-border aspect will need to be familiar with the provisions of the Regulation, and should if necessary raise with the parties the possibility of application of a law other than English law. Secondly, if the parties are content for English law to be applied, the judge should seek to formalize that consensus by appropriate statements in the parties' statements of case, so as to enable the court to apply English law in accordance with Art 14(1)(a) of the Regulation. In the absence of clear statements to this effect (e.g. 'The Claimant/Defendant agrees that English law should apply to this Claim'), it may be doubted whether a choice of English law can be said to have been 'demonstrated with reasonable certainty' by reason only of the fact that neither party has sought to plead a foreign law.[208] Thirdly, and particularly if the case falls within Arts 6(1), 6(3), or 8 of the Regulation with the result that Art 14 does not apply,[209] the court should at least consider exercising its case management powers[210] so as (a) to require the parties to address the question of the applicable law in their statements of case, (b) to bring forward evidence of foreign law, for example (i) by the appointment of an assessor with expertise in the relevant foreign law,[211] (ii) if the law of a Commonwealth country applies, by using the mechanism contained in the British Law Ascertainment Act 1959 to ascertain the law of such country,[212] or (iii) possibly,[213] by letter of request to the competent authority of another State, including (in particular) a State party to the European Convention on information on foreign law, concluded in London in 1968 and commonly referred to as the London Convention.[214] Finally, in

---

[208] **13.36** above.

[209] Text to n 198 above.

[210] See, in particular, CPR, rr 3.1 (general), 32.1 (evidence), and Part 35 (expert evidence).

[211] Supreme Court Act 1981, s 70; County Courts Act 1984, s 63; Civil Procedure Rules, r 35.15.

[212] Dicey, Morris & Collins, paras 9-003 and 9-023. The editors refer (text to footnote 12) to 19th century cases in which orders for the ascertainment of foreign law under the 1859 Act have been made at the court's own motion although the foreign law was not pleaded. Under the Foreign Law Ascertainment Act 1861, similar provision was made to enable the law of non-Commonwealth jurisdictions to be ascertained pursuant to treaty. No relevant convention was ever concluded, however, and the 1861 Act was repealed in 1973.

[213] Layton & Mercer, n 170 above, para 8.014, but compare Dicey, Morris & Collins, para 9-024, text to footnote 31.

[214] Cm 4229 (1969). For the text of the Convention, see <http://conventions.coe.int/Treaty/EN/Treaties/Html/062.htm>. To date, the Convention has been ratified by Albania, Austria, Azerbaijan, Belarus, Belgium, Bulgaria, Costa Rica, Cyprus, Czech Republic, Denmark, Estonia, Finland, France, Georgia, Germany, Greece, Hungary, Iceland, Italy, Latvia, Liechtenstein, Lithuani, Luxembourg, Malta, Mexico, Moldova, Montenegro, Netherland, Norway, Poland, Portugal, Romania, Russia, Serbia, Slovakia, Slovenia, Spain, Sweden, Switzerland, FYR Macedonia, Turkey, Ukraine, and the United Kingdom.

cases in which foreign law has been placed in issue by one of the parties, the court may consider it expedient to exert greater control over the ascertainment of foreign law by exercising its power to require the parties to instruct a single joint expert.[215]

E. FORMAL VALIDITY

Article 21

Formal validity

A unilateral act intended to have legal effect and relating to a non-contractual obligation shall be formally valid if it satisfies the formal requirements of the law governing the non-contractual obligation in question or the law of the country in which the act is performed.

14.77 Art 21 of the Rome II Regulation, which concerns the formal validity of unilateral acts relating to non-contractual obligations, reflects almost exactly[216] Art 16 of the Commission Proposal.

14.78 In this connection, the Commission explained:[217]

Article 16 is inspired by Article 9 of the Rome Convention.[218]

Although the concept of formal validity plays a minor role in the creation of non-contractual obligations, an obligation can well arise as a result of a unilateral act by one or other of the parties.

To promote the validity of such acts, Article 16 provides for an alternative rule along the lines of Article 9 of the Rome Convention, whereby the act is formally valid if it satisfies the formal requirements of the law which governs the non-contractual obligation in question or the law of the country in which this act is done.

14.79 Art 21 is linked to Art 22(2), dealing with the mode of proof of acts intended to have legal effect.[219] The latter provision cross-refers to the laws applicable under Art 21. Art 21, like Art 22, is referred to in Art 1(3) as qualifying the exclusion from the Regulation of matters of evidence and procedure.[220]

---

[215] Civil Procedure Rules, r 35.7.
[216] In the Regulation, the final word 'performed' is substituted for 'done' in the Proposal.
[217] Commission Proposal, 26 (footnote added).
[218] Rome I Regulation, Art 11.
[219] **14.84–14.86** below.
[220] **14.57** above.

From an English law viewpoint, at least, the provision appears of miniscule **14.80** importance. That said, one point of interest emerges from the Commission's commentary, specifically its statement that 'an obligation can well arise as a result of a unilateral act by one or other of the parties'. That is, no doubt, the case in some legal systems, including England (for example, under a deed poll).[221] It is difficult, however, to see obligations of this kind as falling within the scope of the Regulation and, in particular, as arising out of tort/delict, unjust enrichment, *negotiorum gestio*, or *culpa in contrahendo*. Instead, Art 21 will apply (if at all) to unilateral acts that discharge or modify existing non-contractual obligations.

F. BURDEN OF PROOF

Article 22

Burden of proof

1. The law governing a non-contractual obligation under this Regulation shall apply to the extent that, in matters of non-contractual obligations, it contains rules which raise presumptions of law or determine the burden of proof.

2. Acts intended to have legal effect may be proved by any mode of proof recognised by the law of the forum or by any of the laws referred to in Article 21 under which that act is formally valid, provided that such mode of proof can be administered by the forum.

Art 22 of the Rome II Regulation, in line with Art 17 of the Commission **14.81** Proposal, follows very closely the language of Art 14 of the Rome Convention.[222] According to the Commission:[223]

This is a useful provision as questions relating to evidence are basically matters for the procedural law of the *lex fori*.

Art 22(1) requires application of rules of the law applicable under the **14.82** Regulation which raise presumptions or determine the burden of proof. As Professors Giuliano and Lagarde pointed out in their report on the corresponding provision in the Rome Convention, rules of these kinds are really rules of substance that contribute to making clear the obligations of

---

[221] Under Italian law, a separate rule of applicable law provides that unilateral promises are governed by the law of the State in which the promise is made (Law of 31 May 1995, no 218 'Riforma del sistema italiano di diritto internazionale privato', Art 58).

[222] Rome I Regulation, Art 18.

[223] Commission Proposal, 26.

the parties and cannot be separated from the law governing the obligation in question.[224] Nevertheless, as the same authors pointed out, that provision was subject to an important restriction, as follows:[225]

> The burden of proof is not totally subject to the law of the contract. It is only subject to it to the extent that the law of the contract determines it with regard to contractual obligations ('in the law of contract'), that is to say only to the extent to which the rules relating to the burden of proof are in effect rules of substance.

14.83   To the same effect, Art 22(1) of the Rome II Regulation will only import rules raising presumptions of law or determining the burden of proof insofar as those rules specifically concern non-contractual obligations and are not part of the general law of civil procedure or of evidence. An example of a rule falling within the scope of Art 22(1) can be found in s 2(1) of the UK Misrepresentation Act 1967, which provides that:

> Where a person has entered into a contract after a misrepresentation has been made to him by another party thereto and as a result thereof he has suffered loss, then, if the person making the misrepresentation would be liable to damages in respect thereof had the misrepresentation been made fraudulently, that person shall be so liable notwithstanding that the misrepresentation was not made fraudulently, *unless he proves that he had reasonable ground to believe and did believe up to the time the contract was made that the facts represented were true.*

14.84   Art 22(2) of the Regulation concerns the mode of proof of 'acts intended to have legal effect'. The Commission stated that this sub-rule:[226]

> [C]oncerns the admissibility of modes of proving acts intended to have legal effect referred to in Article 16 [*of the Proposal*[227]]. It does not cover evidence of legal facts, which is also covered by the *lex fori*. The very liberal system of Article 14(2) of the Rome Convention is used here, providing for the alternative application of the *lex fori* and the law governing the form of the relevant act.

14.85   The meaning of the reference in this passage to 'evidence of legal facts' is not entirely clear. The French language version of the Commission Proposal uses the phrase '*la preuve des faits juridiques*' which suggests that the Commission wished to emphasize that Art 22 does not apply generally to the proof of legally relevant facts, but instead only to acts intended to have legal effect (for example, a release of liability).

14.86   As to the requirement in the closing words of Art 22(2) that the mode of proof be capable of being administered by the forum, Professors Giuliano

---

[224] Giuliano & Lagarde Report (OJ C282, 36 [31.10.1980]).
[225] Ibid.
[226] Commission Proposal, 26.
[227] Regulation, Art 21 (**14.77–14.80** above).

and Lagarde, commenting on the identical wording in Art 14(2) of the Rome Convention, explained:[228]

Nevertheless this liberalism should not lead to imposing on the trial court modes of proof which its procedural law does not enable it to administer. Article 14 does not deal with the administration of modes of proof, which the legal system of each Contracting State makes subject to the law of the trial court. Admitting the application of a law other than that of the forum to modes of proof ought not to lead to the rules of the law of the forum, as regards the administration of the modes of proof, being rendered nugatory.

This is the explanation of the proviso which in substance enables a court, without reference to public policy, to disregard modes of proof which the law of procedure cannot generally allow, such as an affidavit, the testimony of a party or common knowledge.

G. DIRECT ACTION AGAINST INSURER

Article 18

Direct action against the insurer of the person liable

The person having suffered damage may bring his or her claim directly against the insurer of the person liable to provide compensation if the law applicable to the non-contractual obligation or the law applicable to the insurance contract so provides.

INTRODUCTION

Art 18 of the Rome II Regulation entitles the person suffering damage to bring an action directly against the insurer of the person liable if such action is permitted either by the law applicable under the Regulation to the non-contractual obligation owed to him by the person liable[229] or the law applicable to the contract between insurer and insured.[230] Although expressed differently, this provision (reflecting the Council's Common Position[231]) adopts the solution favoured in Art 14 of the Commission **14.87**

---

[228] Giuliano-Lagarde Report (OJ C282, 37 [31.10.1980]).

[229] Leaving out of account for this purpose any agreement on choice of law under Art 14 (**13.27** above).

[230] The position under the pre-existing English private international law rules was unclear, although the prevailing view favoured the application of the law applicable to the contract of insurance (see Dicey, Morris & Collins, para 35-043). Also **14.94** below.

[231] Common Position Art 18. Compare EP 1st Reading Position, Art 16 (reflecting Amendment 46); Commission Amended Proposal, Art 15.

Proposal, which applied the law applicable under the Regulation subject to the right of the person who has suffered damage to base his claim on the law applicable to the insurance contract. The Commission suggested that:[232]

> The proposed rule strikes a reasonable balance between the interests at stake as it protects the person sustaining damage by giving him the option, while limiting the choice to the two laws which the insurer can legitimately expect to be applied the law applicable to the non-contractual obligation and the law applicable to the insurance contract.

14.88 The Commission's view that the proposed rule was fair was challenged by the UK Government and by the House of Lords' European Union Committee in its report on the Commission Proposal.[233] Despite early criticism,[234] the philosophy underlying Art 14 was agreed in principle at an early stage of discussions in the Council's Rome II Committee.[235] The European Parliament did not make any material amendment to this provision on first or second reading.[236]

LIMITS TO DIRECT ACTION

14.89 The effect of Art 18, in its final form, is to give the person having suffered damage the benefit of the most favourable regime in terms of his right to claim directly against the insurer of the person liable.

14.90 If he chooses to pursue his claim against the insurer of the person liable according to the law applicable to the insurance contract, Art 18 appears to present little difficulty. The claimant must, of course, establish that the insured person owed him a non-contractual obligation by reference to the law applicable to that obligation under the Regulation, that the claim falls within the policy coverage under the insurance contract, and that any other conditions for proceeding directly against the insurer under the law applicable to that contract are satisfied.

14.91 If, on the other hand, the person suffering damage chooses to pursue his claim against the insurer of the person liable according to the law applicable

---

[232] Commission Proposal, 25–6.

[233] Council document 9009/04 ADD 15 [26.5.2004], 8; House of Lords' European Union Committee, *The Rome II Regulation*, 8th Report of Session 2003–2004 (HL Paper 66), paras 147–50.

[234] Council document 8445/04 [19.4.2004].

[235] Commission note of meeting held on 16–17 September 2004 (Commission document (JAI C1 (2004) D9487), 2).

[236] EP 1st Reading Position, Art 16; EP 2nd Reading Position, Art 18.

under the Regulation to the insured's non-contractual obligation to him, an important question is raised as to the ability of the insurer to protect himself by reference to the terms of the insurance contract or the law which applies to it. In the explanatory memorandum accompanying its Proposal, the Commission suggested:[237]

At all events, the scope of the insurer's obligations is determined by the law governing the insurance contract.

Although that will be true if the law applicable to the contract of insurance **14.92** is relied on by the claimant to found his direct claim or if the law applicable to the non-contractual obligation is the same as that which applies to the insurance contract, the assumption may prove incorrect if Art 18 offers the claimant a genuine choice between laws and he opts for the law applicable to the non-contractual obligation. In this case, although the right of action created under that law may well be formulated in terms of a transfer of contractual rights against the insurer[238] or by reference to the content of the insurance contract, there is no necessary correlation. Even if the insurance contract is taken into account in defining the claim, certain of its terms (including limits on the insurer's liability) may be overridden or disregarded.

For example, in the English case of *Through Transport v New India*,[239] an **14.93** insurer sought an anti-suit injunction to restrain proceedings brought against it in Finland, on the ground that the contract of insurance (governed by English law) contained an agreement for arbitration in London. The party bringing the Finnish proceedings, as assignee of the rights of the owner of a lost cargo shipped by the insured, had relied on a provision in the Finnish insurance contracts legislation that conferred on a person suffering damage or loss a direct right to compensation against the

---

[237] Ibid, 26.

[238] e.g. Third Party (Rights Against Insurers) Act 1930, s 1. The transfer of rights contemplated by s 1 arises on bankruptcy, insolvency, and certain related events. If the bankruptcy etc. proceedings fall within the scope of the Insolvency Regulation, the rules of applicable law in that Regulation will, very arguably, displace those in Art 18 (see **16.32** below) on the basis that the availability of a direct action in these circumstances concerns 'the effects of the insolvency proceedings on current contracts to which the debtor is a party' (Insolvency Regulation, Art 4(2)(e)). In an earlier case, *Irish Shipping Ltd v Commercial Union Assurance Co Ltd* [1991] 2 QB 206, 219–21 (EWCA), Staughton LJ considered possible options for limiting the territorial scope of the 1930 Act, without reaching a concluded view.

[239] *Through Transport Mutual Insurance Association (Eurasia) Ltd v New India Insurance Co Ltd (The Hari Bhum)* [2004] EWCA Civ 1598; [2005] 1 Lloyd's Rep 67. Also *Markel International Co Ltd v P M M Craft (The Norseman)* [2006] EWHC 3150 (Comm).

insurer under certain circumstances.[240] An anti-avoidance provision in that legislation provided that:[241]

Any terms or conditions of an insurance contract that deviate from the provisions of this Act to the detriment of an injured person or a person entitled to compensation or benefits other than the policyholder shall be null and void.

14.94 The effect of this provision was understood to be that a 'pay to be paid' clause in the insurance contract, requiring the insured to have paid out to the victim before claiming on the policy, would be overridden under Finnish law in proceedings brought by the victim, although it would have been effective as a matter of English contract law.[242] Both the Commercial Court judge[243] and the Court of Appeal[244] side-stepped the anti-avoidance provision by characterizing the right of action against the insurer as a contractual right to enforce the insurance contract, governed therefore by English law. That line of reasoning will, however, no longer be open to Member State courts in cases in which the claimant relies on a right of action conferred by the law applicable under the Regulation to the non-contractual obligation in question. The only question of characterization in those cases will be whether that right of action enables the claimant to whom a non-contractual obligation is owed to bring his claim for compensation directly against the insurer, so as to bring it within the scope of Art 18. If so, the theoretical basis of that right of action, within its legal system of origin or according to forum's pre-existing rules of private international law, will be irrelevant.

14.95 In the event, although the Court of Appeal in *Through Transport* held that it had jurisdiction to grant the injunction as the subject matter of the action fell outside the Brussels I Regulation, it found that the requirements for the grant of an injunction had not been made out. The question as to the compatibility with the Brussels I Regulation of anti-suit injunctions designed to enforce arbitration agreements has since been referred by the House of Lords to the Court of Justice, and a (negative) ruling is expected in late 2008 or early 2009.[245]

---

[240] Ibid, [10], containing a translation into English of s 67 of the Finnish Insurance Contracts Act 1994.

[241] Ibid, [11], containing a translation of s 3 of the Finnish Act. The quoted extract is from s 3(1). Under s 3(3), the peremptory effect of s 3(1) is stated not to apply to certain types of insurance.

[242] Ibid, [73]. Compare the decision of the House of Lords in *Firma C-Trade SA v Newcastle Protection and Indemnity Association (The Fanti)* [1990] 2 Lloyd's Rep 191.

[243] [2003] EWHC 3158 (Comm); [2004] 1 Lloyd's Rep 206, [18]–[20].

[244] [2005] 1 Lloyd's Rep 67, [53]–[60].

[245] See reference in Case C-185/07, *Allianz SpA (formerly Riunione Adriatica Di Sicurta SpA) v West Tankers Inc*, the decision to refer [2007] UKHL 4; [2007] 1 Lloyd's Rep 391 and the

In the course of discussions in the Council's Rome II Committee, one dele- **14.96** gation (understood to be Sweden) proposed adding a paragraph in terms that:[246]

At all events, the scope of the insurer's obligations shall be determined by the law applicable to the insurance contract.

Although several delegations welcomed that proposal, it was not adopted **14.97** as part of the Council's Common Position. At a meeting of the Council's Rome II Committee in November 2004, the Swedish position was supported by the Netherlands and the UK, but opposed by Germany, Austria, and the Commission on the ground that it would amount to a provision regulating the law applicable to a contractual obligation.[247] That view, however, confuses the categorization of the obligation with the identification of the connecting factor. The insurer's obligation to the person sustaining damage is properly characterized as a non-contractual obligation under the Rome II Regulation, as (a) there is no obligation freely assumed by the insurer towards the victim,[248] and (b) Art 18 specifically treats it as such. The proposition that the law applicable to the insurer's contractual obligation to the insured should also govern this non-contractual obligation, designed to ensure greater foreseeability for the insurer,[249] does not, however, convert the obligation into a contractual one falling outside the Rome II Regulation and within the Rome I Regime. As other provisions of the Rome II Regulation make clear, the law applicable to a non-contractual obligation may be determined by reference to a contractual connecting factor.

At the same meeting, a German proposal to replace the Commission's **14.98** proposed language with the wording carried forward to Art 18 of the Regulation in its final form was widely supported.[250]

Opinion of Adv Gen Kokott (5 September 2008) to the effect that the grant of an injunction was incompatible with the Brussels I Regulation.

[246] Council document 8445/04 [19.4.2004], 2–3. See the similar proposals by the delegations from Sweden (Council document 9009/04 ADD 8 [18.5.2004], 22; Council document 14193/04 [4.11.2004], 7) and Spain (ibid, ADD 10 [18.5.2004], 14). The Polish delegation, on the other hand, suggested that a party suing both insured and insurer in the same set of proceedings should be able to choose the law applicable to the insurance contract to govern both claims (Council document 9009/04 ADD 3 [4.5.2004], 5). Mercifully, this suggestion was not taken up.

[247] Commission note (undated) of meeting held on 10–11 November 2004, 3.

[248] Cf Case C-26/91, *Handte v Traitements Mécano-chimiques des Surfaces* [1992] ECR I-3967, discussed at **3.112–3.115** above.

[249] Council document 8445/04, 2.

[250] Commission note (undated) of meeting of the Council's Rome II Committee held on 10–11 November 2004, 3.

14.99 Art 18 refers only to the claim of the person having suffered damage and not, as elsewhere in the Regulation,[251] to 'the person seeking compensation'. In contrast, the Commission Proposal referred to 'the right of persons who have suffered damage to take direct action'.[252] It is, therefore, unclear whether other claimants (including those claiming by succession or otherwise through the person suffering damage) may take advantage of the choice offered by this Article. As the policy identified by the Commission applies equally to such claimants, it is submitted that the words 'person having suffered damage' should be read broadly as including others claiming through him, such as the Finnish claimant in *Through Transport v New India*.

Motor Insurance—Direct Right of Action under EC Law

14.100 Art 18 is linked to Directive (EC) No 90/232[253] and Directive (EC) No 2000/26[254] on the approximation of the laws of the Member States relating to insurance against civil liability in respect of the use of motor vehicles (respectively the **Third and Fourth Motor Insurance Directives**), which require Member States in certain cases to recognize a direct right of action under EC law against the insurer of a motor vehicle involved in an accident caused by a vehicle insured in a Member State. Art 1(1) of the Fourth Motor Insurance Directive provides:

> The objective of this Directive is to lay down special provisions applicable to injured parties entitled to compensation in respect of any loss or injury resulting from accidents occurring in a Member State other than the Member State of residence of the injured party which are caused by the use of vehicles[255] insured and normally based in a Member State.

---

[251] Arts 6(3)(b) and 7.

[252] A number of delegations in the Council's Rome II Committee had thought even the Commission's wording to be unclear on this point (Council document 8445/04, 3).

[253] OJ L125, 93 [19.5.1990], as amended by Directive (EC) No 2005/14 (OJ L149, 14 [11.6.2005]).

[254] OJ L181, 65 [20.7.2000], as amended by Directive (EC) No 2005/14 (OJ L149, 14).

[255] 'Vehicle' means 'any motor vehicle intended for travel on land and propelled by mechanical power, but not running on rails, and any trailer, whether or not coupled' (see ibid, Art 2(c) referring to Art 1(1) of Directive (EEC) No 72/166 on the approximation of the laws of Member States relating to insurance against civil liability in respect of the use of motor vehicles, and to the enforcement of the obligation to insure against such liability (OJ L103, 1 [2.5.1972]), as amended) (the **First Motor Insurance Directive**). A consolidated version of the First Motor Insurance Directive is available at <http://eur-lex.europa.eu/LexUriServ/LexUriServ.do?uri=CONSLEG:1972L0166:20050611:EN:PDF>.

Accordingly, the Fourth Directive applies specifically to cross-border cases **14.101** within the Community. Art 1(1) continues:

Without prejudice to the legislation of third countries on civil liability and private international law, this Directive shall also apply to injured parties resident in a Member State and entitled to compensation in respect of any loss or injury resulting from accidents occurring in third countries whose national insurer's bureaux . . .[256] have joined the Green Card system whenever such accidents are caused by the use of vehicles insured and normally based in a Member State.

Art 3 of the Fourth Directive requires Member States to establish a direct **14.102** right of action against the insurer of the person responsible for a motor accident as follows:

Each Member State shall ensure that injured parties[257] referred to in Article 1 in accidents within the meaning of that provision enjoy a direct right of action against the insurance undertaking covering the responsible person against civil liability.

This right has been extended to residents of Iceland, Liechtenstein, and **14.103** Norway as participants in the European Economic Area.[258] As appears from Art 1(1), it applies to accidents occurring not only in Member/EEA States (excluding the State of residence of the injured party) but also in certain third countries that are members of the Green Card system.[259] The obligatory language in Art 3 and the reference to 'private international law' only in the second paragraph of Art 1(1), concerning accidents occurring in third countries, indicate that, at least for accidents occurring in Member/EEA States, the right of action conferred by the Directive is intended to have mandatory effect across the EC, irrespective of the law applicable to the contract of insurance or to the law applicable under the Regulation to the claim of the injured party against the responsible person. For accidents occurring outside the EC/EEA in another Green Card System State, it is unclear whether the second paragraph of Art 1(1) refers to 'private international law' generally (including that of the

---

[256] As defined in Article 1(3) of the First Motor Insurance Directive.

[257] 'Injured party' means 'any person entitled to compensation in respect of any loss or injury caused by vehicles' (see Fourth Motor Insurance Directive, Art 2(d) referring to Art 1(2) of the First Motor Insurance Directive).

[258] Decision No 4/2001 of the European Economic Area Joint Committee (OJ L266, 46 [8.3.2001]).

[259] The third country members of the Green Card system are Albania, Belarus, Bosnia and Herzegovina, Former Yugoslav Republic of Macedonia, Islamic Republic of Iran, Israel, Moldova, Montengro, Morocco, Serbia, Switzerland, Tunisia, Turkey, Ukraine. For further information concerning the system, see the website of, the Council des Bureaux, the system administrator, <http://www.cobx.org/>.

Member States) or only to 'legislation of third countries on. . . private international law'. If the former interpretation, which appears the more natural meaning of the words, is correct, Art 3 of the Fourth Directive will only apply in these cases if the Member States' rules of private international law point to the application of the law of a Member State to govern the possibility of a direct claim. As Art 18 of the Rome II Regulation allows such a claim to be brought under the law applicable to the contract of insurance and as the Fourth Directive applies only to vehicles insured and normally based in a Member State, the 'private international law' qualification in the Fourth Directive, would no longer appear to have any significant impact.

14.104 Under Art 4d of the Third Motor Insurance Directive (a provision inserted in 2005 by the Fifth Motor Insurance Directive[260]), the right of action under EC law has been extended to all accidents caused by a vehicle based in the EC.

14.105 Art 3 of the Fourth Motor Insurance Directive was implemented in the UK by the European Communities (Rights against Insurers) Regulations 2002.[261] Under regulation 3(2) of the 2002 Regulations, if an entitled party has a cause of action against an insured person in tort or delict, and that cause of action arises out of an accident, that party 'may, without prejudice to his right to issue proceedings against the insured person, issue proceedings against the insurer that issued the policy of insurance relating to the insured vehicle, and that insurer shall be directly liable to the entitled party to the extent that he is liable to the insured person'. 'Entitled party' means a resident of a Member/EEA State, including the United Kingdom.[262] 'Accident' means an accident on a road or other public place in the United Kingdom caused by, or arising out of, the use of any insured vehicle.[263] 'Vehicle' means any motor vehicle intended for travel on land and propelled by mechanical power, but not running on rails, and any trailer whether or not coupled, which is normally based in the United Kingdom.[264]

14.106 The right of action conferred by the UK Regulations would appear to be narrower than the Motor Insurance Directives require, being limited to the

---

[260] Directive (EC) No 2005/14, n 253 above, Art 4(4).

[261] SI 2002/3061. No further implementing measures were considered necessary for the 2005 amendment to the Third Directive.

[262] Ibid, reg 2(1).

[263] Ibid. Reg 2(3) defines the concept of an 'insured vehicle' as one for which there is in force in relation to the use of that vehicle on a road or other public place in the United Kingdom by the insured person a policy of insurance (including a covering note) that fulfils the requirements of s 145 of the Road Traffic Act 1988 or art 92 of the Road Traffic (Northern Ireland) Order 1981.

[264] Ibid. Rules for determining where a vehicle is 'normally based' are contained in reg 2(2).

UK both in terms of the geographical location of the accident *and* the base of the vehicle causing the accident. If, therefore, proceedings against the insurer are brought in a UK court or the law of a part of the UK applies under Art 18 of the Rome II Regulation, the 2002 Regulations will not assist a person who suffers injury as a result of an accident occurring outside the UK or caused by a non-UK based vehicle. In either case, that may not be significant if the insured's liability to the victim or the relevant contract of insurance is governed by the law of a Member State that recognizes a direct right of action consistently with the terms of the Directives, as Art 18 would require Member State courts to uphold that right. There may, however, be circumstances in which an injured person will be left without a direct right of action in the UK courts against the insurer, for example if an accident occurs outside the UK, but within the territory covered by the Directives, between two vehicles based and insured in the UK and driven by persons habitually resident in the same part of the UK. In this case, both the law applicable to the insurance contract and, probably, the law applicable under the Rome II Regulation to claims between the persons involved[265] will be that of a part of the UK, but the 2002 Regulations give no direct right of action against the insurer of the person liable. The injured person will be left with his remedy against the person liable.[266]

RELATIONSHIP TO THE BRUSSELS I REGULATION

The Brussels I Regulation contains, in Chapter II, Section 3, special rules of **14.107** jurisdiction for matters of insurance, which favour the policyholder, the insured, or a beneficiary, by entitling that person to sue an insurer domiciled[267] in a Member State in several places, including in the Member State of his own domicile.[268] Under Art 11(2), these rules apply to actions brought by the injured party directly against the insurer, where such direct actions are permitted. Under Art 11(3), if the law governing such direct actions provides that the policyholder or the insured may be joined as a party to the action, the

---

[265] By reason of their common habitual residence (Art 4(2)).

[266] As well, possibly, as a claim against the UK for failure to implement the Motor Insurance Directives. Under the circumstances described in the example, the injured party will not be entitled to compensation from the Motor Insurers' Bureau, the body acting as the UK's compensation body under Art 6 of the Directive, as neither Art 6 nor the corresponding provision in the UK implementing regulations apply if the vehicle that caused the accident is insured through an establishment in the injured party's Member State or residence, or normally based there (Fourth Motor Insurance Directive, Art 1(2); Motor Vehicles (Compulsory Insurance) (Information Centre and Compensation Body) Regulations (SI 2003/37), Art 11(1)).

[267] Or deemed to be domiciled (Brussels I Regulation, Art 9(2)).

[268] Brussels I Regulation, Arts 9–10.

same court shall also have jurisdiction over them. Recital (16a) of the Fourth Motor Insurance Directive, inserted by a 2005 amendment,[269] provides:

> Under Article 11(2) read in conjunction with Article 9(1)(b) of [the Brussels I Regulation] injured parties may bring legal proceedings against the civil liability insurance provider in the Member State in which they are domiciled.

14.108 In *FBTO Schadeverzekeringen NV v Odenbreit*, the ECJ held that a person bringing a direct action could rely on these provisions to bring the claim in the courts of his own Member State of domicile, even if he could not be described as a 'beneficiary' of the policy.[270]

H. SUBROGATION

Article 19

Subrogation

Where a person (the creditor) has a non-contractual claim upon another (the debtor), and a third person has a duty to satisfy the creditor, or has in fact satisfied the creditor in discharge of that duty, the law which governs the third person's duty to satisfy the creditor shall determine whether, and the extent to which, the third person is entitled to exercise against the debtor the rights which the creditor had against the debtor under the law governing their relationship.

14.109 Art 19 reflects very closely Art 15(1) of the Commission Proposal.[271] That aspect of the Proposal was criticized by the Swedish delegation on the Council's Rome II Committee as 'so complicated that it is almost unintelligible'.[272] If is fair to say that the provision will win no awards for legislative clarity. Understandably, however, the Commission and, ultimately, the Council and the Parliament were content to mirror the wording of Art 13(1) of the Rome Convention.[273]

14.110 The rule covers, but is not limited to, the relationship between the victim's insurer and the person liable to determine whether the former has the right to bring a non-contractual claim against the latter by way of 'subrogation'.[274] Under Art 19, the third party's (in the example, the insurer's) right to

---

[269] Directive (EC) No 2005/14, n 253 above, Art 5(1).
[270] Case C-463/06 [2007] ECR I-11321, Judgment of 13 December 2007.
[271] The words 'and the extent to which' have been added to the final text of the Regulation.
[272] Council document 9009/04 ADD 8 [18.5.2004], 24 (Sweden).
[273] The Rome I Regulation deals separately with contractual subrogation (alongside voluntary assignment) (Art 14) and legal subrogation (Art 15). Art 15 follows the wording of Art 13(1) of the Rome Convention.
[274] Commission Proposal, 26.

assume the rights of the person (the 'creditor'; in the example, the insured) having a non-contractual claim[275] against another (the 'debtor') must be determined by reference to the law applicable to the third party's duty to satisfy the creditor (the law applicable to the insurance contract). For this purpose, the reference to a 'duty to satisfy' the creditor should not, it is submitted, be taken to require that performance by the third person of that duty would (but for the subrogation) discharge the debtor's non-contractual obligation to that person. Thus, the right of an indemnity insurer under English law to take over the remedies of the assured against a tortfeasor falls within the scope of the Article even though the insurer's payment does not ordinarily discharge the tortfeasor's liability.[276]

In the case of a contractual duty on the part of the third party to satisfy the creditor, the law applicable under Art 19 will (normally) fall to be determined by reference to the rules contained in the Rome Convention and its successor Regulation. Further, as the closing words of Art 19 emphasize, the existence and content of the non-contractual obligation between the debtor and creditor will remain governed by the law which applies to it under Chapters II to IV of the Rome II Regulation. **14.111**

In their assessment of Art 13(1) of the Rome Convention, Professors Giuliano and Lagarde comment:[277] **14.112**

According to the legislation in various Member States of the Community, 'subrogration' involves the vesting of the creditor's rights in the person who, being obliged to pay the debt with or on behalf of others, had an interest in satisfying it: this is so under Article 1251-3 of the French Civil Code and Article 1203-3 of the Italian Civil Code. For example, in a contract of guarantee the guarantor who pays instead of the debtor succeeds to the rights of the creditor. The same occurs when a payment is made by one of a number of debtors who are jointly and severally liable or when an indivisible obligation is discharged.

Article 13 of the Convention embodies the conflict rule in matters of subrogation of a third party to the rights of a creditor. Having regard to the fact that the Convention applies only to contractual obligations, the Group thought it proper to limit the application of the rule adopted in Article 13 to assignments of rights which are contractual in nature. Therefore this rule does not apply to subrogation

---

[275] The French text of Art 19 refers to *'une obligation non-contractuelle'* (a non-contractual obligation). The German text, more consistently with the English version, refers to *'aufgrund eines außervertraglichen Schuldverhältnisses eine Forderung'* (a claim or demand grounded in a non-contractual obligation).

[276] *Esso Petroleum Ltd v Hall, Russell & Co Ltd* [1989] AC 643 (UKHL). For the argument that this right is concerned with the reversal of unjust enrichment, see A Burrows, *The Law of Restitution* (2nd edn, 2002), 107–12.

[277] Giuliano & Lagarde Report, OJ C282, 35 [31.10.1980].

by operation of law when the debt to be paid has its origin in tort (for example, where the insurer succeeds to the rights of the insured against the person causing damage).

14.113 Art 19(1) thus fills the gap left by the Rome Convention. The Giuliano & Lagarde Report continued by considering situations in which a person has paid without being obliged so to do by contract or by law (i.e. without a duty to satisfy the creditor), but having an economic interest recognized by law.[278] They concluded that 'in principle the same rule applies to these situations, but the court has a discretion in this respect'.[279] That view, however, is impossible to reconcile with the wording of Art 13 of the Rome Convention, which requires the discharge of a duty, refers to the law that governs the third party's duty to satisfy the creditor, and does not contemplate any element of discretion on the court's part.[280] For the same reasons, it would appear that the consequences of intervention otherwise than by legal compulsion in the satisfaction of a non-contractual obligation fall outside Art 19(1) of the Rome II Regulation. They should be addressed (a) as between the third party and the payee, by the law governing the relationship between those parties or by the rules in Art 10 of the Rome II Regulation (unjust enrichment), and (b) as between the third party and the person liable to the payee, by the rules for unjust enrichment or, if applicable, the rules contained in Art 11 (*negotiorum gestio*).[281]

14.114 Art 19(1) only applies to situations in which the position as between the third party and the person liable is not regulated by contract (e.g. a contract of indemnity). Contractual claims between these two parties fall outside the scope of the Rome II Regulation.[282]

I. MULTIPLE LIABILITY—INDEMNITY AND CONTRIBUTION

Article 20

Multiple liability

If a creditor has a claim against several debtors who are liable for the same claim, and one of the debtors has already satisfied the claim in whole or in part,

---

[278] The authors referred to Article 1251(3) of the French Civil Code (*Code Civil*) and Article 1203-3 of the Italian Civil Code (*Codice Civile*).

[279] Giuliano & Lagarde Report (OJ C282, 36 [31.10.1980]).

[280] Also Dicey, Morris & Collins, para 32-211.

[281] **Chs 10 and 11** above.

[282] Also Giuliano & Lagarde Report (OJ C282, 36 [31.10.1980]).

the question of that debtor's right to demand compensation from the other debtors shall be governed by the law applicable to that debtor's non-contractual obligation towards the creditor.

In both the Rome Convention and the Commission Proposal, the rule **14.115** dealing with subrogation (now Art 19 of the Regulation[283]) was coupled with a short provision extending its application to situations in which 'several persons are subject to the same claim and one of them has satisfied the creditor'. In the Rome II Regulation in its final form, questions of multiple liability are now dealt with separately and more broadly by Art 20.[284] Even so, this Article uses terminology already defined in Art 19. Thus, 'creditor' means the person with a non-contractual 'claim' and the 'debtors' are the persons liable to the creditor for that 'claim'.

Two conditions must apparently be satisfied in order for Art 20 to apply at **14.116** all. First, the debtors must be liable for the 'same claim'. Secondly, the debtor who seeks compensation must already have satisfied the claim in whole or in part. If Art 20 applies, that debtor's claim against his co-debtors will be governed by the law applicable to *his* non-contractual obligation toward the common creditor, determined in accordance with Arts 4 to 12 of the Regulation. An agreement on choice of law between the debtor and the common creditor as to the law applicable to non-contractual obligations between them should normally be left out of account for this purpose, even if it otherwise meets the requirements of Art 14(1), as such a choice cannot prejudice the rights of the other debtors, assuming that they are not parties to that agreement.[285]

As to the first condition, although the French text, referring to '*la même* **14.117** *obligation*', suggests that both the legal and factual basis of the obligation must be the same, the reference to 'the law applicable to that debtor's non-contractual obligation', as opposed to '*the debtors'* non-contractual obligation' suggests that the rule applies more widely than situations in which the liability of two parties coincides exactly. Instead, Art 20 may be capable of accommodating situations in which several persons are liable to another for the consequences of a tort/delict, unjust enrichment, *negotiorum gestio*, or *culpa in contrahendo*,[286] without the need to show that (1) the legal or

---

[283] **14.109–14.114**.

[284] For comment, influenced by US governmental interest analysis, see T W Dornis, 'Contribution and Indemnification among Joint Tortfeasors in Multi-State Conflict Cases: A Study of Doctrine and the Current Law in the US and Under the Rome II Regulation' (2008) 4 J Priv Int L 237.

[285] **13.27** above.

[286] Regulation, Art 2(1).

factual basis of the claims against those persons is the same, (2) the same law applies to the obligations underlying those claims, and (3) the claims (other than that against the person seeking compensation from a co-debtor under Art 20) are non-contractual obligations falling within the scope of the Regulation.

14.118   Thus, for example, if A receives minor injuries in a traffic accident for which B is responsible but is more severely injured while travelling to hospital in an ambulance driven by C and is there carelessly treated by D resulting in a further deterioration of his condition, Art 20 should apply to the right of B (or his insurer) to recover from C or D, some or all of the amount that he has paid to A to compensate him for his injuries (assuming that he has been held responsible for the injuries caused by the entire sequence of events[287]) even if the obligations underlying A's claims against C or D are contractual in nature or are subject to the law of a different country from A's claim against B. Here, B's claim against C or D would be governed by the law that, under the Rome II Regulation, applies to A's claim against him. For Art 20 to apply, however, B must show that either C or D, as the case may be, was 'liable' to A under the law that applies to the obligation underlying the claim against each of them, determined in accordance with the Regulation or otherwise. If B's liability has not been established by a court decision, he must also establish his own liability.

14.119   As to the second condition, Art 20 would appear narrower than Art 19, which requires that the person seeking to exercise a right of subrogation 'has a duty to satisfy the creditor, *or* has in fact satisfied the creditor in discharge of that duty'. In some legal systems, including England and Wales,[288] an obligation on the part of a person liable to contribute towards a common liability may arise before any one of the persons liable has paid the common creditor. If the person seeking compensation from a co-debtor has already discharged his obligation to the common creditor, Art 20 will apply. If he has not, Art 20 will not apply, leaving open the question as to what law(s) should apply to the existence, and extent, of the obligations between the persons liable in these circumstances. One option would be to apply the rule in Art 20 by analogy, favouring the law applicable to the contribution claimant's non-contractual obligation towards the creditor.[289] It might, however, be objected that there is no reason to give priority to

---

[287] C van Dam, n 31 above, 292.

[288] Civil Liability (Contribution) Act 1978, s 1.

[289] The editors of Dicey, Morris & Collins refer in their commentary on Art 20 to the right to claim a contribution without distinguishing between cases in which the contribution claimant has, and those in which he has not, satisfied the claim (Dicey, Morris & Collins, 1st supplement, paras 34-051 and S35-267).

that law over any other law governing a co-debtor's liability to the common creditor, in circumstances where none of them have actually satisfied that creditor. Alternatively, it may be possible to treat contribution as an aspect of 'division of liability' under Art 15(b).[290] That approach would also favour the law applicable to the non-contractual obligation owed by the contribution claimant to the common creditor, but would leave open the possibility of a counterclaim by the contribution defendant under the law applicable to his own non-contractual obligation to the common creditor. A third possibility would be to treat a claim to contribution as resting on a non-contractual obligation arising out of unjust enrichment, i.e. the contribution defendant's enrichment if the contribution claimant alone were called upon to satisfy the contribution creditor.[291] That would require the application of the rules of applicable law in Art 10, although these appear ill-designed for the purpose.[292] Finally, it would appear possible to characterize the contribution claimant's claim for compensation as concerning not his own liability to the common creditor but the (indirect) consequences to him of the event triggering the contribution defendant's liability to the common creditor.[293] On this view, the contribution claim would fall to be determined by reference to the same law as would govern the contribution defendant's liability to the common creditor under the Regulation or otherwise. That solution may be thought to produce an adequate result if the contribution claimant's obligation is non-contractual (whether arising from tort/delict, unjust enrichment, *negotiorum gestio*, or *culpa in contrahendo*), but not if it is contractual. On balance, the treatment of contribution claims falling outside Art 20 as an aspect of 'division of liability', although complex, seems the best of these options.

Under English law, contribution claims are regulated by the provisions of **14.120** the Civil Liability (Contribution) Act 1978. The provisions of the Act have been held to apply to all contribution claims brought before the English courts between persons liable for the same damage, whether or not there

---

[290] **14.16–14.17** above.
[291] This was the prevailing view as to the treatment of contribution claims under the pre-existing English rules of applicable law (Dicey, Morris & Collins, paras 34-011 and 34-051).
[292] Identification of the country in which the enrichment will take place may cause particular difficulty if no payment has yet been made to the common creditor (cf **10.34** above).
[293] Cf *Hewden Tower Cranes Ltd v Wolffkran GmbH* [2007] EWHC 857 (TCC); [2007] 2 Lloyd's Rep 138, [30]–[32], in which Jackson J treated a contribution claim as a matter relating to tort, delict, or quasi-delict for the purposes of the Brussels I Regulation. The decision can be criticized on the ground that the reasoning does not distinguish sufficiently between the contribution defendant's liability to the common creditor and his liability to the contribution claimant.

is otherwise a close connection to England or to English law. [294] In the terminology of the Regulation, therefore, they have been accorded the status of 'overriding mandatory provisions'.[295] It may be doubted, however, whether this treatment is sustainable under the Regulation, given the limited role that it reserves to the law of the forum.[296]

[294] *Arab Monetary Fund v Hashim (No 9)* (1994) The Times, 11 October (EWHC); *Petroleo Brasiliero SA v Mellitus Shipping Inc* [2001] EWCA Civ 418; [2001] 2 Lloyd's Rep 203, [36] (Potter LJ). Cf the approach taken by the Supreme Court of Victoria in relation to a very similar contribution statute in *Fluor Australia Pty v ASC Engineering Pty Ltd* [2007] VSC 262, [47]–[57] (Bongiorno J).

[295] Art 16.

[296] **15.16–15.18** below. For criticism of the decision in *AMF v Hashim (No 9)* from an English law viewpoint, see C Mitchell, 'The Civil Liability (Contribution) Act 1978' [1997] Restitution L Rev 27, 51–2; R Stevens, 'The Choice of Law Rules of Restitutionary Obligations', in F Rose (ed), *Restitution and the Conflict of Laws* (1995), 209–10; A Briggs, *The Conflict of Laws* (2nd edn, 2008), 215.

15

Public Policy, Mandatory Rules, and Rules of Conduct and Safety

A. INTRODUCTION

Arts 16 and 26 of the Rome II Regulation govern the relationship between **15.01** the law applicable under the Regulation and the law of the forum. Art 26 provides for the overriding effect of the forum's public policy. Art 16 permits the application of 'overriding mandatory provisions' of the law of the forum. Recital (32) emphasizes that these provisions are to be narrowly construed:[1]

Considerations of public interest justify giving the courts of the Member States the possibility, in exceptional circumstances, of applying exceptions based on public policy and overriding mandatory provisions. . . .

A Recital in almost exactly the same terms appeared in the Commission **15.02** Proposal.[2] A restrictive view of the qualifications to the rules of applicable

---

[1] The remainder of the Recital is set out in **14.21** above.
[2] Commission Proposal, Recital (17).

law in the Regulation, so far as possible application of the law of the forum (*lex fori*) is concerned, is supported by the objective of certainty as to the law applicable, and by the perceived need to control forum shopping.[3]

B. PUBLIC POLICY

Article 26

Public policy of the forum

The application of a provision of the law of any country specified by this Regulation may be refused only if such application is manifestly incompatible with the public policy (*ordre public*) of the forum.

15.03 Art 26 follows very closely the wording of Art 16 of the Rome Convention.[4] That provision was described in the Giuliano & Lagarde Report as 'a precise and restrictively worded reservation'.[5]

15.04 The exceptional character of the public policy exception, emphasized in Recital (32),[6] is both necessary and inevitable. Legislators and courts in formulating rules concerning torts and other non-contractual obligations must weigh competing policy interests and consider the interests of the parties alongside the public interest. For example, in cases of civil liability arising from sporting and leisure activities, a balance must be struck, in terms of the public interest, between the protection of personal safety and the promotion of public health and well-being and, in terms of the parties' own interests, between the defendant's freedom to participate in or to offer an activity without being hindered by the fear of liability or excessive costs and the claimant's interest in being protected against and compensated for debilitating physical injury.[7] The fact that a foreign legislator or court, in formulating a rule governing non-contractual liability, has made a policy choice that differs from that made by the legislature or the courts of the forum Member State could not, of itself, justify displacement of the foreign rule in favour of the forum's rule. Otherwise, the *lex fori* would predominate,[8] and the objectives of the Regulation would be frustrated.

---

[3] **2.72–2.73** above.

[4] Also Rome I Regulation, Art 21.

[5] Giuliano & Lagarde Report (OJ C282, 38 [31.10.1980]).

[6] **15.01** above.

[7] See eg *Tomlinson v Congleton BC* [2003] UKHL 47; [2004] 1 AC 46, [45]–[47] (Lord Hoffmann); *Perry v Harris* [2008] EWCA Civ 907, [34] (Lord Phillips CJ).

[8] Note the views of Savigny and others to the effect that delictual liability is either akin to criminal liability, or else so closely connected with the fundamental principles of public policy applicable in the country of the forum, and that it should be entirely governed by the *lex*

This restrictive approach accords with the case law of the Court of Justice **15.05** concerning the public policy exception to the recognition and enforcement of judgments in Art 27(1) of the Brussels Convention.[9] In *Krombach v Bamberski*, the Court stated:[10]

With regard . . . to recourse to the public-policy clause in Article 27, point 1, of the Convention, the Court has made it clear that such recourse is to be had only in exceptional cases.[11]

It follows that, while the Contracting States in principle remain free, by virtue of the proviso in Article 27, point 1, of the Convention, to determine, according to their own conceptions, what public policy requires, the limits of that concept are a matter for interpretation of the Convention.

Consequently, while it is not for the Court to define the content of the public policy of a Contracting State, it is none the less required to review the limits within which the courts of a Contracting State may have recourse to that concept . . .

In *Renault v Maxicar*, a decision issued less than two months after *Krombach*, **15.06** the Court issued the following guidance:[12]

Recourse to the clause on public policy in Article 27, point 1, of the Convention can be envisaged only where recognition or enforcement of the judgment delivered in another Contracting State *would be at variance to an unacceptable degree with the legal order of the State in which enforcement is sought inasmuch as it infringes a fundamental principle.*

This test seems equally apposite in the context of the Rome II Regulation. **15.07** Accordingly, application of a provision of the law of a country specified by one of the rules of applicable law contained in the Regulation may be refused only if its application by the Member State court seised of the dispute would infringe a principle that is fundamental to its legal order.

In its 1st Reading Position, the European Parliament went further by list- **15.08** ing the following specific examples of circumstances that would justify invoking the public policy exception: (a) breach of fundamental rights and

---

fori (M Wolff, *Private International Law* (2nd ed, 1950), para 469; *Regie National des Usines Renault SA v Zhang* [2002] HCA 10; (2002) 210 CLR 491, [46]–[60] (HC Aus)).

   [9] 'A judgment shall not be recognized—1. If such recognition is contrary to public policy in the State in which recognition is sought . . .'.

   [10] Case C-798 [2000] ECR I-1935, paras 21–23.

   [11] The Court referred to Case 145/86, *Hoffmann v Krieg* [1988] ECR 645, para 21 and Case C-78/95, *Henrikman v Magenta Druck & Verlag GmbH* [1996] ECR I-4943, para 23.

   [12] Case C-38/98, *Régie Nationale des Usines Renault SA v Maxicar SpA* [2000] ECR I-2973, para 30 (emphasis added). In this case, the Court concluded that a failure by the court of origin to apply EC law correctly did not (in the circumstances) constitute a manifest breach of a rule of law regarded as essential in the legal order of the State in which enforcement was sought.

freedoms as enshrined in the European Convention on Human Rights, (b) national constitutional provisions, or (c) international humanitarian law.[13] The Commission rejected that approach on the ground that '[e]ven though the public policy of the Member States will inevitably contain common elements, there are variations from one to another'.[14] Similarly, in the view of the Council, '[i]t would be difficult for the time-being to lay down common criteria and reference instruments for the purposes of defining public policy'.[15] Nevertheless, the rights and freedoms enshrined in the European Convention on Human Rights provide the clearest examples of fundamental principles common to the Member States, infringement of which would entitle a Member State court to refuse to apply a rule of foreign law under the Regulation, whether or not the State from which the rule originates is a party to the Convention.[16] In *Krombach v Bamberski*, the ECJ held that a Member State court was entitled, on public policy grounds, to refuse to enforce a judgment from another Member State in circumstances in which there had been an infringement of the defendant's right to a fair trial under Art 6 of the ECHR.[17] In this connection, the Court recognized that:[18]

The Court has consistently held that fundamental rights form an integral part of the general principles of law whose observance the Court ensures . . . [19] For that purpose, the Court draws inspiration from the constitutional traditions common to the Member States and from the guidelines supplied by international treaties for the protection of human rights on which the Member States have collaborated or of which they are signatories. In that regard, the European Convention for the Protection of Human Rights and Fundamental Freedoms (hereinafter the ECHR) has particular significance . . .[20]

15.09   Accordingly, Art 26, in combination with Art 16 (overriding mandatory provisions), addresses concerns raised during the passage of the Rome II Regulation that the general rule for tort/delict did not offer sufficient

---

[13] EP 1st Reading Position, Art 24(4) (Amendment 50).

[14] Commission Amended Proposal, 5.

[15] Statement of reasons accompanying the Council's common position (OJ C289E, 80 [28.11.2006]).

[16] *Pellegrini v Italy* (Application no 30882/96) (2001) 35 EHRR 44.

[17] *Krombach v Bamberski*, n 10 above, paras 35–45.

[18] Ibid, para 25. Also Treaty on European Union, Art 6(2); Charter of Fundamental Rights of the European Union (OJ 364, 1 [18.12.2000]); Treaty on European Union (as amended by the Lisbon Reform Treaty), Art 6.

[19] The Court referred to *Opinion 2/94 on the Accession by the Community to the European Convention for the Protection of Human Rights and Fundamental Freedoms* [1996] ECR I-1759, para 33.

[20] Referring to Case 222/84, *Johnston v Chief Constable of the Royal Ulster Constabulary* [1986] ECR 1651, para 18.

protection against the imposition of 'inhumane laws' and, in particular, did not afford sufficient protection to individual victims of human rights violations.[21] It must, however, be noted that the Rome II Regulation will only apply to civil claims based on alleged violations of human rights insofar as they constitute 'civil . . . matters' within Art 1(1). Liability of the State or of a public authority or office holder for acts and omissions in the exercise of State authority (*acta iure imperii*) is specifically excluded. Claims for compensation against a State or public official with respect to the military action of its armed forces[22] or torture, in violation of Art 1 of the Torture Convention, concern *acta iure imperii* and fall within this exclusion,[23] with the result that the Member States' pre-existing rules of private international law must apply, subject to the forum's public policy.[24]

Art 26, like Art 16 of the Rome Convention, expressly requires that the **15.10** result of applying a provision of the law applicable under the Rome II Regulation must be 'manifestly incompatible' with the forum's public policy. The word 'manifestly', originating in the public policy clauses of the Hague Conventions on private international law matters, emphasizes that the contravention of a fundamental principle of the legal order of the forum State must be 'obvious' and that reliance on public policy must be specifically justified.[25] It might also be taken to require that any doubt be resolved in favour of the application of the law which would otherwise apply under the Regulation.

There is no reason why, in an appropriate case, a court cannot invoke the **15.11** public policy of the forum of its own motion to deny application of a rule of foreign law. At its first reading stage, the European Parliament proposed that the public policy exception could only be applied with respect to a provision of the law of another Member State at the request of one

---

[21] House of Lords' European Union Committee, *The Rome II Regulation* (8th Report of Session 2003–04), HL Paper 66, paras 151–5 and Evidence, 88–9.

[22] Case C-292/05, *Lechouritou v Dimosio tis Omospondiakis Dimokratias tis Germanias* [2007] ECR I-1519.

[23] **3.285** above. The State and those acting in the exercise of State authority may be able to assert immunity from suit in any event (*Jones v Ministry of Interior of the Kingdom of Saudi Arabia* [2006] UKHL 26; [2007] 1 AC 270).

[24] e.g. *R (on the application of Al-Jedda) v Secretary of State for Defence* [2007] UKHL 58.

[25] Giuliano & Lagarde Report (OJ C282, 38 [31.10.1980]). Cf A Briggs and P Rees, *Civil Jurisdiction and Judgments* (4th ed, 2005), para 7.13, footnote 124, suggesting that the insertion of the word 'manifestly' in Art 34(1) of the Brussels I Regulation added little of discernible substance to the pre-existing case law of the ECJ under the Brussels Convention (**15.05–15.06** above).

of the parties.[26] According to the Parliament's JURI Committee, this position would bring the Regulation into line with the Brussels I Regulation 'which forbids the automatic application of such grounds for non-recognition'.[27] In the JURI Committee's view, it was undesirable that the public policy exception should be applied automatically by a judicial body to exclude the law applicable under the Regulation.[28] As to the first of these reasons, the Brussels I Regulation does not, contrary to the JURI Committee's view, preclude Member State courts from raising objections to the recognition or enforcement of a judgment of their own motion.[29] As to the second reason, it appears (on the contrary) wholly desirable to give the court a measure of control over these matters: the parties should not be the final arbiters as to the impact of the fundamental values of the forum. Although it is conceivable that the private international law of the European Community may, in the future, move to a position under which Member State judgments and laws are mutually recognized without the possibility of an exception on public policy grounds,[30] that is not the current state of affairs. Accordingly, Art 26 of the Rome II Regulation cannot be taken to require Member States to delegate to the parties decisions that are, by their nature, in the public interest.[31]

15.12 Recital (32) also refers to a specific application of the forum's public policy in relation to the award of non-compensatory exemplary or punitive damages. This wording has been considered in the commentary on the approach that the Regulation takes to the assessment on damages in the preceding chapter.[32]

---

[26] EP 1st Reading Position, Art 24(4) (Amendment 50). The Spanish delegation, in its initial response to the Commission Proposal, suggested restricting the exception to cases in which the law applicable was that of a non-Member State (Council document 9009/04 ADD 10 [18.5.2004], 10). That proposal supported by Lithuania (ibid, ADD 14 [24.5.2004], 5), but opposed by the majority of delegations (Council document 8445/04 [19.4.2004], 6; Commission note of meeting of Council's Rome II Committee held on 16–17 September 2004 (Commission document JAI C1 (2004) D9487), 2).

[27] EP 1st Reading Report, 33.

[28] Ibid.

[29] U Magnus and P Mankowski, *Brussels I Regulation* (2007), Art 34, paras 7–8. Art 41 excludes any review on the grounds set out in Arts 34 and 35 (including public policy under Art 34(1)) at the first stage of enforcement proceedings, but the mandatory wording of Arts 34 and 35 is entirely consistent with the view that Member State courts may raise objections to the recognition of judgments or to their enforcement at the *inter partes* stage.

[30] See, e.g., A Dickinson, 'Third-Country Mandatory Rules in the Law Applicable to Contractual Obligations: So Long, Farewell, Auf Wiedersehen, Adieu?' (2007) 3 J Priv Int L 53, 60–1.

[31] Commission Amended Proposal, 5.

[32] **14.21–14.23** above.

Under Art 26, it is the *application* of a rule that would otherwise apply **15.13** under the Regulation in the circumstances of the particular case, and not its content in the abstract, that must offend the forum's public policy.[33] Art 26 appears to be entirely negative in its effect. It does not, unlike Art 16 (overriding mandatory provisions),[34] authorize a Member State court to give positive, overriding effect to a rule originating in its own legal system, even if based on the same public policy, or to determine the law applicable by some other means. On the contrary, it must continue to give effect to provisions of the applicable law whose application is not objectionable. On this view, public policy operates under the Regulation as a shield and not a sword.[35] It can be relied on to avoid or restrict non-contractual obligations or grounds for opposing non-contractual liability under the law specified by the Regulation, but not to create obligations or remedies of a kind not recognized under any circumstances by that law.

C. OVERRIDING MANDATORY PROVISIONS

Article 16

Overriding mandatory provisions

Nothing in this Regulation shall restrict the application of the provisions of the law of the forum in a situation where they are mandatory irrespective of the law otherwise applicable to the non-contractual obligation.

INTRODUCTION

Art 16 mirrors almost exactly[36] the wording of Art 7(2) of the Rome **15.14** Convention. That wording was adopted by the Commission in its Proposal, and was not changed during the legislative process.[37]

---

[33] Giuliano & Lagarde Report (OJ C282, 38 [31.10.1980]); Dicey, Morris & Collins, para 32-233 commenting on Art 16 of the Rome Convention.

[34] **15.14–15.21** below.

[35] Cf EP 1st Reading Position, Art 24(2) (Amendment 50) referring to the possibility of invoking public policy to justify applying the law of the forum. Also Council document 8445/04 [19.4.2004], suggesting that it might be possible to replace the rejected law with the internal law of the forum or the general rule in Art 3 of the Commission Proposal.

[36] The word 'Regulation' is substituted for 'Convention' and the words 'non-contractual obligation' for 'contract'.

[37] Commission Proposal, Art 12(2). In their initial responses to the Commission Proposal, Austria and Italy opposed this provision on the ground that the public policy provision (now Art 26) offered sufficient protection (see Council documents 9009/04 ADD 1 [3.5.2004], 4; ibid, ADD 17 [2.6.2004], 6).

CONCEPT OF 'MANDATORY' RULES

15.15 The language of Art 16 suggests that it is for the Member State court seised of the dispute to determine whether particular rules are 'mandatory irrespective of the law otherwise applicable to the non-contractual obligation'.[38] Although English law did not, at the time that the Rome Convention was adopted, have a developed concept of 'mandatory rules' (corresponding to the French term, *lois de police*[39]), the ability of Parliament to lay down statutory rules which apply even to cases with a foreign connection that would otherwise support the application of the law of another country has always been recognized as a fundamental aspect of its sovereignty.[40] Indeed, the pre-existing English statutory rules of applicable law for torts were expressed to be without prejudice to 'any rule of law which either has effect notwithstanding the rules of private international law applicable in the particular circumstances or modifies the rules of private international law that would otherwise be applicable'.[41]

15.16 The English courts have occasionally ascribed mandatory status to the provisions of statutes regulating non-contractual obligations that expressly contemplate proceedings before an English court, or which also contain rules regulating procedural aspects of such claims. The decision of the Court of Appeal in *Roerig v Valiant Trawlers*, which appears best explained on this ground, has been considered in at **14.62** above. A similar approach has been taken to the application of the provisions of the Civil Liability (Contribution) Act 1978, which has been held to confer an entitlement before the English courts to contribution between persons jointly liable to a third person for the same damage, even if the claim for contribution does not otherwise have a close connection with England or with

---

[38] In the French version, '*des dispositions de la loi du for qui régissent impérativement la situation, quelle que soit la loi applicable à l'obligation non contractuelle*'. Contrast the references in Arts 14(2) and 14(3) to provisions of law 'which cannot be derogated from by agreement', reflecting the language used in Art 3(3) of the Rome Convention. Also Rome I Regulation, Recital (37).

[39] This is the title given to Art 7 in the French language version the Rome Convention. In the French version of the Rome II Regulation, the title given to Art 16 is '*dispositions impératives dérogatoires*'. Cf S Knöfel, 'Mandatory Rules and Choice of law: A Comparative Approach to Article 7(2) of the Rome Convention' [1999] JBL 239.

[40] Sir L Collins and others (eds), *Dicey, Morris & Collins: The Conflict of Laws* (14th edn, 2006), paras 1-053 to 1-061; A Briggs, *The Conflict of Laws* (2nd edn, 2008), 51–2.

[41] Private International Law (Miscellaneous Provisions) Act 1995, s 14(4). See Dicey, Morris & Collins, paras 35-120 to 35-121. As a possible example of such rules in tort cases, the editors refer to the Law Reform (Personal Injuries) Act 1948, which limits the extent to which contracts of employment may exclude liability for personal injury.

English law.[42] The approach to statutory construction in these cases will need to be re-considered against the background of the Regulation, and the limited role that it appears to contemplate for the law of the forum. In particular, it appears likely that (consistently with its case law relating to the public policy exception in the Brussels Convention[43]) the Court of Justice will seek to control the extent to which Member State courts can invoke provisions of local law to override the law applicable under the Regulation. The most obvious basis for that control involves giving the word 'mandatory' an independent autonomous meaning that is narrower than it appears hitherto to have been given under Art 7(2) of the Rome Convention.[44] That restriction on the scope of the mandate given by Art 16 of the Rome II Regulation is not evident in the text of the Article itself, but may be supported by the following explanation by the Commission of its Proposal:

In *Arblade*,[45] the Court of Justice gave an initial definition of overriding mandatory rules (also called public-order legislation) as 'national provisions compliance with which has been deemed to be so crucial for the protection of the political, social or economic order in the Member State concerned as to require compliance therewith by all persons present on the national territory of that Member State and all legal relationships within that State'. What is specific about them is that the courts do not even apply their own conflict rules to determine the law applicable to a given situation and to evaluate in practical terms whether its content would be repugnant to the values of the forum, but they apply their own rules as a matter of course.

[Art 12(2) of the Proposal[46]] allows the courts to apply the overriding mandatory rules of the forum. As the Court also held in *Arblade*, in intra-Community relations the application of the mandatory rules of the forum must be compatible with the fundamental freedoms of the internal market.

A similar thought pattern, based on the decision of the ECJ in the *Arblade* **15.17** case, inspired the definition given to 'overriding mandatory provisions' in Art 9(1) of the Rome I Regulation in the following terms:[47]

---

[42] *Arab Monetary Fund v Hashim* (1994) The Times, 11 October (EWHC); *Petroleo Brasiliero SA v Mellitus Shipping Inc* [2001] EWCA Civ 418; [2001] 2 Lloyd's Rep 203, [36] (Potter LJ) discussed at **14.120** above. Cf *Fluor Australia Pty Ltd v ASC Engineering Pty Ltd* [2007] VSC 262, esp at [50]–[57] (Bongiorno J), refusing to accord mandatory status to a local contribution statute in similar terms to the UK Civil Liability (Contribution) Act 1978.

[43] **15.05–15.06** above.

[44] P Nygh, *Autonomy in International Contracts* (1999), 200–5; A Briggs, n 40 above, 173–4; Dicey, Morris & Collins, paras 32-135 to 32-137.

[45] Referring to the decision of the Court of Justice in Joined Cases C-369 & 376/96, [1999] ECR I-8453.

[46] Regulation, Art 16.

[47] See the Commission's explanation of Art 8(1) of its proposal (COM (2005) 650 final, 7).

Overriding mandatory provisions are provisions the respect for which is regarded as crucial by a country for safeguarding its public interests, such as its political, social or economic organisation, to such an extent that they are applicable to any situation falling within their scope, irrespective of the law otherwise applicable to the contract under this Regulation.

15.18 This attempt to reflect the approach taken by the Court of Justice to Member States' imperative requirements restricting the exercise of the fundamental freedoms under the EC Treaty appears incomplete and uncertain.[48] Nevertheless, and even though there is no definition of 'overriding mandatory provisions' in the Rome II Regulation, the ECJ's desire to treat the Rome I and Rome II instruments as a single, harmonious regime[49] and to control the influence of the law of the forum may lead it to insist that Member State courts apply a similar threshold requirement in the application of mandatory provisions under Art 16. If that prediction were to prove correct, it would be difficult to justify the continued mandatory application by the English courts of legislation such as s 4 of the Fatal Accidents Act 1976 (considered in *Roerig v Valiant Trawlers*) and the Civil Liability (Contribution) Act 1978, which cannot be described as 'crucial for the protection of the political, social or economic order' in the UK.

MANDATORY RULES OF EC LAW

15.19 EC law, of course, forms part of the legal order of every Member State. To the extent that a relevant rule of EC law, whether contained in the Treaty or in subordinate legislation (in the case of EC directives, as implemented by the Member States) applies to the subject matter of proceedings before a Member State court, that rule must be applied by a Member State court in the determination of non-contractual obligations (1) if the law applicable under the Rome II Regulation is the law of a Member State, or (2) under Art 16 of the Regulation, if the rule of EC law has overriding effect irrespective of the law applicable under the Regulation.[50] The questions whether a rule of EC law applies to the subject matter of proceedings and whether it is an overriding mandatory provision, or takes effect only if the law applicable under the Rome II Regulation is that of a Member State, must be answered in each case by construing the measure in which the provision is contained, having regard to its context and objectives.[51]

---

[48] A Dickinson, n 30 above, 67.

[49] Recital (7), discussed at **3.33–3.34** above.

[50] See the comments of the Swedish delegation in Council document 9009/04 ADD 8 [24.5.2004], 31–2.

[51] Case C-381/98, *Ingmar GB Ltd v Eaton Leonard Technologies Inc* [2000] ECR I-9305.

Examples of measures imposing or affecting non-contractual obligations[52] **15.20** that may, on their proper construction, be capable of applying even if the law applicable under the Rome II Regulation is that of a non-Member State are Council Regulation (EC) No 2027/97 on air carrier liability in the event of accidents,[53] the Product Liability Directive,[54] the Prospectus Directive,[55] and the Transparency Directive.[56] With respect to the last two named instruments, the Council on adopting the Transparency Directive made the following statement:[57]

> The Council notes that the current rules on the law applicable to non contractual obligations need to be examined further with regard to corporate liability in the situations covered by Article 6 of Directive 2003/71/EC and Article 7 of the present Directive.

Art 7 of the Transparency Directive concerns responsibility and liability for information provided by issuers. Art 6 of the Prospectus Directive concerns responsibility and liability attaching to a prospectus. The relationship of the Rome II Regulation to these rules, and to the civil liability rules of the Member States to which they refer,[58] remains to be settled.[59]

MANDATORY RULES OF INTERNATIONAL LAW

Rules of international law, whether arising from a treaty to which the **15.21** forum Member State is a party or customary international law, may also have overriding effect under Art 16 of the Rome II Regulation, whether directly or through implementing measures adopted under the law of the

---

[52] The relationship between the Rome II Regulation, the E-Commerce Directive, and the UK legislation implementing the E-Commerce Directive is addressed at **16.12–16.12** and **16.33–16.35** below.

[53] OJ L285, 1 [17.10.1997], as amended by Regulation (EC) No 889/2002 (OJ L140, 2 [30.5.2002]) to give effect to the provisions of the Montreal Convention for the Unification of Certain Rules Relating to International Carriage by Air (n 62 below).

[54] **5.48** above.

[55] Directive (EC) No 2003/71 on the prospectus to be published when securities are offered to the public or admitted to trading (OJ L345, 64 [31.12.2003]).

[56] Directive (EC) No 2004/109 on the harmonisation of transparency requirements in relation to information about issuers whose securities are admitted to trading on a regulated market (OJ L390, 38 [31.12.2004]).

[57] Council document 15556/04 ADD 1 [20.1.2005], 5.

[58] For the UK rules implementing the civil liability requirements of the Prospectus and Transparency Directives, see Financial Services and Markets Act 2000, ss 90–90B; Prospectus Rules (FSA), para 5.5.

[59] During discussions in the Council's Rome II Committee, a proposal by the UK to exclude non-contractual obligations arising financial transactions from the scope of the Regulation was not accepted (**3.171–3.172** above).

Member State concerned.[60] Indeed, for treaties that treatment will normally be necessary for the Member State concerned to comply with its international commitments. Relevant examples concerning non-contractual, civil liability include (1) international conventions regulating the liability of carriers by sea,[61] air,[62] and rail[63] for damage to passengers and their property, (2) the Oil Pollution Conventions, discussed in **Chapter 7**,[64] and other conventions concerning civil liability for environmental damage,[65] (3) international conventions concerning salvage,[66] and (4) conventions on limitation of liability for maritime claims.[67]

Mandatory Rules of the Law Applicable under the Regulation

15.22 Rules of the law applicable under the Regulation will apply in accordance with the provisions of Chapter V of the Regulation, defining its vertical scope,[68] whether or not they are 'mandatory' in character.

Third Country Mandatory Rules

15.23 The Commission's Proposal contained an additional provision (Art 12(1)) enabling Member State courts to apply (on a discretionary basis) mandatory rules of another country, in the following terms:

[60] Under UK law, treaties do not have direct effect but must be implemented by legislation (see, e.g., *The Hollandia* [1983] 1 AC 565 (UKHL)).

[61] Convention relating to the carriage of passengers and their luggage by sea (Athens, 13 December 1974), Part I, implemented in the UK by Merchant Shipping Act 1995, s 183 and Sch 6.

[62] Convention for the unification of certain Rules for international carriage by air (Montreal, 28 May 1999), Chapter III, implemented in the UK by Carriage by Air Act 1961, s1 and Sch 1B and under EC law by Council Regulation (EC) No 2027/97 on air carrier liability in the event of accidents, n 53 above.

[63] Title III of the Uniform Rules Concerning the Contract for International Carriage of Passengers and Luggage by Rail, Appendix A to the Convention concerning the international carriage by rail (COTIF) (Berne, 9 May 1980). The Convention, as amended by the Protocol signed at Vilnius on 3 May 1999, is implemented in the UK by the Railways (Convention on International Carriage by Rail Regulations) (SI 2005/2092).

[64] **7.32–7.34** above.

[65] See the list of Conventions in Annex IV of Directive (EC) No 2004/35 on environmental liability with regard to the prevention and remedying of environmental damage.

[66] **11.15–11.17** above.

[67] Convention on limitation of liability for maritime claims (Brussels, 19 November 1976), as amended by the Protocol signed on 3 May 1996, implemented in the UK by Merchant Shipping Act 1995, s 185 and Sch 7.

[68] **Ch 14** above.

Where the law of a specific third country is applicable by virtue of this Regulation, effect may be given to the mandatory rules of another country with which the situation is closely connected, if and in so far as, under the law of the latter country, those rules must be applied whatever the law applicable to the non-contractual obligation. In considering whether to give effect to these mandatory rules, regard shall be had to their nature and purpose and to the consequences of their application or non-application.

This provision followed closely the wording of Art 7(1) of the Rome **15.24** Convention, a provision that had proved unpalatable to the United Kingdom and several other Member States,[69] all of whom chose to exercise the opt-out right conferred by Art 22(1)(a) of that Convention following the failure to reach a consensus during negotiations.[70] Although several Member States had criticized the inclusion of this provision in the Rome II Regulation,[71] and delegations on the Council's Rome II Committee were divided as to its utility,[72] it came as a pleasant surprise when this aspect of the Commission Proposal was rejected by the Council's Rome II Committee.[73] Neither the Commission nor the European Parliament (which had previously supported this aspect of the Proposal[74]) objected to its deletion. Indeed, the Commission noted that:[75]

This provision in the Commission's proposal did not reflect any particular Community interest; it was aiming at consistency as it was inspired by a similar provision in the 1980 Rome Convention on the Law Applicable to Contractual Obligations.

[69] Germany, Ireland, Luxembourg, Portugal, Latvia, and Slovenia.

[70] Giuliano & Lagarde Report (OJ C282, 27 [31.10.1980]). For a critical commentary on Art 7(1) of the Convention and Art 8(3) of the Commission's Rome I proposal, see A Dickinson, n 30 above.

[71] See the comments of Luxembourg (Council document 9009/04 [29.4.2004], 4); Austria (ibid, ADD 1 [3.5.2004], 4); Latvia (ibid, ADD 9 [18.5.2004], p 3; Spain (ibid, ADD 10 [18.5.2004], 7); Germany (ibid, ADD 11 [24.5.2004], 14); Ireland (ibid, ADD 13 [24.5.2004], 6), United Kingdom (ibid, ADD 15 [26.5.2004], 8); Italy (ibid, ADD 17 [2.6.2004], 6). For a spirited defence of the rule, see the arguments presented by the Swedish delegation in Council document 14193/04 ADD 1 [4.11.2004], 5–6.

[72] Council document 7551/06 [22.3.2006], 3.

[73] The Commission's text appears in square brackets in a draft produced by the Austrian Presidency in March 2006 (Council document 7432/06 [16.3.2006]), but was omitted from the overall compromise package sent to COREPER the following month (Council document 7929/06 [10.4.2006]).

[74] EP 1st Reading position, Art 14(2), reversing the order of the mandatory rules provisions in the Commission Proposal.

[75] Commission Communication concerning the Council's Common Position (COM (2006) 566 final [27.9.2006]), 4.

15.25 Accordingly, the Rome II Regulation provides no basis for the application of the law of a country other than the forum or a country whose law is expressly applied by the Regulation's specific rules of applicable law.[76]

D. RULES OF SAFETY AND CONDUCT

Article 17

Rules of safety and conduct

In assessing the conduct of the person claimed to be liable, account shall be taken, as a matter of fact and in so far as is appropriate, of the rules of safety and conduct which were in force at the place and time of the event giving rise to the liability.

INTRODUCTION

15.26 Article 17 of the Rome II Regulation, concerning the role of 'rules of safety and conduct', must be read together with Recital (34), as follows:

> In order to strike a reasonable balance between the parties, account must be taken, in so far as appropriate, of the rules of safety and conduct in operation in the country in which the harmful act was committed, even where the non-contractual obligation is governed by the law of another country. The term 'rules of safety and conduct' should be interpreted as referring to all regulations having any relation to safety and conduct, including, for example, road safety rules in the case of an accident.

15.27 This article, originating in Art 13 of the Commission Proposal,[77] is inspired by Art 7 of the Hague Traffic Accidents Convention[78] and Art 9 of the

---

[76] This probably reflects the position under the pre-existing UK statutory rules of applicable law, although there was a measure of doubt (Dicey, Morris & Collins, para 35-120).

[77] 'Whatever may be the applicable law, in determining liability account shall be taken of the rules of safety and conduct which were in force at the place and time of the event giving rise to damage.' The drafting of the provision was criticized by several Member States in their initial responses to the Commission Proposal (see the comments of the delegations from Belgium (Council document 9009/04 ADD 4 [4.5.2004], 3); Sweden (ibid, ADD 8 [18.5.2004], 21); Latvia (ibid, ADD 9 [18.5.2004], 3–4); Spain (ibid, ADD 10 [18.5.2004], 8); Germany (ibid, ADD 11 [24.5.2004], 14); Ireland (ibid, ADD 13 [24.5.2004], 6); Lithuania (ibid, ADD 14 [24.5.2004], 4); Italy (ibid, ADD 17 [2.6.2004]), 6).

[78] Art 7 of that Convention provides that '[w]hatever may be the applicable law, in determining liability account shall be taken of rules relating to the control and safety of traffic which were in force at the place and time of the accident'.

Hague Products Liability Convention.[79] In this connection, the Commission explained that:[80]

> The rule in Article 13 is based on the fact that the perpetrator must abide by the rules of safety and conduct in force in the country in which he operates, irrespective of the law applicable to the civil consequences of his action, and that these rules must also be taken into consideration when ascertaining liability. Taking account of foreign law is not the same thing as applying it: the court will apply only the law that is applicable under the conflict rule, but it must take account of another law as a point of fact, for example when assessing the seriousness of the fault or the author's good or bad faith for the purposes of the measure of damages.

In considering the corresponding provision of the Hague Traffic Accidents Convention, the rapporteur, Mr Eric W Essén, concluded:[81]   **15.28**

> The evaluation of the tortious nature of the act committed by the author of the accident therefore depends on the combined effect of the local law and the law applicable to liability. The rules of the local highway code are data which play a part in the evaluation of the whole situation. This evaluation is carried out according to the applicable law, but on the basis of factual elements drawn *inter alia* from the local law This law is therefore only of relevance in providing certain factual elements to the judge and so to enable him to apply the law governing liability.

The rapporteur also noted that:[82]   **15.29**

> Local rules relating to control and safety of traffic are only data which a judge will all the same have to take in to account. Yet the reference to 'rules relating to the control and safety of traffic' covers different concepts, in respect of which the *lex loci*[83] does not always assert itself equally strongly. There are very many degrees of these rules and the local law is not exclusive. It is for this reason that a flexible wording has been adopted, conferring on judges wide discretionary powers of evaluation.

---

[79] Art 9 of that Convention provides that the application of the rules of applicable law in Arts 4–6 'shall not preclude consideration being given to the rules of conduct and safety prevailing in the State where the product was introduced into the market'. For the history of this provision, see H Duintjer Tebbens, *International Product Liability* (1979), 350.

[80] Commission Proposal, 25.

[81] English translation of Explanatory Report on the Hague Traffic Accidents Convention, available at <http://www.hcch.net/upload/expl19e.pdf>, 28 (para 6.5). The French original of the Report is published in *Actes et Documents de la Onzième Session* (1968), tome III.

[82] Ibid, 27–8 (para 6).

[83] i.e. the law of the place of the accident.

RULES OF SAFETY AND CONDUCT

15.30 According to Recital (34) of the Rome II Regulation, the term 'rules of safety and conduct' should be interpreted as referring to all regulations having any relation to safety and conduct, including, for example, road safety rules in the case of an accident. For example, if A, while driving his car in England, crashes and injures his passenger B, who like A is habitually resident in Ruritania, Ruritanian law will (in principle) apply to determine the basis and extent of A's liability to B under Art 4(2) of the Regulation. Under Art 17, however, a Member State court must take into account, as it considers appropriate, the facts that, according to English traffic law, A was above (or below) the legal alcohol limit and driving on the wrong (or the correct) side of the road even if the same conduct in Ruritania would have been perfectly legal.

15.31 In describing the corresponding provision of the Hague Products Liability Convention, Mr W L M Reese suggested:[84]

> The word 'rule' should be interpreted in a broad sense to include not only statutes and decisional rules but also municipal ordinances.

15.32 Accordingly, although the Recital refers to 'regulations',[85] Art 17 cannot be taken to exclude 'rules' based on case law, such as *Verkehrspflichten* under German law.[86] It may even extend to non-legally binding conventional standards of behaviour (e.g. professional ethical standards). For example, it may be appropriate to judge the question whether the defendant acted dishonestly, if this is an element in liability under the law applicable to the non-contractual obligation, by taking account of the customs and business practices in the place in which he acted.[87]

THE ROLE OF RULES OF SAFETY AND CONDUCT

15.33 The words 'as a matter of fact and in so far as is appropriate' emphasize, first, that Art 17 is not a rule of applicable law[88] and, secondly, that Member State courts enjoy a wide margin of appreciation in deciding whether and, if so, for what purpose and to what extent to take account of any rule

---

[84] Explanatory Report by W L M Reese on the Hague Products Liability Convention, *Acts and Documents of the Twelfth Session* (1972), tome III, 269. The Report is available at <http://hcch.e-vision.nl/upload/expl22.pdf>.

[85] French text: 'réglementation'; German text: 'Vorschriften'.

[86] C van Dam, *European Tort Law* (2005), para 1503-2.

[87] *Dubai Aluminium Co Ltd v Salaam* [1999] 1 Lloyd's Rep 415, 452–3 (Rix J, EWHC).

[88] On this point, S C Symeonides, 'Rome II and Tort Conflicts: A Missed Opportunity' (2008) 56 AJCL 173, 212–13 and the comments of the Swedish delegation in Council document 9009/04 ADD 8 [24.5.2004], 20–1.

identified by Art 17. As the Commission's explanatory memorandum and the report of Mr Essén on the Hague Traffic Accidents Convention[89] make clear, the rules of safety and conduct fall to be taken into consideration as factual, not legal, elements in the framework for determining non-contractual obligations. They provide part of the context within which the conduct of the person liable must be judged, and their significance will vary according to the nature of that conduct and the other surrounding circumstances, as well as the content of legal rules underlying the non-contractual obligation in question. If liability under the applicable law is strict, the conduct of the person liable may not fall to be assessed at all. In such a case, Art 17 may have little or no effect.[90]

Art 17 refers only to the 'conduct of the person claimed to be liable' and **15.34** the focus of the Commission in the passage quoted at **15.27** above was on the position of the 'perpetrator'. This leads Professor Symeonides to suggest that 'the Rome II drafters seem to envision an even narrower, one-sided role for Article 17' as 'a tool for helping the tortfeasor, but not necessarily the victim'.[91] Art 17 applies, however, equally to non-contractual obligations other than torts, and there would appear to be no reason why a person seeking compensation cannot equally pray in aid breaches of rules of safety and conduct, for example, to establish the defendant's fault. Further, it may be argued that Art 17, in *requiring* that certain rules be taken into account in assessing the conduct of the person claimed to be liable, does not exclude the possibility that a Member State court may consider it appropriate to take into account relevant rules of safety and conduct for other purposes, including in assessing the conduct of the person sustaining damage. For example, returning to the example given above,[92] in considering the question of B's contributory fault (to the extent that this provides a defence under Ruritanian law) the Member State court may consider it appropriate to have regard to the fact that B was not wearing a seat belt, as is mandatory under English law.[93] Equally, although Art 17 refers only to 'rules of safety and conduct which were in force at the place and time of the event giving rise to the liability', that should not be taken to exclude the possibility that the rules in force in other places and at other times might be taken into account as relevant elements in the framework for the determination of non-contractual obligations.

---

[89] **15.27–15.29** above.

[90] **7.29** above.

[91] S C Symeonides, n 88 above, 213. In Professor Symeonides' view (ibid), 'the concern for the perpetrator is excessive, if not misplaced'.

[92] **15.30**.

[93] This fact may not, of course, be decisive (cf *Dawson v Broughton* (2007) unreported, 31 July (Judge Holman, Manchester County Court)).

16

Relationship with EC Law and International Instruments

A. RELATIONSHIP WITH EC LAW

Article 27

Relationship with other provisions of Community law

This Regulation shall not prejudice the application of provisions of Community law which, in relation to particular matters, lay down conflict-of-law rules relating to non-contractual obligations.

INTRODUCTION

Art 27 of the Rome II Regulation, which specifically concerns its relation- **16.01** ship with other provisions of EC law regulating the law applicable to non-contractual obligations, must be read together with Recital (35). That Recital provides:

A situation where conflict-of-law rules are dispersed among several instruments and where there are differences between those rules should be avoided. This Regulation, however, does not exclude the possibility of inclusion of conflict-of-law rules relating to non-contractual obligations in provisions of Community law with regard to particular matters.

This Regulation should not prejudice the application of other instruments laying down provisions designed to contribute to the proper functioning of the internal market in so far as they cannot be applied in conjunction with the law designated by the rules of this Regulation. The application of provisions of the applicable law designated by the rules of this Regulation should not restrict the free movement of goods and services as regulated by Community instruments, such as Directive 2000/31/EC of the European Parliament and of the Council of 8 June 2000 on certain legal aspects of information society services, in particular electronic commerce, in the Internal Market (Directive on electronic commerce).

16.02 Art 27 and Recital (35) constitute the vestiges of the more extensive provisions concerning the relationship between the Regulation and other provisions of EC law contained in the Commission Proposal and Amended Proposal and the European Parliament's 1st and 2nd Reading Positions.[1] For example, the European Parliament's first reading text contained the following provision concerning the relationship between the Regulation and other EC legislation:[2]

This Regulation shall not prejudice the application or adoption of acts of the institutions of the European Communities which:

a) in relation to particular matters, lay down choice-of-law rules relating to non-contractual obligations; or

b) lay down rules which apply irrespective of the national law governing the non-contractual obligation in question by virtue of this Regulation; or

c) prevent application of a provision or provisions of the law of the forum or of the law designated by this Regulation; or

d) lay down provisions designed to contribute to the proper functioning of the internal market in so far as they cannot be applied in conjunction with the law designated by the rules of private international law.

16.03 The final text of Art 27[3] and most of Recital (35) originate in the Council's Common Position.[4] The final sentence of the second paragraph of the Recital was added at a late stage in the conciliation process.

[1] Commission Proposal, Recital (19) and Art 23; EP 1st Reading Position, Recital (6) and Art 1(3); Commission Amended Proposal, Recital (7) and Art 3; EP 2nd Reading Position, Art 28.

[2] EP 1st Reading Position, Art 1(3). Also Recital (6) ('The concern for consistency in Community law requires that this Regulation be without prejudice to provisions relating to or having an effect on the applicable law, contained in instruments of secondary legislation other than this Regulation, such as conflict rules in specific matters, overriding mandatory rules of Community origin, and the basic legal principles of the internal market. As a result, this Regulation should promote the proper functioning of the internal market, in particular the free movement of goods and services.')

[3] Similar provisions appear in Rome Convention, Art 20 and Rome I Regulation, Art 23.

[4] Common Position, Art 27 and Recital (31).

The 'Country of Origin Principle'

Exposition

The evolution of these provisions of the Regulation, concerning its rela- **16.04** tionship with other rules of Community law, can only be explained against the background of the debate surrounding the so-called 'country of origin principle',[5] which figured prominently in the exchanges leading to adoption of the Regulation.[6] The 'principle' is chameleon-like in its appearance, changing according to its context and purpose and in response to the arguments advanced against it. In its essential form, the argument in favour of this 'principle' starts from the (uncontroversial[7]) proposition that Member State rules governing liability in tort, or other non-contractual liability, are a form of State regulation of economic activity that must comply with provisions of the EC Treaty guaranteeing free movement within the Community of products and factors of production.[8]

From this starting point, and building upon the case law of the ECJ apply- **16.05** ing the Treaty rules to other forms of regulation,[9] the argument proceeds that a service provider or manufacturer complying with the liability rules of his home Member State (the 'country of origin') should not be impeded in the exercise of cross-border economic activity by the imposition of the

---

[5] For more detailed discussion and references to other materials, see O Remien, 'European Private International Law, The European Community and its Emerging Area of Freedom, Security and Justice' (2001) Common Market L Rev 53, 81–5; M Wilderspin and X Lewis, *'Les relations entre le droit communitaire et les règles de conflits de lois des États membres'* (2002) 91 *Revue critique de droit international privé* 1; H Muir Watt, 'Choice of law in tort within the internal market: Do the economics of the internal market call for the application of the law of country of origin?', paper produced for the working group organized by the European Parliament's rapporteur on 14 March 2005; R Michaels, 'EU Law as Private International Law? Reconceptualising the Country-of-Origin Principle as Vested-Rights Theory' (2006) 2 J Priv Int L 195; G Vitellino, 'Rome II from an Internal Market Perspective' in A Malatesta (ed), *The Unification of Choice of Law Rules on Torts and Other Non-Contractual Obligations in Europe* (2006), 271–300.

[6] **1.59–1.63** and **1.85** above.

[7] Thus, the Court of Justice has emphasized that the effectiveness of Community law cannot vary according to the various branches of national law that it may affect (Case 20/92 *Hubbard v Hamburger* [1993] ECR I-3777, para 19).

[8] i.e. EC Treaty, Arts 28–29 (goods), 39 (workers), 43 (establishment), 49 (services), and 56 (capital).

[9] In particular, so far as free movement of goods is concerned, Case 8/74 *Procureur du Roi v Dassonville* [1974] ECR 837; Case 120/78 *Rewe-Zentral AG v Bundersmonopolverwaltung für Branntwein ('Cassis de Dijon')* [1979] ECR 649, para 14. In relation to services, see e.g. Case 288/89 *Stichting Collectieve Antennevoorziening Gouda v Commissariat voor de Media* [1991] ECR I-4007, para 13.

more onerous non-contractual liability regime of another Member State. By combining this, the principle of 'mutual recognition',[10] with the argument that (at least in the case of liability for goods) the Member State of origin should regulate exported products no less favorably than products for domestic consumption, so as to avoid creating obstacles to free movement by requiring compliance with two sets of rules,[11] the contention emerges that the internal market freedoms are irreconcilable with the 'private international law approach' to regulating liability for civil wrongs, an approach that uses rules of applicable law both to delimit the scope of local rules governing civil liability and related matters and to import foreign rules in their place using connecting factors that are considered appropriate according to the nature of the particular obligation or issue.

16.06 Instead, according to at least some proponents of the 'country of origin principle', the local civil liability rules of the Member State of origin of goods or services should be applied by the courts of that Member State without distinguishing between purely internal situations and cross-border situations within the EC. Moreover, to avoid hindering cross-border trade by the phenomenon of double regulation, those same rules should be applied by the courts of all other Member States whenever they have jurisdiction over civil claims relating to goods and services imported from other Member States, at least insofar as the rules that they would otherwise apply are more burdensome to the exporter or service provider.[12]

16.07 Taking this version of the 'country of origin principle' at face value, it suggests that the EC Treaty had from the outset established its own applicable law regime for non-contractual liability arising in the exercise of the fundamental freedoms, and that the adoption of an instrument such as the Rome II Regulation laying down specific rules of applicable law for non-contractual obligations was unnecessary and, as it uses connecting factors other than the country of origin, unlawful.

---

[10] Also Commission Communication on the *Cassis de Dijon* judgment (OJ C256, 2 [3.10.80]). Standing alone, application of the mutual recognition principle to the regulation of civil liability appears capable of producing a curious *renvoi*-type result, requiring the courts of Member States other than the Member State of origin to reach the same decision as a court in the latter State.

[11] See e.g. Case 53/76, *Procureur de la République de Besançon v Les Sieurs Bouhelier* [1977] ECR 197. Compare the differently focused 'market access' approach taken in services cases, notably Case C-384/93 *Alpine Investments BV v Minister van Financiën* [1995] ECR I-1141.

[12] A 'best of both worlds' approach or *Günstigkeitprinzip* (J Basedow, '*Der kollisionrechtliche Gehalt der Produktfreiheiten im europäischen Binnenmarkt: favour offerentis*' (1995) 59 Rabels Z 1, 16–17; also R Michaels, n 5 above, 208–9).

This argument, however, rests on insecure foundations. In particular, **16.08** the ECJ has recognized that (a) the principle of home State supervision is not a principle laid down by the EC Treaty from which the Community legislature cannot depart,[13] (b) differences between the regulatory treatment of domestic and cross-border situations can be justified on objective grounds,[14] (c) measures characterized as 'restrictions' on trade between Member States may nevertheless be capable of being justified on the basis of overriding reasons in the public interest, such as public health, consumer protection, protection of the environment, and the integrity of commercial transactions[15] (these being reasons of a kind that commonly inform the development of both private international law and substantive rules concerning non-contractual liability), and (d) the existence of disparities among Member State rules concerning non-contractual liability in cross-border situations or, within a single Member State, between the regulation of non-contractual liability in domestic and cross-border situations does not automatically infringe EC law: the impact of such disparities upon access to EC markets may be too indirect and uncertain to be regarded as liable to hinder trade between Member States.[16]

Furthermore, the process of reasoning by analogy to case law involving **16.09** other kinds of regulation of economic activity seems questionable. Rules of civil liability, which do not simply regulate the conduct of the manufacturer or service provider but instead regulate the relationship between the person liable and the person seeking a remedy,[17] have more in common with 'selling arrangements' to which the ECJ has refused to extend the mutual recognition principle.[18] The bilateral character of civil liability rules also highlights another weakness of the approach, in that the recipients of goods and services also benefit from the fundamental freedoms

---

[13] Case C-233/94, *Germany v Parliament and Council* [1997] ECR I-2405, para 64.

[14] e.g. Case 15/83, *Denkavit Nederland BV v Hoofdprodukschap voor Akkerbouwprodukten* [1984] ECR 2171, para 18.

[15] C Barnard, *The Subtantive Law of the EU* (2nd edn, 2007), 115–19 (goods), 378–80 (services).

[16] **2.29** above.

[17] Thus, even rules of product liability, which may require particular standards to be observed in the manufacture of products, are primarily concerned with damage caused to the end-user of the product who has had insufficient warning of non-compliance with those standards or instructions as to how to use the product safely.

[18] Cases C-267 & 268/91, *Keck and Mithouard* [1993] ECR I-6097, esp para 16, a case concerning free movement of goods. For the influence of the *Keck* judgment on the ECJ's case law relating to the free movement of services, see C Barnard, n 15 above, 262–6, 279–83, 373–8; D Wyatt and others (eds), *Wyatt and Dashwood's European Union Law* (5th edn, 2006), paras 19-018 to 19-019, 19-030.

established by EC law,[19] a phenomenon that emphasizes the need to consider their legitimate expectations as to the law applicable.

16.10 In short, the 'country of origin principle' in the form described above does not withstand close scrutiny—it is too inflexible and one-sided. Although it cannot be denied that the fundamental freedoms recognized in EC law may shape the substantive rules governing non-contractual liability in a particular situation,[20] the better view is that they have no direct or automatic effect upon the operation of private international law in this subject area.[21] So far as the Rome II Regulation is concerned, it is to be expected that the harmonization of rules of applicable law for non-contractual obligations will significantly reduce disparities between the regulation by Member State courts of particular situations, the focus shifting to differences in the overriding effect of the law of the forum through mandatory rules and public policy. Insofar as the rules of applicable law in the Regulation will produce disparities in the treatment by individual Member States of domestic and cross-border situations (for example, where the defendant's activity causes damage in two Member States), that result may be justified on the basis of objective differences between the two situations, and in particular the bilateral character of the relationship that is being regulated, or by reference to other objectives legitimately pursued by the Community legislature.

Rise and Fall of the Country of Origin Principle

16.11 During the passage of the Regulation, most proponents of the 'country of origin principle' tended to deploy it in one of two ways. First, by arguing that sectoral instruments containing a so-called 'internal market clause', referring to rules of the Member State of origin, removed non-contractual obligations falling within their field of application from the reach of both Member States' existing systems of private international law and any future Community private international law instruments, including the Rome II Proposal. Secondly, by arguing that (at least in specific areas) the rules of applicable law contained in a future Rome II instrument should adopt the 'principle' by expressly selecting the law of the country of origin

---

[19] Joined Cases C-286/82 and 26/83, *Luise and Carbone v Ministero del Tesoro* [1984] ECR 377, para 10; Case 186/87, *Cowan v Trésor Public* [1989] ECR 195, para 15. Also C Barnard, n 15 above, 357–8.

[20] **2.29** above.

[21] This was the approach taken by the Commission in its Communication on the freedom to provide services and the general good in the Second Banking Directive (SEC (97) 1193 final), 25–8.

of cross-border activities to govern non-contractual claims arising as a result.

The first type of argument based on the 'principle' manifested itself most **16.12** prominently in connection with the E-Commerce Directive, adopted in 2000.[22] Art 3 of the Directive contains an internal market clause in the following terms:

1   Each Member State shall ensure that the information society services provided by a service provider established on its territory comply with the national provisions applicable in the Member State in question which fall within the co-ordinated field.
2   Member States may not, for reasons falling within the co-ordinated field, restrict the freedom to provide information society services from another Member State.

The 'co-ordinated field', defined by Art 2(h)(i) of the E-Commerce Directive includes 'requirements concerning the liability of the service provider'.

The question put was this: did these provisions in combination require **16.13** that all liability issues be determined by reference to the domestic civil liability regime of the Member State of origin? One might have thought that a negative answer to that question was required by Art 1(4) of the Directive which expressly disclaimed any intention on the part of the legislator to establish additional rules on private international law. On the other hand, Recital (23) of the Directive stated 'provisions of the applicable law designated by rules of private international law must not restrict the freedom to provide information society services as established in this Directive' and Art 3(3) further muddied the waters by excluding several matters from the scope of the internal market clause, including 'the freedom of the parties to choose the law applicable to their contracts' but without making any reference to the law applicable to non-contractual obligations. These provisions were taken by some to support the conclusion that Art 3(1), directly or indirectly, mandated application to non-contractual obligations of the law of the service provider's country of establishment.[23] That view, however,

---

[22] Directive (EC) No 2000/31 on certain legal aspects of information society services, in particular, electronic commerce in the Internal Market (OJ L178, 1) [17.7.2000]). For differing views on the impact of the Directive on private international law, see A Thünken, 'Multi-State Advertising over the Internet and the Private International Law of Unfair Competition' (2002) 51 ICLQ 909; M Hellner, 'The Country of Origin Principle in the E-Commerce Directive—A Conflict with the Conflict of Laws?' (2004) 12 Eur Rev Priv L 193; J Hörnle, 'The UK Perspective on the Country of Origin Rule in the E-Commerce Directive—A Rule of Administrative Law Applicable to Private Law Disputes' (2004) 12 Int J L & IT 333.

[23] This view is evident in the positions taken by DG Markt and DG Information Society in their responses to the Commissions 2001 draft Green Paper (**1.61** above). For references to

not only contradicts Art 1(4), it also (1) requires that the reference to 'national provisions' in Art 3(1) of the E-Commerce Directive be taken as referring only to rules of law originating within the Member State of origin to the exclusion of foreign rules applied by the courts of that Member State in accordance with its rules of private international law, and (2) treats the 'freedom to provide information society services' as an absolute freedom. These two premises may, in turn, be challenged. The first perceives rules of another country that fall to be applied in accordance with a Member State of origin's rules of applicable law as not belonging to that Member State's legal order at all. That perception, however, misapprehends the nature of rules of applicable law. Instead of requiring or authorizing local courts to stand in the shoes of foreign courts in the application of foreign law, rules of applicable law (including those in the Rome II Regulation[24]) take effect by identifying rules, whether of local or foreign origin, to be accommodated within the forum's legal order, to the extent that they are compatible with it. When so applied, they become local rules. The second premise insulates the E-Commerce Directive from the wider freedom to provide services under the EC Treaty that it is intended to facilitate, and from which it feeds. For the reasons already given in analysing the 'country of origin principle',[25] the application by Member State courts of their pre-existing rules of private international law for non-contractual obligations cannot, of itself, be said to constitute a restriction on the freedom to provide services. That argument is weaker still in relation to the harmonized rules introduced by the Rome II Regulation.

16.14 Accordingly, although it will almost certainly require a ruling of the ECJ to settle the debate, the better view is that Art 3 of the E-Commerce Directive did not override or circumvent the Member State's pre-existing rules of applicable law for non-contractual obligations, but instead required that (1) the Member State of origin take steps to ensure compliance with any decision of its courts as to the service provider's civil liability, having regard to its rules of private international law whenever appropriate, and (2) any disparity between the (hypothetical) determination of questions of civil liability by a court in the Member State of origin and the (actual) determination of identical questions by a court in another Member State, in each case with reference to its own rules of applicable law, should be taken into account in determining whether the 'regulation' of the situation by the latter Member State is a 'restriction' on the freedom

similar arguments, see M Hellner, n 22 above, 202–13; N Höning, 'The European Directive on e-Commerce and its Consequences on the Conflict of Laws' (2005) Global Jurist Topics vol 5: issue 2, art 2, 17–36.

[24] **3.39–3.40** above.
[25] **16.08–16.10** above.

to provide information society services. On this view, the E-Commerce Directive and the Rome II Regulation are wholly consistent with one another, and Recital (35) does no more than serve as a reminder that sectoral instruments such as the E-Commerce Directive, where appropriate as implemented under the law of the forum, may override or qualify the substantive rules governing non-contractual liability of the law that applies under the Regulation.

Nevertheless, when implementing the E-Commerce Directive, the UK **16.15** Department of Trade and Industry appeared to subscribe to the 'country of origin as applicable law' view of Art 3(1), and took the (curious) decision to remove from the final text of the Electronic Commerce (EC Directive) Regulations 2002[26] a provision in the draft Regulations that had expressly preserved the effect of existing private international law rules.[27] One might have thought that this amounted to a failure to implement Art 1(4) of the Directive. Whether that is correct, the resulting lack of clarity as to the relationship between the 2002 Regulations, the E-Commerce Directive, and the Rome II Regulation leaves much to be desired.[28]

By contrast, the German Government not only took a different approach **16.16** in its draft implementing Regulations,[29] giving priority to existing rules of private international law, but also went to the lengths of recommending that the Council should consider the issue with a view to implementing the 'country of origin principle' in line with its proposal and not in the form of a rule of applicable law.[30] This, it appears, led to a rebuke by the Commission and to revision of the German implementing Regulations.[31]

The seed having been planted, the argument based on the 'country of **16.17** origin principle' soon began to appear in other contexts.[32] If anything, however, the more that the argument was pressed, the weaker it became. It appeared to lack balance, ignoring factors (and, in particular, the impact of the service provider's conduct on the victim) that pointed towards other

---

[26] SI 2002/2013.

[27] Department of Trade and Industry, Electronic Commerce (EC Directive) Regulations 2002, Public Consultation—Government Response, 31 July 2002 under heading '*Private International Law*'.

[28] The issues are addressed briefly at **16.33–16.35** below.

[29] Council document 10481/01 ADD 1 [10.7.2001].

[30] Council document 10481/01 [2.7.2001].

[31] M Hellner, n 22 above, 204, text to footnotes 43 to 45.

[32] See the reports by the Council's Committee on Civil Law Matters on the proposed Directives on unfair commercial practices (Council document 8821/04 [10.5.2004]), services (Council document 12655/04 [24.9.2004]) and sales promotions (Council document 14402/04 [11.11.2004]). The legislative history of the first of these proposals is considered at **6.35–6.41** above.

solutions, requiring separate treatment of 'domestic' and 'cross-border cases'. In contrast, the Commission Proposal for the Rome II Regulation,[33] with its objective of ensuring closer harmony in civil liability regimes while remaining sensitive to cross-border elements in particular situations and promoting other policy objectives of the EC Treaty (e.g. environmental protection) provided a rallying point for opponents of the 'principle'.

16.18 The high-water mark in terms of recognition of the 'country of origin principle' was reached with the Commission's proposal for a Directive on services in the internal market.[34] The proposal contained an internal market clause (under the heading 'Country of origin principle'), which specified that:[35]

> Member States shall ensure that providers are *subject only to the national provisions of their Member State of origin* which fall within the coordinated field.[36]

> Paragraph 1 shall cover national provisions relating to access to and the exercise of a service activity, in particular those requirements governing the behaviour of the provider, the quality or content of the service, advertising, contracts *and the provider's liability*.

16.19 There followed a list of general derogations from this requirement,[37] including:

> (20) the freedom of parties to choose the law applicable to their contract; . . .
> (23) the non-contractual liability of a provider in the case of an accident involving a person and occurring as a consequence of the service provider's activities in the Member State to which he has moved temporarily.

16.20 The Commission emphasized the proposed subordination of private international law techniques to the application of the country of origin in its explanatory memorandum. Having referred to the Rome II Proposal and the Rome Convention, the Commission commented:[38]

> These instruments could, however, play an important role not only for the activities which are not covered by this Directive but also for the questions which are the object of derogations to the country of origin principle, notably the derogation in relation to contracts concluded by consumers, as well as the derogation relating

---

[33] Led by DG JLS, in contrast to the Services Directive, a proposal led by DG Markt.
[34] COM (2004) 2 final [5.3.2004].
[35] Ibid, Art 16(1) (emphasis and footnote added).
[36] 'Coordinated field' was defined broadly as meaning 'any requirement applicable to access to service activities or to the exercise thereof' (ibid, Art 4(9)). Certain service activities (including financial services) were excluded from the proposed Directive by Art 1.
[37] Ibid, Art 17.
[38] COM (2004) 2 final, 17. See also the 'Technical analysis of the provisions of the Rome I Convention and the Rome II Draft Regulation in light of the Draft Services Directive', produced by the General Secretariat of the Council (Council document 10542/04 [25.6.2004]).

to the non-contractual liability of the provider in the case of an accident occurring in the context of his activity which affects a person in a Member State which a provider visits.

As was widely publicized at the time, the Commission's approach to the **16.21** proposed Services Directive, and in particular its strong preference for regulation of service providers according to their country of origin, was the object of fierce criticism. It must be acknowledged that private international law played a relatively small part in this debate, which was ultimately one of the many reasons cited for the rejection by Dutch and French voters of the proposed EU Constitutional Treaty.[39]

During this period, however, Council's Committee on Civil Law Matters **16.22** issued an opinion opposing the proposed subordination of the Rome Convention and proposed Rome II Regulation to the country of origin rule enshrined in the proposed Services Directive.[40] In the Committee's view:[41]

If the country of origin were rigidly applied in this area, the effect would be to disrupt the application of standards of justice which have a particular importance in this context. . . .

For reasons of legal clarity and in order to avoid providing rules on applicable law over several instruments, the Committee proposes that all factors touching on the law applicable to contractual and non-contractual obligations be concentrated as far as possible respectively in the Rome Convention, which will most likely become a Community act, and in the Rome II Regulation.

Eventually, as appears below,[42] the Committee's view would eventually prevail over that of the Commission.

The second type of argument based on the 'country of origin principle' **16.23** was advanced in the debate as to the law that should be applied to non-contractual obligations arising out of violations of privacy and rights relating to the personality (including defamation).[43] The Commission had proposed that these obligations be subject to the general rule for tort/delict, prioritizing the law of the country of damage, subject to the fundamental principles of the forum as regards freedom of expression and information and a special rule applying the law of the country of the broadcaster's or publisher's habitual residence to the right to reply or

---

[39] R Michaels, n 5 above, 195–6.
[40] Council document 12655/04 [25.9.2004]. See also the comments of the Council legal service in Council document 13858/04 [27.10.2004] (partially accessible) and the Presidency note in Council document 14558/1/04 REV 1 [22.11.2004], 3–4.
[41] Council document 12655/04, paras 19 and 22.
[42] **16.28–16.29.**
[43] **3.217–3.221** above.

equivalent measures.[44] Representatives of the media argued, however, that the law of the 'country of origin' of broadcasts or published works should be applied to all aspects of non-contractual liability, relying on the fundamental freedoms under Community law, on Community instruments that were argued to require or favour application of the law of the country of origin,[45] and on the right to freedom of expression in Art 10 of the European Convention of Human Rights.[46]

16.24 In the early stages of the Regulation's progress, these arguments enjoyed a measure of success. The House of Lords' European Union Committee concluded:[47]

> The media favours a country of origin rule, by which they mean that the applicable law would be the law of the place where the editorial control over publication was exercised. A country of origin rule would have certain advantages, notably simplicity and certainty. It would point to one law. It would not require the amalgam which Article 6 [*of the Commission Proposal*] presently envisages. To adopt a country of origin rule would also accord with, though not necessarily in all cases replicate, the host country/place of establishment regimes found in the E-Commerce and other Single Market measures. A country of origin rule would encourage enterprise, education and the widest dissemination of knowledge, information and opinion.

> We recognise, however, that such a rule would cut across the general scheme of the Regulation, which favours the law either of the place where the damage occurs or the habitual residence of the victim. And it is not difficult to imagine situations where many of the facts of a case are closer to one of those laws than the place where the editorial control is sited. A country of origin rule would also seem to entrust to the law of the publisher rather than the law system of the victim the striking of the balance between the competing interests of the media in freedom of

---

[44] Commission Proposal, Art 6.

[45] In particular, the E-Commerce Directive; Directive (EEC) No 89/552 on the co-ordination of certain provisions laid down by law, regulation or administrative action in Member States concerning the pursuit of television broadcasting activities (OJ L298, 23 [17.10.89]), as amended by Directive (EC) No 97/36 (OJ L202, 60 [30.7.1997]) and, subsequently, by Directive (EC) No 2007/65 (OJ L332, 27 [18.12.2007]) (the 'Television Without Frontiers Directive'); Directive (EEC) No 93/83 on the coordination of certain rules concerning copyright and rights related to copyright applicable to satellite broadcasting and cable retransmission (OJ L148, 15 [6.10.1993]); and Directive (EC) No 95/46 on the protection of individuals with regard to the processing of personal data and the free movement of personal data (OJ L281, 31 [23.11.1995]). With the possible exception of Arts 4 and 22 the Data Protection Directive (**3.228** above), these Directives do not advance the case for applying the law of the country of origin to civil, non-contractual liability.

[46] See the evidence to the House of Lords' European Union Committee, *The Rome II Regulation*, 8th Report of Session 2003–2004 (HL Paper 66), Evidence, 31–45

[47] Ibid, paras 128–9.

expression and of the victim in rights to privacy. But it should be recalled that all Member States are parties to the ECHR and that freedom of expression cannot ride roughshod over rights to privacy. Finally, it should be noted that a country of origin rule is not without risk for publishers, including those in the United Kingdom. A country of origin rule would have the effect of exporting our law. UK publishers might be sued in any other Member State and UK law, including its damages rules, would apply.

The European Parliament's rapporteur, while not accepting the case for applying the law of the 'country of origin' alone,[48] proposed a compromise solution, giving a significantly greater role to the place of habitual residence of a publisher or broadcaster[49] and adjusting the general rules of applicable law in such a way as to favour the country to which the publisher or broadcaster principally directs his activities.[50] That solution gained support from representatives of the media, but was rejected by both the Commission[51] and the Council.[52] To avoid deadlock, non-contractual obligations arising out of violations of privacy and rights of personality were eventually excluded from the scope of the Regulation.[53] **16.25**

Further, the Parliament's rapporteur was plainly influenced in her overall approach by what she saw as the demands of the internal market under EC law. She explained:[54] **16.26**

The rapporteur is conscious that her approach diverges from that of traditional international conventions in the field of private international law, but would point out that the instrument in preparation is a piece of Community legislation and hence has to satisfy different requirements. In contrast to previous instruments where the Community has taken over an existing international convention on private law, in this instance there was no previous convention, which provides a unique opportunity to legislate in a specifically Community context. In particular, your rapporteur has taken pains to ensure that the regulation can co-exist with Internal Market legislation and promote, rather than hamper, the proper functioning of the Internal Market. Particular consideration has been given to the Regulation's relationship with the television without frontiers and the e-commerce directives. Your rapporteur has been anxious to suggest a principled holistic

[48] Ibid, para 180.
[49] Governing not only the right to reply but also preventative measures and prohibitory injunctions (EP 1st Reading Report, Amendment 30 amending Commission Proposal, Art 6(2)).
[50] EP 1st Reading Report, Amendment 30 amending Commission Proposal, Art 6(1).
[51] Commission Amended Proposal, 6, describing the EP position as 'too generous to press editors rather than the victim of alleged defamation in the press'.
[52] Statement of reasons accompanying the Council's Common Position (C289E, 77 [28.11.2006]).
[53] Art 1(2)(g) (**3.217–3.228** above).
[54] EP 1st Reading Report, 39.

approach which should avoid the necessity for confusing carve-outs and special regimes, present or future, as these merely serve to make our legislation more complex to navigate and less transparent.

16.27 That influence manifested itself in the provisions of the European Parliament's first reading text concerning the relationship between the Regulation and other EC legislation.[55]

16.28 By 2006, whether due to a genuine re-appraisal of the validity of the arguments advanced by the rival camps or political expediency following the sinking of the EU Constitution, the 'country of origin principle' had been placed firmly on the back foot. There was no reference to the principle in the final version of the Services Directive, which contained a more detailed and less emphatic clause concerning the freedom to provide services.[56] More significantly for present purposes, it specifically excluded any claim to affect 'provisions regarding contractual and non-contractual obligations . . . determined pursuant to the rules of private international law'.[57] In its amended proposal for the Services Directive, the Commission accepted the need for this last amendment because 'the provision on the freedom to provide services is the provision of this Directive that could possibly conflict with the application of rules of private international law'.[58]

16.29 The retreat extended to the final terms of the Rome II Regulation. Thus, in contrast to the positions of the Commission and the European Parliament,[59] Art 27 and its accompanying Recital are more restrained. Tellingly, the Commission, in its September 2006 Communication in response to the Council's Common Position observed:[60]

In view of the recent developments in the European Parliament and the Council in the context of negotiations of other proposals such specifically tailored provision in this instrument seems no longer necessary.

16.30 Even so, the changes may be more significant from a presentational viewpoint than in terms of their actual effect on the relationship between the Rome II Regulation and other rules of EC law, as the Regulation does not

---

[55] **16.02** above.

[56] Directive (EC) No 2006/123 on services in the internal market (OJ L376, 36 [27.12.2006]), Art 16. Recital (35) to the Rome II Regulation refers to the E-Commerce Directive but not the Services Directive.

[57] Ibid, Art 17(15) and Art 3(2). See Council documents 13643/05 [14.11.2005], 45–6; 15310/05 [6.12.2005], 43–4; 15310/1/05 [21.12.2005], 43–4 recording the positions taken by individual Member States in negotiations on this issue.

[58] COM (2006) 160 final [4.4.2006], 12.

[59] **16.02** above.

[60] COM (2006) 566 final [27.9.2006], 4.

qualify the obligation of Member State courts to give effect to relevant substantive rules of EC law as an integral part of the law applicable under the Regulation (if it is the law of a Member State) or as a mandatory rule[61] or, possibly, as a rule of safety and conduct.[62]

Finally, it may be noted that the rules of applicable law contained in the **16.31** Rome II Regulation (and, in particular, the general rule for torts, favouring the law of the place of damage, and the special rules on product liability and unfair competition) flatly contradict the country of origin approach. In the circumstances, it seems that, if this so-called 'principle' is to prevail in the area of the law applicable to non-contractual obligations, its proponents must adjust their arguments to take account of the endorsement that the Regulation undoubtedly gives to traditional techniques of private international law.

EFFECT OF ARTICLE 27

Under Art 27, the Regulation's rules of applicable law may be overridden **16.32** by 'provisions of Community law which, in relation to particular matters, lay down conflict-of-law rules relating to non-contractual obligations'. There appear to be very few provisions of this character currently in force. The clearest example would appear to be Art 4 of the Insolvency Regulation, which applies to 'insolvency proceedings and their effects', insofar as they fall within its scope, the law of the Member State within the territory of which proceedings are opened.[63] The (non-exhaustive) list of matters to which that law applies in Art 4 includes matters that might otherwise be argued fall within the scope of the Rome II Regulation insofar as they concern non-contractual obligations, including 'the respective powers of the debtor and the liquidator',[64] 'the conditions under which set-offs may be invoked',[65] 'the effects of insolvency proceedings on current contracts to which the debtor is a party',[66] and 'the rules relating to the voidness,

---

[61] Art 14(3) (**13.32–13.33** above) and 16 (**15.19–15.20** above).

[62] Art 17 (**15.26–15.34** above).

[63] Regulation (EC) No 1346/2000 on insolvency proceedings (OJ L160, 1 [30.6.2000]), Art 4. Also, to similar effect, Directive (EC) No 2001/17 on the reorganisation and winding-up of insurance undertakings (OJ L110, 28 [20.4.2001]), Art 9; Directive (EC) No 2001/24 on the reorganisation and winding up of credit institutions (OJ L125, 15 [5.5.2001]), Art 10. The two Directives have been implemented in the UK by the Insurers (Reorganisation and Winding Up) Regulations (SI 2004/353) and by the Credit Institutions (Reorganisation and Winding Up) Regulations (SI 2004/1045).

[64] Ibid, Art 4(2)(c).

[65] Ibid, Art 4(2)(d). Also Art 6.

[66] Ibid, Art 4(2)(e) (**14.92**, text to n 238 above).

voidability or unenforceability of legal acts detrimental to all creditors'.[67] In its initial response to the Commission Proposal, the Irish delegation suggested that matters covered by the Insolvency Regulation be specifically excluded from the scope of the Regulation.[68] Art 27 makes such a provision unnecessary.

16.33 Another possible example, although one whose status and effect is controversial and much less clear, is provided by the 'internal market clause' in Art 3 of the E-Commerce Directive,[69] as implemented in the UK by Reg 4 of the Electronic Commerce (EC Directive) Regulations 2002.[70] Arts 4(1) and 4(3) of the 2002 Regulations provide that, subject to certain exceptions:

(1) [A]ny requirement which falls within the coordinated field shall apply to the provision of an information society service by a service provider established in the United Kingdom irrespective of whether that information society service is provided in the United Kingdom or another member State. . . .

(3) [A]ny requirement shall not be applied to the provision of an information society service by a service provider established in a member State other than the United Kingdom for reasons which fall within the coordinated field where its application would restrict the freedom to provide information society services to a person in the United Kingdom from that member State.

16.34 The 'coordinated field' includes 'requirements applicable to information society service providers or information society services, regardless of whether they are of a general nature or specifically designed for them, and covers requirements with which the service provider has to comply in respect of . . . the liability of the service provider'.[71] 'Requirement' means 'any legal requirement under the law of the United Kingdom, or any part of it, imposed by or under any enactment or otherwise'.

16.35 The English courts have yet to grapple with the effect of the internal market provisions in the 2002 Regulations in relation to the non-contractual liability of the service provider in a cross-border case.[72] It seems clear,

---

[67] Ibid, Art 4(2)(m). Also Art 13. For discussion of the question whether the *action paulienne* under French law and similar claims fall within the scope of the Rome II Regulation, see **4.249–4.258** above.

[68] Council document 9009/04 ADD 13 [24.5.2004], 3.

[69] **16.12–16.14** above, where the view that Art 3(1) operates as a rule of applicable law favouring the 'country of origin' is rejected.

[70] SI 2002/2013.

[71] Electronic Commerce (EC Directive) Regulations 2002, Reg 2(1).

[72] J Hörnle, n 22 above.

however, that Reg 4(1) and 4(3) do not, individually or in combination, operate as a rule of applicable law favouring the law of the service provider's country of establishment, even if (contrary to the view taken above[73]) this is what Art 3 of the E-Commerce Directive is eventually held to require. Instead, if Reg 4 applies to disputes between private parties,[74] it would appear to modify the sphere of application of relevant rules of the UK, or its constituent parts, by giving them the status of overriding mandatory provisions in cases involving service providers established in the UK (Art 4(1)) and by restricting their effect insofar as service providers established in other Member States are concerned (Art 4(3)). On this view, it is Art 16, not Art 27, of the Rome II Regulation, which must be relied on to give priority to Art 4(1). The restriction in Art 4(3) may be given effect as a 'limiting provision' if the law of a part of the UK applies under the Regulation.[75]

B. RELATIONSHIP WITH INTERNATIONAL INSTRUMENTS

Article 28

Relationship with existing international conventions

1. This Regulation shall not prejudice the application of international conventions to which one or more Member States are parties at the time when this Regulation is adopted and which lay down conflict-of-law rules relating to non-contractual obligations.

2. However, this Regulation shall, as between Member States, take precedence over conventions concluded exclusively between two or more of them in so far as such conventions concern matters governed by this Regulation.

Article 29

List of conventions

1. By 11 July 2008, Member States shall notify the Commission of the conventions referred to in Article 28(1). After that date, Member States shall notify the Commission of all denunciations of such conventions.

2. The Commission shall publish in the *Official Journal of the European Union* within six months of receipt:

    (i) a list of the conventions referred to in paragraph 1;
    (ii) the denunciations referred to in paragraph 1.

---

[73] **16.14** above.
[74] For the view that it does not, see J Hörnle, n 22 above.
[75] **3.42** above.

INTRODUCTION

16.36   Arts 28 and 29 regulate the relationship of the rules of applicable law contained in the Rome II Regulation with those contained in international treaties to which the Member States were parties when it was adopted on 11 June 2007.

16.37   In this connection, Recital (36) provides:

> Respect for international commitments entered into by the Member States means that this Regulation should not affect international conventions to which one or more Member States are parties at the time this Regulation is adopted. To make the rules more accessible, the Commission should publish the list of the relevant conventions in the *Official Journal of the European Union* on the basis of information supplied by the Member States.

16.38   Art 28, paragraph 1 and Art 29 are broadly consistent with the terms of the original Commission Proposal.[76] Art 28, paragraph 2, concerning conventions exclusively between the Member States,[77] was introduced by the Council.[78] The German delegation in the Council's Rome II Committee had proposed a specific rule dealing with the relationship between the Regulation and future 'bilateral conventions with a regional territorial scope',[79] but this proposal was not accepted. In reaching these conclusions, the Rome II Committee took account of advice given by the Council Legal Service.[80]

16.39   As at 11 July 2008, the deadline fixed in Art 29(1), it is understood that only a few Member States had notified to the Commission a list of the international conventions referred to in Art 28(1) to which it was a party on 11 July 2007.[81] The UK was not among them. As it is not a party to the Hague Traffic Accidents or Hague Products Liability Conventions,[82] the international instrument that most obviously triggers the UK's obligation to notify under Art 29(1) is the Hague Trusts Convention.[83] The International Convention on Salvage, concluded in London on 28 April 1989,

---

[76] Commission Proposal, Arts 26 and 27.
[77] For these purposes, 'Member State' excludes Denmark (Art 1(4)).
[78] Common Position, Art 28(2).
[79] Council document 5805/06 [31.1.2006].
[80] Council document 7645/06 [22.3.2006].
[81] The Commission's list of these conventions, when published, will appear on the companion website <http://www.romeii.eu>.
[82] **16.41–16.42** below.
[83] **3.174** and **3.201–3.207** above.

also contains (in Art 15(2)) a rule regulating the law applicable to apportionment between salvors.[84]

The approach taken in Art 28 is consistent with Art 307 of the EC Treaty, **16.40** which provides that the rights and obligations of Member States arising from agreements concluded with one or more third countries before the date of their accession to the Community are not affected by the provisions of the Treaty, subject to an obligation to take 'all appropriate steps' to eliminate any incompatibility. The Council Legal Service has taken the view that these principles apply equally to Community legislative instruments with respect to agreements concluded before their entry into force.[85] As a consequence, it would appear that notification by a Member State to the Commission under Art 29 is not a prerequisite to the application by a Member State court of a pre-existing treaty to determine the law applicable to a non-contractual obligation, although the failure to notify may involve a breach of EC law, having other consequences.

THE HAGUE TRAFFIC ACCIDENTS AND PRODUCTS LIABILITY CONVENTIONS

In terms of their subject matter and the participation of Member States, the **16.41** Hague Traffic Accidents and Products Liability Conventions are the most important of the international conventions that will continue to apply under Art 28 in the Member States party to them.[86]

At its first reading stage, the European Parliament had recommended **16.42** that, if all other elements of the situation at the time when the loss is sustained were located in one or more Member States, the rules of applicable law in the Rome II Regulation should take priority over those in the Hague Traffic Accidents Convention, where applicable.[87] At the same time, within the framework of the Regulation, Art 7 of the EP 1st Reading Position could be read as giving all Member States the option of applying either set of rules in traffic accident cases,[88] although it appears that the intention

---

[84] **11.16** above.
[85] Council document 7645/06, para 9 referring to an earlier (unpublished) opinion given by the Legal Service with respect to the Brussels I Regulation.
[86] For analysis of the provisions of these Conventions and their relationship to the rules of applicable law in the Rome II Regulation, see **4.114–4.120** (Hague Traffic Accidents Convention) and **5.49–5.53** (Hague Products Liability Convention).
[87] EP 1st Reading Position, Art 25(3).
[88] EP 1st Reading Position, Art 7(1) (Amendment 32) ('Until such time as the Community adopts detailed legislation on the law applicable to traffic accidents, Member States shall either apply the general rules set out in this Regulation, subject to Article 15, or the Hague Convention of 4 May 1971 on the Law Applicable to Traffic Accidents').

behind the amendment was to give that option only to Member States party to the Hague Convention.[89] In its Amended Proposal, the Commission went further in recommending that, in situations exclusively connected with the Member States, the rules of the Regulation should take priority over both the Hague Traffic Accidents Convention and the Hague Products Liability Convention.[90] Neither of these proposals was carried forward into the final text of the Regulation,[91] with the result that both Hague Conventions take priority over the Rome II Regulation in the Member States party to them.[92] Instead, the review clause in Art 30 requires the Commission to include in its first report on the functioning of the Regulation, due by 20 August 2001, a study on the effects of Art 28 of this Regulation with respect to the Hague Traffic Accidents Convention.

THE COMMUNITY'S EXTERNAL COMPETENCE

16.43 Following the Opinion of the Court of Justice on the competence of the European Community to conclude the Lugano Convention,[93] there is no doubt that the organs of the Community will consider themselves to have exclusive competence going forward to negotiate and conclude international agreements concerning the law applicable to non-contractual obligations falling within the scope of the Regulation. Further, in view of the universal application of the Regulation,[94] it seems likely that any international agreement proposed in this area will affect harmonized Community rules to a sufficient extent to support that exclusive competence.[95]

16.44 That competence, and its consequences in terms of the ability of Member States to conclude bilateral or multilateral agreements with third countries in their own right, is recognized in Recital (37), which provides:[96]

The Commission will make a proposal to the European Parliament and the Council concerning the procedures and conditions according to which Member States would be entitled to negotiate and conclude on their own behalf agreements with

---

[89] EP 1st Reading Report, 40.

[90] Commission Amended Proposal, Art 24(2).

[91] See Council documents 15643/05 [22.12.2005], 2 and 7551/06 [22.3.2006], 4.

[92] Hague Traffic Accidents Convention: Austria, Belgium, Czech Republic, France, Latvia, Lithuania, Luxembourg, Netherlands, Poland, Slovakia, Slovenia, Spain. Hague Products Liability Convention: Finland, France, Luxembourg, Netherlands, Slovenia, Spain.

[93] Opinion 01/03, [2006] ECR I-1145. See F Pocar (ed), *The External Competence of the European Union and Private International Law* (2007).

[94] Art 3 (**3.294–3.295** above).

[95] Opinion 01/03, n 93 above, paras 114–33.

[96] Cf the proposal of the German delegation in Council document 7928/06 [30.3.2006], 2.

third countries in individual and exceptional cases, concerning sectoral matters, containing provisions on the law applicable to non-contractual obligations.

It is understood that this Recital (originally contained in the Council's **16.45** Common Position[97]) was inserted at the request of some Member States who wanted to protect their right to conclude agreements with neighbouring non-Member States in relation to matters that specifically concerned them (for example, accidents in a border area). Interestingly, the text may not reflect the Commission's view as to the extent to which it would be prepared to allow departures from the Community's newly acquired exclusive competence. In its communication responding to the Common Position, the Commission expressed regret that the wording did not accurately reflect the declaration made by it at the JHA Council meeting held in April 2006.[98] That declaration was in the following terms:

The Commission is prepared, in appropriate cases, to examine the possibility of making proposal[99] to the Council authorising Member States to conclude international agreements concerning specific sectoral matters which contain provisions on the law applicable to non-contractual obligations. This remains without prejudice to the possibility of the Community to negotiate and conclude such international agreements in accordance with the provisions of Article 300 EC.

Although the Commission has not clarified its position since adoption of **16.46** the Regulation, this suggests that a general derogation from the Community's external competence will not be forthcoming. Instead, Member States will need to seek exemption on a case-by-case basis.

---

[97] Common Position, Recital (33).
[98] Commission Communication concerning the Council Common Position (COM (2006) 566 final [27.9.2006]), 5, text to footnote 1.
[99] *Sic.*

Conclusion

Putting arguments about necessity and treaty basis to one side, the adoption of the Rome II Regulation should be seen as a positive step for private international law in the UK, Europe and globally. Although the structure and content of some of the Regulation's rules have been criticized in the preceding commentary, the pre-Regulation UK statutory and judge-made rules of applicable law for non-contractual obligations could hardly be said to be a model of clarity or to be satisfactory from a practitioner's point of view. In terms of legal certainty, the Rome II Regulation potentially offers significant advantages for UK courts, litigants and their advisers in the medium to long term through the development of a set of rules in common with at least 25 other Member States. That said, there will be an inevitable delay before ECJ has the opportunity to grapple with the more difficult questions, and it may be many years before the contours of the Regulation can be defined with confidence. As one commentator notes:[1]

Even a superficial reading of the 'Rome II' Regulation reveals that behind nearly any paragraph and even any sentence lurk more than one legal issue that will have to be resolved by the Court of Justice. 'Rome II' will (taken together with 'Rome I') increase the workload of the Court, and it will confront the Court, at least to some extent, with some very 'technical' issues with nevertheless broad implications. This should again stimulate reflections of Court reform.

In the final analysis, one need not share Professor Symeonides' transatlantic view of the strengths and weaknesses of the Regulation, to agree with his conclusion that:[2]

[A]lthough European PIL would have been better off with a 'better' Rome II, the more realistic question is whether it would have been better off without Rome II at all. On balance, this author's answer is in the negative. If nothing else, and despite its flaws, Rome II will unify and thus equalize, the private international law of the member-states of the European Union.

That said, the Rome II Regulation, in combination with the Rome I and Brussels I Regulations and other Title IV instruments, should not be seen as laying the foundations for European private international law code of

---

[1] Editorial Comment, 'Sometimes it takes thirty years and even more . . .' (2007) 44 CML Rev 1567, 1574.
[2] S C Symeonides, 'Rome II and Tort Conflicts: A Missed Opportunity' (2008) 56 AJCL 173, 218.

the kind envisaged by the Benelux nations in 1969. Every future legislative proposal in this area must be considered on its merits, based on a proper assessment of its relationship to the functioning of the internal market and a full impact assessment, and not waved through solely on the ground of an unshakeable belief that harmonized rules will inevitably improve legal certainty or secure greater predictability in the outcome of cross-border litigation. The final form of the Rome II Regulation may be generally satisfactory, but the case presented for and the process leading to its adoption left much to be desired.

Finally, it seems likely that in the coming years the role of private international law in the Member States' legal systems will come under increasing scrutiny in the course of discussions, within and outside the institutions of the European Community, as to whether there should be greater harmony in the Member States' substantive rules regulating contractual and non-contractual liability. If the movement for a 'European Civil Code' or similar instrument is to be repulsed, and national legal autonomy preserved, it is vital that the Rome I and Rome II Regulations should be seen to be successful in promoting access to justice for individuals and businesses alike. Against this background, we must apply ourselves to the challenges that the Regulation presents, knowing that a worse fate may befall us if it fails in its objectives.

Appendices

Appendix 1

Regulation (EC) No 864/2007 of the European Parliament and of the Council of 11 July 2007 on the law applicable to non-contractual obligations (Rome II)

Official Journal L 199, 31/07/2007 P. 0040 – 0049

Regulation (EC) No 864/2007 of the European Parliament and of the Council of 11 July 2007 on the law applicable to non-contractual obligations (Rome II)

THE EUROPEAN PARLIAMENT AND THE COUNCIL OF THE EUROPEAN UNION,

Having regard to the Treaty establishing the European Community, and in particular Articles 61(c) and 67 thereof,

Having regard to the proposal from the Commission,

Having regard to the opinion of the European Economic and Social Committee [1],

Acting in accordance with the procedure laid down in Article 251 of the Treaty in the light of the joint text approved by the Conciliation Committee on 25 June 2007 [2],

Whereas:

(1) The Community has set itself the objective of maintaining and developing an area of freedom, security and justice. For the progressive establishment of such an area, the Community is to adopt measures relating to judicial cooperation in civil matters with a cross-border impact to the extent necessary for the proper functioning of the internal market.

(2) According to Article 65(b) of the Treaty, these measures are to include those promoting the compatibility of the rules applicable in the Member States concerning the conflict of laws and of jurisdiction.

(3) The European Council meeting in Tampere on 15 and 16 October 1999 endorsed the principle of mutual recognition of judgments and other decisions of judicial authorities as the cornerstone of judicial cooperation in civil matters and invited the Council and the Commission to adopt a programme of measures to implement the principle of mutual recognition.

(4) On 30 November 2000, the Council adopted a joint Commission and Council programme of measures for implementation of the principle of mutual recognition of decisions in civil and commercial matters [3]. The programme identifies

measures relating to the harmonisation of conflict-of-law rules as those facilitating the mutual recognition of judgments.

(5) The Hague Programme [4], adopted by the European Council on 5 November 2004, called for work to be pursued actively on the rules of conflict of laws regarding non-contractual obligations (Rome II).

(6) The proper functioning of the internal market creates a need, in order to improve the predictability of the outcome of litigation, certainty as to the law applicable and the free movement of judgments, for the conflict-of-law rules in the Member States to designate the same national law irrespective of the country of the court in which an action is brought.

(7) The substantive scope and the provisions of this Regulation should be consistent with Council Regulation (EC) No 44/2001 of 22 December 2000 on jurisdiction and the recognition and enforcement of judgments in civil and commercial matters [5] (Brussels I) and the instruments dealing with the law applicable to contractual obligations.

(8) This Regulation should apply irrespective of the nature of the court or tribunal seised.

(9) Claims arising out of *acta iure imperii* should include claims against officials who act on behalf of the State and liability for acts of public authorities, including liability of publicly appointed office-holders. Therefore, these matters should be excluded from the scope of this Regulation.

(10) Family relationships should cover parentage, marriage, affinity and collateral relatives. The reference in Article 1(2) to relationships having comparable effects to marriage and other family relationships should be interpreted in accordance with the law of the Member State in which the court is seised.

(11) The concept of a non-contractual obligation varies from one Member State to another. Therefore for the purposes of this Regulation non-contractual obligation should be understood as an autonomous concept. The conflict-of-law rules set out in this Regulation should also cover non-contractual obligations arising out of strict liability.

(12) The law applicable should also govern the question of the capacity to incur liability in tort/delict.

[OJ L199, 41]

(13) Uniform rules applied irrespective of the law they designate may avert the risk of distortions of competition between Community litigants.

(14) The requirement of legal certainty and the need to do justice in individual cases are essential elements of an area of justice. This Regulation provides for the connecting factors which are the most appropriate to achieve these objectives. Therefore, this Regulation provides for a general rule but also for specific rules and, in certain provisions, for an 'escape clause' which allows a departure from these rules where it is clear from all the circumstances of the case that the tort/ delict is manifestly more closely connected with another country. This set of rules

thus creates a flexible framework of conflict-of-law rules. Equally, it enables the court seised to treat individual cases in an appropriate manner.

(15) The principle of the *lex loci delicti commissi* is the basic solution for non-contractual obligations in virtually all the Member States, but the practical application of the principle where the component factors of the case are spread over several countries varies. This situation engenders uncertainty as to the law applicable.

(16) Uniform rules should enhance the foreseeability of court decisions and ensure a reasonable balance between the interests of the person claimed to be liable and the person who has sustained damage. A connection with the country where the direct damage occurred (*lex loci damni*) strikes a fair balance between the interests of the person claimed to be liable and the person sustaining the damage, and also reflects the modern approach to civil liability and the development of systems of strict liability.

(17) The law applicable should be determined on the basis of where the damage occurs, regardless of the country or countries in which the indirect consequences could occur. Accordingly, in cases of personal injury or damage to property, the country in which the damage occurs should be the country where the injury was sustained or the property was damaged respectively.

(18) The general rule in this Regulation should be the *lex loci damni* provided for in Article 4(1). Article 4(2) should be seen as an exception to this general principle, creating a special connection where the parties have their habitual residence in the same country. Article 4(3) should be understood as an 'escape clause' from Article 4(1) and (2), where it is clear from all the circumstances of the case that the tort/delict is manifestly more closely connected with another country.

(19) Specific rules should be laid down for special torts/delicts where the general rule does not allow a reasonable balance to be struck between the interests at stake.

(20) The conflict-of-law rule in matters of product liability should meet the objectives of fairly spreading the risks inherent in a modern high-technology society, protecting consumers' health, stimulating innovation, securing undistorted competition and facilitating trade. Creation of a cascade system of connecting factors, together with a foreseeability clause, is a balanced solution in regard to these objectives. The first element to be taken into account is the law of the country in which the person sustaining the damage had his or her habitual residence when the damage occurred, if the product was marketed in that country. The other elements of the cascade are triggered if the product was not marketed in that country, without prejudice to Article 4(2) and to the possibility of a manifestly closer connection to another country.

(21) The special rule in Article 6 is not an exception to the general rule in Article 4(1) but rather a clarification of it. In matters of unfair competition, the conflict-of-law rule should protect competitors, consumers and the general public and ensure that the market economy functions properly. The connection to the law of the country where competitive relations or the collective interests of consumers are, or are likely to be, affected generally satisfies these objectives.

(22) The non-contractual obligations arising out of restrictions of competition in Article 6(3) should cover infringements of both national and Community competition law. The law applicable to such non-contractual obligations should be the law of the country where the market is, or is likely to be, affected. In cases where the market is, or is likely to be, affected in more than one country, the claimant should be able in certain circumstances to choose to base his or her claim on the law of the court seised.

(23) For the purposes of this Regulation, the concept of restriction of competition should cover prohibitions on agreements between undertakings, decisions by associations of undertakings and concerted practices which have as their object or effect the prevention, restriction or distortion of competition within a Member State or within the internal market, as well as prohibitions on the abuse of a dominant position within a Member State or within the internal market, where such agreements, decisions, concerted practices or abuses are prohibited by Articles 81 and 82 of the Treaty or by the law of a Member State.

(24) 'Environmental damage' should be understood as meaning adverse change in a natural resource, such as water, land or air, impairment of a function performed by that resource for the benefit of another natural resource or the public, or impairment of the variability among living organisms.

[OJ L199, 42]

(25) Regarding environmental damage, Article 174 of the Treaty, which provides that there should be a high level of protection based on the precautionary principle and the principle that preventive action should be taken, the principle of priority for corrective action at source and the principle that the polluter pays, fully justifies the use of the principle of discriminating in favour of the person sustaining the damage. The question of when the person seeking compensation can make the choice of the law applicable should be determined in accordance with the law of the Member State in which the court is seised.

(26) Regarding infringements of intellectual property rights, the universally acknowledged principle of the *lex loci protectionis* should be preserved. For the purposes of this Regulation, the term 'intellectual property rights' should be interpreted as meaning, for instance, copyright, related rights, the *sui generis* right for the protection of databases and industrial property rights.

(27) The exact concept of industrial action, such as strike action or lock-out, varies from one Member State to another and is governed by each Member State's internal rules. Therefore, this Regulation assumes as a general principle that the law of the country where the industrial action was taken should apply, with the aim of protecting the rights and obligations of workers and employers.

(28) The special rule on industrial action in Article 9 is without prejudice to the conditions relating to the exercise of such action in accordance with national law and without prejudice to the legal status of trade unions or of the representative organisations of workers as provided for in the law of the Member States.

(29) Provision should be made for special rules where damage is caused by an act other than a tort/delict, such as unjust enrichment, *negotiorum gestio* and *culpa in contrahendo.*

(30) *Culpa in contrahendo* for the purposes of this Regulation is an autonomous concept and should not necessarily be interpreted within the meaning of national law. It should include the violation of the duty of disclosure and the breakdown of contractual negotiations. Article 12 covers only non-contractual obligations presenting a direct link with the dealings prior to the conclusion of a contract. This means that if, while a contract is being negotiated, a person suffers personal injury, Article 4 or other relevant provisions of this Regulation should apply.

(31) To respect the principle of party autonomy and to enhance legal certainty, the parties should be allowed to make a choice as to the law applicable to a non-contractual obligation. This choice should be expressed or demonstrated with reasonable certainty by the circumstances of the case. Where establishing the existence of the agreement, the court has to respect the intentions of the parties. Protection should be given to weaker parties by imposing certain conditions on the choice.

(32) Considerations of public interest justify giving the courts of the Member States the possibility, in exceptional circumstances, of applying exceptions based on public policy and overriding mandatory provisions. In particular, the application of a provision of the law designated by this Regulation which would have the effect of causing non-compensatory exemplary or punitive damages of an excessive nature to be awarded may, depending on the circumstances of the case and the legal order of the Member State of the court seised, be regarded as being contrary to the public policy (*ordre public*) of the forum.

(33) According to the current national rules on compensation awarded to victims of road traffic accidents, when quantifying damages for personal injury in cases in which the accident takes place in a State other than that of the habitual residence of the victim, the court seised should take into account all the relevant actual circumstances of the specific victim, including in particular the actual losses and costs of after-care and medical attention.

(34) In order to strike a reasonable balance between the parties, account must be taken, in so far as appropriate, of the rules of safety and conduct in operation in the country in which the harmful act was committed, even where the non-contractual obligation is governed by the law of another country. The term 'rules of safety and conduct' should be interpreted as referring to all regulations having any relation to safety and conduct, including, for example, road safety rules in the case of an accident.

(35) A situation where conflict-of-law rules are dispersed among several instruments and where there are differences between those rules should be avoided. This Regulation, however, does not exclude the possibility of inclusion of conflict-of-law

rules relating to non-contractual obligations in provisions of Community law with regard to particular matters.

This Regulation should not prejudice the application of other instruments laying down provisions designed to contribute to the proper functioning of the internal market in so far as they cannot be applied in conjunction with the law designated by the rules of this Regulation. The application of provisions of the applicable law designated by the rules of this Regulation should not restrict the free movement of goods and services as regulated by Community instruments, such as Directive 2000/31/EC of the European Parliament and of the Council of 8 June 2000 on certain legal aspects of information society services, in particular electronic commerce, in the Internal Market (Directive on electronic commerce) [6].

[OJ L199 , 43]

(36) Respect for international commitments entered into by the Member States means that this Regulation should not affect international conventions to which one or more Member States are parties at the time this Regulation is adopted. To make the rules more accessible, the Commission should publish the list of the relevant conventions in the *Official Journal of the European Union* on the basis of information supplied by the Member States.

(37) The Commission will make a proposal to the European Parliament and the Council concerning the procedures and conditions according to which Member States would be entitled to negotiate and conclude on their own behalf agreements with third countries in individual and exceptional cases, concerning sectoral matters, containing provisions on the law applicable to non-contractual obligations.

(38) Since the objective of this Regulation cannot be sufficiently achieved by the Member States, and can therefore, by reason of the scale and effects of this Regulation, be better achieved at Community level, the Community may adopt measures, in accordance with the principle of subsidiarity set out in Article 5 of the Treaty. In accordance with the principle of proportionality set out in that Article, this Regulation does not go beyond what is necessary to attain that objective.

(39) In accordance with Article 3 of the Protocol on the position of the United Kingdom and Ireland annexed to the Treaty on European Union and to the Treaty establishing the European Community, the United Kingdom and Ireland are taking part in the adoption and application of this Regulation.

(40) In accordance with Articles 1 and 2 of the Protocol on the position of Denmark, annexed to the Treaty on European Union and to the Treaty establishing the European Community, Denmark does not take part in the adoption of this Regulation, and is not bound by it or subject to its application,

HAVE ADOPTED THIS REGULATION:

CHAPTER I

SCOPE

Article 1

Scope

1. This Regulation shall apply, in situations involving a conflict of laws, to non-contractual obligations in civil and commercial matters. It shall not apply, in particular, to revenue, customs or administrative matters or to the liability of the State for acts and omissions in the exercise of State authority (*acta iure imperii*).

2. The following shall be excluded from the scope of this Regulation:
(a) non-contractual obligations arising out of family relationships and relationships deemed by the law applicable to such relationships to have comparable effects including maintenance obligations;
(b) non-contractual obligations arising out of matrimonial property regimes, property regimes of relationships deemed by the law applicable to such relationships to have comparable effects to marriage, and wills and succession;
(c) non-contractual obligations arising under bills of exchange, cheques and promissory notes and other negotiable instruments to the extent that the obligations under such other negotiable instruments arise out of their negotiable character;
(d) non-contractual obligations arising out of the law of companies and other bodies corporate or unincorporated regarding matters such as the creation, by registration or otherwise, legal capacity, internal organisation or winding-up of companies and other bodies corporate or unincorporated, the personal liability of officers and members as such for the obligations of the company or body and the personal liability of auditors to a company or to its members in the statutory audits of accounting documents;
(e) non-contractual obligations arising out of the relations between the settlors, trustees and beneficiaries of a trust created voluntarily;
(f) non-contractual obligations arising out of nuclear damage;
(g) non-contractual obligations arising out of violations of privacy and rights relating to personality, including defamation.

3. This Regulation shall not apply to evidence and procedure, without prejudice to Articles 21 and 22.

4. For the purposes of this Regulation, 'Member State' shall mean any Member State other than Denmark.

Article 2

Non-contractual obligations

1. For the purposes of this Regulation, damage shall cover any consequence arising out of tort/delict, unjust enrichment, *negotiorum gestio* or *culpa in contrahendo*.

2. This Regulation shall apply also to non-contractual obligations that are likely to arise.

[OJ L199, 44]

3. Any reference in this Regulation to:

(a) an event giving rise to damage shall include events giving rise to damage that are likely to occur; and

(b) damage shall include damage that is likely to occur.

Article 3

Universal application

Any law specified by this Regulation shall be applied whether or not it is the law of a Member State.

CHAPTER II

TORTS/DELICTS

Article 4

General rule

1. Unless otherwise provided for in this Regulation, the law applicable to a non-contractual obligation arising out of a tort/delict shall be the law of the country in which the damage occurs irrespective of the country in which the event giving rise to the damage occurred and irrespective of the country or countries in which the indirect consequences of that event occur.

2. However, where the person claimed to be liable and the person sustaining damage both have their habitual residence in the same country at the time when the damage occurs, the law of that country shall apply.

3. Where it is clear from all the circumstances of the case that the tort/delict is manifestly more closely connected with a country other than that indicated in paragraphs 1 or 2, the law of that other country shall apply. A manifestly closer connection with another country might be based in particular on a pre-existing relationship between the parties, such as a contract, that is closely connected with the tort/delict in question.

Article 5

Product liability

1. Without prejudice to Article 4(2), the law applicable to a non-contractual obligation arising out of damage caused by a product shall be:

(a) the law of the country in which the person sustaining the damage had his or her habitual residence when the damage occurred, if the product was marketed in that country; or, failing that,

(b) the law of the country in which the product was acquired, if the product was marketed in that country; or, failing that,

(c) the law of the country in which the damage occurred, if the product was marketed in that country.

However, the law applicable shall be the law of the country in which the person claimed to be liable is habitually resident if he or she could not reasonably foresee the marketing of the product, or a product of the same type, in the country the law of which is applicable under (a), (b) or (c).

2. Where it is clear from all the circumstances of the case that the tort/delict is manifestly more closely connected with a country other than that indicated in paragraph 1, the law of that other country shall apply. A manifestly closer connection with another country might be based in particular on a pre-existing relationship between the parties, such as a contract, that is closely connected with the tort/delict in question.

Article 6

Unfair competition and acts restricting free competition

1. The law applicable to a non-contractual obligation arising out of an act of unfair competition shall be the law of the country where competitive relations or the collective interests of consumers are, or are likely to be, affected.

2. Where an act of unfair competition affects exclusively the interests of a specific competitor, Article 4 shall apply.

3. (a) The law applicable to a non-contractual obligation arising out of a restriction of competition shall be the law of the country where the market is, or is likely to be, affected.

(b) When the market is, or is likely to be, affected in more than one country, the person seeking compensation for damage who sues in the court of the domicile of the defendant, may instead choose to base his or her claim on the law of the court seised, provided that the market in that Member State is amongst those directly and substantially affected by the restriction of competition out of which the non-contractual obligation on which the claim is based arises; where the claimant sues, in accordance with the applicable rules on jurisdiction, more than one defendant in that court, he or she can only choose to base his or her claim on the law of that court if the restriction of competition on which the claim against each of these defendants relies directly and substantially affects also the market in the Member State of that court.

4. The law applicable under this Article may not be derogated from by an agreement pursuant to Article 14.

[OJ L199, 45]

Article 7

Environmental damage

The law applicable to a non-contractual obligation arising out of environmental damage or damage sustained by persons or property as a result of such damage shall be the law determined pursuant to Article 4(1), unless the person seeking compensation for damage chooses to base his or her claim on the law of the country in which the event giving rise to the damage occurred.

Article 8

Infringement of intellectual property rights

1. The law applicable to a non-contractual obligation arising from an infringement of an intellectual property right shall be the law of the country for which protection is claimed.

2. In the case of a non-contractual obligation arising from an infringement of a unitary Community intellectual property right, the law applicable shall, for any question that is not governed by the relevant Community instrument, be the law of the country in which the act of infringement was committed.

3. The law applicable under this Article may not be derogated from by an agreement pursuant to Article 14.

Article 9

Industrial action

Without prejudice to Article 4(2), the law applicable to a non-contractual obligation in respect of the liability of a person in the capacity of a worker or an employer or the organisations representing their professional interests for damages caused by an industrial action, pending or carried out, shall be the law of the country where the action is to be, or has been, taken.

CHAPTER III

UNJUST ENRICHMENT, *NEGOTIORUM GESTIO* AND *CULPA IN CONTRAHENDO*

Article 10

Unjust enrichment

1. If a non-contractual obligation arising out of unjust enrichment, including payment of amounts wrongly received, concerns a relationship existing between

the parties, such as one arising out of a contract or a tort/delict, that is closely connected with that unjust enrichment, it shall be governed by the law that governs that relationship.

2. Where the law applicable cannot be determined on the basis of paragraph 1 and the parties have their habitual residence in the same country when the event giving rise to unjust enrichment occurs, the law of that country shall apply.

3. Where the law applicable cannot be determined on the basis of paragraphs 1 or 2, it shall be the law of the country in which the unjust enrichment took place.

4. Where it is clear from all the circumstances of the case that the non-contractual obligation arising out of unjust enrichment is manifestly more closely connected with a country other than that indicated in paragraphs 1, 2 and 3, the law of that other country shall apply.

Article 11

Negotiorum gestio

1. If a non-contractual obligation arising out of an act performed without due authority in connection with the affairs of another person concerns a relationship existing between the parties, such as one arising out of a contract or a tort/delict, that is closely connected with that non-contractual obligation, it shall be governed by the law that governs that relationship.

2. Where the law applicable cannot be determined on the basis of paragraph 1, and the parties have their habitual residence in the same country when the event giving rise to the damage occurs, the law of that country shall apply.

3. Where the law applicable cannot be determined on the basis of paragraphs 1 or 2, it shall be the law of the country in which the act was performed.

4. Where it is clear from all the circumstances of the case that the non-contractual obligation arising out of an act performed without due authority in connection with the affairs of another person is manifestly more closely connected with a country other than that indicated in paragraphs 1, 2 and 3, the law of that other country shall apply.

Article 12

Culpa in contrahendo

1. The law applicable to a non-contractual obligation arising out of dealings prior to the conclusion of a contract, regardless of whether the contract was actually concluded or not, shall be the law that applies to the contract or that would have been applicable to it had it been entered into.

2. Where the law applicable cannot be determined on the basis of paragraph 1, it shall be:
(a) the law of the country in which the damage occurs, irrespective of the country in which the event giving rise to the damage occurred and irrespective of

the country or countries in which the indirect consequences of that event occurred; or

(b) where the parties have their habitual residence in the same country at the time when the event giving rise to the damage occurs, the law of that country; or

(c) where it is clear from all the circumstances of the case that the non-contractual obligation arising out of dealings prior to the conclusion of a contract is manifestly more closely connected with a country other than that indicated in points (a) and (b), the law of that other country.

[OJ L199, 46]

Article 13

Applicability of Article 8

For the purposes of this Chapter, Article 8 shall apply to non-contractual obligations arising from an infringement of an intellectual property right.

CHAPTER IV

FREEDOM OF CHOICE

Article 14

Freedom of choice

1. The parties may agree to submit non-contractual obligations to the law of their choice:

(a) by an agreement entered into after the event giving rise to the damage occurred; or

(b) where all the parties are pursuing a commercial activity, also by an agreement freely negotiated before the event giving rise to the damage occurred.

The choice shall be expressed or demonstrated with reasonable certainty by the circumstances of the case and shall not prejudice the rights of third parties.

2. Where all the elements relevant to the situation at the time when the event giving rise to the damage occurs are located in a country other than the country whose law has been chosen, the choice of the parties shall not prejudice the application of provisions of the law of that other country which cannot be derogated from by agreement.

3. Where all the elements relevant to the situation at the time when the event giving rise to the damage occurs are located in one or more of the Member States, the parties' choice of the law applicable other than that of a Member State shall not prejudice the application of provisions of Community law, where appropriate as implemented in the Member State of the forum, which cannot be derogated from by agreement.

CHAPTER V

Common Rules

Article 15

Scope of the law applicable

The law applicable to non-contractual obligations under this Regulation shall govern in particular:

(a) the basis and extent of liability, including the determination of persons who may be held liable for acts performed by them;

(b) the grounds for exemption from liability, any limitation of liability and any division of liability;

(c) the existence, the nature and the assessment of damage or the remedy claimed;

(d) within the limits of powers conferred on the court by its procedural law, the measures which a court may take to prevent or terminate injury or damage or to ensure the provision of compensation;

(e) the question whether a right to claim damages or a remedy may be transferred, including by inheritance;

(f) persons entitled to compensation for damage sustained personally;

(g) liability for the acts of another person;

(h) the manner in which an obligation may be extinguished and rules of prescription and limitation, including rules relating to the commencement, interruption and suspension of a period of prescription or limitation.

Article 16

Overriding mandatory provisions

Nothing in this Regulation shall restrict the application of the provisions of the law of the forum in a situation where they are mandatory irrespective of the law otherwise applicable to the non-contractual obligation.

Article 17

Rules of safety and conduct

In assessing the conduct of the person claimed to be liable, account shall be taken, as a matter of fact and in so far as is appropriate, of the rules of safety and conduct which were in force at the place and time of the event giving rise to the liability.

Article 18

Direct action against the insurer of the person liable

The person having suffered damage may bring his or her claim directly against the insurer of the person liable to provide compensation if the law applicable to the non-contractual obligation or the law applicable to the insurance contract so provides.

Article 19

Subrogation

Where a person (the creditor) has a non-contractual claim upon another (the debtor), and a third person has a duty to satisfy the creditor, or has in fact satisfied the creditor in discharge of that duty, the law which governs the third person's duty to satisfy the creditor shall determine whether, and the extent to which, the third person is entitled to exercise against the debtor the rights which the creditor had against the debtor under the law governing their relationship.

[OJ L199, 47]

Article 20

Multiple liability

If a creditor has a claim against several debtors who are liable for the same claim, and one of the debtors has already satisfied the claim in whole or in part, the question of that debtor's right to demand compensation from the other debtors shall be governed by the law applicable to that debtor's non-contractual obligation towards the creditor.

Article 21

Formal validity

A unilateral act intended to have legal effect and relating to a non-contractual obligation shall be formally valid if it satisfies the formal requirements of the law governing the non-contractual obligation in question or the law of the country in which the act is performed.

Article 22

Burden of proof

1. The law governing a non-contractual obligation under this Regulation shall apply to the extent that, in matters of non-contractual obligations, it contains rules which raise presumptions of law or determine the burden of proof.

2. Acts intended to have legal effect may be proved by any mode of proof recognised by the law of the forum or by any of the laws referred to in Article 21 under which that act is formally valid, provided that such mode of proof can be administered by the forum.

CHAPTER VI

OTHER PROVISIONS

Article 23

Habitual residence

1. For the purposes of this Regulation, the habitual residence of companies and other bodies, corporate or unincorporated, shall be the place of central administration.

Where the event giving rise to the damage occurs, or the damage arises, in the course of operation of a branch, agency or any other establishment, the place where the branch, agency or any other establishment is located shall be treated as the place of habitual residence.

2. For the purposes of this Regulation, the habitual residence of a natural person acting in the course of his or her business activity shall be his or her principal place of business.

Article 24

Exclusion of renvoi

The application of the law of any country specified by this Regulation means the application of the rules of law in force in that country other than its rules of private international law.

Article 25

States with more than one legal system

1. Where a State comprises several territorial units, each of which has its own rules of law in respect of non-contractual obligations, each territorial unit shall be considered as a country for the purposes of identifying the law applicable under this Regulation.

2. A Member State within which different territorial units have their own rules of law in respect of non-contractual obligations shall not be required to apply this Regulation to conflicts solely between the laws of such units.

Article 26

Public policy of the forum

The application of a provision of the law of any country specified by this Regulation may be refused only if such application is manifestly incompatible with the public policy (*ordre public*) of the forum.

Article 27

Relationship with other provisions of Community law

This Regulation shall not prejudice the application of provisions of Community law which, in relation to particular matters, lay down conflict-of-law rules relating to non-contractual obligations.

Article 28

Relationship with existing international conventions

1. This Regulation shall not prejudice the application of international conventions to which one or more Member States are parties at the time when this Regulation is adopted and which lay down conflict-of-law rules relating to non-contractual obligations.

2. However, this Regulation shall, as between Member States, take precedence over conventions concluded exclusively between two or more of them in so far as such conventions concern matters governed by this Regulation.

[OJ L199, 48]

CHAPTER VII

Final Provisions

Article 29

List of conventions

1. By 11 July 2008, Member States shall notify the Commission of the conventions referred to in Article 28(1). After that date, Member States shall notify the Commission of all denunciations of such conventions.

2. The Commission shall publish in the *Official Journal of the European Union* within six months of receipt:
 (i) a list of the conventions referred to in paragraph 1;
 (ii) the denunciations referred to in paragraph 1.

Article 30

Review clause

1. Not later than 20 August 2011, the Commission shall submit to the European Parliament, the Council and the European Economic and Social Committee a report on the application of this Regulation. If necessary, the report shall be accompanied by proposals to adapt this Regulation. The report shall include:

(i) a study on the effects of the way in which foreign law is treated in the different jurisdictions and on the extent to which courts in the Member States apply foreign law in practice pursuant to this Regulation;

(ii) a study on the effects of Article 28 of this Regulation with respect to the Hague Convention of 4 May 1971 on the law applicable to traffic accidents.

2. Not later than 31 December 2008, the Commission shall submit to the European Parliament, the Council and the European Economic and Social Committee a study on the situation in the field of the law applicable to non-contractual obligations arising out of violations of privacy and rights relating to personality, taking into account rules relating to freedom of the press and freedom of expression in the media, and conflict-of-law issues related to Directive 95/46/EC of the European Parliament and of the Council of 24 October 1995 on the protection of individuals with regard to the processing of personal data and on the free movement of such data [7].

Article 31

Application in time

This Regulation shall apply to events giving rise to damage which occur after its entry into force.

Article 32

Date of application

This Regulation shall apply from 11 January 2009, except for Article 29, which shall apply from 11 July 2008.

This Regulation shall be binding in its entirety and directly applicable in the Member States in accordance with the Treaty establishing the European Community.

Done at Strasbourg, 11 July 2007.

For the European Parliament
The President
H.-G. Pöttering

For the Council
The President
M. Lobo Antunes

[1] OJ C 241, 28.9.2004, p. 1.
[2] Opinion of the European Parliament of 6 July 2005 (OJ C 157 E, 6.7.2006, p. 371), Council Common Position of 25 September 2006 (OJ C 289 E, 28.11.2006, p. 68) and Position of the European Parliament of 18 January 2007 (not yet published in the Official Journal). European Parliament Legislative Resolution of 10 July 2007 and Council Decision of 28 June 2007.
[3] OJ C 12, 15.1.2001, p. 1.
[4] OJ C 53, 3.3.2005, p. 1.
[5] OJ L 12, 16.1.2001, p. 1. Regulation as last amended by Regulation (EC) No 1791/2006 (OJ L 363, 20.12.2006, p. 1).
[6] OJ L 178, 17.7.2000, p. 1.
[7] OJ L 281, 23.11.1995, p. 31.

[OJ L199, 49]

Commission Statement on the review clause (Article 30)

The Commission, following the invitation by the European Parliament and the Council in the frame of Article 30 of the 'Rome II' Regulation, will submit, not later than December 2008, a study on the situation in the field of the law applicable to non-contractual obligations arising out of violations of privacy and rights relating to personality. The Commission will take into consideration all aspects of the situation and take appropriate measures if necessary.

Commission Statement on road accidents

The Commission, being aware of the different practices followed in the Member States as regards the level of compensation awarded to victims of road traffic accidents, is prepared to examine the specific problems resulting for EU residents involved in road traffic accidents in a Member State other than the Member State of their habitual residence. To that end the Commission will make available to the European Parliament and to the Council, before the end of 2008, a study on all options, including insurance aspects, for improving the position of cross-border victims, which would pave the way for a Green Paper.

Commission Statement on the treatment of foreign law

The Commission, being aware of the different practices followed in the Member States as regards the treatment of foreign law, will publish at the latest four years after the entry into force of the 'Rome II' Regulation and in any event as soon as it is available a horizontal study on the application of foreign law in civil and commercial matters by the courts of the Member States, having regard to the aims of the Hague Programme. It is also prepared to take appropriate measures if necessary.

Appendix 2

Commission Proposal

Brussels, 22.7.2003
COM(2003) 427 final
2003/0168 (COD)

Proposal for a

REGULATION OF THE EUROPEAN PARLIAMENT AND THE COUNCIL ON THE LAW APPLICABLE TO NON-CONTRACTUAL OBLIGATIONS ('ROME II')

(presented by the Commission)

EXPLANATORY MEMORANDUM*

1. INTRODUCTION

[2]

1.1. Context

By Article 2 of the Treaty on European Union, the Member States set themselves the objective of maintaining and developing the Union as an area of freedom, security and justice, in which the free movement of persons is assured and litigants can assert their rights in the courts and before the authorities of all the Member States, enjoying facilities equivalent to those they enjoy in their own country.

To establish a genuine European law-enforcement area, the Community, under Articles 61(c) and 65 of the Treaty establishing the European Community, is to adopt measures in the field of judicial cooperation in civil matters in so far as necessary for the proper functioning of the internal market. The Tampere European Council on 15 and 16 October 1999[1] acknowledged the mutual recognition principle as the cornerstone of judicial cooperation in the Union. It asked the Council and the Commission to adopt, by December 2000, a programme of measures to implement the mutual recognition principle.

---

* Author's note: Footnote numbering as original. The bold numbering in square brackets in the text (e.g. **[3]**) refers to the original numbered pages of the Commission Proposal.

[1] Presidency conclusions of 16 October 1999, points 28 to 39.

The joint Commission and Council programme of measures to implement the principle of mutual recognition of decisions in civil and commercial matters, adopted by the Council on 30 November 2000,[2] states that measures relating to harmonisation of conflict-of-law rules, which may sometimes be incorporated in the same instruments as those relating to jurisdiction and the recognition and enforcement of judgments, actually do help facilitate the mutual recognition of judgments. The fact that the courts of the Member States apply the same conflict rules to determine the law applicable to a practical situation reinforces the mutual trust in judicial decisions given in other Member States and is a vital element in attaining the longer-term objective of the free movement of judgments without intermediate review measures.

1.2. Complementarity with instruments of private international law already in force in the Community

This initiative relates to the Community harmonisation of private international law in civil and commercial matters that began late in the 1960s. On 27 September 1968 the six Member States of the European Economic Community concluded a Convention on jurisdiction and the recognition and enforcement of judgments in civil and commercial matters (the 'Brussels Convention') on the basis of the fourth indent of Article 293 (formerly 220) of the EC Treaty. This was drawn up on the idea, already described in the EC Treaty, that the establishment of a common market implied the possibility of having a judgment given in any Member State recognised and enforced as easily as possible. To facilitate the attainment of that objective, the Brussels Convention begins by setting out rules identifying the Member State whose courts have jurisdiction to hear and determine a cross-border dispute.

[3] The mere fact that there are rules governing the jurisdiction of the courts does not generate reasonable foreseeability as to the outcome of a case being heard on the merits. The Brussels Convention and the 'Brussels I' Regulation that superseded it on 1 March 2001[3] contain a number of options enabling claimants to prefer this or that court. The risk is that parties will opt for the courts of one Member State rather than another simply because the law applicable in the courts of this state would be more favourable to them.

That is why work began on codifying the rules on conflicts of laws in the Community in 1967. The Commission convened two meetings of experts in 1969, at which it was agreed to focus initially on questions having the greatest impact on the operation of the common market the law applicable to tangible and intangible

---

[2] OJ C 12, 15.1.2001, p. 1.

[3] Council Regulation (EC) No 44/2001 of 22 December 2000, OJ L 12, 16.1.2001, p. 1, replacing the Brussels Convention of 1968, of which a consolidated version was published in OJ C 27, 26.1.1998, p. 1. But the Brussels Convention remains in force for relations between Denmark and the other Member States.

property, contractual and non-contractual obligations and the form of legal documents. On 23 June 1972, the experts presented a first preliminary draft convention on the law applicable to contractual and non-contractual obligations. Following the accession of the United Kingdom, Ireland and Denmark, the group was expanded in 1973, and that slowed progress. In March 1978, the decision was taken to confine attention to contractual obligations so that negotiations could be completed within a reasonable time and to commence negotiations later for a second convention on non-contractual obligations.

In June 1980 the Convention on the law applicable to contractual obligations (the 'Rome Convention') was opened for signature, and it entered into force on 1 April 1991.[4] As there was no proper legal basis in the EC Treaty at the time of its signing, the convention takes the traditional form of an international treaty. But as it was seen as the indispensable adjunct to the Brussels Convention, the complementarity being referred to expressly in the Preamble, it is treated in the same way as the instruments adopted on the basis of Article 293 (ex-220) and is an integral part of the Community acquis.

Given the substantial difference in scope between the Brussels and Rome Conventions the former covers both contractual and non-contractual obligations whereas the latter covers only contractual obligations the proposed Regulation, commonly known as 'Rome II', will be the natural extension of the unification of the rules of private international law relating to contractual and non-contractual obligations in civil or commercial matters in the Community.

1.3. Resumption of work in the 1990s under the Maastricht and Amsterdam Treaties

Article K.1(6) of the Union Treaty in the Maastricht version classified judicial cooperation in civil matters in the areas of common interest to the Member States of the European Union. In its Resolution of 14 October 1996 laying down the priorities for cooperation in the field of justice and home affairs for the period from 1 July 1996 to 30 June 1998,[5] the Council stated that, in pursuing the objectives set by the European Council, it intended to concentrate during the above period on certain priority areas, which included the 'launching of discussions on the necessity and possibility of drawing up . . . a convention on the law applicable to extra-contractual obligations'.

[4] In February 1998 the Commission sent the Member States a questionnaire on a draft convention on the law applicable to non-contractual obligations. The Austrian Presidency held four working meetings to examine the replies to the questionnaire. It was established that all the Member States supported the principle of an

---

[4] The consolidated text of the Convention as amended by the various Conventions of Accession, and the declarations and protocols annexed to it, is published in OJ C 27, 26.1.1998, p. 34.

[5] OJ C 319, 26 October 1996, p. 1.

instrument on the law applicable to non-contractual obligations. At the same time the Commission financed a GROTIUS project[6] presented by the European Private International Law Group (GEDIP) to examine the feasibility of a European Convention on the law applicable to non-contractual obligations, which culminated in a draft text.[7] The Council's ad hoc 'Rome II' Working Party continued to meet throughout 1999 under the German and Finnish Presidencies, examining the draft texts presented by the Austrian Presidency and by Gedip. An initial consensus emerged on a number of conflict rules, which this proposal for a Regulation duly reflects.

The Amsterdam Treaty, which entered into force on 1 May 1999, having moved cooperation in civil matters into the Community context, the Justice and Home Affairs Council on 3 December 1998 adopted the Action Plan of the Council and the Commission on how best to implement the provisions of the Treaty of Amsterdam on an area of freedom, security and justice.[8] It recalls that principles such as certainty in the law and equal access to justice require among other things '*clear designation of the applicable law*' and states in paragraph 40 that '*The following measures should be taken within two years after the entry into force of the Treaty: . . . b) drawing up a legal instrument on the law applicable to non-contractual obligations (Rome II)*'.

On 3 May 2002, the Commission launched consultations with interested circles on an initial preliminary draft proposal for a 'Rome II' Regulation prepared by the Directorate-General for Justice and Home Affairs. The consultations prompted a very wide response, and the Commission received 80 or so written contributions from the Member States, academics, representatives of industry and consumers' associations.[9] The written consultation procedure was followed by a public hearing in Brussels on 7 January 2003. This proposal duly reflects the comments received.

2. PROPOSAL FOR A EUROPEAN PARLIAMENT AND COUNCIL REGULATION

2.1. General purpose – to improve the foreseeability of solutions regarding the applicable law

The purpose of this proposal for a regulation is to standardise the Member States' rules of conflict of laws regarding non-contractual obligations and thus extend the harmonisation of private international law in relation to civil and commercial obligations which is already well advanced in the Community with the 'Brussels I' Regulation and the Rome Convention of 1980.

---

[6] Project No GR/97/051.
[7] Accessible at <http://www.drt.ucl.ac.be/gedip/gedip_documents.html>.
[8] OJ C 19, 23.1.1999, p. 1.
[9] The contributions received by the Commission can be consulted at:<http://europa.eu.int/comm/justice_home/news/consulting_public/rome_ii/news_summary_rome2_en.htm>.

[5] The harmonisation of conflict rules, which must be distinguished from the harmonisation of substantive law, seeks to harmonise the rules whereby the law applicable to an obligation is determined. This technique is particularly suitable for settling cross-border disputes, as, by stating with reasonable certainty the law applicable to the obligation in question irrespective of the forum, it can help to develop a European area of justice. Instead of having to study often widely differing conflict rules of all the Member States' courts that might have jurisdiction in a case, this proposal allows the parties to confine themselves to studying a single set of conflict rules, thus reducing the cost of litigation and boosting the foreseeability of solutions and certainty as to the law.

These general observations are particularly apt in the case of non-contractual obligations, the importance of which for the internal market is clear from sectoral instruments, in force or in preparation, governing this or that specific aspect (product liability or environmental liability, for example). The approximation of the substantive law of obligations is no more than embryonic. Despite common principles, there are still major divergences between Member States, in particular as regards the following questions: the boundary between strict liability and fault-based liability; compensation for indirect damage and third-party damage; compensation for non-material damage, including third-party damage; compensation in excess of actual damage sustained (punitive and exemplary damages); the liability of minors; and limitation periods. During the consultations undertaken by the Commission, several representatives of industry stated that these divergences made it difficult to exercise fundamental freedoms in the internal market. They realised that harmonisation of the substantive law was not a short-term prospect and stressed the importance of the rules of conflict of laws to improve the foreseeability of solutions.

A comparative law analysis of the rules of conflict of laws reveals that the present situation does not meet economic operators' need for foreseeability and that the differences are markedly wider than was the case for contracts before the harmonisation achieved by the Rome Convention. Admittedly, the Member States virtually all give pride of place to the *lex loci delicti commissi*, whereby torts/delicts are governed by the law of the place where the act was committed. The application of this rule is problematic, however, in the case of what are known as 'complex' torts/delicts, where the harmful event and the place where the loss is sustained are spread over several countries.[10] There are variations between national laws as regards the practical impact of the *lex loci delicti commissi* rule in the case of cross-border non-contractual obligations. While certain Member States still take the traditional solution of applying the law of the country where the event giving rise to the damage occurred, recent developments more commonly tend to support the law of the country where the damage is sustained. But to understand the law in force in a Member State, it is not enough to ascertain whether the harmful event or the

---

[10] See the decision of the Court of Justice in the following notes as regards the account to be taken of this spreading of factors for the international jurisdiction of the courts.

damage sustained is the dominant factor. The basic rule needs to be combined with other criteria. A growing number of Member States allow a claimant to opt for the law that is most favourable to him. Others leave it to the courts to determine the country with which the situation is most closely connected, either as a basic rule or exceptionally where the basic rule turns out to be inappropriate in the individual case. Generally speaking most Member States use a sometimes complex combination of the different solutions. Apart from the diversity of solutions, their legibility is not improved by the fact that only some of the Member States have codified their conflict-of-laws rules; in the others, solutions emerge gradually from the decisions of the courts and often remain uncertain, particularly as regards special torts/delicts.

[6] There is no doubt that replacing more than fifteen national systems of conflict rules[11] by a single set of uniform rules would represent considerable progress for economic operators and the general public in terms of certainty as to the law.

The next need is to analyse the conflict rules in the context of the rules governing the international jurisdiction of the courts. Apart from the basic jurisdiction of the courts for the place of the defendant's habitual residence, provided for by Article 2 of the 'Brussels I' Regulation, Article 5(3) provides for a special head of jurisdiction in relation to torts/delicts and quasi-delict in the form of *'the courts for the place where the harmful event occurred. . .'*. The Court of Justice has always held that where the place where the harmful act occurred and the place where the loss is sustained are not the same, the defendant can be sued, at the claimant's choice, in the courts either of the place where the harmful act occurred or of the place where the loss is sustained.[12] Admittedly, the Court acknowledged that each of the two places could constitute a meaningful connecting factor for jurisdiction purposes, since each could be of significance in terms of evidence and organisation of the proceedings, but it is also true that the number of forums available to the claimant generates a risk of forum-shopping.

This proposal for a Regulation would allow parties to determine the rule applicable to a given legal relationship in advance, and with reasonable certainty, especially as the proposed uniform rules will receive a uniform interpretation from the Court of Justice. This initiative would accordingly help to boost certainty in the law and promote the proper functioning of the internal market. It is also in the Commission's programme of measures to facilitate the extra-judicial settlement of disputes, since the fact that the parties have a clear vision of their situation makes it all the easier to come to an amicable agreement.

2.2. Legal basis

Since the Amsterdam Treaty came into force, conflict rules have been governed by Article 61(c) of the EC Treaty. Under Article 67 of the EC Treaty, as amended by

---

[11] There are more than fifteen national systems because the United Kingdom does not have a unitary system.

[12] Case 21/76 *Mines de Potasse d'Alsace* [1976] ECR 1735 (judgment given on 30.11.1976).

the Nice Treaty that entered into force on 1 February 2003, the Regulation will be adopted by the codecision procedure laid down by Article 251 of the EC Treaty.

Article 65(b) provides: *'Measures in the field of judicial cooperation in civil matters having cross-border implications, to be taken . . . in so far as necessary for the proper functioning of the internal market, shall include: promoting the compatibility of the rules applicable in the Member States concerning the conflict of laws. . .'*

The Community legislature has the power to put flesh on the bones of this Article and the discretion to determine whether a measure is necessary for the proper functioning of the internal market. The Council exercised this power when adopting the Vienna action plan of 3 December 1998[13] on how best to implement the provisions of the Treaty of Amsterdam on an area of freedom, security and justice, point 40(c) of which calls expressly for a 'Rome II' instrument.

[7] Harmonisation of the conflict rules helps to promote equal treatment between economic operators and individuals involved in cross-border litigation in the internal market. It is the necessary adjunct to the harmonisation already achieved by the 'Brussels I' Regulation as regards the rules governing the international jurisdiction of the courts and the mutual recognition of judgments. Given that there are more than fifteen different systems of conflict rules, two firms in distinct Member States, A and B, bringing the same dispute between them and a third firm in country C before their respective courts would have different conflict rules applied to them, which could provoke a distortion of competition. Such a distortion could also incite operators to go forum-shopping.

But the harmonisation of the conflict rules also facilitates the implementation of the principle of the mutual recognition of judgments in civil and commercial matters. The mutual recognition programme[14] calls for the reduction and ultimately the abolition of intermediate measures for recognition of a judgment given in another Member State. But the removal of all intermediate measures calls for a degree of mutual trust between Member States which is not conceivable if their courts do not all apply the same conflict rule in the same situation.

Title IV of the EC Treaty, which covers the matters to which this proposal for a Regulation applies, does not apply to Denmark by virtue of the Protocol concerning it. Nor does it apply to the United Kingdom or Ireland, unless those countries exercise their option of joining the initiative (opt-in clause) on the conditions set out in the Protocol annexed to the Treaty. At the Council meeting (Justice and Home Affairs) on 12 March 1999, these two Member States announced their intention of being fully associated with Community activities in relation to judicial cooperation in civil matters. They were also fully associated with the work of the ad hoc Council working party before the Amsterdam Treaty entered into force.

[13] OJ C 19, 23.1.1999, p. 1.
[14] OJ C 12, 15.1.2001, p. 8.

2.3. Justification for proposal in terms of proportionality and subsidiarity principles

The technique of harmonising conflict-of-laws rules fully respects the subsidiarity and proportionality principles since it enhances certainty in the law without demanding harmonisation of the substantive rules of domestic law.

As for the choice of instrument, point 6 of the Protocol on the application of the principles of subsidiarity and proportionality provides that *'Other things being equal, directives should be preferred to regulations and framework directives to detailed measures.'* But for the purposes of this proposal a Regulation is the most appropriate instrument. It lays down uniform rules for the applicable law. These rules are detailed, precise and unconditional and require no measures by the Member States for their transposal into national law. They are therefore self-executing. The nature of these rules is the direct result of the objective set for them, which is to enhance certainty in the law and the foreseeability of the solutions adopted as regards the law applicable to a given legal relationship. If the Member States had room for manoeuvre in transposing these rules, uncertainty would be reintroduced into the law, and that is precisely what the harmonisation is supposed to abolish. The Regulation is therefore the instrument that must be chosen to guarantee uniform application in the Member States.

3. INDIVIDUAL PROVISIONS

[8] Article 1 – Material scope

Like the Brussels Convention and the 'Brussels I' Regulation, the proposed Regulation covers civil and commercial obligations. This is an autonomous concept of Community law that has been interpreted by the Court of Justice. The reference to this makes it clear that the 'Brussels I' Regulation, the Rome Convention and the Regulation proposed here constitute a coherent set of instruments covering the general field of private international law in matters of civil and commercial obligations.

The scope of the Regulation covers all non-contractual obligations except those in matters listed in paragraph 2. Non-contractual obligations are in two major categories, those that arise out of a tort or delict and those that do not. The first category comprises obligations relating to tort or delict, and the second comprises obligations relating to what in some jurisdictions is termed 'quasi-delict' or 'quasi-contract', including in particular unjust enrichment and agency without authority or *negotiorum gestio*. The latter category is governed by section 2. But the demarcation line between contractual obligations and obligations based on tort or delict is not identical in all the Member States, and there may be doubts as to which instrument the Rome Convention or the proposed Regulation should be applied in a given dispute, for example in the event of pre-contractual liability, of *culpa in contrahendo* or of actions by creditors to have certain transactions by their debtors declared void as prejudicial to their interests. The Court of Justice, in actions under Articles 5(1) and (3) of the Brussels Convention, has already had occasion to rule that tort/delict cases are residual in relation to contract cases, which must be defined in strict terms.[15] It will no doubt refine its analysis when interpreting the proposed Regulation.

The proposed Regulation would apply to all situations involving a conflict of laws, i.e. situations in which there are one or more elements that are alien to the domestic social life of a country that entail applying several systems of law. Under Article 1(2), the following are excluded from the scope of the proposed Regulation:

a) non-contractual obligations arising out of family or similar relationships: family obligations do not in general arise from a tort or delict. But such obligations can occasionally appear in the family context, as is the case of an action for compensation for damage caused by late payment of a maintenance obligation. Some commentators have suggested including these obligations within the scope of the Regulation on the grounds that they are governed by the exception clause in Article 3(3), which expressly refers to the mechanism of the 'secondary connection' that places them under the same law as the underlying family relationship. Since there are so far no harmonised conflict-of-laws rules in the Community as regards family law, it has been found preferable to exclude non-contractual obligations arising out of such relationships from the scope of the proposed Regulation.

b) Non-contractual obligations arising in connection with matrimonial property regimes and successions: these are excluded for similar reasons to those given at point a).

[9] c) Non-contractual obligations arising out of bills of exchange, cheques and promissory notes and other negotiable instruments to the extent that the obligations under such other negotiable instruments arise out of their negotiable character; this point is taken over from Article 1(2)(c) of the Rome Convention. It is incorporated here for the same reasons as are given in the Giuliano-Lagarde Report,[16] namely that the Regulation is not the proper instrument for such obligations, that the Geneva Conventions of 7 June 1930 and 19 March 1931 regulate much of this matter and that these obligations are not dealt with uniformly in the Member States.

d) The personal legal liability of officers and members as such for the debts of a company or firm or other body corporate or unincorporate, and the personal legal liability of persons responsible for carrying out the statutory audits of accounting documents: this question cannot be separated from the law governing companies or firms or other bodies corporate or unincorporate that is applicable to the company or firm or other body corporate or unincorporate in connection with whose management the question of liability arises.

---

[15] Case 34/82 *Martin Peters* [1983] ECR I-987 (judgment given on 22 March 1983); Case C-26/91 *Jacob Handte* [1992] ECR I-3697 (judgment given on 17 June 1992); Case C-334/00 *Fonderie Officine Meccaniche Tacconi* [202] ECR I-7357 (judgment given on 17.9.2002).

[16] Report on the Convention on the law applicable to contractual obligations, OJ C 282, 31.10.1980, p. 1.

e) Non-contractual obligations among the settlers, trustees and beneficiaries of a trust: trusts are a *sui generis* institution and should be excluded from the scope of this Regulation as previously from the Rome Convention.

f) non-contractual obligations arising out of nuclear damage: this exclusion is explained by the importance of the economic and State interests at stake and the Member States' contribution to measures to compensate for nuclear damage in the international scheme of nuclear liability established by the Paris Convention of 29 July 1960 and the Additional Convention of Brussels of 31 January 1963, the Vienna Convention of 21 May 1963, the Convention on Supplementary Compensation of 12 September 1997 and the Protocol of 21 September 1988.

These being exceptions, the exclusions will have to be interpreted strictly.

The proposed Regulation does not take over the exclusion in Article 1(2)(h) of the Rome Convention, which concerns rules of evidence and procedure. It is clear from Article 11 that, subject to the exceptions mentioned, these rules are matters for the *lex fori*. They would be out of place in a list of non-contractual obligations excluded from the scope of this Regulation.

Article 2 – Universal application

Under Article 2, this is a universal Regulation, meaning that the uniform conflict rules can designate the law of a Member State of the European Union or of a third country.

This is a firmly-rooted principle of the law concerning conflict of laws and already exists in the Rome Convention, the conventions concluded in the Hague Conference and the domestic law of the Member States.

Given the complementarily between 'Brussels I' and the proposed Regulation, the universal nature of the latter is necessary for the proper functioning of the internal market as avoiding distortions of competition between Community litigants. If the 'Brussels I' Regulation distinguishes *a priori* between situations in which the defendant is habitually resident in the **[10]** territory of a Member State and those in which he is habitually resident in a third country,[17] it still governs both purely 'intra-Community' situations and situations involving a 'foreign' element. For the rules of recognition and enforcement, first of all, all judgments given by a court in a Member State that are within the scope of the 'Brussels I' Regulation qualify for the simplified recognition and enforcement scheme; the law under which the judgment was given the law of a Member State or of a third country therefore has very little impact. As for the rules of jurisdiction, the 'Brussels I' Regulation also applies where the defendant is habitually resident outside Community territory: this is the case where the dispute is within an exclusive jurisdiction rule,[18] where the

---

[17] Article 2(1).
[18] Article 22.

jurisdiction of the court proceeds from a jurisdiction clause,[19] where the defendant enters an appearance[20] and where the *lis pendens* rule applies;[21] in general, Article 4(2) specifies that where the defendant is habitually resident in a third country, the claimant, if habitually resident in a Member States, may rely on exorbitant rules of the law of the country where he is habitually resident, irrespective of his nationality. It follows from all these provisions that the 'Brussels I' Regulation applies both to 'intra-Community' situations and to situations involving an 'extra-Community' element.

What must be sought, therefore, is equal treatment for Community litigants, even in situations that are not purely 'intra-Community'. If there continue to be more than fifteen different systems of conflict rules, two firms in distinct Member States, A and B, bringing the same dispute between them and a third firm in country C before their respective courts, would have different conflict rules applied to them, which could provoke a distortion of competition as in purely intra-Community situations.

Moreover, the separation between 'intra-Community' and 'extra-Community' disputes is by now artificial. How, for instance, are we to describe a dispute that initially concerns only a national of a Member State and a national of a third country but subsequently develops into a dispute concerning several Member States, for instance where the Community party joins an insurer established in another Member State or the debt in issue is assigned. Given the extent to which economic relations in the internal market are now intertwined, all disputes potentially have an intra-Community nature.

And on purely practical grounds, evidence presented to the Commission by the legal professions – both bench and bar – in the course of the written consultation emphasised that private international law in general and the conflict rules in particular are perceived as highly complex. This complexity would be even greater if this measure had the effect of doubling the sources of conflict rules and if practitioners now had to deal not only with Community uniform rules but also with distinct national rules in situations not connected as required with Community territory. The universal nature of the proposed Regulation accordingly meets the concern for certainty in the law and the Union's commitment in favour of transparent legislation.

[11] Article 3 – General rules

Article 3 lays down general rules for determining the law applicable to non-contractual obligations arising out of a tort or delict. It covers all obligations for which the following Articles lay down no special rule.

---

[19] Article 23.
[20] Article 24.
[21] Article 27.

The Commission's objectives in confirming the *lex loci delicti commissi* rule are to guarantee certainty in the law and to seek to strike a reasonable balance between the person claimed to be liable and the person sustaining the damage. The solutions adopted here also reflect recent developments in the Member States' conflict rules.

Paragraph 1 – General rule

Article 3(1) takes as the basic rule the law of the place where the direct damage arises or is likely to arise. In most cases this corresponds to the law of the injured party's country of residence. The expression 'is likely to arise' shows that the proposed Regulation, like Article 5(3) of the 'Brussels I' Regulation, also covers preventive actions such as actions for a prohibitive injunction.

The place or places where indirect damage, if any, was sustained are not relevant for determining the applicable law. In the event of a traffic accident, for example, the place of the direct damage is the place where the collision occurs, irrespective of financial or non-material damage sustained in another country. In a Brussels Convention case the Court of Justice held that the '*place where the harmful event occurred*' does not include the place where the victim suffered financial damage following upon initial damage arising and suffered by him in another Contracting State.[22]

The rule entails, where damage is sustained in several countries, that the laws of all the countries concerned will have to be applied on a distributive basis, applying what is known as 'Mosaikbetrachtung' in German law.

The proposed Regulation also reflects recent developments in the Member States' conflict rules. While the absence of codification in several Member States makes it impossible to give a clear answer for the more than fifteen systems, the connection to the law of the place where the damage was sustained has been adopted by those Member States where the rules have recently been codified. The solution applies to the Netherlands, the United Kingdom and France, but also in Switzerland. In Germany, Italy and Poland, the victim may opt for this law among others.

The solution in Article 3(1) meets the concern for certainty in the law. It diverges from the solution in the draft Convention of 1972, which takes as its basic rule the place where the 'harmful event' occurred. But the Court of Justice has held that the 'harmful event' covers both the act itself and the resultant damage. This solution reflects the specific objectives of international jurisdiction but it does not enable the parties to foresee the law that will be applicable to their situation with reasonable certainty.

The rule also reflects the need to strike a reasonable balance between the various interests at stake. The Commission has not adopted the principle of favouring the victim as a basic rule, which would give the victim the option of choosing the law

---

[22] Case C-364/93 *Marinari v Lloyds Bank* [1995] ECR I–2719 (judgment given on 19.9.1995).

most favourable to him. It considers that this solution would go beyond the victim's legitimate expectations and would **[12]** reintroduce uncertainty in the law, contrary to the general objective of the proposed Regulation. The solution in Article 3 is therefore a compromise between the two extreme solutions of applying the law of the place where the event giving rise to the damage occurs and giving the victim the option.

Article 3(1), which establishes an objective link between the damage and the applicable law, further reflects the modern concept of the law of civil liability which is no longer, as it was in the first half of the last century, oriented towards punishing for fault-based conduct: nowadays, it is the compensation function that dominates, as can be seen from the proli feration of no-fault strict liability schemes.

But the application of the basic rule might well be inappropriate where the situation has only a tenuous connection with the country where the damage occurs. The following paragraphs therefore exclude it in specified circumstances.

Paragraph 2 – Law of the common place of residence
Paragraph 2 introduces a special rule where the person claimed to be liable and the person who has allegedly sustained damage are habitually resident in the same country, the law of that country being applicable. This is the solution adopted by virtually all the Member States, either by means of a special rule or by the rule concerning connecting factors applied in the courts. It reflects the legitimate expectations of the two parties.

Paragraph 3 – General exception and secondary connection
Like Article 4(5) of the Rome Convention, paragraph 3 is a general exception clause which aims to bring a degree of flexibility, enabling the court to adapt the rigid rule to an individual case so as to apply the law that reflects the centre of gravity of the situation.

Since this clause generates a degree of unforeseeability as to the law that will be applicable, it must remain exceptional. Experience with the Rome Convention, which begins by setting out presumptions, has shown that the courts in some Member States tend to begin in fact with the exception clause and seek the law that best meets the proximity criterion, rather than starting from these presumptions.[23] That is why the rules in Article 3(1) and (2) of the proposed Regulation are drafted in the form of rules and not of mere presumptions. To make clear that the exception clause really must be exceptional, paragraph 3 requires the obligation to be '*manifestly more closely connected*' with another country.

Paragraph 3 then allows the court to be guided, for example, by the fact that the parties are already bound by a pre-existing relationship. This is a factor that can be taken into account to determine whether there is a manifestly closer connection

---

[23] Cf. point 3.2.5 of the Green Paper on converting the Convention of Rome of 1980 on the law applicable to contractual obligations into a Community instrument and its modernisation.

with a country other than the one designated by the strict rules. But the law applicable to the pre-existing relationship does not apply automatically, and the court enjoys a degree of discretion to decide whether there is a significant connection between the non-contractual obligations and the law applicable to the pre-existing relationship.

The text states that the pre-existing relationship may consist of a contract that is closely connected with the non-contractual obligations in question. This solution is particularly interesting for Member States whose legal system allows both contractual and non-contractual **[13]** obligations between the same parties. But the text is flexible enough to allow the court to take account of a contractual relationship that is still only contemplated, as in the case of the breakdown of negotiations or of annulment of a contract, or of a family relationship. By having the same law apply to all their relationships, this solution respects the parties' legitimate expectations and meets the need for sound administration of justice. On a more technical level, it means that the consequences of the fact that one and the same relationship may be covered by the law of contract in one Member State and the law of tort/delict in another can be mitigated, until such time as the Court of Justice comes up with its own autonomous response to the situation. The same reasoning applies to the consequences of the nullity of a contract, already covered by a special rule in Article 10(1)(e) of the Rome Convention. Certain Member States having expressed a reservation as to this Article, the use of the secondary connection mechanism will overcome the difficulties that might flow from the application of two separate instruments.

But where the pre-existing relationship consists of a consumer or employment contract and the contract contains a choice-of-law clause in favour of a law other than the law of the consumer's habitual place of residence, the place where the employment contract is habitually performed or, exceptionally, the place where the employee was hired, the secondary connection mechanism cannot have the effect of depriving the weaker party of the protection of the law otherwise applicable. The proposed Regulation does not contain an express rule to this effect since the Commission considers that the solution is already implicit in the protective rules of the Rome Convention: Articles 5 and 6 would be deflected from their objective if the secondary connection validated the choice of the parties as regards non-contractual obligations but their choice was at least partly invalid as regards their contract.

Article 4 – Product liability

Article 4 introduces a specific rule for non-contractual obligations in the event of damage caused by a defective product. For the definition of product and defective product for the purposes of Article 4, Articles 2 and 6 of Directive 85/374 will apply. [24]

---

[24] Council Directive 85/374/EEC of 25.7.1985 on the approximation of the laws, regulations and administrative provisions of the Member States concerning liability for defective

Directive 85/374 approximated the Member States' substantive law regarding strict liability, i.e. no-fault liability. But there is no full harmonisation, as the Member States are authorised to exercise certain options. The Directive does not affect national law concerning fault-based liability, which the victim can always rely on, and covers only certain types of damage. The scope of the special rule in Article 4 is consequently broader than the scope of Directive 85/374, as it also applies to actions based on purely national provisions governing product liability that do not emanate from the Directive.

Apart from respecting the parties' legitimate expectations, the conflict rule regarding product liability must reflect also the wide scatter of possible connecting factors (producer's headquarters, place of manufacture, place of first marketing, place of acquisition by the victim, victim's habitual residence), accentuated by the development of international trade, tourism and the mobility of persons and goods in the Union. Connection solely to the place of **[14]** the direct damage is not suitable here as the law thus designated could be unrelated to the real situation, unforeseeable for the producer and no source of adequate protection for the victim.[25]

Countries in which there are special rules thus tend to provide for a rule requiring several elements to be present in the same country for that country's law to be applicable. This is also the approach taken in the Hague Convention 1973 on the law applicable to products liability, in force in five Member States.[26] Under Article 25 of the proposed Regulation, the Convention will remain in force in the Member States that have ratified it when the Regulation comes into force. The 1973 Convention determines the law applicable to the liability of manufacturers, producers, suppliers and repairers on the basis of the following factors, whether distributed or combined on a complex basis: the place of damage, place of the habitual residence of the victim, principal place of business of the manufacturer or producer, place where the product was acquired.

The proposed Regulation acknowledges the specific constraints inherent in the subject-matter in issue but nevertheless proceeds from the need for a rule to avoid being unnecessarily complex.

Under Article 4, the applicable law is basically the law of the place of where the person sustaining damage has his habitual residence. But this solution is conditional on the product having been marketed in that country with the consent of the person claimed to be liable. In the absence of consent, the applicable law is the law of the country in which the person claimed to be liable has his habitual residence. Article 3(2) (common habitual residence) and (3) (general exception clause) also apply.

---

products (OJ L 210, 7.8.1985, p. 29), as amended by Directive 1999/34/EC of 10 May 1999 (OJ L 141, 4.6.1999, p. 20).

[25] Such a case might be a German tourist buying French-made goods in Rome airport to take to an African country, where they explode and cause him to sustain damage.

[26] Finland, France, Luxembourg the Netherlands and Spain. The convention is also in force in Norway, Croatia, Macedonia, Slovenia and Yugoslavia.

The fact that this is a simple and predictable rule means that it is particularly suitable in an area where the number of out-of-court settlements is very high, partly because insurers are so often involved. Article 4 strikes a reasonable balance between the interests in issue. Given the requirement that the product be marketed in the country of the victim's habitual residence for his law to be applicable, the solution is foreseeable for the producer, who has control over his sales network. It also reflects the legitimate interests of the person sustaining damage, who will generally have acquired a product that is lawfully marketed in his country of residence.

Where the victim acquires the product in a country other than that of his habitual residence, perhaps while travelling, two hypotheses need to be distinguished: the first is where the victim acquired abroad a product also marketed in their country of residence, for instance in order to enjoy a special offer. In this case the producer had already foreseen that his activity might be evaluated by the yardstick of the rules in force in that country, and Article 4 designates the law of that country, since both parties could foresee that it would be applicable.

In the second hypothesis, by contrast, where the victim acquired abroad a product that is not lawfully marketed in their country of habitual residence, none of the parties would have expected that law to be applied. A subsidiary rule is consequently needed. The two connecting factors discussed during the Commission's consultations were the place where the damage is sustained and the habitual residence of the person claimed to be liable. Since the large-scale mobility of consumer goods means that the connection to the place where the damage is [15] sustained no longer meets the need for certainty in the law or for protection of the victim, the Commission has opted for the second solution.

The rule in Article 4 corresponds not only to the parties' expectations but also to the European Union's more general objectives of a high level of protection of consumers' health and the preservation of fair competition on a given market. By ensuring that all competitors on a given market are subject to the same safety standards, producers established in a low-protection country could no longer export their low standards to other countries, which will be a general incentive to innovation and scientific and technical development.

The expression *'person claimed to be liable'* does not necessarily mean the manufacturer of a finished product; it might also be the producer of a component or commodity, or even an intermediary or a retailer. Anybody who imports a product into the Community is considered in certain conditions to be responsible for the safety of the products in the same way as the producer.[27]

Article 5 – Unfair competition

Article 5 provides for an autonomous connection for actions for damage arising out of an act of unfair competition.

---

[27] Directive 85/374, Article 3(2).

The purpose of the rules against unfair competition is to protect fair competition by obliging all participants to play the game by the same rules. Among other things they outlaw acts calculated to influence demand (misleading advertising, forced sales, etc.), acts that impede competing supplies (disruption of deliveries by competitors, enticing away a competitor's staff, boycotts), and acts that exploit a competitor's value (passing off and the like). The modern competition law seeks to protect not only competitors (horizontal dimension) but also consumers and the public in general (vertical relations). This three-dimensional function of competition law must be reflected in a modern conflict-of-laws instrument.

Article 5 reflects this triple objective since it refers to the effect on the market in general, the effect on competitors' interests and the effect on the broad and rather vague interests of consumers (as opposed to the individual interests of a specific consumer). This last concept is taken over from a number of Community consumer-protection directives, in particular Directive 98/27 of 19 May 1998.[28] This is not to say that the concept relates solely to actions brought by a consumers' association; given the triple objective of competition law, virtually any act of unfair competition also affects the collective interests of consumers, and it is neither here nor there whether the action is brought by a competitor or an association. But Article 5 applies also to actions for injunctions brought by consumer associations. The proposed Regulation thus sits well with recent decisions of the Court of Justice on the Brussels Convention holding, for instance, that *'a preventive action brought by a consumer protection organisation for the purpose of preventing a trader from using terms considered to be unfair in contracts with private individuals is a matter relating to tort, delict or quasi-delict within the meaning of Article 5(3) of that convention'.*[29]

[16] Comparative analysis of the Member States' private international law shows that there is a broad consensus in favour of applying the law of the country in which the market is distorted by competitive acts. This result is obtained either through the general principle of the *lex loci delicti* or by a specific connection (Austria, Netherlands, Spain and also Switzerland) and corresponds to recommendations extensively made by academic writers and by the Ligue internationale du droit de la concurrence en matière de publicité.[30] The current situation, however, is one of uncertainty, particularly in countries where the courts have not had an opportunity to rule on how the *lex loci delicti* rule should operate in practice. The establishment of a uniform conflict rule here would thus enhance the foreseeability of court decisions.

Article 5 provides for connection to the law of the State in whose territory *'competitive relations or the collective interests of consumers are affected or are likely to be affected'*

[28] Parliament and Council Directive 98/27/EC of 19 May 1998 on injunctions for the protection of consumers' interests: OJ L 166, 11.6.1998, p. 51.

[29] Case C-167/2000 *Henkel* (judgment given on 1.10.2002).

[30] Resolution passed at the Amsterdam congress in October 1992, published in the *Revue internationale de la concurrence* 1992 (No 168), p. 51, this Resolution having also called for an effort to harmonise the substantive rules here.

by '*an act of unfair competition*'. This is the market where competitors are seeking to gain the customer's favour. This solution corresponds to the victims' expectations since the rule generally designates the law governing their economic environment. But it also secures equal treatment for all operators on the same market. The purpose of competition law is to protect a market; it pursues a macro-economic objective. Actions for compensation are purely secondary and must be dependent on the overall judgement of how the market functions.

Regarding the assessment of the impact on the market, academic writers generally acknowledge that only the direct substantial effects of an act of unfair competition should be taken into account. This is particularly important in international situations since anti-competitive conduct commonly has an impact on several markets and gives rise to the distributive application of the laws involved.

The need for a special rule here is sometimes disputed on the ground that it would lead to the same solution as the general rule in Article 3, the damage for which compensation is sought being assimilated to the anti-competitive effect on which the application of competition law depends. While the two very often coincide in territorial terms, they will not automatically do so: for instance, the question of the place where the damage is sustained is tricky where two firms from State A both operate on market B. Moreover, the rules of secondary connection, of the common residence and the exception clause are not adapted to this matter in general.

Paragraph 2 deals with situations where an act of unfair competition targets a specific competitor, as in the case of enticing away a competitor's staff, corruption, industrial espionage, disclosure of business secrets or inducing breach of contract. It is not entirely excluded that such conduct may also have a negative impact on a given market, but these are situations that have to be regarded as bilateral. There is consequently no reason why the victim should not enjoy the benefit of Article 3 relating to the common residence or the general exception clause. This solution is in conformity with recent developments in private international law: there is a similar provision in section 4(2) of the Dutch Act of 2001 and section 136(2) of the Swiss Act. The German courts take the same approach.

[17] Article 6 – Violations of privacy and rights relating to the personality

The Regulation follows the approach generally taken by the law of the Member States nowadays and classifies violations of privacy and rights relating to the personality, particularly in the event of defamation by the mass media, in the category of non-contractual obligations rather than matters of personal status, except as regards rights to the use of a name.

There are specific provisions on respect for privacy and freedom of expression and information, also covering respect for media freedom and pluralism, in the Charter of Fundamental Rights of the European Union and in the Council of Europe Convention on the Protection of Human Rights and Fundamental Freedoms. The Community institutions and the Member States are required to respect these fundamental values. The European Court of Human Rights has already given valuable pointers to how to reconcile the two principles in the event of defamation proceedings. International conventions have helped to approximate the rules governing freedom of the press in the Member States, but differences remain as regards the practical application of that freedom. Operators regard the foresee-ability of the law applicable to their business as of the greatest importance.

A study of the conflict rules in the Member States shows that there is not only a degree of diversity in the solutions adopted but also considerable uncertainty as to the law. In the absence of codification, court decisions laying down general rules are still lacking in many Member States.[31] The connecting factors in the other Member States vary widely: the publisher's headquarters or the place where the product was published (Germany and Italy, at the victim's option); the place where the product was distributed and brought to the knowledge of third parties (Belgium, France, Luxembourg); the place where the victim enjoys a reputation, presumed to be his habitual residence (Austria). Other Member States follow the principle of favouring the victim, by giving the victim the option (Germany, Italy), or applying the law of the place where the damage is sustained where the *lex loci delicti* does not provide for compensation (Portugal). The UK solution is very differ-ent from the solutions applied in other Member States, for it differentiates depend-ing whether the publication is distributed in the UK or elsewhere: in the former case the only law applicable is the law of the place of distribution; in the latter case the court applies both the law of the place of distribution and the *lex fori* ('double actionability rule'). This rule protects the national press, as the English courts can-not give judgment against it if there is no provision for this in English law.[32]

Given the diversity and the uncertainties of the current situation, harmonising the conflict rule in the Community will increase certainty in the law.

The content of the uniform rule must reflect the rules of international jurisdiction in the 'Brussels I' Regulation. The effect of the *Mines de Potasse d'Alsace* and *Fiona Shevill* judgments[33] is that the victim may sue for damages either in the courts of the State where the publisher of the defamatory material is established, which have full jurisdiction to compensate for all damage sustained, or in the courts of each State in which the publication was **[18]** distributed and the victim claims to have suffered a loss of reputation, with jurisdiction to award damages only for damage sustained in their own State. Consequently, if the victim decides to bring the action in a court in a State where the publication is distributed, that court will apply its own law to the damage sustained in that State. But if the victim brings the action in the court for the place where the publisher is headquartered, that court will have jurisdiction to rule on the entire claim for damages: the *lex fori* will then

---

[31] Denmark, Finland, Greece, Ireland (doctrine of the 'proper law of the tort'), Netherlands, Spain and Sweden.

[32] Some academic writers in England doubt, however, whether invasions of privacy are also covered by this rule.

[33] Case C 68/93 *Fiona Shevill and others v Press Alliance SA* [1995] ECR I-415 (judgment given on 7 March 1995).

govern the damage sustained in that country and the court will apply the laws involved on a distributive basis if the victim also claims compensation for damage sustained in other States.

In view of the practical difficulties in the distributive application of several laws to a given situation, the Commission proposed, in its draft proposal for a Council Regulation of May 2002, that the law of the victim's habitual residence be applied. But there was extensive criticism of this during the consultations, one of the grounds being that it is not always easy to ascertain the habitual residence of a celebrity and another being that the combination of rules of jurisdiction and conflict rules could produce a situation in which the courts of the State of the publisher's establishment would have to give judgment against the publisher under the law of the victim's habitual residence even though the product was perfectly in conformity with the rules of the publisher's State of establishment and no single copy of the product was distributed in the victim's State of residence. The Commission has taken these criticisms on board and reviewed its proposal.

Article 6(1) of the proposed Regulation now provides for the law applicable to violations of privacy and rights relating to the personality to be determined in accordance with the rules in Article 3, which posit the law of the place where the direct damage is sustained, unless the parties reside in the same State or the dispute is more closely connected with another country.

In *Fiona Shevill* the Court of Justice ruled on the actual determination of the place where the damage was sustained in the event of defamation by the press, opting for the '*State in which the publication was distributed and where the victim claims to have suffered injury to his reputation*'. The place where a publication is distributed is the place where it comes to the knowledge of third parties and a person's reputation is liable to be harmed. This solution is in conformity with the victim's legitimate expectations without neglecting those of media firms. A publication can be regarded as distributed in a country only if is actually distributed there on a commercial basis.

But the Commission has been sensitive to concerns expressed both in the press and by certain Member States regarding situations in which a court in Member State A might be obliged to give judgment against a publisher with its own nationality A under the laws of Member State B, or even a third country, even though the publication in dispute was perfectly in conformity with the rules applicable in Member State A. It has been pointed out that the application of law B could be unconstitutional in country A as violating the freedom of the press. Given that this is a sensitive issue, where the Member States' constitutional rules diverge quite considerably, the Commission has felt that Article 6(1) should make it explicitly clear that the law designated by Article 3 must be disapplied in favour of the *lex fori* if it is incompatible with the public policy of the forum in relation to freedom of the press.

The law designated by Article 6(1) does not seem to provide a proper basis for settling the question whether and in what conditions the victim can oblige the publisher to issue a corrected version and exercise a right of reply. Paragraph 2 accordingly provides that the right of reply and equivalent measures will be governed by the law of the country in which the broadcaster or publisher is established.

[19] Article 7 – Violation of the environment

Article 7 lays down a special rule for civil liability in relation to violations of the environment. Reflecting recent developments in the substantive law, the rule covers both damage to property and persons and damage to the ecology itself, provided it is the result of human activity.

European or even international harmonisation is particularly important here as so many environmental disasters have an international dimension. But the instruments adopted so far deal primarily with questions of substantive law or international jurisdiction rather than with harmonisation of the conflict rules. And they address only selected types of cross-border pollution. In spite of this gradual approximation of the substantive law, not only in the Community, major differences subsist – for example in determining the damage giving rise to compensation, limitation periods, indemnity and insurance rules, the right of associations to bring actions and the amounts of compensation. The question of the applicable law has thus lost none of its importance.

Analysis of the current conflict rules shows that the solutions vary widely. The *lex fori* and the law of the place where the dangerous activity is exercised play a certain role, particularly in the international Conventions, but the most commonly applied solution is the law of the place where the loss is sustained (France, United Kingdom, Netherlands, Spain, Japan, Switzerland, Romania, Turkey, Quebec) or one of the variants of the principle of the law that is most favourable to the victim (Germany, Austria, Italy, Czech Republic, Yugoslavia, Estonia, Turkey, Nordic Convention of 1974 on the protection of the environment, Convention between Germany and Austria of 19 December 1967 concerning nuisances generated by the operation of Salzburg airport in Germany). The Hague Conference has also put an international convention on cross-border environmental damage on its work programme, and preparatory work seems to be moving towards a major role for the place where the damage is sustained, though the merits of the principle of favouring the victim are acknowledged.

The uniform rule proposed in Article 7 takes as its primary solution the application of the general rule in Article 3(1), applying the law of the place where the damage is sustained but giving the victim the option of selecting the law of the place where the event giving rise to the damage occurred.

The basic connection to the law of the place where the damage was sustained is in conformity with recent objectives of environmental protection policy, which tends to support strict liability. The solution is also conducive to a policy of prevention, obliging operators established in countries with a low level of protection to abide by the higher levels of protection in neighbouring countries, which removes the incentive for an operator to opt for low-protection countries. The rule thus contributes to raising the general level of environmental protection.

But the exclusive connection to the place where the damage is sustained would also mean that a victim in a low-protection country would not enjoy the higher level of protection available in neighbouring countries. Considering the Union's more general objectives in environmental matters, the point is not only to respect the victim's legitimate interests but also to establish a legislative policy that contributes to raising the general level of environmental protection, especially as the author of the environmental damage, unlike other torts or delicts, generally derives an economic benefit from his harmful activity. Applying exclusively the law of the place where the damage is sustained could give an operator an incentive to establish his [20] facilities at the border so as to discharge toxic substances into a river and enjoy the benefit of the neighbouring country's laxer rules. This solution would be contrary to the underlying philosophy of the European substantive law of the environment and the 'polluter pays' principle.

Article 7 accordingly allows the victim to make his claim on the basis of the law of the country in which the event giving rise to the damage occurred. It will therefore be for the victim rather than the court to determine the law that is most favourable to him. The question of the stage in proceedings at which the victim must exercise his option is a question for the procedural law of the forum, each Member State having its own rules to determine the moment from which it is no longer possible to file new claims.

A further difficulty regarding civil liability for violations of the environment lies in the close link with the public-law rules governing the operator's conduct and the safety rules with which he is required to comply. One of the most frequently asked questions concerns the consequences of an activity that is authorised and legitimate in State A (where, for example, a certain level of toxic emissions is tolerated) but causes damage to be sustained in State B, where it is not authorised (and where the emissions exceed the tolerated level). Under Article 13, the court must then be able to have regard to the fact that the perpetrator has complied with the rules in force in the country in which he is in business.

Article 8 – Infringement of intellectual property rights

Article 8 lays down special rules for non-contractual obligations flowing from an infringement of intellectual property rights. According to Recital 14 the term intellectual property rights means copyright, related rights, *sui generis* right for protection of databases and industrial property rights.

The treatment of intellectual property was one of the questions that came in for intense debate during the Commission's consultations. Many contributions recalled the existence of the universally recognised principle of the *lex loci protectionis*, meaning the law of the country in which protection is claimed on which e.g. the Bern Convention for the Protection of Literary and Artistic Works of 1886 and the Paris Convention for the Protection of Industrial Property of 1883 are built. This rule, also known as the 'territorial principle', enables each country to apply its own law to an infringement of an intellectual property right which is in force in its territory: counterfeiting an industrial property right is governed by the law of the country in which the patent was issued or the trade mark or model was registered; in copyright cases the courts apply the law of the country where the violation was committed. This solution confirms that the rights held in each country are independent.

The general rule contained in Article 3(1) does not appear to be compatible with the specific requirements in the field of intellectual property. To reflect this incompatibility, two approaches were discussed in the course of preparatory work. The first is to exclude the subject from the scope of the proposed Regulation, either by means of an express exclusion in Article 1 or by means of Article 25, which preserves current international conventions. The second is to lay down a special rule, and this is the approach finally adopted by the Commission with Article 8.

Article 8(1) enshrines the *lex loci protectionis* principle for infringements of intellectual property rights conferred under national legislation or international conventions.

[21] Paragraph 2 concerns infringements of unitary Community rights such as the Community trade mark, Community designs and models and other rights that might be created in future such as the Community patent for which the Commission has adopted a proposal for a Council regulation[34] on 1 August 2000. The *locus protectionis* referring to the Community as a whole, the non contractual obligations that are covered by the present proposal for a regulation are directly governed by the unitary Community law. In case of infringements and where for a specific question the Community instrument neither contains a provision of substantive law nor a special conflict of laws' rule, Article 8(2) of the proposed regulation contains a subsidiary rule according to which the applicable law is the law of the Member State in which an act of infringement of the Community right has been committed.

Article 9 – Law applicable to non-contractual obligations arising out of an act other than a tort or delict

In all the Member States' legal systems there are obligations that arise neither out of a contract nor out of a tort or delict. The situations that are familiar to all the Member States are payments made by mistake and services rendered by a person that enable another person to avoid sustaining personal injury or loss of assets.

Since these obligations are clearly distinguished by their own features from torts and delicts, it has been decided that there should be a special section for them.

To reflect the wide divergences between national systems here, technical terms need to be avoided. This Regulation refers therefore to '*non-contractual obligations arising out of an act other than a tort or delict*'. In most Member States there are subcategories for repayment of amounts wrongly received or unjust enrichment on

[34] OJ C 337 E, 28.11.2000, p. 78.

the one hand and agency without authority (*negotiorum gestion*) on the other. Both the substantive law and the conflict rules are still evolving rapidly in most of the Member States, which means that the law is far from certain. The uniform conflict rule must reflect the divergences in the substantive rules. The difficulty is in laying down rules that are neither so precise that they cannot be applied in a Member State whose substantive law makes no distinction between the various relevant hypotheses nor so general that they might be open to challenge as serving no obvious purpose. Article 9 seeks to overcome the problem by laying down specific rules for the two sub-categories, unjust enrichment and agency without authority, while leaving the courts with sufficient flexibility to adapt the rule their national systems.

The secondary connection technique, confirmed by paragraph 1, is particularly important here, for example where an agent exceeds his authority or where a third-party debt is settled. The rule is accordingly a strict one. The obligation is so closely connected with the pre-existing relationship between the parties that it is preferable for the entire legal situation to be governed by the same law. As in the case of the general exception clause in Article 3(3), the expression 'pre-existing relationship' applies particularly to pre-contractual relationships and to void contracts.

Paragraph 2 reflects the legitimate expectations of the parties where they are habitually resident in the same country.

[22] Paragraph 3 concerns unjust enrichment in the absence of a pre-existing relationship between the parties, in which case the non-contractual obligation is governed by the law of the country in which the enrichment occurs. The proposed rule is a conventional one, found also in the GEDIP draft and the Swiss legislation.

Paragraph 4, concerning *negotiorum gestio* (agency without authority), distinguishes between measures to be described as assistance and measures that might be described as interference. Measures of assistance mean one-off initiatives taken on an exceptional basis by the 'agent', who deserves special protection since he acted in order to preserve the interests of the 'principal', which justifies a local connection to the law of the property or person assisted. In the case of measures of interference in the assets of another person, as in the case of payment of a third-party debt, it is the 'principal' who deserves protection. The applicable law is therefore generally the law of the latter's place of habitual residence.

Paragraph 5, like the first sentence of Article 3, provides an exception clause.

To ensure that several different laws are not applicable to one and the same dispute, paragraph 6 excludes from this Article non-contractual obligations relating to intellectual property, to which Article 8 alone applies. E.g. an obligation based on unjust enrichment arising from an infringement of an intellectual property right is accordingly governed by the same law as the infringement itself.

Article 10 – Freedom of choice

Paragraph 1 allows the parties to choose the law applicable to the non-contractual obligation after the dispute has arisen. The proposed Regulation thus follows recent developments in national private international law, which likewise tend to encourage greater freedom of will,[35] even if the situation is less frequent that in contract cases. For this reason, the rule is based on objective connecting factors, unlike the Rome Convention.

Freedom of will is not accepted, however, for intellectual property, where it would not be appropriate.

As in Article 3 of the Rome Convention, it is stated that the choice must either be explicit or emerge clearly from the circumstances of the case. Since the proposed Regulation does not allow an *ex ante* choice, there is no need for special provisions to protect a weaker party.

Paragraph 1 further specifies that the parties' choice may not affect the rights of third parties. The typical example is the insurer's obligation to reimburse damages payable by the insured.

Paragraph 2 puts a restriction on freedom of will, which is inspired by Article 3(3) of the Rome Convention and applies where all the elements of the situation (except the choice of law) are located in a country other than the one whose law is chosen. In reality this is a purely internal situation regarding a Member State and is within the scope of the Regulation only because the parties have agreed on a choice of law. The choice by the parties is not deactivated, but it may not operate to the detriment of such mandatory provisions of the law which might otherwise be applicable.

[23] In this Article the concept of 'mandatory rules', unlike the overriding mandatory rules referred to in Article 12, refers to a country's rules of internal public policy. These are rules from which the parties cannot derogate by contract, particularly those designed to protect weaker parties. But internal public policy rules are not necessarily mandatory in an international context. They must be distinguished from the rules of international public policy of the forum referred to in Article 22 and from the overriding mandatory rules referred to in Article 12.

Paragraph 3 represents an extension by analogy of the limit provided for by paragraph 2 and applies where all the elements of the case apart from the choice of law are located in two or more Member States. It has the same objective, i.e. to prevent the parties frustrating the application of mandatory rules of Community law through the choice of the law of a third country.

Article 11 – Scope of the law applicable to non-contractual obligations

Article 11 defines the scope of the law determined under Articles 3 to 10 of the proposed Regulation. It lists the questions to be settled by that law. The approach taken in the Member States is not entirely uniform: while certain questions, such

---

[35] Examples include section 6 of the Dutch Act of 11 April 2001 and section 42 of the German EGBGB.

as the conditions for liability, are generally governed by the applicable law, others, such as limitation periods, the burden of proof, the measure of damages etc., may fall to be treated by the *lex fori*. Like Article 10 of the Rome Convention, Article 11 accordingly lists the questions to be settled by the law that is actually designated.

In line with the general concern for certainty in the law, Article 11 confers a very wide function on the law designated. It broadly takes over Article 10 of the Rome Convention, with a few changes of detail:

a) 'The conditions and extent of liability, including the determination of persons who are liable for acts performed by them'; the expression 'conditions. . . of liability' refers to intrinsic factors of liability. The following questions are particularly concerned: nature of liability (strict or fault-based); the definition of fault, including the question whether an omission can constitute a fault; the causal link between the event giving rise to the damage and the damage; the persons potentially liable; etc. 'Extent of liability' refers to the limitations laid down by law on liability, including the maximum extent of that liability and the contribution to be made by each of the persons liable for the damage which is to be compensated for. The expression also includes division of liability between joint perpetrators.

b) 'The grounds for exemption from liability, any limitation of liability and any division of liability': these are extrinsic factors of liability. The grounds for release from liability include *force majeure*; necessity; third-party fault and fault by the victim. The concept also includes the inadmissibility of actions between spouses and the exclusion of the perpetrator's liability in relation to certain categories of persons.

c) 'The existence and kinds of damage for which compensation may be due': this is to determine the damage for which compensation may be due, such as personal injury, damage to property, moral damage and environmental damage, and financial loss or loss of an opportunity.

[24] d) 'the measures which a court has power to take under its procedural law to prevent or terminate damage or to ensure the provision of compensation': this refers to forms of compensation, such as the question whether the damage can be repaired by payment of damages, and ways of preventing or halting the damage, such as an interlocutory injunction, though without actually obliging the court to order measures that are unknown in the procedural law of the forum.

e) 'the measure of damages in so far as prescribed by law': if the applicable law provides for rules on the measure of damages, the court must apply them.

f) 'the question whether a right to compensation may be assigned or inherited': this is self-explanatory. In succession cases, the designated law governs the question whether an action can be brought by a victim's heir to obtain compensation for damage sustained by the victim.[36] In assignment cases, the designated

---

[36] It goes without saying that the law governing the injured party's succession applies to the determination of the heirs, this being a preliminary to the main action.

law governs the question whether a claim is assignable[37] and the relationship between assignor and debtor.

g) The law that is designated will also determine the 'persons entitled to compensation for damage sustained personally': this concept particularly refers to the question whether a person other than the 'direct victim' can obtain compensation for damage sustained on a 'knock-on' basis, following damage sustained by the victim. Such damage might be non-material, as in the pain and suffering caused by a bereavement, or financial, as in the loss sustained by the children or spouse of a deceased person.

h) 'liability for the acts of another person': this concept concerns provisions in the law designated for vicarious liability. It covers the liability of parents for their children and of principals for their agents.

i) 'the manners in which an obligation may be extinguished and rules of prescription and limitation, including rules relating to the commencement of a period of prescription or limitation and the interruption and suspension of the period'; the law designated governs the loss of a right following failure to exercise it, on the conditions set by the law.

Article 12 – Overriding mandatory rules

This Article closely follows the corresponding Article of the Rome Convention.

In *Arblade*, the Court of Justice gave an initial definition of overriding mandatory rules (also called public-order legislation) as *'national provisions compliance with which has been deemed to be so crucial for the protection of the political, social or economic order in the Member State concerned as to require compliance therewith by all persons present on the national territory of that Member State and all legal relationships within that State'*.[38] What is specific about them is that the courts do not even apply their own conflict rules to determine the law applicable to a given situation and to evaluate in practical terms whether its **[25]** content would be repugnant to the values of the forum, but they apply their own rules as a matter of course.[39]

Paragraph 2 allows the courts to apply the overriding mandatory rules of the forum. As the Court also held in *Arblade*, in intra-Community relations the application of the mandatory rules of the forum must be compatible with the fundamental freedoms of the internal market.[40]

---

[37] Article 12(2) of the Rome Convention.

[38] Cases C-369/96 and C-376/96 [1999] ECR I-8453 (judgment given on 23.11.1999).

[39] This is the international public policy exception, to which Article 22 is devoted.

[40] Paragraph 31 of the judgment states that *'The fact that national rules are categorised as public-order legislation does not mean that they are exempt from compliance with the provisions of the Treaty'* and that *'The considerations underlying such national legislation can be taken into account by Community law only in terms of the exceptions to Community freedoms expressly provided for by the Treaty and, where appropriate, on the ground that they constitute overriding reasons relating to the public interest'*.

Paragraph 1 refers to foreign mandatory rules, where the court enjoys considerable discretion if there is a close connection with the situation, depending on its nature, its purposes and the consequences of applying it. Under the Rome Convention, Germany, Luxembourg and the United Kingdom have exercised their right to refrain from applying Article 7(1), relating to foreign mandatory rules. But the Commission like most of the contributors during the written consultations sees no reason to exclude this possibility since references to foreign mandatory rules have been perfectly exceptional hitherto.

Article 13 – Rules of safety and conduct

Where the law that is designated is not the law of the country in which the event giving rise to the damage occurred, Article 13 of the proposed Regulation requires the court to take account of the rules of safety and conduct which were in force at the place and time of the relevant event.

This article is based on the corresponding articles of the Hague Conventions on traffic accidents (Article 7) and product liability (Article 9). There are equivalent principles in the conflict systems of virtually all the Member States, either in express statutory provisions or in the decided cases.

The rule in Article 13 is based on the fact that the perpetrator must abide by the rules of safety and conduct in force in the country in which he operates, irrespective of the law applicable to the civil consequences of his action, and that these rules must also be taken into consideration when ascertaining liability. Taking account of foreign law is not the same thing as applying it: the court will apply only the law that is applicable under the conflict rule, but it must take account of another law as a point of fact, for example when assessing the seriousness of the fault or the author's good or bad faith for the purposes of the measure of damages.

Article 14 – Direct action

Article 14 determines the law applicable to the question whether the person sustaining damage may bring a direct action against the insurer of the person liable. The proposed rule strikes a reasonable balance between the interests at stake as it protects the person sustaining damage by giving him the option, while limiting the choice to the two laws which the insurer [26] can legitimately expect to be applied the law applicable to the non-contractual obligation and the law applicable to the insurance contract.

At all events, the scope of the insurer's obligations is determined by the law governing the insurance contract.

As in Article 7, relating to the environment, the form of words used here will avert the risk of doubts where the victim does not exercise his right of option.

Article 15 – Subrogation and multiple liability

This Article is identical to Article 13 of the Rome Convention.

It applies in particular to the relationship between insurer and perpetrator to determine whether the form has a right of action by way of subrogation against the latter.

Where there are several perpetrators, it also applies where one of the joint and several debtors makes a payment.

Article 16 – Formal validity

Article 16 is inspired by Article 9 of the Rome Convention.

Although the concept of formal validity plays a minor role in the creation of non-contractual obligations, an obligation can well arise as a result of a unilateral act by one or other of the parties.

To promote the validity of such acts, Article 16 provides for an alternative rule along the lines of Article 9 of the Rome Convention, whereby the act is formally valid if it satisfies the formal requirements of the law which governs the non-contractual obligation in question or the law of the country in which this act is done.

Article 17 – Burden of proof

Article 17 is identical to Article 14 of the Rome Convention.

It provides that the law governing non-contractual obligations applies to the extent that it contains, in matters of non-contractual obligations, rules which raise presumptions of law or determine the burden of proof. This is a useful provision as questions relating to evidence are basically matters for the procedural law of the *lex fori*.

Paragraph 2 concerns the admissibility of modes of proving acts intended to have legal effect referred to in Article 16. It does not cover evidence of legal facts, which is also covered by the *lex fori*. The very liberal system of Article 14(2) of the Rome Convention is used here, providing for the alternative application of the *lex fori* and the law governing the form of the relevant act.

[27] Article 18 – Assimilation to the territory of a State

Article 18 applies to situations in which one or more of the connecting factors in the conflict rules of the proposed Regulation relate to an area that is not subject to territorial sovereignty.

The text proposed by the Commission in the written consultation procedure in May 2002 contained a special conflict rule. One of the difficulties with this rule lay in the diversity of the situations concerned. It is by no means certain that a single rule will adequately cover the position of a collision between ships on the high seas, the explosion of an electronic device or the breakdown of negotiations in an aircraft in flight, pollution caused by a ship at sea etc.

The contributions received by the Commission have made it aware that the proposed rule made it all too easy to designate the law of a flag of convenience, which would be contrary to the more general objectives of Community policy. Many contributors had doubts about the value added by a rule which, where two or more laws are potentially involved, as in collision cases, merely refers to the principle of the closest connection.

Rather than introducing a special rule here, Article 18 offers a definition of the 'territory of a State'. This solution is founded on the need to strike a reasonable balance between divergent interests by means of the different conflict rules in the proposed Regulation where one or more connecting factors are located in an area subject to no sovereignty. The general rule in Article 3 and the special conflict rules accordingly apply.

The definitions in the proposed text are inspired by section 1 of the Dutch Act on conflicts of laws in relation to obligations arising out of unlawful acts (11 April 2001).

Article 19 – Assimilation to habitual residence

This article deals with the concept of habitual residence for companies and firms and other bodies corporate or unincorporate and for natural persons exercising a liberal profession or business activity in a self-employed capacity.

In general terms the proposed Regulation is distinguished from the 'Brussels I' Regulation by the fact that, in accordance with the generally accepted solution in conflict matters, the criterion used here is not domicile but the more flexible criterion of habitual residence.

With regard to companies and firms and other bodies corporate or unincorporate, simply taking over the alternative rule in Article 60 of the 'Brussels I' Regulation, whereby the domicile of a body corporate is either its registered office, or its central administration, or its principal establishment, would not make the applicable law adequately foreseeable.

Article 19(1) accordingly provides that the principal establishment of a company or firms or other body corporate or unincorporate is considered to be its habitual residence. However, the second sentence of paragraph 1 states that where the event giving rise to the damage occurs or the damage is sustained in the course of operation of a subsidiary, a branch or any other establishment, the establishment takes the place of the habitual residence. Like Article 5(5) of the 'Brussels I' Regulation, the purpose of this is to respect the legitimate expectations of the parties.

Paragraph 2 determines the habitual residence of a natural person exercising a liberal profession or business activity in a self-employed capacity, for whom the professional establishment operates as habitual residence.

[28] Article 20 – Exclusion of renvoi

This Article is identical to Article 15 of the Rome Convention.

To avoid jeopardising the objective of certainty in the law that is the main inspiration for the conflict rules in the proposed Regulation, Article 20 excludes renvoi. Consequently, designating a law under uniform conflict rules means designating the substantive rules of that law but not its rules of private international law, even where the law thus designated is that of a third country.

Article 21 – States with more than one legal system

This Article is identical to Article 19 of the Rome Convention.

The uniform rules also apply where several legal systems coexist in a single State. Where a State has several territorial units each with its own rules of law, each of those units is considered a country for the purposes of private international law. Examples of those States are the United Kingdom, Canada, the United States and Australia. For example, if damage is sustained in Scotland, the law designated by Article 3(1) is Scots law.

Article 22 – Public policy of the forum

This Article corresponds to Article 16 of the Rome Convention relating to the mechanism of the public policy exception. Like the Rome Convention, this concerns a State's public policy in the private international law sense, a more restrictive concept than public policy in the domestic law sense. The words 'of the forum' have been added to distinguish the rules of public policy in the private international law sense, which proceed solely from the national law of a State, from those flowing from Community law, to which the specific rule of Article 23 applies.

The mechanism of the public policy exception allows the court to disapply rules of the foreign law designated by the conflict rule and to replace it by the *lex fori* where the application of the foreign law in a given case would be contrary to the public policy of the forum. This is distinguished from overriding mandatory rules: in the latter case, the courts apply the law of the forum automatically, without first looking at the content of the foreign law. The word 'manifestly' incompatible with the public policy of the forum means that the use of the public policy exception must be exceptional.

In a Brussels Convention case the Court of Justice held that the concept of public policy remains a national concept and that '. . . *it is not for the Court to define the content of the public policy of a Contracting State* . . .', but it must none the less '*review the limits within which the courts of a Contracting State may have recourse to that concept for the purpose of refusing recognition of a judgment emanating from another Contracting State*'.[41]

---

[41] Case C-38/98 *Renault v Maxicar* [2000] ECR I-2973 (judgment given on 11.5.2000).

[29] Article 23 – Relationship with other provisions of Community law

Paragraph 1 refers to the traditional mechanisms of private international law that can be found in the treaties and the secondary legislation and entail special conflict rules in specific matters, mandatory rules of Community and the Community public policy exception.

Paragraph 2 refers more particularly to the specific principles of the internal market relating to the free movement of goods and services, commonly known as the 'mutual recognition' and 'home-country control' principles.

Article 24 – Non-compensatory damages

Article 24 is the practical application of the Community public policy exception provided for by the third indent of Article 23(1) in the form of a special rule.

In the written consultation, many contributors expressed concern at the idea of applying the law of a third country providing for damages not calculated to compensate for damage sustained. It was suggested that it would be preferable to adopt a specific rule rather than to apply the public policy exception of the forum, as is the case of section 40-III of the German EGBGB.

The effect of Article 24 is accordingly that application of a provision of the law designated by this Regulation which has the effect of causing non-compensatory damages, such as exemplary or punitive damages, to be awarded will be contrary to Community public policy.

The words used are descriptive rather than technical legal terms, too loosely tied to a specific legal system. Compensatory damages serve to compensate for damage sustained by the victim or liable to be sustained by him at a future date. Non-compensatory damages serve a punitive or deterrent function.

Article 25 – Relationship with existing international conventions

Article 25 allows Member States to go on applying choice of law rules laid down in international conventions to which they are party when this Regulation is adopted.

These conventions include the Hague Conventions on traffic accidents (4 May 1971) and product liability (2 October 1973).

Article 26 – List of conventions referred to in Article 25

To make it easier to identify the conventions to which Article 25 applies, Article 26 provides that the Member States are to notify the Commission of the list, which the Commission is then to publish in the *Official Journal of the European Union*. The Member States are also to notify the Commission of denunciations of these conventions so that it can update the list.

[30]

2003/0168 (COD)

Proposal for a

REGULATION OF THE EUROPEAN PARLIAMENT AND THE COUNCIL ON THE LAW APPLICABLE TO NON-CONTRACTUAL OBLIGATIONS ('ROME II')

THE EUROPEAN PARLIAMENT AND THE COUNCIL OF THE EUROPEAN UNION,

Having regard to the Treaty establishing the European Community, and in Article 61(c) thereof,

Having regard to the proposal from the Commission,[42]

Having regard to the opinion of the European Economic and Social Committee,[43]

Acting in accordance with the procedure laid down in Article 251 of the Treaty,[44]

Whereas:

(1) The Union has set itself the objective of establishing an area of freedom, security and justice. To that end the Community must adopt measures relating to judicial cooperation in civil matters with a cross-border impact to the extent necessary for the proper functioning of the internal market, including measures promoting the compatibility of the rules applicable in the Member States concerning the conflict of laws and of jurisdiction.

(2) For the purposes of effectively implementing the relevant provisions of the Amsterdam Treaty, the Council (Justice and Home Affairs) on 3 December 1998 adopted a plan of action specifying that the preparation of a legal instrument on the law applicable to non-contractual obligations is among the measures to be taken within two years following the entry into force of the Amsterdam Treaty.[45]

(3) The Tampere European Council on 15 and 16 October 1999[46] approved the principle of mutual recognition of judgments as a priority matter in the establishment of a European law-enforcement area. The Mutual Recognition Programme[47] states that measures relating to harmonisation of conflict-of-law rules are measures that 'actually do help facilitate the implementation of the principle'.

---

[42] OJ C [. . .], [. . .], p. [. . .].

[43] OJ C [. . .], [. . .], p. [. . .].

[44] Opinion of the European Parliament of [. . .] (OJ C [. . .], [. . .], p. [. . .].

[45] Action Plan of the Council and the Commission on how best to implement the provisions of the Treaty of Amsterdam on an area of freedom, security and justice: OJ C 19, 23.1.1999.

[46] Presidency conclusions of 16 October 1999, points 28 to 39.

[47] OJ C 12, 15.1.2001, p. 1.

[31]](4) The proper functioning of the internal market creates a need, in order to improve the predictability of the outcome of litigation, certainty as to the law and the free movement of judgments, for the rules of conflict of laws in the Member States to designate the same national law irrespective of the country of the court in which an action is brought.

(5) The scope of the Regulation must be determined in such a way as to be consistent with Regulation (EC) No 44/2001[48] and the Rome Convention of 1980.[49]

(6) Only uniform rules applied irrespective of the law they designate can avert the risk of distortions of competition between Community litigants.

(7) The principle of the lex loci delicti commissi is the basic solution for non-contractual obligations in virtually all the Member States, but the practical application of the principle where the component factors of the case are spread over several countries is handled differently. This situation engenders uncertainty in the law.

(8) The uniform rule must serve to improve the foreseeability of court decisions and ensure a reasonable balance between the interests of the person claimed to be liable and the person who has sustained damage. A connection with the country where the direct damage occurred (lex loci delicti commissi) strikes a fair balance between the interests of the person causing the damage and the person sustaining the damage, and also reflects the modern approach to civil liability and the development of systems of strict liability.

(9) Specific rules should be laid down for special torts/delicts where the general rule does not allow a reasonable balance to be struck between the interests at stake.

(10) Regarding product liability, the conflict rule must meet the objectives of fairly spreading the risks inherent in a modern high-technology society, protecting consumers' health, stimulating innovation, securing undistorted competition and facilitating trade. Connection to the law of the place where the person sustaining the damage has his habitual residence, together with a foreseeability clause, is a balanced solution in regard to these objectives.

(11) In matters of unfair competition, the conflict rule must protect competitors, consumers and the general public and ensure that the market economy functions properly. The connection to the law of the relevant market generally satisfies these objectives, though in specific circumstances other rules might be appropriate.

(12) In view of the Charter of Fundamental Rights of the European Union and the Council of Europe Convention for the Protection of Human Rights and Fundamental Freedoms, the conflict must strike a reasonable balance as regards violations of privacy and rights in the personality. Respect for the fundamental principles that

---

[48] OJ L 12, 16.1.2001, p. 1.

[49] The consolidated text of the Convention as amended by the various Conventions of Accession, and the declarations and protocols annexed to it, is published in OJ C 27, 26.1.1998, p. 34.

apply in the Member States as regards freedom of the press must be secured by a specific safeguard clause.

[32](13) Regarding violations of the environment, Article 174 of the Treaty, which provides that there must a high level of protection based on the precautionary principle and the principle that preventive action must be taken, the principle of priority for corrective action at source and the principle that the polluter pays, fully justifies the use of the principle of discriminating in favour of the person sustaining the damage.

(14) Regarding violations of intellectual property rights, the universally acknowledged principle of the *lex loci protectionis* should be preserved. For the purposes of the present Regulation, the term intellectual property rights means copyright, related rights, sui generis right for the protection of databases and industrial property rights.

(15) Similar rules should be provided for where damage is caused by an act other than a tort or delict, such as unjust enrichment and agency without authority.

(16) To preserve their freedom of will, the parties should be allowed to determine the law applicable to a non-contractual obligation. Protection should be given to weaker parties by imposing certain conditions on the choice.

(17) Considerations of the public interest warrant giving the courts of the Member States the possibility, in exceptional circumstances, of applying exceptions based on public policy and overriding mandatory rules.

(18) The concern to strike a reasonable balance between the parties means that account must be taken of the rules of safety and conduct in operation in the country in which the harmful act was committed, even where the non-contractual obligations is governed by another law.

(19) The concern for consistency in Community law requires that this Regulation be without prejudice to provisions relating to or having an effect on the applicable law, contained in the treaties or instruments of secondary legislation other than this Regulation, such as the conflict rules in specific matters, overriding mandatory rules of Community origin, the Community public policy exception and the specific principles of the internal market. Furthermore, this regulation is not intended to create, nor shall its application lead to obstacles to the proper functioning of the internal market, in particular free movement of goods and services.

(20) Respect for international commitments entered into by the Member States means that this Regulation should not affect conventions relating to specific matters to which the Member States are parties. To make the rules easier to read, the Commission will publish the list of the relevant conventions in the *Official Journal of the European Union* on the basis of information supplied by the Member States.

(21) Since the objective of the proposed action, namely better foreseeability of court judgments requiring genuinely uniform rules determined by a mandatory and directly applicable Community legal instrument, cannot be adequately attained by the Member States, who cannot lay down uniform Community rules,

and can therefore, by reason of its effects throughout the Community, be better achieved at Community level, the Community can take measures, in accordance with the subsidiarity principle set out in Article 5 of the Treaty. In accordance with the proportionality principle set out in that Article, a Regulation, which increases certainty in the law without requiring harmonisation of the substantive rules of domestic law, does not go beyond what is necessary to attain that objective.

[33](22) [In accordance with Article 3 of the Protocol on the position of the United Kingdom and Ireland, annexed to the Treaty on European Union and the Treaty establishing the European Community, these Member States have stated their intention of participating in the adoption and application of this Regulation. / In accordance with Articles 1 and 2 of the Protocol on the position of the United Kingdom and Ireland, annexed to the Treaty on European Union and the Treaty establishing the European Community, these Member States are not participating in the adoption of this Regulation, which will accordingly not be binding on those Member States.]

(23) In accordance with Articles 1 and 2 of the Protocol on the position of Denmark, annexed to the Treaty on European Union and the Treaty establishing the European Community, that Member State is not participating in the adoption of this Regulation, which will accordingly not be binding on that Member State,

HAVE ADOPTED THIS REGULATION:

CHAPTER I – SCOPE

Article 1 – Material scope

1. This Regulation shall apply, in situations involving a conflict of laws, to non-contractual obligations in civil and commercial matters.

It shall not apply to revenue, customs or administrative matters.

2. The following are excluded from the scope of this Regulation:
a) non-contractual obligations arising out of family relationships and relationships deemed to be equivalent, including maintenance obligations;
b) non-contractual obligations arising out of matrimonial property regimes and successions;
c) obligations arising under bills of exchange, cheques and promissory notes and other negotiable instruments to the extent that the obligations under such other negotiable instruments arise out of their negotiable character;
d) the personal legal liability of officers and members as such for the debts of a company or firm or other body corporate or incorporate, and the personal legal liability of pers ons responsible for carrying out the statutory audits of accounting documents;
e) non-contractual obligations among the settlers, trustees and beneficiaries of a trust;
f) non-contractual obligations arising out of nuclear damage.

3. For the purposes of this Regulation, 'Member State' means any Member State other than [the United Kingdom, Ireland or] Denmark.

[34] Article 2 – Universal application

Any law specified by this Regulation shall be applied whether or not it is the law of a Member State.

CHAPTER II – UNIFORM RULES

SECTION 1
RULES APPLICABLE TO NON-CONTRACTUAL OBLIGATIONS ARISING OUT OF A TORT OR DELICT

Article 3 – General rule

1. The law applicable to a non-contractual obligation shall be the law of the country in which the damage arises or is likely to arise, irrespective of the country in which the event giving rise to the damage occurred and irrespective of the country or countries in which the indirect consequences of that event arise.

2. However, where the perso n claimed to be liable and the person sustaining damage both have their habitual residence in the same country when the damage occurs, the non-contractual obligation shall be governed by the law of that country.

3. Notwithstanding paragraphs 1 and 2, where it is clear from all the circumstances of the case that the non-contractual obligation is manifestly more closely connected with another country, the law of that other country shall apply. A manifestly closer connection with another country may be based in particular on a pre-existing relationship between the parties, such as a contract that is closely connected with the non-contractual obligation in question.

Article 4 – Product liability

Without prejudice to Article 3(2) and (3), the law applicable to a non-contractual obligation arising out of damage or a risk of damage caused by a defective product shall be that of the country in which the person sustaining the damage is habitually resident, unless the person claimed to be liable can show that the product was marketed in that country without his consent, in which case the applicable law shall be that of the country in which the person claimed to be liable is habitually resident.

Article 5 – Unfair competition

1. The law applicable to a non-contractual obligation arising out of an act of unfair competition shall be the law of the country where competitive relations or the

collective interests of consumers are or are likely to be directly and substantially affected.

2. Where an act of unfair competition affects exclusively the interests of a specific competitor, Article 3(2) and (3) shall apply.

[35] Article 6 – Violations of privacy and rights relating to the personality

1. The law applicable to a non-contractual obligation arising out of a violation of privacy or rights relating to the personality shall be the law of the forum where the application of the law designated by Article 3 would be contrary to the fundamental principles of the forum as regards freedom of expression and information.

2. The law applicable to the right of reply or equivalent measures shall be the law of the country in which the broadcaster or publisher has its habitual residence.

Article 7 – Violation of the environment

The law applicable to a non-contractual obligation arising out of a violation of the environment shall be the law determined by the application of Article 3(1), unless the person sustaining damage prefers to base his claim on the law of the country in which the event giving rise to the damage occurred.

Article 8 – Infringement of intellectual property rights

1. The law applicable to a non-contractual obligation arising from an infringement of a intellectual property right shall be the law of the country for which protection is sought.

2. In the case of a non-contractual obligation arising from an infringement of a unitary Community industrial property right, the relevant Community instrument shall apply. For any question that is not governed by that instrument, the applicable law shall be the law of the Member State in which the act of infringement is committed.

SECTION 2

RULES APPLICABLE TO NON-CONTRACTUAL OBLIGATIONS
ARISING OUT OF AN ACT OTHER THAN A TORT OR DELICT

Article 9 – Determination of the applicable law

1. If a non-contractual obligation arising out of an act other than a tort or delict concerns a relationship previously existing between the parties, such as a contract closely connected with the non-contractual obligation, it shall be governed by the law that governs that relationship.

2. Without prejudice to paragraph 1, where the parties have their habitual residence in the same country when the event giving rise to the damage occurs, the law applicable to the non-contractual obligation shall be the law of that country.

3. Without prejudice to paragraphs 1 and 2, a non-contractual obligation arising out of unjust enrichment shall be governed by the law of the country in which the enrichment takes place.

4. Without prejudice to paragraphs 1 and 2, the law applicable to a non-contractual obligation arising out of actions performed without due authority in connection with the affairs of another person shall be the law of the country in which the beneficiary has his [36] habitual residence at the time of the unauthorised action. However, where a non-contractual obligation arising out of actions performed without due authority in connection with the affairs of another person relates to the physical protection of a person or of specific tangible property, the law applicable shall be the law of the country in which the beneficiary or property was situated at the time of the unauthorised action.

5. Notwithstanding paragraphs 1, 2, 3 and 4, where it is clear from all the circumstances of the case that the non-contractual obligation is manifestly more closely connected with another country, the law of that other country shall apply.

6. Nowithstanding the present Article, all non-contractual obligations in the field of intellectual property shall be governed by Article 8.

SECTION 3
COMMON RULES APPLICABLE TO NON-CONTRACTUAL OBLIGATIONS ARISING OUT OF A TORT OR DELICT AND OUT OF AN ACT OTHER THAN A TORT OR DELICT

Article 10 – Freedom of choice

1. The parties may agree, by an agreement entered into after their dispute arose, to submit non-contractual obligations other than the obligations to which Article 8 applies to the law of their choice. The choice must be expressed or demonstrated with reasonable certainty by the circumstances of the case. It may not affect the rights of third parties.

2. If all the other elements of the situation at the time when the loss is sustained are located in a country other than the country whose law has been chosen, the choice of the parties shall be without prejudice to the application of rules of the law of that country which cannot be derogated from by contract.

3. The parties' choice of the applicable law shall not debar the application of provisions of Community law where the other elements of the situation were located in one of the Member States of the European Community at the time when the loss was sustained.

Article 11 – Scope of the law applicable to non-contractual obligations

The law applicable to non-contractual obligations under Articles 3 to 10 of this Regulation shall govern in particular:

a) the conditions and extent of liability, including the determination of persons who are liable for acts performed by them;

b) the grounds for exemption from liability, any limitation of liability and any division of liability;

c) the existence and kinds of injury or damage for which compensation may be due;

d) within the limits of its powers, the measures which a court has power to take under its procedural law to prevent or terminate injury or damage or to ensure the provision of compensation;

[37]e) the assessment of the damage in so far as prescribed by law;

f) the question whether a right to compensation may be assigned or inherited;

g) persons entitled to compensation for damage sustained personally;

h) liability for the acts of another person;

i) the manners in which an obligation may be extinguished and rules of prescription and limitation, including rules relating to the commencement of a period of prescription or limitation and the interruption and suspension of the period.

Article 12 – Overriding mandatory rules

1. Where the law of a specific third country is applicable by virtue of this Regulation, effect may be given to the mandatory rules of another country with which the situation is closely connected, if and in so far as, under the law of the latter country, those rules must be applied whatever the law applicable to the non-contractual obligation. In considering whether to give effect to these mandatory rules, regard shall be had to their nature and purpose and to the consequences of their application or non-application.

2. Nothing in this Regulation shall restrict the application of the rules of the law of the forum in a situation where they are mandatory irrespective of the law otherwise applicable to the non-contractual obligation.

Article 13 – Rules of safety and conduct

Whatever may be the applicable law, in determining liability account shall be taken of the rules of safety and conduct which were in force at the place and time of the event giving rise to the damage.

Article 14 – Direct action against the insurer of the person liable

The right of persons who have suffered damage to take direct action against the insurer of the person claimed to be liable shall be governed by the law applicable to the non-contractual obligation unless the person who has suffered damage prefers to base his claims on the law applicable to the insurance contract.

Article 15 – Subrogation and multiple liability

1. Where a person ('the creditor') has a non-contractual claim upon another ('the debtor'), and a third person has a duty to satisfy the creditor, or has in fact satisfied the creditor in discharge of that duty, the law which governs the third person's duty to satisfy the creditor shall determine whether the third person is entitled to exercise against the debtor the rights which the creditor had against the debtor under the law governing their relationship in whole or in part.

2. The same rule shall apply where several persons are subject to the same claim and one of them has satisfied the creditor.

[38] Article 16 – Formal validity

A unilateral act intended to have legal effect and relating to a non-contractual obligation is formally valid if it satisfies the formal requirements of the law which governs the non-contractual obligation in question or the law of the country in which this act is done.

Article 17 – Burden of proof

1. The law governing a non-contractual obligation under this Regulation applies to the extent that, in matters of non-contractual obligations, it contains rules which raise presumptions of law or determine the burden of proof.

2. Acts intended to have legal effect may be proved by any mode of proof recognised by the law of the forum or by any of the laws referred to in Article 16 under which that act is formally valid, provided that such mode of proof can be administered by the forum.

CHAPTER III – OTHER PROVISIONS

Article 18 – Assimilation to the territory of a State

For the purposes of this Regulation, the following shall be treated as being the territory of a State:

a) installations and other facilities for the exploration and exploitation of natural resources in, on or below the part of the seabed situated outside the State's territorial waters if the State, under international law, enjoys sovereign rights to explore and exploit natural resources there;

b) a ship on the high seas which is registered in the State or bears lettres de mer or a comparable document issued by it or on its behalf, or which, not being registered or bearing lettres de mer or a comparable document, is owned by a national of the State;

c) an aircraft in the airspace, which is registered in or on behalf of the State or entered in its register of nationality, or which, not being registered or entered in the register of nationality, is owned by a national of the State.

Article 19 – Assimilation to habitual residence

1. For companies or firms and other bodies or incorporate or unincorporate, the principal establishment shall be considered to be the habitual residence. However, where the event giving rise to the damage occurs or the damage arises in the course of operation of a subsidiary, a branch or any other establishment, the establishment shall take the place of the habitual residence.

2. Where the event giving rise to the damage occurs or the damage arises in the course of the business activity of a natural person, that natural person's establishment shall take the place of the habitual residence.

[39]3. For the purpose of Article 6(2), the place where the broadcaster is established within the meaning of the directive 89/552/EEC, as amended by the directive 97/36/EC, shall take the place of the habitual residence.

Article 20 – Exclusion of *renvoi*

The application of the law of any country specified by this Regulation means the application of the rules of law in force in that country other than its rules of private international law.

Article 21 – States with more than one legal system

1. Where a State comprises several territorial units, each of which has its own rules of law in respect of non-contractual obligations, each territorial unit shall be considered as a country for the purposes of identifying the law applicable under this Regulation.

2. A State within which different territorial units have their own rules of law in respect of non-contractual obligations shall not be bound to apply this Regulation to conflicts solely between the laws of such units.

Article 22 – Public policy of the forum

The application of a rule of the law of any country specified by this Regulation may be refused only if such application is manifestly incompatible with the public policy ('*ordre public*') of the forum.

Article 23 – Relationship with other provisions of Community law

1. This Regulation shall not prejudice the application of provisions contained in the Treaties establishing the European Communities or in acts of the institutions of the European Communities which:

- in relation to particular matters, lay down choice-of-law rules relating to non-contractual obligations; or
- lay down rules which apply irrespective of the national law governing the non-contractual obligation in question by virtue of this Regulation; or
- prevent application of a provision or provisions of the law of the forum or of the law designated by this Regulation.

2. This regulation shall not prejudice the application of Community instruments which, in relation to particular matters and in areas coordinated by such instruments, subject the supply of services or goods to the laws of the Member State where the service-provider is established and, in the area coordinated, allow restrictions on freedom to provide services or goods originating in another Member State only in limited circumstances.

[40] Article 24 – Non-compensatory damages

The application of a provision of the law designated by this Regulation which has the effect of causing non-compensatory damages, such as exemplary or punitive damages, to be awarded shall be contrary to Community public policy.

Article 25 – Relationship with existing international conventions

This Regulation shall not prejudice the application of international conventions to which the Member States are parties when this Regulation is adopted and which, in relation to particular matters, lay down conflict-of-law rules relating to non-contractual obligations.

CHAPTER IV – FINAL PROVISIONS

Article 26 – List of conventions referred to in Article 25

1. The Member States shall notify the Commission, no later than 30 June 2004, of the list of conventions referred to in Article 25. After that date, the Member States shall notify the Commission of all denunciations of such conventions.

2. The Commission shall publish the list of conventions referred to in paragraph 1 in the *Official Journal of the European Union* within six months of receiving the full list.

Article 27 – Entry into force and application in time

This Regulation shall enter into force on 1 January 2005.

It shall apply to non-contractual obligations arising out of acts occurring after its entry into force.

This Regulation shall be binding in its entirety and directly applicable in all Member States in accordance with the Treaty establishing the European Community.

Done at Brussels, [. . .].

For the European Parliament   *For the Council*

The President   *The President*

Appendix 3

Commission Amended Proposal

Amended proposal for a

EUROPEAN PARLIAMENT AND COUNCIL REGULATION

ON THE LAW APPLICABLE TO NON-CONTRACTUAL
OBLIGATIONS('ROME II')

(presented by the Commission pursuant to Article 250 (2) of the
EC Treaty)

EXPLANATORY MEMORANDUM*

1. Backround

[2]

The proposal[1] was adopted by the Commission on 22 July 2003 and transmitted to the European Parliament and the Council on the same date.

The European Economic and Social Committee adopted its Opinion on the Commission proposal on 30 June and I July 2004.[2]

The European Parliament adopted 54 amendments at first reading in plenary session on 6 July 2005.[3]

2. Objective of the Amended Proposal

The amended proposal adapts the original proposal for a Regulation on the law applicable to non-contractual obligations in the light of certain amendments passed by Parliament while reflecting proceedings in the Council.

---

* Author's note: Footnote numbering as original. The bold numbering in square brackets in the text (e.g. **[3]**) refers to the original numbered pages of the Commission Proposal.

[1] COM (2003) 427 final – 2003/0168 (COD); not yet published in the OJ.

[2] OJ C 241, 28.9.2004, p. 1.

[3] A6-0211/2005.

3. Commission Opinion on the Amendments Adopted by Parliament

3.1 *Amendments accepted in their entirety by the Commission*

Amendments 2, 12, 17, 19, 22, 24, 35, 38, 39, 40, 44, 45, 48, 51, 52 and 53 can be accepted as presented by Parliament since they make improvements relating either to the clarity of the instrument or to questions of detail, or add material that will be potentially useful in implementing the initial proposal.

3.2 *Amendments accepted by the Commission as to substance, subject to redrafting*

Amendments 1, 5, 18, 20, 21, 23, 25, 28, 34, 36, 37, 46 and 49 can be accepted in principle, subject to redrafting.

Amendment 1 refers to the Rome I Regulation. But until the Regulation has been adopted, it would be preferable to refer to the future Community instrument that will replace the Rome Convention of 1980.

Amendment 5 brings non-contractual obligations based on strict liability and the capacity to incur liability in tort/delict within the scope of the Regulation. While the Commission can accept this analysis, it prefers to combine all the points concerning the scope of the Regulation in a single recital – recital 5 – without repeating all the questions already covered expressly by Article 12 (scope of the applicable law).

[3] **Amendment 18** specifies that unjust enrichment and administration of others' affairs without a mandate are to be considered as breaches of non-contractual obligations for the purposes of the Regulation. The Commission agrees with this. But to avoid making the text more cumbersome, it prefers to combine all the points concerning the scope of the Regulation in a single recital. Above all the Commission feels it is preferable to restate that there should be an autonomous and coherent interpretation of the legal concepts used in the Brussels I and Rome II instruments and the Rome Convention of 1980 – or the Community instrument that will replace it – by the Court of Justice rather than a long but inevitably incomplete list of details. This amendment also aims to exclude the liability of public administrations in respect of acts or omissions occurring in the performance of their duties from the scope of the Regulation. The Commission accepts the amendment as regards the substance but prefers the forms of words commonly used in international conventions.

Amendment 20 aims to exclude non-contractual obligations governed by specific provisions of company law or specific provisions applicable to other bodies corporate such as associations. The Commission accepts this amendment as regards the substance but proposes drafting it in simpler terms.

Amendment 21 would exclude non-contractual obligations arising from a trust. The Commission accepts the principle of the amendment but prefers to adopt the wording of the Hague Convention of 1 July 1985.

Amendment 23 would exclude liability for acts of public authority, including liability of publicly appointed office-holders. The Commission can accept the proposed solution as regards the substance but considers the amendment to be redundant in view of amendment 18.

Amendment 25 would allow certain parties who are already in a contractual relationship to choose the law applicable to their non-contractual obligation before the loss or damage is sustained. The Commission can accept the principle of an *ex ante* choice and agrees that the choice should be subject to strict conditions, in particular to protect the weaker party. But the conditions for the choice should be expressed in clear and simple terms. If the legal terms are not precise enough, parties might feel they were being given an incentive to litigate, which would make the procedure more cumbersome in terms of duration and cost and thus run counter to the objective pursued by the Regulation. The wording proposed by the Commission would both protect consumers and employees from ill-thought-out choices and exclude the possibility of such choices being imposed in standard contracts.

The Commission can accept the principle of **amendments 28 and 34**, which would change the structure and title of the sections to make a clearer distinction between the general rule and special rules for certain categories of liability. To reflect proceedings in the Council and the differences between the Member States' legal systems, the Commission proposal makes an additional distinction between the special rules applicable to certain categories of liability and the specific rules governing unjust enrichment and administration of others' affairs.

Amendments 36 and 37 replace the single rule of Article 9 of the initial Commission proposal, applicable to all quasi-contracts, by two specific rules, one applying to unjust enrichment and the other to administration of others' affairs. The Commission can accept this additional distinction. In its amended proposal, however, it wishes to reflect certain technical improvements in the text emerging from Council proceedings.

Amendment 46 seeks to clarify the rule on direct actions against the insurer of the person liable without modifying it as to the substance. The Commission can accept the principle of redrafting the rule to make it easier to understand. But it prefers the form of words that emerged from the Council, which pursues the same objective.

[4] Amendment 49 seeks to clarify the place where a natural person working from home has his habitual residence. The Commission can accept the principle of this clarification, but it prefers a form of words that is closer to what emerged from the Council, whereby the court would prefer the actual place where an occupation is exercised rather than an official address which might turn out to be purely fictitious.

3.3 Amendments accepted by the Commission in part

Amendment 3 would adapt recital 7 **of the initial proposal** to the changes made by amendment 26 relating to the general rule in Article 3. Since the Commission can only accept part of amendment 26, it will have to reject the corresponding amendment to the recital. As regards the final sentence of the amendment, restating the need to respect the intentions of the parties, the idea is already covered by recital 8 in the Commission's amended proposal.

Amendment 14 relating to rules of safety and conduct in the country where the loss or damage is sustained serves two purposes: first, to add the words *"in so far as is appropriate"* so as to emphasise even further that the application of these rules is in the discretion of the court, and second, to exclude this possibility in matters of defamation and unfair competition. The Commission can accept the proposed clarification for the first sentence of the recital. But Parliament's report offers no justification for excluding the rule in matters of defamation and unfair competition. The Commission accordingly sees no reason for depriving the perpetrators of these two categories of liability of the protection which this rule gives them.

Amendment 26 relating to the general rule in Article 3 of the initial Commission proposal can be accepted as regards the drafting improvements to paragraph 1, which confirms the rule proposed by the Commission. On the other hand, the Commission cannot accept the changes to paragraphs 2 and 3. Paragraph 2 brings in a specific rule concerning traffic accidents which would subject to two different laws the non-contractual obligation and the amount of damages. The Commission appreciates Parliament's efforts to find a fair solution for so many people who are the victims of traffic accidents but this solution, which would diverge sharply from the law in force in the Member States, cannot be adopted without prior in-depth analysis. It is accordingly proposed that the question be considered in detail in the report on the application of the Regulation, provided for by amendment 54. As regards paragraph 3, the amendment would substantially alter the spirit of the instrument. While it is specified that the exception clause available to the court really would be applied *'by way of exception'*, the current wording runs the risk of sending a message that is contrary to the foreseeability objective pursued by the Regulation. The mere fact that the paragraph lists no less than five factors that can be taken into consideration to justify activating the exception clause means that the parties and the courts will routinely check the justification for the solution that the general rule would have generated even where it is at first sight satisfactory. The Commission therefore cannot accept this part of amendment 26 and maintains its initial approach, which the Council also appears to have endorsed. But the Commission does acknowledge the significance of some of the factors listed in paragraph 3, in particular as regards the parties' shared habitual residence, a pre-existing *de facto* or *de jure* relationship or the legitimate expectations of the parties. As the first two of these are already mentioned expressly in paragraphs 2 and 3 of the initial proposal, Article 5(3) of the amended proposal now contains an express reference to the legitimate expectations of the parties.

Amendment 50, which concerns the mechanism for the public policy (*ordre public*) exception, first inserts a new paragraph 1a) to spell out the concept of public policy of the forum by listing reference instruments. Even though the public policy of the Member States [5] will inevitably contain common elements, there are variations from one to another. Consequently the Commission cannot accept such a list. The proposed new paragraph 1b) addresses the issue of damages in amounts regarded as excessive, such as certain types of exemplary or punitive damages, already covered by a specific rule in Article 24 of the initial Commission proposal. Subject to drafting changes to make clear that punitive damages are not *ipso facto* excessive, the Commission can accept this rule being incorporated in the Article concerning the public policy of the forum. Under the proposed new paragraph 1c), only the parties would be able to rely on the exception clause. But it is for the court to ensure compliance with the fundamental values of the forum, and that task cannot be delegated to the parties, especially as they are not always legally represented. The Brussels I Regulation provides for the possibility for the court to withhold the *exequatur* from a judgment given in another Member State if it would be contrary to the public policy of the forum. The Commission accordingly cannot accept the proposed paragraph 1c).

Amendment 54 provides for an obligation for the Commission to report on the application of the Regulation after it is in force. While the Commission acknowledges the value of such a report, it cannot accept all the conditions provided for by the amendment. For one thing, the period of three years after adoption of the Regulation would not allow an adequate number of judgments to be given as the basis for an effective evaluation. As in the Brussels I Regulation, the Commission proposes a period of five years after the Regulation enters into force. As for the content of the report, the question of the amount of damages awarded by the courts and the elaboration of a code of ethics for the European media are way out of place in a conflict-of-laws regulation. The Commission accordingly cannot accept that these questions should be dealt with in a report on the application of this Regulation. On the other hand the Commission agrees with Parliament on the need to consider how to achieve a more uniform approach to applying foreign law in the courts of the Member States. It does not believe that the time is ripe for a legislative initiative in this respect (see amendment 43), but it can accept the idea of looking into the question in depth in the application report.

3.4 *Amendments rejected*

Amendments 4, 9, 10, 15 and 16 are not acceptable to the Commission as it rejects amendments 26, 30, 54 (paragraph 3), 31 and 42 to which they correspond.

Amendments 6, 7, 8, 11 and 13 would adapt the recitals to reflect the removal of several special rules for specific forms of liability as proposed in amendments 27, 29 and 33. Since the Commission cannot accept the deletion of these special rules (see above), it must logically reject the corresponding changes to the recitals. In its report, however, Parliament does not exclude the possibility of keeping the special rules, as long as their scope is clearly defined, particular as regards unfair trading practices and damage to the environment. Recitals 12, 13 and 14 of the amended proposal now accordingly refer to the relevant Community secondary legislation. The legal terminology of these Articles has also been changed to align it on that used in the secondary legislation. But while the concepts are thus better defined in Community law, it must still be borne in mind that they may be defined in broader terms than in Community law when they are used for the determination of a tort/ delict for the purposes of private international law.

Amendment 27 would abolish the special rule for product liability. As in the case of the other torts/delicts such as unfair competition and environmental damage, the Commission considers that the general rule would not make it possible to foresee the applicable law with reasonable certainty. The place where the damage arises may be the result of pure chance in view of the **[6]** great mobility of consumer goods (imagine a Dutch-made hairdryer, owned by a German tourist travelling in Thailand). Since in this area there are very often amicable settlements between insurers, it is particularly important to come up with a clear, foreseeable rule to facilitate such agreements. The Commission accordingly cannot accept the proposed deletion.

Amendment 29 would abolish the special rule for anti-competitive practices. The Commission cannot accept this amendment: Article 5 of the initial proposal did not seek to introduce a rule differing from the general rule on the substance but simply to determine more accurately the place where the damage arises, which is not always an easy matter. Article 7 has been slightly reworded in the amended proposal to make clear that the aim is solely to determine more accurately where the damage arises. To meet the European Parliament's requests regarding definitions, the Commission has also opted to use terminology in Article 7 of the amended proposal that is directly inspired by Directive 2005/29 of 11 May 2005. The result, *a contrario*, is that non-contractual obligations arising from anti-competitive practices outlawed under Articles 81 and 82 of the Treaty or equivalent rules in the Member States are not covered by Article 7; they are consequently subject to the general rule in Article 5. But in its Green Paper *'Damages actions for breach of the EC antitrust rules'*, scheduled for publication in December 2005, the Commission is planning to provoke debate on the question of the law applicable to civil actions for compensation for damage arising from an anti competitive practice. Depending on the replies, the Commission may wish to support a different solution in the course of the codecision procedure.

Amendment 57 would change the substance of the rule applicable to violations of privacy, particularly by the press. The Commission cannot accept this amendment, which is too generous to press editors rather than the victim of alleged defamation in the press and does not reflect the solution taken by a large majority of Member States. Since it is not possible to reconcile the Council's text and the text adopted by Parliament at first reading, the Commission considers that the best solution to this controversial question is to exclude all press offences and the like from the proposal and delete Article 6 of the original proposal. Other privacy violations would be covered by Article 5.

Amendment 31 would bring in a new special rule concerning damage arising from the exercise of the right to strike by employed people. The Commission is sensitive to the underlying political arguments but it cannot accept this amendment as the proposed rule is too rigid.

Amendment 32 restates that, until such time as the Community adopts detailed legislation on the law applicable to traffic accidents, Member States will either apply the 1971 Hague Convention or the general rules of the Rome II Convention. Since it is quite possible that the implementation report provided for by Article 26 of the amended proposal will confirm that the general rules of the Regulation provide a satisfactory solution, the Commission cannot commit itself now to a future legislative proposal and accordingly rejects this amendment. Paragraph 2 of this amendment reiterates the proposal made in amendment 26 as regards the introduction of a new special rule on the evaluation of the damage arising from a traffic accident, which the Commission cannot accept (see above under amendment 26).

Amendment 33 would delete the special rule for damage to the environment. The Commission cannot accept this amendment as the proposed rule reflects the 'polluter pays' principle promoted by the Community and already applied in several Member States. The Greens, incidentally, abstained from voting on this amendment in plenary.

Amendment 41 again raises the question of the evaluation of the damages, which would generally (except as regards traffic accidents) be governed by the *lex fori*. The Commission [7] cannot accept this amendment. This is a vital question for victims not only of traffic accidents but of any other situations, in particular personal injury, and the rules laid down by the Regulation offer a fair solution reflecting, the legitimate expectations both of the victim and of the person causing the damage.

Amendments 42 and 43 address the question of the application of foreign law by the court. The former would require the parties to indicate the law applicable in their statement of claim. The Commission is in favour of making things easier for courts dealing with international litigation, but this rule would be too difficult to implement as parties are not all capable of stating what law is applicable to their situation, in particular when they are not legally represented. The purpose of the latter is to formalise the rule already in operation in some Member States that the court must itself determine the content of the foreign law, though it can seek help from the parties. The Commission is of the opinion that, as matters stand, most Member States would not be able to apply the rule as they do not have proper structures in place to enable the courts to apply the foreign law in this way, and it rejects this amendment. But it agrees that this is an avenue well worth exploring and that special attention should be paid to it in the implementation report.

Amendment 47 is redundant with amendment 22, which the Commission prefers on drafting grounds. Amendment 47 is accordingly rejected.

4. Conclusion

Acting under Article 250(2) of the EC Treaty, the Commission amends its proposal as follows.

Amended proposal for a

EUROPEAN PARLIAMENT AND COUNCIL REGULATION ON THE LAW APPLICABLE TO NON-CONTRACTUAL OBLIGATIONS ('ROME II')

THE EUROPEAN PARLIAMENT AND THE COUNCIL OF THE EUROPEAN UNION,

Having regard to the Treaty establishing the European Community, and in particular Article 61(c) thereof,

Having regard to the proposal from the Commission,4

Having regard to the opinion of the European Economic and Social Committee,5

Acting in accordance with the procedure laid down in Article 251 of the Treaty,6

Whereas:

(1) The Union has set itself the objective of establishing an area of freedom, security and justice. To that end the Community must adopt measures relating to judicial cooperation in civil matters with a cross-border impact to the extent necessary for the proper functioning of the internal market, including measures promoting the compatibility of the rules applicable in the Member States concerning the conflict of laws and of jurisdiction.

(2) For the purposes of effectively implementing the relevant provisions of the Amsterdam Treaty, the Council (Justice and Home Affairs) on 3 December 1998 adopted a plan of action specifying that the preparation of a legal instrument on the law applicable to non-contractual obligations is among the measures to be taken within two years following the entry into force of the Amsterdam Treaty.7

(3) The Tampere European Council on 15 and 16 October 1999⁸ approved the principle of mutual recognition of judgments as a priority matter in the establishment of a European law-enforcement area. The mutual recognition programme⁹ states that measures relating to harmonisation of conflict-of-law rules are measures that actually do help facilitate the implementation of the principle.

---

⁴ ~~OJ C [...], [...], p. [...]p.~~ **Not yet published in the OJ.**

⁵ OJ C **241, 28.9.2004,** p.1

⁶ Opinion of the European Parliament of ~~[...] (JO C [...] du [...], [...]~~ **6 July 2005**.

⁷ Action plan of the Council and the Commission on how best to implement the provisions of the Treaty of Amsterdam on an area of freedom, security and justice: OJ C 19, 23.1.1999, p. 1.

⁸ Presidency conclusions of 16 October 1999, points 28 to 39.

⁹ OJ C 12, 15.1.2001, p. 1.

[9]

(4) The proper functioning of the internal market creates a need, in order to improve the foreseeability of the outcome of litigation, certainty as to the law and the free movement of judgments, for the rules of conflict of laws in the Member States to designate the same national law irrespective of the country of the court in which an action is brought.

(5) The scope **and provisions** of ~~the~~ **this** Regulation**, which are subject to autonomous interpretation by the Court of Justice,** must be determined in such a way as to be consistent with Regulation (EC) No 44/2001[10] **of 22 December 2000 on jurisdiction and the recognition and enforcement of judgments in civil and commercial matters (Brussels I),**[11] the Rome Convention of 1980[~~12~~13]**.** **and the Community instrument which will replace it. This Regulation will accordingly apply not only to actions for compensation for damage that has already arisen but also to actions to prevent likely future damage. It also covers obligations based on rules imposing strict liability.**

(6) Only uniform rules applied irrespective of the law they designate can avert the risk of distortions of competition between Community litigants.

~~(7) The principle of the lex loci delicti commissi is the basic solution for non-contractual obligations in virtually all the Member States, but the practical application of the principle where the component factors of the case are spread over several countries is handled differently. This situation engenders uncertainty in the law.~~

(7) **The concern for consistency in Community law requires that this Regulation be without prejudice to provisions relating to or having an effect on the applicable law, contained in the treaties or instruments of secondary legislation other than this Regulation, such as conflict rules in specific matters, overriding mandatory rules of Community origin, and the basic legal principles of the internal market. As a result, this Regulation should promote the proper functioning of the internal market, in particular the free movement of goods and services.**

(8) **To respect the intentions of the parties, they must be able to make an express choice as to the law applicable to a non-contractual obligation. However, their choice should be subject to certain conditions, and consumers and employees should have no possibility of choosing the applicable law before the event from which the damage occurs.**

(9) **The principle of the *lex loci delicti commissi* is the basic solution for non-contractual obligations in virtually all the Member States, but the practical**

---

[10] ~~OJ L 12, 16.1.2001, p. 1.~~

[11] **OJ L 12, 16.1.2001, p.1**

[12] ~~The consolidated text of the Convention as amended by the various Conventions of Accession, and the declarations and protocols annexed to it, is published in OJ C 27, 26.1.1998, p. 34.~~

[13] **The consolidated text of the Convention, as amended by the various Conventions of Accession, and the declarations and protocols annexed to it, is published in OJ C 27, 26.1.1998, p. 34.**

application of the principle where the component factors of the case are spread over several countries is handled differently. This situation engenders uncertainty in the law.

[10]

(8 **10**) The uniform rule must serve to improve the foreseeability of court decisions and ensure a reasonable balance between the interests of the person claimed to be liable and the person who has sustained damage. A connection with the country where the direct damage occurred (*lex loci delicti commissi*) strikes a fair balance between the interests of the person causing the damage and the person sustaining the damage, and also reflects the modern approach to civil liability and the development of systems of strict liability.

(9 **11**) Specific rules should be laid down for special torts/delicts where the general rule does not allow a reasonable balance to be struck between the interests at stake.

(10 **12**) Regarding product liability, **as penalised under Directive 374/1985/EEC of 25 July 1985 on the approximation of the laws, regulations and administrative provisions of the Member States concerning liability for defective products,[14]** the conflict rule must meet the objectives of fairly spreading the risks inherent in a modern high-technology society, protecting consumers' health, stimulating innovation, securing undistorted competition and facilitating trade. Connection to the law of the place where the person sustaining the damage has his habitual residence, together with a foreseeability clause, is a balanced solution in regard to these objectives.

(11 **13**) In matters of unfair ~~competition~~ **commercial practices, as penalised under Directive 29/2005/EC of 11 May 2005 concerning unfair business-to-consumer commercial practices in the internal market,[15]** the **general** conflict rule ~~must~~ **makes it possible to** protect competitors, consumers and the general public and ensure that the market economy functions properly. ~~The connection to the law of the relevant market generally satisfies these objectives, though in specific circumstances other rules might be appropriate~~ **The provision in a specific Article that the place where the damage occurs is the place where the market is affected helps to increase certainty as to the law**.

(12) ~~In view of the Charter of Fundamental Rights of the European Union and the Council of Europe Convention for the Protection of Human Rights and Fundamental Freedoms, the conflict must strike a reasonable balance as regards violations of privacy and rights in the personality. Respect for the fundamental principles that apply in the Member States as regards freedom of the press must be secured by a specific safeguard clause.~~

---

[14] **OJ L 210, 7.8.1985, p. 29, as amended by Directive 34/1999/EC of 10 May 1999, JO L 141, 4.6.1999, p. 20.**
[15] **OJ L 149, 11.6.2005, p. 22.**

(~~13~~14) Regarding ~~violations of the environment,~~**environmental damage to which Directive 35/2004/EC of 21 April 2004 on environmental liability with regard to the prevention and remedying of environmental damage**[16] **applies, the solution of allowing the person sustaining the loss to choose the applicable law is fully compliant with** Article 174 of the Treaty, which provides that there must a high level of protection based on the precautionary principle and the principle that preventive action must be taken, the principle of priority for corrective action at source and the principle that the polluter pays ~~fully justifies the use of the principle of discriminating in favour of the person sustaining the damage~~.

[11]

(~~14~~15) Regarding violations of intellectual property rights, the universally acknowledged principle of the *lex loci protectionis* should be preserved. For the purposes of this Regulation, the term intellectual property rights means copyright, related rights, *sui generis* right for the protection of databases and industrial property rights.

(~~15~~16) ~~Similar~~ **Special** rules should be **laid down for non-contractual obligations arising from** ~~provided for where damage is caused by an act other than a tort or delict, such as~~ unjust enrichment and agency without authority.

~~(16) To preserve their freedom of will, the parties should be allowed to determine the law applicable to a non-contractual obligation. Protection should be given to weaker parties by imposing certain conditions on the choice.~~

(17) Considerations of the public interest warrant giving the courts of the Member States the possibility, in exceptional circumstances, of applying exceptions based on public policy and overriding mandatory rules

(18) The concern to strike a reasonable balance between the parties means that account must be taken of the rules of safety and conduct in operation in the country in which the harmful act was committed, even where the non-contractual obligation is governed by another law**, in so far as is appropriate**.

~~(19) The concern for consistency in Community law requires that this Regulation be without prejudice to provisions relating to or having an effect on the applicable law, contained in the treaties or instruments of secondary legislation other than this Regulation, such as the conflict rules in specific matters, overriding mandatory rules of Community origin, the Community public policy exception and the specific principles of the internal market. Furthermore, this regulation is not intended to create, nor shall its application lead to obstacles to the proper functioning of the internal market, in particular free movement of goods and services.~~

(~~20~~19) Respect for international commitments entered into by the Member States means that this Regulation should not affect conventions relating to specific matters to which the Member States are parties. To make the rules easier to read,

---

[16] **OJ L 143, 30.4.2004, p. 56.**

the Commission will publish the list of the relevant conventions in the *Official Journal of the European Union* on the basis of information supplied by the Member States.

(~~21~~20) Since the objective of the proposed action, namely better foreseeability of court judgments requiring genuinely uniform rules determined by a mandatory and directly applicable Community legal instrument, cannot be adequately attained by the Member States, who cannot lay down uniform Community rules, and can therefore, by reason of its effects throughout the Community, be better achieved at Community level, the Community can take measures, in accordance with the subsidiarity principle set out in Article 5 of the Treaty. In accordance with the proportionality principle set out in that Article, a regulation, which increases certainty in the law without requiring harmonisation of the substantive rules of domestic law, does not go beyond what is necessary to attain that objective.

(~~22~~21) [In accordance with Article 3 of the Protocol on the position of the United Kingdom and Ireland, annexed to the Treaty on European Union and the Treaty establishing the European Community, these Member States have stated their intention of participating **[12]** in the adoption and application of this Regulation.~~/ In accordance with Articles 1 and 2 of the Protocol on the position of the United Kingdom and Ireland, annexed to the Treaty on European Union and the Treaty establishing the European Community, these Member States are not participating in the adoption of this Regulation, which will accordingly not be binding on those Member States.~~]

(~~23~~22) In accordance with Articles 1 and 2 of the Protocol on the position of Denmark, annexed to the Treaty on European Union and the Treaty establishing the European Community, that Member State is not participating in the adoption of this Regulation, which will accordingly not be binding on that Member State,

HAVE ADOPTED THIS REGULATION:

CHAPTER I – SCOPE

Article 1 – Material scope

1. This Regulation shall apply, in situations involving a conflict of laws, to non-contractual obligations in civil and commercial matters.

It shall not apply to revenue, customs or administrative matters.

2. The following are excluded from the scope of this Regulation:
   a) non-contractual obligations arising out of family relationships and relationships ~~deemed to be equivalent, including~~ **having comparable effects under the law applicable to such relationships, including** maintenance obligations;
   b) non-contractual obligations arising out of matrimonial property regimes and successions **or regimes having comparable effects under the law applicable to such relationships**;

c) **non-contractual** obligations arising under bills of exchange, cheques and promissory notes and other negotiable instruments to the extent that the obligations under such other instruments arise out of their negotiable character;

d) ~~the personal legal liability of officers and members as such for the debts of a company or firm or other body corporate or incorporate, and the personal legal liability of persons responsible for carrying out the statutory audits of accounting documents~~ **non-contractual obligations, in particular the liability of partners, management bodies and persons responsible for carrying out the statutory audits of accounting documents of an association, a company or firm or other body corporate or incorporate, provided they are subject to specific rules of company law or other specific provisions applicable to such persons or bodies;**

e) non-contractual obligations ~~among~~ **arising from relationships between** the settlers, trustees and beneficiaries of a trust **created voluntarily and evidenced in writing;**

f) non-contractual obligations arising out of nuclear damage;

[13] **g) non-contractual obligations arising in connection with the liability of the State for acts done in the exercise of public authority ('*acta iure imperii*');**

h) violations of privacy and of personal rights by the media;

i) evidence and procedure, without prejudice to Article 19.

3. For the purposes of this Regulation, 'Member State' means any Member State other than ~~[the United Kingdom, Ireland or]~~ Denmark.

Article 2 – ~~Universal application~~ *Application of the law of a third country*

Any law specified by this Regulation shall be applied whether or not it is the law of a Member State.

Article 3 – *Relationship with other provisions of Community law*

1. This Regulation shall not prejudice the application or adoption of acts of the institutions of the European Communities which:

a) in relation to particular matters, lay down choice-of-law rules relating to non-contractual obligations; or

b) lay down rules which apply irrespective of the national law governing the relevant non-contractual obligation by virtue of this Regulation; or

c) preclude the application of one or more provisions of the law of the forum or the law designated by this Regulation;

d) lay down rules to promote the smooth operation of the internal market, where such rules cannot apply at the same time as the law designated by the rules of private international law.

CHAPTER II – UNIFORM RULES

~~Rules applicable to non-contractual obligations arising out of a tort or delict~~ Freedom of choice

~~Article 3 – General rule~~ *Article 4 – Freedom of choice*

1. The **parties may agree, by an agreement entered into after their dispute arose, to submit non-contractual obligations to the law of their choice. The choice must be expressed or demonstrated with reasonable certainty by the circumstances of the case. It may not affect the rights and obligations of third parties.**

[14] 2. **Where all the parties exercise a commercial activity, such choice may also be made by an agreement freely negotiated before the event from which the damage arises occurs.**

3. **If all the other elements of the situation at the time when the loss is sustained are located in a country other than the country whose law has been chosen, the choice of the parties shall be without prejudice to the application of rules of the law of that country which cannot be derogated from by contract ('mandatory provisions').**

4. **The parties' choice of the applicable law shall not debar the application of provisions of Community law where the other elements of the situation were located in one of the Member States of the European Community at the time when the loss was sustained.**

Section 2

General rule applicable to non-contractual obligations arising out of a tort or delict

Article 5 – General rule

1. **Where no choice has been made under Article 4, the** law applicable to a non-contractual obligation shall be the law of the country in which the damage arises or is likely to arise, irrespective of the country in which the event giving rise to the damage occurred and irrespective of the country or countries in which the indirect consequences of that event arise.

2. However, where the person claimed to be liable and the person sustaining damage both have their habitual residence in the same country when the damage occurs, the non-contractual obligation shall be governed by the law of that country.

3. Notwithstanding paragraphs 1 and 2, where it is clear from all the circumstances of the case that the non-contractual obligation is manifestly more closely connected with another country, the law of that other country shall apply. A manifestly closer connection with another country may be based in particular on a

pre-existing relationship between the parties, such as a contract that is closely connected with the non-contractual obligation in question. **For the purpose of assessing the existence of a manifestly closer connection with another country, account shall be taken *inter alia* of the expectations of the parties regarding the applicable law.**

SECTION 3

RULES APPLICABLE TO NON-CONTRACTUAL OBLIGATIONS ARISING FROM SPECIFIC TORTS/DELICTS

Article 4 6 – Product liability

Without prejudice to Article 3 5(2) and (3), the law applicable to a non-contractual obligation arising out of damage ~~or a risk of damage~~ caused by a defective product shall be that of the **[15]** country in which the person sustaining the damage is habitually resident **at the time when the damage occurs,** unless the person claimed to be liable can show that the product was marketed in that country without his consent, in which case the applicable law shall be that of the country in which the person claimed to be liable is habitually resident.

~~*Article 5 – Unfair competition*~~ *Article 7 – Unfair commercial practices*

1. The law applicable to a non-contractual obligation arising out of an ~~act of unfair competition~~ **unfair commercial practice** shall be **designated by Article 5(1). The country where the damage occurs or threatens to occur shall be** the country where competitive relations or the collective interests of consumers are or are likely to be directly and substantially affected.

2. Where an act of unfair competition affects exclusively the interests of a specific competitor, Article 3 5(2) and (3) shall **also** apply.

~~*Article 6 - Violations of privacy and rights relating to the personality*~~

~~1. The law applicable to a non-contractual obligation arising out of a violation of privacy or rights relating to the personality shall be the law of the forum where the application of the law designated by Article 3 would be contrary to the fundamental principles of the forum as regards freedom of expression and information.~~

~~2. The law applicable to the right of reply or equivalent measures shall be the law of the country in which the broadcaster or publisher has its habitual residence.~~

~~*Article 7 - Violation of the environment*~~ *Article 8 – Environmental damage*

The law applicable to a non-contractual obligation arising out of ~~a violation of the environment~~ **environmental damage or damage sustained by persons or** property as a result of such damage shall be the law determined by the application of Article 3̶5(1), unless the person sustaining damage prefers to base his claim on the law of the country in which the event giving rise to the damage occurred.

Article 8̶9 – Infringement of intellectual property rights

1. The law applicable to a non-contractual obligation arising from an infringement of a̶ **an** intellectual property right shall be the law of the country for which protection is sought.

2. In the case of a non-contractual obligation arising from an infringement of a unitary Community industrial property right, the relevant Community instrument shall apply. For any question that is not governed by that instrument, the applicable law shall be the law of the Member State in which the act of infringement is committed.

3. Notwithstanding Sections 1, 2 and 4, this Article shall apply to all non-contractual obligations arising from an infringement of an intellectual property right.

[16]   SECTION 2
RULES APPLICABLE TO NON-CONTRACTUAL OBLIGATIONS ARISING OUT OF AN ACT
OTHER THAN A TORT OR DELICT

Article 9 – Determination of the applicable law

SECTION 4
SPECIAL RULES APPLICABLE TO NON-CONTRACTUAL OBLIGATIONS ARISING OUT OF
UNJUST ENRICHMENT AND NEGOTIORUM GESTIO

Article 10 – Unjust enrichment

1. If a non-contractual obligation arising out of a̶n̶ a̶c̶t̶ o̶t̶h̶e̶r̶ t̶h̶a̶n̶ a̶ t̶o̶r̶t̶ o̶r̶ d̶e̶l̶i̶c̶t̶ **unjust enrichment, including payment of amounts wrongly received,** concerns a relationship previously existing between the parties, such as a contract **or a tort or delict to which section 2 or 3 applies, which is** closely connected with the non-contractual obligation, it shall be governed by the law that governs that relationship.

2. W̶i̶t̶h̶o̶u̶t̶ p̶r̶e̶j̶u̶d̶i̶c̶e̶ t̶o̶ **Where the applicable law cannot be determined on the basis of** paragraph 1,̶ **and** the parties have their habitual residence in the same country w̶h̶e̶n̶ t̶h̶e̶ e̶v̶e̶n̶t̶ g̶i̶v̶i̶n̶g̶ r̶i̶s̶e̶ t̶o̶ t̶h̶e̶ d̶a̶m̶a̶g̶e̶ o̶c̶c̶u̶r̶s̶ **when the event giving rise to unjust enrichment occurs**, the law applicable to the non-contractual obligation shall be the law of that country.

3. W̶i̶t̶h̶o̶u̶t̶ p̶r̶e̶j̶u̶d̶i̶c̶e̶ t̶o̶ **Where the applicable law cannot be determined on the basis of** paragraphs 1 and 2, a non-contractual obligation arising out of unjust

enrichment shall be governed by the law of the country in which ~~the enrichment takes place~~ **the event giving rise to unjust enrichment substantially occurs**.

~~4. Without prejudice to paragraphs 1 and 2, the law applicable to a non-contractual obligation arising out of actions performed without due authority in connection with the affairs of another person shall be the law of the country in which the beneficiary has his habitual residence at the time of the unauthorised action. However, where a non-contractual obligation arising out of actions performed without due authority in connection with the affairs of another person relates to the physical protection of a person or of specific tangible property, the law applicable shall be the law of the country in which the beneficiary or property was situated at the time of the unauthorised action.~~

~~5. Notwithstanding paragraphs 1, 2, 3 and 4, where it is clear from all the circumstances of the case that the non-contractual obligation is manifestly more closely connected with another country, the law of that other country shall apply.~~

~~6. Notwithstanding the present Article, all non-contractual obligations in the field of intellectual property shall be governed by Article 8.~~

4. Where it is clear from all the circumstances of the case that the non-contractual obligation arising out of unjust enrichment is manifestly more closely connected with a country other than the one indicated by paragraphs 1, 2 or 3, the law of that other country shall apply.

[17] *Article 11 – Negotiorum gestio*

1. If a non-contractual obligation arising out of an action or actions performed without due authority in connection with the affairs of another person concerns a relationship previously existing between the parties, such as a contract or a tort or delict to which section 2 or 3 applies, which is closely connected with that non-contractual obligation, it shall be governed by the law that governs that relationship.

2. Where the applicable law cannot be determined on the basis of paragraph 1 and the parties have their habitual residence in the same country when the event giving rise to the loss or damage occurs, the applicable law shall be the law of that country.

3. Where the applicable law cannot be determined on the basis of paragraphs 1 and 2, the applicable law shall be the law of the country in which the action took place.

4. Where it is clear from all the circumstances of the case that the non-contractual obligation is manifestly more closely connected with a country other than the one indicated by paragraphs 1, 2 or 3, the law of that other country shall apply.

~~**Section 3**~~

~~**Common rules applicable to non-contractual obligations arising out of a tort or delict and out of an act other than a tort or delict**~~

~~Article 10 – Freedom of choice~~

~~1. The parties may agree, by an agreement entered into after their dispute arose, to submit non-contractual obligations other than the obligations to which Article 8 applies to the law of their choice. The choice must be expressed or demonstrated with reasonable certainty by the circumstances of the case. It may not affect the rights of third parties.~~

~~2. If all the other elements of the situation at the time when the loss is sustained are located in a country other than the country whose law has been chosen, the choice of the parties shall be without prejudice to the application of rules of the law of that country which cannot be derogated from by contract.~~

~~3. The parties' choice of the applicable law shall not debar the application of provisions of Community law where the other elements of the situation were located in one of the Member States of the European Community at the time when the loss was sustained.~~

SECTION 5
COMMON RULES

Article ~~11~~12 – Scope of the law applicable to non-contractual obligations

The law applicable to non-contractual obligations under Articles ~~3~~4 to ~~10~~11 of this Regulation shall govern in particular:

[18] a) the conditions and extent of liability, including the determination of persons who are liable for acts performed by them;
b) the grounds for exemption from liability, any limitation of liability and any division of liability;
c) the existence and kinds of injury or damage for which compensation may be due;
d) within the limits of its powers, the measures which a court has power to take under its procedural law to prevent or terminate injury or damage or to ensure the provision of compensation;
e) the assessment of the damage in so far as prescribed by law;
f) the question whether a right to compensation may be assigned or inherited;
g) persons entitled to compensation for damage sustained personally;
h) liability for the acts of another person;
i) the manners in which an obligation may be extinguished and rules of prescription and limitation, including rules relating to the commencement of a period of prescription or limitation and the interruption and suspension of the period.

Article ~~12~~13 – Overriding mandatory rules

~~2~~1. Nothing in this Regulation shall restrict the application of the rules of the law of the forum in a situation where they are mandatory irrespective of the law otherwise applicable to the non-contractual obligation.

~~1.~~2. Where the law of a specific country is applicable by virtue of this Regulation, effect may be given to the mandatory rules of another country with which the situation is closely connected, if and in so far as, under the law of the latter country, those rules must be applied whatever the law applicable to the non-contractual obligation. In considering whether to give effect to these mandatory rules, regard shall be had to their nature and purpose and to the consequences of their application or non-application.

Article ~~13~~14 – Rules of safety and conduct

Whatever may be the applicable law, in determining liability account shall be taken**, as a matter of fact, and in so far as is appropriate,** of the rules of safety and conduct which were in force at the place and time of the event giving rise to the damage.

Article ~~14~~15 – Direct action against the insurer of the person liable

~~The right of~~ Persons who have suffered damage ~~to~~ **may** take direct action against the insurer of the person claimed to be liable ~~shall be governed by~~ **where such actions are provided for either by** the law applicable to the non-contractual obligation ~~unless the person who has~~ [19] ~~suffered damage prefers to base his claims on~~ **or by** the law applicable to the insurance contract.

Article ~~15~~16 – Statutory subrogation ~~and multiple liability~~

~~1. Where a person ('the creditor') has a non-contractual claim upon another ('the debtor'), and a third person has a duty to satisfy the creditor, or has in fact satisfied the creditor in discharge of that duty, the law which governs the third person's duty to satisfy the creditor shall determine whether the third person is entitled to exercise against the debtor the rights which the creditor had against the debtor under the law governing their relationship in whole or in part.~~

~~2. The same rule shall apply where several persons are subject to the same claim and one of them has satisfied the creditor.~~

Where a third person, for example an insurer, has a duty to satisfy a creditor in respect of a non-contractual obligation, the right of that third person to take action against the person owing the non-contractual obligation shall be governed by the law applicable to the duty to satisfy the third person's claim, for example under an insurance contract.

Article ~~16~~17 – Multiple liability

Where a person has a claim upon several debtors who are jointly liable and one of those debtors has already satisfied the creditor, the right of that debtor to take action against the other debtors shall be governed by the law applicable to that debtor's duty to satisfy the creditor.

Article 18 – Formal validity

A unilateral act intended to have legal effect and relating to a non-contractual obligation is formally valid if it satisfies the formal requirements of the law which governs the non-contractual obligation in question or the law of the country in which this act is done.

Article ~~17~~19 – Evidence

1. The law governing a non-contractual obligation under this Regulation applies to the extent that, in matters of non-contractual obligations, it contains rules which raise presumptions of law or determine the burden of proof.

2. Acts intended to have legal effect may be proved by any mode of proof recognised by the law of the forum or by any of the laws referred to in Article ~~16~~18 under which that act is formally valid, provided that such mode of proof can be administered by the forum.

[20]

CHAPTER III – OTHER PROVISIONS

~~Article18 - Assimilation to the territory of a State~~

~~For the purposes of this Regulation, the following shall be treated as being the territory of a State:~~

~~a) installations and other facilities for the exploration and exploitation of natural resources in, on or below the part of the seabed situated outside the State's territorial waters if the State, under international law, enjoys sovereign rights to explore and exploit natural resources there;~~

~~b) a ship on the high seas which is registered in the State or bears lettres de mer or a comparable document issued by it or on its behalf, or which, not being registered or bearing lettres de mer or a comparable document, is owned by a national of the State;~~

~~c) an aircraft in the airspace, which is registered in or on behalf of the State or entered in its register of nationality, or which, not being registered or entered in the register of nationality, is owned by a national of the State.~~

Article ~~19~~20 – *Assimilation to habitual residence*

1. For companies or firms and other bodies or incorporate or unincorporate, the principal place of business shall be considered to be the habitual residence. However, where the event giving rise to the damage occurs or the damage arises in the course of operation of a subsidiary, a branch or any other establishment, the place of business shall take the place of the habitual residence.

2. Where the event giving rise to the damage occurs or the damage arises in the course of the business activity of a natural person, that natural person's **principal** place of business shall take the place of the habitual residence.

~~3. For the purpose of Article 6(2), the place where the broadcaster is established within the meaning of the directive 89/552/EEC, as amended by the directive 97/36/EC, shall take the place of the habitual residence.~~

Article ~~20~~21 – *Exclusion of renvoi*

The application of the law of any country specified by this Regulation means the application of the rules of law in force in that country other than its rules of private international law.

Article ~~21~~22 – *States with more than one legal system*

1. Where a State comprises several territorial units, each of which has its own rules of law in respect of non-contractual obligations, each territorial unit shall be considered as a country for the purposes of identifying the law applicable under this Regulation.

[21] 2. A State within which different territorial units have their own rules of law in respect of non-contractual obligations shall not be bound to apply this Regulation to conflicts solely between the laws of such units.

Article ~~22~~23 – *Public policy of the forum*

The application of a rule of the law of any country specified by this Regulation may be refused only if such application is manifestly incompatible with the public policy (*'ordre public'*) of the forum. **In particular, the application under this Regulation of a law that would have the effect of causing non-compensatory damages to be awarded that would be excessive may be considered incompatible with the public policy of the forum.**

Article ~~23~~24 – *Relationship with ~~other provisions of Community law~~* **international conventions**

~~1. This Regulation shall not prejudice the application of provisions contained in the Treaties establishing the European Communities or in acts of the institutions~~

of the European Communities which: **This Regulation shall not prejudice the application of multilateral international conventions to which the Member States are parties when this Regulation is adopted and which, in relation to particular matters, lay down conflict-of-law rules relating to non-contractual obligations and of which the Commission has been notified in accordance with Article 26.**

‑in relation to particular matters, lay down choice-of-law rules relating to non-contractual obligations; or

‑lay down rules which apply irrespective of the national law governing the non-contractual obligation in question by virtue of this Regulation; or

‑prevent application of a provision or provisions of the law of the forum or of the law designated by this Regulation.

2. This Regulation shall not prejudice the application of Community instruments which, in relation to particular matters and in areas coordinated by such instruments, subject the supply of services or goods to the laws of the Member State where the service-provider is established and, in the area coordinated, allow restrictions on freedom to provide services or goods originating in another Member State only in limited circumstances.

Article 24 ‑ Non-compensatory damages

The application of a provision of the law designated by this Regulation which has the effect of causing non-compensatory damages, such as exemplary or punitive damages, to be awarded shall be contrary to Community public policy.

[22] *Article 25 ‑ Relationship with existing international conventions*

This Regulation shall not prejudice the application of international conventions to which the Member States are parties when this Regulation is adopted and which, in relation to particular matters, lay down conflict-of-law rules relating to non-contractual obligations.

2. However, where, at the time of conclusion of the contract, all the material aspects of the situation are located in one or more Member States, this Regulation shall take precedence over the following Conventions:

– the Hague Convention of 4 May 1971 on the Law Applicable to Traffic Accidents;

–the Hague Convention of 2 October 1973 on the Law Applicable to Products Liability.

CHAPTER IV – FINAL PROVISIONS

Article ~~26~~25 – List of conventions referred to in Article ~~25~~24

1. The Member States shall notify the Commission, no later than ~~30 June 2004~~ ..., of the list of conventions referred to in Article ~~25~~24. After that date, the Member States shall notify the Commission of all denunciations of such conventions.

2. The Commission shall publish the list of conventions referred to in paragraph 1 in the *Official Journal of the European Union* within six months of receiving ~~the full~~ **that** list.

Article ~~27~~26 – Implementation report

Not later than five years after this Regulation enters into force, the Commission shall submit to the European Parliament, the Council and the European Economic and Social Committee a report on its application. If necessary, this report shall be accompanied by proposals to adapt the Regulation.

In making its report, the Commission shall pay particular attention to the effects of the way in which foreign law is treated in the courts of the Member States. If necessary, the report shall include recommendations as to the desirability of a common approach to the application of foreign law.

The report shall consider whether Community legislation specifically dealing with the law applicable to traffic accidents ought to be proposed.

Article 27 – Entry into force and application in time

This Regulation shall enter into force on ~~1 January 2005~~....

It shall apply to non-contractual obligations arising out of acts occurring after its entry into force.

[23] This Regulation shall be binding in its entirety and directly applicable in all Member States in accordance with the Treaty establishing the European Community.

Done at Brussels,

For the European Parliament   *For the Council*

The President   *The President*

Appendix 4

Statement of Reasons Accompanying Council's Common Position
[Official Journal C289, 28.11.2006, P.0068–0083]

COMMON POSITION (EC) No 22/2006
adopted by the Council on 25 September 2006
with a view to adopting Regulation (EC) No . . ./. . . of the European
Parliament and of the Council of . . . on the law applicable to
non-contractual obligations (ROME II)
(2006/C 289 E/04)

[The text of the Council's Common Position (OJ C289E, 68–75) has been omitted]

[OJ C289E, 75]

STATEMENT OF THE COUNCIL'S REASONS

I. INTRODUCTION

The Council reached general agreement on the text of the draft Regulation on the law applicable to non-contractual obligations on 1–2 June 2006. This led to the adoption of a common position on 25 September 2006 under the co-decision procedure.

The Council took its decision by qualified majority. The delegations of Estonia and Latvia voted against due to their reservations on Article 9 on industrial action and its implications for the freedom to provide services. [1]

When adopting its position, the Council took into account the opinion of the European Parliament delivered at first reading on 6 July 2005. [2]

The purpose of this proposal is to lay down a uniform set of rules of law applicable to non-contractual obligations, irrespective of the country of the court in which an action is brought. This should increase certainty as to the applicable law and improve the predictability of legal disputes and the free movement of judgements.

---

[1] See ref to I/A-item note 12219/2006 CODEC 838 JUSTCIV 181;
[2] See 10812/05 CODEC 590 JUSTCIV 132;

II. ANALYSIS OF THE COMMON POSITION

1. General

The Council's common position follows largely the same line as the Commission's original proposal as modified by the amended proposal submitted to the Council on 22 February 2006.[1]

The principal changes made to the text are as follows:

1. In comparison with the original Commission proposal the scope of the instrument has been clarified and further elaborated. Civil and commercial matters do not cover liability of the State for acts and omissions in the exercise of state authority ('acta iure imperii'). An additional exclusion has been added to Article 1(2)(g) to reflect the discussions and the final compromise on violations of privacy and rights relating to personality.

2. The Regulation follows the same logic as the original Commission proposal in the sense that the Regulation sets out a general rule for the law applicable to a tort/delict. The general rule consists of applying the law of the country where damage occurred. This has not changed as compared to the original Commission proposal. Article 4(2) sets out an exception from the general principle, creating a special connection where the parties have their habitual residence in the same country. Article 4(3) should be understood as an 'escape clause' from Articles 4(1) and 4(2), where it is clear from all the circumstances of the case that the tort/delict is manifestly more closely connected with another country.

As a matter of principle, the general rule should be applicable to all non-contractual obligations covered by the Regulation. Only in certain limited, duly justified circumstances should the general rule be derogated from and special rules applied. In accordance with the conditions specified in Article 14 the parties may agree to submit non-contractual obligations to the law of their choice.

3. In comparison with the original Commission proposal, the scope of the special rules has been further clarified in order to facilitate their practical application. The Regulation currently contains special rules in matters of product liability, unfair competition, environmental damage, infringements of intellectual property and industrial action.

4. Negotiations over violations of privacy and rights relating to personality caused difficulties to many delegations. The Council examined this issue on numerous occasions and carefully considered all options on the negotiating table, including the proposal by the European Parliament.

[OJ C289E, 77]

Nevertheless, as a final compromise and in an attempt to reconcile the conflicting interests, the Council decided to delete the special rule on violations of privacy

---

[1] See 6622/06 JUSTCIV 32 CODEC 171;

and rights relating to personality at this stage. As indicated above, such matters are currently excluded from the scope of the Regulation by Article 1(2)(g).

However, this has to be read together with Article 30. The review clause, proposed by the European Parliament and currently contained in Article 30, makes provision for a report to be submitted by the Commission at the latest four years after the date of entry into force of the Regulation. The report should consider in particular non-contractual obligations arising out of violations of privacy and rights relating to personality, including defamation.

5. Differently from the original Commission proposal, the Regulation now also contains a rule on industrial action in line with the proposal of the European Parliament. With the aim of balancing the interests of workers and employers, this rule consists of applying the law of the country where the industrial action was taken. However, this provision caused such difficulties to two delegations that they voted against the common position.

6. The original proposal of the Commission contained one provision for non-contractual obligations arising out of acts other than torts/delicts. The Regulation now includes a specific chapter with separate provisions on unjust enrichment, *negotiorum gestio* and *culpa in contrahendo*.

7. The Articles on mandatory provisions, relationship with other Community law provisions and relationship with existing international conventions have further been simplified.

8. The Regulation now contains, as requested by the European Parliament, a review clause, which obliges the Commission to submit to the European Parliament, the Council and the European Economic and Social Committee a report on the application of the Regulation. In particular, the report shall consider non-contractual obligations arising out of traffic accidents and out of violations of privacy and rights relating to personality, including defamation.

Other amendments are of a more formal nature and have been made to render the text easier to read.

After revision by Legal/Linguistic Experts, the text and the recitals have been re-numbered. A table in the Annex sets out the respective numbers as set out in the common position and as they were indicated in the original proposal.

2. Parliament's amendments

The Council has accepted many of European Parliament's amendments. In some cases, however, the discussions in the Council and the revision of the text by Legal/Linguistic Experts showed the need for certain technical clarifications. In order to ensure correspondence to the provisions of the Regulation, the recitals have been adapted and updated.

The changes made to Articles 1, 2, 4, 9, 10, 11, 12, 28 and 30 require the inclusion of additional recitals.

Recitals 1–5 have been updated in order to take account of the latest developments at political level. Accordingly, the reference to the 1998 Action Plan has been replaced by guidelines contained in the Hague Programme adopted by the European Council in 2004.

a) Amendments accepted in their entirety

Amendments 12, 17, 21, 22, 35, 37, 39, 40, 45, 51, 52 and the oral amendments can be accepted as presented by the European Parliament since they contribute either to the clarity and consistency of the instrument or to questions of detail.

b) Amendments accepted in substance

Amendments 2, 15, 18, 19, 20, 23, 24, 28, 31, 34, 38, 45, 54 can be accepted in substance subject to re-drafting.

[OJ C289E, 78]

Amendment 2 is covered by current recitals (29) and (31).

The substance of amendment 15 is taken over by recital (24).

The changes proposed by amendment 18 are reflected in substance in Articles 2 and 1(1).

Amendments 19 and 20 are included in the text of Articles 1(2) b and 1(2) d. However, the drafting has been simplified, in particular due to the inclusion of Article 2.

Amendment 23 is accepted in substance. However, the Council considers that in view of the changes made to recital (9) and Article 1(1) this amendment is redundant.

The Council consider that the changes proposed by amendment 24 are covered in substance by the changes made to Articles 16, 26 and 27, as well as recital (31).

The Council can accept the principle of amendments 28 and 34, which would change the structure and the title of the sections. The Council considers that this is reflected in the current structure of the Regulation, which is divided into, Chapter I — Scope, Chapter II — Torts/delicts, Chapter III — Unjust enrichment, negotiorum gestio and culpa in contrahendo, Chapter IV — Freedom of choice and Chapter V — Common provisions, and would serve the same purpose.

Amendment 31 introduces a new provision on industrial action. This is in line with the negotiations in the Council. However, the substance of the rule has been further elaborated in Article 9 and by recitals (24) and (25).

The substance of amendment 38 is taken over by Article 14. However, the Council has tried to simplify the wording and render it more flexible.

The substance of amendment 46 is taken over by Article 18.

c) Amendments accepted in part

Amendment 3, 14, 25, 26, 36, 44, 53 and 54 can be accepted in part.

Amendment 3 is only partly acceptable since the recital relates to Article 4 and amendment 26 on Article 4 is not fully accepted. The first sentence of the amendment is reflected in substance in the current text of recitals (13) and (14). The last part of the amendment is reflected in the current text of recital (28).

Amendment 14 proposes, firstly, to add the words 'in so far as appropriate' so as to add emphasis to the discretion of the court and, secondly, to exclude this possibility in matters of violations of privacy and unfair competition. While the Council can accept the first part of the amendment, matters of violations of privacy have been excluded from the scope, and the Council sees no justification for making an exception for cases of unfair competition.

Amendment 25 is acceptable in principle. However, the conditions for expressing ex ante choice should in view of the Council be laid down in clear and unequivocal terms.

Amendment 26 relates to the general rule contained in Article 4.

With regard to Article 4(1) the Council can accept the changes proposed.

On the other hand, the Council cannot accept the changes to paragraph 2. Paragraph 2 brings in a specific rule on traffic accidents which would subject the non-contractual obligation and the amount of damages to two different laws. As the Commission has stated in its revised proposal [1] this solution diverges from the law in force in the Member States and cannot therefore be adopted without prior in-depth analysis. It is accordingly proposed that the question be considered in detail in the report foreseen by Article 30.

[OJ C289E, 79]

As to Article 4(3), it should be seen as an escape clause from Articles 4(1) and (2), where it is clear from all the circumstances of the case that the tort/delict is manifestly more closely connected with another country. In the light of this, the Council sees no need for listing specific factors.

Amendment 36 relates to the new Article 10. While in principle the changes proposed are acceptable, the Council considers that the law of the country in which enrichment took place is a more appropriate connecting factor in case the applicable law cannot be determined on the basis of Article 10(1) or (2).

The first part of amendment 44 is acceptable to the Council. However, in the course of the negotiations it was agreed to delete paragraph (2) that would create fundamental problems to certain Member States and therefore the Council cannot accept this part of the amendment.

Amendment 53 is accepted in part. The Council considers that it would be more appropriate to have the Regulation take automatically precedence over conventions concluded exclusively between two or more of the Member States insofar as such conventions concern matters governed by the Regulation. The amendment proposed to Article 28(3) is not accepted since the Hague Convention provides for a specific regime on traffic accidents and many of the Member States that are contracting parties to the Convention expressed their wish to preserve this regime. In this context, regard should be had to the review clause in Article 30, which makes a specific reference to traffic accidents.

---

[1] See 6622/06 JUSTCIV 32 CODEC 171;

The Council welcomes the review clause as proposed by amendment 54. However, the Council suggests that a more generic review clause is more appropriate to ensure effective evaluation in the framework of the existing competencies (see Article 30).

d) Amendments rejected

Amendments 1, 4, 5, 6, 8, 10, 11, 13, 16, 27, 29, 32, 33, 41, 42, 43, 47, 49, 50, 56 and 57 are rejected.

Amendment 1 refers to the Rome I Regulation. However, until the Regulation is adopted, it is more appropriate to refer to the existing 1980 Rome I Convention on the law applicable to contractual obligations.

Amendment 4 relates to the changes proposed to the general rule (amendment 26). Since amendment 26 was rejected in part, the corresponding changes to the recital would have to be rejected.

In view of the changes made to the scope of the Regulation, the Council sees no need for amendment 5.

Amendment 6, 8, 11 and 13 would adapt the recitals to reflect the deletion of several special rules from the Regulation as proposed by amendments 27 (product liability), 29 (unfair competition and acts restricting free competition) and 33 (violations of the environment). The Council cannot accept the deletion of these special rules, therefore the corresponding amendments to the recitals would have to be rejected as well. However, the Council has made an effort to clearly define the scope of these special rules in order to facilitate their practical application.

Amendments 10 and 56 would have to be rejected since non-contractual obligations arising out of violations of privacy and rights relating to personality, including defamation, have been excluded from the scope of the Regulation

Amendment 16 is not acceptable to the Council, since the Council rejects amendment 42 to which this amendment corresponds.

Amendment 27 would abolish the special rule on product liability. The Council considers that the application of the general rules in cases of product liability would not allow foreseeing the applicable law with reasonable certainty. Creation of a cascade system of connecting factors, together with a foreseeability clause, appears to be a balanced solution in view of this objective.

[OJ C289E, 80]

Amendment 29 proposes to delete the specific rule on unfair competition. The Council cannot accept that. The rule in Article 6 is not an exception to the general rule contained in Article 4(1) but rather clarifies it in order to determine where the damage arises. In matters of unfair competition, the rule should protect competitors, consumers and the general public and ensure that the market economy functions properly. The connection to the place where the competitive relations or the collective interests of consumers are affected, or in case of restrictions of competition, the country where the restriction has or is likely to have effect, generally satisfy these objectives. The non-contractual obligations arising out of restrictions of competition in Article 6(3) should cover infringements of both Community and national competition law.

Amendment 32 is related to amendment 26 which is rejected by the Council to the extent it relates to traffic accidents. For the same reasons as indicated above, this amendment is rejected.

The Council cannot accept the deletion of the special rule for environmental damage as proposed by amendment 33. The proposed rule reflects the 'polluter pays' principle promoted by the Community and already applied in several Member States.

The Council cannot accept amendment 41 since it would appear to be in contradiction with the changes proposed by amendment 40 which the Council accepts.

Amendments 42 and 43 address the question of the application of foreign law by the court. The Council rejects these amendments since this question should be tackled in a different context.

Since amendment 22 was accepted, amendment 47 is redundant in the view of the Council.

The Council considers that the clarification contained in Article 23(2) is sufficient for the purposes of natural persons acting in the course of their business activities. Thus, amendment 49 is rejected.

Amendment 50 aims at clarifying the concept of public policy. It would be difficult for the time being to lay down common criteria and reference instruments for the purposes of defining public policy. For these reasons amendment 50 is rejected.

Amendment 57 relates to Article 6 of the original Commission proposal. The Council examined this issue on numerous occasions and carefully considered all options on the negotiating table, including the solution proposed by the European Parliament. However, as a final compromise and in an attempt to reconcile the conflicting interests, the Council proposes to delete the special rule on violations of privacy and rights relating to personality at this stage. Accordingly amendment 57 has to be rejected. Instead the Regulation provides in Article 1(2)(g) for an exclusion from the scope.

However, this should be read together with Article 30. The review clause contained in Article 30 makes provision for a report to be submitted by the Commission at the latest four years after the date of entry into force of the Regulation. The report shall consider in particular non-contractual obligations arising out of violations of privacy and rights relating to personality, including defamation.

III. Conclusion

The Council considers that the text of the common position on Regulation on the law applicable to non-contractual obligations creates a balanced system of conflict-of-law rules in the field of noncontractual obligations and achieves the desired uniformity of rules of applicable law. Furthermore, the common position is in broad terms in line with the original proposal of the Commission and the opinion of the European Parliament.

[OJ C289E, 81]

ANNEX
TABLE OF CORRESPONDENCE

The original Commission proposal	The Council's common position
Recital (1)	Recital (1)
new	Recital (2)
Recital (2)	deleted
Recital (3)	Recital (3)
new	Recital (4)
new	Recital (5)
Recital (4)	Recital (6)
Recital (5)	Recital (7)
new	Recital (8)
new	Recital (9)
new	Recital (10)
new	Recital (11)
Recital (6)	Recital (12)
Recital (7)	Recital (13)
Recital (8)	Recital (14)
new	Recital (15)
new	Recital (16)
Recital (9)	Recital (17)
Recital (10)	Recital (18)
Recital (11)	Recital (19)
new	Recital (20)
new	Recital (21)

The original Commission proposal	The Council's common position
Recital (12)	deleted
Recital (13)	Recital (22)
Recital (14)	Recital (23)
new	Recital (24)
new	Recital (25)
Recital (15)	Recital (26)
new	Recital (27)
Recital (16)	Recital (28)
Recital (17)	Recital (29)
Recital (18)	Recital (30)
Recital (19)	Recital (31)
Recital (20)	Recital (32)
new	Recital (33)
Recital (21)	Recital (34)
Recital (22)	Recital (35)
Recital (23)	Recital (36)
Article 1	Article 1
new	Article 2
Article 2	Article 3
Article 3	Article 4
Article 4	Article 5
Article 5	Article 6
Article 6	deleted
Article 7	Article 7
Article 8	Article 8
new	Article 9
Article 9(1)	Article 12

The original Commission proposal	The Council's common position
Article 9(2)	Article 10(2), 11(2), 12(2)b
Article 9(3)	Article 10
Article 9(4)	Article 11
Article 9(5)	Article 10(4), 11(4), 12(2)c
Article 9(6)	Article 13
Article 10	Article 14
Article 11	Article 15
Article 12	Article 16
Article 13	Article 17
Article 14	Article 18
Article 15(1)	Article 19
Article 15(2)	Article 20
Article 16	Article 21
Article 17	Article 22
Article 18	deleted
Article 19	Article 23
Article 20	Article 24
Article 21	Article 25
Article 22	Article 26
Article 23	Article 27
Article 24	deleted
Article 25	Article 28
Article 26	Article 29
new	Article 30
Article 27 second section	Article 31
Article 27 first and third sections	Article 32

Appendix 5

Chronology

Date	Document/ OJ reference	Event	Ref
8 September 1967		Letter from the Ambassador Joseph van der Meulen, Permanent Representative of Belgium to the EEC, regarding the proposed unification of the conflict of laws rules within the Community	**1.45**
27 September 1968	OJ L299, 32 [31.12.1972]	Signature of Brussels Convention on jurisdiction and the enforcement of judgments in civil and commercial matters	
26–28 February 1969		First meeting of the group of experts appointed to consider the Benelux proposal	**1.46**
20–22 October 1969		Second meeting of group of experts recommends giving priority to certain areas, including contractual and non-contractual obligations	**1.48**
15 January 1970		COREPER mandates group of experts to continue work, giving priority to the areas suggested	**1.48**
2–3 February 1970		Group of experts reconvenes, chaired by Professor Jenard. Professor Giuliano (Milan), Professor Lagarde (Paris), and Mr Th van Sasse van Ysselt (Netherlands Ministry of Justice) appointed as rapporteurs for contractual/non-contractual obligations project[1]	**1.48**
21–23 June 1972	Commission XIV/398/72	Group of experts finalizes preliminary draft convention on the law applicable to contractual and non-contractual obligations	**1.48**

---

[1] For a list of the meetings of the group of experts between 1970 and 1972, see the Report of Professors M Giuliano and P Lagarde (OJ C282, 6 [31.10.1980], footnote 8) (**Giuliano & Lagarde Report**). The rapporteurs also met from 1–4 June 1970.

Date	Document/ OJ reference	Event	Ref
27–28 September 1972	Commission XIV/408/72	Meeting of rapporteurs to finalize reports on preliminary draft convention on the law applicable to contractual and non-contractual obligations. Draft convention and reports submitted to COREPER.	
1 January 1973		UK, Ireland, and Denmark join EEC	
August 1974		English and Scottish Law Commissions issue joint consultative document on the draft convention	
22–23 September 1975		Expanded group of experts resumes work on draft convention[2]	
6–10 March 1978		Group of experts decides to limit the proposed convention to contractual negotiations, leaving the subject of non-conventions to a later stage	1.50
17 March 1980	OJ L94, 39 [11.4.1980]	Commission opinion on the draft convention on the law applicable to contractual obligations	
21–25 April 1980		Ad hoc working party finalizes text of convention on law applicable to contractual obligations	
19 June 1980	OJ L266, 1 [9.10.1980]	(Rome) Convention on the law applicable to contractual obligations opened for signature	1.50
1 January 1993	OJ C191, 1 [29.7.1992]	Treaty on European Union (Maastricht) comes into force promoting wider cooperation between Member States in the area of judicial cooperation in civil matters	1.51
14 October 1996	OJ C319, 1 [26.10.1996]	Council resolution laying down priorities for cooperation in the field of justice and home affairs identifies a convention on the law applicable to extra-contractual obligations as a priority area	1.51

[2] For a list of the meetings of the group of experts between 1975 and 1979, see the Giuliano & Lagarde Report, ibid, 7, footnote 10.

Date	Document/ OJ reference	Event	Ref
2 October 1997	OJ C340, 1 [10.11.1997]	Treaty of Amsterdam signed, including in Title IV new Community competence in the field of judicial cooperation in civil matters. Art 65(d) specifically refers to measures 'promoting the compatibility of the rules applicable in the Member States concerning the conflict of laws'.	**1.52**
16 February 1998	For questions and Member State responses, see Council document 12544/98	Commission questionnaire on draft convention on law applicable to non-contractual obligations sent to Member States	**1.53**
15 July 1998	Council document 9755/98	Austrian Presidency presents a document on the principal questions to be addressed by a convention on the law applicable to non-contractual obligations	**1.53**
25–27 September 1998		GEDIP adopts proposal for a European convention on the law applicable to non-contractual obligations[3]	**1.54**
3 October 1998	OJ C19, 1 [23.1.1999]	JHA Council adopts (Vienna) action plan of Council and Commission on how best to implement the provisions of the Treaty of Amsterdam on an area of freedom, security and justice requiring the drawing up of a legal instrument on the law applicable to non-contractual obligations within two years of entry into force of the Treaty of Amsterdam	**1.56**
November 1998		First meeting of the Council working group on the draft convention	
1 May 1999		Treaty of Amsterdam comes into force	

[3] (1998) 45 Neth Int L Rev 465.

Date	Document/ OJ reference	Event	Ref
15–16 October 1999		European Council meeting in Tampere endorses principle of mutual recognition as the cornerstone of judicial cooperation in civil matters	**1.57**
9 December 1999	Council document 11892/99	State of work draft of proposed convention on law applicable to non-contractual obligations produced by Council working group	**1.58**
8 June 2000	OJ L178, 1 [17.7.2000]		
10 November 2000	OJ C12, 1 [15.1.2001]	Council adopts joint Commission and Council programme of measures for the implementation of the principle of mutual recognition of decisions in civil and commercial matters	**1.58**
18 January 2001		Unpublished Commission Green Paper on the law applicable to non-contractual obligations (in French)	**1.61**
3 May 2002		Commission publishes preliminary draft proposal for a Council Regulation on the law applicable to non-contractual obligations and launches public consultation	**1.64**
7 January 2003		Public hearing on the proposed Rome II Regulation (Brussels)	**1.67**
1 February 2003	OJ C80, 1 [10.3.2001], Art. 2.4	Treaty of Nice comes into force introducing qualified majority voting by the co-decision procedure (EC Treaty, Art 251) for measures falling within Art 65 (including those relating to conflict of laws)	**1.68**
22 July 2003	COM (2003) 427 final	Commission proposal for a Regulation of the European Parliament and the Council on the law applicable to non-contractual obligations (Rome II)	**1.69**
20 October 2003	Council document 13903/03	UK opts in to the Rome II proposal	**1.80**

Date	Document/ OJ reference	Event	Ref
28 October 2003	Council document 14119/03	Ireland opts in to the Rome II proposal	**1.80**
5 February 2004	EP document PE 338.502	EP JURI Committee working document on the Rome II proposal (part 1) (rapporteur: Diana Wallis MEP)	
2 March 2004	Council document 7015/04	Opinion of the Council Legal Service on the legal basis for the Rome II proposal	**1.80, 2.94– 2.100**
15 March 2004	EP document PE 338.465	Draft EP JURI Committee provisional report on Rome II proposal (revised 5.4.2004)	
7 April 2004	8th Report of Session 2003– 2004 (HL Paper 66) (2004)	UK House of Lords' European Union Committee publishes report on Rome II proposal	**1.72**
2–3 June 2004	OJ C241, 1 [28.9.2004]	Opinion of the European Economic and Social Committee on the Rome II proposal	**1.78**
5 November 2004	OJ C 53, 1 [3.3.2005]	Council adopts 'Hague Programme' requiring work on the Rome II proposal to be 'actively pursued'	
11 November 2004	EP document PE 349.977v01-00	Further revised draft EP JURI Committee report on the Rome II proposal	
29 March 2005	EP document PE 349.977v02-00	Final draft EP JURI Committee report (first reading)	
15 April 2005	EP document PE 357.649v01-00	Draft opinion of the EP LIBE Committee on the Rome II proposal (rapporteur: Barbara Kudrycka MEP)	
27 June 2005	EP document A6-0211/2005 FINAL	EP JURI Committee report on the Rome II proposal	**1.74**

Date	Document/ OJ reference	Event	Ref
6 July 2005	OJ C157 E, 371 [6.7.2006]	EP adopts first reading position on the Rome II proposal	**1.75**
15 December 2005	COM (2005) 650 final	Commission proposal for a Regulation on the law applicable to contractual obligations (Rome I)	
21 February 2006	COM (2006) 83 final	Commission publishes amended proposal for Rome II Regulation	**1.86**
27–28 April 2006	Council document 8417/06 + ADD1 + ADD2	JHA Council reaches agreement on compromise package for Rome II proposal	**1.87**
1–2 June 2006	Council document 9143/06 + ADD1 + ADD2	Council reaches general political agreement on Rome II proposal	**1.88**
25 September 2006	OJ C289 E, 68 [28.11.2006]	Common Position adopted by the Council on the Rome II proposal (Estonia and Latvia voting against)	**1.88**
27 September 2006	COM (2006) 0566	Commission communication on the Council's Common Position	**1.89**
8 November 2006	EP document PE 378.872v01-00	EP JURI Committee provisional draft recommendation for second reading	
22 December 2006	EP document A6-0481/2006 FINAL	EP JURI Committee recommendation for second reading	**1.90**
18 January 2007	OJ C244E, 194 [18.10.2007]	EP adopts 2nd Reading Position on Rome II proposal	**1.90**
6 March 2007		First 'trilogue' of EP-Council Conciliation Commiteee	
14 March 2007	COM (2007) 0126	Commission opinion on the EP 2nd Reading Position	**1.93**

Date	Document/ OJ reference	Event	Ref
27 March 2007		Second 'trialogue' of EP-Council Conciliation Committee	
19 April 2007	8569/07 COR1 [4.6.2007]	Council rejects EP 2nd Reading Position	
24 April 2007		Third 'trialogue' of EP-Council Conciliation Committee	
15 May 2007	Council document 9713/07 (Presse 111)	EP-Council Conciliation Committee reaches agreement on Rome II Regulation	**1.95**
12 June 2007	EP document PE390.527	Draft report by EP delegation to the Conciliation Committee	
22 June 2007	PE-CONS 3619/07	EP-Council joint text	
28 June 2007	Council document 11313/07	Council approves Rome II Regulation (Estonia and Latvia voting against)	**1.96**
28 June 2007	EP document A6-0267/2007	EP report on joint Conciliation Committee text for Rome II Regulation	
10 July 2007	EP document T6-0317/2007	EP approves Rome II Regulation	**1.96**
11 July 2007	OJ L199, 40 [31.7.2007]	Regulation (EC) No 864/2007 on the law applicable to non-contractual obligations (Rome II) adopted	
17 June 2008	OJ L177, 6 [4.7.2008]	Regulation (EC) No 593/2008 on the law applicable to contractual obligations (Rome I) adopted	
11 January 2009		Rome II Regulation applies	

Appendix 6

Published Materials[1]

HISTORICAL BACKGROUND (THE 1972 DRAFT CONVENTION)

'EEC Preliminary Draft Convention on the Law Applicable to Contractual and Non-Contractual Obligations'; Joint Consultative Document issued by the English and Scottish Law Commissions (August 1974)

I G F Karsten, 'Tort: General Principles'; C G J Morse, 'The Draft Convention and Torts—Special Provisions'; J G Collier, 'The Draft Convention and Restitution or Quasi-Contract', all in K Lipstein (ed), *Harmonisation of Private International Law by the EEC* (London: IALS, 1978)

K H Nadelmann, 'Impression and Unification of Law: The EEC Draft Convention on the Law Applicable to Contractual and Non-Contractual Obligations' (1976) 24 AJCL 1

K Siehr, 'General Report on Non-Contractual Obligations, General Problems and the Final Provisions', pp 42–74 in O Lando, B von Hoffmann and K Siehr (eds), *European Private International Law of Obligations* (1975)

THE COMMISSION'S PRELIMINARY DRAFT PROPOSAL

A Dickinson, 'Cross-Border Torts in EC Courts—A Response to the Proposed "Rome II" Regulation' (2002) 13 EBLR 367

V C Nourissat and E Treppoz, '*Quelques observations sur l'avant project de proposition du règlement du Conseil sur la loi applicable aux obligations non contractuelles (Rome II)*' (2003) 130 *Journal du droit international* 7

---

[1] Sources for the articles listed below include the catalogues of the European Peace Palace Library (<http://www.ppl.nl>) and the European Commission Library Automated System (ECLAS) (<http://ec.europa.eu/eclas/>).

THE COMMISSION PROPOSAL

M Benecke, *'Auf dem Weg zu "Rom II": der Vorschlag für eine Verordnung zur Angleichung des IPR der außertragliche Schuldverhältnisse'* (2003) *Recht der internationalen Wirtschaft* 830

D Busse, *'Internationales Bereicherungsrecht zwischen EGBGB-Reform und "Rom II"'* (2003) 49 *Recht der internationalen Wirtschaft* 406

J M Carruthers and E B Crawford, 'Variations on a Theme of Rome II: Reflections on Proposed Choice of Law Rules for Non-Contractual Obligations' (2005) 9 Edin LR 65 (part 1), 238 (part 2)

A Fuchs, *'Zum Kommisionsvorschlag einer "Rom II'-Verordnung"* (2004) 50 *Recht der internationalen Wirtschaft* 100

Hamburg Group for Private International Law, Comments on the European Commission's Draft Proposal for a Council Regulation on the Law Applicable to Non-Contractual Obligations (Hamburg Group for Private International Law) (2003) *Rabels Zeitschrift für auslandisches und internationales Privatrecht* 1

P Huber and I Bach, *'Die Rome II – VO: Kommissionsentwurf und aktuelle Entwicklungen'* (2005) 25 *Praxis des internationalen Privat- und Vehrfahrensrechts (IPRax)* 73

S Leible and A Engel, *'Der Vorschlag der EG-Kommission für eine Rom-II Verordnung'* (2004) 15 *Europäische Zeitschrift für Wirtschaftsrecht* 7

P Stone, 'The Rome II Proposal on the Law Applicable to Non-Contractual Obligations' [2004] European Legal Forum 213

S C Symeonides, 'Tort Conflicts and Rome II: A View from Across', pp 935–54 in H P Mansel and others (eds), *Festscrift für Erik Jayme* (Munich: Sellier, 2004)

P de Vareilles-Sommières, *'La responsabilité civile dans la proposition de règlement communautaire sur la loi applicable aux obligations non contractuelles (Rome II)'* in A Fuchs, H Muir-Watt, and E Pataut (eds), *Les conflits de lois et le système juridique communautaire* (Paris: Dalloz, 2004)

THE LEGISLATIVE PROCESS

S Bariatti, 'The Future Community Rules in the Framework of the Communitarization of Private International Law' and other papers (see below) in A Malatesta (ed), *The Unification of Choice of Law Rules on Torts and Other Non-Contractual Obligations in Europe* (CEDAM, 2003)

P Beaumont, 'Private International Law of the European Union: Competence Questions Arising from the Proposed Rome II Regulation on Choice of Law in Non-Contractual Obligations' in R Brand (ed) *Private law, private international law & judicial co-operation in the EU-US relationship* (Eagan: Thomson/West, 2005)

F J Garcimartín Alférez, 'The Rome II Regulation: on the way towards a European Private International Law Code' [2007] European Legal Forum I-77

T Petch, 'The Rome II Regulation: An Update' [2006] JIBLR 449 (part 1), 509 (part 2)

W Posch, 'The "Draft Regulation Rome II" in 2004: its Past and Future Perspectives' (2004) 6 Yearbook of Private International Law 129

G Wagner, *'Internationales Deliksrecht, die Arbeiten an der Rom-II Verordnung unter der Europäische Deliktsgerichtsstand'* (2005) 26 *Praxis des internationalen Privat- und Vehrfahrensrechts (IPRax)* 372

A Warshaw, 'Uncertainty from Abroad: Rome II and the Choice of Law for Defamation Claims' (2006) 32 Brooklyn J Int L 269

R Weintraub, 'Rome II and the Tension between Predictability and Flexibility', in H Rasmussen-Bonne, R Freer, and W Lüke (eds), *Balancing of Interests: Liber Amoricum Peter Hay* (Frankfurt: Verlag Recht und Wirtschaft, 2005)

COMMENT

GENERAL

S Corneloup and N Joubert, *Le règlement communautaire 'Rome II' sur la loi applicable aux obligations non contractuelles* (Paris: Litec, 2008)

C Brière, *'Le règlement (CE) no 864/2007 du 11 juillet 2007 sur la loi applicable aux obligations non contractuelles (Rome II)'* (2008) 138 *Journal du droit international* 31

Sir L Collins and others (eds), *Dicey, Morris & Collins: The Conflict of Laws* (14th edn, 2006), 1st supplement (2007), update to ch 34 and paras S35-165 to S35-273

C Fresnedo de Aguirre and D P Fernandez Arroyo, 'A Quick Latin American Look at the Rome II Regulation' (2007) 9 Yearbook of Private International Law 193

C W Fröhlich, *The Private International Law of Non-Contractual Obligations According to the Rome-II Regulation* (Hamburg: Verlag Dr Kovač, 2008)

F Guerchoun and S Piedelièvre, *'Le règlement sur la loi applicable aux obligations non contractuelles ("Rome II")'* (2007) 127 *La gazette du palais /Recueil bimestriel* 3106–30

H Heiss and L Loacker, *'Die Vergemeinschaftung des Kollisionsrechts der außervertraglichen Schuldverhältnisse durch Rom II'* (2007) *Juristische Blätter* 613

P J Kozyris, 'Rome II: Tort Conflicts on the Right Track! A Postscript to Symeon Symeonides' "Missed Opportunity"' (2008) 56 AJCL 471

G Légier, *'Le règlement "Rome II" sur la loi applicable aux obligations non contractuelles'*, *JCP/La Semaine Juridique—Edition Générale*, 21 November 2007, I-207

S Leible and M Lehman, *'Die neue EG-Verordnung über das auf außervertragliche Schuldverhältnisse anzuwendende Recht ('Rom II')'* (2007) 53 *Recht der internationalen Wirtschaft* 721–35

L de Lima Pinheiro, 'Choice of Law on Non-Contractual Obligations between Communitarization and Globalization: a first Assessment of EC Regulation Rome II' (2008) 44 *Rivista di diritto internazionale privato e processuale* 5

J Meeusen, '*Rome II: nieuw Europees conflictenrecht voor niet-contractuele verbintenissen*' (2008) 114 *Revue de droit commercial belge* 471

R Mortensen, 'A Common Law Cocoon: Australia and the Rome II Regulation' (2007) 9 Yearbook of Private International Law 203

Y Nishitani, 'The Rome II Regulation from a Japanese Point of View' (2007) 9 Yearbook of Private International Law 175

H Ofner, '*Die Rom II-Verordnung: neues Internationales Privatrecht für außervertragliche Schuldverhältnisse in der Europäischen Union*' (2008) 49 *Zeitschrift für Rechtsvergleichung, Internationales Privatrecht und Europarecht* 13

P Stone, 'The Rome II Regulation on Choice of Law in Tort' (2007) 4 Ankara LR 95.

S C Symeonides, 'Rome II: A Centrist Critique' (2007) 9 Yearbook of Private International Law 149

S C Symeonides, 'Rome II and Tort Conflicts: A Missed Opportunity' (2008) 56 AJCL 173

Editorial Comment, 'Sometimes it takes thirty years and even more . . .' (2007) 44 Common Market L Rev 1567

B Volders, '*Niet-contractuele verbintenissen en Rome II*' (2008) 114 *Revue de droit commercial belge* 482

F Wagner, '*Die Neue Rom-II Verordnung*' (2008) 28 *Praxis des internationalen Privat- und Vehrfahrensrechts (IPRax)* 1

R Weintraub, 'The Choice of Law Rules of the European Community Regulation on the Law Applicable to Non-Contractual Obligations: Simple and Predictable, Consequences Based, or Neither?' (2008) 43 Texas Int LJ 401

ART 4 (TORTS/DELICTS)

G Hohloch, 'Place of Injury, Habitual Residence, Closer Connections and Substantive Scope—the Basic Principles' (2007) 9 Yearbook of Private International Law 1

A Junker, '*Die Rom II-Verordnung: neues internationales Deliktsrecht auf europäischer Grundlage*' (2007) 60 *Neue Juristische Wochenschrift* 3675

H Koziol and T Thiede, '*Kritische Bemerkungen zum derzeitigen Stand des Entwurfs einer Rom II-Verordnung*' (2007) 106 ZVgiR Wiss 235

K Kreuzer, 'Tort Liability in General' in Malatesta, *Unification*

A Nuyts, '*La règle générale de conflit de lois en matière non contractuelle dans le Règlement Rome II*' (2008) 114 *Revue de droit commercial belge* 489

ART 5 (PRODUCT LIABILITY)

P Huber and Martin Illmer, 'International Product Liability. A Commentary on Article 5 of the Rome II Regulation' (2007) 9 Yearbook of Private International Law 31

T Kadner Graziano, 'The Law Applicable to Product Liability: The Present State of the Law in Europe and Current Proposals for Reform' (2005) 54 ICLQ 475

A Saraville, 'The Law Applicable to Products Liability: Hopping Off the Endless Merry-Go-Round' in Malatesta, *Unification*

ART 6 (UNFAIR COMPETITION/RESTRICTIONS OF COMPETITION)

M Danov, 'Awarding exemplary (or punitive) antitrust damages in EC competition cases with an international element' [2008] ECLR 430.

Christian Handig, *'Rom II-VO: Auswirkungen auf das Internationale Wettbewerbs- und Immaterialgüterrecht'* (2008) 22 *Wirtschaftsrechtliche Blätter* 1

M Hellner, 'Unfair Competition and Acts Restricting Free Competition. A Commentary on Article 6 of the Rome II Regulation' (2007) 9 Yearbook of Private International Law 49

C Honorati, 'The Law Applicable to Unfair Competition' in Malatesta, *Unification*

P Mankowski, *'Das neue Internationale Kartellrecht des Art 6 Abs. 3 der Rom II-Verordnung'* (2008) 54 *Recht der internationalen Wirtschaft* 177

V Pironon, *'L'entrée du droit de la concurrence dans le règlement 'Rome II': bonne ou mauvaise idée?'* (2008) 18 *Europe* 6

C Wadlow, 'Trade secrets and the Rome II Regulation on the law applicable to non-contravtual obligations' [2006] EIPR 309

ART 7 (ENVIRONMENTAL DAMAGE)

L Enneking, 'The common denominator of the *Trafigura* case, foreign direct liability cases and the Rome II Regulation' (2008) 16 Eur Rev Priv L 283.

K Fach Gómez, 'The Law Applicable to Cross-Border Environmental Damage: from the European National Systems to Rome II' (2004) 6 Yearbook of Private International Law 291

T Kadner Graziano, 'The Law Applicable to Cross-Border Damage to the Environment. A Commentary on Article 7 of the Rome II Regulation' (2007) 9 Yearbook of Private International Law 71

F Munari and L Schiano di Pepe, 'Liability for Environmental Torts in Europe' in Malatesta, *Unification*

ART 8 (*INFRINGEMENTS OF INTELLECTUAL PROPERTY RIGHTS*)

J Drexl, 'The Proposed Rome II Regulation: European Choice of Law in the Field of Intellectual Property' in J Drexl and A Kur (eds), *Intellectual Property and Private International Law: Heading for the Future* (2005)

N Boschiero, 'Infringement of Intellectual Property Rights. A Commentary on Article 8 of the Rome II Regulation' (2007) 9 Yearbook of Private International Law 87

G Dinwoodie, 'Conflicts and International Copyright Litigation: The Role of International Norms', in J Basedow, J Drexl, A Kur, and A Metzger (eds), *Intellectual Property in the Conflict of Laws* (Tübingen: Mohr Siebeck, 2005)

C Hahn and O Tell, 'The European Commission's Agenda: The Future "Rome I and Rome II" Regulations', in Basedow, *Intellectual Property*

A Kur, 'Trademark Conflicts on the Internet: Territorality Redefined?', in Basedow, *Intellectual Property*

S Leible, '*Rechtswahl im IPR der außervertraglichen Schuldverhältnisse nach der Rom II-Verordnung*' (2008) 54 *Recht der internationalen Wirtschaft* 257

M Leistner, 'Comments: The Rome II Regulation Proposal and its Relation to the European Country-of-Origin Principle' in J Drexl and A Kur (eds), *Intellectual Property and Private International Law: Heading for the Future* (2005)

A Metzger, 'Community Rights & Conflict of Laws: Community Trademark, Community Design, Community Patent—Applicable Law for Claims of Damages', in J Drexl and A Kur (eds), *Intellectual Property and Private International Law: Heading for the Future* (2005)

M Pertegás, 'Intellectual Property and Choice of Law Rules' in Malatesta, *Unification*

M Pertagás, 'Patent Infringement: Choice of Laws, and the Forthcoming Rome II Regulation', in Basedow, *Intellectual Property*

E Schaper, 'Choice-of-Law Rules in the EU: Special Issues with Respect to Community Rights—Infringement of Community Trade Marks and Applicable Law' in J Drexl and A Kur (eds), *Intellectual Property and Private International Law: Heading for the Future* (2005)

W Tilmann, 'Community IP Rights and Conflict of Laws', in Basedow, *Intellectual Property*

F Wenzel Bulst and C Heinze, 'Discussion: Non-Contractual Obligations', in Basedow, *Intellectual Property*

ART 9 (INDUSTRIAL ACTION)

F Dorssemont and A van Hoek, '*De collectieve actie bij arbeidsconflicten in Rome II*' (2008) 114 *Revue de droit commercial belge* 515

G Palao Moreno, 'The Law Applicable to a Non-Contractual Obligation with Respect to an Industrial Action. A Commentary on Article 9 of the Rome II Regulation' (2007) 9 Yearbook of Private International Law 115

CHAPTER III (UNJUST ENRICHMENT, NEGOTIORUM GESTIO, AND CULPA IN CONTRAHENDO)

G Carella, 'The Law Applicable to Non-Contractual Obligations other than Tort or Delict' in Malatesta, *Unification*

A Chong, 'Choice of Law for Unjust Enrichment/Restitution and the Rome II Regulation' (2008) 56 ICLQ 1

J Lüttringhaus, '*Das internationale Privatrecht der culpa in contrahendo nach den EG-Verordnungen "Rom I" und "Rom II"*' (2008) 54 *Recht der internationalen Wirtschaft* 193

B Volders, '*Culpa in Contrahendo* in the Conflict of Laws. A Commentary on Article 12 of the Rome II Regulation' (2007) 9 Yearbook of Private International Law 127

OTHER PROVISIONS AND TOPICS

P Beaumont and Z Tang, 'Classification of Delictual Damages—*Harding v Wealands* and the Rome II Regulation' (2008) 12 Edin LR 135.

M Bogdan, 'General Aspects of the Future Regulation' in Malatesta, *Unification*

M Bona, 'Personal Injuries, Fatal Accidents and Rome II' in Malatesta, *Unification*

Th M De Boer, 'Party Autonomy and its Limitations in the Rome II Regulation' (2007) 9 Yearbook of Private International Law 19

C Brière, '*Réflexions sur les interactions entre la proposition de règlement "Rome II" et les conventions internationales*' (2005) 132 *Journal du droit international* 677

T W Dorris, 'Contribution and Indemnification among Joint Tortfeasors in Multi-State Conflict Cases: A Study of Doctrine and Current Law in the US and Under the Rome II Regulation' (2008) 4 J Pr Int L 237

M van Eechoud, 'The Position of Broadcasters and other Media under "Rome II": Proposed Regulation on the Law Applicable to Non-Contractual Obligations' (2006) European Audiovisual Observatory, Iris plus, Issue 2006-10, 1

M Fallon, '*La relation du règlement Rome II avec d'autres règles de conflit de lois*' (2008) 114 Revue de droit commercial belge 549

G Garriga, 'Relationship between Rome II and Other International Instruments. A Commentary on Article 28 of the Rome II Regulation' (2007) 9 Yearbook of Private International Law 137

A Junker, *'Das Internationale Privatrecht der Straßenverkehrsunfälle nach der Rom II-Verordnung'* (2008) 63 *Juristenzeitung* 169

C Kunke, 'Rome II and Defamation: Will the Tail Wag the Dog?' (2005) 19 Emory Int L Rev 1733

A Malatesta, 'The Law Applicable to Traffic Accidents' in Malatesta, *Unification*

A Staudinger, 'Rome II and Traffic Accidents' [2005] European Legal Forum I-61

T Thiede and M Kellner, *'"Forum shopping" zwischen dem Haager Übereinkommen über das auf Verkehrsunfälle anzuwndende Recht und der Rom-II-Verordnung'*, VersR 2007, 1624

G Vitellino, 'Rome II from an Internal Market Perspective' in Malatesta, *Unification*

Appendix 7

Table of Recitals

Article	Related Recitals
1	7, 8, 9, 11
1(2)(a)	10
3	13
4	16, 17, 18, 19
5	20
6	21
6(3)	22, 23
7	24, 25
8	26
9	27, 28
10	29
11	29
12	29, 30
14	31
15	12, 33
16	32
17	34
26	32
27	35
28	36, 37

Index

Index